X-MEN

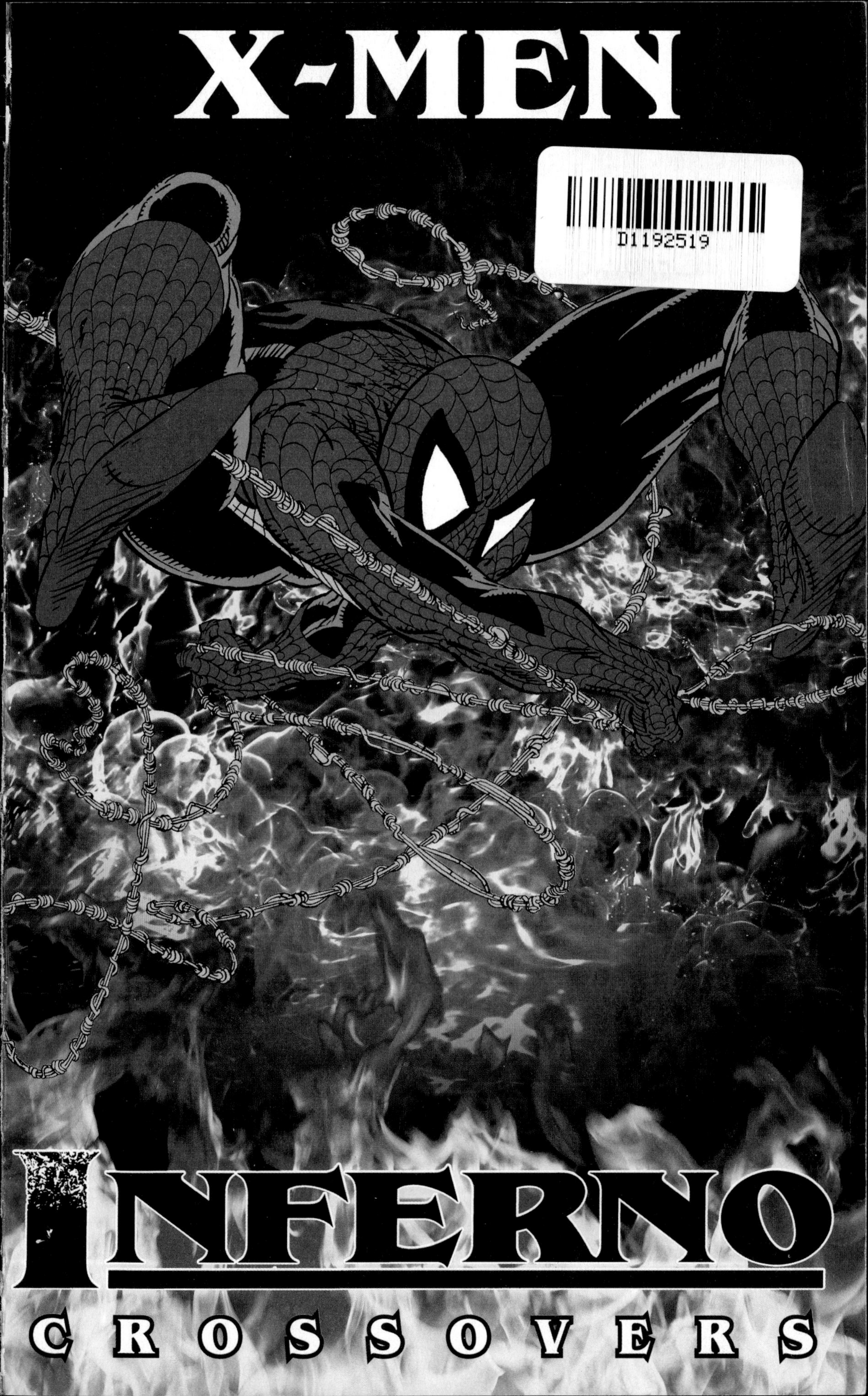

INFERNO

CROSSOVERS

X-MEN

INFERNO

CROSSOVERS

WRITERS

Walter Simonson, Steve Englehart, David Michelinie, Gerry Conway & Ann Nocenti with Ralph Macchio

PENCILERS

John Buscema, Keith Pollard, Todd McFarlane, Sal Buscema, Alex Saviuk & John Romita Jr. with Walter Simonson

INKERS

Tom Palmer, Joe Sinnott, Romeo Tanghal, Todd McFarlane, Sal Buscema, Keith Williams & Al Williamson with Walter Simonson

LETTERERS

Bill Oakley, John Workman, Joe Rosen & Rick Parker with Ken Lopez

COLORISTS

Eliot R. Brown, Christie Scheele, Paul Becton, Marc Siry, George Roussos, Bob Sharen, Janice Cohen & John Wilcox with Walter Simonson & Gregory Wright

ASSISTANT EDITORS

Gregory Wright, Marc Siry & Glenn Herdling

EDITORS

Mark Gruenwald, Ralph Macchio & Jim Salicrup

FRONT COVER ARTISTS

Marc Silvestri, Dan Green & Veronica Gandini

BACK COVER ARTISTS

Todd McFarlane & Chris Sotomayor

X-MEN CREATED BY Stan Lee & Jack Kirby

COLLECTION EDITOR: Mark D. Beazley ASSOCIATE MANAGING EDITOR: Kateri Woody
ASSOCIATE MANAGER, DIGITAL ASSETS: Joe Hochstein ASSOCIATE EDITOR: Sarah Brunstad
EDITOR, SPECIAL PROJECTS: Jennifer Grünwald VP PRODUCTION & SPECIAL PROJECTS: Jeff Youngquist
RESEARCH & LAYOUT: Jeph York PRODUCTION: Jerron Quality Color, ColorTek & Joe Frontirre
COLOR RECONSTRUCTION: Digikore, Tom Smith, Tom Ziuko, John Barber, Jason Lewis, ColorTek, Jameson Services & Wilson Ramos BOOK DESIGNER: Rodolfo Muraguchi
SVP PRINT, SALES & MARKETING: David Gabriel
EDITOR IN CHIEF: Axel Alonso CHIEF CREATIVE OFFICER: Joe Quesada
PUBLISHER: Dan Buckley EXECUTIVE PRODUCER: Alan Fine

Special Thanks to Mike Hansen

X-MEN: INFERNO CROSSOVERS. Contains material originally published in magazine form as AVENGERS #298-300, FANTASTIC FOUR #322-324, AMAZING SPIDER-MAN #311-313, SPECTACULAR SPIDER-MAN #146-148, WEB OF SPIDER-MAN #47-48, and DAREDEVIL #262-263 and #265. First printing 2016. ISBN# 978-0-7851-9551-1. Published by MARVEL WORLDWIDE, INC., a subsidiary of MARVEL ENTERTAINMENT, LLC. OFFICE OF PUBLICATION: 135 West 50th Street, New York, NY 10020. **Printed in the U.S.A.** ALAN FINE, President, Marvel Entertainment; DAN BUCKLEY, President, TV, Publishing & Brand Management; JOE QUESADA, Chief Creative Officer; TOM BREVOORT, SVP of Publishing; DAVID BOGART, SVP of Business Affairs & Operations, Publishing & Partnership; C.B. CEBULSKI, VP of Brand Management & Development, Asia; DAVID GABRIEL, SVP of Sales & Marketing, Publishing; JEFF YOUNGQUIST, VP of Production & Special Projects; DAN CARR, Executive Director of Publishing Technology; ALEX MORALES, Director of Publishing Operations; SUSAN CRESPI, Production Manager; STAN LEE, Chairman Emeritus. For information regarding advertising in Marvel Comics or on Marvel.com, please contact Vit DeBellis, Integrated Sales Manager, at vdebellis@marvel.com. For Marvel subscription inquiries, please call 888-511-5480. **Manufactured between 10/21/2016 and 11/28/2016 by LSC COMMUNICATIONS INC., SALEM, VA, USA.**

10 9 8 7 6 5 4 3 2 1

The demonic dimension of Limbo was ruled over by Illyana Rasputin, the New Mutants member known as Magik. But arch-demons S'ym and N'astirh sought to depose her — and so the two hatched a plan to merge Limbo with Earth. S'ym corrupted Madelyne Pryor, estranged wife of X-Factor leader Cyclops, transforming her into the Goblin Queen — and channeled her newfound magic powers to begin transforming New York, bringing inanimate objects to life and twisting the landscape as an unnatural heat wave rose across the city.

Meanwhile, N'astirh traveled to Earth and gathered thirteen mutant infants — including Madelyne's son, Nathan Christopher Summers — and used them to power a pentagram-shaped gate over Times Square. N'astirh then tricked Magik into opening the gate with her teleportation powers, and a horde of demons rained down on the city. For one hellish night, New York City burned...transformed into a demonic Inferno.

X-Factor and the X-Men eventually defeated N'astirh and Madelyne, while the New Mutants and the fledging X-Terminators team defeated S'ym and closed the portal. The demon horde was banished back to Limbo, and the city slowly reverted to normal.

But Earth's mutants weren't the only heroes to face the Inferno. While they fought against Limbo's invasion at the source, a multitude of other heroes heeded the call to battle — dealing with animated objects, goblin infestations and old foes corrupted by Limbo's magics. The Avengers, the Fantastic Four, Spider-Man and Daredevil have all proven themselves heroes beyond doubt, time and again — but Inferno's demonic fires may test them to their breaking points...

X-MEN
MARVEL
INFERNO

X-MEN
MARVEL
INFERNO

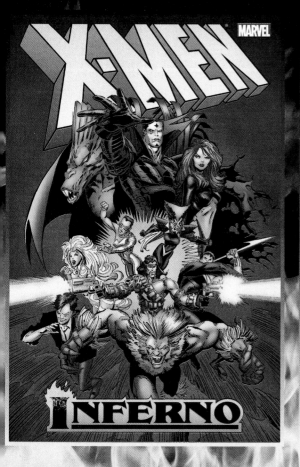

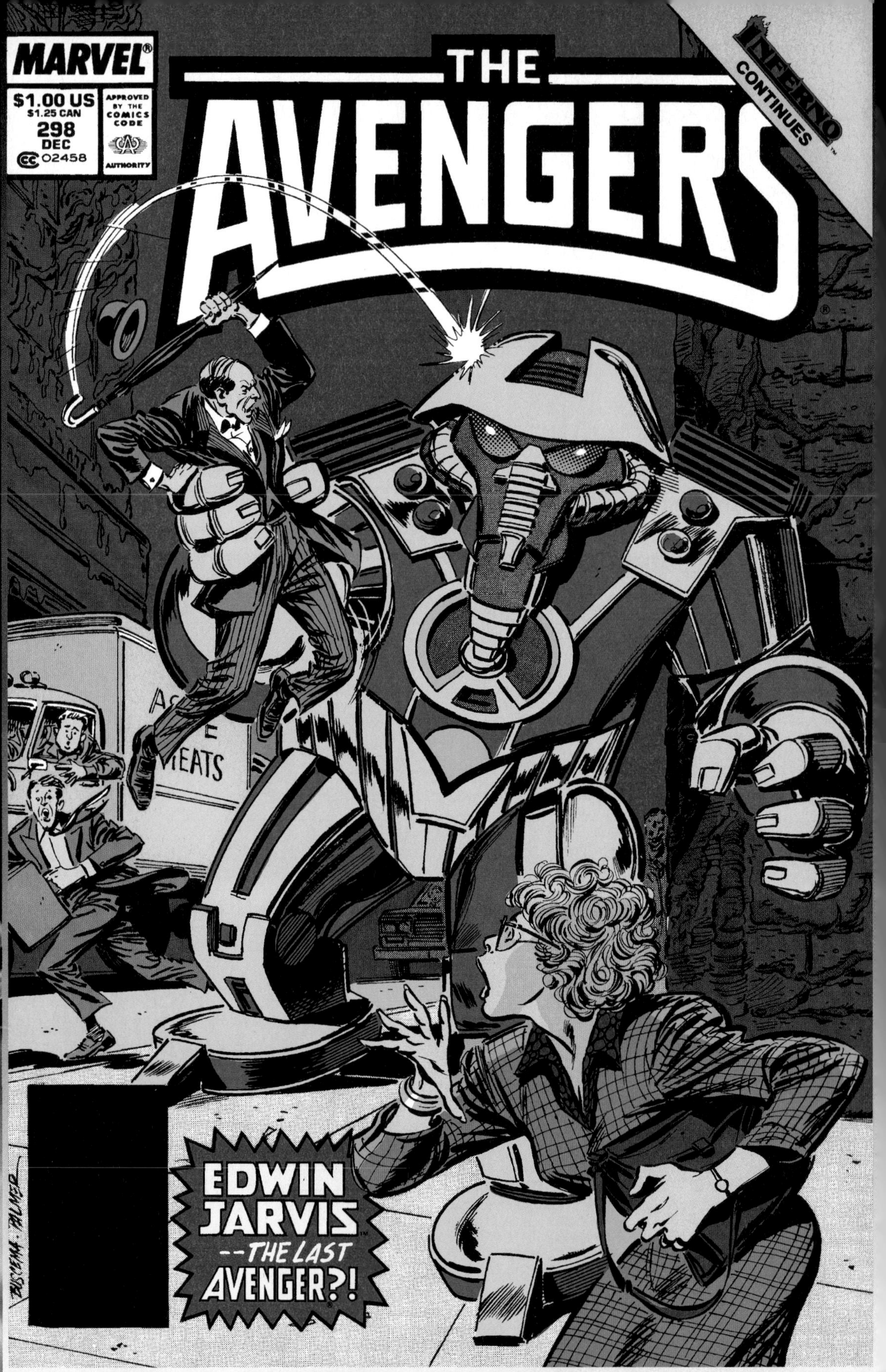
MARVEL
$1.00 US
$1.25 CAN
298
DEC
02458
APPROVED BY THE COMICS CODE AUTHORITY
THE AVENGERS
INFERNO CONTINUES
EDWIN JARVIS --THE LAST AVENGER?!

Stan Lee PRESENTS: THE MIGHTY AVENGERS!

DISASTER!!!

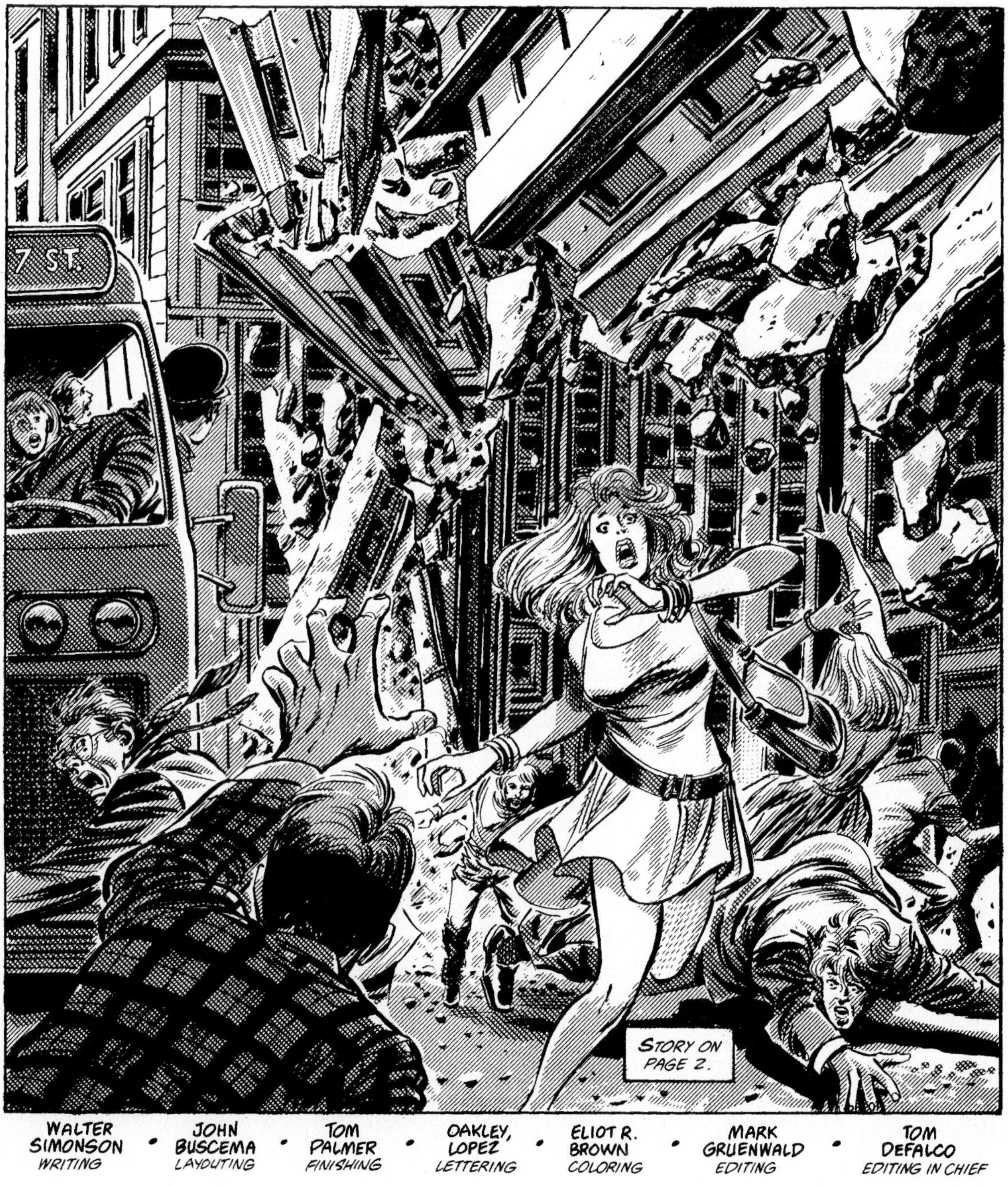
7 ST.
STORY ON PAGE 2.

WALTER SIMONSON *WRITING* • JOHN BUSCEMA *LAYOUTING* • TOM PALMER *FINISHING* • OAKLEY, LOPEZ *LETTERING* • ELIOT R. BROWN *COLORING* • MARK GRUENWALD *EDITING* • TOM DEFALCO *EDITING IN CHIEF*

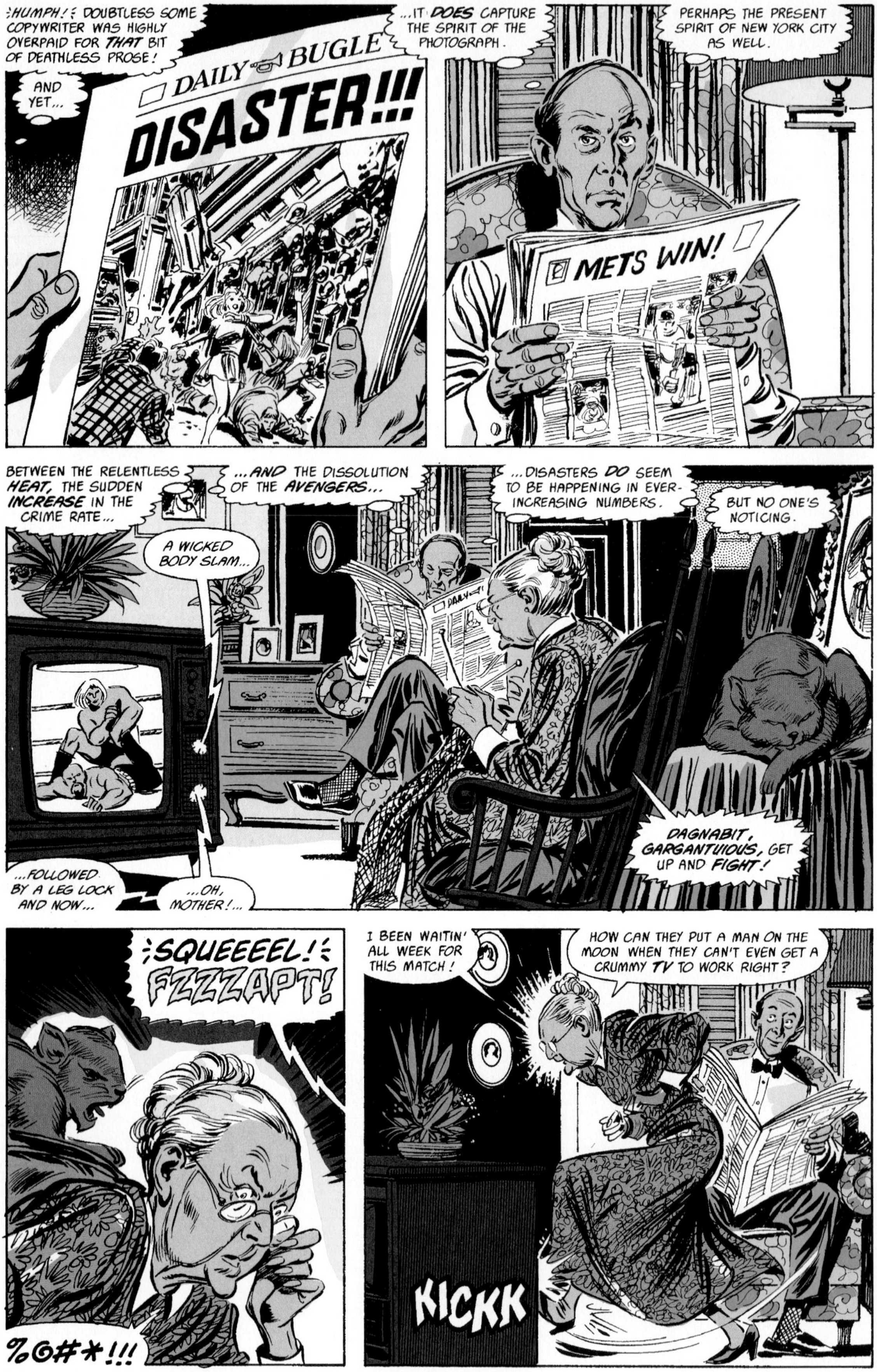
¡HUMPH! ¡ DOUBTLESS SOME COPYWRITER WAS HIGHLY OVERPAID FOR THAT BIT OF DEATHLESS PROSE!
AND YET...
DAILY BUGLE
DISASTER!!!
...IT DOES CAPTURE THE SPIRIT OF THE PHOTOGRAPH.
PERHAPS THE PRESENT SPIRIT OF NEW YORK CITY AS WELL.
METS WIN!
BETWEEN THE RELENTLESS HEAT, THE SUDDEN INCREASE IN THE CRIME RATE...
...AND THE DISSOLUTION OF THE AVENGERS...
...DISASTERS DO SEEM TO BE HAPPENING IN EVER-INCREASING NUMBERS.
BUT NO ONE'S NOTICING.
A WICKED BODY SLAM...
...FOLLOWED BY A LEG LOCK AND NOW...
...OH, MOTHER!...
DAGNABIT, GARGANTUIOUS, GET UP AND FIGHT!
¡SQUEEEEL! ¡ FZZZAPT!
%@#*!!!
I BEEN WAITIN' ALL WEEK FOR THIS MATCH!
HOW CAN THEY PUT A MAN ON THE MOON WHEN THEY CAN'T EVEN GET A CRUMMY TV TO WORK RIGHT?
KICKK

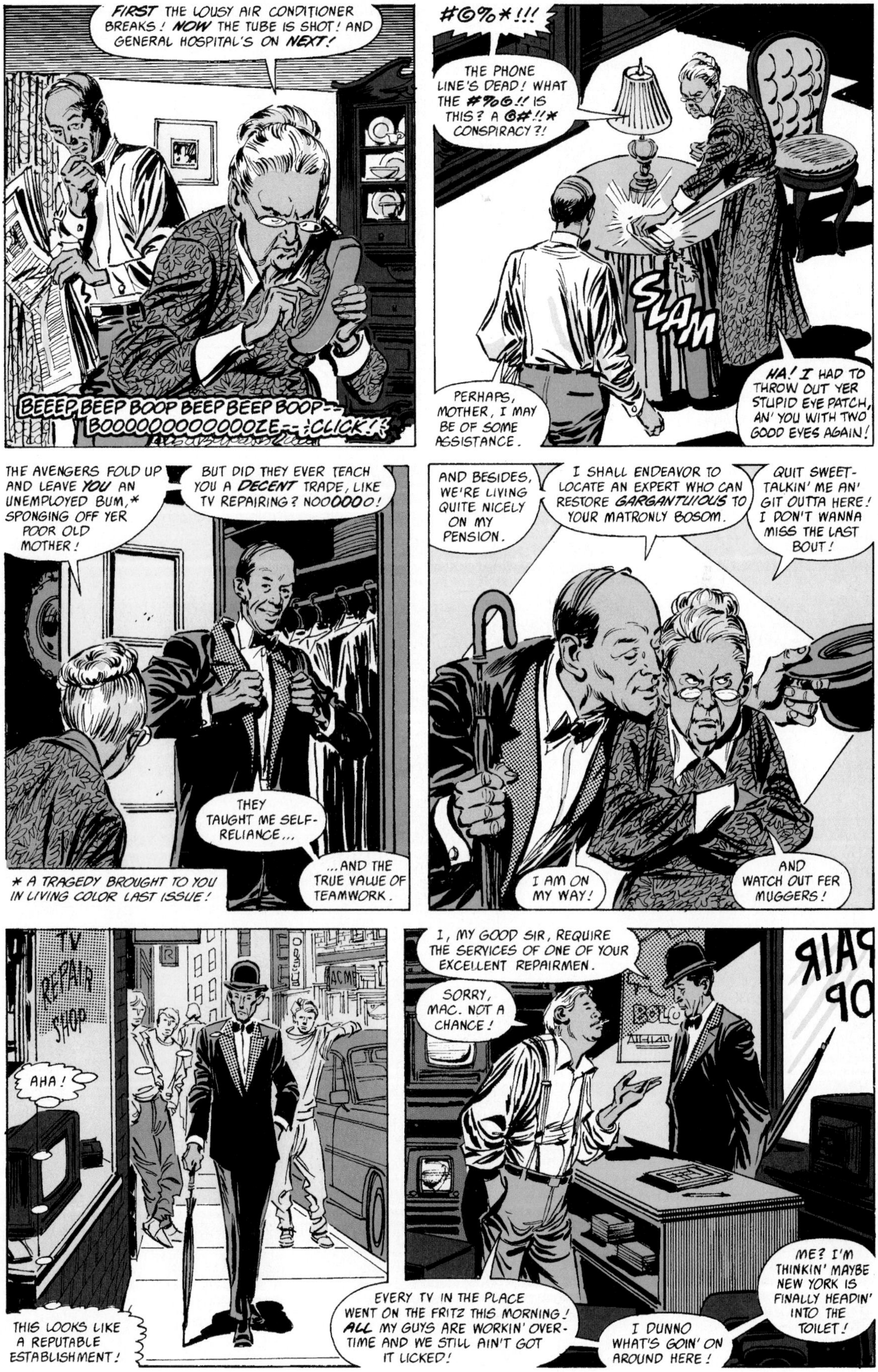
FIRST THE LOUSY AIR CONDITIONER BREAKS! NOW THE TUBE IS SHOT! AND GENERAL HOSPITAL'S ON NEXT!
BEEEP BEEP BOOP BEEP BEEP BOOP-- BOOOOOOOOOOOOZE--CLICK!
#@%*!!!
THE PHONE LINE'S DEAD! WHAT THE #%@!! IS THIS? A @#!!* CONSPIRACY?!
SLAM
PERHAPS, MOTHER, I MAY BE OF SOME ASSISTANCE.
HA! I HAD TO THROW OUT YER STUPID EYE PATCH, AN' YOU WITH TWO GOOD EYES AGAIN!
THE AVENGERS FOLD UP AND LEAVE YOU AN UNEMPLOYED BUM,* SPONGING OFF YER POOR OLD MOTHER!
BUT DID THEY EVER TEACH YOU A DECENT TRADE, LIKE TV REPAIRING? NOOOOOO!
THEY TAUGHT ME SELF-RELIANCE...
...AND THE TRUE VALUE OF TEAMWORK.
* A TRAGEDY BROUGHT TO YOU IN LIVING COLOR LAST ISSUE!
AND BESIDES, WE'RE LIVING QUITE NICELY ON MY PENSION.
I SHALL ENDEAVOR TO LOCATE AN EXPERT WHO CAN RESTORE GARGANTUIOUS TO YOUR MATRONLY BOSOM.
QUIT SWEET-TALKIN' ME AN' GIT OUTTA HERE! I DON'T WANNA MISS THE LAST BOUT!
I AM ON MY WAY!
AND WATCH OUT FER MUGGERS!
TV REPAIR SHOP
AHA!
THIS LOOKS LIKE A REPUTABLE ESTABLISHMENT!
I, MY GOOD SIR, REQUIRE THE SERVICES OF ONE OF YOUR EXCELLENT REPAIRMEN.
SORRY, MAC. NOT A CHANCE!
EVERY TV IN THE PLACE WENT ON THE FRITZ THIS MORNING! ALL MY GUYS ARE WORKIN' OVER-TIME AND WE STILL AIN'T GOT IT LICKED!
I DUNNO WHAT'S GOIN' ON AROUND HERE!
ME? I'M THINKIN' MAYBE NEW YORK IS FINALLY HEADIN' INTO THE TOILET!

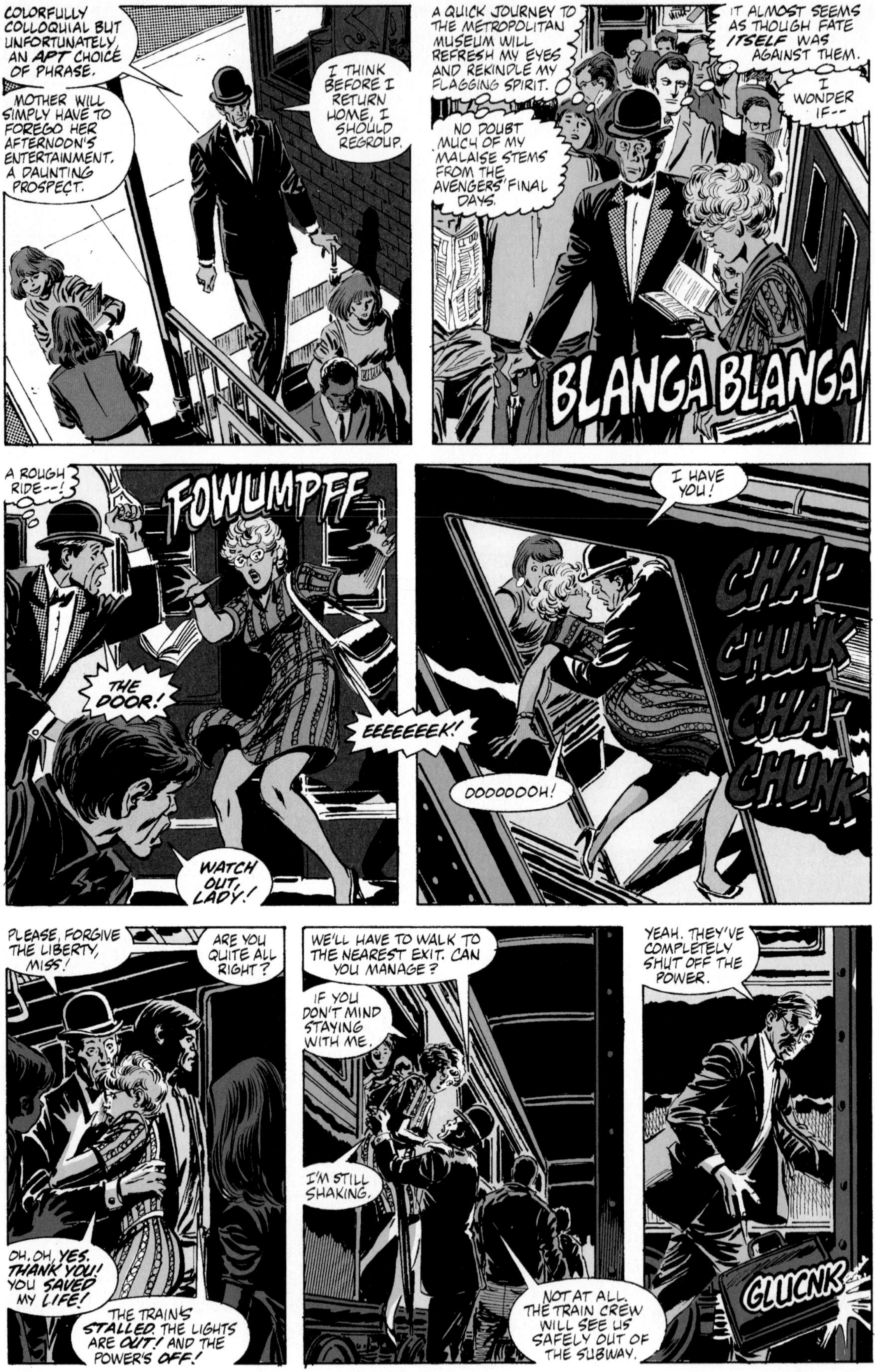
COLORFULLY COLLOQUIAL BUT UNFORTUNATELY, AN APT CHOICE OF PHRASE.
MOTHER WILL SIMPLY HAVE TO FOREGO HER AFTERNOON'S ENTERTAINMENT. A DAUNTING PROSPECT.
I THINK BEFORE I RETURN HOME, I SHOULD REGROUP.
A QUICK JOURNEY TO THE METROPOLITAN MUSEUM WILL REFRESH MY EYES AND REKINDLE MY FLAGGING SPIRIT.
NO DOUBT MUCH OF MY MALAISE STEMS FROM THE AVENGERS' FINAL DAYS.
IT ALMOST SEEMS AS THOUGH FATE ITSELF WAS AGAINST THEM.
I WONDER IF--
BLANGA BLANGA
A ROUGH RIDE--!
FOWUMPFF
THE DOOR!
EEEEEEEK!
WATCH OUT, LADY!
I HAVE YOU!
CHA-CHUNK CHA-CHUNK
OOOOOOOH!
PLEASE, FORGIVE THE LIBERTY, MISS!
ARE YOU QUITE ALL RIGHT?
OH, OH, YES. THANK YOU! YOU SAVED MY LIFE!
THE TRAIN'S STALLED. THE LIGHTS ARE OUT! AND THE POWER'S OFF!
WE'LL HAVE TO WALK TO THE NEAREST EXIT. CAN YOU MANAGE?
IF YOU DON'T MIND STAYING WITH ME.
I'M STILL SHAKING.
NOT AT ALL. THE TRAIN CREW WILL SEE US SAFELY OUT OF THE SUBWAY.
YEAH. THEY'VE COMPLETELY SHUT OFF THE POWER.
GLUCNK

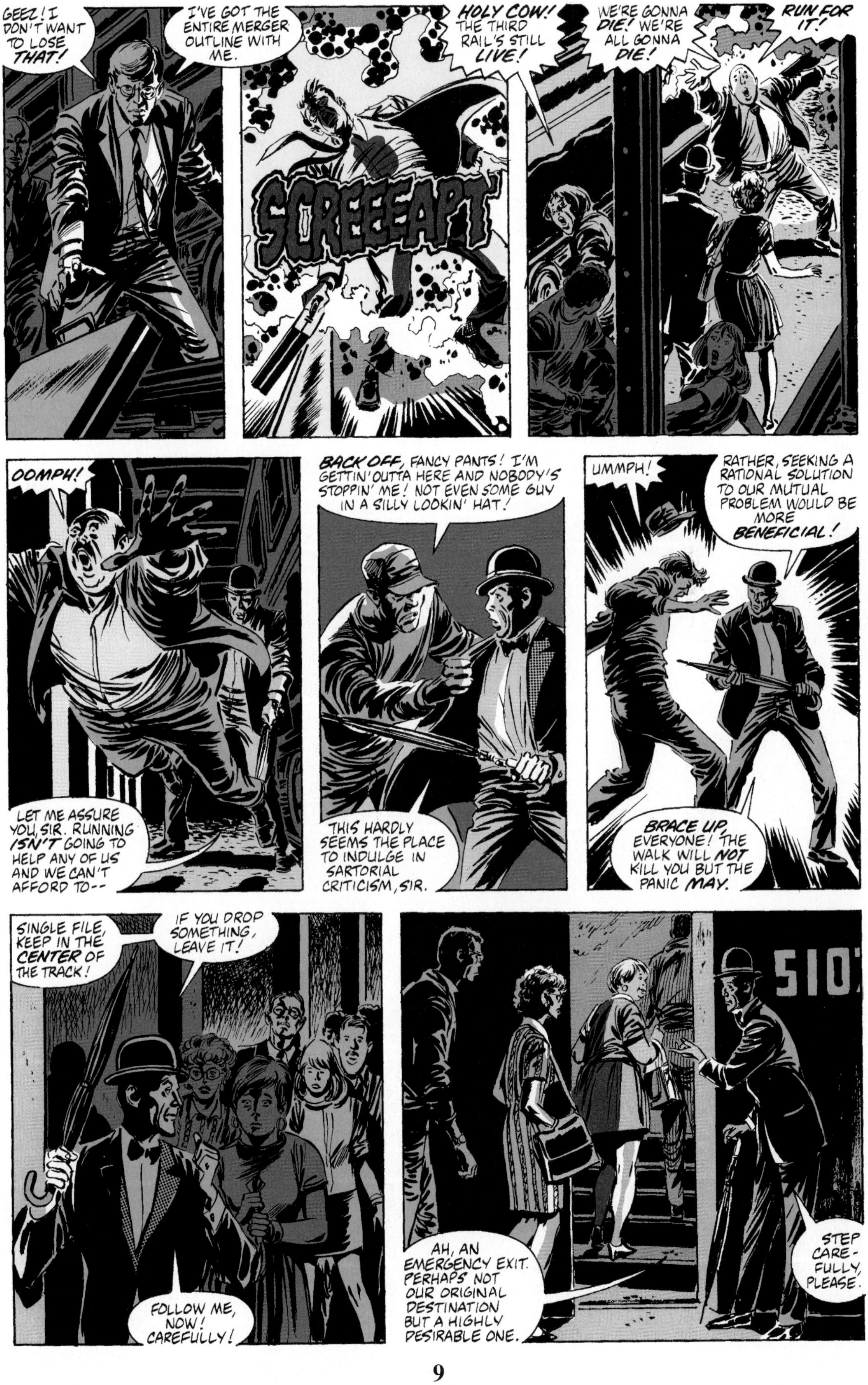
GEEZ! I DON'T WANT TO LOSE THAT!
I'VE GOT THE ENTIRE MERGER OUTLINE WITH ME.
SCREEEAPT
HOLY COW! THE THIRD RAIL'S STILL LIVE!
WE'RE GONNA DIE! WE'RE ALL GONNA DIE!
RUN FOR IT!
OOMPH!
LET ME ASSURE YOU, SIR. RUNNING ISN'T GOING TO HELP ANY OF US AND WE CAN'T AFFORD TO--
BACK OFF, FANCY PANTS! I'M GETTIN' OUTTA HERE AND NOBODY'S STOPPIN' ME! NOT EVEN SOME GUY IN A SILLY LOOKIN' HAT!
THIS HARDLY SEEMS THE PLACE TO INDULGE IN SARTORIAL CRITICISM, SIR.
UMMPH!
RATHER, SEEKING A RATIONAL SOLUTION TO OUR MUTUAL PROBLEM WOULD BE MORE BENEFICIAL!
BRACE UP, EVERYONE! THE WALK WILL NOT KILL YOU BUT THE PANIC MAY.
SINGLE FILE, KEEP IN THE CENTER OF THE TRACK!
IF YOU DROP SOMETHING, LEAVE IT!
FOLLOW ME, NOW! CAREFULLY!
AH, AN EMERGENCY EXIT. PERHAPS NOT OUR ORIGINAL DESTINATION BUT A HIGHLY DESIRABLE ONE.
STEP CARE-FULLY, PLEASE.

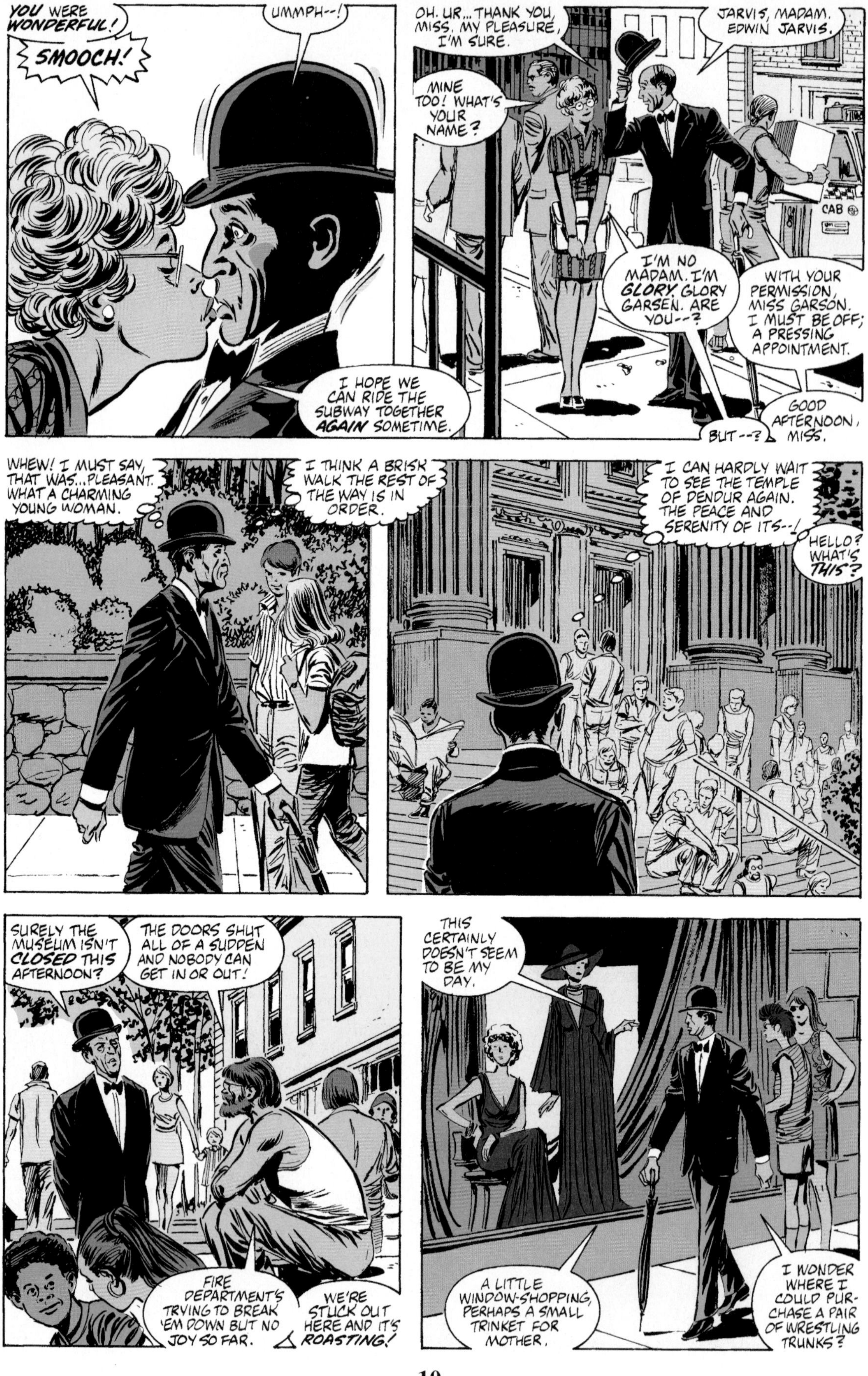
YOU WERE WONDERFUL!
SMOOCH!
UMMPH--!
I HOPE WE CAN RIDE THE SUBWAY TOGETHER AGAIN SOMETIME.
OH. UR... THANK YOU, MISS. MY PLEASURE, I'M SURE.
MINE TOO! WHAT'S YOUR NAME?
JARVIS, MADAM. EDWIN JARVIS.
I'M NO MADAM. I'M GLORY. GLORY GARSEN. ARE YOU--?
WITH YOUR PERMISSION, MISS GARSON. I MUST BE OFF; A PRESSING APPOINTMENT.
BUT--?
GOOD AFTERNOON, MISS.
WHEW! I MUST SAY, THAT WAS...PLEASANT. WHAT A CHARMING YOUNG WOMAN.
I THINK A BRISK WALK THE REST OF THE WAY IS IN ORDER.
I CAN HARDLY WAIT TO SEE THE TEMPLE OF DENDUR AGAIN. THE PEACE AND SERENITY OF ITS--!
HELLO? WHAT'S THIS?
SURELY THE MUSEUM ISN'T CLOSED THIS AFTERNOON?
THE DOORS SHUT ALL OF A SUDDEN AND NOBODY CAN GET IN OR OUT!
FIRE DEPARTMENT'S TRYING TO BREAK 'EM DOWN BUT NO JOY SO FAR.
WE'RE STUCK OUT HERE AND IT'S ROASTING!
THIS CERTAINLY DOESN'T SEEM TO BE MY DAY.
A LITTLE WINDOW-SHOPPING, PERHAPS A SMALL TRINKET FOR MOTHER.
I WONDER WHERE I COULD PURCHASE A PAIR OF WRESTLING TRUNKS?

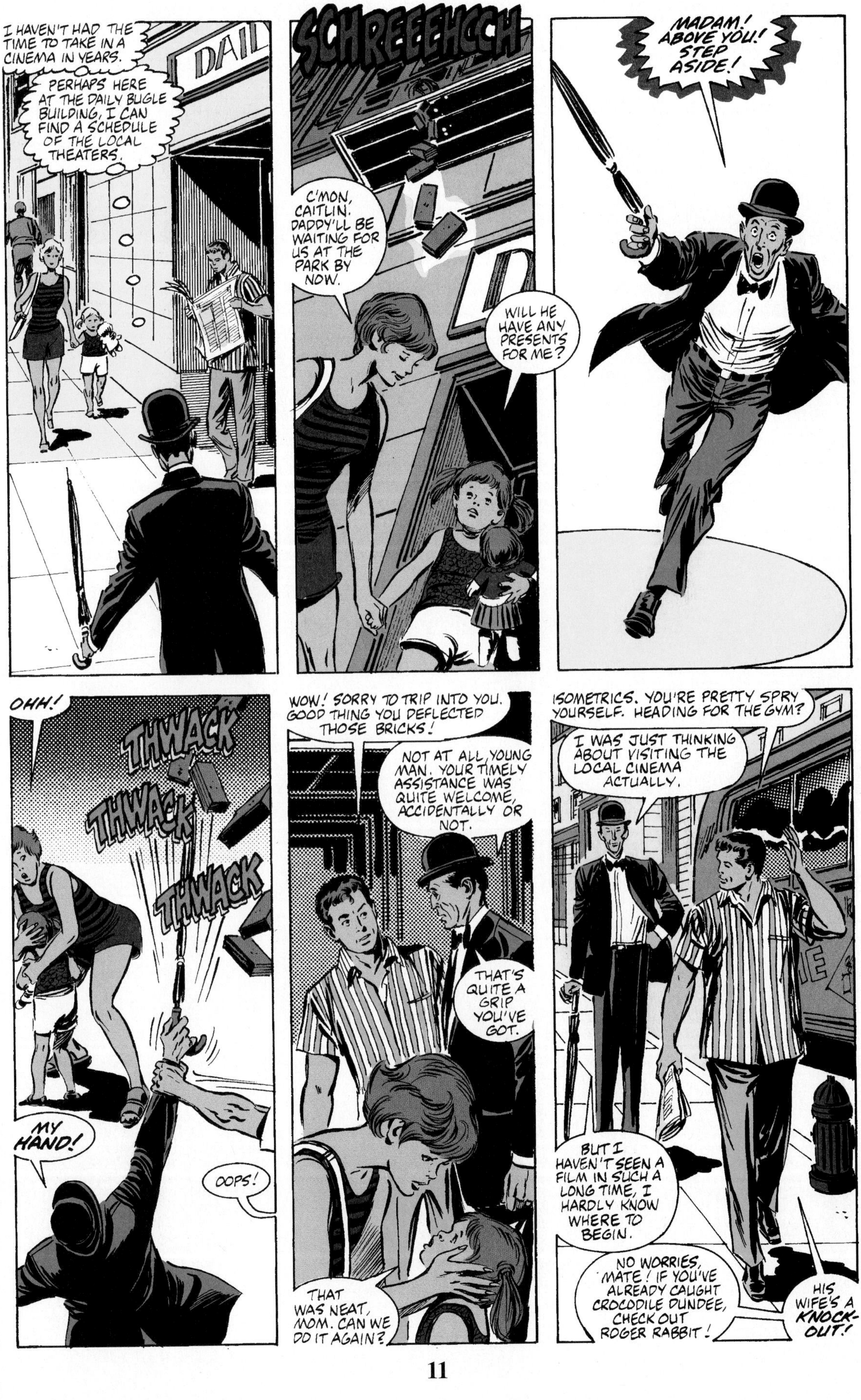
I HAVEN'T HAD THE TIME TO TAKE IN A CINEMA IN YEARS.
PERHAPS HERE AT THE DAILY BUGLE BUILDING, I CAN FIND A SCHEDULE OF THE LOCAL THEATERS.
DAIL
SCHREEEHCCH
C'MON, CAITLIN. DADDY'LL BE WAITING FOR US AT THE PARK BY NOW.
WILL HE HAVE ANY PRESENTS FOR ME?
MADAM! ABOVE YOU! STEP ASIDE!
OHH!
THWACK
THWACK
THWACK
MY HAND!
OOPS!
WOW! SORRY TO TRIP INTO YOU. GOOD THING YOU DEFLECTED THOSE BRICKS!
NOT AT ALL, YOUNG MAN. YOUR TIMELY ASSISTANCE WAS QUITE WELCOME, ACCIDENTALLY OR NOT.
THAT'S QUITE A GRIP YOU'VE GOT.
THAT WAS NEAT, MOM. CAN WE DO IT AGAIN?
ISOMETRICS. YOU'RE PRETTY SPRY YOURSELF. HEADING FOR THE GYM?
I WAS JUST THINKING ABOUT VISITING THE LOCAL CINEMA ACTUALLY.
BUT I HAVEN'T SEEN A FILM IN SUCH A LONG TIME, I HARDLY KNOW WHERE TO BEGIN.
NO WORRIES, MATE! IF YOU'VE ALREADY CAUGHT CROCODILE DUNDEE, CHECK OUT ROGER RABBIT!
HIS WIFE'S A KNOCK-OUT!

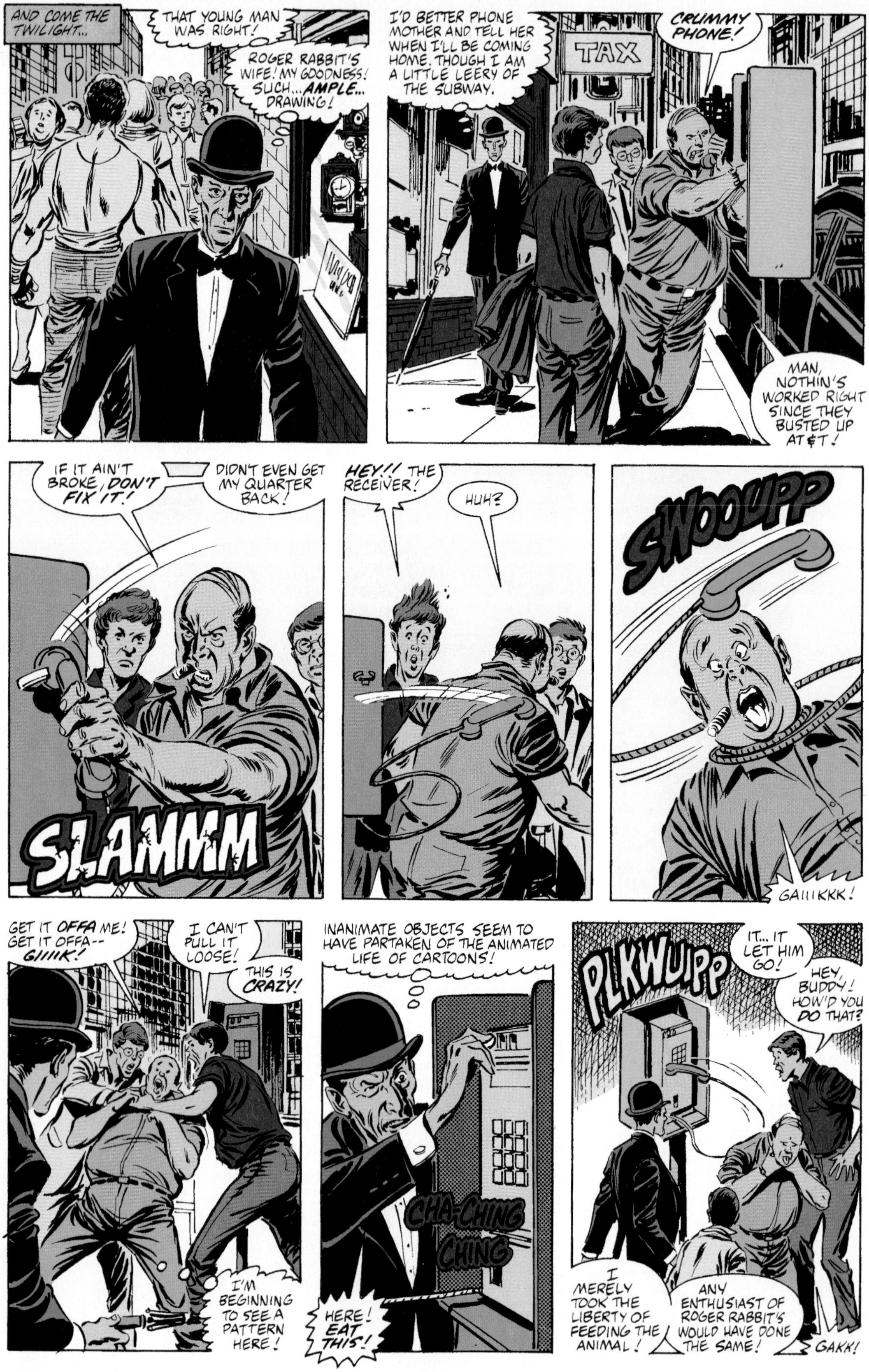
AND COME THE TWILIGHT...
THAT YOUNG MAN WAS RIGHT!
ROGER RABBIT'S WIFE! MY GOODNESS! SUCH... AMPLE... DRAWING!
I'D BETTER PHONE MOTHER AND TELL HER WHEN I'LL BE COMING HOME. THOUGH I AM A LITTLE LEERY OF THE SUBWAY.
TAX
CRUMMY PHONE!
MAN, NOTHIN'S WORKED RIGHT SINCE THEY BUSTED UP AT&T!
IF IT AIN'T BROKE, DON'T FIX IT!
DIDN'T EVEN GET MY QUARTER BACK!
SLAMMM
HEY!! THE RECEIVER!
HUH?
SWOOUPP
GAIIIKKK!
GET IT OFFA ME! GET IT OFFA-- GIIIIK!
I CAN'T PULL IT LOOSE!
THIS IS CRAZY!
I'M BEGINNING TO SEE A PATTERN HERE!
INANIMATE OBJECTS SEEM TO HAVE PARTAKEN OF THE ANIMATED LIFE OF CARTOONS!
CHA-CHING CHING
HERE! EAT THIS!
PLKWUIPP
IT... IT LET HIM GO!
HEY, BUDDY! HOW'D YOU DO THAT?
I MERELY TOOK THE LIBERTY OF FEEDING THE ANIMAL!
ANY ENTHUSIAST OF ROGER RABBIT'S WOULD HAVE DONE THE SAME!
GAKK!

THIS IS DEFINITELY TOO STRANGE TO BE IGNORED. EVEN THE BUILDINGS SEEM TO BE SWEATING!

WATCHING A CARTOON IS ONE THING; REAL LIFE *SHOULD* BE ANOTHER!

AND I KNOW *JUST* THE PARTY TO CALL.

HOWEVER, I SHALL ENDEAVOR TO PREVENT THE PHONE FROM STRANGLING ME SHOULD IT DECIDE TO ATTEMPT FURTHER VIOLENCE.

THE AVENGERS ARE NO MORE BUT I THINK I MUST ESSAY A PHONE CALL MYSELF.

BZZZZZT! PLEASE DEPOSIT $429.45 TO COMPLETE YOUR CALL... BZZZZT!

THIS IS RECORDING 19; PLEASE STATE YOUR NAME AND NUMBER AND CREDIT WILL BE ARRANGED! BZZZZZZZZZT!

BZZZZZT! I'M SORRY. YOUR CALL CANNOT BE COMPLETED AS DIALED... BZZZZZT!

I SEE. WELL, MY TECHNOLOGICAL FRIEND, *TWO* CAN PLAY AT *THIS* GAME!

COMPLETE THIS CALL AND I SHALL FEED YOU ALL THE CHANGE I POSSESS!

FRUSTRATE THAT EFFORT AND I SHALL RETURN MOMENTARILY WITH BOLT CUTTERS...

...AND *SEVER* YOUR RECEIVER! YOU'LL NEVER EAT IN THIS TOWN AGAIN!

CLICK.... BZZZZZZZT... RING... RING... RING...

AHH.

SOMETIME LATER, AS THE SUN BEGINS TO SET BEHIND THE SKYSCRAPERS OF MANHATTAN...

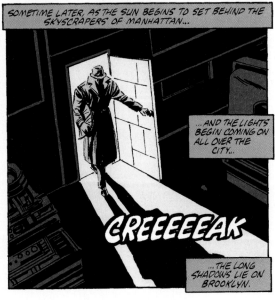

...AND THE LIGHTS BEGIN COMING ON ALL OVER THE CITY...

CREEEEEEAK

...THE LONG SHADOWS LIE ON BROOKLYN.

13

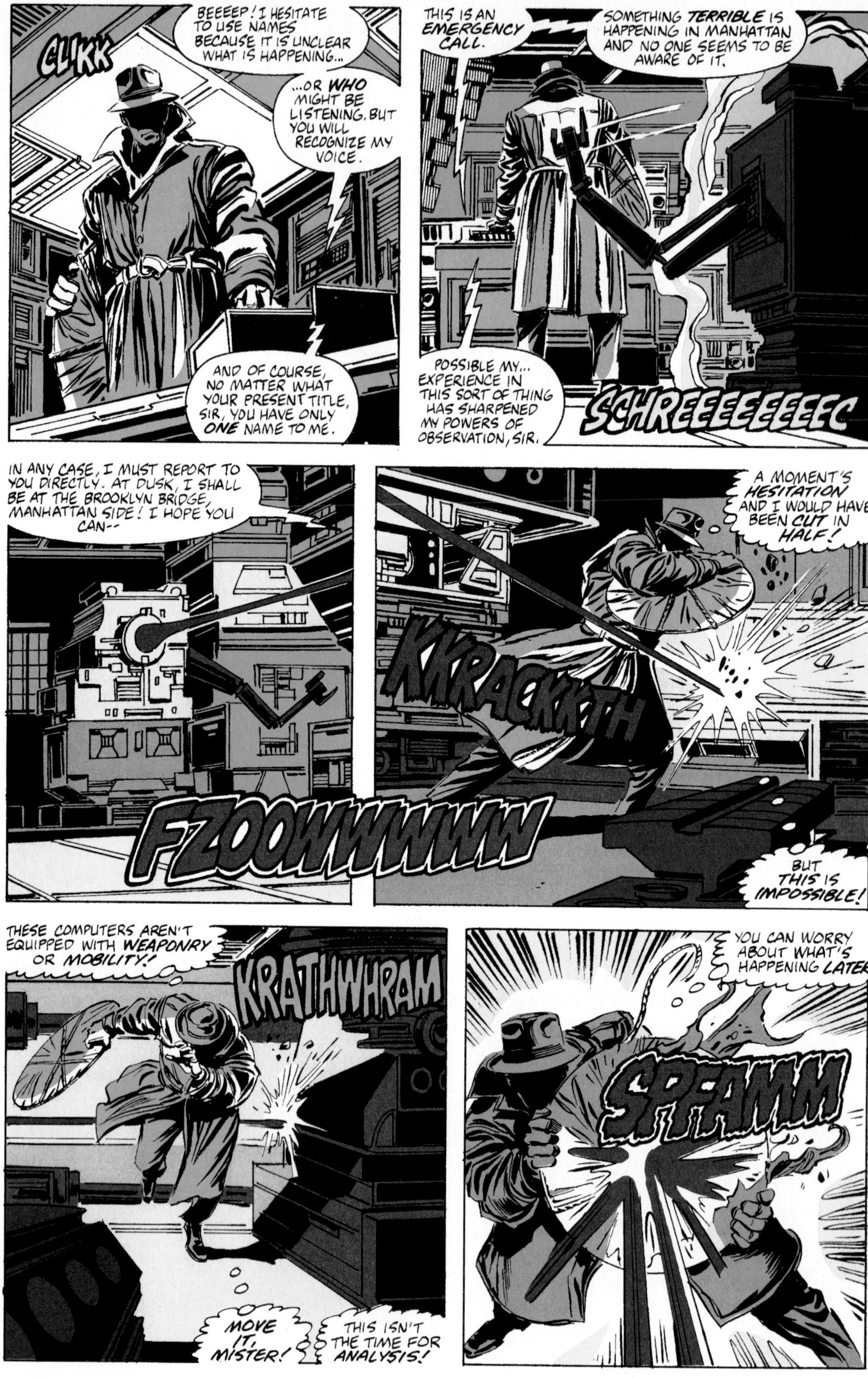
CLIKK
BEEEEP! I HESITATE TO USE NAMES BECAUSE IT IS UNCLEAR WHAT IS HAPPENING...
...OR WHO MIGHT BE LISTENING, BUT YOU WILL RECOGNIZE MY VOICE.
AND OF COURSE, NO MATTER WHAT YOUR PRESENT TITLE, SIR, YOU HAVE ONLY ONE NAME TO ME.
THIS IS AN EMERGENCY CALL.
SOMETHING TERRIBLE IS HAPPENING IN MANHATTAN AND NO ONE SEEMS TO BE AWARE OF IT.
POSSIBLE MY... EXPERIENCE IN THIS SORT OF THING HAS SHARPENED MY POWERS OF OBSERVATION, SIR.
SCHREEEEEEEEEC
IN ANY CASE, I MUST REPORT TO YOU DIRECTLY. AT DUSK, I SHALL BE AT THE BROOKLYN BRIDGE, MANHATTAN SIDE! I HOPE YOU CAN--
FZOOWWWWWN
A MOMENT'S HESITATION AND I WOULD HAVE BEEN CUT IN HALF!
KKRACKKTH
BUT THIS IS IMPOSSIBLE!
THESE COMPUTERS AREN'T EQUIPPED WITH WEAPONRY OR MOBILITY!
KRATHWHRAM
MOVE IT, MISTER!
THIS ISN'T THE TIME FOR ANALYSIS!
YOU CAN WORRY ABOUT WHAT'S HAPPENING LATER!
SPFAMM

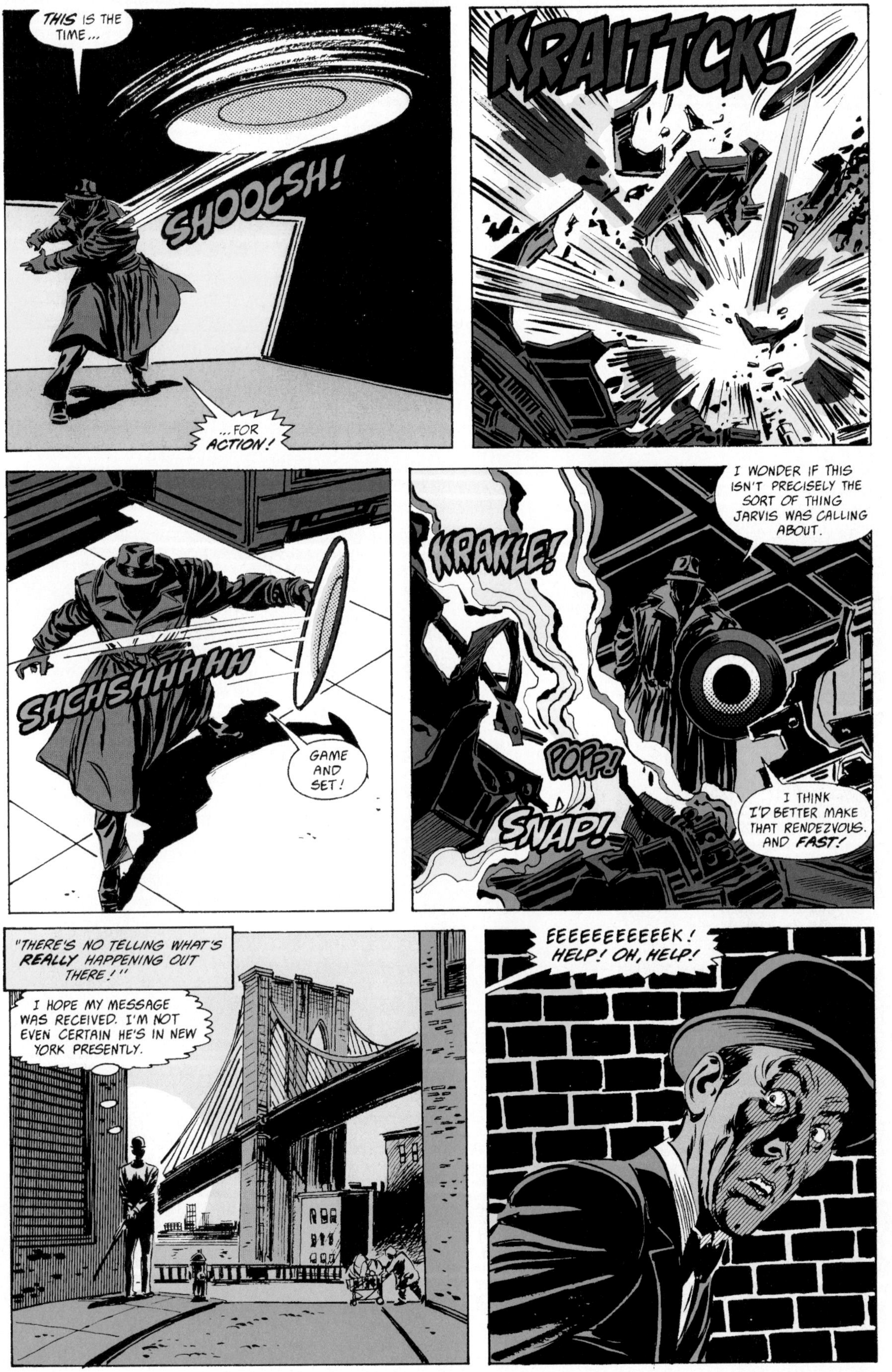
THIS IS THE TIME...
SHOOCSH!
...FOR ACTION!
KRAITTCK!
SHCHSHHHHH
GAME AND SET!
KRAKLE!
I WONDER IF THIS ISN'T PRECISELY THE SORT OF THING JARVIS WAS CALLING ABOUT.
POPP!
SNAP!
I THINK I'D BETTER MAKE THAT RENDEZVOUS. AND FAST!
"THERE'S NO TELLING WHAT'S REALLY HAPPENING OUT THERE!"
I HOPE MY MESSAGE WAS RECEIVED. I'M NOT EVEN CERTAIN HE'S IN NEW YORK PRESENTLY.
EEEEEEEEEEEK! HELP! OH, HELP!

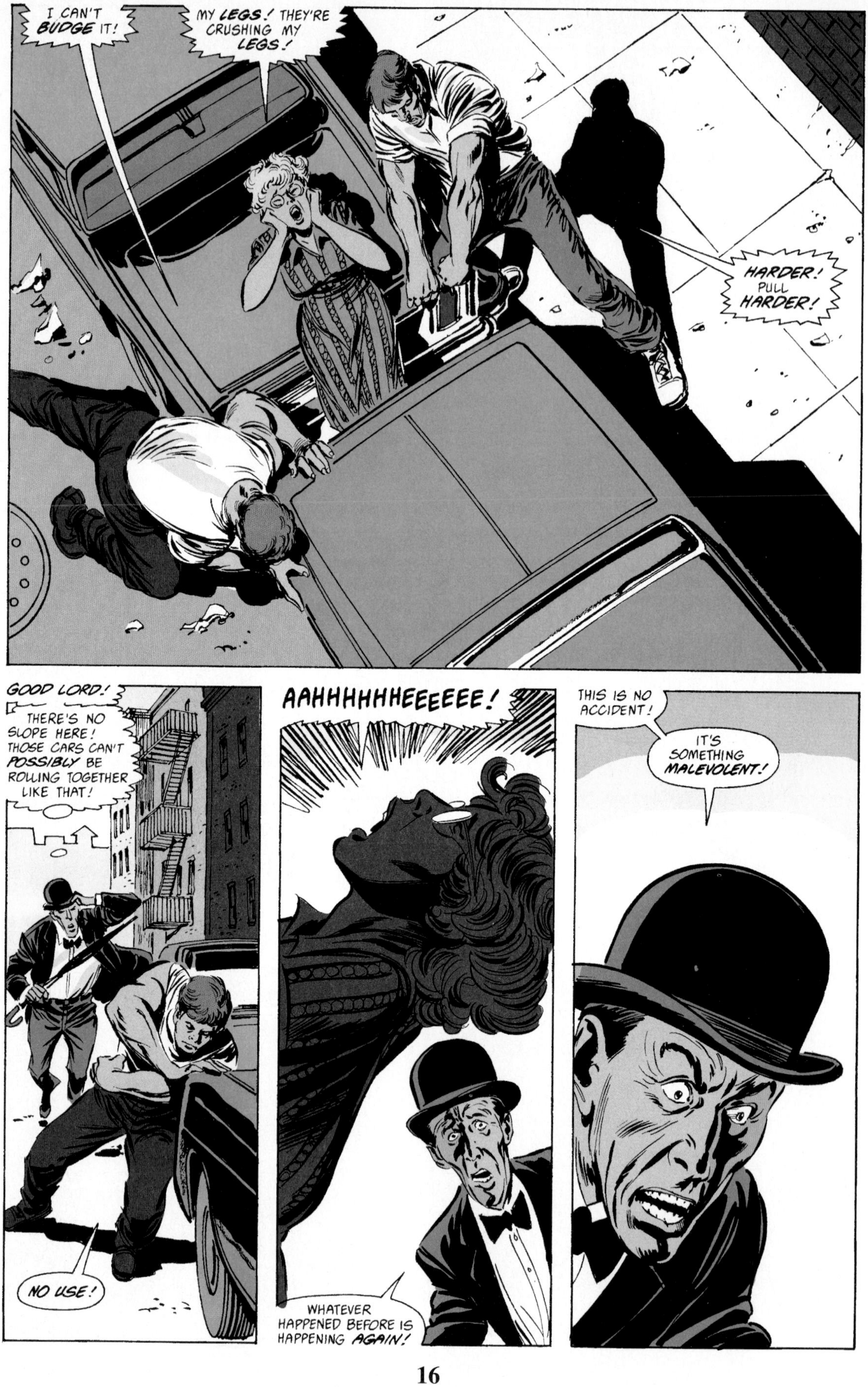
I CAN'T BUDGE IT!
MY LEGS! THEY'RE CRUSHING MY LEGS!
HARDER! PULL HARDER!
GOOD LORD!
THERE'S NO SLOPE HERE! THOSE CARS CAN'T POSSIBLY BE ROLLING TOGETHER LIKE THAT!
NO USE!
AAHHHHHHEEEEEE!
WHATEVER HAPPENED BEFORE IS HAPPENING AGAIN!
THIS IS NO ACCIDENT!
IT'S SOMETHING MALEVOLENT!

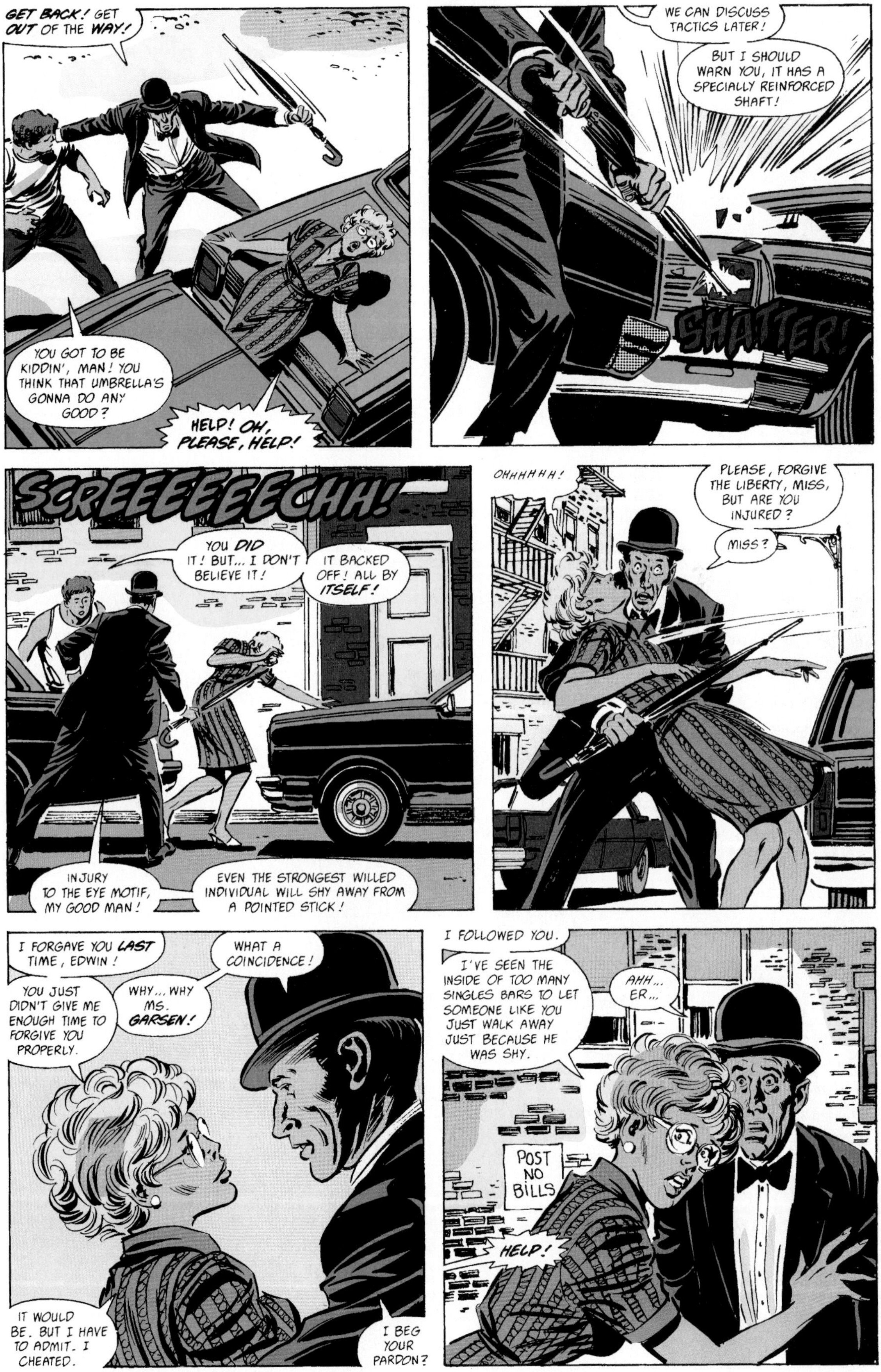

GET BACK! GET OUT OF THE WAY!
YOU GOT TO BE KIDDIN', MAN! YOU THINK THAT UMBRELLA'S GONNA DO ANY GOOD?
HELP! OH, PLEASE, HELP!
WE CAN DISCUSS TACTICS LATER!
BUT I SHOULD WARN YOU, IT HAS A SPECIALLY REINFORCED SHAFT!
SHATTER!
SCREEEEEEECHH!
YOU DID IT! BUT... I DON'T BELIEVE IT!
IT BACKED OFF! ALL BY ITSELF!
INJURY TO THE EYE MOTIF, MY GOOD MAN!
EVEN THE STRONGEST WILLED INDIVIDUAL WILL SHY AWAY FROM A POINTED STICK!
OHHHHHH!
PLEASE, FORGIVE THE LIBERTY, MISS, BUT ARE YOU INJURED?
MISS?
I FORGAVE YOU LAST TIME, EDWIN!
WHAT A COINCIDENCE!
YOU JUST DIDN'T GIVE ME ENOUGH TIME TO FORGIVE YOU PROPERLY.
WHY... WHY MS. GARSEN!
IT WOULD BE. BUT I HAVE TO ADMIT. I CHEATED.
I BEG YOUR PARDON?
I FOLLOWED YOU.
I'VE SEEN THE INSIDE OF TOO MANY SINGLES BARS TO LET SOMEONE LIKE YOU JUST WALK AWAY JUST BECAUSE HE WAS SHY.
AHH... ER...
POST NO BILLS
HELP!

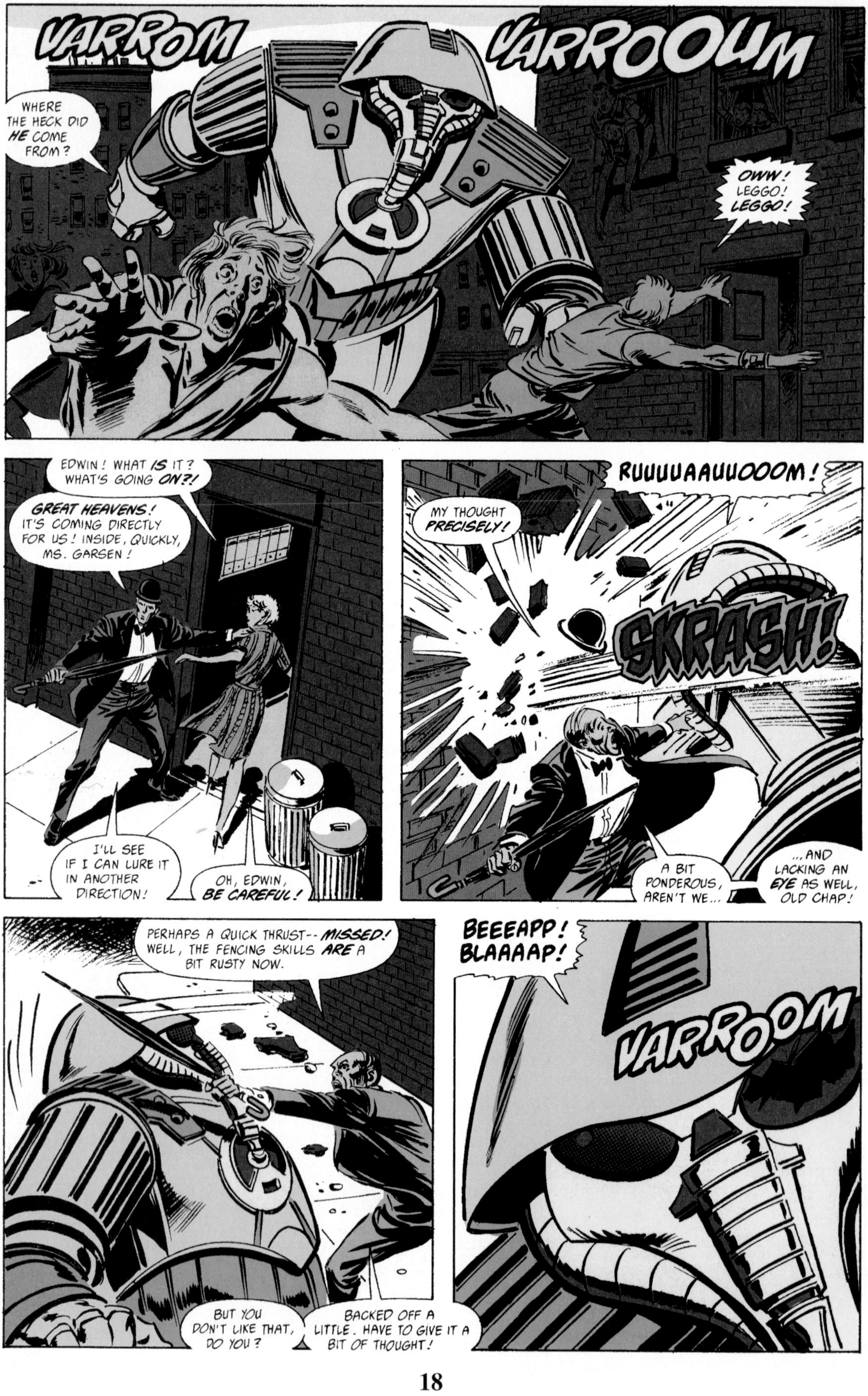
VARROM
VARROOUM
WHERE THE HECK DID HE COME FROM?
OWW! LEGGO! LEGGO!
EDWIN! WHAT IS IT? WHAT'S GOING ON?!
GREAT HEAVENS! IT'S COMING DIRECTLY FOR US! INSIDE, QUICKLY, MS. GARSEN!
I'LL SEE IF I CAN LURE IT IN ANOTHER DIRECTION!
OH, EDWIN, BE CAREFUL!
RUUUUAAUUOOOM!
MY THOUGHT PRECISELY!
SKRASH!
A BIT PONDEROUS, AREN'T WE...
...AND LACKING AN EYE AS WELL, OLD CHAP!
PERHAPS A QUICK THRUST-- MISSED! WELL, THE FENCING SKILLS ARE A BIT RUSTY NOW.
BUT YOU DON'T LIKE THAT, DO YOU?
BACKED OFF A LITTLE. HAVE TO GIVE IT A BIT OF THOUGHT!
BEEEAPP! BLAAAAP!
VARROOM

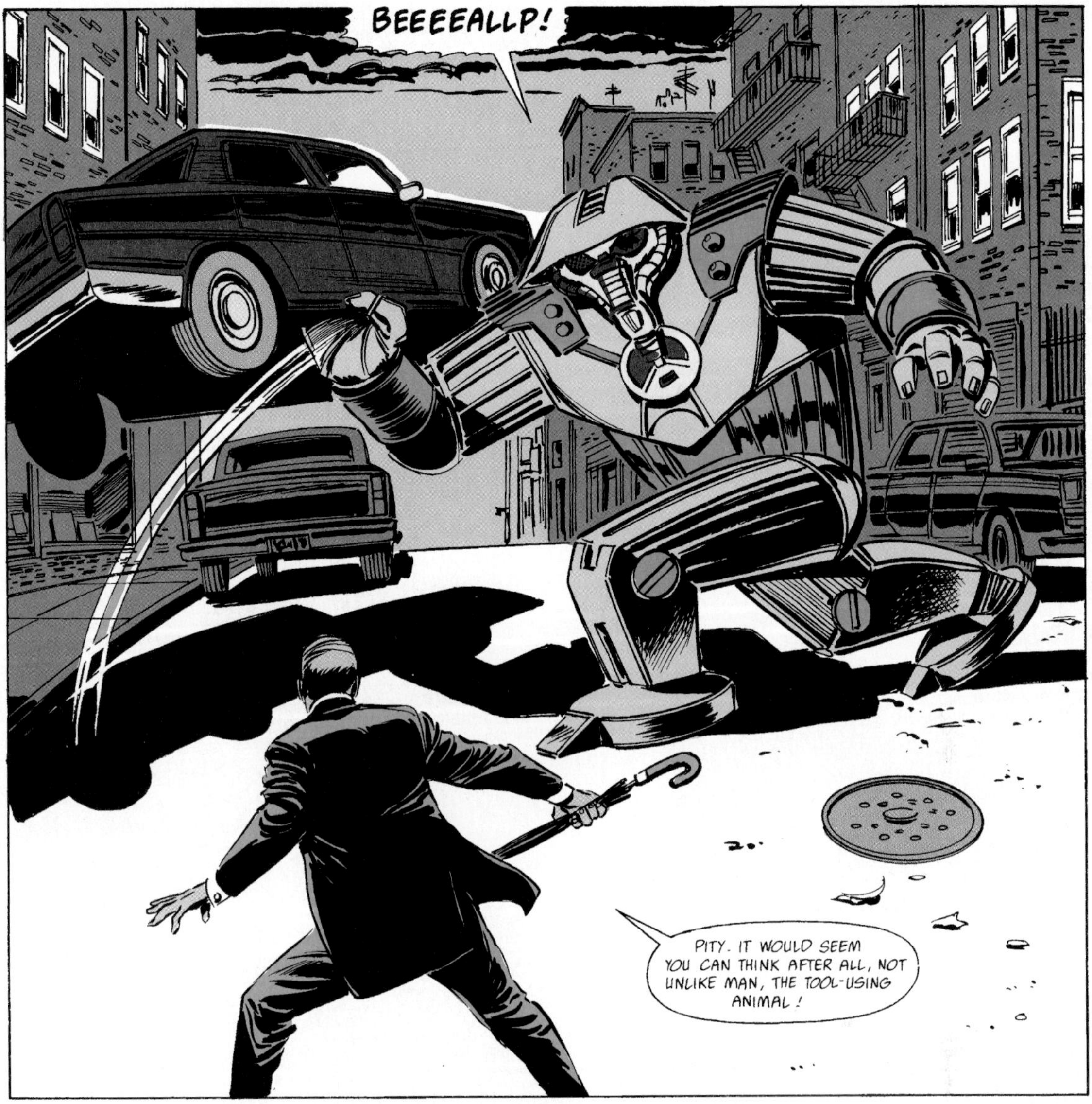
BEEEEALLP!
PITY. IT WOULD SEEM YOU CAN THINK AFTER ALL, NOT UNLIKE MAN, THE TOOL-USING ANIMAL!

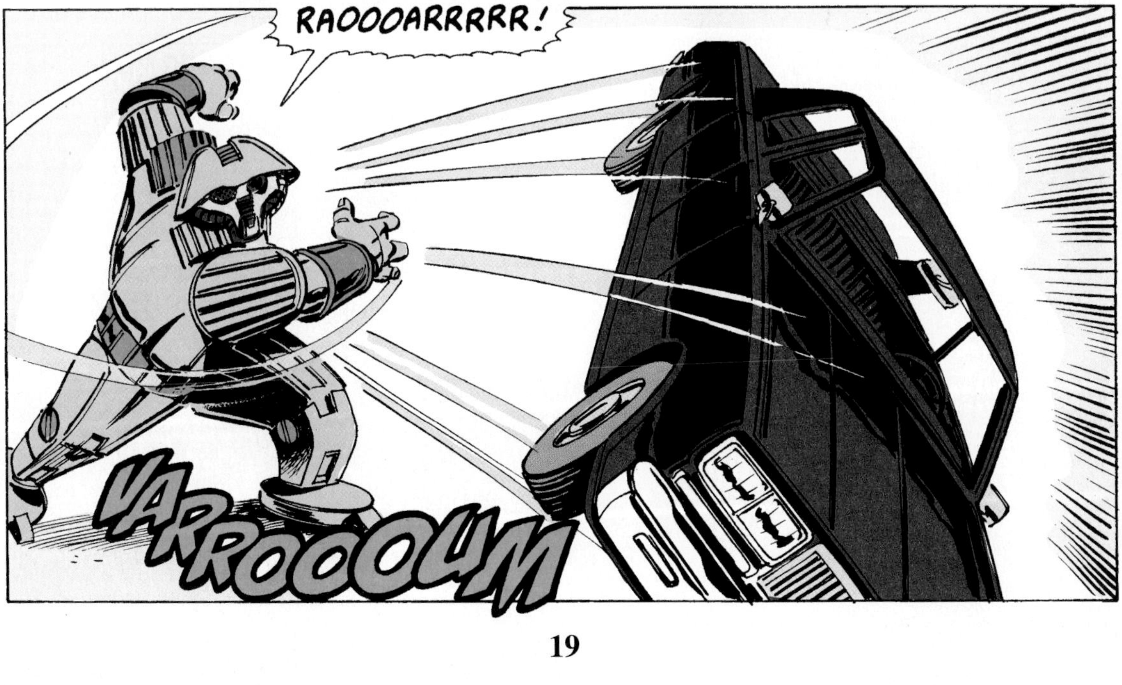
RAOOOARRRRR!
VARROOOUM

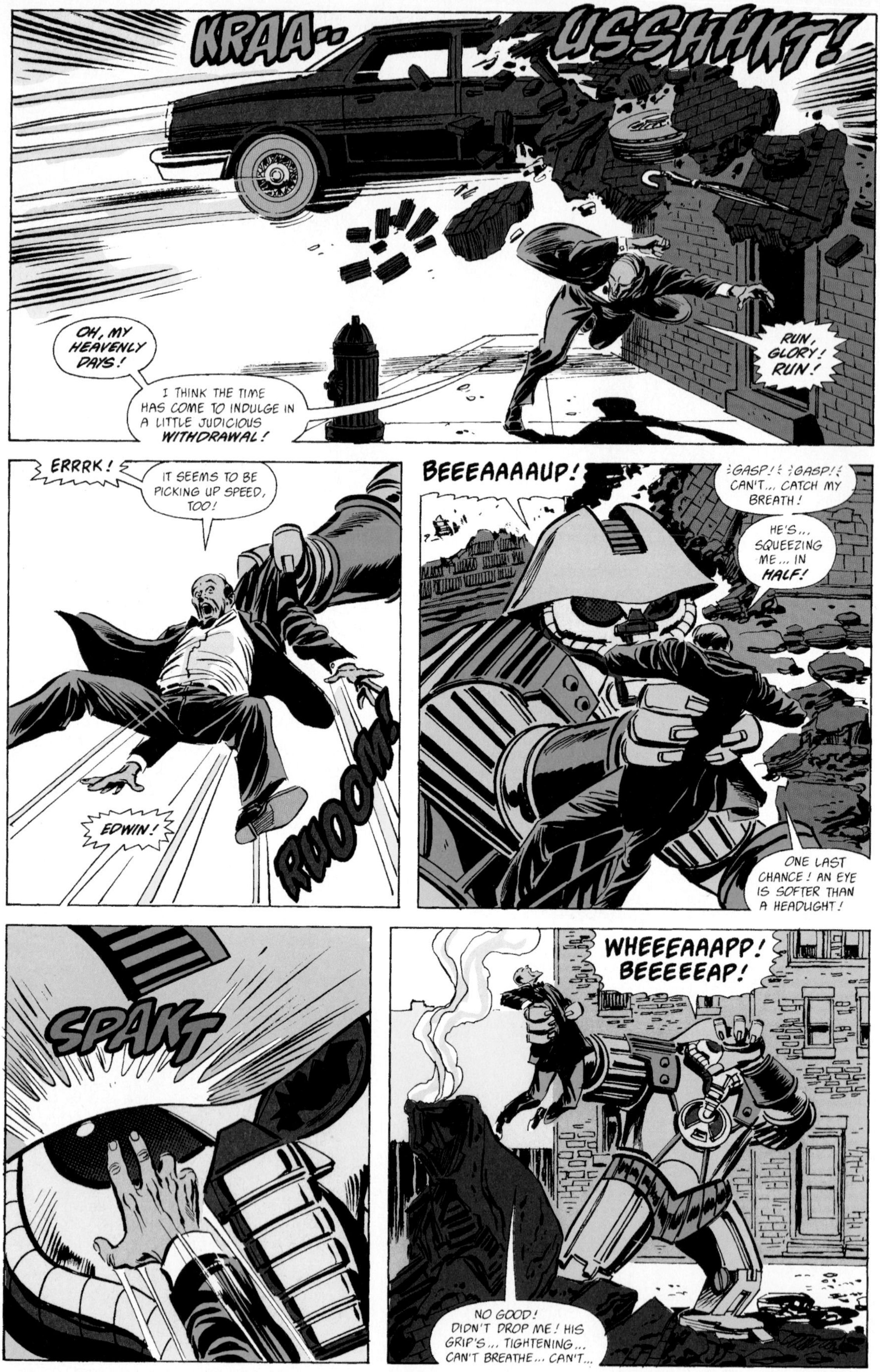
KRAA--USSHHKT!
OH, MY HEAVENLY DAYS!
I THINK THE TIME HAS COME TO INDULGE IN A LITTLE JUDICIOUS WITHDRAWAL!
RUN, GLORY! RUN!
ERRRK!
IT SEEMS TO BE PICKING UP SPEED, TOO!
EDWIN!
RUOOM!
BEEEAAAAUP!
GASP! GASP! CAN'T... CATCH MY BREATH!
HE'S... SQUEEZING ME... IN HALF!
ONE LAST CHANCE! AN EYE IS SOFTER THAN A HEADLIGHT!
SPAKT
WHEEEAAAPP! BEEEEEAP!
NO GOOD! DIDN'T DROP ME! HIS GRIP'S... TIGHTENING... CAN'T BREATHE... CAN'T...

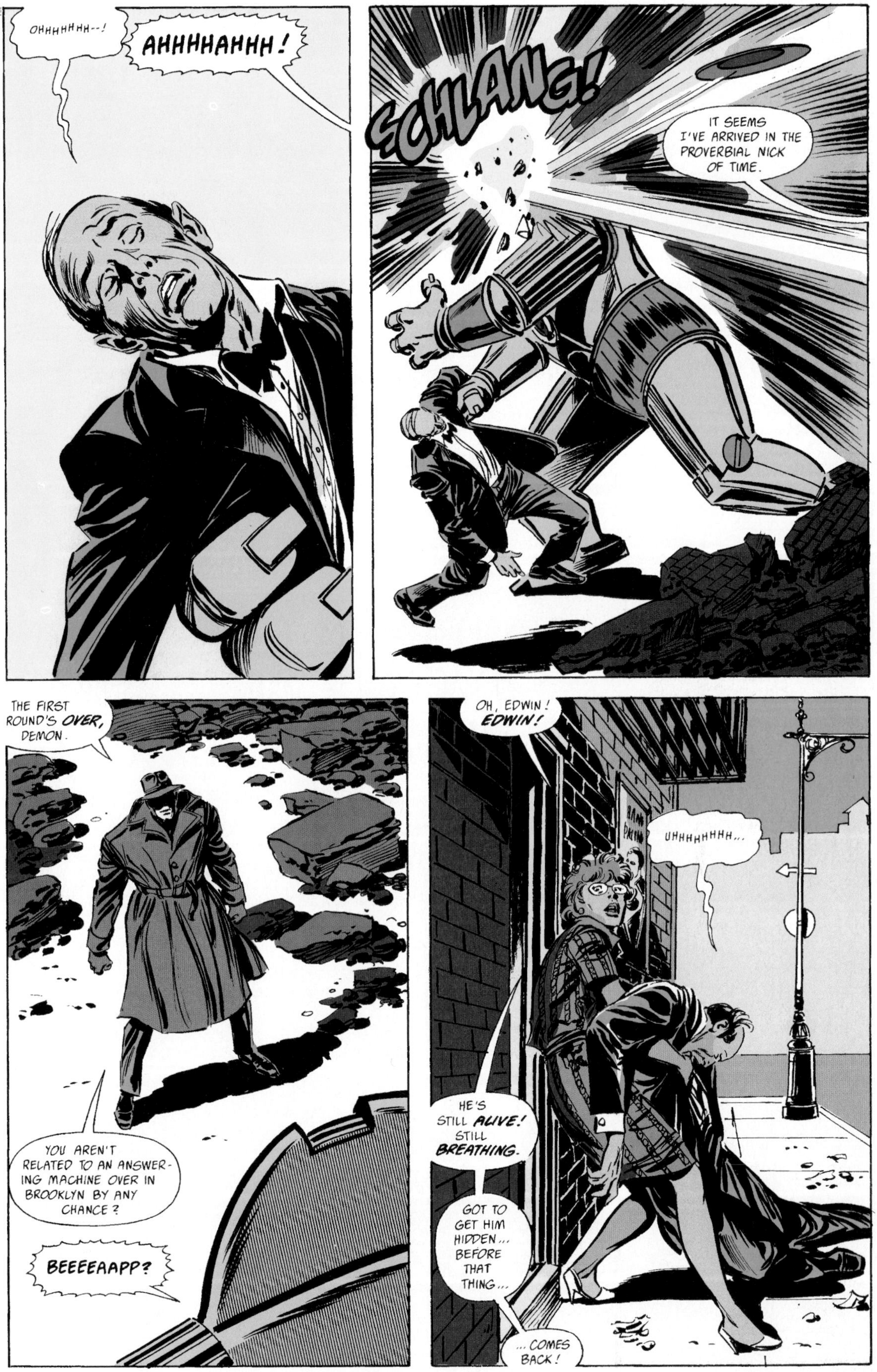

OHHHHHHH--!
AHHHHAHHH!
SCHLANG!
IT SEEMS I'VE ARRIVED IN THE PROVERBIAL NICK OF TIME.
THE FIRST ROUND'S OVER, DEMON.
YOU AREN'T RELATED TO AN ANSWERING MACHINE OVER IN BROOKLYN BY ANY CHANCE?
BEEEEAAPP?
OH, EDWIN! EDWIN!
UHHHHHHHH...
HE'S STILL ALIVE! STILL BREATHING.
GOT TO GET HIM HIDDEN... BEFORE THAT THING...
...COMES BACK!

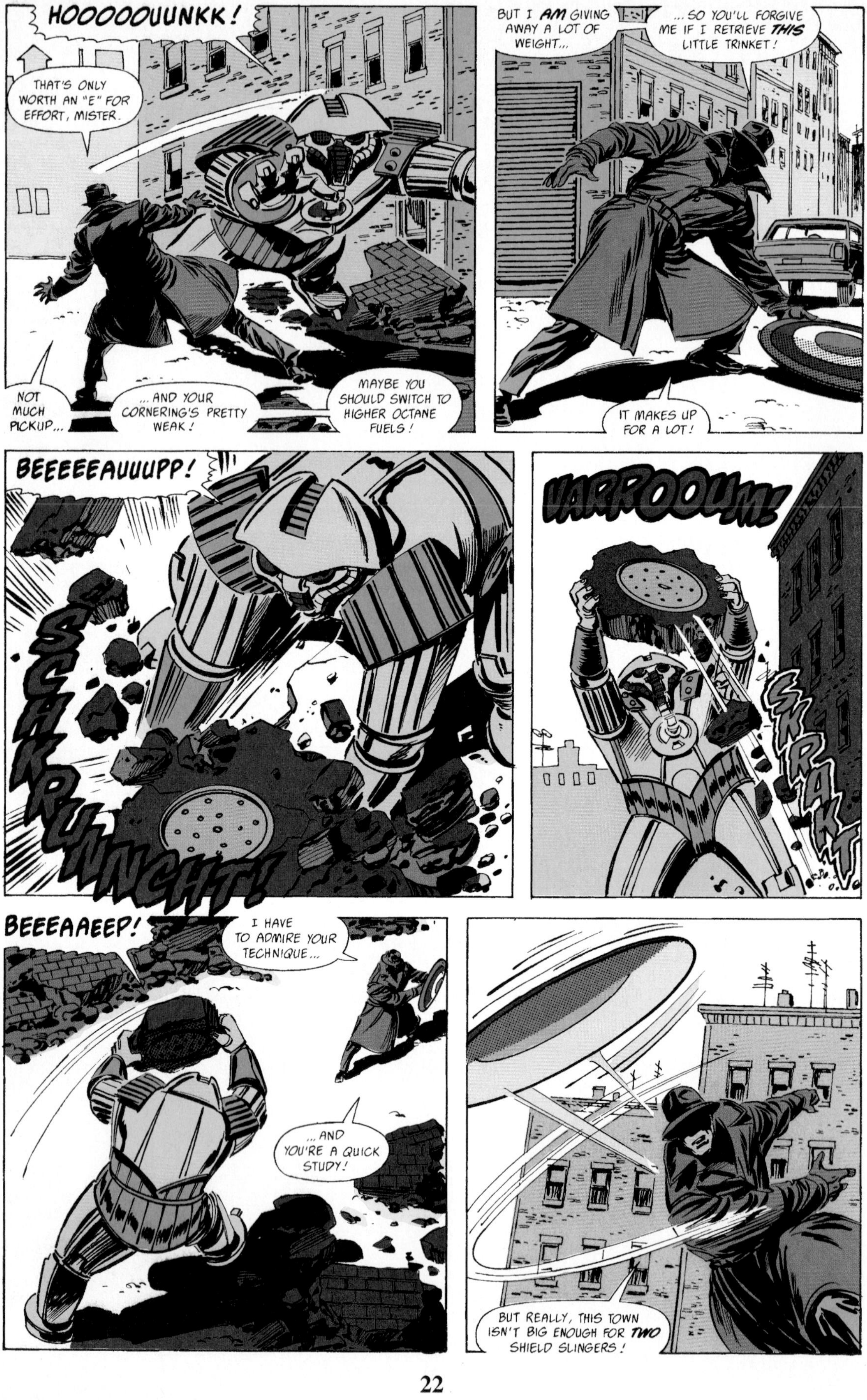
HOOOOOUUNKK!
THAT'S ONLY WORTH AN "E" FOR EFFORT, MISTER.
NOT MUCH PICKUP...
...AND YOUR CORNERING'S PRETTY WEAK!
MAYBE YOU SHOULD SWITCH TO HIGHER OCTANE FUELS!
BUT I AM GIVING AWAY A LOT OF WEIGHT...
...SO YOU'LL FORGIVE ME IF I RETRIEVE THIS LITTLE TRINKET!
IT MAKES UP FOR A LOT!
BEEEEEAUUUPP!
SCHKRUNNCHT!
VARROOUM!
SKRAKT
BEEEAAEEP!
I HAVE TO ADMIRE YOUR TECHNIQUE...
...AND YOU'RE A QUICK STUDY!
BUT REALLY, THIS TOWN ISN'T BIG ENOUGH FOR TWO SHIELD SLINGERS!

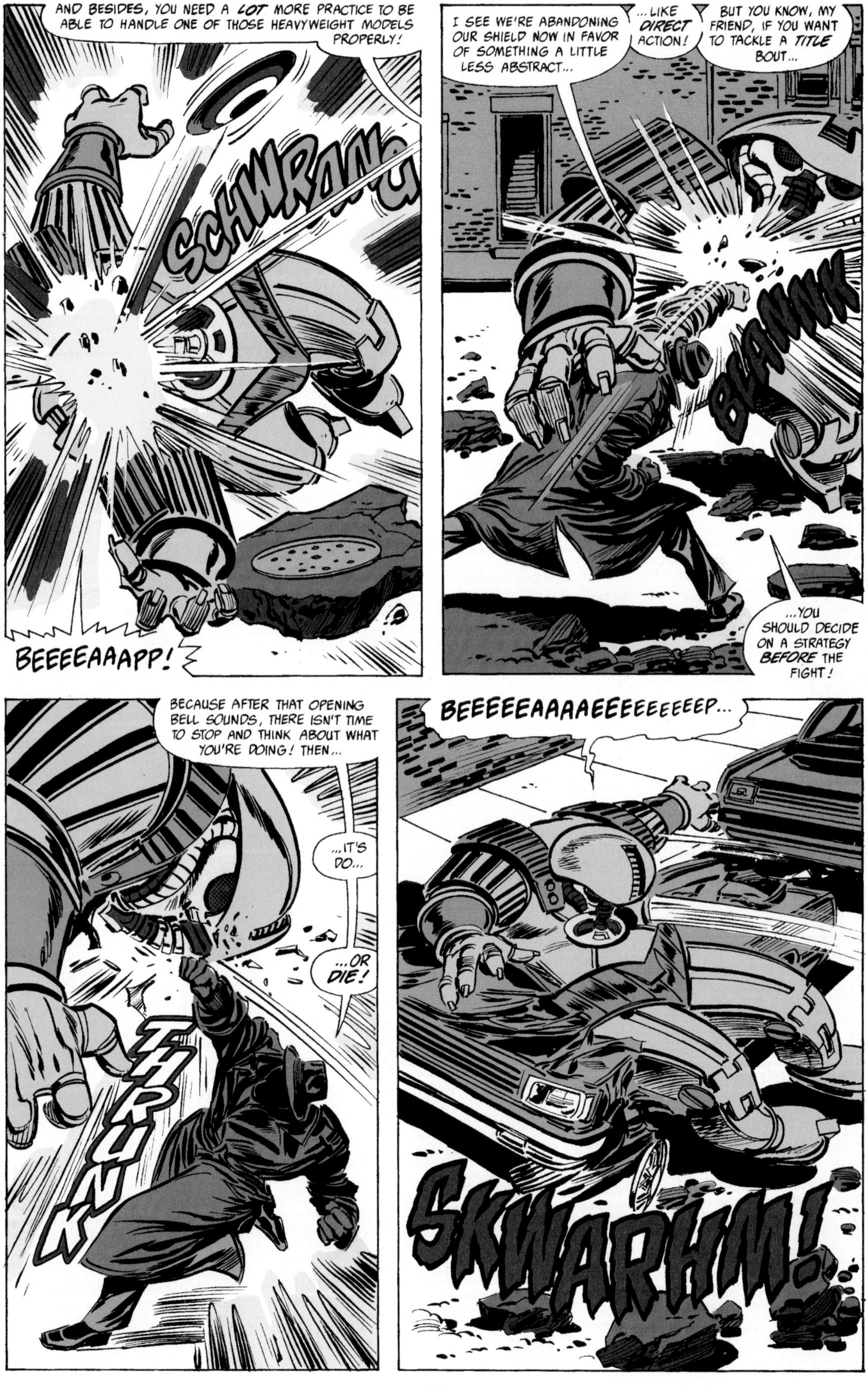
AND BESIDES, YOU NEED A LOT MORE PRACTICE TO BE ABLE TO HANDLE ONE OF THOSE HEAVYWEIGHT MODELS PROPERLY!
SCHWRANG
BEEEEAAAPP!
I SEE WE'RE ABANDONING OUR SHIELD NOW IN FAVOR OF SOMETHING A LITTLE LESS ABSTRACT...
...LIKE DIRECT ACTION!
BUT YOU KNOW, MY FRIEND, IF YOU WANT TO TACKLE A TITLE BOUT...
BLANNK
...YOU SHOULD DECIDE ON A STRATEGY BEFORE THE FIGHT!
BECAUSE AFTER THAT OPENING BELL SOUNDS, THERE ISN'T TIME TO STOP AND THINK ABOUT WHAT YOU'RE DOING! THEN...
...IT'S DO...
...OR DIE!
THRUNK
BEEEEEAAAAEEEEEEEEEP...
SKWARHM!

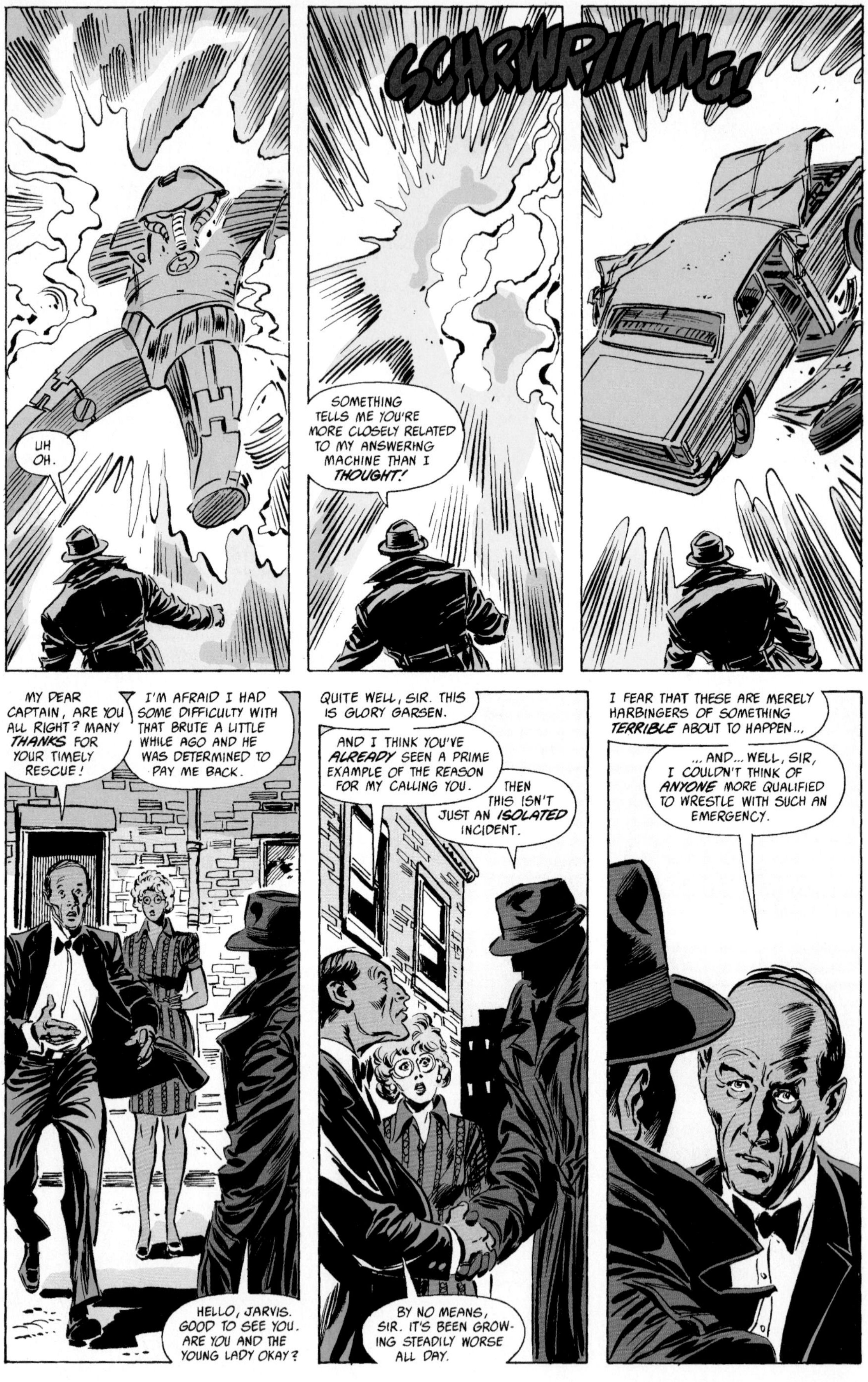
UH OH.
SCHRWRIINNG!
SOMETHING TELLS ME YOU'RE MORE CLOSELY RELATED TO MY ANSWERING MACHINE THAN I THOUGHT!
MY DEAR CAPTAIN, ARE YOU ALL RIGHT? MANY THANKS FOR YOUR TIMELY RESCUE!
I'M AFRAID I HAD SOME DIFFICULTY WITH THAT BRUTE A LITTLE WHILE AGO AND HE WAS DETERMINED TO PAY ME BACK.
HELLO, JARVIS. GOOD TO SEE YOU. ARE YOU AND THE YOUNG LADY OKAY?
QUITE WELL, SIR. THIS IS GLORY GARSEN.
AND I THINK YOU'VE ALREADY SEEN A PRIME EXAMPLE OF THE REASON FOR MY CALLING YOU.
THEN THIS ISN'T JUST AN ISOLATED INCIDENT.
BY NO MEANS, SIR. IT'S BEEN GROWING STEADILY WORSE ALL DAY.
I FEAR THAT THESE ARE MERELY HARBINGERS OF SOMETHING TERRIBLE ABOUT TO HAPPEN...
... AND... WELL, SIR, I COULDN'T THINK OF ANYONE MORE QUALIFIED TO WRESTLE WITH SUCH AN EMERGENCY.

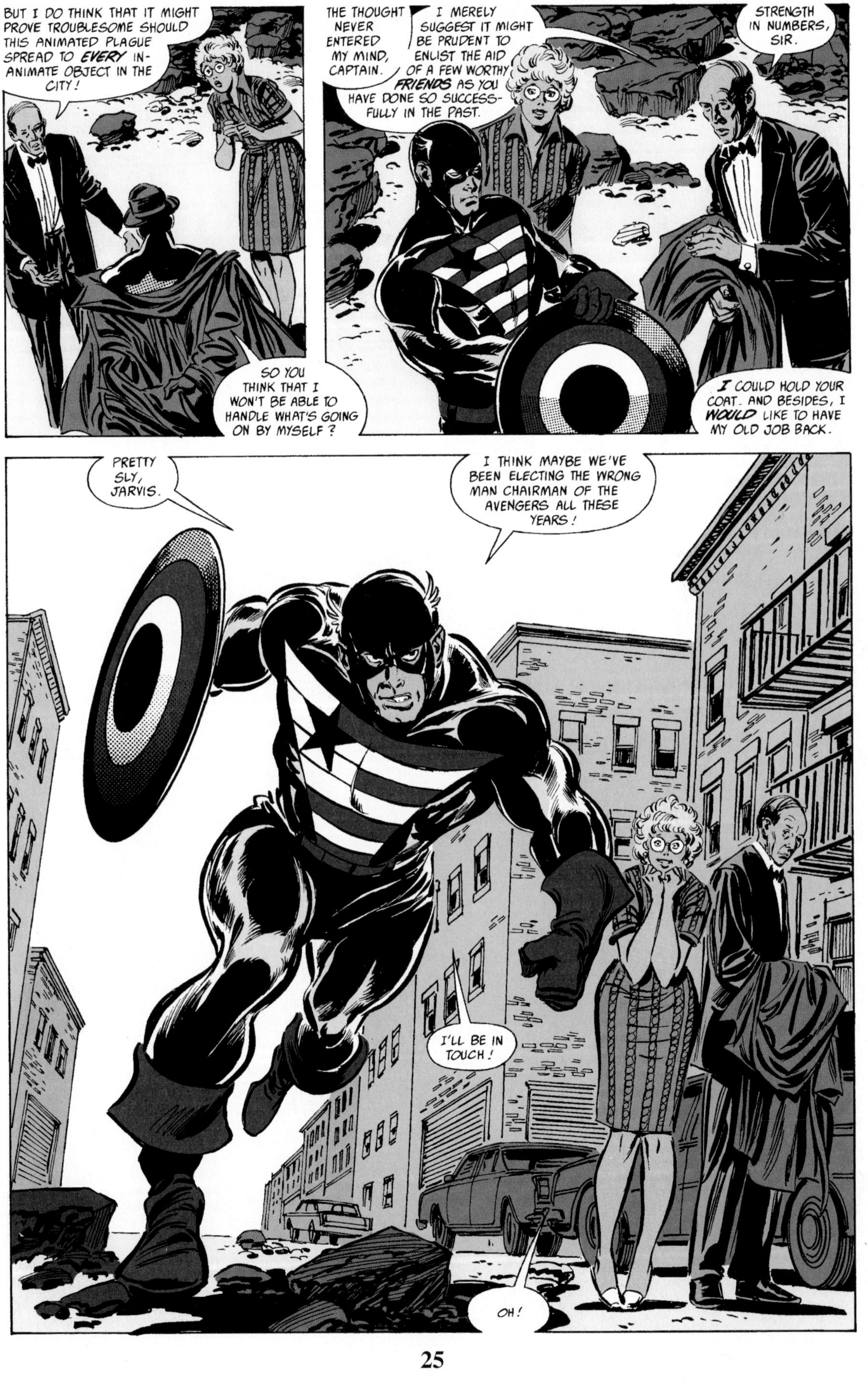
BUT I DO THINK THAT IT MIGHT PROVE TROUBLESOME SHOULD THIS ANIMATED PLAGUE SPREAD TO EVERY INANIMATE OBJECT IN THE CITY!
SO YOU THINK THAT I WON'T BE ABLE TO HANDLE WHAT'S GOING ON BY MYSELF?
THE THOUGHT NEVER ENTERED MY MIND, CAPTAIN.
I MERELY SUGGEST IT MIGHT BE PRUDENT TO ENLIST THE AID OF A FEW WORTHY FRIENDS AS YOU HAVE DONE SO SUCCESSFULLY IN THE PAST.
STRENGTH IN NUMBERS, SIR.
I COULD HOLD YOUR COAT. AND BESIDES, I WOULD LIKE TO HAVE MY OLD JOB BACK.
PRETTY SLY, JARVIS.
I THINK MAYBE WE'VE BEEN ELECTING THE WRONG MAN CHAIRMAN OF THE AVENGERS ALL THESE YEARS!
I'LL BE IN TOUCH!
OH!

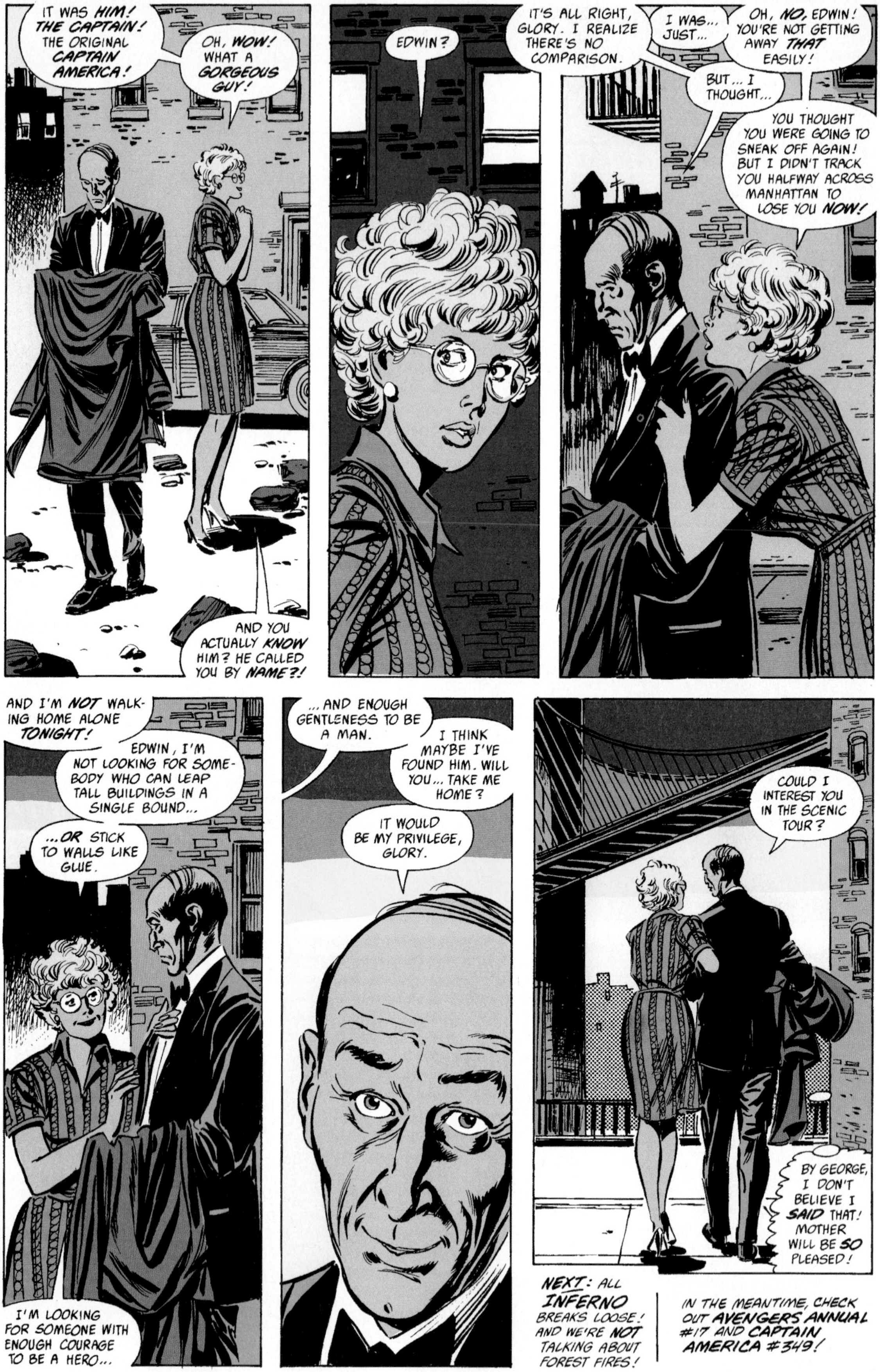

IT WAS HIM! THE CAPTAIN! THE ORIGINAL CAPTAIN AMERICA!
OH, WOW! WHAT A GORGEOUS GUY!
AND YOU ACTUALLY KNOW HIM? HE CALLED YOU BY NAME?!
EDWIN?
IT'S ALL RIGHT, GLORY. I REALIZE THERE'S NO COMPARISON.
I WAS... JUST...
OH, NO, EDWIN! YOU'RE NOT GETTING AWAY THAT EASILY!
BUT... I THOUGHT...
YOU THOUGHT YOU WERE GOING TO SNEAK OFF AGAIN! BUT I DIDN'T TRACK YOU HALFWAY ACROSS MANHATTAN TO LOSE YOU NOW!
AND I'M NOT WALKING HOME ALONE TONIGHT!
EDWIN, I'M NOT LOOKING FOR SOMEBODY WHO CAN LEAP TALL BUILDINGS IN A SINGLE BOUND...
...OR STICK TO WALLS LIKE GLUE.
I'M LOOKING FOR SOMEONE WITH ENOUGH COURAGE TO BE A HERO...
...AND ENOUGH GENTLENESS TO BE A MAN.
I THINK MAYBE I'VE FOUND HIM. WILL YOU... TAKE ME HOME?
IT WOULD BE MY PRIVILEGE, GLORY.
COULD I INTEREST YOU IN THE SCENIC TOUR?
BY GEORGE, I DON'T BELIEVE I SAID THAT! MOTHER WILL BE SO PLEASED!
NEXT: ALL INFERNO BREAKS LOOSE! AND WE'RE NOT TALKING ABOUT FOREST FIRES!
IN THE MEANTIME, CHECK OUT AVENGERS ANNUAL #17 AND CAPTAIN AMERICA #349!

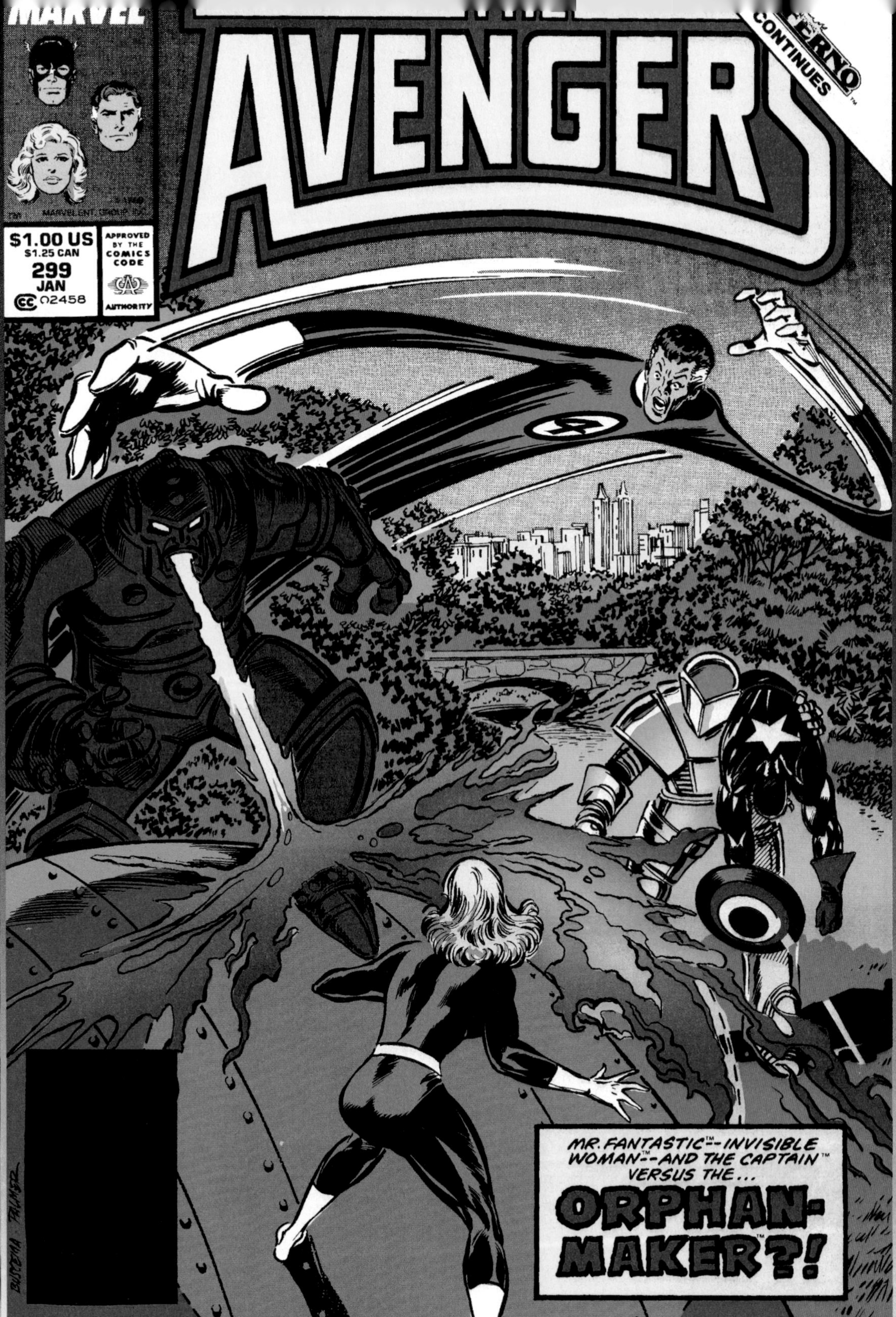
MARVEL
AVENGERS
CONTINUES
$1.00 US
$1.25 CAN
299
JAN
APPROVED BY THE COMICS CODE AUTHORITY
MR. FANTASTIC--INVISIBLE WOMAN--AND THE CAPTAIN VERSUS THE...
ORPHAN-MAKER?!

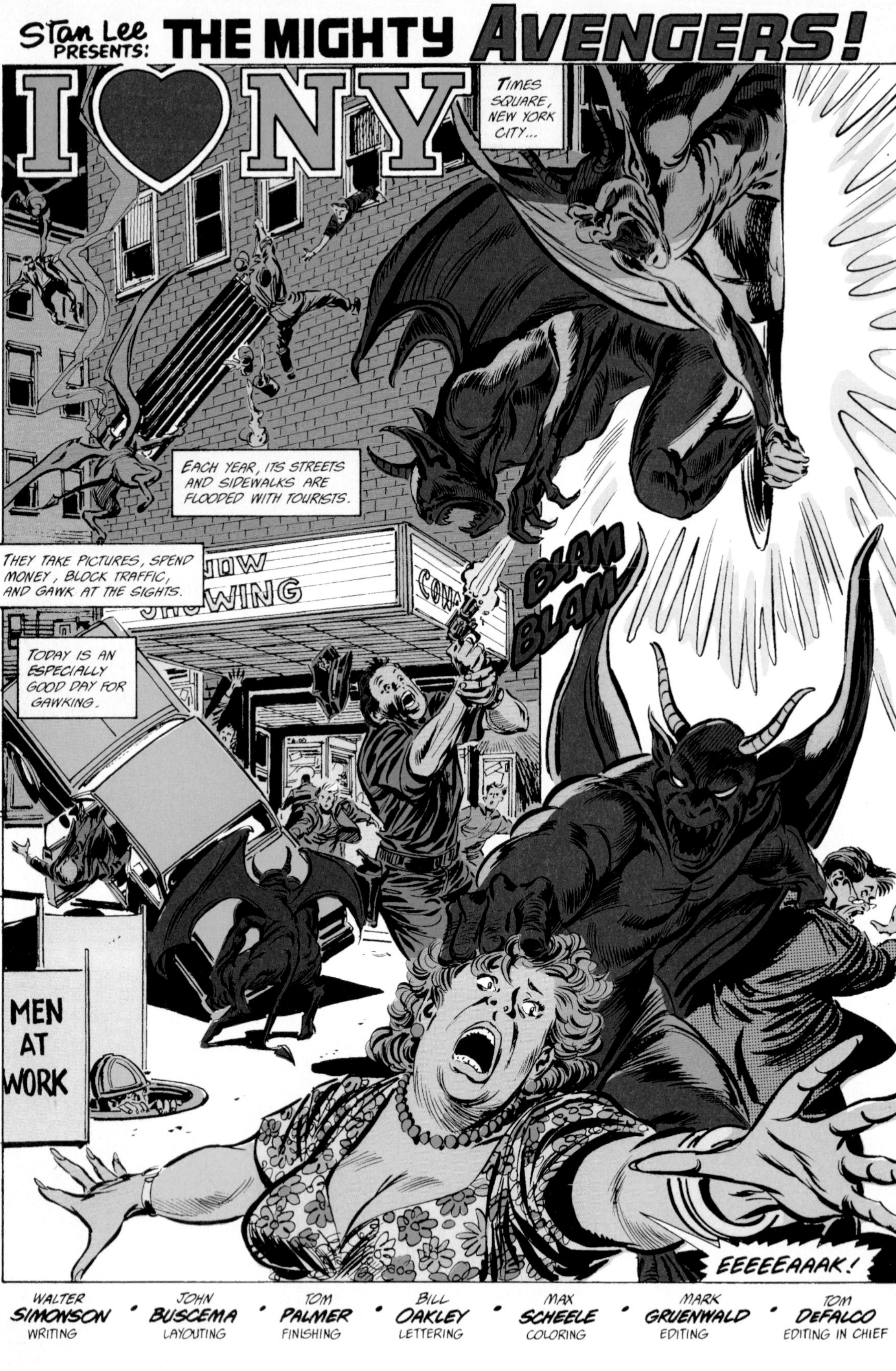
Stan Lee PRESENTS: THE MIGHTY AVENGERS!
I ♥ NY
TIMES SQUARE, NEW YORK CITY...
EACH YEAR, ITS STREETS AND SIDEWALKS ARE FLOODED WITH TOURISTS.
THEY TAKE PICTURES, SPEND MONEY, BLOCK TRAFFIC, AND GAWK AT THE SIGHTS.
TODAY IS AN ESPECIALLY GOOD DAY FOR GAWKING.
BLAM BLAM
MEN AT WORK
EEEEEAAAK!
WALTER SIMONSON WRITING • JOHN BUSCEMA LAYOUTING • TOM PALMER FINISHING • BILL OAKLEY LETTERING • MAX SCHEELE COLORING • MARK GRUENWALD EDITING • TOM DEFALCO EDITING IN CHIEF

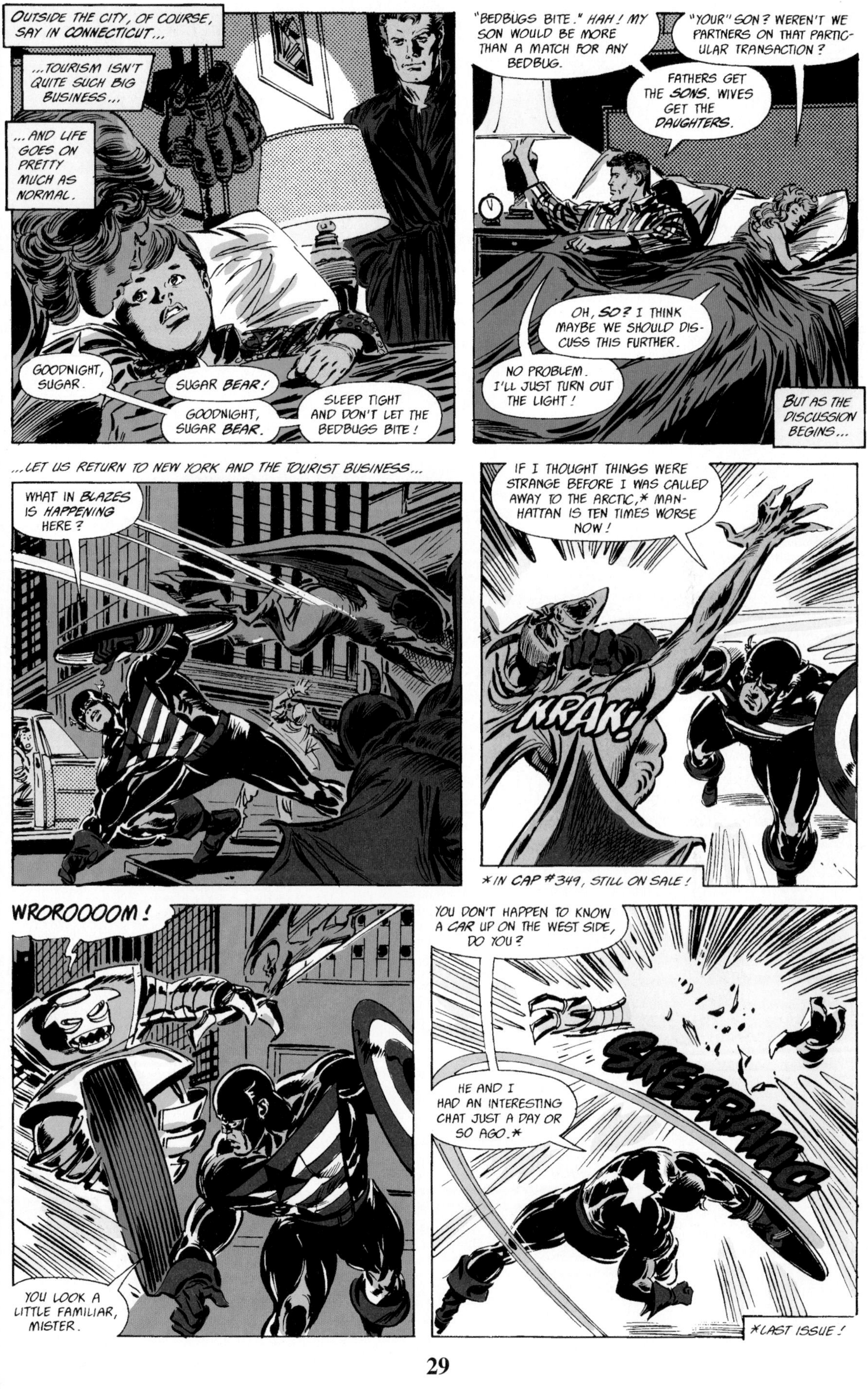

OUTSIDE THE CITY, OF COURSE, SAY IN CONNECTICUT...
...TOURISM ISN'T QUITE SUCH BIG BUSINESS...
...AND LIFE GOES ON PRETTY MUCH AS NORMAL.
GOODNIGHT, SUGAR.
SUGAR BEAR!
GOODNIGHT, SUGAR BEAR.
SLEEP TIGHT AND DON'T LET THE BEDBUGS BITE!
"BEDBUGS BITE." HAH! MY SON WOULD BE MORE THAN A MATCH FOR ANY BEDBUG.
"YOUR" SON? WEREN'T WE PARTNERS ON THAT PARTICULAR TRANSACTION?
FATHERS GET THE SONS. WIVES GET THE DAUGHTERS.
OH, SO? I THINK MAYBE WE SHOULD DISCUSS THIS FURTHER.
NO PROBLEM. I'LL JUST TURN OUT THE LIGHT!
BUT AS THE DISCUSSION BEGINS...
...LET US RETURN TO NEW YORK AND THE TOURIST BUSINESS...
WHAT IN BLAZES IS HAPPENING HERE?
IF I THOUGHT THINGS WERE STRANGE BEFORE I WAS CALLED AWAY TO THE ARCTIC,* MANHATTAN IS TEN TIMES WORSE NOW!
KRAK!
*IN CAP #349, STILL ON SALE!
WROROOOOM!
YOU LOOK A LITTLE FAMILIAR, MISTER.
YOU DON'T HAPPEN TO KNOW A CAR UP ON THE WEST SIDE, DO YOU?
HE AND I HAD AN INTERESTING CHAT JUST A DAY OR SO AGO.*
SKEERANG
*LAST ISSUE!

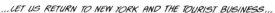

ANOTHER ONE! IT LOOKS LIKE TRANSFORMERS ARE ALL THE RAGE THIS WEEK!

ZINNG!

JUST LIKE THAT CAR!

AND JUST IN TIME, TOO!

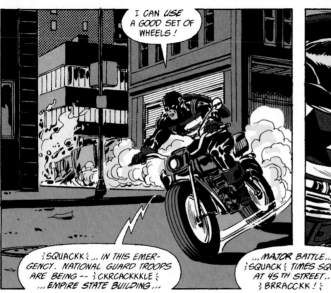

I CAN USE A GOOD SET OF WHEELS!

§SQUACKK§ ...IN THIS EMERGENCY. NATIONAL GUARD TROOPS ARE BEING -- §CKRCACKKKLE§ ...EMPIRE STATE BUILDING ...

THAT'S ONLY A FEW BLOCKS FROM HERE!

...MAJOR BATTLE... §SQUACK§ TIMES SQUARE AT 45TH STREET... §BRRACCKK!§

AND MOMENTS LATER...

·UP AHEAD! THAT MUST BE THE BATTLE... BUT IT LOOKS LIKE THESE CREATURES ARE HAVING A TOUGH TIME OF IT!

SO WHO'S GIVING IT TO THEM?

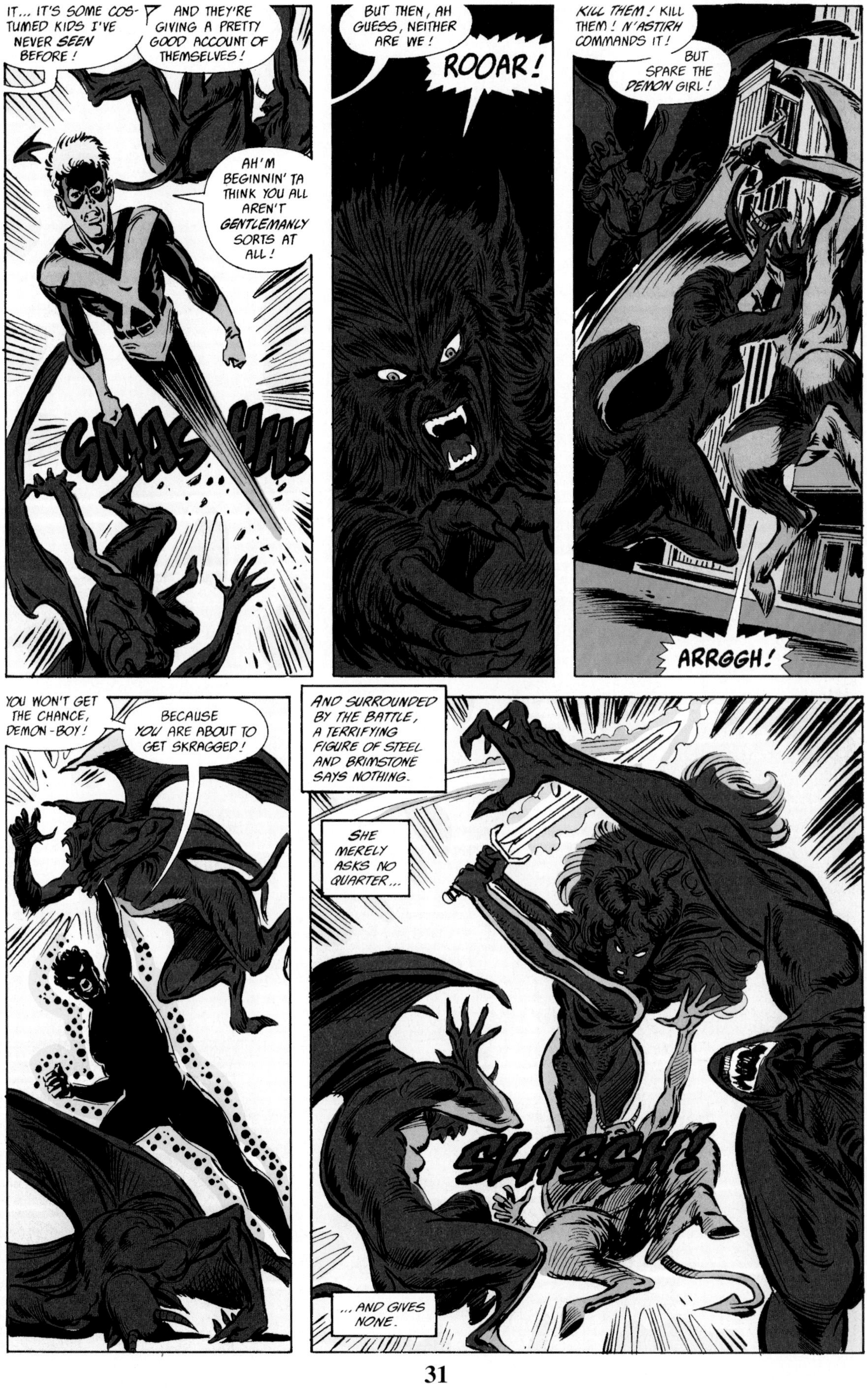
IT... IT'S SOME COS-TUMED KIDS I'VE NEVER SEEN BEFORE!
AND THEY'RE GIVING A PRETTY GOOD ACCOUNT OF THEMSELVES!
AH'M BEGINNIN' TA THINK YOU ALL AREN'T GENTLEMANLY SORTS AT ALL!
SMASHHH!
BUT THEN, AH GUESS, NEITHER ARE WE!
ROOAR!
KILL THEM! KILL THEM! N'ASTIRH COMMANDS IT!
BUT SPARE THE DEMON GIRL!
ARRGGH!
YOU WON'T GET THE CHANCE, DEMON-BOY!
BECAUSE YOU ARE ABOUT TO GET SKRAGGED!
AND SURROUNDED BY THE BATTLE, A TERRIFYING FIGURE OF STEEL AND BRIMSTONE SAYS NOTHING.
SHE MERELY ASKS NO QUARTER...
SLASSH!
...AND GIVES NONE.

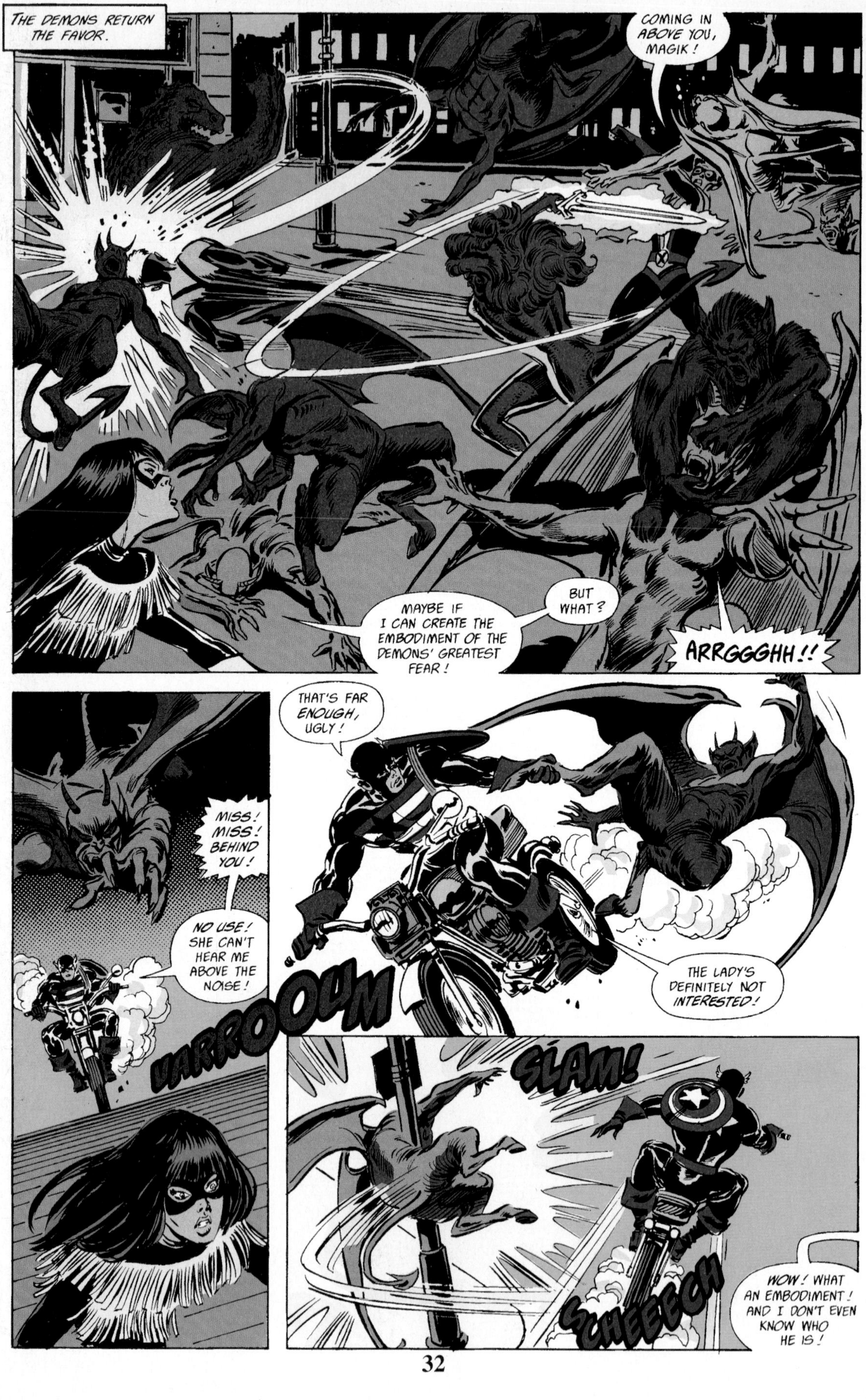
THE DEMONS RETURN THE FAVOR.
COMING IN ABOVE YOU, MAGIK!
MAYBE IF I CAN CREATE THE EMBODIMENT OF THE DEMONS' GREATEST FEAR!
BUT WHAT?
ARRGGGHH!!
MISS! MISS! BEHIND YOU!
NO USE! SHE CAN'T HEAR ME ABOVE THE NOISE!
VARROOOUM
THAT'S FAR ENOUGH, UGLY!
THE LADY'S DEFINITELY NOT INTERESTED!
SLAM!
SCHEEECH
WOW! WHAT AN EMBODIMENT! AND I DON'T EVEN KNOW WHO HE IS!

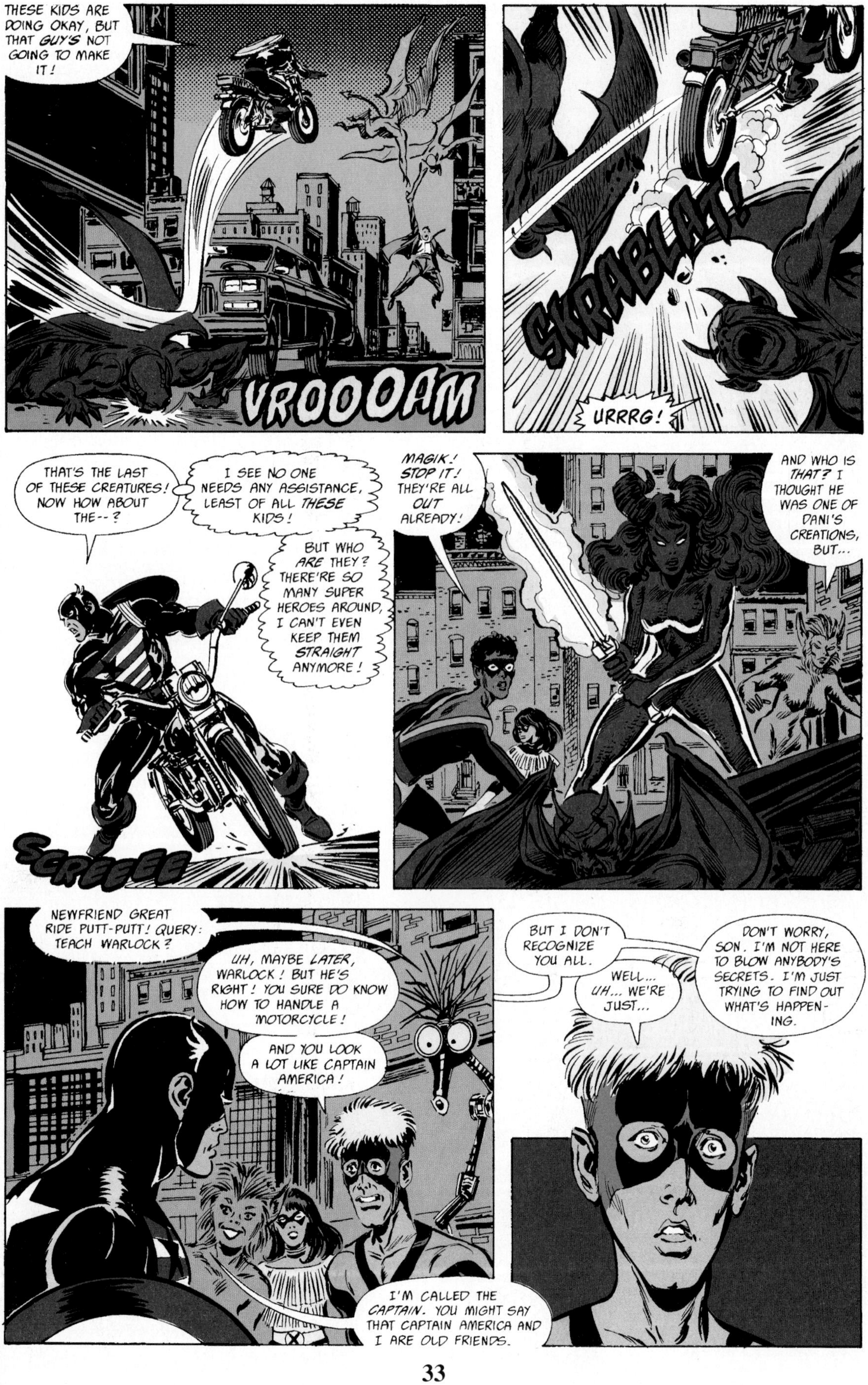
THESE KIDS ARE DOING OKAY, BUT THAT GUY'S NOT GOING TO MAKE IT!
VROOOAM
SKRABLAT!
URRRG!
THAT'S THE LAST OF THESE CREATURES! NOW HOW ABOUT THE--?
I SEE NO ONE NEEDS ANY ASSISTANCE, LEAST OF ALL THESE KIDS!
BUT WHO ARE THEY? THERE'RE SO MANY SUPER HEROES AROUND, I CAN'T EVEN KEEP THEM STRAIGHT ANYMORE!
SCREEEEE
MAGIK! STOP IT! THEY'RE ALL OUT ALREADY!
AND WHO IS THAT? I THOUGHT HE WAS ONE OF DANI'S CREATIONS, BUT...
NEWFRIEND GREAT RIDE PUTT-PUTT! QUERY: TEACH WARLOCK?
UH, MAYBE LATER, WARLOCK! BUT HE'S RIGHT! YOU SURE DO KNOW HOW TO HANDLE A MOTORCYCLE!
AND YOU LOOK A LOT LIKE CAPTAIN AMERICA!
I'M CALLED THE CAPTAIN. YOU MIGHT SAY THAT CAPTAIN AMERICA AND I ARE OLD FRIENDS.
BUT I DON'T RECOGNIZE YOU ALL.
WELL... UH... WE'RE JUST...
DON'T WORRY, SON. I'M NOT HERE TO BLOW ANYBODY'S SECRETS. I'M JUST TRYING TO FIND OUT WHAT'S HAPPENING.

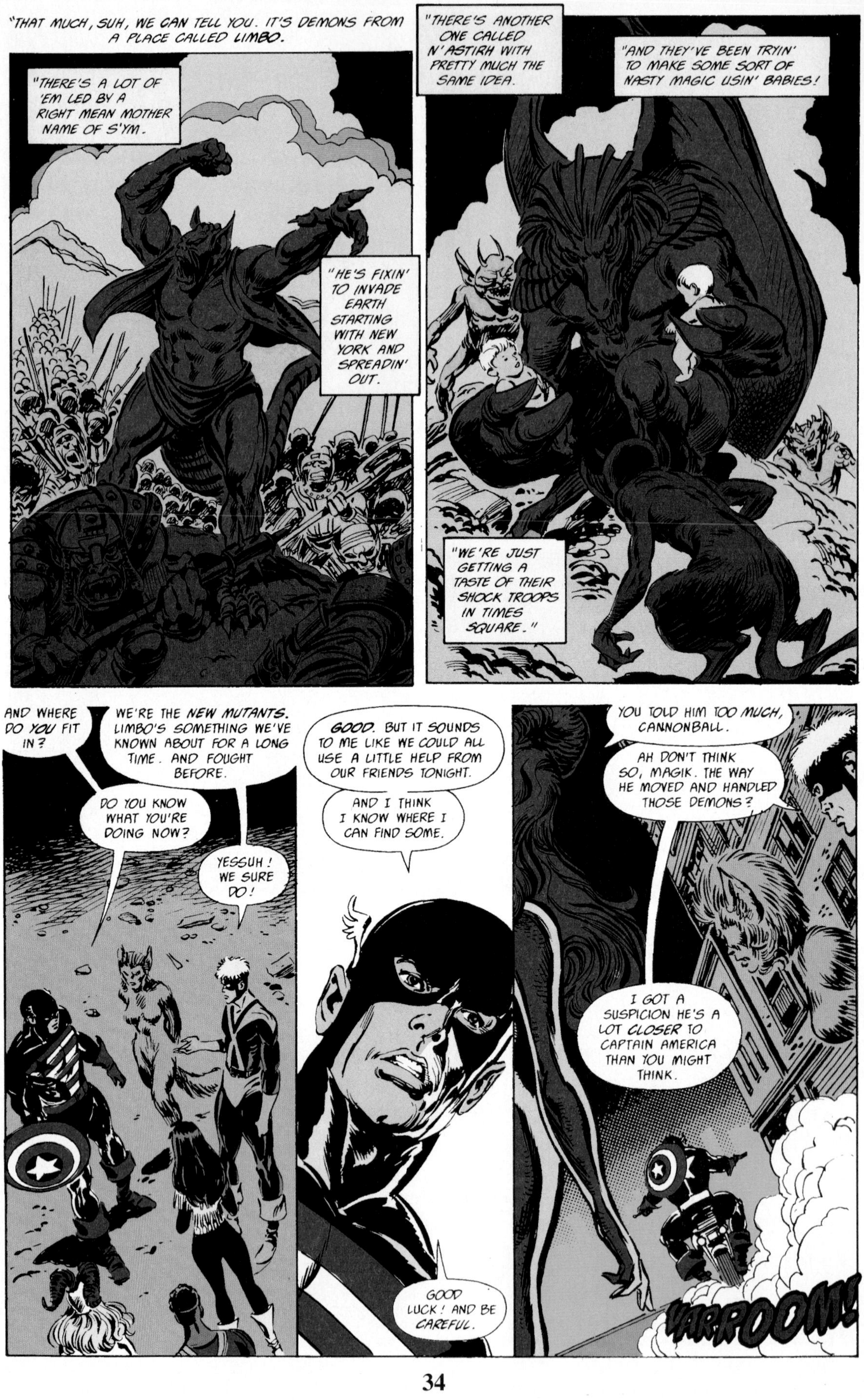
"THAT MUCH, SUH, WE CAN TELL YOU. IT'S DEMONS FROM A PLACE CALLED LIMBO.
"THERE'S A LOT OF 'EM LED BY A RIGHT MEAN MOTHER NAME OF S'YM.
"HE'S FIXIN' TO INVADE EARTH STARTING WITH NEW YORK AND SPREADIN' OUT.
"THERE'S ANOTHER ONE CALLED N'ASTIRH WITH PRETTY MUCH THE SAME IDEA.
"AND THEY'VE BEEN TRYIN' TO MAKE SOME SORT OF NASTY MAGIC USIN' BABIES!
"WE'RE JUST GETTING A TASTE OF THEIR SHOCK TROOPS IN TIMES SQUARE."
AND WHERE DO YOU FIT IN?
WE'RE THE NEW MUTANTS. LIMBO'S SOMETHING WE'VE KNOWN ABOUT FOR A LONG TIME. AND FOUGHT BEFORE.
DO YOU KNOW WHAT YOU'RE DOING NOW?
YESSUH! WE SURE DO!
GOOD. BUT IT SOUNDS TO ME LIKE WE COULD ALL USE A LITTLE HELP FROM OUR FRIENDS TONIGHT.
AND I THINK I KNOW WHERE I CAN FIND SOME.
GOOD LUCK! AND BE CAREFUL.
YOU TOLD HIM TOO MUCH, CANNONBALL.
AH DON'T THINK SO, MAGIK. THE WAY HE MOVED AND HANDLED THOSE DEMONS?
I GOT A SUSPICION HE'S A LOT CLOSER TO CAPTAIN AMERICA THAN YOU MIGHT THINK.
VARROOM!

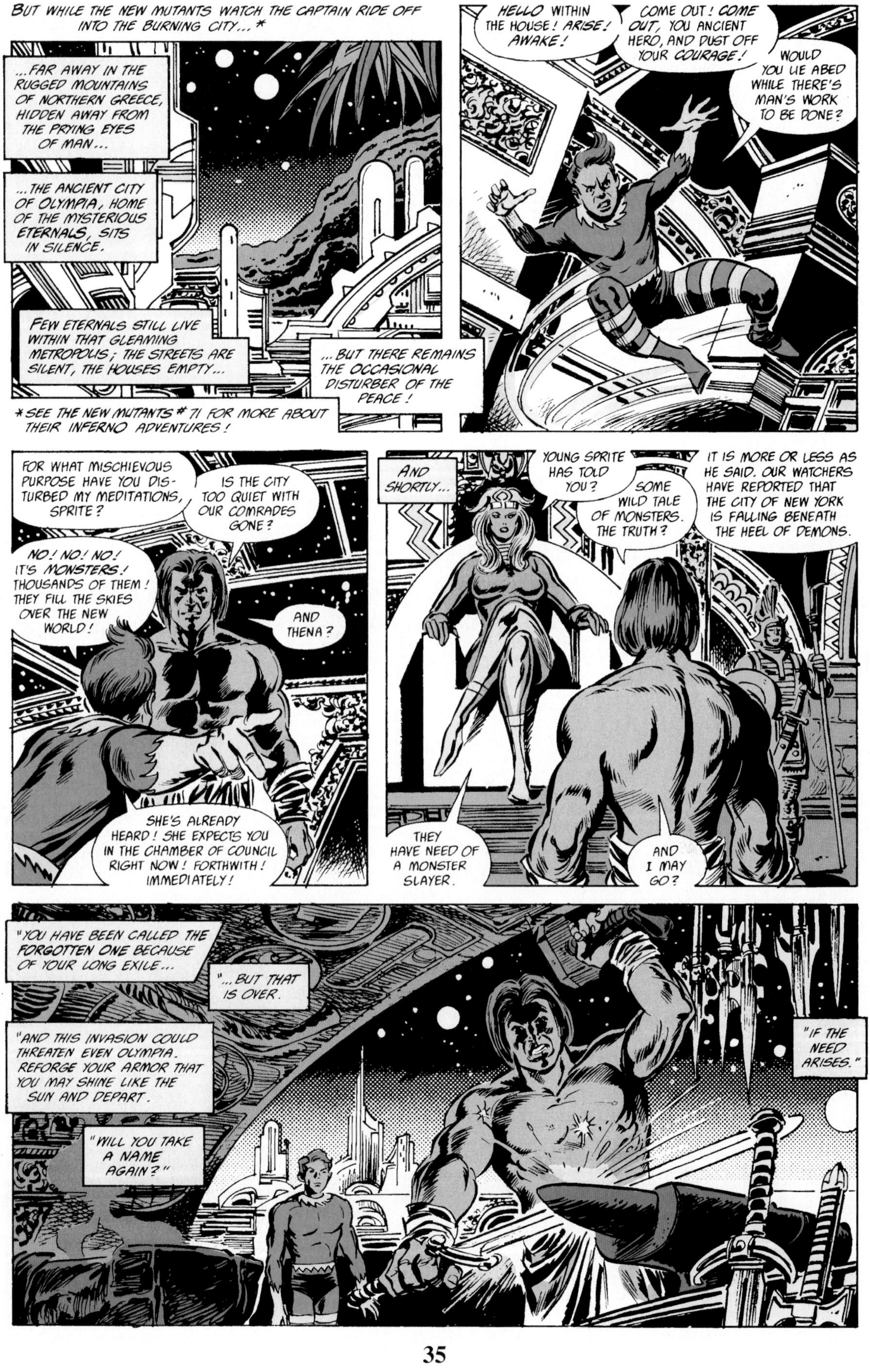

BUT WHILE THE NEW MUTANTS WATCH THE CAPTAIN RIDE OFF INTO THE BURNING CITY... *
...FAR AWAY IN THE RUGGED MOUNTAINS OF NORTHERN GREECE, HIDDEN AWAY FROM THE PRYING EYES OF MAN...
...THE ANCIENT CITY OF OLYMPIA, HOME OF THE MYSTERIOUS ETERNALS, SITS IN SILENCE.
FEW ETERNALS STILL LIVE WITHIN THAT GLEAMING METROPOLIS; THE STREETS ARE SILENT, THE HOUSES EMPTY...
...BUT THERE REMAINS THE OCCASIONAL DISTURBER OF THE PEACE!
* SEE THE NEW MUTANTS # 71 FOR MORE ABOUT THEIR INFERNO ADVENTURES!
HELLO WITHIN THE HOUSE! ARISE! AWAKE!
COME OUT! COME OUT, YOU ANCIENT HERO, AND DUST OFF YOUR COURAGE!
WOULD YOU LIE ABED WHILE THERE'S MAN'S WORK TO BE DONE?
FOR WHAT MISCHIEVOUS PURPOSE HAVE YOU DISTURBED MY MEDITATIONS, SPRITE?
IS THE CITY TOO QUIET WITH OUR COMRADES GONE?
NO! NO! NO! IT'S MONSTERS! THOUSANDS OF THEM! THEY FILL THE SKIES OVER THE NEW WORLD!
AND THENA?
SHE'S ALREADY HEARD! SHE EXPECTS YOU IN THE CHAMBER OF COUNCIL RIGHT NOW! FORTHWITH! IMMEDIATELY!
AND SHORTLY...
YOUNG SPRITE HAS TOLD YOU?
SOME WILD TALE OF MONSTERS. THE TRUTH?
IT IS MORE OR LESS AS HE SAID. OUR WATCHERS HAVE REPORTED THAT THE CITY OF NEW YORK IS FALLING BENEATH THE HEEL OF DEMONS.
THEY HAVE NEED OF A MONSTER SLAYER.
AND I MAY GO?
"YOU HAVE BEEN CALLED THE FORGOTTEN ONE BECAUSE OF YOUR LONG EXILE...
"...BUT THAT IS OVER.
"AND THIS INVASION COULD THREATEN EVEN OLYMPIA. REFORGE YOUR ARMOR THAT YOU MAY SHINE LIKE THE SUN AND DEPART.
"WILL YOU TAKE A NAME AGAIN?"
"IF THE NEED ARISES."

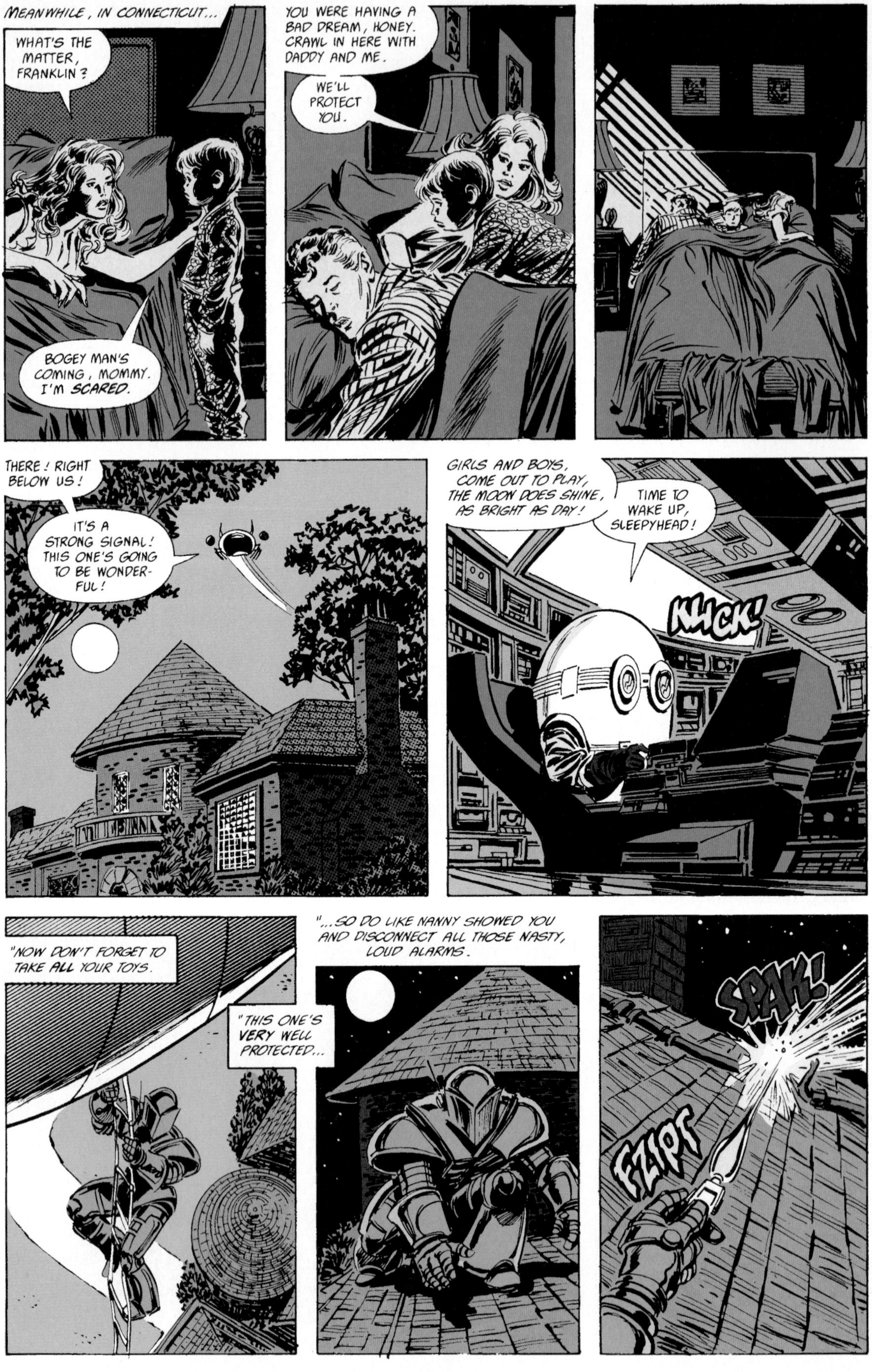
MEANWHILE, IN CONNECTICUT...
WHAT'S THE MATTER, FRANKLIN?
BOGEY MAN'S COMING, MOMMY. I'M SCARED.
YOU WERE HAVING A BAD DREAM, HONEY. CRAWL IN HERE WITH DADDY AND ME.
WE'LL PROTECT YOU.
THERE! RIGHT BELOW US!
IT'S A STRONG SIGNAL! THIS ONE'S GOING TO BE WONDERFUL!
GIRLS AND BOYS, COME OUT TO PLAY, THE MOON DOES SHINE, AS BRIGHT AS DAY!
TIME TO WAKE UP, SLEEPYHEAD!
KLICK!
"NOW DON'T FORGET TO TAKE ALL YOUR TOYS.
"...SO DO LIKE NANNY SHOWED YOU AND DISCONNECT ALL THOSE NASTY, LOUD ALARMS.
"THIS ONE'S VERY WELL PROTECTED...
SPAK!
FZIPT

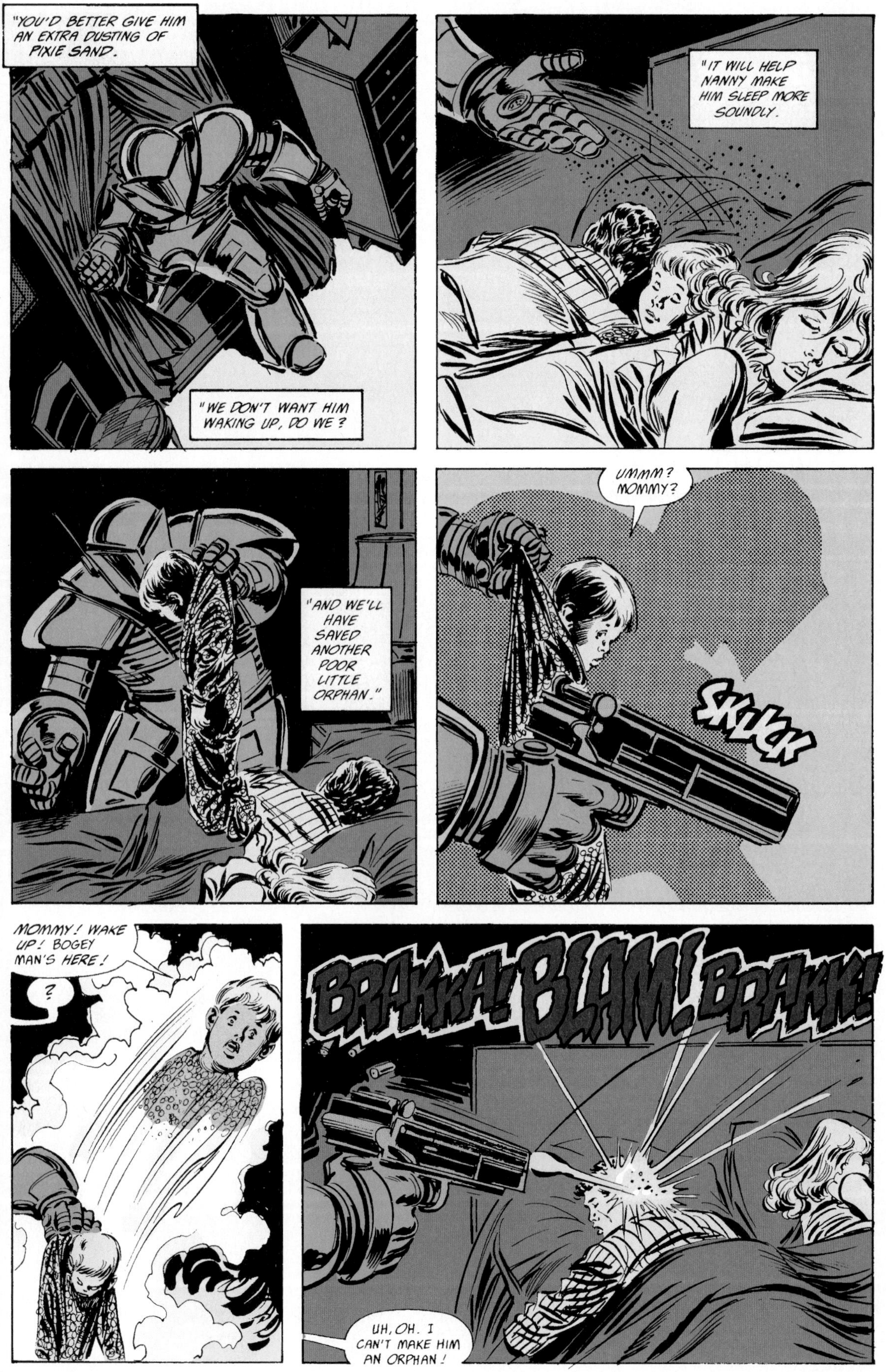
"YOU'D BETTER GIVE HIM AN EXTRA DUSTING OF PIXIE SAND.
"WE DON'T WANT HIM WAKING UP, DO WE?
"IT WILL HELP NANNY MAKE HIM SLEEP MORE SOUNDLY.
"AND WE'LL HAVE SAVED ANOTHER POOR LITTLE ORPHAN."
UMMM? MOMMY?
SKLICK
MOMMY! WAKE UP! BOGEY MAN'S HERE!
?
BRAKKA! BLAM! BRAKK!
UH, OH. I CAN'T MAKE HIM AN ORPHAN!

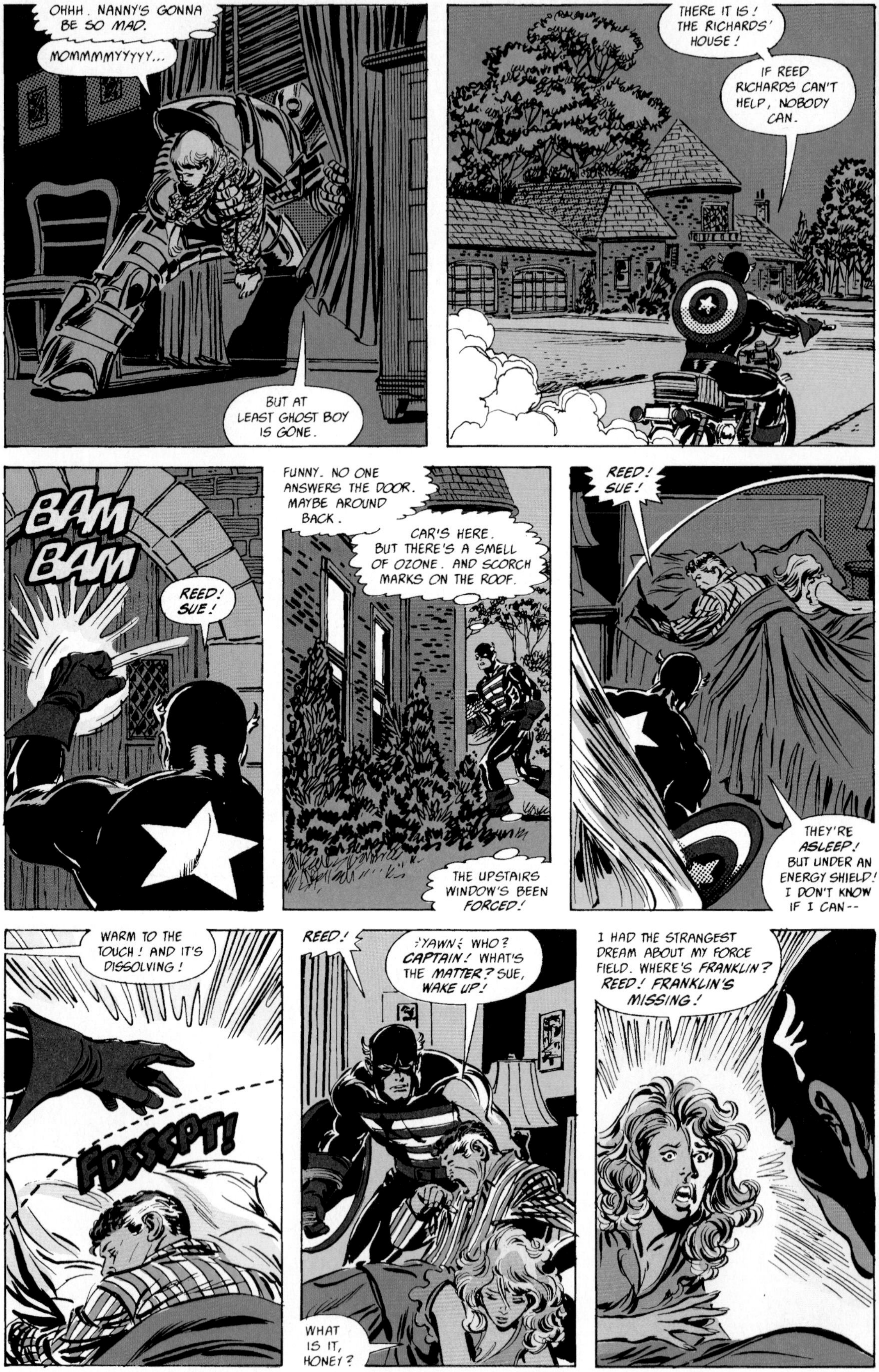
OHHH. NANNY'S GONNA BE SO MAD.
MOMMMMYYYYY...
BUT AT LEAST GHOST BOY IS GONE.
THERE IT IS! THE RICHARDS' HOUSE!
IF REED RICHARDS CAN'T HELP, NOBODY CAN.
BAM BAM
REED! SUE!
FUNNY. NO ONE ANSWERS THE DOOR. MAYBE AROUND BACK.
CAR'S HERE. BUT THERE'S A SMELL OF OZONE. AND SCORCH MARKS ON THE ROOF.
THE UPSTAIRS WINDOW'S BEEN FORCED!
REED! SUE!
THEY'RE ASLEEP! BUT UNDER AN ENERGY SHIELD! I DON'T KNOW IF I CAN--
WARM TO THE TOUCH! AND IT'S DISSOLVING!
FDSSSPT!
REED!
;YAWN; WHO? CAPTAIN! WHAT'S THE MATTER? SUE, WAKE UP!
WHAT IS IT, HONEY?
I HAD THE STRANGEST DREAM ABOUT MY FORCE FIELD. WHERE'S FRANKLIN? REED! FRANKLIN'S MISSING!

CHECK HIS BED, HONEY! *HURRY!*

WHAT'S *GOING ON,* CAPTAIN?

YOU... *KNOW* WHO I AM?

I WASN'T THE LEADER OF THE FANTASTIC FOUR FOR YEARS WITHOUT LEARNING HOW TO KEEP TRACK OF SUPER HEROES, CAPTAIN.

EVEN WHEN THEY HAVE NEW NAMES AND COSTUMES.

MY PROBLEM WILL KEEP, REED.

HE'S *NOWHERE* IN THE *HOUSE!* OH, REED! WHAT'S *HAPPENED* TO HIM?

STAY CALM, HONEY. WE'LL KNOW IN A MINUTE AS SOON AS I ACTIVATE THE MONITORS.

THERE! LESS THAN AN HOUR AGO! FRANKLIN'S BEEN *KIDNAPED!*

OH, NO! BUT *WHY?*

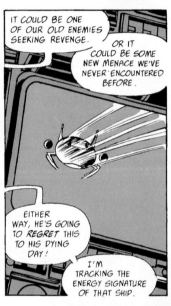

IT COULD BE ONE OF OUR OLD ENEMIES SEEKING REVENGE.

OR IT COULD BE SOME NEW MENACE WE'VE NEVER ENCOUNTERED BEFORE.

EITHER WAY, HE'S GOING TO *REGRET* THIS TO HIS DYING DAY!

I'M TRACKING THE ENERGY SIGNATURE OF THAT SHIP.

IT'S HEADING INTO NEW YORK CITY, CAPTAIN?

THAT'S WHERE *MY* PROBLEM IS, TOO.

THERE'S SOME SORT OF DIMENSIONAL DISLOCATION OCCURRING IN NEW YORK, REED. ALIEN CREATURES LIKE DEMONS ARE FLOODING IN.

I CAME FOR HELP. I DIDN'T EXPECT TO FIND *YOU* NEEDING SOME AS WELL!

LET'S MOVE IT!

MAYBE WE CAN HELP EACH OTHER.

ELSEWHERE, IN OLYMPIA...

EXCELLENT.

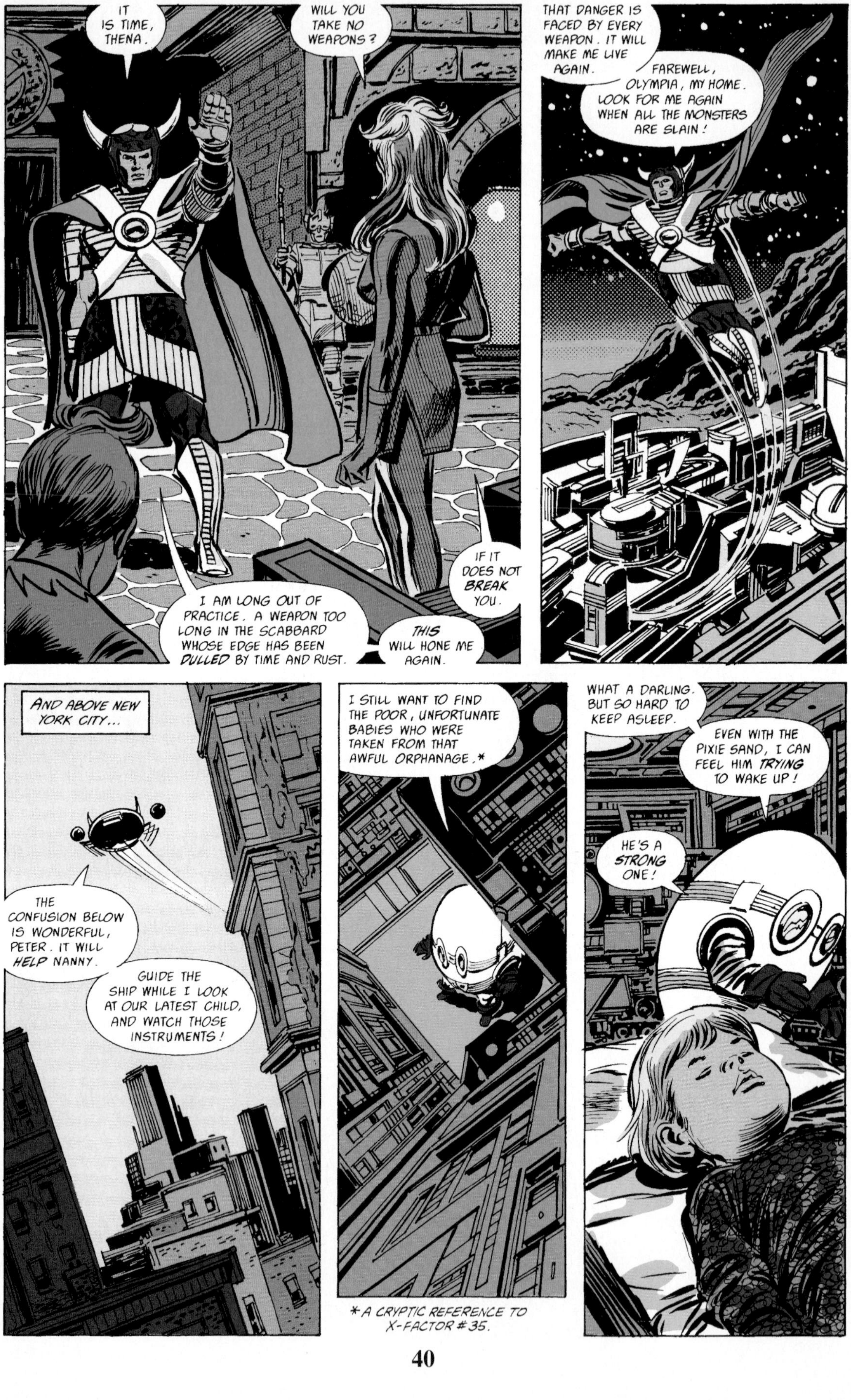
IT IS TIME, THENA.
WILL YOU TAKE NO WEAPONS?
I AM LONG OUT OF PRACTICE. A WEAPON TOO LONG IN THE SCABBARD WHOSE EDGE HAS BEEN DULLED BY TIME AND RUST.
THIS WILL HONE ME AGAIN.
IF IT DOES NOT BREAK YOU.
THAT DANGER IS FACED BY EVERY WEAPON. IT WILL MAKE ME LIVE AGAIN.
FAREWELL, OLYMPIA, MY HOME. LOOK FOR ME AGAIN WHEN ALL THE MONSTERS ARE SLAIN!
AND ABOVE NEW YORK CITY...
THE CONFUSION BELOW IS WONDERFUL, PETER. IT WILL HELP NANNY.
GUIDE THE SHIP WHILE I LOOK AT OUR LATEST CHILD, AND WATCH THOSE INSTRUMENTS!
I STILL WANT TO FIND THE POOR, UNFORTUNATE BABIES WHO WERE TAKEN FROM THAT AWFUL ORPHANAGE.*
WHAT A DARLING. BUT SO HARD TO KEEP ASLEEP.
EVEN WITH THE PIXIE SAND, I CAN FEEL HIM TRYING TO WAKE UP!
HE'S A STRONG ONE!
*A CRYPTIC REFERENCE TO X-FACTOR #35.

WHAT ARE LITTLE BOYS MADE OF? FROGS AND SNAILS AND PUPPY DOG TAILS, THAT'S WHAT LITTLE BOYS ARE MADE OF.
CELLULAR PROBES ENGAGED, RECORDING ON.
DNA STRUCTURE... CHROMOSOMAL DEPARTURES ...MUTATIONS INCLUDING... INCREDIBLE!
I MUST KNOW MORE, CHILD. YOU MUST SING FOR YOUR SUPPER.
TELL NANNY WHO YOU ARE.
FRANKLIN.
FRANKLIN WHO?
FRANKLIN RICHARDS.
OH, NO!
AND YOUR MOMMY AND DADDY'S NAMES?
SUSAN AND REED.
PETER! COME HERE AT ONCE!
YES, NANNY?
TELL ME TRULY. IS THIS CHILD AN ORPHAN?
OH, YES, NANNY!
BAD! BAD BOY! NANNY HAS TOLD YOU NEVER TO LIE!
I COULDN'T KILL THEM, NANNY! THEY WERE INSIDE A CLEAR LITTLE HOUSE!
HOLD OUT YOUR HAND!
BAD! BAD! BAD!
SKRETZH! SKRETZH!
I'M SORRY, NANNY! I'M SORRY!

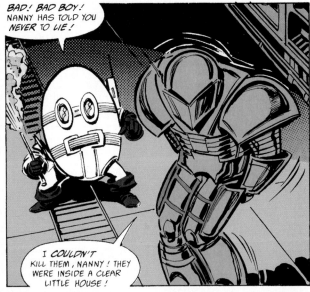

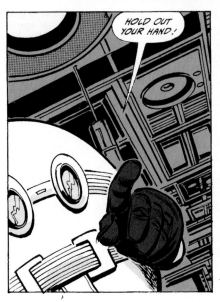

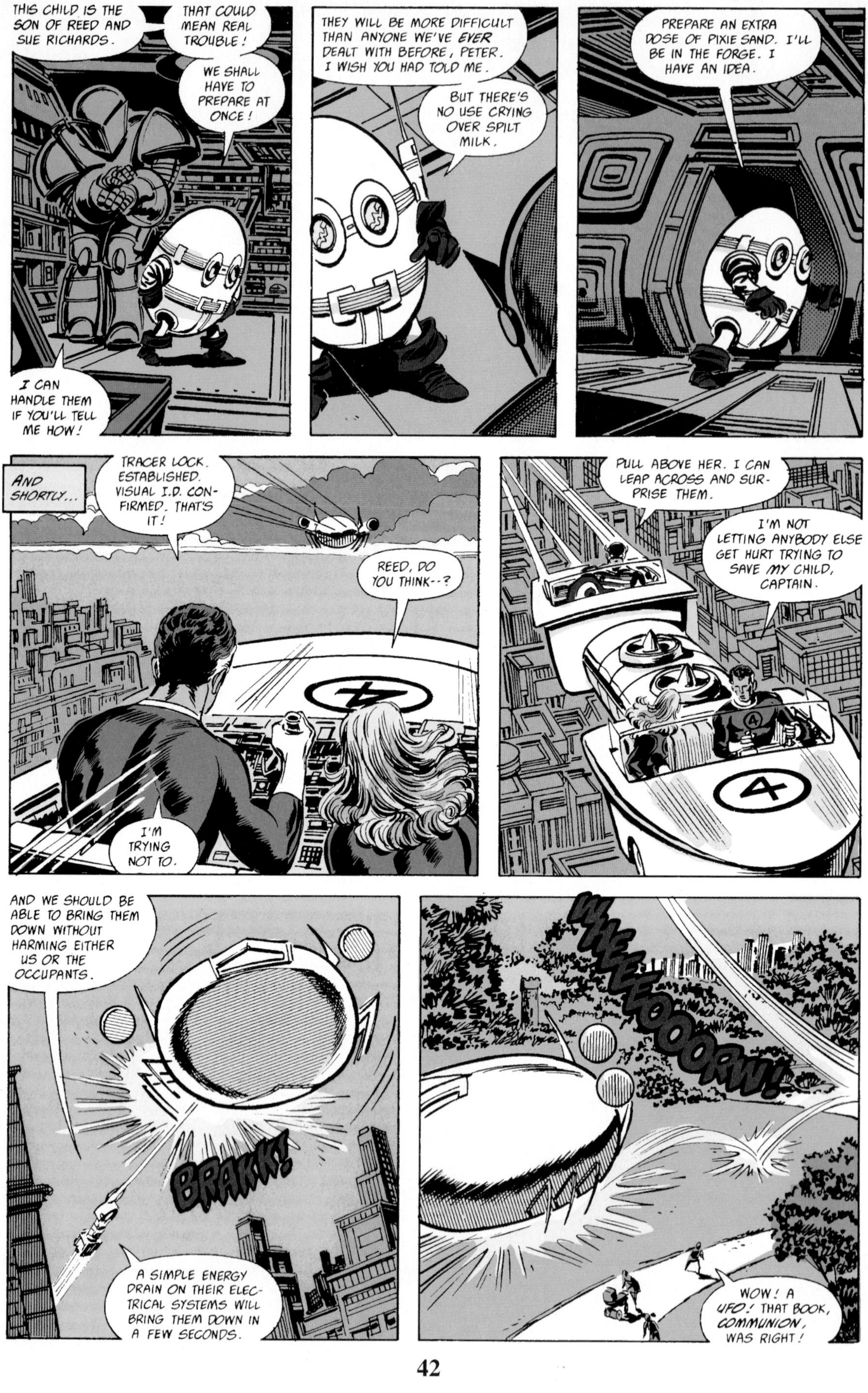
THIS CHILD IS THE SON OF REED AND SUE RICHARDS.
THAT COULD MEAN REAL TROUBLE!
WE SHALL HAVE TO PREPARE AT ONCE!
I CAN HANDLE THEM IF YOU'LL TELL ME HOW!
THEY WILL BE MORE DIFFICULT THAN ANYONE WE'VE EVER DEALT WITH BEFORE, PETER. I WISH YOU HAD TOLD ME.
BUT THERE'S NO USE CRYING OVER SPILT MILK.
PREPARE AN EXTRA DOSE OF PIXIE SAND. I'LL BE IN THE FORGE. I HAVE AN IDEA.
AND SHORTLY...
TRACER LOCK. ESTABLISHED. VISUAL I.D. CONFIRMED. THAT'S IT!
REED, DO YOU THINK--?
I'M TRYING NOT TO.
PULL ABOVE HER. I CAN LEAP ACROSS AND SURPRISE THEM.
I'M NOT LETTING ANYBODY ELSE GET HURT TRYING TO SAVE MY CHILD, CAPTAIN.
AND WE SHOULD BE ABLE TO BRING THEM DOWN WITHOUT HARMING EITHER US OR THE OCCUPANTS.
BRAKK!
A SIMPLE ENERGY DRAIN ON THEIR ELECTRICAL SYSTEMS WILL BRING THEM DOWN IN A FEW SECONDS.
WHEEEOOOORW!
WOW! A UFO! THAT BOOK, COMMUNION, WAS RIGHT!

NICELY DONE, REED! NOW IT'S MY TURN!
CAPTAIN!
PREPARE TO LAND, SUE, AND DON'T WORRY ABOUT HIM.
THERE'S NO STOPPING AN OLD WARHORSE LIKE CAP!
KATHUMP!
THE WELCOME WAGON'S READY, I SEE!
YOU'LL FIND ME A DIFFERENT KETTLE OF FISH THAN A DEFENSELESS CHILD, MISTER!
TOO SLOW!
KRANG!
I GOT UNDER HIS GUARD BUT EVEN MY SHIELD DOESN'T SEEM TO DENT WHATEVER THIS STUFF IS HE'S WEARING!
THAT ARMOR'S GOING TO MAKE IT TOUGH TO SCORE POINTS AGAINST THIS BIRD!
UHH!
AND IT DOESN'T SEEM TO SLOW HIM DOWN! BARELY ABLE TO ROLL WITH THAT PUNCH!
REED! I CAN'T WRAP A FORCE BUBBLE AROUND HIM! HE'S PROTECTED BY SOME KIND OF SCREENING DEVICE!
TRY TO LIFT HIM, HONEY!
TOO LATE!
HIS GRIP'S UNBREAKABLE!
HAVE TO BE READY TO ROLL WITH HIS THROW!
AND HOPE HE DOESN'T DECIDE TO TAKE A LITTLE TARGET PRACTICE AGAINST THE TREES!

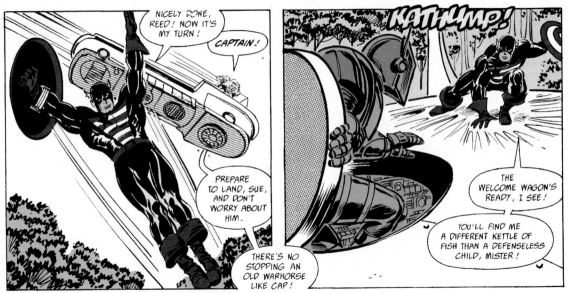

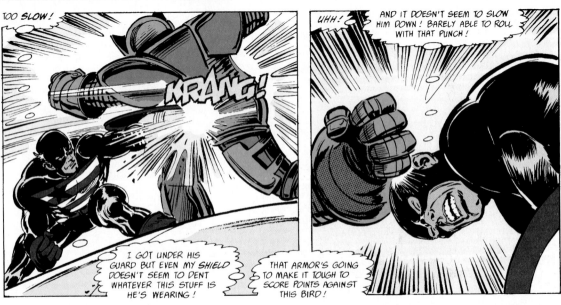

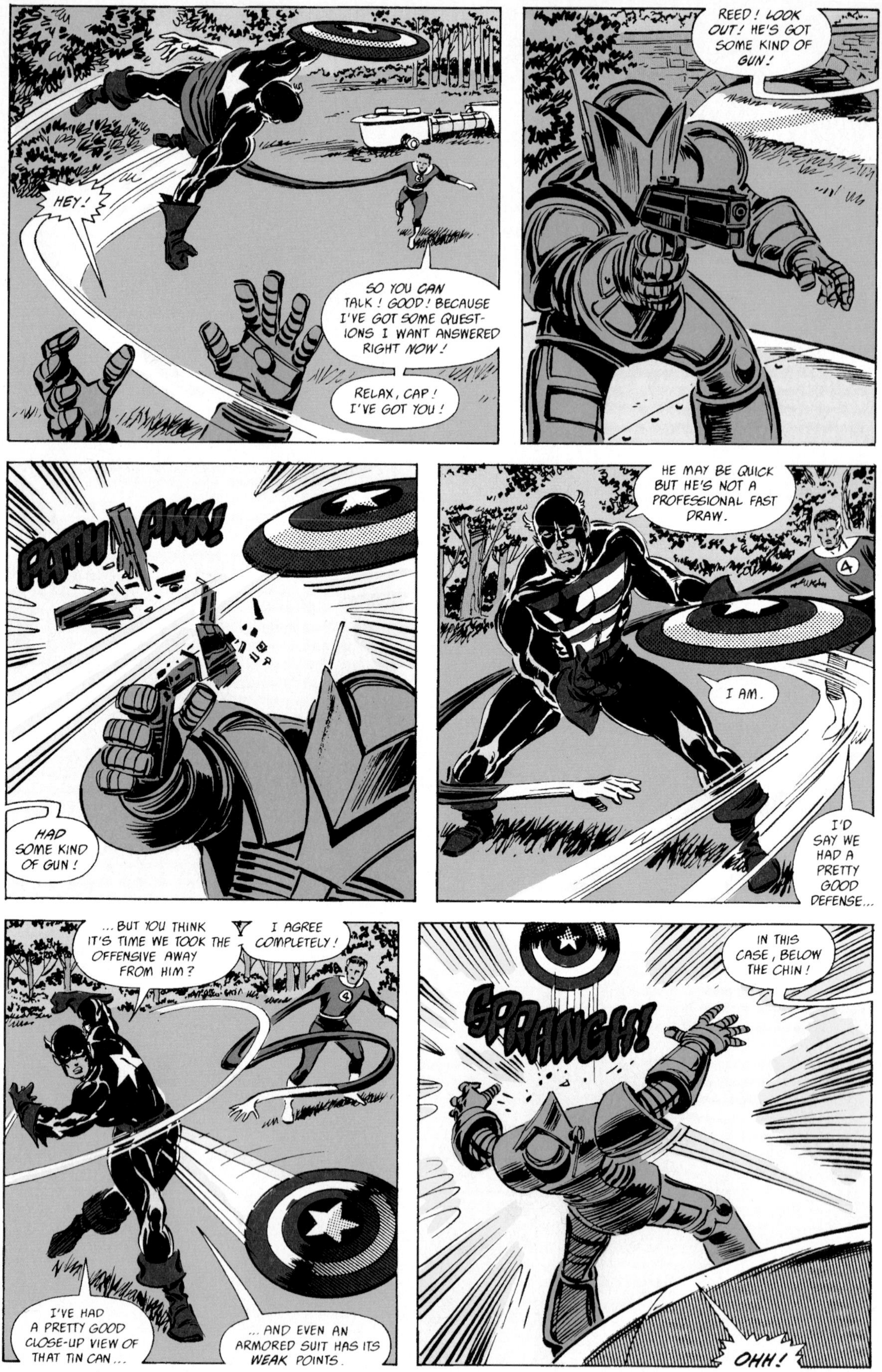
HEY!
SO YOU CAN TALK! GOOD! BECAUSE I'VE GOT SOME QUESTIONS I WANT ANSWERED RIGHT NOW!
RELAX, CAP! I'VE GOT YOU!
REED! LOOK OUT! HE'S GOT SOME KIND OF GUN!
PTTTH ... AKK!
HAD SOME KIND OF GUN!
HE MAY BE QUICK BUT HE'S NOT A PROFESSIONAL FAST DRAW.
I AM.
I'D SAY WE HAD A PRETTY GOOD DEFENSE...
...BUT YOU THINK IT'S TIME WE TOOK THE OFFENSIVE AWAY FROM HIM?
I AGREE COMPLETELY!
I'VE HAD A PRETTY GOOD CLOSE-UP VIEW OF THAT TIN CAN...
...AND EVEN AN ARMORED SUIT HAS ITS WEAK POINTS.
IN THIS CASE, BELOW THE CHIN!
SPRANGH!
OHH!

PLATHUNK!

OOOOFF!

WAAAAHH!

I'M HURT! I WANT NANNY! NANNY!

WAAAAHH!

WHAT IN THE WORLD?

NANNY! HELP ME!

WAAAH!

IT... IT SOUNDS LIKE A SMALL CHILD!

BUT HOW CAN THAT--

SKLIKT

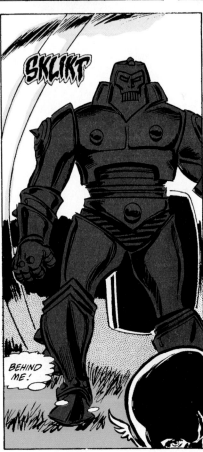

BEHIND ME!

BUT THE CAPTAIN'S SIXTH SENSE WARNS HIM A SPLIT SECOND TOO LATE! AS...

THWRAHnn!

UGGH!

45

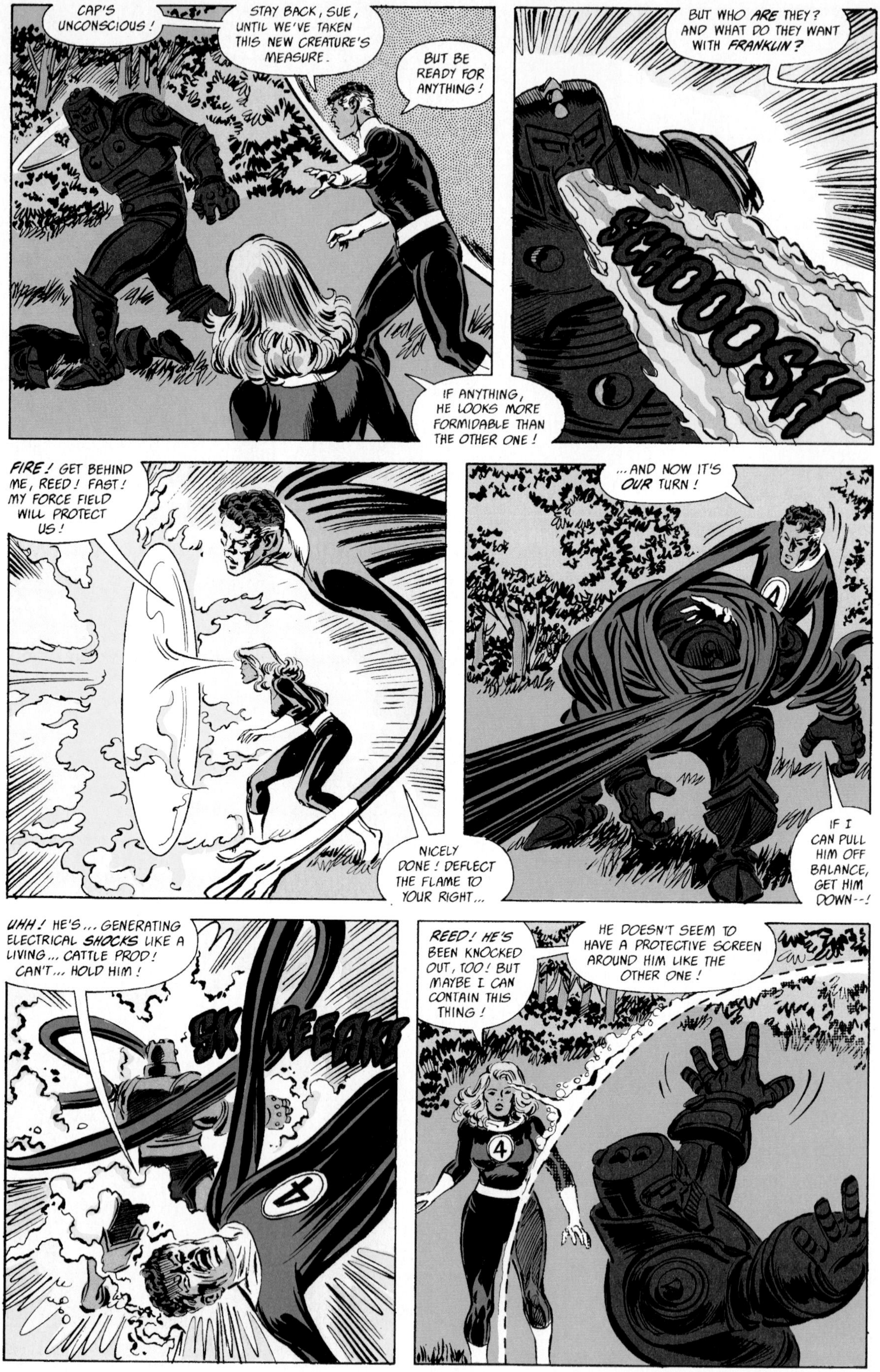
CAP'S UNCONSCIOUS!
STAY BACK, SUE, UNTIL WE'VE TAKEN THIS NEW CREATURE'S MEASURE.
BUT BE READY FOR ANYTHING!
IF ANYTHING, HE LOOKS MORE FORMIDABLE THAN THE OTHER ONE!
BUT WHO ARE THEY? AND WHAT DO THEY WANT WITH FRANKLIN?
SCHOOOSH
FIRE! GET BEHIND ME, REED! FAST! MY FORCE FIELD WILL PROTECT US!
NICELY DONE! DEFLECT THE FLAME TO YOUR RIGHT...
...AND NOW IT'S OUR TURN!
IF I CAN PULL HIM OFF BALANCE, GET HIM DOWN--!
UHH! HE'S... GENERATING ELECTRICAL SHOCKS LIKE A LIVING... CATTLE PROD! CAN'T... HOLD HIM!
REED! HE'S BEEN KNOCKED OUT, TOO! BUT MAYBE I CAN CONTAIN THIS THING!
HE DOESN'T SEEM TO HAVE A PROTECTIVE SCREEN AROUND HIM LIKE THE OTHER ONE!

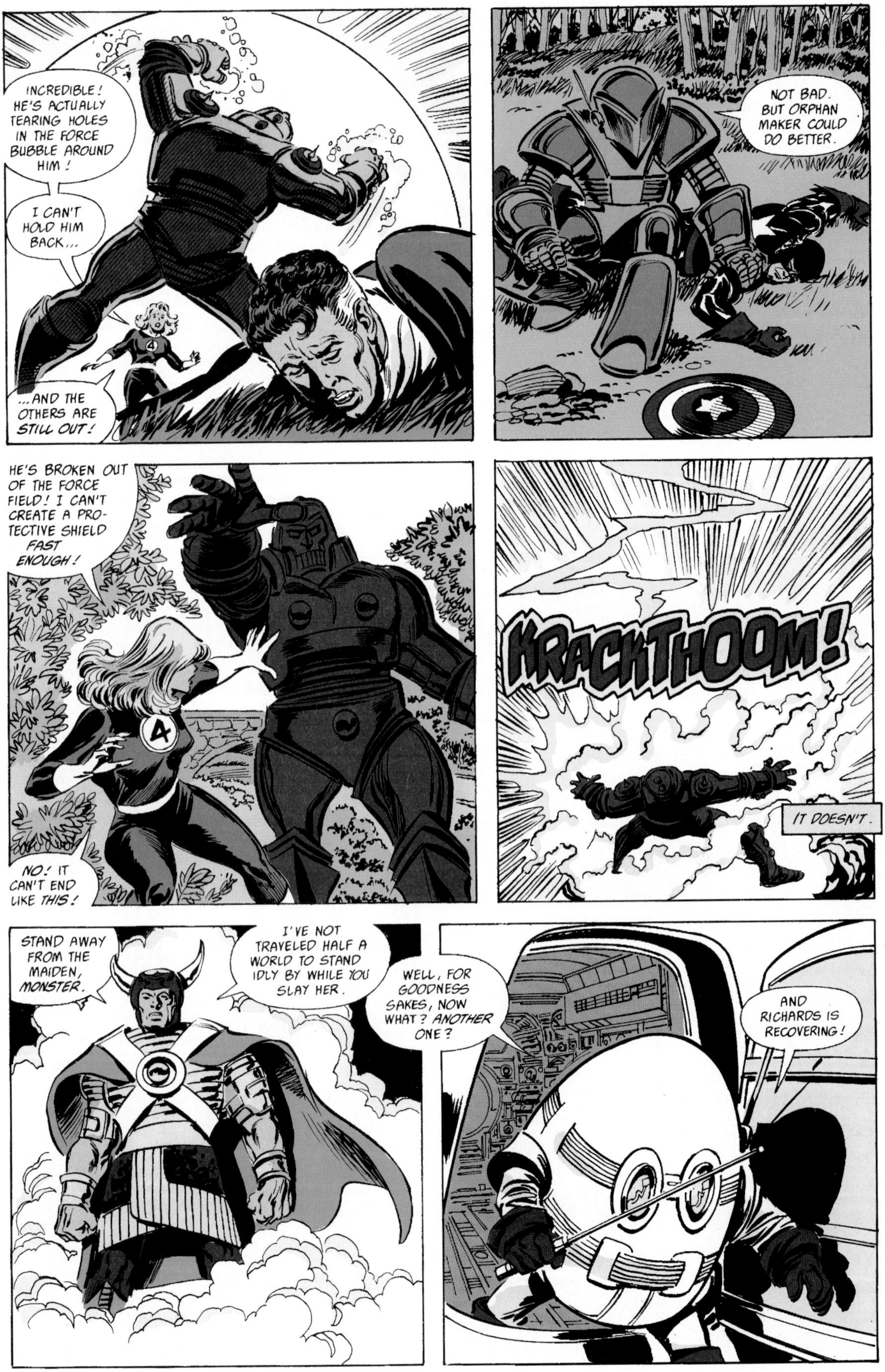
INCREDIBLE! HE'S ACTUALLY TEARING HOLES IN THE FORCE BUBBLE AROUND HIM!
I CAN'T HOLD HIM BACK...
...AND THE OTHERS ARE STILL OUT!
NOT BAD. BUT ORPHAN MAKER COULD DO BETTER.
HE'S BROKEN OUT OF THE FORCE FIELD! I CAN'T CREATE A PROTECTIVE SHIELD FAST ENOUGH!
NO! IT CAN'T END LIKE THIS!
KRACKTHOOM!
IT DOESN'T.
STAND AWAY FROM THE MAIDEN, MONSTER.
I'VE NOT TRAVELED HALF A WORLD TO STAND IDLY BY WHILE YOU SLAY HER.
WELL, FOR GOODNESS SAKES, NOW WHAT? ANOTHER ONE?
AND RICHARDS IS RECOVERING!

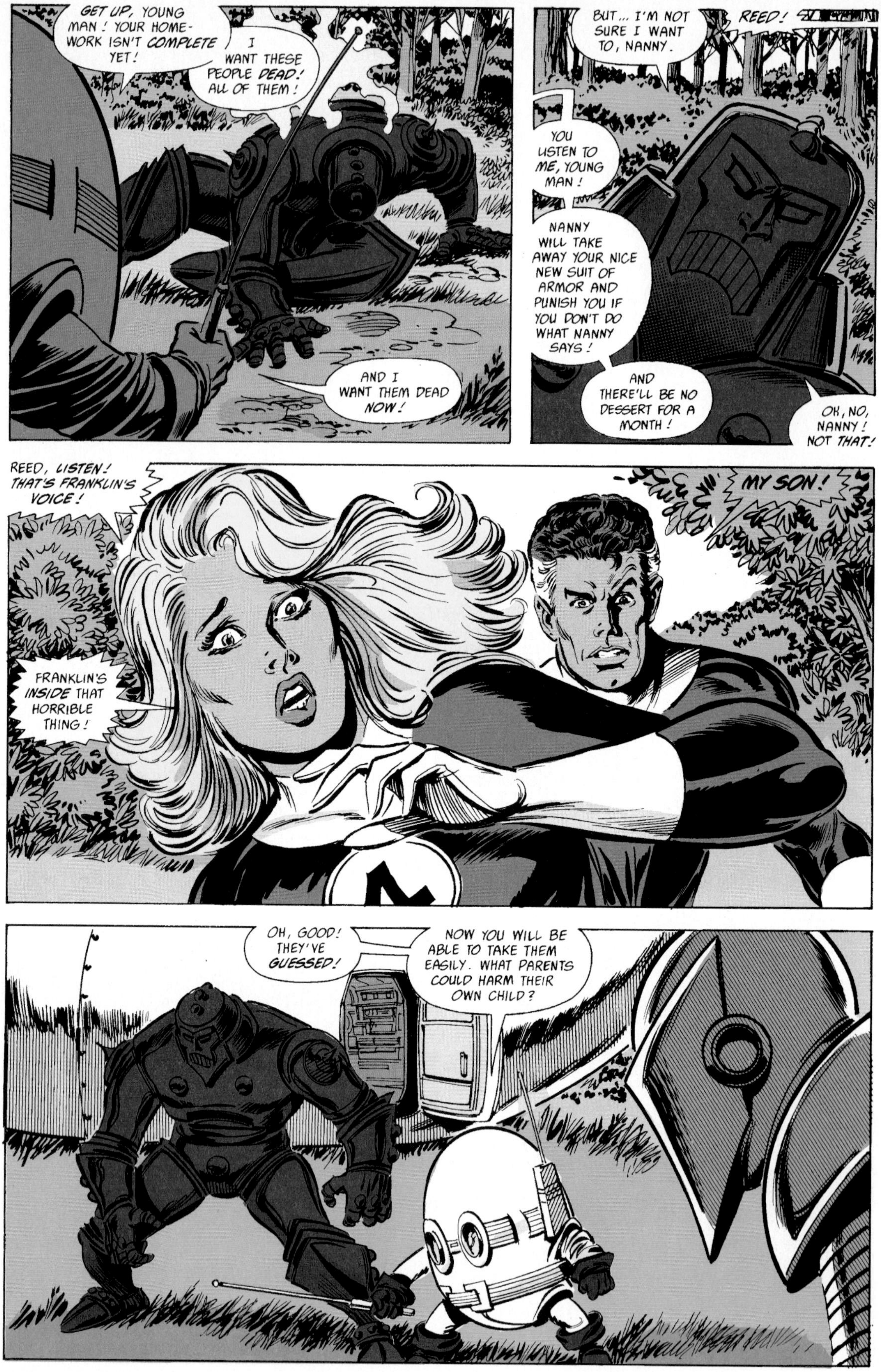
GET UP, YOUNG MAN! YOUR HOME-WORK ISN'T COMPLETE YET!
I WANT THESE PEOPLE DEAD! ALL OF THEM!
AND I WANT THEM DEAD NOW!
BUT... I'M NOT SURE I WANT TO, NANNY.
REED!
YOU LISTEN TO ME, YOUNG MAN!
NANNY WILL TAKE AWAY YOUR NICE NEW SUIT OF ARMOR AND PUNISH YOU IF YOU DON'T DO WHAT NANNY SAYS!
AND THERE'LL BE NO DESSERT FOR A MONTH!
OH, NO, NANNY! NOT THAT!
REED, LISTEN! THAT'S FRANKLIN'S VOICE!
MY SON!
FRANKLIN'S INSIDE THAT HORRIBLE THING!
OH, GOOD! THEY'VE GUESSED!
NOW YOU WILL BE ABLE TO TAKE THEM EASILY. WHAT PARENTS COULD HARM THEIR OWN CHILD?

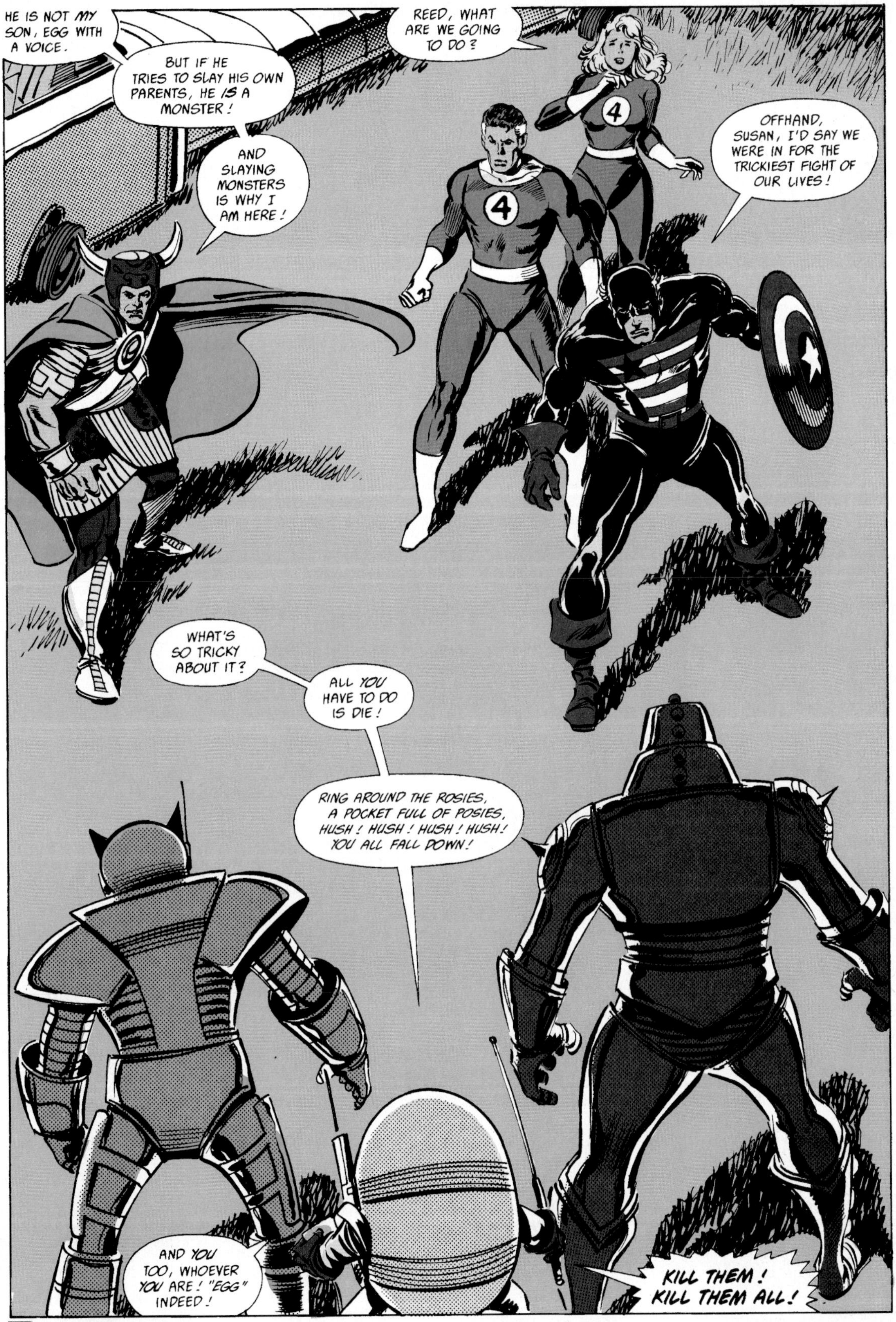
HE IS NOT MY SON, EGG WITH A VOICE.
BUT IF HE TRIES TO SLAY HIS OWN PARENTS, HE IS A MONSTER!
AND SLAYING MONSTERS IS WHY I AM HERE!
REED, WHAT ARE WE GOING TO DO?
OFFHAND, SUSAN, I'D SAY WE WERE IN FOR THE TRICKIEST FIGHT OF OUR LIVES!
WHAT'S SO TRICKY ABOUT IT?
ALL YOU HAVE TO DO IS DIE!
RING AROUND THE ROSIES, A POCKET FULL OF POSIES, HUSH! HUSH! HUSH! HUSH! YOU ALL FALL DOWN!
AND YOU TOO, WHOEVER YOU ARE! "EGG" INDEED!
KILL THEM! KILL THEM ALL!

NEXT **INFERNO CUBED!** IN WHICH MANY FIGHTS ARE FOUGHT, DEMONS TOUR THE WORLD TRADE CENTER, AND A PACT IS SEALED! ALL YOURS IN **AVENGERS #300!**

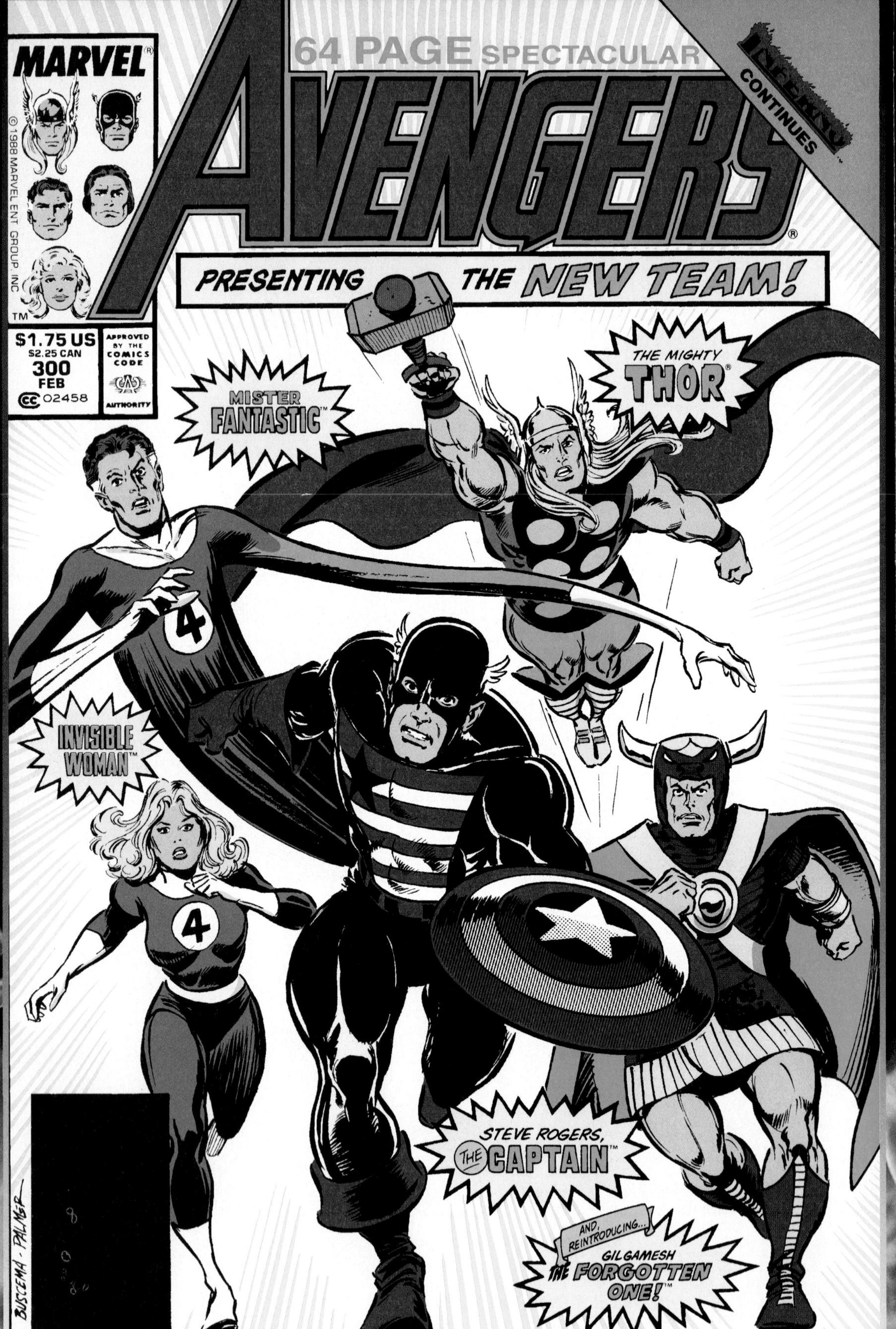
MARVEL
64 PAGE SPECTACULAR
CONTINUES
AVENGERS
© 1988 MARVEL ENT GROUP INC
TM
PRESENTING THE NEW TEAM!
$1.75 US
$2.25 CAN
300
FEB
CC 02458
APPROVED BY THE COMICS CODE AUTHORITY
MISTER FANTASTIC
THE MIGHTY THOR
INVISIBLE WOMAN
STEVE ROGERS, THE CAPTAIN
AND, REINTRODUCING... GILGAMESH THE FORGOTTEN ONE!
BUSCEMA - PALMER

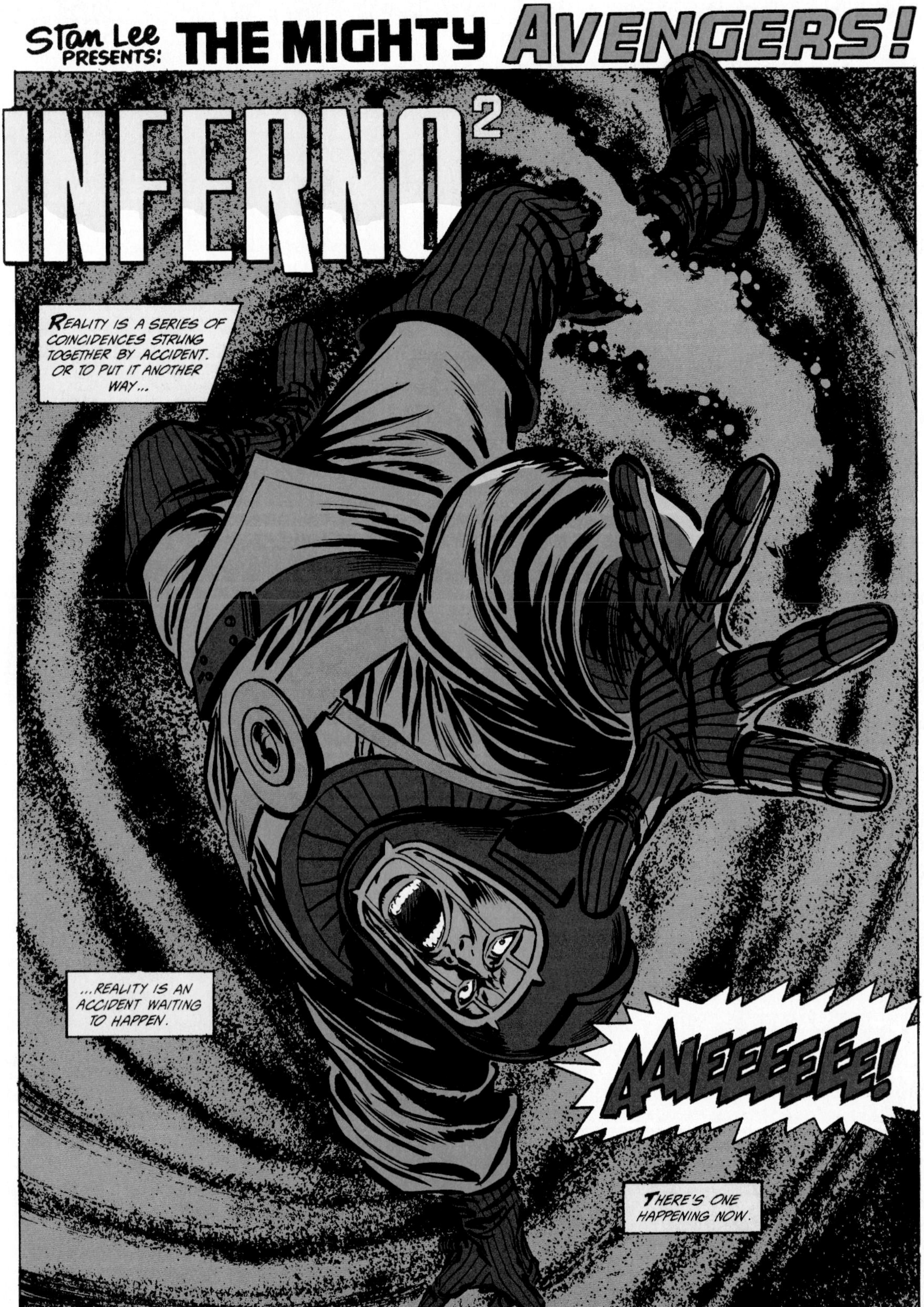

STAN LEE PRESENTS: THE MIGHTY AVENGERS!
INFERNO²
REALITY IS A SERIES OF COINCIDENCES STRUNG TOGETHER BY ACCIDENT. OR TO PUT IT ANOTHER WAY...
...REALITY IS AN ACCIDENT WAITING TO HAPPEN.
AAIEEEEEEE!
THERE'S ONE HAPPENING NOW.

WALTER SIMONSON WRITING • JOHN BUSCEMA LAYOUTING • TOM PALMER FINISHING • BILL OAKLEY LETTERING • BECTON & SIRY COLORING • MARK GRUENWALD EDITING • TOM DEFALCO EDITING IN CHIEF

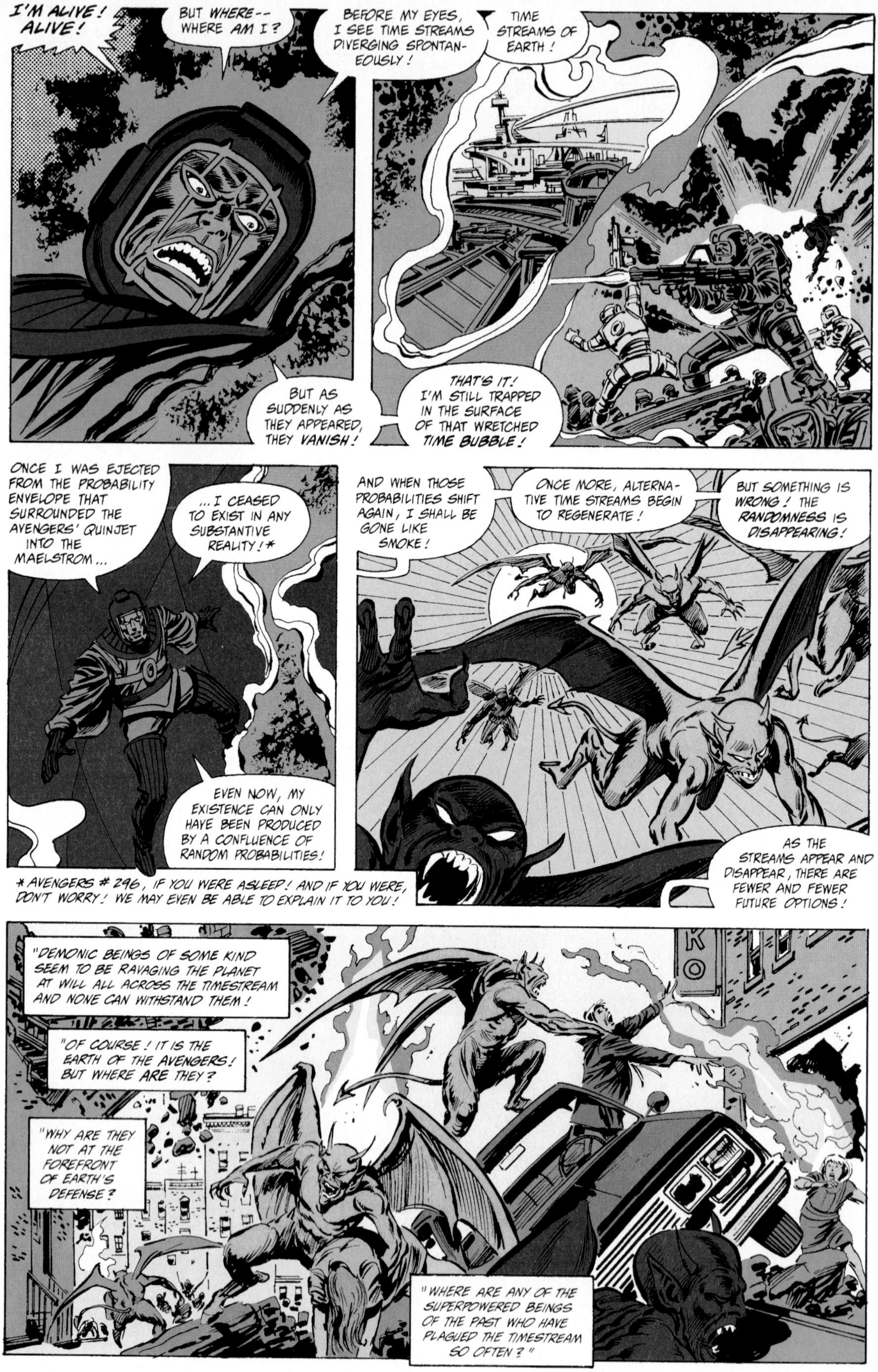
I'M ALIVE! ALIVE!
BUT WHERE-- WHERE AM I?
BEFORE MY EYES, I SEE TIME STREAMS DIVERGING SPONTANEOUSLY!
TIME STREAMS OF EARTH!
BUT AS SUDDENLY AS THEY APPEARED, THEY VANISH!
THAT'S IT! I'M STILL TRAPPED IN THE SURFACE OF THAT WRETCHED TIME BUBBLE!
ONCE I WAS EJECTED FROM THE PROBABILITY ENVELOPE THAT SURROUNDED THE AVENGERS' QUINJET INTO THE MAELSTROM...
...I CEASED TO EXIST IN ANY SUBSTANTIVE REALITY! *
EVEN NOW, MY EXISTENCE CAN ONLY HAVE BEEN PRODUCED BY A CONFLUENCE OF RANDOM PROBABILITIES!
* AVENGERS # 296, IF YOU WERE ASLEEP! AND IF YOU WERE, DON'T WORRY! WE MAY EVEN BE ABLE TO EXPLAIN IT TO YOU!
AND WHEN THOSE PROBABILITIES SHIFT AGAIN, I SHALL BE GONE LIKE SMOKE!
ONCE MORE, ALTERNATIVE TIME STREAMS BEGIN TO REGENERATE!
BUT SOMETHING IS WRONG! THE RANDOMNESS IS DISAPPEARING!
AS THE STREAMS APPEAR AND DISAPPEAR, THERE ARE FEWER AND FEWER FUTURE OPTIONS!
"DEMONIC BEINGS OF SOME KIND SEEM TO BE RAVAGING THE PLANET AT WILL ALL ACROSS THE TIMESTREAM AND NONE CAN WITHSTAND THEM!
"OF COURSE! IT IS THE EARTH OF THE AVENGERS! BUT WHERE ARE THEY?
"WHY ARE THEY NOT AT THE FOREFRONT OF EARTH'S DEFENSE?
"WHERE ARE ANY OF THE SUPERPOWERED BEINGS OF THE PAST WHO HAVE PLAGUED THE TIMESTREAM SO OFTEN?"

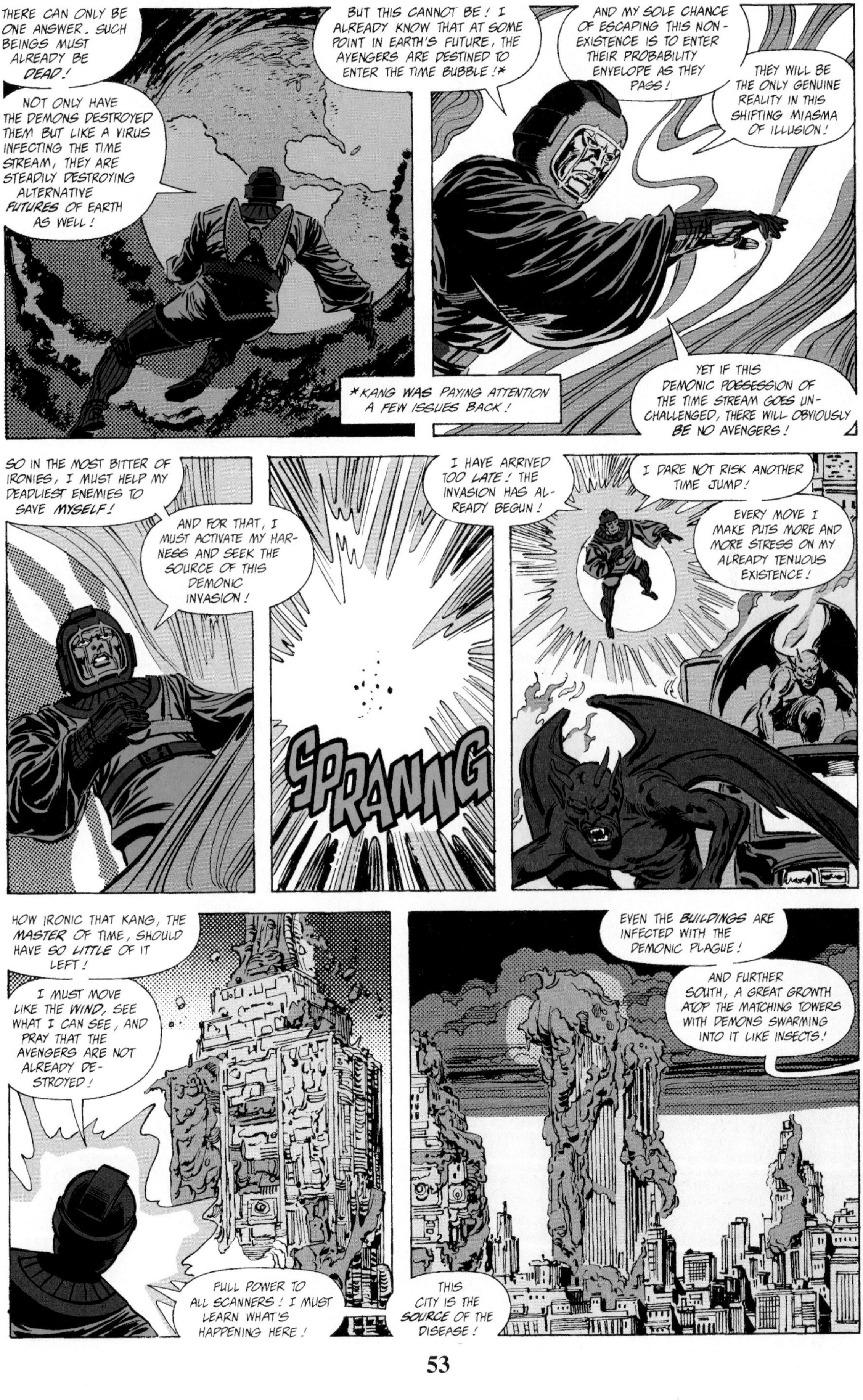
THERE CAN ONLY BE ONE ANSWER. SUCH BEINGS MUST ALREADY BE DEAD!
NOT ONLY HAVE THE DEMONS DESTROYED THEM BUT LIKE A VIRUS INFECTING THE TIME STREAM, THEY ARE STEADILY DESTROYING ALTERNATIVE FUTURES OF EARTH AS WELL!
BUT THIS CANNOT BE! I ALREADY KNOW THAT AT SOME POINT IN EARTH'S FUTURE, THE AVENGERS ARE DESTINED TO ENTER THE TIME BUBBLE!*
AND MY SOLE CHANCE OF ESCAPING THIS NON-EXISTENCE IS TO ENTER THEIR PROBABILITY ENVELOPE AS THEY PASS!
THEY WILL BE THE ONLY GENUINE REALITY IN THIS SHIFTING MIASMA OF ILLUSION!
*KANG WAS PAYING ATTENTION A FEW ISSUES BACK!
YET IF THIS DEMONIC POSSESSION OF THE TIME STREAM GOES UNCHALLENGED, THERE WILL OBVIOUSLY BE NO AVENGERS!
SO IN THE MOST BITTER OF IRONIES, I MUST HELP MY DEADLIEST ENEMIES TO SAVE MYSELF!
AND FOR THAT, I MUST ACTIVATE MY HARNESS AND SEEK THE SOURCE OF THIS DEMONIC INVASION!
SPRANNG
I HAVE ARRIVED TOO LATE! THE INVASION HAS ALREADY BEGUN!
I DARE NOT RISK ANOTHER TIME JUMP!
EVERY MOVE I MAKE PUTS MORE AND MORE STRESS ON MY ALREADY TENUOUS EXISTENCE!
HOW IRONIC THAT KANG, THE MASTER OF TIME, SHOULD HAVE SO LITTLE OF IT LEFT!
I MUST MOVE LIKE THE WIND, SEE WHAT I CAN SEE, AND PRAY THAT THE AVENGERS ARE NOT ALREADY DESTROYED!
FULL POWER TO ALL SCANNERS! I MUST LEARN WHAT'S HAPPENING HERE!
THIS CITY IS THE SOURCE OF THE DISEASE!
EVEN THE BUILDINGS ARE INFECTED WITH THE DEMONIC PLAGUE!
AND FURTHER SOUTH, A GREAT GROWTH ATOP THE MATCHING TOWERS WITH DEMONS SWARMING INTO IT LIKE INSECTS!

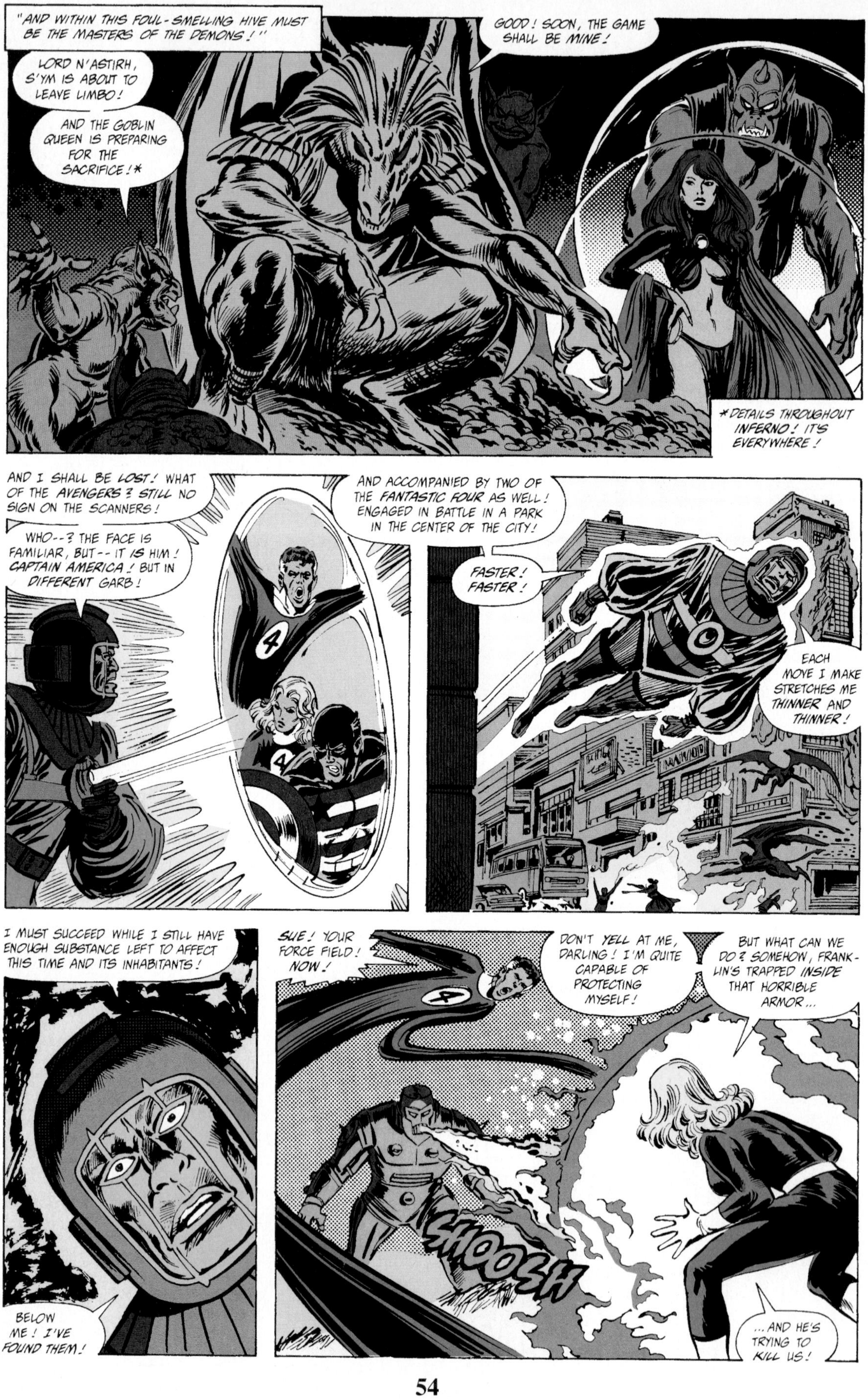

"AND WITHIN THIS FOUL-SMELLING HIVE MUST BE THE MASTERS OF THE DEMONS!"
LORD N'ASTIRH, S'YM IS ABOUT TO LEAVE LIMBO!
AND THE GOBLIN QUEEN IS PREPARING FOR THE SACRIFICE!*
GOOD! SOON, THE GAME SHALL BE MINE!
*DETAILS THROUGHOUT INFERNO! IT'S EVERYWHERE!
AND I SHALL BE LOST! WHAT OF THE AVENGERS? STILL NO SIGN ON THE SCANNERS!
WHO--? THE FACE IS FAMILIAR, BUT-- IT IS HIM! CAPTAIN AMERICA! BUT IN DIFFERENT GARB!
AND ACCOMPANIED BY TWO OF THE FANTASTIC FOUR AS WELL! ENGAGED IN BATTLE IN A PARK IN THE CENTER OF THE CITY!
FASTER! FASTER!
EACH MOVE I MAKE STRETCHES ME THINNER AND THINNER!
I MUST SUCCEED WHILE I STILL HAVE ENOUGH SUBSTANCE LEFT TO AFFECT THIS TIME AND ITS INHABITANTS!
BELOW ME! I'VE FOUND THEM!
SUE! YOUR FORCE FIELD! NOW!
DON'T YELL AT ME, DARLING! I'M QUITE CAPABLE OF PROTECTING MYSELF!
BUT WHAT CAN WE DO? SOMEHOW, FRANKLIN'S TRAPPED INSIDE THAT HORRIBLE ARMOR...
SHOOOSH
...AND HE'S TRYING TO KILL US!

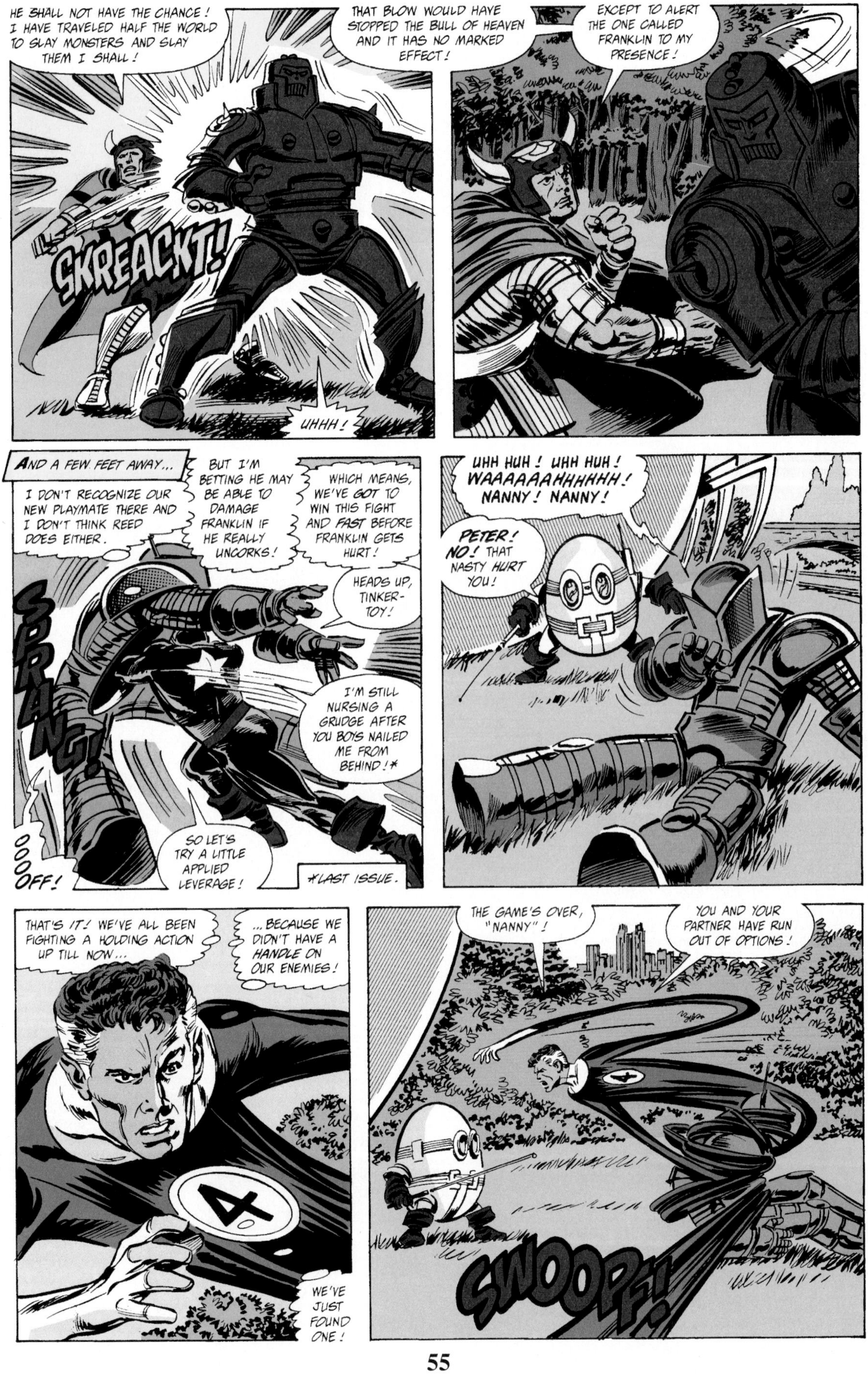
HE SHALL NOT HAVE THE CHANCE! I HAVE TRAVELED HALF THE WORLD TO SLAY MONSTERS AND SLAY THEM I SHALL!
SKREACKT!
UHHH!
THAT BLOW WOULD HAVE STOPPED THE BULL OF HEAVEN AND IT HAS NO MARKED EFFECT!
EXCEPT TO ALERT THE ONE CALLED FRANKLIN TO MY PRESENCE!
AND A FEW FEET AWAY...
I DON'T RECOGNIZE OUR NEW PLAYMATE THERE AND I DON'T THINK REED DOES EITHER.
BUT I'M BETTING HE MAY BE ABLE TO DAMAGE FRANKLIN IF HE REALLY UNCORKS!
WHICH MEANS, WE'VE GOT TO WIN THIS FIGHT AND FAST BEFORE FRANKLIN GETS HURT!
HEADS UP, TINKER-TOY!
SPRANG!
I'M STILL NURSING A GRUDGE AFTER YOU BOYS NAILED ME FROM BEHIND!*
OOOOFF!
SO LET'S TRY A LITTLE APPLIED LEVERAGE!
*LAST ISSUE.
UHH HUH! UHH HUH! WAAAAAAHHHHHH! NANNY! NANNY!
PETER! NO! THAT NASTY HURT YOU!
THAT'S IT! WE'VE ALL BEEN FIGHTING A HOLDING ACTION UP TILL NOW...
...BECAUSE WE DIDN'T HAVE A HANDLE ON OUR ENEMIES!
WE'VE JUST FOUND ONE!
THE GAME'S OVER, "NANNY"!
YOU AND YOUR PARTNER HAVE RUN OUT OF OPTIONS!
SWOOPF!

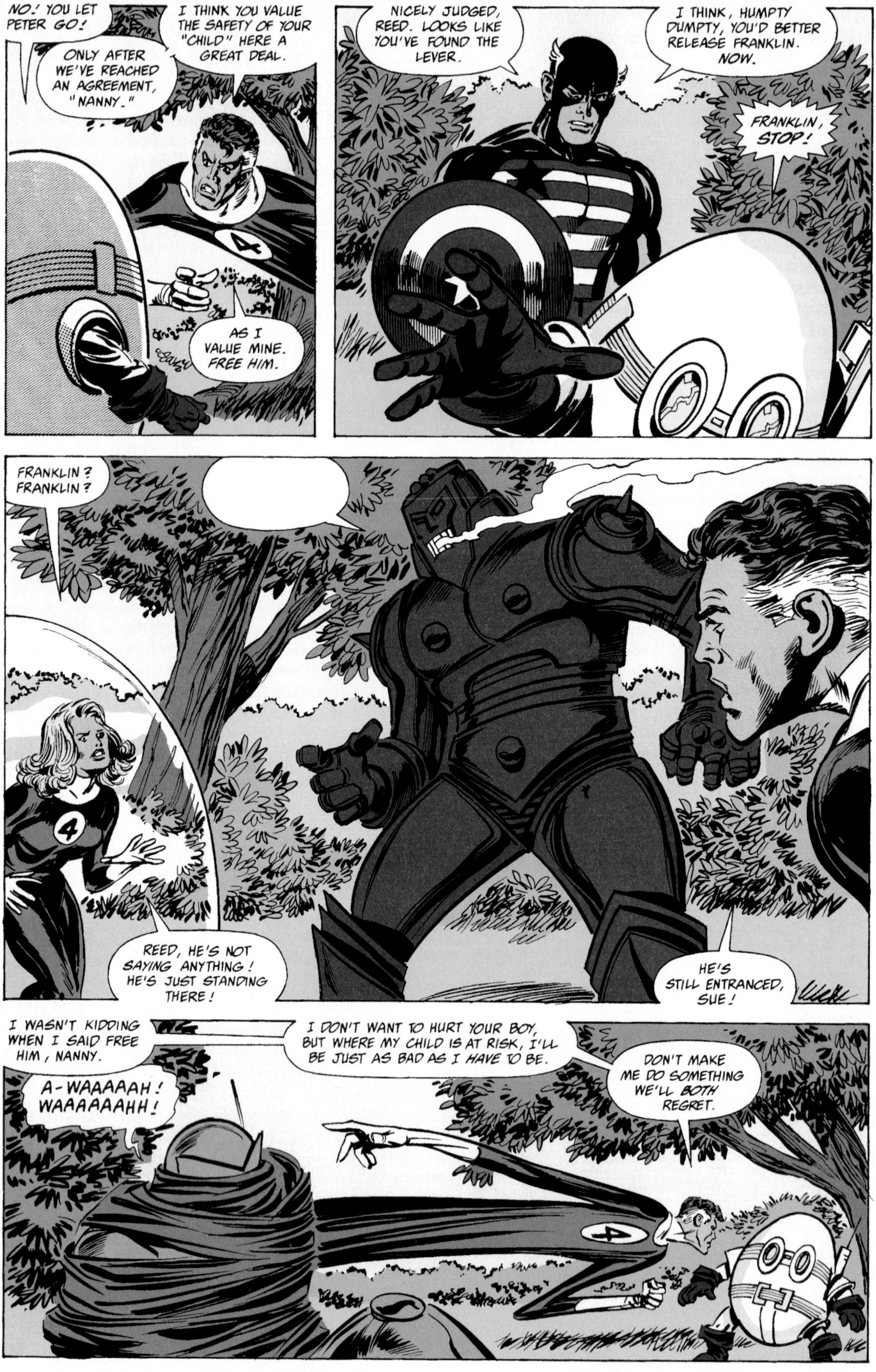
NO! YOU LET PETER GO!
I THINK YOU VALUE THE SAFETY OF YOUR "CHILD" HERE A GREAT DEAL.
ONLY AFTER WE'VE REACHED AN AGREEMENT, "NANNY."
AS I VALUE MINE. FREE HIM.
NICELY JUDGED, REED. LOOKS LIKE YOU'VE FOUND THE LEVER.
I THINK, HUMPTY DUMPTY, YOU'D BETTER RELEASE FRANKLIN. NOW.
FRANKLIN, STOP!
FRANKLIN? FRANKLIN?
REED, HE'S NOT SAYING ANYTHING! HE'S JUST STANDING THERE!
HE'S STILL ENTRANCED, SUE!
I WASN'T KIDDING WHEN I SAID FREE HIM, NANNY.
I DON'T WANT TO HURT YOUR BOY, BUT WHERE MY CHILD IS AT RISK, I'LL BE JUST AS BAD AS I HAVE TO BE.
A-WAAAAAH! WAAAAAAHH!
DON'T MAKE ME DO SOMETHING WE'LL BOTH REGRET.

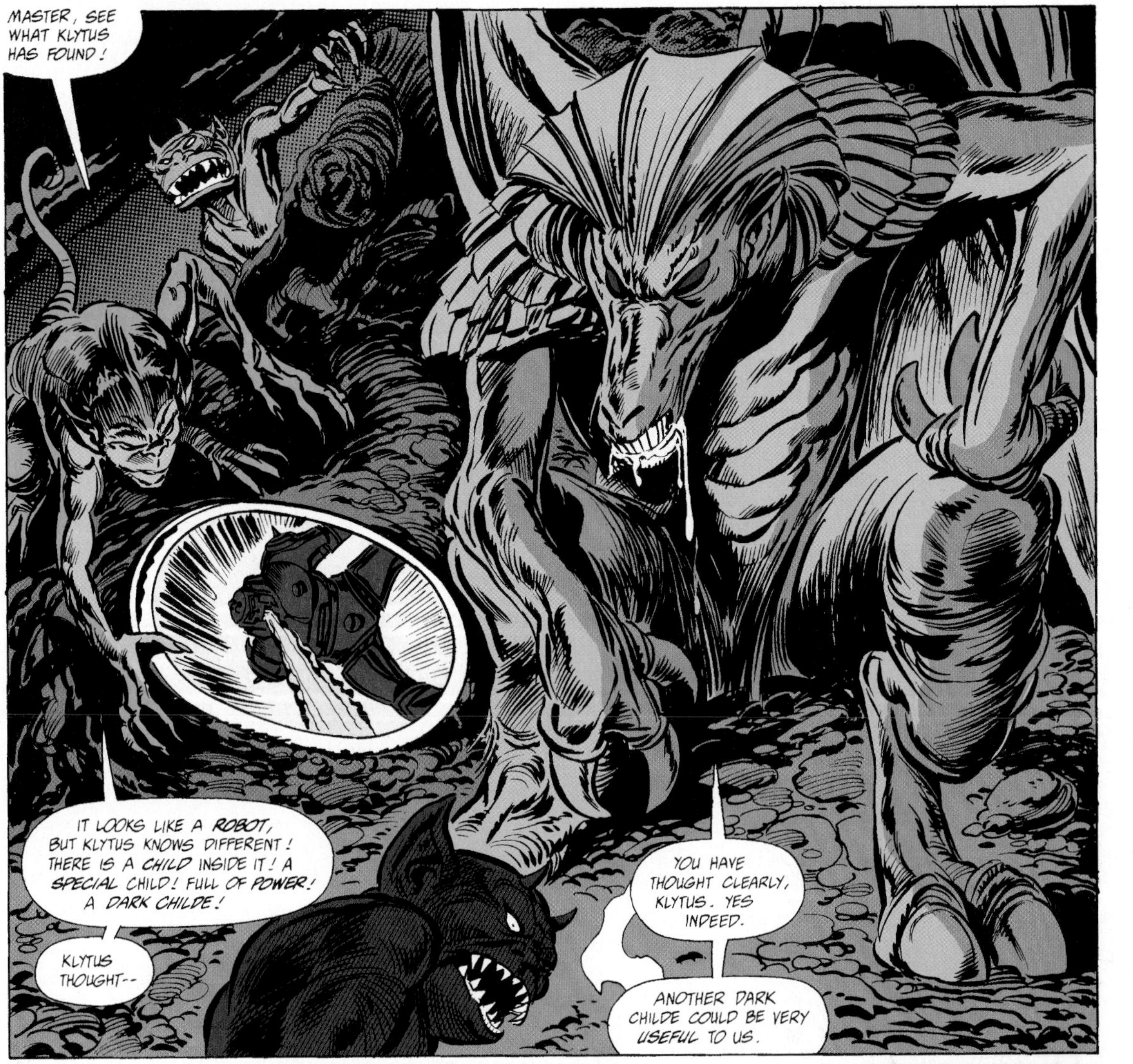
MASTER, SEE WHAT KLYTUS HAS FOUND!
IT LOOKS LIKE A ROBOT, BUT KLYTUS KNOWS DIFFERENT! THERE IS A CHILD INSIDE IT! A SPECIAL CHILD! FULL OF POWER! A DARK CHILDE!
KLYTUS THOUGHT--
YOU HAVE THOUGHT CLEARLY, KLYTUS. YES INDEED.
ANOTHER DARK CHILDE COULD BE VERY USEFUL TO US.

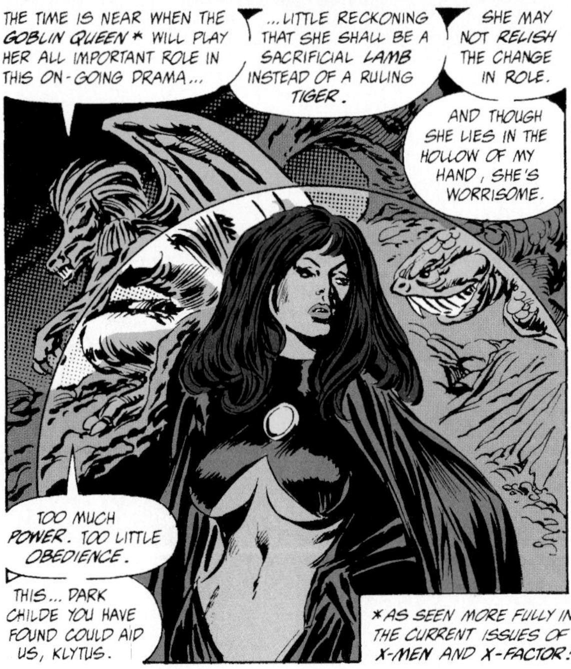
THE TIME IS NEAR WHEN THE GOBLIN QUEEN* WILL PLAY HER ALL IMPORTANT ROLE IN THIS ON-GOING DRAMA...
...LITTLE RECKONING THAT SHE SHALL BE A SACRIFICIAL LAMB INSTEAD OF A RULING TIGER.
SHE MAY NOT RELISH THE CHANGE IN ROLE.
AND THOUGH SHE LIES IN THE HOLLOW OF MY HAND, SHE'S WORRISOME.
TOO MUCH POWER. TOO LITTLE OBEDIENCE.
THIS... DARK CHILDE YOU HAVE FOUND COULD AID US, KLYTUS.
*AS SEEN MORE FULLY IN THE CURRENT ISSUES OF X-MEN AND X-FACTOR!

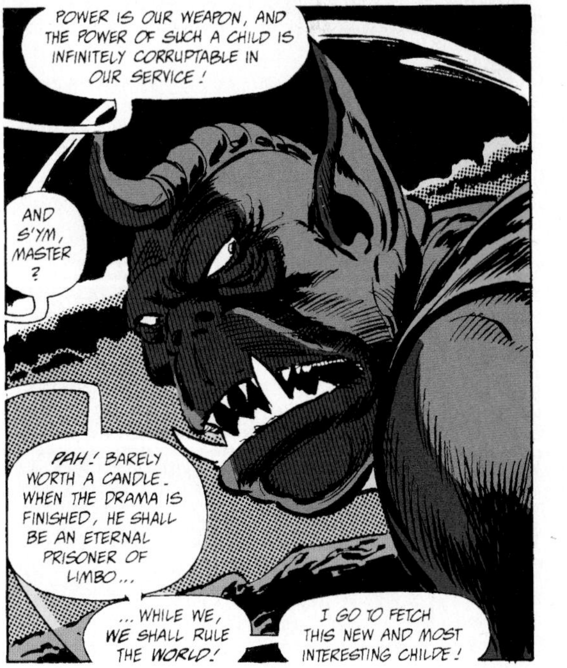
POWER IS OUR WEAPON, AND THE POWER OF SUCH A CHILD IS INFINITELY CORRUPTABLE IN OUR SERVICE!
AND S'YM, MASTER?
PAH! BARELY WORTH A CANDLE. WHEN THE DRAMA IS FINISHED, HE SHALL BE AN ETERNAL PRISONER OF LIMBO...
...WHILE WE, WE SHALL RULE THE WORLD!
I GO TO FETCH THIS NEW AND MOST INTERESTING CHILDE!

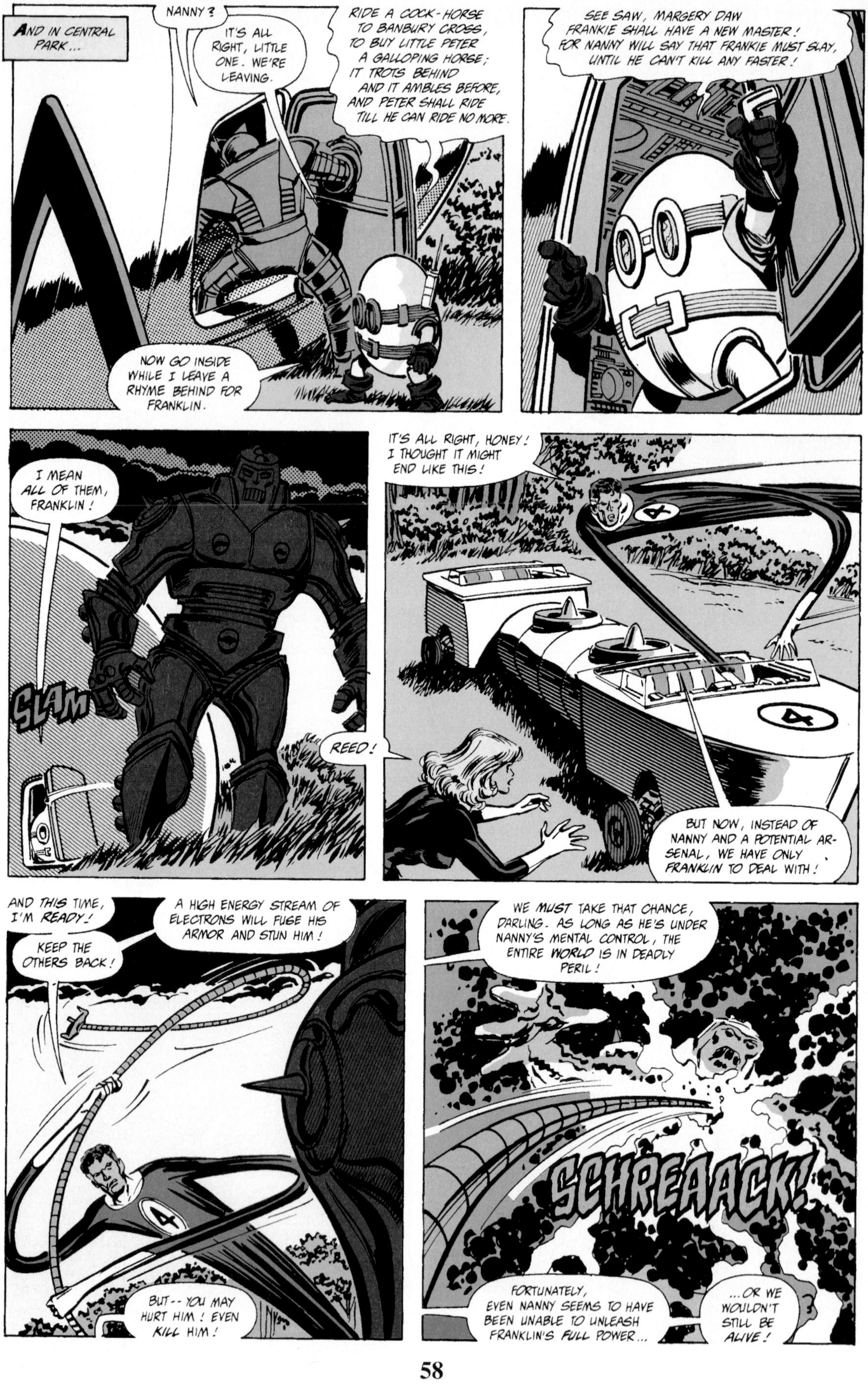
AND IN CENTRAL PARK...
NANNY?
IT'S ALL RIGHT, LITTLE ONE. WE'RE LEAVING.
RIDE A COCK-HORSE TO BANBURY CROSS, TO BUY LITTLE PETER A GALLOPING HORSE; IT TROTS BEHIND AND IT AMBLES BEFORE, AND PETER SHALL RIDE TILL HE CAN RIDE NO MORE.
NOW GO INSIDE WHILE I LEAVE A RHYME BEHIND FOR FRANKLIN.
SEE SAW, MARGERY DAW FRANKIE SHALL HAVE A NEW MASTER! FOR NANNY WILL SAY THAT FRANKIE MUST SLAY, UNTIL HE CAN'T KILL ANY FASTER!
I MEAN ALL OF THEM, FRANKLIN!
SLAM
IT'S ALL RIGHT, HONEY! I THOUGHT IT MIGHT END LIKE THIS!
REED!
BUT NOW, INSTEAD OF NANNY AND A POTENTIAL AR-SENAL, WE HAVE ONLY FRANKLIN TO DEAL WITH!
AND THIS TIME, I'M READY!
KEEP THE OTHERS BACK!
A HIGH ENERGY STREAM OF ELECTRONS WILL FUSE HIS ARMOR AND STUN HIM!
BUT--YOU MAY HURT HIM! EVEN KILL HIM!
WE MUST TAKE THAT CHANCE, DARLING. AS LONG AS HE'S UNDER NANNY'S MENTAL CONTROL, THE ENTIRE WORLD IS IN DEADLY PERIL!
SCHREAACK!
FORTUNATELY, EVEN NANNY SEEMS TO HAVE BEEN UNABLE TO UNLEASH FRANKLIN'S FULL POWER...
...OR WE WOULDN'T STILL BE ALIVE!

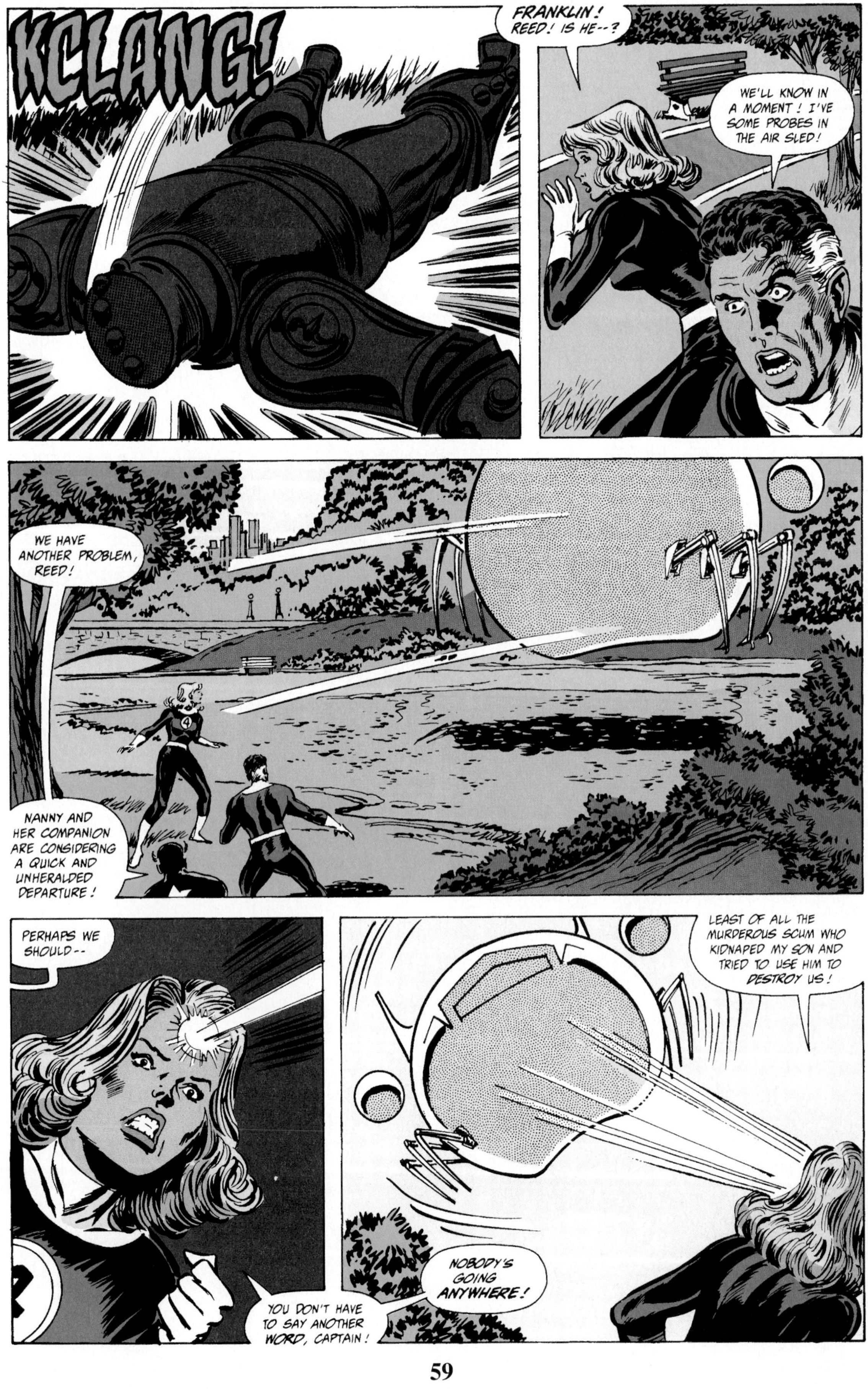
KCLANG!
FRANKLIN! REED! IS HE--?
WE'LL KNOW IN A MOMENT! I'VE SOME PROBES IN THE AIR SLED!
WE HAVE ANOTHER PROBLEM, REED!
NANNY AND HER COMPANION ARE CONSIDERING A QUICK AND UNHERALDED DEPARTURE!
PERHAPS WE SHOULD--
YOU DON'T HAVE TO SAY ANOTHER WORD, CAPTAIN!
NOBODY'S GOING ANYWHERE!
LEAST OF ALL THE MURDEROUS SCUM WHO KIDNAPED MY SON AND TRIED TO USE HIM TO DESTROY US!

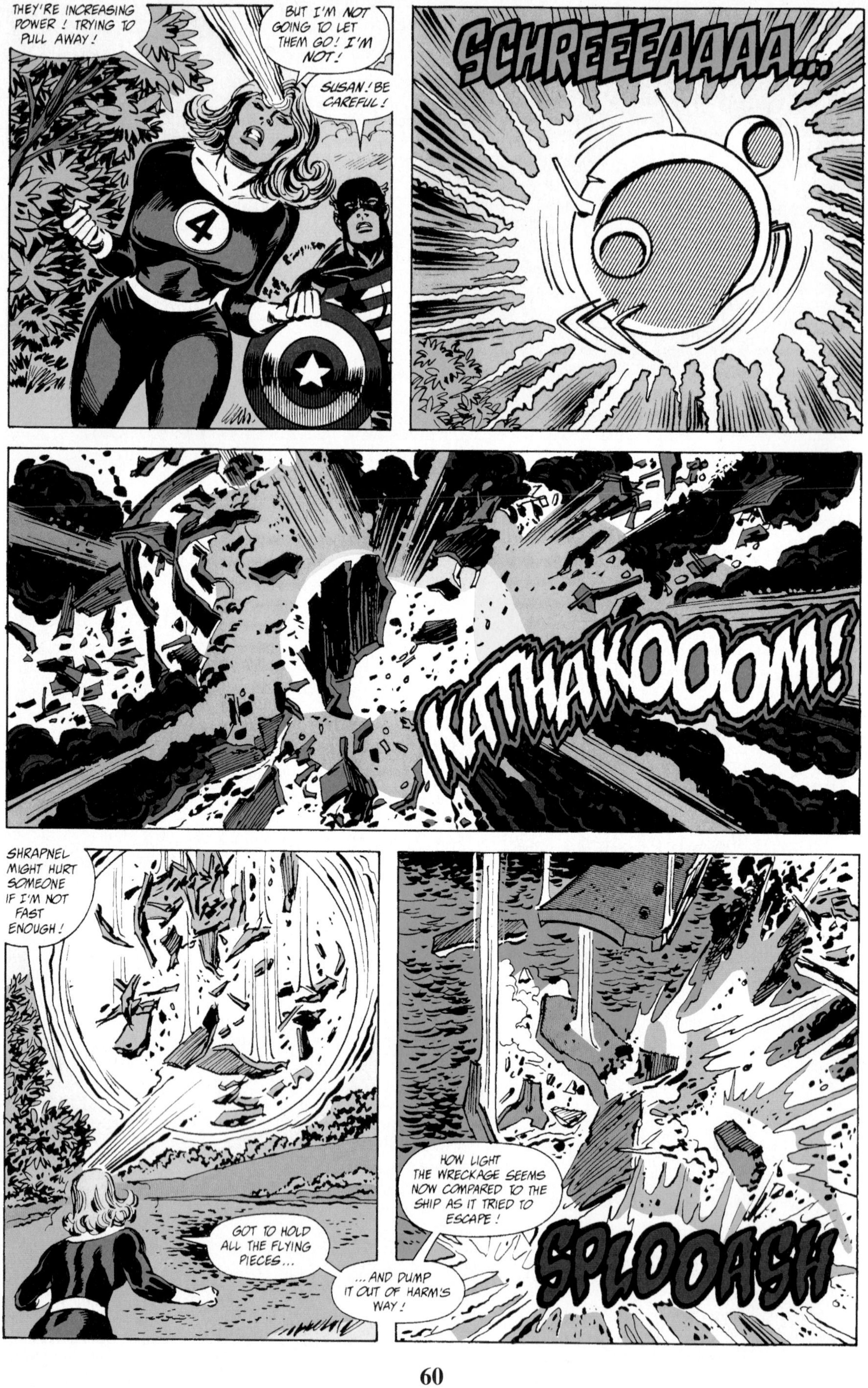
THEY'RE INCREASING POWER! TRYING TO PULL AWAY!
BUT I'M NOT GOING TO LET THEM GO! I'M NOT!
SUSAN! BE CAREFUL!
SCHREEEAAAA...
KATHAKOOOM!
SHRAPNEL MIGHT HURT SOMEONE IF I'M NOT FAST ENOUGH!
GOT TO HOLD ALL THE FLYING PIECES...
...AND DUMP IT OUT OF HARM'S WAY!
HOW LIGHT THE WRECKAGE SEEMS NOW COMPARED TO THE SHIP AS IT TRIED TO ESCAPE!
SPLOOASH

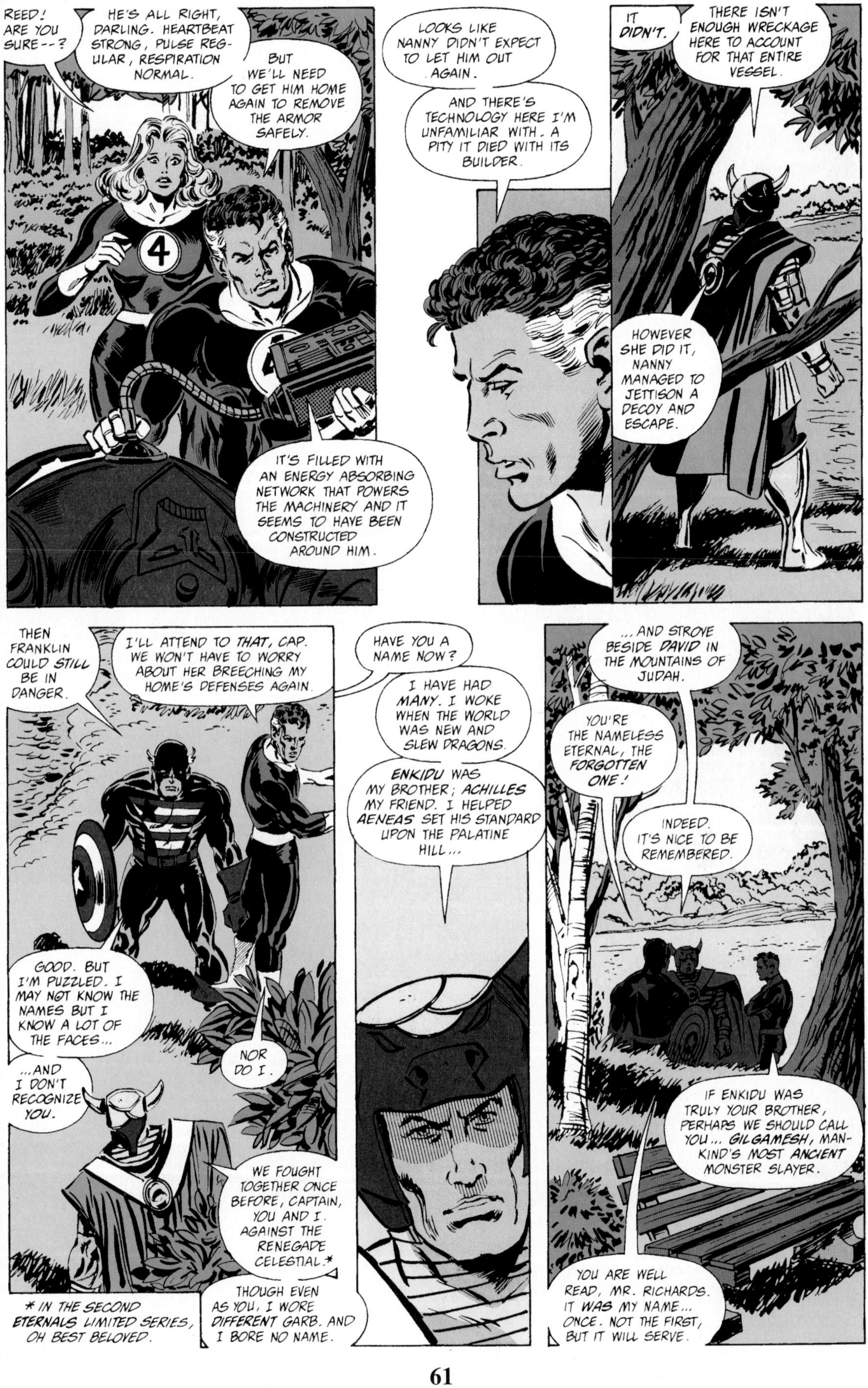
REED! ARE YOU SURE--?
HE'S ALL RIGHT, DARLING. HEARTBEAT STRONG, PULSE REGULAR, RESPIRATION NORMAL.
BUT WE'LL NEED TO GET HIM HOME AGAIN TO REMOVE THE ARMOR SAFELY.
IT'S FILLED WITH AN ENERGY ABSORBING NETWORK THAT POWERS THE MACHINERY AND IT SEEMS TO HAVE BEEN CONSTRUCTED AROUND HIM.
LOOKS LIKE NANNY DIDN'T EXPECT TO LET HIM OUT AGAIN.
AND THERE'S TECHNOLOGY HERE I'M UNFAMILIAR WITH. A PITY IT DIED WITH ITS BUILDER.
IT DIDN'T.
THERE ISN'T ENOUGH WRECKAGE HERE TO ACCOUNT FOR THAT ENTIRE VESSEL.
HOWEVER SHE DID IT, NANNY MANAGED TO JETTISON A DECOY AND ESCAPE.
THEN FRANKLIN COULD STILL BE IN DANGER.
I'LL ATTEND TO THAT, CAP. WE WON'T HAVE TO WORRY ABOUT HER BREECHING MY HOME'S DEFENSES AGAIN.
GOOD. BUT I'M PUZZLED. I MAY NOT KNOW THE NAMES BUT I KNOW A LOT OF THE FACES...
NOR DO I.
...AND I DON'T RECOGNIZE YOU.
WE FOUGHT TOGETHER ONCE BEFORE, CAPTAIN, YOU AND I. AGAINST THE RENEGADE CELESTIAL.*
THOUGH EVEN AS YOU, I WORE DIFFERENT GARB. AND I BORE NO NAME.
* IN THE SECOND ETERNALS LIMITED SERIES, OH BEST BELOVED.
HAVE YOU A NAME NOW?
I HAVE HAD MANY. I WOKE WHEN THE WORLD WAS NEW AND SLEW DRAGONS.
ENKIDU WAS MY BROTHER; ACHILLES MY FRIEND. I HELPED AENEAS SET HIS STANDARD UPON THE PALATINE HILL...
...AND STROVE BESIDE DAVID IN THE MOUNTAINS OF JUDAH.
YOU'RE THE NAMELESS ETERNAL, THE FORGOTTEN ONE!
INDEED. IT'S NICE TO BE REMEMBERED.
IF ENKIDU WAS TRULY YOUR BROTHER, PERHAPS WE SHOULD CALL YOU... GILGAMESH, MANKIND'S MOST ANCIENT MONSTER SLAYER.
YOU ARE WELL READ, MR. RICHARDS. IT WAS MY NAME... ONCE. NOT THE FIRST, BUT IT WILL SERVE.

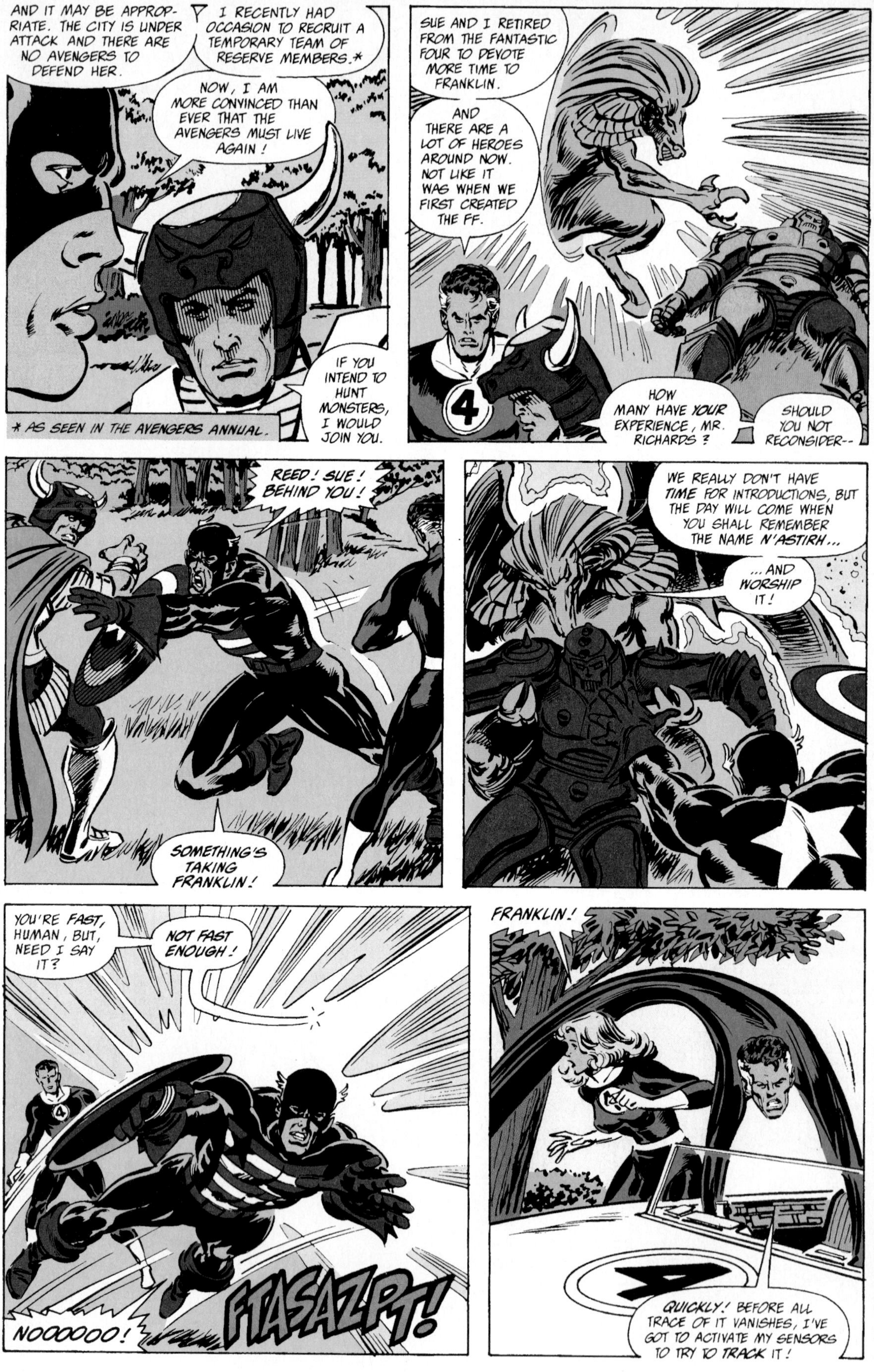
AND IT MAY BE APPROPRIATE. THE CITY IS UNDER ATTACK AND THERE ARE NO AVENGERS TO DEFEND HER.
I RECENTLY HAD OCCASION TO RECRUIT A TEMPORARY TEAM OF RESERVE MEMBERS.*
NOW, I AM MORE CONVINCED THAN EVER THAT THE AVENGERS MUST LIVE AGAIN!
IF YOU INTEND TO HUNT MONSTERS, I WOULD JOIN YOU.
* AS SEEN IN THE AVENGERS ANNUAL.
SUE AND I RETIRED FROM THE FANTASTIC FOUR TO DEVOTE MORE TIME TO FRANKLIN.
AND THERE ARE A LOT OF HEROES AROUND NOW. NOT LIKE IT WAS WHEN WE FIRST CREATED THE FF.
HOW MANY HAVE YOUR EXPERIENCE, MR. RICHARDS?
SHOULD YOU NOT RECONSIDER--
REED! SUE! BEHIND YOU!
SOMETHING'S TAKING FRANKLIN!
WE REALLY DON'T HAVE TIME FOR INTRODUCTIONS, BUT THE DAY WILL COME WHEN YOU SHALL REMEMBER THE NAME N'ASTIRH...
...AND WORSHIP IT!
YOU'RE FAST, HUMAN, BUT, NEED I SAY IT?
NOT FAST ENOUGH!
FTASAZPT!
NOOOOOO!
FRANKLIN!
QUICKLY! BEFORE ALL TRACE OF IT VANISHES, I'VE GOT TO ACTIVATE MY SENSORS TO TRY TO TRACK IT!

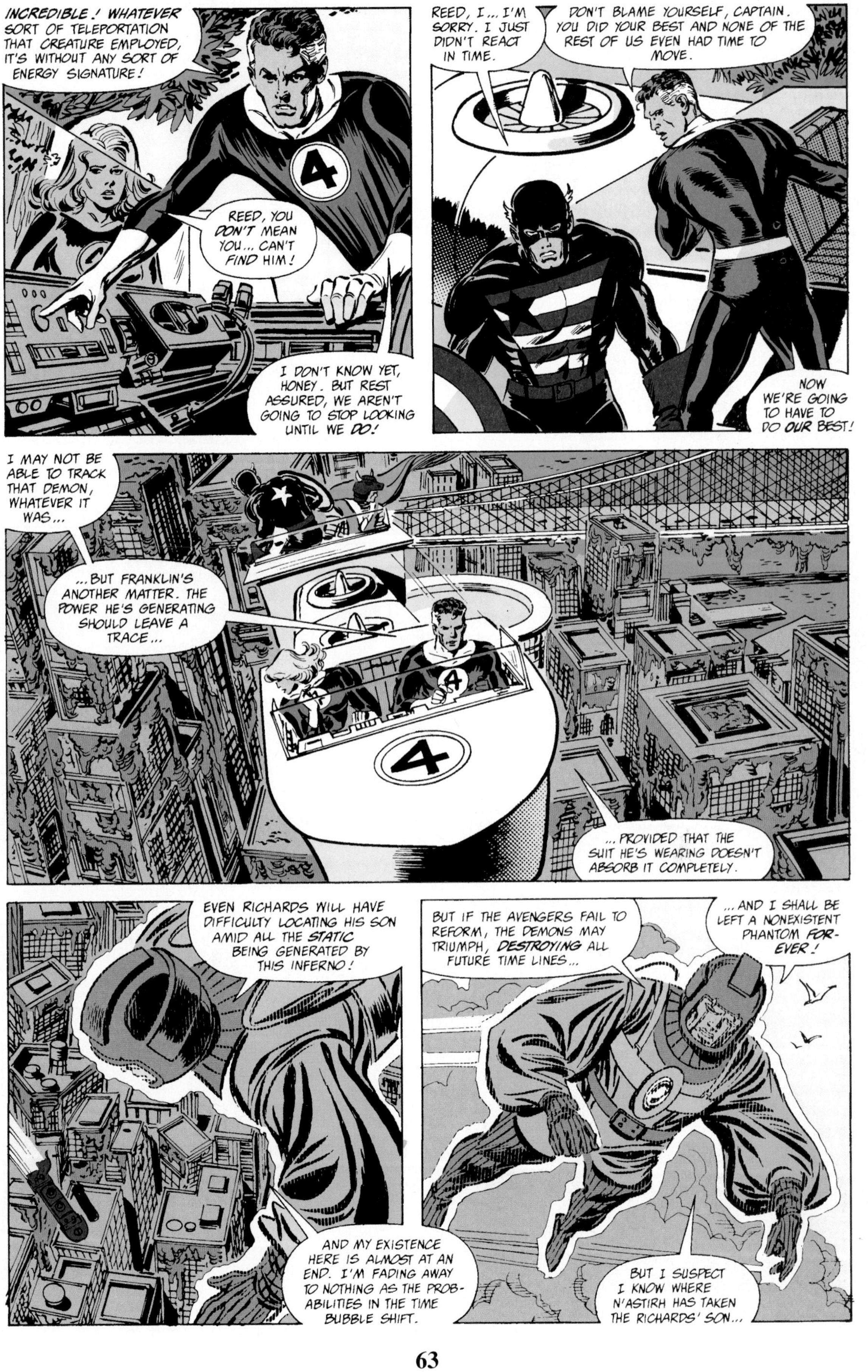
INCREDIBLE! WHATEVER SORT OF TELEPORTATION THAT CREATURE EMPLOYED, IT'S WITHOUT ANY SORT OF ENERGY SIGNATURE!
REED, YOU DON'T MEAN YOU... CAN'T FIND HIM!
I DON'T KNOW YET, HONEY. BUT REST ASSURED, WE AREN'T GOING TO STOP LOOKING UNTIL WE DO!
REED, I... I'M SORRY. I JUST DIDN'T REACT IN TIME.
DON'T BLAME YOURSELF, CAPTAIN. YOU DID YOUR BEST AND NONE OF THE REST OF US EVEN HAD TIME TO MOVE.
NOW WE'RE GOING TO HAVE TO DO OUR BEST!
I MAY NOT BE ABLE TO TRACK THAT DEMON, WHATEVER IT WAS...
...BUT FRANKLIN'S ANOTHER MATTER. THE POWER HE'S GENERATING SHOULD LEAVE A TRACE...
...PROVIDED THAT THE SUIT HE'S WEARING DOESN'T ABSORB IT COMPLETELY.
EVEN RICHARDS WILL HAVE DIFFICULTY LOCATING HIS SON AMID ALL THE STATIC BEING GENERATED BY THIS INFERNO!
AND MY EXISTENCE HERE IS ALMOST AT AN END. I'M FADING AWAY TO NOTHING AS THE PROBABILITIES IN THE TIME BUBBLE SHIFT.
BUT IF THE AVENGERS FAIL TO REFORM, THE DEMONS MAY TRIUMPH, DESTROYING ALL FUTURE TIME LINES...
...AND I SHALL BE LEFT A NONEXISTENT PHANTOM FOREVER!
BUT I SUSPECT I KNOW WHERE N'ASTIRH HAS TAKEN THE RICHARDS' SON...

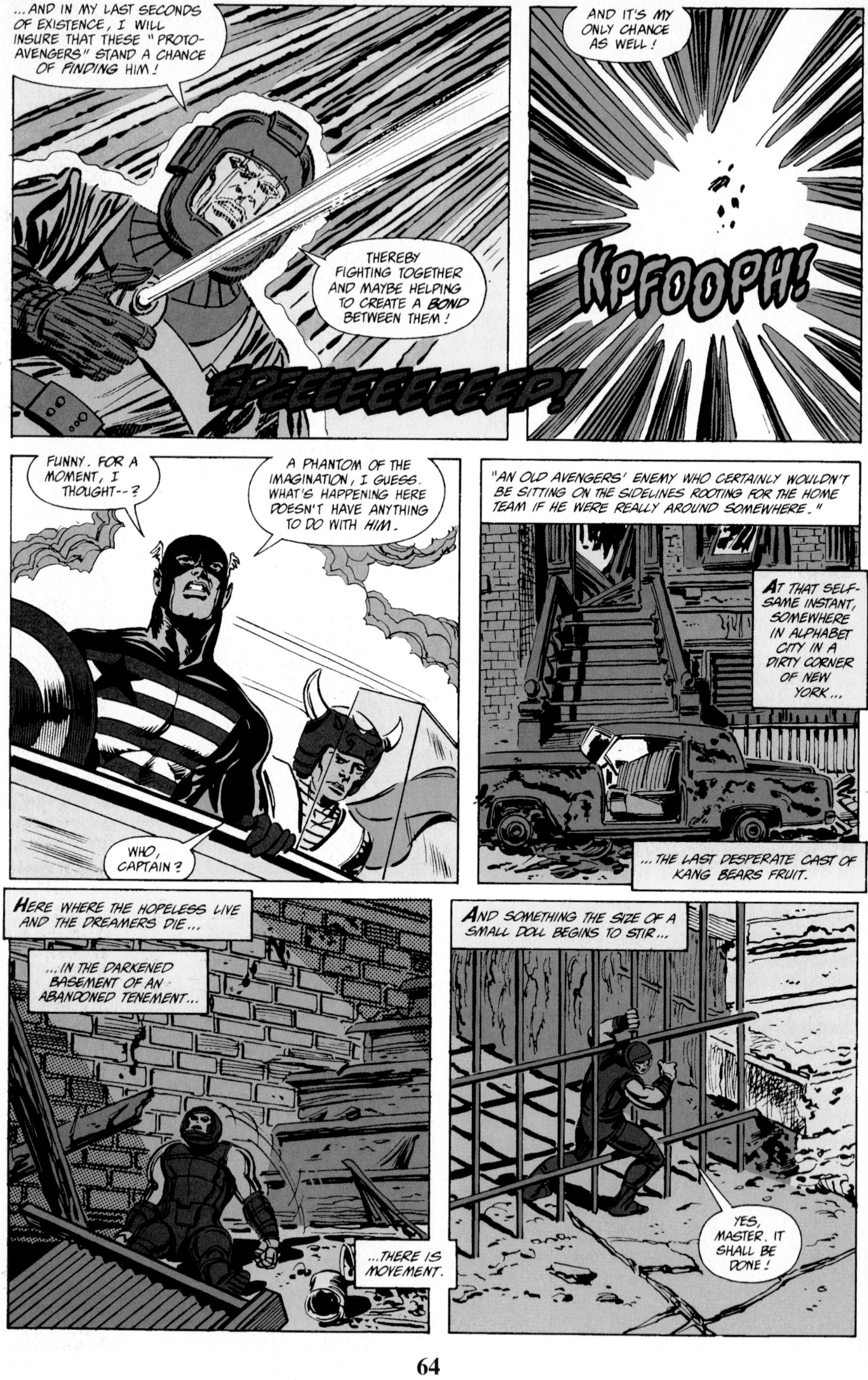
...AND IN MY LAST SECONDS OF EXISTENCE, I WILL INSURE THAT THESE "PROTO-AVENGERS" STAND A CHANCE OF FINDING HIM!
THEREBY FIGHTING TOGETHER AND MAYBE HELPING TO CREATE A BOND BETWEEN THEM!
SPEEEEEEEEEP!
AND IT'S MY ONLY CHANCE AS WELL!
KPFOOPH!
FUNNY. FOR A MOMENT, I THOUGHT--?
A PHANTOM OF THE IMAGINATION, I GUESS. WHAT'S HAPPENING HERE DOESN'T HAVE ANYTHING TO DO WITH HIM.
WHO, CAPTAIN?
"AN OLD AVENGERS' ENEMY WHO CERTAINLY WOULDN'T BE SITTING ON THE SIDELINES ROOTING FOR THE HOME TEAM IF HE WERE REALLY AROUND SOMEWHERE."
AT THAT SELF-SAME INSTANT, SOMEWHERE IN ALPHABET CITY IN A DIRTY CORNER OF NEW YORK...
...THE LAST DESPERATE CAST OF KANG BEARS FRUIT.
HERE WHERE THE HOPELESS LIVE AND THE DREAMERS DIE...
...IN THE DARKENED BASEMENT OF AN ABANDONED TENEMENT...
...THERE IS MOVEMENT.
AND SOMETHING THE SIZE OF A SMALL DOLL BEGINS TO STIR...
YES, MASTER. IT SHALL BE DONE!

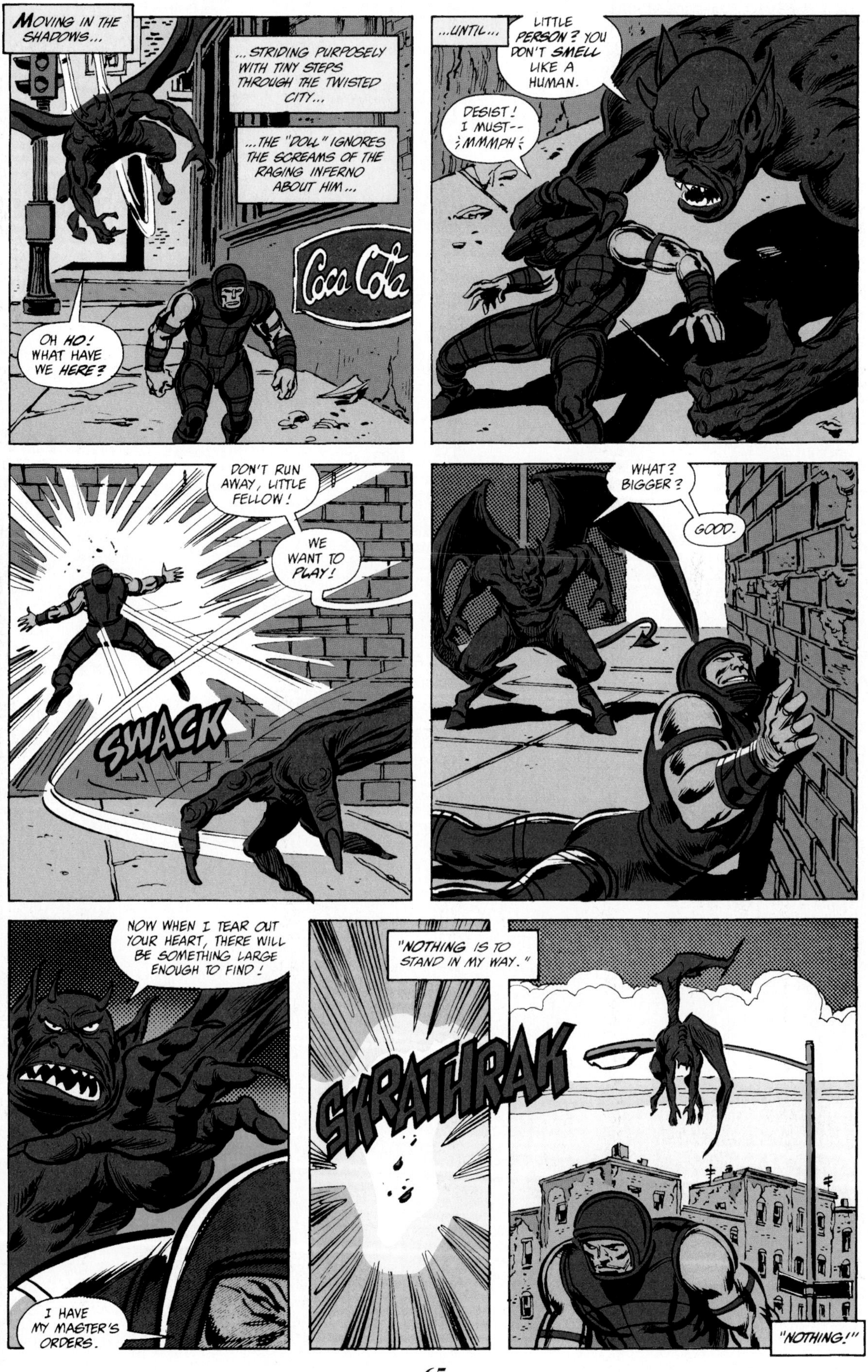
MOVING IN THE SHADOWS...
...STRIDING PURPOSELY WITH TINY STEPS THROUGH THE TWISTED CITY...
...THE "DOLL" IGNORES THE SCREAMS OF THE RAGING INFERNO ABOUT HIM...
Coca Cola
OH HO! WHAT HAVE WE HERE?
...UNTIL...
LITTLE PERSON? YOU DON'T SMELL LIKE A HUMAN.
DESIST! I MUST-- MMMPH
DON'T RUN AWAY, LITTLE FELLOW!
WE WANT TO PLAY!
SWACK
WHAT? BIGGER?
GOOD.
NOW WHEN I TEAR OUT YOUR HEART, THERE WILL BE SOMETHING LARGE ENOUGH TO FIND!
I HAVE MY MASTER'S ORDERS.
"NOTHING IS TO STAND IN MY WAY."
SKRATHRAK
"NOTHING!"

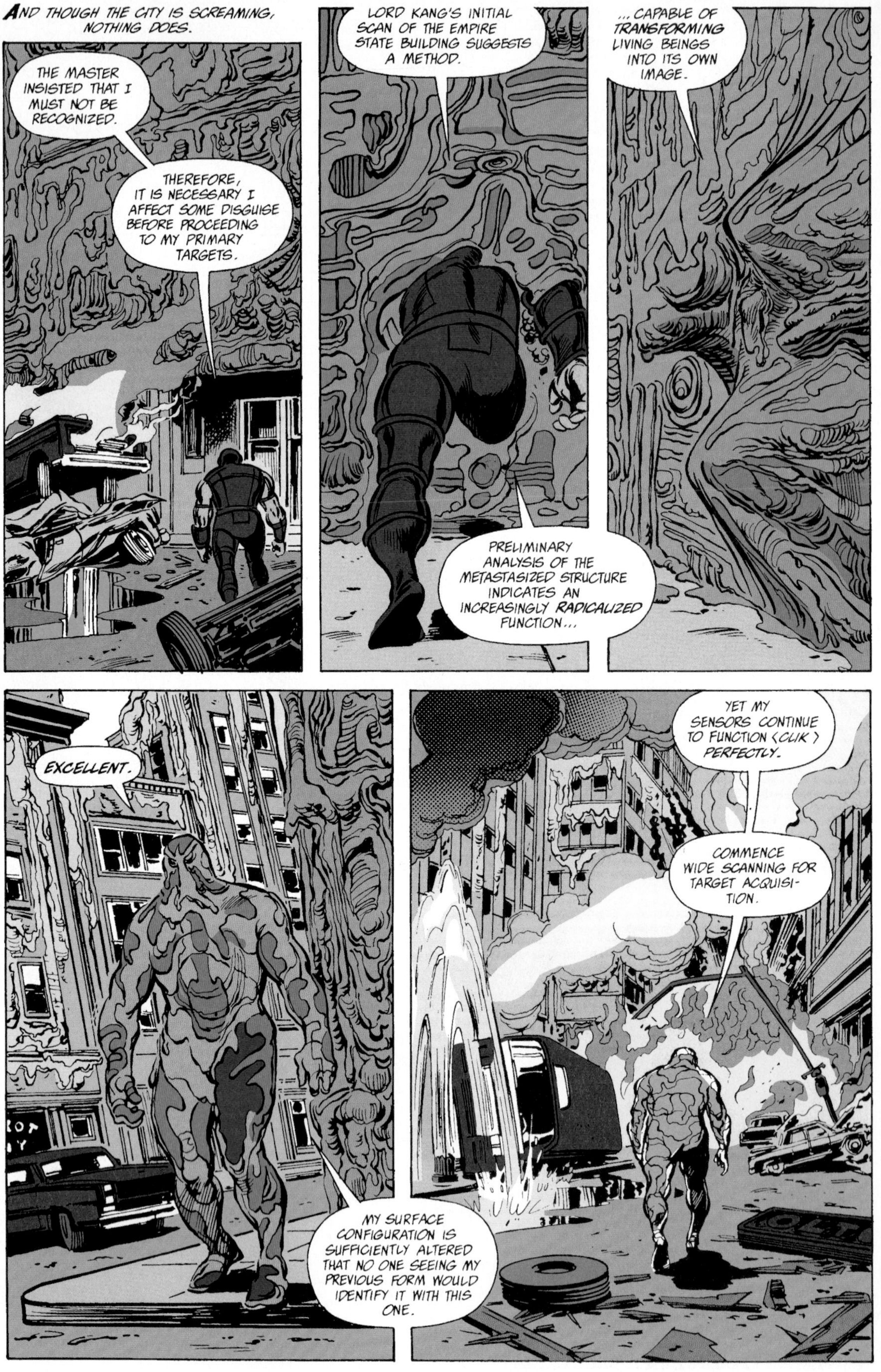
AND THOUGH THE CITY IS SCREAMING, NOTHING DOES.
THE MASTER INSISTED THAT I MUST NOT BE RECOGNIZED.
THEREFORE, IT IS NECESSARY I AFFECT SOME DISGUISE BEFORE PROCEEDING TO MY PRIMARY TARGETS.
LORD KANG'S INITIAL SCAN OF THE EMPIRE STATE BUILDING SUGGESTS A METHOD.
PRELIMINARY ANALYSIS OF THE METASTASIZED STRUCTURE INDICATES AN INCREASINGLY RADICALIZED FUNCTION...
...CAPABLE OF TRANSFORMING LIVING BEINGS INTO ITS OWN IMAGE.
EXCELLENT.
MY SURFACE CONFIGURATION IS SUFFICIENTLY ALTERED THAT NO ONE SEEING MY PREVIOUS FORM WOULD IDENTIFY IT WITH THIS ONE.
YET MY SENSORS CONTINUE TO FUNCTION <CLIK> PERFECTLY.
COMMENCE WIDE SCANNING FOR TARGET ACQUISITION.

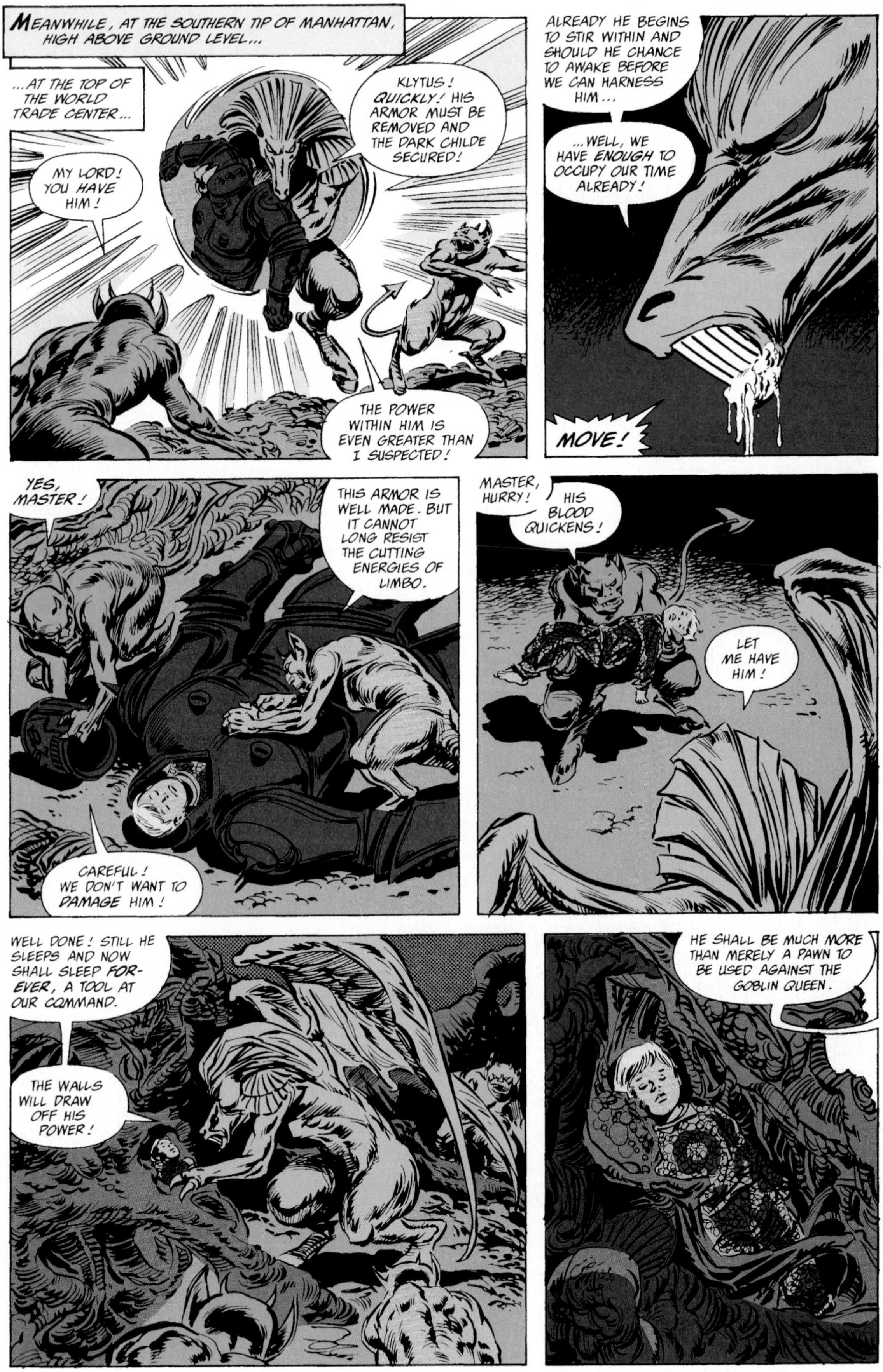
MEANWHILE, AT THE SOUTHERN TIP OF MANHATTAN, HIGH ABOVE GROUND LEVEL...
...AT THE TOP OF THE WORLD TRADE CENTER...
MY LORD! YOU HAVE HIM!
KLYTUS! QUICKLY! HIS ARMOR MUST BE REMOVED AND THE DARK CHILDE SECURED!
THE POWER WITHIN HIM IS EVEN GREATER THAN I SUSPECTED!
ALREADY HE BEGINS TO STIR WITHIN AND SHOULD HE CHANCE TO AWAKE BEFORE WE CAN HARNESS HIM...
...WELL, WE HAVE ENOUGH TO OCCUPY OUR TIME ALREADY!
MOVE!
YES, MASTER!
THIS ARMOR IS WELL MADE. BUT IT CANNOT LONG RESIST THE CUTTING ENERGIES OF LIMBO.
CAREFUL! WE DON'T WANT TO DAMAGE HIM!
MASTER, HURRY!
HIS BLOOD QUICKENS!
LET ME HAVE HIM!
WELL DONE! STILL HE SLEEPS AND NOW SHALL SLEEP FOREVER, A TOOL AT OUR COMMAND.
THE WALLS WILL DRAW OFF HIS POWER!
HE SHALL BE MUCH MORE THAN MERELY A PAWN TO BE USED AGAINST THE GOBLIN QUEEN.

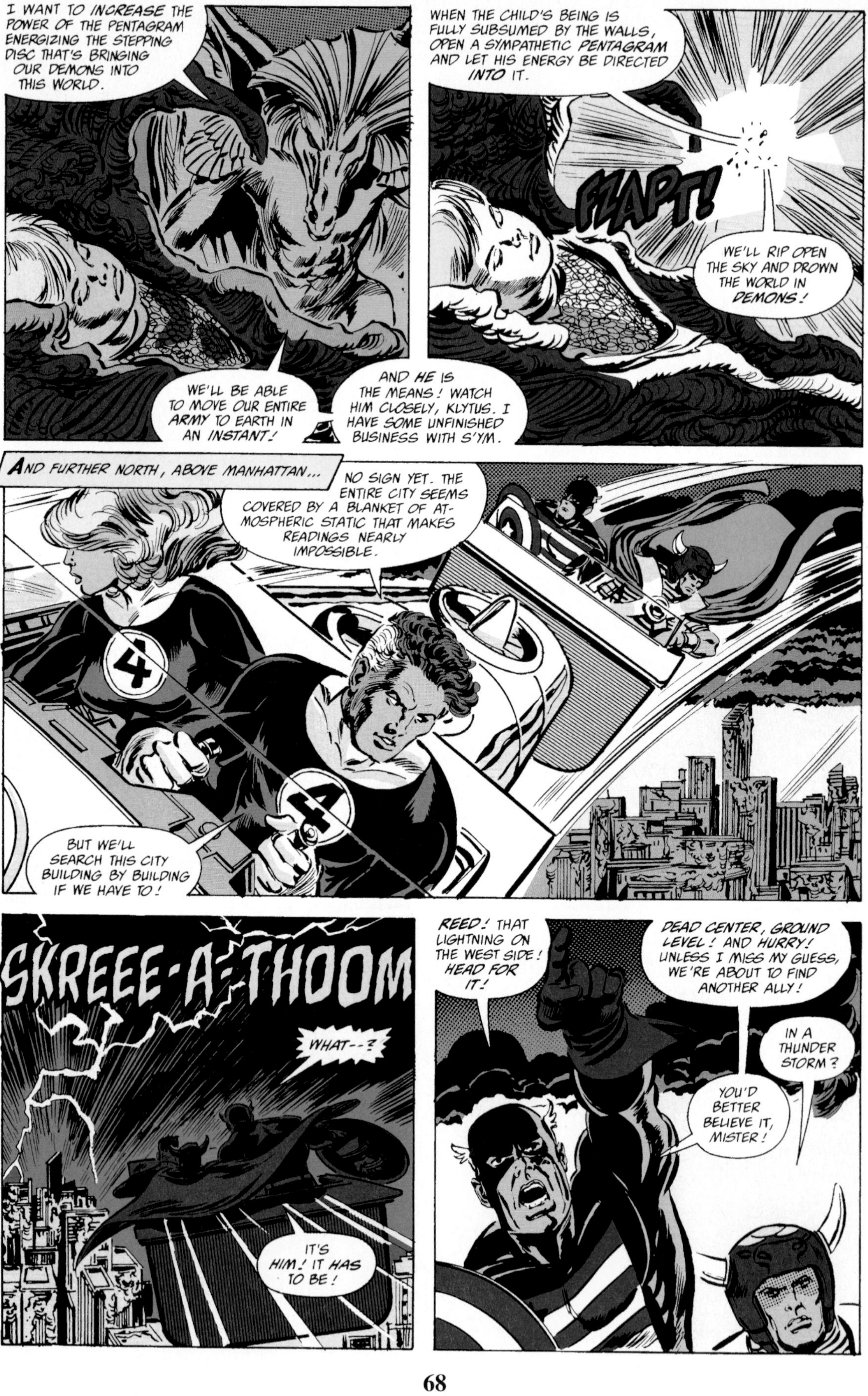
I WANT TO INCREASE THE POWER OF THE PENTAGRAM ENERGIZING THE STEPPING DISC THAT'S BRINGING OUR DEMONS INTO THIS WORLD.
WE'LL BE ABLE TO MOVE OUR ENTIRE ARMY TO EARTH IN AN INSTANT!
AND HE IS THE MEANS! WATCH HIM CLOSELY, KLYTUS. I HAVE SOME UNFINISHED BUSINESS WITH S'YM.
WHEN THE CHILD'S BEING IS FULLY SUBSUMED BY THE WALLS, OPEN A SYMPATHETIC PENTAGRAM AND LET HIS ENERGY BE DIRECTED INTO IT.
FZAPT!
WE'LL RIP OPEN THE SKY AND DROWN THE WORLD IN DEMONS!
AND FURTHER NORTH, ABOVE MANHATTAN...
NO SIGN YET. THE ENTIRE CITY SEEMS COVERED BY A BLANKET OF AT-MOSPHERIC STATIC THAT MAKES READINGS NEARLY IMPOSSIBLE.
BUT WE'LL SEARCH THIS CITY BUILDING BY BUILDING IF WE HAVE TO!
SKREEE-A-THOOM
WHAT--?
IT'S HIM! IT HAS TO BE!
REED! THAT LIGHTNING ON THE WEST SIDE! HEAD FOR IT!
DEAD CENTER, GROUND LEVEL! AND HURRY! UNLESS I MISS MY GUESS, WE'RE ABOUT TO FIND ANOTHER ALLY!
IN A THUNDER STORM?
YOU'D BETTER BELIEVE IT, MISTER!

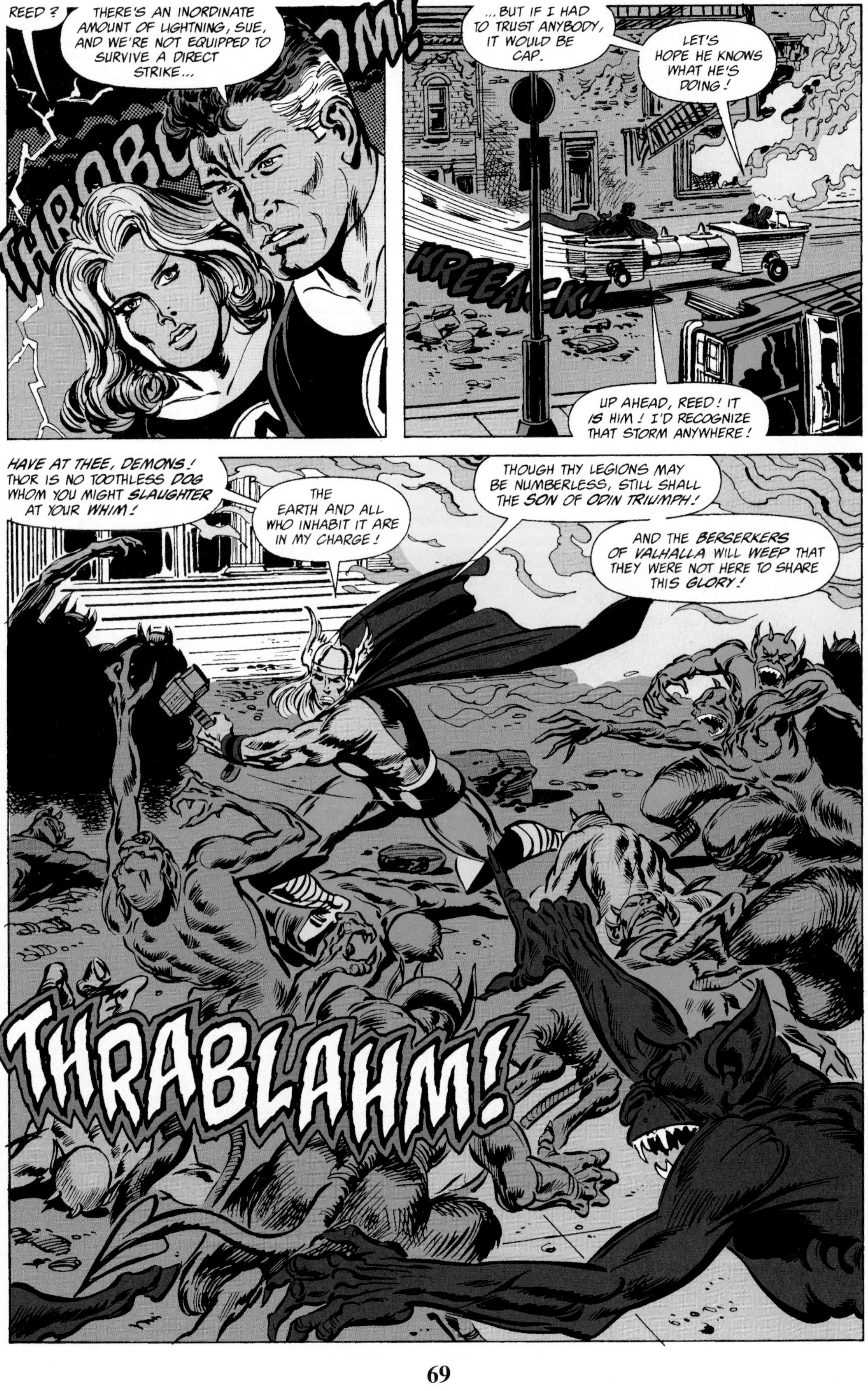
REED?
THERE'S AN INORDINATE AMOUNT OF LIGHTNING, SUE, AND WE'RE NOT EQUIPPED TO SURVIVE A DIRECT STRIKE...
THROBOOM!
...BUT IF I HAD TO TRUST ANYBODY, IT WOULD BE CAP.
LET'S HOPE HE KNOWS WHAT HE'S DOING!
KREEACK!
UP AHEAD, REED! IT IS HIM! I'D RECOGNIZE THAT STORM ANYWHERE!
HAVE AT THEE, DEMONS! THOR IS NO TOOTHLESS DOG WHOM YOU MIGHT SLAUGHTER AT YOUR WHIM!
THE EARTH AND ALL WHO INHABIT IT ARE IN MY CHARGE!
THOUGH THY LEGIONS MAY BE NUMBERLESS, STILL SHALL THE SON OF ODIN TRIUMPH!
AND THE BERSERKERS OF VALHALLA WILL WEEP THAT THEY WERE NOT HERE TO SHARE THIS GLORY!
THRABLAHM!

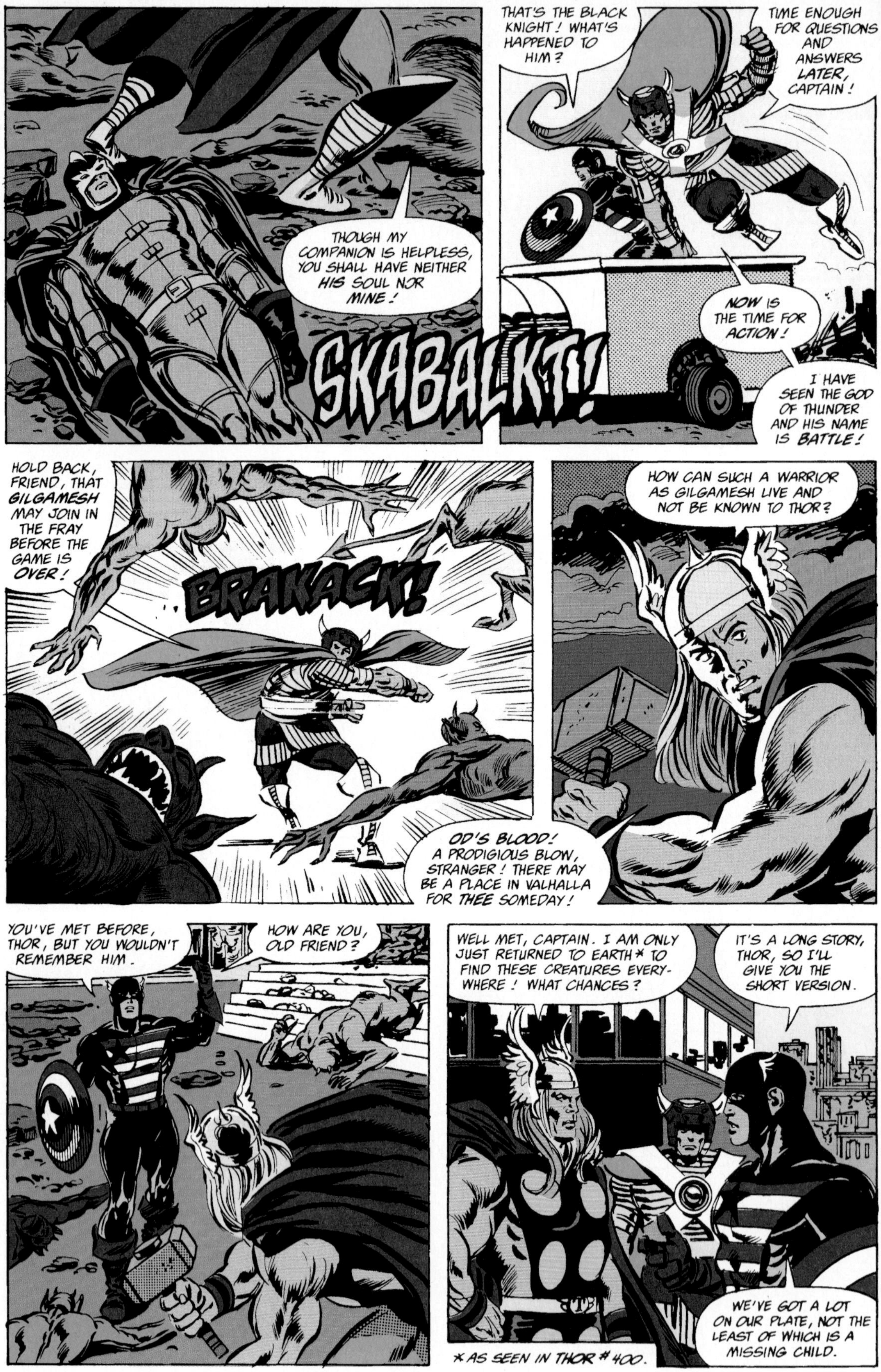
THOUGH MY COMPANION IS HELPLESS, YOU SHALL HAVE NEITHER HIS SOUL NOR MINE!
SKABALKT!
THAT'S THE BLACK KNIGHT! WHAT'S HAPPENED TO HIM?
TIME ENOUGH FOR QUESTIONS AND ANSWERS LATER, CAPTAIN!
NOW IS THE TIME FOR ACTION!
I HAVE SEEN THE GOD OF THUNDER AND HIS NAME IS BATTLE!
HOLD BACK, FRIEND, THAT GILGAMESH MAY JOIN IN THE FRAY BEFORE THE GAME IS OVER!
BRAKACK!
OD'S BLOOD! A PRODIGIOUS BLOW, STRANGER! THERE MAY BE A PLACE IN VALHALLA FOR THEE SOMEDAY!
HOW CAN SUCH A WARRIOR AS GILGAMESH LIVE AND NOT BE KNOWN TO THOR?
YOU'VE MET BEFORE, THOR, BUT YOU WOULDN'T REMEMBER HIM.
HOW ARE YOU, OLD FRIEND?
WELL MET, CAPTAIN. I AM ONLY JUST RETURNED TO EARTH* TO FIND THESE CREATURES EVERYWHERE! WHAT CHANCES?
IT'S A LONG STORY, THOR, SO I'LL GIVE YOU THE SHORT VERSION.
WE'VE GOT A LOT ON OUR PLATE, NOT THE LEAST OF WHICH IS A MISSING CHILD.
*AS SEEN IN THOR #400.

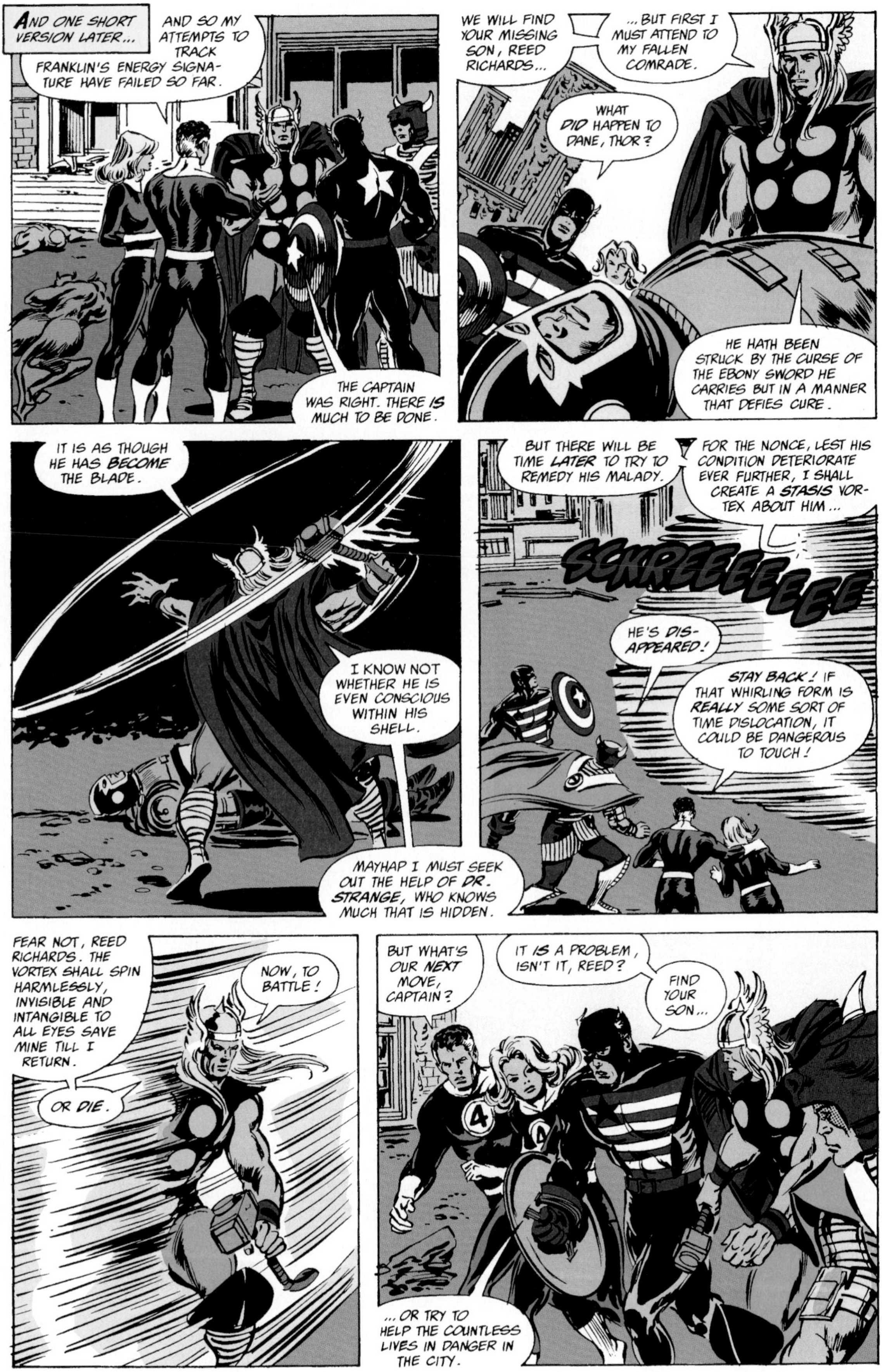

AND ONE SHORT VERSION LATER...
AND SO MY ATTEMPTS TO TRACK FRANKLIN'S ENERGY SIGNATURE HAVE FAILED SO FAR.
THE CAPTAIN WAS RIGHT. THERE IS MUCH TO BE DONE.
WE WILL FIND YOUR MISSING SON, REED RICHARDS...
...BUT FIRST I MUST ATTEND TO MY FALLEN COMRADE.
WHAT DID HAPPEN TO DANE, THOR?
HE HATH BEEN STRUCK BY THE CURSE OF THE EBONY SWORD HE CARRIES BUT IN A MANNER THAT DEFIES CURE.
IT IS AS THOUGH HE HAS BECOME THE BLADE.
I KNOW NOT WHETHER HE IS EVEN CONSCIOUS WITHIN HIS SHELL.
MAYHAP I MUST SEEK OUT THE HELP OF DR. STRANGE, WHO KNOWS MUCH THAT IS HIDDEN.
BUT THERE WILL BE TIME LATER TO TRY TO REMEDY HIS MALADY.
FOR THE NONCE, LEST HIS CONDITION DETERIORATE EVER FURTHER, I SHALL CREATE A STASIS VORTEX ABOUT HIM...
SCHREEEEEEEE
HE'S DISAPPEARED!
STAY BACK! IF THAT WHIRLING FORM IS REALLY SOME SORT OF TIME DISLOCATION, IT COULD BE DANGEROUS TO TOUCH!
FEAR NOT, REED RICHARDS. THE VORTEX SHALL SPIN HARMLESSLY, INVISIBLE AND INTANGIBLE TO ALL EYES SAVE MINE TILL I RETURN.
OR DIE.
NOW, TO BATTLE!
BUT WHAT'S OUR NEXT MOVE, CAPTAIN?
IT IS A PROBLEM, ISN'T IT, REED?
FIND YOUR SON...
...OR TRY TO HELP THE COUNTLESS LIVES IN DANGER IN THE CITY.

I THINK WE MUST SPLIT UP, CAPTAIN.

WE *CAN'T* ASK THE THREE OF YOU TO AID US IN FINDING FRANKLIN WHILE THE CITY IS UNDER SIEGE.

BUT WE CAN'T ABANDON THE SEARCH OURSELVES.

TAKE THE AIR CAR TO HELP YOU SEEK OUT THE SOURCE OF THE DEMONS.

TRACKING LOCK. ⟨CLIK⟩ TARGET AQUISITION!

I'VE GOT A PORTABLE ENERGY ANALYZER TO HELP US LOCATE FRANKLIN.

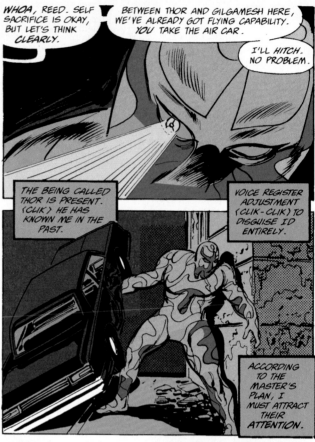

WHOA, REED. SELF SACRIFICE IS OKAY, BUT LET'S THINK *CLEARLY*.

BETWEEN THOR AND GILGAMESH HERE, WE'VE ALREADY GOT FLYING CAPABILITY. *YOU* TAKE THE AIR CAR.

I'LL *HITCH*. NO PROBLEM.

THE BEING CALLED THOR IS PRESENT. ⟨CLIK⟩ HE HAS KNOWN ME IN THE PAST.

VOICE REGISTER ADJUSTMENT ⟨CLIK-CLIK⟩ TO DISGUISE ID ENTIRELY.

ACCORDING TO THE MASTER'S PLAN, I MUST ATTRACT THEIR ATTENTION.

GREAT ZURAS! DUCK!

SMACKSH

THE DEMONS JUST INCREASED THE STAKES!

OUR IMMEDIATE PROBLEM COULD BE SIMPLY STAYING ALIVE!

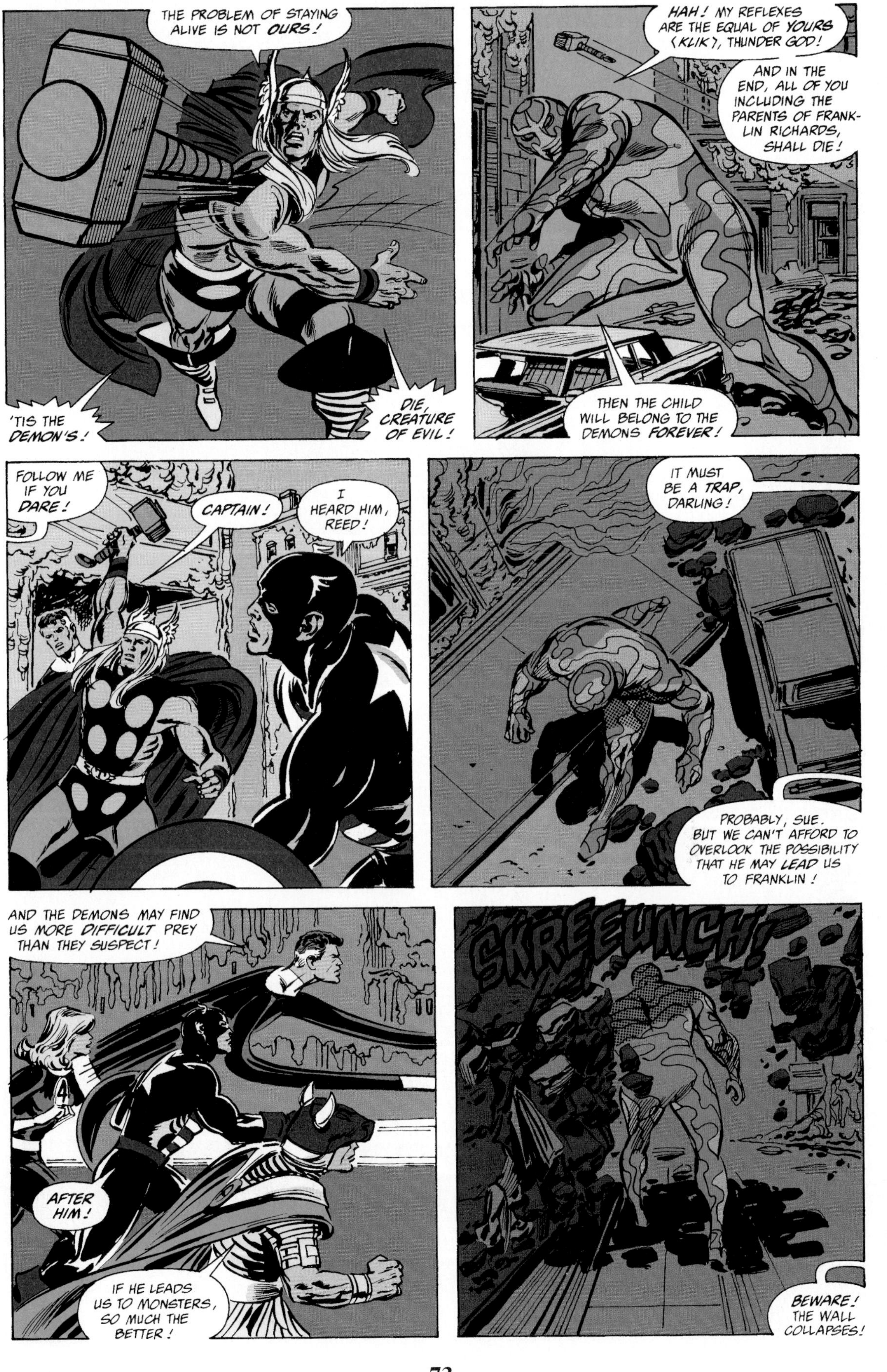
THE PROBLEM OF STAYING ALIVE IS NOT OURS!
'TIS THE DEMON'S!
DIE, CREATURE OF EVIL!
HAH! MY REFLEXES ARE THE EQUAL OF YOURS (KLIK), THUNDER GOD!
AND IN THE END, ALL OF YOU INCLUDING THE PARENTS OF FRANKLIN RICHARDS, SHALL DIE!
THEN THE CHILD WILL BELONG TO THE DEMONS FOREVER!
FOLLOW ME IF YOU DARE!
CAPTAIN!
I HEARD HIM, REED!
IT MUST BE A TRAP, DARLING!
PROBABLY, SUE. BUT WE CAN'T AFFORD TO OVERLOOK THE POSSIBILITY THAT HE MAY LEAD US TO FRANKLIN!
AND THE DEMONS MAY FIND US MORE DIFFICULT PREY THAN THEY SUSPECT!
AFTER HIM!
IF HE LEADS US TO MONSTERS, SO MUCH THE BETTER!
SKREEUNCH!
BEWARE! THE WALL COLLAPSES!

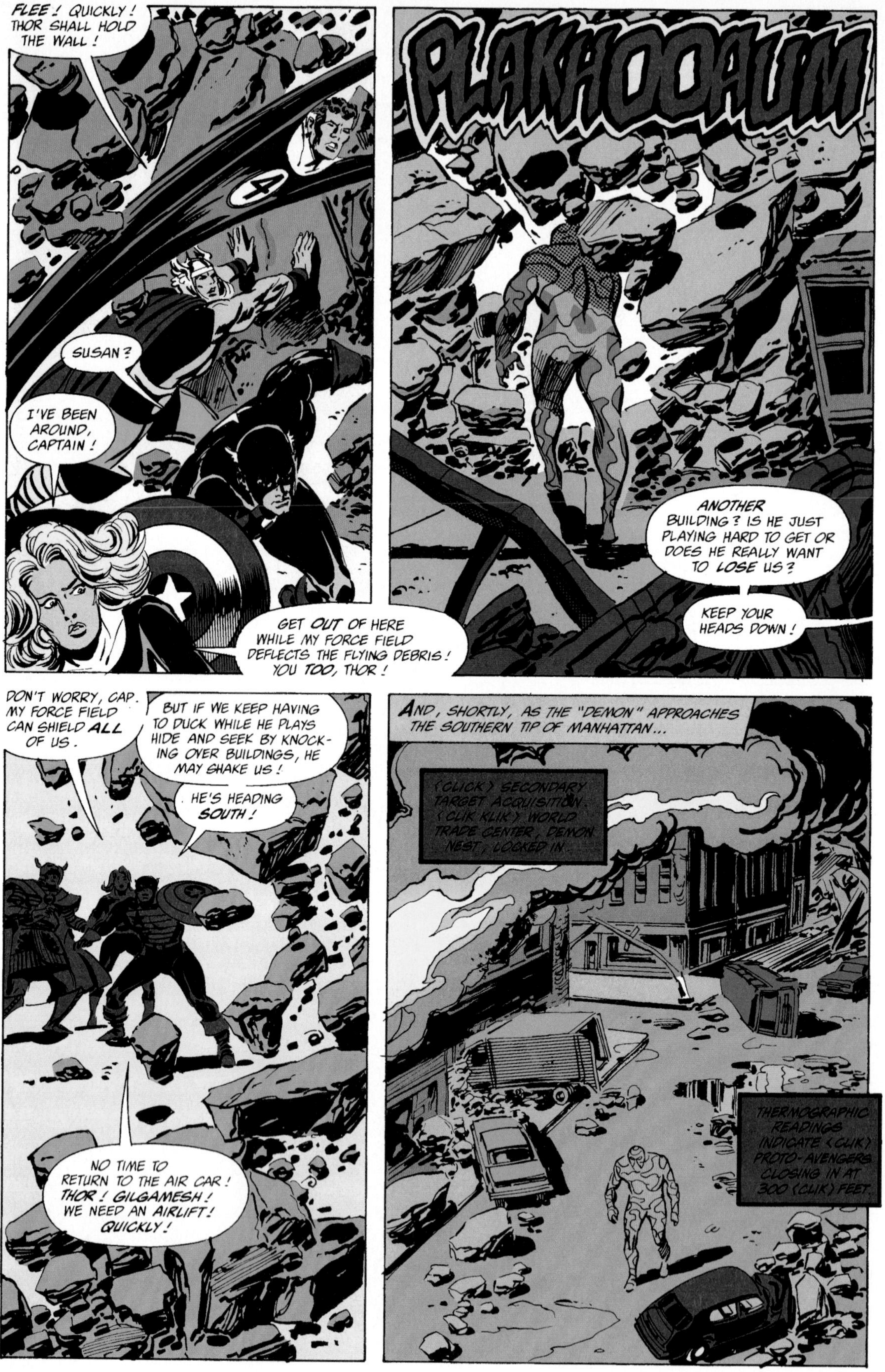
FLEE! QUICKLY! THOR SHALL HOLD THE WALL!
SUSAN?
I'VE BEEN AROUND, CAPTAIN!
GET OUT OF HERE WHILE MY FORCE FIELD DEFLECTS THE FLYING DEBRIS! YOU TOO, THOR!
PLAKHOOAUM
ANOTHER BUILDING? IS HE JUST PLAYING HARD TO GET OR DOES HE REALLY WANT TO LOSE US?
KEEP YOUR HEADS DOWN!
DON'T WORRY, CAP. MY FORCE FIELD CAN SHIELD ALL OF US.
BUT IF WE KEEP HAVING TO DUCK WHILE HE PLAYS HIDE AND SEEK BY KNOCKING OVER BUILDINGS, HE MAY SHAKE US!
HE'S HEADING SOUTH!
NO TIME TO RETURN TO THE AIR CAR! THOR! GILGAMESH! WE NEED AN AIRLIFT! QUICKLY!
AND, SHORTLY, AS THE "DEMON" APPROACHES THE SOUTHERN TIP OF MANHATTAN...
‹CLICK› SECONDARY TARGET ACQUISITION. ‹CLIK KLIK› WORLD TRADE CENTER. DEMON NEST, LOCKED IN.
THERMOGRAPHIC READINGS INDICATE ‹CLIK› PROTO-AVENGERS CLOSING IN AT 300 ‹CLIK› FEET.

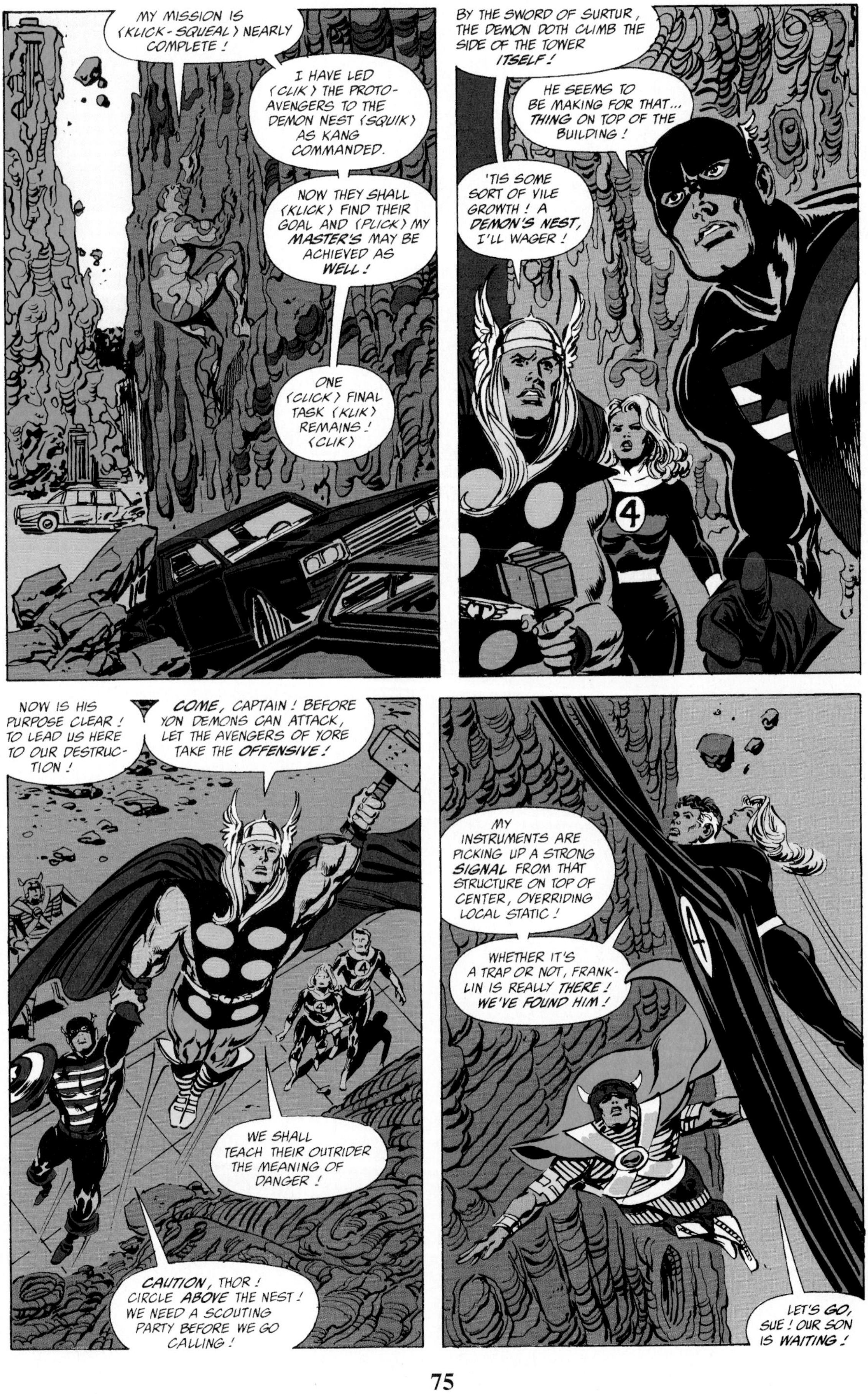
MY MISSION IS (KLICK-SQUEAL) NEARLY COMPLETE!
I HAVE LED (CLIK) THE PROTO-AVENGERS TO THE DEMON NEST (SQUIK) AS KANG COMMANDED.
NOW THEY SHALL (KLICK) FIND THEIR GOAL AND (PLICK) MY MASTER'S MAY BE ACHIEVED AS WELL!
ONE (CLICK) FINAL TASK (KLIK) REMAINS! (CLIK)
BY THE SWORD OF SURTUR, THE DEMON DOTH CLIMB THE SIDE OF THE TOWER ITSELF!
HE SEEMS TO BE MAKING FOR THAT... THING ON TOP OF THE BUILDING!
'TIS SOME SORT OF VILE GROWTH! A DEMON'S NEST, I'LL WAGER!
NOW IS HIS PURPOSE CLEAR! TO LEAD US HERE TO OUR DESTRUCTION!
COME, CAPTAIN! BEFORE YON DEMONS CAN ATTACK, LET THE AVENGERS OF YORE TAKE THE OFFENSIVE!
WE SHALL TEACH THEIR OUTRIDER THE MEANING OF DANGER!
CAUTION, THOR! CIRCLE ABOVE THE NEST! WE NEED A SCOUTING PARTY BEFORE WE GO CALLING!
MY INSTRUMENTS ARE PICKING UP A STRONG SIGNAL FROM THAT STRUCTURE ON TOP OF CENTER, OVERRIDING LOCAL STATIC!
WHETHER IT'S A TRAP OR NOT, FRANKLIN IS REALLY THERE! WE'VE FOUND HIM!
LET'S GO, SUE! OUR SON IS WAITING!

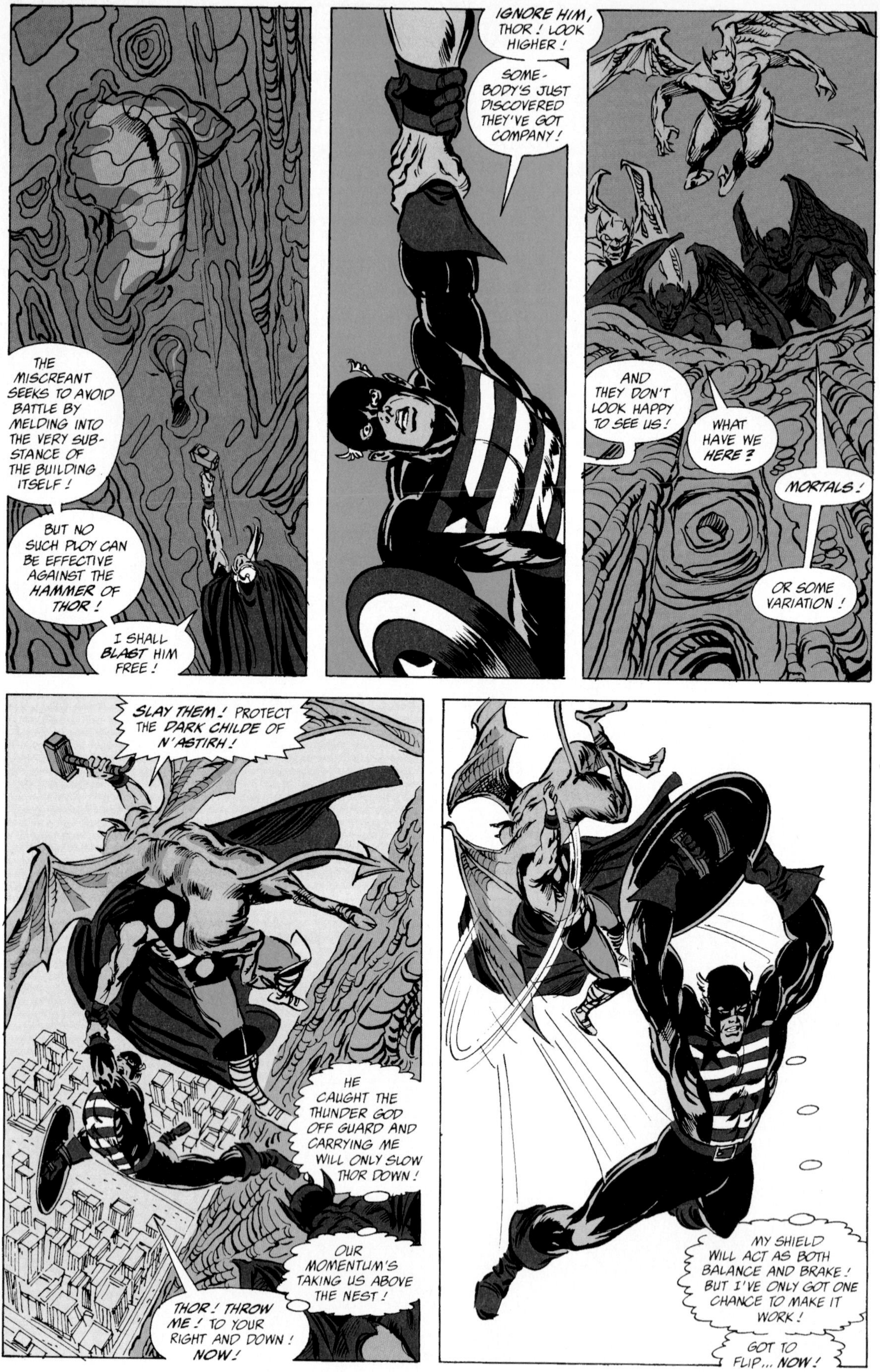

THE MISCREANT SEEKS TO AVOID BATTLE BY MELDING INTO THE VERY SUBSTANCE OF THE BUILDING ITSELF!
BUT NO SUCH PLOY CAN BE EFFECTIVE AGAINST THE HAMMER OF THOR!
I SHALL BLAST HIM FREE!
IGNORE HIM, THOR! LOOK HIGHER!
SOMEBODY'S JUST DISCOVERED THEY'VE GOT COMPANY!
AND THEY DON'T LOOK HAPPY TO SEE US!
WHAT HAVE WE HERE?
MORTALS!
OR SOME VARIATION!
SLAY THEM! PROTECT THE DARK CHILDE OF N'ASTIRH!
HE CAUGHT THE THUNDER GOD OFF GUARD AND CARRYING ME WILL ONLY SLOW THOR DOWN!
OUR MOMENTUM'S TAKING US ABOVE THE NEST!
THOR! THROW ME! TO YOUR RIGHT AND DOWN! NOW!
MY SHIELD WILL ACT AS BOTH BALANCE AND BRAKE! BUT I'VE ONLY GOT ONE CHANCE TO MAKE IT WORK!
GOT TO FLIP... NOW!

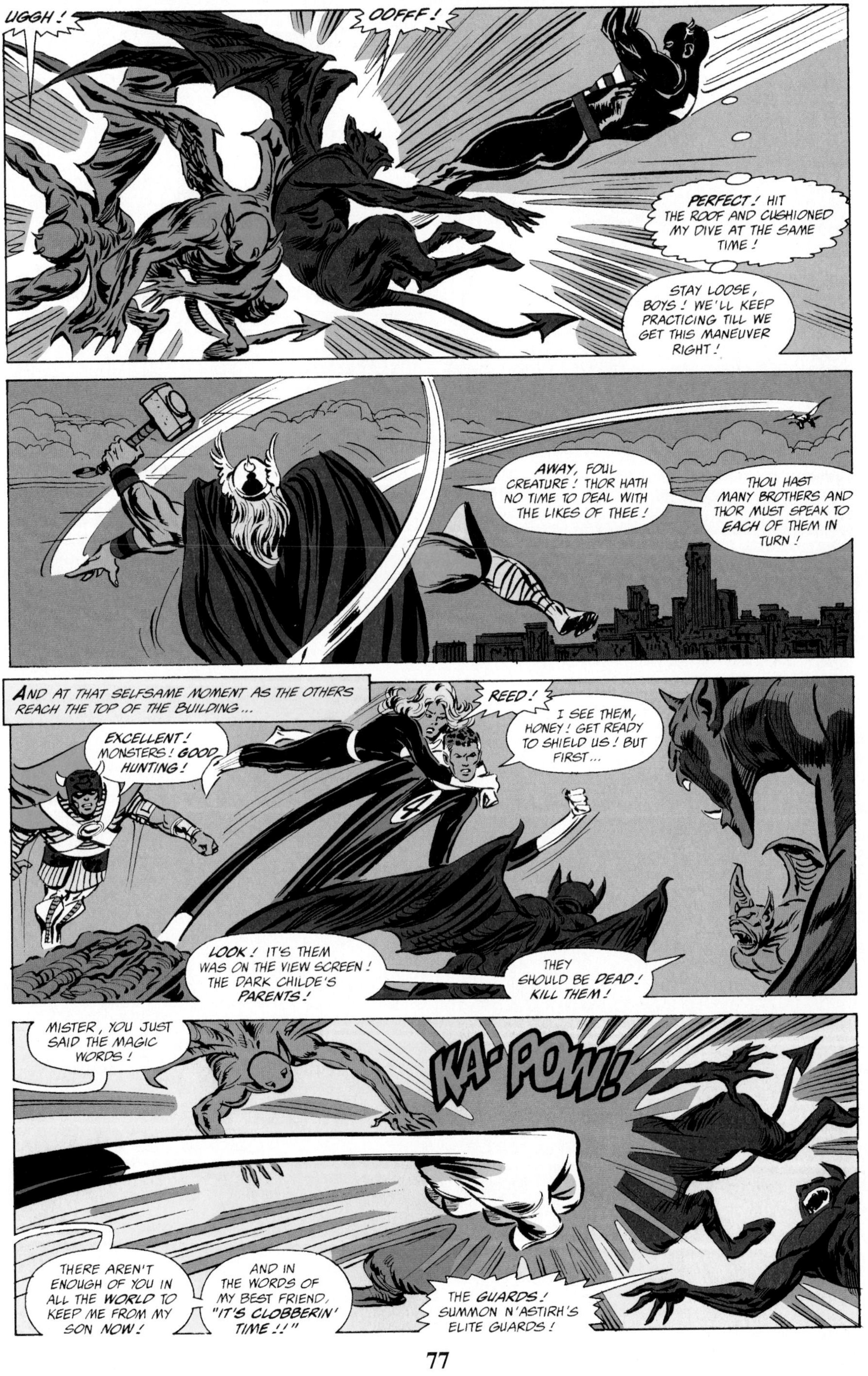
UGGH!
OOFFF!
PERFECT! HIT THE ROOF AND CUSHIONED MY DIVE AT THE SAME TIME!
STAY LOOSE, BOYS! WE'LL KEEP PRACTICING TILL WE GET THIS MANEUVER RIGHT!
AWAY, FOUL CREATURE! THOR HATH NO TIME TO DEAL WITH THE LIKES OF THEE!
THOU HAST MANY BROTHERS AND THOR MUST SPEAK TO EACH OF THEM IN TURN!
AND AT THAT SELFSAME MOMENT AS THE OTHERS REACH THE TOP OF THE BUILDING...
EXCELLENT! MONSTERS! GOOD HUNTING!
REED!
I SEE THEM, HONEY! GET READY TO SHIELD US! BUT FIRST...
LOOK! IT'S THEM WAS ON THE VIEW SCREEN! THE DARK CHILDE'S PARENTS!
THEY SHOULD BE DEAD! KILL THEM!
MISTER, YOU JUST SAID THE MAGIC WORDS!
KA-POW!
THERE AREN'T ENOUGH OF YOU IN ALL THE WORLD TO KEEP ME FROM MY SON NOW!
AND IN THE WORDS OF MY BEST FRIEND, "IT'S CLOBBERIN' TIME!!"
THE GUARDS! SUMMON N'ASTIRH'S ELITE GUARDS!

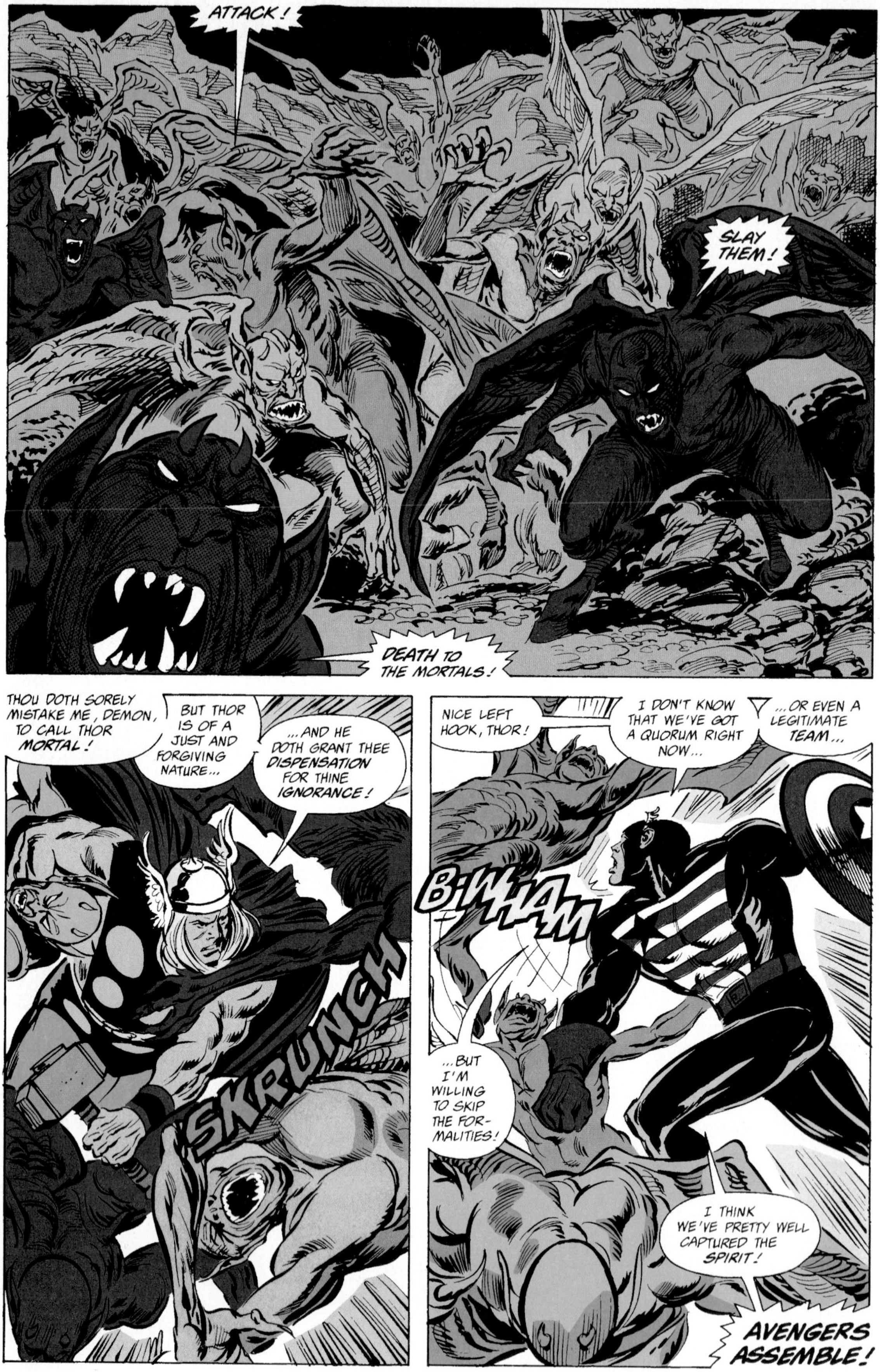
ATTACK!
SLAY THEM!
DEATH TO THE MORTALS!
THOU DOTH SORELY MISTAKE ME, DEMON, TO CALL THOR MORTAL!
BUT THOR IS OF A JUST AND FORGIVING NATURE...
...AND HE DOTH GRANT THEE DISPENSATION FOR THINE IGNORANCE!
SKRUNCH
NICE LEFT HOOK, THOR!
I DON'T KNOW THAT WE'VE GOT A QUORUM RIGHT NOW...
...OR EVEN A LEGITIMATE TEAM...
B-WHAM
...BUT I'M WILLING TO SKIP THE FOR-MALITIES!
I THINK WE'VE PRETTY WELL CAPTURED THE SPIRIT!
AVENGERS ASSEMBLE!

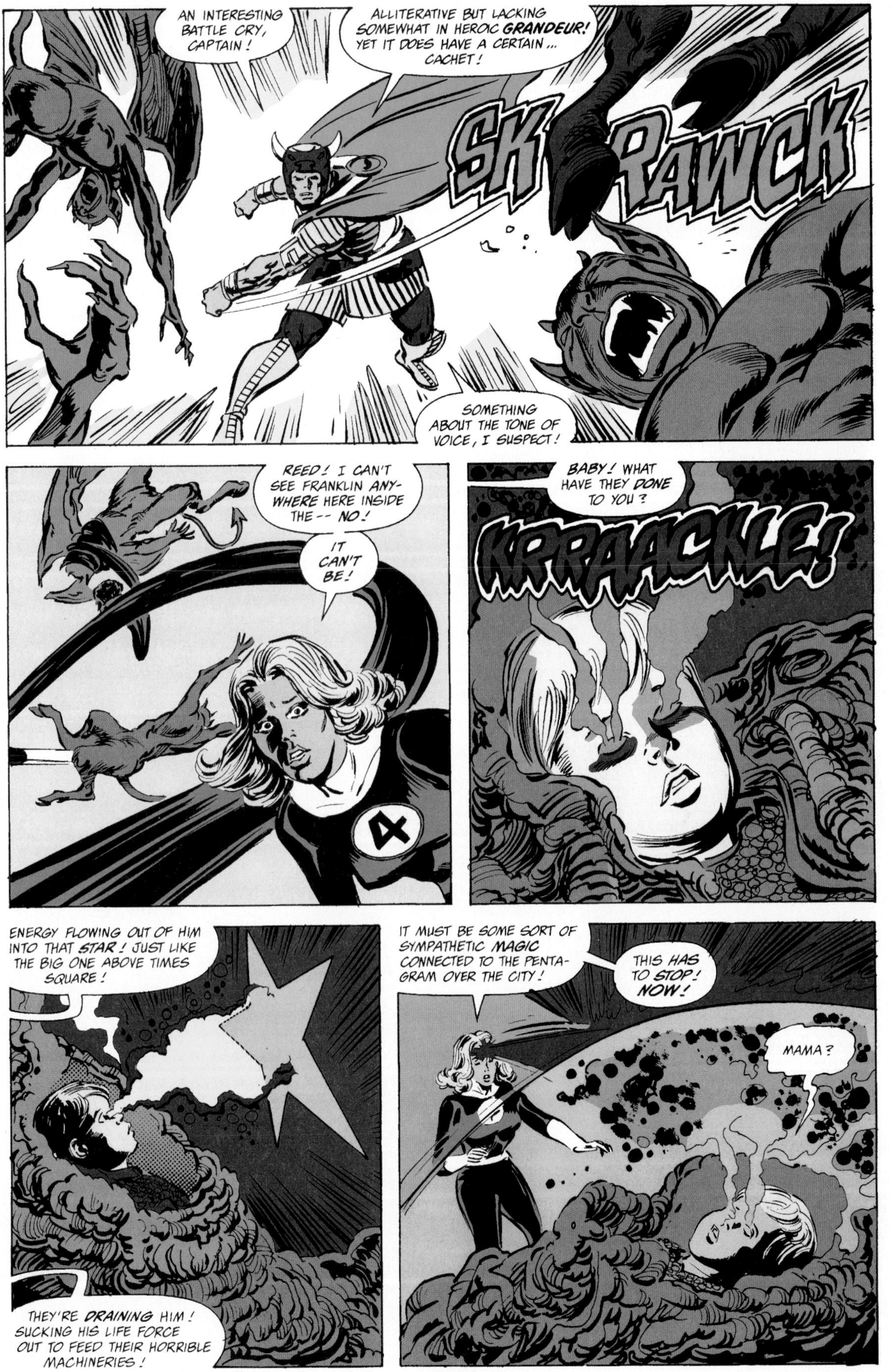
AN INTERESTING BATTLE CRY, CAPTAIN!
ALLITERATIVE BUT LACKING SOMEWHAT IN HEROIC GRANDEUR! YET IT DOES HAVE A CERTAIN... CACHET!
SKRAWCK
SOMETHING ABOUT THE TONE OF VOICE, I SUSPECT!
REED! I CAN'T SEE FRANKLIN ANYWHERE HERE INSIDE THE -- NO!
IT CAN'T BE!
BABY! WHAT HAVE THEY DONE TO YOU?
KRRAACKLE!
ENERGY FLOWING OUT OF HIM INTO THAT STAR! JUST LIKE THE BIG ONE ABOVE TIMES SQUARE!
THEY'RE DRAINING HIM! SUCKING HIS LIFE FORCE OUT TO FEED THEIR HORRIBLE MACHINERIES!
IT MUST BE SOME SORT OF SYMPATHETIC MAGIC CONNECTED TO THE PENTAGRAM OVER THE CITY!
THIS HAS TO STOP! NOW!
MAMA?

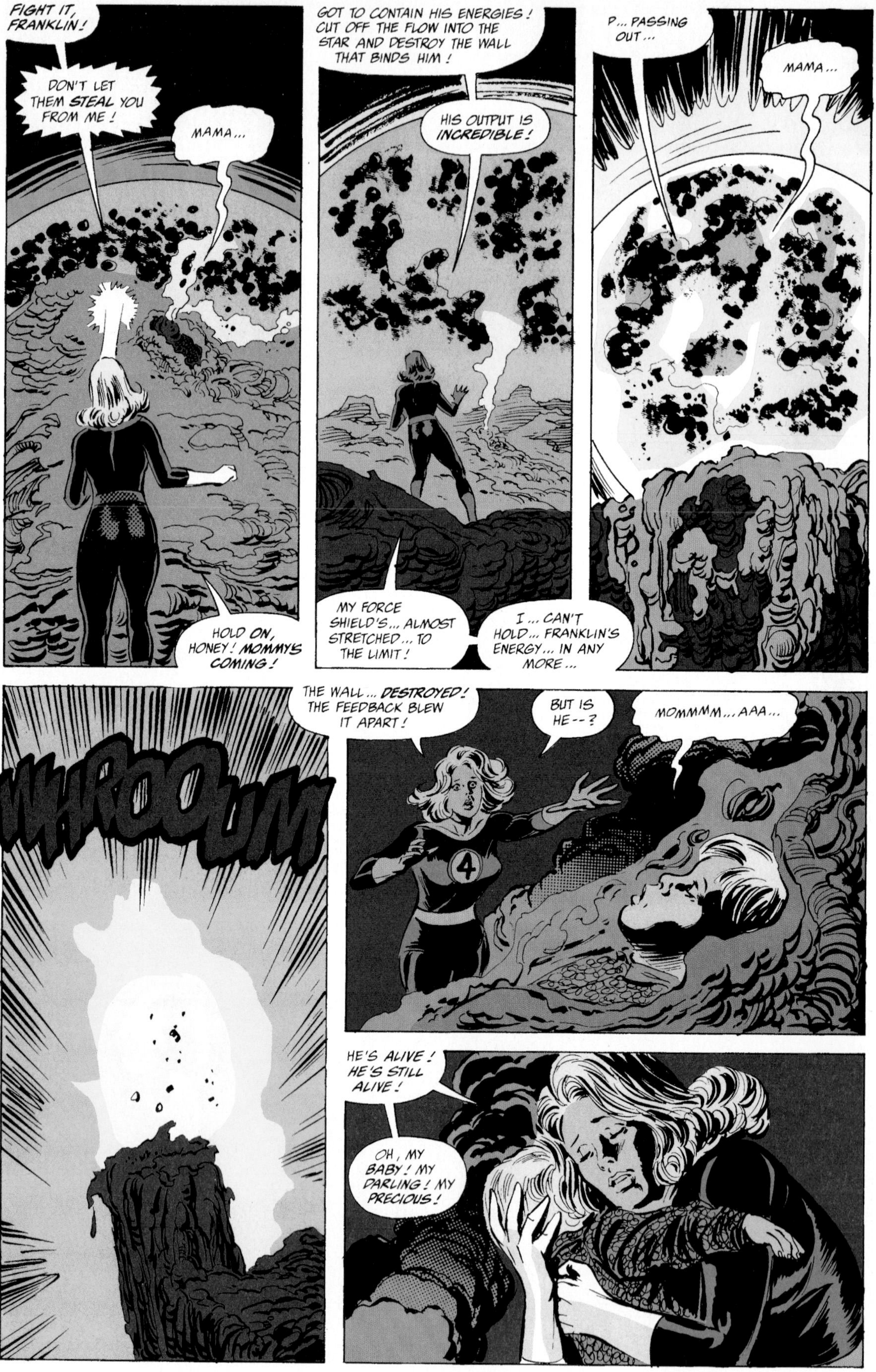
FIGHT IT, FRANKLIN!
DON'T LET THEM STEAL YOU FROM ME!
MAMA...
HOLD ON, HONEY! MOMMY'S COMING!
GOT TO CONTAIN HIS ENERGIES! CUT OFF THE FLOW INTO THE STAR AND DESTROY THE WALL THAT BINDS HIM!
HIS OUTPUT IS INCREDIBLE!
MY FORCE SHIELD'S... ALMOST STRETCHED... TO THE LIMIT!
P... PASSING OUT...
MAMA...
I... CAN'T HOLD... FRANKLIN'S ENERGY... IN ANY MORE...
WHROOOM
THE WALL... DESTROYED! THE FEEDBACK BLEW IT APART!
BUT IS HE--?
MOMMMM... AAA...
HE'S ALIVE! HE'S STILL ALIVE!
OH, MY BABY! MY DARLING! MY PRECIOUS!

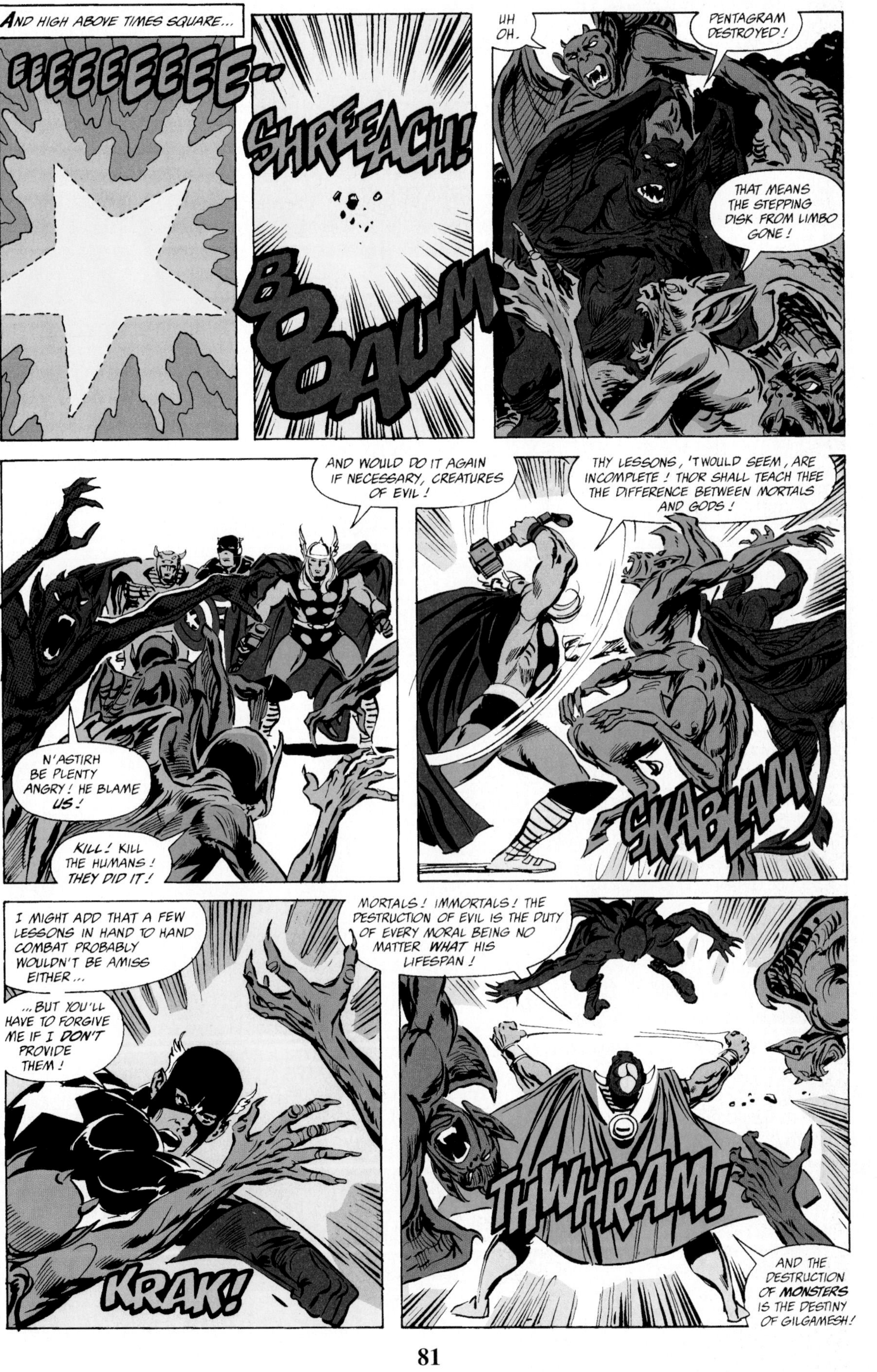

AND HIGH ABOVE TIMES SQUARE...
EEEEEEEEEE--
SHREEACH!
BOOAUM!
UH OH.
PENTAGRAM DESTROYED!
THAT MEANS THE STEPPING DISK FROM LIMBO GONE!
AND WOULD DO IT AGAIN IF NECESSARY, CREATURES OF EVIL!
N'ASTIRH BE PLENTY ANGRY! HE BLAME US!
KILL! KILL THE HUMANS! THEY DID IT!
THY LESSONS, 'TWOULD SEEM, ARE INCOMPLETE! THOR SHALL TEACH THEE THE DIFFERENCE BETWEEN MORTALS AND GODS!
SKABLAM
I MIGHT ADD THAT A FEW LESSONS IN HAND TO HAND COMBAT PROBABLY WOULDN'T BE AMISS EITHER...
...BUT YOU'LL HAVE TO FORGIVE ME IF I DON'T PROVIDE THEM!
KRAK!
MORTALS! IMMORTALS! THE DESTRUCTION OF EVIL IS THE DUTY OF EVERY MORAL BEING NO MATTER WHAT HIS LIFESPAN!
THWHRAM!
AND THE DESTRUCTION OF MONSTERS IS THE DESTINY OF GILGAMESH!

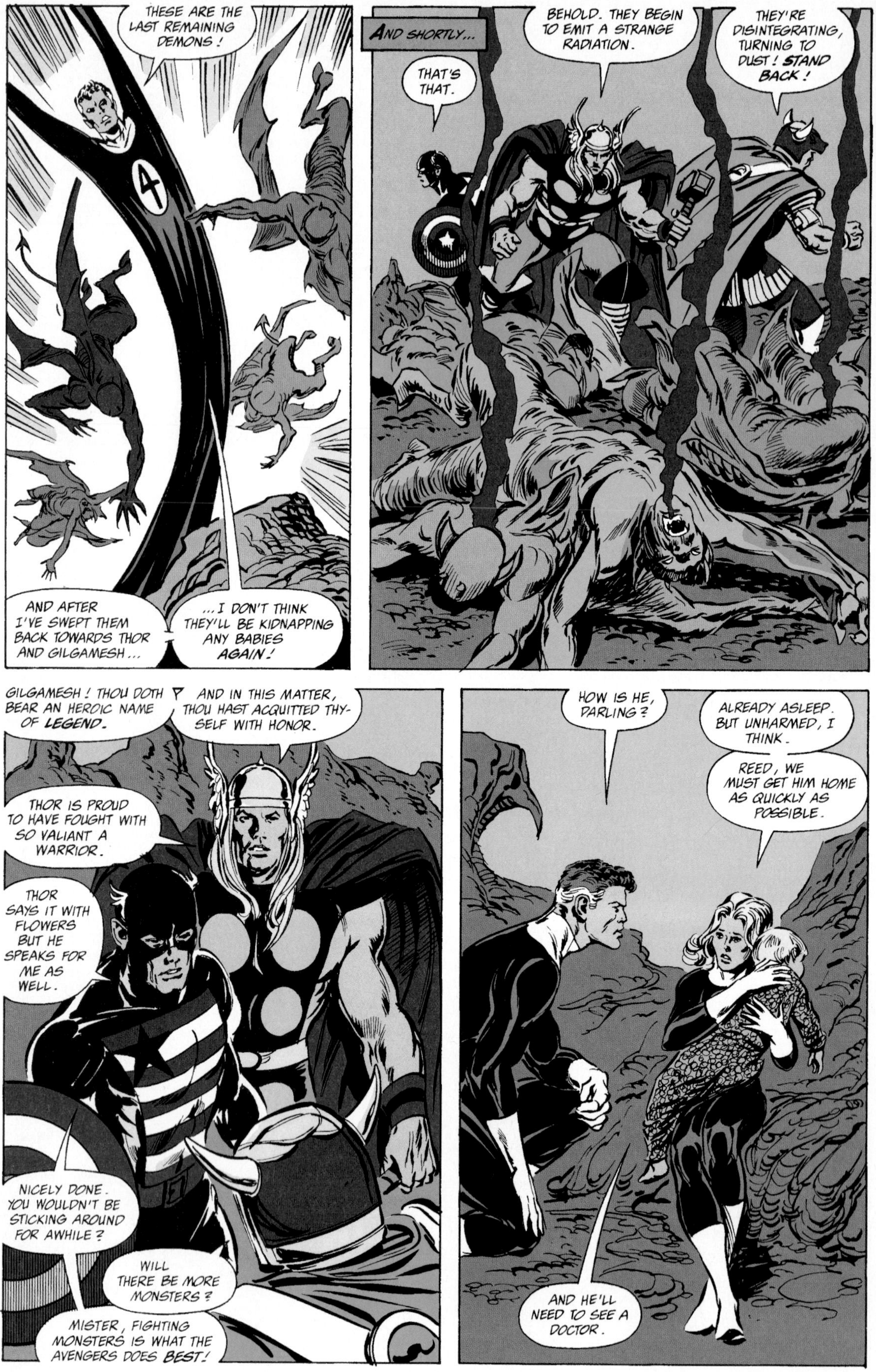

THESE ARE THE LAST REMAINING DEMONS!
AND AFTER I'VE SWEPT THEM BACK TOWARDS THOR AND GILGAMESH...
...I DON'T THINK THEY'LL BE KIDNAPPING ANY BABIES AGAIN!
AND SHORTLY...
THAT'S THAT.
BEHOLD. THEY BEGIN TO EMIT A STRANGE RADIATION.
THEY'RE DISINTEGRATING, TURNING TO DUST! STAND BACK!
GILGAMESH! THOU DOTH BEAR AN HEROIC NAME OF LEGEND.
AND IN THIS MATTER, THOU HAST ACQUITTED THYSELF WITH HONOR.
THOR IS PROUD TO HAVE FOUGHT WITH SO VALIANT A WARRIOR.
THOR SAYS IT WITH FLOWERS BUT HE SPEAKS FOR ME AS WELL.
NICELY DONE. YOU WOULDN'T BE STICKING AROUND FOR AWHILE?
WILL THERE BE MORE MONSTERS?
MISTER, FIGHTING MONSTERS IS WHAT THE AVENGERS DOES BEST!
HOW IS HE, DARLING?
ALREADY ASLEEP. BUT UNHARMED, I THINK.
REED, WE MUST GET HIM HOME AS QUICKLY AS POSSIBLE.
AND HE'LL NEED TO SEE A DOCTOR.

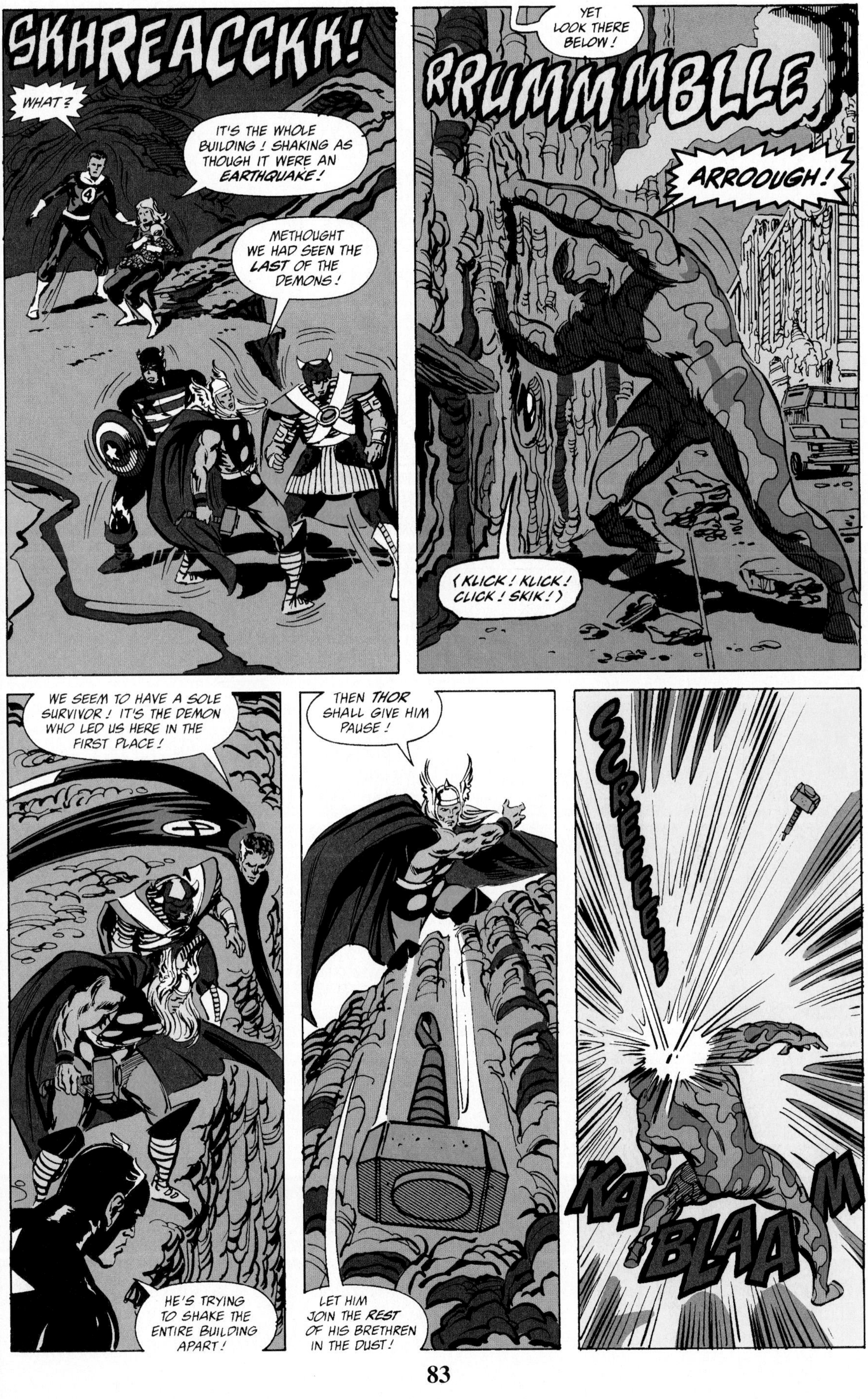
SKHREACCKK!
WHAT?
IT'S THE WHOLE BUILDING! SHAKING AS THOUGH IT WERE AN EARTHQUAKE!
METHOUGHT WE HAD SEEN THE LAST OF THE DEMONS!
YET LOOK THERE BELOW!
RRUMMMBLLE
ARROOUGH!
(KLICK! KLICK! CLICK! SKIK!)
WE SEEM TO HAVE A SOLE SURVIVOR! IT'S THE DEMON WHO LED US HERE IN THE FIRST PLACE!
HE'S TRYING TO SHAKE THE ENTIRE BUILDING APART!
THEN THOR SHALL GIVE HIM PAUSE!
LET HIM JOIN THE REST OF HIS BRETHREN IN THE DUST!
KA BLAAM

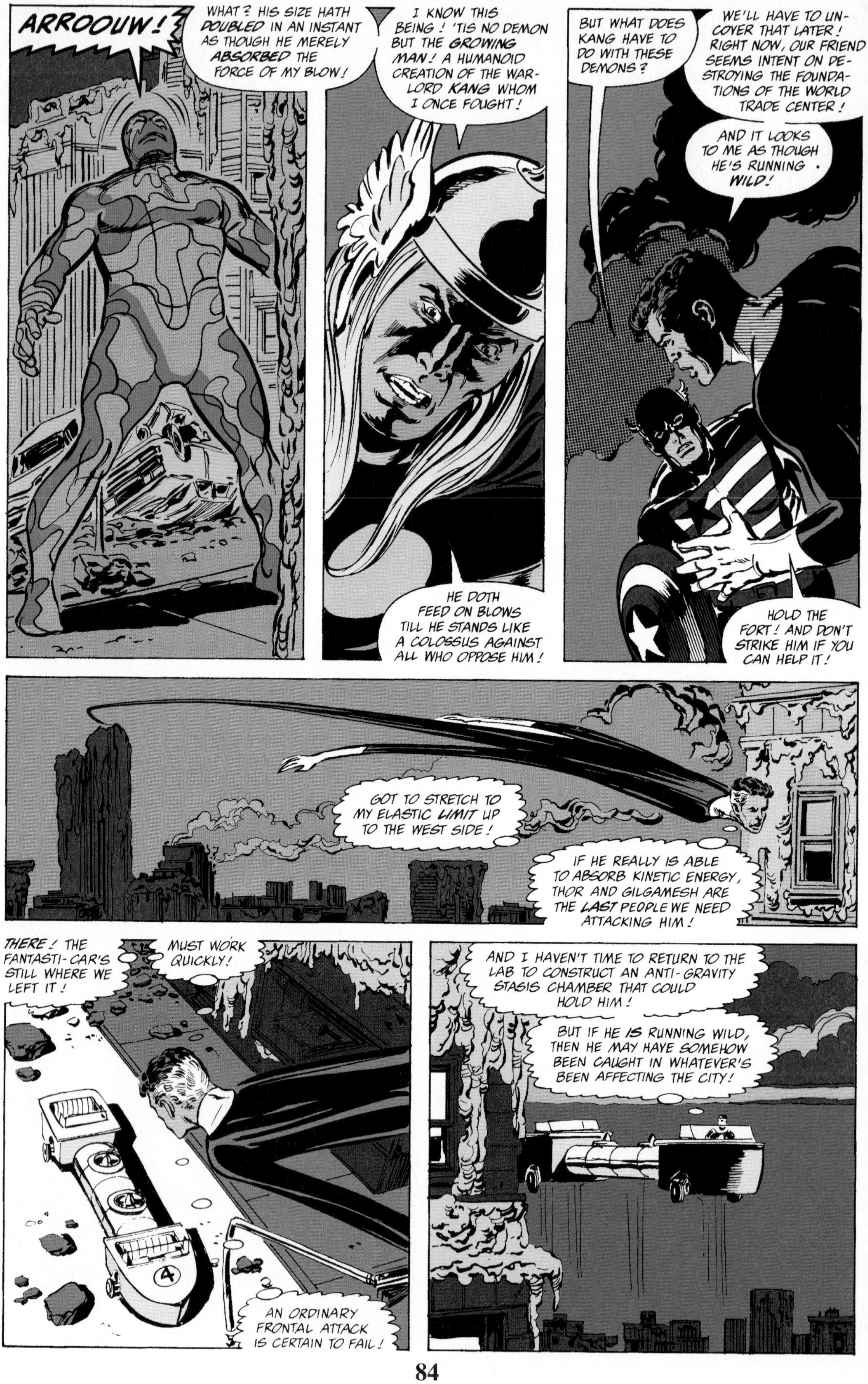
ARROOUW!
WHAT? HIS SIZE HATH DOUBLED IN AN INSTANT AS THOUGH HE MERELY ABSORBED THE FORCE OF MY BLOW!
I KNOW THIS BEING! 'TIS NO DEMON BUT THE GROWING MAN! A HUMANOID CREATION OF THE WAR-LORD KANG WHOM I ONCE FOUGHT!
HE DOTH FEED ON BLOWS TILL HE STANDS LIKE A COLOSSUS AGAINST ALL WHO OPPOSE HIM!
BUT WHAT DOES KANG HAVE TO DO WITH THESE DEMONS?
WE'LL HAVE TO UNCOVER THAT LATER! RIGHT NOW, OUR FRIEND SEEMS INTENT ON DESTROYING THE FOUNDATIONS OF THE WORLD TRADE CENTER!
AND IT LOOKS TO ME AS THOUGH HE'S RUNNING WILD!
HOLD THE FORT! AND DON'T STRIKE HIM IF YOU CAN HELP IT!
GOT TO STRETCH TO MY ELASTIC LIMIT UP TO THE WEST SIDE!
IF HE REALLY IS ABLE TO ABSORB KINETIC ENERGY, THOR AND GILGAMESH ARE THE LAST PEOPLE WE NEED ATTACKING HIM!
THERE! THE FANTASTI-CAR'S STILL WHERE WE LEFT IT!
MUST WORK QUICKLY!
AN ORDINARY FRONTAL ATTACK IS CERTAIN TO FAIL!
AND I HAVEN'T TIME TO RETURN TO THE LAB TO CONSTRUCT AN ANTI-GRAVITY STASIS CHAMBER THAT COULD HOLD HIM!
BUT IF HE IS RUNNING WILD, THEN HE MAY HAVE SOMEHOW BEEN CAUGHT IN WHATEVER'S BEEN AFFECTING THE CITY!

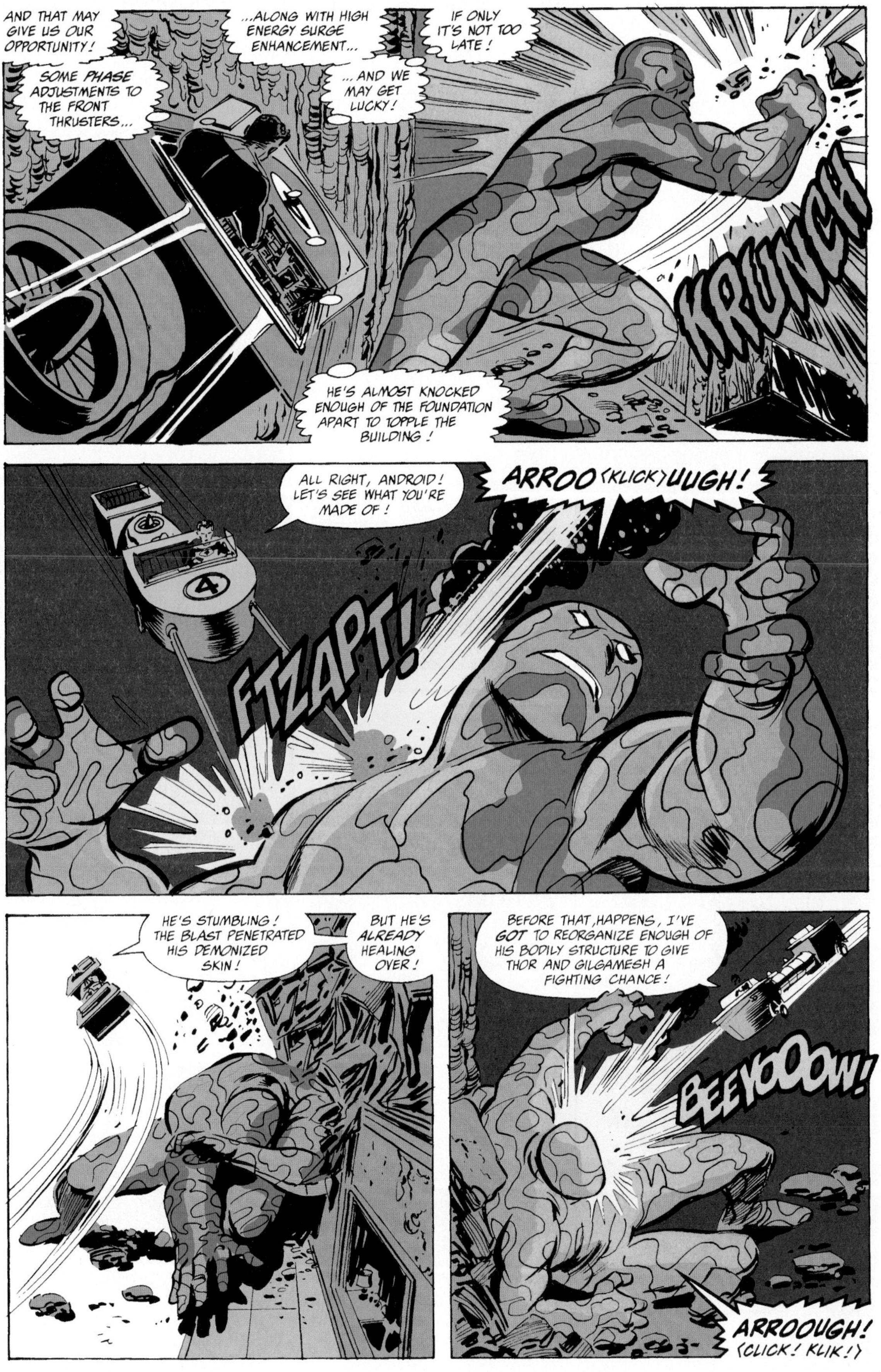
AND THAT MAY GIVE US OUR OPPORTUNITY!
SOME PHASE ADJUSTMENTS TO THE FRONT THRUSTERS...
...ALONG WITH HIGH ENERGY SURGE ENHANCEMENT...
...AND WE MAY GET LUCKY!
IF ONLY IT'S NOT TOO LATE!
KRUNCH
HE'S ALMOST KNOCKED ENOUGH OF THE FOUNDATION APART TO TOPPLE THE BUILDING!
ALL RIGHT, ANDROID! LET'S SEE WHAT YOU'RE MADE OF!
ARROO (KLICK) UUGH!
FTZAPT!
HE'S STUMBLING! THE BLAST PENETRATED HIS DEMONIZED SKIN!
BUT HE'S ALREADY HEALING OVER!
BEFORE THAT HAPPENS, I'VE GOT TO REORGANIZE ENOUGH OF HIS BODILY STRUCTURE TO GIVE THOR AND GILGAMESH A FIGHTING CHANCE!
BEEYOOOW!
ARROOUGH! (CLICK! KLIK!)

AND QUICKLY! THE THUNDER GOD ISN'T RENOWN FOR HIS PATIENCE!

RICHARDS HATH DONE HIS BEST BUT STILL THE THING MOVES!

'TIS TIME OTHER HANDS JOINED IN THE FRAY!

COME, GILGAMESH! THE MONSTER AWAITS!

THEN HE'LL WAIT NO LONGER!

THE ANDROID'S SKIN BURNS WITH ENERGY!

I SHALL LAND BEFORE THE CREATURE TO DISTRACT HIM!

SCHREEE

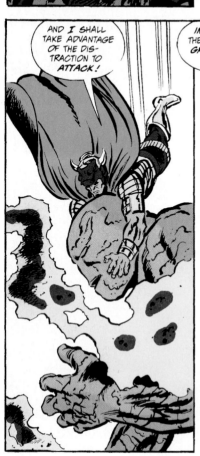

AND I SHALL TAKE ADVANTAGE OF THE DISTRACTION TO ATTACK!

INCREDIBLE! UNDER THE IMPACT OF MY FALL, THE GROWING MAN HAS GROWN SMALLER!

ARROOUGHH!

THIS WAS RICHARDS' DOING! THE CREATURE IS NO LONGER THE GROWING MAN...

...BUT THE SHRINKING MAN!

MR. FANTASTIC HATH TURNED HIS OWN ENERGIES AGAINST HIM!

86

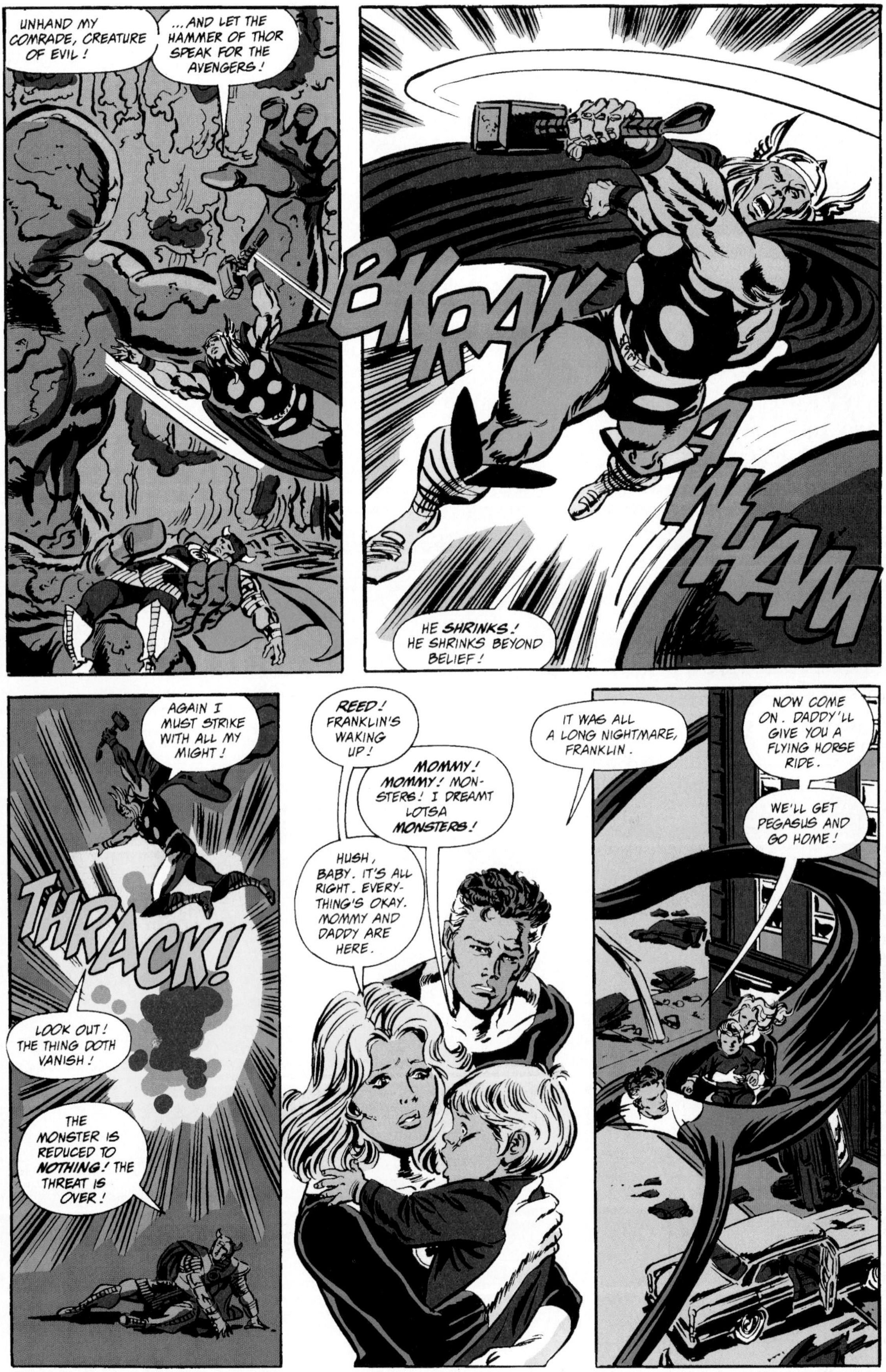

UNHAND MY COMRADE, CREATURE OF EVIL!
...AND LET THE HAMMER OF THOR SPEAK FOR THE AVENGERS!
BKRAK
WHAM
HE SHRINKS! HE SHRINKS BEYOND BELIEF!
AGAIN I MUST STRIKE WITH ALL MY MIGHT!
THRACK!
LOOK OUT! THE THING DOTH VANISH!
THE MONSTER IS REDUCED TO NOTHING! THE THREAT IS OVER!
REED! FRANKLIN'S WAKING UP!
MOMMY! MOMMY! MONSTERS! I DREAMT LOTSA MONSTERS!
HUSH, BABY. IT'S ALL RIGHT. EVERYTHING'S OKAY. MOMMY AND DADDY ARE HERE.
IT WAS ALL A LONG NIGHTMARE, FRANKLIN.
NOW COME ON. DADDY'LL GIVE YOU A FLYING HORSE RIDE.
WE'LL GET PEGASUS AND GO HOME!

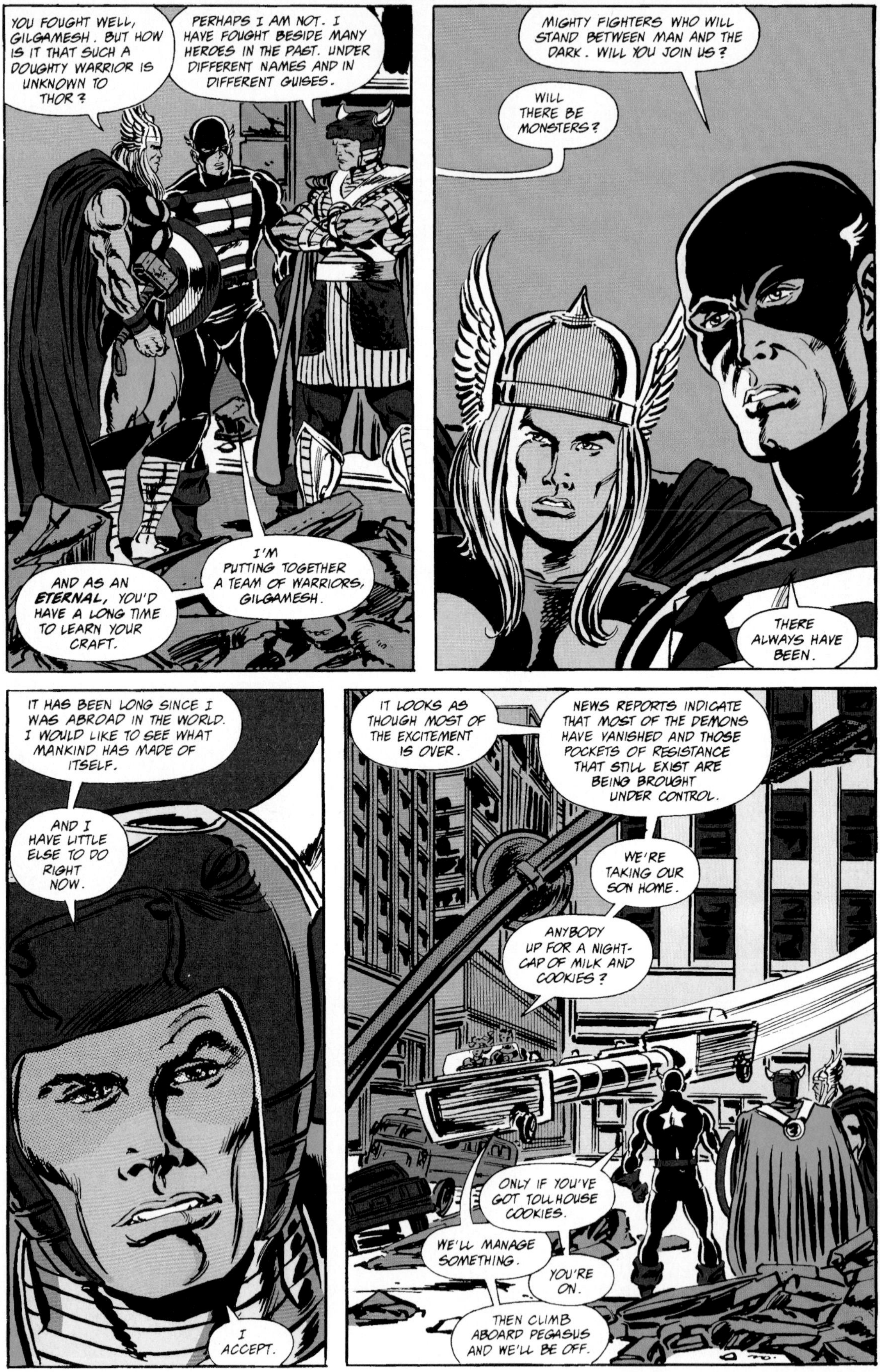

YOU FOUGHT WELL, GILGAMESH. BUT HOW IS IT THAT SUCH A DOUGHTY WARRIOR IS UNKNOWN TO THOR?
PERHAPS I AM NOT. I HAVE FOUGHT BESIDE MANY HEROES IN THE PAST. UNDER DIFFERENT NAMES AND IN DIFFERENT GUISES.
I'M PUTTING TOGETHER A TEAM OF WARRIORS, GILGAMESH.
AND AS AN ETERNAL, YOU'D HAVE A LONG TIME TO LEARN YOUR CRAFT.
MIGHTY FIGHTERS WHO WILL STAND BETWEEN MAN AND THE DARK. WILL YOU JOIN US?
WILL THERE BE MONSTERS?
THERE ALWAYS HAVE BEEN.
IT HAS BEEN LONG SINCE I WAS ABROAD IN THE WORLD. I WOULD LIKE TO SEE WHAT MANKIND HAS MADE OF ITSELF.
AND I HAVE LITTLE ELSE TO DO RIGHT NOW.
I ACCEPT.
IT LOOKS AS THOUGH MOST OF THE EXCITEMENT IS OVER.
NEWS REPORTS INDICATE THAT MOST OF THE DEMONS HAVE VANISHED AND THOSE POCKETS OF RESISTANCE THAT STILL EXIST ARE BEING BROUGHT UNDER CONTROL.
WE'RE TAKING OUR SON HOME.
ANYBODY UP FOR A NIGHT-CAP OF MILK AND COOKIES?
ONLY IF YOU'VE GOT TOLLHOUSE COOKIES.
WE'LL MANAGE SOMETHING.
YOU'RE ON.
THEN CLIMB ABOARD PEGASUS AND WE'LL BE OFF.

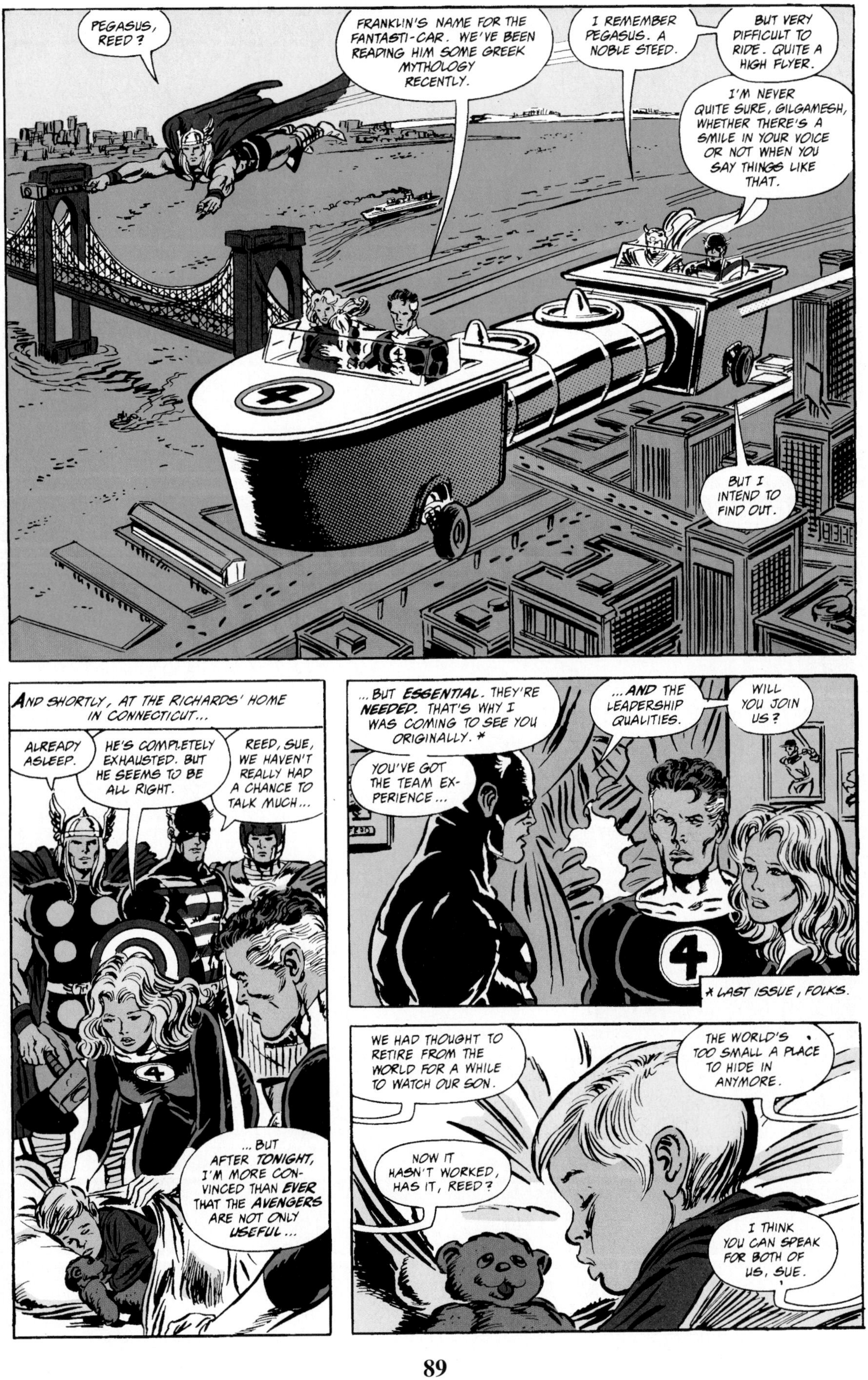
PEGASUS, REED?
FRANKLIN'S NAME FOR THE FANTASTI-CAR. WE'VE BEEN READING HIM SOME GREEK MYTHOLOGY RECENTLY.
I REMEMBER PEGASUS. A NOBLE STEED.
BUT VERY DIFFICULT TO RIDE. QUITE A HIGH FLYER.
I'M NEVER QUITE SURE, GILGAMESH, WHETHER THERE'S A SMILE IN YOUR VOICE OR NOT WHEN YOU SAY THINGS LIKE THAT.
BUT I INTEND TO FIND OUT.
AND SHORTLY, AT THE RICHARDS' HOME IN CONNECTICUT...
ALREADY ASLEEP.
HE'S COMPLETELY EXHAUSTED. BUT HE SEEMS TO BE ALL RIGHT.
REED, SUE, WE HAVEN'T REALLY HAD A CHANCE TO TALK MUCH...
...BUT AFTER TONIGHT, I'M MORE CONVINCED THAN EVER THAT THE AVENGERS ARE NOT ONLY USEFUL...
...BUT ESSENTIAL. THEY'RE NEEDED. THAT'S WHY I WAS COMING TO SEE YOU ORIGINALLY.*
YOU'VE GOT THE TEAM EXPERIENCE...
...AND THE LEADERSHIP QUALITIES.
WILL YOU JOIN US?
*LAST ISSUE, FOLKS.
WE HAD THOUGHT TO RETIRE FROM THE WORLD FOR A WHILE TO WATCH OUR SON.
THE WORLD'S TOO SMALL A PLACE TO HIDE IN ANYMORE.
NOW IT HASN'T WORKED, HAS IT, REED?
I THINK YOU CAN SPEAK FOR BOTH OF US, SUE.

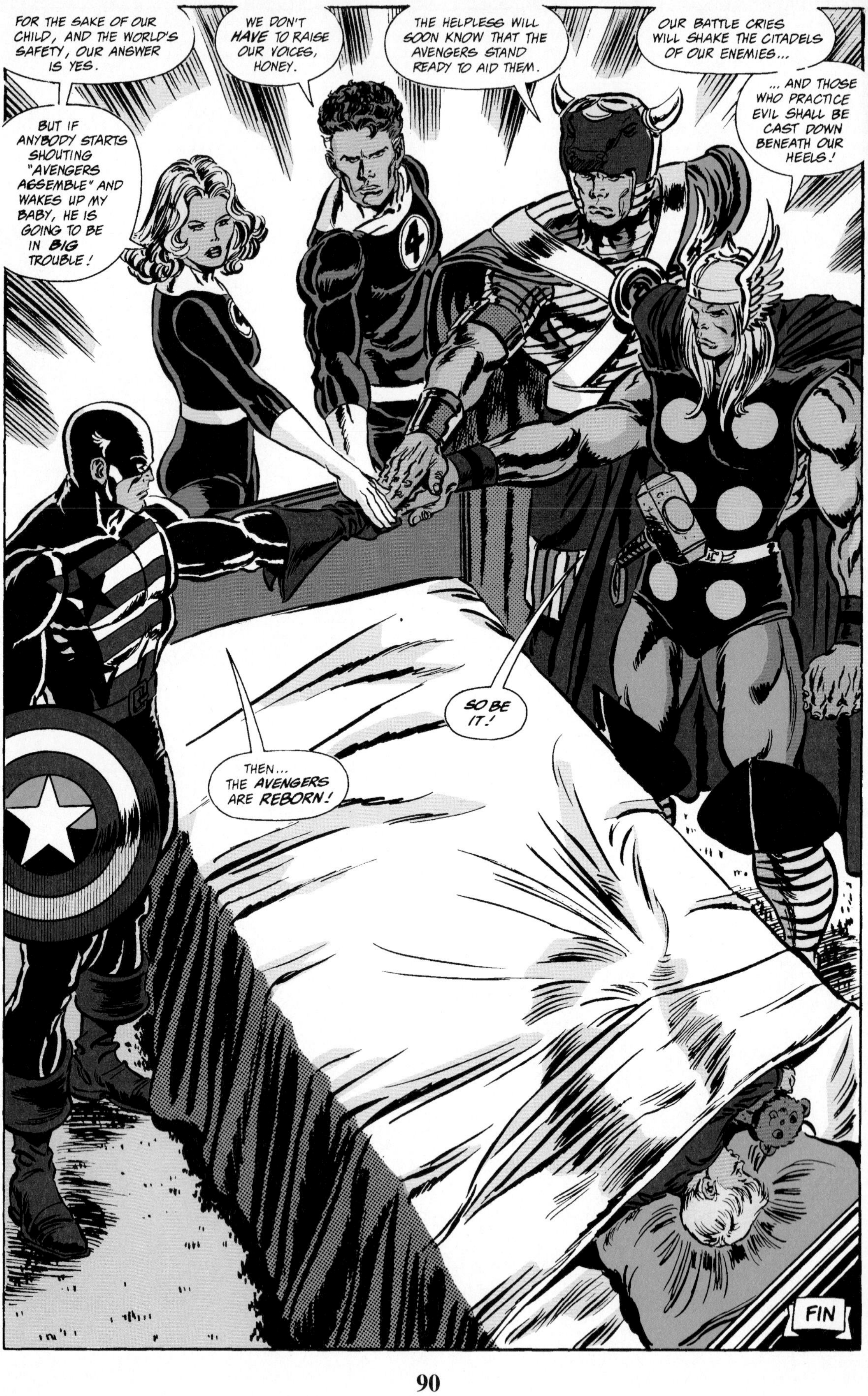
FOR THE SAKE OF OUR CHILD, AND THE WORLD'S SAFETY, OUR ANSWER IS YES.
BUT IF ANYBODY STARTS SHOUTING "AVENGERS ASSEMBLE" AND WAKES UP MY BABY, HE IS GOING TO BE IN BIG TROUBLE!
WE DON'T HAVE TO RAISE OUR VOICES, HONEY.
THE HELPLESS WILL SOON KNOW THAT THE AVENGERS STAND READY TO AID THEM.
OUR BATTLE CRIES WILL SHAKE THE CITADELS OF OUR ENEMIES...
... AND THOSE WHO PRACTICE EVIL SHALL BE CAST DOWN BENEATH OUR HEELS!
SO BE IT!
THEN... THE AVENGERS ARE REBORN!
FIN

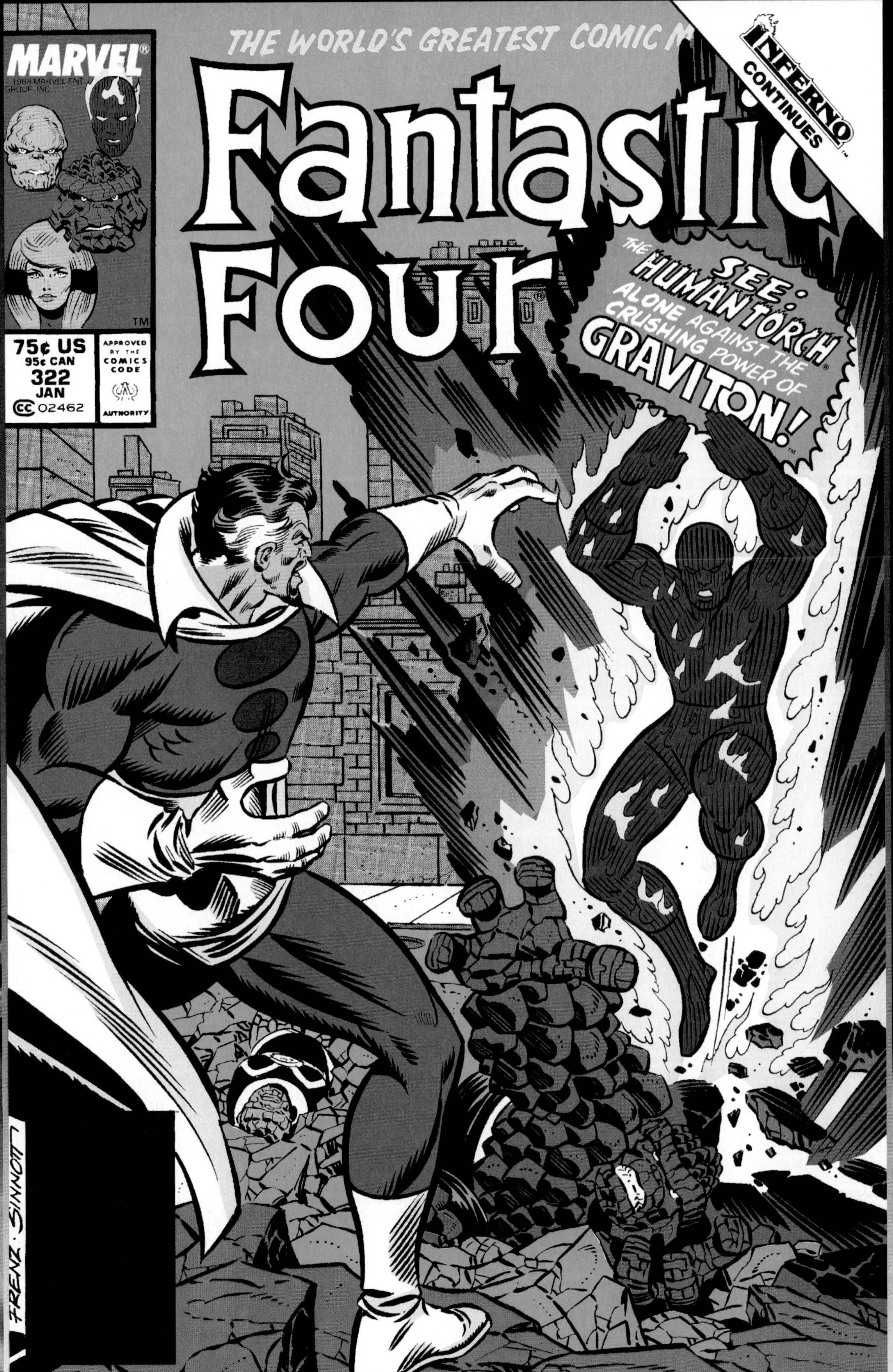
THE WORLD'S GREATEST COMIC M
MARVEL
© 1988 MARVEL ENT. GROUP, INC.
Fantastic Four
INFERNO CONTINUES
SEE: THE HUMAN TORCH ALONE AGAINST THE CRUSHING POWER OF GRAVITON!
75¢ US
95¢ CAN
322
JAN
02462
APPROVED BY THE COMICS CODE AUTHORITY
FRENZ · SINNOTT

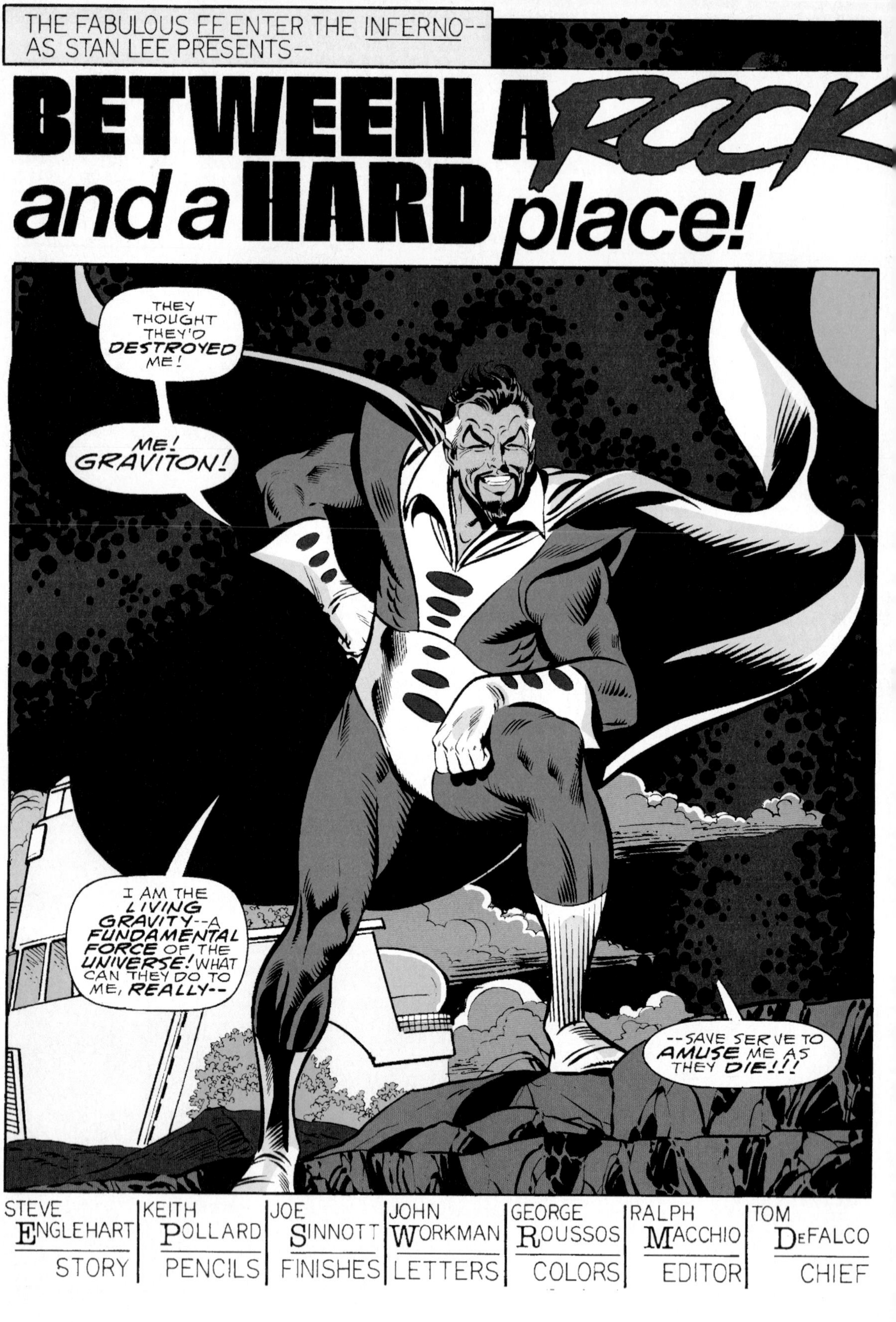
THE FABULOUS FF ENTER THE INFERNO--
AS STAN LEE PRESENTS--
BETWEEN A ROCK and a HARD place!
THEY THOUGHT THEY'D DESTROYED ME!
ME! GRAVITON!
I AM THE LIVING GRAVITY--A FUNDAMENTAL FORCE OF THE UNIVERSE! WHAT CAN THEY DO TO ME, REALLY--
--SAVE SERVE TO AMUSE ME AS THEY DIE!!!
STEVE ENGLEHART STORY
KEITH POLLARD PENCILS
JOE SINNOTT FINISHES
JOHN WORKMAN LETTERS
GEORGE ROUSSOS COLORS
RALPH MACCHIO EDITOR
TOM DEFALCO CHIEF

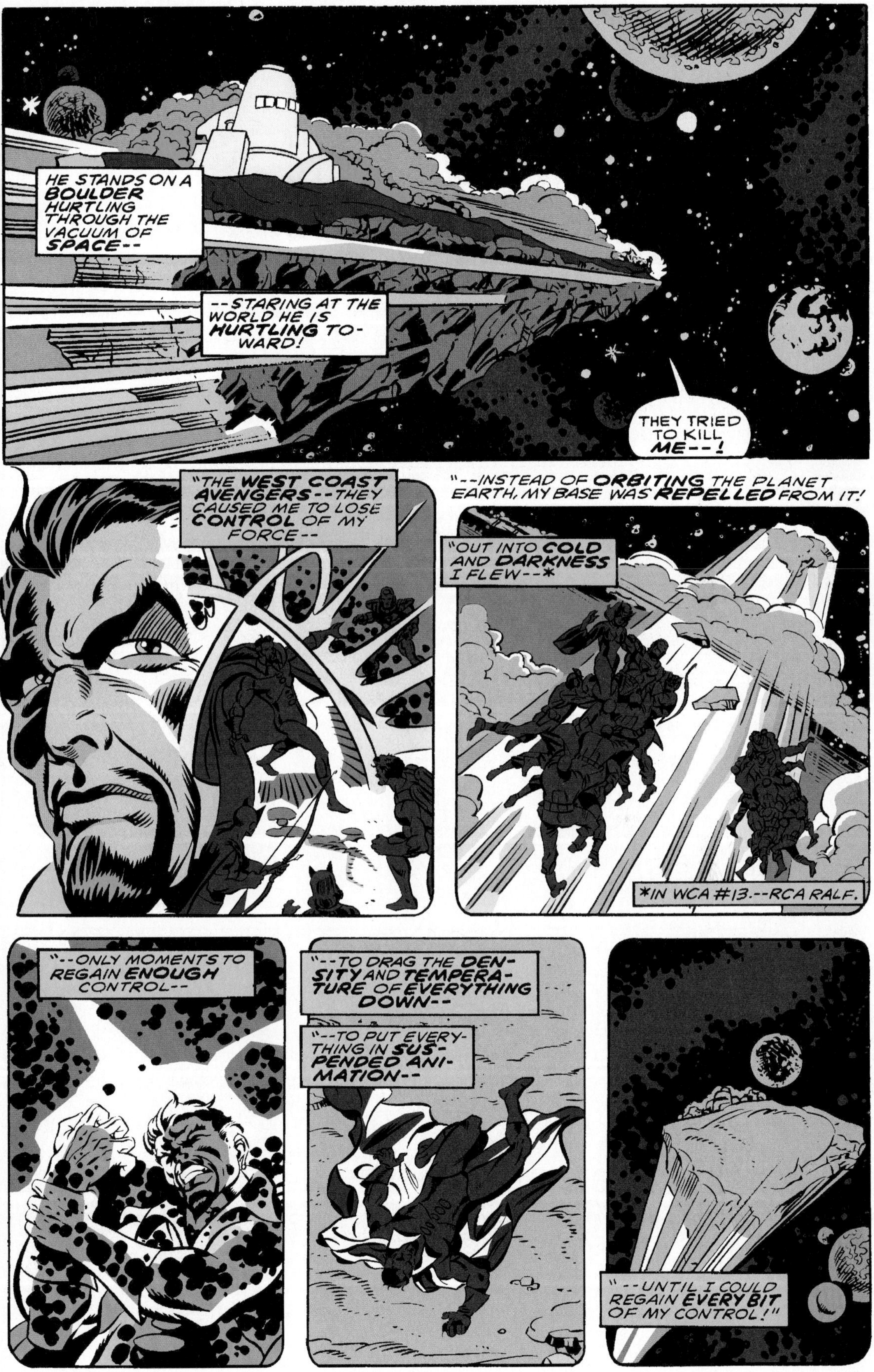

HE STANDS ON A BOULDER HURTLING THROUGH THE VACUUM OF SPACE--
--STARING AT THE WORLD HE IS HURTLING TOWARD!
THEY TRIED TO KILL ME--!
"THE WEST COAST AVENGERS--THEY CAUSED ME TO LOSE CONTROL OF MY FORCE--
"--INSTEAD OF ORBITING THE PLANET EARTH, MY BASE WAS REPELLED FROM IT!
"OUT INTO COLD AND DARKNESS I FLEW--*
*IN WCA #13.--RCA RALF.
"--ONLY MOMENTS TO REGAIN ENOUGH CONTROL--
"--TO DRAG THE DENSITY AND TEMPERATURE OF EVERYTHING DOWN--
"--TO PUT EVERYTHING IN SUSPENDED ANIMATION--
"--UNTIL I COULD REGAIN EVERY BIT OF MY CONTROL!"

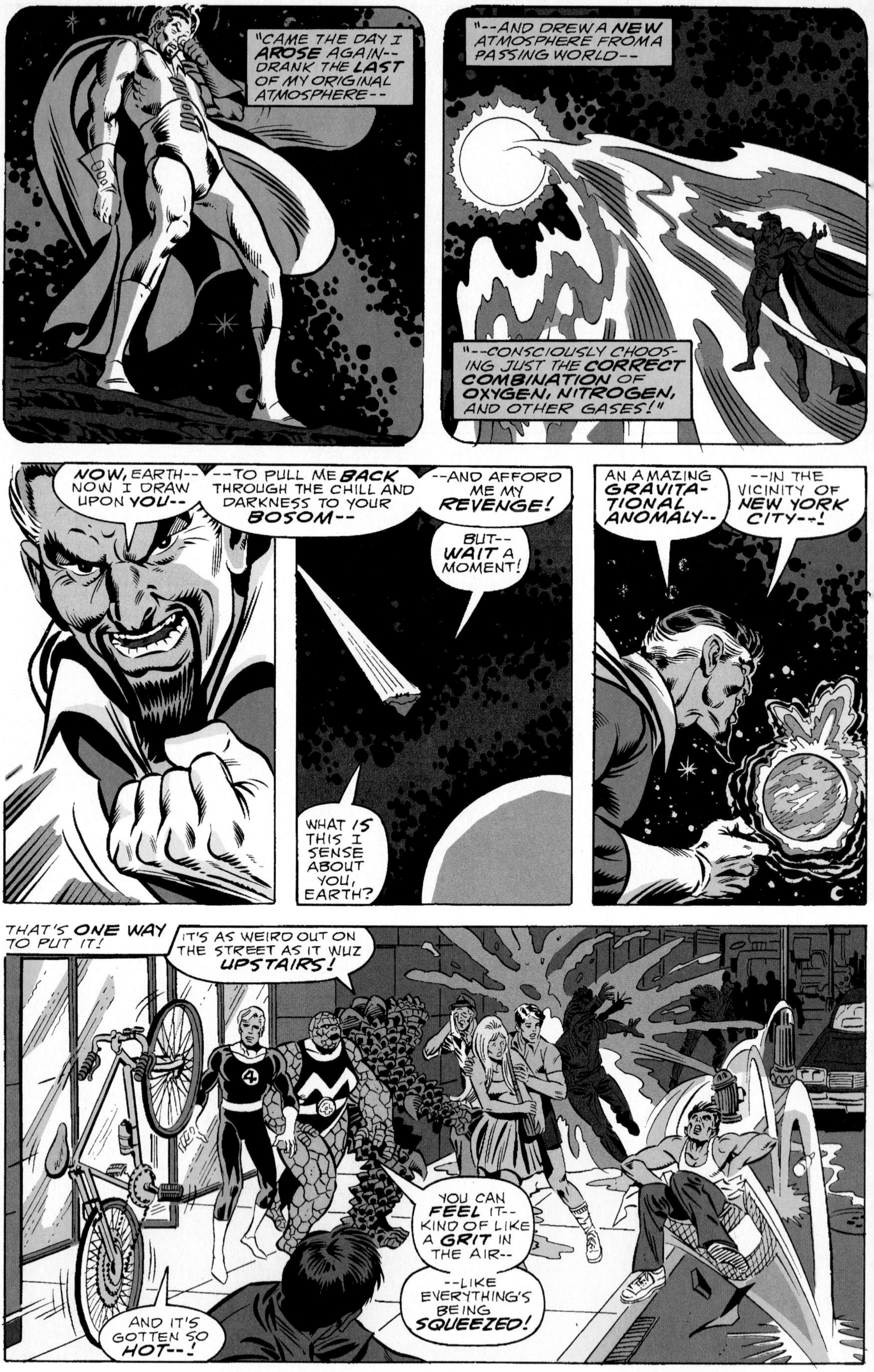
"CAME THE DAY I AROSE AGAIN-- DRANK THE LAST OF MY ORIGINAL ATMOSPHERE--
"--AND DREW A NEW ATMOSPHERE FROM A PASSING WORLD--
"--CONSCIOUSLY CHOOSING JUST THE CORRECT COMBINATION OF OXYGEN, NITROGEN, AND OTHER GASES!"
NOW, EARTH-- NOW I DRAW UPON YOU--
--TO PULL ME BACK THROUGH THE CHILL AND DARKNESS TO YOUR BOSOM--
--AND AFFORD ME MY REVENGE!
BUT-- WAIT A MOMENT!
WHAT IS THIS I SENSE ABOUT YOU, EARTH?
AN AMAZING GRAVITATIONAL ANOMALY--
--IN THE VICINITY OF NEW YORK CITY--!
THAT'S ONE WAY TO PUT IT!
IT'S AS WEIRD OUT ON THE STREET AS IT WUZ UPSTAIRS!
YOU CAN FEEL IT-- KIND OF LIKE A GRIT IN THE AIR--
--LIKE EVERYTHING'S BEING SQUEEZED!
AND IT'S GOTTEN SO HOT--!

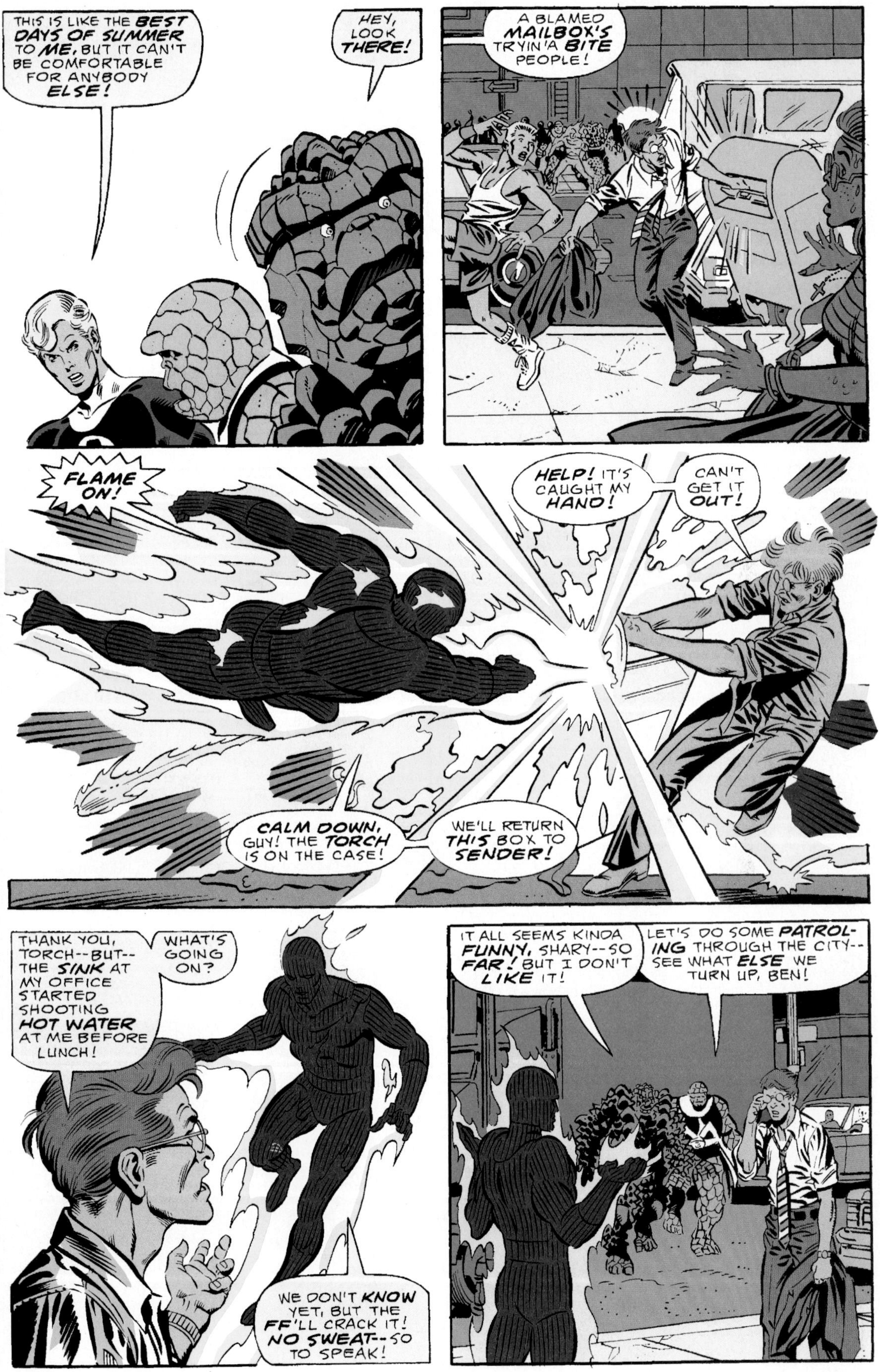

THIS IS LIKE THE BEST DAYS OF SUMMER TO ME, BUT IT CAN'T BE COMFORTABLE FOR ANYBODY ELSE!
HEY, LOOK THERE!
A BLAMED MAILBOX'S TRYIN'A BITE PEOPLE!
FLAME ON!
HELP! IT'S CAUGHT MY HAND!
CAN'T GET IT OUT!
CALM DOWN, GUY! THE TORCH IS ON THE CASE!
WE'LL RETURN THIS BOX TO SENDER!
THANK YOU, TORCH--BUT--THE SINK AT MY OFFICE STARTED SHOOTING HOT WATER AT ME BEFORE LUNCH!
WHAT'S GOING ON?
WE DON'T KNOW YET, BUT THE FF'LL CRACK IT! NO SWEAT--SO TO SPEAK!
IT ALL SEEMS KINDA FUNNY, SHARY--SO FAR! BUT I DON'T LIKE IT!
LET'S DO SOME PATROLING THROUGH THE CITY--SEE WHAT ELSE WE TURN UP, BEN!

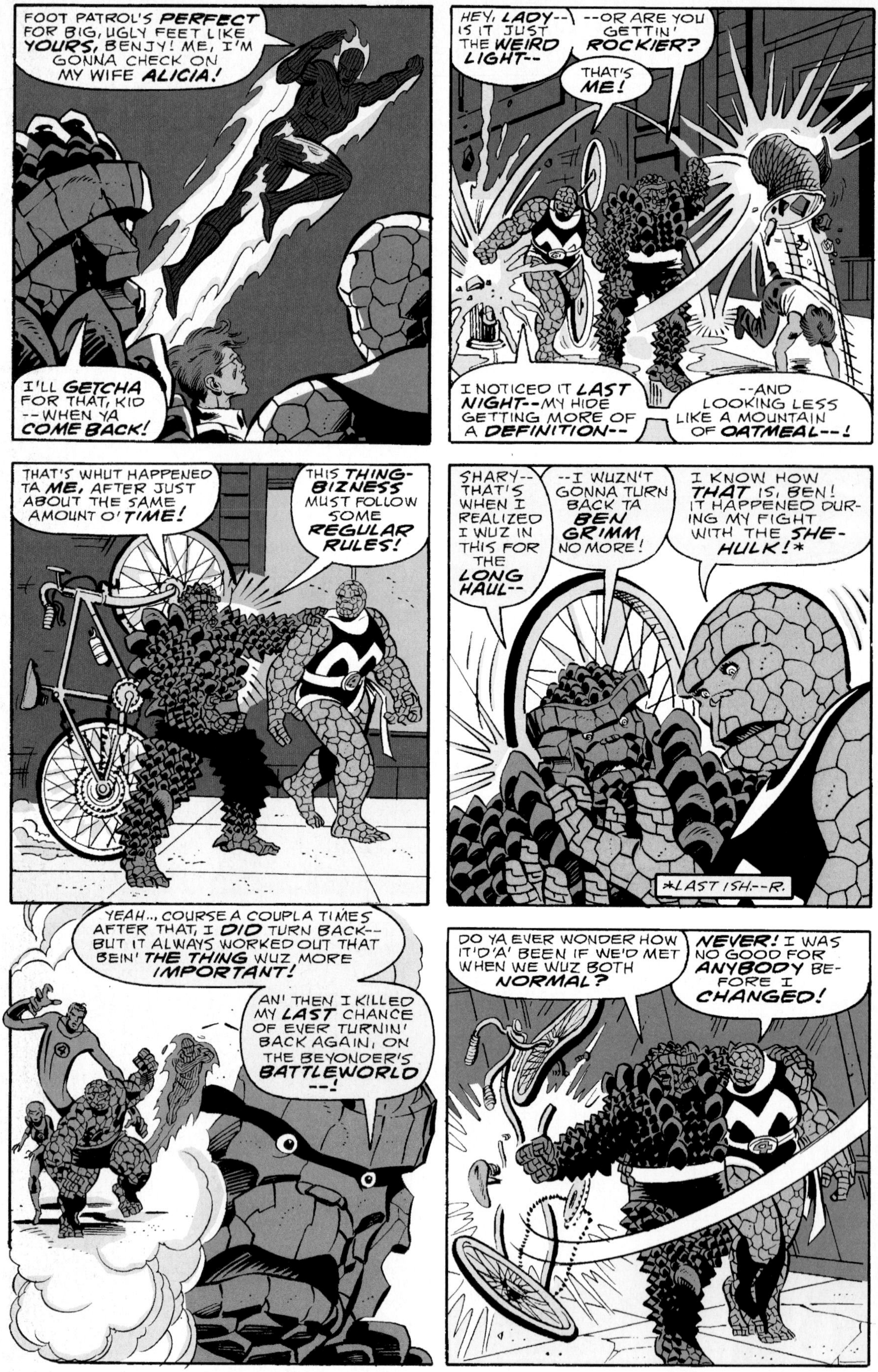
FOOT PATROL'S PERFECT FOR BIG, UGLY FEET LIKE YOURS, BENJY! ME, I'M GONNA CHECK ON MY WIFE ALICIA!
I'LL GETCHA FOR THAT, KID --WHEN YA COME BACK!
HEY, LADY-- IS IT JUST THE WEIRD LIGHT--
--OR ARE YOU GETTIN' ROCKIER?
THAT'S ME!
I NOTICED IT LAST NIGHT--MY HIDE GETTING MORE OF A DEFINITION--
--AND LOOKING LESS LIKE A MOUNTAIN OF OATMEAL--!
THAT'S WHUT HAPPENED TA ME, AFTER JUST ABOUT THE SAME AMOUNT O' TIME!
THIS THING-BIZNESS MUST FOLLOW SOME REGULAR RULES!
SHARY-- THAT'S WHEN I REALIZED I WUZ IN THIS FOR THE LONG HAUL--
--I WUZN'T GONNA TURN BACK TA BEN GRIMM NO MORE!
I KNOW HOW THAT IS, BEN! IT HAPPENED DURING MY FIGHT WITH THE SHE-HULK!*
*LAST ISH.--R.
YEAH... COURSE A COUPLA TIMES AFTER THAT, I DID TURN BACK-- BUT IT ALWAYS WORKED OUT THAT BEIN' THE THING WUZ MORE IMPORTANT!
AN' THEN I KILLED MY LAST CHANCE OF EVER TURNIN' BACK AGAIN, ON THE BEYONDER'S BATTLEWORLD--!
DO YA EVER WONDER HOW IT'D 'A' BEEN IF WE'D MET WHEN WE WUZ BOTH NORMAL?
NEVER! I WAS NO GOOD FOR ANYBODY BEFORE I CHANGED!

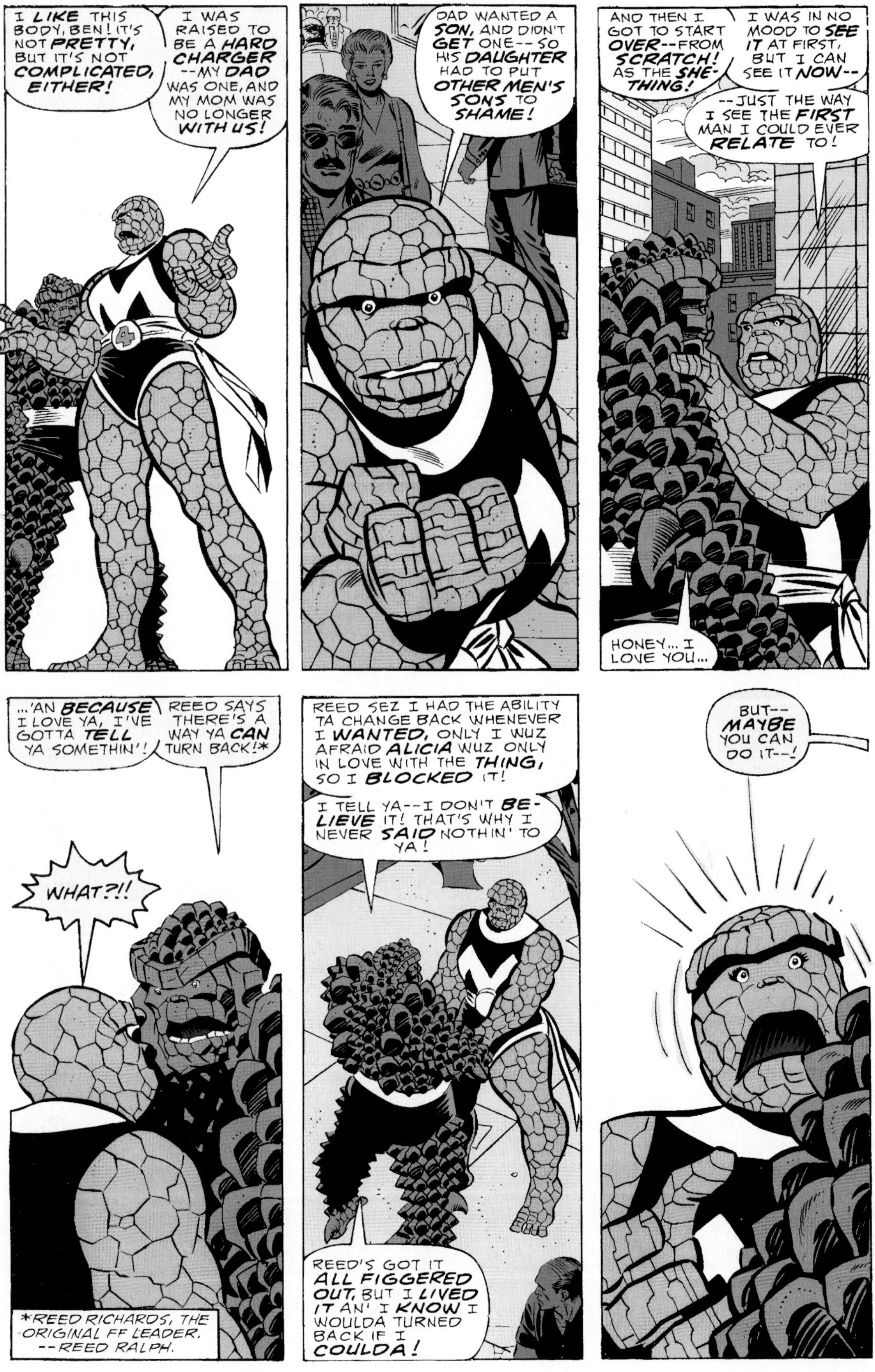
I LIKE THIS BODY, BEN! IT'S NOT PRETTY, BUT IT'S NOT COMPLICATED, EITHER!
I WAS RAISED TO BE A HARD CHARGER --MY DAD WAS ONE, AND MY MOM WAS NO LONGER WITH US!
DAD WANTED A SON, AND DIDN'T GET ONE-- SO HIS DAUGHTER HAD TO PUT OTHER MEN'S SONS TO SHAME!
AND THEN I GOT TO START OVER--FROM SCRATCH! AS THE SHE-THING!
I WAS IN NO MOOD TO SEE IT AT FIRST, BUT I CAN SEE IT NOW--
--JUST THE WAY I SEE THE FIRST MAN I COULD EVER RELATE TO!
HONEY... I LOVE YOU...
...'AN BECAUSE I LOVE YA, I'VE GOTTA TELL YA SOMETHIN'!
REED SAYS THERE'S A WAY YA CAN TURN BACK!*
WHAT?!!
*REED RICHARDS, THE ORIGINAL FF LEADER. --REED RALPH.
REED SEZ I HAD THE ABILITY TA CHANGE BACK WHENEVER I WANTED, ONLY I WUZ AFRAID ALICIA WUZ ONLY IN LOVE WITH THE THING, SO I BLOCKED IT!
I TELL YA--I DON'T BE-LIEVE IT! THAT'S WHY I NEVER SAID NOTHIN' TO YA!
REED'S GOT IT ALL FIGGERED OUT, BUT I LIVED IT AN' I KNOW I WOULDA TURNED BACK IF I COULDA!
BUT-- MAYBE YOU CAN DO IT--!

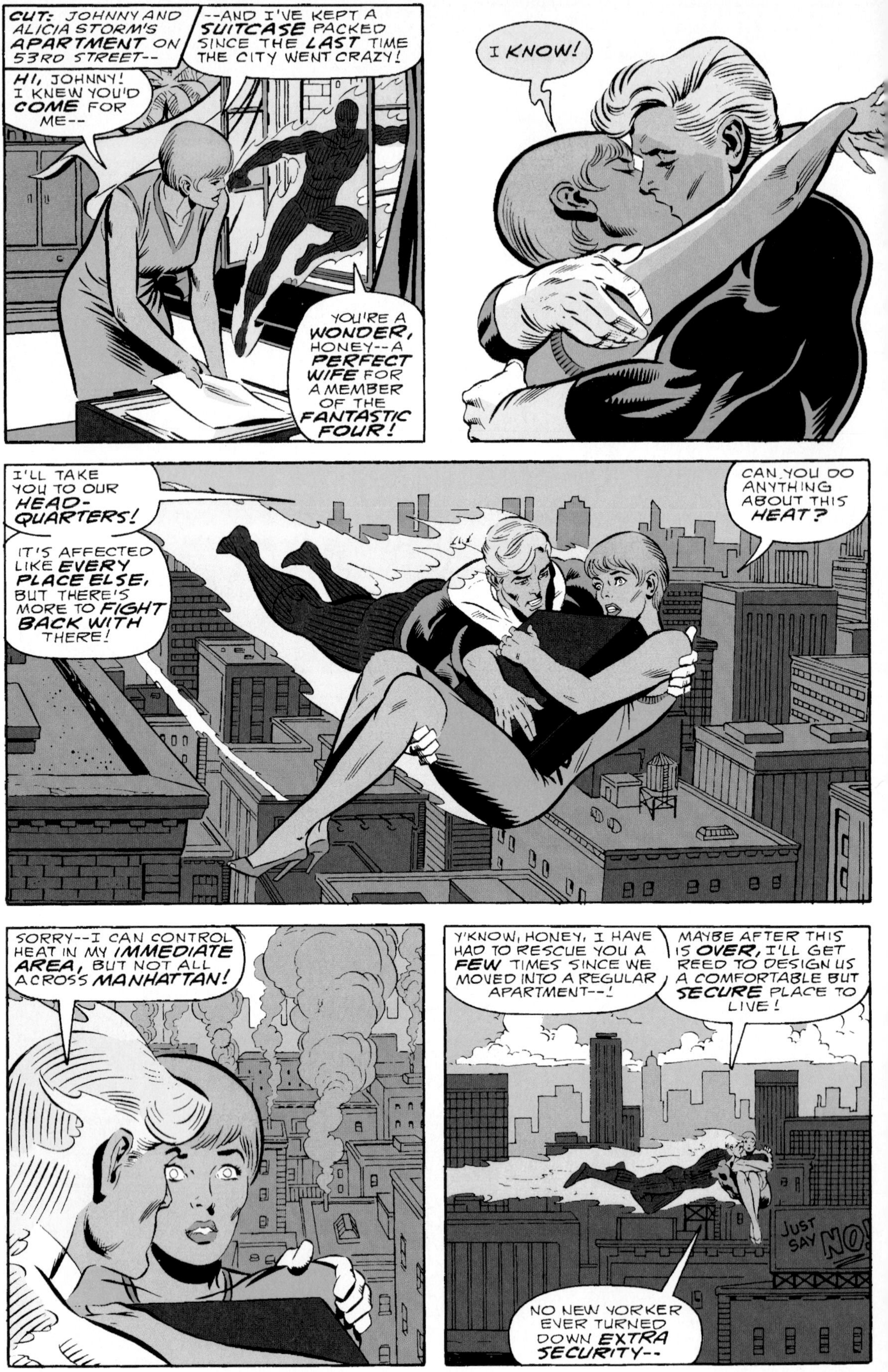
CUT: JOHNNY AND ALICIA STORM'S APARTMENT ON 53RD STREET--
--AND I'VE KEPT A SUITCASE PACKED SINCE THE LAST TIME THE CITY WENT CRAZY!
HI, JOHNNY! I KNEW YOU'D COME FOR ME--
YOU'RE A WONDER, HONEY--A PERFECT WIFE FOR A MEMBER OF THE FANTASTIC FOUR!
I KNOW!
I'LL TAKE YOU TO OUR HEAD-QUARTERS!
IT'S AFFECTED LIKE EVERY PLACE ELSE, BUT THERE'S MORE TO FIGHT BACK WITH THERE!
CAN YOU DO ANYTHING ABOUT THIS HEAT?
SORRY--I CAN CONTROL HEAT IN MY IMMEDIATE AREA, BUT NOT ALL ACROSS MANHATTAN!
Y'KNOW, HONEY, I HAVE HAD TO RESCUE YOU A FEW TIMES SINCE WE MOVED INTO A REGULAR APARTMENT--!
MAYBE AFTER THIS IS OVER, I'LL GET REED TO DESIGN US A COMFORTABLE BUT SECURE PLACE TO LIVE!
JUST SAY NO!
NO NEW YORKER EVER TURNED DOWN EXTRA SECURITY--

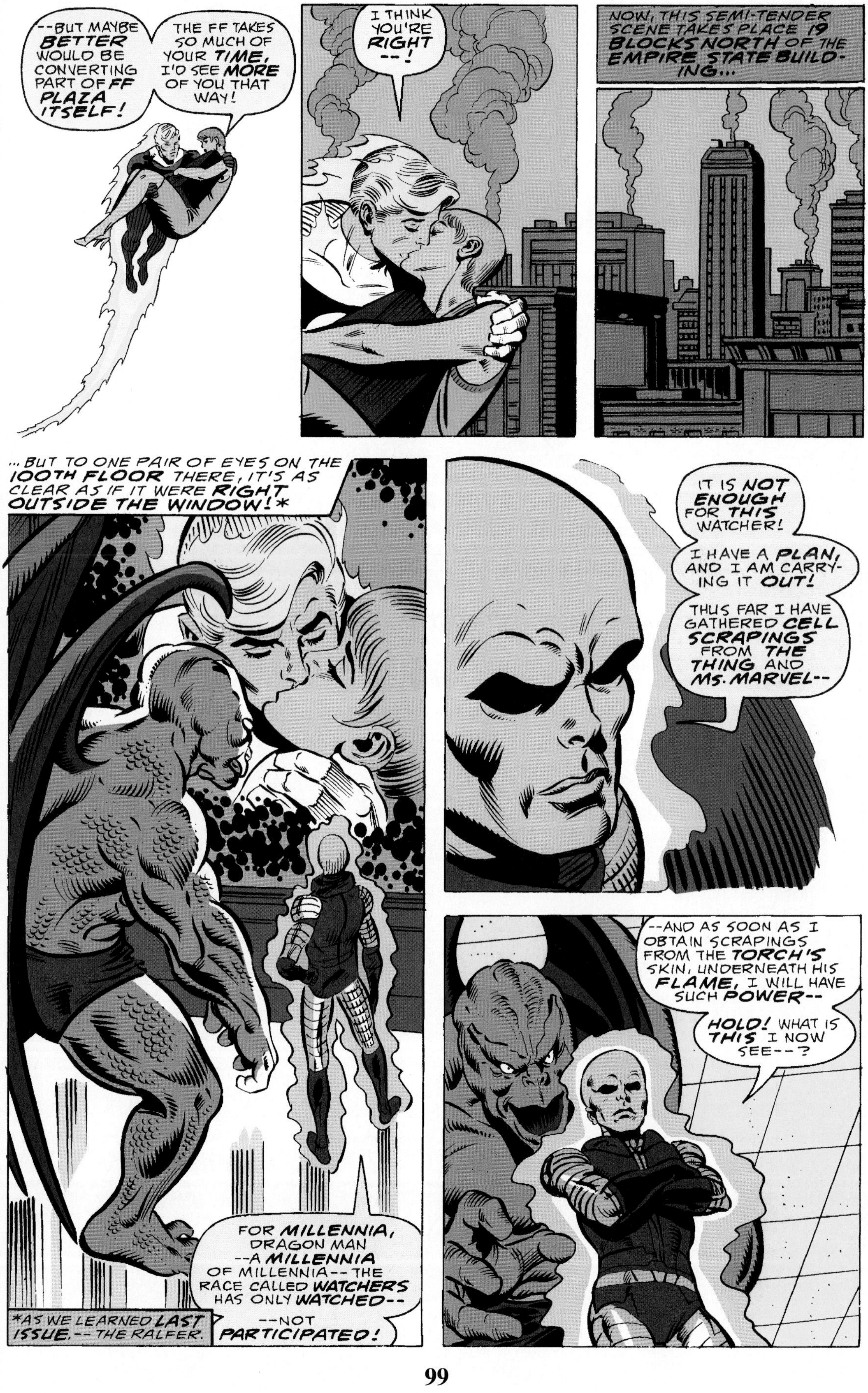
--BUT MAYBE BETTER WOULD BE CONVERTING PART OF FF PLAZA ITSELF!
THE FF TAKES SO MUCH OF YOUR TIME, I'D SEE MORE OF YOU THAT WAY!
I THINK YOU'RE RIGHT --!
NOW, THIS SEMI-TENDER SCENE TAKES PLACE 19 BLOCKS NORTH OF THE EMPIRE STATE BUILD-ING...
...BUT TO ONE PAIR OF EYES ON THE 100TH FLOOR THERE, IT'S AS CLEAR AS IF IT WERE RIGHT OUTSIDE THE WINDOW!*
FOR MILLENNIA, DRAGON MAN --A MILLENNIA OF MILLENNIA-- THE RACE CALLED WATCHERS HAS ONLY WATCHED--
--NOT PARTICIPATED!
*AS WE LEARNED LAST ISSUE. -- THE RALFER.
IT IS NOT ENOUGH FOR THIS WATCHER!
I HAVE A PLAN, AND I AM CARRY-ING IT OUT!
THUS FAR I HAVE GATHERED CELL SCRAPINGS FROM THE THING AND MS. MARVEL--
--AND AS SOON AS I OBTAIN SCRAPINGS FROM THE TORCH'S SKIN, UNDERNEATH HIS FLAME, I WILL HAVE SUCH POWER--
HOLD! WHAT IS THIS I NOW SEE--?

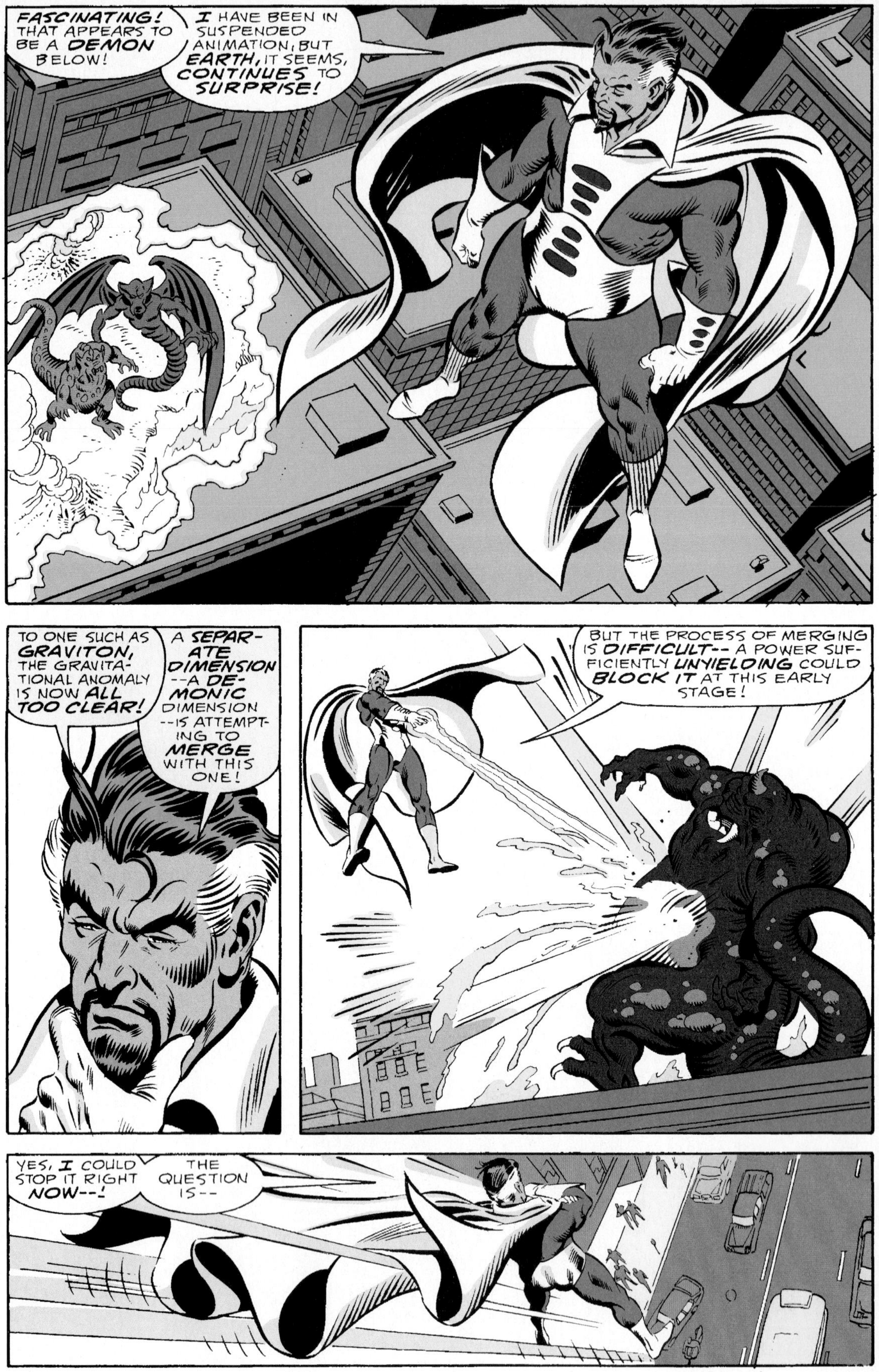
FASCINATING! THAT APPEARS TO BE A DEMON BELOW!
I HAVE BEEN IN SUSPENDED ANIMATION, BUT EARTH, IT SEEMS, CONTINUES TO SURPRISE!
TO ONE SUCH AS GRAVITON, THE GRAVITATIONAL ANOMALY IS NOW ALL TOO CLEAR!
A SEPARATE DIMENSION --A DEMONIC DIMENSION --IS ATTEMPTING TO MERGE WITH THIS ONE!
BUT THE PROCESS OF MERGING IS DIFFICULT-- A POWER SUFFICIENTLY UNYIELDING COULD BLOCK IT AT THIS EARLY STAGE!
YES, I COULD STOP IT RIGHT NOW--!
THE QUESTION IS--

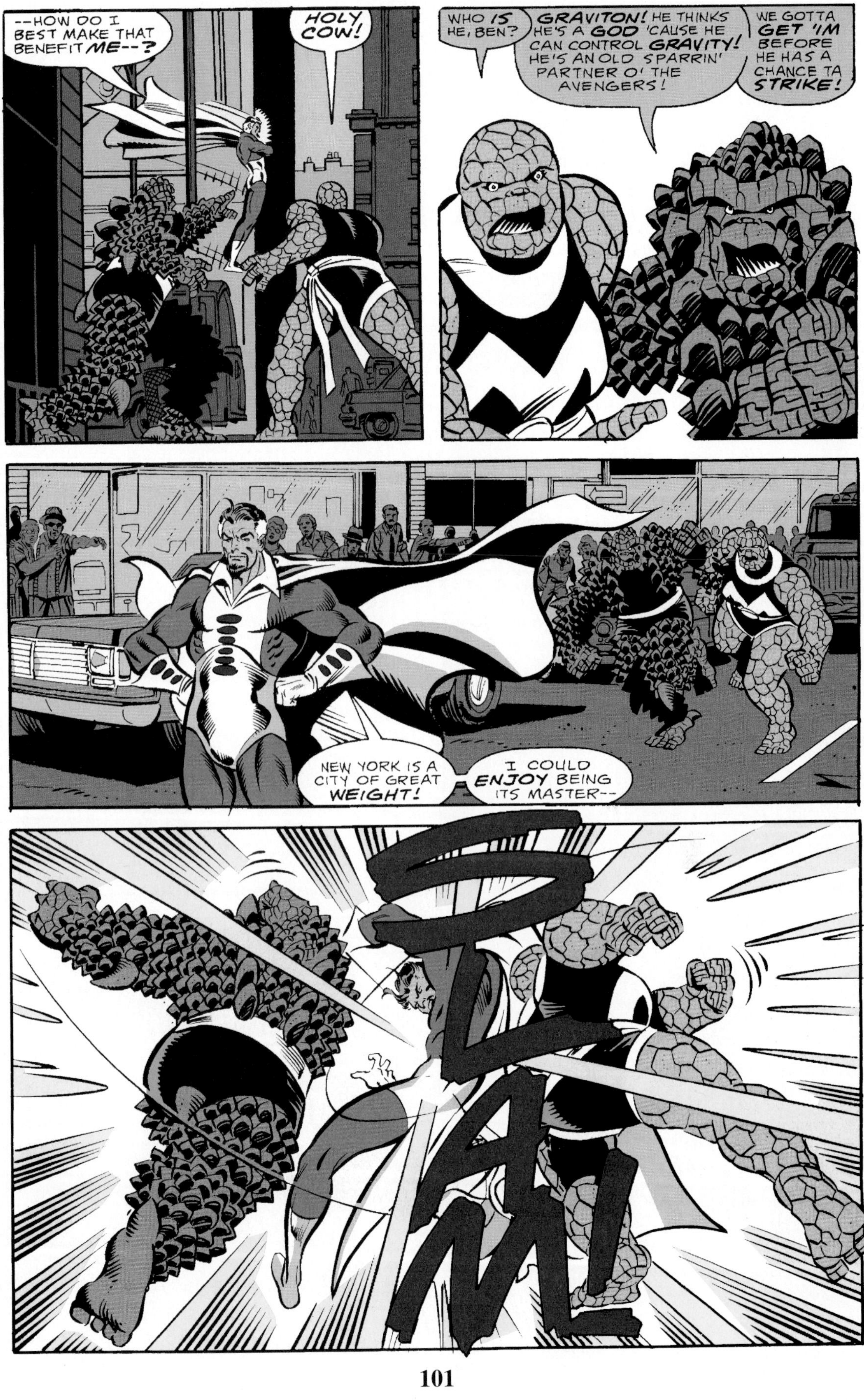
--HOW DO I BEST MAKE THAT BENEFIT ME--?
HOLY COW!
WHO IS HE, BEN?
GRAVITON! HE THINKS HE'S A GOD 'CAUSE HE CAN CONTROL GRAVITY! HE'S AN OLD SPARRIN' PARTNER O' THE AVENGERS!
WE GOTTA GET 'IM BEFORE HE HAS A CHANCE TA STRIKE!
NEW YORK IS A CITY OF GREAT WEIGHT!
I COULD ENJOY BEING ITS MASTER--

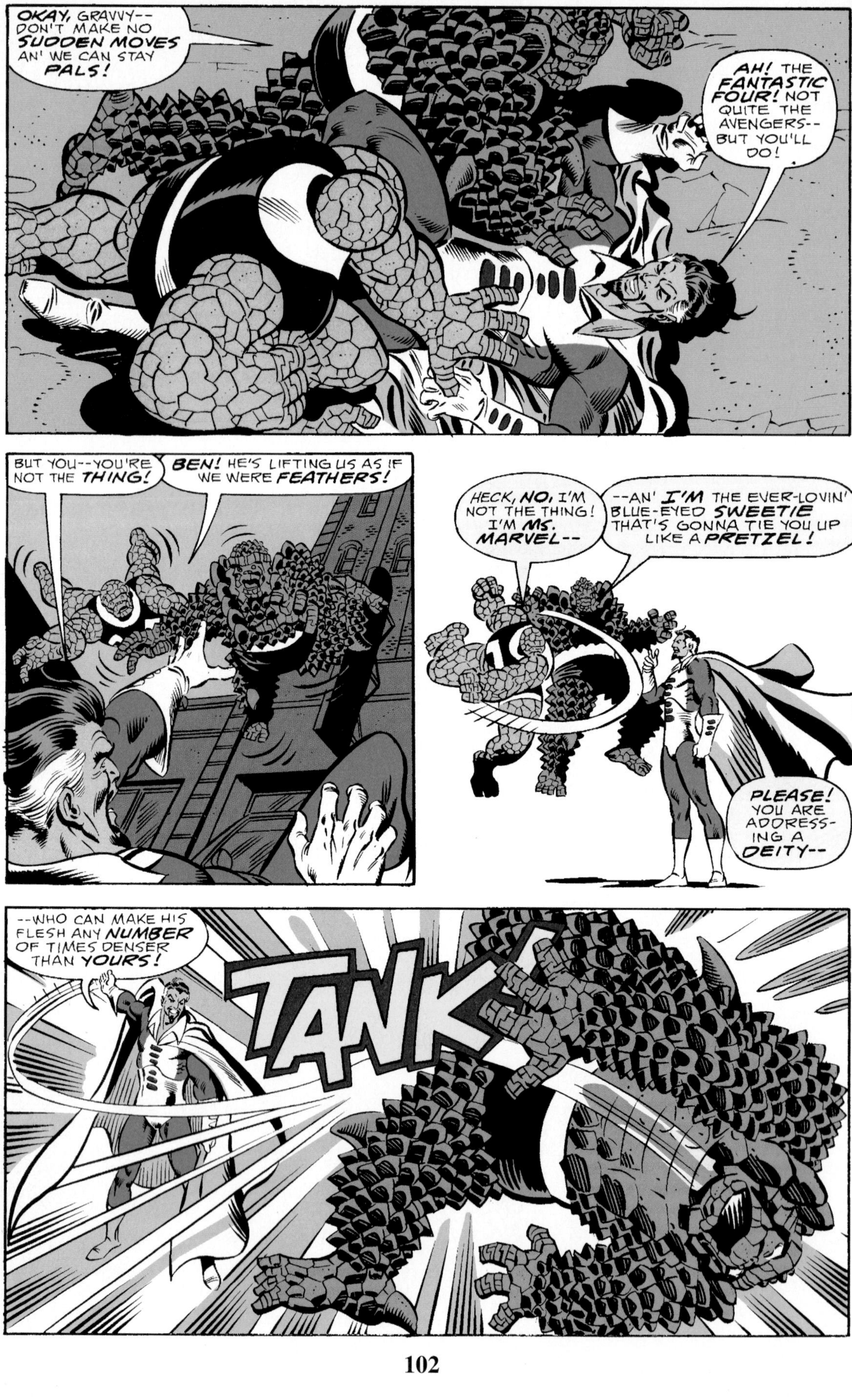
OKAY, GRAVVY--
DON'T MAKE NO
SUDDEN MOVES
AN' WE CAN STAY
PALS!
AH! THE FANTASTIC FOUR! NOT QUITE THE AVENGERS-- BUT YOU'LL DO!
BUT YOU--YOU'RE NOT THE THING!
BEN! HE'S LIFTING US AS IF WE WERE FEATHERS!
HECK, NO, I'M NOT THE THING! I'M MS. MARVEL--
--AN' I'M THE EVER-LOVIN' BLUE-EYED SWEETIE THAT'S GONNA TIE YOU UP LIKE A PRETZEL!
PLEASE! YOU ARE ADDRESS-ING A DEITY--
--WHO CAN MAKE HIS FLESH ANY NUMBER OF TIMES DENSER THAN YOURS!
TANK

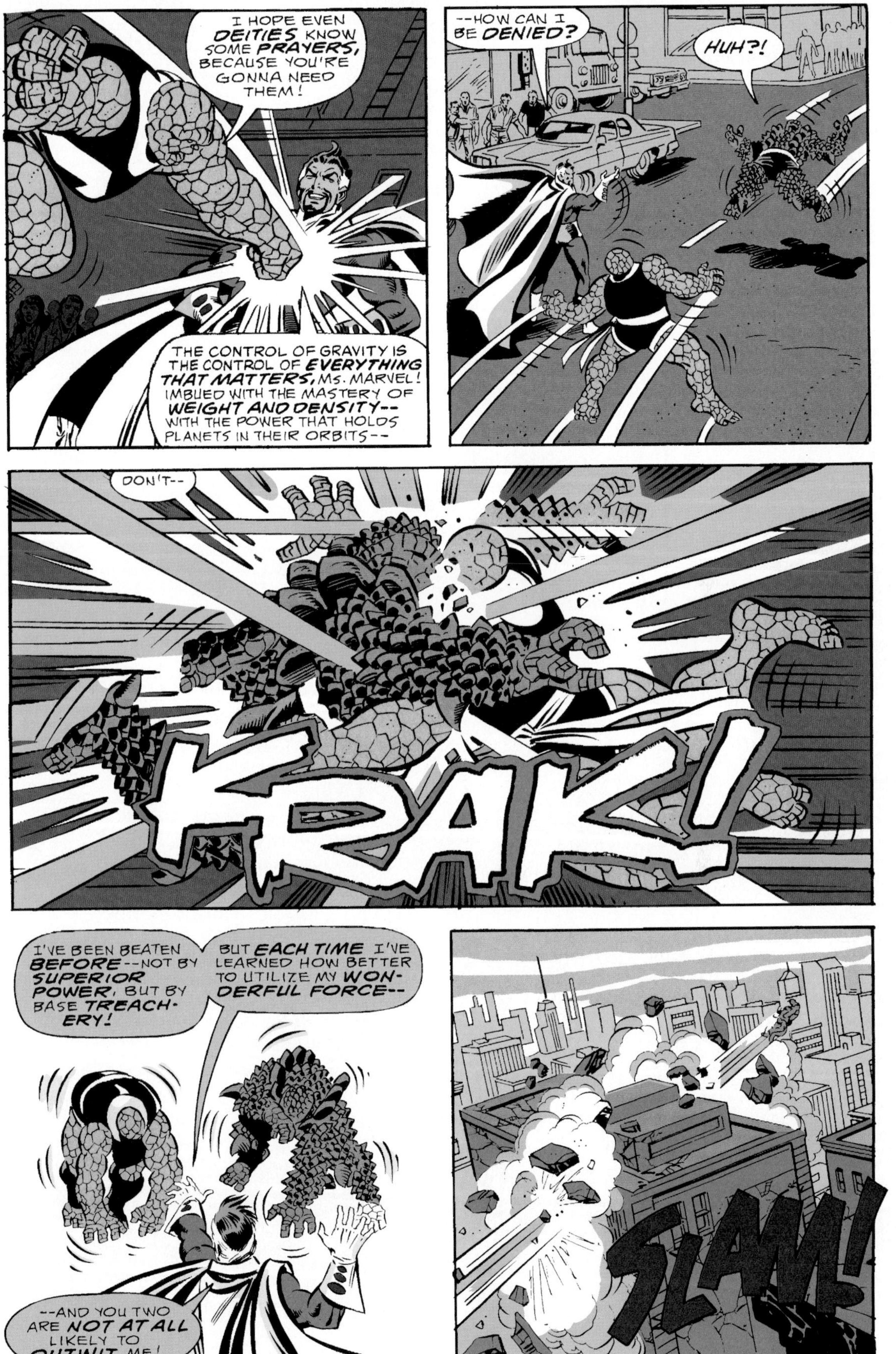
I HOPE EVEN DEITIES KNOW SOME PRAYERS, BECAUSE YOU'RE GONNA NEED THEM!
THE CONTROL OF GRAVITY IS THE CONTROL OF EVERYTHING THAT MATTERS, Ms. MARVEL! IMBUED WITH THE MASTERY OF WEIGHT AND DENSITY-- WITH THE POWER THAT HOLDS PLANETS IN THEIR ORBITS--
--HOW CAN I BE DENIED?
HUH?!
DON'T--
KRAK!
I'VE BEEN BEATEN BEFORE--NOT BY SUPERIOR POWER, BUT BY BASE TREACHERY!
BUT EACH TIME I'VE LEARNED HOW BETTER TO UTILIZE MY WONDERFUL FORCE--
--AND YOU TWO ARE NOT AT ALL LIKELY TO OUTWIT ME!
SLAM!

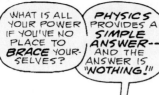

HOLY TOLEDO!

WHAT IS IT, JOHNNY?

I WISH YOU COULD SEE, HONEY --SO YOU COULD TELL ME IF I'M DREAMING--!

WHAT IS ALL YOUR POWER IF YOU'VE NO PLACE TO BRACE YOURSELVES?

PHYSICS PROVIDES A SIMPLE ANSWER-- AND THE ANSWER IS "NOTHING!"

NEW THING --OLD THING--

--YOU ARE NO-THING!!

KRAM!

OR AM I WRONG?

WHY NOT JUST STAND UP AND TELL ME SO?

YER A SICKO, YA --SICKO--!

BEN! THE HARDER I PUSH--

--THE MORE PRESSURE --HE APPLIES--

:UNNGH!:

DON'T-- CHA WORRY, GRAVVY--!

I'LL GET UP--AND WHEN I DO--!

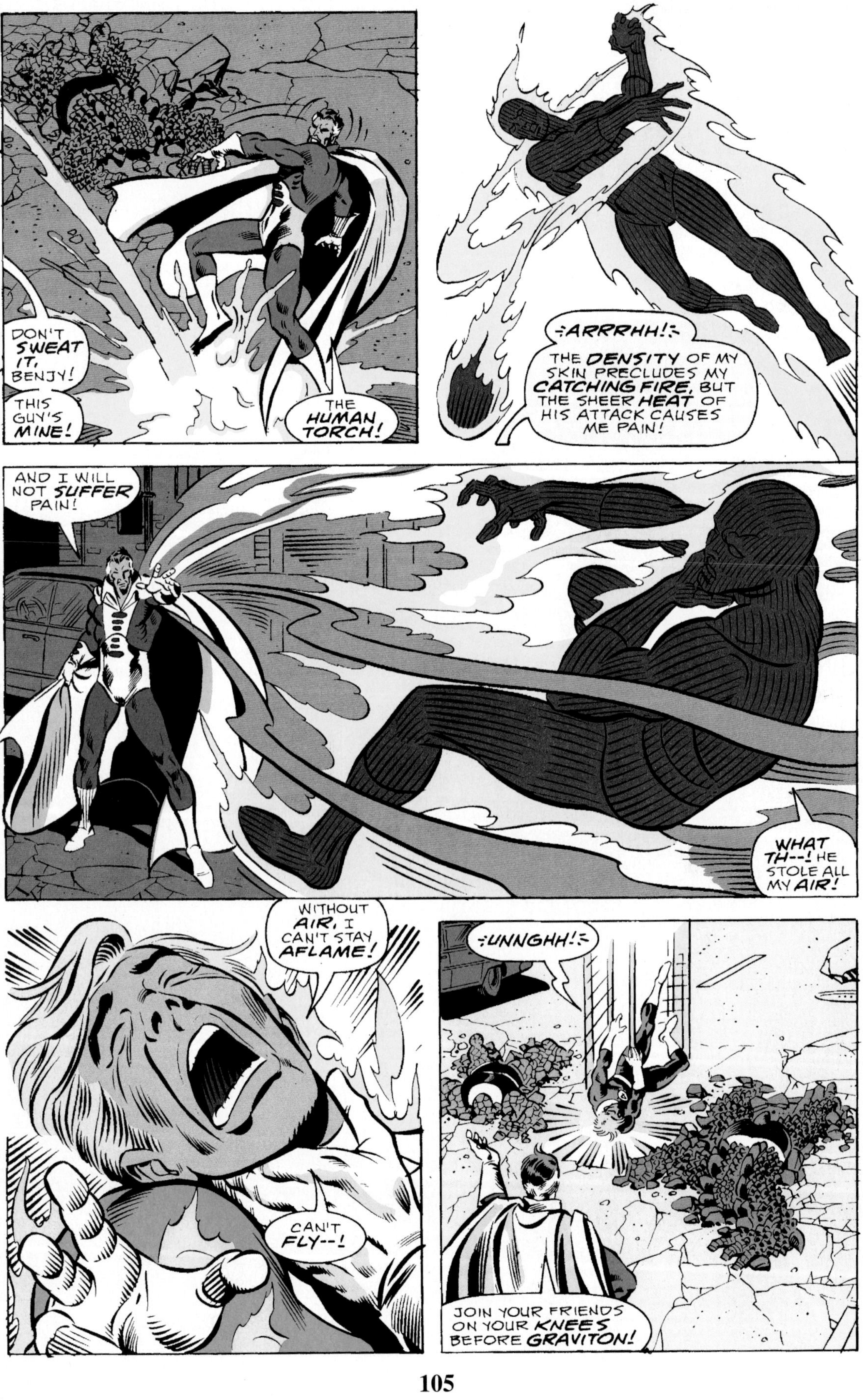

DON'T SWEAT IT, BENJY!
THIS GUY'S MINE!
THE HUMAN TORCH!
-ARRRHH!-
THE DENSITY OF MY SKIN PRECLUDES MY CATCHING FIRE, BUT THE SHEER HEAT OF HIS ATTACK CAUSES ME PAIN!
AND I WILL NOT SUFFER PAIN!
WHAT TH--! HE STOLE ALL MY AIR!
WITHOUT AIR, I CAN'T STAY AFLAME!
CAN'T FLY--!
-UNNGHH!-
JOIN YOUR FRIENDS ON YOUR KNEES BEFORE GRAVITON!

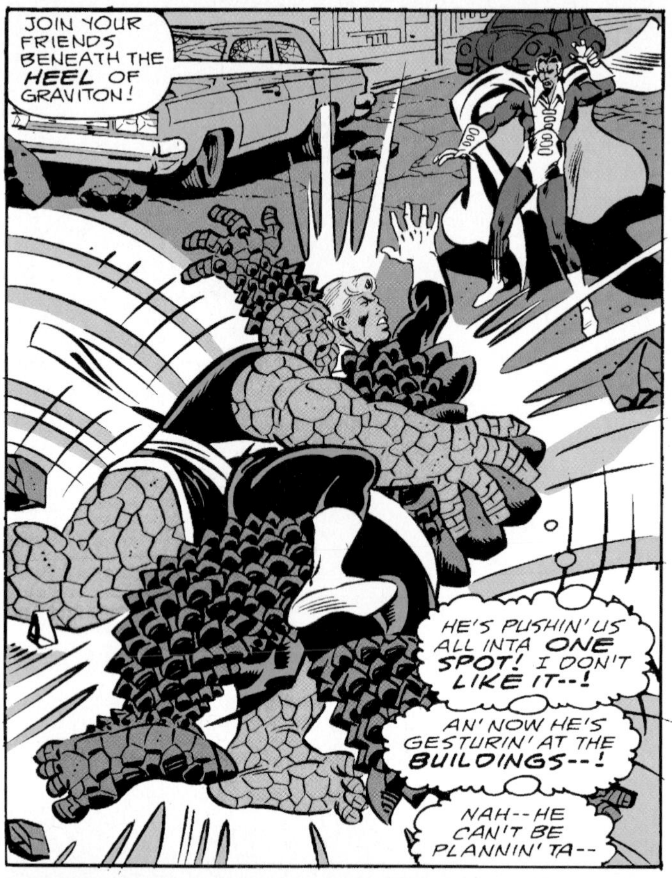
JOIN YOUR FRIENDS BENEATH THE HEEL OF GRAVITON!
HE'S PUSHIN' US ALL INTA ONE SPOT! I DON'T LIKE IT--!
AN' NOW HE'S GESTURIN' AT THE BUILDINGS--!
NAH--HE CAN'T BE PLANNIN' TA--

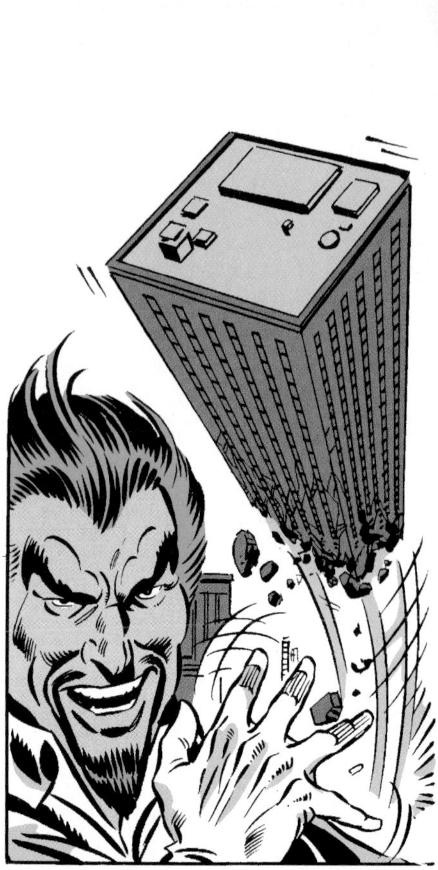

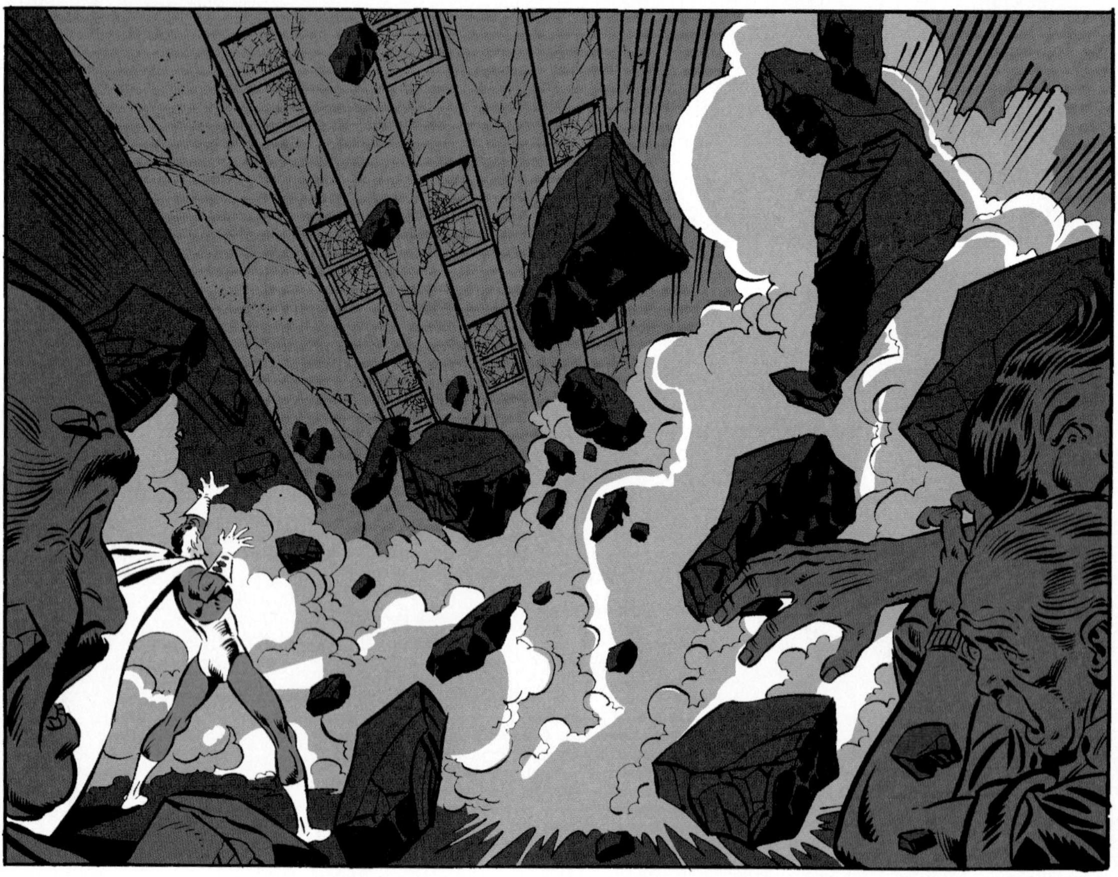

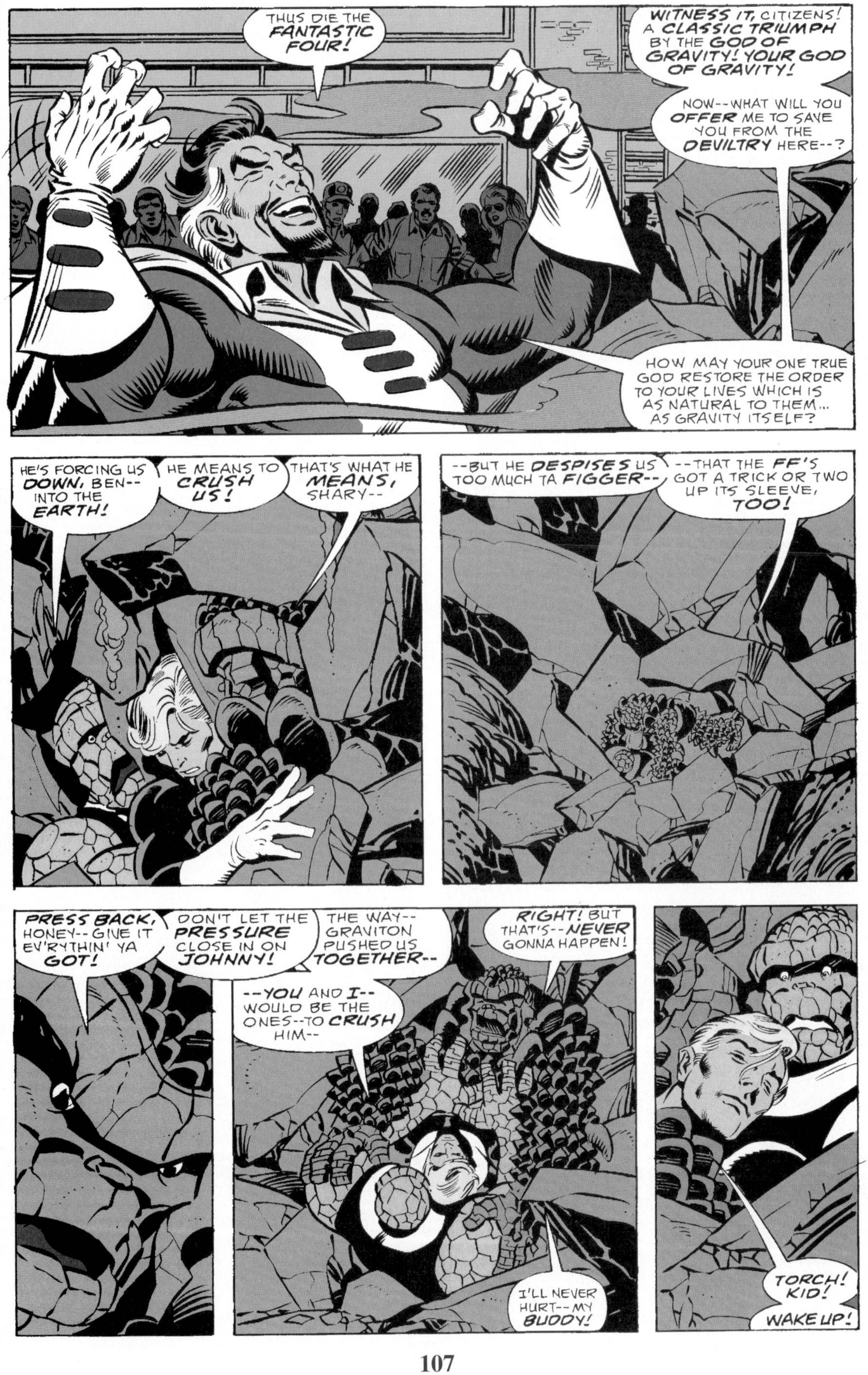
THUS DIE THE FANTASTIC FOUR!
WITNESS IT, CITIZENS! A CLASSIC TRIUMPH BY THE GOD OF GRAVITY! YOUR GOD OF GRAVITY!
NOW--WHAT WILL YOU OFFER ME TO SAVE YOU FROM THE DEVILTRY HERE--?
HOW MAY YOUR ONE TRUE GOD RESTORE THE ORDER TO YOUR LIVES WHICH IS AS NATURAL TO THEM... AS GRAVITY ITSELF?
HE'S FORCING US DOWN, BEN--INTO THE EARTH!
HE MEANS TO CRUSH US!
THAT'S WHAT HE MEANS, SHARY--
--BUT HE DESPISES US TOO MUCH TA FIGGER--
--THAT THE FF'S GOT A TRICK OR TWO UP ITS SLEEVE, TOO!
PRESS BACK, HONEY-- GIVE IT EV'RYTHIN' YA GOT!
DON'T LET THE PRESSURE CLOSE IN ON JOHNNY!
THE WAY-- GRAVITON PUSHED US TOGETHER--
--YOU AND I-- WOULD BE THE ONES--TO CRUSH HIM--
RIGHT! BUT THAT'S--NEVER GONNA HAPPEN!
I'LL NEVER HURT--MY BUDDY!
TORCH! KID!
WAKE UP!

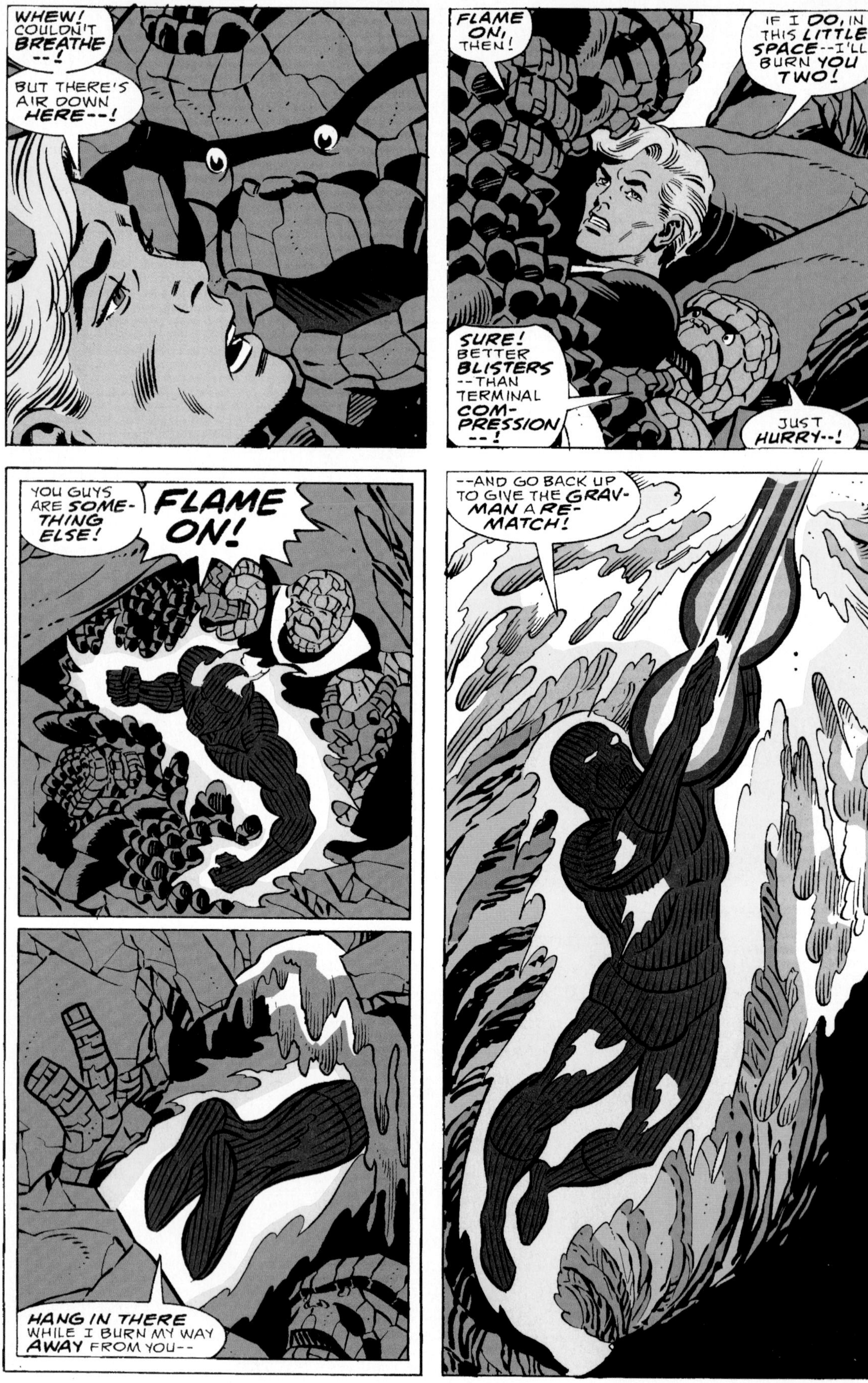
WHEW! COULDN'T BREATHE --!
BUT THERE'S AIR DOWN HERE--!
FLAME ON, THEN!
IF I DO, IN THIS LITTLE SPACE--I'LL BURN YOU TWO!
SURE! BETTER BLISTERS --THAN TERMINAL COM-PRESSION --!
JUST HURRY--!
YOU GUYS ARE SOME-THING ELSE!
FLAME ON!
HANG IN THERE WHILE I BURN MY WAY AWAY FROM YOU--
--AND GO BACK UP TO GIVE THE GRAV-MAN A RE-MATCH!

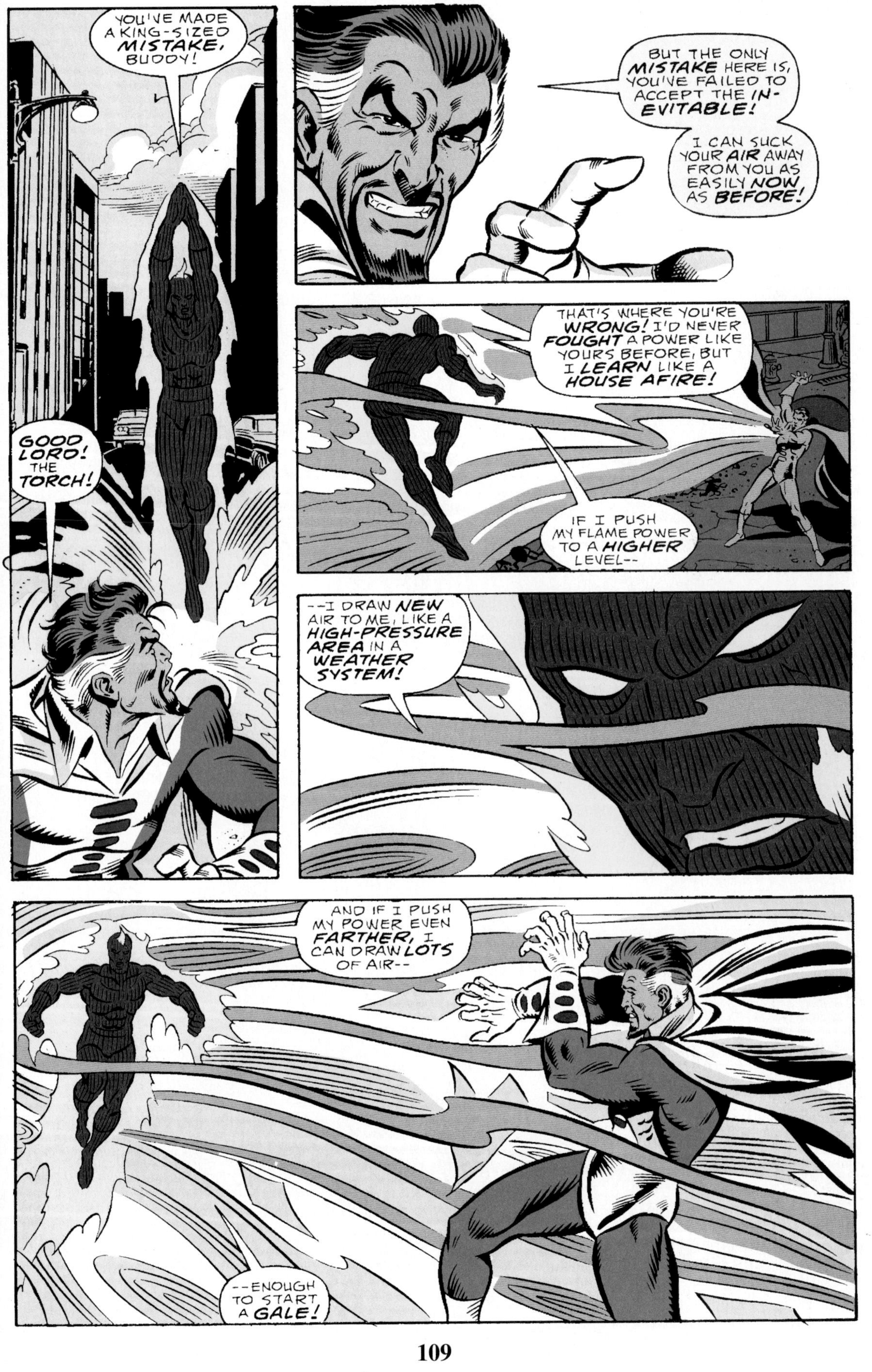
YOU'VE MADE A KING-SIZED MISTAKE, BUDDY!
GOOD LORD! THE TORCH!
BUT THE ONLY MISTAKE HERE IS, YOU'VE FAILED TO ACCEPT THE IN-EVITABLE!
I CAN SUCK YOUR AIR AWAY FROM YOU AS EASILY NOW, AS BEFORE!
THAT'S WHERE YOU'RE WRONG! I'D NEVER FOUGHT A POWER LIKE YOURS BEFORE, BUT I LEARN LIKE A HOUSE AFIRE!
IF I PUSH MY FLAME POWER TO A HIGHER LEVEL--
--I DRAW NEW AIR TO ME, LIKE A HIGH-PRESSURE AREA IN A WEATHER SYSTEM!
AND IF I PUSH MY POWER EVEN FARTHER, I CAN DRAW LOTS OF AIR--
--ENOUGH TO START A GALE!

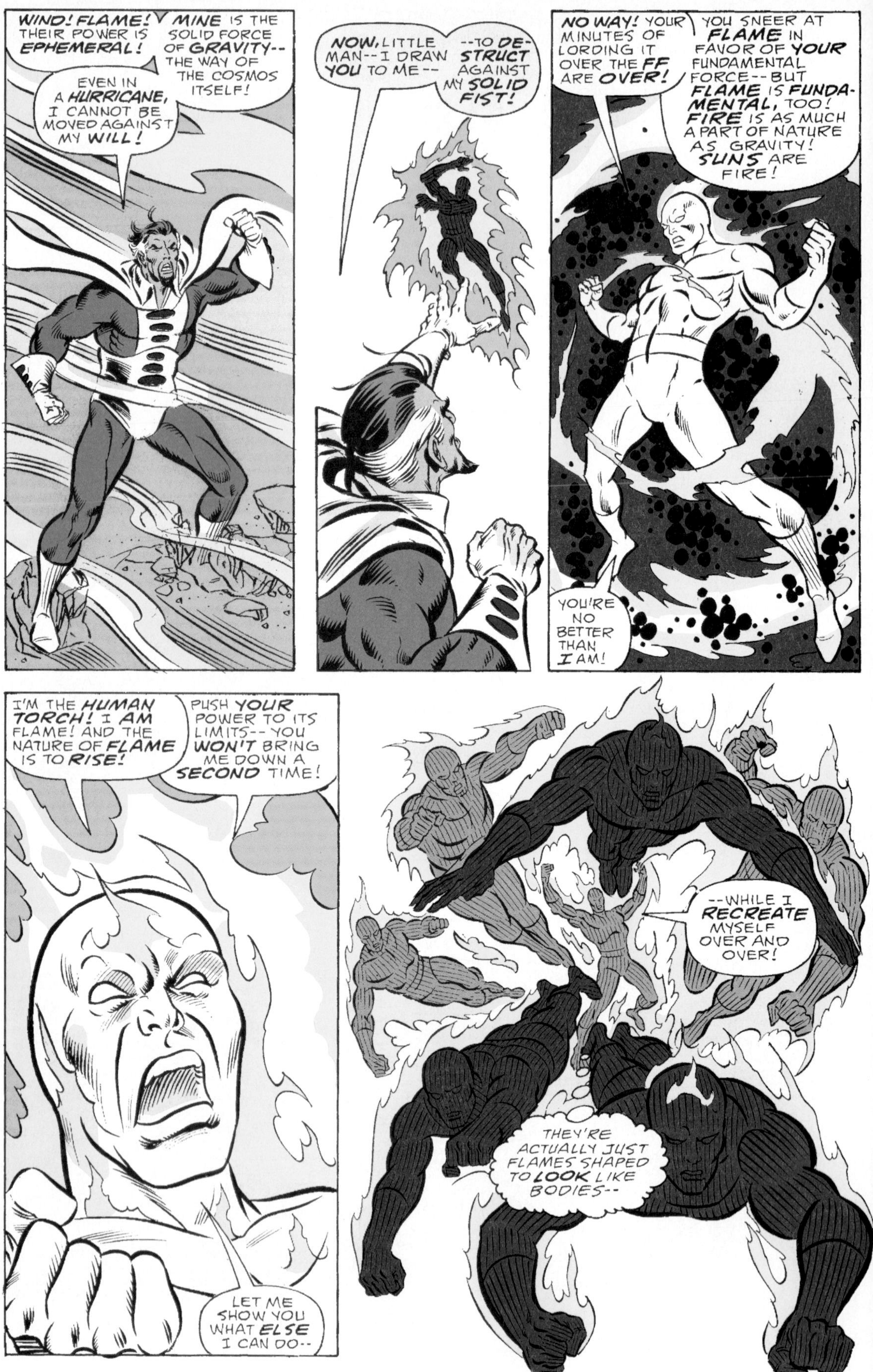
WIND! FLAME! THEIR POWER IS EPHEMERAL!
MINE IS THE SOLID FORCE OF GRAVITY-- THE WAY OF THE COSMOS ITSELF!
EVEN IN A HURRICANE, I CANNOT BE MOVED AGAINST MY WILL!
NOW, LITTLE MAN--I DRAW YOU TO ME--
--TO DESTRUCT AGAINST MY SOLID FIST!
NO WAY! YOUR MINUTES OF LORDING IT OVER THE FF ARE OVER!
YOU SNEER AT FLAME IN FAVOR OF YOUR FUNDAMENTAL FORCE--BUT FLAME IS FUNDAMENTAL, TOO! FIRE IS AS MUCH A PART OF NATURE AS GRAVITY! SUNS ARE FIRE!
YOU'RE NO BETTER THAN I AM!
I'M THE HUMAN TORCH! I AM FLAME! AND THE NATURE OF FLAME IS TO RISE!
PUSH YOUR POWER TO ITS LIMITS--YOU WON'T BRING ME DOWN A SECOND TIME!
LET ME SHOW YOU WHAT ELSE I CAN DO--
--WHILE I RECREATE MYSELF OVER AND OVER!
THEY'RE ACTUALLY JUST FLAMES SHAPED TO LOOK LIKE BODIES--

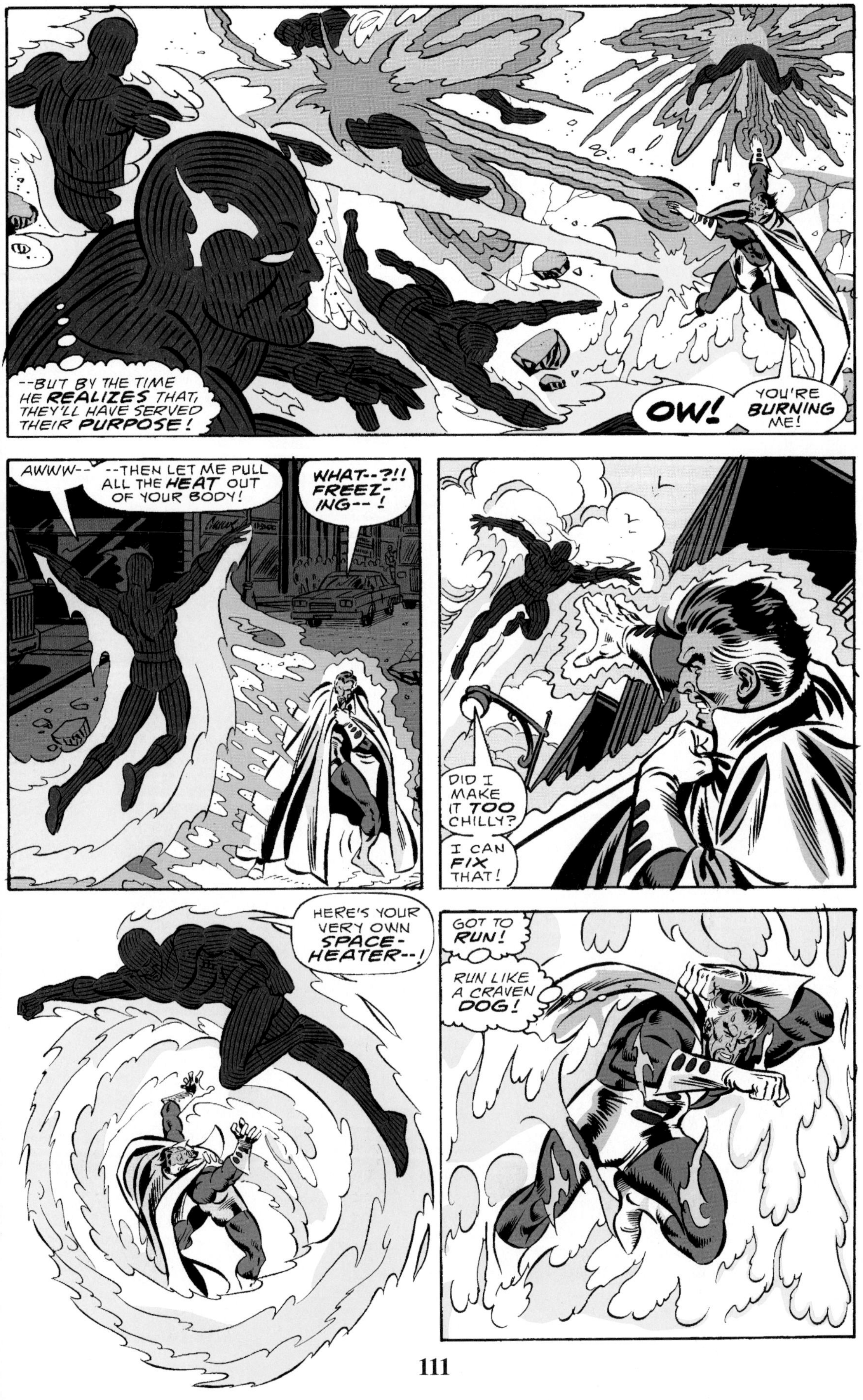
--BUT BY THE TIME HE REALIZES THAT, THEY'LL HAVE SERVED THEIR PURPOSE!
OW!
YOU'RE BURNING ME!
AWWW--
--THEN LET ME PULL ALL THE HEAT OUT OF YOUR BODY!
WHAT--?!! FREEZ-ING--!
DID I MAKE IT TOO CHILLY?
I CAN FIX THAT!
HERE'S YOUR VERY OWN SPACE-HEATER--!
GOT TO RUN!
RUN LIKE A CRAVEN DOG!

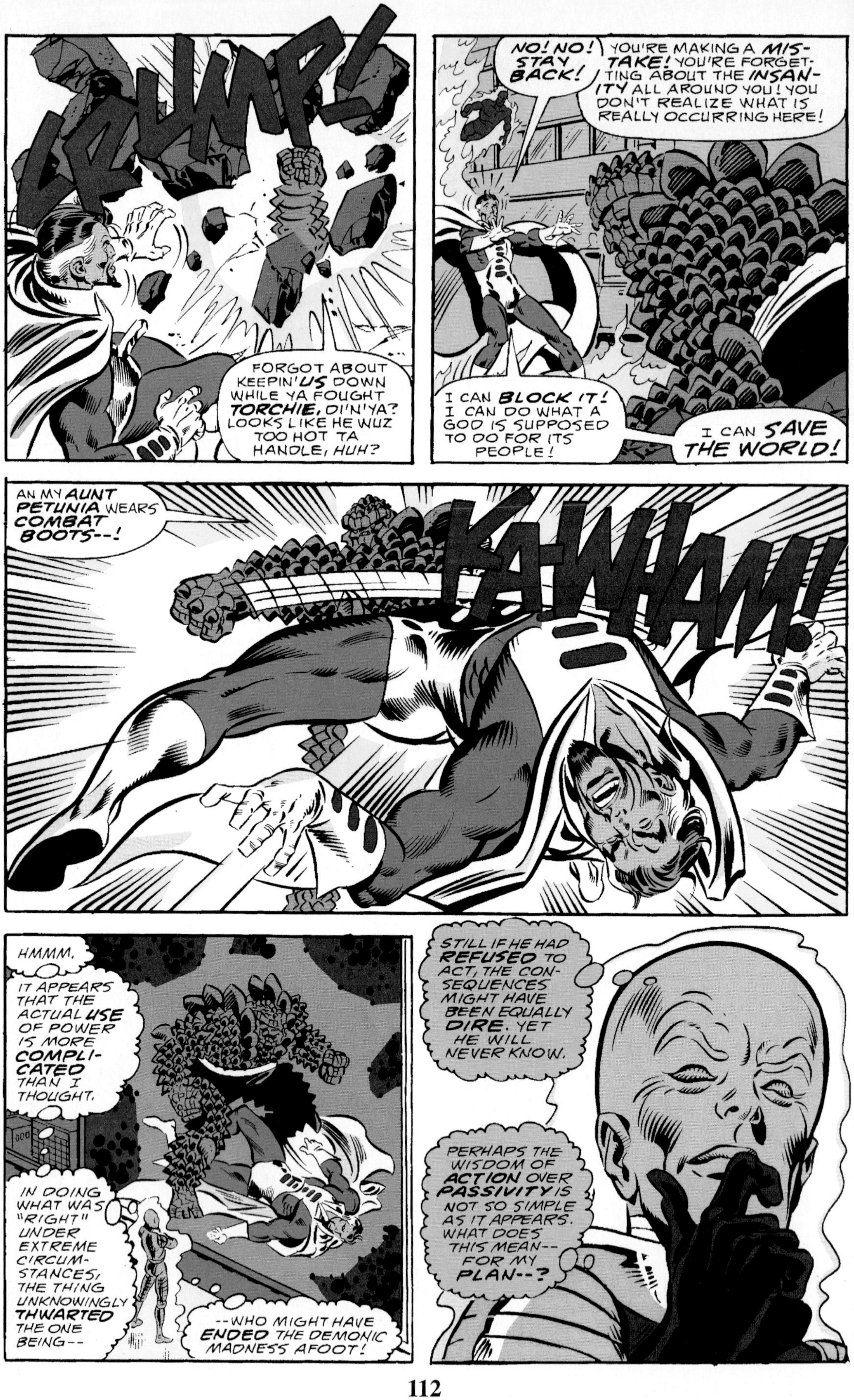
KRUMP!
FORGOT ABOUT KEEPIN' US DOWN WHILE YA FOUGHT TORCHIE, DI'N'YA? LOOKS LIKE HE WUZ TOO HOT TA HANDLE, HUH?
NO! NO! STAY BACK!
YOU'RE MAKING A MIS-TAKE! YOU'RE FORGET-TING ABOUT THE INSAN-ITY ALL AROUND YOU! YOU DON'T REALIZE WHAT IS REALLY OCCURRING HERE!
I CAN BLOCK IT! I CAN DO WHAT A GOD IS SUPPOSED TO DO FOR ITS PEOPLE!
I CAN SAVE THE WORLD!
AN MY AUNT PETUNIA WEARS COMBAT BOOTS--!
KA-WHAM!
HMMM.
IT APPEARS THAT THE ACTUAL USE OF POWER IS MORE COMPLI-CATED THAN I THOUGHT.
IN DOING WHAT WAS "RIGHT" UNDER EXTREME CIRCUM-STANCES, THE THING UNKNOWINGLY THWARTED THE ONE BEING--
--WHO MIGHT HAVE ENDED THE DEMONIC MADNESS AFOOT!
STILL IF HE HAD REFUSED TO ACT, THE CON-SEQUENCES MIGHT HAVE BEEN EQUALLY DIRE. YET HE WILL NEVER KNOW.
PERHAPS THE WISDOM OF ACTION OVER PASSIVITY IS NOT SO SIMPLE AS IT APPEARS. WHAT DOES THIS MEAN-- FOR MY PLAN--?

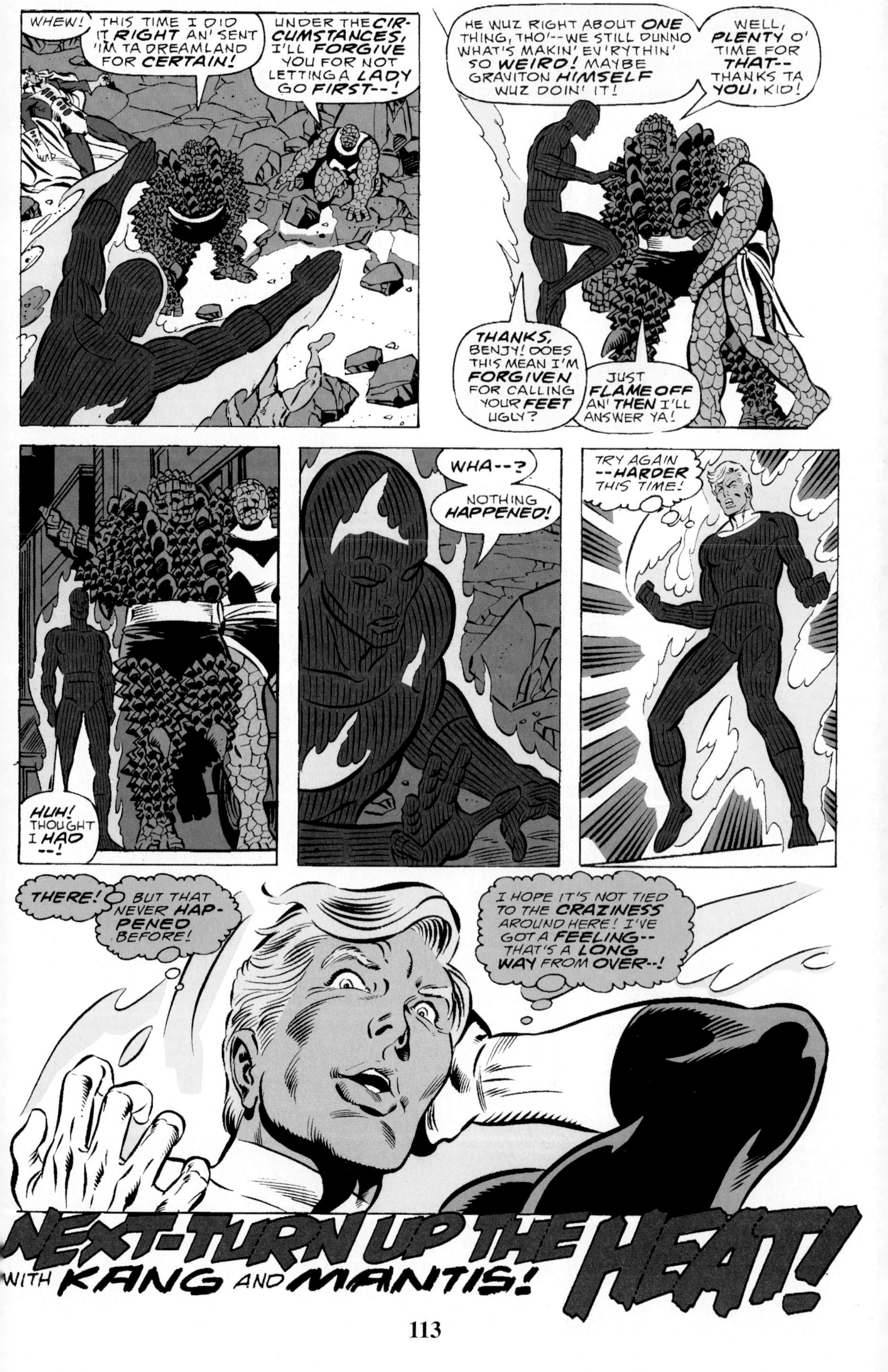
WHEW!
THIS TIME I DID IT RIGHT AN' SENT 'IM TA DREAMLAND FOR CERTAIN!
UNDER THE CIR-CUMSTANCES, I'LL FORGIVE YOU FOR NOT LETTING A LADY GO FIRST--!
HE WUZ RIGHT ABOUT ONE THING, THO'--WE STILL DUNNO WHAT'S MAKIN' EV'RYTHIN' SO WEIRD! MAYBE GRAVITON HIMSELF WUZ DOIN' IT!
WELL, PLENTY O' TIME FOR THAT--THANKS TA YOU, KID!
THANKS, BENJY! DOES THIS MEAN I'M FORGIVEN FOR CALLING YOUR FEET UGLY?
JUST FLAME OFF AN' THEN I'LL ANSWER YA!
HUH! THOUGHT I HAD--!
WHA--?
NOTHING HAPPENED!
TRY AGAIN --HARDER THIS TIME!
THERE!
BUT THAT NEVER HAP-PENED BEFORE!
I HOPE IT'S NOT TIED TO THE CRAZINESS AROUND HERE! I'VE GOT A FEELING--THAT'S A LONG WAY FROM OVER--!
NEXT-TURN UP THE HEAT!
WITH KANG AND MANTIS!

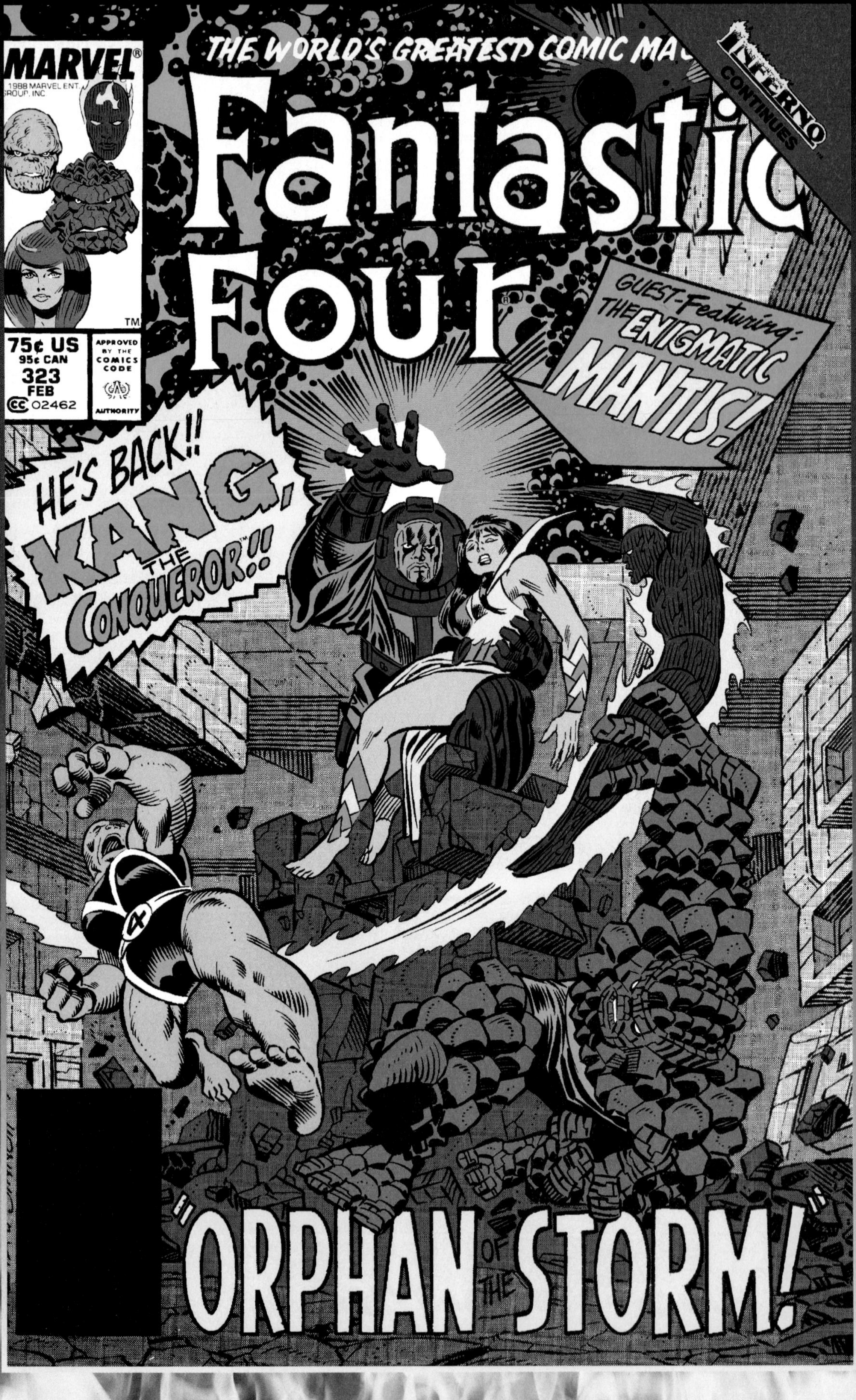
MARVEL
©1988 MARVEL ENT. GROUP, INC.
THE WORLD'S GREATEST COMIC MA
INFERNO CONTINUES
Fantastic Four
75¢ US
95¢ CAN
323
FEB
02462
APPROVED BY THE COMICS CODE AUTHORITY
GUEST-Featuring: THE ENIGMATIC MANTIS!
HE'S BACK!! KANG THE CONQUEROR!!
"ORPHAN OF THE STORM!"

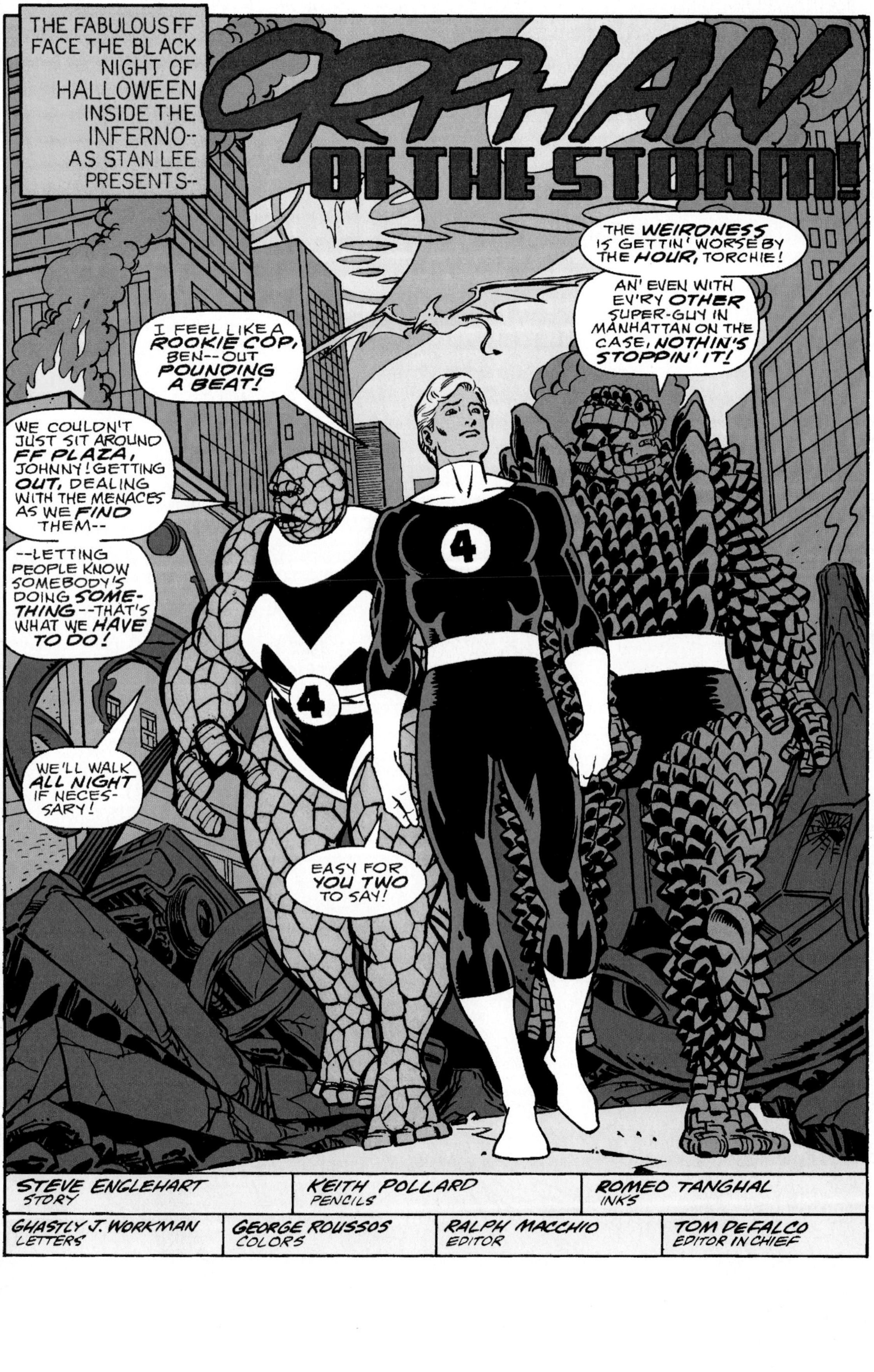
THE FABULOUS FF FACE THE BLACK NIGHT OF HALLOWEEN INSIDE THE INFERNO-- AS STAN LEE PRESENTS--
ORPHAN OF THE STORM!
THE WEIRDNESS IS GETTIN' WORSE BY THE HOUR, TORCHIE!
AN' EVEN WITH EV'RY OTHER SUPER-GUY IN MANHATTAN ON THE CASE, NOTHIN'S STOPPIN' IT!
I FEEL LIKE A ROOKIE COP, BEN--OUT POUNDING A BEAT!
WE COULDN'T JUST SIT AROUND FF PLAZA, JOHNNY! GETTING OUT, DEALING WITH THE MENACES AS WE FIND THEM--
--LETTING PEOPLE KNOW SOMEBODY'S DOING SOME-THING--THAT'S WHAT WE HAVE TO DO!
WE'LL WALK ALL NIGHT IF NECES-SARY!
EASY FOR YOU TWO TO SAY!
STEVE ENGLEHART STORY
KEITH POLLARD PENCILS
ROMEO TANGHAL INKS
GHASTLY J. WORKMAN LETTERS
GEORGE ROUSSOS COLORS
RALPH MACCHIO EDITOR
TOM DEFALCO EDITOR IN CHIEF

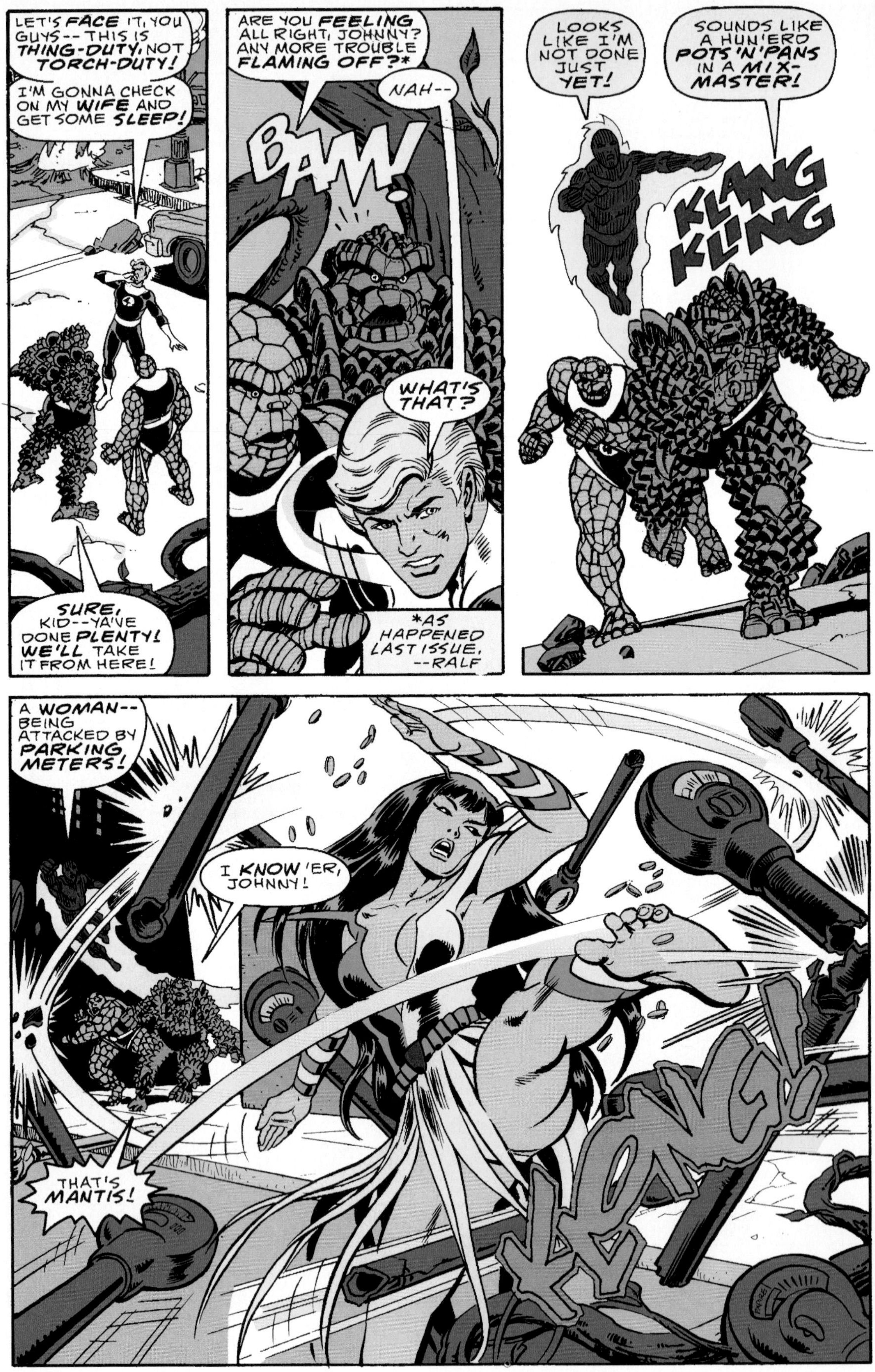
LET'S FACE IT, YOU GUYS -- THIS IS THING-DUTY, NOT TORCH-DUTY!
I'M GONNA CHECK ON MY WIFE AND GET SOME SLEEP!
SURE, KID--YA'VE DONE PLENTY! WE'LL TAKE IT FROM HERE!
ARE YOU FEELING ALL RIGHT, JOHNNY? ANY MORE TROUBLE FLAMING OFF?*
NAH--
BAM!
WHAT'S THAT?
*AS HAPPENED LAST ISSUE. --RALF
LOOKS LIKE I'M NOT DONE JUST YET!
SOUNDS LIKE A HUN'ERD POTS 'N' PANS IN A MIX-MASTER!
KLANG KLING
A WOMAN-- BEING ATTACKED BY PARKING METERS!
I KNOW 'ER, JOHNNY!
THAT'S MANTIS!

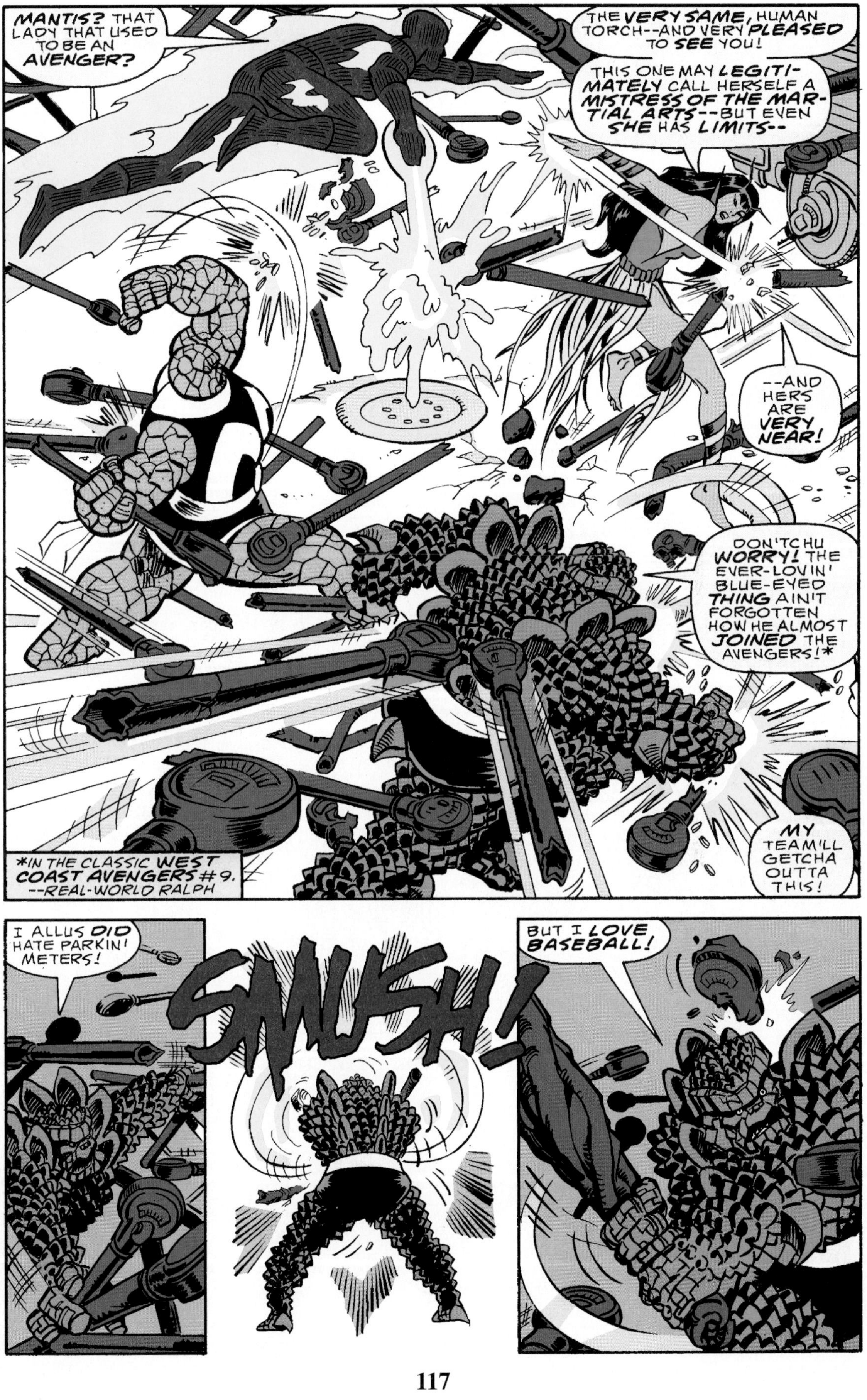
MANTIS? THAT LADY THAT USED TO BE AN AVENGER?
THE VERY SAME, HUMAN TORCH--AND VERY PLEASED TO SEE YOU!
THIS ONE MAY LEGITIMATELY CALL HERSELF A MISTRESS OF THE MARTIAL ARTS--BUT EVEN SHE HAS LIMITS--
--AND HERS ARE VERY NEAR!
DON'TCHU WORRY! THE EVER-LOVIN' BLUE-EYED THING AIN'T FORGOTTEN HOW HE ALMOST JOINED THE AVENGERS!*
MY TEAM'LL GETCHA OUTTA THIS!
*IN THE CLASSIC WEST COAST AVENGERS #9. --REAL-WORLD RALPH
I ALLUS DID HATE PARKIN' METERS!
SMUSH!
BUT I LOVE BASEBALL!

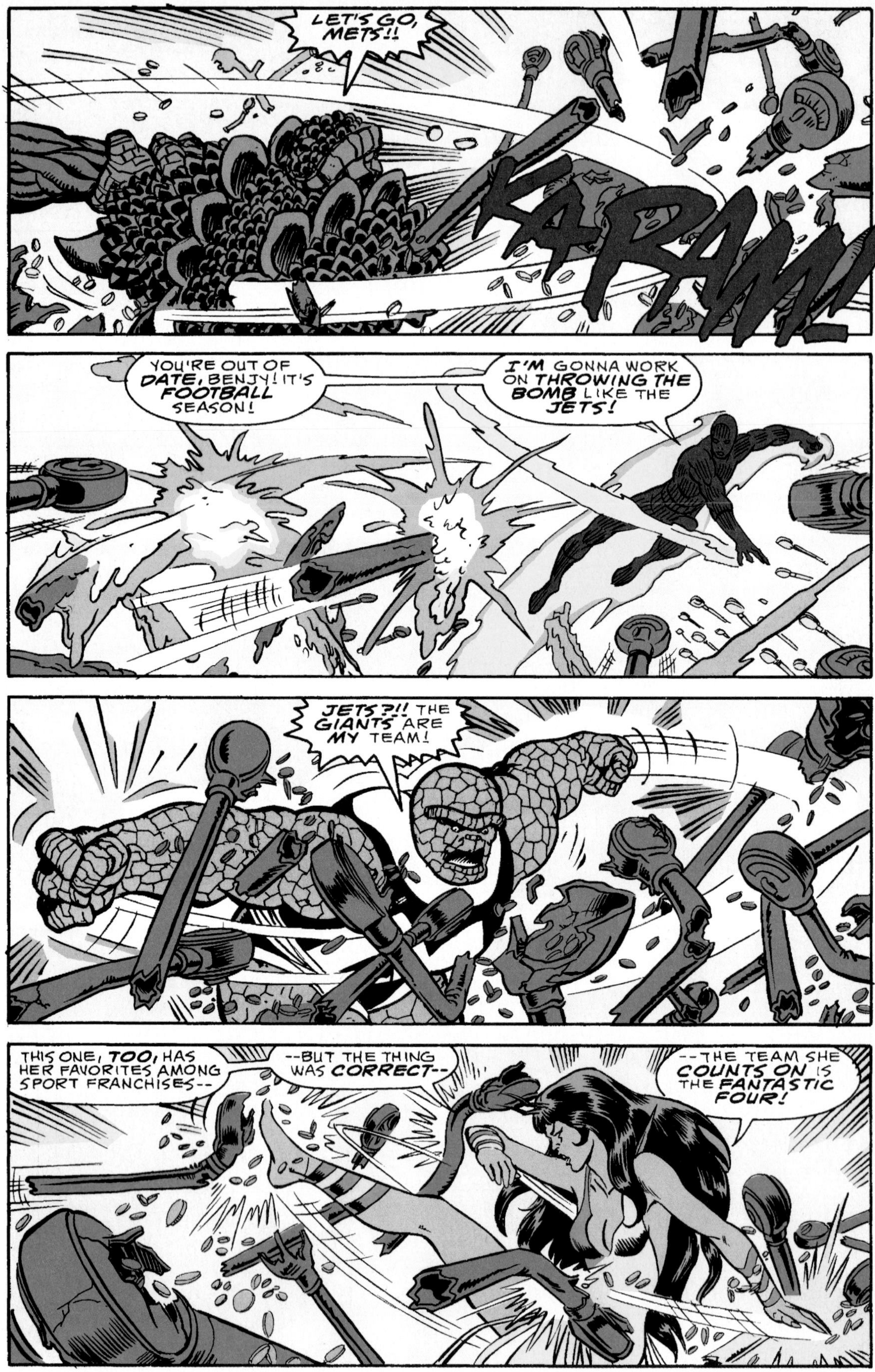

LET'S GO, METS!!
KA-RAWW!
YOU'RE OUT OF DATE, BENJY! IT'S FOOTBALL SEASON!
I'M GONNA WORK ON THROWING THE BOMB LIKE THE JETS!
JETS?!! THE GIANTS ARE MY TEAM!
THIS ONE, TOO, HAS HER FAVORITES AMONG SPORT FRANCHISES--
--BUT THE THING WAS CORRECT--
--THE TEAM SHE COUNTS ON IS THE FANTASTIC FOUR!

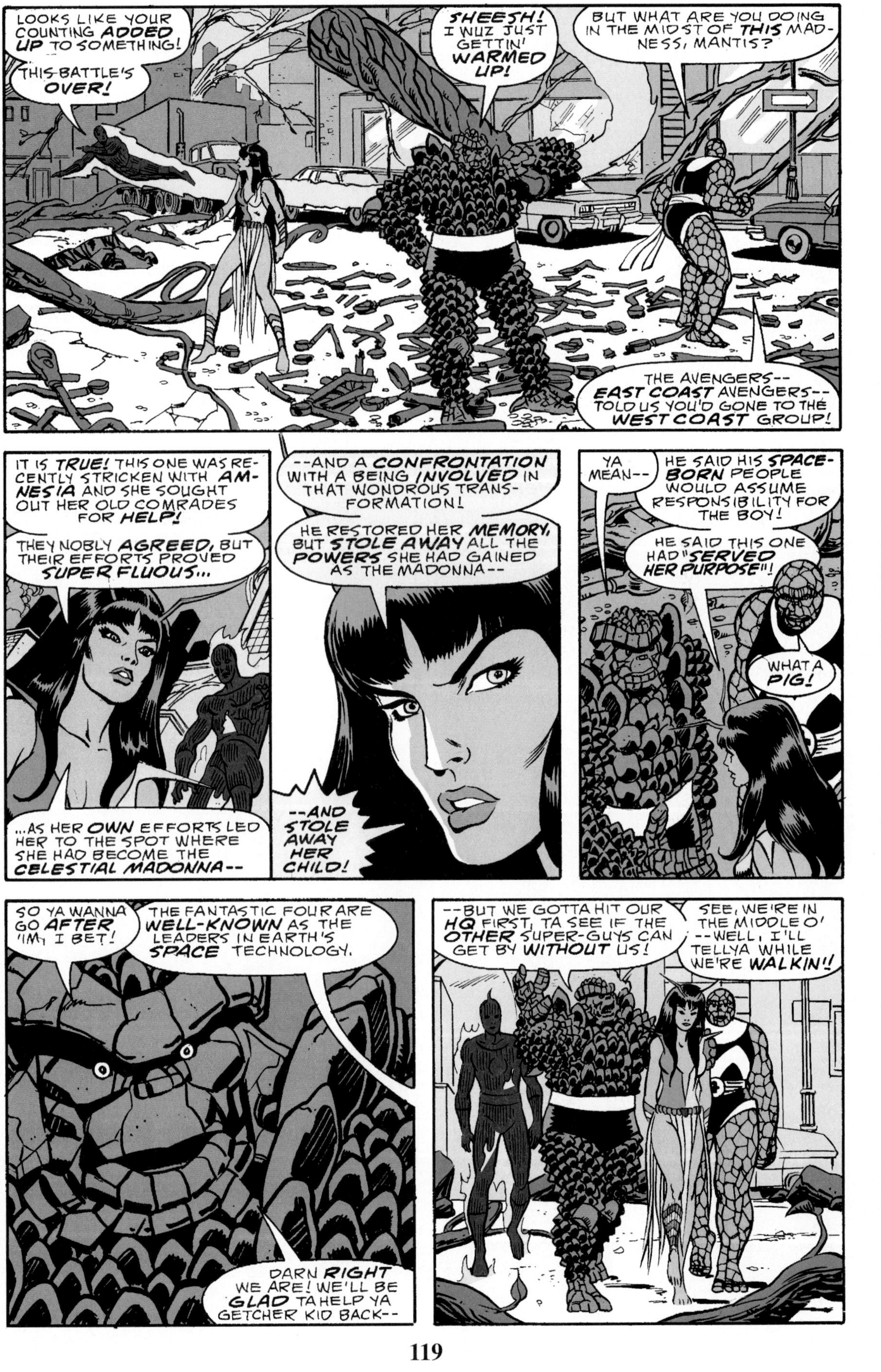
LOOKS LIKE YOUR COUNTING ADDED UP TO SOMETHING!
THIS BATTLE'S OVER!
SHEESH! I WUZ JUST GETTIN' WARMED UP!
BUT WHAT ARE YOU DOING IN THE MIDST OF THIS MADNESS, MANTIS?
THE AVENGERS-- EAST COAST AVENGERS-- TOLD US YOU'D GONE TO THE WEST COAST GROUP!
IT IS TRUE! THIS ONE WAS RECENTLY STRICKEN WITH AMNESIA AND SHE SOUGHT OUT HER OLD COMRADES FOR HELP!
THEY NOBLY AGREED, BUT THEIR EFFORTS PROVED SUPERFLUOUS...
...AS HER OWN EFFORTS LED HER TO THE SPOT WHERE SHE HAD BECOME THE CELESTIAL MADONNA--
--AND A CONFRONTATION WITH A BEING INVOLVED IN THAT WONDROUS TRANSFORMATION!
HE RESTORED HER MEMORY, BUT STOLE AWAY ALL THE POWERS SHE HAD GAINED AS THE MADONNA--
--AND STOLE AWAY HER CHILD!
YA MEAN--
HE SAID HIS SPACE-BORN PEOPLE WOULD ASSUME RESPONSIBILITY FOR THE BOY!
HE SAID THIS ONE HAD "SERVED HER PURPOSE"!
WHAT A PIG!
SO YA WANNA GO AFTER 'IM, I BET!
THE FANTASTIC FOUR ARE WELL-KNOWN AS THE LEADERS IN EARTH'S SPACE TECHNOLOGY.
DARN RIGHT WE ARE! WE'LL BE GLAD TA HELP YA GETCHER KID BACK--
--BUT WE GOTTA HIT OUR HQ FIRST, TA SEE IF THE OTHER SUPER-GUYS CAN GET BY WITHOUT US!
SEE, WE'RE IN THE MIDDLE O' --WELL, I'LL TELLYA WHILE WE'RE WALKIN'!

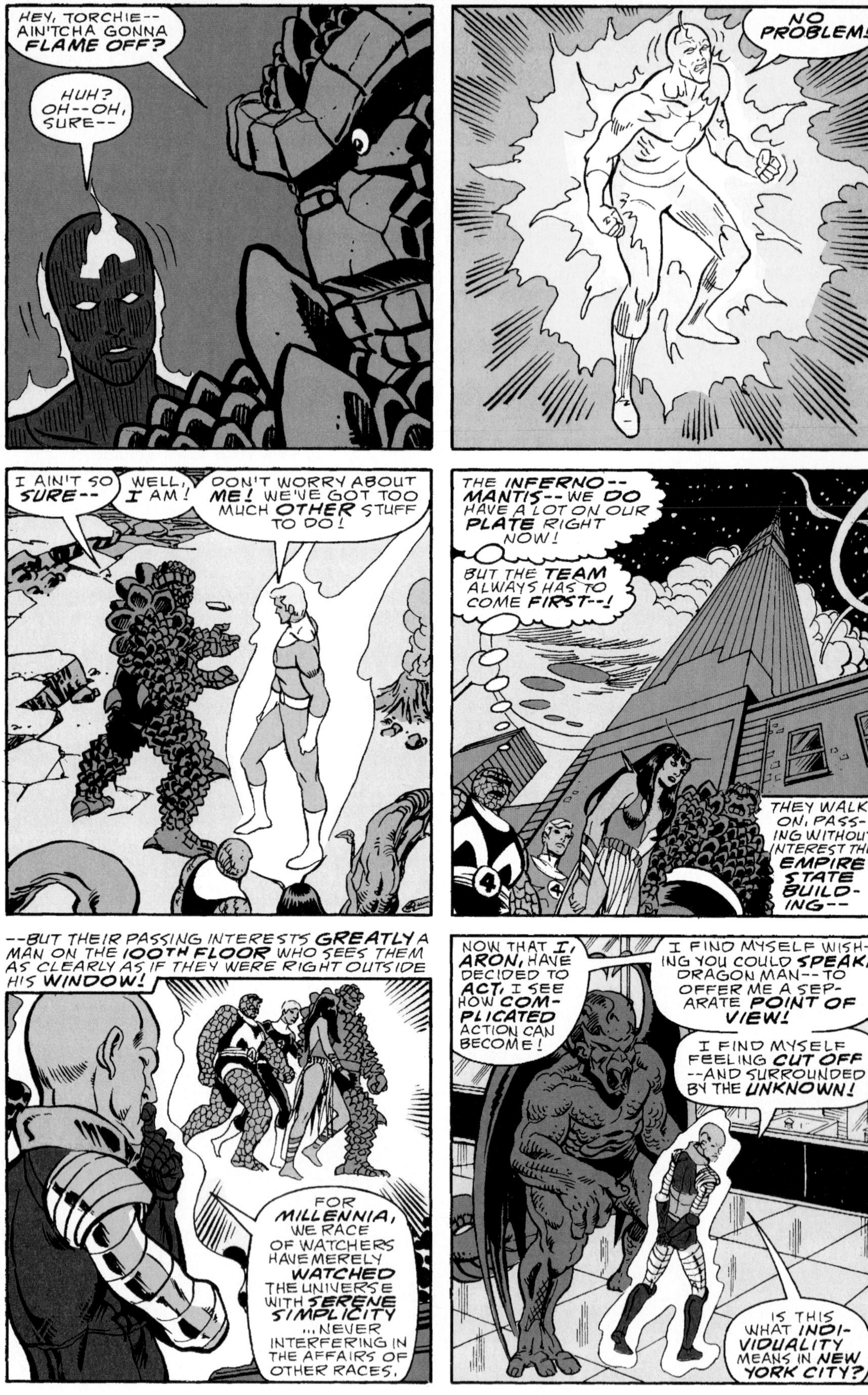
HEY, TORCHIE-- AIN'TCHA GONNA FLAME OFF?
HUH? OH--OH, SURE--
NO PROBLEM!
I AIN'T SO SURE--
WELL, I AM!
DON'T WORRY ABOUT ME! WE'VE GOT TOO MUCH OTHER STUFF TO DO!
THE INFERNO-- MANTIS--WE DO HAVE A LOT ON OUR PLATE RIGHT NOW!
BUT THE TEAM ALWAYS HAS TO COME FIRST--!
THEY WALK ON, PASSING WITHOUT INTEREST THE EMPIRE STATE BUILDING--
--BUT THEIR PASSING INTERESTS GREATLY A MAN ON THE 100TH FLOOR WHO SEES THEM AS CLEARLY AS IF THEY WERE RIGHT OUTSIDE HIS WINDOW!
FOR MILLENNIA, WE RACE OF WATCHERS HAVE MERELY WATCHED THE UNIVERSE WITH SERENE SIMPLICITY ...NEVER INTERFERING IN THE AFFAIRS OF OTHER RACES.
NOW THAT I, ARON, HAVE DECIDED TO ACT, I SEE HOW COMPLICATED ACTION CAN BECOME!
I FIND MYSELF WISHING YOU COULD SPEAK, DRAGON MAN--TO OFFER ME A SEPARATE POINT OF VIEW!
I FIND MYSELF FEELING CUT OFF --AND SURROUNDED BY THE UNKNOWN!
IS THIS WHAT INDIVIDUALITY MEANS IN NEW YORK CITY?

BY THE STANDARDS BRED *INTO* ME, I AM A *WONDROUS BEING*, BUT SINCE DESCENDING INTO THIS VICIOUS AND *FINITE MILIEU* I HAVE BEEN BUFFETED BY SUCH UNEXPECTED *EVILS--!*

MORE AND MORE, I FEAR FOR MY VERY *SOUL!*

WOULD A *MORTAL* MAN KNOW WHAT TO DO NOW--?

OR--AM I MERELY *IMAGINING* THESE DANGERS...?

...LEERS!

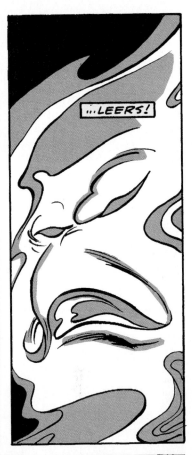

IN THE FAR CORNER OF THE MAMMOTH CHAMBER...SOMETHING AS FORMLESS AS THE WATCHER'S FEARS...

AND THAT'S ONLY *HALF* OF IT!

IN WHAT PASSES FOR *SIMULTANEITY*, IN A DIMENSION WITHOUT TIME--

--KANG THE CONQUEROR IS *ALSO* PERUSING THE EVENTS ON EARTH!

THIS IS THE *MOMENT* FOR THE *MASTER OF TIME* TO *STRIKE!*

THIS IS THE *MOMENT* TO TAKE MY *REVENGE* ON THE *CELESTIAL MADONNA* AND INSURE MY *ETERNAL SURVIVAL!*

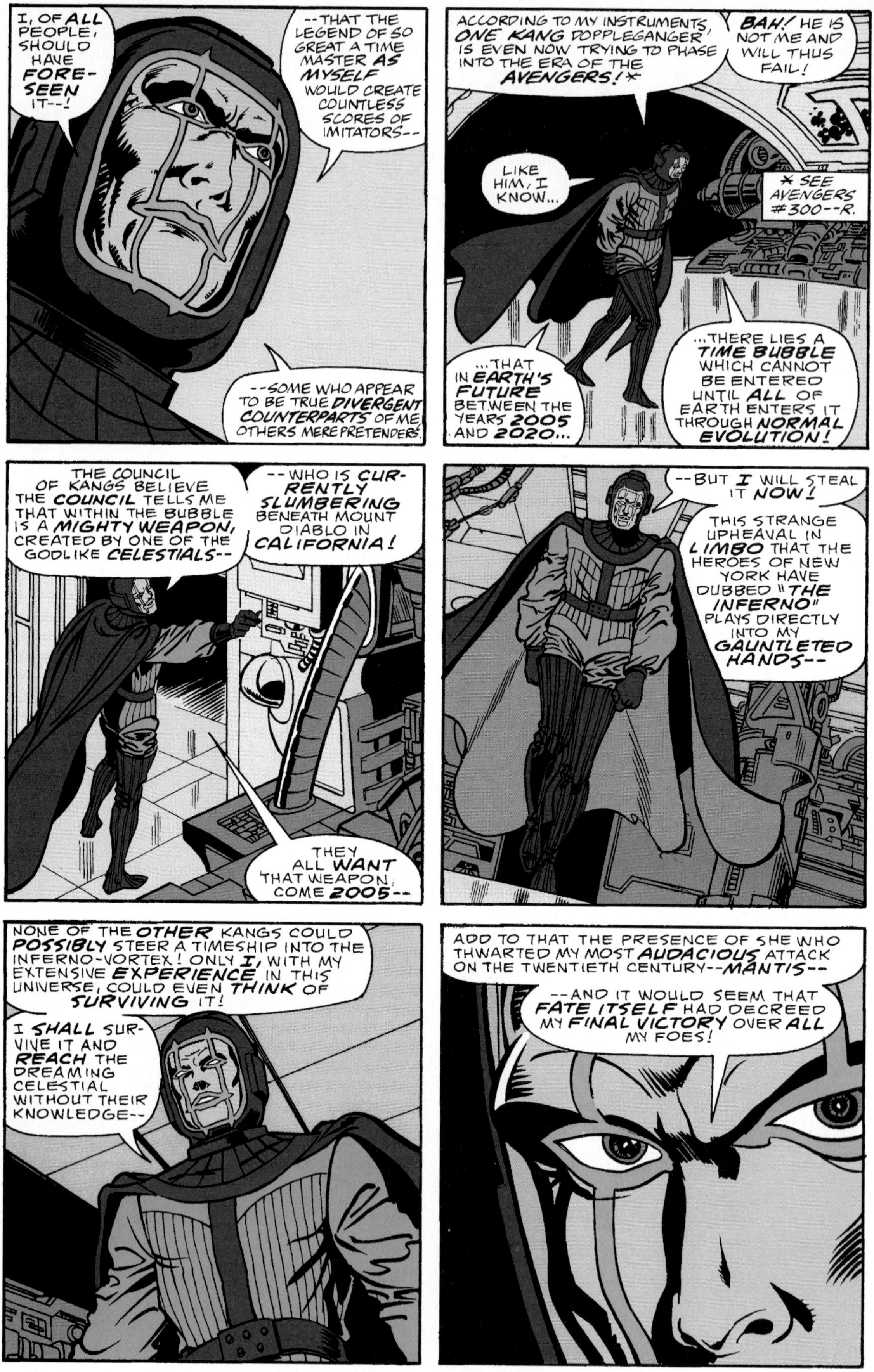
I, OF ALL PEOPLE, SHOULD HAVE FORESEEN IT--!
--THAT THE LEGEND OF SO GREAT A TIME MASTER AS MYSELF WOULD CREATE COUNTLESS SCORES OF IMITATORS--
--SOME WHO APPEAR TO BE TRUE DIVERGENT COUNTERPARTS OF ME! OTHERS MERE PRETENDERS!
ACCORDING TO MY INSTRUMENTS, ONE KANG DOPPLEGANGER IS EVEN NOW TRYING TO PHASE INTO THE ERA OF THE AVENGERS! *
BAH! HE IS NOT ME AND WILL THUS FAIL!
LIKE HIM, I KNOW...
* SEE AVENGERS #300--R.
...THAT IN EARTH'S FUTURE BETWEEN THE YEARS 2005 AND 2020...
...THERE LIES A TIME BUBBLE WHICH CANNOT BE ENTERED UNTIL ALL OF EARTH ENTERS IT THROUGH NORMAL EVOLUTION!
THE COUNCIL OF KANGS BELIEVE THE COUNCIL TELLS ME THAT WITHIN THE BUBBLE IS A MIGHTY WEAPON, CREATED BY ONE OF THE GODLIKE CELESTIALS--
--WHO IS CURRENTLY SLUMBERING BENEATH MOUNT DIABLO IN CALIFORNIA!
THEY ALL WANT THAT WEAPON, COME 2005--
--BUT I WILL STEAL IT NOW!
THIS STRANGE UPHEAVAL IN LIMBO THAT THE HEROES OF NEW YORK HAVE DUBBED "THE INFERNO" PLAYS DIRECTLY INTO MY GAUNTLETED HANDS--
NONE OF THE OTHER KANGS COULD POSSIBLY STEER A TIMESHIP INTO THE INFERNO-VORTEX! ONLY I, WITH MY EXTENSIVE EXPERIENCE IN THIS UNIVERSE, COULD EVEN THINK OF SURVIVING IT!
I SHALL SURVIVE IT AND REACH THE DREAMING CELESTIAL WITHOUT THEIR KNOWLEDGE--
ADD TO THAT THE PRESENCE OF SHE WHO THWARTED MY MOST AUDACIOUS ATTACK ON THE TWENTIETH CENTURY--MANTIS--
--AND IT WOULD SEEM THAT FATE ITSELF HAD DECREED MY FINAL VICTORY OVER ALL MY FOES!

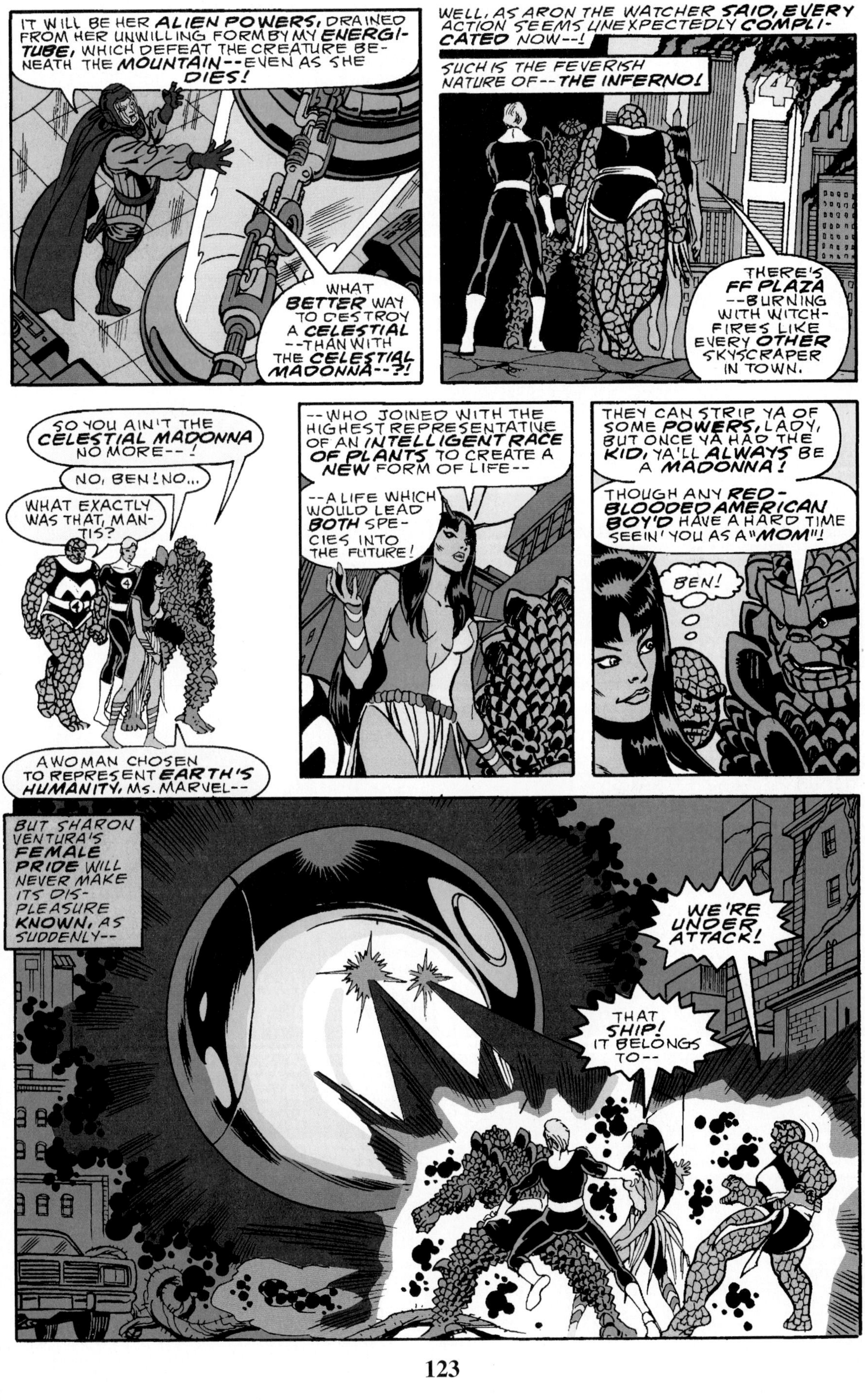
IT WILL BE HER ALIEN POWERS, DRAINED FROM HER UNWILLING FORM BY MY ENERGI-TUBE, WHICH DEFEAT THE CREATURE BENEATH THE MOUNTAIN--EVEN AS SHE DIES!
WHAT BETTER WAY TO DESTROY A CELESTIAL --THAN WITH THE CELESTIAL MADONNA--?!
WELL, AS ARON THE WATCHER SAID, EVERY ACTION SEEMS UNEXPECTEDLY COMPLICATED NOW--!
SUCH IS THE FEVERISH NATURE OF--THE INFERNO!
THERE'S FF PLAZA --BURNING WITH WITCH-FIRES LIKE EVERY OTHER SKYSCRAPER IN TOWN.
SO YOU AIN'T THE CELESTIAL MADONNA NO MORE--!
NO, BEN! NO...
WHAT EXACTLY WAS THAT, MANTIS?
A WOMAN CHOSEN TO REPRESENT EARTH'S HUMANITY, Ms. MARVEL--
--WHO JOINED WITH THE HIGHEST REPRESENTATIVE OF AN INTELLIGENT RACE OF PLANTS TO CREATE A NEW FORM OF LIFE--
--A LIFE WHICH WOULD LEAD BOTH SPECIES INTO THE FUTURE!
THEY CAN STRIP YA OF SOME POWERS, LADY, BUT ONCE YA HAD THE KID, YA'LL ALWAYS BE A MADONNA!
THOUGH ANY RED-BLOODED AMERICAN BOY'D HAVE A HARD TIME SEEIN' YOU AS A "MOM"!
BEN!
BUT SHARON VENTURA'S FEMALE PRIDE WILL NEVER MAKE ITS DISPLEASURE KNOWN, AS SUDDENLY--
WE'RE UNDER ATTACK!
THAT SHIP! IT BELONGS TO--

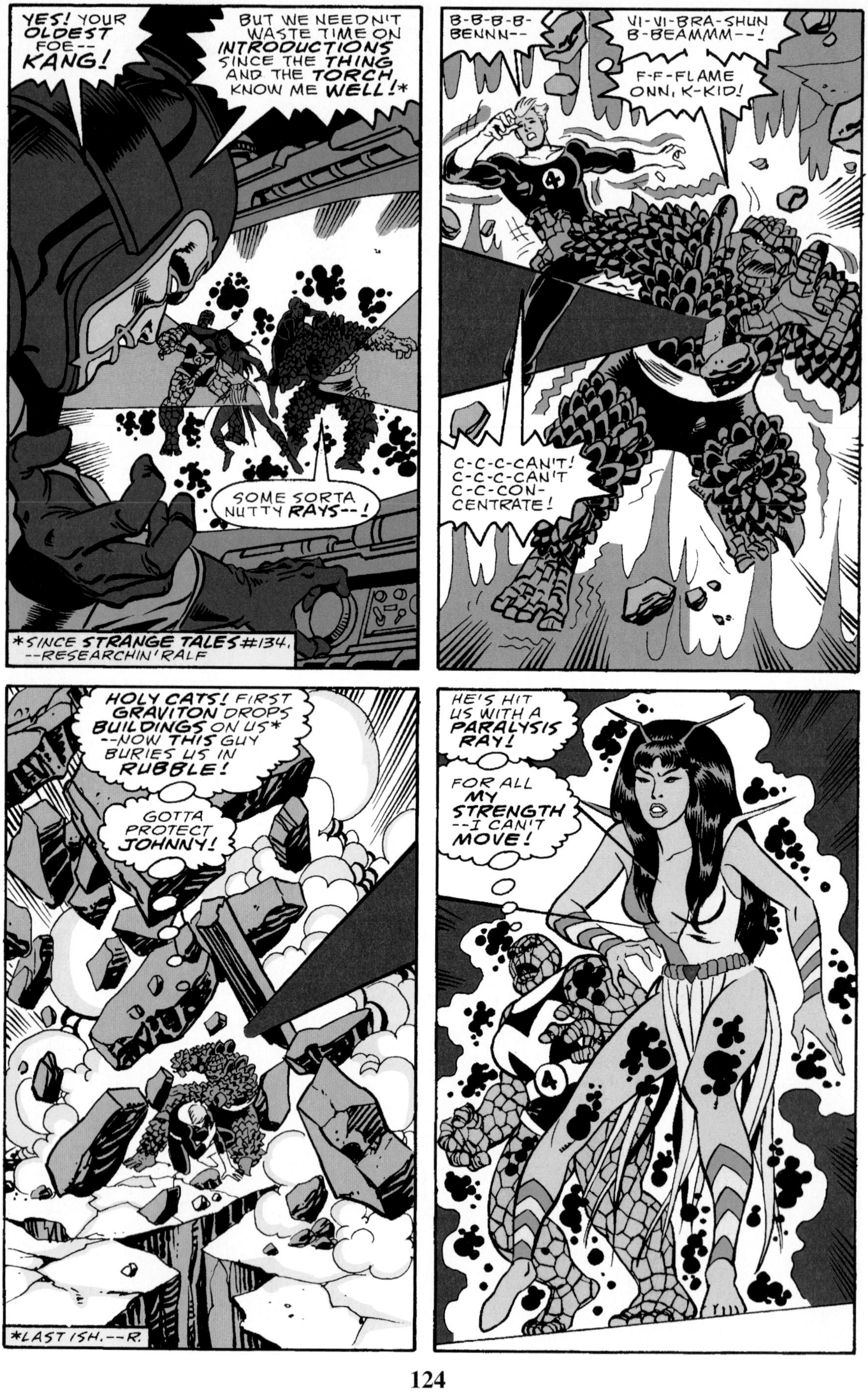
YES! YOUR OLDEST FOE-- KANG!
BUT WE NEEDN'T WASTE TIME ON INTRODUCTIONS SINCE THE THING AND THE TORCH KNOW ME WELL!*
SOME SORTA NUTTY RAYS--!
*SINCE STRANGE TALES #134. --RESEARCHIN' RALF
B-B-B-B-BENNN--
VI-VI-BRA-SHUN B-BEAMMM--!
F-F-FLAME ONN, K-KID!
C-C-C-CAN'T! C-C-C-CAN'T C-C-CON-CENTRATE!
HOLY CATS! FIRST GRAVITON DROPS BUILDINGS ON US* --NOW THIS GUY BURIES US IN RUBBLE!
GOTTA PROTECT JOHNNY!
*LAST ISH.--R.
HE'S HIT US WITH A PARALYSIS RAY!
FOR ALL MY STRENGTH --I CAN'T MOVE!

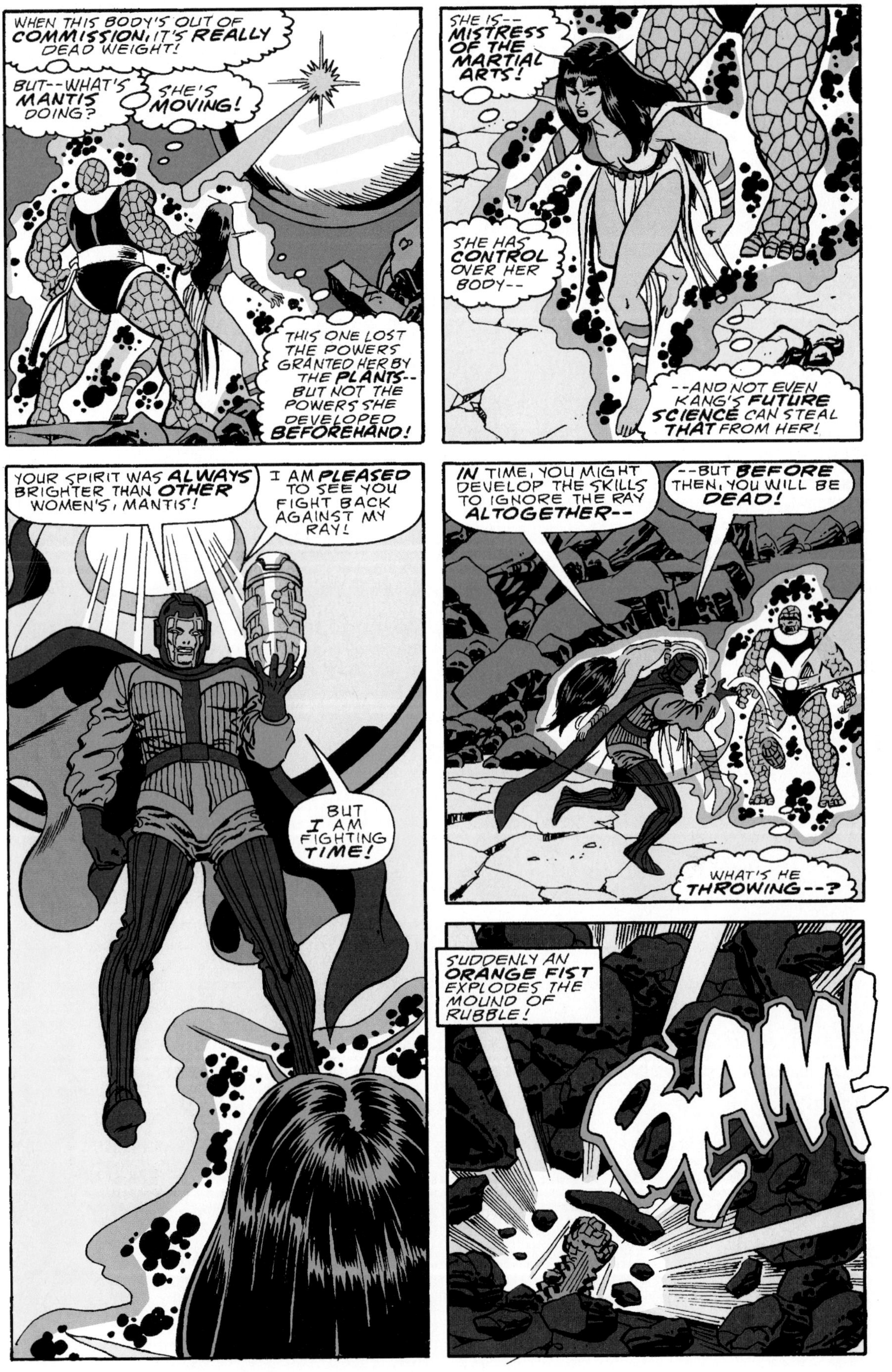
WHEN THIS BODY'S OUT OF COMMISSION, IT'S REALLY DEAD WEIGHT!
BUT--WHAT'S MANTIS DOING?
SHE'S MOVING!
THIS ONE LOST THE POWERS GRANTED HER BY THE PLANTS-- BUT NOT THE POWERS SHE DEVELOPED BEFOREHAND!
SHE IS-- MISTRESS OF THE MARTIAL ARTS!
SHE HAS CONTROL OVER HER BODY--
--AND NOT EVEN KANG'S FUTURE SCIENCE CAN STEAL THAT FROM HER!
YOUR SPIRIT WAS ALWAYS BRIGHTER THAN OTHER WOMEN'S, MANTIS!
I AM PLEASED TO SEE YOU FIGHT BACK AGAINST MY RAY!
BUT I AM FIGHTING TIME!
IN TIME, YOU MIGHT DEVELOP THE SKILLS TO IGNORE THE RAY ALTOGETHER--
--BUT BEFORE THEN, YOU WILL BE DEAD!
WHAT'S HE THROWING--?
SUDDENLY AN ORANGE FIST EXPLODES THE MOUND OF RUBBLE!
BAM

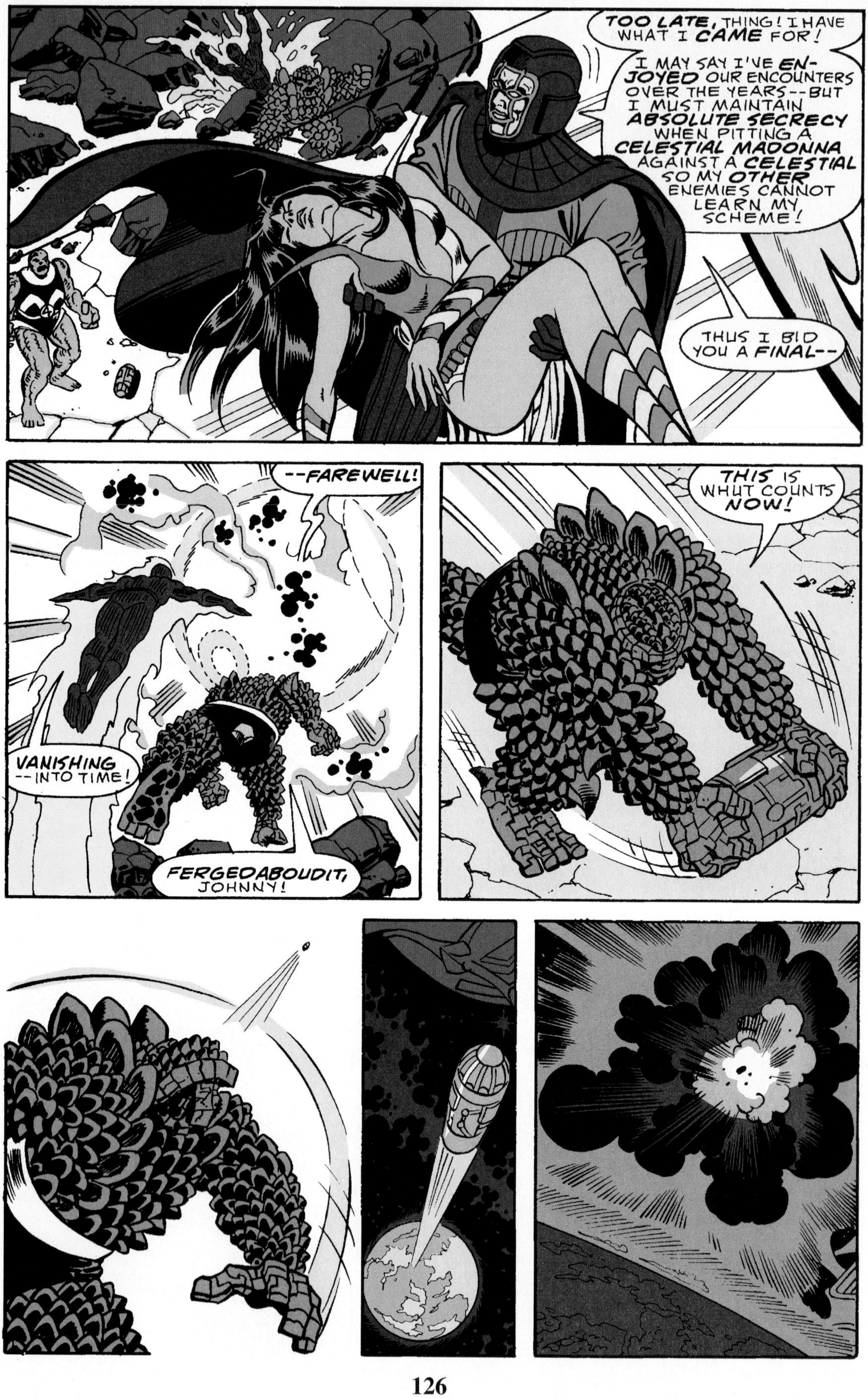
TOO LATE, THING! I HAVE WHAT I CAME FOR!
I MAY SAY I'VE ENJOYED OUR ENCOUNTERS OVER THE YEARS--BUT I MUST MAINTAIN ABSOLUTE SECRECY WHEN PITTING A CELESTIAL MADONNA AGAINST A CELESTIAL SO MY OTHER ENEMIES CANNOT LEARN MY SCHEME!
THUS I BID YOU A FINAL--
--FAREWELL!
VANISHING --INTO TIME!
FERGEDABOUDIT, JOHNNY!
THIS IS WHUT COUNTS NOW!

THAT *BOMB* WOULD'VE LEVELED THE *ENTIRE CITY!*

IF YOU HADN'T GAINED SO MUCH STRENGTH FROM YOUR *NEW MUTATION*--!

BUT WHAT ABOUT *MANTIS?*

WE TOLD HER WE'D *HELP* HER, BUT KANG'S *TAKEN* HER, AND WE DON'T KNOW *WHERE!*

MAYBE WE *DO,* SHARY! HE TALKED ABOUT A *CELESTIAL,* AND I REMEMBER THE *AVENGERS* FOUND ONE O' THEM UNDER SOME MOUNTAIN IN *CALIFORNIA!*

WE CAN LOOK IT UP ON THE *FANTASTI-CAR'S COMPUTER* WHILE WE'RE FLYIN' *OUT* THERE!

ALL RIGHT!

YOU TWO TAKE THE PLANE! I WANT TO FLY ON MY *OWN!* BESIDES, WE CAN'T SEEM TO DO MUCH IN NEW YORK ABOUT ALL THESE CRAZY HAPPENINGS.

I'LL *MEET* YOU THERE!

HUH?

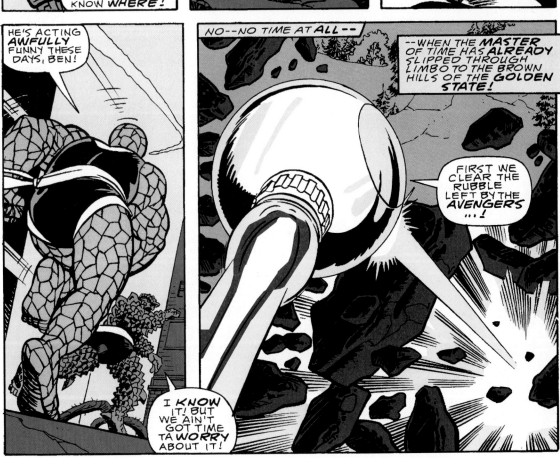

HE'S ACTING *AWFULLY* FUNNY THESE DAYS, BEN!

I *KNOW* IT! BUT WE AIN'T GOT TIME TA *WORRY* ABOUT IT!

NO--NO TIME AT *ALL*--

--WHEN THE *MASTER OF TIME* HAS *ALREADY* SLIPPED THROUGH LIMBO TO THE BROWN HILLS OF THE *GOLDEN STATE!*

FIRST WE CLEAR THE RUBBLE LEFT BY THE *AVENGERS* ...!

127

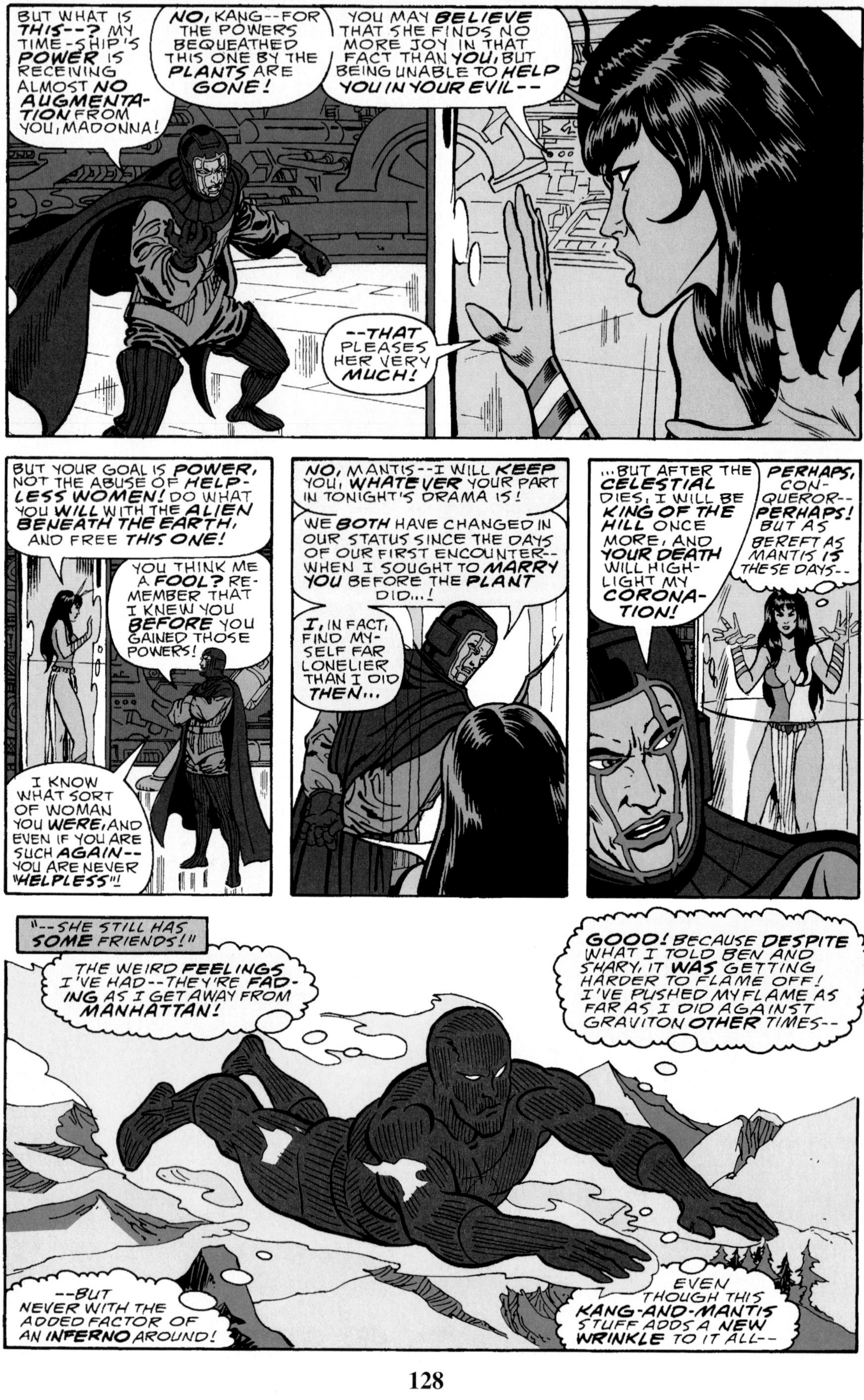

BUT WHAT IS THIS--? MY TIME-SHIP'S POWER IS RECEIVING ALMOST NO AUGMENTATION FROM YOU, MADONNA!
NO, KANG--FOR THE POWERS BEQUEATHED THIS ONE BY THE PLANTS ARE GONE!
YOU MAY BELIEVE THAT SHE FINDS NO MORE JOY IN THAT FACT THAN YOU, BUT BEING UNABLE TO HELP YOU IN YOUR EVIL--
--THAT PLEASES HER VERY MUCH!
BUT YOUR GOAL IS POWER, NOT THE ABUSE OF HELPLESS WOMEN! DO WHAT YOU WILL WITH THE ALIEN BENEATH THE EARTH, AND FREE THIS ONE!
YOU THINK ME A FOOL? REMEMBER THAT I KNEW YOU BEFORE YOU GAINED THOSE POWERS!
I KNOW WHAT SORT OF WOMAN YOU WERE, AND EVEN IF YOU ARE SUCH AGAIN--YOU ARE NEVER "HELPLESS"!
NO, MANTIS--I WILL KEEP YOU, WHATEVER YOUR PART IN TONIGHT'S DRAMA IS!
WE BOTH HAVE CHANGED IN OUR STATUS SINCE THE DAYS OF OUR FIRST ENCOUNTER--WHEN I SOUGHT TO MARRY YOU BEFORE THE PLANT DID...!
I, IN FACT, FIND MYSELF FAR LONELIER THAN I DID THEN...
...BUT AFTER THE CELESTIAL DIES, I WILL BE KING OF THE HILL ONCE MORE, AND YOUR DEATH WILL HIGHLIGHT MY CORONATION!
PERHAPS, CONQUEROR--PERHAPS! BUT AS BEREFT AS MANTIS IS THESE DAYS--
"--SHE STILL HAS SOME FRIENDS!"
THE WEIRD FEELINGS I'VE HAD--THEY'RE FADING AS I GET AWAY FROM MANHATTAN!
GOOD! BECAUSE DESPITE WHAT I TOLD BEN AND SHARY, IT WAS GETTING HARDER TO FLAME OFF! I'VE PUSHED MY FLAME AS FAR AS I DID AGAINST GRAVITON OTHER TIMES--
--BUT NEVER WITH THE ADDED FACTOR OF AN INFERNO AROUND!
EVEN THOUGH THIS KANG-AND-MANTIS STUFF ADDS A NEW WRINKLE TO IT ALL--

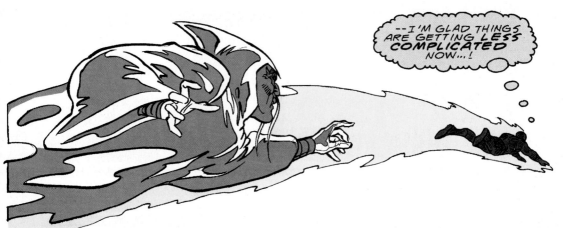

--I'M GLAD THINGS ARE GETTING *LESS* **COMPLICATED** NOW...!

AND SPEAKING OF *"LESS COMPLICATED"*--

--HI, BENJY!

HI *YER-SELF*, KID!

IF YA'VE HAD ENUFF *EXERCISE*, HOP *IN!*

NOW THAT WE'VE *CAUGHT UPTA* YA, THERE'S NO NEED TA BE A *STRANGER!*

THANKS *ANYWAY*, BUT I'M KINDA LIKE A *STREET ROD* WITH A *DIRTY CARBURETOR*, GETTING OUT ON THE TRACK TO RUN *FULL THROTTLE* FOR A WHILE!

SAY *WHUT?*

I'M *CLEAN-ING OUT!*

YOU *HEAD ON!* I'LL BE THERE TO *BACK YOU UP!*

BUT WILL *ANY* OF THE FABULOUS FF BE THERE -- IN *TIME?*

FINALLY-- THE DOOR TO THE DREAMING CELESTIAL LIES *RE-VEALED* ONCE MORE!

NO ONE *UNDERESTIMATES* YOU, KANG--BUT THIS ONE HAS LIVED AMONG THE *STARS*, AT THE SIDE OF THE *SILVER SURFER!* SHE KNOWS THE *LEGENDS* OF THE CELESTIALS!

ARE YOU CERTAIN *YOU* KNOW WHAT YOU FACE WHEN YOU ATTACK A *SPACE GOD?*

YOU KNOW THE LEGENDS OF *SPACE!*

KANG KNOWS THE LEGENDS OF *TIME!*

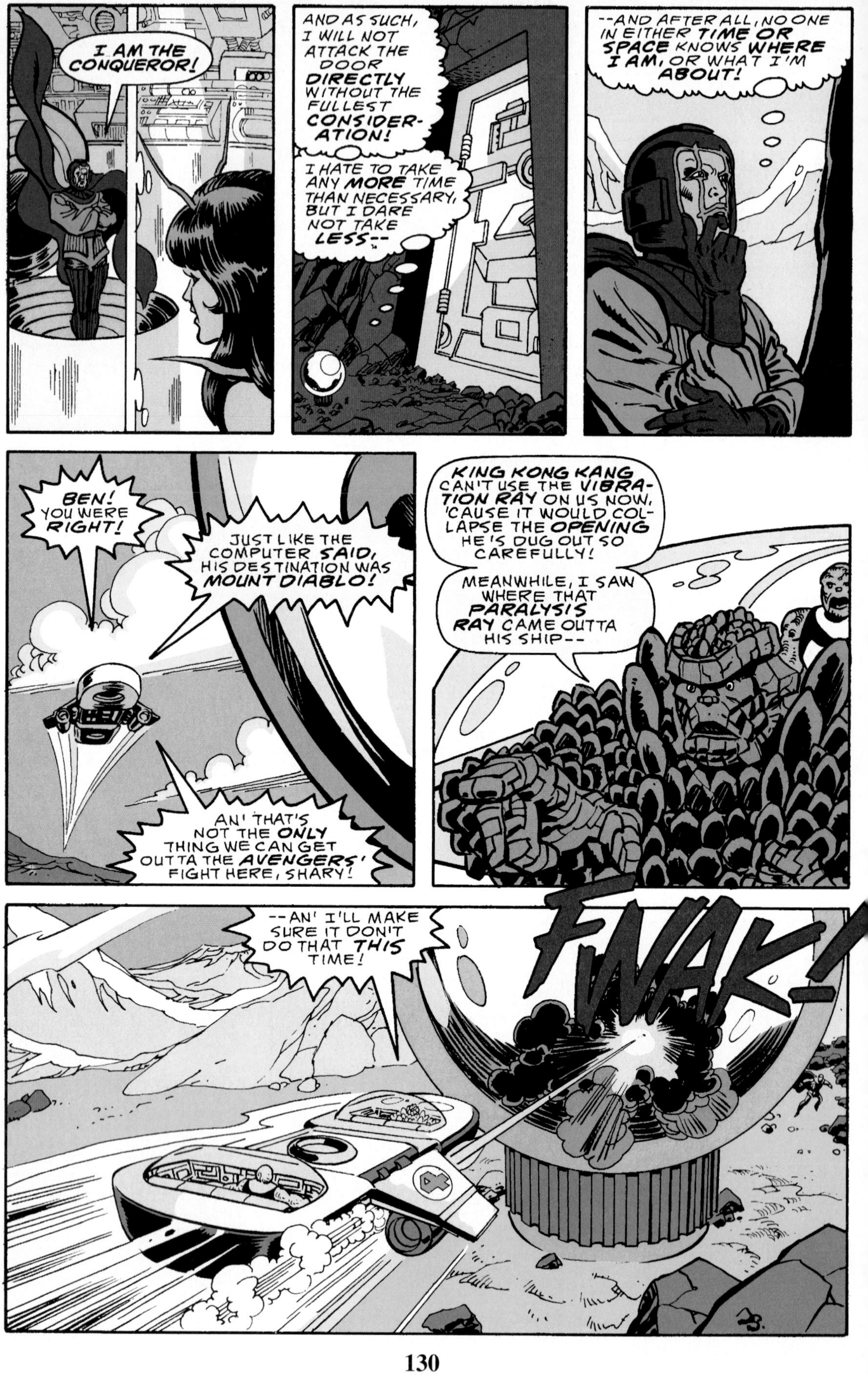
I AM THE CONQUEROR!
AND AS SUCH, I WILL NOT ATTACK THE DOOR DIRECTLY WITHOUT THE FULLEST CONSIDER-ATION!
I HATE TO TAKE ANY MORE TIME THAN NECESSARY, BUT I DARE NOT TAKE LESS--
--AND AFTER ALL, NO ONE IN EITHER TIME OR SPACE KNOWS WHERE I AM, OR WHAT I'M ABOUT!
BEN! YOU WERE RIGHT!
JUST LIKE THE COMPUTER SAID, HIS DESTINATION WAS MOUNT DIABLO!
AN' THAT'S NOT THE ONLY THING WE CAN GET OUTTA THE AVENGERS' FIGHT HERE, SHARY!
KING KONG KANG CAN'T USE THE VIBRA-TION RAY ON US NOW, 'CAUSE IT WOULD COL-LAPSE THE OPENING HE'S DUG OUT SO CAREFULLY!
MEANWHILE, I SAW WHERE THAT PARALYSIS RAY CAME OUTTA HIS SHIP--
--AN' I'LL MAKE SURE IT DON'T DO THAT THIS TIME!
FWAK-!

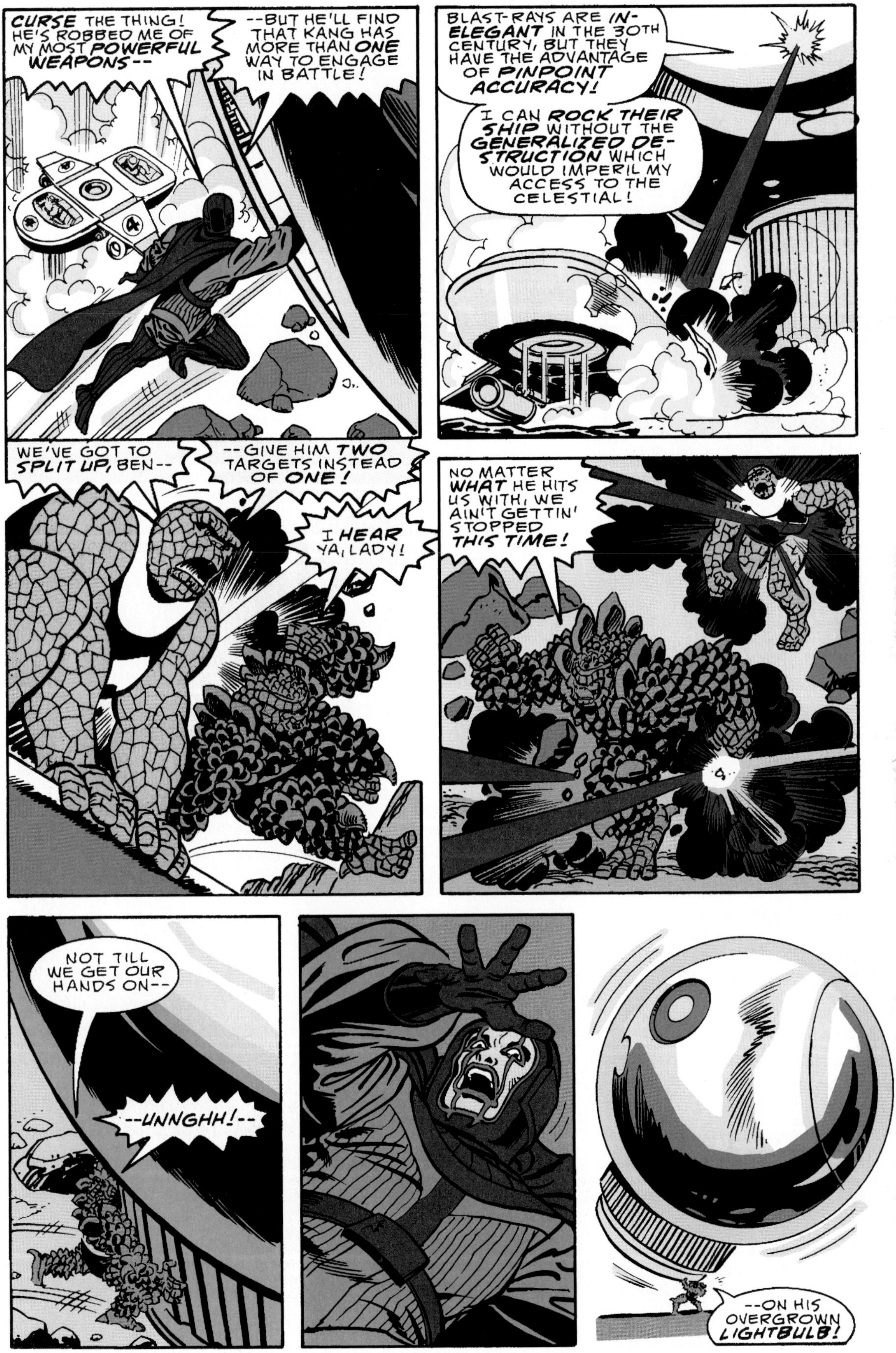
CURSE THE THING! HE'S ROBBED ME OF MY MOST POWERFUL WEAPONS--
--BUT HE'LL FIND THAT KANG HAS MORE THAN ONE WAY TO ENGAGE IN BATTLE!
BLAST-RAYS ARE INELEGANT IN THE 30TH CENTURY, BUT THEY HAVE THE ADVANTAGE OF PINPOINT ACCURACY!
I CAN ROCK THEIR SHIP WITHOUT THE GENERALIZED DESTRUCTION WHICH WOULD IMPERIL MY ACCESS TO THE CELESTIAL!
WE'VE GOT TO SPLIT UP, BEN--
--GIVE HIM TWO TARGETS INSTEAD OF ONE!
I HEAR YA, LADY!
NO MATTER WHAT HE HITS US WITH, WE AIN'T GETTIN' STOPPED THIS TIME!
NOT TILL WE GET OUR HANDS ON--
--UNNGHH!--
--ON HIS OVERGROWN LIGHTBULB!

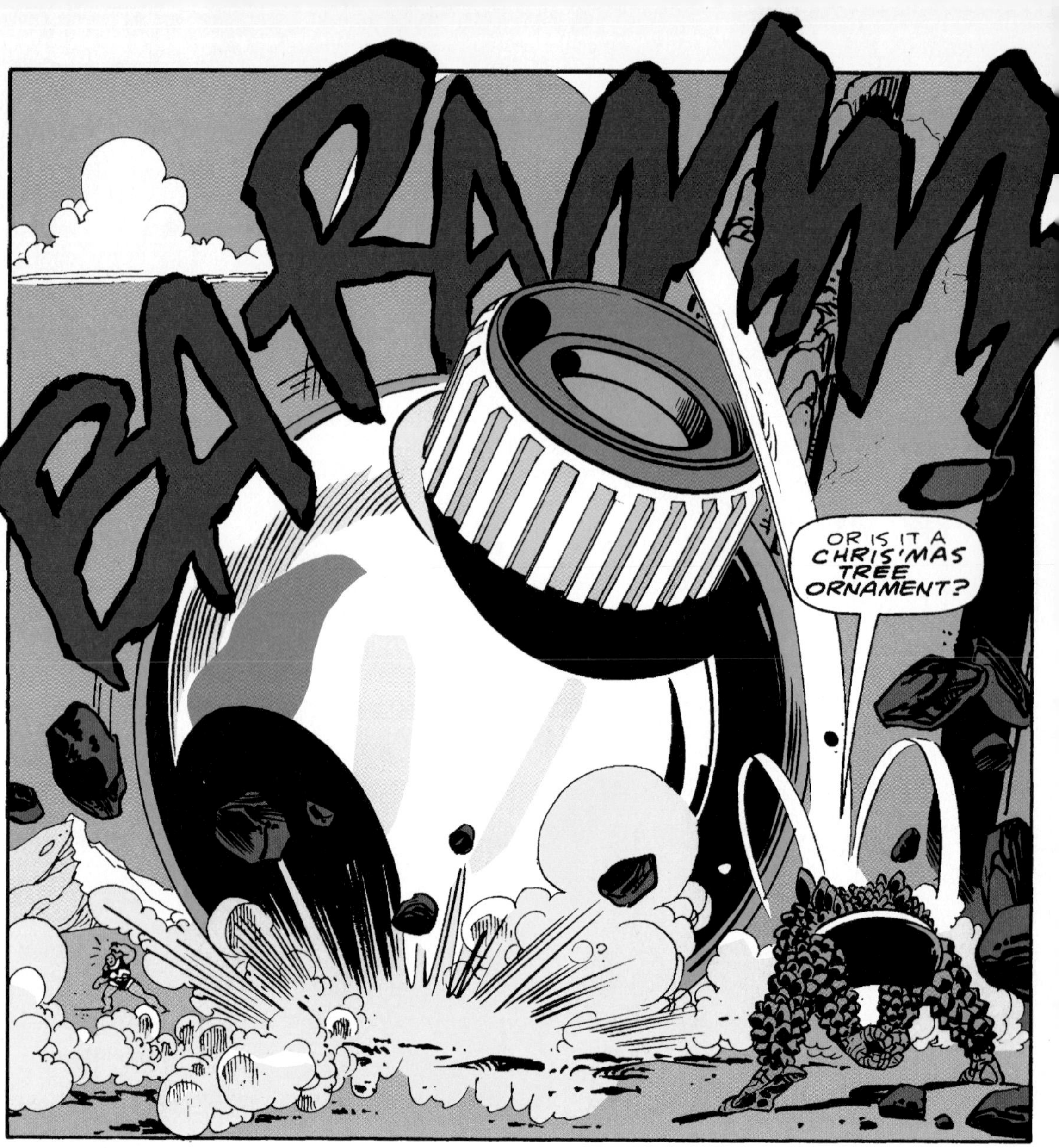
BA-RAMM!
OR IS IT A CHRIS'MAS TREE ORNAMENT?

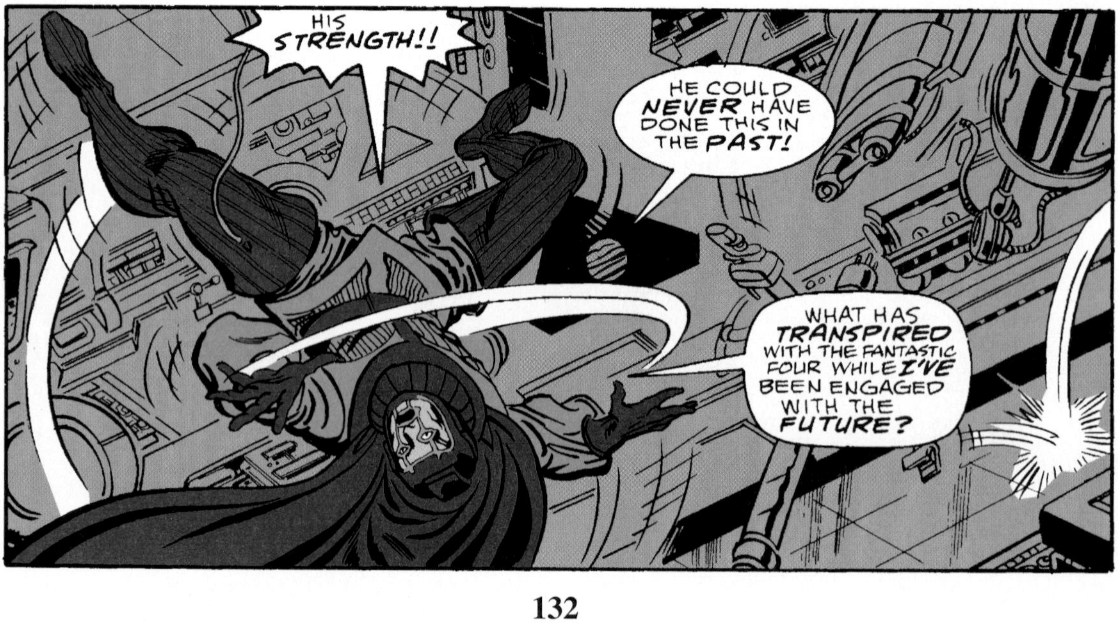
HIS STRENGTH!!
HE COULD NEVER HAVE DONE THIS IN THE PAST!
WHAT HAS TRANSPIRED WITH THE FANTASTIC FOUR WHILE I'VE BEEN ENGAGED WITH THE FUTURE?

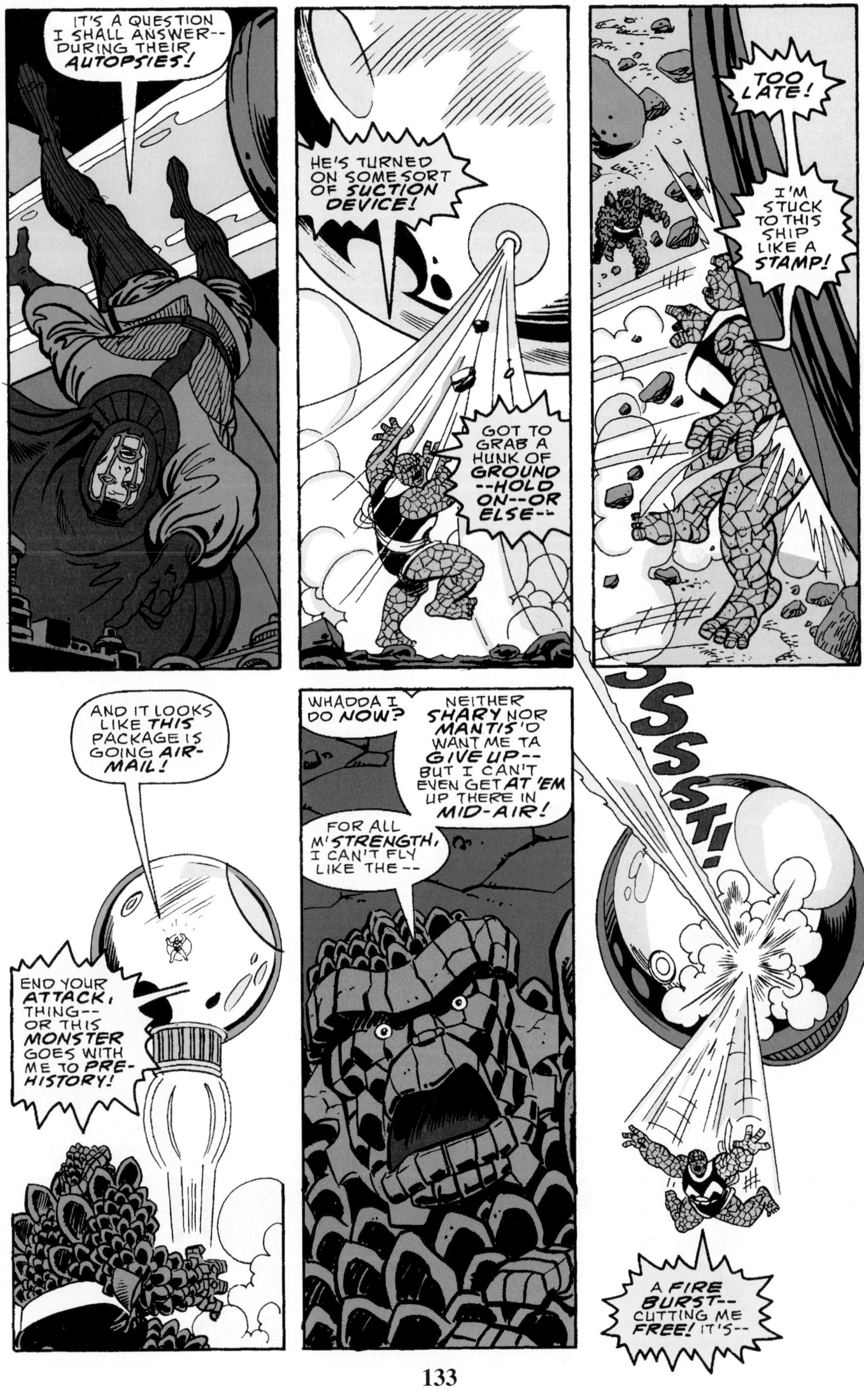

IT'S A QUESTION I SHALL ANSWER-- DURING THEIR AUTOPSIES!
HE'S TURNED ON SOME SORT OF SUCTION DEVICE!
GOT TO GRAB A HUNK OF GROUND --HOLD ON--OR ELSE--
TOO LATE!
I'M STUCK TO THIS SHIP LIKE A STAMP!
AND IT LOOKS LIKE THIS PACKAGE IS GOING AIR-MAIL!
END YOUR ATTACK, THING-- OR THIS MONSTER GOES WITH ME TO PRE-HISTORY!
WHADDA I DO NOW?
NEITHER SHARY NOR MANTIS 'D WANT ME TA GIVE UP-- BUT I CAN'T EVEN GET AT 'EM UP THERE IN MID-AIR!
FOR ALL M'STRENGTH, I CAN'T FLY LIKE THE--
SSSSK!
A FIRE BURST-- CUTTING ME FREE! IT'S--

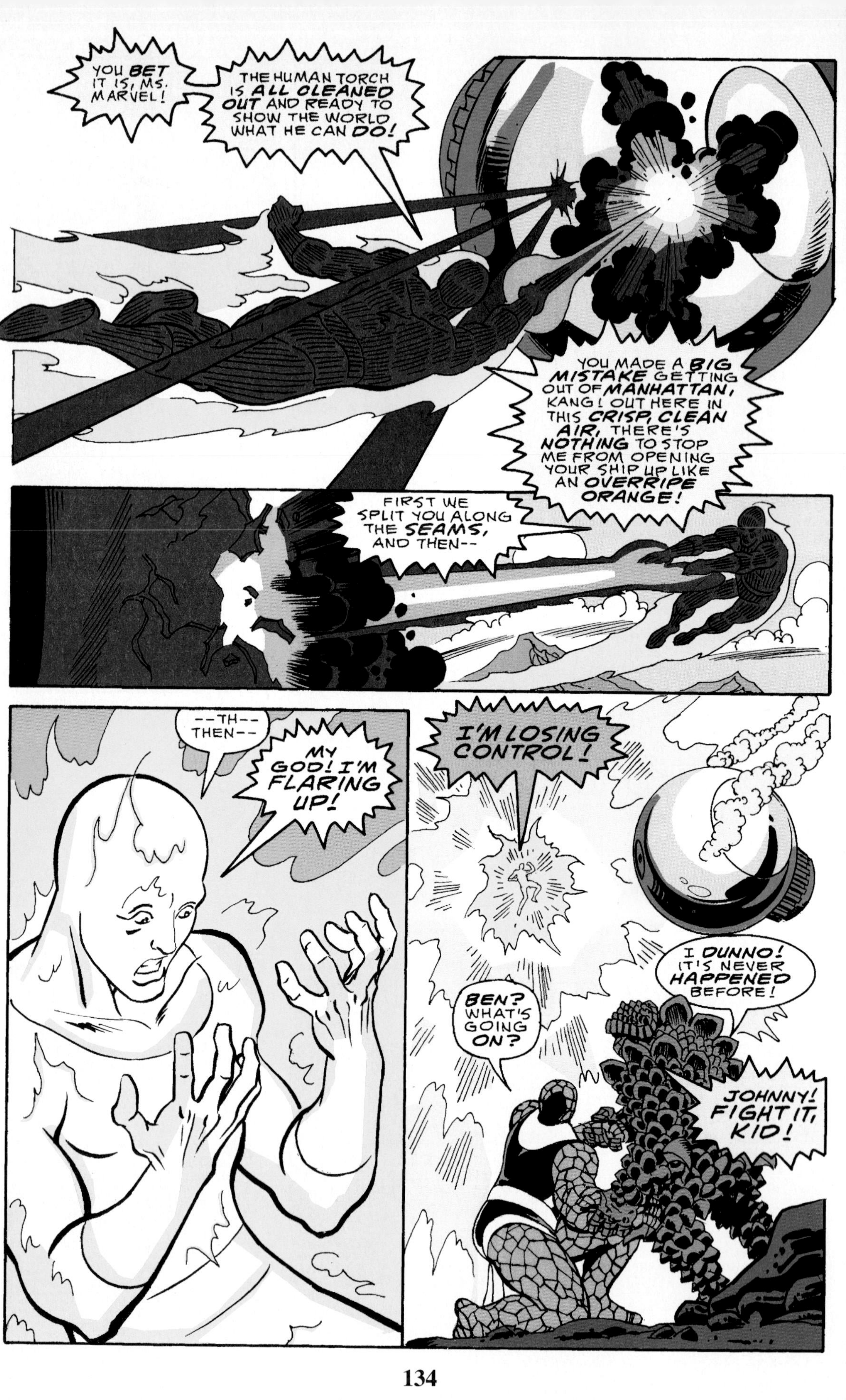
YOU BET IT IS, MS. MARVEL!
THE HUMAN TORCH IS ALL CLEANED OUT AND READY TO SHOW THE WORLD WHAT HE CAN DO!
YOU MADE A BIG MISTAKE GETTING OUT OF MANHATTAN, KANG! OUT HERE IN THIS CRISP, CLEAN AIR, THERE'S NOTHING TO STOP ME FROM OPENING YOUR SHIP UP LIKE AN OVERRIPE ORANGE!
FIRST WE SPLIT YOU ALONG THE SEAMS, AND THEN--
--TH-- THEN--
MY GOD! I'M FLARING UP!
I'M LOSING CONTROL!
BEN? WHAT'S GOING ON?
I DUNNO! IT'S NEVER HAPPENED BEFORE!
JOHNNY! FIGHT IT, KID!

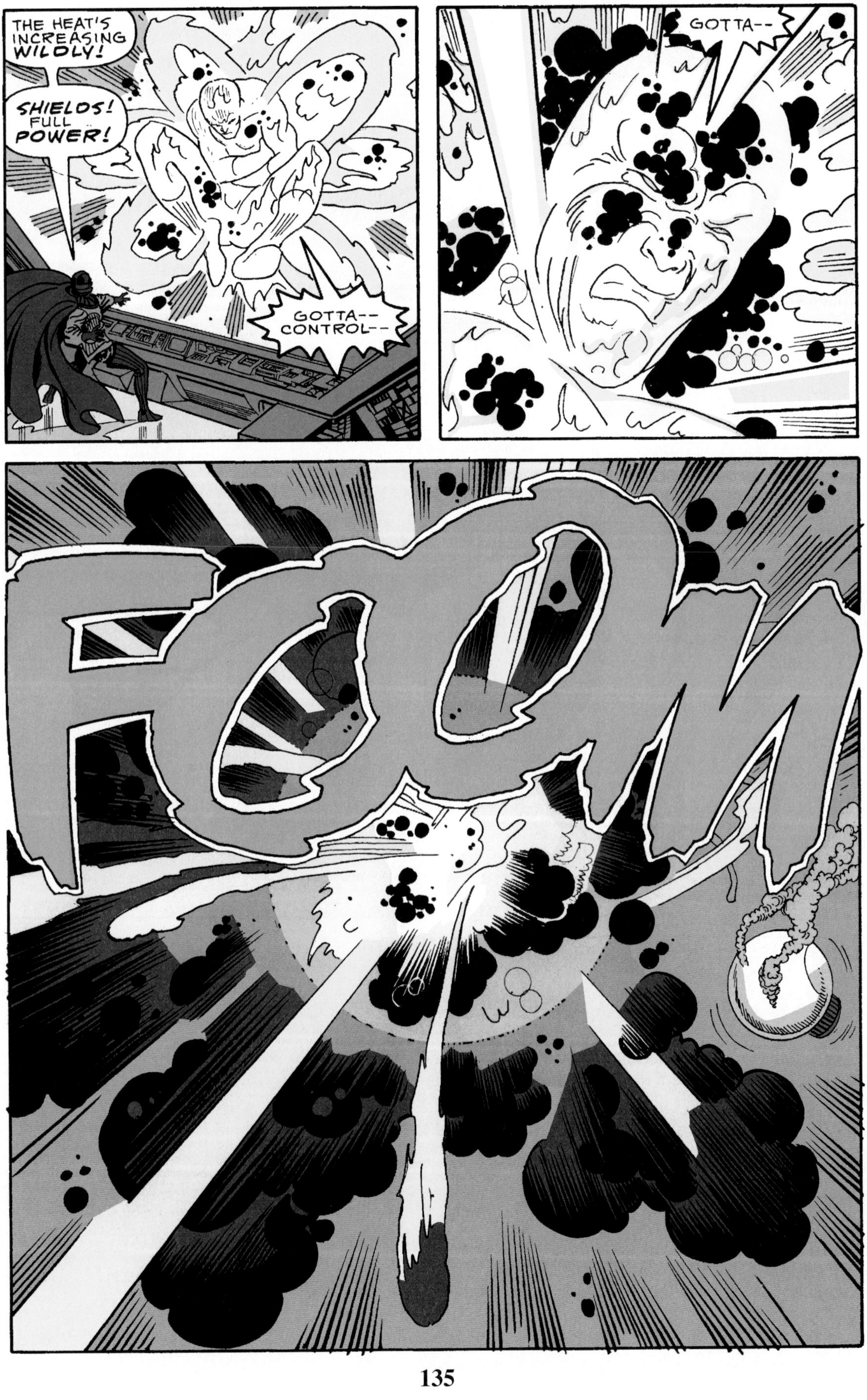
THE HEAT'S INCREASING WILDLY!
SHIELDS! FULL POWER!
GOTTA-- CONTROL--
GOTTA--
FOOM

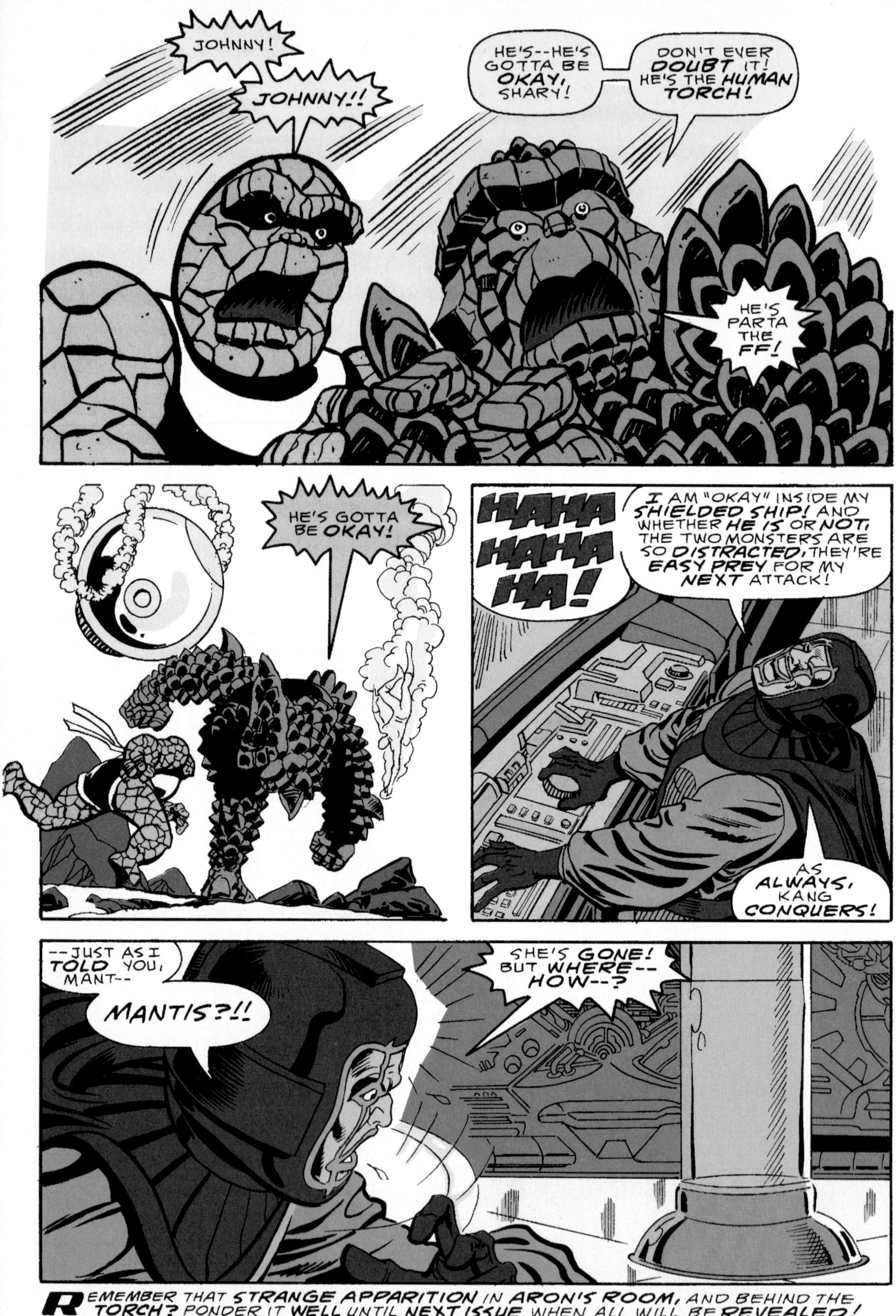
JOHNNY!
JOHNNY!!
HE'S--HE'S GOTTA BE OKAY, SHARY!
DON'T EVER DOUBT IT! HE'S THE HUMAN TORCH!
HE'S PARTA THE FF!
HE'S GOTTA BE OKAY!
HAHA HAHA HA!
I AM "OKAY" INSIDE MY SHIELDED SHIP! AND WHETHER HE IS OR NOT, THE TWO MONSTERS ARE SO DISTRACTED, THEY'RE EASY PREY FOR MY NEXT ATTACK!
AS ALWAYS, KANG CONQUERS!
--JUST AS I TOLD YOU, MANT--
MANTIS?!!
SHE'S GONE! BUT WHERE-- HOW--?
REMEMBER THAT STRANGE APPARITION IN ARON'S ROOM, AND BEHIND THE TORCH? PONDER IT WELL UNTIL NEXT ISSUE WHEN ALL WILL BE REVEALED!
INFERNO PART III: CELESTIAL SLAUGHTER!

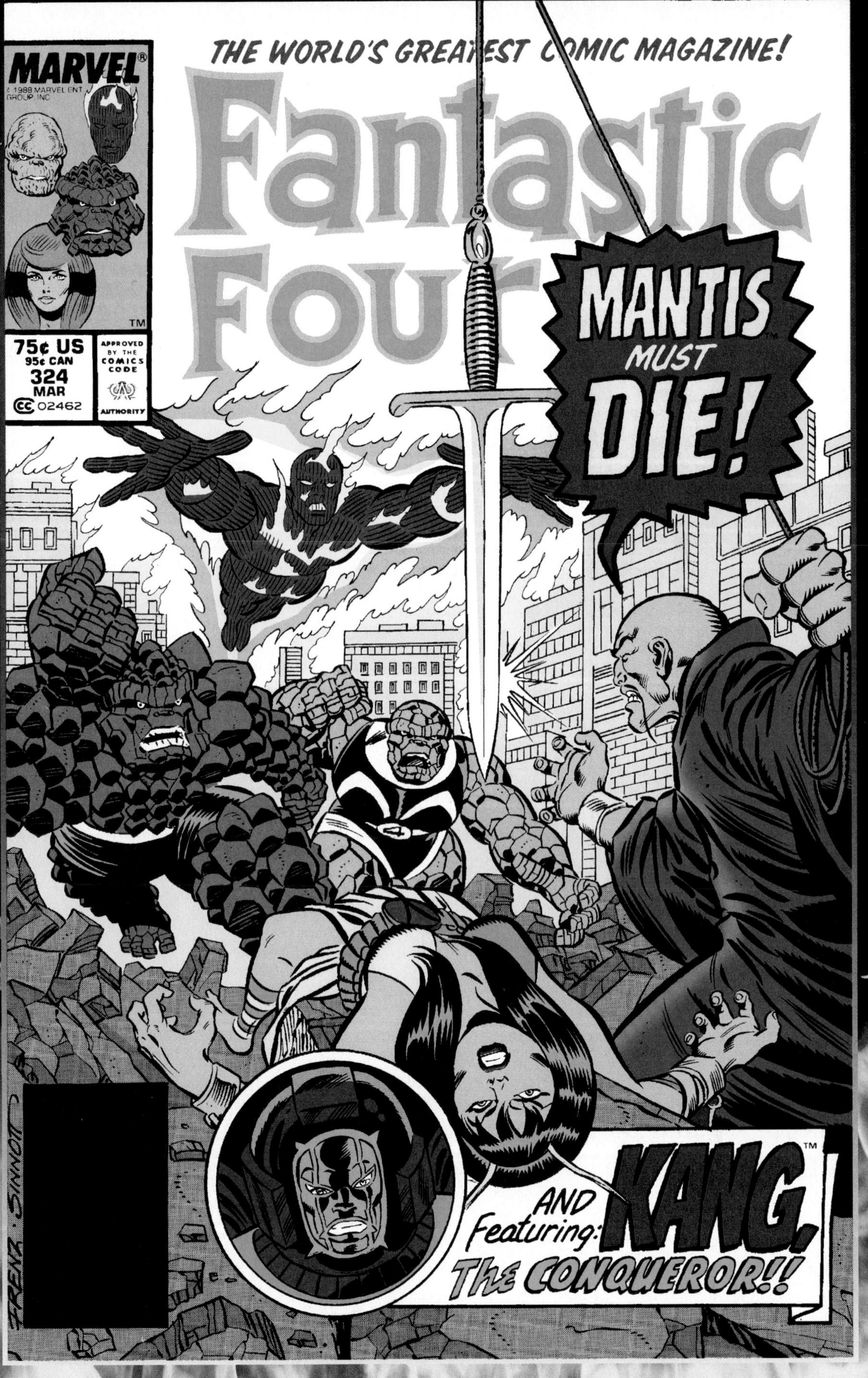
MARVEL®
© 1988 MARVEL ENT. GROUP, INC.
THE WORLD'S GREATEST COMIC MAGAZINE!
Fantastic Four
TM
75¢ US
95¢ CAN
324
MAR
CC 02462
APPROVED BY THE COMICS CODE AUTHORITY
MANTIS MUST DIE!
TM
AND Featuring: KANG, The CONQUEROR!!
TM
FRENZ • SINNOTT

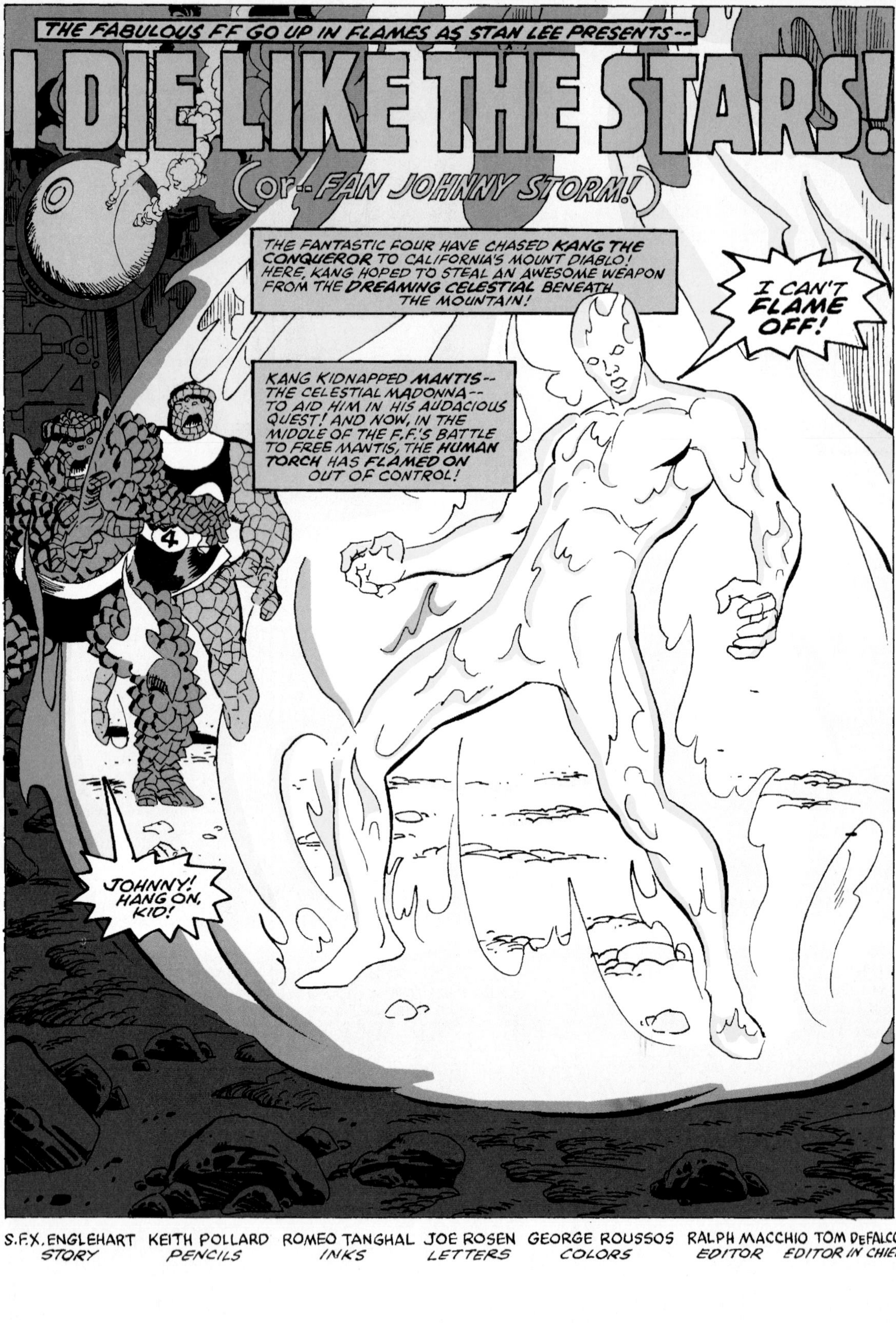
THE FABULOUS FF GO UP IN FLAMES AS STAN LEE PRESENTS--
I DIE LIKE THE STARS!
(or-- FAN JOHNNY STORM!)
THE FANTASTIC FOUR HAVE CHASED KANG THE CONQUEROR TO CALIFORNIA'S MOUNT DIABLO! HERE, KANG HOPED TO STEAL AN AWESOME WEAPON FROM THE DREAMING CELESTIAL BENEATH THE MOUNTAIN!
I CAN'T FLAME OFF!
KANG KIDNAPPED MANTIS-- THE CELESTIAL MADONNA-- TO AID HIM IN HIS AUDACIOUS QUEST! AND NOW, IN THE MIDDLE OF THE F.F.'S BATTLE TO FREE MANTIS, THE HUMAN TORCH HAS FLAMED ON OUT OF CONTROL!
4
JOHNNY! HANG ON, KID!

S.F.X. ENGLEHART *STORY* KEITH POLLARD *PENCILS* ROMEO TANGHAL *INKS* JOE ROSEN *LETTERS* GEORGE ROUSSOS *COLORS* RALPH MACCHIO *EDITOR* TOM DEFALCO *EDITOR IN CHIEF*

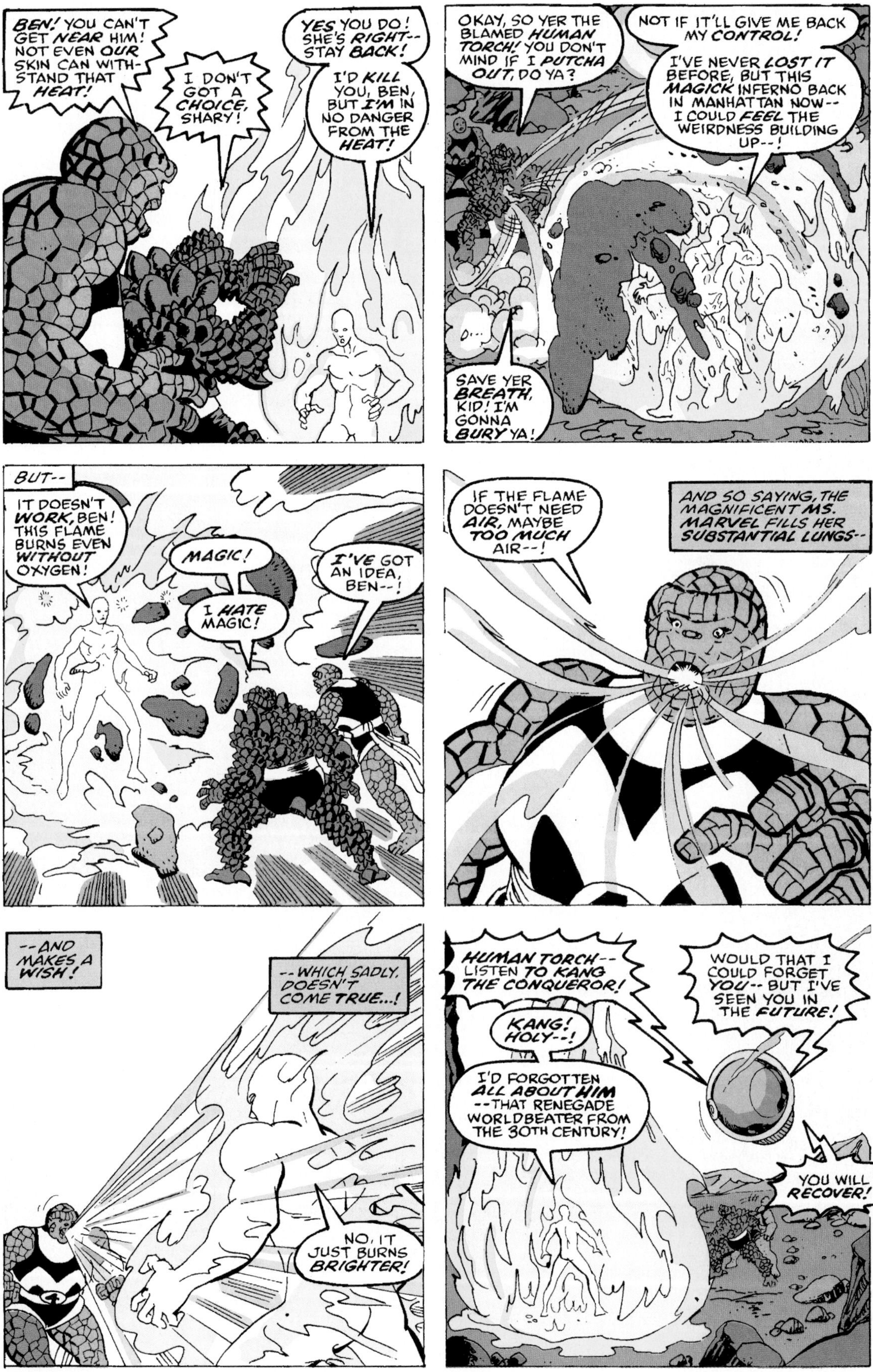
BEN! YOU CAN'T GET NEAR HIM! NOT EVEN OUR SKIN CAN WITH-STAND THAT HEAT!
I DON'T GOT A CHOICE, SHARY!
YES YOU DO! SHE'S RIGHT-- STAY BACK!
I'D KILL YOU, BEN, BUT I'M IN NO DANGER FROM THE HEAT!
OKAY, SO YER THE BLAMED HUMAN TORCH! YOU DON'T MIND IF I PUTCHA OUT, DO YA?
NOT IF IT'LL GIVE ME BACK MY CONTROL!
I'VE NEVER LOST IT BEFORE, BUT THIS MAGICK INFERNO BACK IN MANHATTAN NOW-- I COULD FEEL THE WEIRDNESS BUILDING UP--!
SAVE YER BREATH, KID! I'M GONNA BURY YA!
BUT--
IT DOESN'T WORK, BEN! THIS FLAME BURNS EVEN WITHOUT OXYGEN!
MAGIC!
I HATE MAGIC!
I'VE GOT AN IDEA, BEN--!
IF THE FLAME DOESN'T NEED AIR, MAYBE TOO MUCH AIR--!
AND SO SAYING, THE MAGNIFICENT MS. MARVEL FILLS HER SUBSTANTIAL LUNGS--
--AND MAKES A WISH!
--WHICH SADLY, DOESN'T COME TRUE...!
NO, IT JUST BURNS BRIGHTER!
HUMAN TORCH-- LISTEN TO KANG THE CONQUEROR!
KANG! HOLY--!
I'D FORGOTTEN ALL ABOUT HIM --THAT RENEGADE WORLDBEATER FROM THE 30TH CENTURY!
WOULD THAT I COULD FORGET YOU-- BUT I'VE SEEN YOU IN THE FUTURE!
YOU WILL RECOVER!

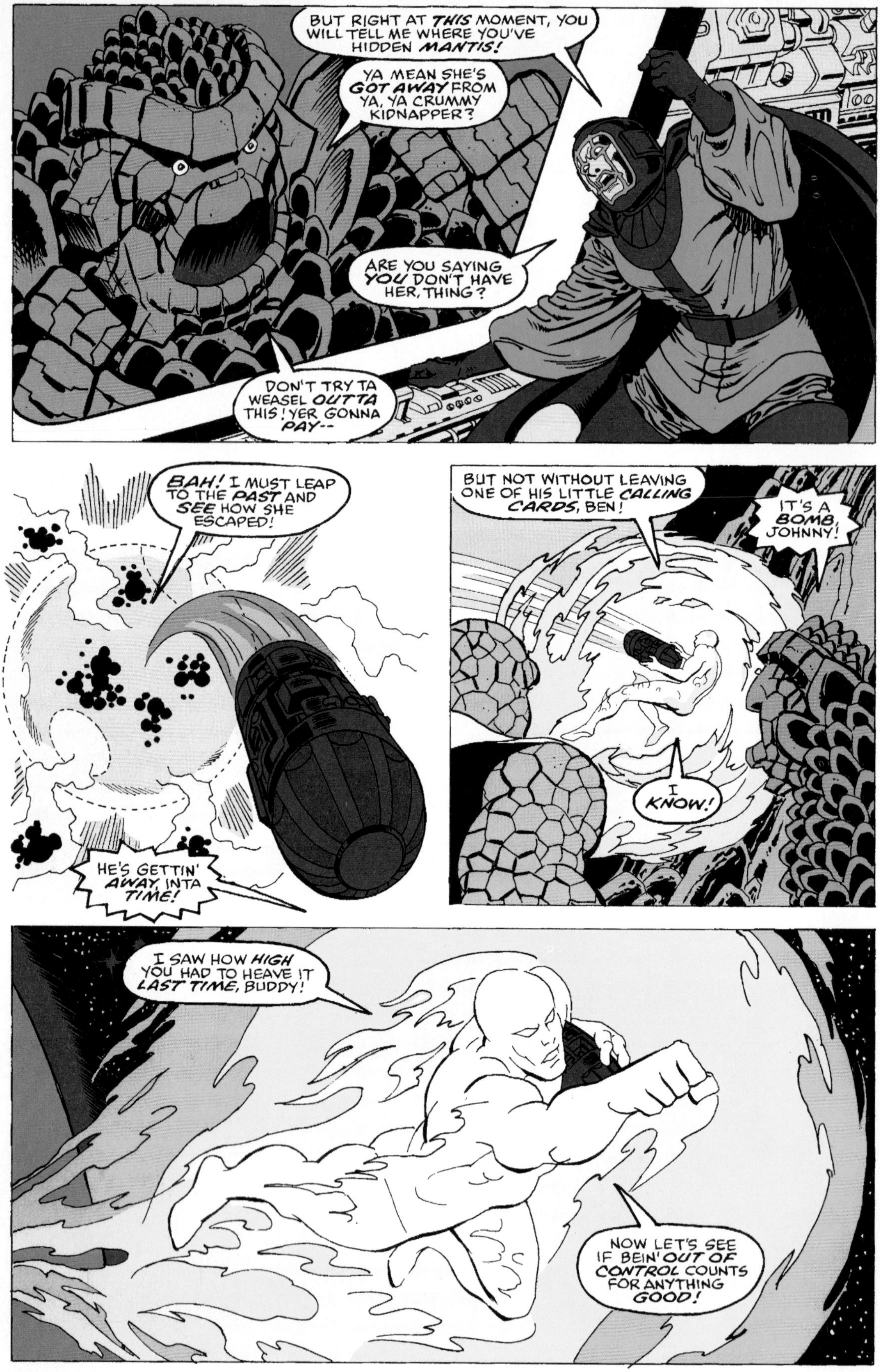
BUT RIGHT AT THIS MOMENT, YOU WILL TELL ME WHERE YOU'VE HIDDEN MANTIS!
YA MEAN SHE'S GOT AWAY FROM YA, YA CRUMMY KIDNAPPER?
ARE YOU SAYING YOU DON'T HAVE HER, THING?
DON'T TRY TA WEASEL OUTTA THIS! YER GONNA PAY--
BAH! I MUST LEAP TO THE PAST AND SEE HOW SHE ESCAPED!
HE'S GETTIN' AWAY, INTA TIME!
BUT NOT WITHOUT LEAVING ONE OF HIS LITTLE CALLING CARDS, BEN!
IT'S A BOMB, JOHNNY!
I KNOW!
I SAW HOW HIGH YOU HAD TO HEAVE IT LAST TIME, BUDDY!
NOW LET'S SEE IF BEIN' OUT OF CONTROL COUNTS FOR ANYTHING GOOD!

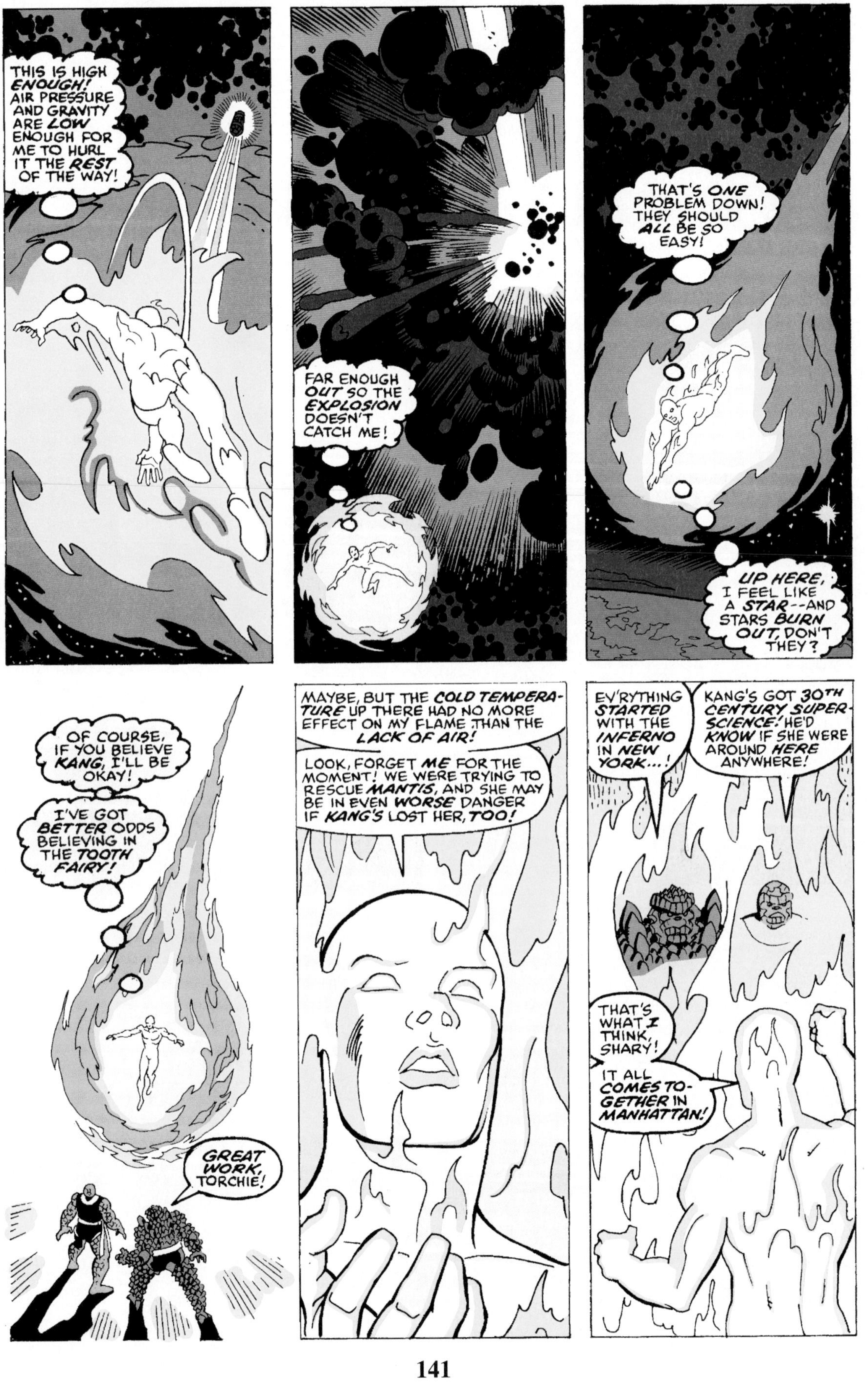
THIS IS HIGH ENOUGH! AIR PRESSURE AND GRAVITY ARE LOW ENOUGH FOR ME TO HURL IT THE REST OF THE WAY!
FAR ENOUGH OUT SO THE EXPLOSION DOESN'T CATCH ME!
THAT'S ONE PROBLEM DOWN! THEY SHOULD ALL BE SO EASY!
UP HERE, I FEEL LIKE A STAR--AND STARS BURN OUT, DON'T THEY?
OF COURSE, IF YOU BELIEVE KANG, I'LL BE OKAY!
I'VE GOT BETTER ODDS BELIEVING IN THE TOOTH FAIRY!
GREAT WORK, TORCHIE!
MAYBE, BUT THE COLD TEMPERATURE UP THERE HAD NO MORE EFFECT ON MY FLAME THAN THE LACK OF AIR!
LOOK, FORGET ME FOR THE MOMENT! WE WERE TRYING TO RESCUE MANTIS, AND SHE MAY BE IN EVEN WORSE DANGER IF KANG'S LOST HER, TOO!
EV'RYTHING STARTED WITH THE INFERNO IN NEW YORK...!
KANG'S GOT 30TH CENTURY SUPER-SCIENCE! HE'D KNOW IF SHE WERE AROUND HERE ANYWHERE!
THAT'S WHAT I THINK, SHARY!
IT ALL COMES TOGETHER IN MANHATTAN!

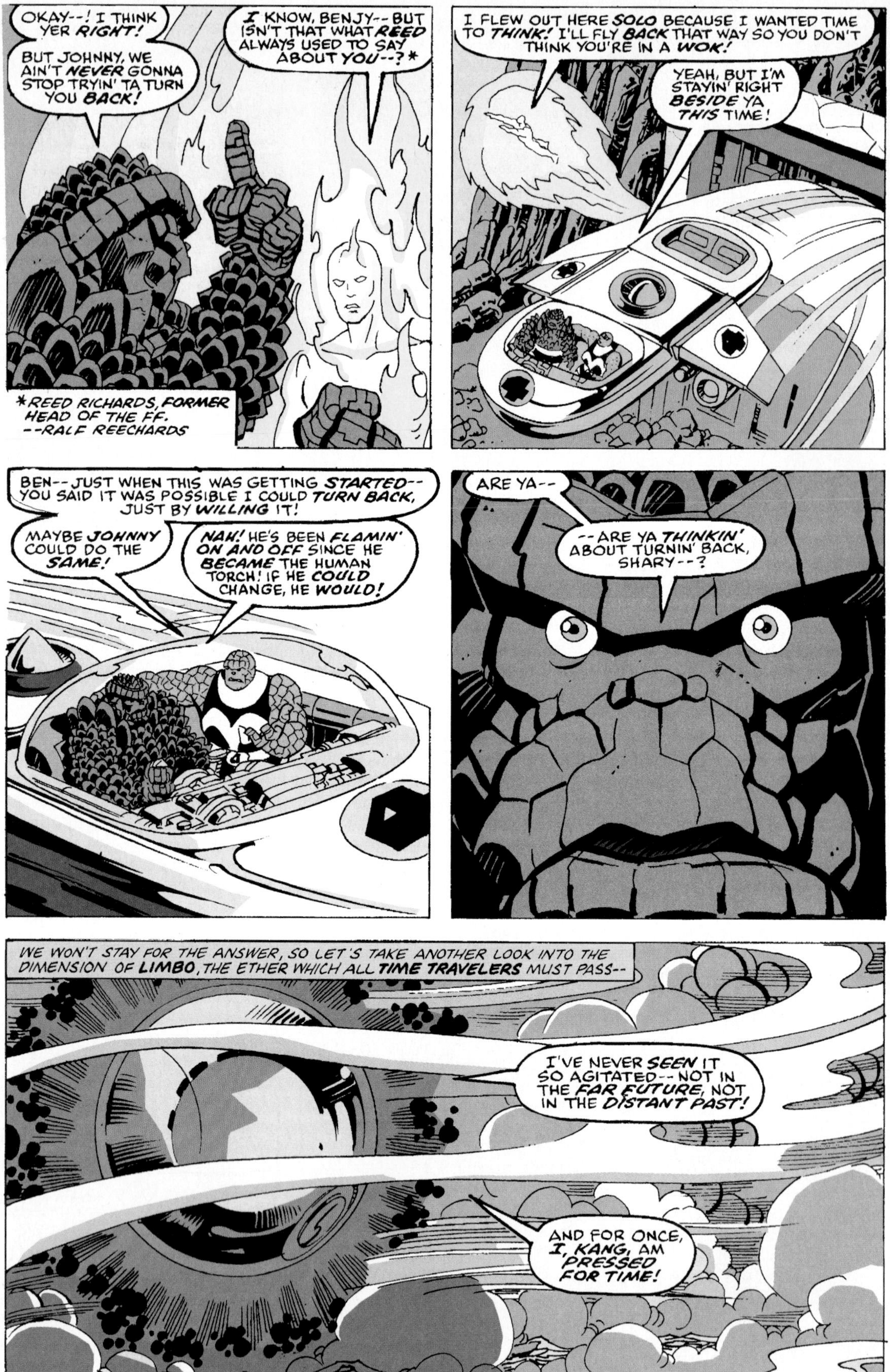
OKAY--! I THINK YER RIGHT!
BUT JOHNNY, WE AIN'T NEVER GONNA STOP TRYIN' TA TURN YOU BACK!
I KNOW, BENJY-- BUT ISN'T THAT WHAT REED ALWAYS USED TO SAY ABOUT YOU--?*
*REED RICHARDS, FORMER HEAD OF THE FF. --RALF REECHARDS
I FLEW OUT HERE SOLO BECAUSE I WANTED TIME TO THINK! I'LL FLY BACK THAT WAY SO YOU DON'T THINK YOU'RE IN A WOK!
YEAH, BUT I'M STAYIN' RIGHT BESIDE YA THIS TIME!
BEN--JUST WHEN THIS WAS GETTING STARTED--YOU SAID IT WAS POSSIBLE I COULD TURN BACK, JUST BY WILLING IT!
MAYBE JOHNNY COULD DO THE SAME!
NAH! HE'S BEEN FLAMIN' ON AND OFF SINCE HE BECAME THE HUMAN TORCH! IF HE COULD CHANGE, HE WOULD!
ARE YA--
--ARE YA THINKIN' ABOUT TURNIN' BACK, SHARY--?
WE WON'T STAY FOR THE ANSWER, SO LET'S TAKE ANOTHER LOOK INTO THE DIMENSION OF LIMBO, THE ETHER WHICH ALL TIME TRAVELERS MUST PASS--
I'VE NEVER SEEN IT SO AGITATED--NOT IN THE FAR FUTURE, NOT IN THE DISTANT PAST!
AND FOR ONCE, I, KANG, AM PRESSED FOR TIME!

I KNOW THAT THIS *INFERNO* WILL *END* SOON, AND IT'S ONLY *DURING* THIS TEMPORAL CONFUSION THAT I CAN EXECUTE MY PLAN WITHOUT THE COUNCIL OF CROSS-TIME KANGS LEARNING OF IT! *

BUT THE *RECENT PAST* IS IMPOSSIBLE TO *NAVIGATE* NOW! I CANNOT SEE WHAT *HAPPENED* TO MY PRISONER!

*SEE AVENGERS #295-300.

PERHAPS I SHOULD NEVER HAVE ATTEMPTED *SO MUCH*--TAKING MY REVENGE ON *MANTIS* FOR PAST INDISCRETIONS AGAINST ME., *AND* USING HER TO AID ME--

--IN DEFEATING THE *DREAMING CELESTIAL*, THEREBY FORCING HIM TO GIVE ME THE WEAPON ALL THE *OTHER* KANGS EXPECT TO FIND IN THE *NEXT CENTURY!* YET, WITHOUT MANTIS, MY PLAN IS STALLED.

BUT THIS *INVASION OF EARTH* BY THE *DEMON-CASTE OF LIMBO* WAS A ONCE-IN-A-LIFETIME *CHANCE* FOR AN *UNPARALLELED COUP!*

THE *FOCUS* OF THE INFERNO IS *NEW YORK CITY* -- IF THERE ARE *ANSWERS* TO BE HAD, THEY LIE *THERE*--

--OR SHOULD I SAY *"HERE"*?

HOW CAN THIS MADNESS HAVE AFFECTED *THIS* TIME--?

PETTY *BARBARIANS!* ALWAYS READY TO REVERT TO THEIR PRIMITIVE WAYS!

THEY ARE NOT THE ONES WHO'VE STOLEN MY PRIZE! THEY--

WAIT! MY *INSTRUMENTS* DETECT-- AN ANOMALY *WITHIN* THE ANOMALY!

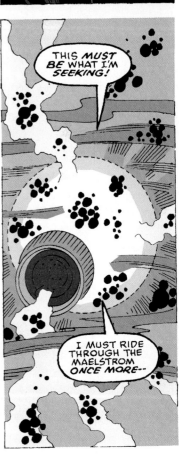

THIS *MUST* BE WHAT I'M *SEEKING!*

I MUST RIDE THROUGH THE MAELSTROM *ONCE MORE*--

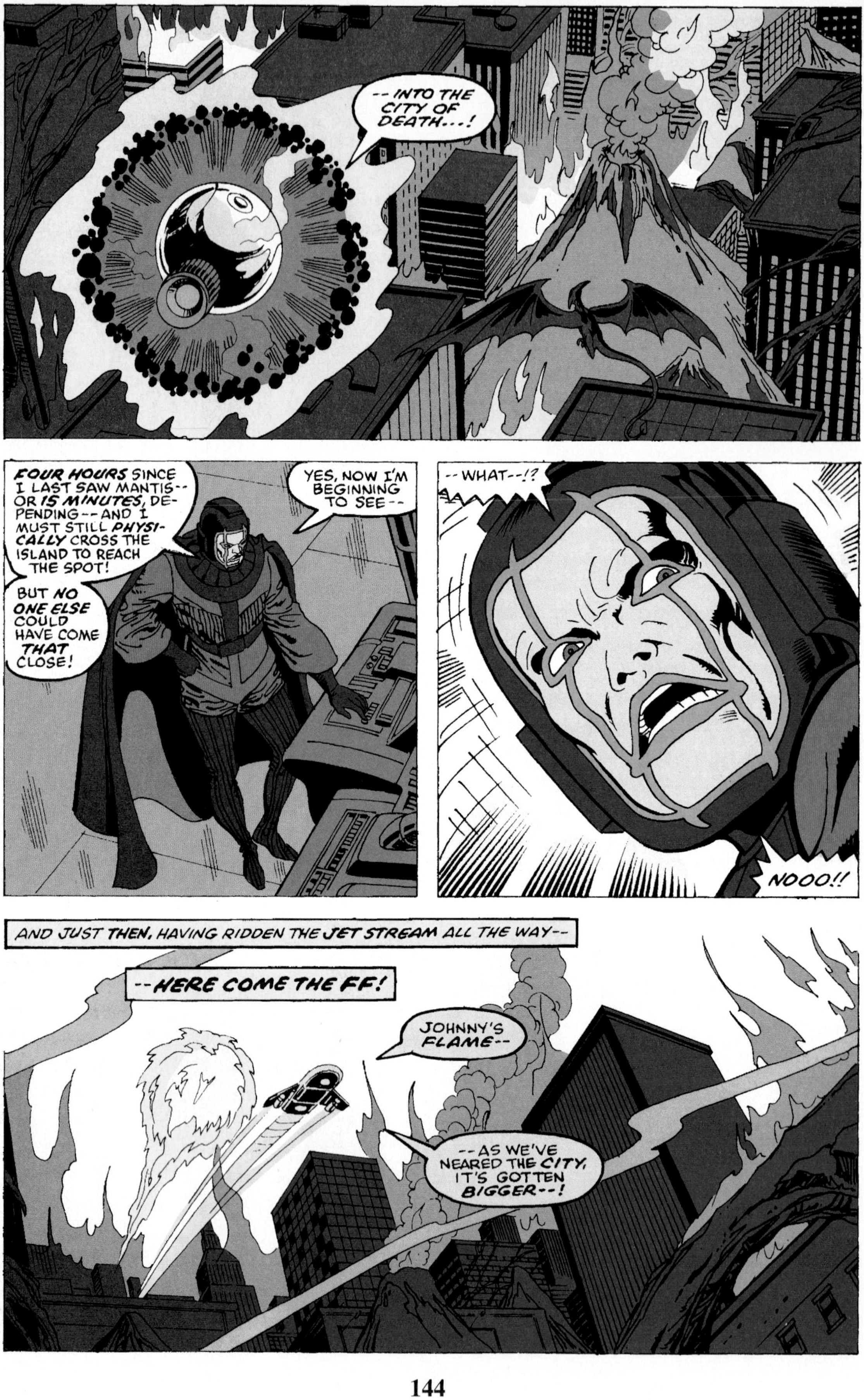
--INTO THE CITY OF DEATH...!
FOUR HOURS SINCE I LAST SAW MANTIS--OR 15 MINUTES, DEPENDING--AND I MUST STILL PHYSICALLY CROSS THE ISLAND TO REACH THE SPOT!
BUT NO ONE ELSE COULD HAVE COME THAT CLOSE!
YES, NOW I'M BEGINNING TO SEE--
--WHAT--!?
NOOO!!
AND JUST THEN, HAVING RIDDEN THE JET STREAM ALL THE WAY--
--HERE COME THE FF!
JOHNNY'S FLAME--
--AS WE'VE NEARED THE CITY, IT'S GOTTEN BIGGER--!

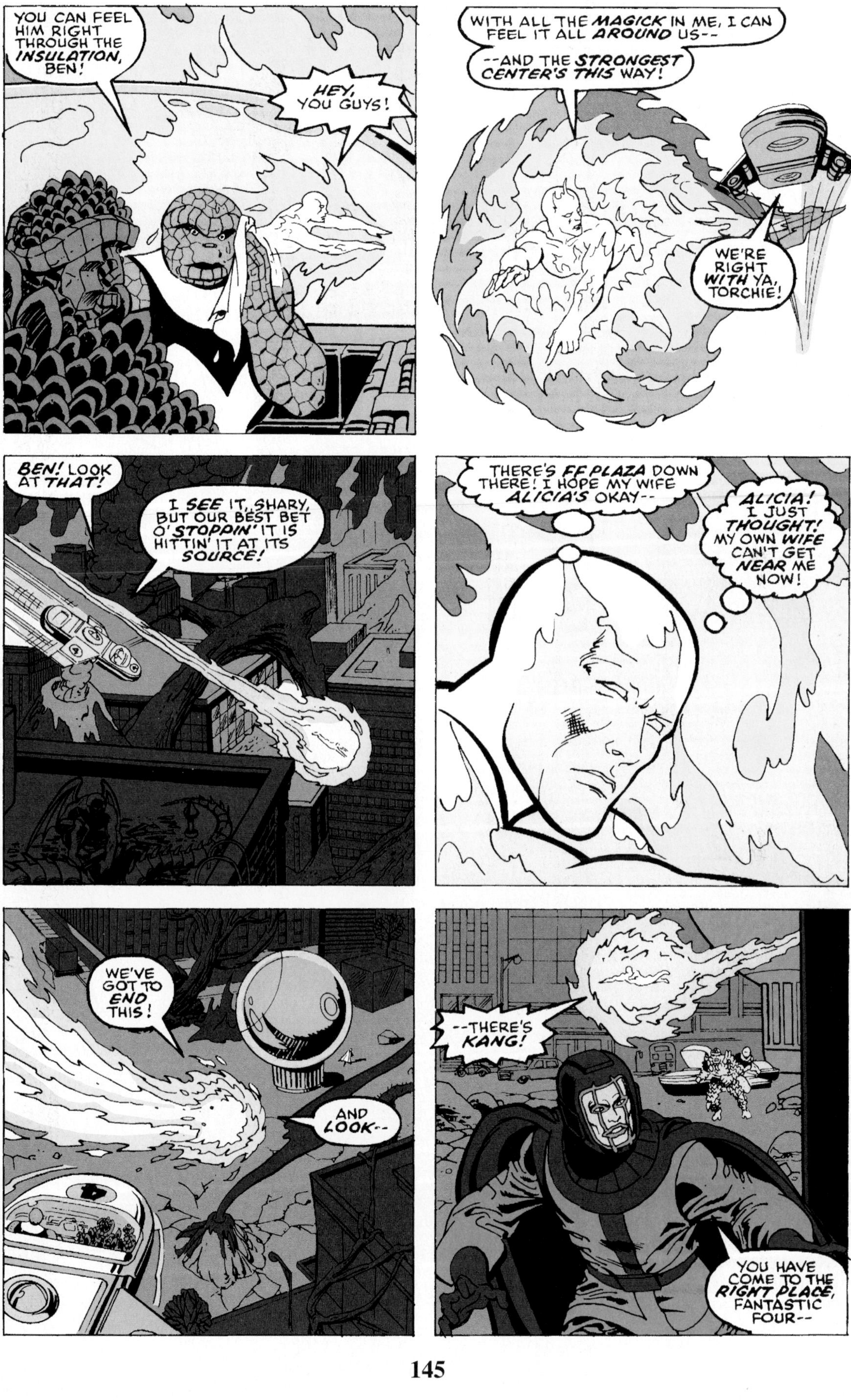
YOU CAN FEEL HIM RIGHT THROUGH THE INSULATION, BEN!
HEY, YOU GUYS!
WITH ALL THE MAGICK IN ME, I CAN FEEL IT ALL AROUND US--
--AND THE STRONGEST CENTER'S THIS WAY!
WE'RE RIGHT WITH YA, TORCHIE!
BEN! LOOK AT THAT!
I SEE IT, SHARY, BUT OUR BEST BET O' STOPPIN' IT IS HITTIN' IT AT ITS SOURCE!
THERE'S FF PLAZA DOWN THERE! I HOPE MY WIFE ALICIA'S OKAY--
ALICIA! I JUST THOUGHT! MY OWN WIFE CAN'T GET NEAR ME NOW!
WE'VE GOT TO END THIS!
AND LOOK--
--THERE'S KANG!
YOU HAVE COME TO THE RIGHT PLACE, FANTASTIC FOUR--

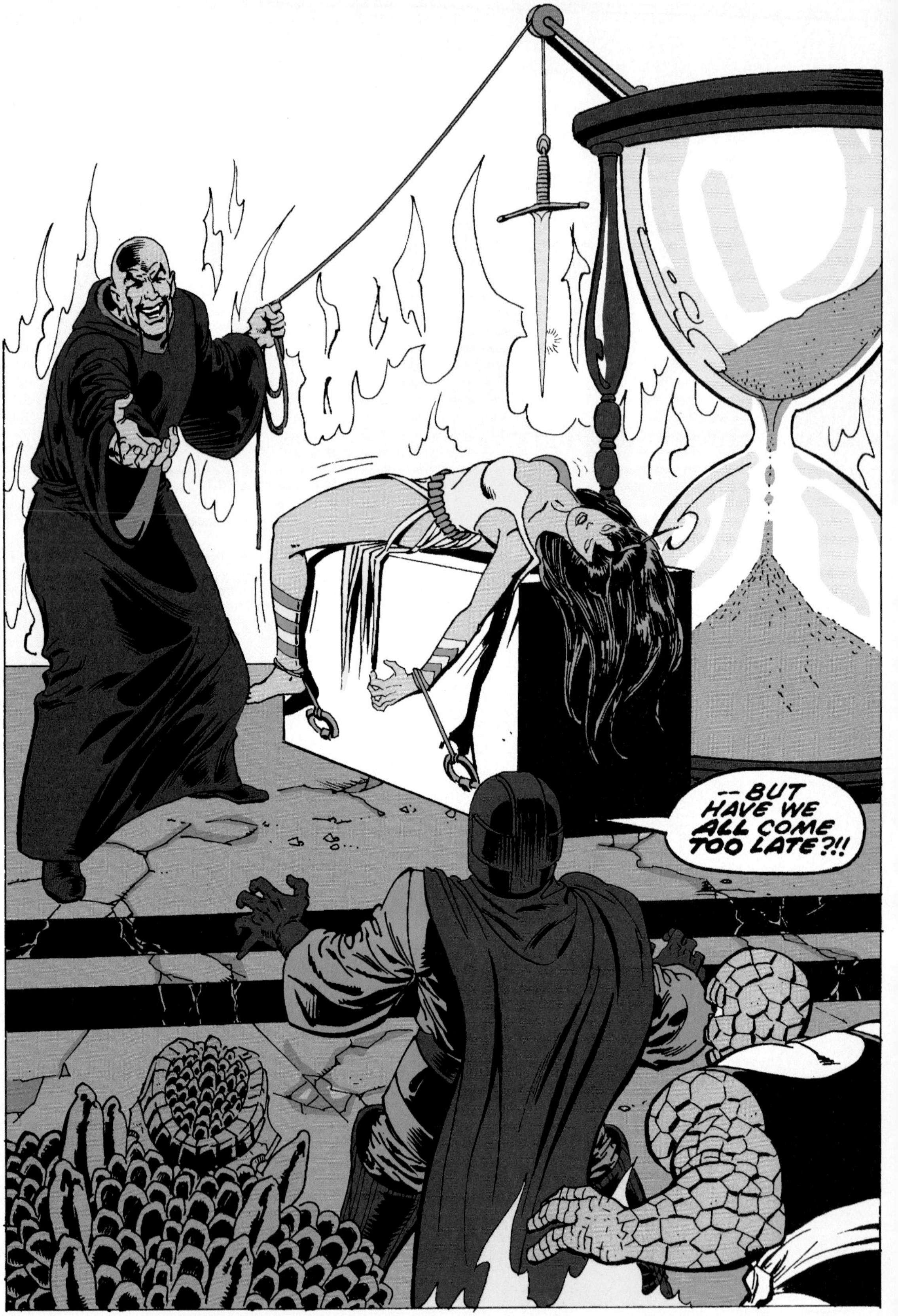
--BUT HAVE WE ALL COME TOO LATE?!!

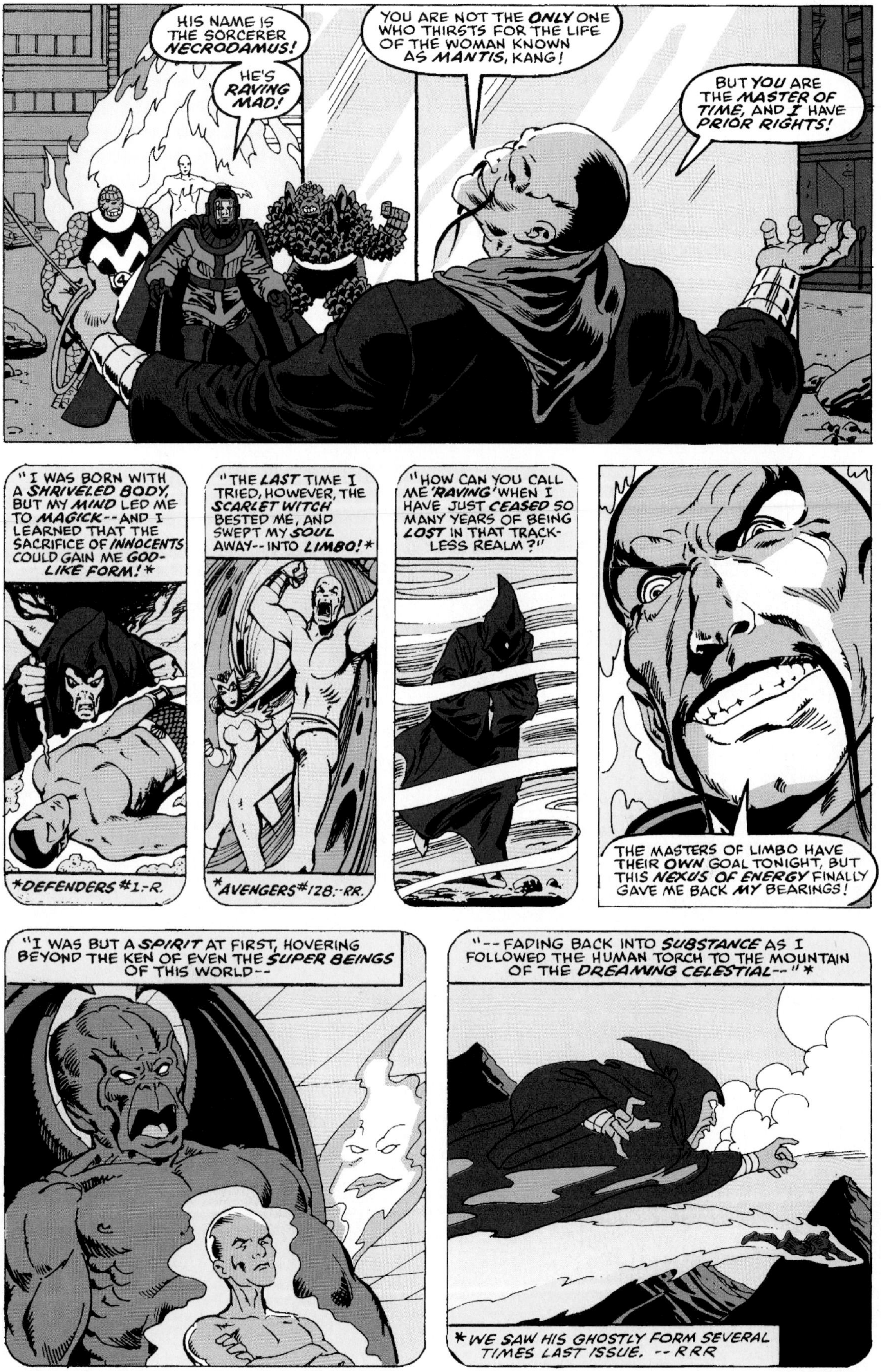
HIS NAME IS THE SORCERER NECRODAMUS!
HE'S RAVING MAD!
YOU ARE NOT THE ONLY ONE WHO THIRSTS FOR THE LIFE OF THE WOMAN KNOWN AS MANTIS, KANG!
BUT YOU ARE THE MASTER OF TIME, AND I HAVE PRIOR RIGHTS!
"I WAS BORN WITH A SHRIVELED BODY, BUT MY MIND LED ME TO MAGICK--AND I LEARNED THAT THE SACRIFICE OF INNOCENTS COULD GAIN ME GOD-LIKE FORM! *
*DEFENDERS #1.-R.
"THE LAST TIME I TRIED, HOWEVER, THE SCARLET WITCH BESTED ME, AND SWEPT MY SOUL AWAY--INTO LIMBO! *
*AVENGERS #128.-RR.
"HOW CAN YOU CALL ME 'RAVING' WHEN I HAVE JUST CEASED SO MANY YEARS OF BEING LOST IN THAT TRACK-LESS REALM?"
THE MASTERS OF LIMBO HAVE THEIR OWN GOAL TONIGHT, BUT THIS NEXUS OF ENERGY FINALLY GAVE ME BACK MY BEARINGS!
"I WAS BUT A SPIRIT AT FIRST, HOVERING BEYOND THE KEN OF EVEN THE SUPER BEINGS OF THIS WORLD--
"--FADING BACK INTO SUBSTANCE AS I FOLLOWED THE HUMAN TORCH TO THE MOUNTAIN OF THE DREAMING CELESTIAL--" *
* WE SAW HIS GHOSTLY FORM SEVERAL TIMES LAST ISSUE. --RRR

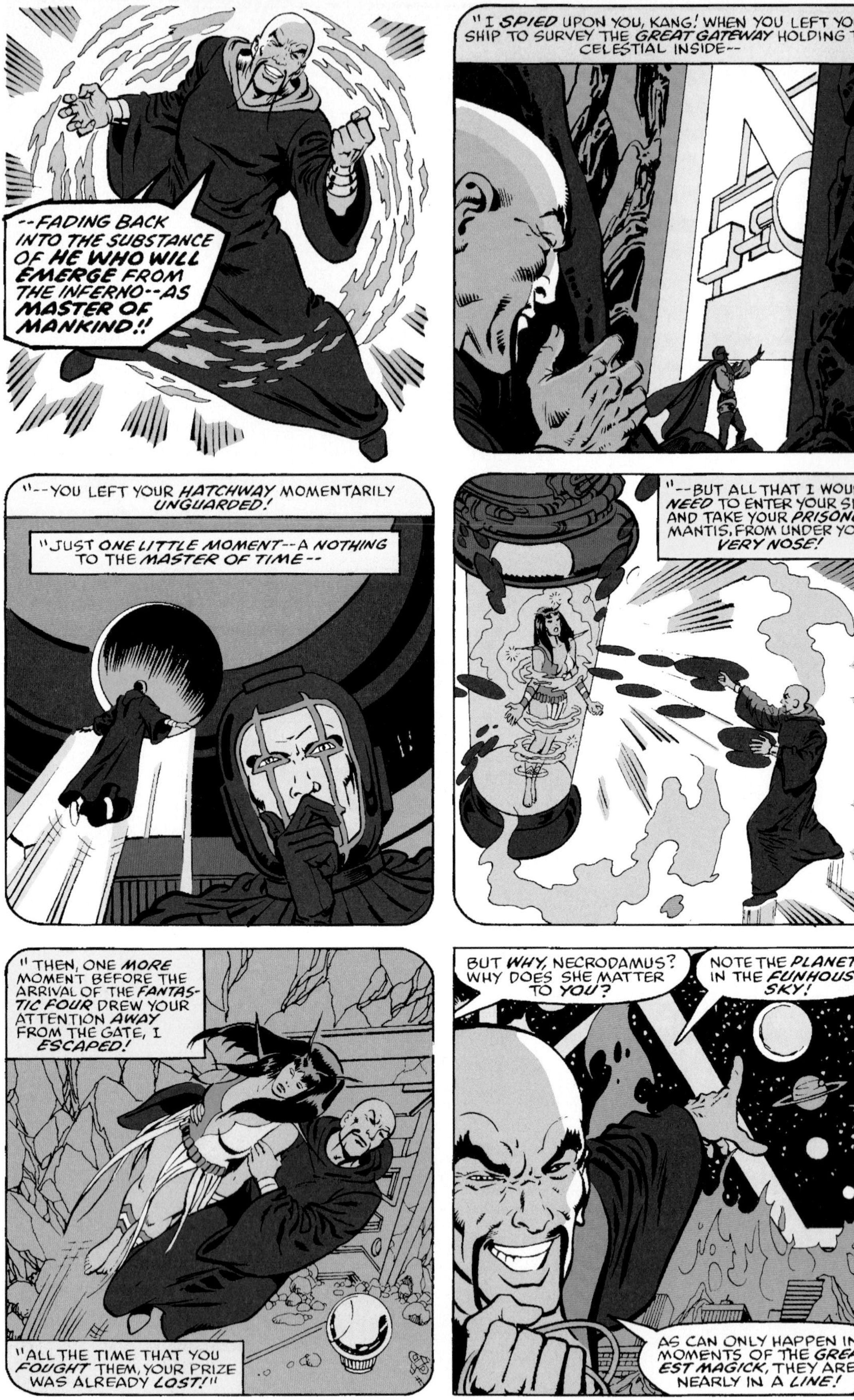
--FADING BACK INTO THE SUBSTANCE OF HE WHO WILL EMERGE FROM THE INFERNO--AS MASTER OF MANKIND!!
"I SPIED UPON YOU, KANG! WHEN YOU LEFT YOUR SHIP TO SURVEY THE GREAT GATEWAY HOLDING THE CELESTIAL INSIDE--
"--YOU LEFT YOUR HATCHWAY MOMENTARILY UNGUARDED!
"JUST ONE LITTLE MOMENT--A NOTHING TO THE MASTER OF TIME--
"--BUT ALL THAT I WOULD NEED TO ENTER YOUR SHIP AND TAKE YOUR PRISONER, MANTIS, FROM UNDER YOUR VERY NOSE!
"THEN, ONE MORE MOMENT BEFORE THE ARRIVAL OF THE FANTASTIC FOUR DREW YOUR ATTENTION AWAY FROM THE GATE, I ESCAPED!
"ALL THE TIME THAT YOU FOUGHT THEM, YOUR PRIZE WAS ALREADY LOST!"
BUT WHY, NECRODAMUS? WHY DOES SHE MATTER TO YOU?
NOTE THE PLANETS IN THE FUNHOUSE SKY!
AS CAN ONLY HAPPEN IN MOMENTS OF THE GREATEST MAGICK, THEY ARE NEARLY IN A LINE!

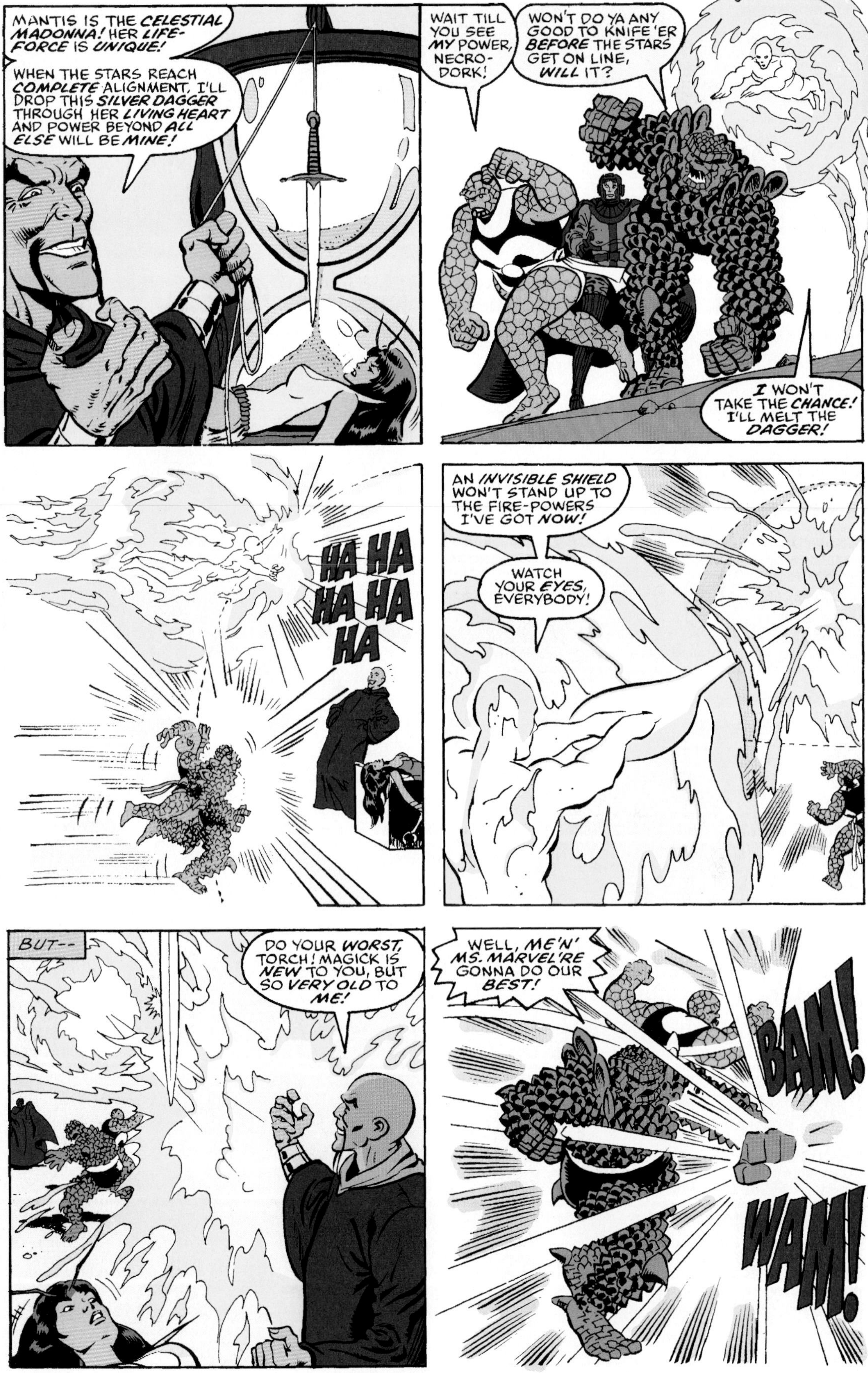
MANTIS IS THE CELESTIAL MADONNA! HER LIFE-FORCE IS UNIQUE!
WHEN THE STARS REACH COMPLETE ALIGNMENT, I'LL DROP THIS SILVER DAGGER THROUGH HER LIVING HEART AND POWER BEYOND ALL ELSE WILL BE MINE!
WAIT TILL YOU SEE MY POWER, NECRO-DORK!
WON'T DO YA ANY GOOD TO KNIFE 'ER BEFORE THE STARS GET ON LINE, WILL IT?
I WON'T TAKE THE CHANCE! I'LL MELT THE DAGGER!
HA HA HA HA HA
AN INVISIBLE SHIELD WON'T STAND UP TO THE FIRE-POWERS I'VE GOT NOW!
WATCH YOUR EYES, EVERYBODY!
BUT--
DO YOUR WORST, TORCH! MAGICK IS NEW TO YOU, BUT SO VERY OLD TO ME!
WELL, ME'N' MS. MARVEL'RE GONNA DO OUR BEST!
BAM!
WAM!

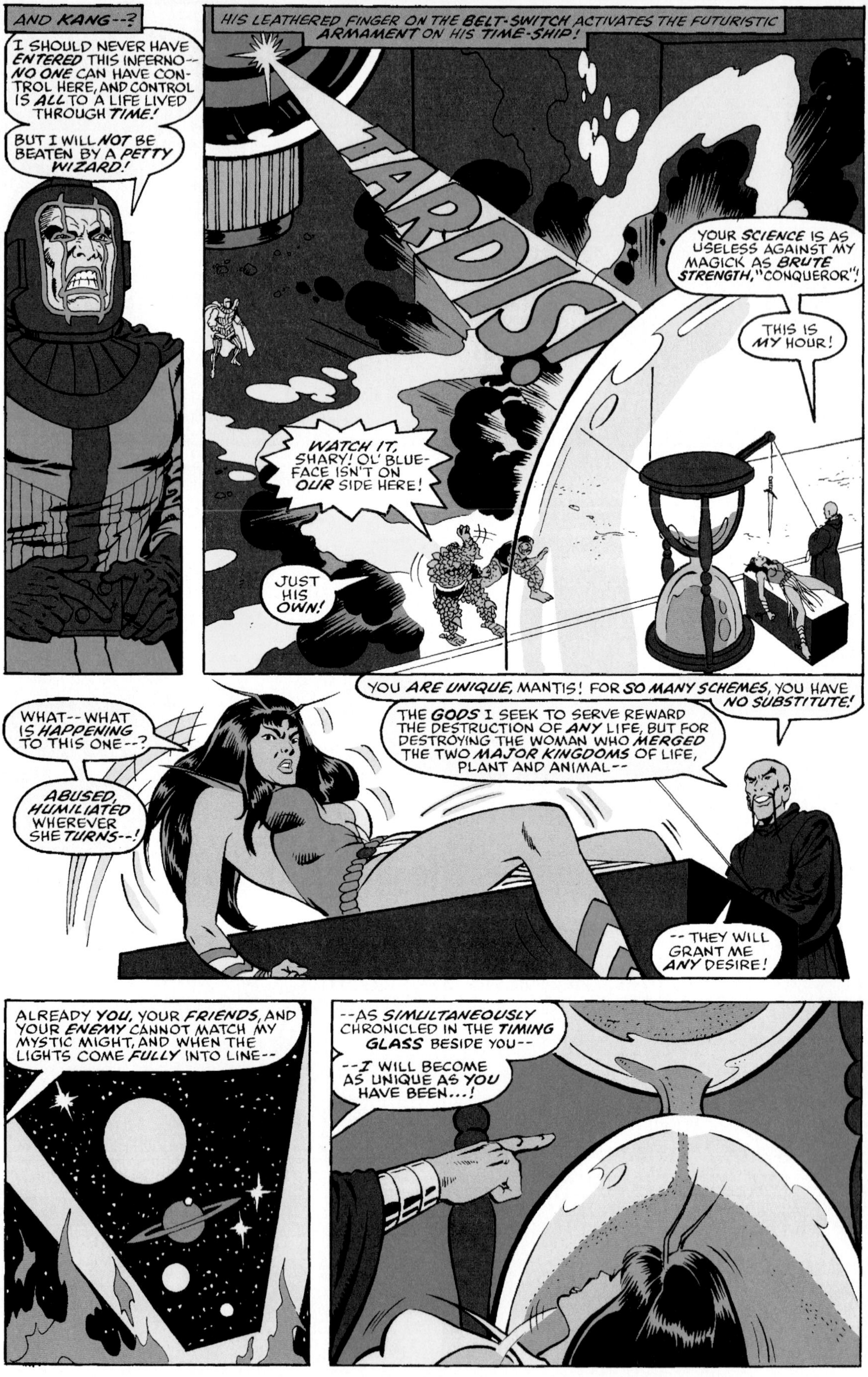
AND KANG--?
I SHOULD NEVER HAVE ENTERED THIS INFERNO-- NO ONE CAN HAVE CONTROL HERE, AND CONTROL IS ALL TO A LIFE LIVED THROUGH TIME!
BUT I WILL NOT BE BEATEN BY A PETTY WIZARD!
HIS LEATHERED FINGER ON THE BELT-SWITCH ACTIVATES THE FUTURISTIC ARMAMENT ON HIS TIME-SHIP!
TARDIS!
YOUR SCIENCE IS AS USELESS AGAINST MY MAGICK AS BRUTE STRENGTH, "CONQUEROR"!
THIS IS MY HOUR!
WATCH IT, SHARY! OL' BLUE-FACE ISN'T ON OUR SIDE HERE!
JUST HIS OWN!
WHAT--WHAT IS HAPPENING TO THIS ONE--?
ABUSED, HUMILIATED WHEREVER SHE TURNS--!
YOU ARE UNIQUE, MANTIS! FOR SO MANY SCHEMES, YOU HAVE NO SUBSTITUTE!
THE GODS I SEEK TO SERVE REWARD THE DESTRUCTION OF ANY LIFE, BUT FOR DESTROYING THE WOMAN WHO MERGED THE TWO MAJOR KINGDOMS OF LIFE, PLANT AND ANIMAL--
--THEY WILL GRANT ME ANY DESIRE!
ALREADY YOU, YOUR FRIENDS, AND YOUR ENEMY CANNOT MATCH MY MYSTIC MIGHT, AND WHEN THE LIGHTS COME FULLY INTO LINE--
--AS SIMULTANEOUSLY CHRONICLED IN THE TIMING GLASS BESIDE YOU--
--I WILL BECOME AS UNIQUE AS YOU HAVE BEEN...!

GOOD LORD!

I'VE GOT IT!

SNAT!

KANG-- I KNOW A WAY TO *STOP* THIS LUNATIC!

STAND BACK, WOMAN! I WILL BROOK NO *TREACHERY!*

OH, *SHUT UP!* LISTEN...

DOUBLE-M? WHOSE SIDE ARE YOU *ON?*

SHARY--?

BY MY WASTED YEARS AS THE PHARAOH RAMA-TUT! YOU ARE *CORRECT*, WOMAN!

TORCH! COME WITH ME AND I'LL *EXPLAIN!*

YEAH, SURE-- MAYBE A WEEK FROM *SUNDAY*--!

NO, JOHNNY --IT'S *OKAY!*

IS IT, SHARY? I CAN'T TRUST *KANG, EVER*--AND I CAN'T TRUST *YOU*-- NOT *COMPLETELY!* NOT *YET!*

YOU HAVEN'T LET US *DOWN* SINCE YOU RECOVERED FROM TURNING INTO A *THING*--*

*FF #312-- RIGHTEOUS RALF.

--BUT *THIS* IS ONE I HAVE TO MAKE UP MY *OWN* MIND ON!

TORCH! I MUST HAVE YOUR HELP FOR MS. MARVEL'S PLAN!

JOIN ME AND I'LL SUB- DUE YOUR *RUNAWAY FLAME!*

THERE IS NO TIME TO *WASTE!* IF YOU *REFUSE* ME YOUR WORLD DIES! I AM THE ONE *HOPE!*

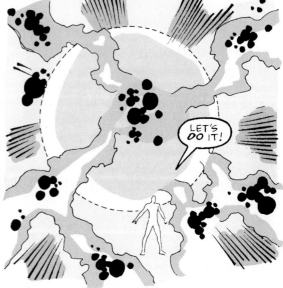

LET'S *DO* IT!

151

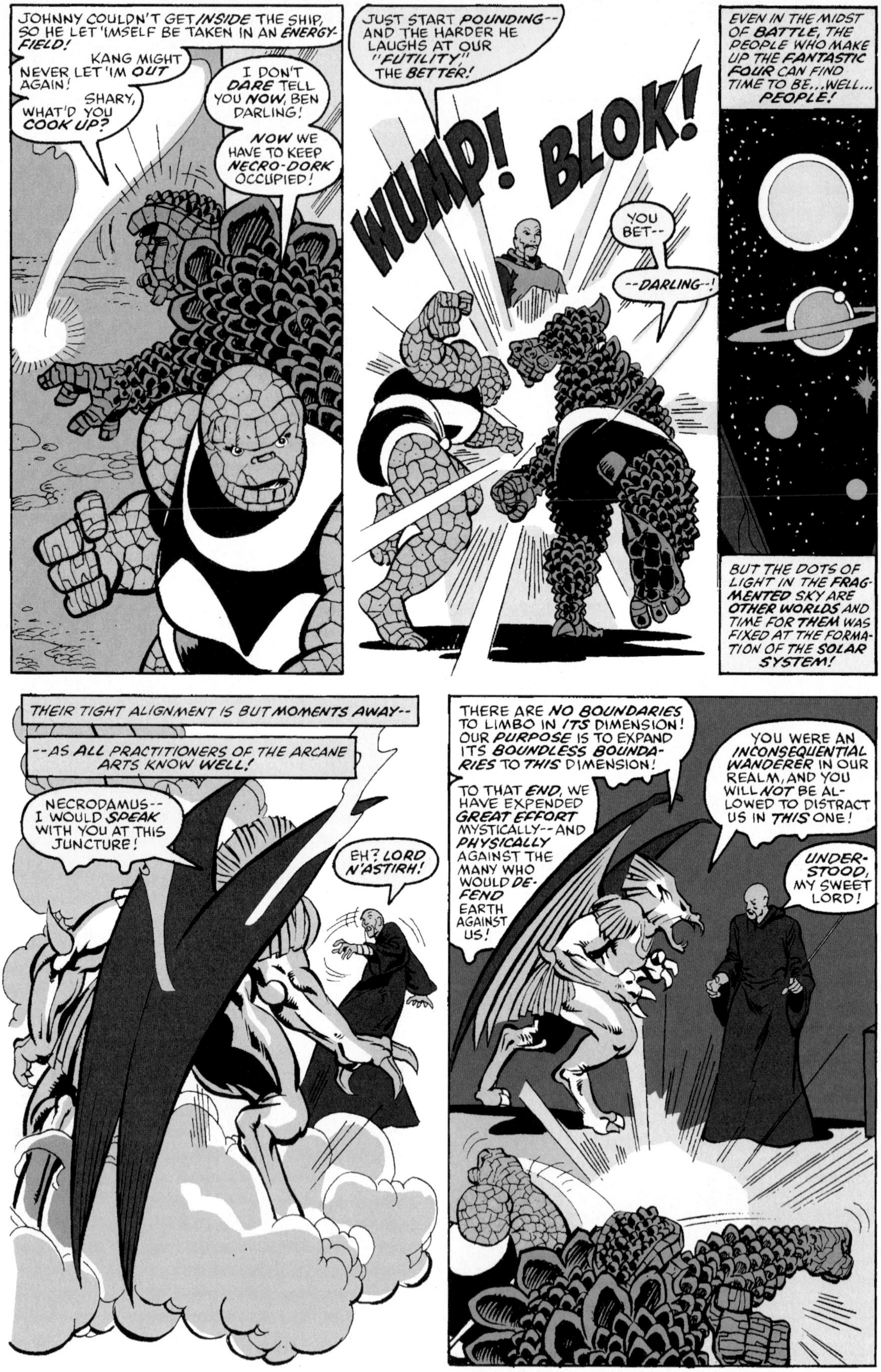
JOHNNY COULDN'T GET INSIDE THE SHIP, SO HE LET 'IMSELF BE TAKEN IN AN ENERGY-FIELD!
KANG MIGHT NEVER LET 'IM OUT AGAIN!
SHARY, WHAT'D YOU COOK UP?
I DON'T DARE TELL YOU NOW, BEN DARLING!
NOW WE HAVE TO KEEP NECRO-DORK OCCUPIED!
JUST START POUNDING-- AND THE HARDER HE LAUGHS AT OUR "FUTILITY," THE BETTER!
WUMP! BLOK!
YOU BET--
--DARLING--!
EVEN IN THE MIDST OF BATTLE, THE PEOPLE WHO MAKE UP THE FANTASTIC FOUR CAN FIND TIME TO BE...WELL... PEOPLE!
BUT THE DOTS OF LIGHT IN THE FRAGMENTED SKY ARE OTHER WORLDS AND TIME FOR THEM WAS FIXED AT THE FORMATION OF THE SOLAR SYSTEM!
THEIR TIGHT ALIGNMENT IS BUT MOMENTS AWAY--
--AS ALL PRACTITIONERS OF THE ARCANE ARTS KNOW WELL!
NECRODAMUS-- I WOULD SPEAK WITH YOU AT THIS JUNCTURE!
EH? LORD N'ASTIRH!
THERE ARE NO BOUNDARIES TO LIMBO IN ITS DIMENSION! OUR PURPOSE IS TO EXPAND ITS BOUNDLESS BOUNDARIES TO THIS DIMENSION!
TO THAT END, WE HAVE EXPENDED GREAT EFFORT MYSTICALLY--AND PHYSICALLY AGAINST THE MANY WHO WOULD DEFEND EARTH AGAINST US!
YOU WERE AN INCONSEQUENTIAL WANDERER IN OUR REALM, AND YOU WILL NOT BE ALLOWED TO DISTRACT US IN THIS ONE!
UNDERSTOOD, MY SWEET LORD!

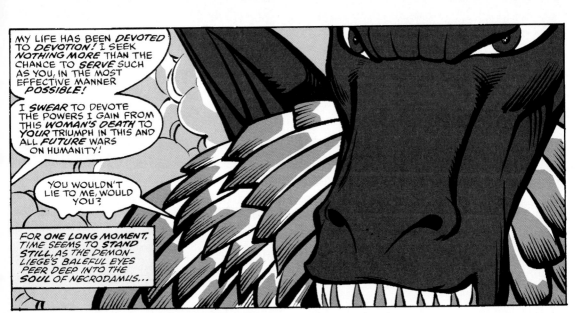

MY LIFE HAS BEEN *DEVOTED* TO *DEVOTION!* I SEEK *NOTHING MORE* THAN THE CHANCE TO *SERVE* SUCH AS YOU, IN THE MOST EFFECTIVE MANNER *POSSIBLE!*

I *SWEAR* TO DEVOTE THE POWERS I GAIN FROM THIS *WOMAN'S DEATH* TO *YOUR* TRIUMPH IN THIS AND ALL *FUTURE* WARS ON HUMANITY!

YOU WOULDN'T *LIE* TO ME, WOULD YOU?

FOR *ONE LONG MOMENT,* TIME SEEMS TO *STAND STILL,* AS THE DEMON-LIEGE'S BALEFUL EYES PEER DEEP INTO THE *SOUL* OF NECRODAMUS...

...BUT TIME CANNOT STOP FOR *LONG NOW!*

YOU HAVE MY *BLESSING,* WIZARD!

HEY! *SNAGGLETOOTH!* YOU WANT A *WAR,* JUST OPEN HIS *BARRIER* AN' WE'LL GIVE YA ALL THE WAR YA *WANT!*

WOMP!

NICE *TRY,* BEN!

HECK, I'LL TRY *ANYTHING* NOW!

THAT OVERGROWN *EGG-TIMER* IN THERE IS *JUST ABOUT EMPTIED OUT!*

I SURE HOPE YOUR *PLAN'S* GONNA WORK!

LET'S FIND *OUT!*

MASTER OF TIME *AND SPACE* AM I, HUMAN *TORCH!*

BEHOLD THE PLANET *MERCURY!* THE NEAREST WORLD TO YOUR SUN!

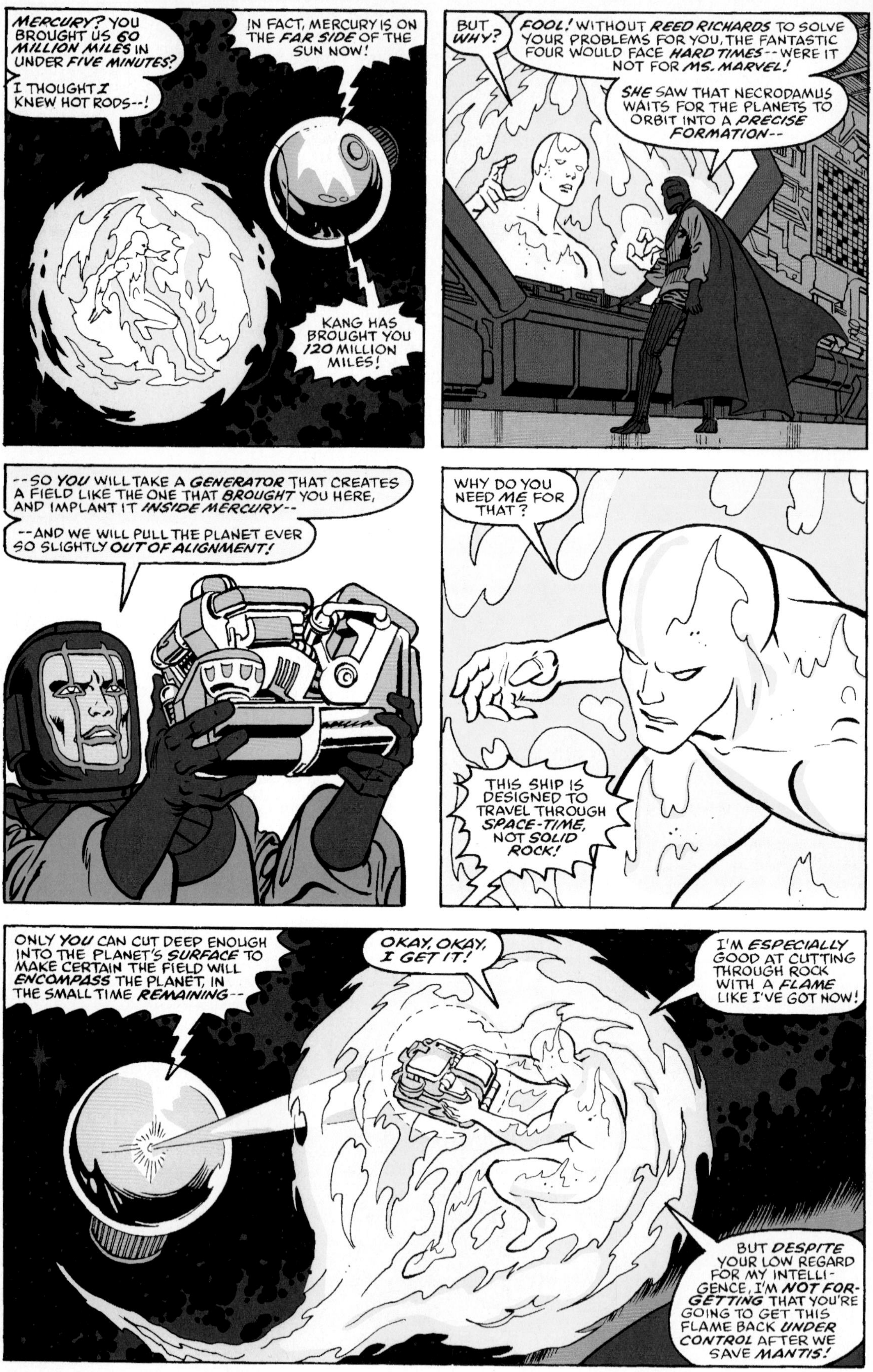
MERCURY? YOU BROUGHT US 60 MILLION MILES IN UNDER FIVE MINUTES?
I THOUGHT I KNEW HOT RODS--!
IN FACT, MERCURY IS ON THE FAR SIDE OF THE SUN NOW!
KANG HAS BROUGHT YOU 120 MILLION MILES!
BUT WHY?
FOOL! WITHOUT REED RICHARDS TO SOLVE YOUR PROBLEMS FOR YOU, THE FANTASTIC FOUR WOULD FACE HARD TIMES--WERE IT NOT FOR MS. MARVEL!
SHE SAW THAT NECRODAMUS WAITS FOR THE PLANETS TO ORBIT INTO A PRECISE FORMATION--
--SO YOU WILL TAKE A GENERATOR THAT CREATES A FIELD LIKE THE ONE THAT BROUGHT YOU HERE, AND IMPLANT IT INSIDE MERCURY--
--AND WE WILL PULL THE PLANET EVER SO SLIGHTLY OUT OF ALIGNMENT!
WHY DO YOU NEED ME FOR THAT?
THIS SHIP IS DESIGNED TO TRAVEL THROUGH SPACE-TIME, NOT SOLID ROCK!
ONLY YOU CAN CUT DEEP ENOUGH INTO THE PLANET'S SURFACE TO MAKE CERTAIN THE FIELD WILL ENCOMPASS THE PLANET, IN THE SMALL TIME REMAINING--
OKAY, OKAY, I GET IT!
I'M ESPECIALLY GOOD AT CUTTING THROUGH ROCK WITH A FLAME LIKE I'VE GOT NOW!
BUT DESPITE YOUR LOW REGARD FOR MY INTELLI-GENCE, I'M NOT FOR-GETTING THAT YOU'RE GOING TO GET THIS FLAME BACK UNDER CONTROL AFTER WE SAVE MANTIS!

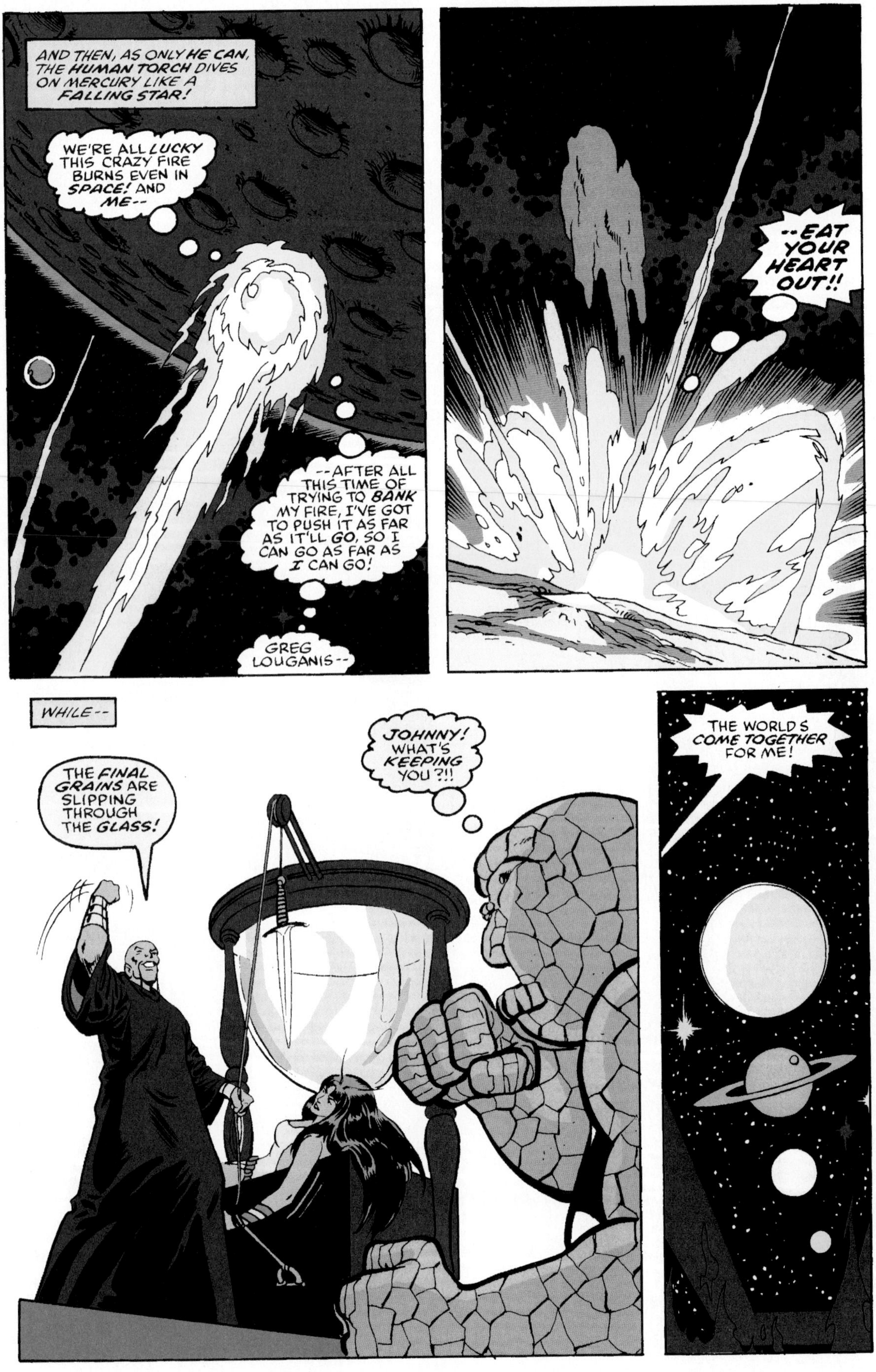
AND THEN, AS ONLY HE CAN, THE HUMAN TORCH DIVES ON MERCURY LIKE A FALLING STAR!
WE'RE ALL LUCKY THIS CRAZY FIRE BURNS EVEN IN SPACE! AND ME--
--AFTER ALL THIS TIME OF TRYING TO BANK MY FIRE, I'VE GOT TO PUSH IT AS FAR AS IT'LL GO, SO I CAN GO AS FAR AS I CAN GO!
GREG LOUGANIS--
--EAT YOUR HEART OUT!!
WHILE--
THE FINAL GRAINS ARE SLIPPING THROUGH THE GLASS!
JOHNNY! WHAT'S KEEPING YOU?!!
THE WORLDS COME TOGETHER FOR ME!

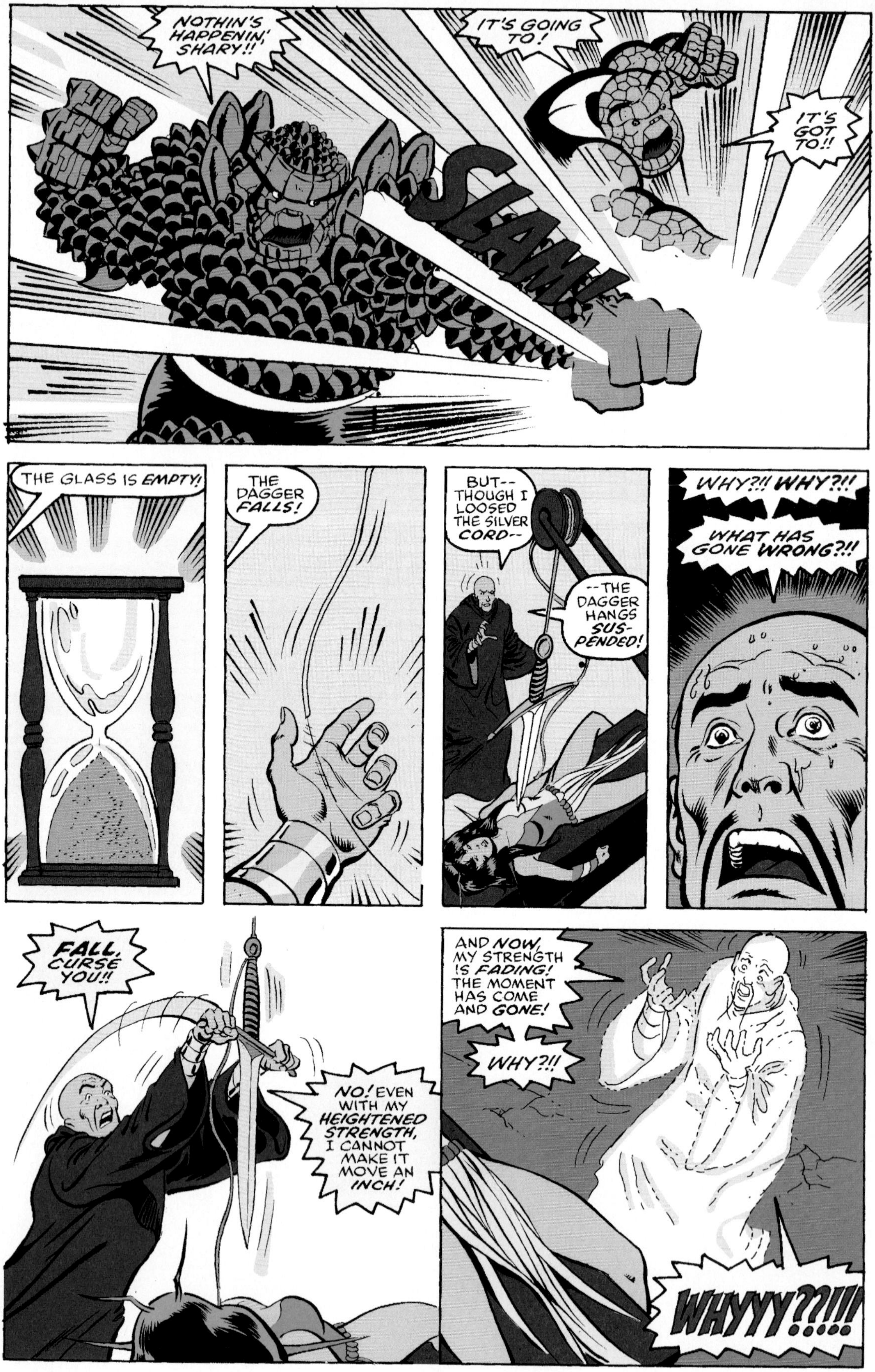
NOTHIN'S HAPPENIN', SHARY!!
IT'S GOING TO!
IT'S GOT TO!!
SLAM!
THE GLASS IS EMPTY!
THE DAGGER FALLS!
BUT-- THOUGH I LOOSED THE SILVER CORD--
--THE DAGGER HANGS SUS-PENDED!
WHY?!! WHY?!!
WHAT HAS GONE WRONG?!!
FALL, CURSE YOU!!
NO! EVEN WITH MY HEIGHTENED STRENGTH, I CANNOT MAKE IT MOVE AN INCH!
AND NOW, MY STRENGTH IS FADING! THE MOMENT HAS COME AND GONE!
WHY?!!
WHYYY??!!!

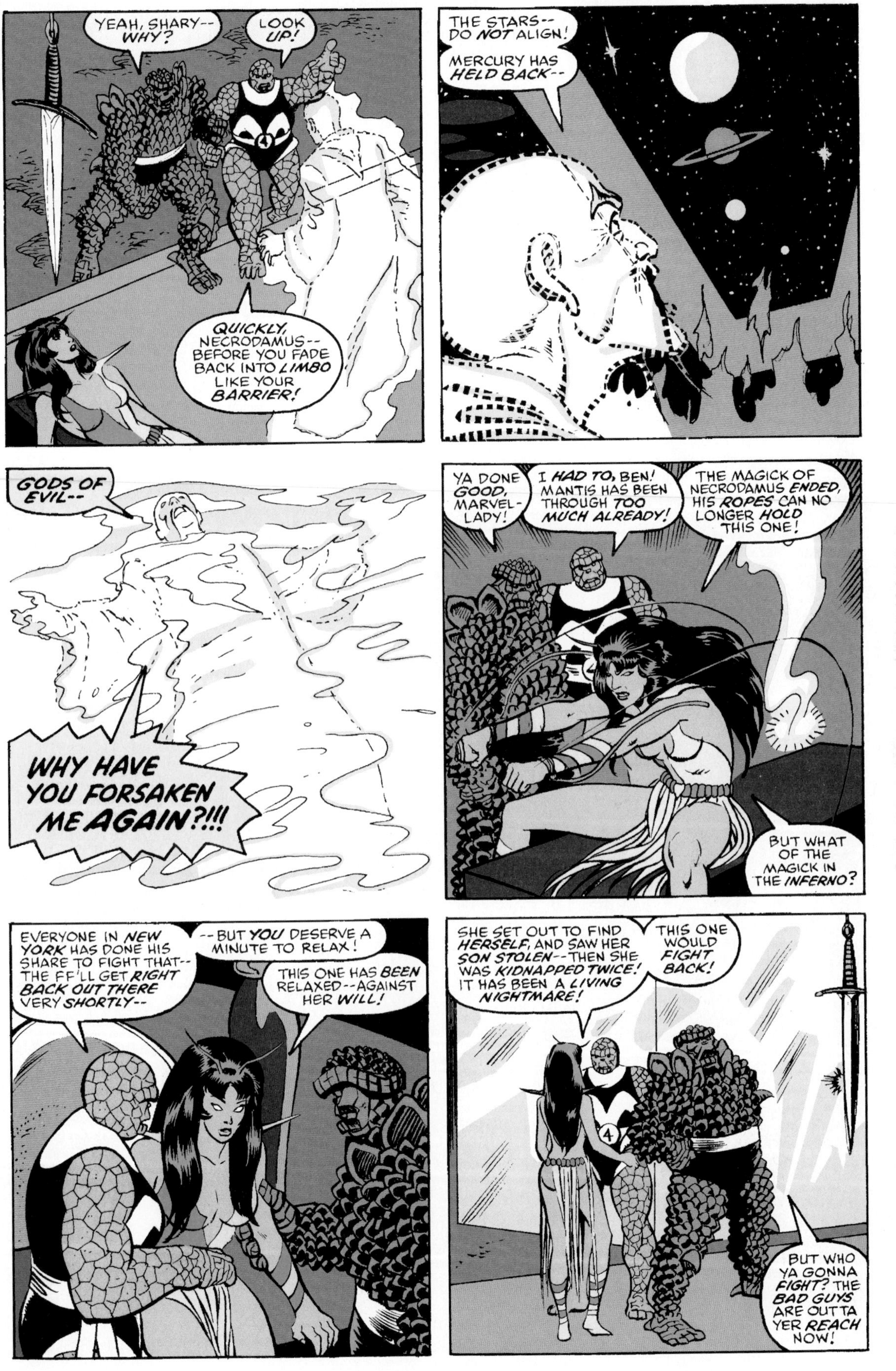
YEAH, SHARY-- WHY?
LOOK UP!
QUICKLY, NECRODAMUS-- BEFORE YOU FADE BACK INTO LIMBO LIKE YOUR BARRIER!
THE STARS-- DO NOT ALIGN!
MERCURY HAS HELD BACK--
GODS OF EVIL--
WHY HAVE YOU FORSAKEN ME AGAIN?!!!
YA DONE GOOD, MARVEL-LADY!
I HAD TO, BEN! MANTIS HAS BEEN THROUGH TOO MUCH ALREADY!
THE MAGICK OF NECRODAMUS ENDED, HIS ROPES CAN NO LONGER HOLD THIS ONE!
BUT WHAT OF THE MAGICK IN THE INFERNO?
EVERYONE IN NEW YORK HAS DONE HIS SHARE TO FIGHT THAT-- THE FF'LL GET RIGHT BACK OUT THERE VERY SHORTLY--
--BUT YOU DESERVE A MINUTE TO RELAX!
THIS ONE HAS BEEN RELAXED--AGAINST HER WILL!
SHE SET OUT TO FIND HERSELF, AND SAW HER SON STOLEN--THEN SHE WAS KIDNAPPED TWICE! IT HAS BEEN A LIVING NIGHTMARE!
THIS ONE WOULD FIGHT BACK!
BUT WHO YA GONNA FIGHT? THE BAD GUYS ARE OUTTA YER REACH NOW!

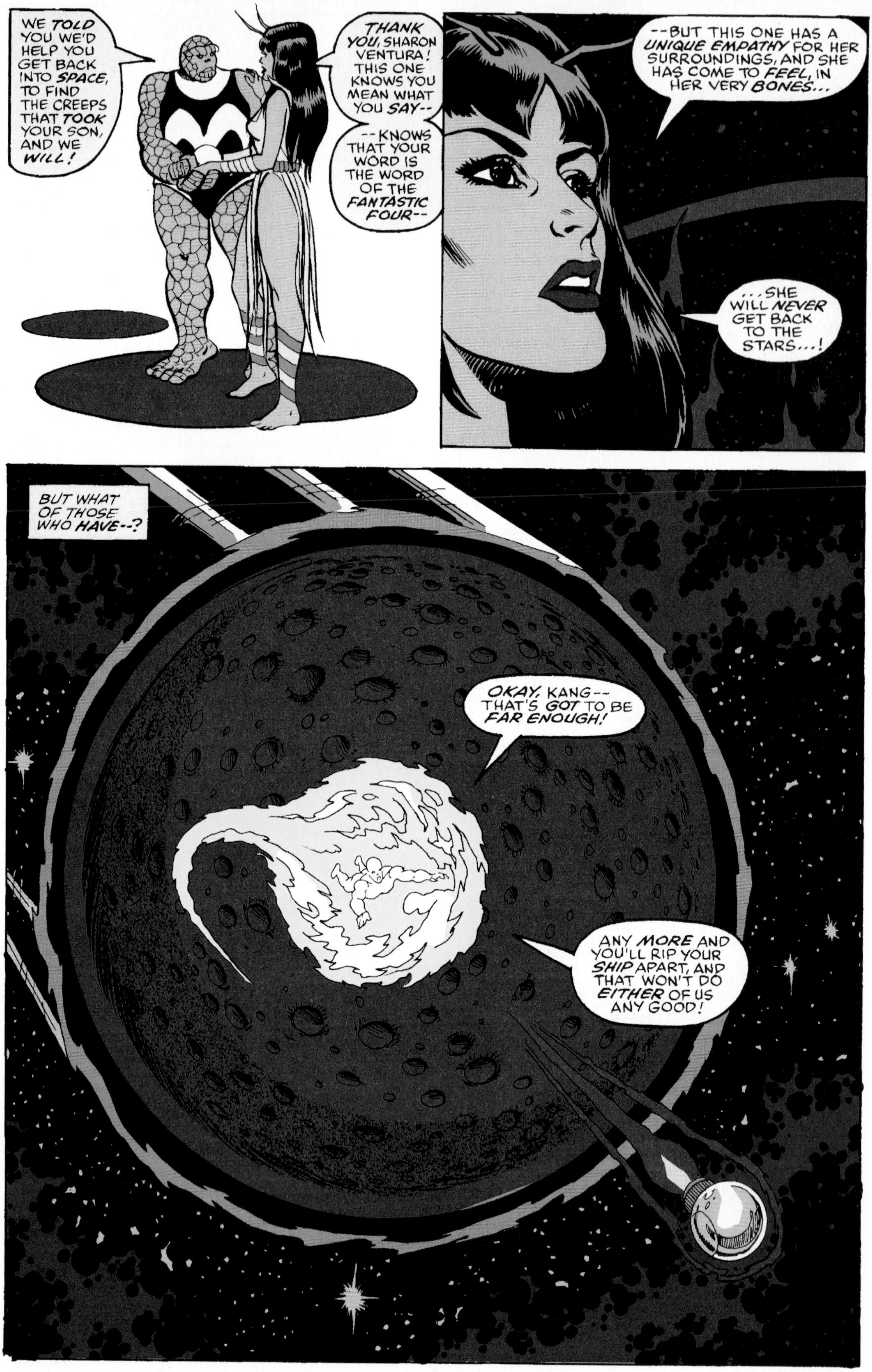
WE TOLD YOU WE'D HELP YOU GET BACK INTO SPACE, TO FIND THE CREEPS THAT TOOK YOUR SON, AND WE WILL!
THANK YOU, SHARON VENTURA! THIS ONE KNOWS YOU MEAN WHAT YOU SAY--
--KNOWS THAT YOUR WORD IS THE WORD OF THE FANTASTIC FOUR--
--BUT THIS ONE HAS A UNIQUE EMPATHY FOR HER SURROUNDINGS, AND SHE HAS COME TO FEEL, IN HER VERY BONES...
...SHE WILL NEVER GET BACK TO THE STARS...!
BUT WHAT OF THOSE WHO HAVE--?
OKAY, KANG-- THAT'S GOT TO BE FAR ENOUGH!
ANY MORE AND YOU'LL RIP YOUR SHIP APART, AND THAT WON'T DO EITHER OF US ANY GOOD!

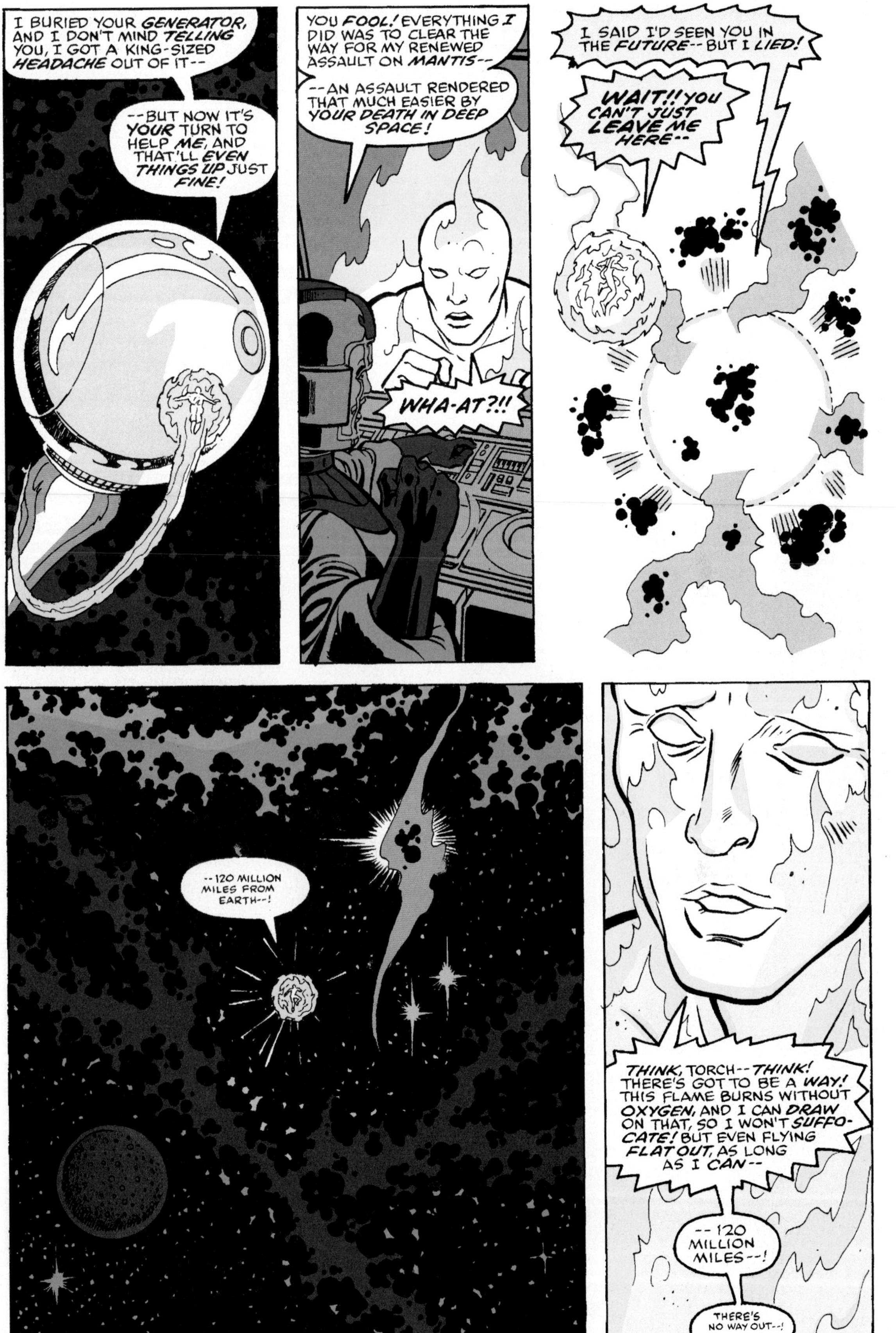
I BURIED YOUR GENERATOR, AND I DON'T MIND TELLING YOU, I GOT A KING-SIZED HEADACHE OUT OF IT--
--BUT NOW IT'S YOUR TURN TO HELP ME, AND THAT'LL EVEN THINGS UP JUST FINE!
YOU FOOL! EVERYTHING I DID WAS TO CLEAR THE WAY FOR MY RENEWED ASSAULT ON MANTIS--
--AN ASSAULT RENDERED THAT MUCH EASIER BY YOUR DEATH IN DEEP SPACE!
WHA-AT?!!
I SAID I'D SEEN YOU IN THE FUTURE-- BUT I LIED!
WAIT!! YOU CAN'T JUST LEAVE ME HERE--
--120 MILLION MILES FROM EARTH--!
THINK, TORCH--THINK! THERE'S GOT TO BE A WAY! THIS FLAME BURNS WITHOUT OXYGEN, AND I CAN DRAW ON THAT, SO I WON'T SUFFOCATE! BUT EVEN FLYING FLAT OUT, AS LONG AS I CAN--
--120 MILLION MILES--!
THERE'S NO WAY OUT--!

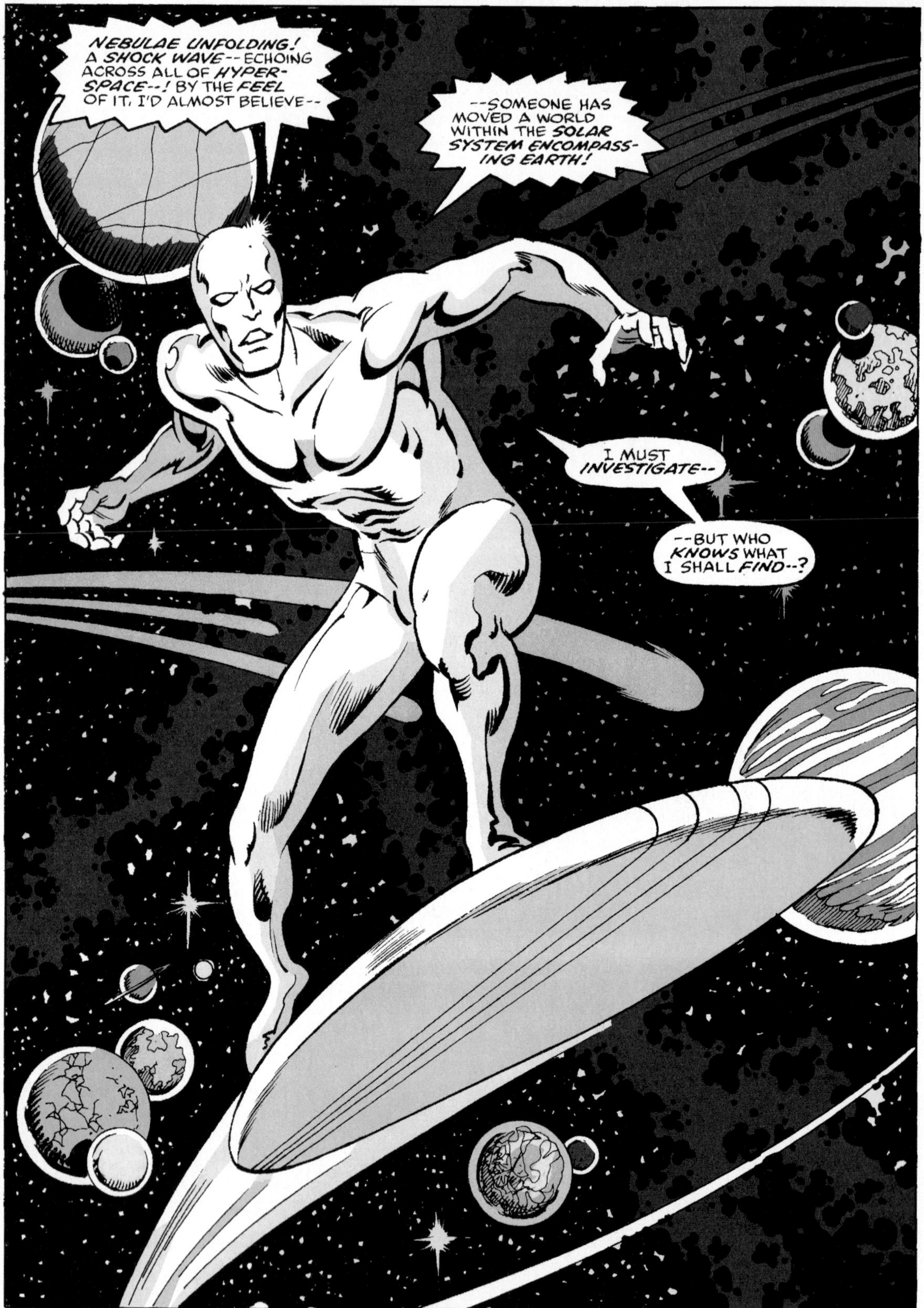
NEBULAE UNFOLDING! A SHOCK WAVE--ECHOING ACROSS ALL OF HYPER-SPACE--! BY THE FEEL OF IT, I'D ALMOST BELIEVE--
--SOMEONE HAS MOVED A WORLD WITHIN THE SOLAR SYSTEM ENCOMPASS-ING EARTH!
I MUST INVESTIGATE--
--BUT WHO KNOWS WHAT I SHALL FIND--?

FOR MONTHS, THE SILVER SURFER HAS BELIEVED HIS **LOST LOVE, MANTIS, DEAD!** NEXT MONTH IN FF #325--

WHEN YOU WISH UPON A STAR...

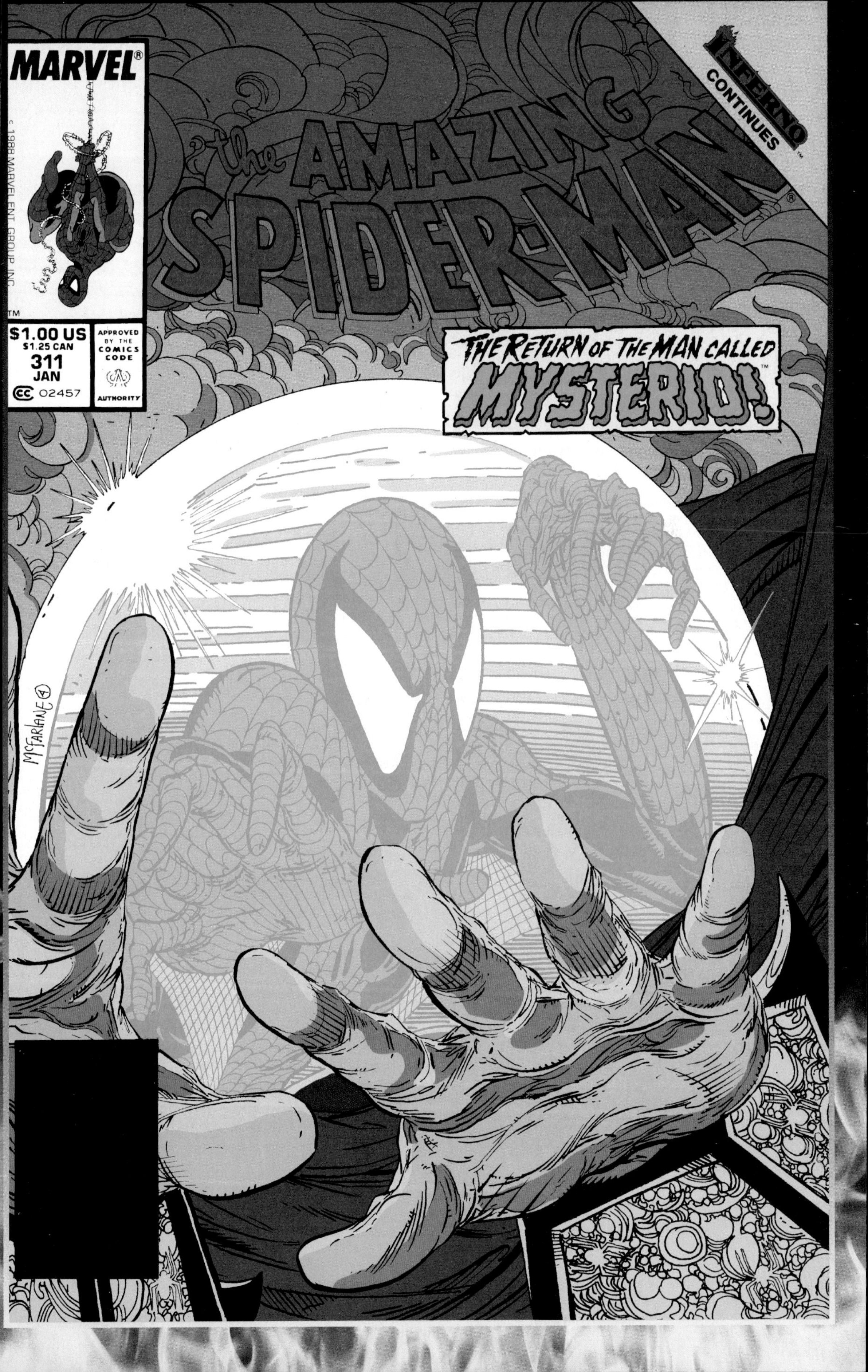
MARVEL
© 1988 MARVEL ENT. GROUP INC.
the AMAZING SPIDER-MAN
INFERNO CONTINUES
$1.00 US
$1.25 CAN
311
JAN
02457
APPROVED BY THE COMICS CODE AUTHORITY
THE RETURN OF THE MAN CALLED MYSTERIO!
McFARLANE

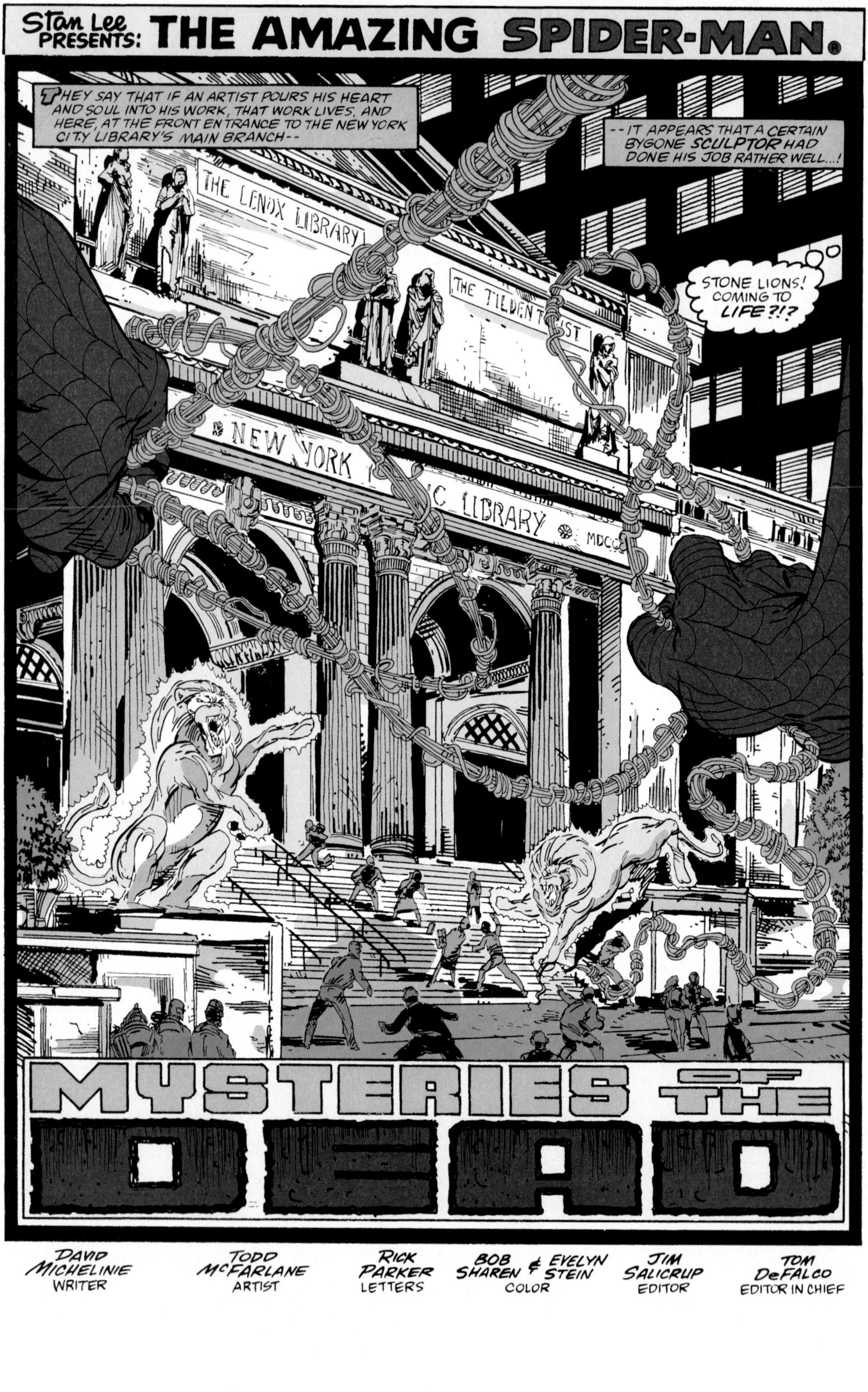
Stan Lee PRESENTS: THE AMAZING SPIDER-MAN.
THEY SAY THAT IF AN ARTIST POURS HIS HEART AND SOUL INTO HIS WORK, THAT WORK LIVES, AND HERE, AT THE FRONT ENTRANCE TO THE NEW YORK CITY LIBRARY'S MAIN BRANCH--
--IT APPEARS THAT A CERTAIN BYGONE SCULPTOR HAD DONE HIS JOB RATHER WELL...!
THE LENOX LIBRARY
THE TILDEN TRUST
STONE LIONS! COMING TO LIFE?!?
NEW YORK
LIBRARY
MYSTERIES OF THE DEAD
DAVID MICHELINIE WRITER
TODD McFARLANE ARTIST
RICK PARKER LETTERS
BOB SHAREN & EVELYN STEIN COLOR
JIM SALICRUP EDITOR
TOM DeFALCO EDITOR IN CHIEF

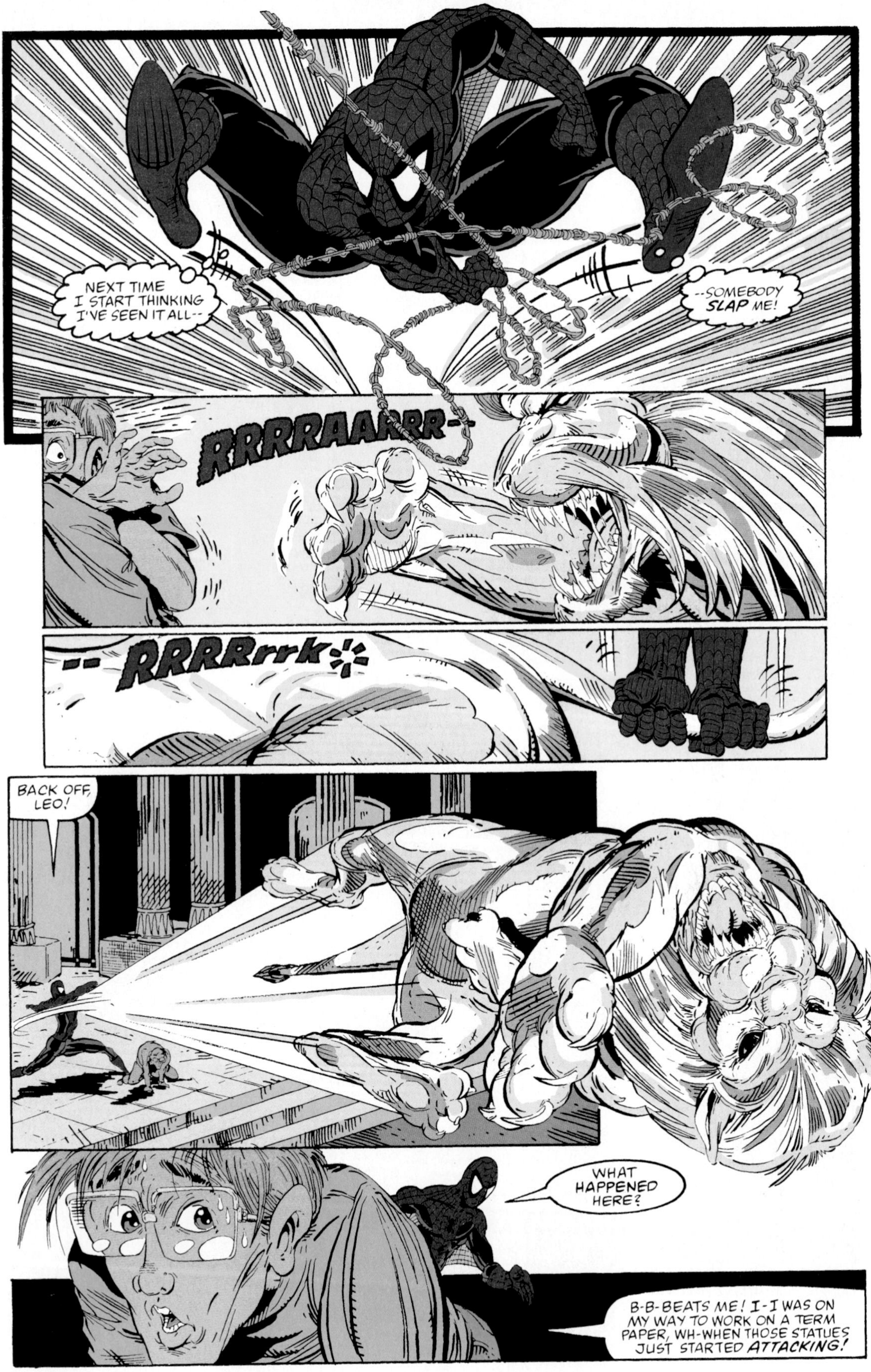
NEXT TIME I START THINKING I'VE SEEN IT ALL--
--SOMEBODY SLAP ME!
RRRRAARRR--
--RRRRrrk
BACK OFF, LEO!
WHAT HAPPENED HERE?
B-B-BEATS ME! I-I WAS ON MY WAY TO WORK ON A TERM PAPER, WH-WHEN THOSE STATUES JUST STARTED ATTACKING!

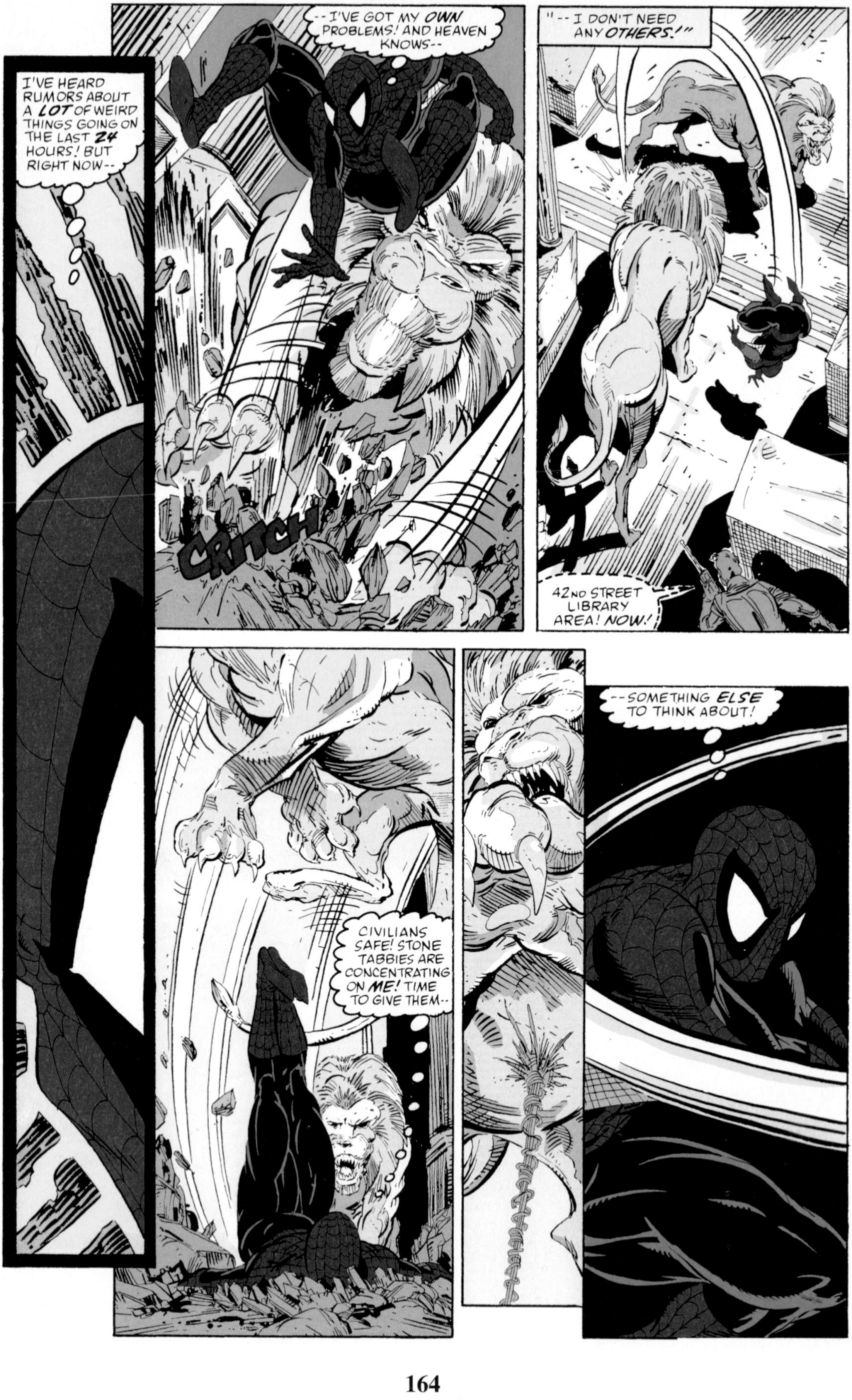
I'VE HEARD RUMORS ABOUT A LOT OF WEIRD THINGS GOING ON THE LAST 24 HOURS! BUT RIGHT NOW--
--I'VE GOT MY OWN PROBLEMS! AND HEAVEN KNOWS--
CRTCH
"--I DON'T NEED ANY OTHERS!"
42ND STREET LIBRARY AREA! NOW!
CIVILIANS SAFE! STONE TABBIES ARE CONCENTRATING ON ME! TIME TO GIVE THEM--
--SOMETHING ELSE TO THINK ABOUT!

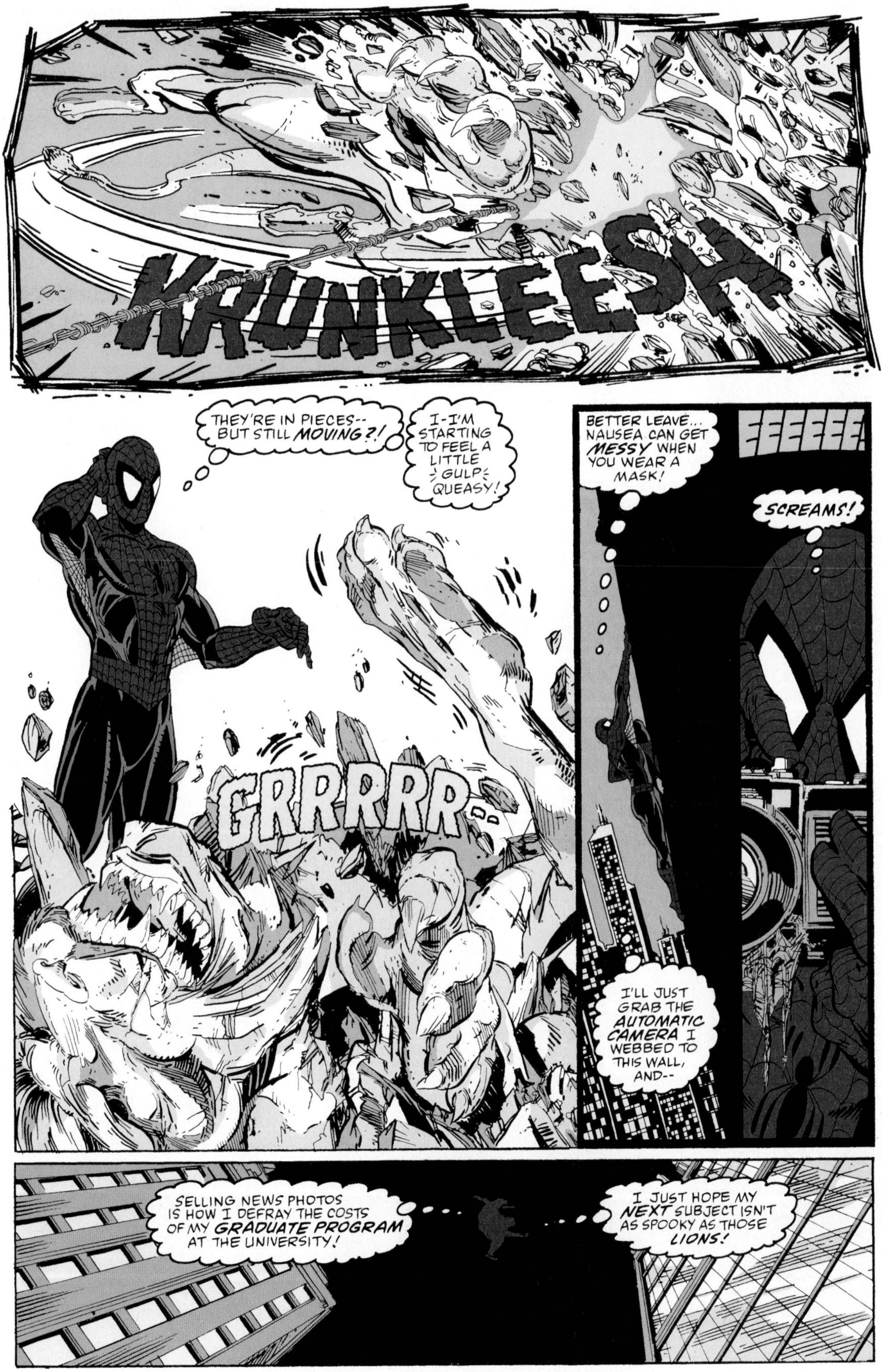
KRUNKLEESH
THEY'RE IN PIECES-- BUT STILL MOVING?!
I-I'M STARTING TO FEEL A LITTLE -GULP- QUEASY!
GRRRRR--
BETTER LEAVE... NAUSEA CAN GET MESSY WHEN YOU WEAR A MASK!
EEEEEE!
SCREAMS!
I'LL JUST GRAB THE AUTOMATIC CAMERA I WEBBED TO THIS WALL, AND--
SELLING NEWS PHOTOS IS HOW I DEFRAY THE COSTS OF MY GRADUATE PROGRAM AT THE UNIVERSITY!
I JUST HOPE MY NEXT SUBJECT ISN'T AS SPOOKY AS THOSE LIONS!

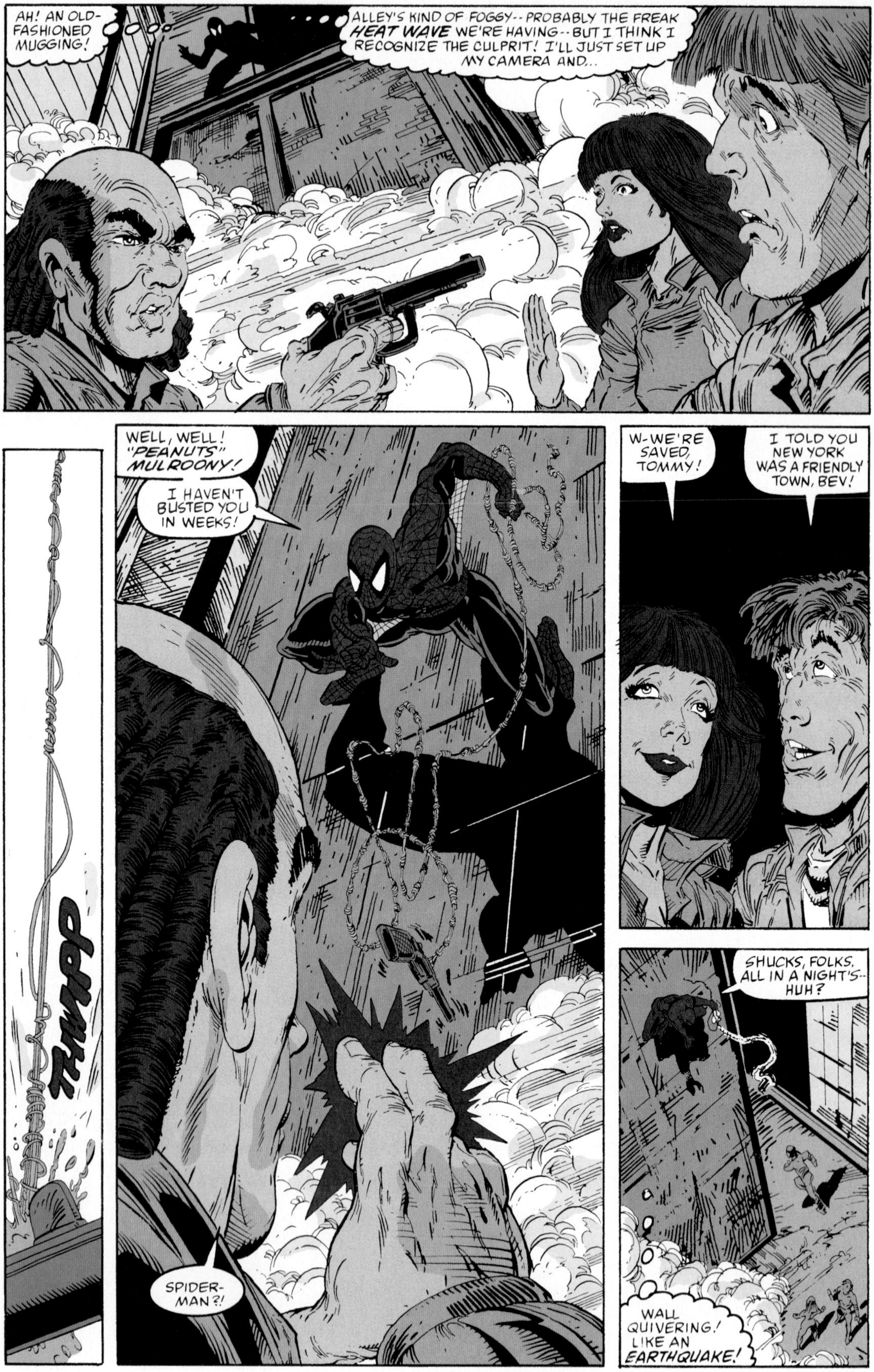
AH! AN OLD-FASHIONED MUGGING!
ALLEY'S KIND OF FOGGY-- PROBABLY THE FREAK HEAT WAVE WE'RE HAVING-- BUT I THINK I RECOGNIZE THE CULPRIT! I'LL JUST SET UP MY CAMERA AND...
THWPP
WELL, WELL! "PEANUTS" MULROONY!
I HAVEN'T BUSTED YOU IN WEEKS!
SPIDER-MAN?!
W-WE'RE SAVED, TOMMY!
I TOLD YOU NEW YORK WAS A FRIENDLY TOWN, BEV!
SHUCKS, FOLKS. ALL IN A NIGHT'S-- HUH?
WALL QUIVERING! LIKE AN EARTHQUAKE!

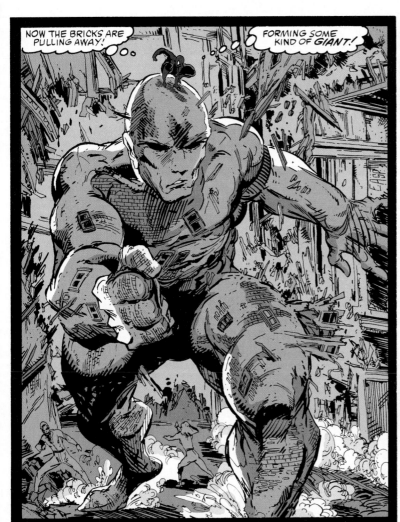

NOW THE BRICKS ARE PULLING AWAY!

FORMING SOME KIND OF *GIANT!*

WHAT THE DEVIL IS *GOING ON?!*

THOK

PRUNCH

HITTING THIS GUY IS LIKE HITTING A BRICK WALL!

WHAT AM I *SAYING?!* HE *IS* A BRICK WALL!

TOMMY! WH-WHAT ARE YOU DOING?

SPIDER-MAN HELPED *US*, SWEETHEART! NOW WE'VE GOT TO HELP--

BAP

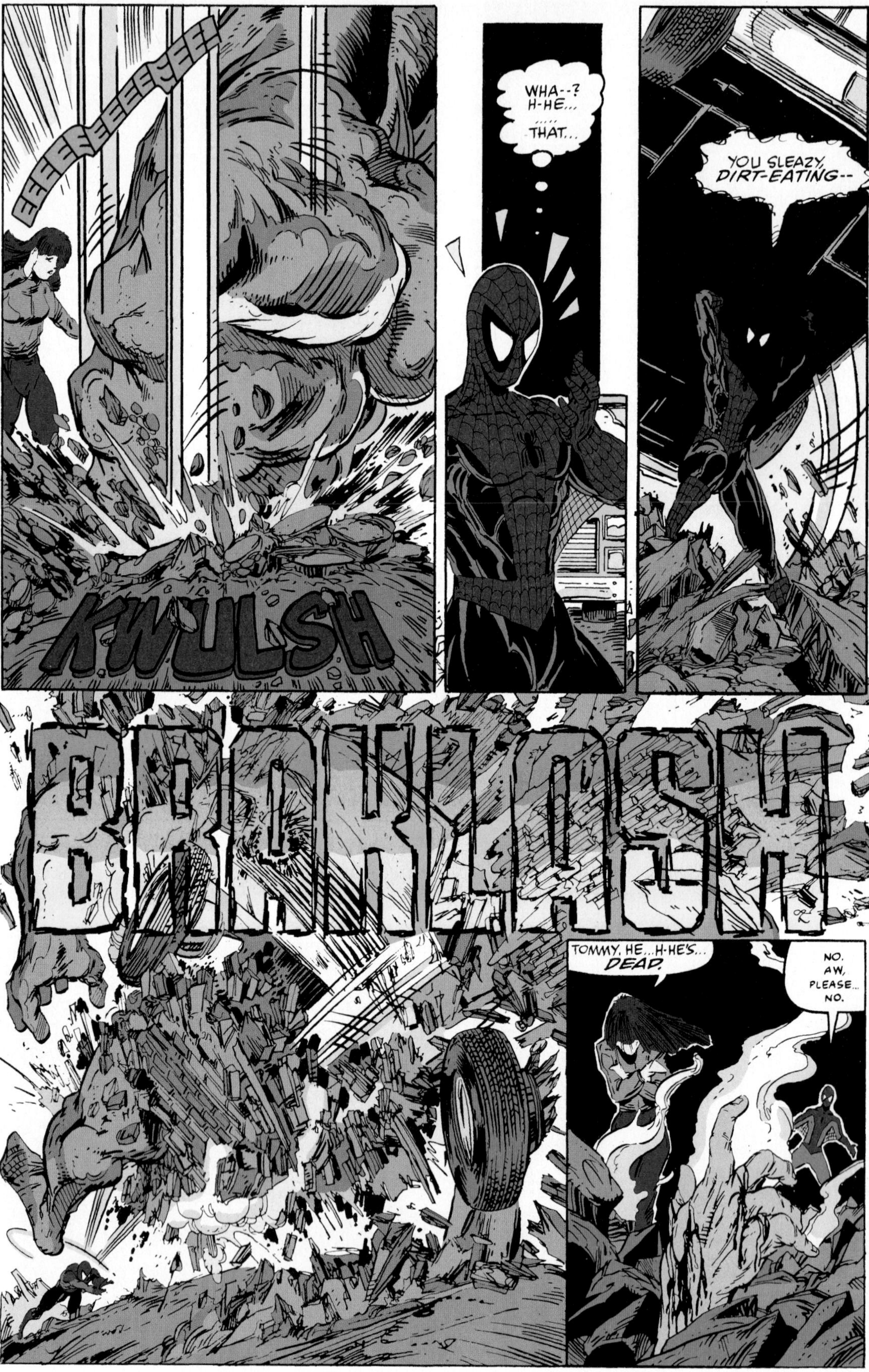
EEEEEEEEEEEEE!
KWULSH
WHA--? H-HE... ..... THAT...
YOU SLEAZY, DIRT-EATING--
TOMMY, HE...H-HE'S... DEAD.
NO. AW, PLEASE... NO.

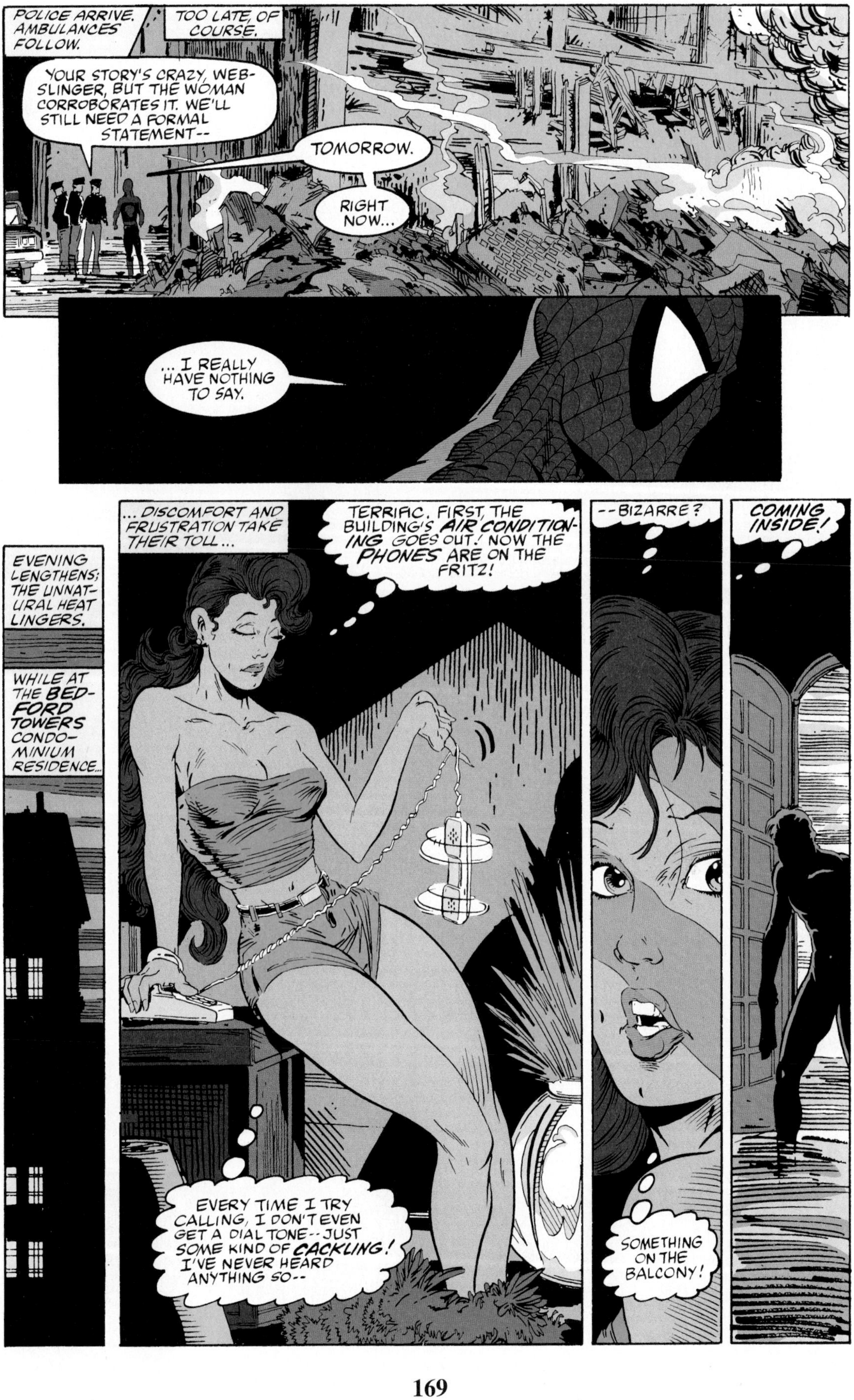

POLICE ARRIVE. AMBULANCES FOLLOW.
TOO LATE, OF COURSE.
YOUR STORY'S CRAZY, WEB-SLINGER, BUT THE WOMAN CORROBORATES IT. WE'LL STILL NEED A FORMAL STATEMENT--
TOMORROW.
RIGHT NOW...
...I REALLY HAVE NOTHING TO SAY.
EVENING LENGTHENS; THE UNNATURAL HEAT LINGERS.
WHILE AT THE BEDFORD TOWERS CONDOMINIUM RESIDENCE...
...DISCOMFORT AND FRUSTRATION TAKE THEIR TOLL...
TERRIFIC. FIRST, THE BUILDING'S AIR CONDITIONING GOES OUT! NOW THE PHONES ARE ON THE FRITZ!
EVERY TIME I TRY CALLING, I DON'T EVEN GET A DIAL TONE--JUST SOME KIND OF CACKLING! I'VE NEVER HEARD ANYTHING SO--
--BIZARRE?
SOMETHING ON THE BALCONY!
COMING INSIDE!

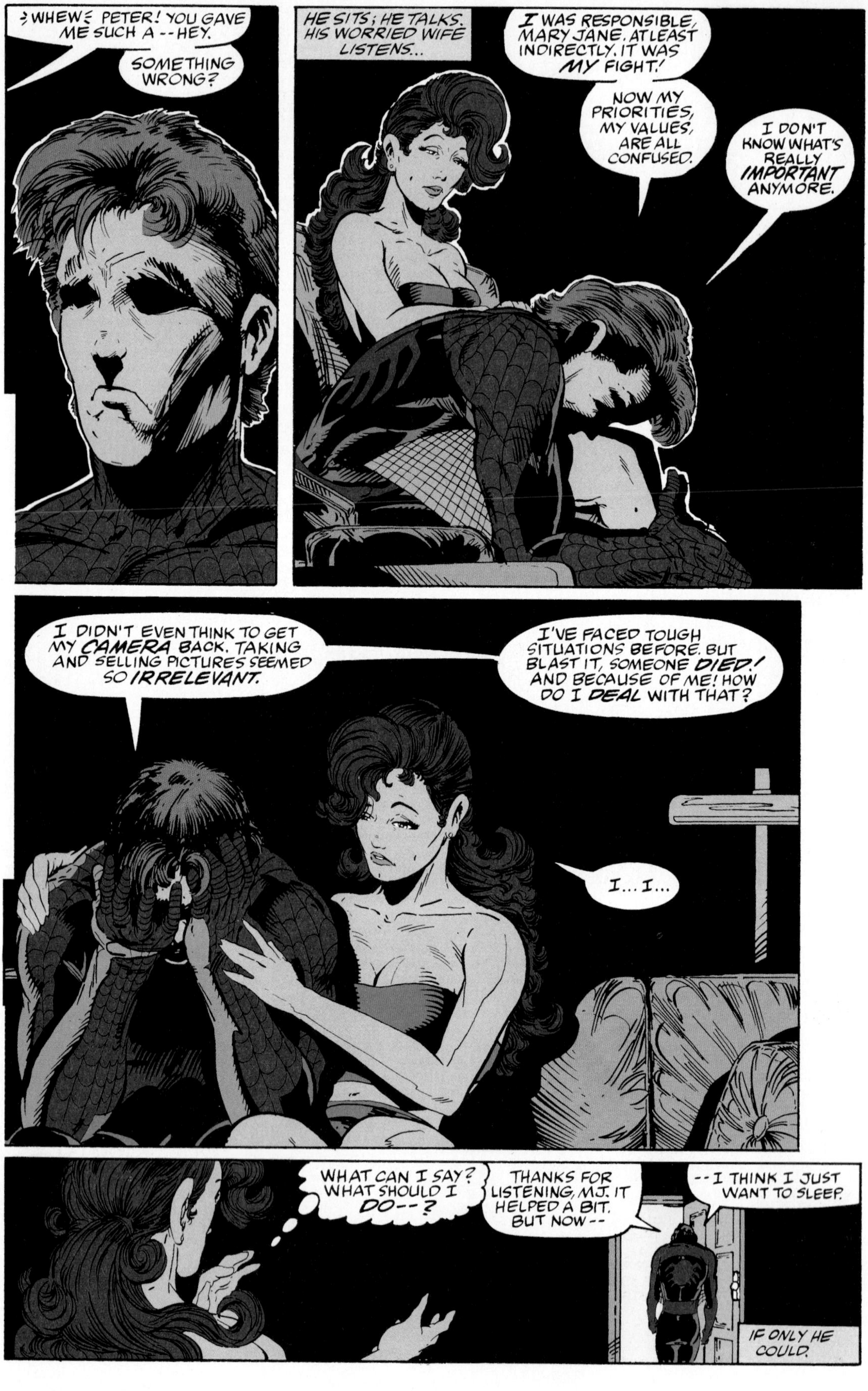

WHEW! PETER! YOU GAVE ME SUCH A --HEY.
SOMETHING WRONG?
HE SITS; HE TALKS. HIS WORRIED WIFE LISTENS...
I WAS RESPONSIBLE, MARY JANE. AT LEAST INDIRECTLY. IT WAS MY FIGHT!
NOW MY PRIORITIES, MY VALUES, ARE ALL CONFUSED.
I DON'T KNOW WHAT'S REALLY IMPORTANT ANYMORE.
I DIDN'T EVEN THINK TO GET MY CAMERA BACK. TAKING AND SELLING PICTURES SEEMED SO IRRELEVANT.
I'VE FACED TOUGH SITUATIONS BEFORE. BUT BLAST IT, SOMEONE DIED! AND BECAUSE OF ME! HOW DO I DEAL WITH THAT?
I... I...
WHAT CAN I SAY? WHAT SHOULD I DO--?
THANKS FOR LISTENING, MJ. IT HELPED A BIT. BUT NOW--
--I THINK I JUST WANT TO SLEEP.
IF ONLY HE COULD.

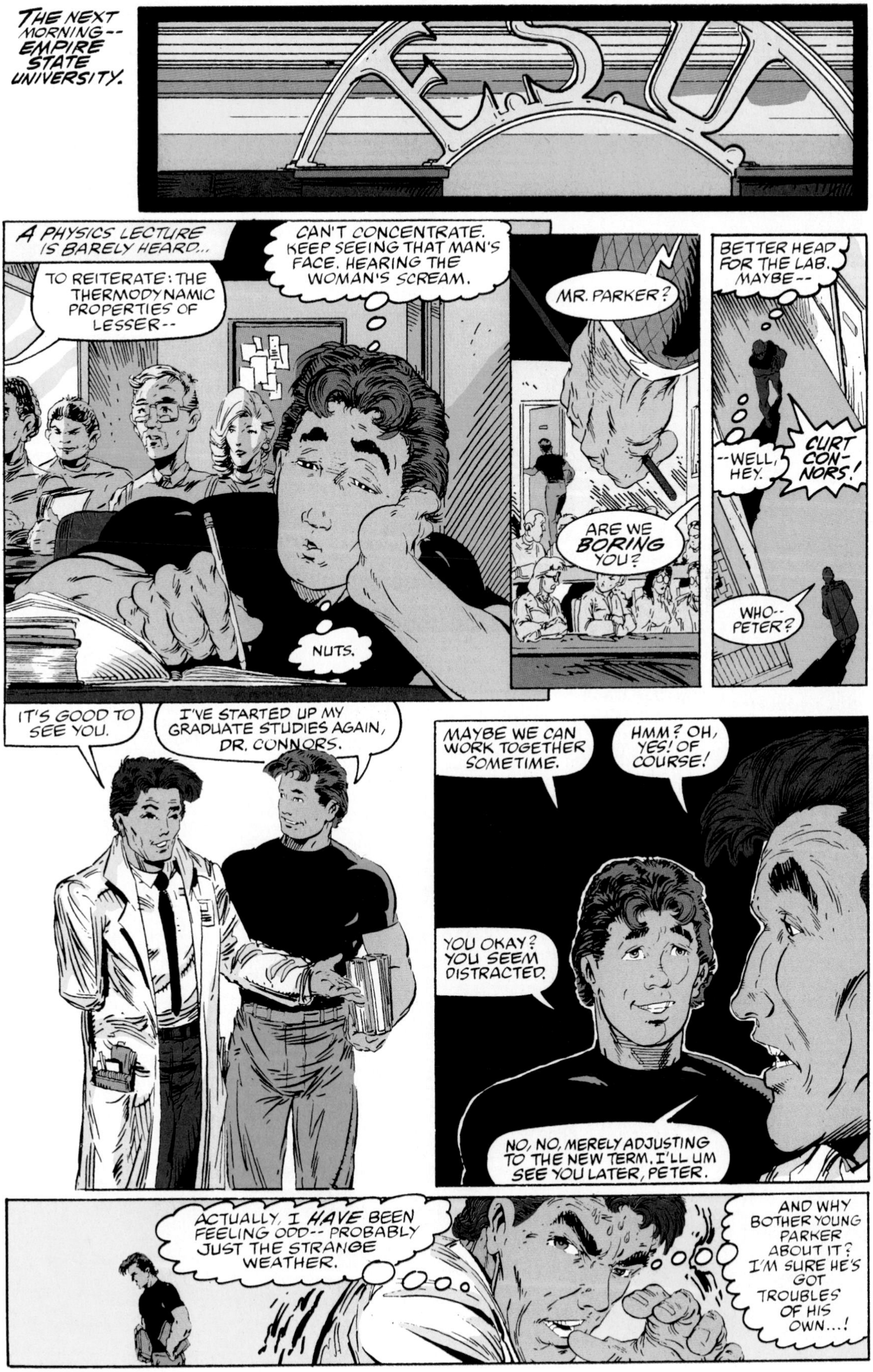
THE NEXT MORNING-- EMPIRE STATE UNIVERSITY.
E.S.U.
A PHYSICS LECTURE IS BARELY HEARD...
TO REITERATE: THE THERMODYNAMIC PROPERTIES OF LESSER--
CAN'T CONCENTRATE. KEEP SEEING THAT MAN'S FACE. HEARING THE WOMAN'S SCREAM.
NUTS.
MR. PARKER?
ARE WE BORING YOU?
BETTER HEAD FOR THE LAB. MAYBE--
--WELL, HEY.
CURT CONNORS!
WHO-- PETER?
IT'S GOOD TO SEE YOU.
I'VE STARTED UP MY GRADUATE STUDIES AGAIN, DR. CONNORS.
MAYBE WE CAN WORK TOGETHER SOMETIME.
HMM? OH, YES! OF COURSE!
YOU OKAY? YOU SEEM DISTRACTED.
NO, NO, MERELY ADJUSTING TO THE NEW TERM. I'LL UM SEE YOU LATER, PETER.
ACTUALLY, I HAVE BEEN FEELING ODD-- PROBABLY JUST THE STRANGE WEATHER.
AND WHY BOTHER YOUNG PARKER ABOUT IT? I'M SURE HE'S GOT TROUBLES OF HIS OWN...!

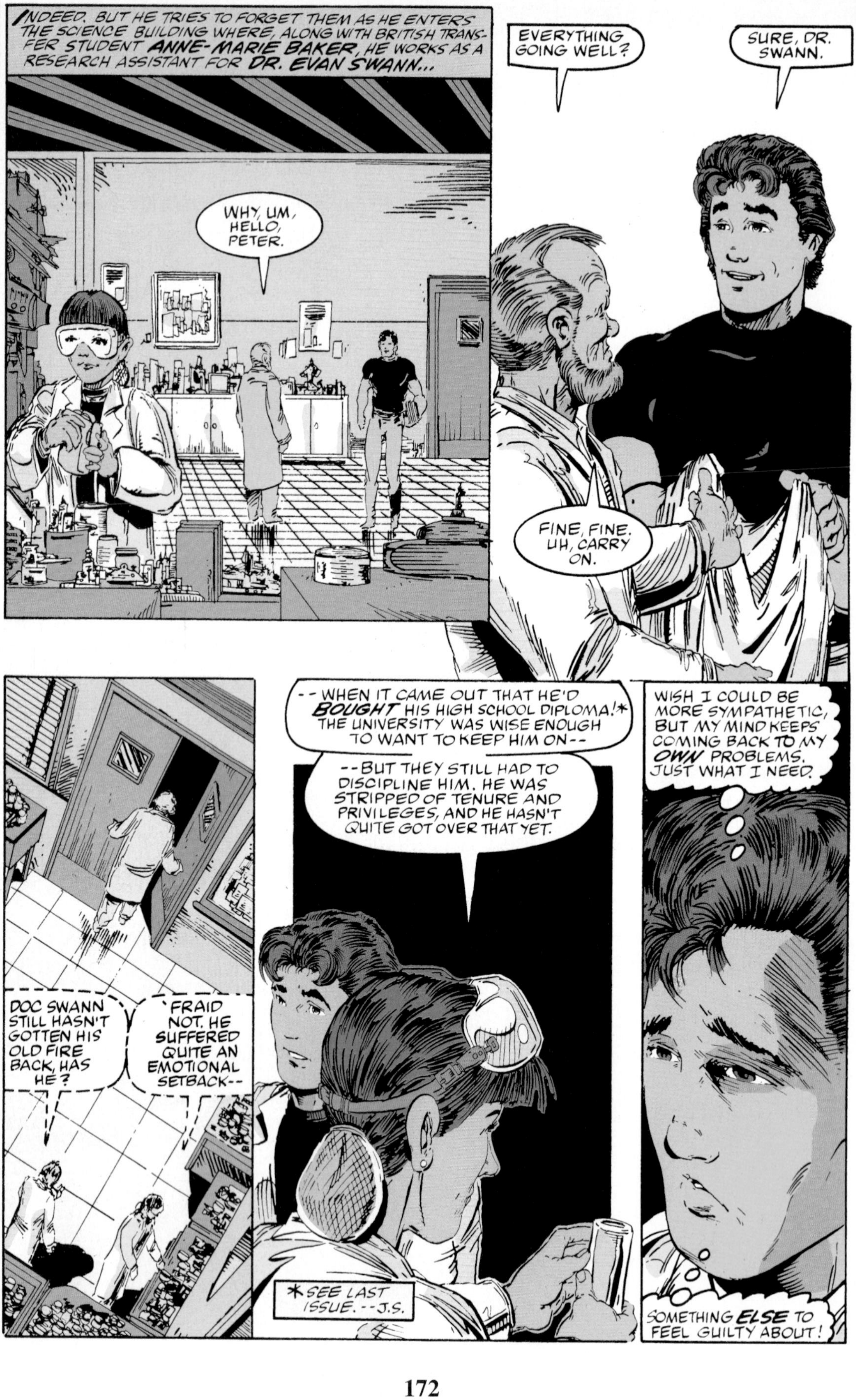
INDEED. BUT HE TRIES TO FORGET THEM AS HE ENTERS THE SCIENCE BUILDING WHERE, ALONG WITH BRITISH TRANSFER STUDENT ANNE-MARIE BAKER, HE WORKS AS A RESEARCH ASSISTANT FOR DR. EVAN SWANN...
WHY, UM, HELLO, PETER.
EVERYTHING GOING WELL?
SURE, DR. SWANN.
FINE, FINE. UH, CARRY ON.
DOC SWANN STILL HASN'T GOTTEN HIS OLD FIRE BACK, HAS HE?
'FRAID NOT. HE SUFFERED QUITE AN EMOTIONAL SETBACK--
--WHEN IT CAME OUT THAT HE'D BOUGHT HIS HIGH SCHOOL DIPLOMA!* THE UNIVERSITY WAS WISE ENOUGH TO WANT TO KEEP HIM ON--
--BUT THEY STILL HAD TO DISCIPLINE HIM. HE WAS STRIPPED OF TENURE AND PRIVILEGES, AND HE HASN'T QUITE GOT OVER THAT YET.
*SEE LAST ISSUE. --J.S.
WISH I COULD BE MORE SYMPATHETIC, BUT MY MIND KEEPS COMING BACK TO MY OWN PROBLEMS. JUST WHAT I NEED.
SOMETHING ELSE TO FEEL GUILTY ABOUT!

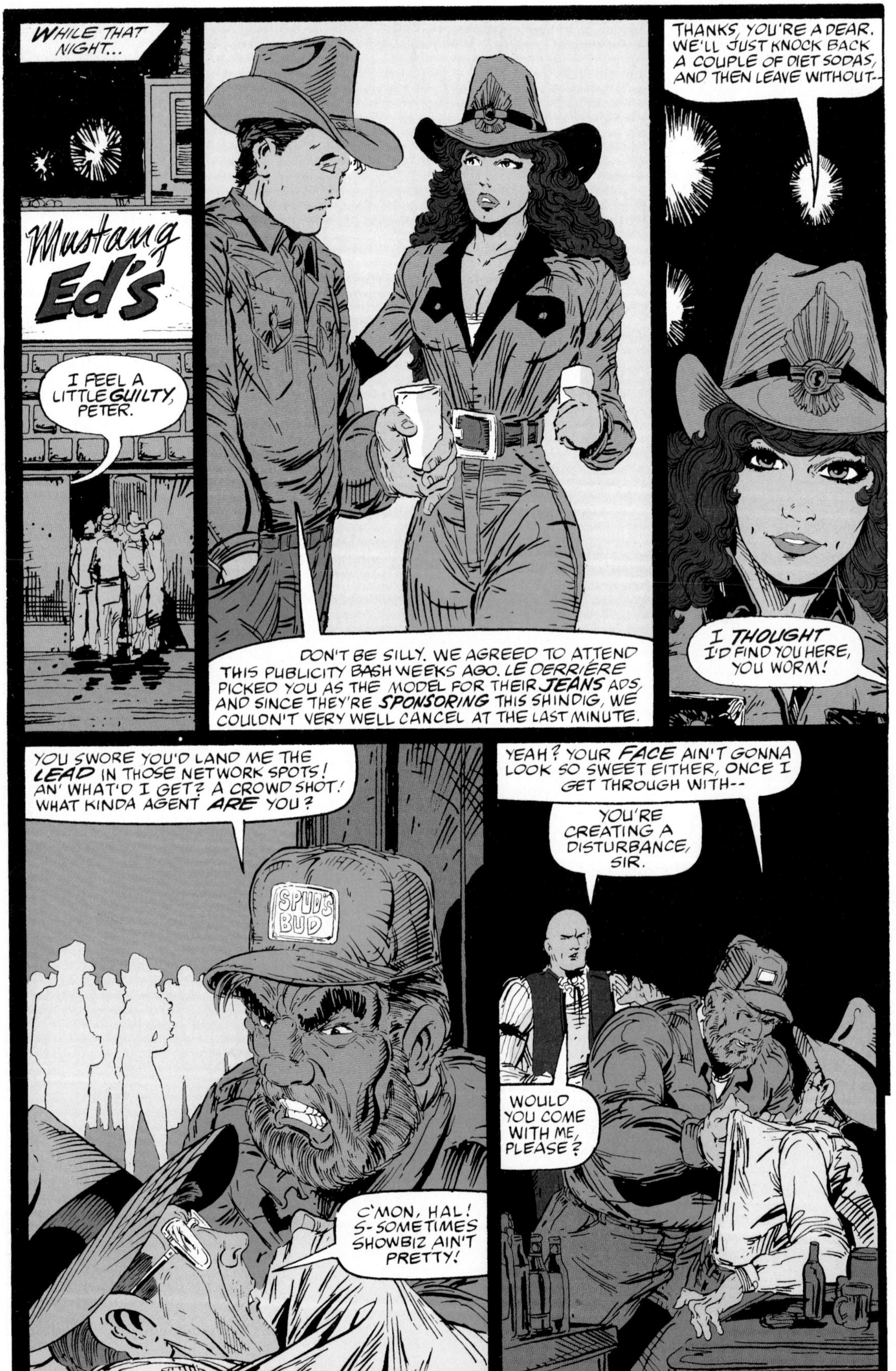
WHILE THAT NIGHT...
Mustang Ed's
I FEEL A LITTLE GUILTY, PETER.
DON'T BE SILLY. WE AGREED TO ATTEND THIS PUBLICITY BASH WEEKS AGO. LE DERRIÉRE PICKED YOU AS THE MODEL FOR THEIR JEANS ADS, AND SINCE THEY'RE SPONSORING THIS SHINDIG, WE COULDN'T VERY WELL CANCEL AT THE LAST MINUTE.
THANKS, YOU'RE A DEAR. WE'LL JUST KNOCK BACK A COUPLE OF DIET SODAS, AND THEN LEAVE WITHOUT--
I THOUGHT I'D FIND YOU HERE, YOU WORM!
YOU SWORE YOU'D LAND ME THE LEAD IN THOSE NETWORK SPOTS! AN' WHAT'D I GET? A CROWD SHOT! WHAT KINDA AGENT ARE YOU?
SPUD'S BUD
C'MON, HAL! S-SOMETIMES SHOWBIZ AIN'T PRETTY!
YEAH? YOUR FACE AIN'T GONNA LOOK SO SWEET EITHER, ONCE I GET THROUGH WITH--
YOU'RE CREATING A DISTURBANCE, SIR.
WOULD YOU COME WITH ME, PLEASE?

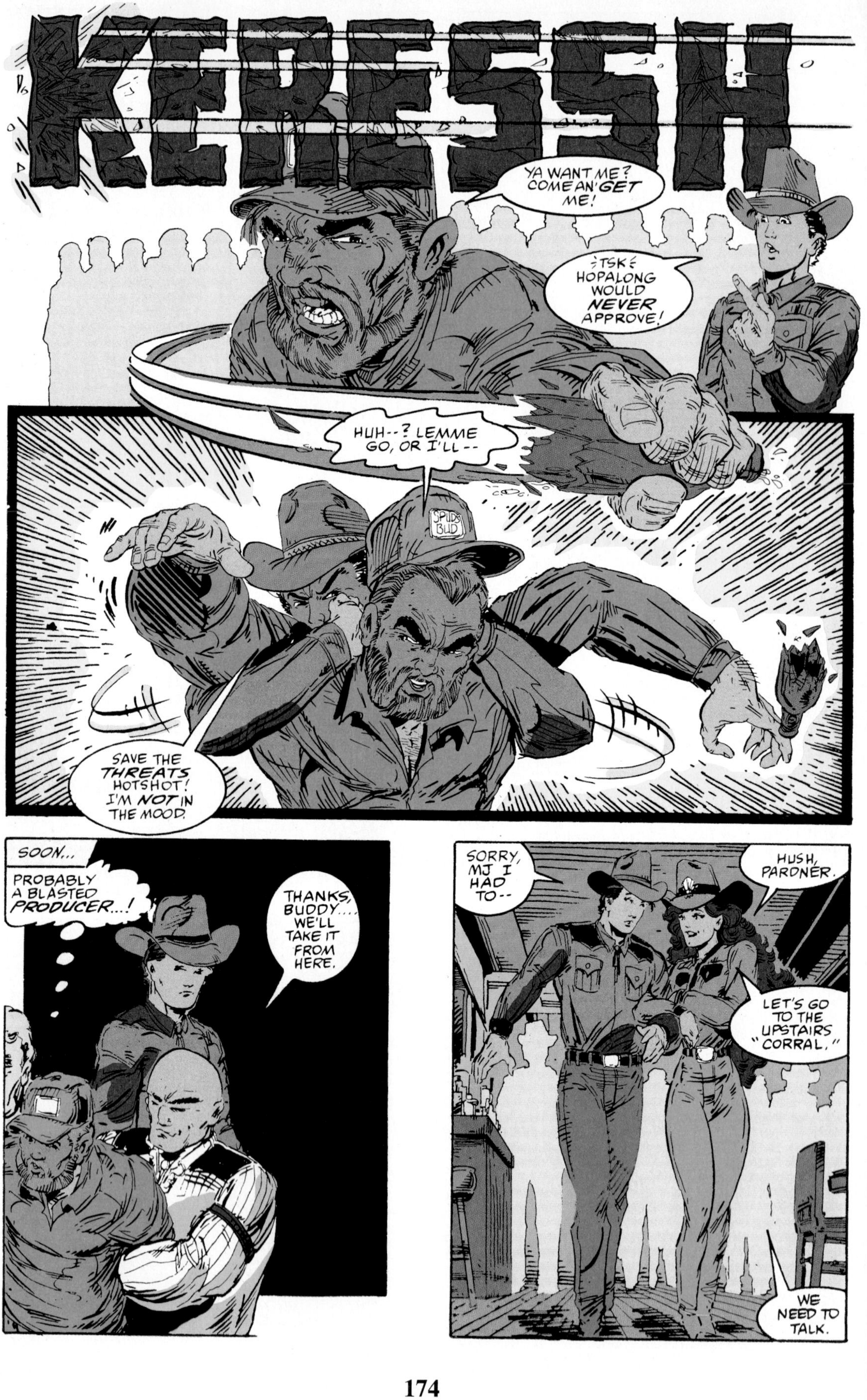
KERSSH
YA WANT ME? COME AN' GET ME!
TSK HOPALONG WOULD NEVER APPROVE!
HUH--? LEMME GO, OR I'LL--
SPUDS BUD
SAVE THE THREATS HOTSHOT! I'M NOT IN THE MOOD.
SOON...
PROBABLY A BLASTED PRODUCER...!
THANKS, BUDDY.... WE'LL TAKE IT FROM HERE.
SORRY, MJ I HAD TO--
HUSH, PARDNER.
LET'S GO TO THE UPSTAIRS "CORRAL."
WE NEED TO TALK.

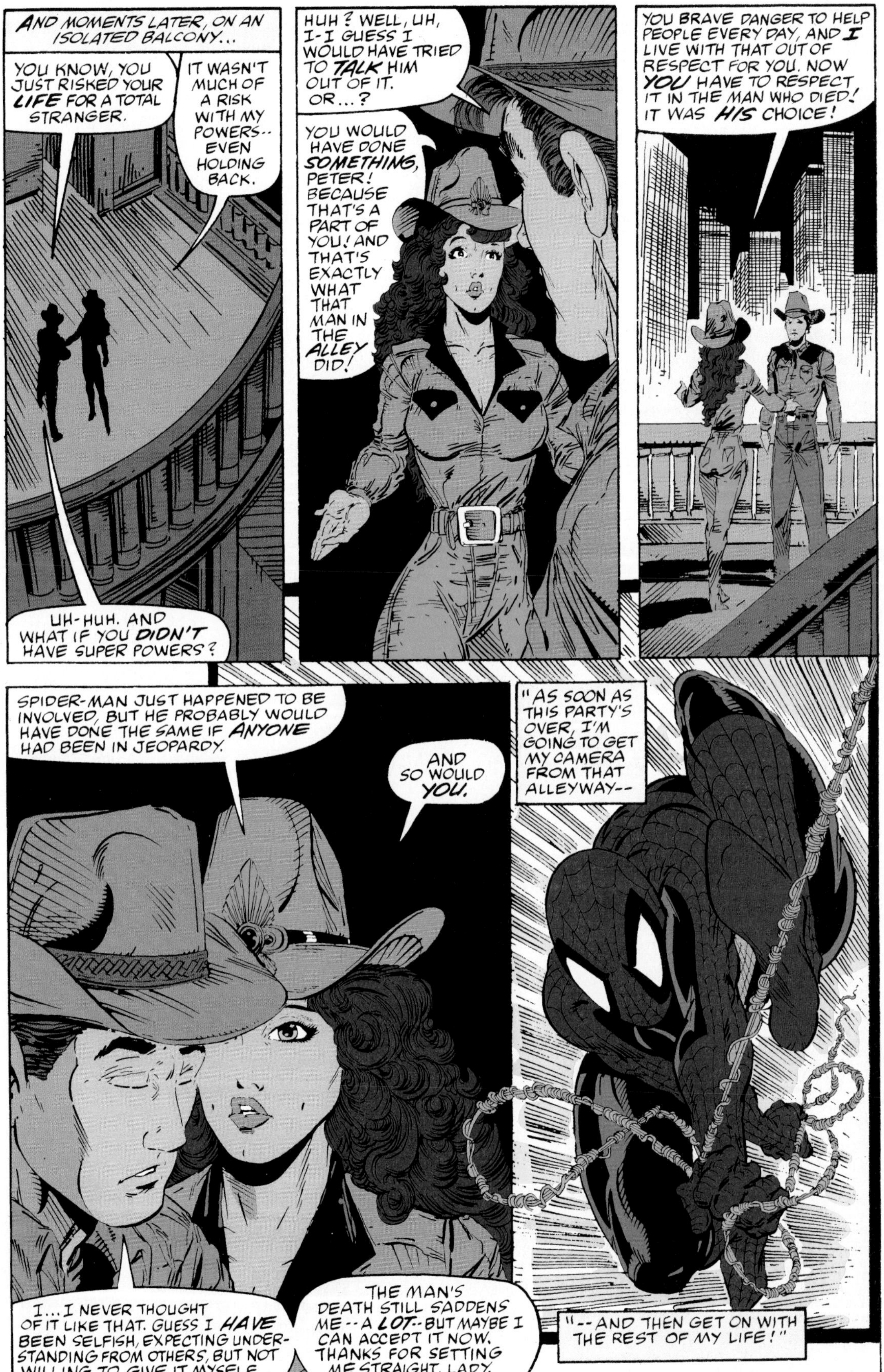
AND MOMENTS LATER, ON AN ISOLATED BALCONY...
YOU KNOW, YOU JUST RISKED YOUR LIFE FOR A TOTAL STRANGER.
IT WASN'T MUCH OF A RISK WITH MY POWERS.. EVEN HOLDING BACK.
UH-HUH. AND WHAT IF YOU DIDN'T HAVE SUPER POWERS?
HUH? WELL, UH, I-I GUESS I WOULD HAVE TRIED TO TALK HIM OUT OF IT. OR...?
YOU WOULD HAVE DONE SOMETHING, PETER! BECAUSE THAT'S A PART OF YOU! AND THAT'S EXACTLY WHAT THAT MAN IN THE ALLEY DID!
YOU BRAVE DANGER TO HELP PEOPLE EVERY DAY, AND I LIVE WITH THAT OUT OF RESPECT FOR YOU. NOW YOU HAVE TO RESPECT IT IN THE MAN WHO DIED! IT WAS HIS CHOICE!
SPIDER-MAN JUST HAPPENED TO BE INVOLVED, BUT HE PROBABLY WOULD HAVE DONE THE SAME IF ANYONE HAD BEEN IN JEOPARDY.
AND SO WOULD YOU.
I... I NEVER THOUGHT OF IT LIKE THAT. GUESS I HAVE BEEN SELFISH, EXPECTING UNDER-STANDING FROM OTHERS, BUT NOT WILLING TO GIVE IT MYSELF.
THE MAN'S DEATH STILL SADDENS ME -- A LOT-- BUT MAYBE I CAN ACCEPT IT NOW. THANKS FOR SETTING ME STRAIGHT, LADY.
"AS SOON AS THIS PARTY'S OVER, I'M GOING TO GET MY CAMERA FROM THAT ALLEYWAY--
"-- AND THEN GET ON WITH THE REST OF MY LIFE!"

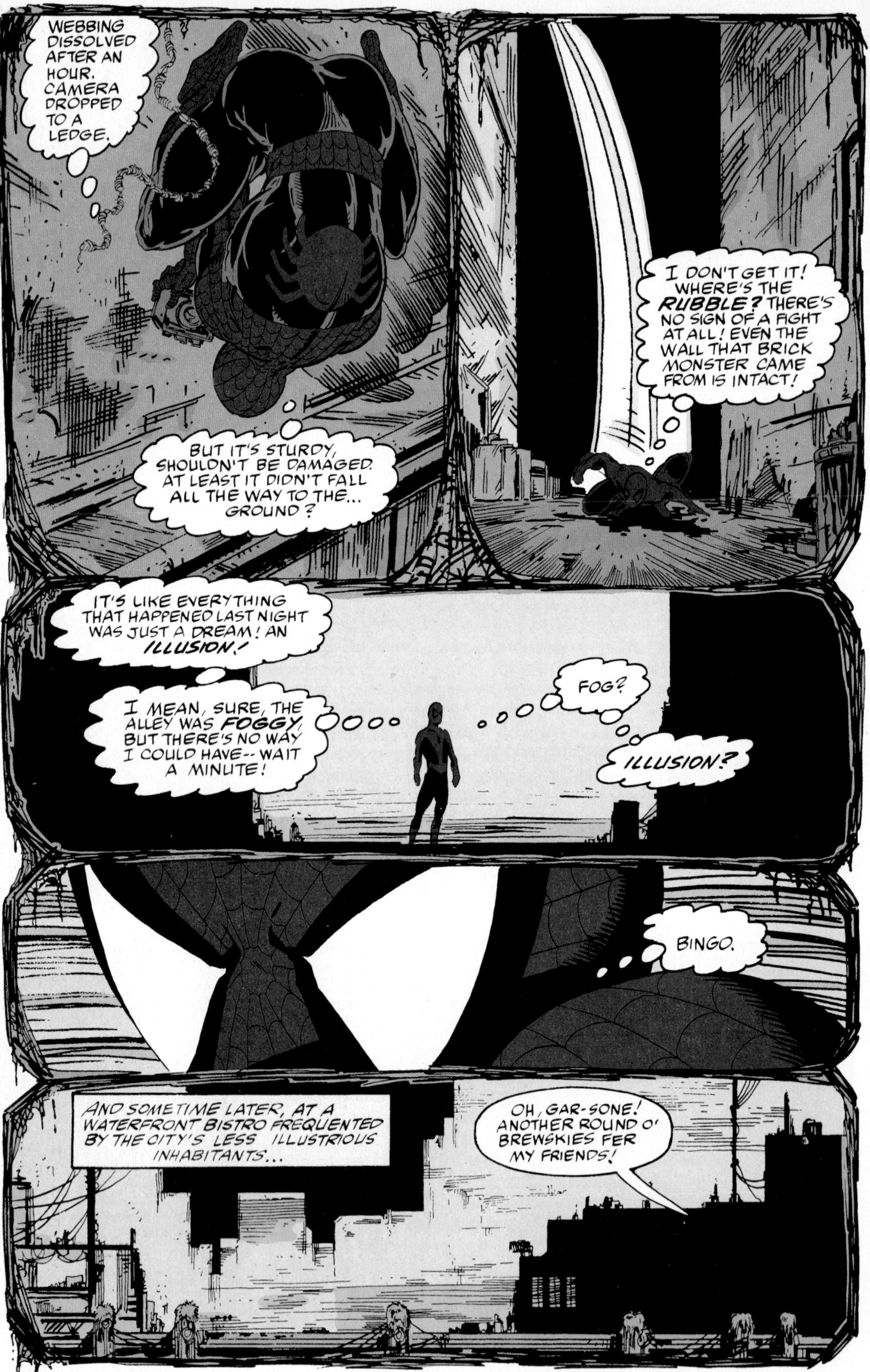
WEBBING DISSOLVED AFTER AN HOUR. CAMERA DROPPED TO A LEDGE.
BUT IT'S STURDY, SHOULDN'T BE DAMAGED. AT LEAST IT DIDN'T FALL ALL THE WAY TO THE... GROUND?
I DON'T GET IT! WHERE'S THE RUBBLE? THERE'S NO SIGN OF A FIGHT AT ALL! EVEN THE WALL THAT BRICK MONSTER CAME FROM IS INTACT!
IT'S LIKE EVERYTHING THAT HAPPENED LAST NIGHT WAS JUST A DREAM! AN ILLUSION!
I MEAN, SURE, THE ALLEY WAS FOGGY, BUT THERE'S NO WAY I COULD HAVE-- WAIT A MINUTE!
FOG?
ILLUSION?
BINGO.
AND SOMETIME LATER, AT A WATERFRONT BISTRO FREQUENTED BY THE CITY'S LESS ILLUSTRIOUS INHABITANTS...
OH, GAR-SONE! ANOTHER ROUND O' BREWSKIES FER MY FRIENDS!

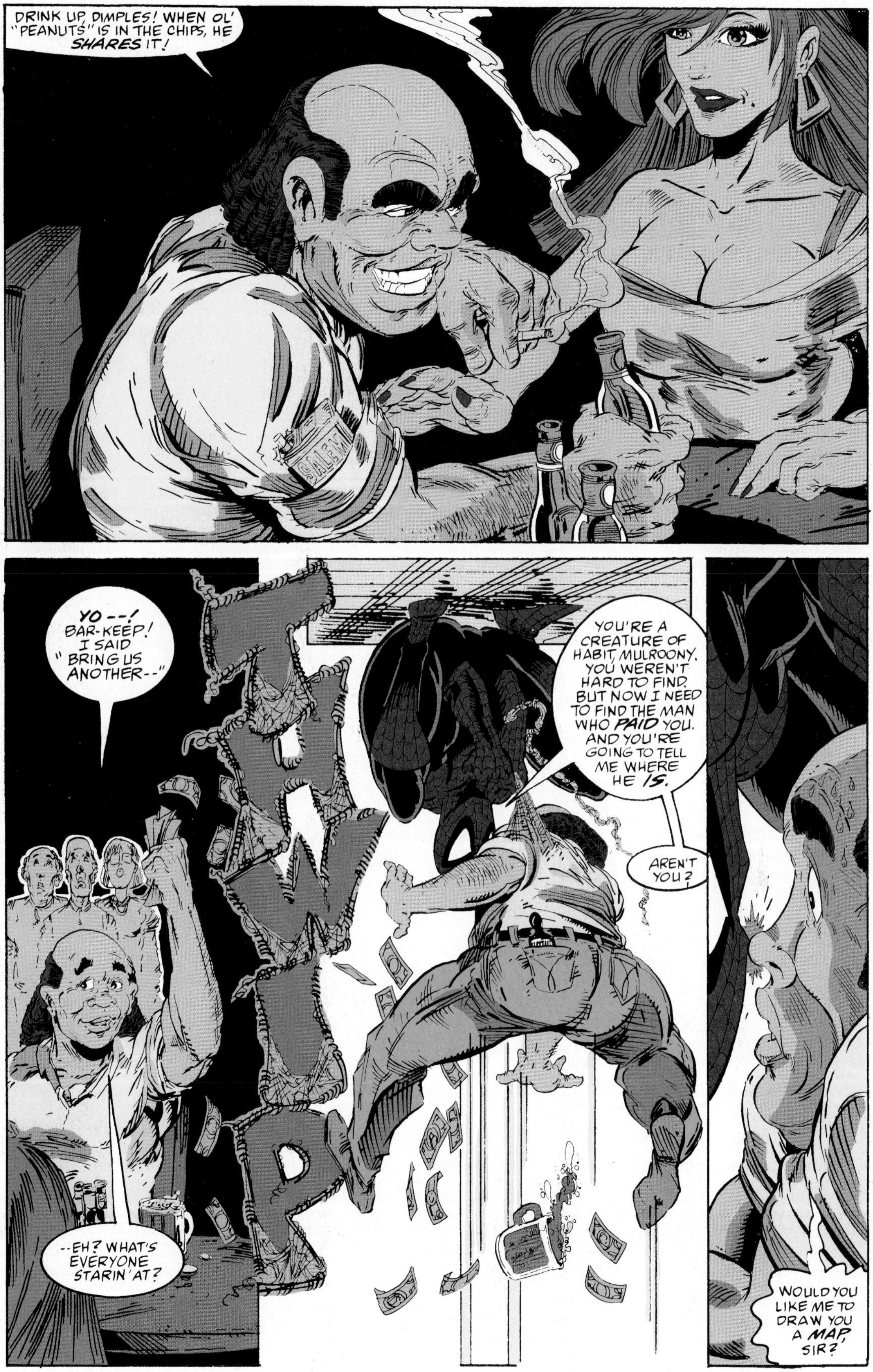
DRINK UP, DIMPLES! WHEN OL' "PEANUTS" IS IN THE CHIPS, HE SHARES IT!
YO--! BAR-KEEP! I SAID "BRING US ANOTHER--"
--EH? WHAT'S EVERYONE STARIN' AT?
YOU'RE A CREATURE OF HABIT, MULROONY. YOU WEREN'T HARD TO FIND. BUT NOW I NEED TO FIND THE MAN WHO PAID YOU. AND YOU'RE GOING TO TELL ME WHERE HE IS.
AREN'T YOU?
WOULD YOU LIKE ME TO DRAW YOU A MAP, SIR?

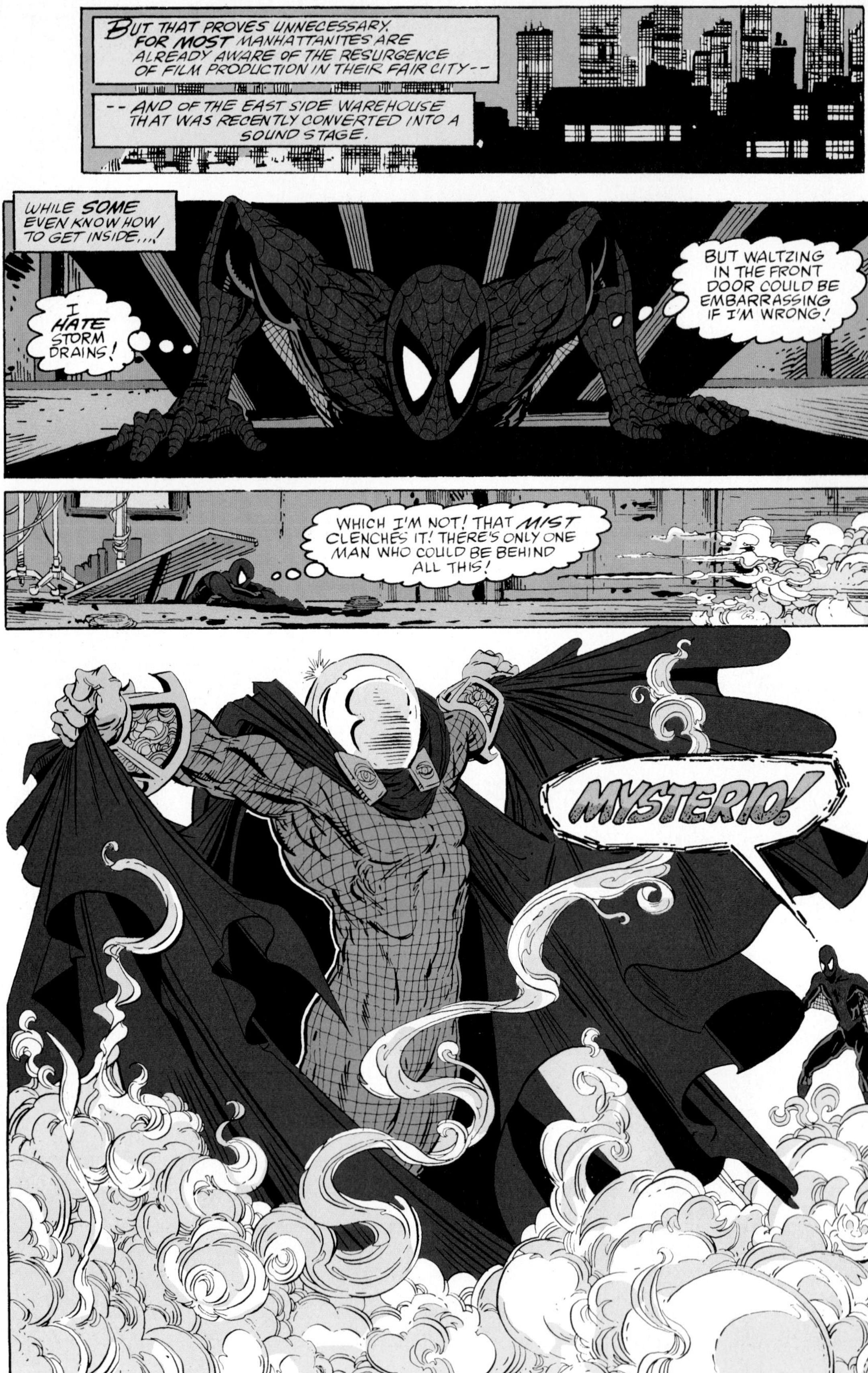
BUT THAT PROVES UNNECESSARY. FOR MOST MANHATTANITES ARE ALREADY AWARE OF THE RESURGENCE OF FILM PRODUCTION IN THEIR FAIR CITY--
-- AND OF THE EAST SIDE WAREHOUSE THAT WAS RECENTLY CONVERTED INTO A SOUND STAGE.
WHILE SOME EVEN KNOW HOW TO GET INSIDE...!
I HATE STORM DRAINS!
BUT WALTZING IN THE FRONT DOOR COULD BE EMBARRASSING IF I'M WRONG!
WHICH I'M NOT! THAT MIST CLENCHES IT! THERE'S ONLY ONE MAN WHO COULD BE BEHIND ALL THIS!
MYSTERIO!

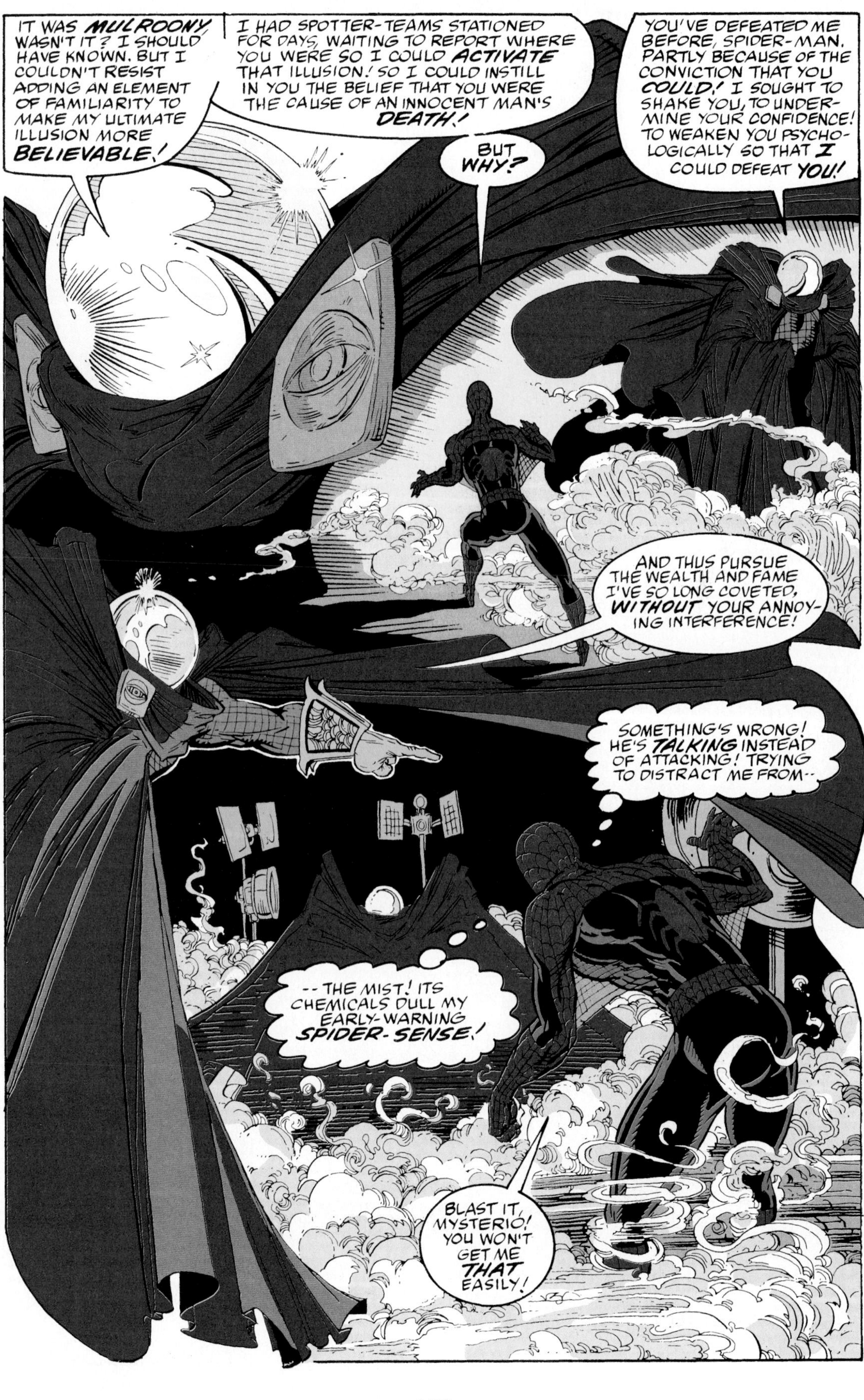

IT WAS MULROONY, WASN'T IT? I SHOULD HAVE KNOWN. BUT I COULDN'T RESIST ADDING AN ELEMENT OF FAMILIARITY TO MAKE MY ULTIMATE ILLUSION MORE BELIEVABLE!
I HAD SPOTTER-TEAMS STATIONED FOR DAYS, WAITING TO REPORT WHERE YOU WERE SO I COULD ACTIVATE THAT ILLUSION! SO I COULD INSTILL IN YOU THE BELIEF THAT YOU WERE THE CAUSE OF AN INNOCENT MAN'S DEATH!
BUT WHY?
YOU'VE DEFEATED ME BEFORE, SPIDER-MAN, PARTLY BECAUSE OF THE CONVICTION THAT YOU COULD! I SOUGHT TO SHAKE YOU, TO UNDERMINE YOUR CONFIDENCE! TO WEAKEN YOU PSYCHOLOGICALLY SO THAT I COULD DEFEAT YOU!
AND THUS PURSUE THE WEALTH AND FAME I'VE SO LONG COVETED, WITHOUT YOUR ANNOYING INTERFERENCE!
SOMETHING'S WRONG! HE'S TALKING INSTEAD OF ATTACKING! TRYING TO DISTRACT ME FROM--
--THE MIST! ITS CHEMICALS DULL MY EARLY-WARNING SPIDER-SENSE!
BLAST IT, MYSTERIO! YOU WON'T GET ME THAT EASILY!

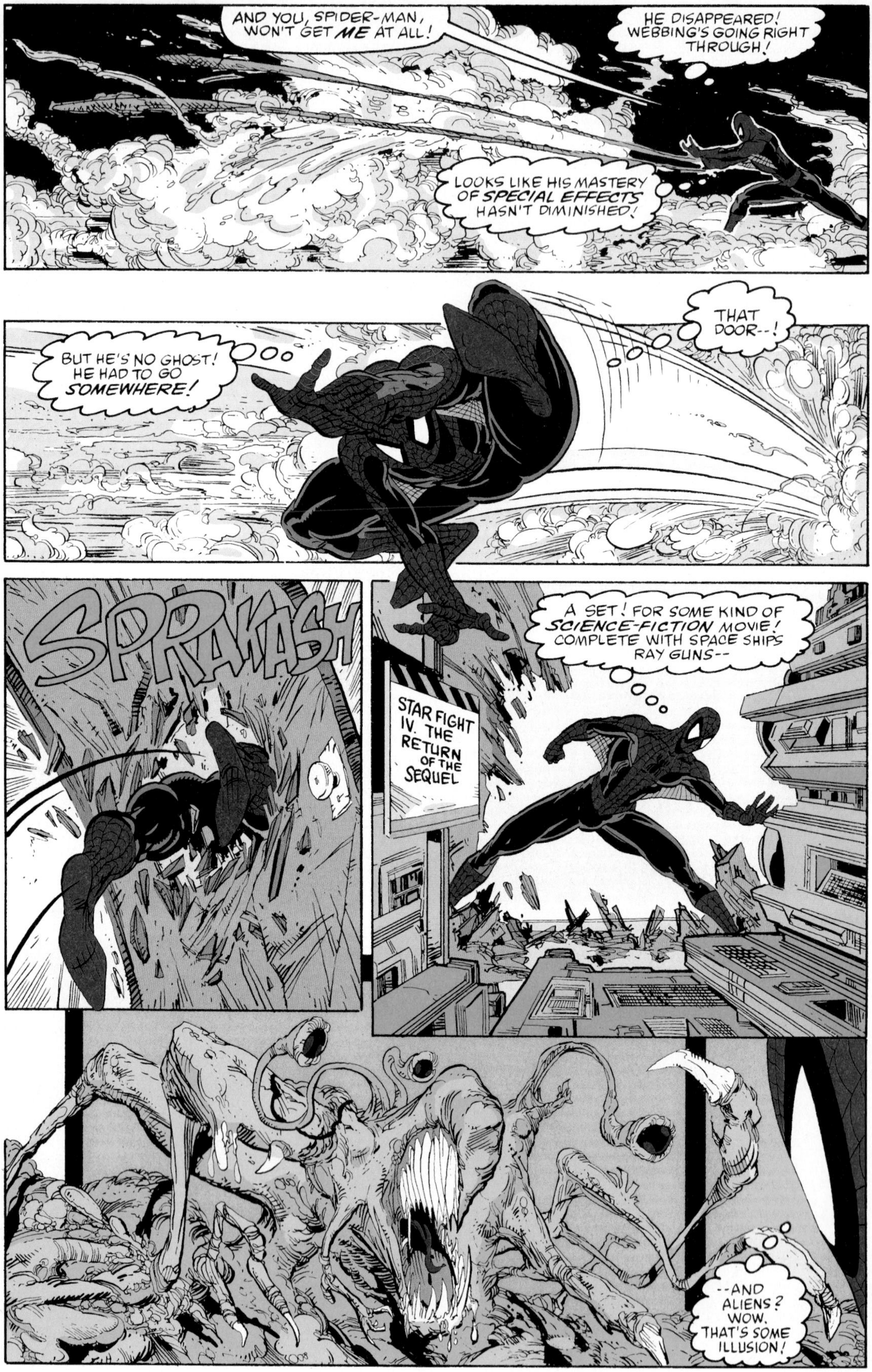
AND YOU, SPIDER-MAN, WON'T GET ME AT ALL!
HE DISAPPEARED! WEBBING'S GOING RIGHT THROUGH!
LOOKS LIKE HIS MASTERY OF SPECIAL EFFECTS HASN'T DIMINISHED!
BUT HE'S NO GHOST! HE HAD TO GO SOMEWHERE!
THAT DOOR--!
SPRAKASH
A SET! FOR SOME KIND OF SCIENCE-FICTION MOVIE! COMPLETE WITH SPACE SHIPS RAY GUNS--
STAR FIGHT IV. THE RETURN OF THE SEQUEL
--AND ALIENS? WOW. THAT'S SOME ILLUSION!

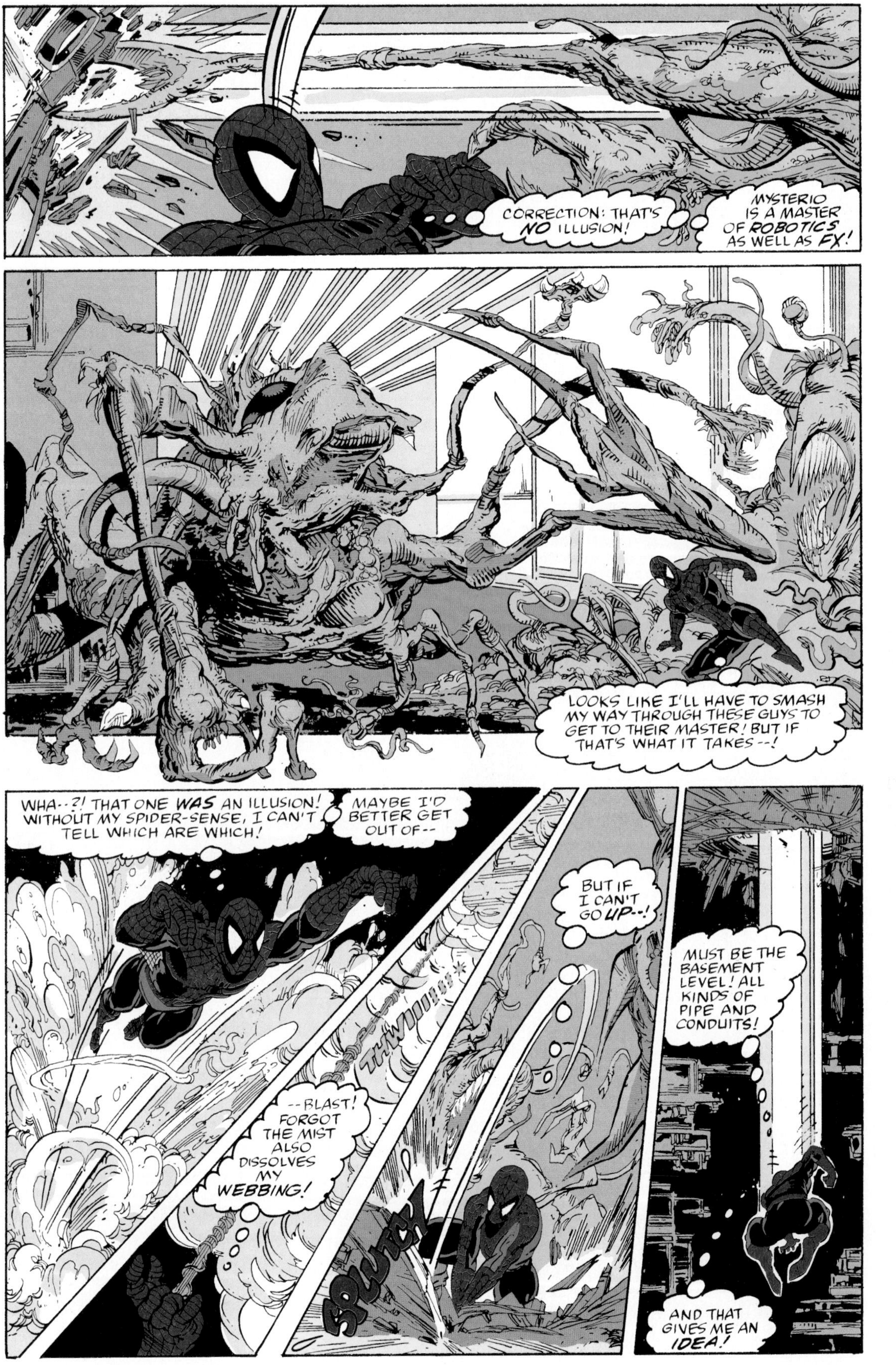
CORRECTION: THAT'S NO ILLUSION!
MYSTERIO IS A MASTER OF ROBOTICS AS WELL AS FX!
LOOKS LIKE I'LL HAVE TO SMASH MY WAY THROUGH THESE GUYS TO GET TO THEIR MASTER! BUT IF THAT'S WHAT IT TAKES--!
WHA--?! THAT ONE WAS AN ILLUSION! WITHOUT MY SPIDER-SENSE, I CAN'T TELL WHICH ARE WHICH!
MAYBE I'D BETTER GET OUT OF--
THWIIIIIIII*
--BLAST! FORGOT THE MIST ALSO DISSOLVES MY WEBBING!
SPLUTCH
BUT IF I CAN'T GO UP--!
MUST BE THE BASEMENT LEVEL! ALL KINDS OF PIPE AND CONDUITS!
AND THAT GIVES ME AN IDEA!

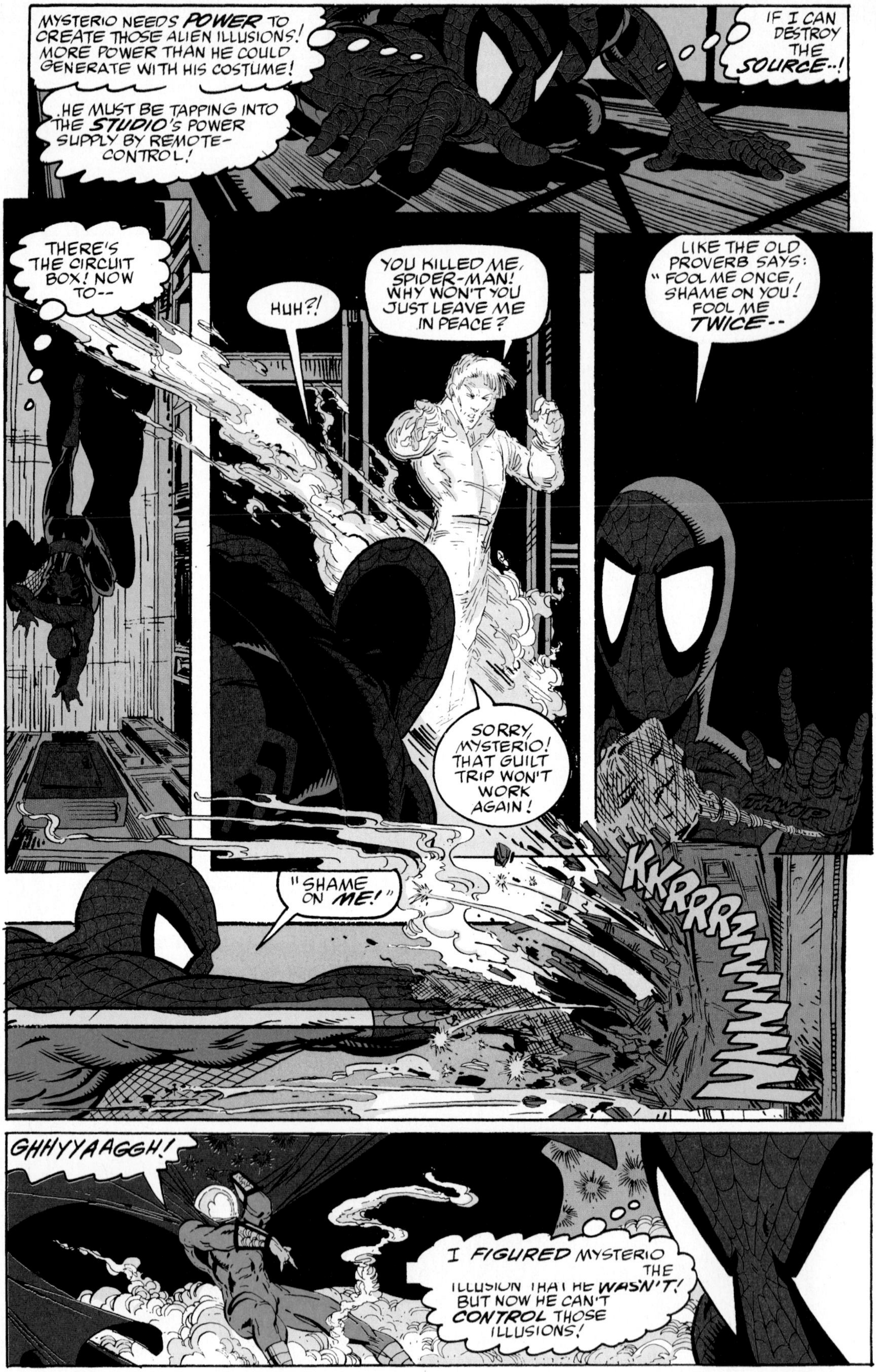
MYSTERIO NEEDS POWER TO CREATE THOSE ALIEN ILLUSIONS! MORE POWER THAN HE COULD GENERATE WITH HIS COSTUME!
.HE MUST BE TAPPING INTO THE STUDIO'S POWER SUPPLY BY REMOTE-CONTROL!
IF I CAN DESTROY THE SOURCE..!
THERE'S THE CIRCUIT BOX! NOW TO--
HUH?!
YOU KILLED ME, SPIDER-MAN! WHY WON'T YOU JUST LEAVE ME IN PEACE?
SORRY, MYSTERIO! THAT GUILT TRIP WON'T WORK AGAIN!
LIKE THE OLD PROVERB SAYS: "FOOL ME ONCE, SHAME ON YOU! FOOL ME TWICE--
THWIP
"SHAME ON ME!"
KKRRRRWWWWW
GHHYYAAGGH!
I FIGURED MYSTERIO
THE
ILLUSION THAT HE WASN'T! BUT NOW HE CAN'T CONTROL THOSE ILLUSIONS!

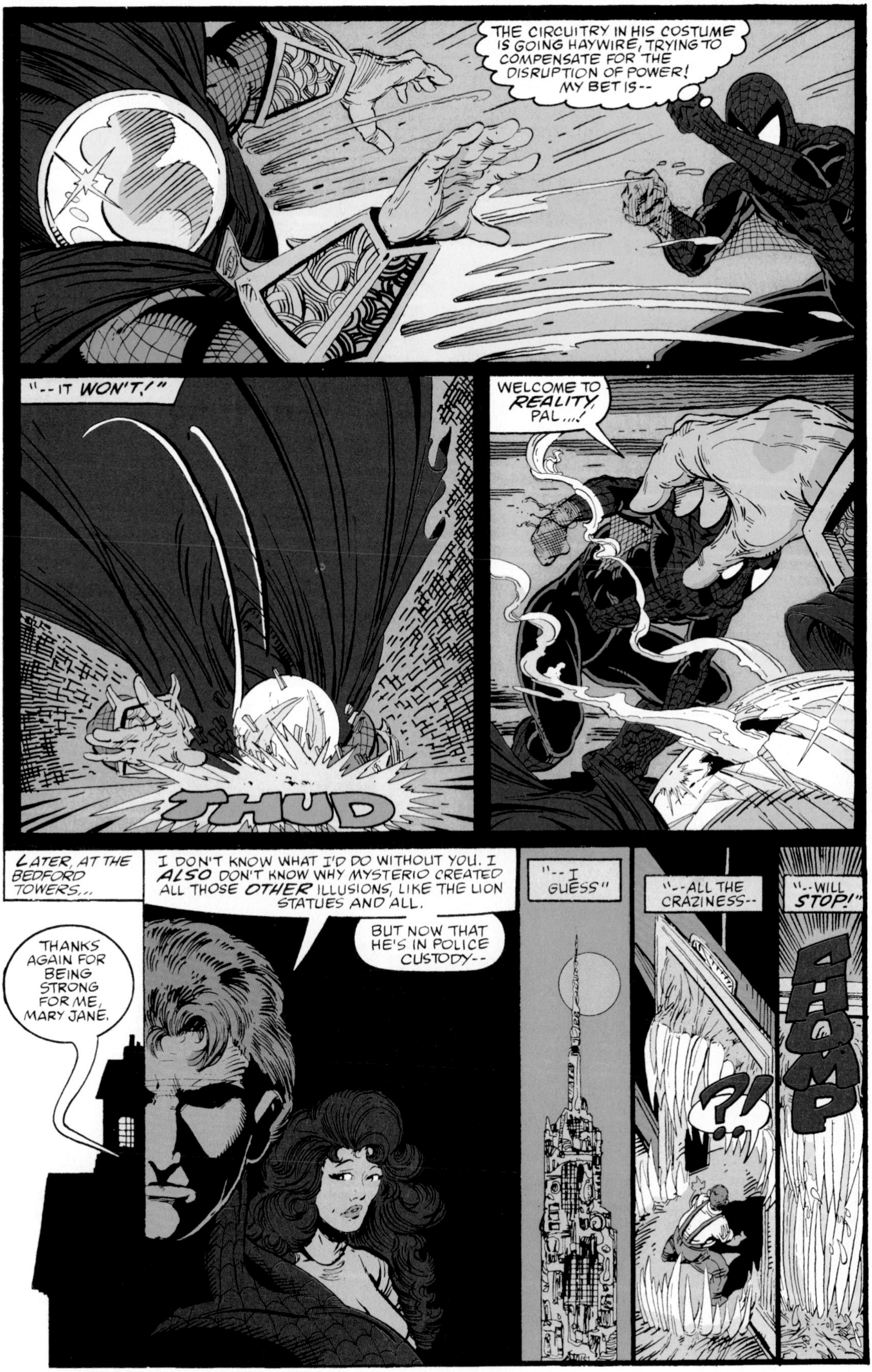
THE CIRCUITRY IN HIS COSTUME IS GOING HAYWIRE, TRYING TO COMPENSATE FOR THE DISRUPTION OF POWER! MY BET IS--
"--IT WON'T!"
THUD
WELCOME TO REALITY, PAL...!
LATER, AT THE BEDFORD TOWERS...
THANKS AGAIN FOR BEING STRONG FOR ME, MARY JANE.
I DON'T KNOW WHAT I'D DO WITHOUT YOU. I ALSO DON'T KNOW WHY MYSTERIO CREATED ALL THOSE OTHER ILLUSIONS, LIKE THE LION STATUES AND ALL.
BUT NOW THAT HE'S IN POLICE CUSTODY--
"--I GUESS"
"--ALL THE CRAZINESS--
?!
"--WILL STOP!"
CHOMP

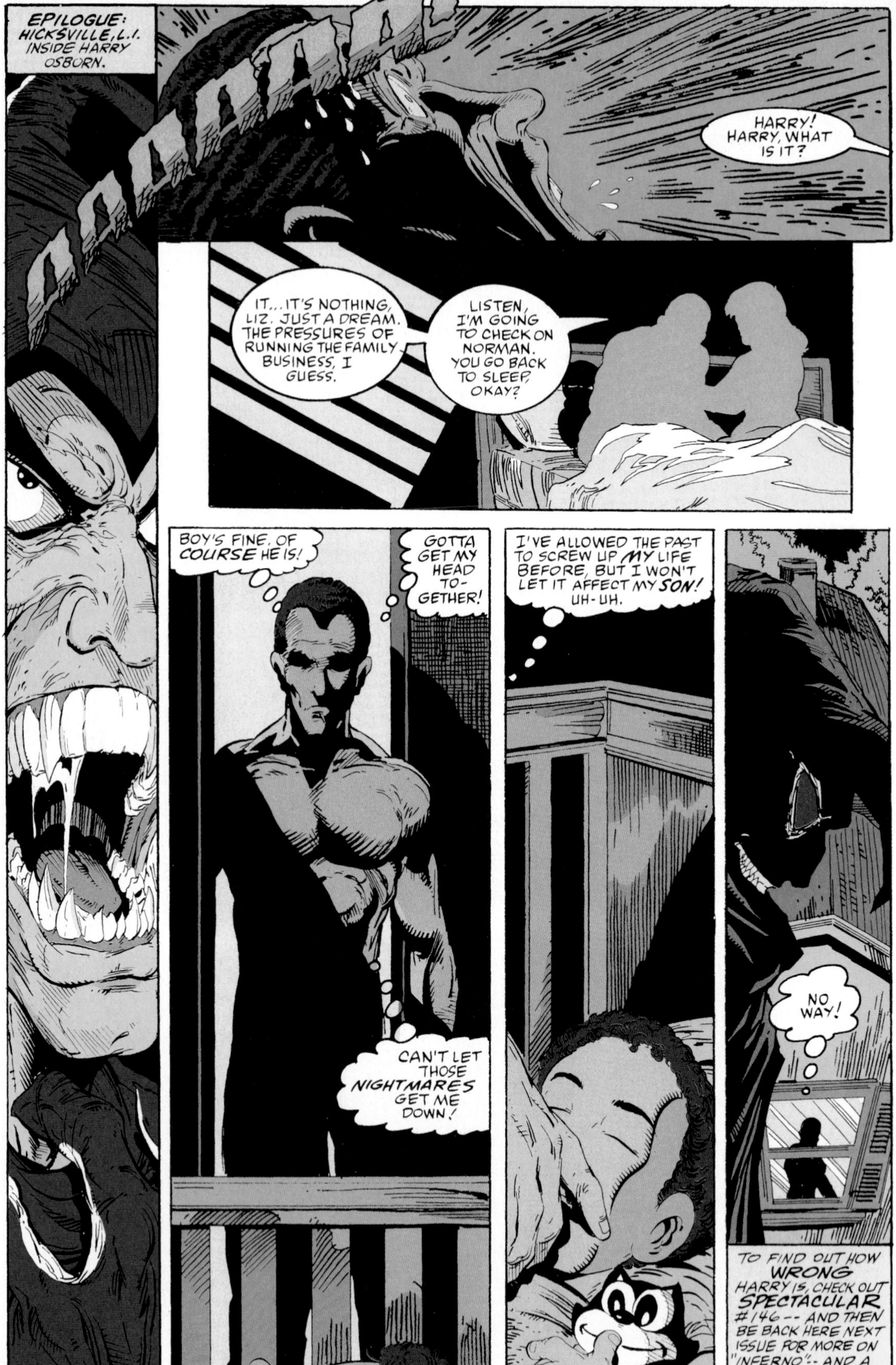
EPILOGUE: HICKSVILLE, L.I. INSIDE HARRY OSBORN.
HARRY! HARRY, WHAT IS IT?
IT... IT'S NOTHING, LIZ. JUST A DREAM. THE PRESSURES OF RUNNING THE FAMILY BUSINESS, I GUESS.
LISTEN, I'M GOING TO CHECK ON NORMAN. YOU GO BACK TO SLEEP, OKAY?
BOY'S FINE. OF COURSE HE IS!
GOTTA GET MY HEAD TO-GETHER!
CAN'T LET THOSE NIGHTMARES GET ME DOWN!
I'VE ALLOWED THE PAST TO SCREW UP MY LIFE BEFORE, BUT I WON'T LET IT AFFECT MY SON! UH-UH.
NO WAY!
TO FIND OUT HOW WRONG HARRY IS, CHECK OUT SPECTACULAR #146 -- AND THEN BE BACK HERE NEXT ISSUE FOR MORE ON "INFERNO"-- AND A FIGHT YOU NEVER THOUGHT YOU'D SEE!

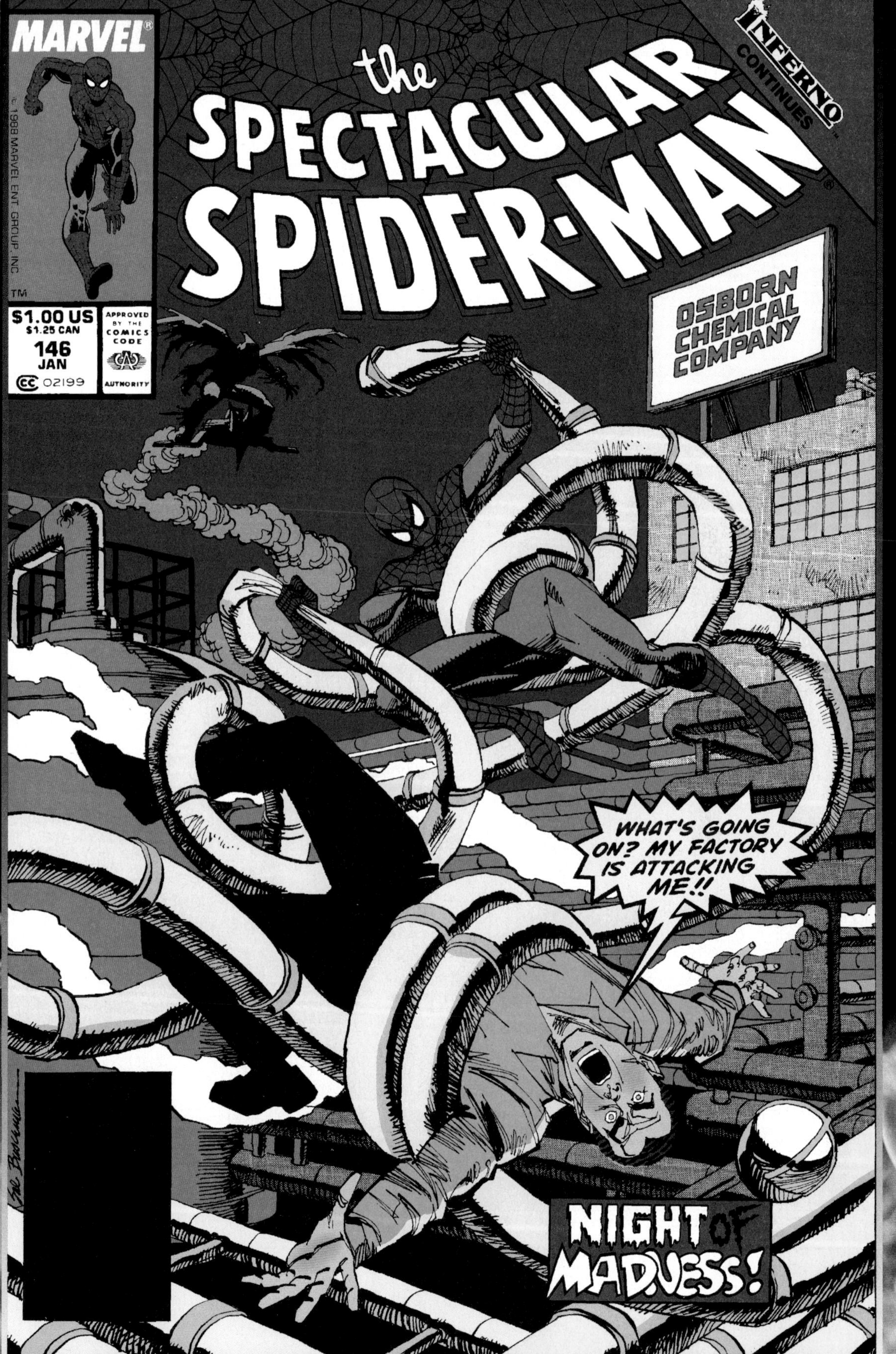
MARVEL
the SPECTACULAR SPIDER-MAN
INFERNO CONTINUES
© 1988 MARVEL ENT. GROUP, INC.
TM
$1.00 US
$1.25 CAN
146
JAN
APPROVED BY THE COMICS CODE AUTHORITY
CC 02199
OSBORN CHEMICAL COMPANY
WHAT'S GOING ON? MY FACTORY IS ATTACKING ME!!
NIGHT OF MADNESS!

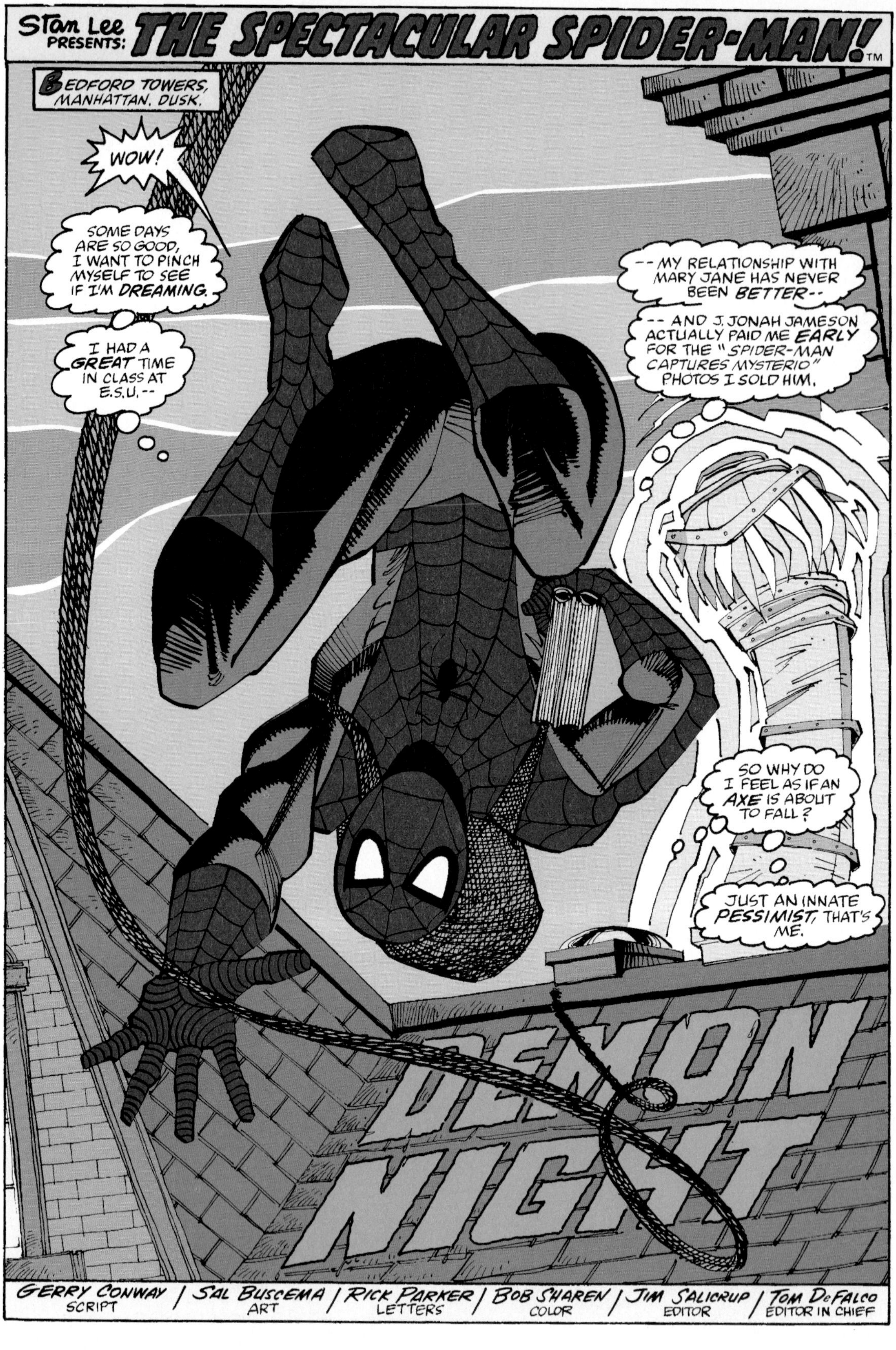
Stan Lee PRESENTS: THE SPECTACULAR SPIDER-MAN! TM
BEDFORD TOWERS, MANHATTAN, DUSK.
WOW!
SOME DAYS ARE SO GOOD, I WANT TO PINCH MYSELF TO SEE IF I'M DREAMING.
I HAD A GREAT TIME IN CLASS AT E.S.U.--
--MY RELATIONSHIP WITH MARY JANE HAS NEVER BEEN BETTER--
--AND J. JONAH JAMESON ACTUALLY PAID ME EARLY FOR THE "SPIDER-MAN CAPTURES MYSTERIO" PHOTOS I SOLD HIM.
SO WHY DO I FEEL AS IF AN AXE IS ABOUT TO FALL?
JUST AN INNATE PESSIMIST, THAT'S ME.
DEMON NIGHT
GERRY CONWAY SCRIPT / SAL BUSCEMA ART / RICK PARKER LETTERS / BOB SHAREN COLOR / JIM SALICRUP EDITOR / TOM DeFALCO EDITOR IN CHIEF

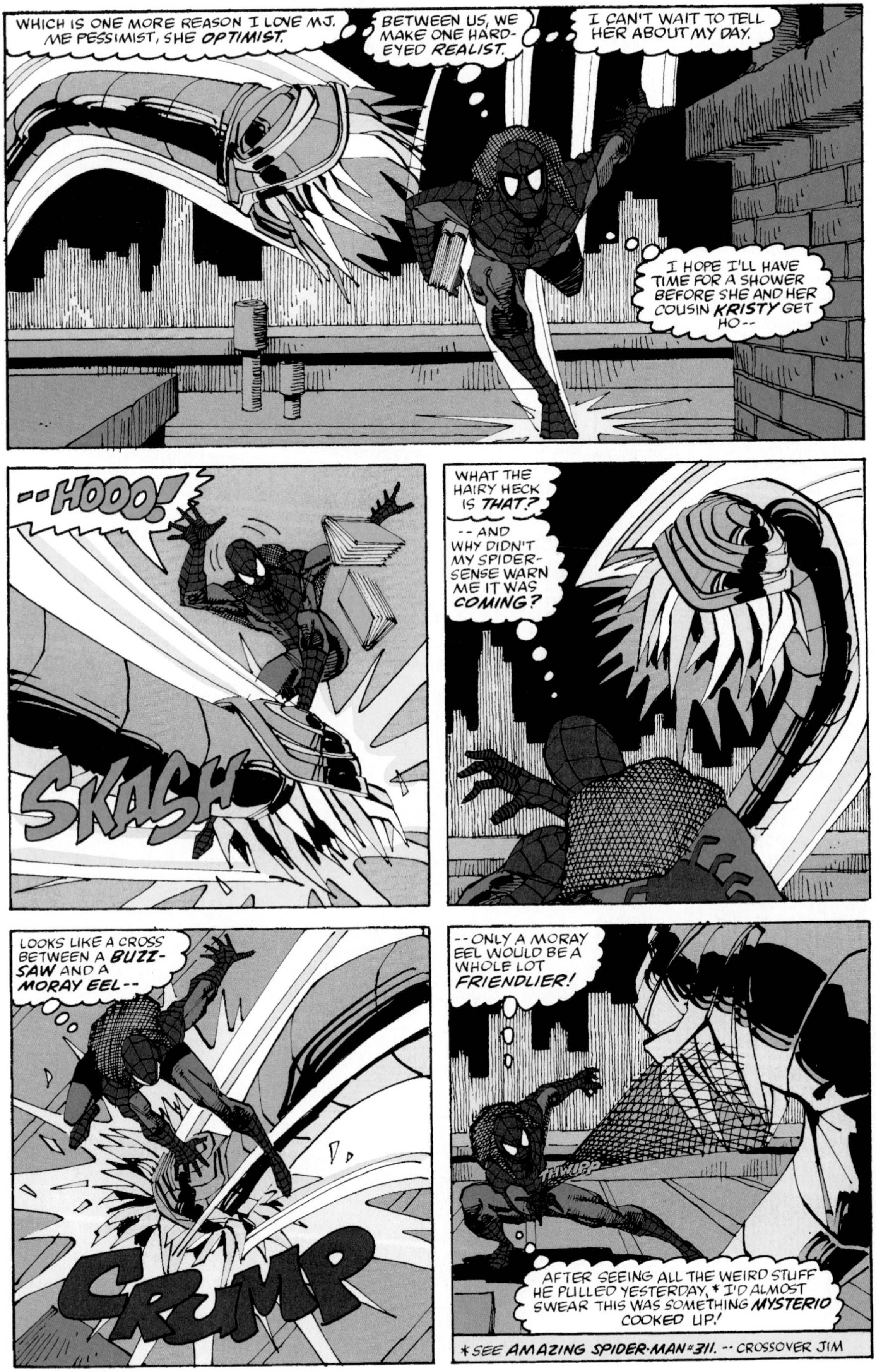
WHICH IS ONE MORE REASON I LOVE MJ. ME PESSIMIST, SHE OPTIMIST.
BETWEEN US, WE MAKE ONE HARD-EYED REALIST.
I CAN'T WAIT TO TELL HER ABOUT MY DAY.
I HOPE I'LL HAVE TIME FOR A SHOWER BEFORE SHE AND HER COUSIN KRISTY GET HO--
--HOOO!
SKASH
WHAT THE HAIRY HECK IS THAT?
--AND WHY DIDN'T MY SPIDER-SENSE WARN ME IT WAS COMING?
LOOKS LIKE A CROSS BETWEEN A BUZZ-SAW AND A MORAY EEL--
CRUMP
--ONLY A MORAY EEL WOULD BE A WHOLE LOT FRIENDLIER!
THWIPP
AFTER SEEING ALL THE WEIRD STUFF HE PULLED YESTERDAY,* I'D ALMOST SWEAR THIS WAS SOMETHING MYSTERIO COOKED UP!
*SEE AMAZING SPIDER-MAN #311. --CROSSOVER JIM

A KILLER MUTANT FAN-VENT WOULD BE JUST HIS IDEA OF FUN.

CORNY AND CRAZY.

ONLY ONE SMALL, MODERATELY INSIGNIFICANT *PROBLEM*:

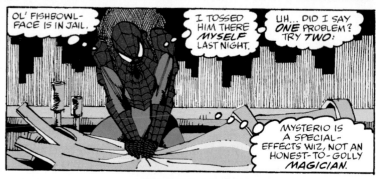

OL' FISHBOWL-FACE IS IN JAIL.

I TOSSED HIM THERE *MYSELF* LAST NIGHT.

UH... DID I SAY *ONE* PROBLEM? TRY *TWO*:

MYSTERIO IS A SPECIAL-EFFECTS WIZ, NOT AN HONEST-TO-GOLLY *MAGICIAN*.

RRRRIP

THERE SHOULD BE ELECTRONICS INSIDE THIS THING-- CIRCUITS, COMPUTERS, *ROBOT* STUFF.

BUT IT'S *EMPTY*.

THERE'S NOTHING IN THIS VENT BUT...

...VENT.

I DON'T BELIEVE IT.

EVEN IN NEW YORK, WEIRD AS IT SOMETIMES IS, FAN-VENTS DON'T JUST COME ALIVE AND *ATTACK* YOU.

USUALLY YOU HAVE TO INSULT THEM FIRST.

NERVOUS HA-HA.

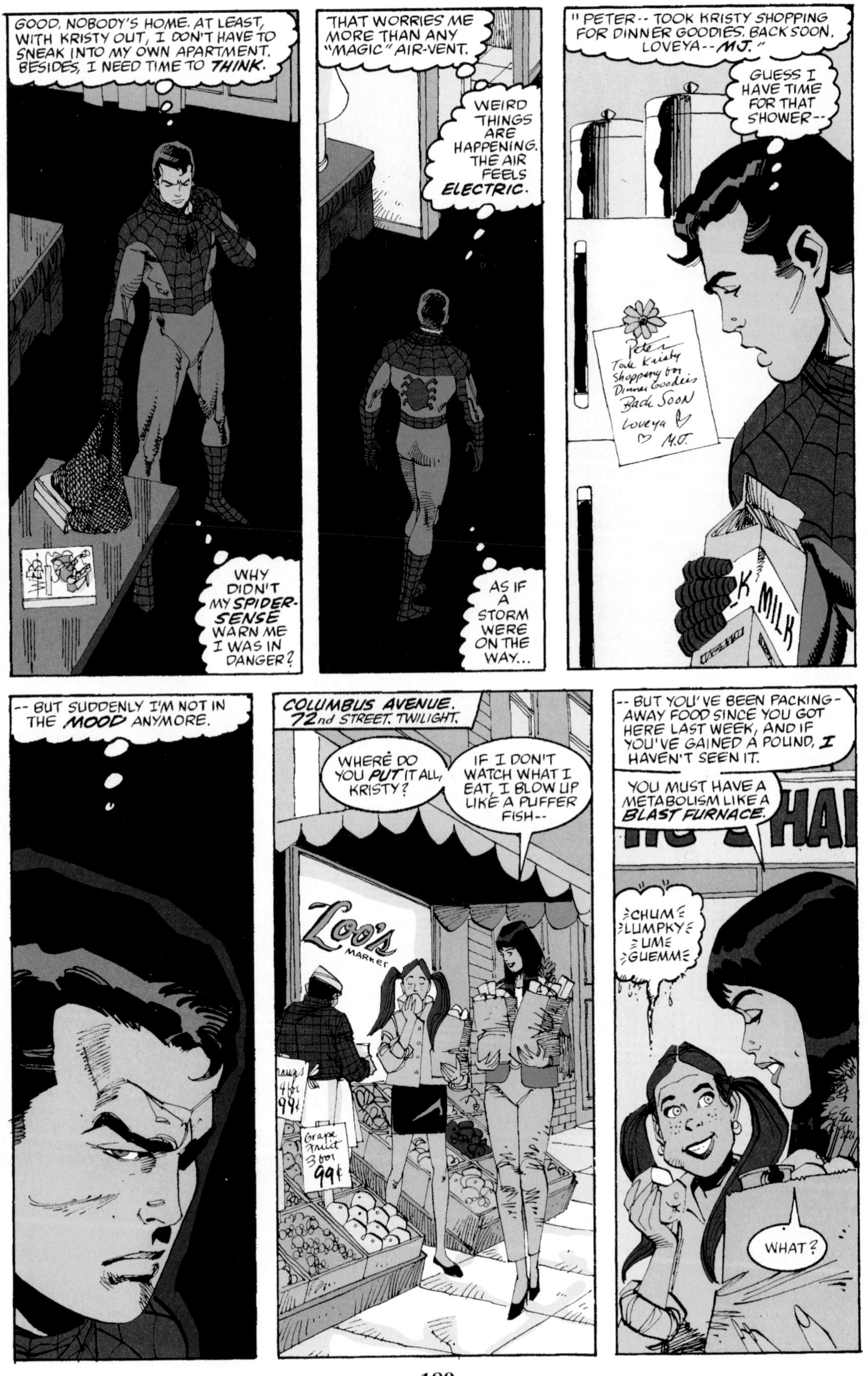
GOOD, NOBODY'S HOME. AT LEAST, WITH KRISTY OUT, I DON'T HAVE TO SNEAK INTO MY OWN APARTMENT. BESIDES, I NEED TIME TO THINK.
WHY DIDN'T MY SPIDER-SENSE WARN ME I WAS IN DANGER?
THAT WORRIES ME MORE THAN ANY "MAGIC" AIR-VENT.
WEIRD THINGS ARE HAPPENING. THE AIR FEELS ELECTRIC.
AS IF A STORM WERE ON THE WAY...
"PETER -- TOOK KRISTY SHOPPING FOR DINNER GOODIES. BACK SOON. LOVEYA -- MJ."
GUESS I HAVE TIME FOR THAT SHOWER --
Peter
Took Kristy
Shopping for
Dinner Goodies
Back SOON
Loveya
M.J.
MILK
-- BUT SUDDENLY I'M NOT IN THE MOOD ANYMORE.
COLUMBUS AVENUE. 72nd STREET. TWILIGHT.
WHERE DO YOU PUT IT ALL, KRISTY?
IF I DON'T WATCH WHAT I EAT, I BLOW UP LIKE A PUFFER FISH --
Loo's
MARKET
Grape Fruit 3 for 99¢
4 for 99¢
-- BUT YOU'VE BEEN PACKING-AWAY FOOD SINCE YOU GOT HERE LAST WEEK, AND IF YOU'VE GAINED A POUND, I HAVEN'T SEEN IT.
YOU MUST HAVE A METABOLISM LIKE A BLAST FURNACE.
CHUM LUMPKY UM GUEMM
WHAT?

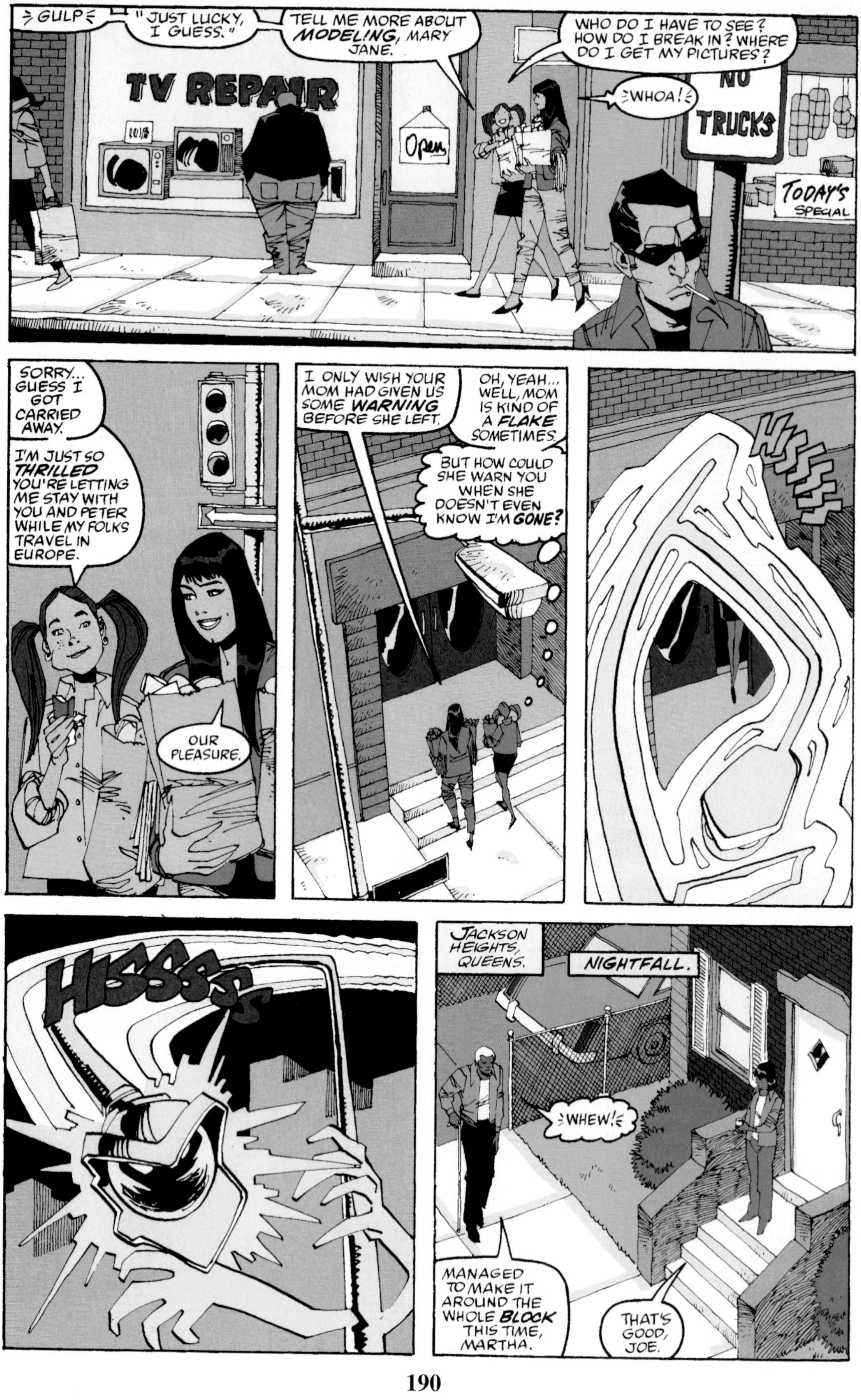

GULP
"JUST LUCKY, I GUESS."
TELL ME MORE ABOUT MODELING, MARY JANE.
WHO DO I HAVE TO SEE? HOW DO I BREAK IN? WHERE DO I GET MY PICTURES?
WHOA!
TV REPAIR
Open
NO TRUCKS
TODAY'S SPECIAL
SORRY... GUESS I GOT CARRIED AWAY.
I'M JUST SO THRILLED YOU'RE LETTING ME STAY WITH YOU AND PETER WHILE MY FOLKS TRAVEL IN EUROPE.
OUR PLEASURE.
I ONLY WISH YOUR MOM HAD GIVEN US SOME WARNING BEFORE SHE LEFT.
OH, YEAH... WELL, MOM IS KIND OF A FLAKE SOMETIMES.
BUT HOW COULD SHE WARN YOU WHEN SHE DOESN'T EVEN KNOW I'M GONE?
HISSSS
HISSSSS
JACKSON HEIGHTS, QUEENS.
NIGHTFALL.
WHEW!
MANAGED TO MAKE IT AROUND THE WHOLE BLOCK THIS TIME, MARTHA.
THAT'S GOOD, JOE.

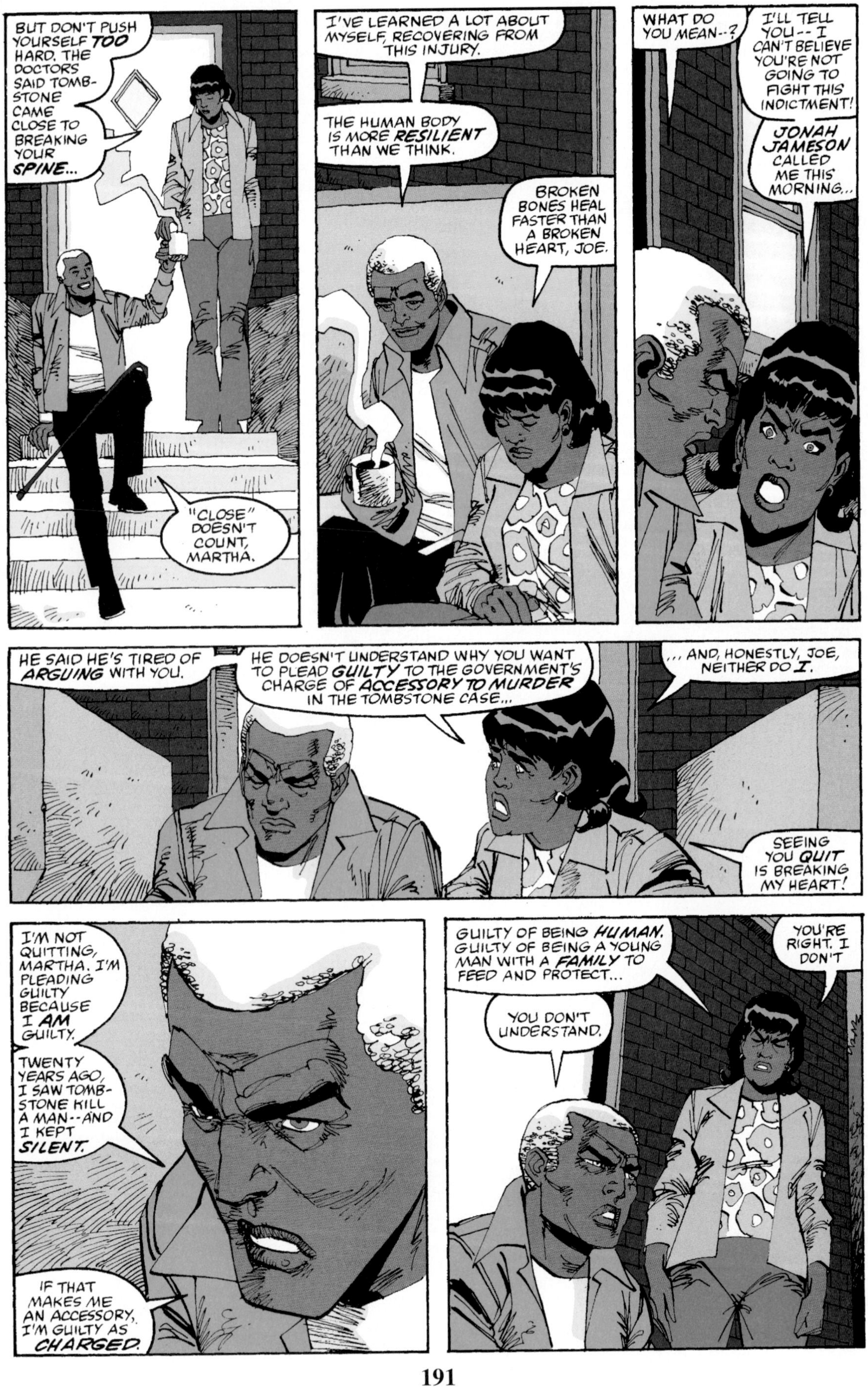
BUT DON'T PUSH YOURSELF TOO HARD. THE DOCTORS SAID TOMBSTONE CAME CLOSE TO BREAKING YOUR SPINE...
"CLOSE" DOESN'T COUNT, MARTHA.
I'VE LEARNED A LOT ABOUT MYSELF, RECOVERING FROM THIS INJURY.
THE HUMAN BODY IS MORE RESILIENT THAN WE THINK.
BROKEN BONES HEAL FASTER THAN A BROKEN HEART, JOE.
WHAT DO YOU MEAN--?
I'LL TELL YOU-- I CAN'T BELIEVE YOU'RE NOT GOING TO FIGHT THIS INDICTMENT!
JONAH JAMESON CALLED ME THIS MORNING...
HE SAID HE'S TIRED OF ARGUING WITH YOU.
HE DOESN'T UNDERSTAND WHY YOU WANT TO PLEAD GUILTY TO THE GOVERNMENT'S CHARGE OF ACCESSORY TO MURDER IN THE TOMBSTONE CASE...
... AND, HONESTLY, JOE, NEITHER DO I.
SEEING YOU QUIT IS BREAKING MY HEART!
I'M NOT QUITTING, MARTHA. I'M PLEADING GUILTY BECAUSE I AM GUILTY.
TWENTY YEARS AGO, I SAW TOMBSTONE KILL A MAN--AND I KEPT SILENT.
IF THAT MAKES ME AN ACCESSORY, I'M GUILTY AS CHARGED.
YOU DON'T UNDERSTAND.
YOU'RE RIGHT. I DON'T
GUILTY OF BEING HUMAN. GUILTY OF BEING A YOUNG MAN WITH A FAMILY TO FEED AND PROTECT...

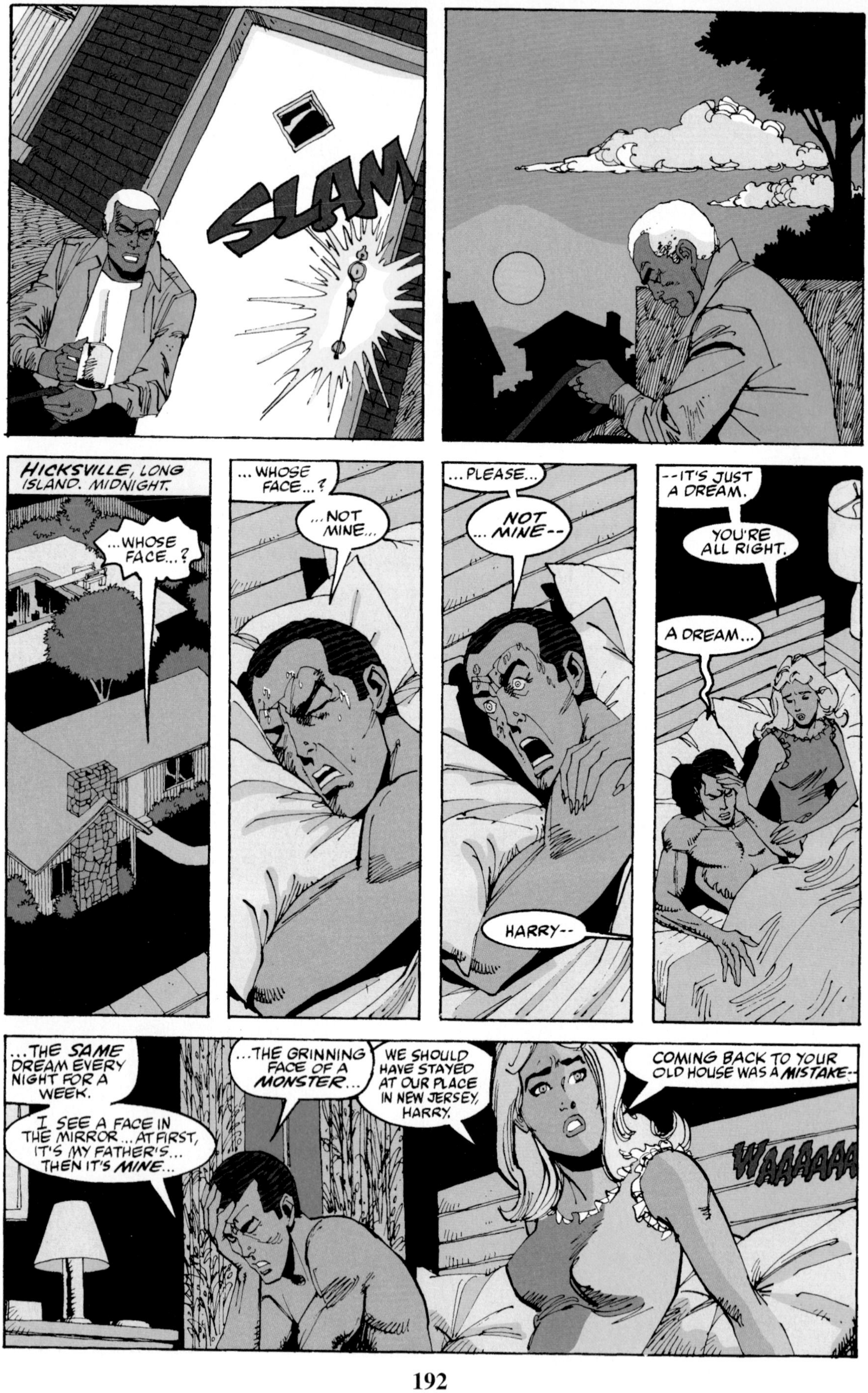
SLAM
HICKSVILLE, LONG ISLAND. MIDNIGHT.
...WHOSE FACE...?
...WHOSE FACE...?
...NOT MINE...
...PLEASE...
NOT ...MINE--
HARRY--
--IT'S JUST A DREAM.
YOU'RE ALL RIGHT.
A DREAM...
...THE SAME DREAM EVERY NIGHT FOR A WEEK.
I SEE A FACE IN THE MIRROR...AT FIRST, IT'S MY FATHER'S... THEN IT'S MINE...
...THE GRINNING FACE OF A MONSTER...
WE SHOULD HAVE STAYED AT OUR PLACE IN NEW JERSEY, HARRY.
COMING BACK TO YOUR OLD HOUSE WAS A MISTAKE--
WAAAAA

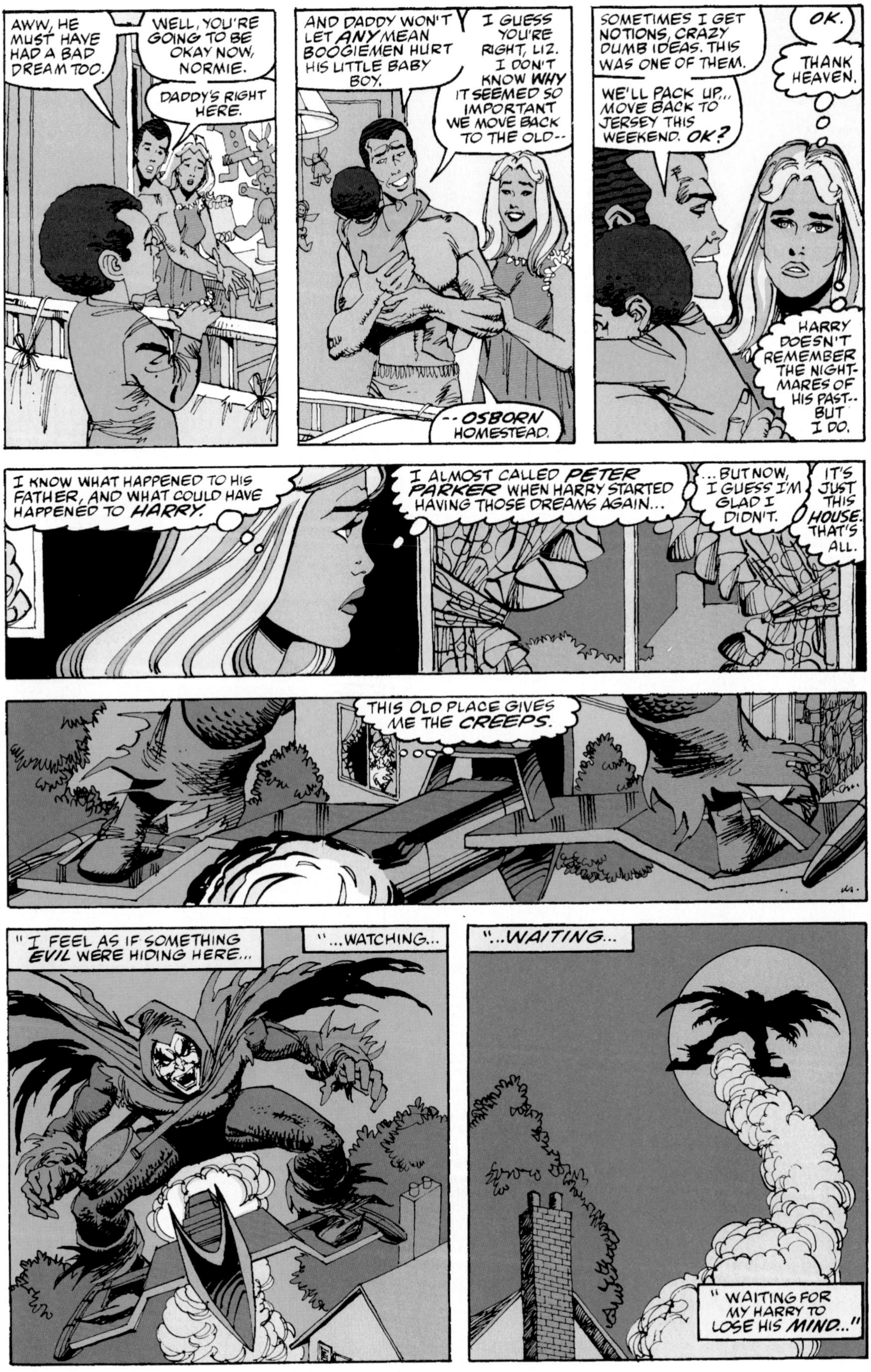
AWW, HE MUST HAVE HAD A BAD DREAM TOO.
WELL, YOU'RE GOING TO BE OKAY NOW, NORMIE.
DADDY'S RIGHT HERE.
AND DADDY WON'T LET ANY MEAN BOOGIEMEN HURT HIS LITTLE BABY BOY.
I GUESS YOU'RE RIGHT, LIZ. I DON'T KNOW WHY IT SEEMED SO IMPORTANT WE MOVE BACK TO THE OLD--
--OSBORN HOMESTEAD.
SOMETIMES I GET NOTIONS, CRAZY DUMB IDEAS. THIS WAS ONE OF THEM.
WE'LL PACK UP... MOVE BACK TO JERSEY THIS WEEKEND. OK?
OK.
THANK HEAVEN.
HARRY DOESN'T REMEMBER THE NIGHTMARES OF HIS PAST-- BUT I DO.
I KNOW WHAT HAPPENED TO HIS FATHER, AND WHAT COULD HAVE HAPPENED TO HARRY.
I ALMOST CALLED PETER PARKER WHEN HARRY STARTED HAVING THOSE DREAMS AGAIN...
...BUT NOW, I GUESS I'M GLAD I DIDN'T.
IT'S JUST THIS HOUSE. THAT'S ALL.
THIS OLD PLACE GIVES ME THE CREEPS.
"I FEEL AS IF SOMETHING EVIL WERE HIDING HERE...
"...WATCHING...
"...WAITING...
"WAITING FOR MY HARRY TO LOSE HIS MIND..."

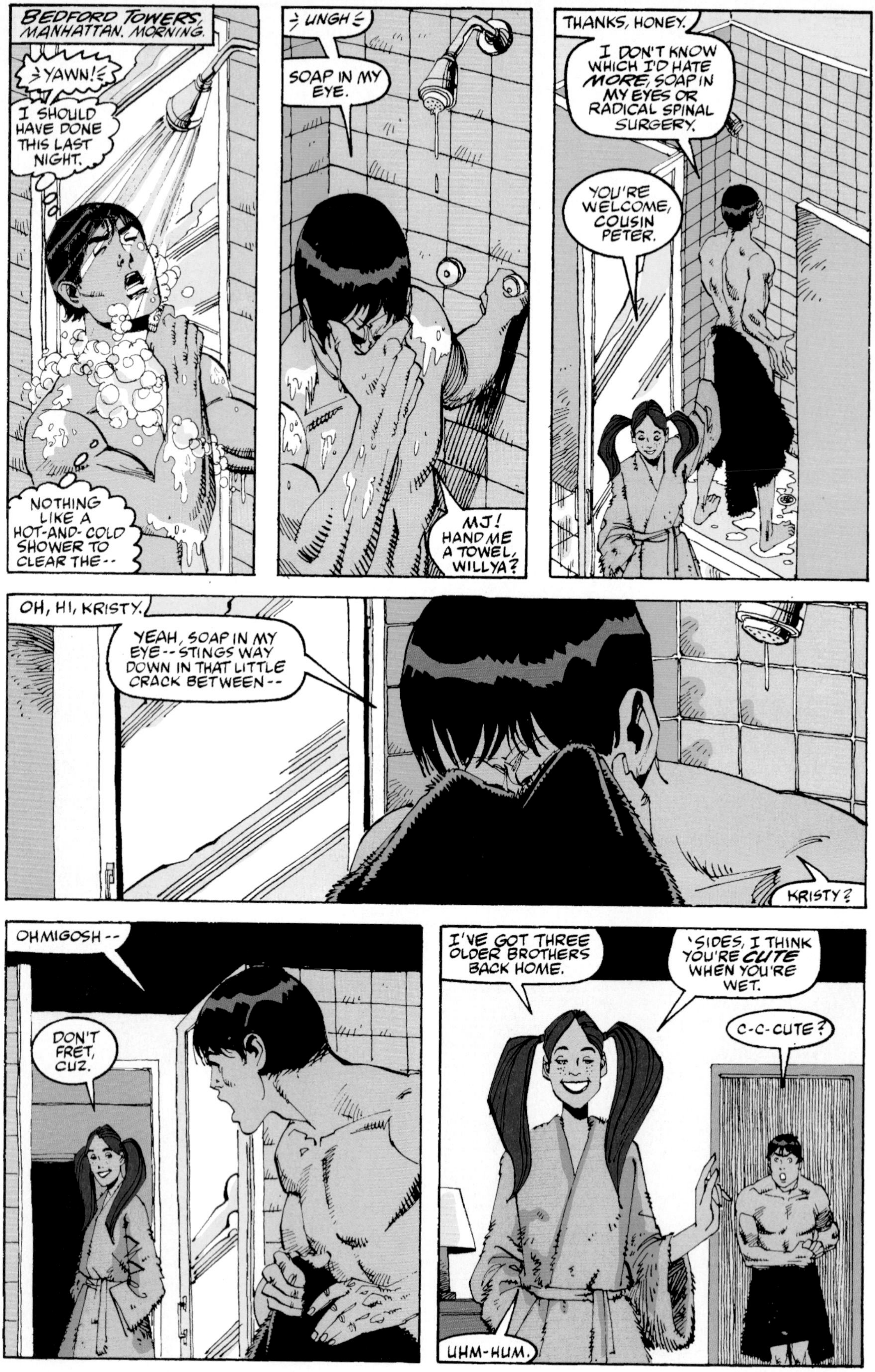
BEDFORD TOWERS, MANHATTAN. MORNING.
YAWN!
I SHOULD HAVE DONE THIS LAST NIGHT.
NOTHING LIKE A HOT-AND-COLD SHOWER TO CLEAR THE--
UNGH
SOAP IN MY EYE.
MJ! HAND ME A TOWEL, WILLYA?
THANKS, HONEY.
I DON'T KNOW WHICH I'D HATE MORE, SOAP IN MY EYES OR RADICAL SPINAL SURGERY.
YOU'RE WELCOME, COUSIN PETER.
OH, HI, KRISTY.
YEAH, SOAP IN MY EYE--STINGS WAY DOWN IN THAT LITTLE CRACK BETWEEN--
KRISTY?
OHMIGOSH--
DON'T FRET, CUZ.
I'VE GOT THREE OLDER BROTHERS BACK HOME.
'SIDES, I THINK YOU'RE CUTE WHEN YOU'RE WET.
C-C-CUTE?
UHM-HUM.

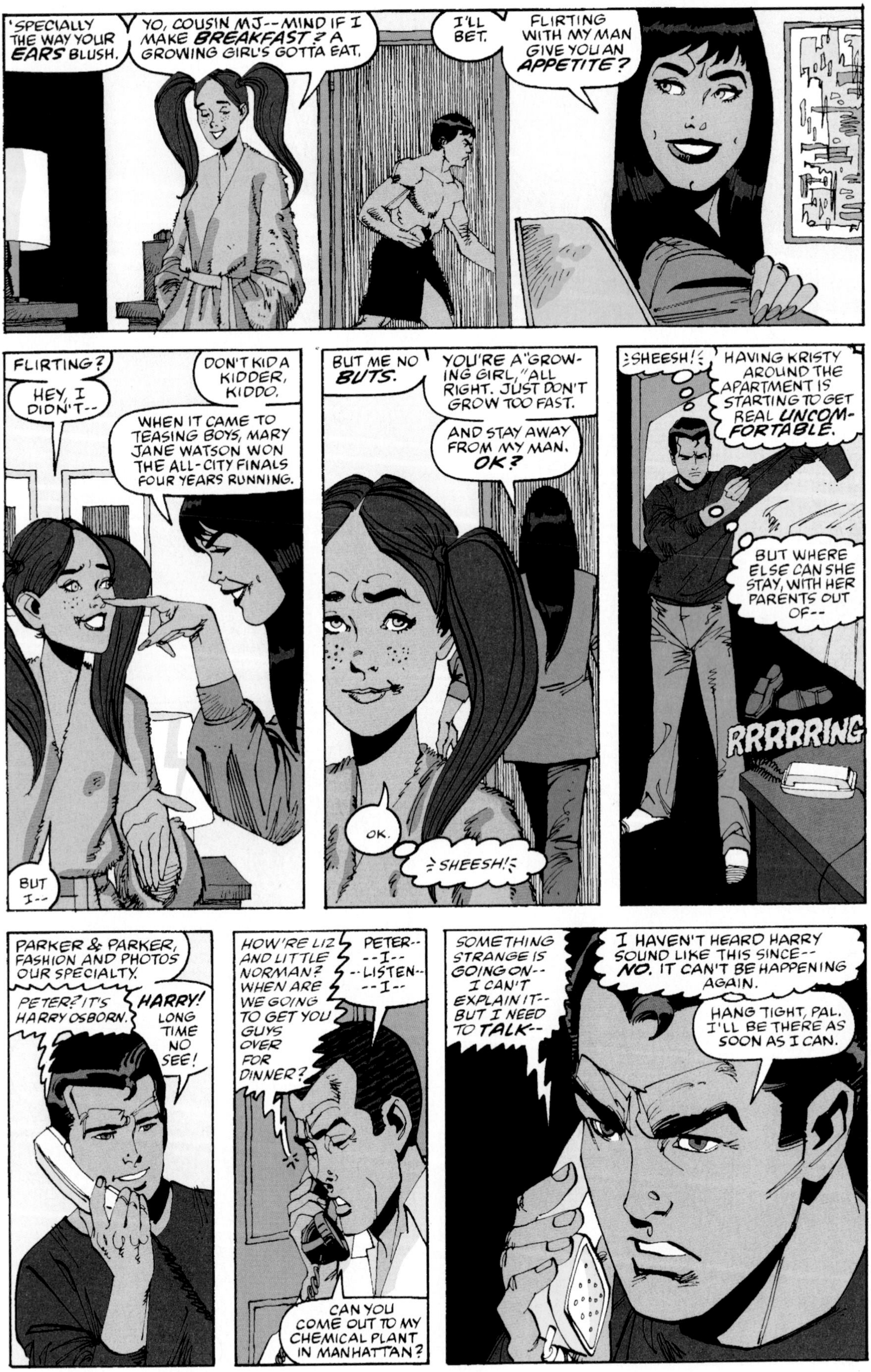

'SPECIALLY THE WAY YOUR EARS BLUSH.
YO, COUSIN MJ--MIND IF I MAKE BREAKFAST? A GROWING GIRL'S GOTTA EAT.
I'LL BET.
FLIRTING WITH MY MAN GIVE YOU AN APPETITE?
FLIRTING?
HEY, I DIDN'T--
DON'T KID A KIDDER, KIDDO.
WHEN IT CAME TO TEASING BOYS, MARY JANE WATSON WON THE ALL-CITY FINALS FOUR YEARS RUNNING.
BUT I--
BUT ME NO BUTS.
YOU'RE A "GROWING GIRL," ALL RIGHT. JUST DON'T GROW TOO FAST.
AND STAY AWAY FROM MY MAN. OK?
OK.
SHEESH!
SHEESH!
HAVING KRISTY AROUND THE APARTMENT IS STARTING TO GET REAL UNCOMFORTABLE.
BUT WHERE ELSE CAN SHE STAY, WITH HER PARENTS OUT OF--
RRRRRING
PARKER & PARKER, FASHION AND PHOTOS OUR SPECIALTY.
PETER? IT'S HARRY OSBORN.
HARRY! LONG TIME NO SEE!
HOW'RE LIZ AND LITTLE NORMAN? WHEN ARE WE GOING TO GET YOU GUYS OVER FOR DINNER?
PETER-- --I-- --LISTEN-- --I--
CAN YOU COME OUT TO MY CHEMICAL PLANT IN MANHATTAN?
SOMETHING STRANGE IS GOING ON-- I CAN'T EXPLAIN IT-- BUT I NEED TO TALK--
I HAVEN'T HEARD HARRY SOUND LIKE THIS SINCE-- NO. IT CAN'T BE HAPPENING AGAIN.
HANG TIGHT, PAL. I'LL BE THERE AS SOON AS I CAN.

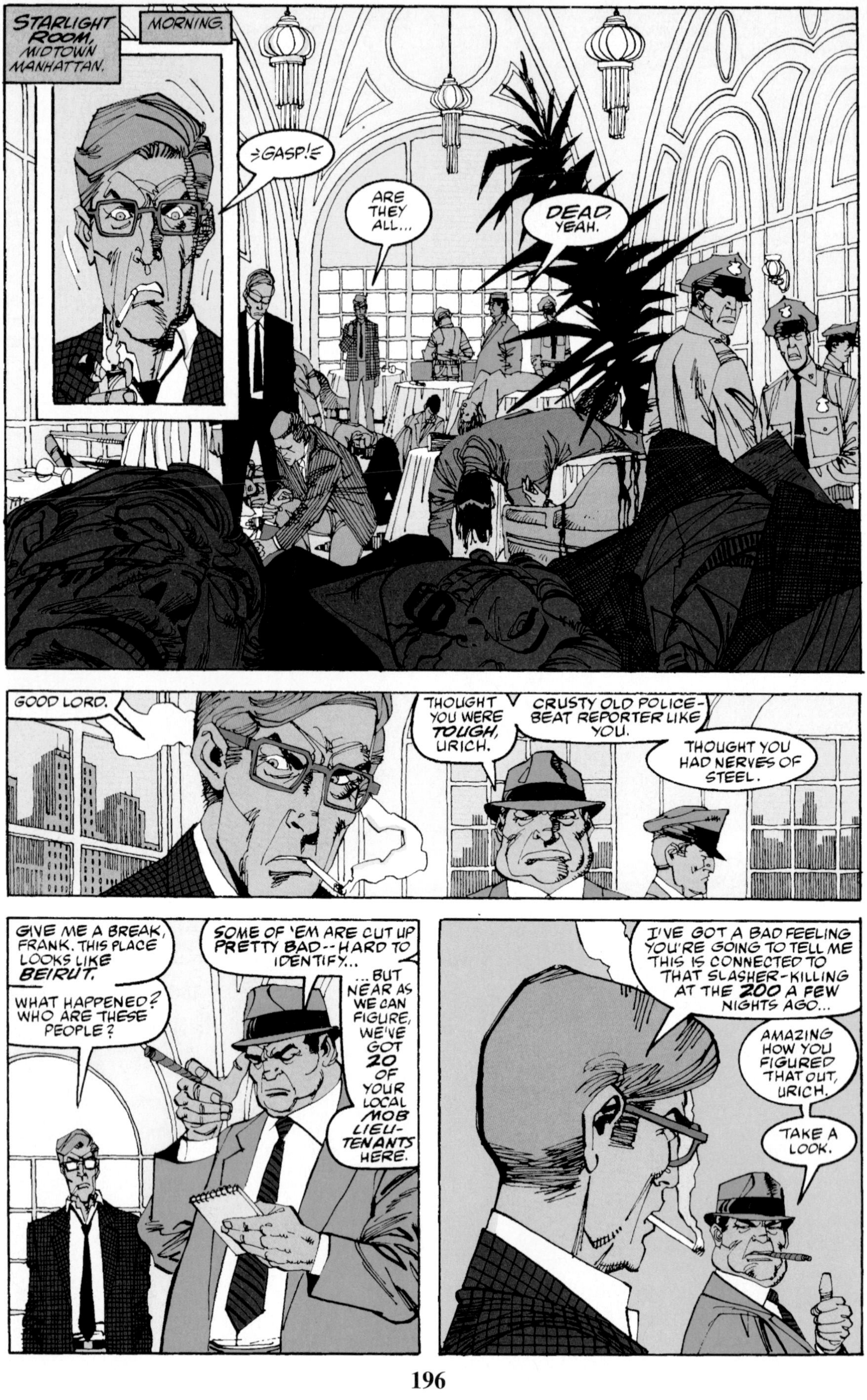
STARLIGHT ROOM, MIDTOWN MANHATTAN.
MORNING.
≥GASP!≤
ARE THEY ALL...
DEAD, YEAH.
GOOD LORD.
THOUGHT YOU WERE TOUGH, URICH.
CRUSTY OLD POLICE-BEAT REPORTER LIKE YOU.
THOUGHT YOU HAD NERVES OF STEEL.
GIVE ME A BREAK, FRANK. THIS PLACE LOOKS LIKE BEIRUT.
WHAT HAPPENED? WHO ARE THESE PEOPLE?
SOME OF 'EM ARE CUT UP PRETTY BAD--HARD TO IDENTIFY...
...BUT NEAR AS WE CAN FIGURE, WE'VE GOT 20 OF YOUR LOCAL MOB LIEU-TENANTS HERE.
I'VE GOT A BAD FEELING YOU'RE GOING TO TELL ME THIS IS CONNECTED TO THAT SLASHER-KILLING AT THE ZOO A FEW NIGHTS AGO...
AMAZING HOW YOU FIGURED THAT OUT, URICH.
TAKE A LOOK.

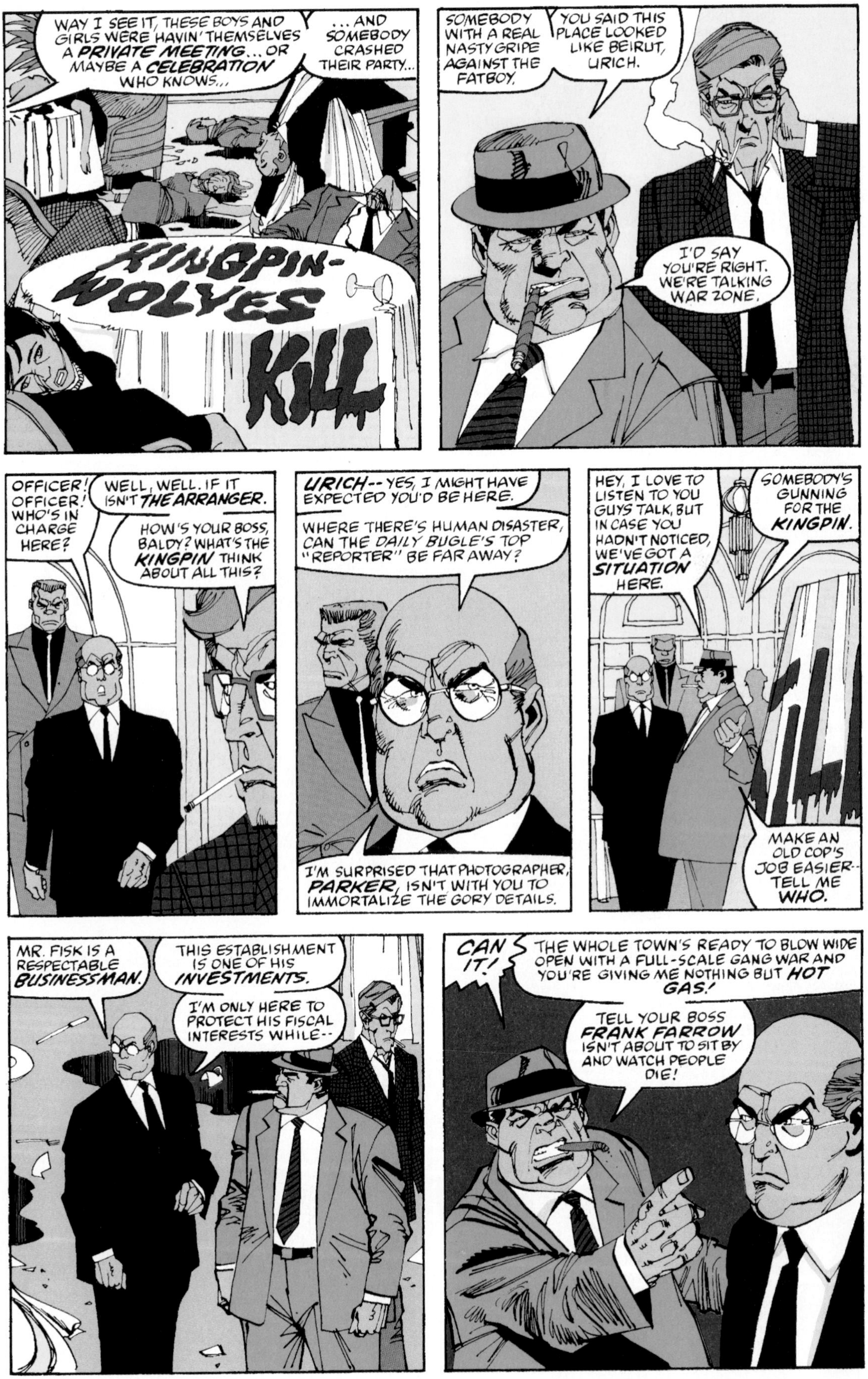
WAY I SEE IT, THESE BOYS AND GIRLS WERE HAVIN' THEMSELVES A PRIVATE MEETING... OR MAYBE A CELEBRATION WHO KNOWS...
...AND SOMEBODY CRASHED THEIR PARTY...
KINGPIN-WOLVES KILL
SOMEBODY WITH A REAL NASTY GRIPE AGAINST THE FATBOY.
YOU SAID THIS PLACE LOOKED LIKE BEIRUT, URICH.
I'D SAY YOU'RE RIGHT. WE'RE TALKING WAR ZONE.
OFFICER! OFFICER! WHO'S IN CHARGE HERE?
WELL, WELL. IF IT ISN'T THE ARRANGER.
HOW'S YOUR BOSS, BALDY? WHAT'S THE KINGPIN THINK ABOUT ALL THIS?
URICH-- YES, I MIGHT HAVE EXPECTED YOU'D BE HERE.
WHERE THERE'S HUMAN DISASTER, CAN THE DAILY BUGLE'S TOP "REPORTER" BE FAR AWAY?
I'M SURPRISED THAT PHOTOGRAPHER, PARKER, ISN'T WITH YOU TO IMMORTALIZE THE GORY DETAILS.
HEY, I LOVE TO LISTEN TO YOU GUYS TALK, BUT IN CASE YOU HADN'T NOTICED, WE'VE GOT A SITUATION HERE.
SOMEBODY'S GUNNING FOR THE KINGPIN.
MAKE AN OLD COP'S JOB EASIER-- TELL ME WHO.
MR. FISK IS A RESPECTABLE BUSINESSMAN.
THIS ESTABLISHMENT IS ONE OF HIS INVESTMENTS.
I'M ONLY HERE TO PROTECT HIS FISCAL INTERESTS WHILE--
CAN IT!
THE WHOLE TOWN'S READY TO BLOW WIDE OPEN WITH A FULL-SCALE GANG WAR AND YOU'RE GIVING ME NOTHING BUT HOT GAS!
TELL YOUR BOSS FRANK FARROW ISN'T ABOUT TO SIT BY AND WATCH PEOPLE DIE!

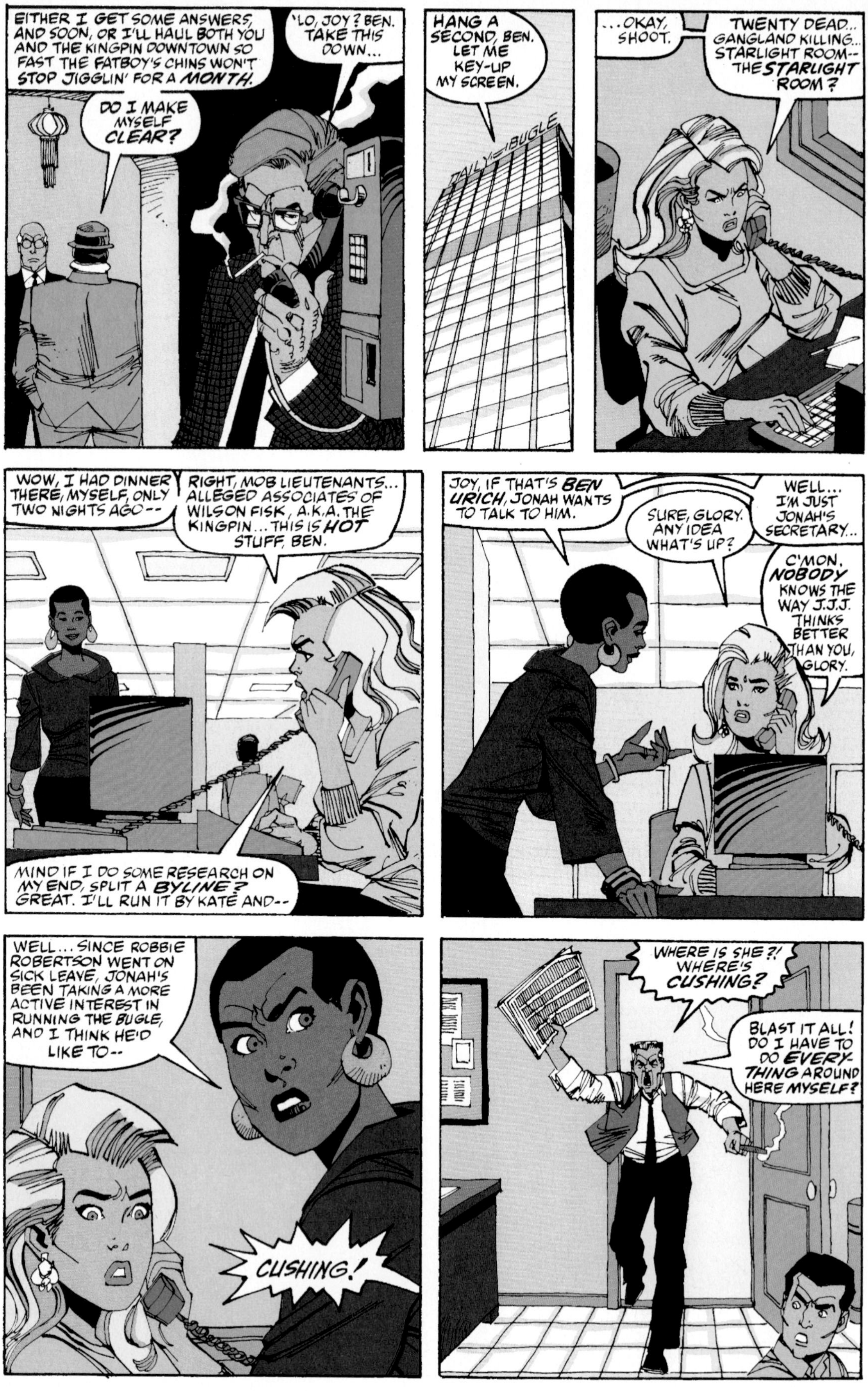
EITHER I GET SOME ANSWERS, AND SOON, OR I'LL HAUL BOTH YOU AND THE KINGPIN DOWNTOWN SO FAST THE FATBOY'S CHINS WON'T STOP JIGGLIN' FOR A MONTH.
DO I MAKE MYSELF CLEAR?
'LO, JOY? BEN. TAKE THIS DOWN...
HANG A SECOND, BEN. LET ME KEY-UP MY SCREEN.
DAILY BUGLE
...OKAY, SHOOT.
TWENTY DEAD... GANGLAND KILLING... STARLIGHT ROOM-- THE STARLIGHT ROOM?
WOW, I HAD DINNER THERE, MYSELF, ONLY TWO NIGHTS AGO--
RIGHT, MOB LIEUTENANTS... ALLEGED ASSOCIATES OF WILSON FISK, A.K.A. THE KINGPIN... THIS IS HOT STUFF, BEN.
MIND IF I DO SOME RESEARCH ON MY END, SPLIT A BYLINE? GREAT. I'LL RUN IT BY KATE AND--
JOY, IF THAT'S BEN URICH, JONAH WANTS TO TALK TO HIM.
SURE, GLORY. ANY IDEA WHAT'S UP?
WELL... I'M JUST JONAH'S SECRETARY...
C'MON, NOBODY KNOWS THE WAY J.J.J. THINKS BETTER THAN YOU, GLORY.
WELL... SINCE ROBBIE ROBERTSON WENT ON SICK LEAVE, JONAH'S BEEN TAKING A MORE ACTIVE INTEREST IN RUNNING THE BUGLE, AND I THINK HE'D LIKE TO--
CUSHING!
WHERE IS SHE?! WHERE'S CUSHING?
BLAST IT ALL! DO I HAVE TO DO EVERYTHING AROUND HERE MYSELF?

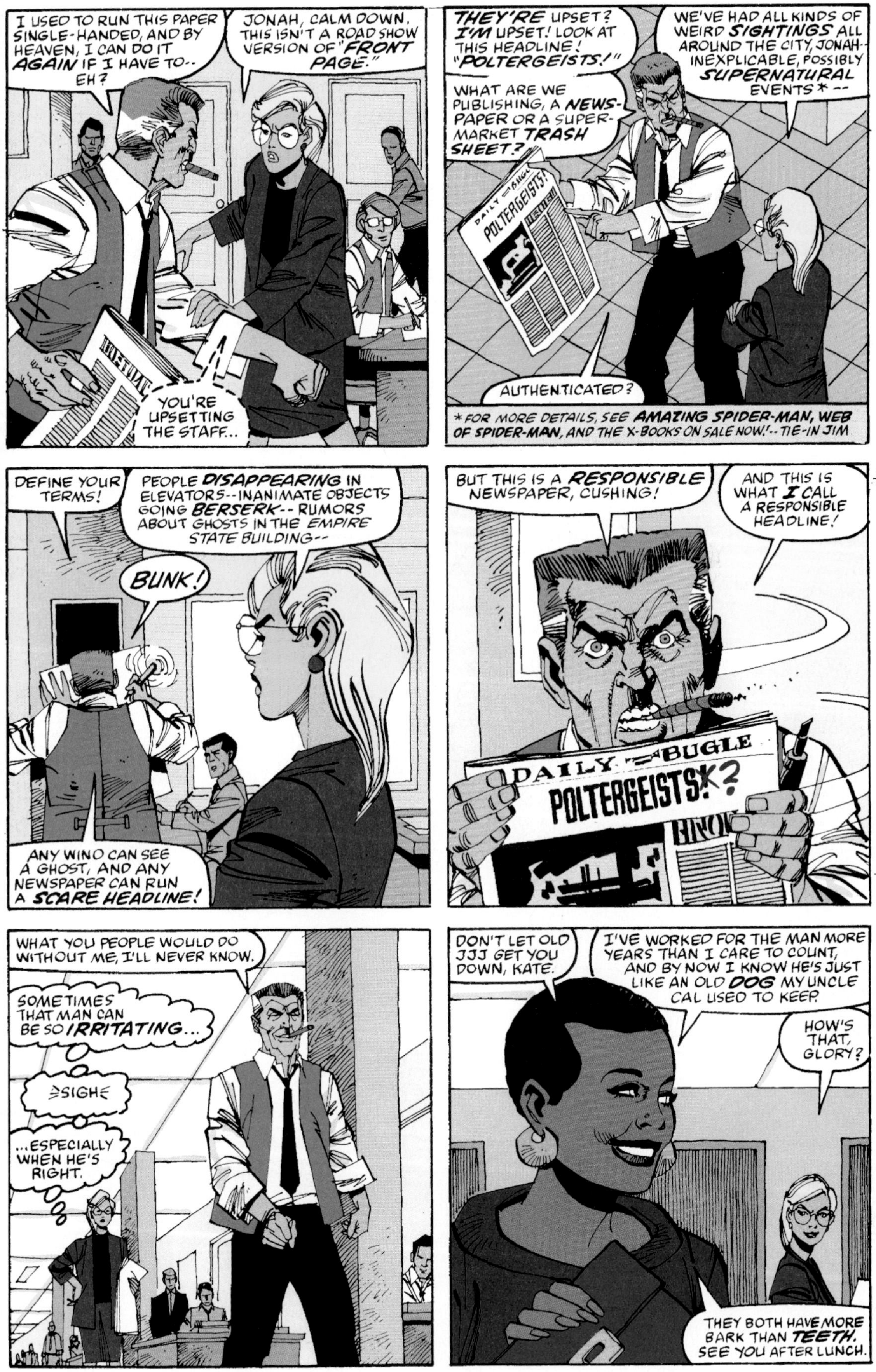
I USED TO RUN THIS PAPER SINGLE-HANDED, AND BY HEAVEN, I CAN DO IT AGAIN IF I HAVE TO-- EH?
JONAH, CALM DOWN. THIS ISN'T A ROAD SHOW VERSION OF "FRONT PAGE."
YOU'RE UPSETTING THE STAFF...
THEY'RE UPSET? I'M UPSET! LOOK AT THIS HEADLINE! "POLTERGEISTS!"
WHAT ARE WE PUBLISHING, A NEWSPAPER OR A SUPERMARKET TRASH SHEET?
DAILY BUGLE
POLTERGEISTS!
WE'VE HAD ALL KINDS OF WEIRD SIGHTINGS ALL AROUND THE CITY, JONAH--INEXPLICABLE, POSSIBLY SUPERNATURAL EVENTS* --
AUTHENTICATED?
*FOR MORE DETAILS, SEE AMAZING SPIDER-MAN, WEB OF SPIDER-MAN, AND THE X-BOOKS ON SALE NOW!--TIE-IN JIM
DEFINE YOUR TERMS!
PEOPLE DISAPPEARING IN ELEVATORS--INANIMATE OBJECTS GOING BERSERK--RUMORS ABOUT GHOSTS IN THE EMPIRE STATE BUILDING--
BUNK!
ANY WINO CAN SEE A GHOST, AND ANY NEWSPAPER CAN RUN A SCARE HEADLINE!
BUT THIS IS A RESPONSIBLE NEWSPAPER, CUSHING!
AND THIS IS WHAT I CALL A RESPONSIBLE HEADLINE!
DAILY BUGLE
POLTERGEISTS!?
WHAT YOU PEOPLE WOULD DO WITHOUT ME, I'LL NEVER KNOW.
SOMETIMES THAT MAN CAN BE SO IRRITATING...
SIGH
...ESPECIALLY WHEN HE'S RIGHT.
DON'T LET OLD JJJ GET YOU DOWN, KATE.
I'VE WORKED FOR THE MAN MORE YEARS THAN I CARE TO COUNT, AND BY NOW I KNOW HE'S JUST LIKE AN OLD DOG MY UNCLE CAL USED TO KEEP.
HOW'S THAT, GLORY?
THEY BOTH HAVE MORE BARK THAN TEETH. SEE YOU AFTER LUNCH.

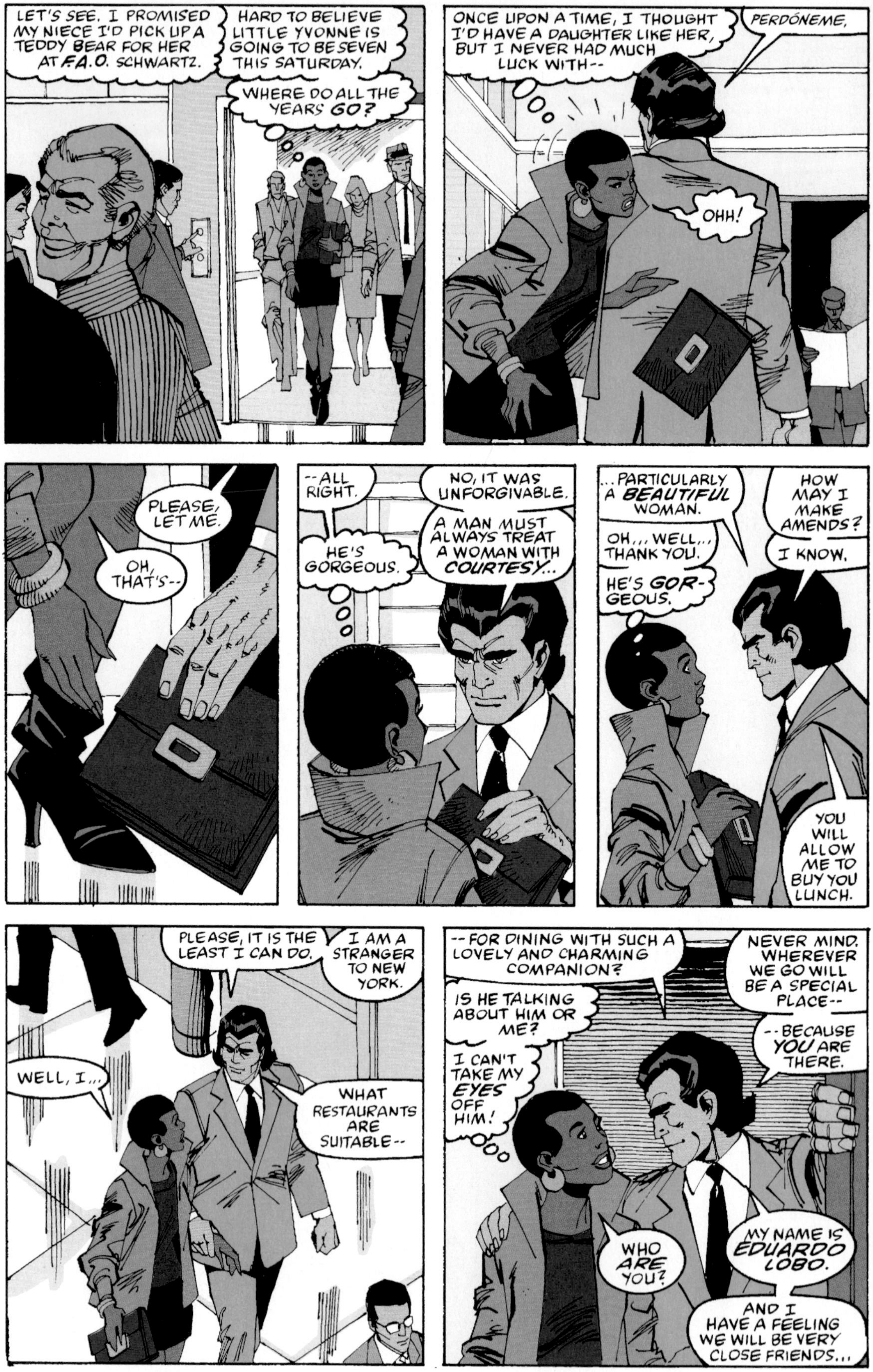
LET'S SEE. I PROMISED MY NIECE I'D PICK UP A TEDDY BEAR FOR HER AT F.A.O. SCHWARTZ.
HARD TO BELIEVE LITTLE YVONNE IS GOING TO BE SEVEN THIS SATURDAY.
WHERE DO ALL THE YEARS GO?
ONCE UPON A TIME, I THOUGHT I'D HAVE A DAUGHTER LIKE HER, BUT I NEVER HAD MUCH LUCK WITH--
PERDÓNEME,
OHH!
PLEASE, LET ME.
OH, THAT'S--
--ALL RIGHT.
HE'S GORGEOUS.
NO, IT WAS UNFORGIVABLE.
A MAN MUST ALWAYS TREAT A WOMAN WITH COURTESY...
...PARTICULARLY A BEAUTIFUL WOMAN.
OH,,, WELL,,, THANK YOU.
HE'S GORGEOUS.
HOW MAY I MAKE AMENDS?
I KNOW.
YOU WILL ALLOW ME TO BUY YOU LUNCH.
PLEASE, IT IS THE LEAST I CAN DO.
I AM A STRANGER TO NEW YORK.
WELL, I...
WHAT RESTAURANTS ARE SUITABLE--
--FOR DINING WITH SUCH A LOVELY AND CHARMING COMPANION?
IS HE TALKING ABOUT HIM OR ME?
I CAN'T TAKE MY EYES OFF HIM!
NEVER MIND. WHEREVER WE GO WILL BE A SPECIAL PLACE--
--BECAUSE YOU ARE THERE.
WHO ARE YOU?
MY NAME IS EDUARDO LOBO.
AND I HAVE A FEELING WE WILL BE VERY CLOSE FRIENDS...

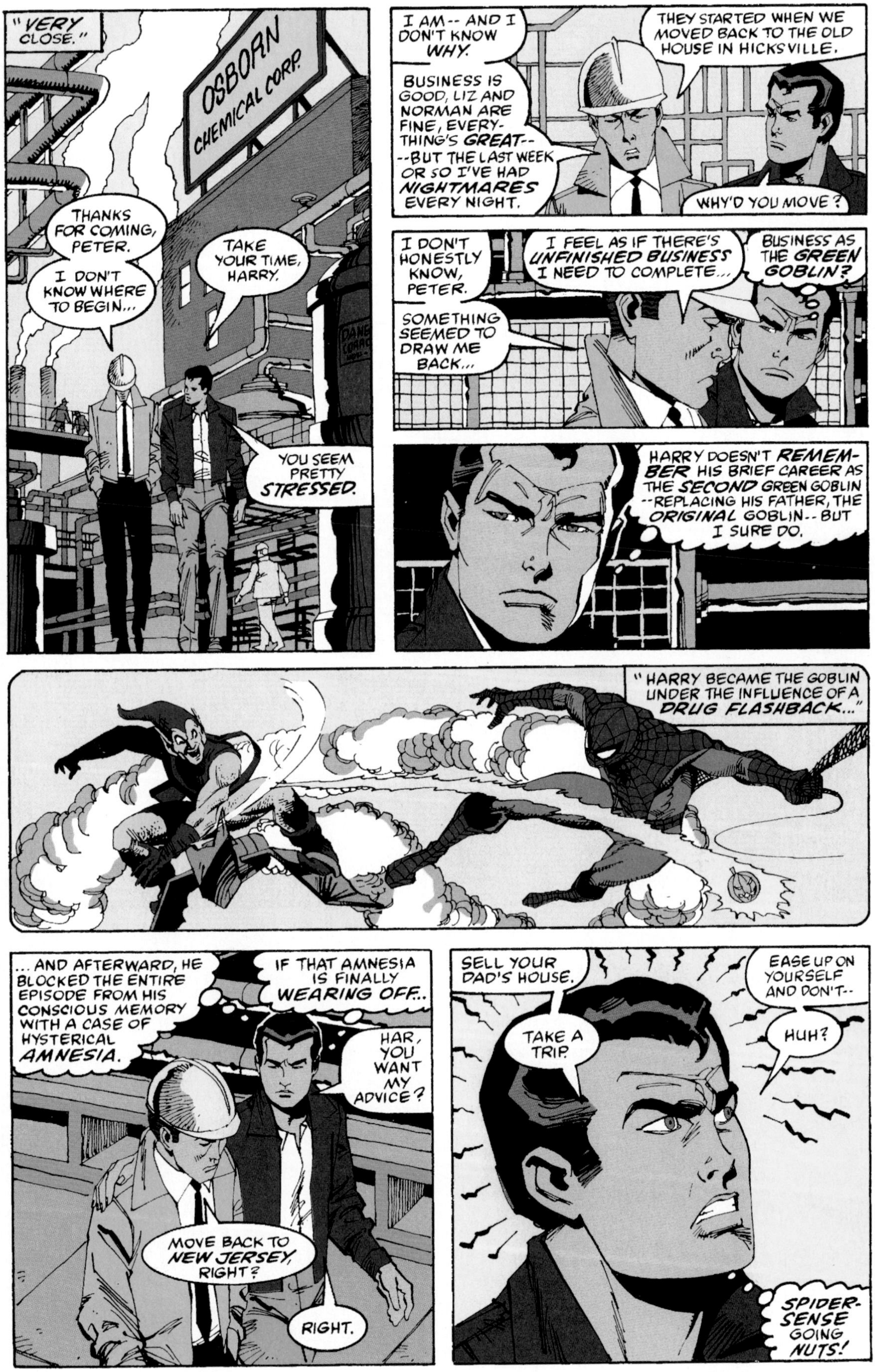
"VERY CLOSE."
OSBORN CHEMICAL CORP.
THANKS FOR COMING, PETER.
I DON'T KNOW WHERE TO BEGIN...
TAKE YOUR TIME, HARRY.
YOU SEEM PRETTY STRESSED.
I AM -- AND I DON'T KNOW WHY.
BUSINESS IS GOOD, LIZ AND NORMAN ARE FINE, EVERYTHING'S GREAT--
--BUT THE LAST WEEK OR SO I'VE HAD NIGHTMARES EVERY NIGHT.
THEY STARTED WHEN WE MOVED BACK TO THE OLD HOUSE IN HICKSVILLE.
WHY'D YOU MOVE?
I DON'T HONESTLY KNOW, PETER.
SOMETHING SEEMED TO DRAW ME BACK...
I FEEL AS IF THERE'S UNFINISHED BUSINESS I NEED TO COMPLETE...
BUSINESS AS THE GREEN GOBLIN?
HARRY DOESN'T REMEMBER HIS BRIEF CAREER AS THE SECOND GREEN GOBLIN --REPLACING HIS FATHER, THE ORIGINAL GOBLIN-- BUT I SURE DO.
"HARRY BECAME THE GOBLIN UNDER THE INFLUENCE OF A DRUG FLASHBACK..."
...AND AFTERWARD, HE BLOCKED THE ENTIRE EPISODE FROM HIS CONSCIOUS MEMORY WITH A CASE OF HYSTERICAL AMNESIA.
IF THAT AMNESIA IS FINALLY WEARING OFF...
HAR, YOU WANT MY ADVICE?
MOVE BACK TO NEW JERSEY, RIGHT?
RIGHT.
SELL YOUR DAD'S HOUSE.
TAKE A TRIP.
EASE UP ON YOURSELF AND DON'T--
HUH?
SPIDER-SENSE GOING NUTS!

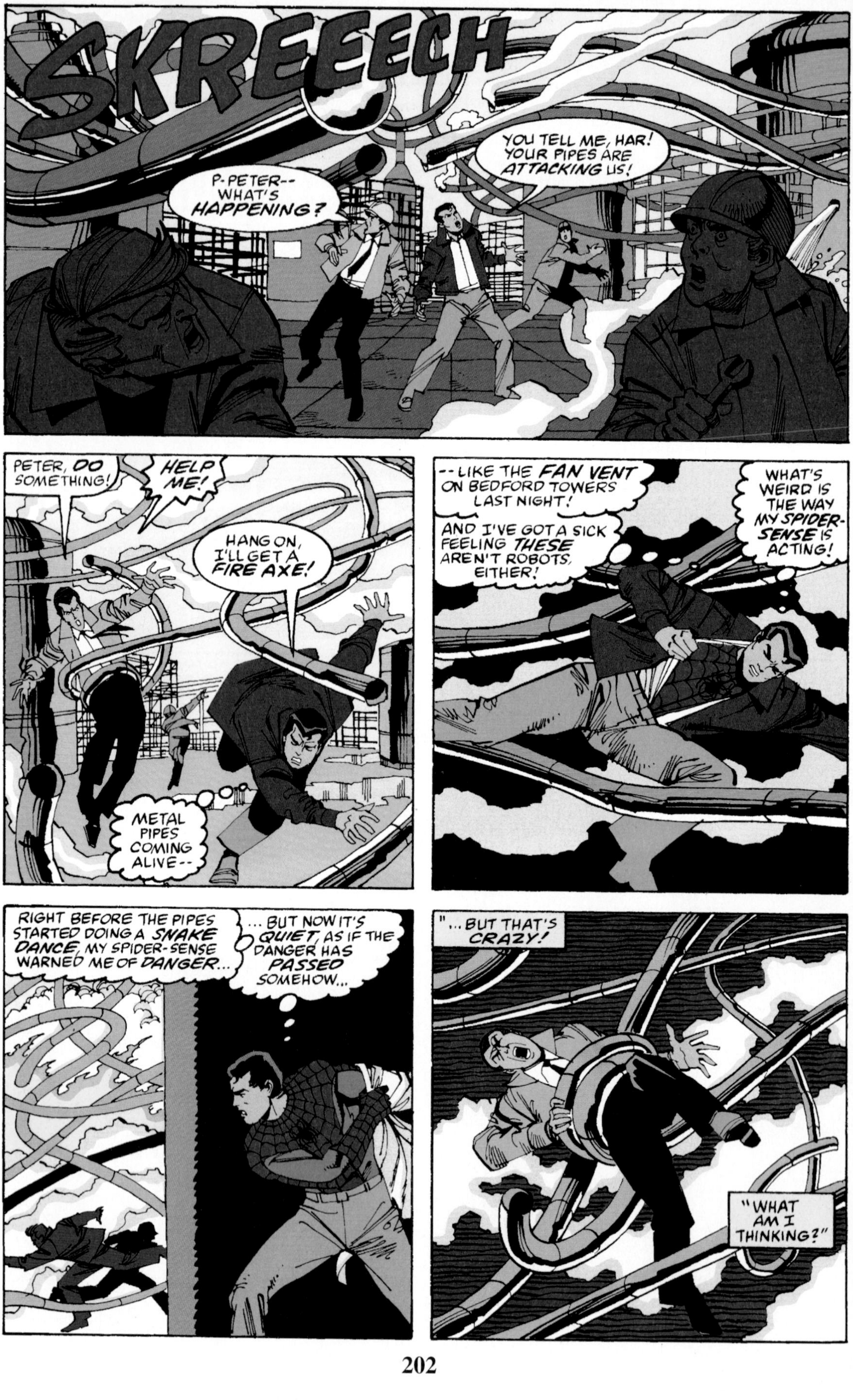
SKREEEECH
P-PETER--
WHAT'S
HAPPENING?
YOU TELL ME, HAR!
YOUR PIPES ARE
ATTACKING US!
PETER, DO
SOMETHING!
HELP
ME!
HANG ON,
I'LL GET A
FIRE AXE!
METAL
PIPES
COMING
ALIVE--
--LIKE THE FAN VENT
ON BEDFORD TOWERS
LAST NIGHT!
AND I'VE GOT A SICK
FEELING THESE
AREN'T ROBOTS,
EITHER!
WHAT'S
WEIRD IS
THE WAY
MY SPIDER-
SENSE IS
ACTING!
RIGHT BEFORE THE PIPES
STARTED DOING A SNAKE
DANCE, MY SPIDER-SENSE
WARNED ME OF DANGER...
...BUT NOW IT'S
QUIET, AS IF THE
DANGER HAS
PASSED
SOMEHOW...
"...BUT THAT'S
CRAZY!
"WHAT
AM I
THINKING?"

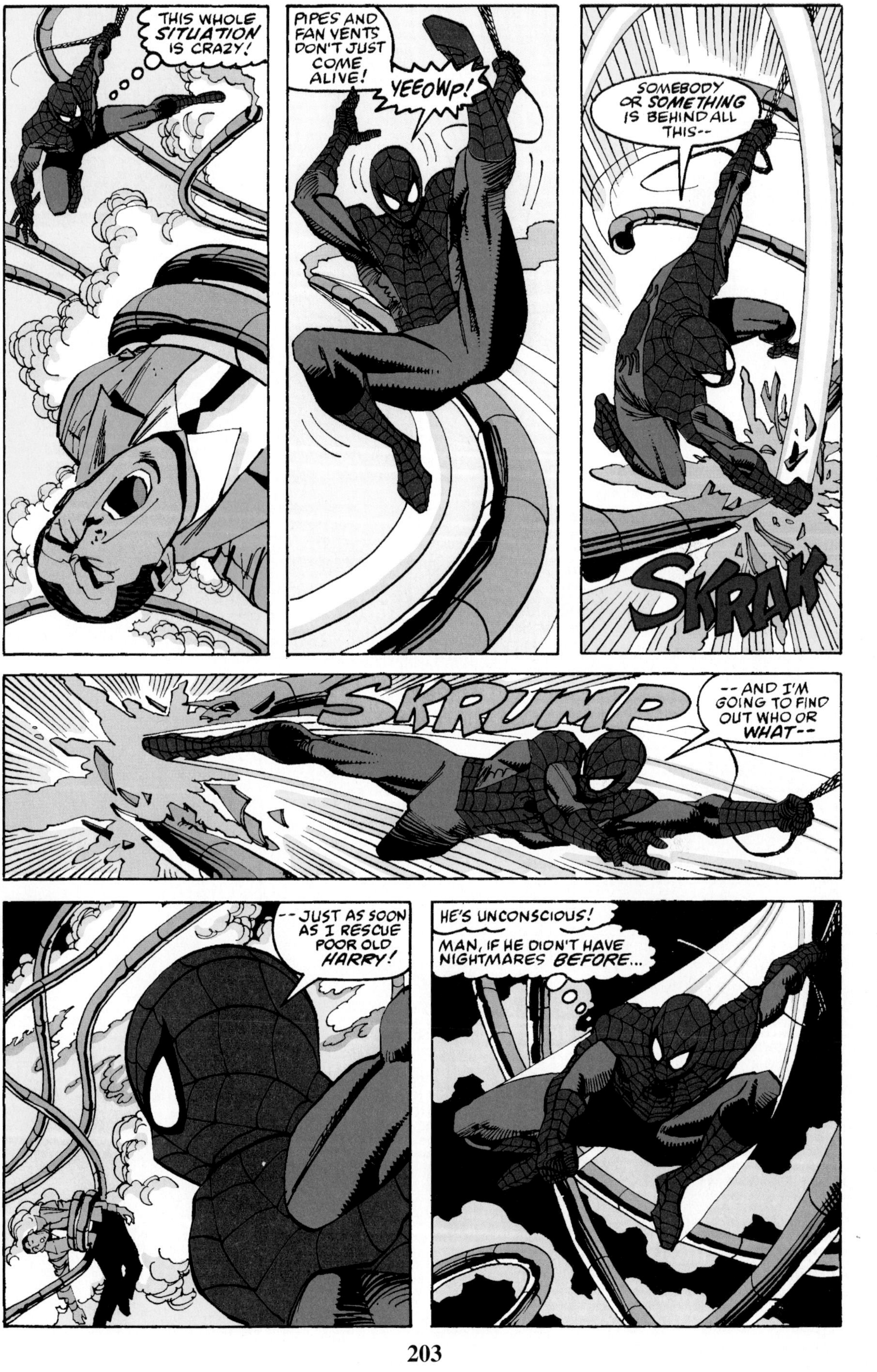
THIS WHOLE SITUATION IS CRAZY!
PIPES AND FAN VENTS DON'T JUST COME ALIVE!
YEEOWP!
SOMEBODY OR SOMETHING IS BEHIND ALL THIS--
SKRAK
SKRUMP
--AND I'M GOING TO FIND OUT WHO OR WHAT--
--JUST AS SOON AS I RESCUE POOR OLD HARRY!
HE'S UNCONSCIOUS!
MAN, IF HE DIDN'T HAVE NIGHTMARES BEFORE...

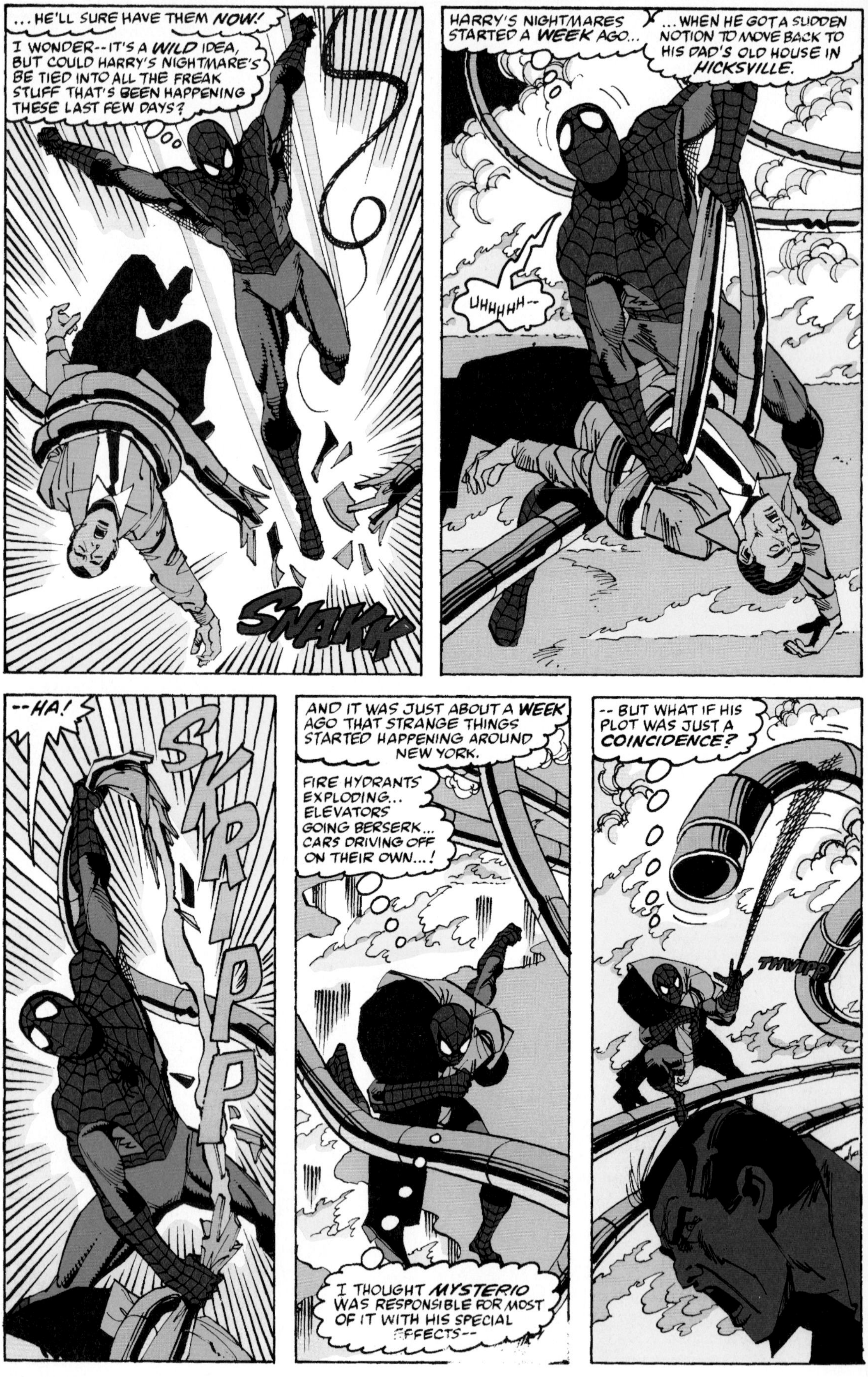
...HE'LL SURE HAVE THEM NOW!
I WONDER--IT'S A WILD IDEA, BUT COULD HARRY'S NIGHTMARE'S BE TIED INTO ALL THE FREAK STUFF THAT'S BEEN HAPPENING THESE LAST FEW DAYS?
SNAKK
HARRY'S NIGHTMARES STARTED A WEEK AGO...
...WHEN HE GOT A SUDDEN NOTION TO MOVE BACK TO HIS DAD'S OLD HOUSE IN HICKSVILLE.
UHHHHH--
--HA!
SKRIPPP
AND IT WAS JUST ABOUT A WEEK AGO THAT STRANGE THINGS STARTED HAPPENING AROUND NEW YORK.
FIRE HYDRANTS EXPLODING... ELEVATORS GOING BERSERK... CARS DRIVING OFF ON THEIR OWN...!
I THOUGHT MYSTERIO WAS RESPONSIBLE FOR MOST OF IT WITH HIS SPECIAL EFFECTS--
-- BUT WHAT IF HIS PLOT WAS JUST A COINCIDENCE?
THWIPP

I DON'T KNOW--

--SOMETHING **BIG** IS GOING ON, BUT EITHER I'M TOO CLOSE TO SEE IT-- OR TOO FAR AWAY!

ALL I CAN DO IS HOPE--

MY **SPIDER-SENSE!** THERE IT GOES **AGAIN!**

DANGER NEARBY...

"...UP IN THE **SMOKE...**

"...SOMEONE **FLYING...** "

"...GONE."

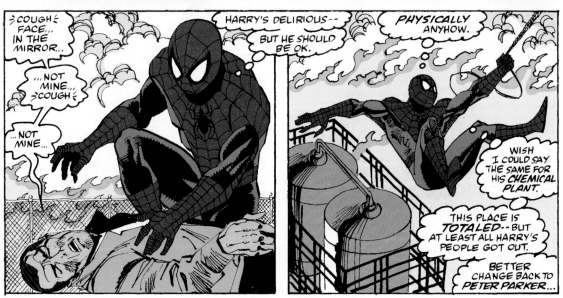

≥COUGH≤ FACE... IN THE MIRROR...

...NOT MINE... ≥COUGH≤

...NOT MINE...

HARRY'S DELIRIOUS-- BUT HE SHOULD BE OK.

PHYSICALLY ANYHOW.

WISH I COULD SAY THE SAME FOR HIS **CHEMICAL PLANT.**

THIS PLACE IS **TOTALED**--BUT AT LEAST ALL HARRY'S PEOPLE GOT OUT.

BETTER CHANGE BACK TO **PETER PARKER...**

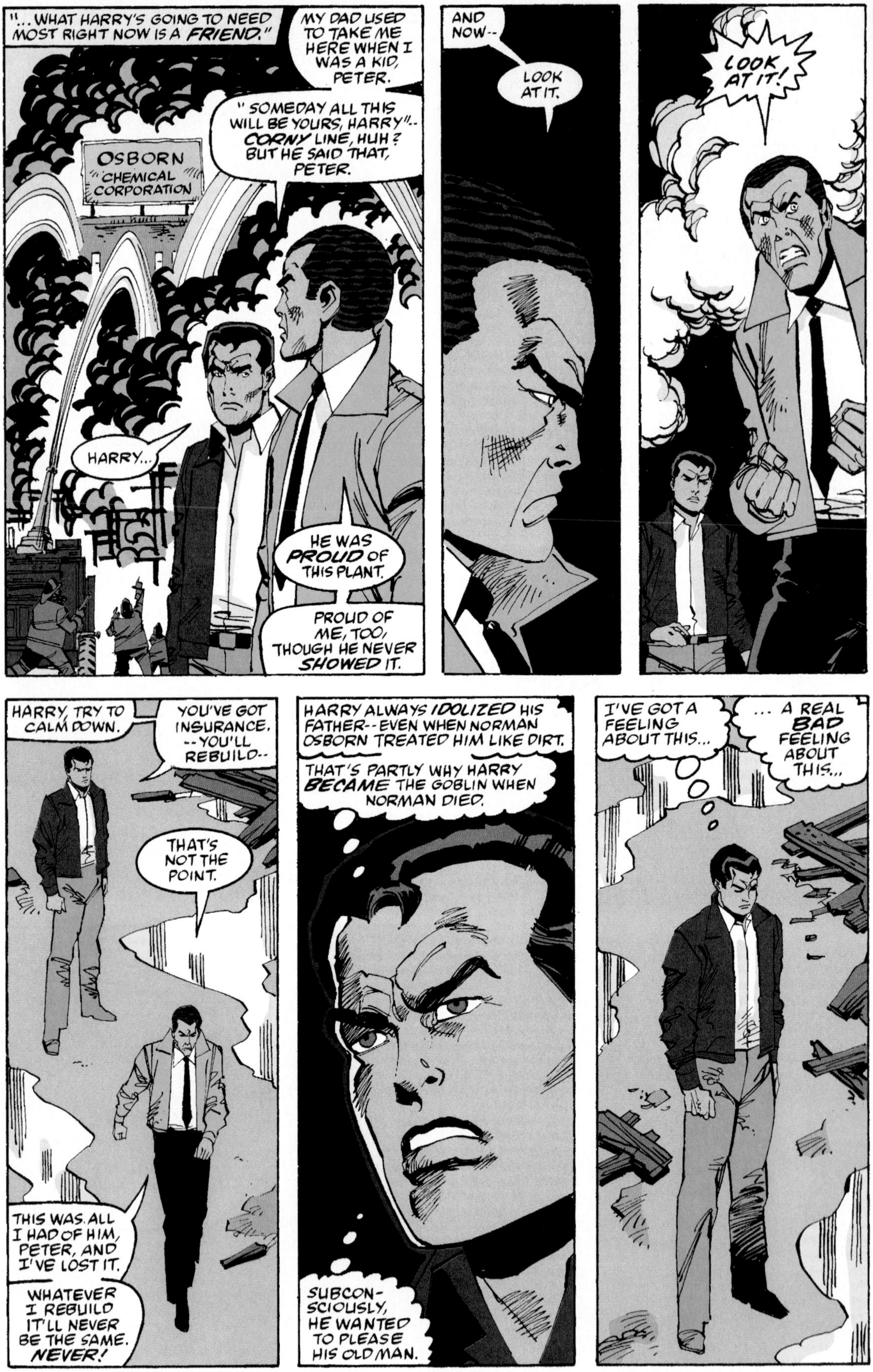
"...WHAT HARRY'S GOING TO NEED MOST RIGHT NOW IS A FRIEND."
MY DAD USED TO TAKE ME HERE WHEN I WAS A KID, PETER.
"SOMEDAY ALL THIS WILL BE YOURS, HARRY"-- CORNY LINE, HUH? BUT HE SAID THAT, PETER.
OSBORN CHEMICAL CORPORATION
HARRY...
HE WAS PROUD OF THIS PLANT.
PROUD OF ME, TOO, THOUGH HE NEVER SHOWED IT.
AND NOW--
LOOK AT IT.
LOOK AT IT!
HARRY, TRY TO CALM DOWN.
YOU'VE GOT INSURANCE. --YOU'LL REBUILD--
THAT'S NOT THE POINT.
THIS WAS ALL I HAD OF HIM, PETER, AND I'VE LOST IT.
WHATEVER I REBUILD IT'LL NEVER BE THE SAME. NEVER!
HARRY ALWAYS IDOLIZED HIS FATHER--EVEN WHEN NORMAN OSBORN TREATED HIM LIKE DIRT.
THAT'S PARTLY WHY HARRY BECAME THE GOBLIN WHEN NORMAN DIED.
SUBCON- SCIOUSLY, HE WANTED TO PLEASE HIS OLD MAN.
I'VE GOT A FEELING ABOUT THIS...
... A REAL BAD FEELING ABOUT THIS...

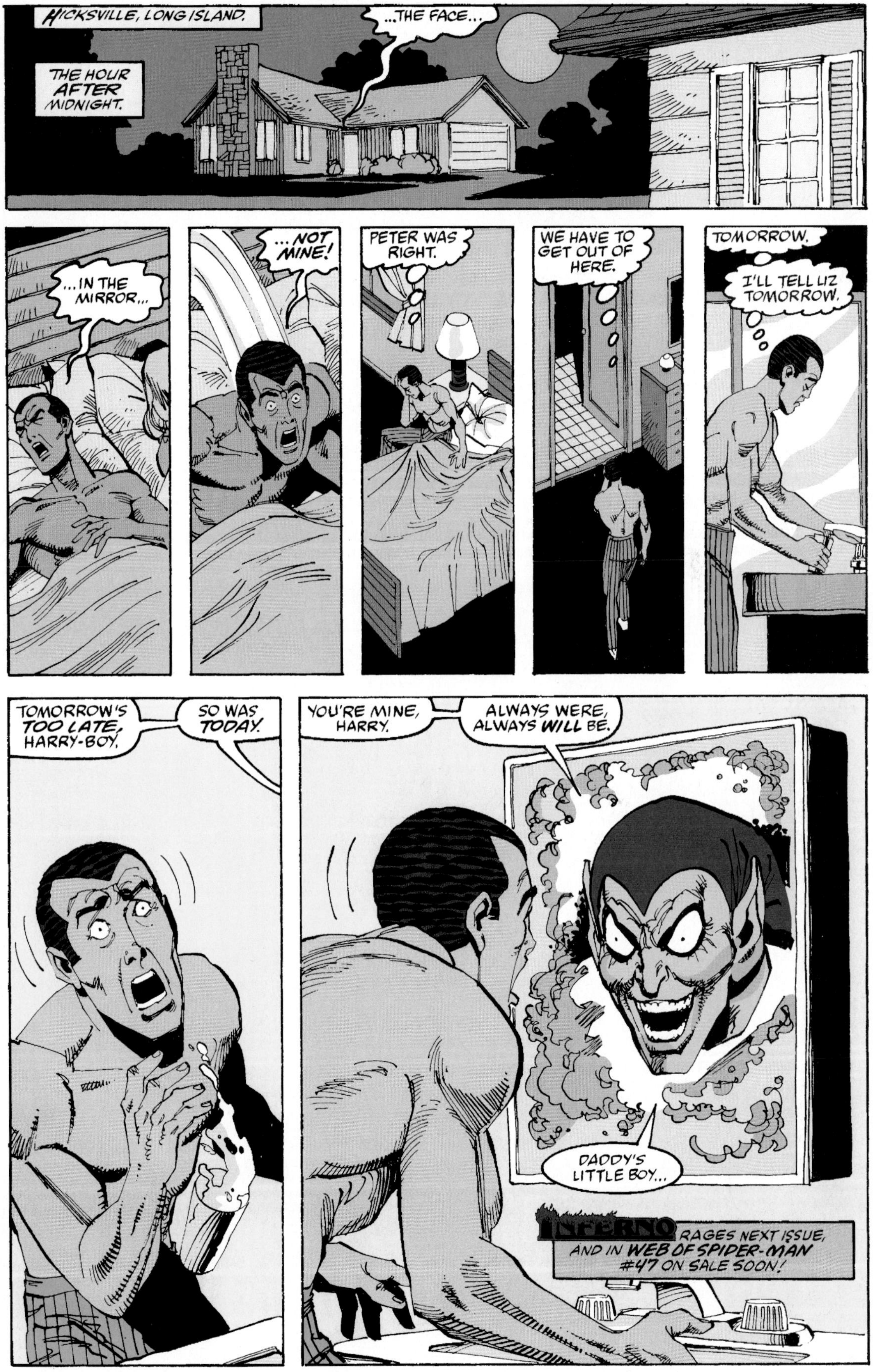
HICKSVILLE, LONG ISLAND.
THE HOUR AFTER MIDNIGHT.
...THE FACE...
...IN THE MIRROR...
...NOT MINE!
PETER WAS RIGHT.
WE HAVE TO GET OUT OF HERE.
TOMORROW.
I'LL TELL LIZ TOMORROW.
TOMORROW'S TOO LATE, HARRY-BOY.
SO WAS TODAY.
YOU'RE MINE, HARRY.
ALWAYS WERE, ALWAYS WILL BE.
DADDY'S LITTLE BOY...
INFERNO RAGES NEXT ISSUE, AND IN WEB OF SPIDER-MAN #47 ON SALE SOON!

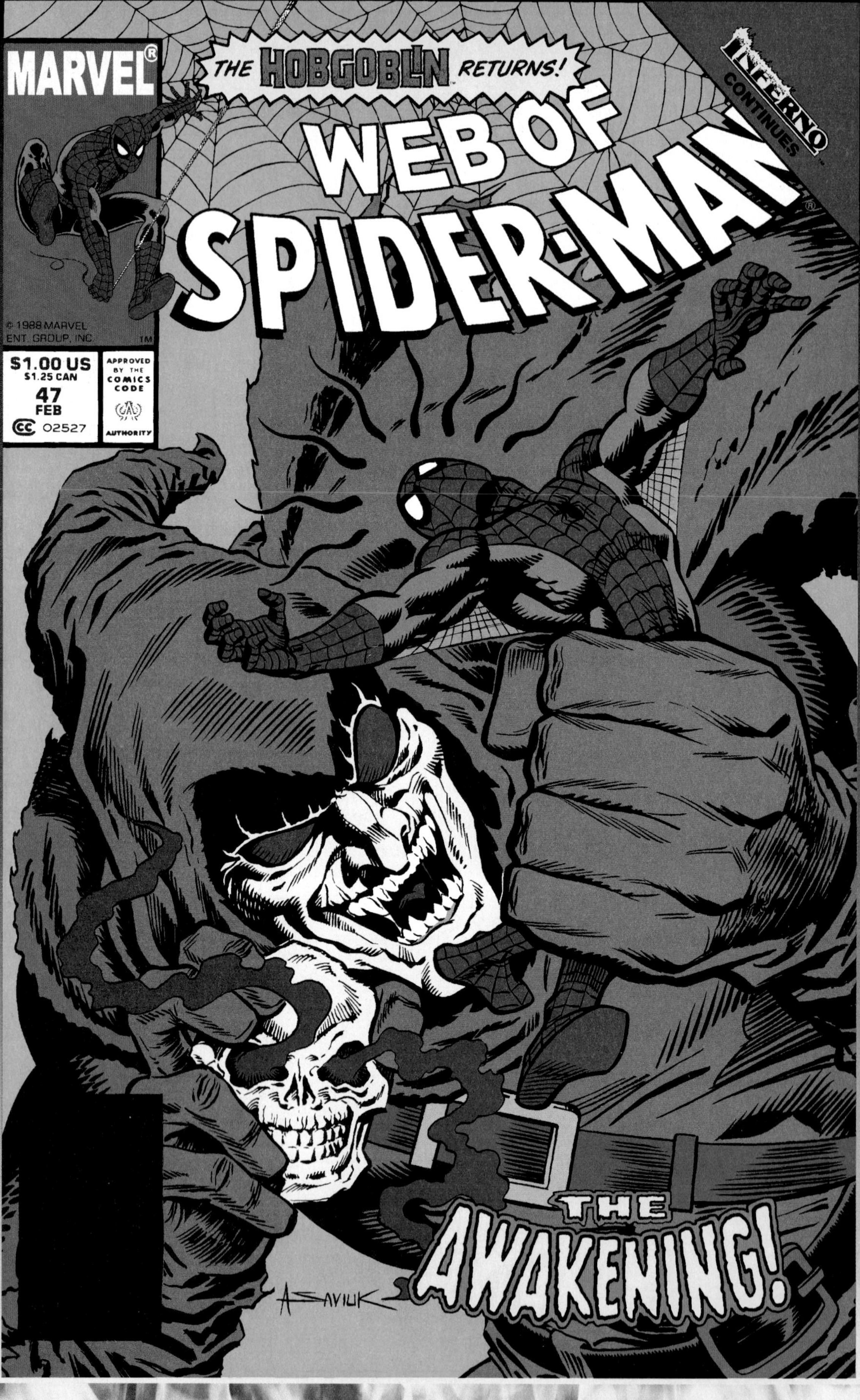
MARVEL®
THE HOBGOBLIN RETURNS!
INFERNO CONTINUES
WEB OF SPIDER-MAN®
© 1988 MARVEL ENT. GROUP, INC. TM
$1.00 US
$1.25 CAN
47
FEB
CC 02527
APPROVED BY THE COMICS CODE AUTHORITY
THE AWAKENING!
A SAVIUK

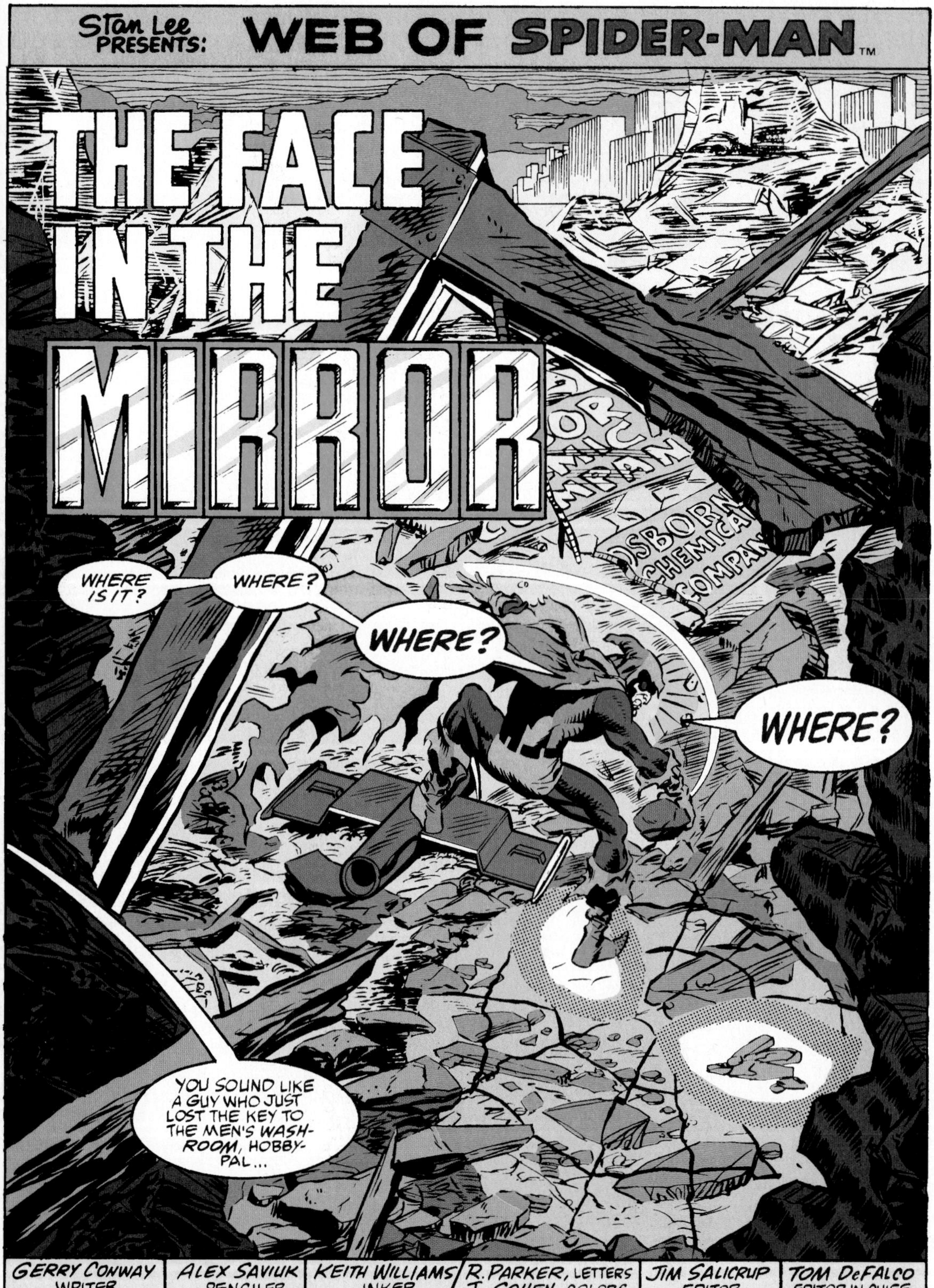
Stan Lee PRESENTS: WEB OF SPIDER-MAN™
THE FACE IN THE MIRROR
WHERE IS IT?
WHERE?
WHERE?
WHERE?
YOU SOUND LIKE A GUY WHO JUST LOST THE KEY TO THE MEN'S WASH-ROOM, HOBBY-PAL...
GERRY CONWAY WRITER
ALEX SAVIUK PENCILER
KEITH WILLIAMS INKER
R. PARKER, LETTERS J. COHEN, COLORS
JIM SALICRUP EDITOR
TOM DeFALCO EDITOR IN CHIEF

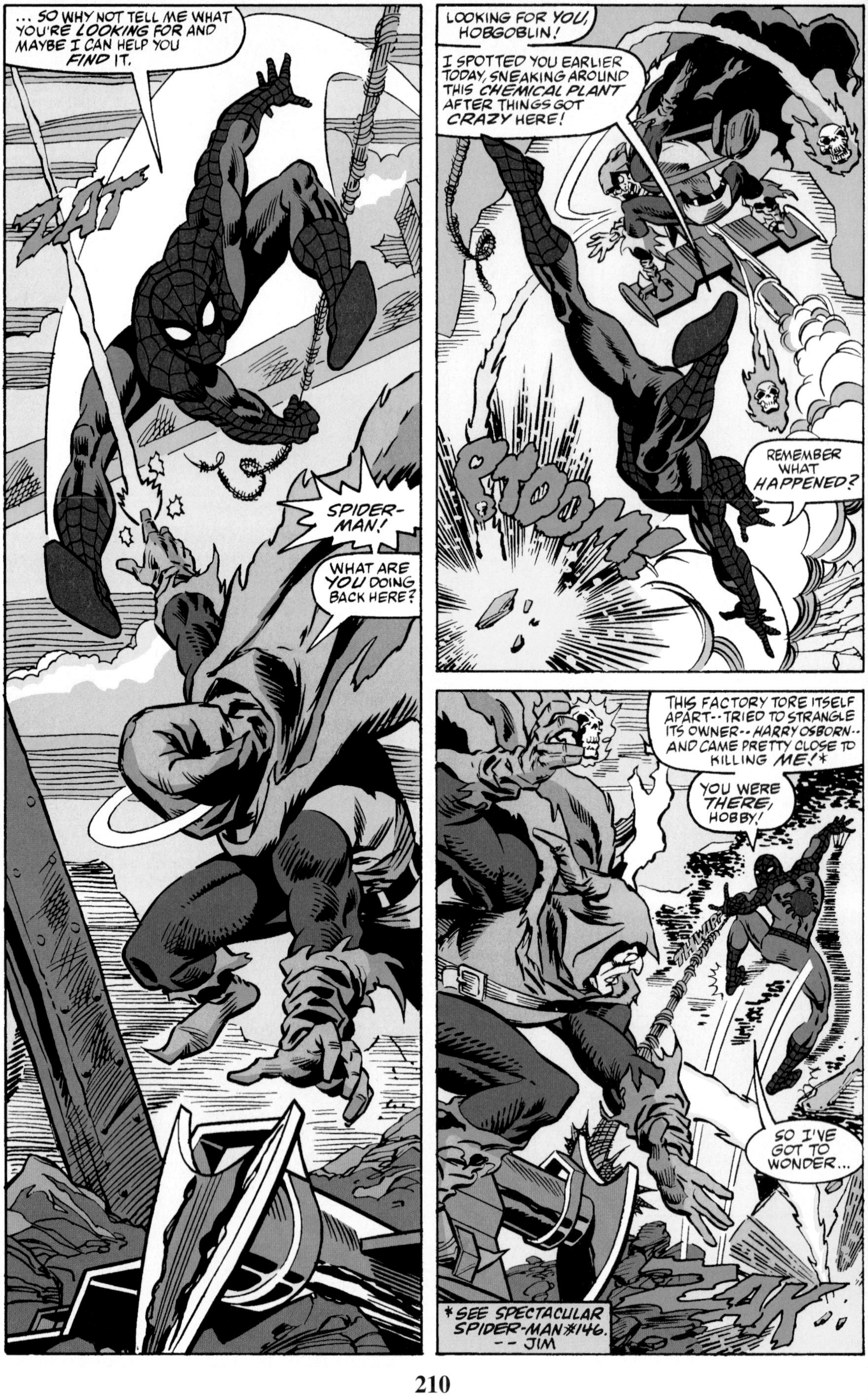
... SO WHY NOT TELL ME WHAT YOU'RE LOOKING FOR AND MAYBE I CAN HELP YOU FIND IT.
ZAT
SPIDER-MAN!
WHAT ARE YOU DOING BACK HERE?
LOOKING FOR YOU, HOBGOBLIN!
I SPOTTED YOU EARLIER TODAY, SNEAKING AROUND THIS CHEMICAL PLANT AFTER THINGS GOT CRAZY HERE!
PTOOM!
REMEMBER WHAT HAPPENED?
THIS FACTORY TORE ITSELF APART--TRIED TO STRANGLE ITS OWNER--HARRY OSBORN--AND CAME PRETTY CLOSE TO KILLING ME!*
YOU WERE THERE, HOBBY!
SO I'VE GOT TO WONDER...
*SEE SPECTACULAR SPIDER-MAN #146. --JIM

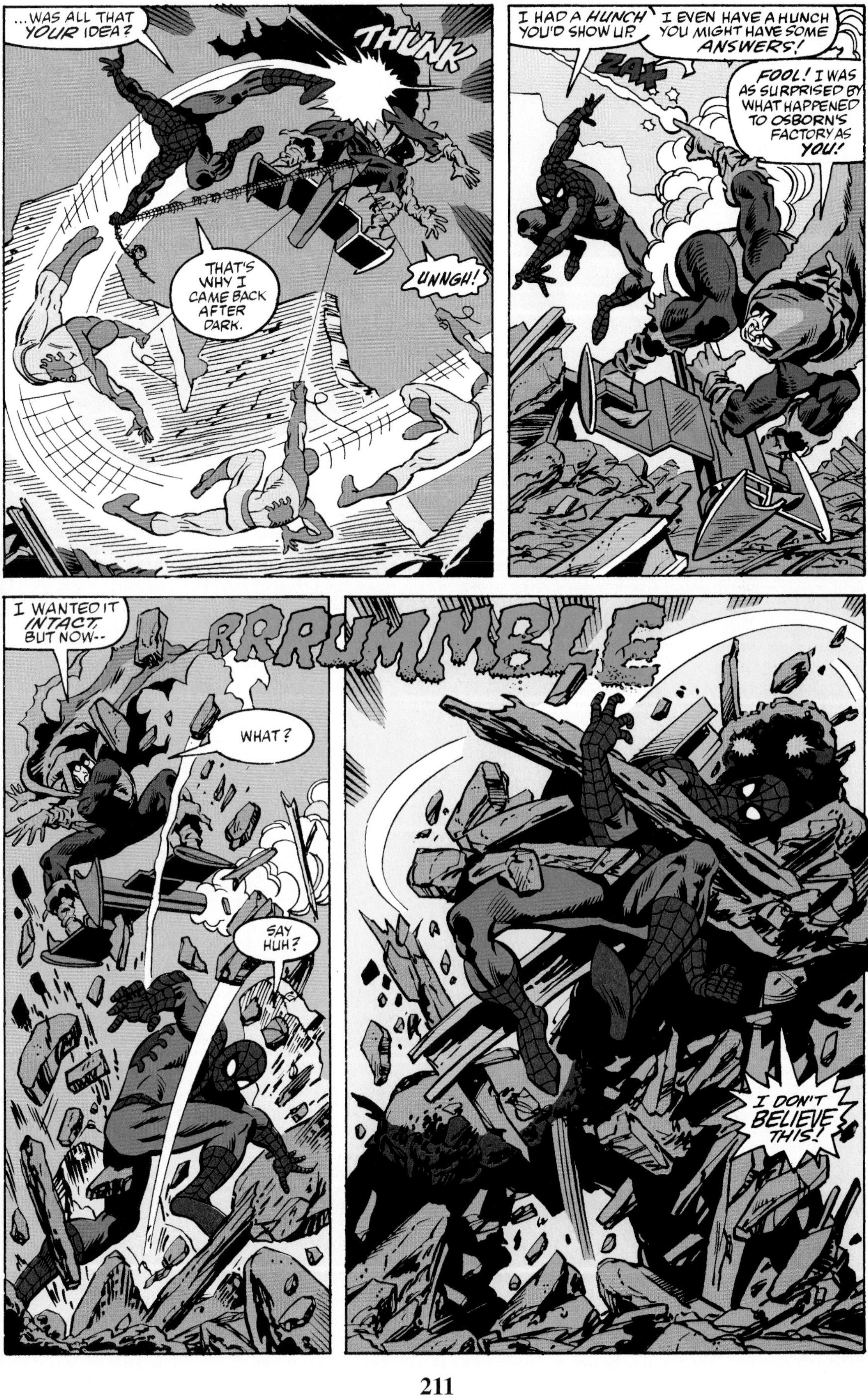

...WAS ALL THAT YOUR IDEA?
THUNK
THAT'S WHY I CAME BACK AFTER DARK.
UNNGH!
I HAD A HUNCH YOU'D SHOW UP.
I EVEN HAVE A HUNCH YOU MIGHT HAVE SOME ANSWERS!
ZAX
FOOL! I WAS AS SURPRISED BY WHAT HAPPENED TO OSBORN'S FACTORY AS YOU!
I WANTED IT INTACT, BUT NOW--
RRRUMMBLE
WHAT?
SAY HUH?
I DON'T BELIEVE THIS!

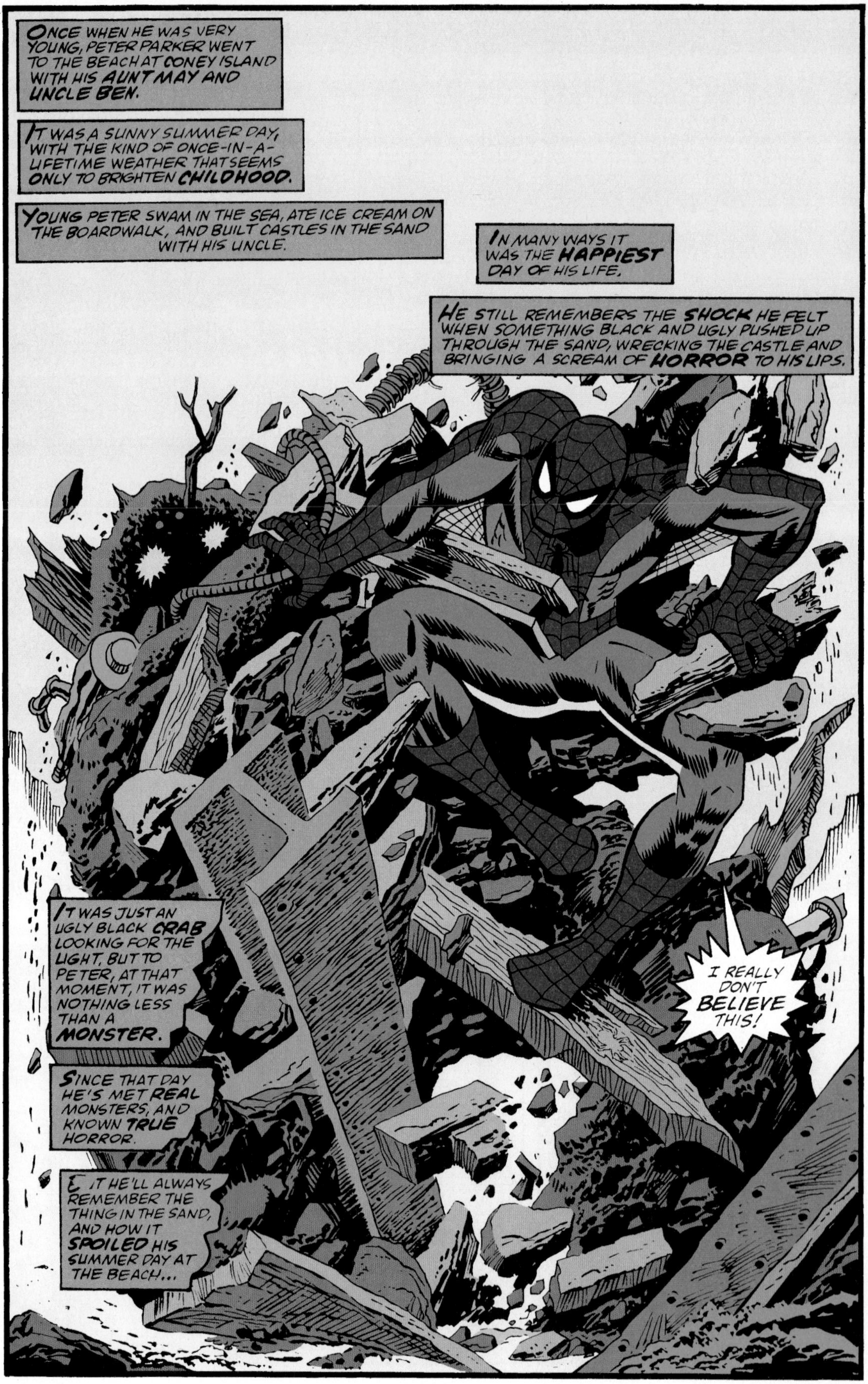

ONCE WHEN HE WAS VERY YOUNG, PETER PARKER WENT TO THE BEACH AT CONEY ISLAND WITH HIS AUNT MAY AND UNCLE BEN.
IT WAS A SUNNY SUMMER DAY, WITH THE KIND OF ONCE-IN-A-LIFETIME WEATHER THAT SEEMS ONLY TO BRIGHTEN CHILDHOOD.
YOUNG PETER SWAM IN THE SEA, ATE ICE CREAM ON THE BOARDWALK, AND BUILT CASTLES IN THE SAND WITH HIS UNCLE.
IN MANY WAYS IT WAS THE HAPPIEST DAY OF HIS LIFE.
HE STILL REMEMBERS THE SHOCK HE FELT WHEN SOMETHING BLACK AND UGLY PUSHED UP THROUGH THE SAND, WRECKING THE CASTLE AND BRINGING A SCREAM OF HORROR TO HIS LIPS.
IT WAS JUST AN UGLY BLACK CRAB LOOKING FOR THE LIGHT, BUT TO PETER, AT THAT MOMENT, IT WAS NOTHING LESS THAN A MONSTER.
I REALLY DON'T BELIEVE THIS!
SINCE THAT DAY HE'S MET REAL MONSTERS, AND KNOWN TRUE HORROR.
T HE'LL ALWAYS REMEMBER THE THING IN THE SAND, AND HOW IT SPOILED HIS SUMMER DAY AT THE BEACH...

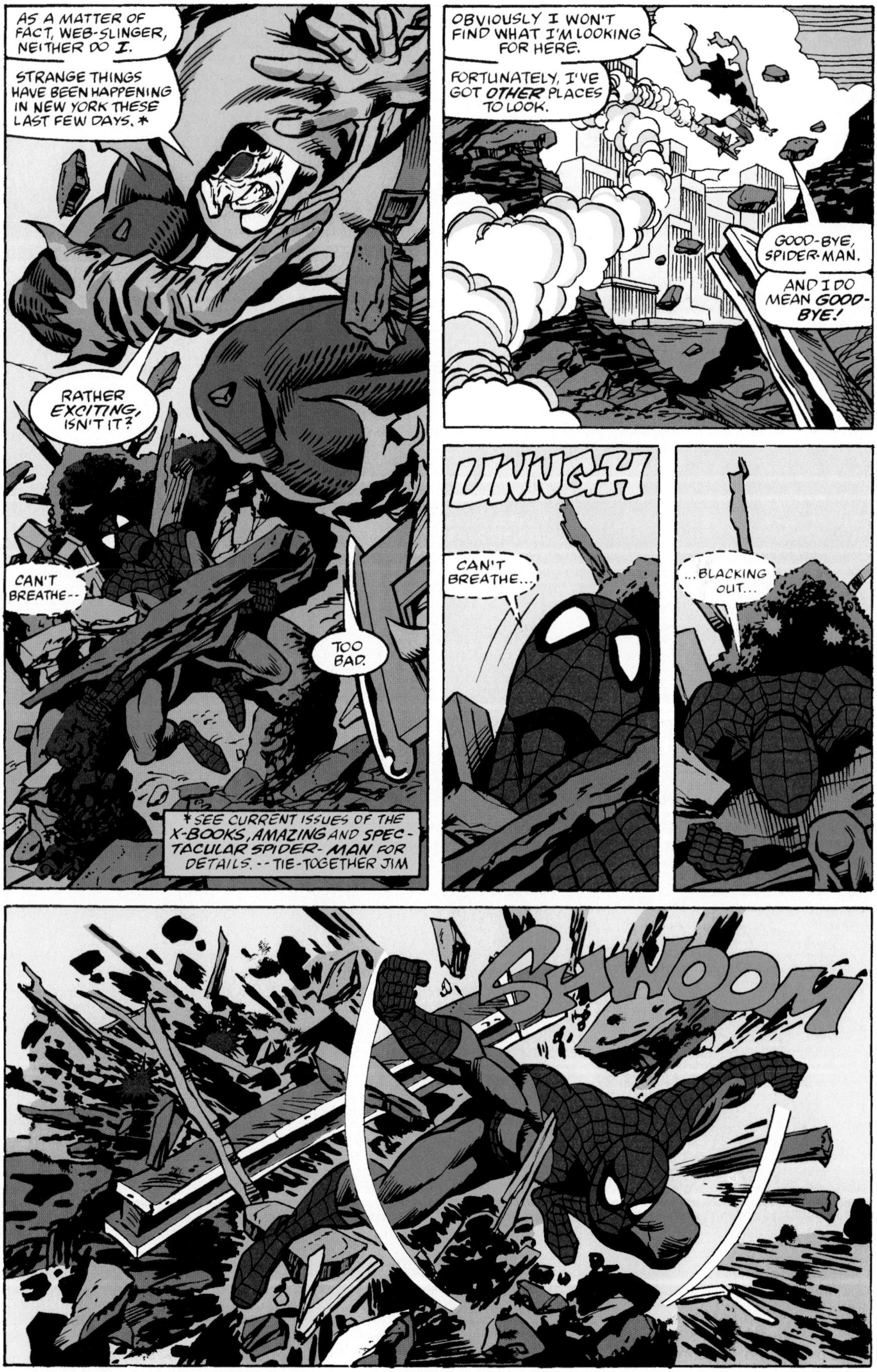

AS A MATTER OF FACT, WEB-SLINGER, NEITHER DO I.
STRANGE THINGS HAVE BEEN HAPPENING IN NEW YORK THESE LAST FEW DAYS. *
RATHER EXCITING, ISN'T IT?
CAN'T BREATHE--
TOO BAD.
* SEE CURRENT ISSUES OF THE X-BOOKS, AMAZING AND SPECTACULAR SPIDER-MAN FOR DETAILS. --TIE-TOGETHER JIM
OBVIOUSLY I WON'T FIND WHAT I'M LOOKING FOR HERE.
FORTUNATELY, I'VE GOT OTHER PLACES TO LOOK.
GOOD-BYE, SPIDER-MAN.
AND I DO MEAN GOOD-BYE!
UNNGH
CAN'T BREATHE...
...BLACKING OUT...
SHWOOM

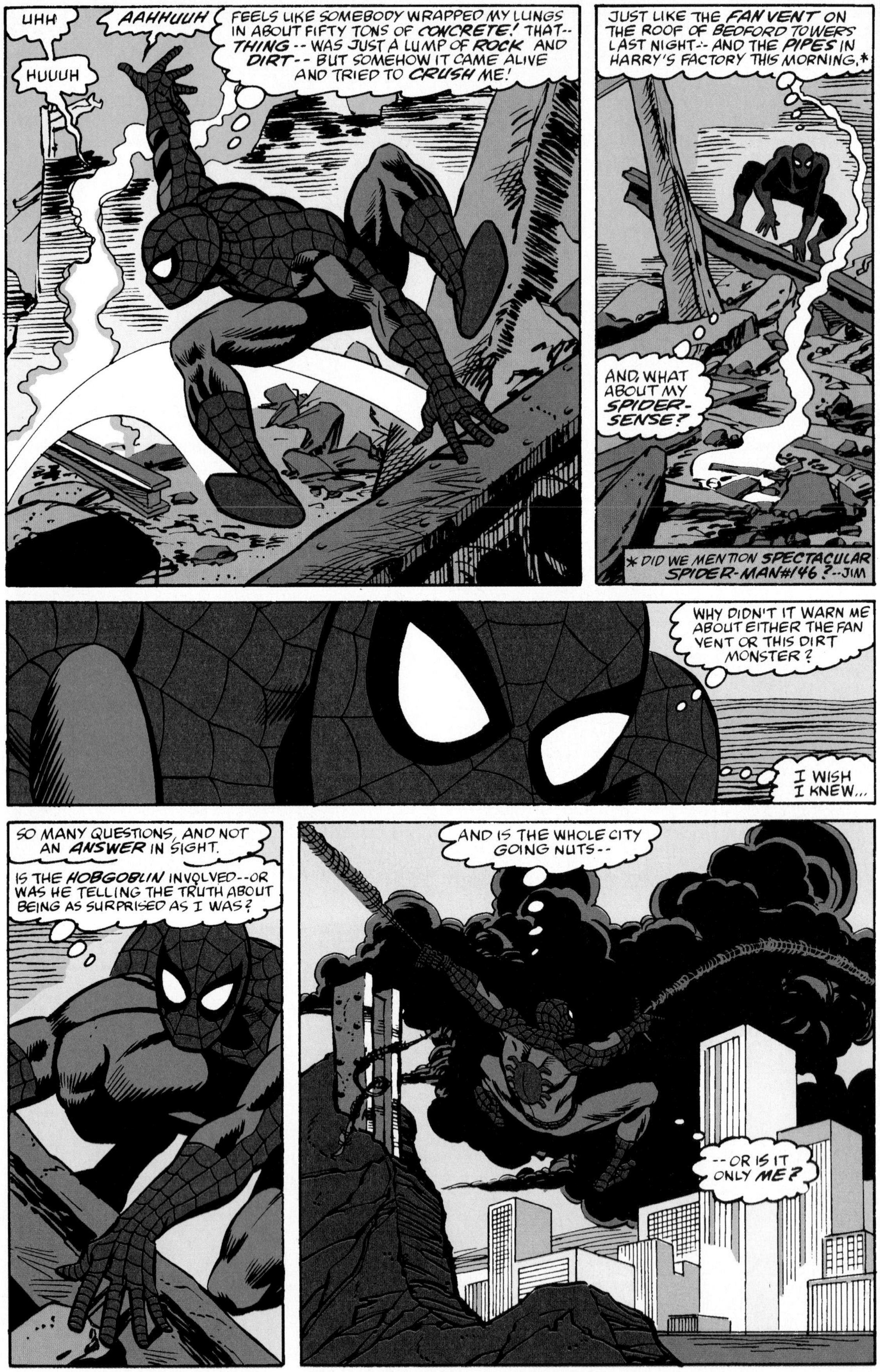
UHH
HUUUH
AAHHUUH
FEELS LIKE SOMEBODY WRAPPED MY LUNGS IN ABOUT FIFTY TONS OF CONCRETE! THAT-- THING -- WAS JUST A LUMP OF ROCK AND DIRT -- BUT SOMEHOW IT CAME ALIVE AND TRIED TO CRUSH ME!
JUST LIKE THE FAN VENT ON THE ROOF OF BEDFORD TOWERS LAST NIGHT-- AND THE PIPES IN HARRY'S FACTORY THIS MORNING.*
AND, WHAT ABOUT MY SPIDER-SENSE?
* DID WE MENTION SPECTACULAR SPIDER-MAN #146? --JIM
WHY DIDN'T IT WARN ME ABOUT EITHER THE FAN VENT OR THIS DIRT MONSTER?
I WISH I KNEW...
SO MANY QUESTIONS, AND NOT AN ANSWER IN SIGHT.
IS THE HOBGOBLIN INVOLVED--OR WAS HE TELLING THE TRUTH ABOUT BEING AS SURPRISED AS I WAS?
AND IS THE WHOLE CITY GOING NUTS--
--OR IS IT ONLY ME?

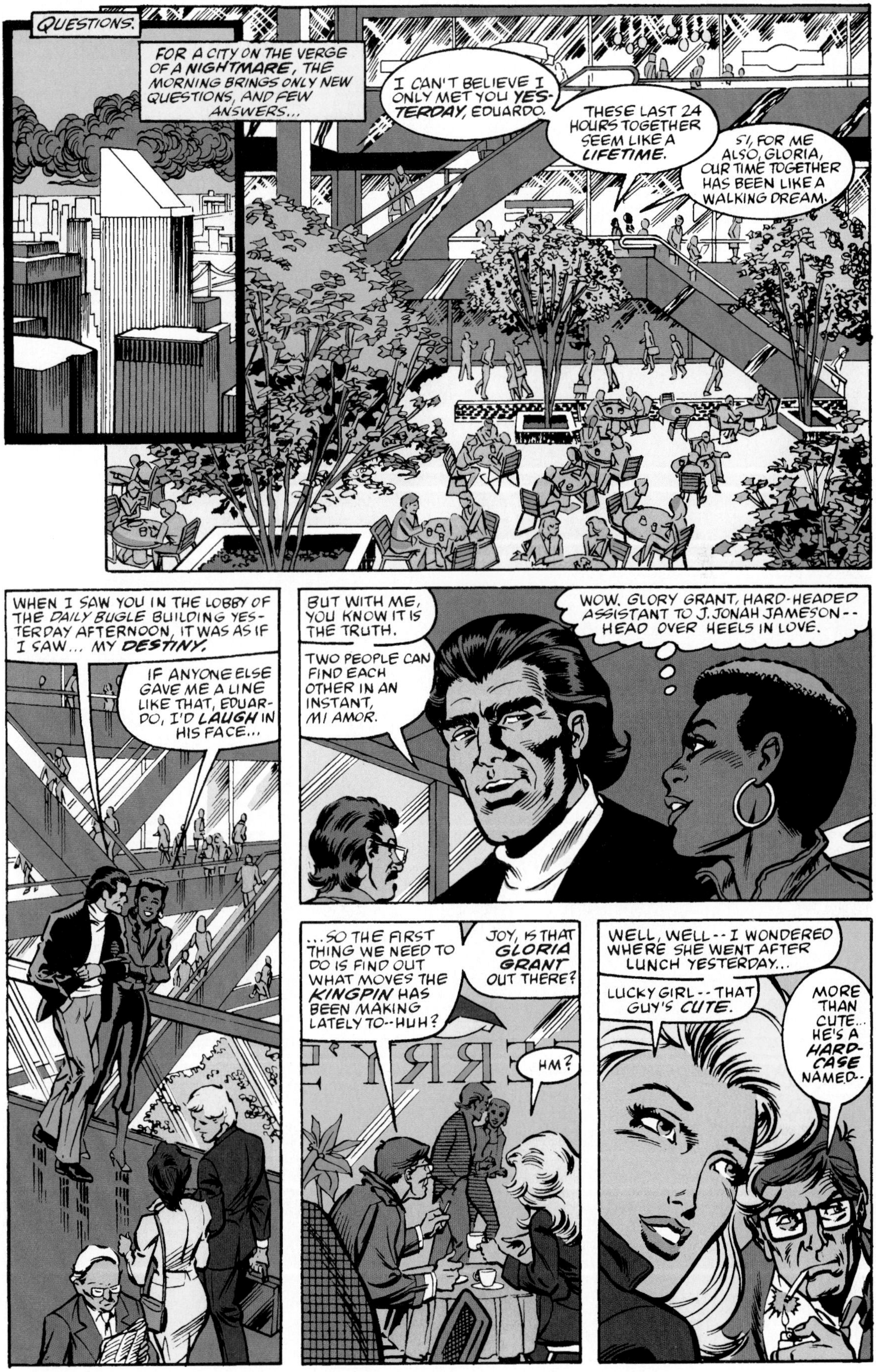
QUESTIONS:
FOR A CITY ON THE VERGE OF A NIGHTMARE, THE MORNING BRINGS ONLY NEW QUESTIONS, AND FEW ANSWERS...
I CAN'T BELIEVE I ONLY MET YOU YESTERDAY, EDUARDO.
THESE LAST 24 HOURS TOGETHER SEEM LIKE A LIFETIME.
SÍ, FOR ME ALSO, GLORIA, OUR TIME TOGETHER HAS BEEN LIKE A WALKING DREAM.
WHEN I SAW YOU IN THE LOBBY OF THE DAILY BUGLE BUILDING YESTERDAY AFTERNOON, IT WAS AS IF I SAW... MY DESTINY.
IF ANYONE ELSE GAVE ME A LINE LIKE THAT, EDUARDO, I'D LAUGH IN HIS FACE...
BUT WITH ME, YOU KNOW IT IS THE TRUTH.
TWO PEOPLE CAN FIND EACH OTHER IN AN INSTANT, MI AMOR.
WOW. GLORY GRANT, HARD-HEADED ASSISTANT TO J. JONAH JAMESON-- HEAD OVER HEELS IN LOVE.
...SO THE FIRST THING WE NEED TO DO IS FIND OUT WHAT MOVES THE KINGPIN HAS BEEN MAKING LATELY TO--HUH?
JOY, IS THAT GLORIA GRANT OUT THERE?
HM?
WELL, WELL-- I WONDERED WHERE SHE WENT AFTER LUNCH YESTERDAY...
LUCKY GIRL-- THAT GUY'S CUTE.
MORE THAN CUTE... HE'S A HARD-CASE NAMED--

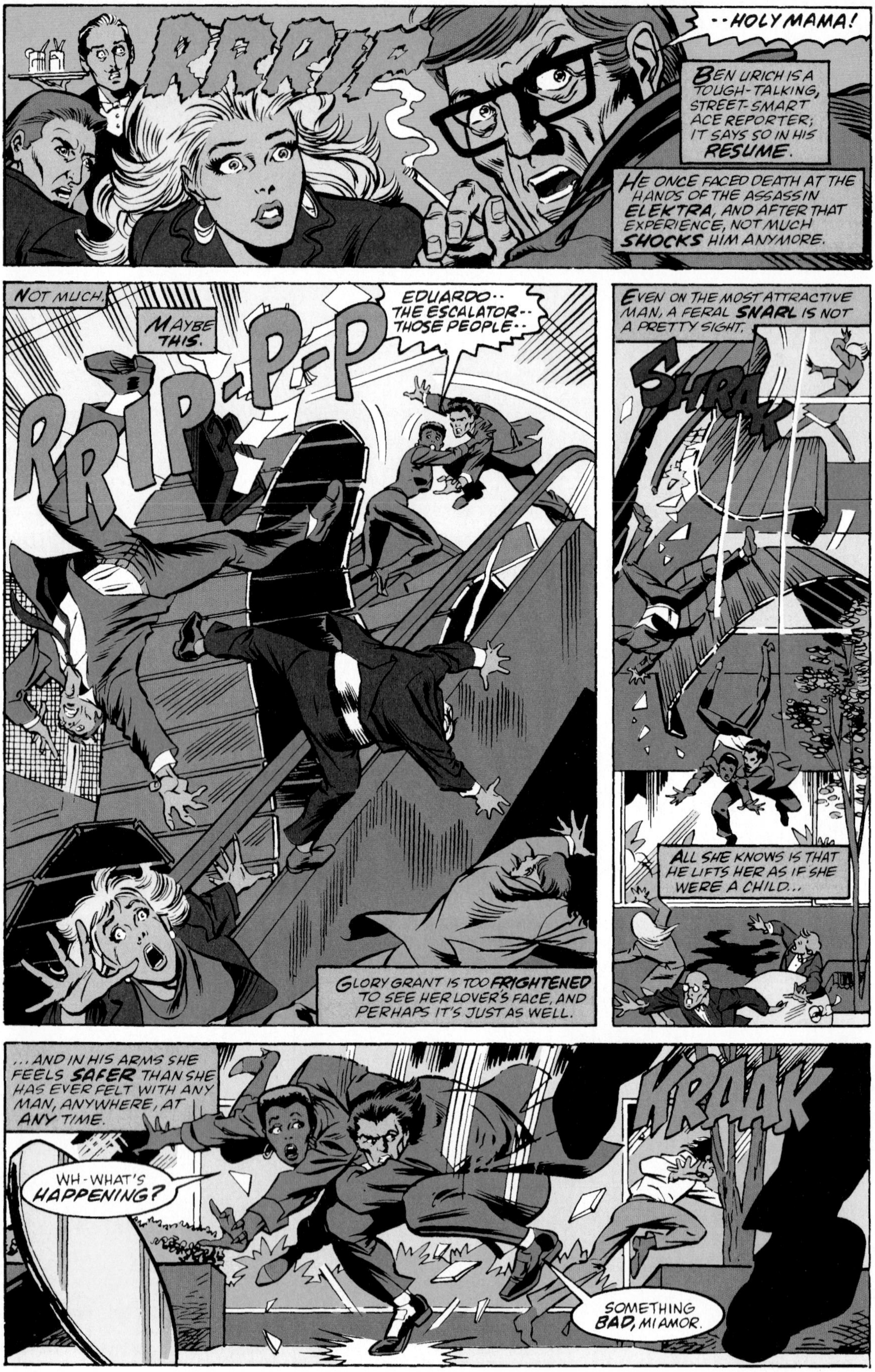
RRRIP
..HOLY MAMA!
BEN URICH IS A TOUGH-TALKING, STREET-SMART ACE REPORTER; IT SAYS SO IN HIS RESUME.
HE ONCE FACED DEATH AT THE HANDS OF THE ASSASSIN ELEKTRA, AND AFTER THAT EXPERIENCE, NOT MUCH SHOCKS HIM ANYMORE.
NOT MUCH.
MAYBE THIS.
RRIP-P-P
EDUARDO-- THE ESCALATOR-- THOSE PEOPLE--
GLORY GRANT IS TOO FRIGHTENED TO SEE HER LOVER'S FACE, AND PERHAPS IT'S JUST AS WELL.
EVEN ON THE MOST ATTRACTIVE MAN, A FERAL SNARL IS NOT A PRETTY SIGHT.
SHRAAK
ALL SHE KNOWS IS THAT HE LIFTS HER AS IF SHE WERE A CHILD...
...AND IN HIS ARMS SHE FEELS SAFER THAN SHE HAS EVER FELT WITH ANY MAN, ANYWHERE, AT ANY TIME.
KRAAK
WH-WHAT'S HAPPENING?
SOMETHING BAD, MI AMOR.

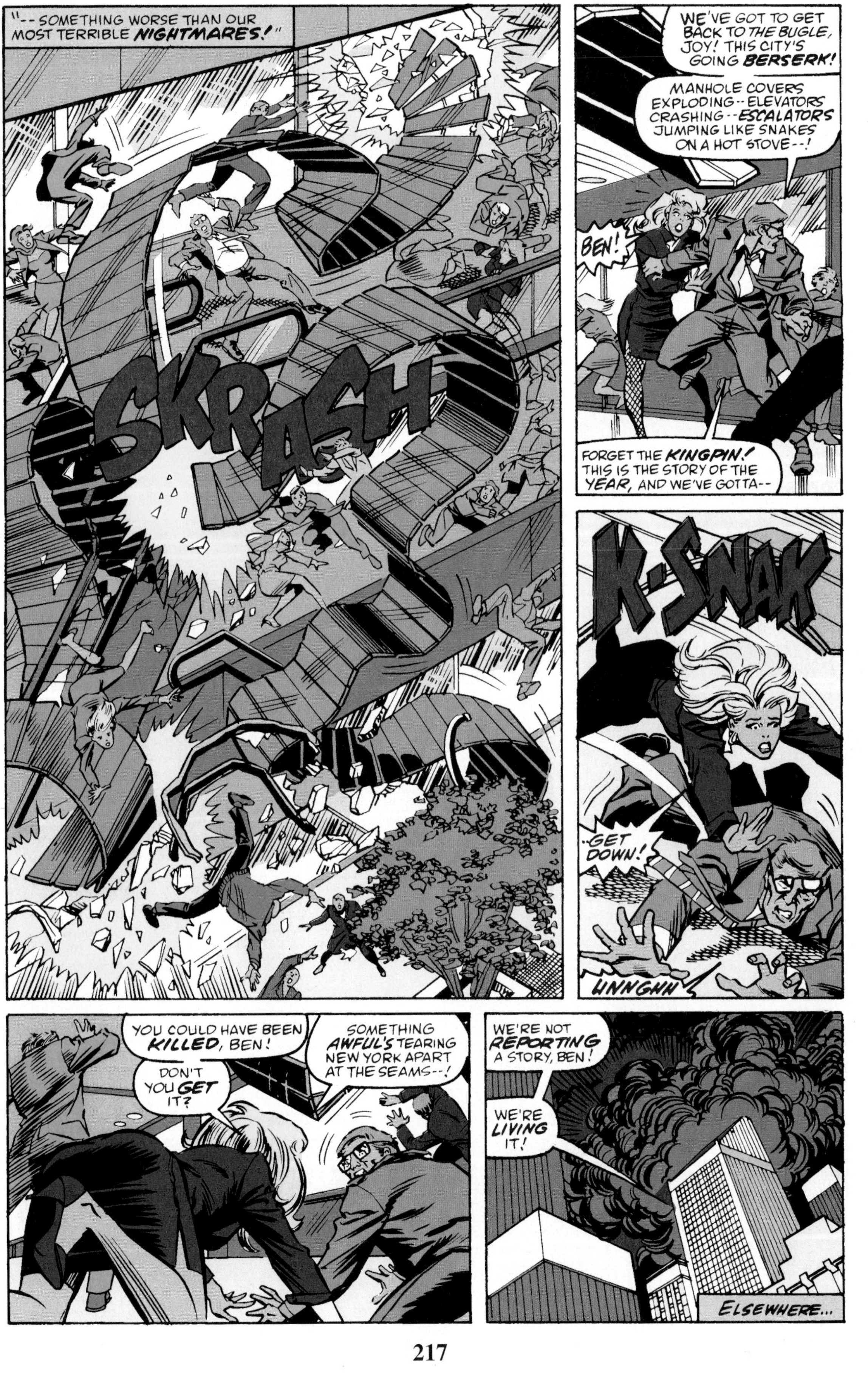
"--SOMETHING WORSE THAN OUR MOST TERRIBLE NIGHTMARES!"
SKRASH
WE'VE GOT TO GET BACK TO THE BUGLE, JOY! THIS CITY'S GOING BERSERK!
MANHOLE COVERS EXPLODING--ELEVATORS CRASHING--ESCALATORS JUMPING LIKE SNAKES ON A HOT STOVE--!
BEN!
FORGET THE KINGPIN! THIS IS THE STORY OF THE YEAR, AND WE'VE GOTTA--
K-SNAK
..GET DOWN!
UNNGHH
YOU COULD HAVE BEEN KILLED, BEN!
DON'T YOU GET IT?
SOMETHING AWFUL'S TEARING NEW YORK APART AT THE SEAMS--!
WE'RE NOT REPORTING A STORY, BEN!
WE'RE LIVING IT!
ELSEWHERE...

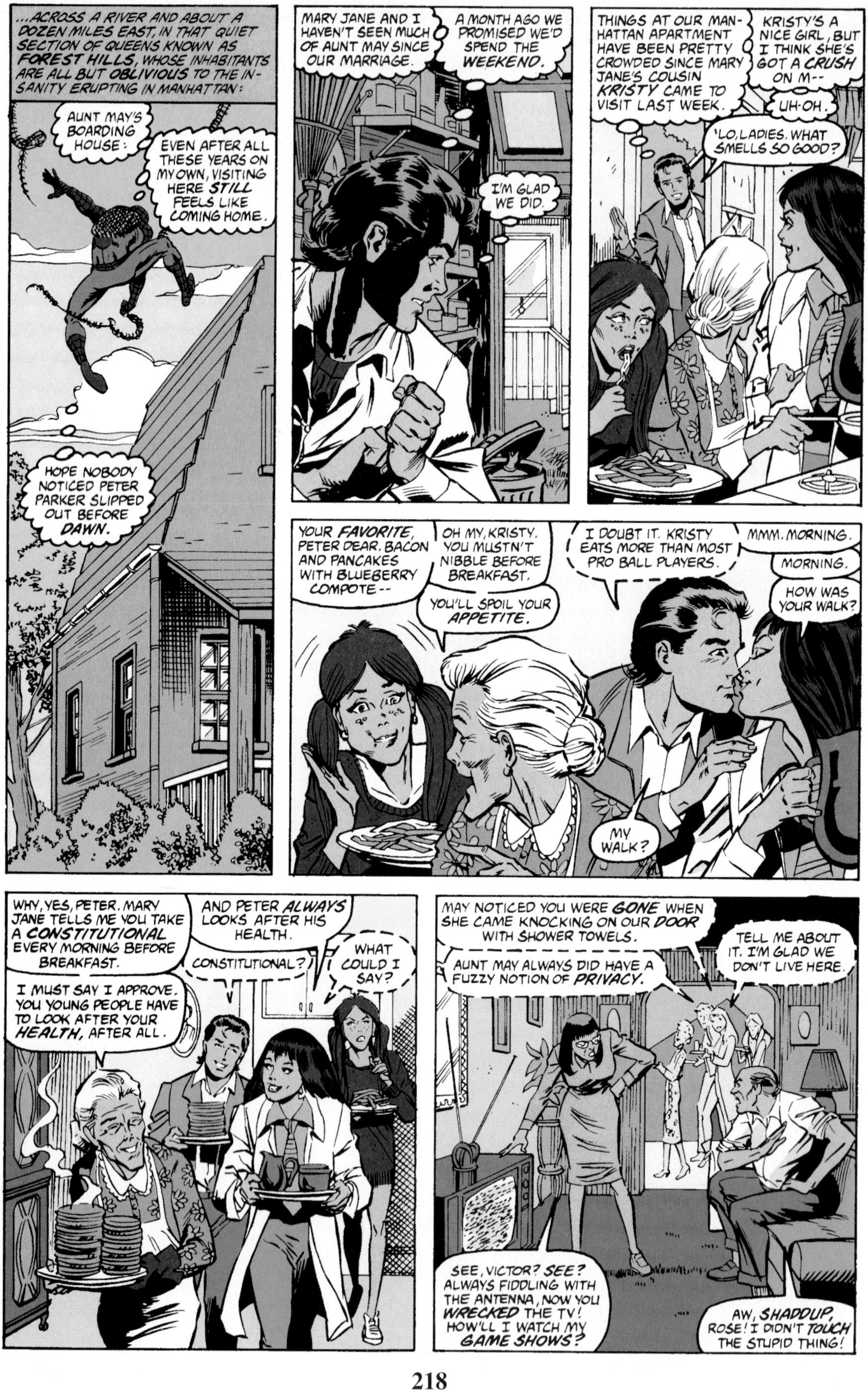
...ACROSS A RIVER AND ABOUT A DOZEN MILES EAST, IN THAT QUIET SECTION OF QUEENS KNOWN AS FOREST HILLS, WHOSE INHABITANTS ARE ALL BUT OBLIVIOUS TO THE INSANITY ERUPTING IN MANHATTAN:
AUNT MAY'S BOARDING HOUSE:
EVEN AFTER ALL THESE YEARS ON MY OWN, VISITING HERE STILL FEELS LIKE COMING HOME.
HOPE NOBODY NOTICED PETER PARKER SLIPPED OUT BEFORE DAWN.
MARY JANE AND I HAVEN'T SEEN MUCH OF AUNT MAY SINCE OUR MARRIAGE.
A MONTH AGO WE PROMISED WE'D SPEND THE WEEKEND.
I'M GLAD WE DID.
THINGS AT OUR MANHATTAN APARTMENT HAVE BEEN PRETTY CROWDED SINCE MARY JANE'S COUSIN KRISTY CAME TO VISIT LAST WEEK.
KRISTY'S A NICE GIRL, BUT I THINK SHE'S GOT A CRUSH ON M--
UH-OH.
'LO, LADIES. WHAT SMELLS SO GOOD?
YOUR FAVORITE, PETER DEAR. BACON AND PANCAKES WITH BLUEBERRY COMPOTE--
OH MY, KRISTY. YOU MUSTN'T NIBBLE BEFORE BREAKFAST.
YOU'LL SPOIL YOUR APPETITE.
I DOUBT IT. KRISTY EATS MORE THAN MOST PRO BALL PLAYERS.
MMM. MORNING.
MORNING.
HOW WAS YOUR WALK?
MY WALK?
WHY, YES, PETER. MARY JANE TELLS ME YOU TAKE A CONSTITUTIONAL EVERY MORNING BEFORE BREAKFAST.
AND PETER ALWAYS LOOKS AFTER HIS HEALTH.
CONSTITUTIONAL?
WHAT COULD I SAY?
I MUST SAY I APPROVE. YOU YOUNG PEOPLE HAVE TO LOOK AFTER YOUR HEALTH, AFTER ALL.
MAY NOTICED YOU WERE GONE WHEN SHE CAME KNOCKING ON OUR DOOR WITH SHOWER TOWELS.
AUNT MAY ALWAYS DID HAVE A FUZZY NOTION OF PRIVACY.
TELL ME ABOUT IT. I'M GLAD WE DON'T LIVE HERE.
SEE, VICTOR? SEE? ALWAYS FIDDLING WITH THE ANTENNA, NOW YOU WRECKED THE TV! HOW'LL I WATCH MY GAME SHOWS?
AW, SHADDUP, ROSE! I DIDN'T TOUCH THE STUPID THING!

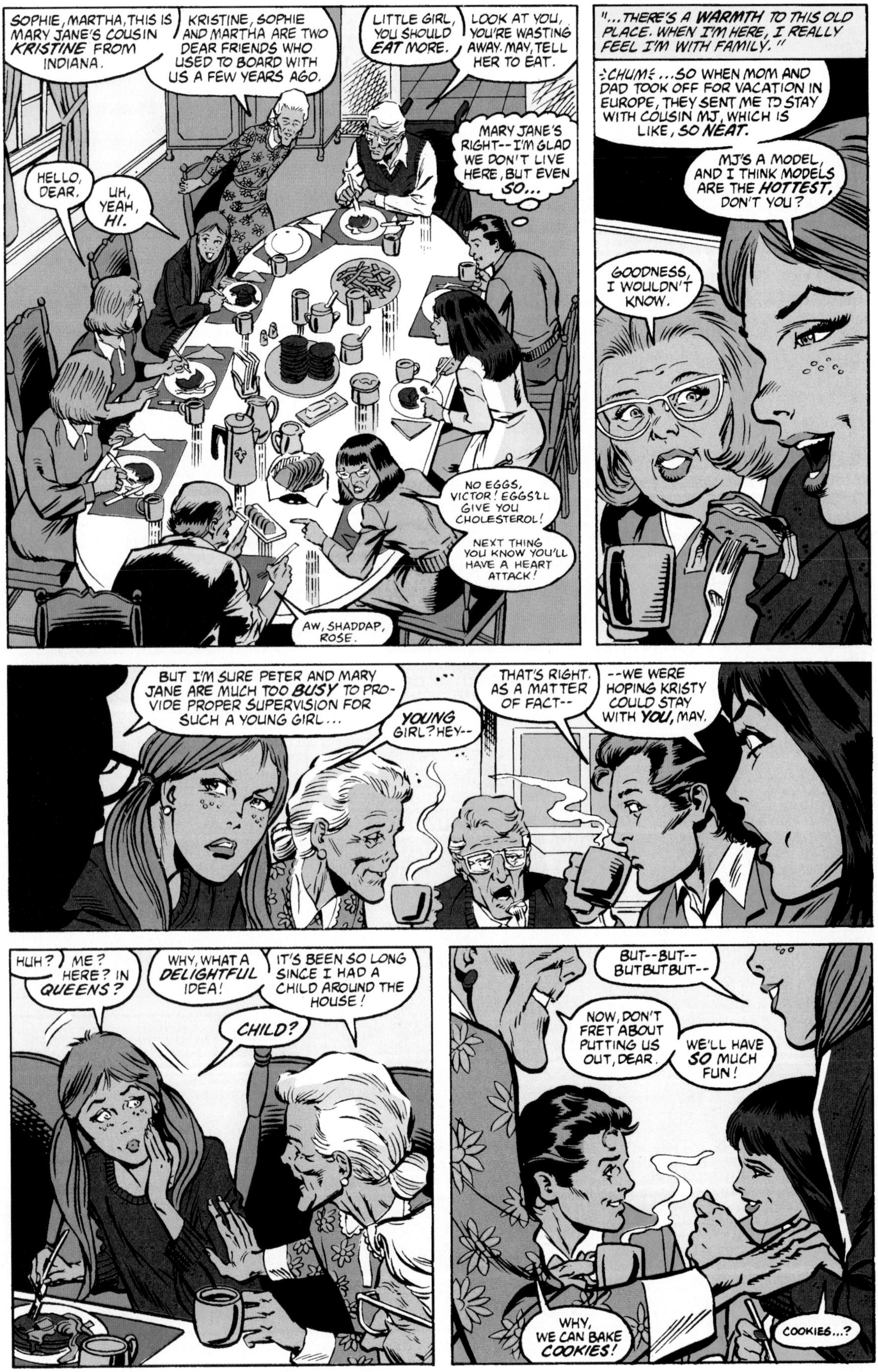
SOPHIE, MARTHA, THIS IS MARY JANE'S COUSIN KRISTINE FROM INDIANA.
KRISTINE, SOPHIE AND MARTHA ARE TWO DEAR FRIENDS WHO USED TO BOARD WITH US A FEW YEARS AGO.
LITTLE GIRL, YOU SHOULD EAT MORE.
LOOK AT YOU, YOU'RE WASTING AWAY. MAY, TELL HER TO EAT.
HELLO, DEAR.
UH, YEAH, HI.
MARY JANE'S RIGHT-- I'M GLAD WE DON'T LIVE HERE, BUT EVEN SO...
NO EGGS, VICTOR! EGGS'LL GIVE YOU CHOLESTEROL!
NEXT THING YOU KNOW YOU'LL HAVE A HEART ATTACK!
AW, SHADDAP, ROSE.
"...THERE'S A WARMTH TO THIS OLD PLACE. WHEN I'M HERE, I REALLY FEEL I'M WITH FAMILY."
CHUM ...SO WHEN MOM AND DAD TOOK OFF FOR VACATION IN EUROPE, THEY SENT ME TO STAY WITH COUSIN MJ, WHICH IS LIKE, SO NEAT.
MJ'S A MODEL, AND I THINK MODELS ARE THE HOTTEST, DON'T YOU?
GOODNESS, I WOULDN'T KNOW.
BUT I'M SURE PETER AND MARY JANE ARE MUCH TOO BUSY TO PROVIDE PROPER SUPERVISION FOR SUCH A YOUNG GIRL...
YOUNG GIRL? HEY--
THAT'S RIGHT. AS A MATTER OF FACT--
--WE WERE HOPING KRISTY COULD STAY WITH YOU, MAY.
HUH?
ME? HERE? IN QUEENS?
WHY, WHAT A DELIGHTFUL IDEA!
IT'S BEEN SO LONG SINCE I HAD A CHILD AROUND THE HOUSE!
CHILD?
BUT--BUT-- BUTBUTBUT--
NOW, DON'T FRET ABOUT PUTTING US OUT, DEAR.
WE'LL HAVE SO MUCH FUN!
WHY, WE CAN BAKE COOKIES!
COOKIES...?

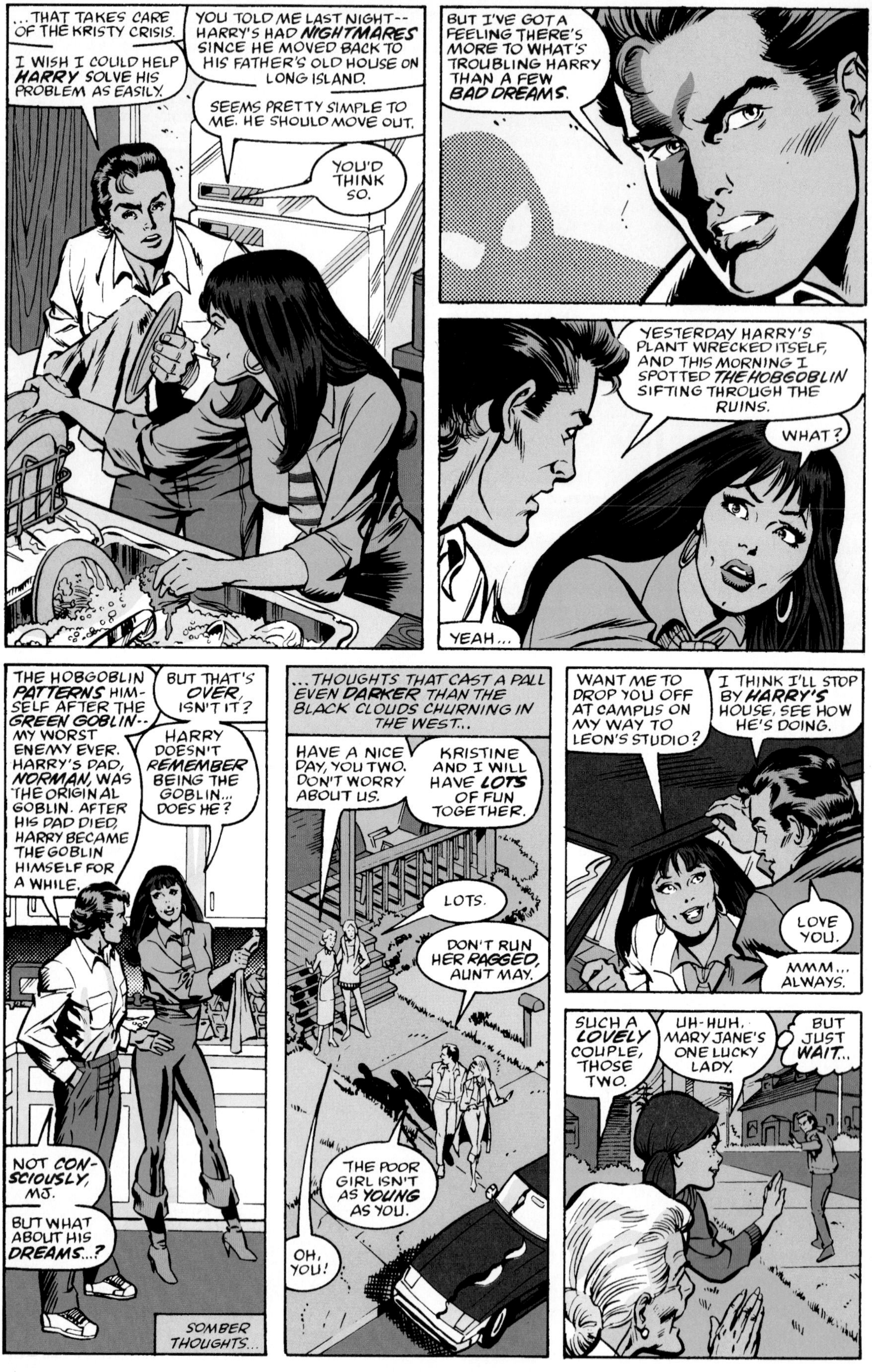
...THAT TAKES CARE OF THE KRISTY CRISIS.
I WISH I COULD HELP HARRY SOLVE HIS PROBLEM AS EASILY.
YOU TOLD ME LAST NIGHT-- HARRY'S HAD NIGHTMARES SINCE HE MOVED BACK TO HIS FATHER'S OLD HOUSE ON LONG ISLAND.
SEEMS PRETTY SIMPLE TO ME. HE SHOULD MOVE OUT.
YOU'D THINK SO.
BUT I'VE GOT A FEELING THERE'S MORE TO WHAT'S TROUBLING HARRY THAN A FEW BAD DREAMS.
YESTERDAY HARRY'S PLANT WRECKED ITSELF, AND THIS MORNING I SPOTTED THE HOBGOBLIN SIFTING THROUGH THE RUINS.
WHAT?
YEAH...
THE HOBGOBLIN PATTERNS HIMSELF AFTER THE GREEN GOBLIN-- MY WORST ENEMY EVER. HARRY'S DAD, NORMAN, WAS THE ORIGINAL GOBLIN. AFTER HIS DAD DIED, HARRY BECAME THE GOBLIN HIMSELF FOR A WHILE.
BUT THAT'S OVER, ISN'T IT?
HARRY DOESN'T REMEMBER BEING THE GOBLIN... DOES HE?
NOT CONSCIOUSLY, MJ.
BUT WHAT ABOUT HIS DREAMS...?
SOMBER THOUGHTS...
...THOUGHTS THAT CAST A PALL EVEN DARKER THAN THE BLACK CLOUDS CHURNING IN THE WEST...
HAVE A NICE DAY, YOU TWO. DON'T WORRY ABOUT US.
KRISTINE AND I WILL HAVE LOTS OF FUN TOGETHER.
LOTS.
DON'T RUN HER RAGGED, AUNT MAY.
THE POOR GIRL ISN'T AS YOUNG AS YOU.
OH, YOU!
WANT ME TO DROP YOU OFF AT CAMPUS ON MY WAY TO LEON'S STUDIO?
I THINK I'LL STOP BY HARRY'S HOUSE, SEE HOW HE'S DOING.
LOVE YOU.
MMM... ALWAYS.
SUCH A LOVELY COUPLE, THOSE TWO.
UH-HUH. MARY JANE'S ONE LUCKY LADY.
BUT JUST WAIT...

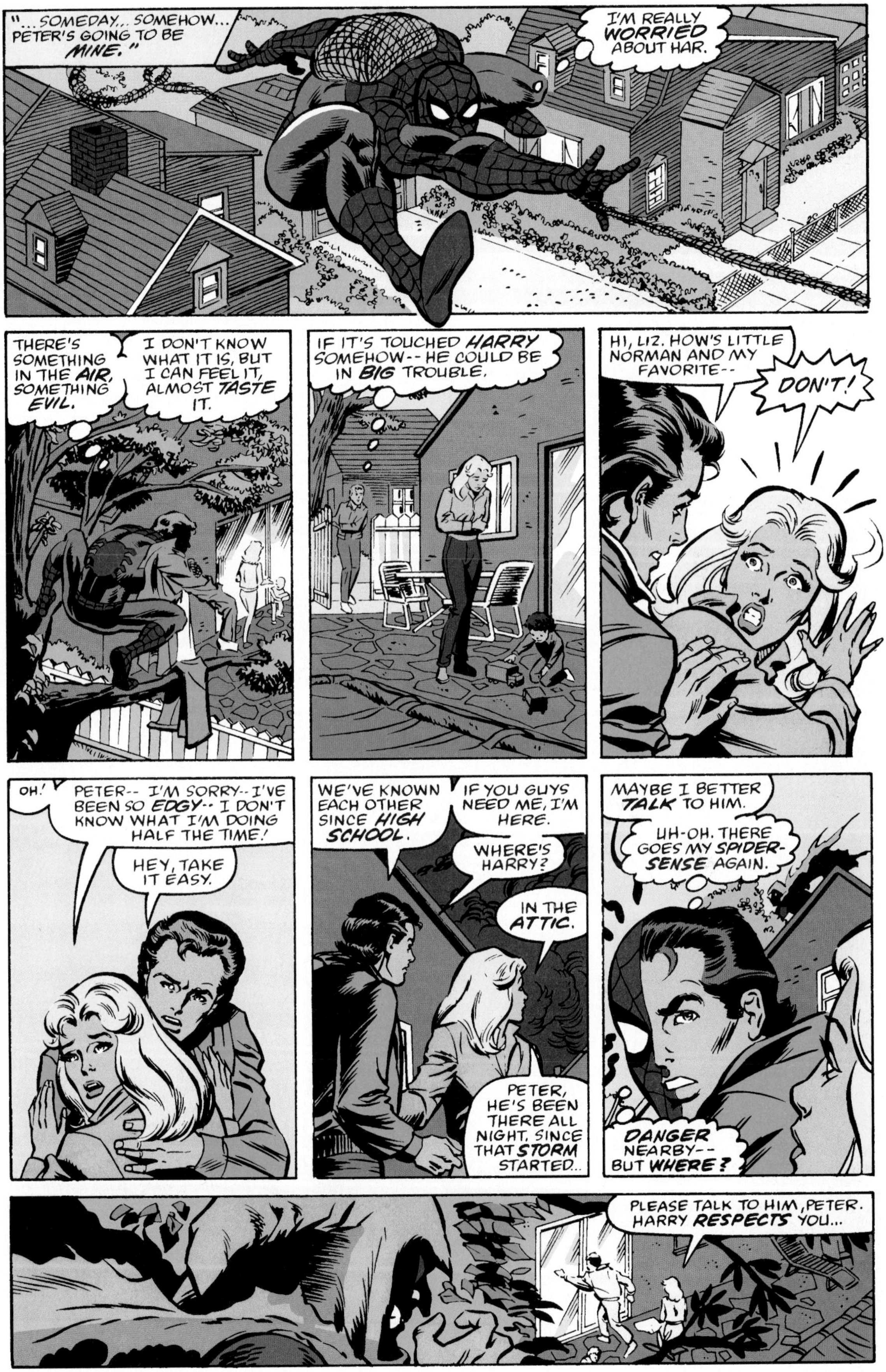
"...SOMEDAY... SOMEHOW... PETER'S GOING TO BE MINE."
I'M REALLY WORRIED ABOUT HAR.
THERE'S SOMETHING IN THE AIR, SOMETHING EVIL.
I DON'T KNOW WHAT IT IS, BUT I CAN FEEL IT, ALMOST TASTE IT.
IF IT'S TOUCHED HARRY SOMEHOW-- HE COULD BE IN BIG TROUBLE.
HI, LIZ. HOW'S LITTLE NORMAN AND MY FAVORITE--
DON'T!
OH!
PETER-- I'M SORRY-- I'VE BEEN SO EDGY-- I DON'T KNOW WHAT I'M DOING HALF THE TIME!
HEY, TAKE IT EASY.
WE'VE KNOWN EACH OTHER SINCE HIGH SCHOOL.
IF YOU GUYS NEED ME, I'M HERE.
WHERE'S HARRY?
IN THE ATTIC.
PETER, HE'S BEEN THERE ALL NIGHT, SINCE THAT STORM STARTED...
MAYBE I BETTER TALK TO HIM.
UH-OH. THERE GOES MY SPIDER-SENSE AGAIN.
DANGER NEARBY-- BUT WHERE?
PLEASE TALK TO HIM, PETER. HARRY RESPECTS YOU...

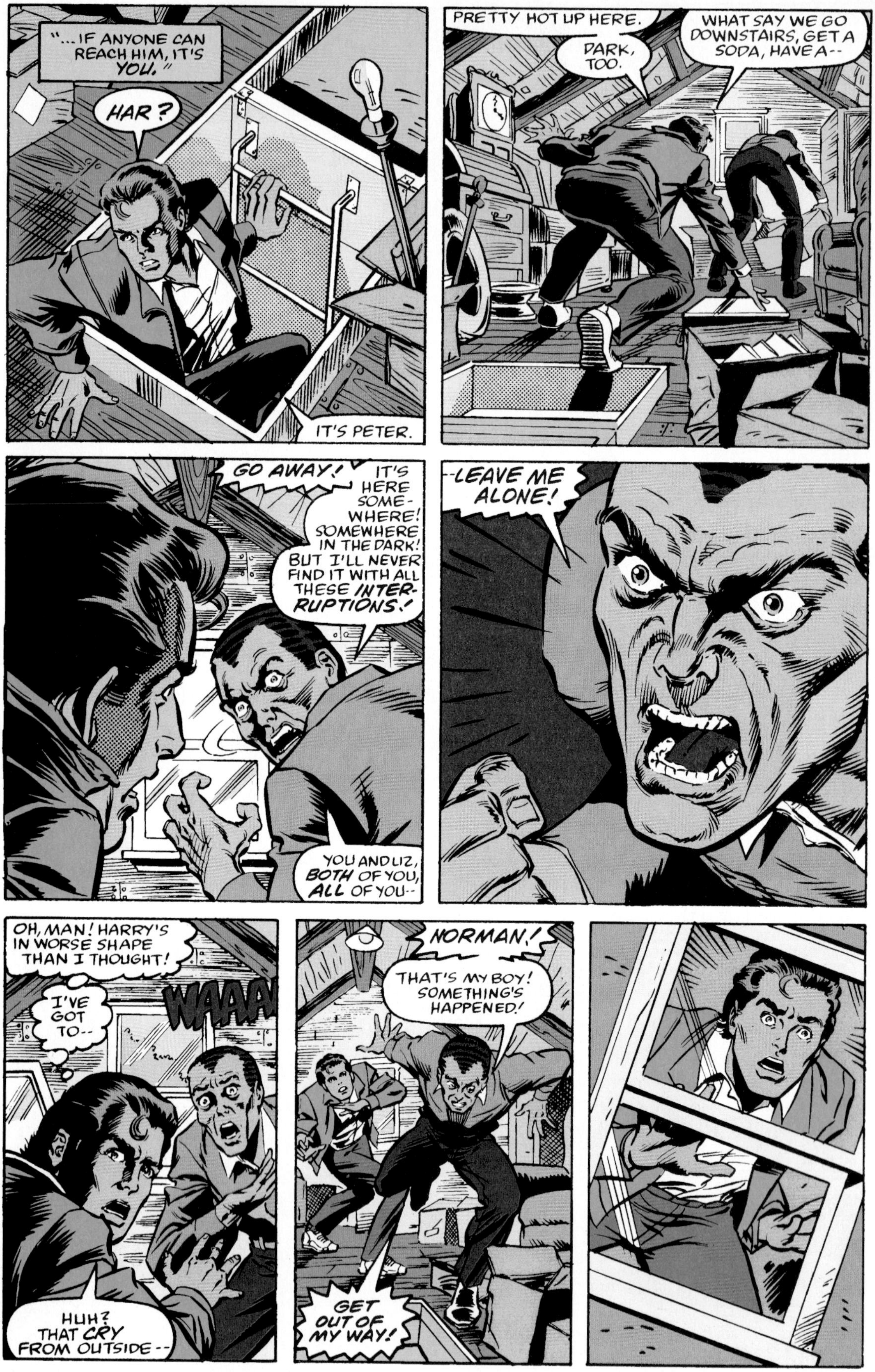
"...IF ANYONE CAN REACH HIM, IT'S YOU."
HAR?
IT'S PETER.
PRETTY HOT UP HERE.
DARK, TOO.
WHAT SAY WE GO DOWNSTAIRS, GET A SODA, HAVE A--
GO AWAY!
IT'S HERE SOME-WHERE! SOMEWHERE IN THE DARK! BUT I'LL NEVER FIND IT WITH ALL THESE INTER-RUPTIONS!
YOU AND LIZ, BOTH OF YOU, ALL OF YOU--
--LEAVE ME ALONE!
OH, MAN! HARRY'S IN WORSE SHAPE THAN I THOUGHT!
I'VE GOT TO--
WAAA
HUH? THAT CRY FROM OUTSIDE--
NORMAN!
THAT'S MY BOY! SOMETHING'S HAPPENED!
GET OUT OF MY WAY!

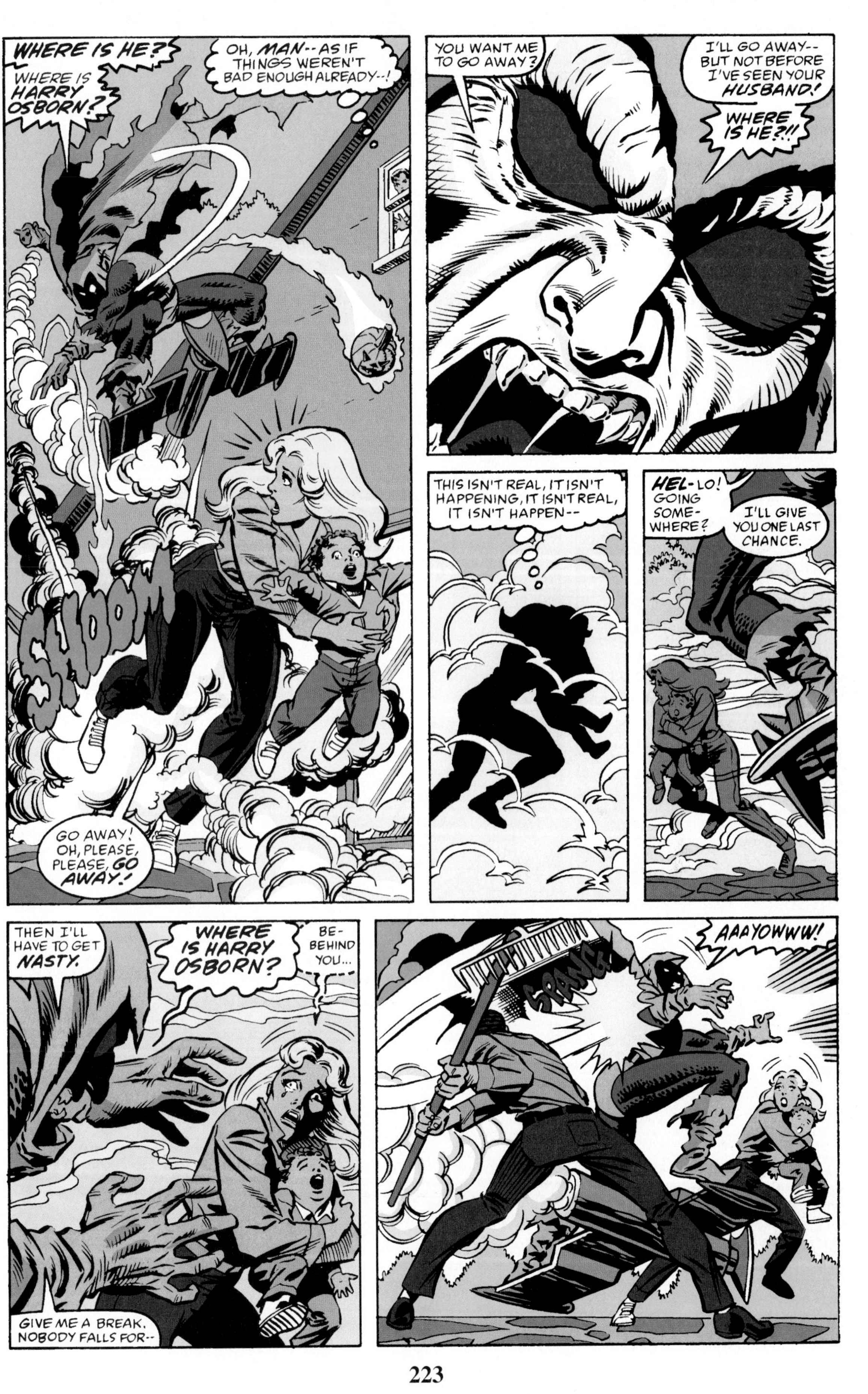

WHERE IS HE?
WHERE IS HARRY OSBORN?
OH, MAN--AS IF THINGS WEREN'T BAD ENOUGH ALREADY--!
SHOOM
GO AWAY! OH, PLEASE, PLEASE, GO AWAY!
YOU WANT ME TO GO AWAY?
I'LL GO AWAY--BUT NOT BEFORE I'VE SEEN YOUR HUSBAND!
WHERE IS HE?!!
THIS ISN'T REAL, IT ISN'T HAPPENING, IT ISN'T REAL, IT ISN'T HAPPEN--
HEL-LO! GOING SOME-WHERE?
I'LL GIVE YOU ONE LAST CHANCE.
THEN I'LL HAVE TO GET NASTY.
WHERE IS HARRY OSBORN?
BE-BEHIND YOU...
GIVE ME A BREAK. NOBODY FALLS FOR--
SPANG!
AAAYOWWW!

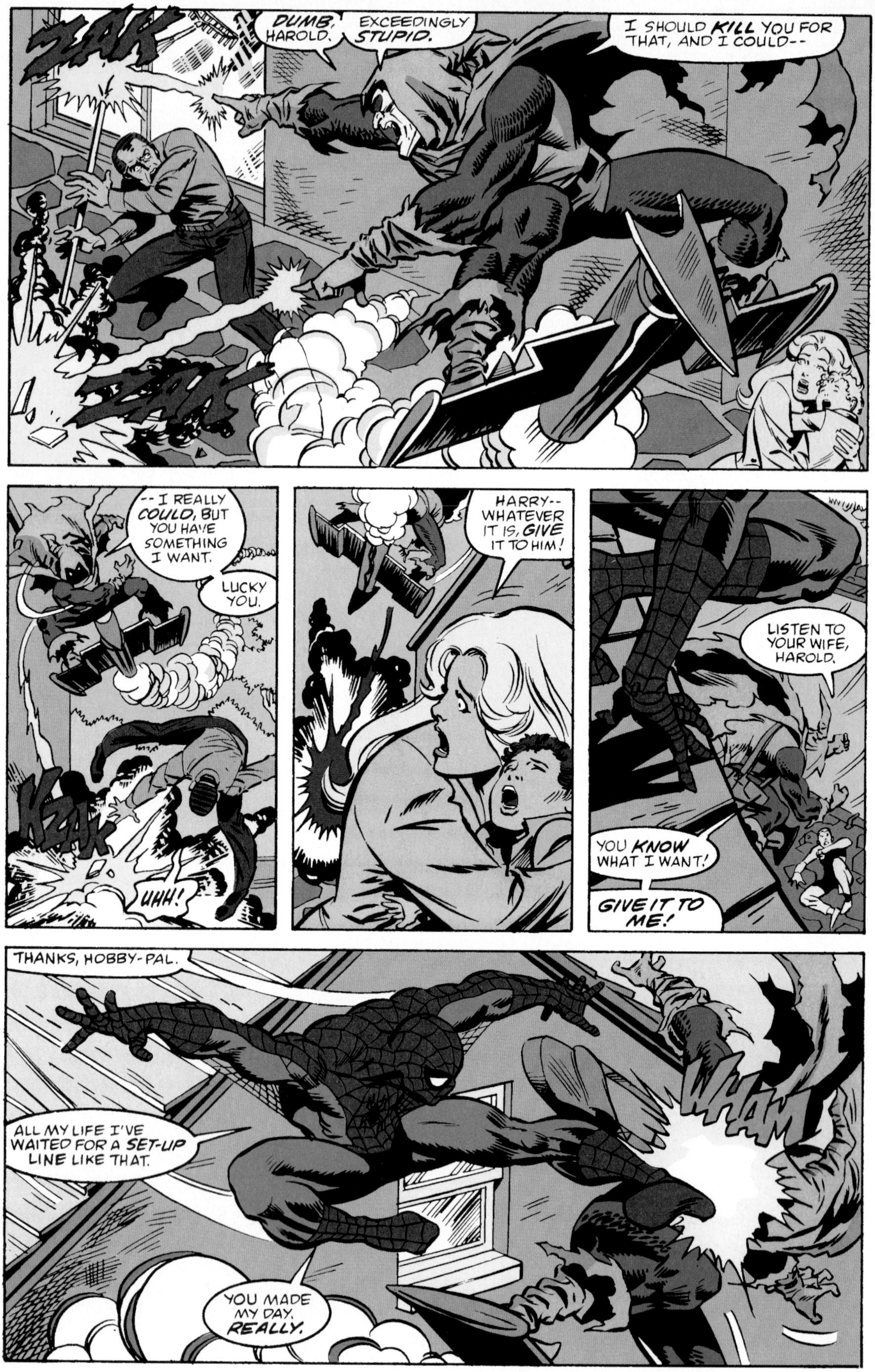
ZAK
DUMB, HAROLD.
EXCEEDINGLY STUPID.
I SHOULD KILL YOU FOR THAT, AND I COULD--
ZAK
--I REALLY COULD, BUT YOU HAVE SOMETHING I WANT.
LUCKY YOU.
KZAK
UHH!
HARRY--WHATEVER IT IS, GIVE IT TO HIM!
LISTEN TO YOUR WIFE, HAROLD.
YOU KNOW WHAT I WANT!
GIVE IT TO ME!
THANKS, HOBBY-PAL.
ALL MY LIFE I'VE WAITED FOR A SET-UP LINE LIKE THAT.
WHAM
YOU MADE MY DAY. REALLY.

ξMMNGGξ

HARRY'S FALLING APART! CAN'T BLAME HIM!

I'M FEELING PRETTY STRESSED MYSELF!

OSBORN! EARTH TO OSBORN!

--NO MORE-- --PLEASE--

YOUR WIFE AND KID NEED YOU, PAL!

GET THEM OUT FAST, BEFORE HOBBY RECOVERS--

UH-OH.

...LET ME RE-PHRASE THAT...

K-AAM

BUTOOM

TOO BAD ABOUT YOUR POOL, HAROLD.

IF YOU DON'T WANT YOUR FAMILY TO BE NEXT--

--GIVE ME YOUR FATHER'S FORMULA!

BEFORE I LOSE MY PATIENCE!

ZRAK

KNOW SOMETHING, HOBS? YOU REMIND ME OF A QUACK *DOCTOR* I USED TO KNOW

HE KEPT LOSING *HIS* PATIENTS, TOO!

THINK YOU'RE *AMUSING*, DON'T YOU?

ACTUALLY...

...YEAH.

NOW'S YOUR CHANCE, HAR!

RUN, WHILE I'VE GOT HOBBY DISTRACTED!

LIZ, GET IN THE *TOOL SHED*--

HARRY, PLEASE-- YOU'VE GOT TO *TELL* ME--

THAT MAN-- WHAT DOES HE *WANT*--?

HE SAID--MY FATHER'S *FORMULA*?

MY FATHER-- HIS FORMULA--

THE FACE-- THE *FACE* IN MY MIRROR...

HARRY...?

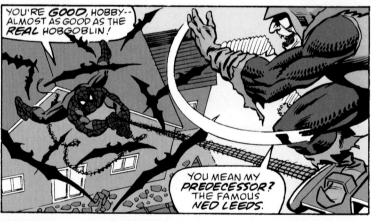

YOU'RE *GOOD*, HOBBY-- ALMOST AS GOOD AS THE *REAL HOBGOBLIN!*

YOU MEAN MY *PREDECESSOR?* THE FAMOUS *NED LEEDS.*

OH, YES, DEAR NED--HE WAS SO GOOD HE GOT HIMSELF *KILLED.*

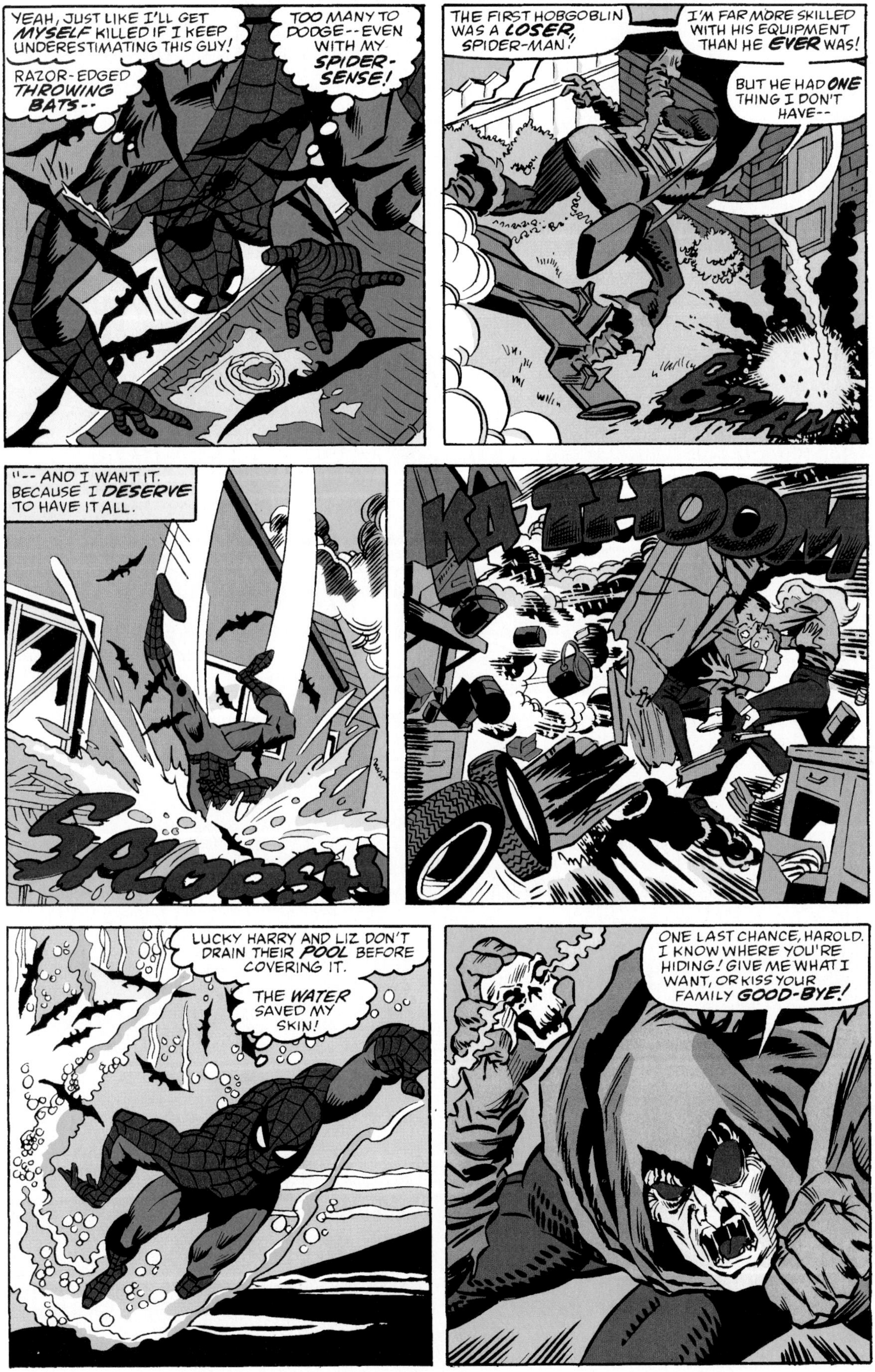
YEAH, JUST LIKE I'LL GET MYSELF KILLED IF I KEEP UNDERESTIMATING THIS GUY!
RAZOR-EDGED THROWING BATS--
TOO MANY TO DODGE--EVEN WITH MY SPIDER-SENSE!
THE FIRST HOBGOBLIN WAS A LOSER, SPIDER-MAN!
I'M FAR MORE SKILLED WITH HIS EQUIPMENT THAN HE EVER WAS!
BUT HE HAD ONE THING I DON'T HAVE--
BRAM
"--AND I WANT IT. BECAUSE I DESERVE TO HAVE IT ALL.
SPLOOSH
KA-THOOM
LUCKY HARRY AND LIZ DON'T DRAIN THEIR POOL BEFORE COVERING IT.
THE WATER SAVED MY SKIN!
ONE LAST CHANCE, HAROLD. I KNOW WHERE YOU'RE HIDING! GIVE ME WHAT I WANT, OR KISS YOUR FAMILY GOOD-BYE!

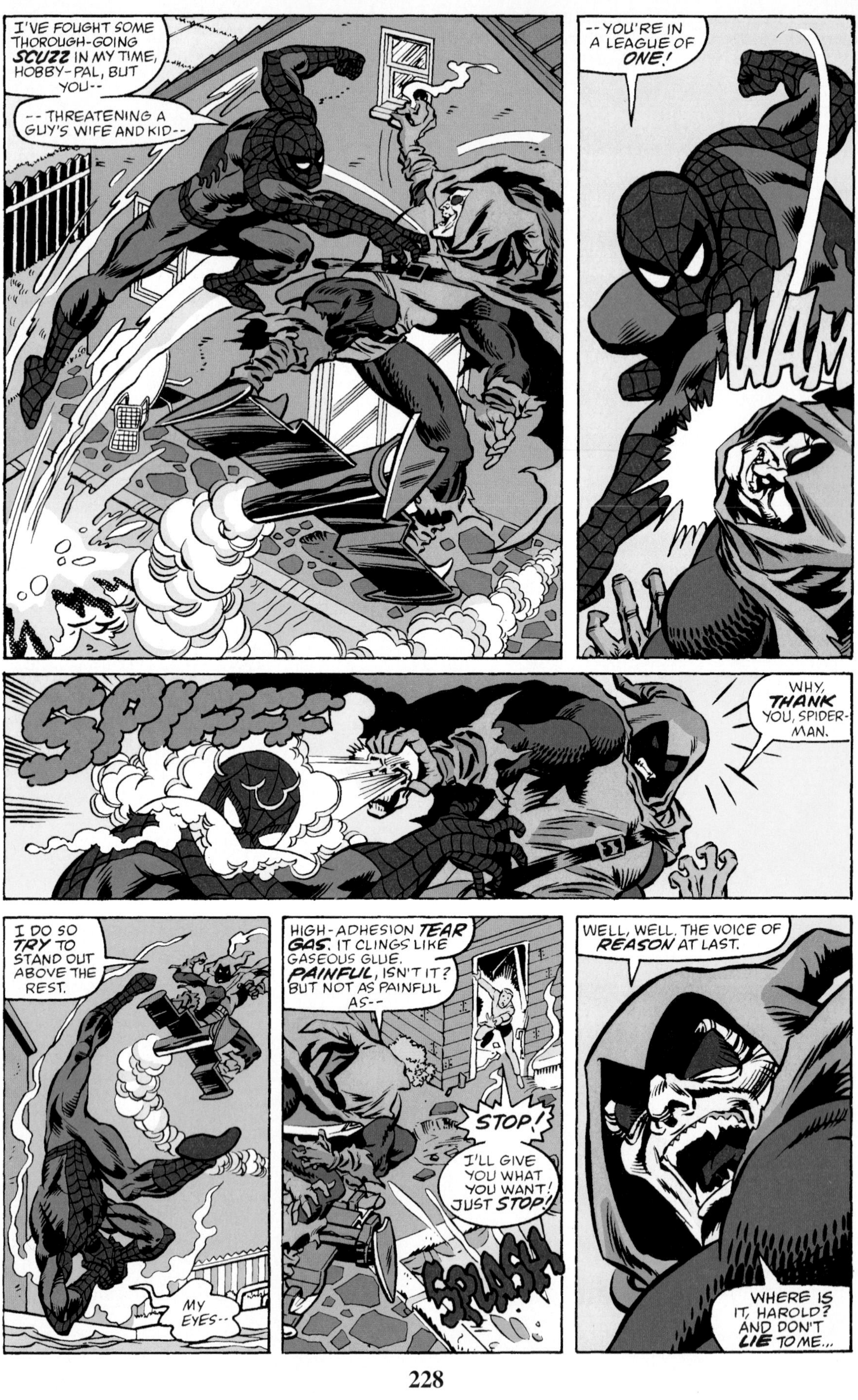
I'VE FOUGHT SOME THOROUGH-GOING SCUZZ IN MY TIME, HOBBY-PAL, BUT YOU--
-- THREATENING A GUY'S WIFE AND KID--
--YOU'RE IN A LEAGUE OF ONE!
WAM
SPIFFF
WHY, THANK YOU, SPIDER-MAN.
I DO SO TRY TO STAND OUT ABOVE THE REST.
MY EYES--
HIGH-ADHESION TEAR GAS. IT CLINGS LIKE GASEOUS GLUE. PAINFUL, ISN'T IT? BUT NOT AS PAINFUL AS--
STOP!
I'LL GIVE YOU WHAT YOU WANT! JUST STOP!
SPLASH
WELL, WELL. THE VOICE OF REASON AT LAST.
WHERE IS IT, HAROLD? AND DON'T LIE TO ME...

MY FATHER'S OLD OFFICE-- *MY* OFFICE NOW-- DOWNTOWN MAN- HATTAN-- THE SAFE--

YOU'LL FIND IT *THERE.*

I'M WARNING YOU, HAROLD--

--IF IT ISN'T THERE, I'LL BE *BACK!*

FIND *WHAT,* HARRY? WHAT DOES HE WANT?

I-I DON'T KNOW, LIZ! I JUST WANTED TO GET RID OF HIM!

I FELT SO *HELPLESS...*

÷AAUGGH÷

÷COUGH÷ WATER CLEARED MY MASK...SECOND TIME YOUR *POOL* SAVED ME.

I SHOULD GET ONE FOR MY APARTMENT.

SO WHERE'D HE *GO?*

MANHATTAN. MY FATHER'S OLD OFFICE DOWNTOWN.

MY *FATHER* WOULDN'T HAVE LET HOBGOBLIN THREATEN HIS FAMILY THIS WAY.

I SHOULD HAVE *DONE* SOMETHING...

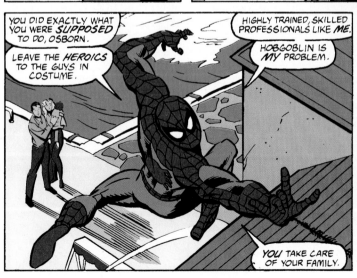

YOU DID EXACTLY WHAT YOU WERE *SUPPOSED* TO DO, OSBORN.

LEAVE THE *HEROICS* TO THE GUYS IN COSTUME.

HIGHLY TRAINED, SKILLED PROFESSIONALS LIKE *ME.*

HOBGOBLIN IS *MY* PROBLEM.

YOU TAKE CARE OF YOUR FAMILY.

WHY DO I HAVE THE SINKING SENSATION HARRY WASN'T *LISTENING?*

ANYWAY, I CAN'T WORRY ABOUT HIM NOW.

I'VE GOT TROUBLE WAITING IN *MANHATTAN...*

229

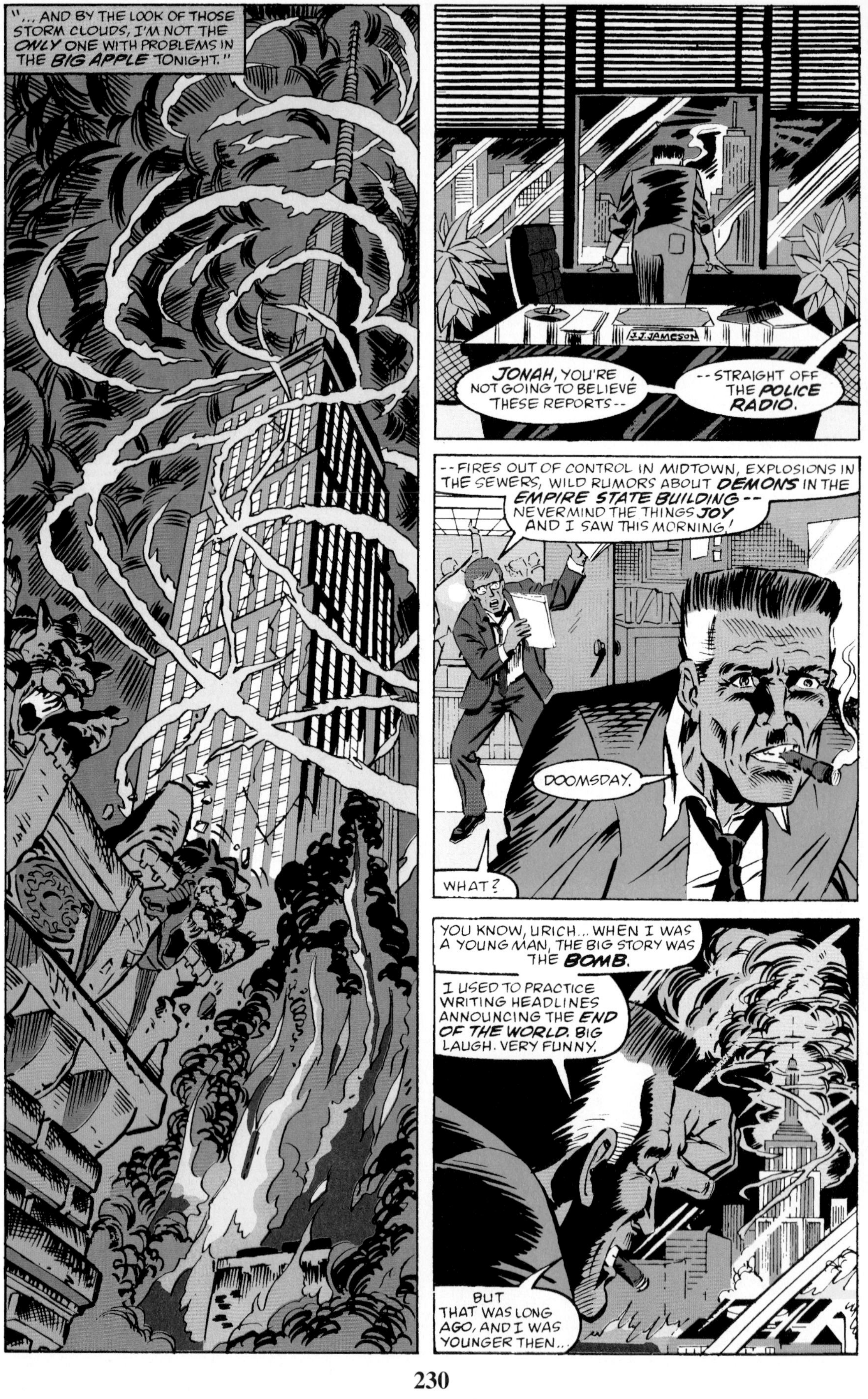
"... AND BY THE LOOK OF THOSE STORM CLOUDS, I'M NOT THE ONLY ONE WITH PROBLEMS IN THE BIG APPLE TONIGHT."
J.J. JAMESON
JONAH, YOU'RE NOT GOING TO BELIEVE THESE REPORTS--
--STRAIGHT OFF THE POLICE RADIO.
--FIRES OUT OF CONTROL IN MIDTOWN, EXPLOSIONS IN THE SEWERS, WILD RUMORS ABOUT DEMONS IN THE EMPIRE STATE BUILDING--
NEVERMIND THE THINGS JOY AND I SAW THIS MORNING!
DOOMSDAY.
WHAT?
YOU KNOW, URICH... WHEN I WAS A YOUNG MAN, THE BIG STORY WAS THE BOMB.
I USED TO PRACTICE WRITING HEADLINES ANNOUNCING THE END OF THE WORLD. BIG LAUGH. VERY FUNNY.
BUT THAT WAS LONG AGO, AND I WAS YOUNGER THEN...

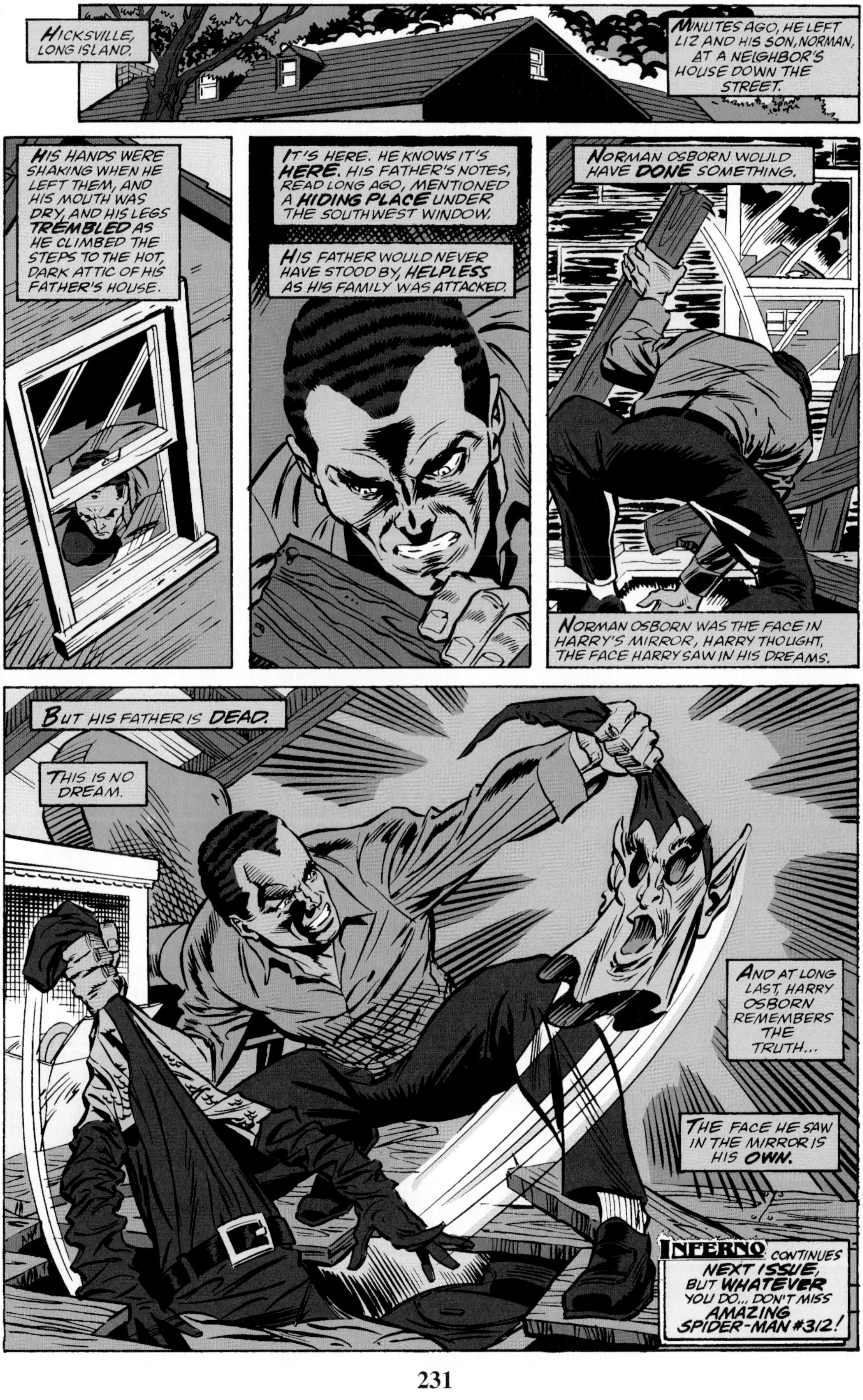
HICKSVILLE, LONG ISLAND.
MINUTES AGO, HE LEFT LIZ AND HIS SON, NORMAN, AT A NEIGHBOR'S HOUSE DOWN THE STREET.
HIS HANDS WERE SHAKING WHEN HE LEFT THEM, AND HIS MOUTH WAS DRY, AND HIS LEGS TREMBLED AS HE CLIMBED THE STEPS TO THE HOT, DARK ATTIC OF HIS FATHER'S HOUSE.
IT'S HERE. HE KNOWS IT'S HERE. HIS FATHER'S NOTES, READ LONG AGO, MENTIONED A HIDING PLACE UNDER THE SOUTHWEST WINDOW.
HIS FATHER WOULD NEVER HAVE STOOD BY, HELPLESS AS HIS FAMILY WAS ATTACKED.
NORMAN OSBORN WOULD HAVE DONE SOMETHING.
NORMAN OSBORN WAS THE FACE IN HARRY'S MIRROR, HARRY THOUGHT, THE FACE HARRY SAW IN HIS DREAMS.
BUT HIS FATHER IS DEAD.
THIS IS NO DREAM.
AND AT LONG LAST, HARRY OSBORN REMEMBERS THE TRUTH...
THE FACE HE SAW IN THE MIRROR IS HIS OWN.
INFERNO CONTINUES NEXT ISSUE, BUT WHATEVER YOU DO... DON'T MISS AMAZING SPIDER-MAN #312!

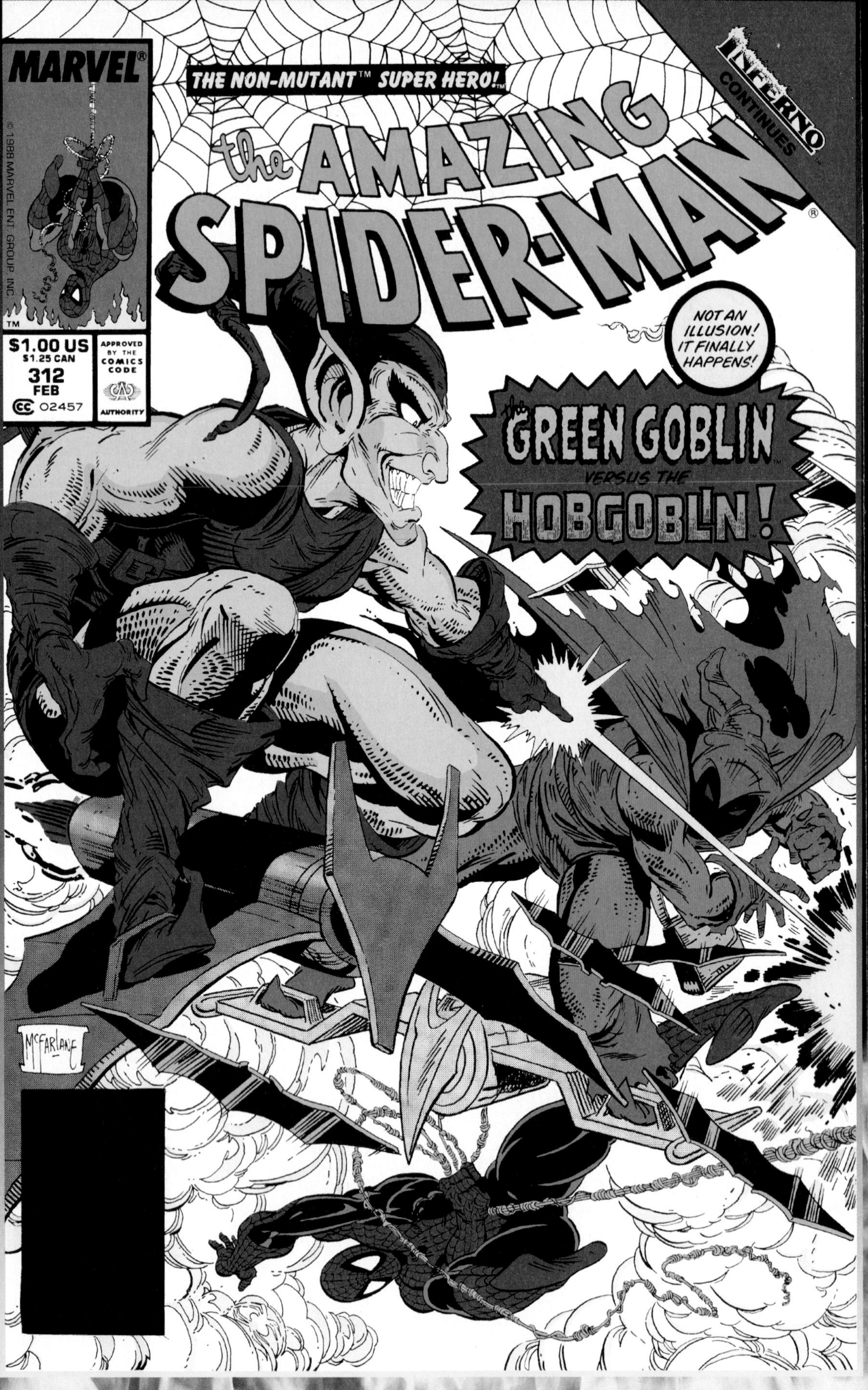
MARVEL®
THE NON-MUTANT™ SUPER HERO!
the AMAZING SPIDER-MAN®
INFERNO CONTINUES
© 1988 MARVEL ENT. GROUP, INC.
TM
$1.00 US
$1.25 CAN
312
FEB
02457
APPROVED BY THE COMICS CODE AUTHORITY
NOT AN ILLUSION! IT FINALLY HAPPENS!
the GREEN GOBLIN versus the HOBGOBLIN!
McFARLANE

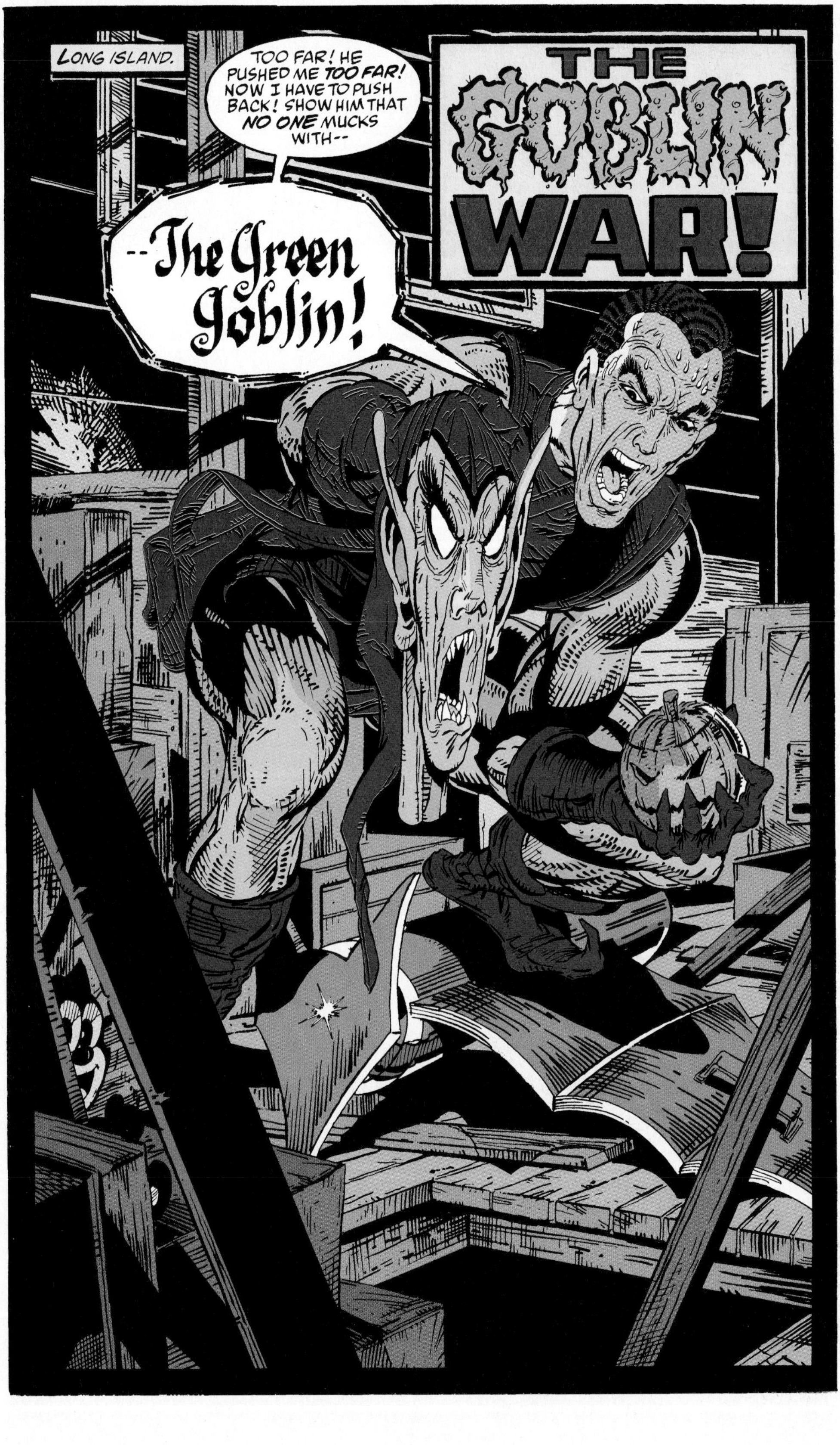
LONG ISLAND.
TOO FAR! HE PUSHED ME TOO FAR! NOW I HAVE TO PUSH BACK! SHOW HIM THAT NO ONE MUCKS WITH--
--The Green Goblin!
THE GOBLIN WAR!

STAN LEE PRESENTS

•

THE AMAZING SPIDER-MAN

•

DAVID MICHELINIE
WRITER

•

TODD McFARLANE
ARTIST

•

RICK PARKER
LETTERER

•

BOB SHAREN
COLORIST

•

JIM SALICRUP
EDITOR

•

TOM DeFALCO
EDITOR IN CHIEF

•

A TALE of INFERNO

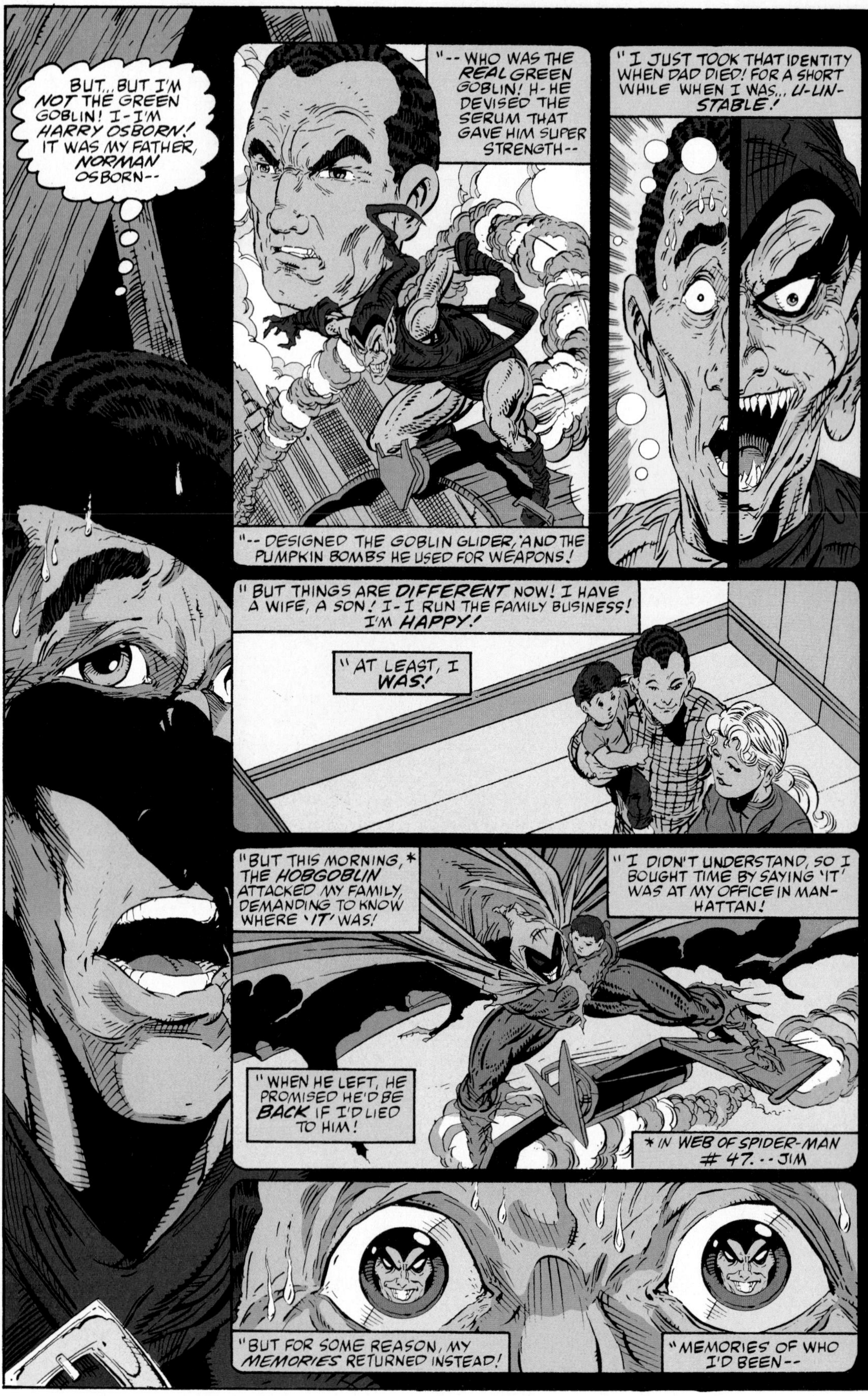

BUT... BUT I'M NOT THE GREEN GOBLIN! I-I'M HARRY OSBORN! IT WAS MY FATHER, NORMAN OSBORN--
"--WHO WAS THE REAL GREEN GOBLIN! H-HE DEVISED THE SERUM THAT GAVE HIM SUPER STRENGTH--
"--DESIGNED THE GOBLIN GLIDER, AND THE PUMPKIN BOMBS HE USED FOR WEAPONS!
"I JUST TOOK THAT IDENTITY WHEN DAD DIED! FOR A SHORT WHILE WHEN I WAS... U-UNSTABLE!
"BUT THINGS ARE DIFFERENT NOW! I HAVE A WIFE, A SON! I-I RUN THE FAMILY BUSINESS! I'M HAPPY!
"AT LEAST, I WAS!
"BUT THIS MORNING,* THE HOBGOBLIN ATTACKED MY FAMILY, DEMANDING TO KNOW WHERE 'IT' WAS!
"I DIDN'T UNDERSTAND, SO I BOUGHT TIME BY SAYING 'IT' WAS AT MY OFFICE IN MANHATTAN!
"WHEN HE LEFT, HE PROMISED HE'D BE BACK IF I'D LIED TO HIM!
*IN WEB OF SPIDER-MAN #47. --JIM
"BUT FOR SOME REASON, MY MEMORIES RETURNED INSTEAD!
"MEMORIES OF WHO I'D BEEN--

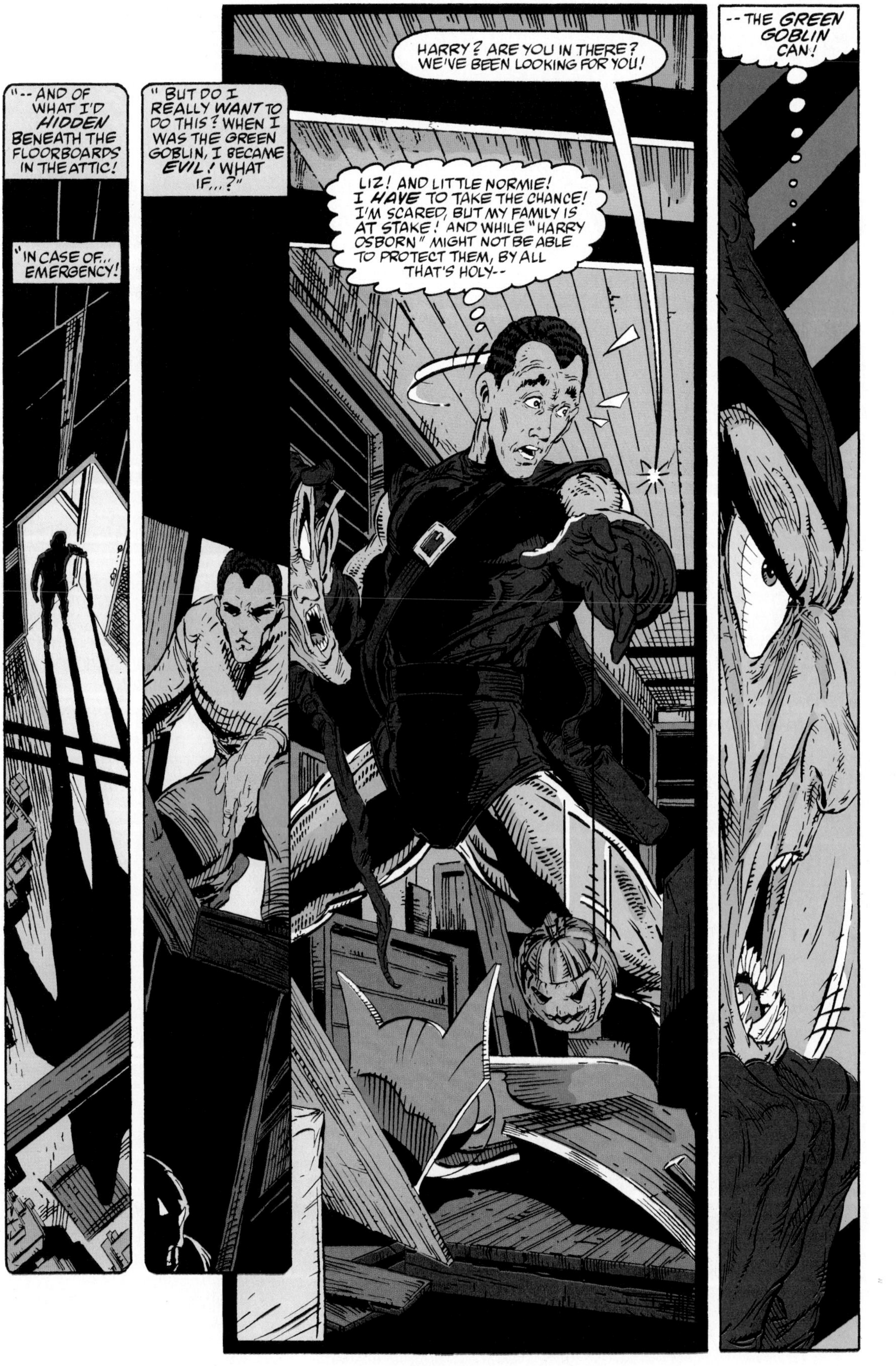
"--AND OF WHAT I'D HIDDEN BENEATH THE FLOORBOARDS IN THE ATTIC!
"IN CASE OF... EMERGENCY!
"BUT DO I REALLY WANT TO DO THIS? WHEN I WAS THE GREEN GOBLIN, I BECAME EVIL! WHAT IF...?"
HARRY? ARE YOU IN THERE? WE'VE BEEN LOOKING FOR YOU!
LIZ! AND LITTLE NORMIE! I HAVE TO TAKE THE CHANCE! I'M SCARED, BUT MY FAMILY IS AT STAKE! AND WHILE "HARRY OSBORN" MIGHT NOT BE ABLE TO PROTECT THEM, BY ALL THAT'S HOLY--
--THE GREEN GOBLIN CAN!

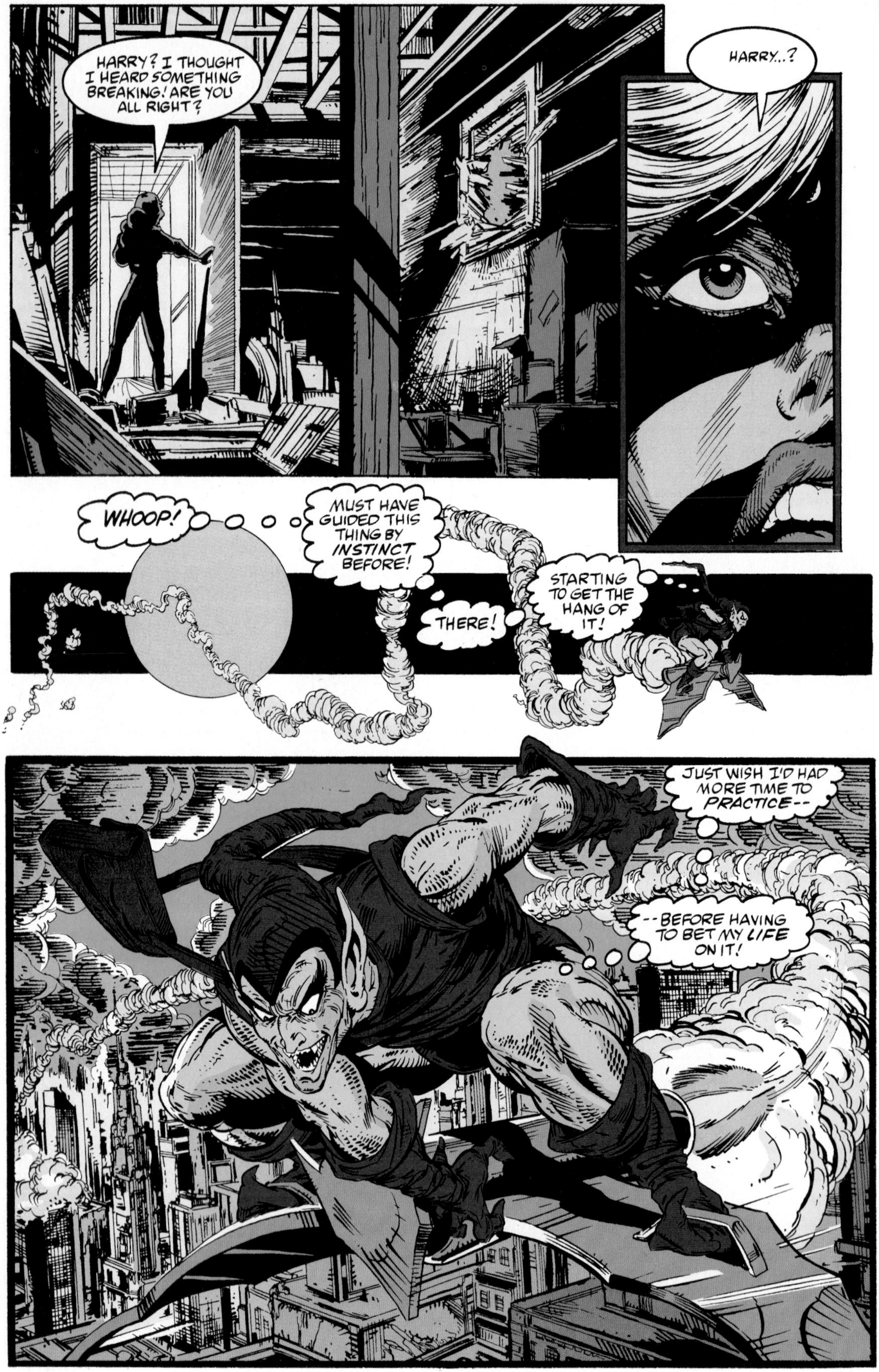

HARRY? I THOUGHT I HEARD SOMETHING BREAKING! ARE YOU ALL RIGHT?
HARRY..?
WHOOP!
MUST HAVE GUIDED THIS THING BY INSTINCT BEFORE!
THERE!
STARTING TO GET THE HANG OF IT!
JUST WISH I'D HAD MORE TIME TO PRACTICE--
--BEFORE HAVING TO BET MY LIFE ON IT!

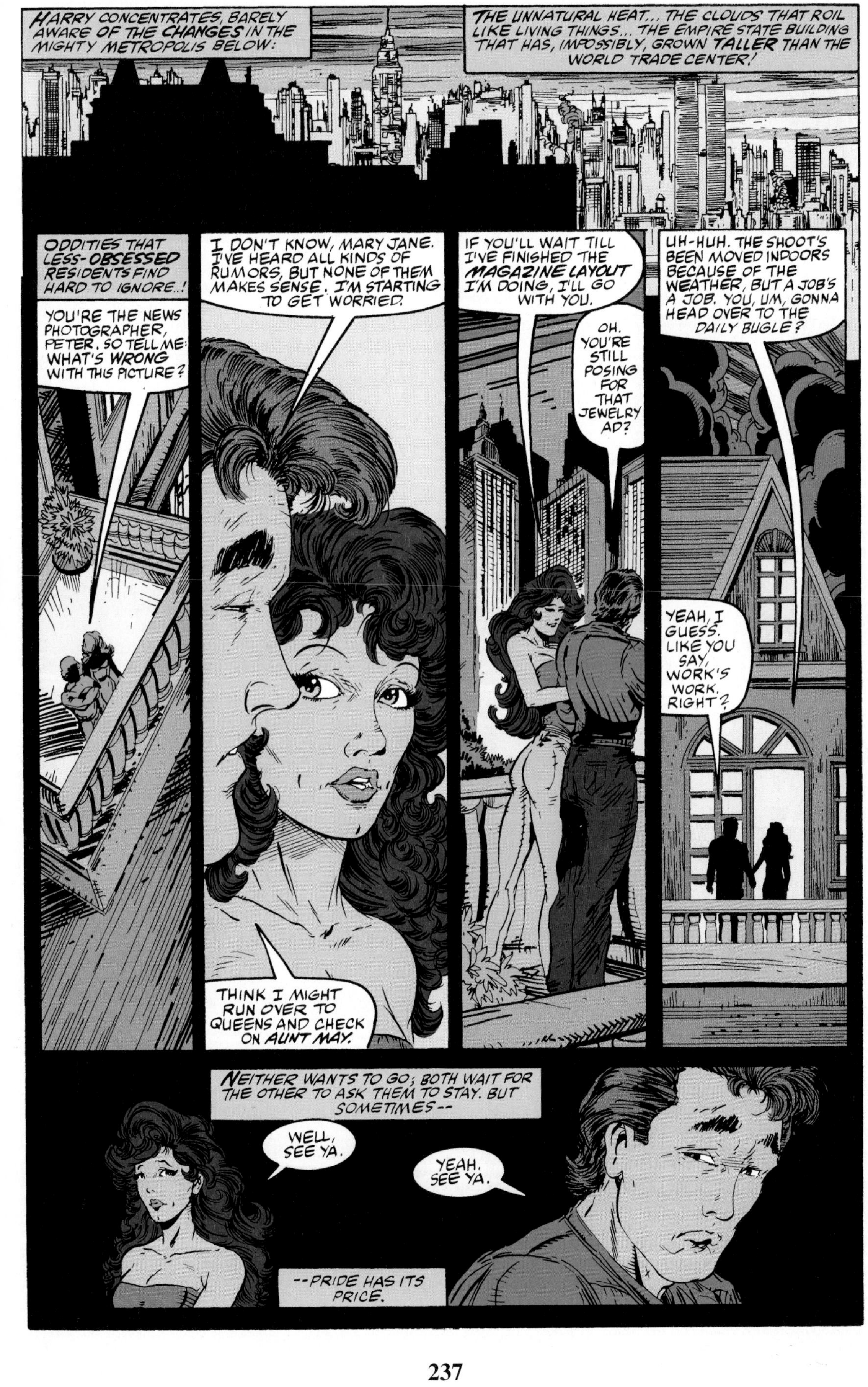
HARRY CONCENTRATES, BARELY AWARE OF THE CHANGES IN THE MIGHTY METROPOLIS BELOW:
THE UNNATURAL HEAT... THE CLOUDS THAT ROIL LIKE LIVING THINGS... THE EMPIRE STATE BUILDING THAT HAS, IMPOSSIBLY, GROWN TALLER THAN THE WORLD TRADE CENTER!
ODDITIES THAT LESS-OBSESSED RESIDENTS FIND HARD TO IGNORE...!
YOU'RE THE NEWS PHOTOGRAPHER, PETER. SO TELL ME: WHAT'S WRONG WITH THIS PICTURE?
I DON'T KNOW, MARY JANE. I'VE HEARD ALL KINDS OF RUMORS, BUT NONE OF THEM MAKES SENSE. I'M STARTING TO GET WORRIED.
THINK I MIGHT RUN OVER TO QUEENS AND CHECK ON AUNT MAY.
IF YOU'LL WAIT TILL I'VE FINISHED THE MAGAZINE LAYOUT I'M DOING, I'LL GO WITH YOU.
OH. YOU'RE STILL POSING FOR THAT JEWELRY AD?
UH-HUH. THE SHOOT'S BEEN MOVED INDOORS BECAUSE OF THE WEATHER, BUT A JOB'S A JOB. YOU, UM, GONNA HEAD OVER TO THE DAILY BUGLE?
YEAH, I GUESS. LIKE YOU SAY, WORK'S WORK. RIGHT?
NEITHER WANTS TO GO; BOTH WAIT FOR THE OTHER TO ASK THEM TO STAY. BUT SOMETIMES--
WELL, SEE YA.
YEAH. SEE YA.
--PRIDE HAS ITS PRICE.

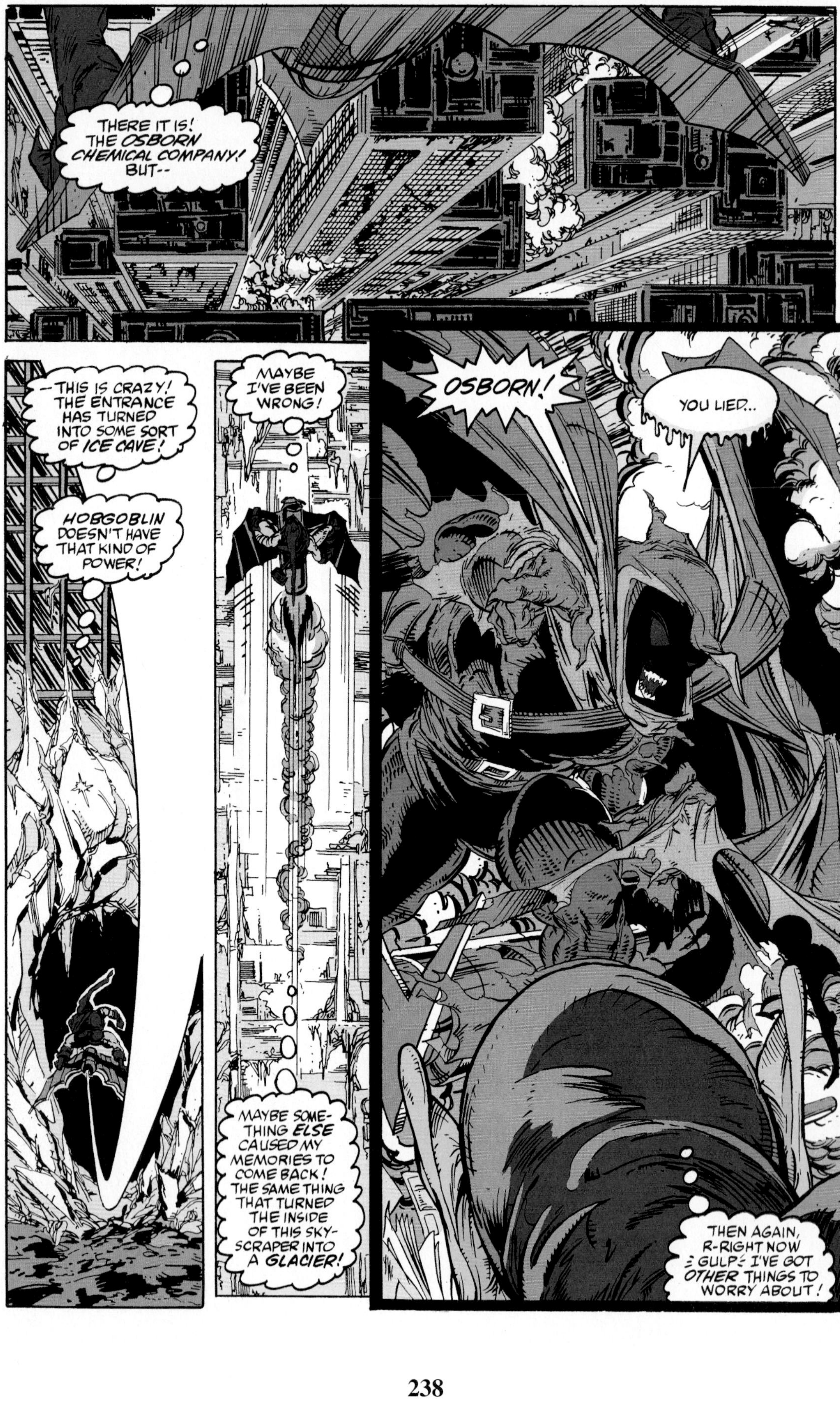
THERE IT IS! THE OSBORN CHEMICAL COMPANY! BUT--
--THIS IS CRAZY! THE ENTRANCE HAS TURNED INTO SOME SORT OF ICE CAVE!
HOBGOBLIN DOESN'T HAVE THAT KIND OF POWER!
MAYBE I'VE BEEN WRONG!
MAYBE SOME-THING ELSE CAUSED MY MEMORIES TO COME BACK! THE SAME THING THAT TURNED THE INSIDE OF THIS SKY-SCRAPER INTO A GLACIER!
OSBORN!
YOU LIED...
THEN AGAIN, R-RIGHT NOW =GULP= I'VE GOT OTHER THINGS TO WORRY ABOUT!

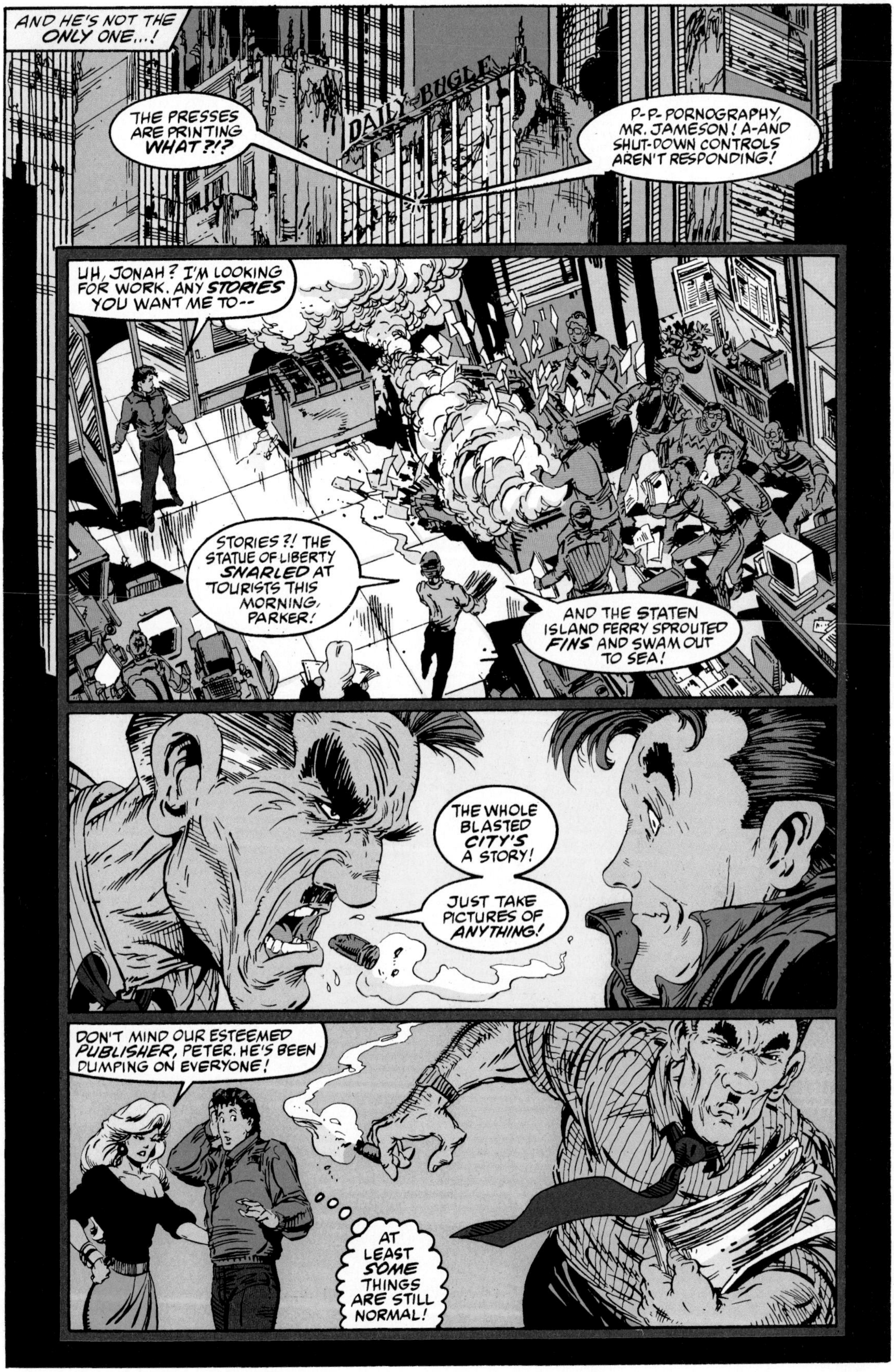
AND HE'S NOT THE ONLY ONE...!
DAILY BUGLE
THE PRESSES ARE PRINTING WHAT?!?
P-P-PORNOGRAPHY, MR. JAMESON! A-AND SHUT-DOWN CONTROLS AREN'T RESPONDING!
UH, JONAH? I'M LOOKING FOR WORK. ANY STORIES YOU WANT ME TO--
STORIES?! THE STATUE OF LIBERTY SNARLED AT TOURISTS THIS MORNING, PARKER!
AND THE STATEN ISLAND FERRY SPROUTED FINS AND SWAM OUT TO SEA!
THE WHOLE BLASTED CITY'S A STORY!
JUST TAKE PICTURES OF ANYTHING!
DON'T MIND OUR ESTEEMED PUBLISHER, PETER. HE'S BEEN DUMPING ON EVERYONE!
AT LEAST SOME THINGS ARE STILL NORMAL!

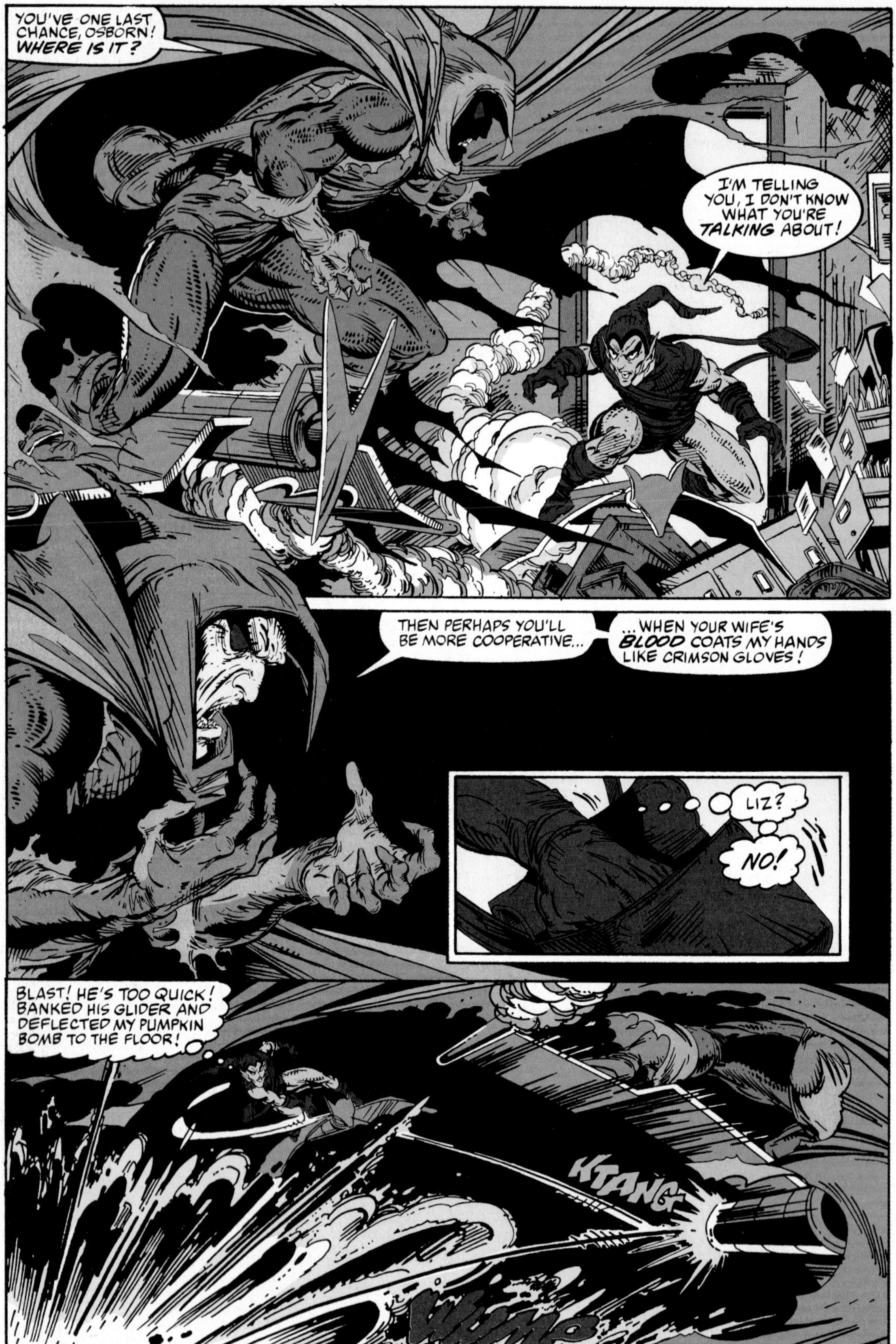
YOU'VE ONE LAST CHANCE, OSBORN! WHERE IS IT?
I'M TELLING YOU, I DON'T KNOW WHAT YOU'RE TALKING ABOUT!
THEN PERHAPS YOU'LL BE MORE COOPERATIVE...
...WHEN YOUR WIFE'S BLOOD COATS MY HANDS LIKE CRIMSON GLOVES!
LIZ?
NO!
BLAST! HE'S TOO QUICK! BANKED HIS GLIDER AND DEFLECTED MY PUMPKIN BOMB TO THE FLOOR!
KTANG
WUMP

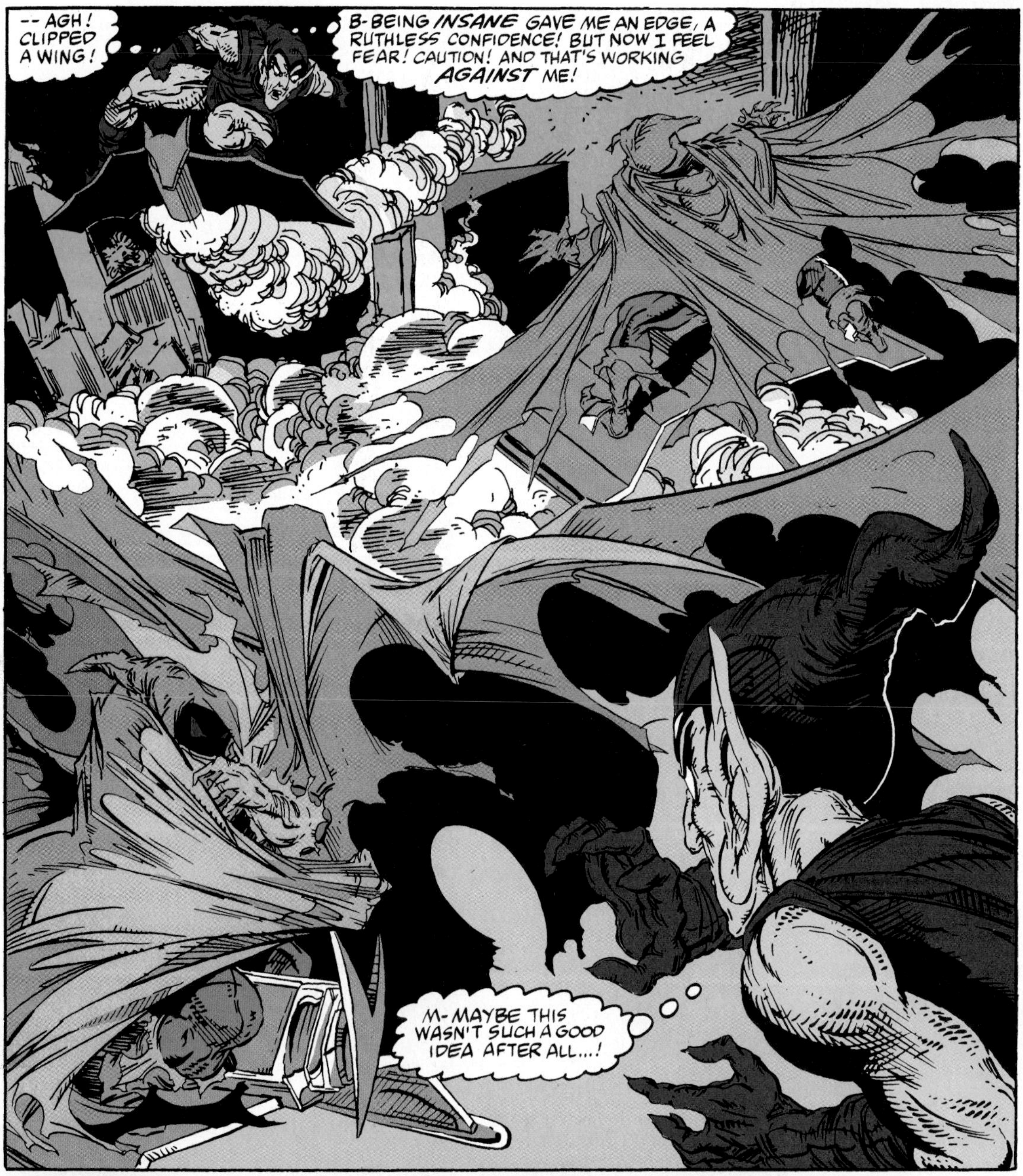
-- AGH! CLIPPED A WING!
B-BEING INSANE GAVE ME AN EDGE, A RUTHLESS CONFIDENCE! BUT NOW I FEEL FEAR! CAUTION! AND THAT'S WORKING AGAINST ME!
M-MAYBE THIS WASN'T SUCH A GOOD IDEA AFTER ALL...!

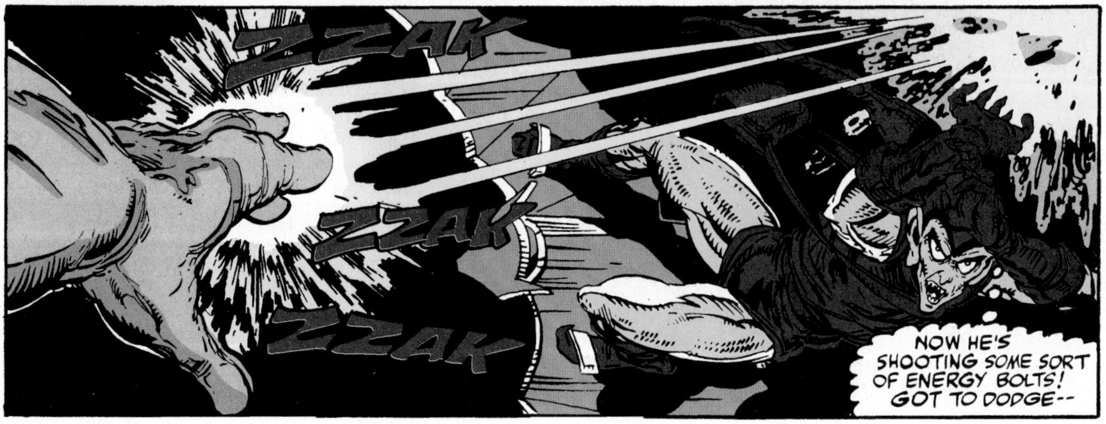
ZZAK
ZZAK
ZZAK
NOW HE'S SHOOTING SOME SORT OF ENERGY BOLTS! GOT TO DODGE--

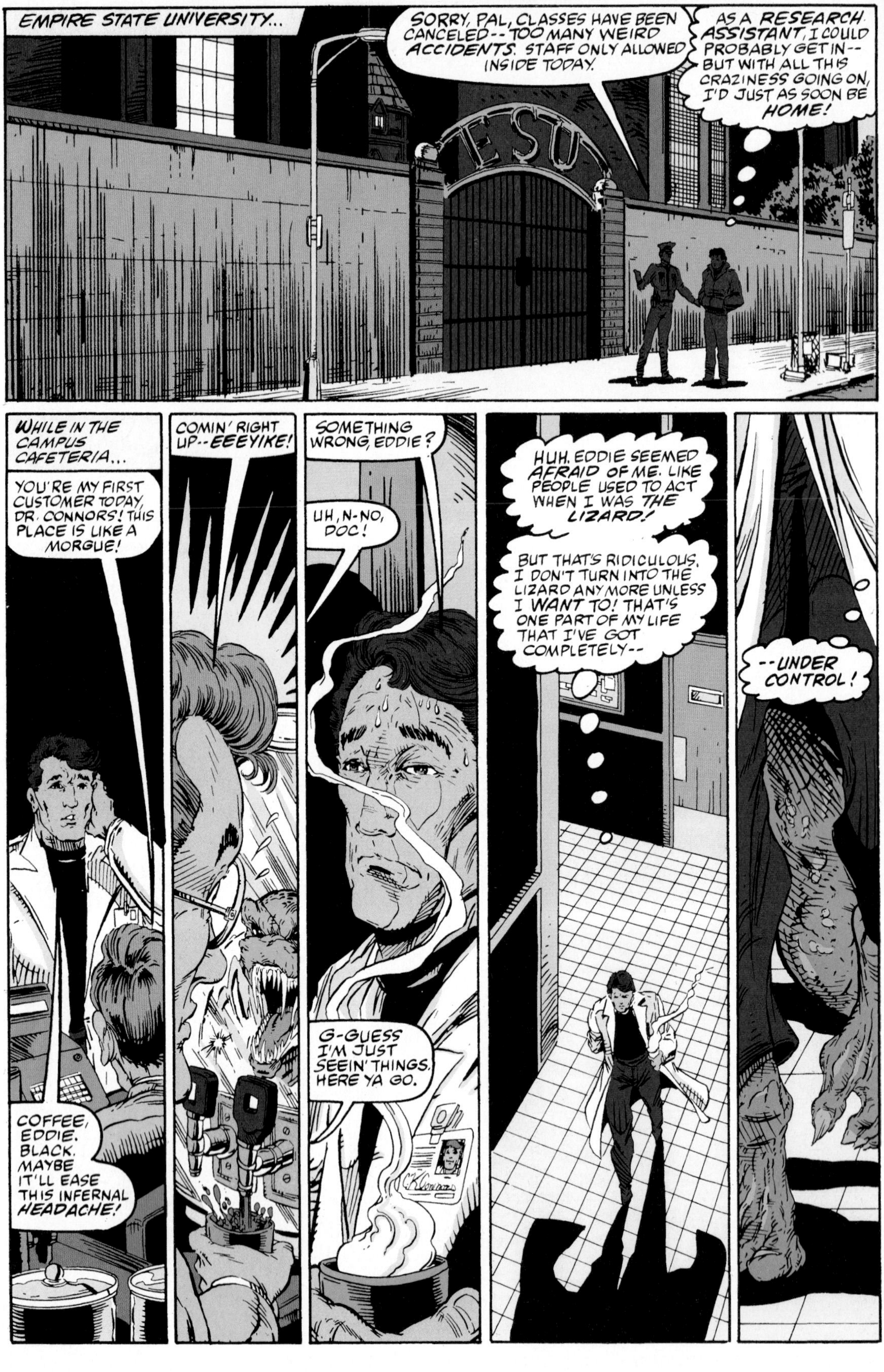
EMPIRE STATE UNIVERSITY...
SORRY, PAL, CLASSES HAVE BEEN CANCELED-- TOO MANY WEIRD ACCIDENTS. STAFF ONLY ALLOWED INSIDE TODAY.
AS A RESEARCH ASSISTANT, I COULD PROBABLY GET IN-- BUT WITH ALL THIS CRAZINESS GOING ON, I'D JUST AS SOON BE HOME!
ESU
WHILE IN THE CAMPUS CAFETERIA...
YOU'RE MY FIRST CUSTOMER TODAY, DR. CONNORS! THIS PLACE IS LIKE A MORGUE!
COFFEE, EDDIE. BLACK. MAYBE IT'LL EASE THIS INFERNAL HEADACHE!
COMIN' RIGHT UP-- EEEYIKE!
SOMETHING WRONG, EDDIE?
UH, N-NO, DOC!
G-GUESS I'M JUST SEEIN' THINGS. HERE YA GO.
HUH, EDDIE SEEMED AFRAID OF ME. LIKE PEOPLE USED TO ACT WHEN I WAS THE LIZARD!
BUT THAT'S RIDICULOUS. I DON'T TURN INTO THE LIZARD ANYMORE UNLESS I WANT TO! THAT'S ONE PART OF MY LIFE THAT I'VE GOT COMPLETELY--
--UNDER CONTROL!

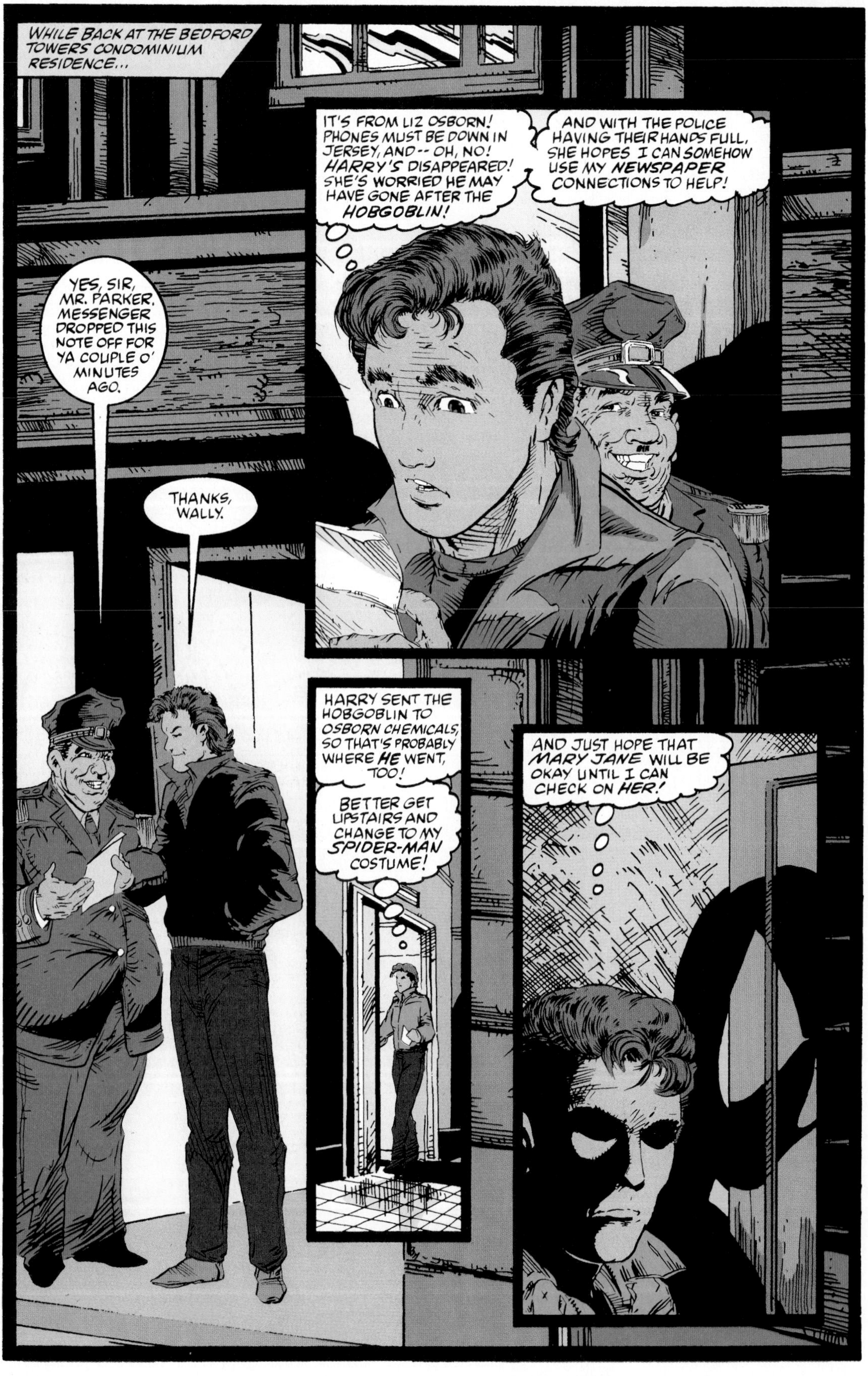
WHILE BACK AT THE BEDFORD TOWERS CONDOMINIUM RESIDENCE...
YES, SIR, MR. PARKER. MESSENGER DROPPED THIS NOTE OFF FOR YA COUPLE O' MINUTES AGO.
THANKS, WALLY.
IT'S FROM LIZ OSBORN! PHONES MUST BE DOWN IN JERSEY, AND-- OH, NO! HARRY'S DISAPPEARED! SHE'S WORRIED HE MAY HAVE GONE AFTER THE HOBGOBLIN!
AND WITH THE POLICE HAVING THEIR HANDS FULL, SHE HOPES I CAN SOMEHOW USE MY NEWSPAPER CONNECTIONS TO HELP!
HARRY SENT THE HOBGOBLIN TO OSBORN CHEMICALS, SO THAT'S PROBABLY WHERE HE WENT, TOO!
BETTER GET UPSTAIRS AND CHANGE TO MY SPIDER-MAN COSTUME!
AND JUST HOPE THAT MARY JANE WILL BE OKAY UNTIL I CAN CHECK ON HER!

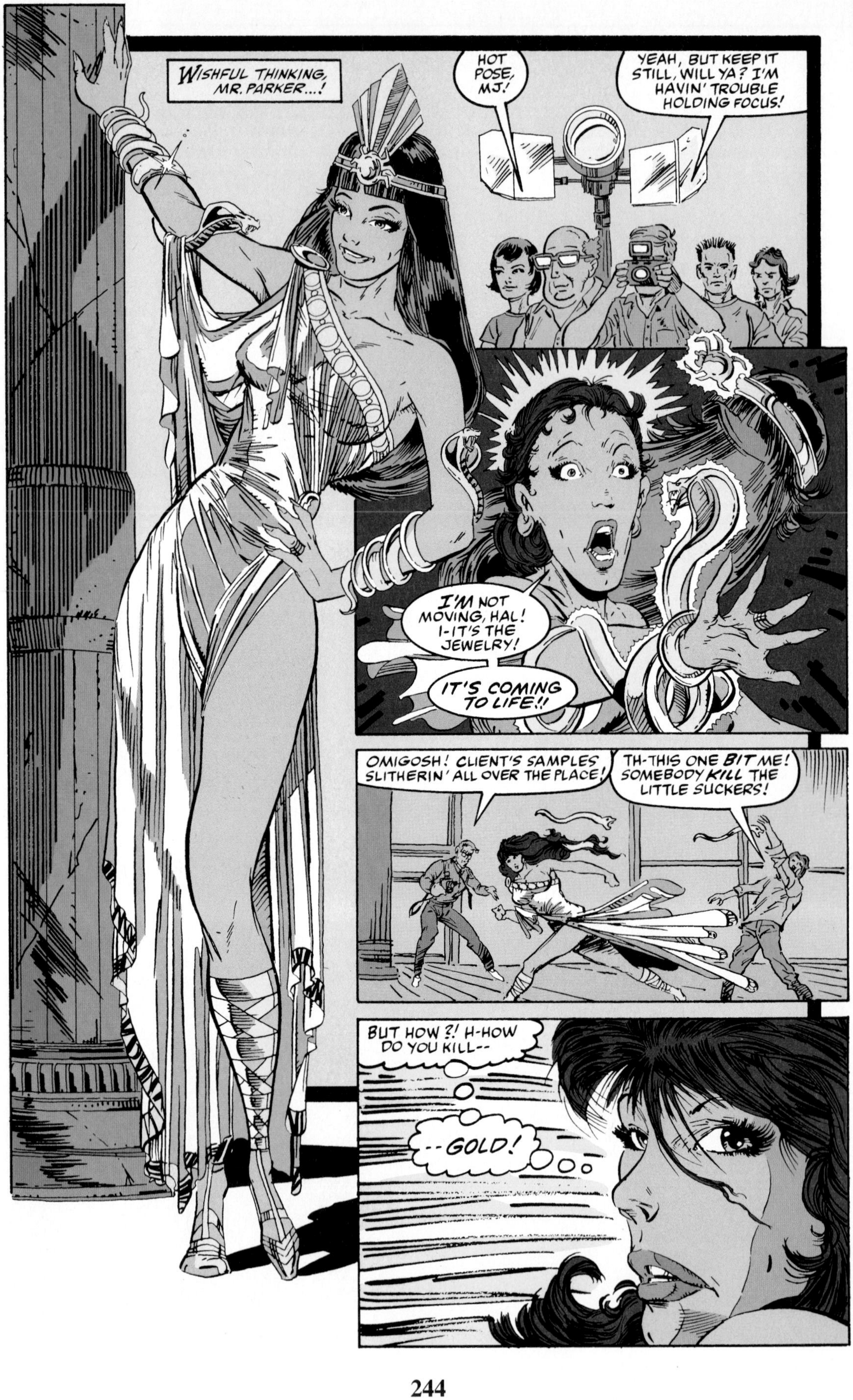

WISHFUL THINKING, MR. PARKER...!
HOT POSE, MJ!
YEAH, BUT KEEP IT STILL, WILL YA? I'M HAVIN' TROUBLE HOLDING FOCUS!
I'M NOT MOVING, HAL! I-IT'S THE JEWELRY!
IT'S COMING TO LIFE!!
OMIGOSH! CLIENT'S SAMPLES SLITHERIN' ALL OVER THE PLACE!
TH-THIS ONE BIT ME! SOMEBODY KILL THE LITTLE SUCKERS!
BUT HOW?! H-HOW DO YOU KILL--
--GOLD!

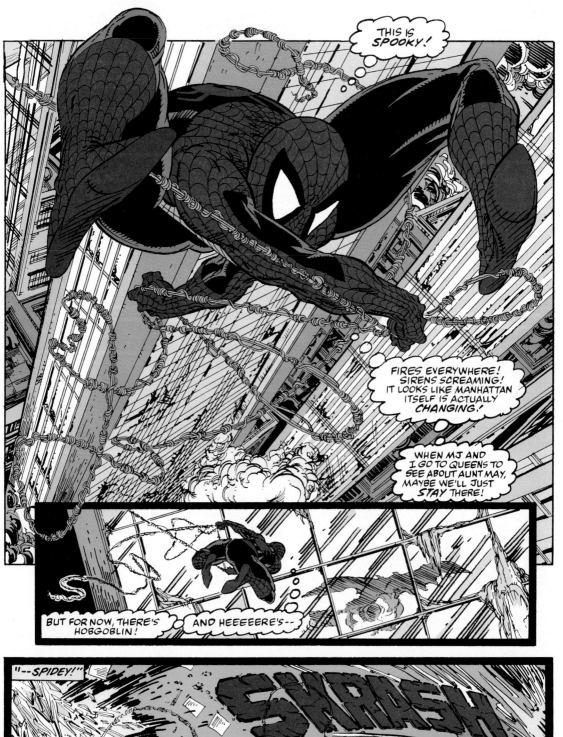

THIS IS SPOOKY!

FIRES EVERYWHERE! SIRENS SCREAMING! IT LOOKS LIKE MANHATTAN ITSELF IS ACTUALLY CHANGING!

WHEN MJ AND I GO TO QUEENS TO SEE ABOUT AUNT MAY, MAYBE WE'LL JUST STAY THERE!

BUT FOR NOW, THERE'S HOBGOBLIN!

AND HEEEEERE'S--

"--SPIDEY!"

SKRASH

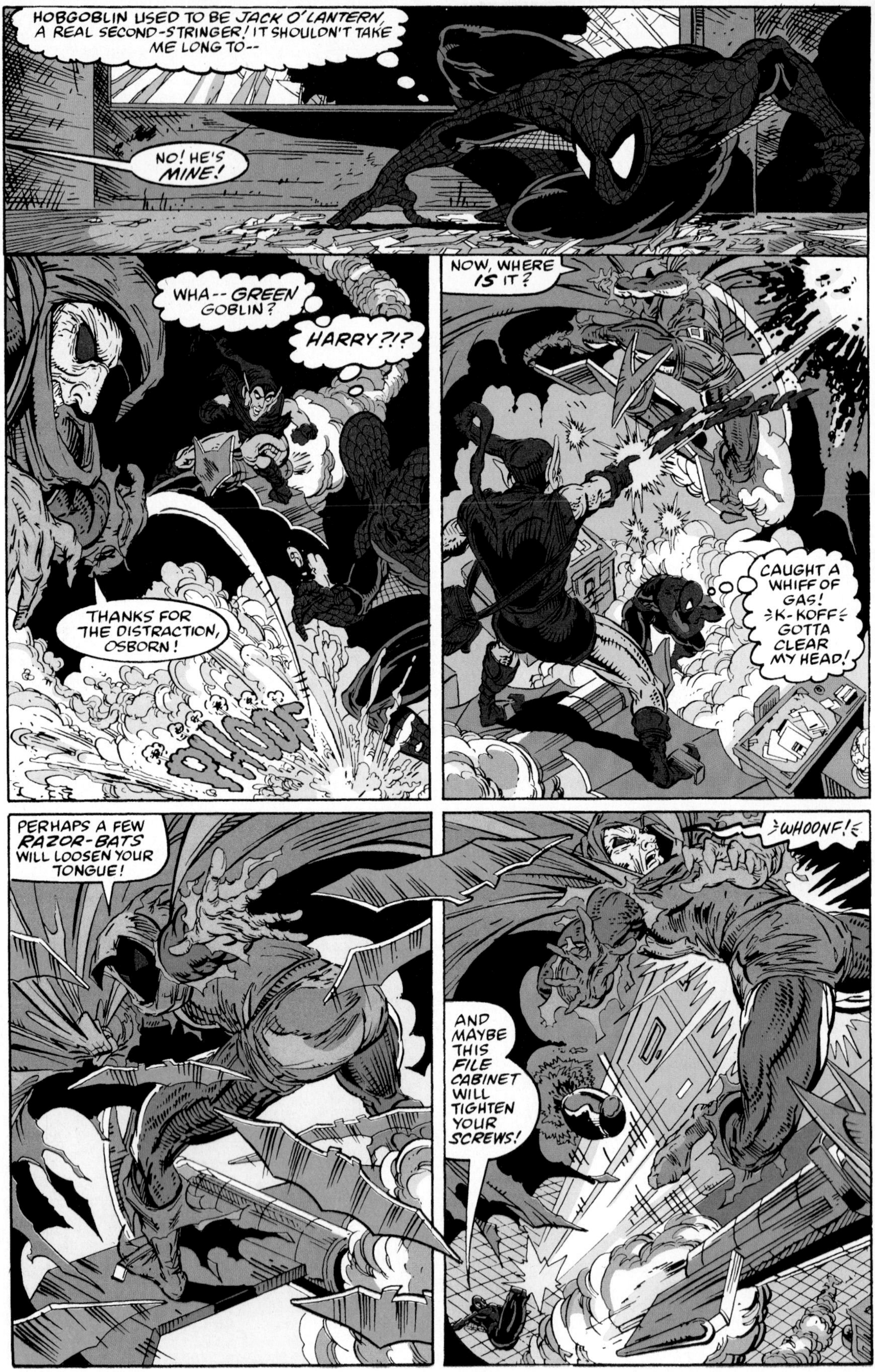
HOBGOBLIN USED TO BE JACK O'LANTERN, A REAL SECOND-STRINGER! IT SHOULDN'T TAKE ME LONG TO--
NO! HE'S MINE!
WHA-- GREEN GOBLIN?
HARRY?!?
THANKS FOR THE DISTRACTION, OSBORN!
PHOOF
NOW, WHERE IS IT?
CAUGHT A WHIFF OF GAS! K-KOFF GOTTA CLEAR MY HEAD!
PERHAPS A FEW RAZOR-BATS WILL LOOSEN YOUR TONGUE!
WHOONF!
AND MAYBE THIS FILE CABINET WILL TIGHTEN YOUR SCREWS!

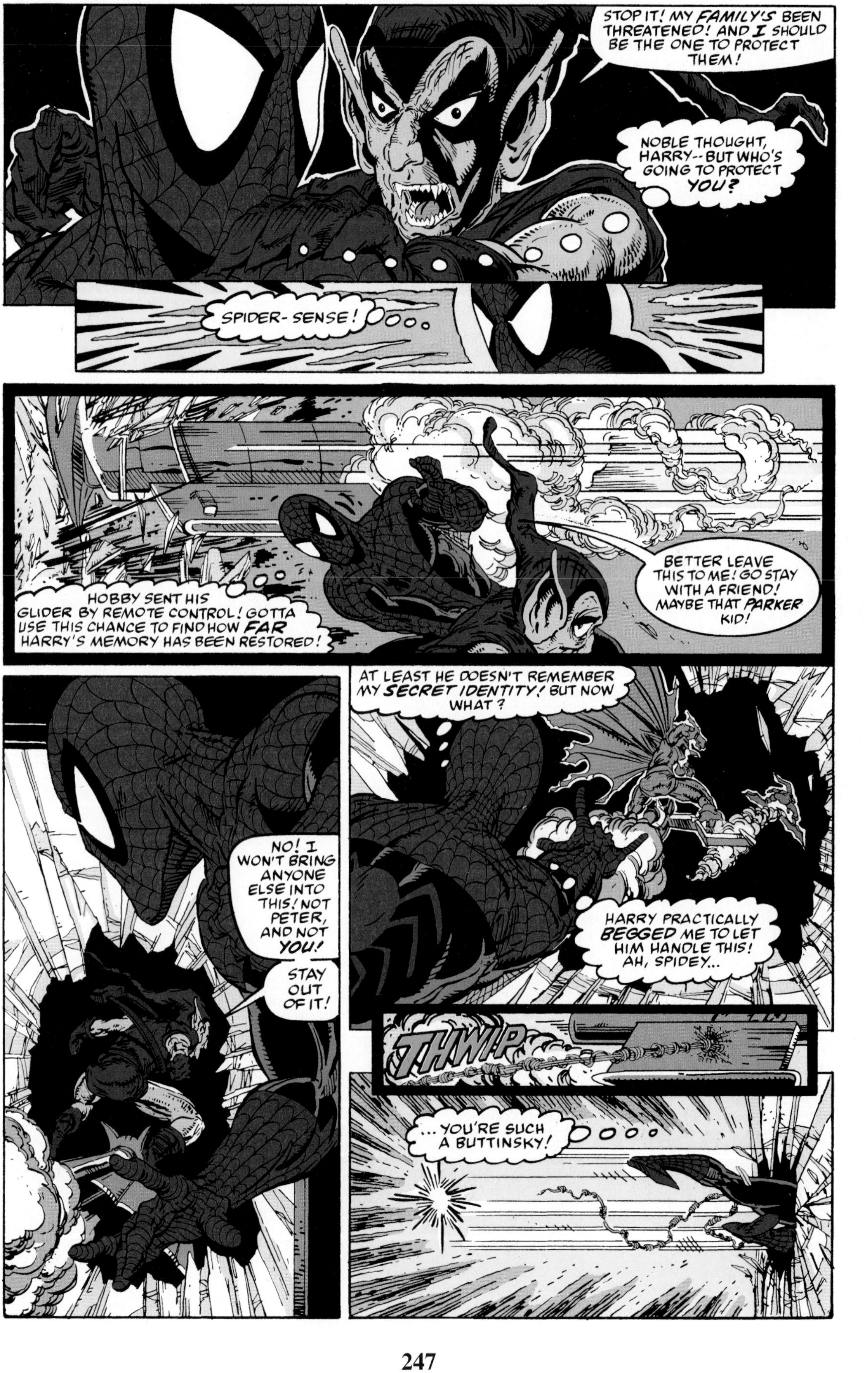
STOP IT! MY FAMILY'S BEEN THREATENED! AND I SHOULD BE THE ONE TO PROTECT THEM!
NOBLE THOUGHT, HARRY-- BUT WHO'S GOING TO PROTECT YOU?
SPIDER-SENSE!
HOBBY SENT HIS GLIDER BY REMOTE CONTROL! GOTTA USE THIS CHANCE TO FIND HOW FAR HARRY'S MEMORY HAS BEEN RESTORED!
BETTER LEAVE THIS TO ME! GO STAY WITH A FRIEND! MAYBE THAT PARKER KID!
NO! I WON'T BRING ANYONE ELSE INTO THIS! NOT PETER, AND NOT YOU!
STAY OUT OF IT!
AT LEAST HE DOESN'T REMEMBER MY SECRET IDENTITY! BUT NOW WHAT?
HARRY PRACTICALLY BEGGED ME TO LET HIM HANDLE THIS! AH, SPIDEY...
THWIP
...YOU'RE SUCH A BUTTINSKY!

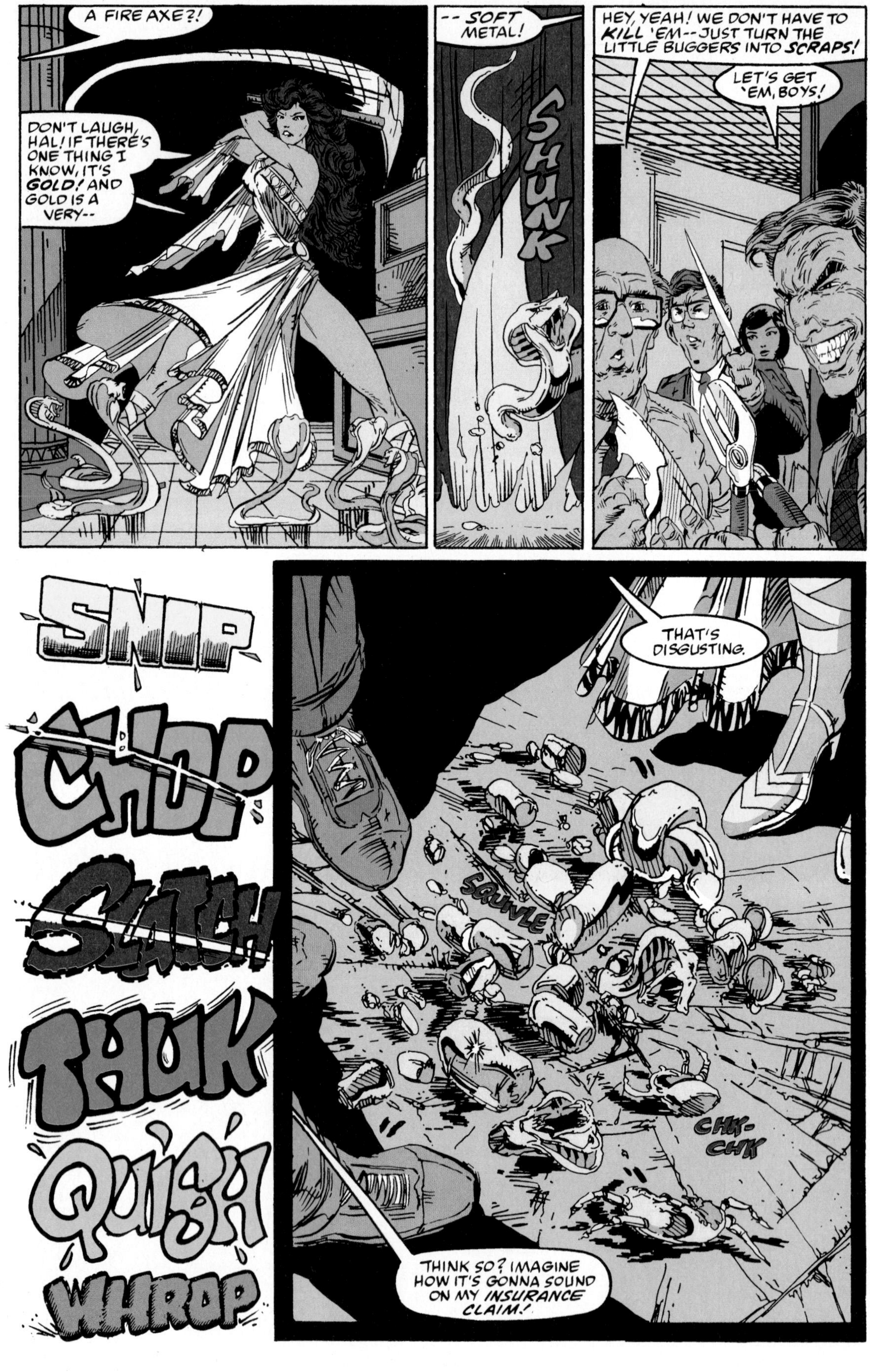
A FIRE AXE?!
DON'T LAUGH, HAL! IF THERE'S ONE THING I KNOW, IT'S GOLD! AND GOLD IS A VERY--
--SOFT METAL!
SHUNK
HEY, YEAH! WE DON'T HAVE TO KILL 'EM--JUST TURN THE LITTLE BUGGERS INTO SCRAPS!
LET'S GET 'EM, BOYS!
SNIP
CHOP
SLATCH
THUK
QUISH
WHROP
THAT'S DISGUSTING.
SQUVLE
CHK-CHK
THINK SO? IMAGINE HOW IT'S GONNA SOUND ON MY INSURANCE CLAIM!

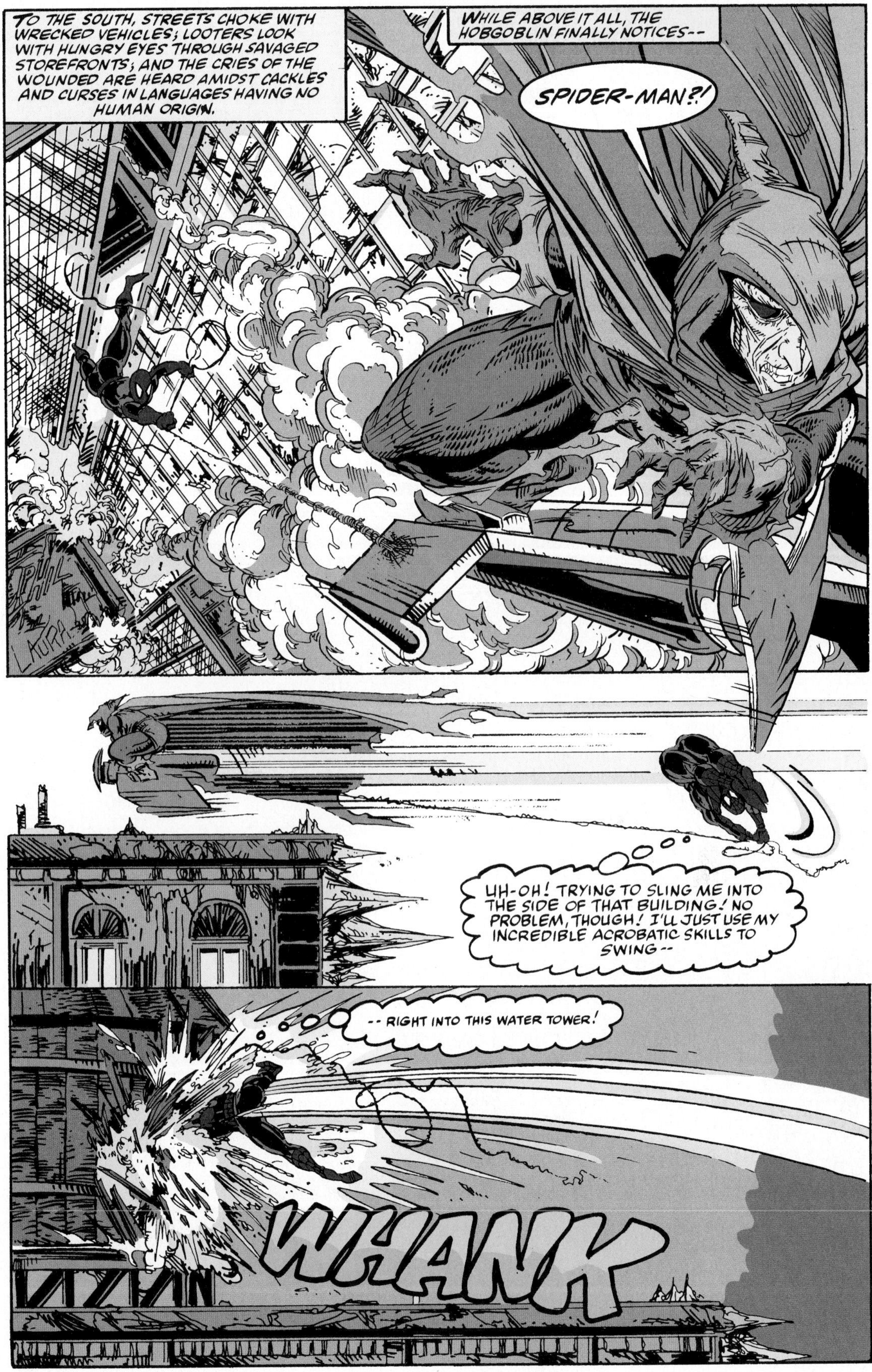
TO THE SOUTH, STREETS CHOKE WITH WRECKED VEHICLES; LOOTERS LOOK WITH HUNGRY EYES THROUGH SAVAGED STOREFRONTS; AND THE CRIES OF THE WOUNDED ARE HEARD AMIDST CACKLES AND CURSES IN LANGUAGES HAVING NO HUMAN ORIGIN.
WHILE ABOVE IT ALL, THE HOBGOBLIN FINALLY NOTICES--
SPIDER-MAN?!
UH-OH! TRYING TO SLING ME INTO THE SIDE OF THAT BUILDING! NO PROBLEM, THOUGH! I'LL JUST USE MY INCREDIBLE ACROBATIC SKILLS TO SWING--
--RIGHT INTO THIS WATER TOWER!
WHANK

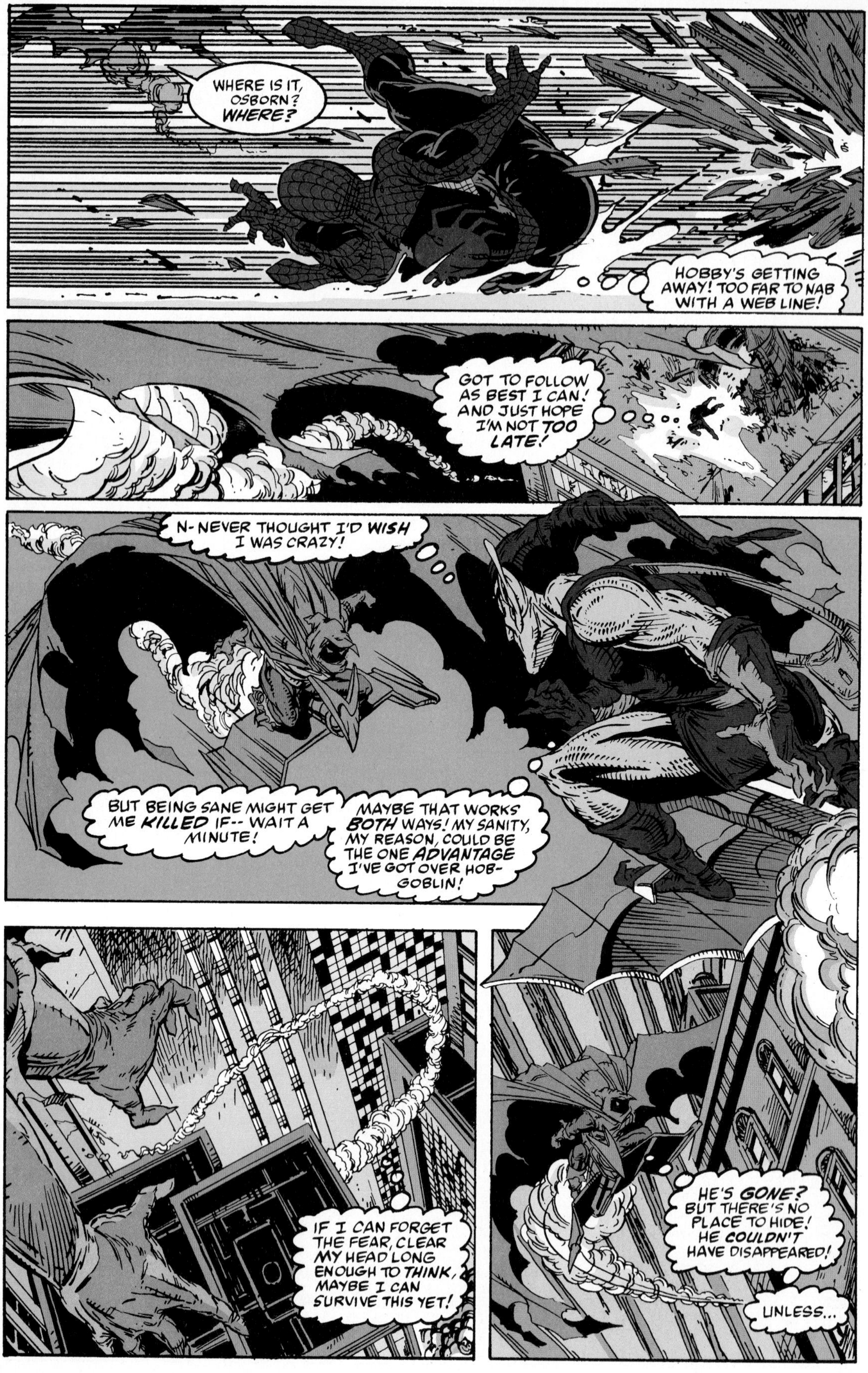
WHERE IS IT, OSBORN? WHERE?
HOBBY'S GETTING AWAY! TOO FAR TO NAB WITH A WEB LINE!
GOT TO FOLLOW AS BEST I CAN! AND JUST HOPE I'M NOT TOO LATE!
N-NEVER THOUGHT I'D WISH I WAS CRAZY!
BUT BEING SANE MIGHT GET ME KILLED IF-- WAIT A MINUTE!
MAYBE THAT WORKS BOTH WAYS! MY SANITY, MY REASON, COULD BE THE ONE ADVANTAGE I'VE GOT OVER HOB-GOBLIN!
IF I CAN FORGET THE FEAR, CLEAR MY HEAD LONG ENOUGH TO THINK, MAYBE I CAN SURVIVE THIS YET!
HE'S GONE? BUT THERE'S NO PLACE TO HIDE! HE COULDN'T HAVE DISAPPEARED!
UNLESS...

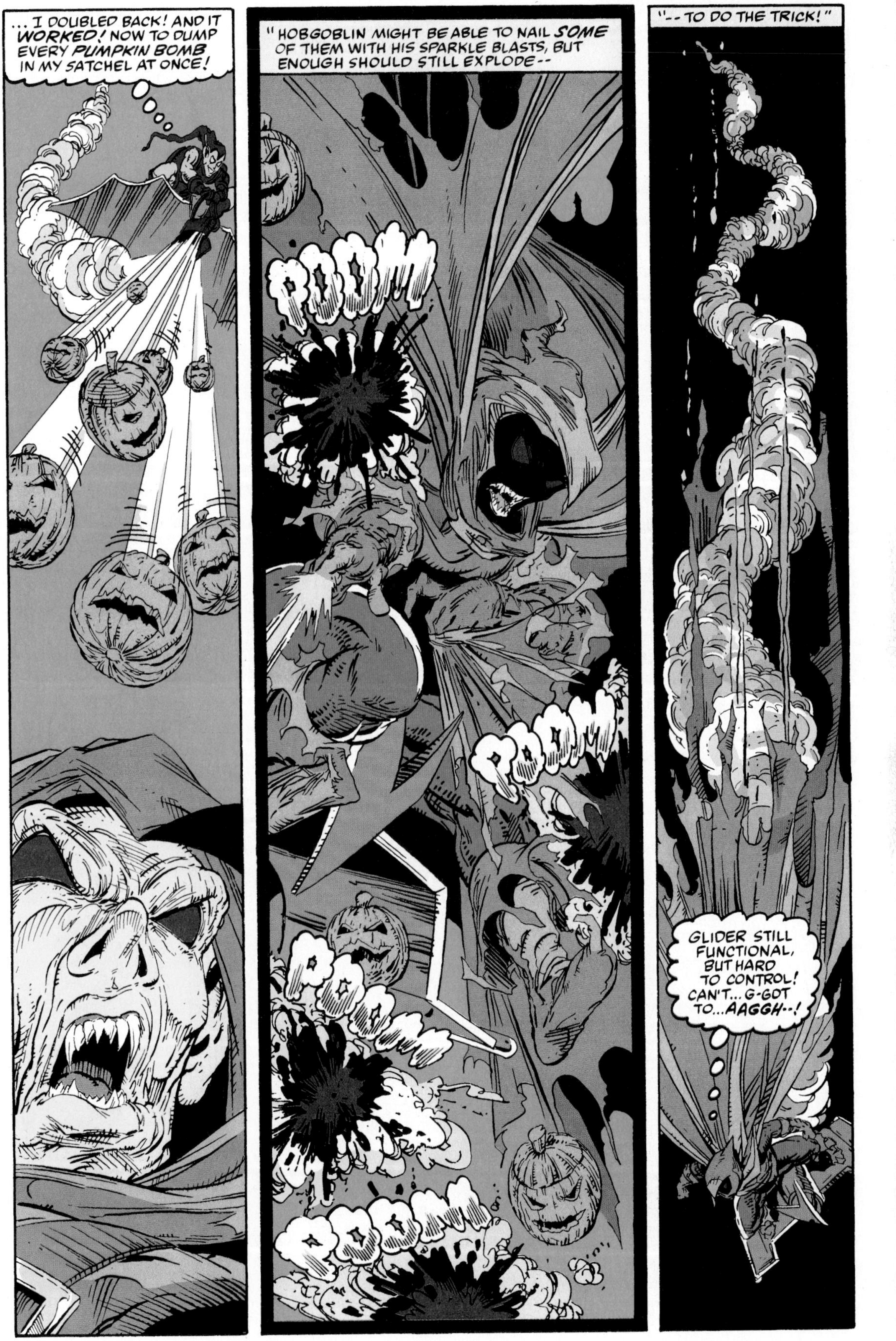
... I DOUBLED BACK! AND IT WORKED! NOW TO DUMP EVERY PUMPKIN BOMB IN MY SATCHEL AT ONCE!
"HOBGOBLIN MIGHT BE ABLE TO NAIL SOME OF THEM WITH HIS SPARKLE BLASTS, BUT ENOUGH SHOULD STILL EXPLODE --
POOOM
POOOM
POOOM
POOOM
"-- TO DO THE TRICK!"
GLIDER STILL FUNCTIONAL, BUT HARD TO CONTROL! CAN'T... G-GOT TO... AAGGH--!

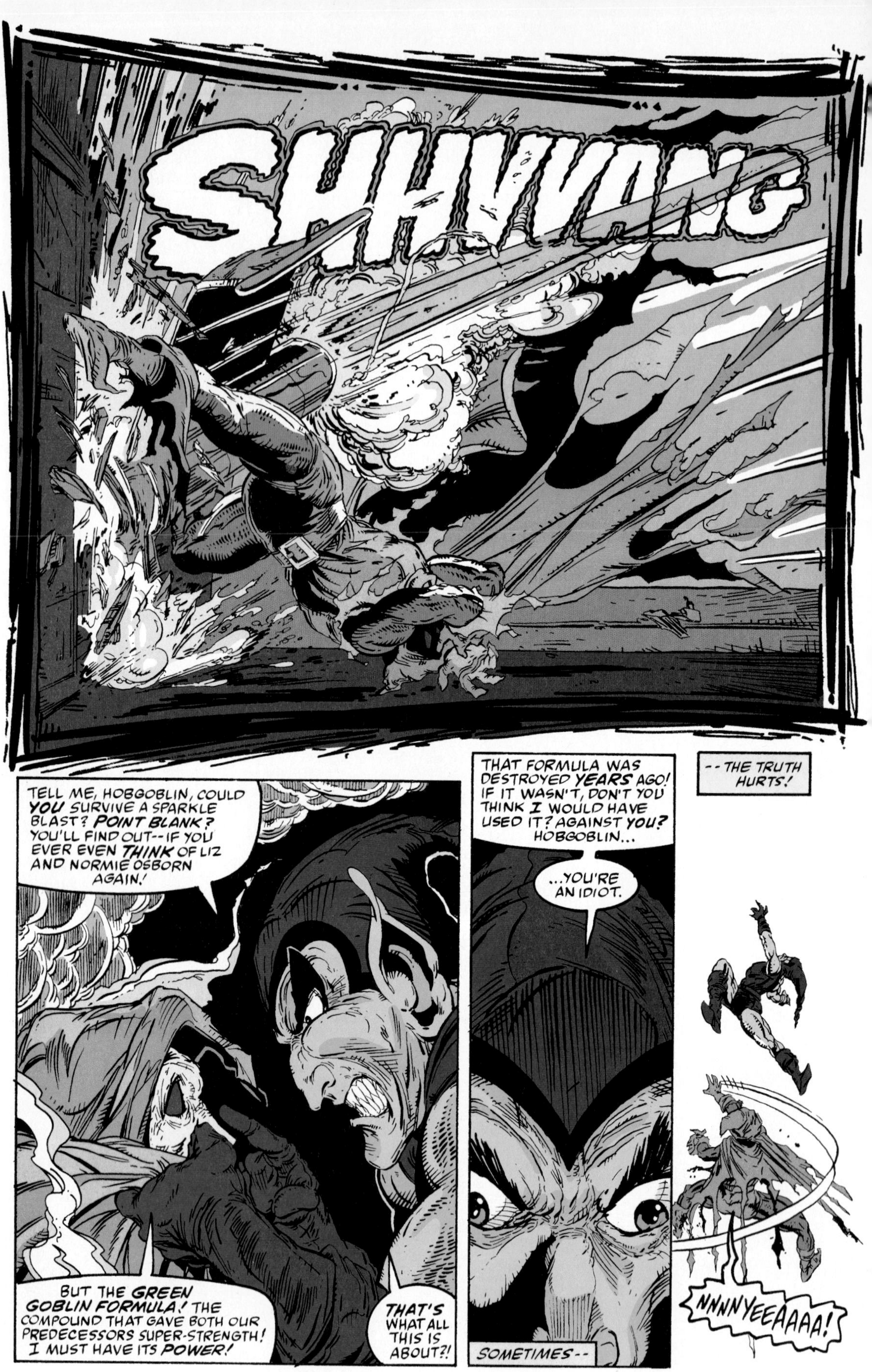
SHHVANG
TELL ME, HOBGOBLIN, COULD YOU SURVIVE A SPARKLE BLAST? POINT BLANK? YOU'LL FIND OUT--IF YOU EVER EVEN THINK OF LIZ AND NORMIE OSBORN AGAIN!
BUT THE GREEN GOBLIN FORMULA! THE COMPOUND THAT GAVE BOTH OUR PREDECESSORS SUPER-STRENGTH! I MUST HAVE ITS POWER!
THAT'S WHAT ALL THIS IS ABOUT?!
THAT FORMULA WAS DESTROYED YEARS AGO! IF IT WASN'T, DON'T YOU THINK I WOULD HAVE USED IT? AGAINST YOU? HOBGOBLIN...
...YOU'RE AN IDIOT.
SOMETIMES--
--THE TRUTH HURTS!
NNNNYEEAAAA!

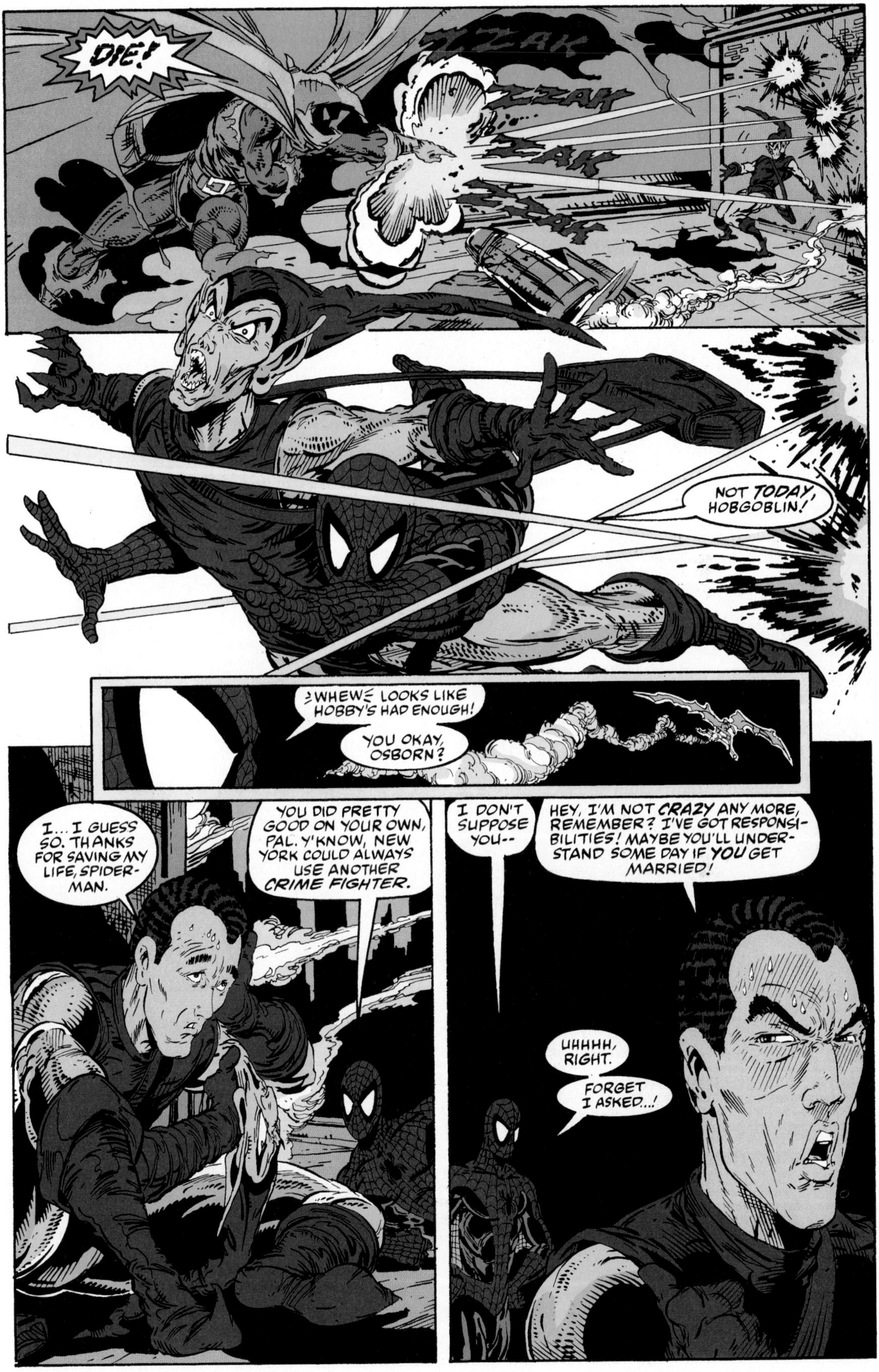

DIE!
TZZAK
TZZAK
ZAK
ZAK
NOT TODAY, HOBGOBLIN!
WHEW LOOKS LIKE HOBBY'S HAD ENOUGH!
YOU OKAY, OSBORN?
I... I GUESS SO. THANKS FOR SAVING MY LIFE, SPIDER-MAN.
YOU DID PRETTY GOOD ON YOUR OWN, PAL. Y'KNOW, NEW YORK COULD ALWAYS USE ANOTHER CRIME FIGHTER.
I DON'T SUPPOSE YOU--
HEY, I'M NOT CRAZY ANY MORE, REMEMBER? I'VE GOT RESPONSI-BILITIES! MAYBE YOU'LL UNDER-STAND SOME DAY IF YOU GET MARRIED!
UHHHH, RIGHT.
FORGET I ASKED...!

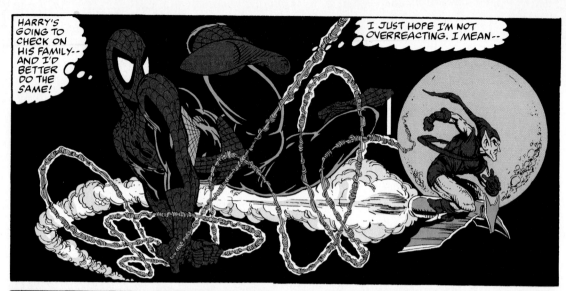

HARRY'S GOING TO CHECK ON HIS FAMILY-- AND I'D BETTER DO THE SAME!

I JUST HOPE I'M NOT OVERREACTING. I MEAN--

"-- SOMETHING *EVIL* IS HAPPENING TO MANHATTAN, THAT'S OBVIOUS! IN THE LAST COUPLE OF DAYS I'VE FOUGHT LIVING STATUES, ASH MONSTERS, EVEN SENTIENT VENT PIPES!"

" BUT AFTER ALL THAT, I JUST HAVE TO WONDER--

" -- COULD THINGS POSSIBLY GET ANY *WORSE?*"

HOT DOGS

HOT DOG 1.25
COKE .50

DR. CONNORS

YESSSSSSSSS....!

"INFERNO" ...CONTINUES NEXT ISSUE!

254

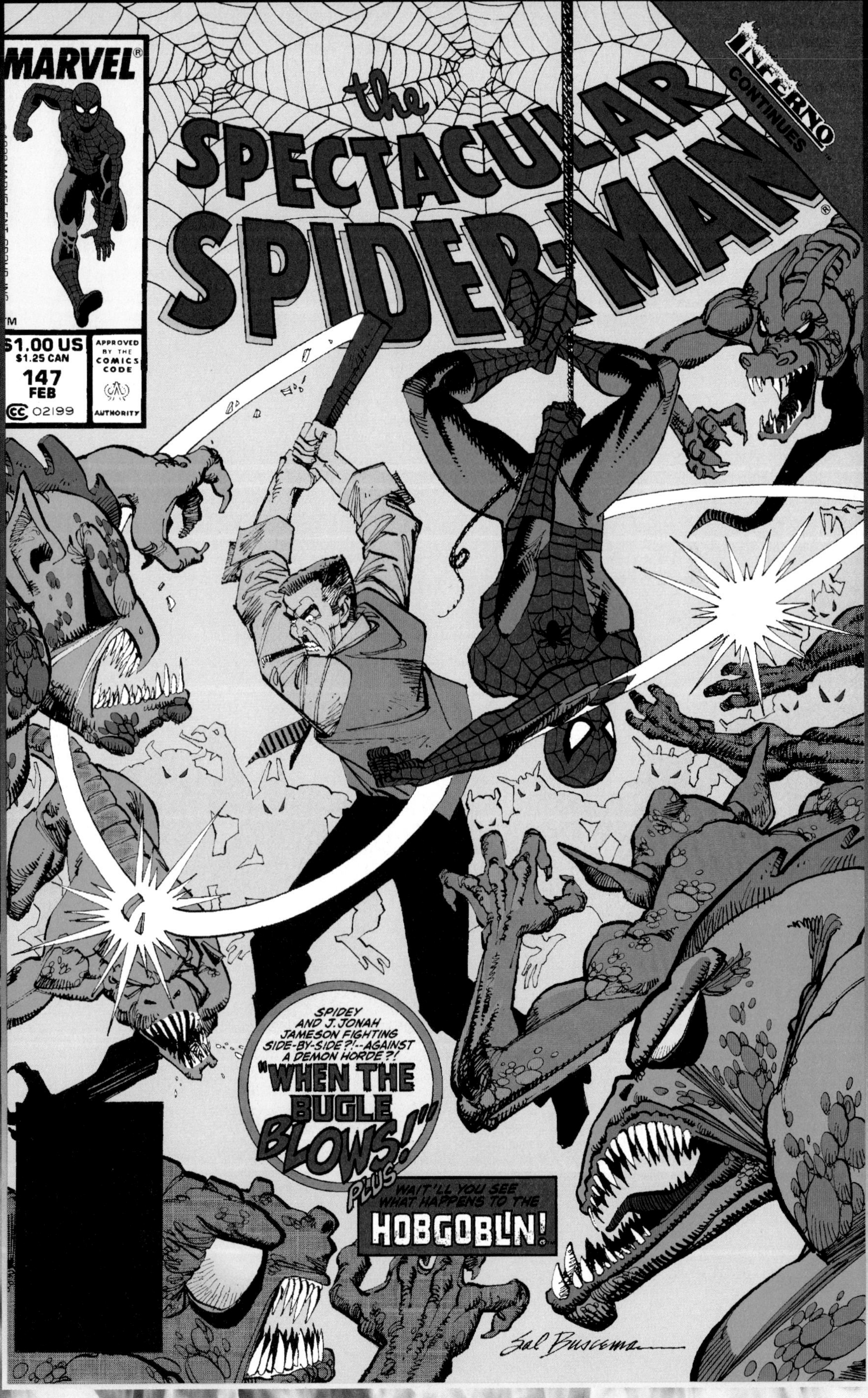
MARVEL®
the SPECTACULAR SPIDER-MAN®
INFERNO CONTINUES™
$1.00 US
$1.25 CAN
147
FEB
CC 02199
APPROVED BY THE COMICS CODE AUTHORITY
SPIDEY AND J. JONAH JAMESON FIGHTING SIDE-BY-SIDE?!--AGAINST A DEMON HORDE?!
"WHEN THE BUGLE BLOWS!"
PLUS: WAIT'LL YOU SEE WHAT HAPPENS TO THE
HOBGOBLIN!
Sal Buscema

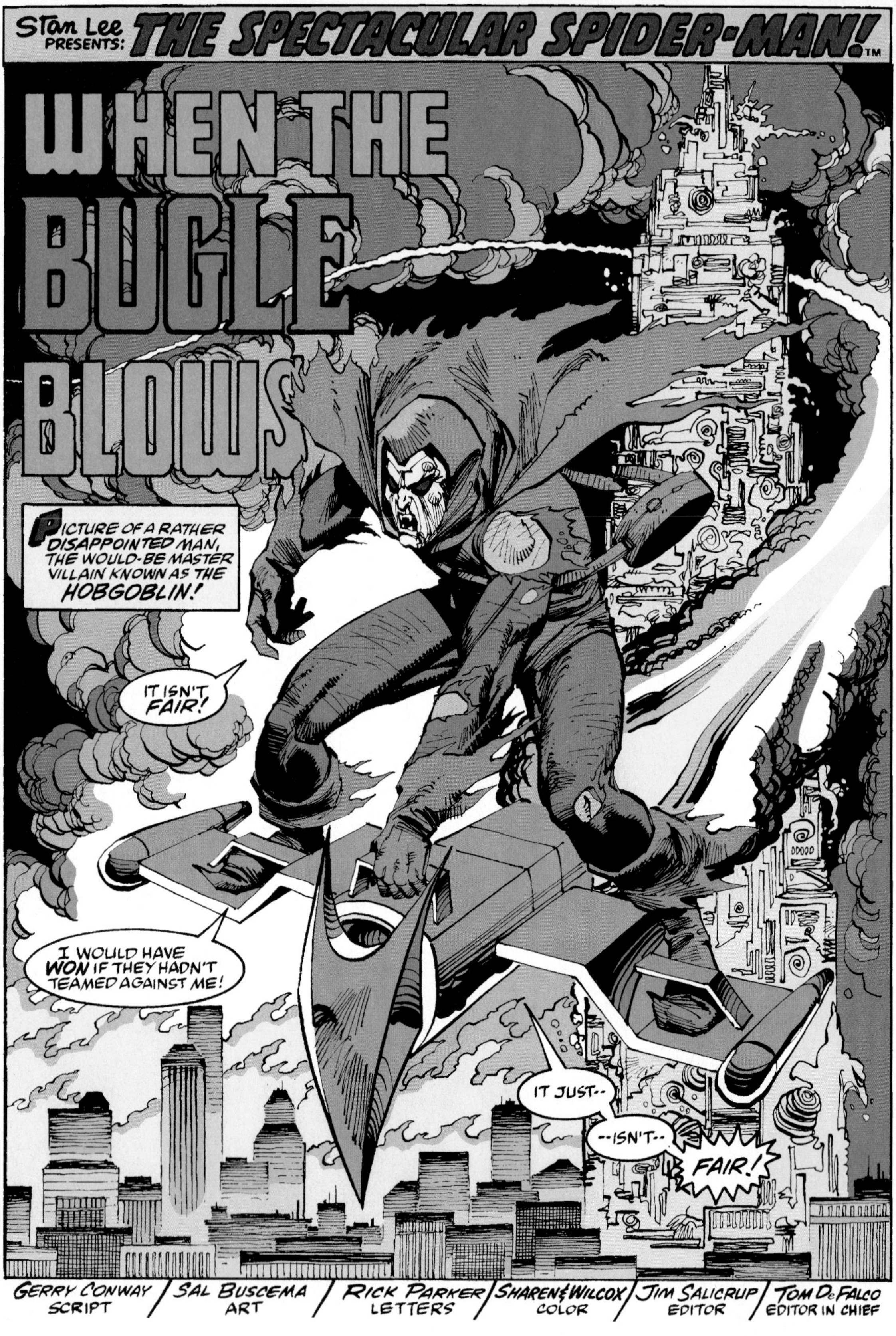
Stan Lee PRESENTS: THE SPECTACULAR SPIDER-MAN!™
WHEN THE BUGLE BLOWS
PICTURE OF A RATHER DISAPPOINTED MAN, THE WOULD-BE MASTER VILLAIN KNOWN AS THE HOBGOBLIN!
IT ISN'T FAIR!
I WOULD HAVE WON IF THEY HADN'T TEAMED AGAINST ME!
IT JUST--
--ISN'T--
FAIR!
GERRY CONWAY SCRIPT
SAL BUSCEMA ART
RICK PARKER LETTERS
SHAREN & WILCOX COLOR
JIM SALICRUP EDITOR
TOM DeFALCO EDITOR IN CHIEF

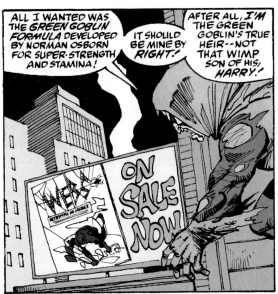

ALL I WANTED WAS THE *GREEN GOBLIN FORMULA* DEVELOPED BY NORMAN OSBORN FOR SUPER-STRENGTH AND STAMINA!

IT SHOULD BE MINE BY *RIGHT!*

AFTER ALL, *I'M* THE GREEN GOBLIN'S TRUE HEIR--NOT THAT WIMP SON OF HIS, *HARRY!*

ALL MY TECHNOLOGY, ALL MY WEAPONS, ALL MY TECHNIQUES ARE *ADAPTED* AND *IMPROVED* FROM THE GOBLIN'S ORIGINAL PLANS!

WHEN THE *FIRST* HOBGOBLIN DIED, I STOLE HIS EQUIPMENT FAIR AND SQUARE!

THE REST OF THE GOBLIN HERITAGE SHOULD BE MINE *TOO!*

AND IT *WOULD* HAVE BEEN, IF HARRY OSBORN AND SPIDER-MAN HADN'T *TRICKED* ME! *

BLAST THEM BOTH!

SP-AK

* ROUGH RECAP OF *AMAZING #312,* STILL ON SALE. (HINT-HINT.) --JM

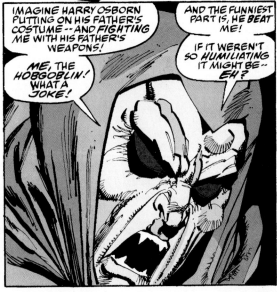

IMAGINE HARRY OSBORN PUTTING ON HIS FATHER'S COSTUME -- AND *FIGHTING* ME WITH HIS FATHER'S WEAPONS!

ME, THE HOBGOBLIN! WHAT A JOKE!

AND THE FUNNIEST PART IS, HE *BEAT* ME!

IF IT WEREN'T SO *HUMILIATING* IT MIGHT BE-- *EH?*

ROWRR

DEMONS!

IN MY ANGER I'D ALMOST *FORGOTTEN* THE MADNESS ASSAILING THIS CITY!

TASTY HUMAN! DRESS LIKE DEMON!

BUT YOU DON'T *FOOL* US!

WE EAT YOU UP!

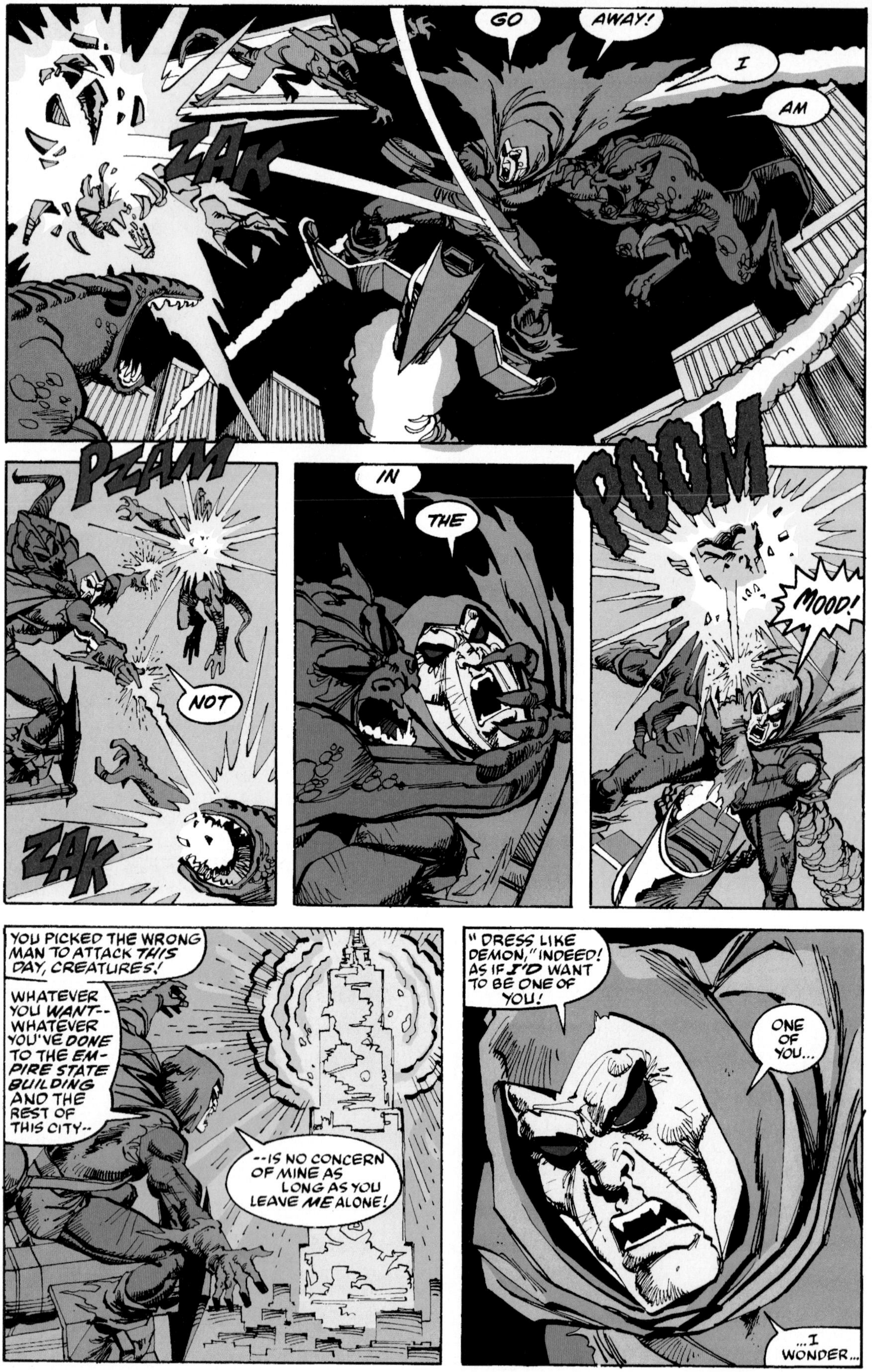
ZAK
GO
AWAY!
I
AM
PZAM
NOT
ZAK
IN
THE
POOM
MOOD!
YOU PICKED THE WRONG MAN TO ATTACK THIS DAY, CREATURES!
WHATEVER YOU WANT-- WHATEVER YOU'VE DONE TO THE EMPIRE STATE BUILDING AND THE REST OF THIS CITY--
--IS NO CONCERN OF MINE AS LONG AS YOU LEAVE ME ALONE!
"DRESS LIKE DEMON," INDEED! AS IF I'D WANT TO BE ONE OF YOU!
ONE OF YOU...
...I WONDER...

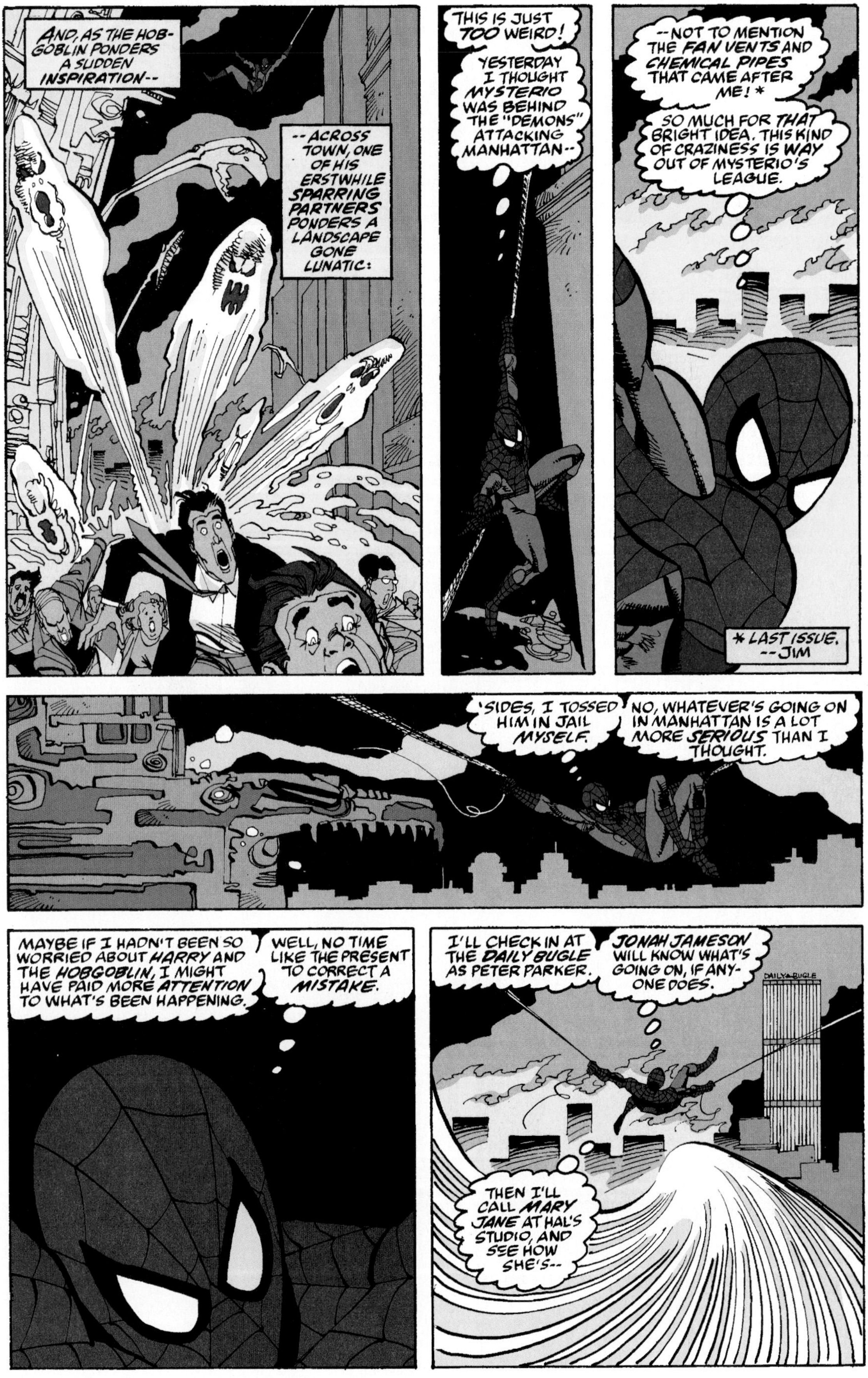

AND, AS THE HOBGOBLIN PONDERS A SUDDEN INSPIRATION--
--ACROSS TOWN, ONE OF HIS ERSTWHILE SPARRING PARTNERS PONDERS A LANDSCAPE GONE LUNATIC:
THIS IS JUST TOO WEIRD!
YESTERDAY I THOUGHT MYSTERIO WAS BEHIND THE "DEMONS" ATTACKING MANHATTAN--
--NOT TO MENTION THE FAN VENTS AND CHEMICAL PIPES THAT CAME AFTER ME! *
SO MUCH FOR THAT BRIGHT IDEA. THIS KIND OF CRAZINESS IS WAY OUT OF MYSTERIO'S LEAGUE.
* LAST ISSUE. --JIM
'SIDES, I TOSSED HIM IN JAIL MYSELF.
NO, WHATEVER'S GOING ON IN MANHATTAN IS A LOT MORE SERIOUS THAN I THOUGHT.
MAYBE IF I HADN'T BEEN SO WORRIED ABOUT HARRY AND THE HOBGOBLIN, I MIGHT HAVE PAID MORE ATTENTION TO WHAT'S BEEN HAPPENING.
WELL, NO TIME LIKE THE PRESENT TO CORRECT A MISTAKE.
I'LL CHECK IN AT THE DAILY BUGLE AS PETER PARKER.
JONAH JAMESON WILL KNOW WHAT'S GOING ON, IF ANYONE DOES.
DAILY BUGLE
THEN I'LL CALL MARY JANE AT HAL'S STUDIO, AND SEE HOW SHE'S--

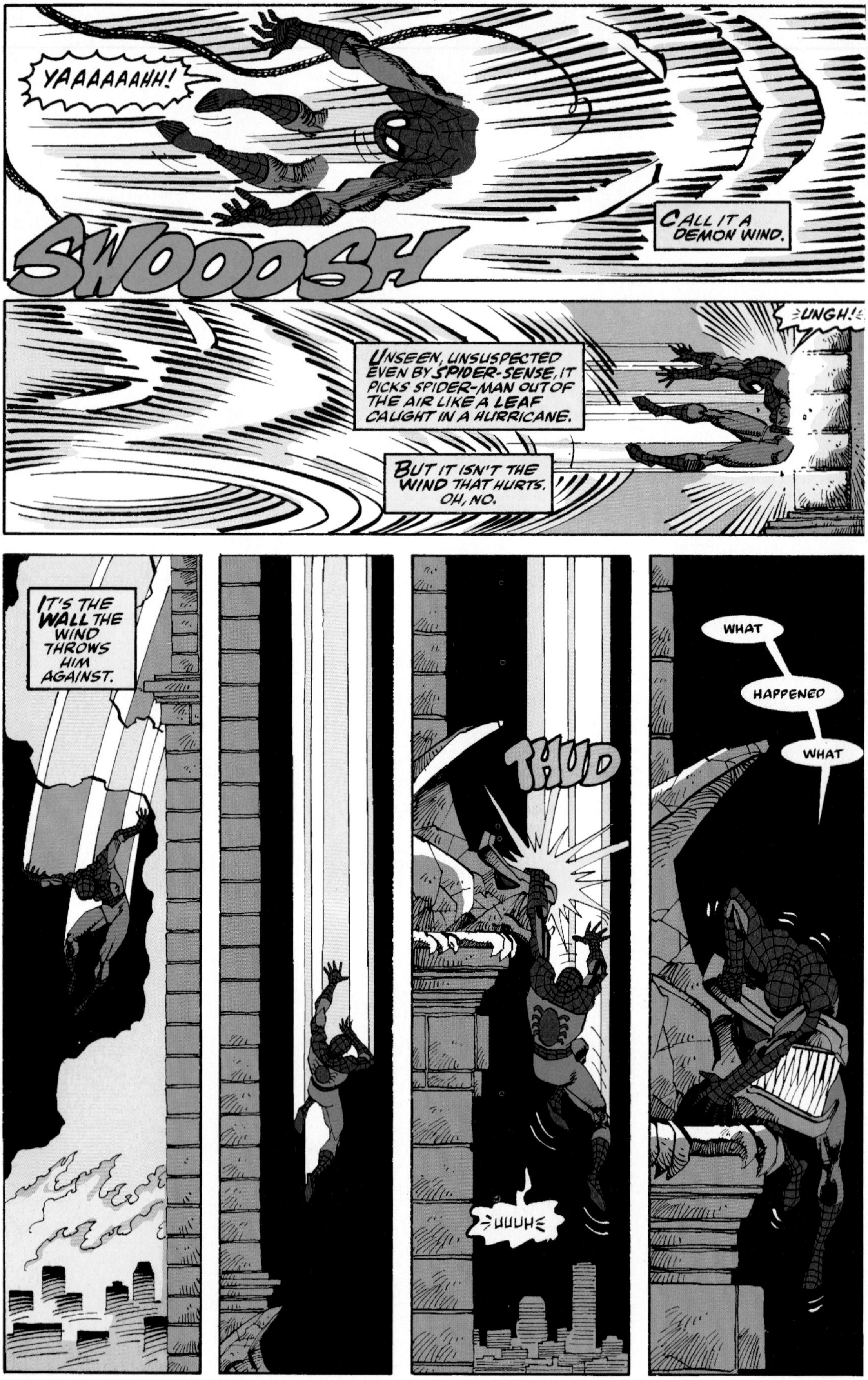
YAAAAAAHH!
SWOOOSH
CALL IT A DEMON WIND.
UNGH!
UNSEEN, UNSUSPECTED EVEN BY SPIDER-SENSE, IT PICKS SPIDER-MAN OUT OF THE AIR LIKE A LEAF CAUGHT IN A HURRICANE.
BUT IT ISN'T THE WIND THAT HURTS. OH, NO.
IT'S THE WALL THE WIND THROWS HIM AGAINST.
THUD
UUUH
WHAT
HAPPENED
WHAT

HAPPENED... CRAZY... IT WAS CRAZY!

THE WIND CAME ALIVE-- ATTACKED ME! AND MY SPIDER-SENSE DIDN'T WARN ME!

BARELY CAUGHT MYSELF ON THIS--

--GARGOYLE!

CHOMP

≈AAAAHH!≈

TA-THUMP

HOW LONG HE LIES UNCON-SCIOUS, HE'LL NEVER KNOW FOR SURE.

LONG ENOUGH.

AND WHEN CONSCIOUSNESS FINALLY RETURNS, THE WORLD IS A CRIMSON BLUR.

THROUGH A HAZE OF PAIN, HE RECOG-NIZES A PLACE NEARBY.

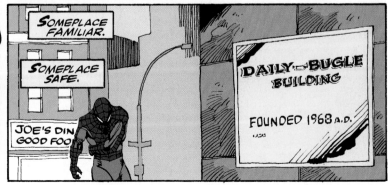

SOMEPLACE FAMILIAR.

SOMEPLACE SAFE.

JOE'S DIN GOOD FOO

DAILY BUGLE BUILDING

FOUNDED 1968 A.D.

261

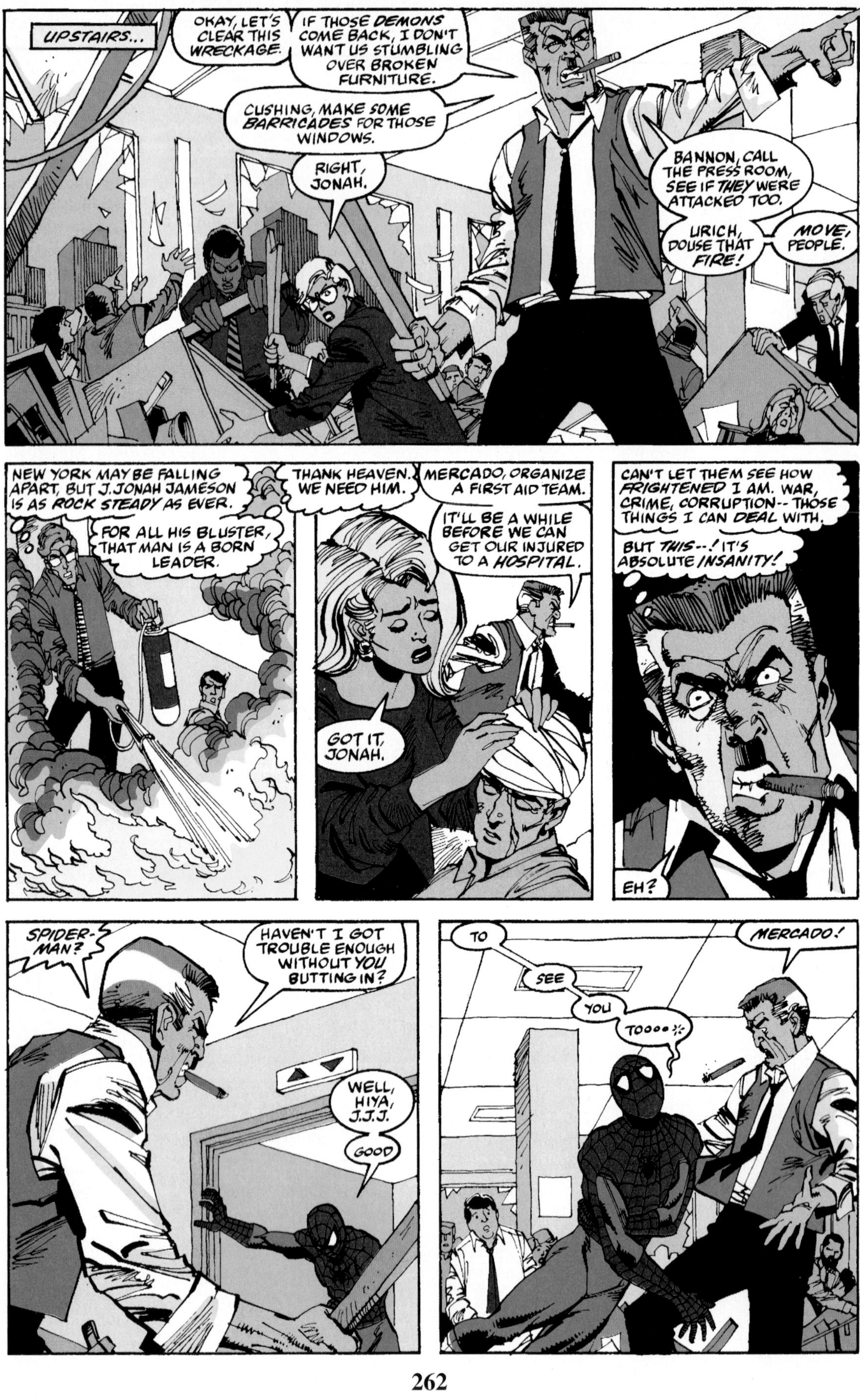
UPSTAIRS...
OKAY, LET'S CLEAR THIS WRECKAGE.
IF THOSE DEMONS COME BACK, I DON'T WANT US STUMBLING OVER BROKEN FURNITURE.
CUSHING, MAKE SOME BARRICADES FOR THOSE WINDOWS.
RIGHT, JONAH.
BANNON, CALL THE PRESS ROOM, SEE IF THEY WERE ATTACKED TOO.
URICH, DOUSE THAT FIRE!
MOVE, PEOPLE.
NEW YORK MAY BE FALLING APART, BUT J. JONAH JAMESON IS AS ROCK STEADY AS EVER.
FOR ALL HIS BLUSTER, THAT MAN IS A BORN LEADER.
THANK HEAVEN. WE NEED HIM.
MERCADO, ORGANIZE A FIRST AID TEAM.
IT'LL BE A WHILE BEFORE WE CAN GET OUR INJURED TO A HOSPITAL.
GOT IT, JONAH.
CAN'T LET THEM SEE HOW FRIGHTENED I AM. WAR, CRIME, CORRUPTION-- THOSE THINGS I CAN DEAL WITH.
BUT THIS--! IT'S ABSOLUTE INSANITY!
EH?
SPIDER-MAN?
HAVEN'T I GOT TROUBLE ENOUGH WITHOUT YOU BUTTING IN?
WELL, HIYA, J.J.J.
GOOD
TO
SEE
YOU
TOOOO!
MERCADO!

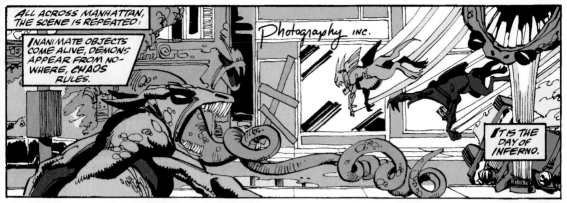

ALL ACROSS MANHATTAN, THE SCENE IS REPEATED:

INANIMATE OBJECTS COME ALIVE, DEMONS APPEAR FROM NO-WHERE, CHAOS RULES.

Photography INC.

IT IS THE DAY OF INFERNO.

AND FOR MARY JANE WATSON-PARKER, CAUGHT IN THE MADNESS WHILE SHOOTING AN EGYPTIAN-MOTIF PHOTO SPREAD, THE DAY HAS GONE FROM BAD TO MUCH, MUCH WORSE...

C'MON, YOU GUYS! BLOCK THAT DOOR!

YOU KNOW WHAT'S OUT THERE!

WHAT'S THE USE? WE DON'T STAND A CHANCE!

YOU CAN'T FIGHT MAGIC! WE'RE ALL DOOMED!

WE'RE GOING TO DIE.

SHUT UP, WEXLER!

NOBODY IS GOING TO--

KRASH

YIII!

MUNCHIE-MUNCHIE! NICE FAT HUMAN FOR HUNGRY ME!

YUMMY!

HEY, WEXLER--

DUCK!

POOM

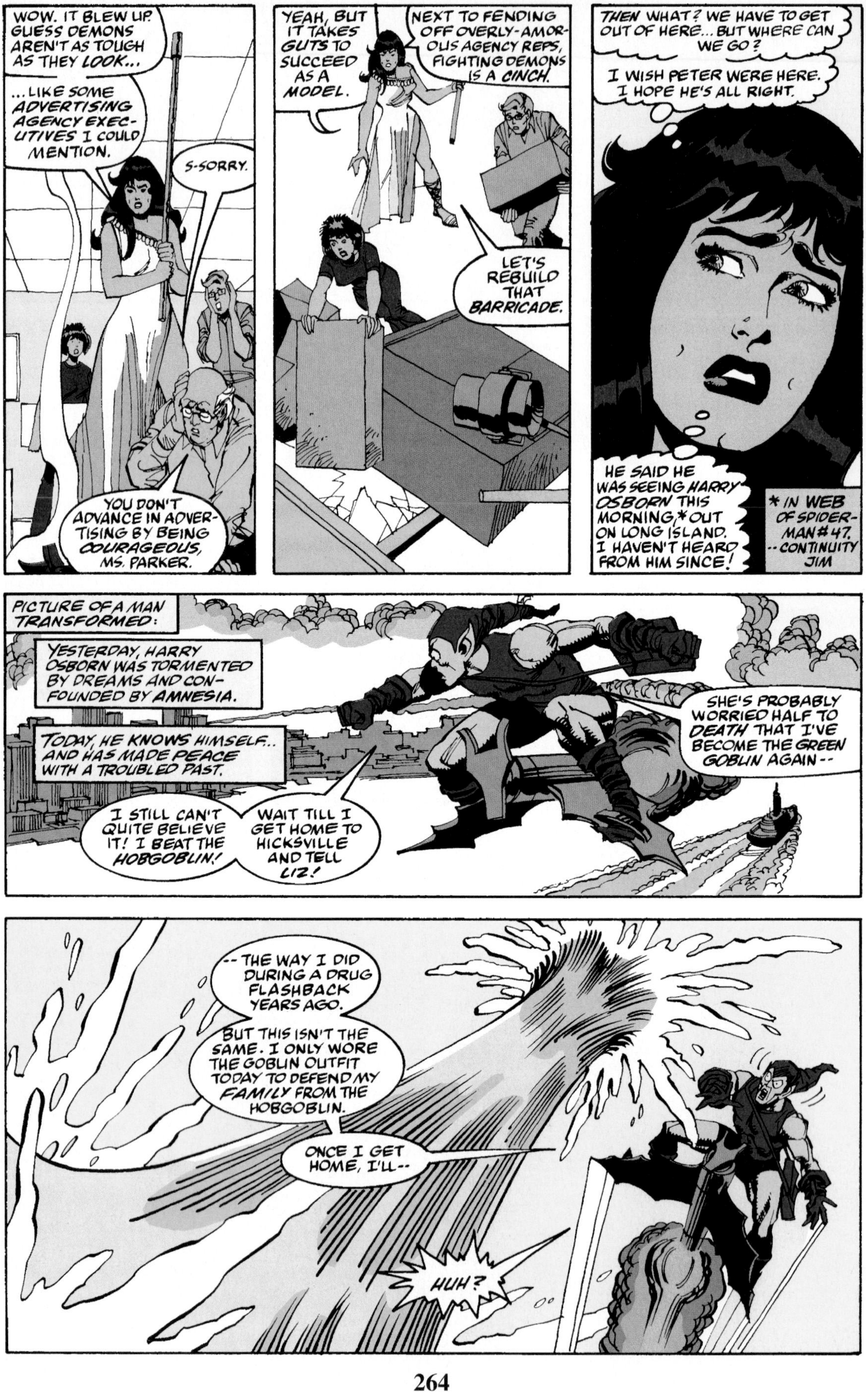
WOW. IT BLEW UP. GUESS DEMONS AREN'T AS TOUGH AS THEY LOOK...
...LIKE SOME ADVERTISING AGENCY EXECUTIVES I COULD MENTION.
S-SORRY.
YOU DON'T ADVANCE IN ADVERTISING BY BEING COURAGEOUS, MS. PARKER.
YEAH, BUT IT TAKES GUTS TO SUCCEED AS A MODEL.
NEXT TO FENDING OFF OVERLY-AMOROUS AGENCY REPS, FIGHTING DEMONS IS A CINCH.
LET'S REBUILD THAT BARRICADE.
THEN WHAT? WE HAVE TO GET OUT OF HERE... BUT WHERE CAN WE GO?
I WISH PETER WERE HERE. I HOPE HE'S ALL RIGHT.
HE SAID HE WAS SEEING HARRY OSBORN THIS MORNING,* OUT ON LONG ISLAND. I HAVEN'T HEARD FROM HIM SINCE!
* IN WEB OF SPIDER-MAN #47. --CONTINUITY JIM
PICTURE OF A MAN TRANSFORMED:
YESTERDAY, HARRY OSBORN WAS TORMENTED BY DREAMS AND CONFOUNDED BY AMNESIA.
TODAY, HE KNOWS HIMSELF... AND HAS MADE PEACE WITH A TROUBLED PAST.
I STILL CAN'T QUITE BELIEVE IT! I BEAT THE HOBGOBLIN!
WAIT TILL I GET HOME TO HICKSVILLE AND TELL LIZ!
SHE'S PROBABLY WORRIED HALF TO DEATH THAT I'VE BECOME THE GREEN GOBLIN AGAIN--
--THE WAY I DID DURING A DRUG FLASHBACK YEARS AGO.
BUT THIS ISN'T THE SAME. I ONLY WORE THE GOBLIN OUTFIT TODAY TO DEFEND MY FAMILY FROM THE HOBGOBLIN.
ONCE I GET HOME, I'LL--
HUH?

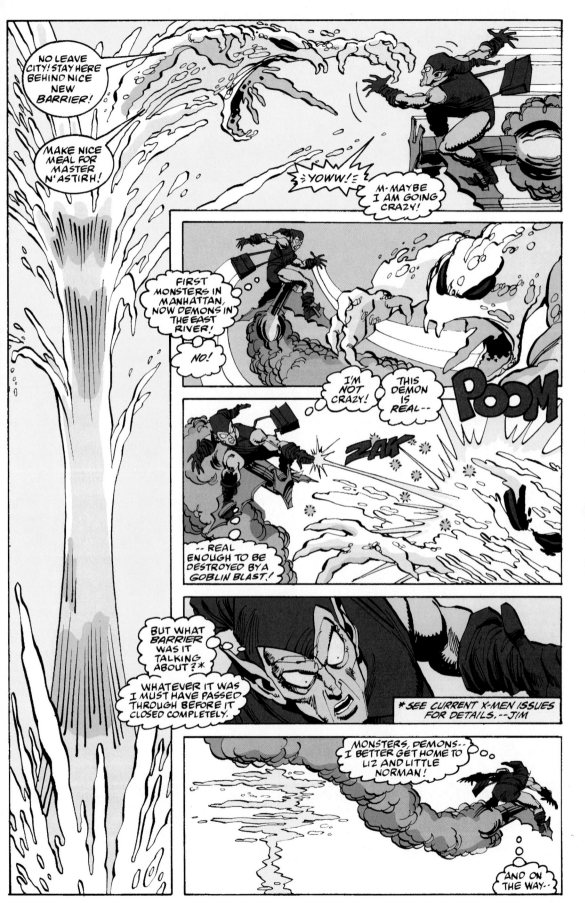

NO LEAVE CITY! STAY HERE BEHIND NICE NEW BARRIER!

MAKE NICE MEAL FOR MASTER N'ASTIRH!

≲YOWW!≳

M-MAYBE I AM GOING CRAZY!

FIRST MONSTERS IN MANHATTAN, NOW DEMONS IN THE EAST RIVER!

NO!

I'M NOT CRAZY!

THIS DEMON IS REAL--

POOM

ZAK

-- REAL ENOUGH TO BE DESTROYED BY A GOBLIN BLAST!

BUT WHAT BARRIER WAS IT TALKING ABOUT?*

WHATEVER IT WAS I MUST HAVE PASSED THROUGH BEFORE IT CLOSED COMPLETELY.

*SEE CURRENT X-MEN ISSUES FOR DETAILS. --JIM

MONSTERS, DEMONS-- I BETTER GET HOME TO LIZ AND LITTLE NORMAN!

AND ON THE WAY--

265

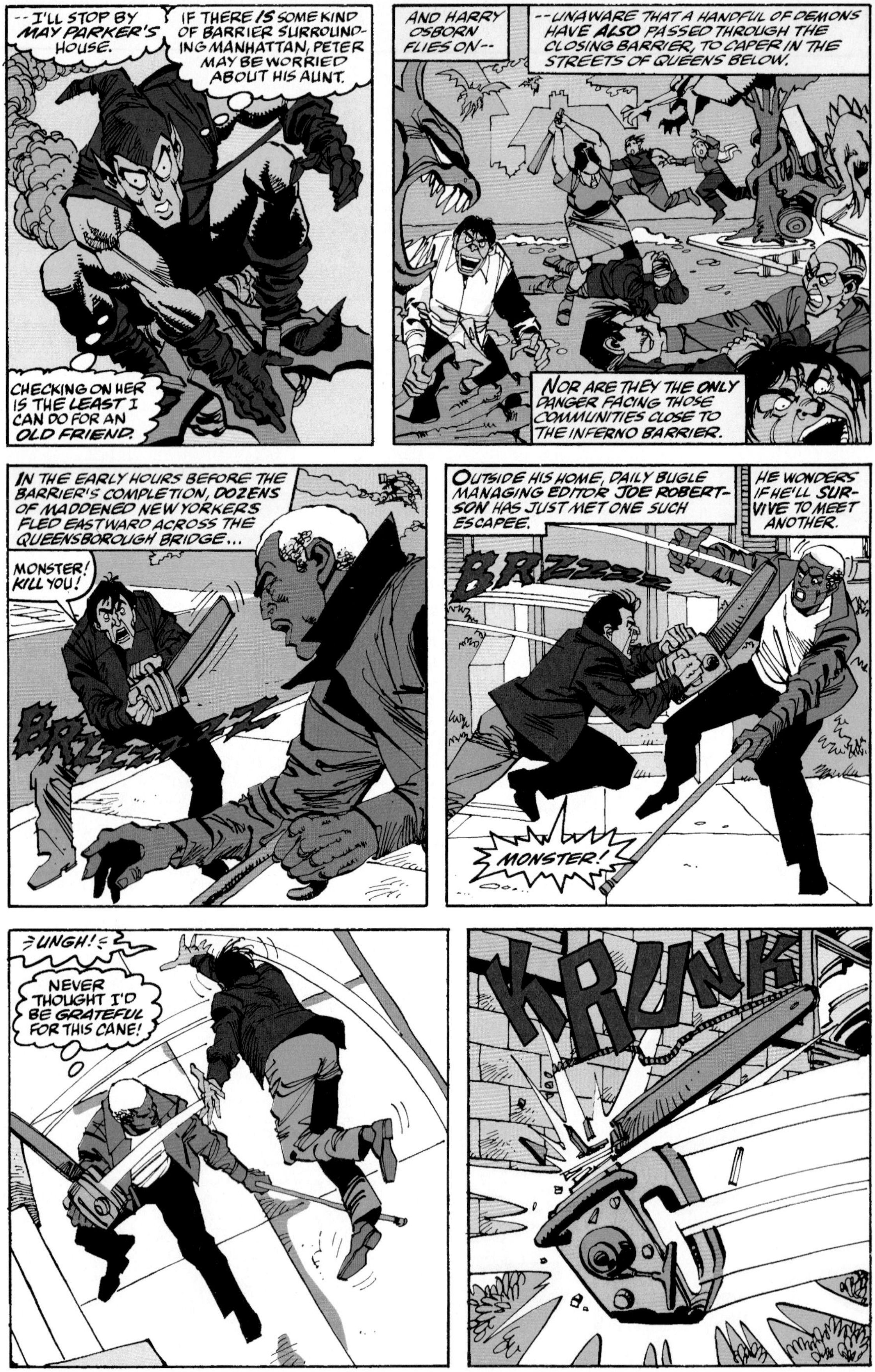
--I'LL STOP BY MAY PARKER'S HOUSE.
IF THERE IS SOME KIND OF BARRIER SURROUNDING MANHATTAN, PETER MAY BE WORRIED ABOUT HIS AUNT.
CHECKING ON HER IS THE LEAST I CAN DO FOR AN OLD FRIEND.
AND HARRY OSBORN FLIES ON--
--UNAWARE THAT A HANDFUL OF DEMONS HAVE ALSO PASSED THROUGH THE CLOSING BARRIER, TO CAPER IN THE STREETS OF QUEENS BELOW.
NOR ARE THEY THE ONLY DANGER FACING THOSE COMMUNITIES CLOSE TO THE INFERNO BARRIER.
IN THE EARLY HOURS BEFORE THE BARRIER'S COMPLETION, DOZENS OF MADDENED NEW YORKERS FLED EASTWARD ACROSS THE QUEENSBOROUGH BRIDGE...
MONSTER! KILL YOU!
OUTSIDE HIS HOME, DAILY BUGLE MANAGING EDITOR JOE ROBERTSON HAS JUST MET ONE SUCH ESCAPEE.
HE WONDERS IF HE'LL SURVIVE TO MEET ANOTHER.
BRZZZZZ
MONSTER!
UNGH!
NEVER THOUGHT I'D BE GRATEFUL FOR THIS CANE!
KRUNK

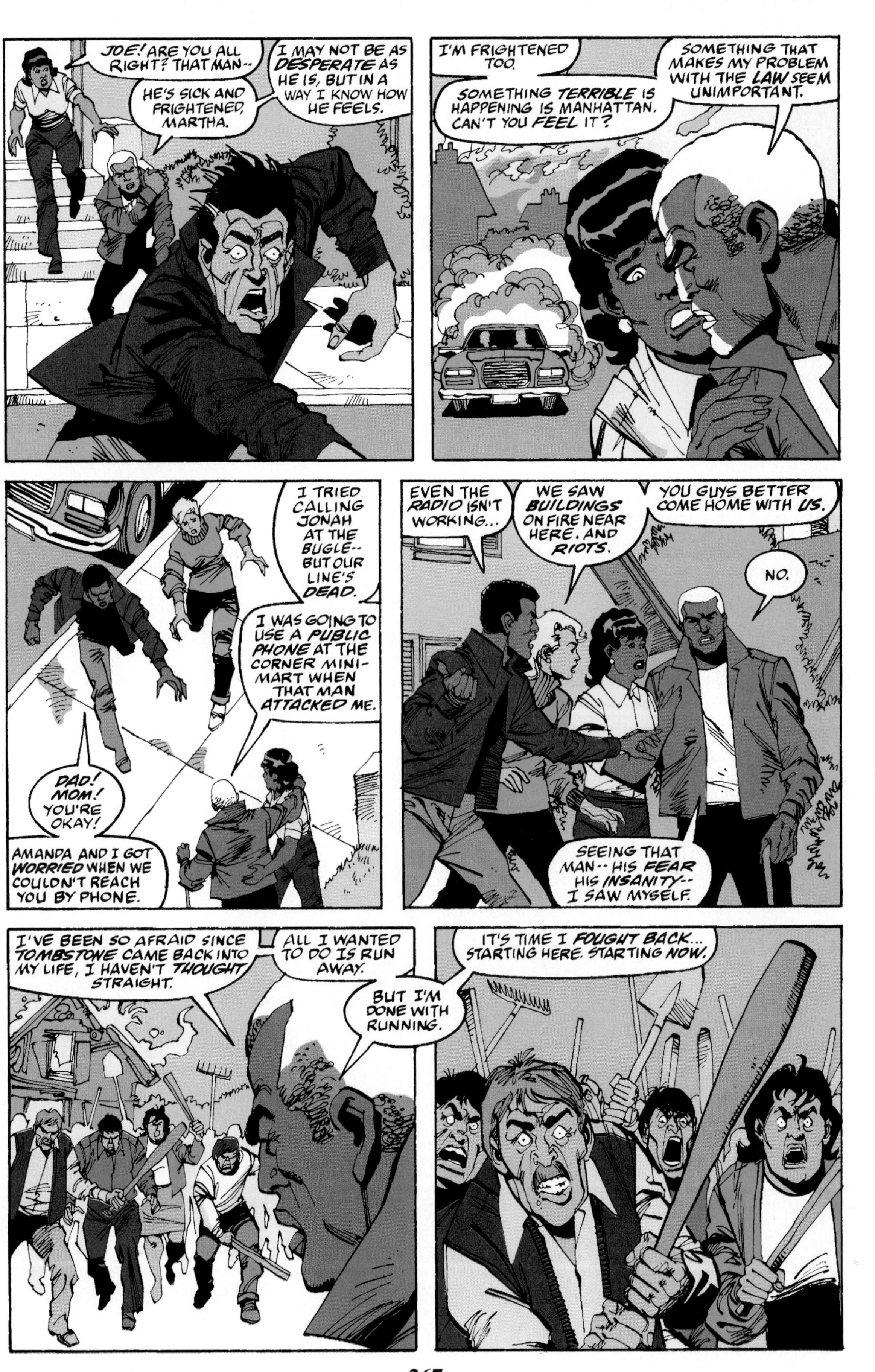
JOE! ARE YOU ALL RIGHT? THAT MAN--
HE'S SICK AND FRIGHTENED, MARTHA.
I MAY NOT BE AS DESPERATE AS HE IS, BUT IN A WAY I KNOW HOW HE FEELS.
I'M FRIGHTENED TOO.
SOMETHING TERRIBLE IS HAPPENING IS MANHATTAN. CAN'T YOU FEEL IT?
SOMETHING THAT MAKES MY PROBLEM WITH THE LAW SEEM UNIMPORTANT.
DAD! MOM! YOU'RE OKAY!
AMANDA AND I GOT WORRIED WHEN WE COULDN'T REACH YOU BY PHONE.
I TRIED CALLING JONAH AT THE BUGLE-- BUT OUR LINE'S DEAD.
I WAS GOING TO USE A PUBLIC PHONE AT THE CORNER MINI-MART WHEN THAT MAN ATTACKED ME.
EVEN THE RADIO ISN'T WORKING...
WE SAW BUILDINGS ON FIRE NEAR HERE. AND RIOTS.
YOU GUYS BETTER COME HOME WITH US.
NO.
SEEING THAT MAN-- HIS FEAR HIS INSANITY-- I SAW MYSELF.
I'VE BEEN SO AFRAID SINCE TOMBSTONE CAME BACK INTO MY LIFE, I HAVEN'T THOUGHT STRAIGHT.
ALL I WANTED TO DO IS RUN AWAY.
BUT I'M DONE WITH RUNNING.
IT'S TIME I FOUGHT BACK... STARTING HERE. STARTING NOW.

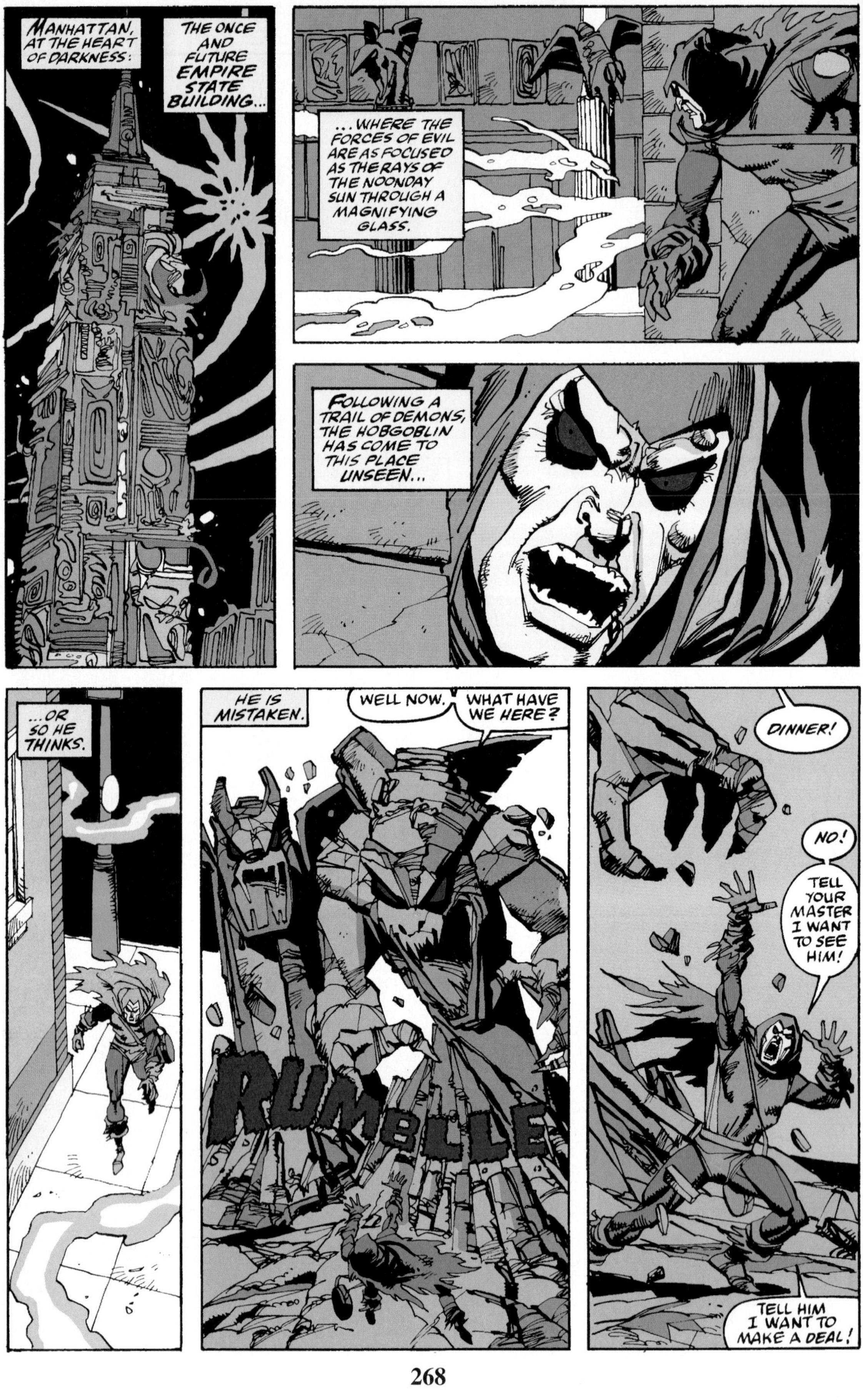
MANHATTAN, AT THE HEART OF DARKNESS:
THE ONCE AND FUTURE EMPIRE STATE BUILDING...
...WHERE THE FORCES OF EVIL ARE AS FOCUSED AS THE RAYS OF THE NOONDAY SUN THROUGH A MAGNIFYING GLASS.
FOLLOWING A TRAIL OF DEMONS, THE HOBGOBLIN HAS COME TO THIS PLACE UNSEEN...
...OR SO HE THINKS.
HE IS MISTAKEN.
WELL NOW.
WHAT HAVE WE HERE?
RUMBLLE
DINNER!
NO!
TELL YOUR MASTER I WANT TO SEE HIM!
TELL HIM I WANT TO MAKE A DEAL!

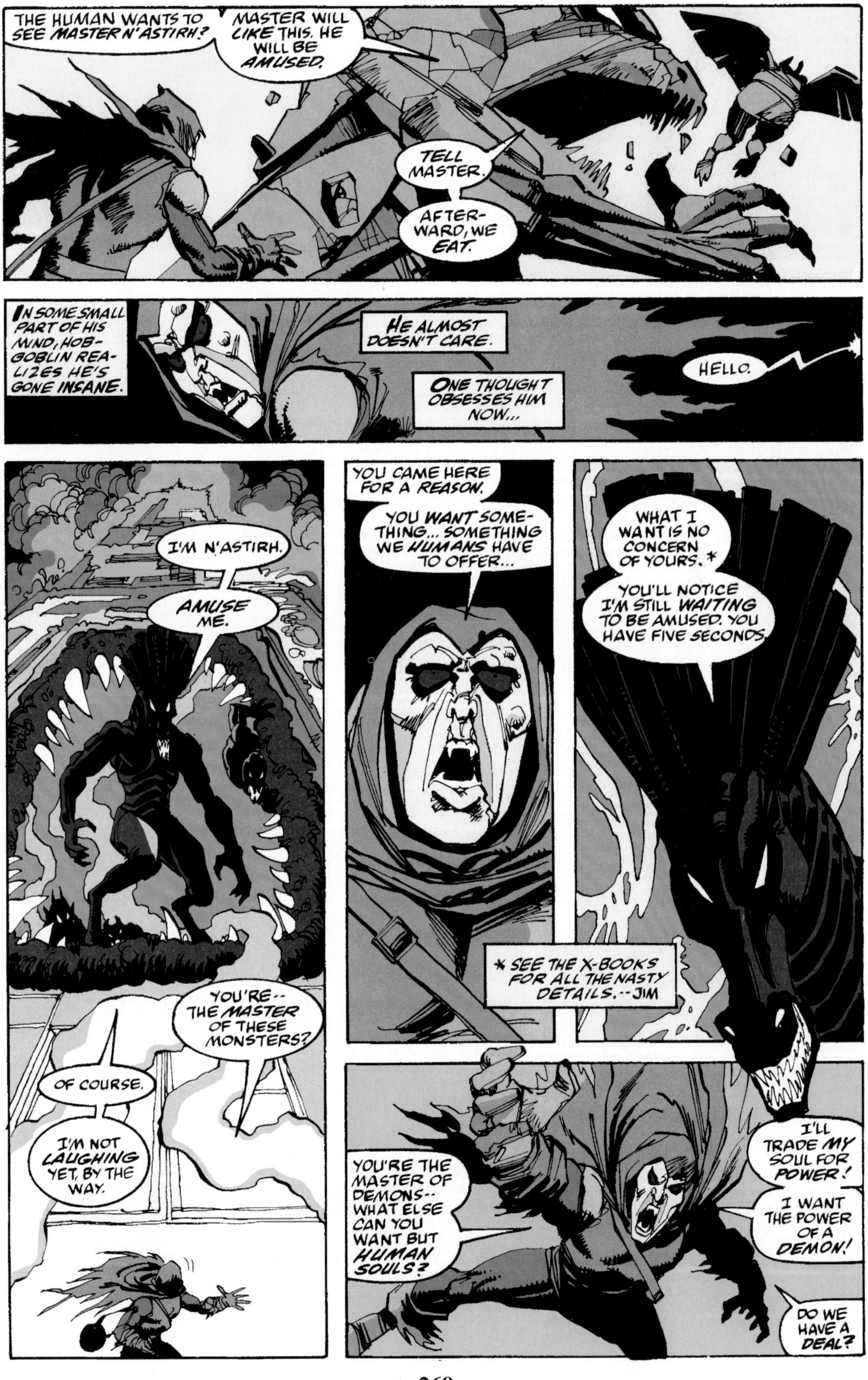
THE HUMAN WANTS TO SEE MASTER N'ASTIRH?
MASTER WILL LIKE THIS. HE WILL BE AMUSED.
TELL MASTER.
AFTER-WARD, WE EAT.
IN SOME SMALL PART OF HIS MIND, HOBGOBLIN REALIZES HE'S GONE INSANE.
HE ALMOST DOESN'T CARE.
ONE THOUGHT OBSESSES HIM NOW...
HELLO.
I'M N'ASTIRH.
AMUSE ME.
YOU'RE-- THE MASTER OF THESE MONSTERS?
OF COURSE.
I'M NOT LAUGHING YET, BY THE WAY.
YOU CAME HERE FOR A REASON.
YOU WANT SOMETHING... SOMETHING WE HUMANS HAVE TO OFFER...
WHAT I WANT IS NO CONCERN OF YOURS.*
YOU'LL NOTICE I'M STILL WAITING TO BE AMUSED. YOU HAVE FIVE SECONDS.
* SEE THE X-BOOKS FOR ALL THE NASTY DETAILS. --JIM
YOU'RE THE MASTER OF DEMONS-- WHAT ELSE CAN YOU WANT BUT HUMAN SOULS?
I'LL TRADE MY SOUL FOR POWER!
I WANT THE POWER OF A DEMON!
DO WE HAVE A DEAL?

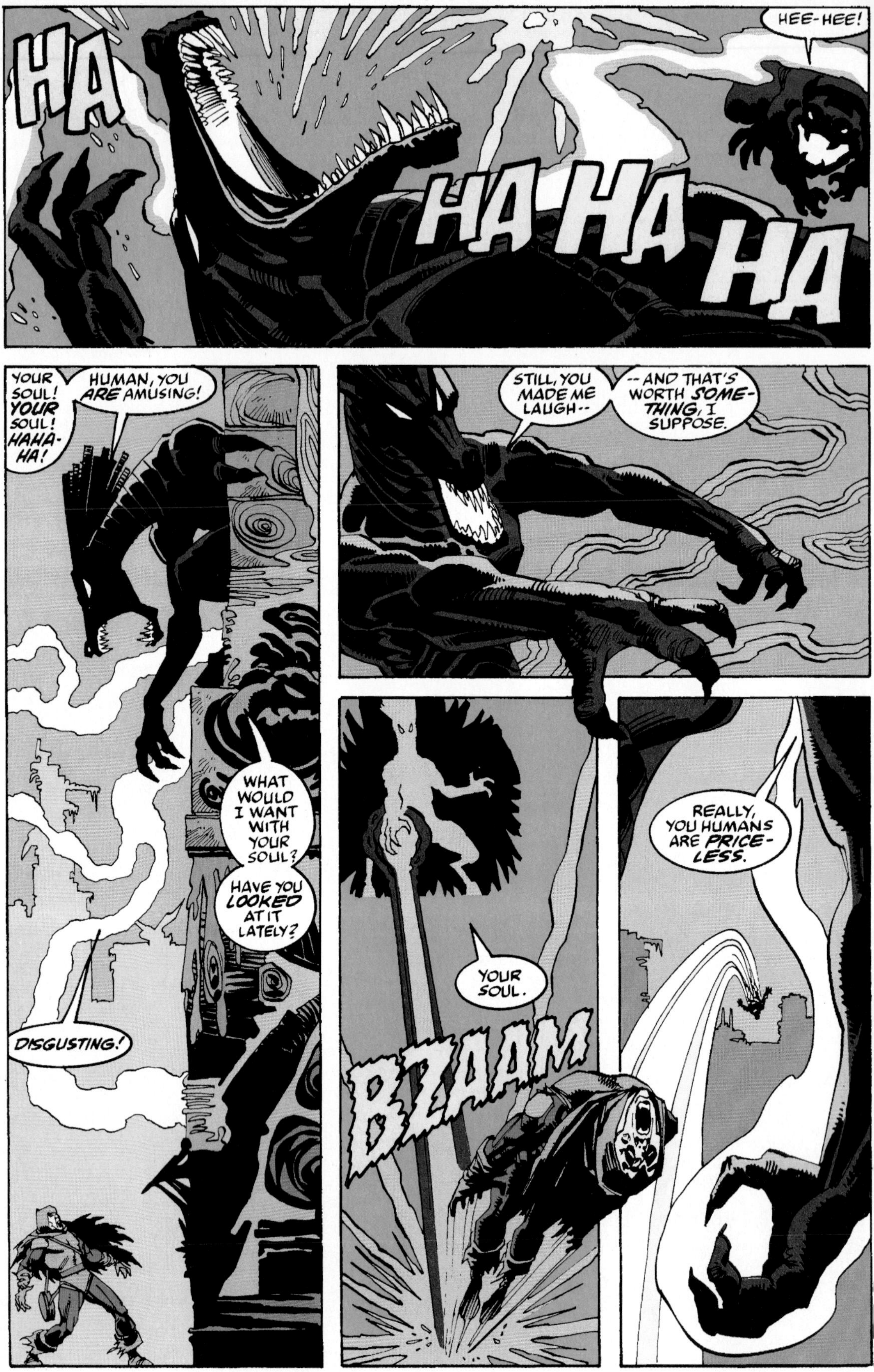

HA
HEE-HEE!
HA HA HA HA
YOUR SOUL! YOUR SOUL! HAHA-HA!
HUMAN, YOU ARE AMUSING!
WHAT WOULD I WANT WITH YOUR SOUL?
HAVE YOU LOOKED AT IT LATELY?
DISGUSTING!
STILL, YOU MADE ME LAUGH--
--AND THAT'S WORTH SOME-THING, I SUPPOSE.
YOUR SOUL.
BZAAM
REALLY, YOU HUMANS ARE PRICE-LESS.

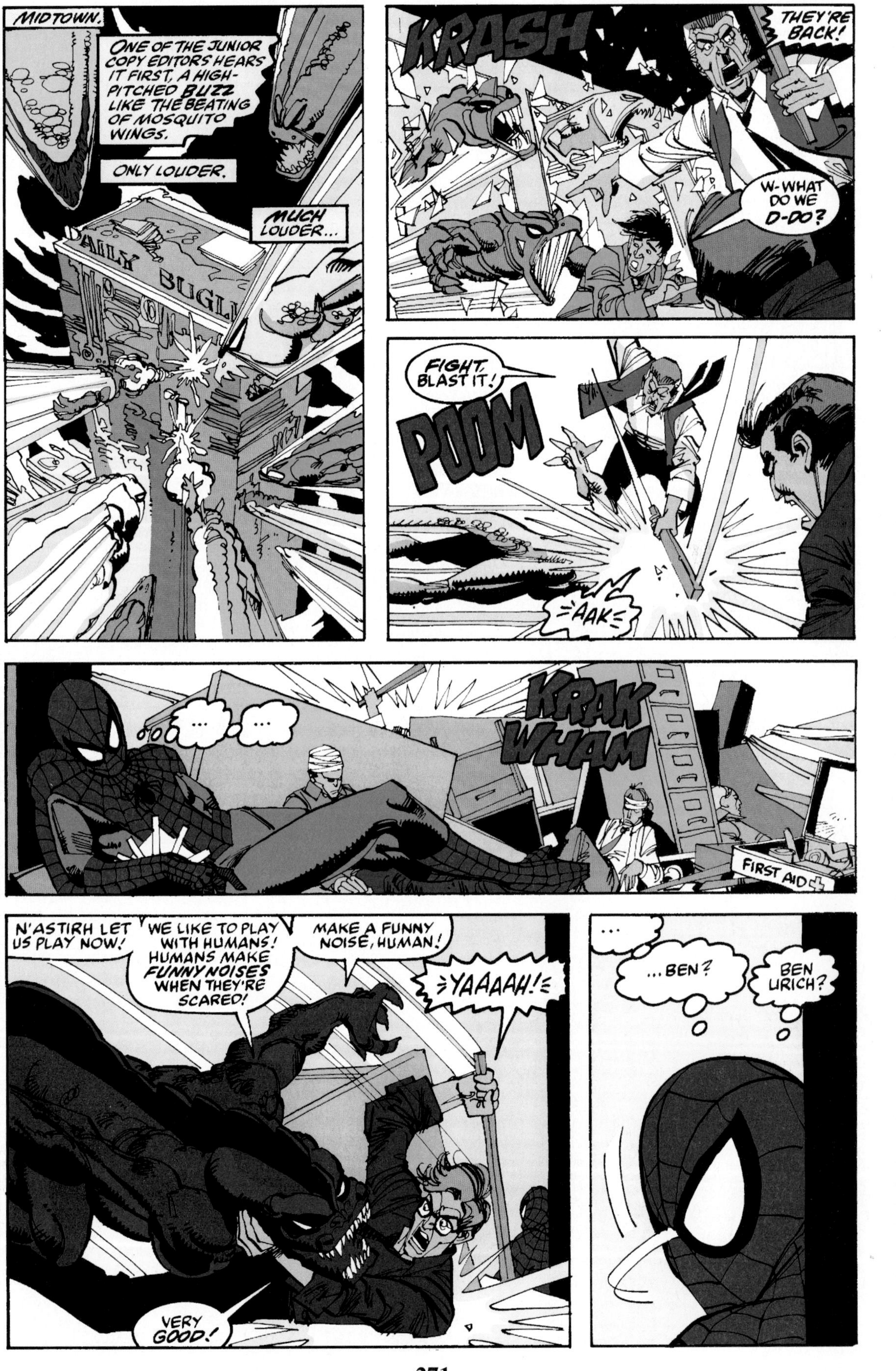
MIDTOWN.
ONE OF THE JUNIOR COPY EDITORS HEARS IT FIRST, A HIGH-PITCHED BUZZ LIKE THE BEATING OF MOSQUITO WINGS.
ONLY LOUDER.
MUCH LOUDER...
DAILY BUGLE
KRASH
THEY'RE BACK!
W-WHAT DO WE D-DO?
FIGHT, BLAST IT!
POOM
AAK
...
...
KRAK
WHAM
FIRST AID
N'ASTIRH LET US PLAY NOW!
WE LIKE TO PLAY WITH HUMANS! HUMANS MAKE FUNNY NOISES WHEN THEY'RE SCARED!
MAKE A FUNNY NOISE, HUMAN!
YAAAAH!
VERY GOOD!
...
...BEN?
BEN URICH?

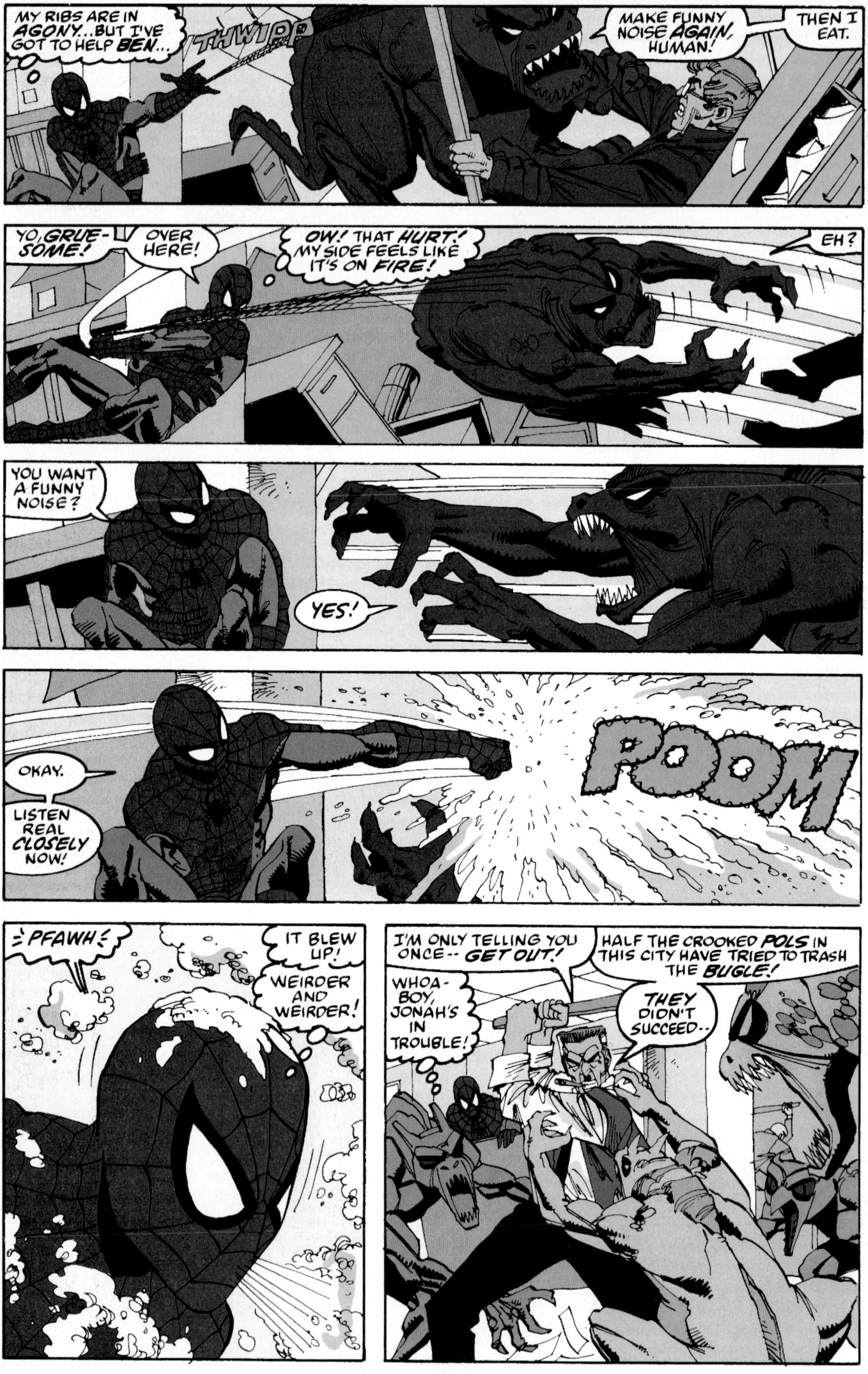
MY RIBS ARE IN AGONY...BUT I'VE GOT TO HELP BEN...
THWIPP
MAKE FUNNY NOISE AGAIN, HUMAN!
THEN I EAT.
YO, GRUESOME!
OVER HERE!
OW! THAT HURT! MY SIDE FEELS LIKE IT'S ON FIRE!
EH?
YOU WANT A FUNNY NOISE?
YES!
OKAY.
LISTEN REAL CLOSELY NOW!
POOM
PFAWH
IT BLEW UP!
WEIRDER AND WEIRDER!
I'M ONLY TELLING YOU ONCE-- GET OUT!
HALF THE CROOKED POLS IN THIS CITY HAVE TRIED TO TRASH THE BUGLE!
WHOA-BOY, JONAH'S IN TROUBLE!
THEY DIDN'T SUCCEED--

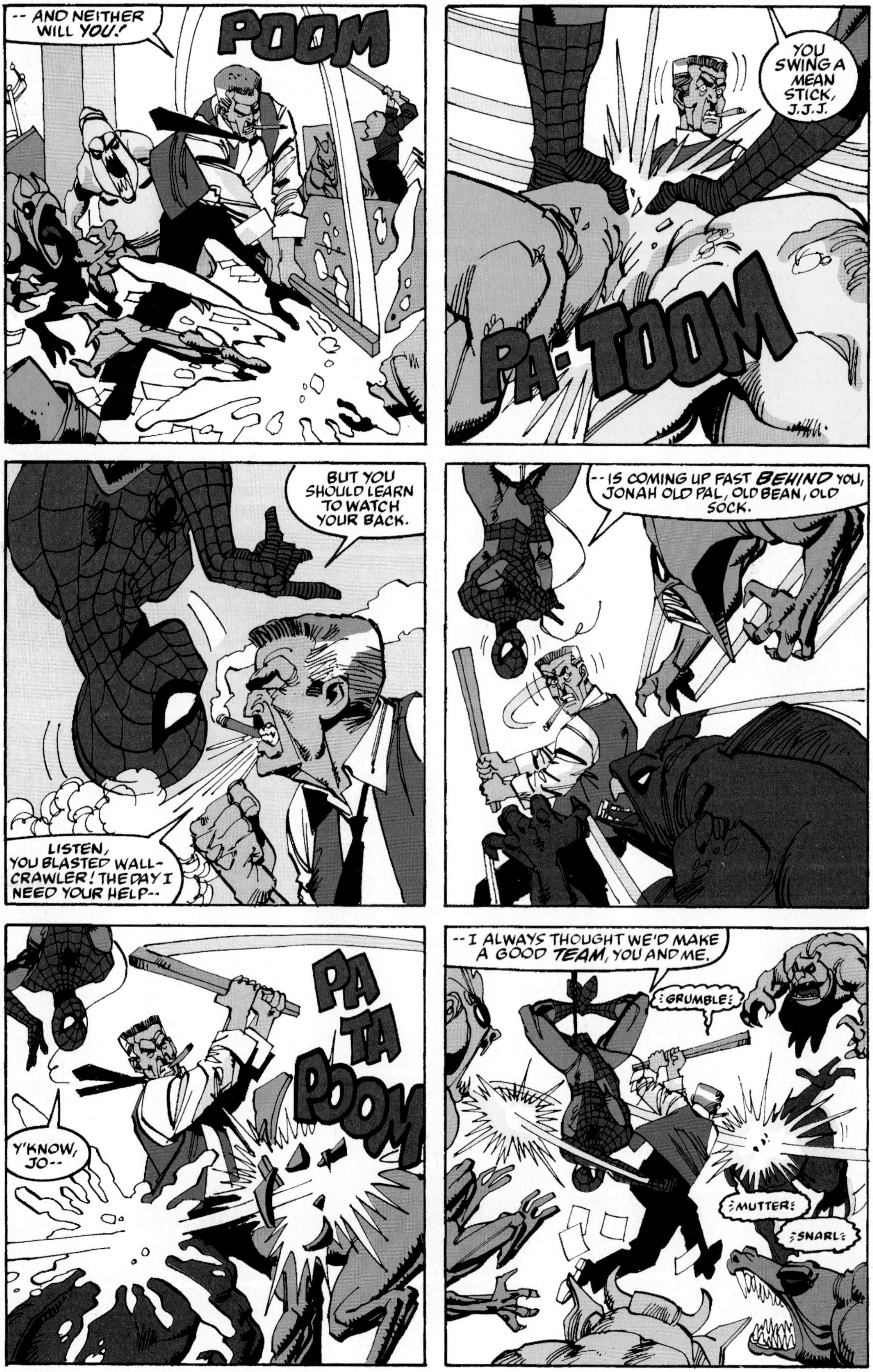
-- AND NEITHER WILL YOU!
POOM
YOU SWING A MEAN STICK, J.J.J.
PA-TOOM
BUT YOU SHOULD LEARN TO WATCH YOUR BACK.
LISTEN, YOU BLASTED WALL-CRAWLER! THE DAY I NEED YOUR HELP--
--IS COMING UP FAST BEHIND YOU, JONAH OLD PAL, OLD BEAN, OLD SOCK.
PA TA POOM
Y'KNOW, JO--
--I ALWAYS THOUGHT WE'D MAKE A GOOD TEAM, YOU AND ME.
GRUMBLE
MUTTER
SNARL

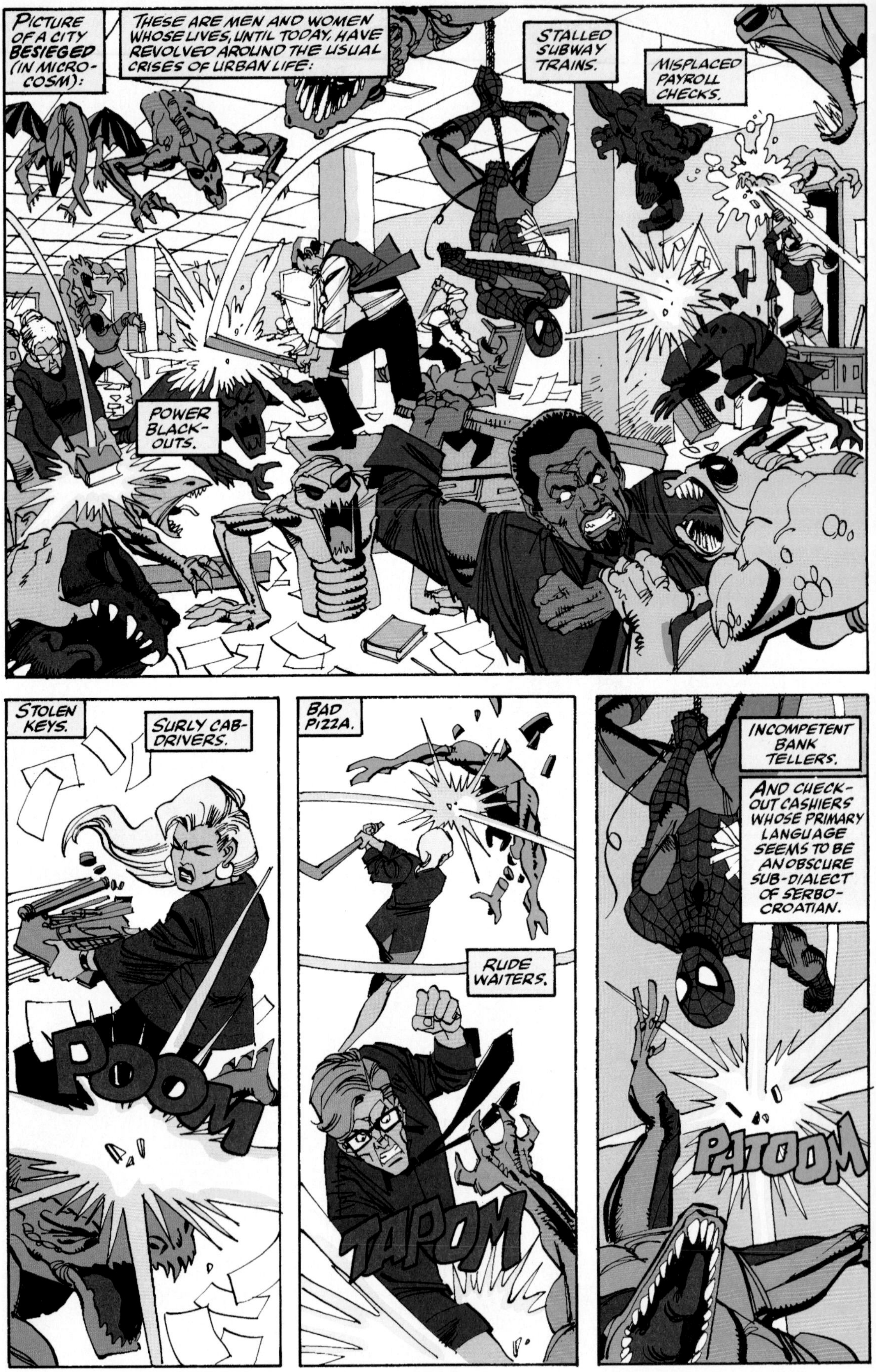

PICTURE OF A CITY BESIEGED (IN MICROCOSM):
THESE ARE MEN AND WOMEN WHOSE LIVES, UNTIL TODAY, HAVE REVOLVED AROUND THE USUAL CRISES OF URBAN LIFE:
STALLED SUBWAY TRAINS.
MISPLACED PAYROLL CHECKS.
POWER BLACK-OUTS.
STOLEN KEYS.
SURLY CAB-DRIVERS.
POOM
BAD PIZZA.
RUDE WAITERS.
TAPOM
INCOMPETENT BANK TELLERS.
AND CHECK-OUT CASHIERS WHOSE PRIMARY LANGUAGE SEEMS TO BE AN OBSCURE SUB-DIALECT OF SERBO-CROATIAN.
PATOOM

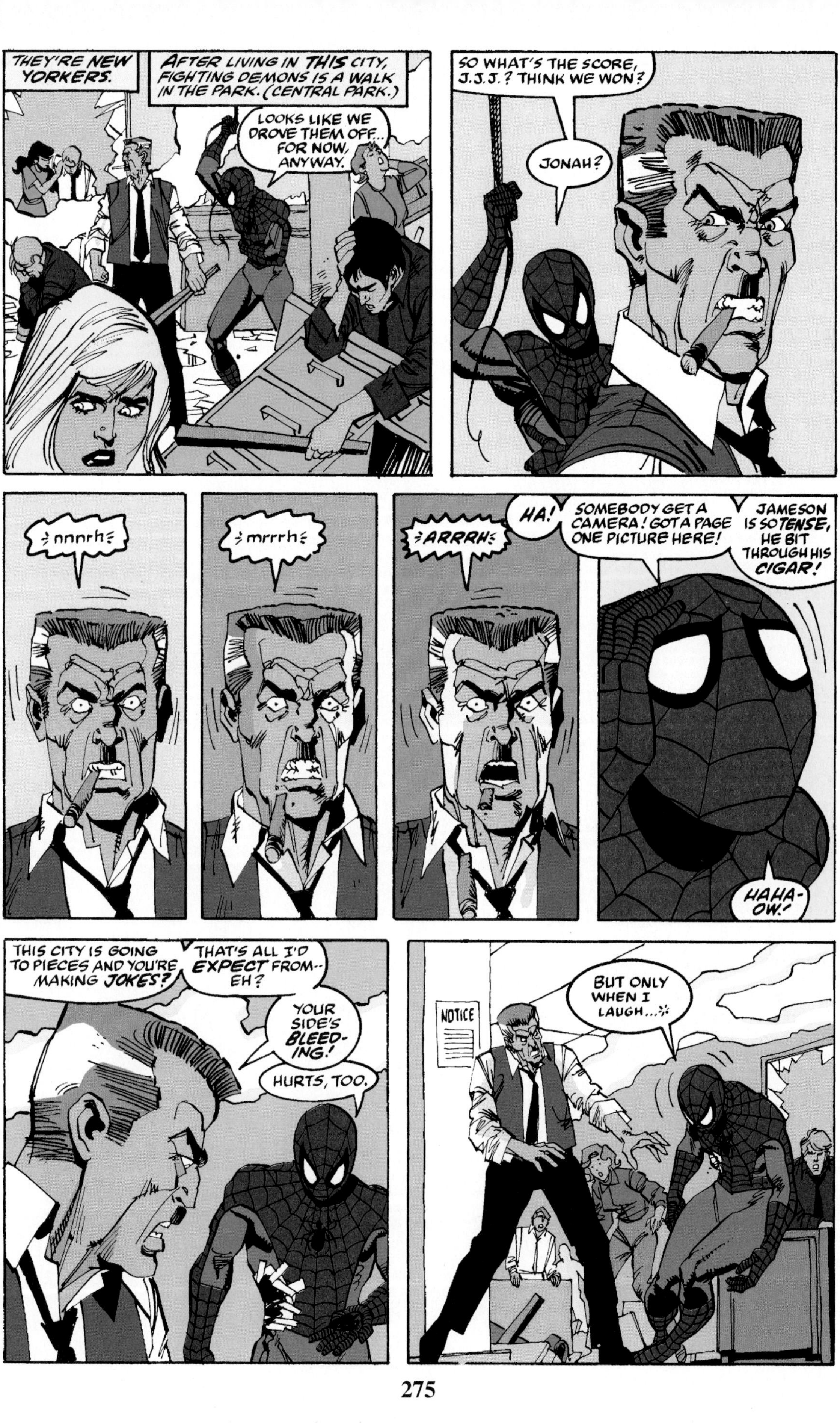
THEY'RE NEW YORKERS.
AFTER LIVING IN THIS CITY, FIGHTING DEMONS IS A WALK IN THE PARK. (CENTRAL PARK.)
LOOKS LIKE WE DROVE THEM OFF... FOR NOW, ANYWAY.
SO WHAT'S THE SCORE, J.J.J.? THINK WE WON?
JONAH?
nnnrh
mrrrh
ARRRH
HA!
SOMEBODY GET A CAMERA! GOT A PAGE ONE PICTURE HERE!
JAMESON IS SO TENSE, HE BIT THROUGH HIS CIGAR!
HAHA-OW!
THIS CITY IS GOING TO PIECES AND YOU'RE MAKING JOKES?
THAT'S ALL I'D EXPECT FROM-- EH?
YOUR SIDE'S BLEEDING!
HURTS, TOO.
NOTICE
BUT ONLY WHEN I LAUGH...

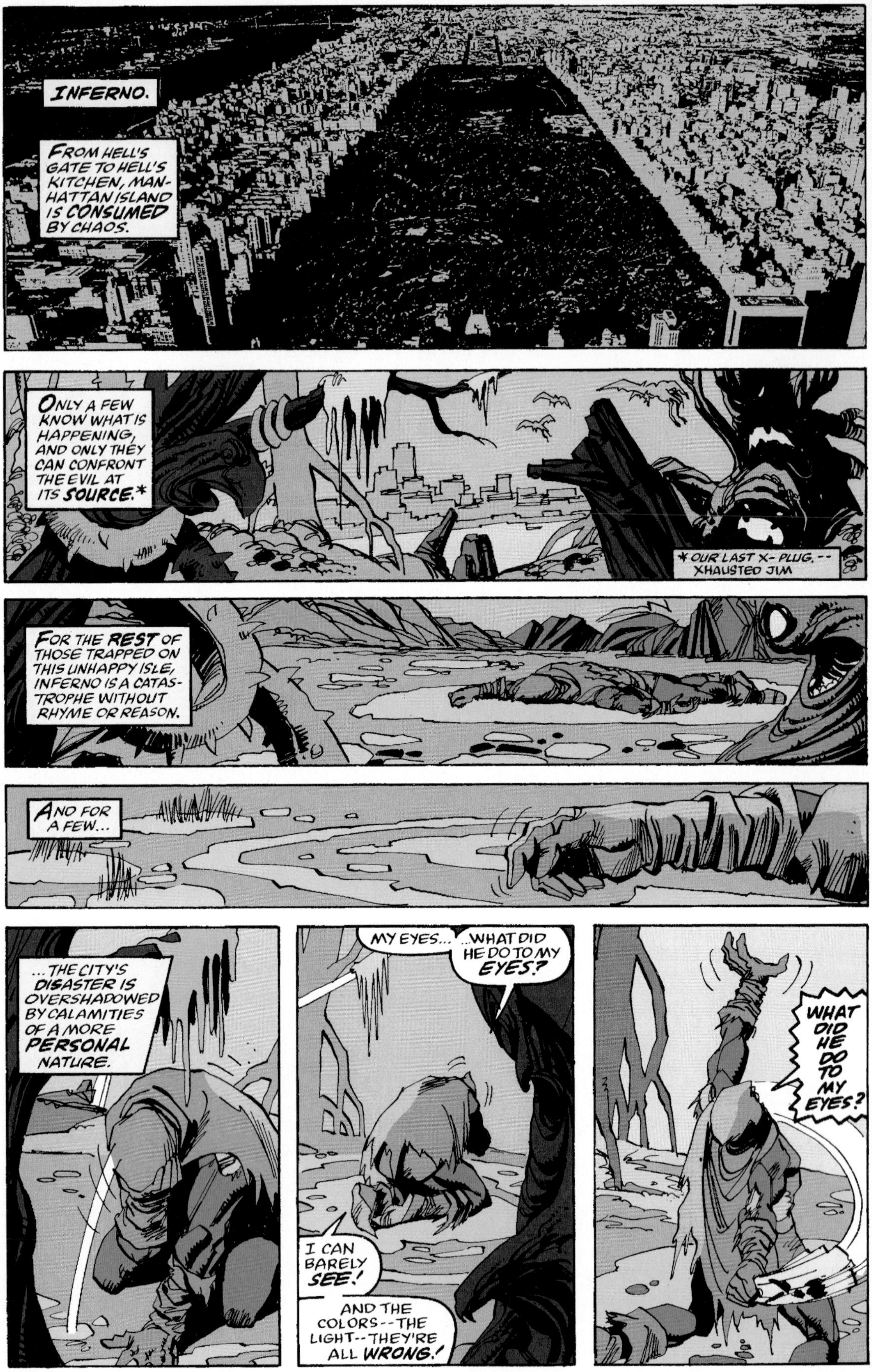
INFERNO.
FROM HELL'S GATE TO HELL'S KITCHEN, MANHATTAN ISLAND IS CONSUMED BY CHAOS.
ONLY A FEW KNOW WHAT IS HAPPENING, AND ONLY THEY CAN CONFRONT THE EVIL AT ITS SOURCE.*
* OUR LAST X-PLUG. -- XHAUSTED JIM
FOR THE REST OF THOSE TRAPPED ON THIS UNHAPPY ISLE, INFERNO IS A CATASTROPHE WITHOUT RHYME OR REASON.
AND FOR A FEW...
...THE CITY'S DISASTER IS OVERSHADOWED BY CALAMITIES OF A MORE PERSONAL NATURE.
MY EYES...
...WHAT DID HE DO TO MY EYES?
I CAN BARELY SEE!
AND THE COLORS--THE LIGHT--THEY'RE ALL WRONG!
WHAT DID HE DO TO MY EYES?

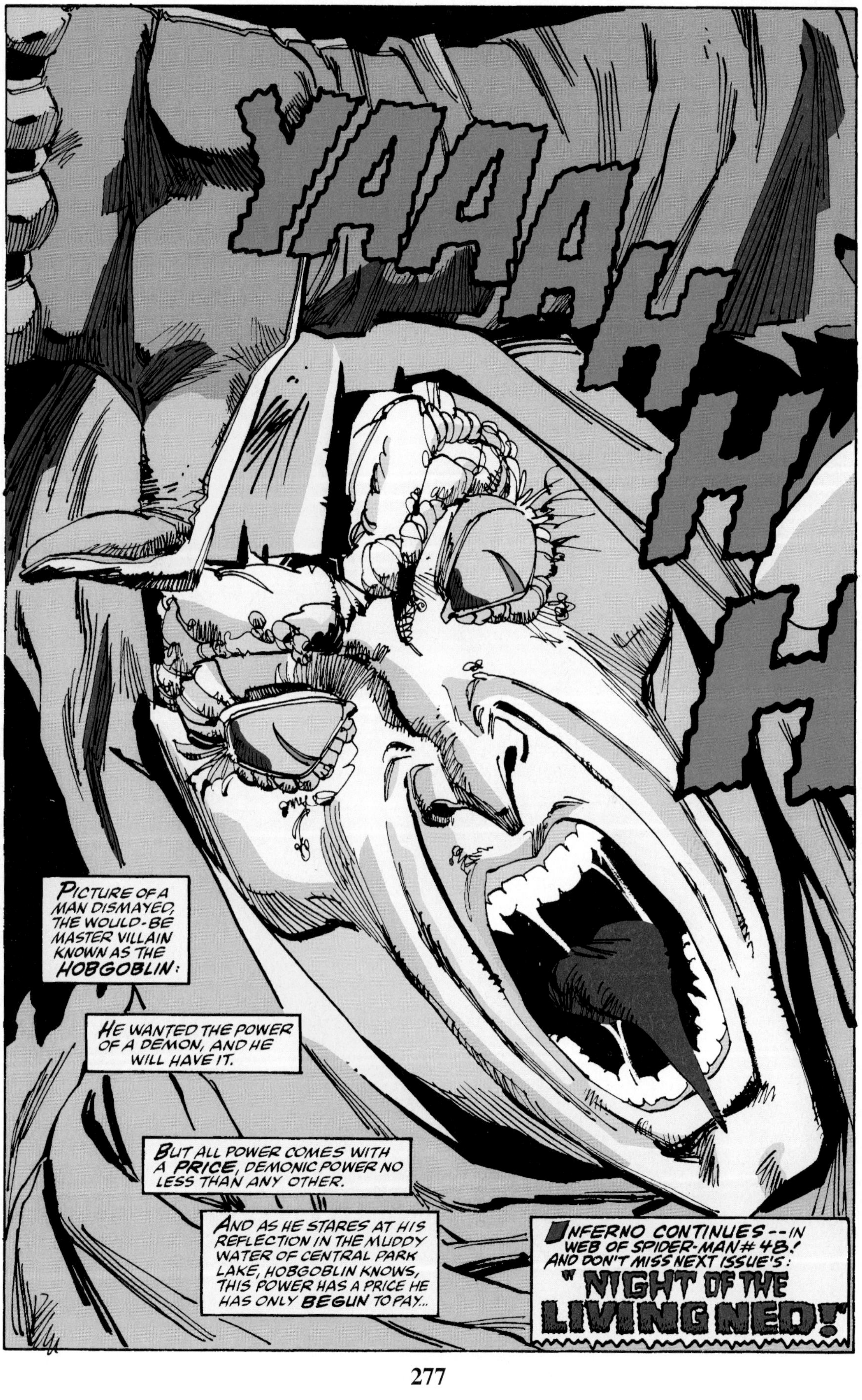
YAAAHHHH
PICTURE OF A MAN DISMAYED, THE WOULD-BE MASTER VILLAIN KNOWN AS THE HOBGOBLIN:
HE WANTED THE POWER OF A DEMON, AND HE WILL HAVE IT.
BUT ALL POWER COMES WITH A PRICE, DEMONIC POWER NO LESS THAN ANY OTHER.
AND AS HE STARES AT HIS REFLECTION IN THE MUDDY WATER OF CENTRAL PARK LAKE, HOBGOBLIN KNOWS, THIS POWER HAS A PRICE HE HAS ONLY BEGUN TO PAY...
INFERNO CONTINUES--IN WEB OF SPIDER-MAN #48! AND DON'T MISS NEXT ISSUE'S: "NIGHT OF THE LIVING NED!"

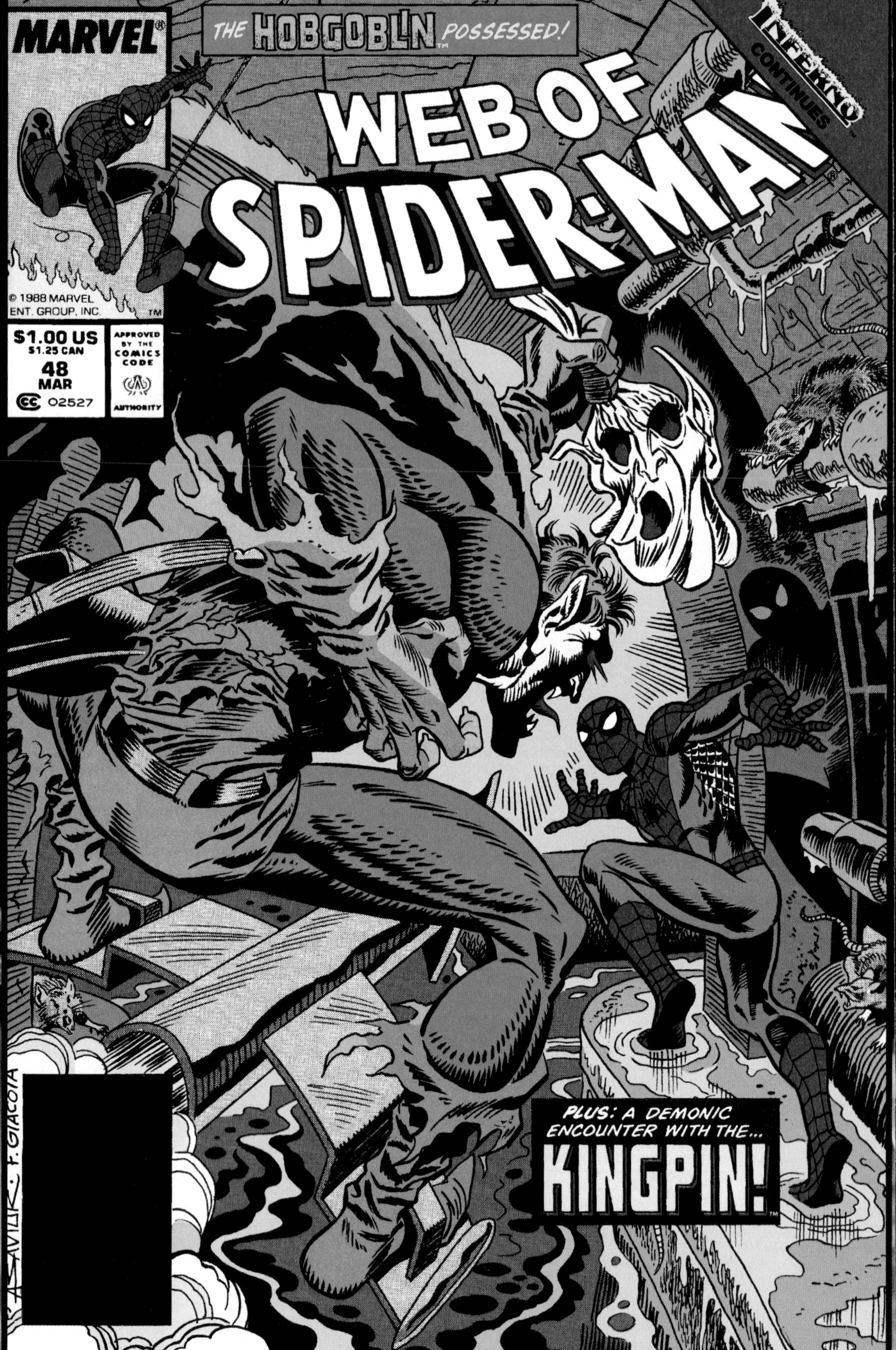
MARVEL
THE HOBGOBLIN POSSESSED!
INFERNO CONTINUES
WEB OF SPIDER-MAN
© 1988 MARVEL ENT. GROUP, INC.
$1.00 US $1.25 CAN
48 MAR
02527
APPROVED BY THE COMICS CODE AUTHORITY
PLUS: A DEMONIC ENCOUNTER WITH THE...
KINGPIN!
SAVIUK - F. GIACOIA

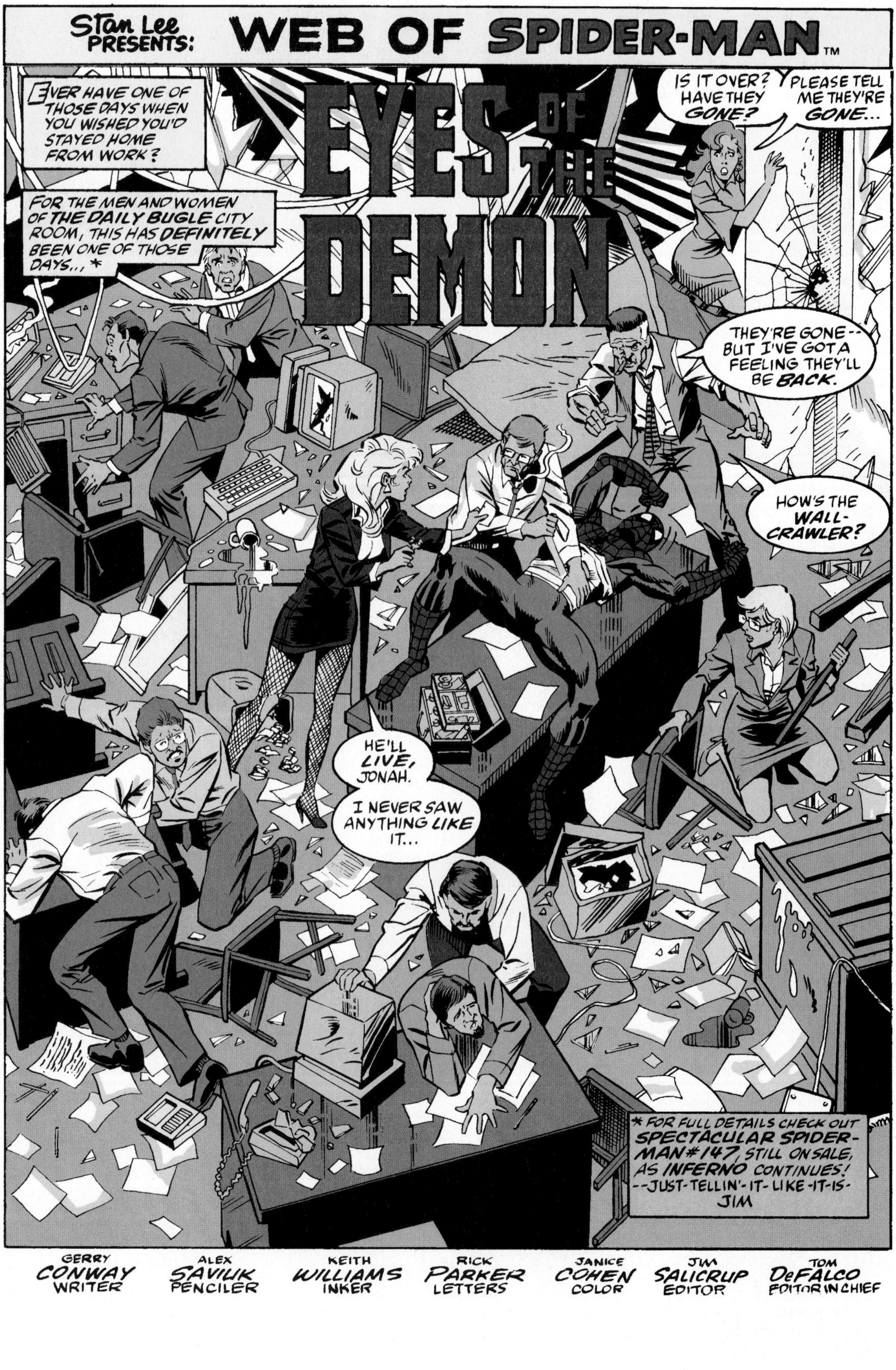

Stan Lee PRESENTS: WEB OF SPIDER-MAN™
EYES OF THE DEMON
EVER HAVE ONE OF THOSE DAYS WHEN YOU WISHED YOU'D STAYED HOME FROM WORK?
FOR THE MEN AND WOMEN OF THE DAILY BUGLE CITY ROOM, THIS HAS DEFINITELY BEEN ONE OF THOSE DAYS... *
IS IT OVER? HAVE THEY GONE?
PLEASE TELL ME THEY'RE GONE...
THEY'RE GONE-- BUT I'VE GOT A FEELING THEY'LL BE BACK.
HOW'S THE WALL-CRAWLER?
HE'LL LIVE, JONAH.
I NEVER SAW ANYTHING LIKE IT...
* FOR FULL DETAILS CHECK OUT SPECTACULAR SPIDER-MAN #147, STILL ON SALE, AS INFERNO CONTINUES! --JUST-TELLIN'-IT-LIKE-IT-IS- JIM

GERRY CONWAY WRITER · ALEX SAVIUK PENCILER · KEITH WILLIAMS INKER · RICK PARKER LETTERS · JANICE COHEN COLOR · JIM SALICRUP EDITOR · TOM DeFALCO EDITOR IN CHIEF

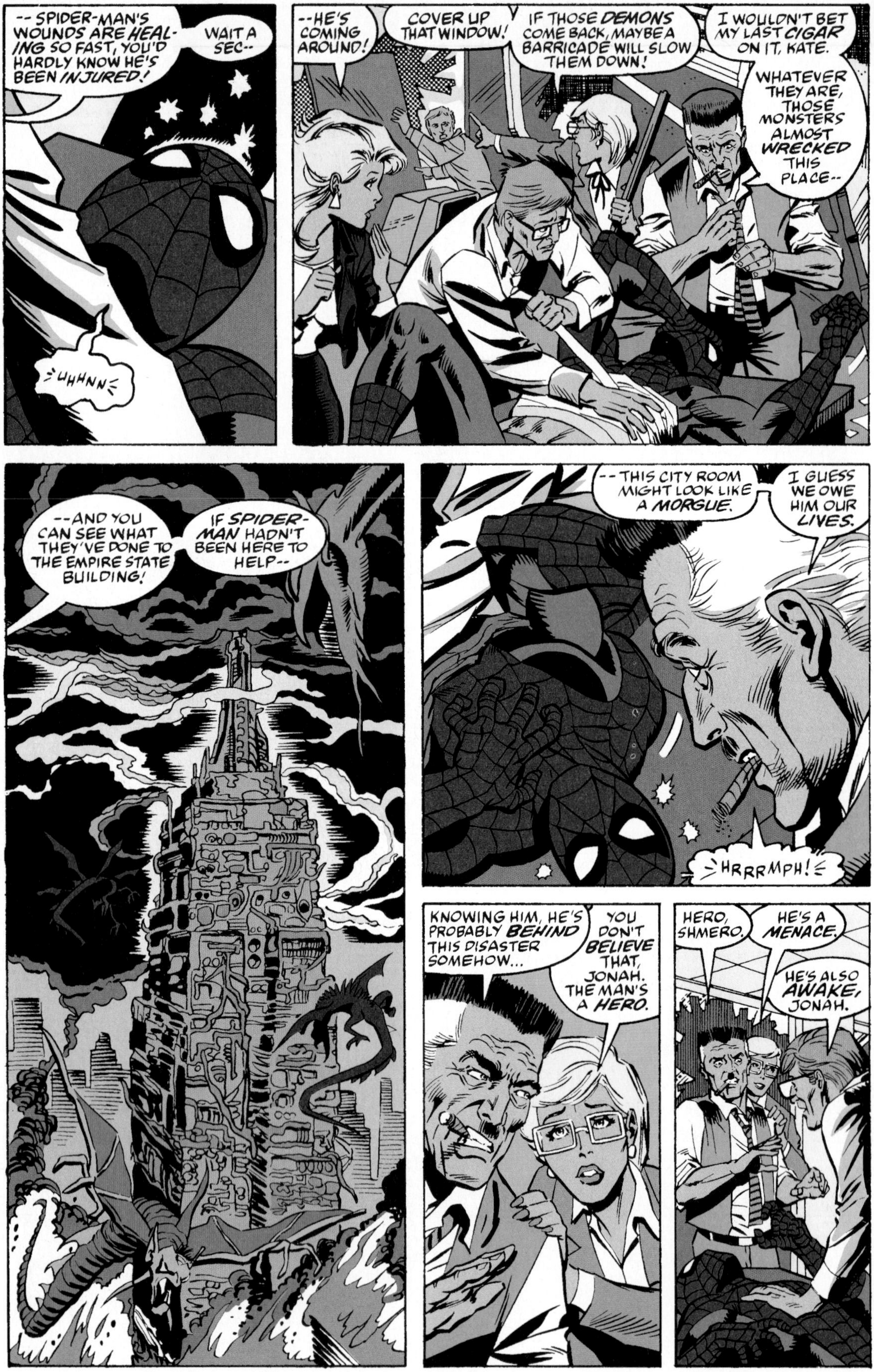
-- SPIDER-MAN'S WOUNDS ARE HEALING SO FAST, YOU'D HARDLY KNOW HE'S BEEN INJURED!
WAIT A SEC--
UHHNN
--HE'S COMING AROUND!
COVER UP THAT WINDOW!
IF THOSE DEMONS COME BACK, MAYBE A BARRICADE WILL SLOW THEM DOWN!
I WOULDN'T BET MY LAST CIGAR ON IT, KATE.
WHATEVER THEY ARE, THOSE MONSTERS ALMOST WRECKED THIS PLACE--
--AND YOU CAN SEE WHAT THEY'VE DONE TO THE EMPIRE STATE BUILDING!
IF SPIDER-MAN HADN'T BEEN HERE TO HELP--
--THIS CITY ROOM MIGHT LOOK LIKE A MORGUE.
I GUESS WE OWE HIM OUR LIVES.
HRRRMPH!
KNOWING HIM, HE'S PROBABLY BEHIND THIS DISASTER SOMEHOW...
YOU DON'T BELIEVE THAT, JONAH. THE MAN'S A HERO.
HERO, SHMERO.
HE'S A MENACE.
HE'S ALSO AWAKE, JONAH.

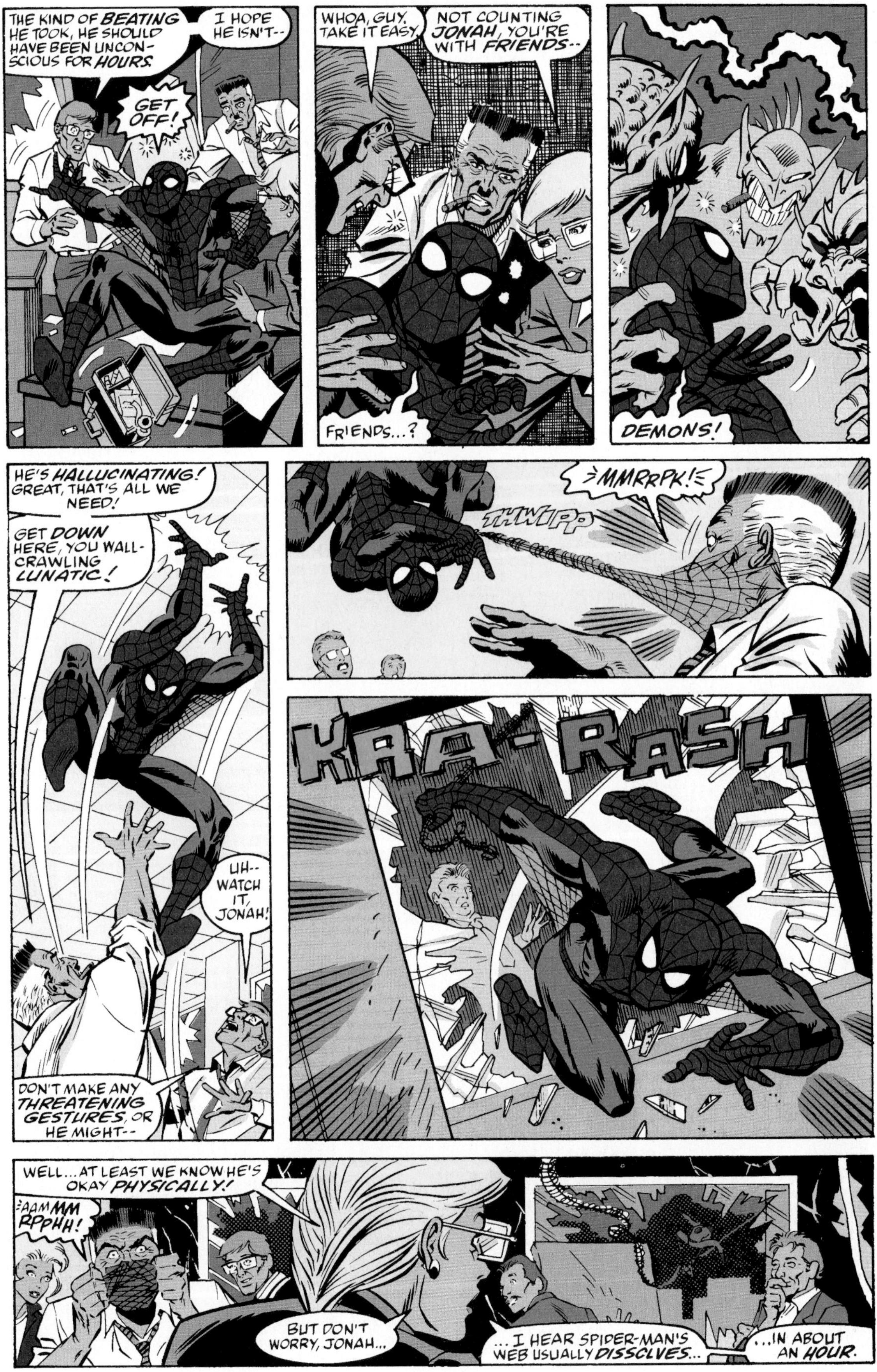

THE KIND OF BEATING HE TOOK, HE SHOULD HAVE BEEN UNCONSCIOUS FOR HOURS.
I HOPE HE ISN'T--
GET OFF!
WHOA, GUY, TAKE IT EASY.
NOT COUNTING JONAH, YOU'RE WITH FRIENDS..
FRIENDS...?
DEMONS!
HE'S HALLUCINATING! GREAT, THAT'S ALL WE NEED!
GET DOWN HERE, YOU WALL-CRAWLING LUNATIC!
UH-- WATCH IT, JONAH!
DON'T MAKE ANY THREATENING GESTURES, OR HE MIGHT--
MMRRPK!
THWIPP
KRA-RASH
WELL... AT LEAST WE KNOW HE'S OKAY PHYSICALLY!
AAMMM RPPHH!
BUT DON'T WORRY, JONAH...
... I HEAR SPIDER-MAN'S WEB USUALLY DISSOLVES...
...IN ABOUT AN HOUR.

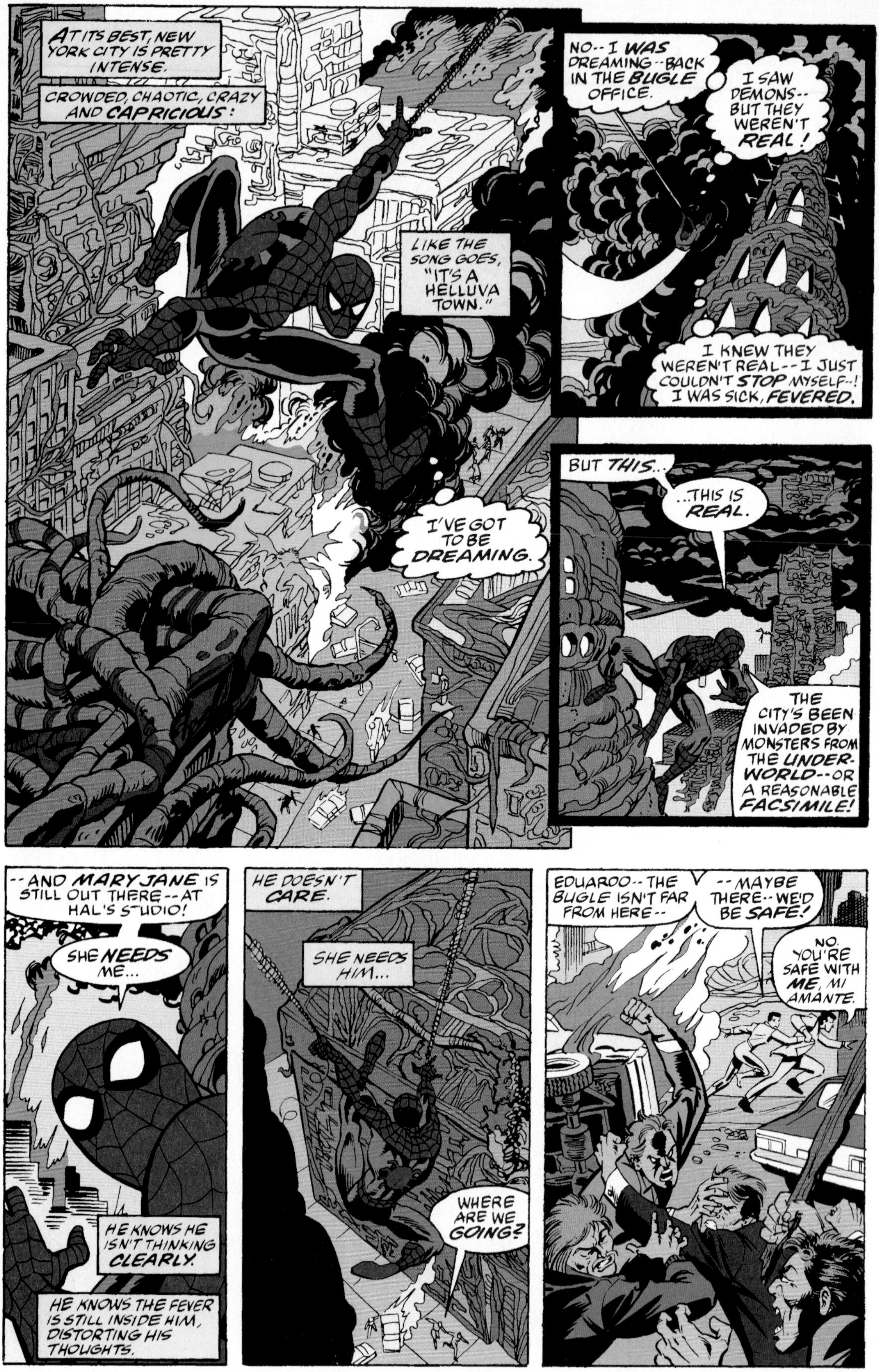
AT ITS BEST, NEW YORK CITY IS PRETTY INTENSE.
CROWDED, CHAOTIC, CRAZY AND CAPRICIOUS:
LIKE THE SONG GOES, "IT'S A HELLUVA TOWN."
I'VE GOT TO BE DREAMING.
NO-- I WAS DREAMING--BACK IN THE BUGLE OFFICE.
I SAW DEMONS-- BUT THEY WEREN'T REAL!
I KNEW THEY WEREN'T REAL--I JUST COULDN'T STOP MYSELF--! I WAS SICK, FEVERED.
BUT THIS...
...THIS IS REAL.
THE CITY'S BEEN INVADED BY MONSTERS FROM THE UNDER-WORLD--OR A REASONABLE FACSIMILE!
--AND MARY JANE IS STILL OUT THERE--AT HAL'S STUDIO!
SHE NEEDS ME...
HE KNOWS HE ISN'T THINKING CLEARLY.
HE KNOWS THE FEVER IS STILL INSIDE HIM, DISTORTING HIS THOUGHTS.
HE DOESN'T CARE.
SHE NEEDS HIM...
WHERE ARE WE GOING?
EDUAROO--THE BUGLE ISN'T FAR FROM HERE--
--MAYBE THERE--WE'D BE SAFE!
NO. YOU'RE SAFE WITH ME, MI AMANTE.

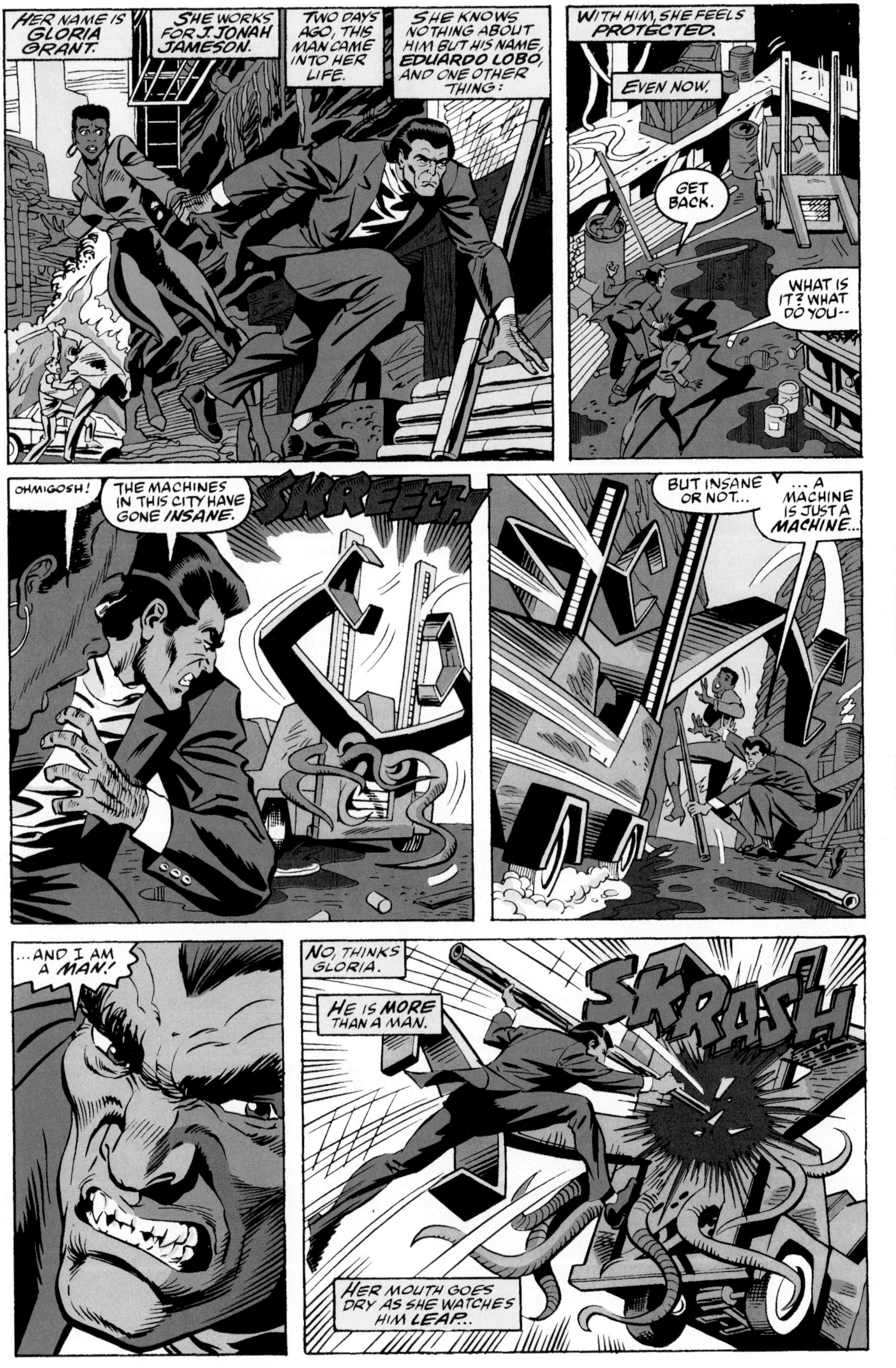
HER NAME IS GLORIA GRANT.
SHE WORKS FOR J. JONAH JAMESON.
TWO DAYS AGO, THIS MAN CAME INTO HER LIFE.
SHE KNOWS NOTHING ABOUT HIM BUT HIS NAME, EDUARDO LOBO, AND ONE OTHER THING:
WITH HIM, SHE FEELS PROTECTED.
EVEN NOW.
GET BACK.
WHAT IS IT? WHAT DO YOU--
OHMIGOSH!
THE MACHINES IN THIS CITY HAVE GONE INSANE.
SKREECH
BUT INSANE OR NOT...
... A MACHINE IS JUST A MACHINE...
...AND I AM A MAN!
NO, THINKS GLORIA.
HE IS MORE THAN A MAN.
SKRASH
HER MOUTH GOES DRY AS SHE WATCHES HIM LEAP...

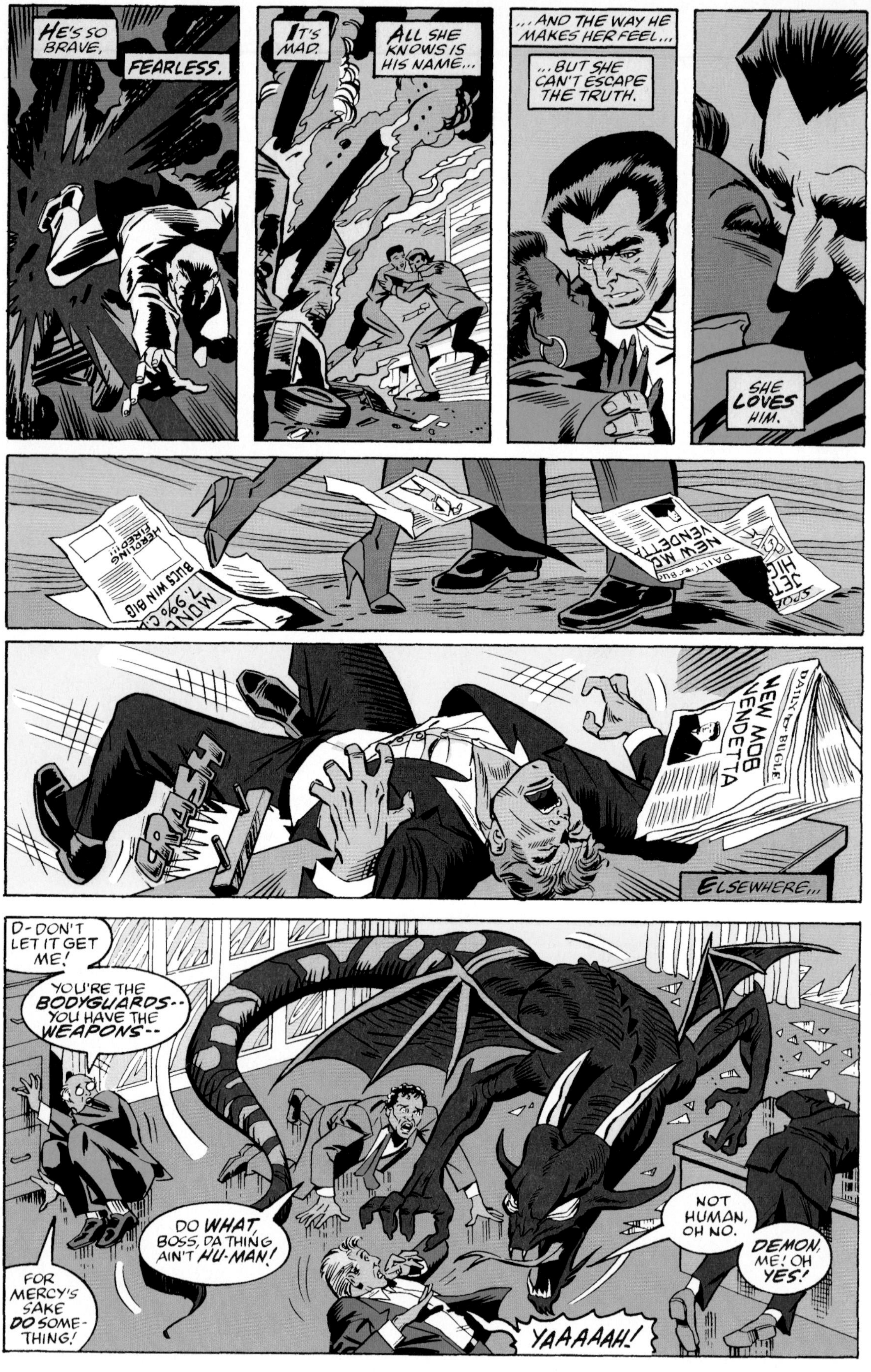

HE'S SO BRAVE,
FEARLESS.
IT'S MAD.
ALL SHE KNOWS IS HIS NAME...
...AND THE WAY HE MAKES HER FEEL...
...BUT SHE CAN'T ESCAPE THE TRUTH.
SHE LOVES HIM.
BUCS WIN BIG
NEW MOB VENDETTA
CRASH
ELSEWHERE...
D-DON'T LET IT GET ME!
YOU'RE THE BODYGUARDS-- YOU HAVE THE WEAPONS--
DO WHAT, BOSS, DA THING AIN'T HU-MAN!
NOT HUMAN, OH NO.
DEMON, ME! OH YES!
FOR MERCY'S SAKE DO SOME-THING!
YAAAAAH!

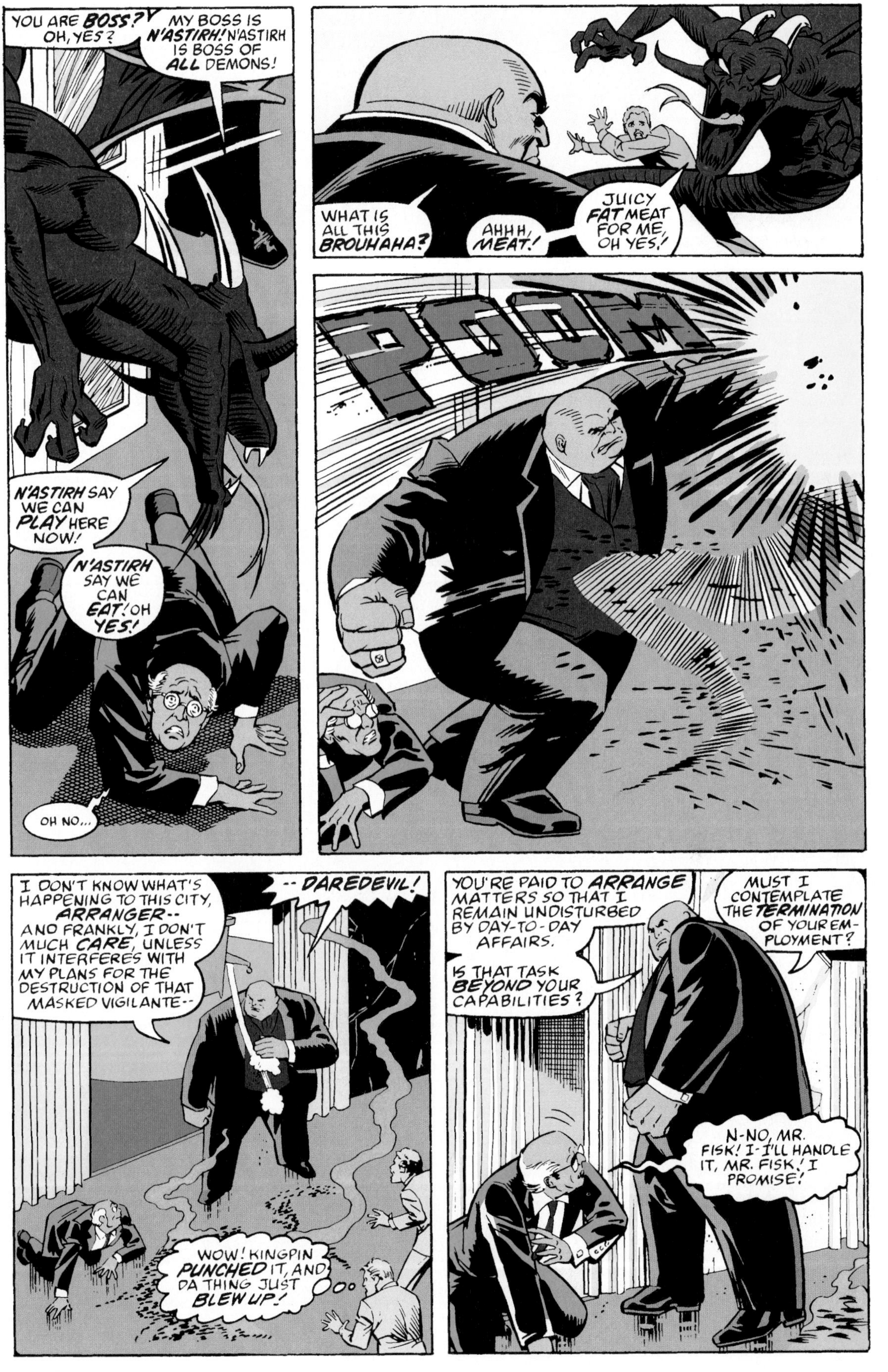

YOU ARE BOSS? OH, YES?
MY BOSS IS N'ASTIRH! N'ASTIRH IS BOSS OF ALL DEMONS!
N'ASTIRH SAY WE CAN PLAY HERE NOW!
N'ASTIRH SAY WE CAN EAT! OH YES!
OH NO...
WHAT IS ALL THIS BROUHAHA?
AHHH, MEAT!
JUICY FAT MEAT FOR ME, OH YES!
POOM
I DON'T KNOW WHAT'S HAPPENING TO THIS CITY, ARRANGER-- AND FRANKLY, I DON'T MUCH CARE, UNLESS IT INTERFERES WITH MY PLANS FOR THE DESTRUCTION OF THAT MASKED VIGILANTE--
--DAREDEVIL!
WOW! KINGPIN PUNCHED IT, AND DA THING JUST BLEW UP!
YOU'RE PAID TO ARRANGE MATTERS SO THAT I REMAIN UNDISTURBED BY DAY-TO-DAY AFFAIRS.
IS THAT TASK BEYOND YOUR CAPABILITIES?
MUST I CONTEMPLATE THE TERMINATION OF YOUR EMPLOYMENT?
N-NO, MR. FISK! I-I'LL HANDLE IT, MR. FISK! I PROMISE!

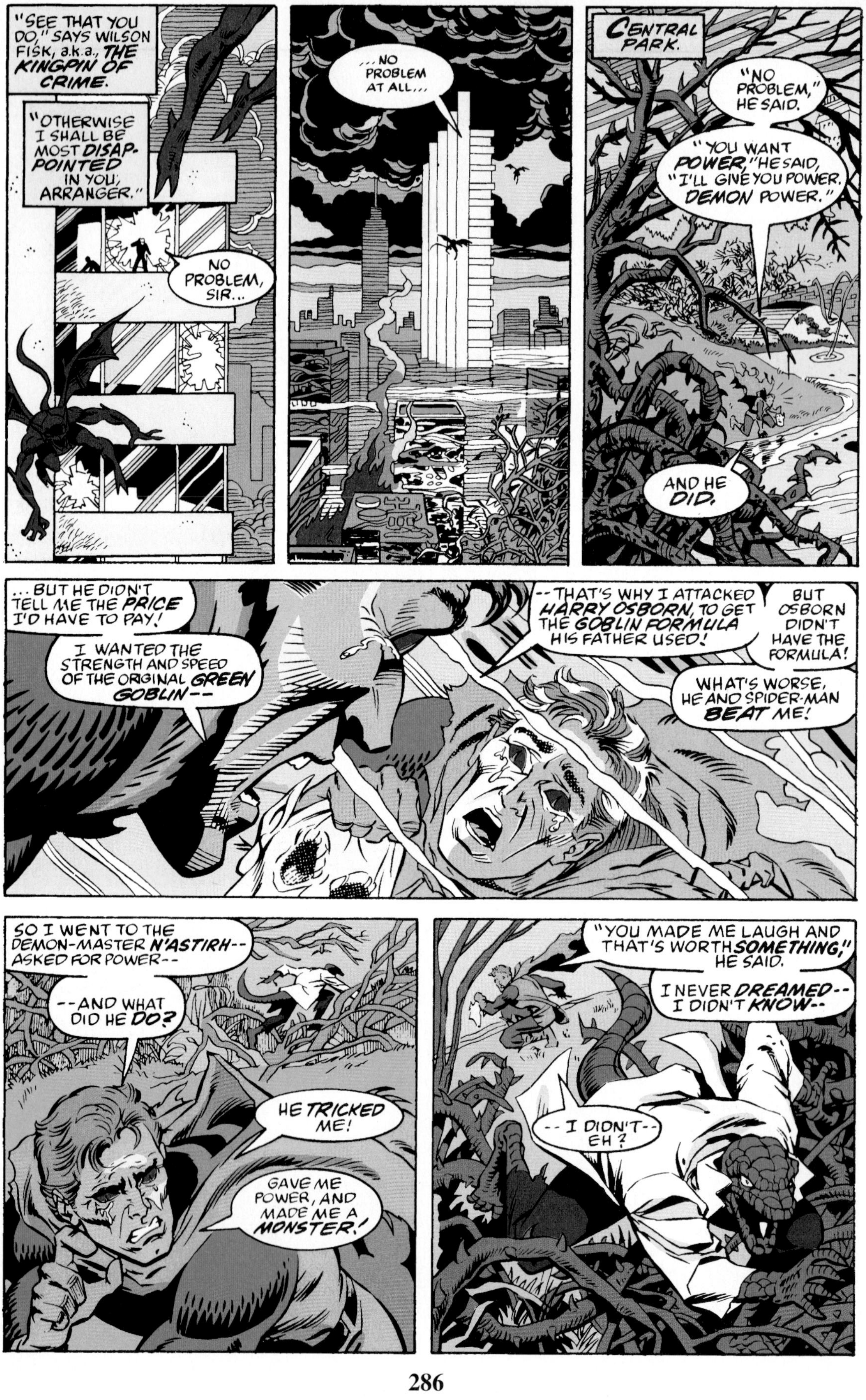
"SEE THAT YOU DO," SAYS WILSON FISK, a.k.a., THE KINGPIN OF CRIME.
"OTHERWISE I SHALL BE MOST DISAPPOINTED IN YOU, ARRANGER."
NO PROBLEM, SIR...
...NO PROBLEM AT ALL...
CENTRAL PARK.
"NO PROBLEM," HE SAID.
"YOU WANT POWER," HE SAID, "I'LL GIVE YOU POWER. DEMON POWER."
AND HE DID.
...BUT HE DIDN'T TELL ME THE PRICE I'D HAVE TO PAY!
I WANTED THE STRENGTH AND SPEED OF THE ORIGINAL GREEN GOBLIN--
--THAT'S WHY I ATTACKED HARRY OSBORN, TO GET THE GOBLIN FORMULA HIS FATHER USED!
BUT OSBORN DIDN'T HAVE THE FORMULA!
WHAT'S WORSE, HE AND SPIDER-MAN BEAT ME!
SO I WENT TO THE DEMON-MASTER N'ASTIRH-- ASKED FOR POWER--
--AND WHAT DID HE DO?
HE TRICKED ME!
GAVE ME POWER, AND MADE ME A MONSTER!
"YOU MADE ME LAUGH AND THAT'S WORTH SOMETHING," HE SAID.
I NEVER DREAMED-- I DIDN'T KNOW--
--I DIDN'T-- EH?

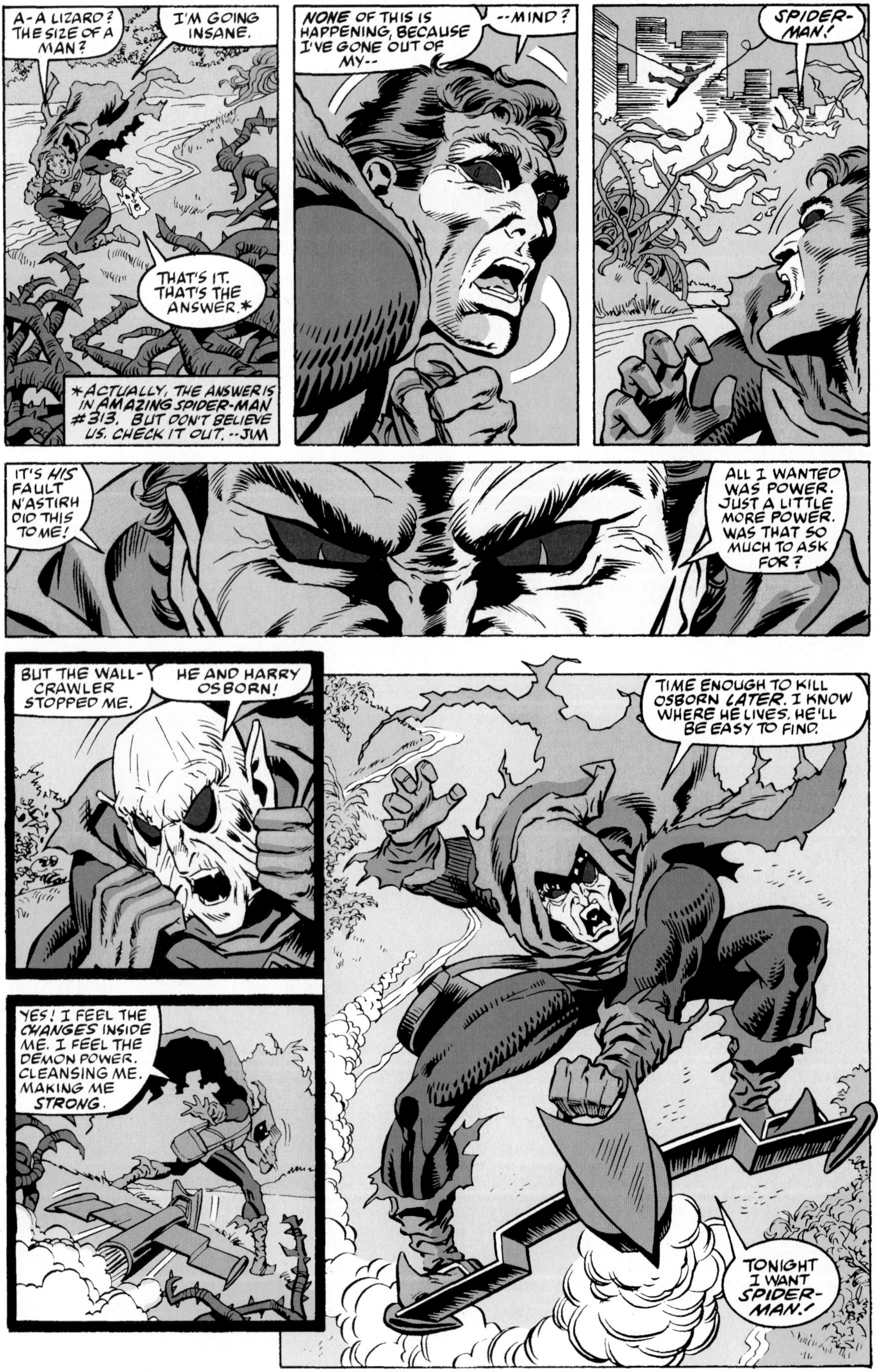

A-A LIZARD? THE SIZE OF A MAN?
I'M GOING INSANE.
THAT'S IT. THAT'S THE ANSWER.*
*ACTUALLY, THE ANSWER IS IN AMAZING SPIDER-MAN #313. BUT DON'T BELIEVE US. CHECK IT OUT. --JIM
NONE OF THIS IS HAPPENING, BECAUSE I'VE GONE OUT OF MY--
--MIND?
SPIDER-MAN!
IT'S HIS FAULT N'ASTIRH DID THIS TO ME!
ALL I WANTED WAS POWER. JUST A LITTLE MORE POWER. WAS THAT SO MUCH TO ASK FOR?
BUT THE WALL-CRAWLER STOPPED ME.
HE AND HARRY OSBORN!
YES! I FEEL THE CHANGES INSIDE ME. I FEEL THE DEMON POWER. CLEANSING ME. MAKING ME STRONG.
TIME ENOUGH TO KILL OSBORN LATER. I KNOW WHERE HE LIVES. HE'LL BE EASY TO FIND.
TONIGHT I WANT SPIDER-MAN!

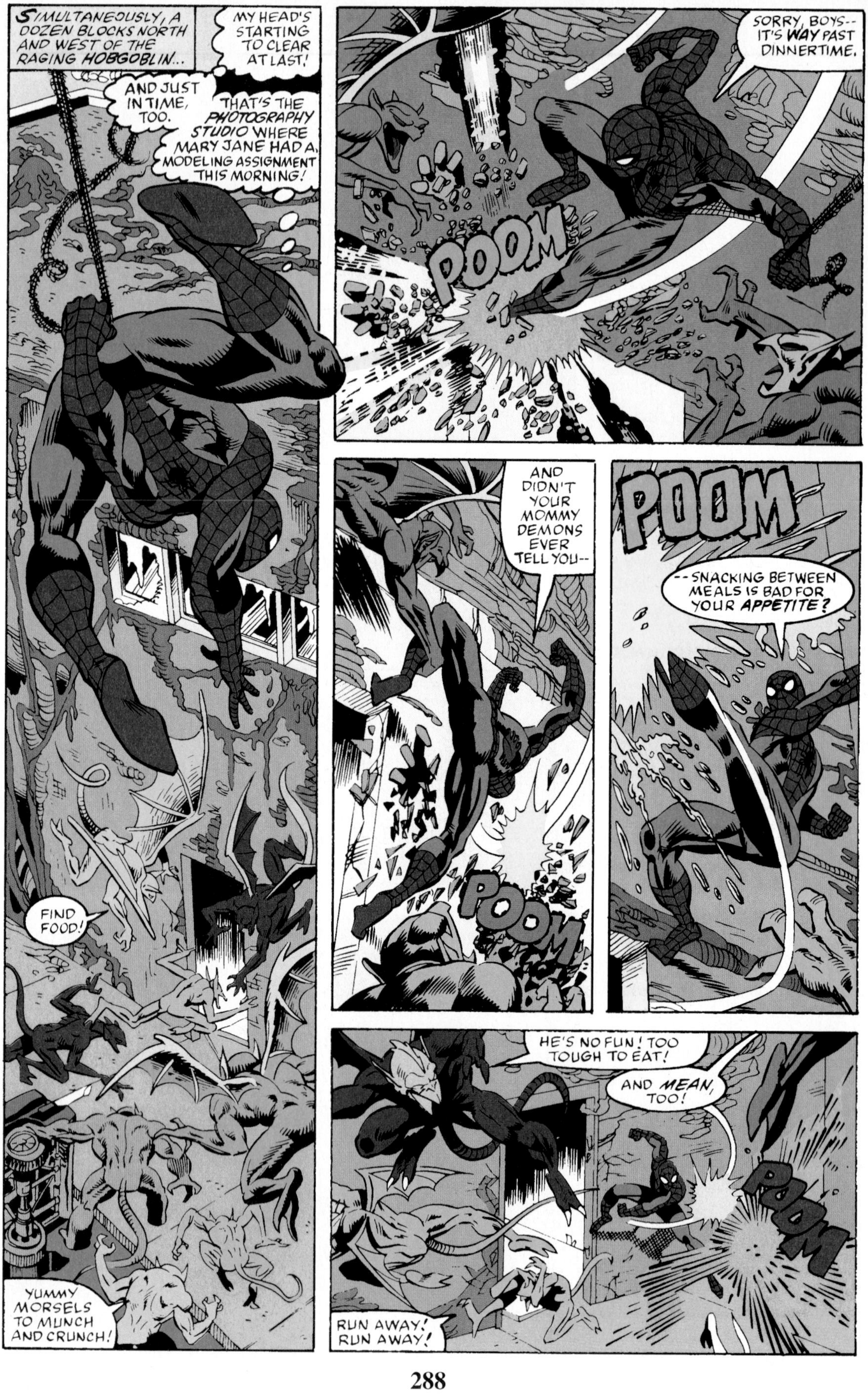
SIMULTANEOUSLY, A DOZEN BLOCKS NORTH AND WEST OF THE RAGING HOBGOBLIN...
MY HEAD'S STARTING TO CLEAR AT LAST!
AND JUST IN TIME, TOO.
THAT'S THE PHOTOGRAPHY STUDIO WHERE MARY JANE HAD A MODELING ASSIGNMENT THIS MORNING!
FIND FOOD!
YUMMY MORSELS TO MUNCH AND CRUNCH!
SORRY, BOYS-- IT'S WAY PAST DINNERTIME.
POOM
AND DIDN'T YOUR MOMMY DEMONS EVER TELL YOU--
POOM
POOM
--SNACKING BETWEEN MEALS IS BAD FOR YOUR APPETITE?
HE'S NO FUN! TOO TOUGH TO EAT!
AND MEAN, TOO!
POOM
RUN AWAY! RUN AWAY!

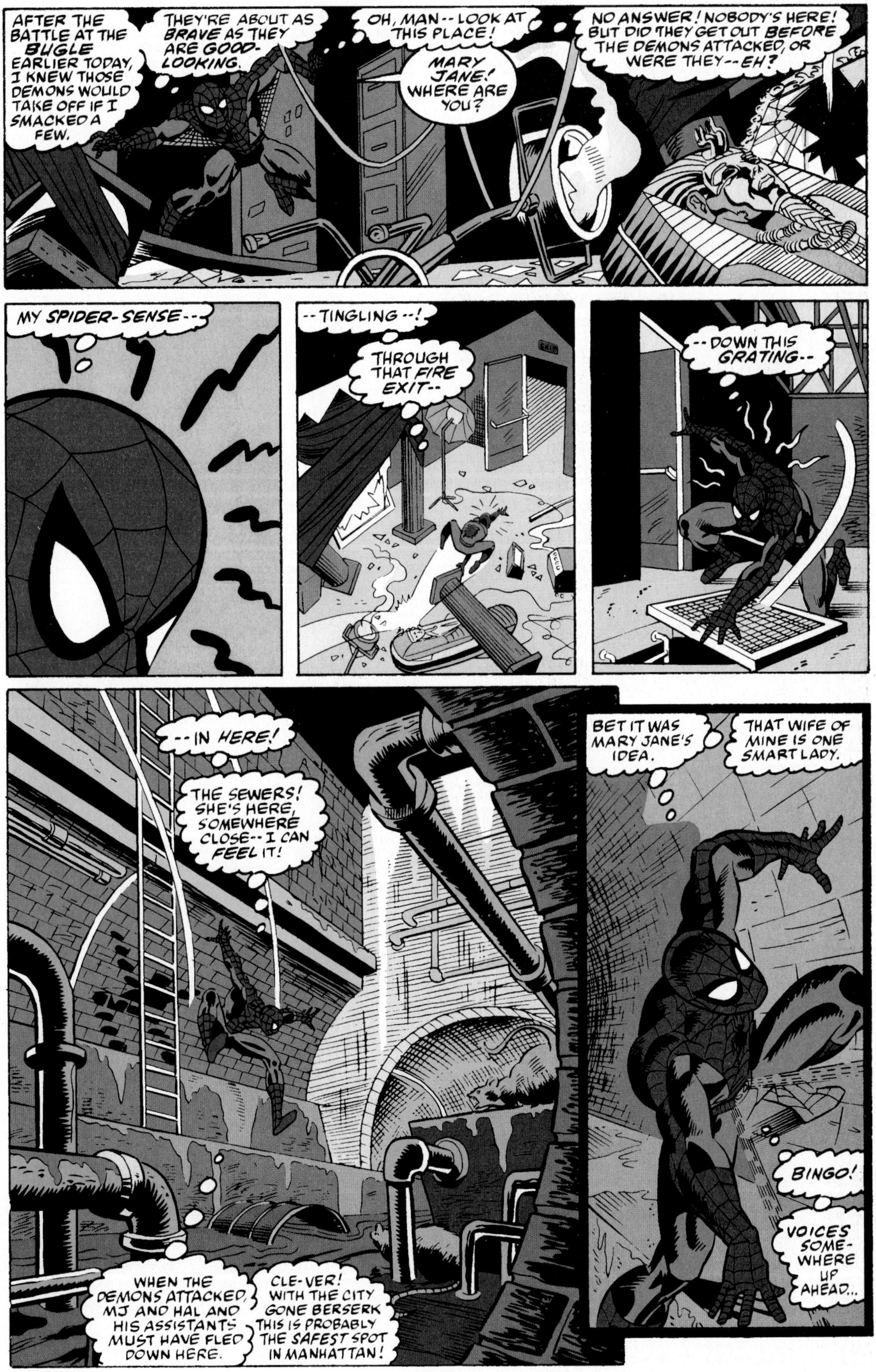
AFTER THE BATTLE AT THE BUGLE EARLIER TODAY, I KNEW THOSE DEMONS WOULD TAKE OFF IF I SMACKED A FEW.
THEY'RE ABOUT AS BRAVE AS THEY ARE GOOD-LOOKING.
OH, MAN -- LOOK AT THIS PLACE!
MARY JANE! WHERE ARE YOU?
NO ANSWER! NOBODY'S HERE! BUT DID THEY GET OUT BEFORE THE DEMONS ATTACKED, OR WERE THEY -- EH?
MY SPIDER-SENSE --
-- TINGLING --!
THROUGH THAT FIRE EXIT --
-- DOWN THIS GRATING --
-- IN HERE!
THE SEWERS! SHE'S HERE, SOMEWHERE CLOSE -- I CAN FEEL IT!
WHEN THE DEMONS ATTACKED, MJ AND HAL AND HIS ASSISTANTS MUST HAVE FLED DOWN HERE.
CLE-VER! WITH THE CITY GONE BERSERK THIS IS PROBABLY THE SAFEST SPOT IN MANHATTAN!
BET IT WAS MARY JANE'S IDEA.
THAT WIFE OF MINE IS ONE SMART LADY.
BINGO!
VOICES SOMEWHERE UP AHEAD...

"... BUT THERE ARE SO MANY ECHOES, SO MANY TUNNELS... THEY COULD BE *ANYWHERE.*"

" ALL I CAN DO IS KEEP LOOKING, AND HOPE I FIND THEM BEFORE ANY STRAY *DEMONS* DO."

OH GREAT, WE'RE LOST. WHICH WAY DO WE GO NOW, MARY JANE?

JUST HEAD INTO THAT *BREEZE,* HAL--

--AND BE CAREFUL WITH YOUR *LIGHTER.*

THOSE ARE GAS PIPES OVERHEAD.

ONE LITTLE LEAK NEAR AN *OPEN FLAME* AND--

OH, RIGHT.

BOOM.

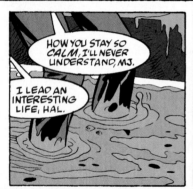

HOW YOU STAY SO *CALM,* I'LL NEVER UNDERSTAND, M.J.

I LEAD AN INTERESTING LIFE, HAL.

YOU MUST.

THE MOST EXCITEMENT I EVER GOT BEFORE TODAY WAS WINNING FIVE BUCKS IN THE *LOTTERY* LAST--

OH, MY.

L-LOOK...

I WON'T SCREAM, I WON'T SCREAM, I *WON'T!*

OH, SPIT...

EEEEEEEEE

⸘EEP!‽

290

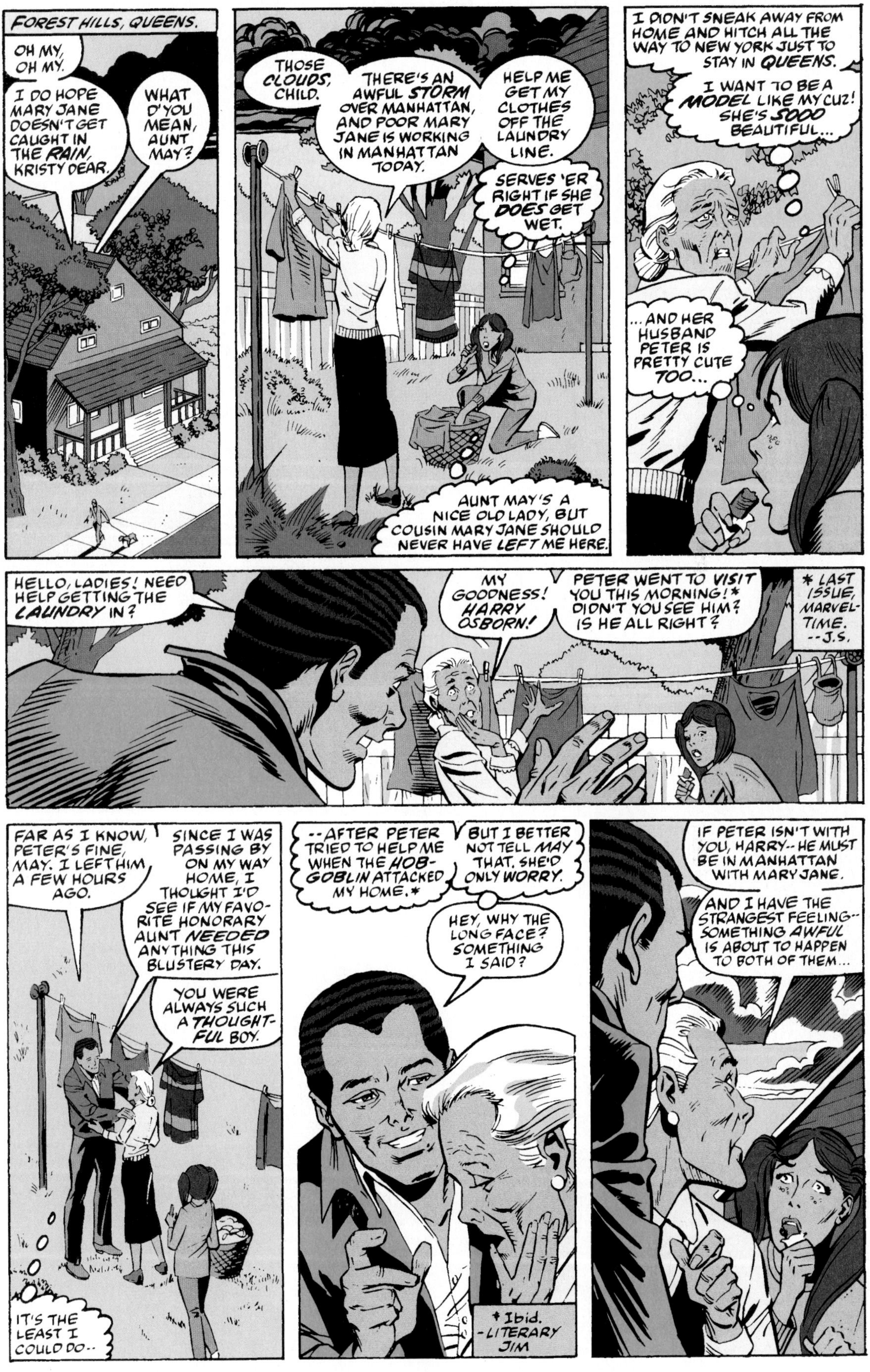
FOREST HILLS, QUEENS.
OH MY, OH MY.
I DO HOPE MARY JANE DOESN'T GET CAUGHT IN THE RAIN, KRISTY DEAR.
WHAT D'YOU MEAN, AUNT MAY?
THOSE CLOUDS, CHILD.
THERE'S AN AWFUL STORM OVER MANHATTAN, AND POOR MARY JANE IS WORKING IN MANHATTAN TODAY.
HELP ME GET MY CLOTHES OFF THE LAUNDRY LINE.
SERVES 'ER RIGHT IF SHE DOES GET WET.
AUNT MAY'S A NICE OLD LADY, BUT COUSIN MARY JANE SHOULD NEVER HAVE LEFT ME HERE.
I DIDN'T SNEAK AWAY FROM HOME AND HITCH ALL THE WAY TO NEW YORK JUST TO STAY IN QUEENS.
I WANT TO BE A MODEL LIKE MY CUZ! SHE'S SOOO BEAUTIFUL...
...AND HER HUSBAND PETER IS PRETTY CUTE TOO...
HELLO, LADIES! NEED HELP GETTING THE LAUNDRY IN?
MY GOODNESS! HARRY OSBORN!
PETER WENT TO VISIT YOU THIS MORNING!* DIDN'T YOU SEE HIM? IS HE ALL RIGHT?
* LAST ISSUE, MARVEL-TIME. --J.S.
FAR AS I KNOW, PETER'S FINE, MAY. I LEFT HIM A FEW HOURS AGO.
SINCE I WAS PASSING BY ON MY WAY HOME, I THOUGHT I'D SEE IF MY FAVORITE HONORARY AUNT NEEDED ANYTHING THIS BLUSTERY DAY.
YOU WERE ALWAYS SUCH A THOUGHTFUL BOY.
IT'S THE LEAST I COULD DO--
--AFTER PETER TRIED TO HELP ME WHEN THE HOBGOBLIN ATTACKED MY HOME.*
BUT I BETTER NOT TELL MAY THAT. SHE'D ONLY WORRY.
HEY, WHY THE LONG FACE? SOMETHING I SAID?
* Ibid. -LITERARY JIM
IF PETER ISN'T WITH YOU, HARRY-- HE MUST BE IN MANHATTAN WITH MARY JANE.
AND I HAVE THE STRANGEST FEELING-- SOMETHING AWFUL IS ABOUT TO HAPPEN TO BOTH OF THEM...

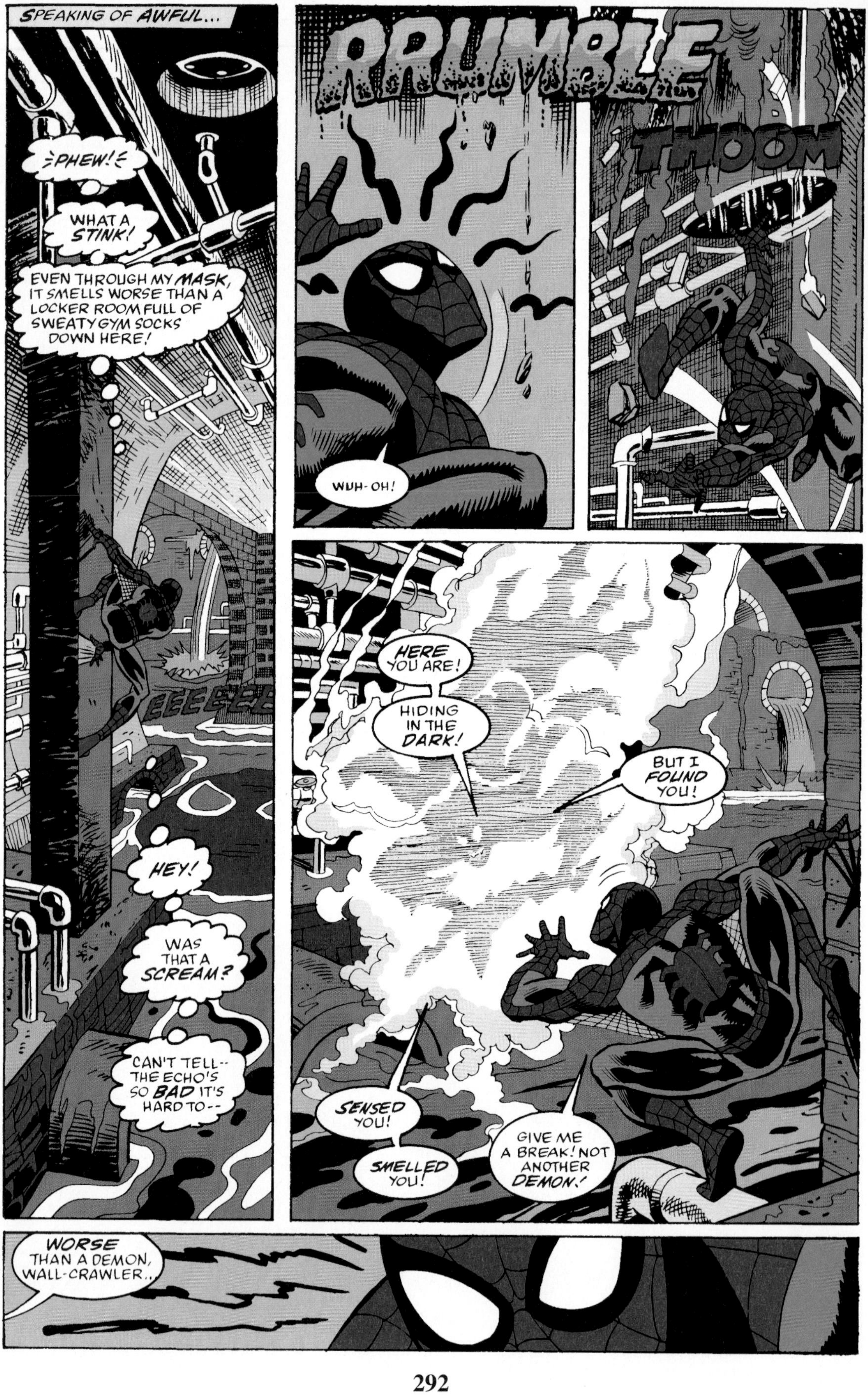
SPEAKING OF AWFUL...
PHEW!
WHAT A STINK!
EVEN THROUGH MY MASK, IT SMELLS WORSE THAN A LOCKER ROOM FULL OF SWEATY GYM SOCKS DOWN HERE!
EEEEEEEE
HEY!
WAS THAT A SCREAM?
CAN'T TELL-- THE ECHO'S SO BAD IT'S HARD TO--
RRUMBLE
WUH-OH!
THOOM
HERE YOU ARE!
HIDING IN THE DARK!
BUT I FOUND YOU!
SENSED YOU!
SMELLED YOU!
GIVE ME A BREAK! NOT ANOTHER DEMON!
WORSE THAN A DEMON, WALL-CRAWLER...

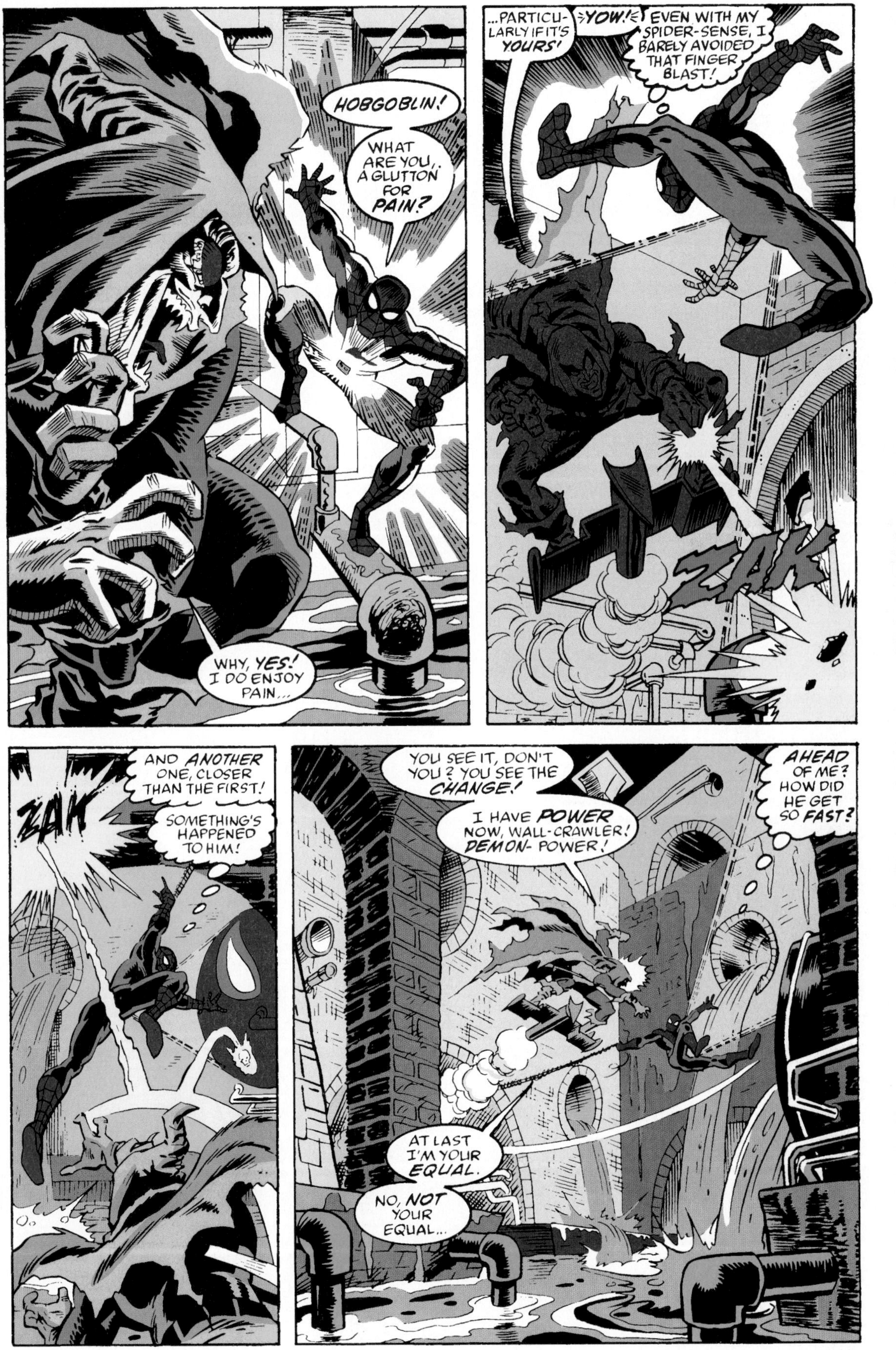
HOBGOBLIN!
WHAT ARE YOU, A GLUTTON FOR PAIN?
WHY, YES! I DO ENJOY PAIN...
...PARTICULARLY IF IT'S YOURS!
YOW!
EVEN WITH MY SPIDER-SENSE, I BARELY AVOIDED THAT FINGER BLAST!
ZAK
ZAK
AND ANOTHER ONE, CLOSER THAN THE FIRST!
SOMETHING'S HAPPENED TO HIM!
YOU SEE IT, DON'T YOU? YOU SEE THE CHANGE!
I HAVE POWER NOW, WALL-CRAWLER! DEMON-POWER!
AHEAD OF ME? HOW DID HE GET SO FAST?
AT LAST I'M YOUR EQUAL.
NO, NOT YOUR EQUAL...

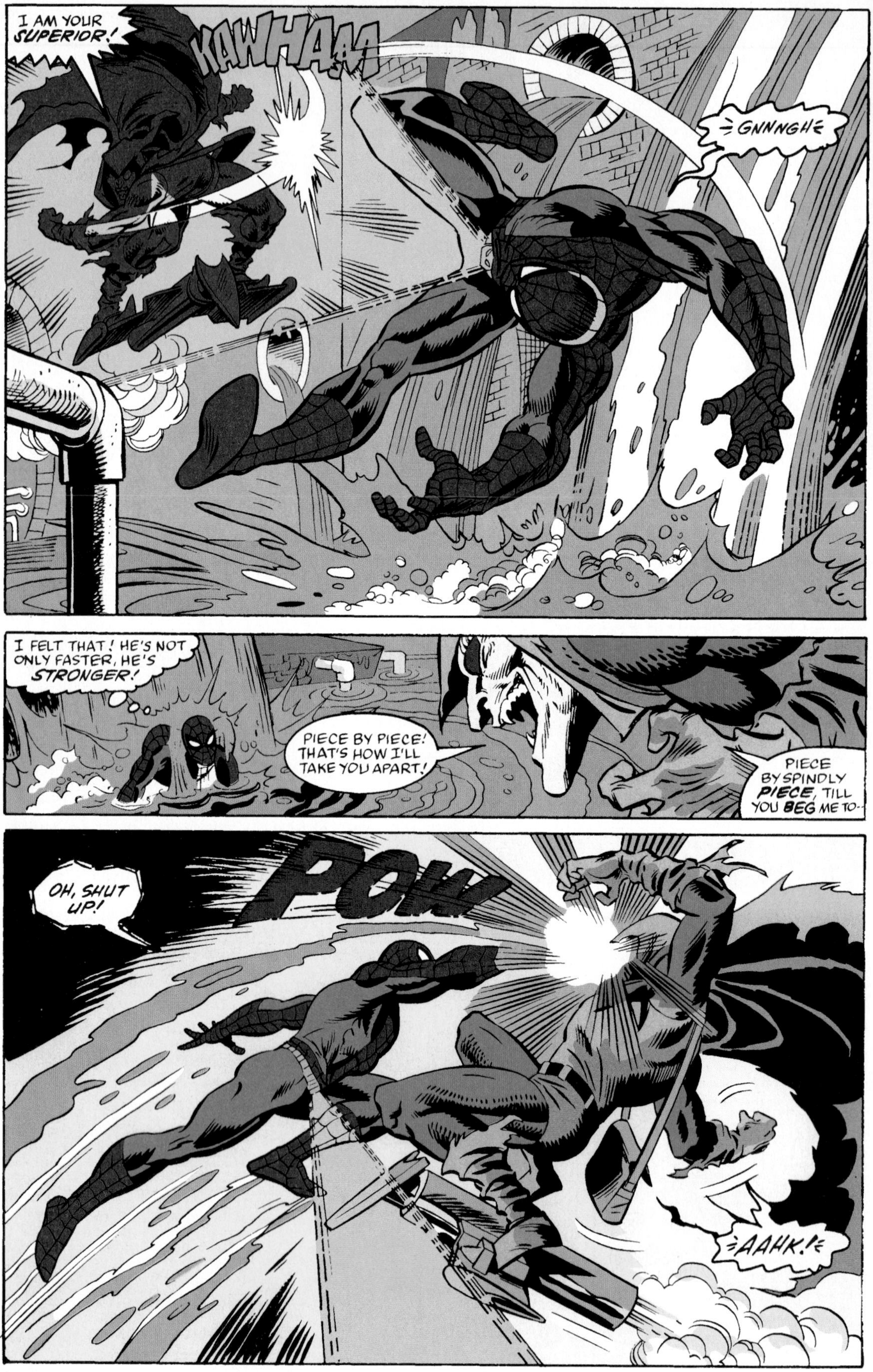
I AM YOUR SUPERIOR!
KAWHAAM
GNNNGH
I FELT THAT! HE'S NOT ONLY FASTER, HE'S STRONGER!
PIECE BY PIECE! THAT'S HOW I'LL TAKE YOU APART!
PIECE BY SPINDLY PIECE, TILL YOU BEG ME TO--
POW
OH, SHUT UP!
AAHK!

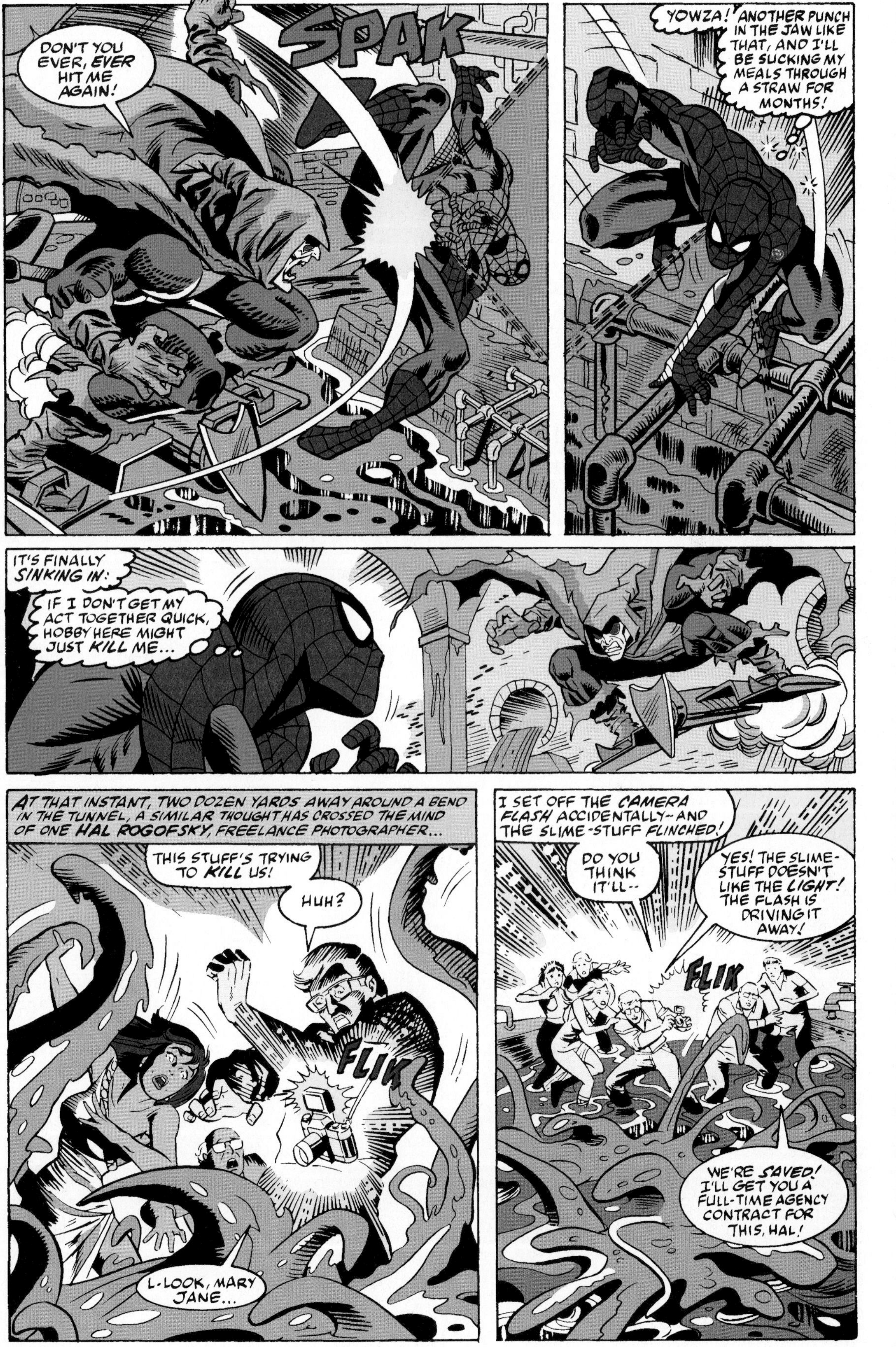
SPAK
DON'T YOU EVER, EVER HIT ME AGAIN!
YOWZA!
ANOTHER PUNCH IN THE JAW LIKE THAT, AND I'LL BE SUCKING MY MEALS THROUGH A STRAW FOR MONTHS!
IT'S FINALLY SINKING IN:
IF I DON'T GET MY ACT TOGETHER QUICK, HOBBY HERE MIGHT JUST KILL ME...
AT THAT INSTANT, TWO DOZEN YARDS AWAY AROUND A BEND IN THE TUNNEL, A SIMILAR THOUGHT HAS CROSSED THE MIND OF ONE HAL ROGOFSKY, FREELANCE PHOTOGRAPHER...
THIS STUFF'S TRYING TO KILL US!
HUH?
FLIK
L-LOOK, MARY JANE...
I SET OFF THE CAMERA FLASH ACCIDENTALLY-- AND THE SLIME-STUFF FLINCHED!
DO YOU THINK IT'LL--
YES! THE SLIME-STUFF DOESN'T LIKE THE LIGHT! THE FLASH IS DRIVING IT AWAY!
FLIK
WE'RE SAVED! I'LL GET YOU A FULL-TIME AGENCY CONTRACT FOR THIS, HAL!

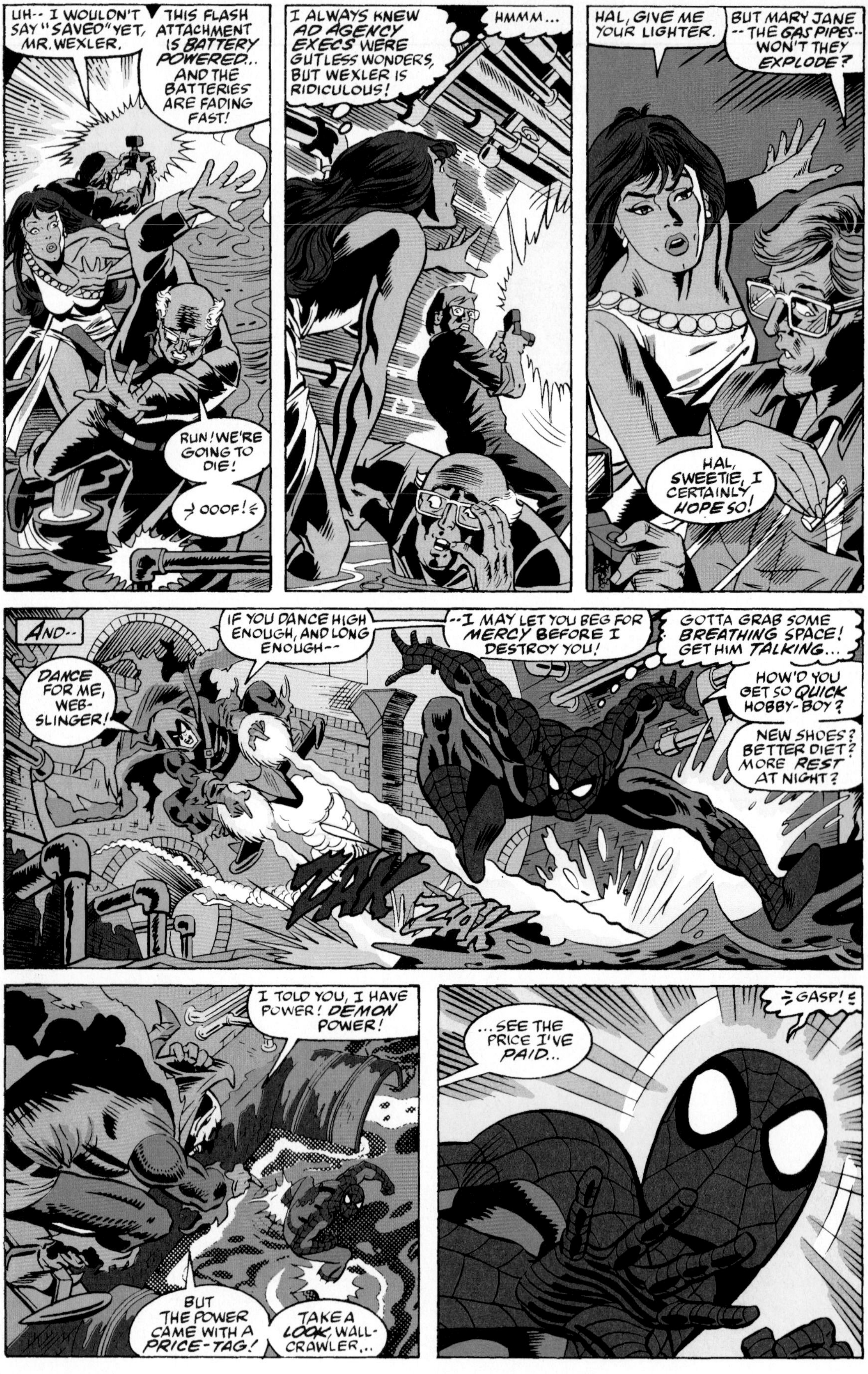
UH-- I WOULDN'T SAY "SAVED" YET, MR. WEXLER.
THIS FLASH ATTACHMENT IS BATTERY POWERED.. AND THE BATTERIES ARE FADING FAST!
RUN! WE'RE GOING TO DIE!
OOOF!
I ALWAYS KNEW AD AGENCY EXECS WERE GUTLESS WONDERS, BUT WEXLER IS RIDICULOUS!
HMMM...
HAL, GIVE ME YOUR LIGHTER.
BUT MARY JANE -- THE GAS PIPES-- WON'T THEY EXPLODE?
HAL, SWEETIE, I CERTAINLY HOPE SO!
AND--
DANCE FOR ME, WEB-SLINGER!
IF YOU DANCE HIGH ENOUGH, AND LONG ENOUGH--
--I MAY LET YOU BEG FOR MERCY BEFORE I DESTROY YOU!
GOTTA GRAB SOME BREATHING SPACE! GET HIM TALKING...
HOW'D YOU GET SO QUICK HOBBY-BOY?
NEW SHOES? BETTER DIET? MORE REST AT NIGHT?
I TOLD YOU, I HAVE POWER! DEMON POWER!
BUT THE POWER CAME WITH A PRICE-TAG!
TAKE A LOOK, WALL-CRAWLER...
...SEE THE PRICE I'VE PAID...
GASP!

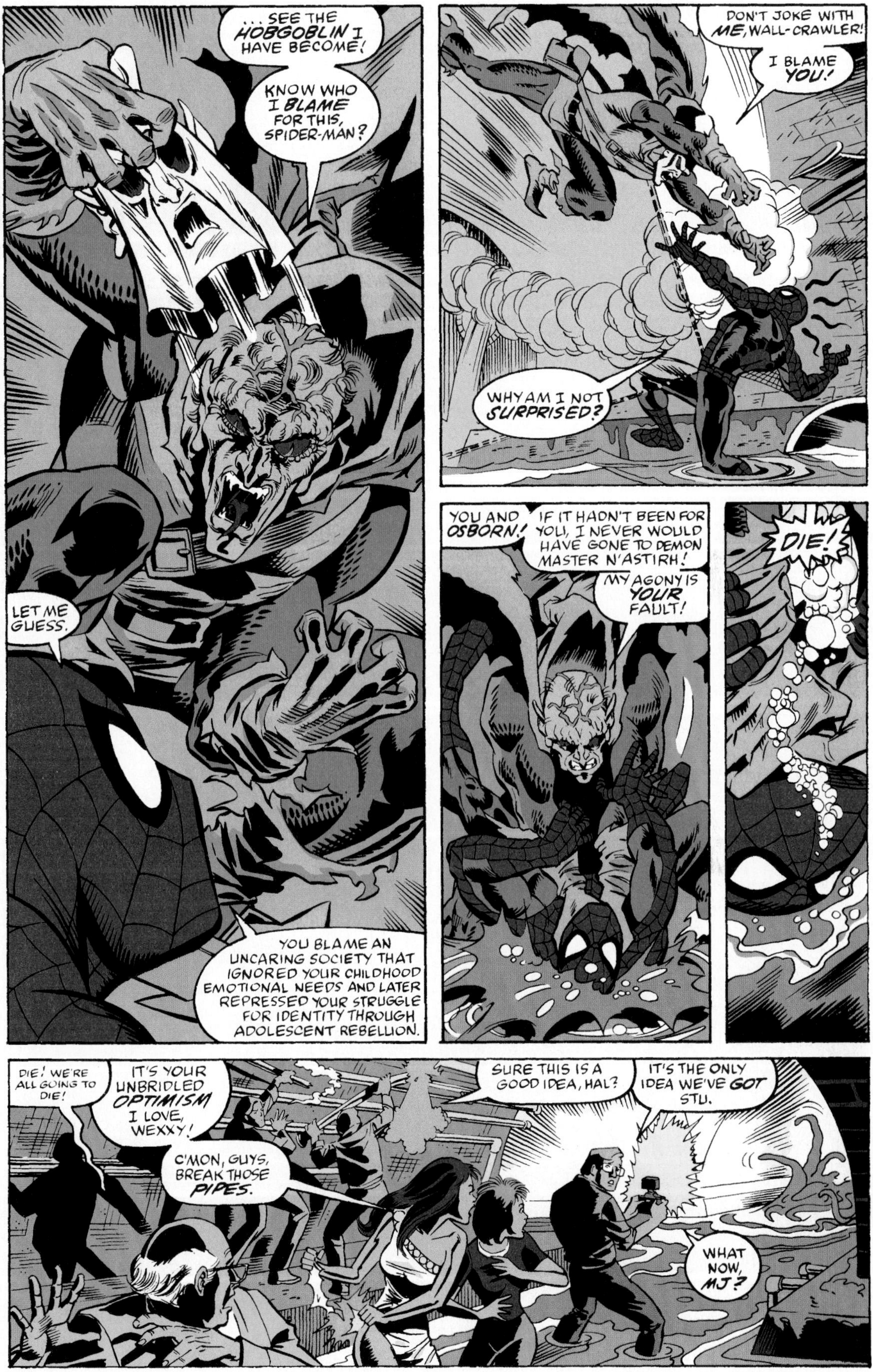
...SEE THE HOBGOBLIN I HAVE BECOME!
KNOW WHO I BLAME FOR THIS, SPIDER-MAN?
LET ME GUESS.
YOU BLAME AN UNCARING SOCIETY THAT IGNORED YOUR CHILDHOOD EMOTIONAL NEEDS AND LATER REPRESSED YOUR STRUGGLE FOR IDENTITY THROUGH ADOLESCENT REBELLION.
DON'T JOKE WITH ME, WALL-CRAWLER!
I BLAME YOU!
WHY AM I NOT SURPRISED?
YOU AND OSBORN!
IF IT HADN'T BEEN FOR YOU, I NEVER WOULD HAVE GONE TO DEMON MASTER N'ASTIRH!
MY AGONY IS YOUR FAULT!
DIE!
DIE! WE'RE ALL GOING TO DIE!
IT'S YOUR UNBRIDLED OPTIMISM I LOVE, WEXXY!
C'MON, GUYS, BREAK THOSE PIPES.
SURE THIS IS A GOOD IDEA, HAL?
IT'S THE ONLY IDEA WE'VE GOT STU.
WHAT NOW, MJ?

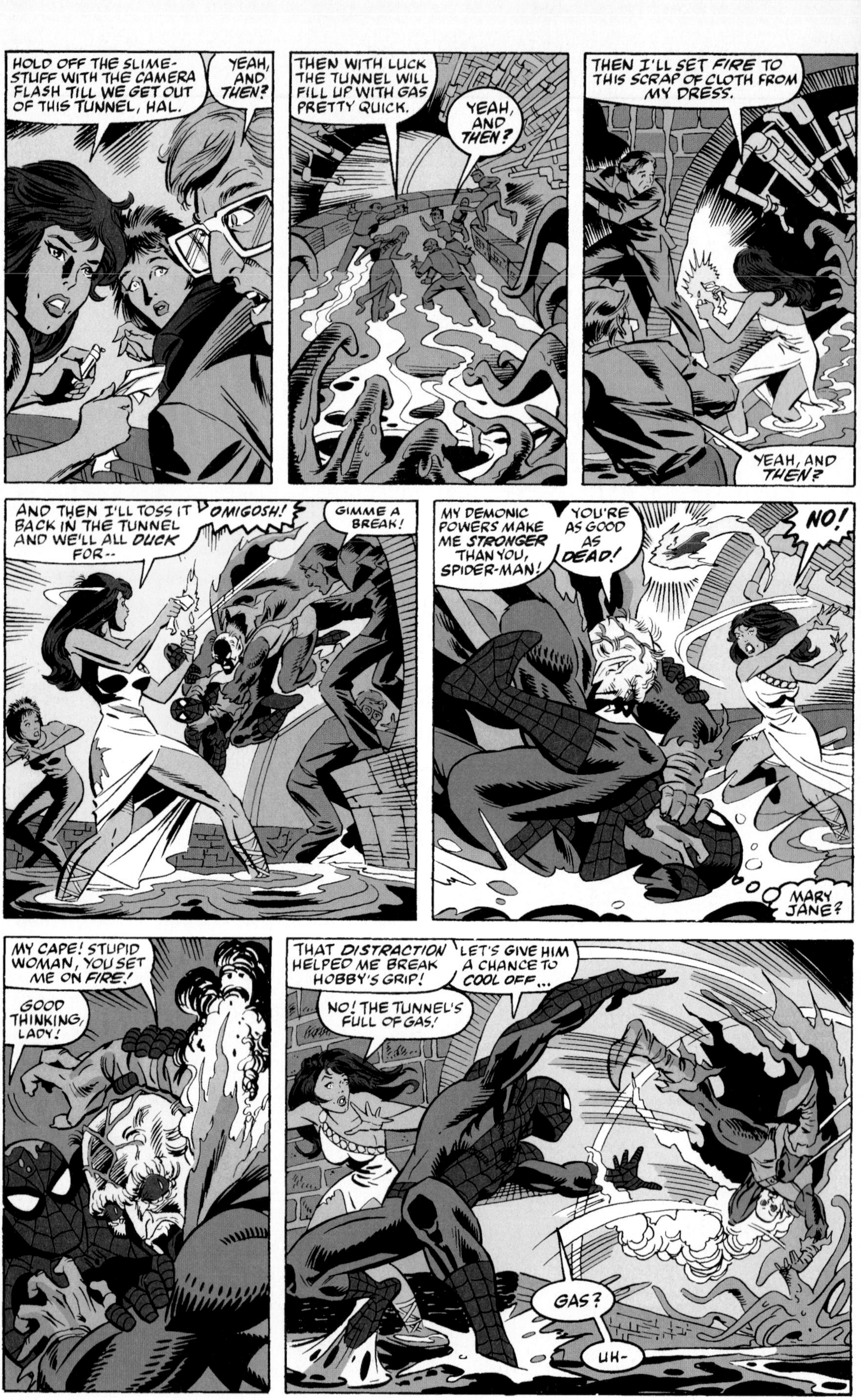
HOLD OFF THE SLIME-STUFF WITH THE CAMERA FLASH TILL WE GET OUT OF THIS TUNNEL, HAL.
YEAH, AND THEN?
THEN WITH LUCK THE TUNNEL WILL FILL UP WITH GAS PRETTY QUICK.
YEAH, AND THEN?
THEN I'LL SET FIRE TO THIS SCRAP OF CLOTH FROM MY DRESS.
YEAH, AND THEN?
AND THEN I'LL TOSS IT BACK IN THE TUNNEL AND WE'LL ALL DUCK FOR--
OMIGOSH!
GIMME A BREAK!
MY DEMONIC POWERS MAKE ME STRONGER THAN YOU, SPIDER-MAN!
YOU'RE AS GOOD AS DEAD!
NO!
MARY JANE?
MY CAPE! STUPID WOMAN, YOU SET ME ON FIRE!
GOOD THINKING, LADY!
THAT DISTRACTION HELPED ME BREAK HOBBY'S GRIP!
LET'S GIVE HIM A CHANCE TO COOL OFF...
NO! THE TUNNEL'S FULL OF GAS!
GAS?
UH-

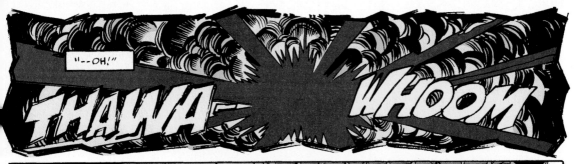

"--OH!"

THAWA WHOOM

WE'RE GOING TO DIE, WE'RE GOING TO DIE, WE'RE GOING TO--

SHRACK

--LIVE?

LOOK! THE CEILING'S CRACKED OPEN! THERE'S A WAY OUT!

MUST BE YOUR LUCKY DAY, BOYS!

I'LL BE BACK FOR YOU IN A MINUTE.

MMMM.

I DIDN'T KNOW YOU COULD SWING THIS HIGH, TIGER.

NEITHER DID I, LADY LOVE.

BUT WHEN I'M WITH YOU, I'M ABOUT AS HIGH AS A GUY CAN GET AND STILL BE LEGAL.

299

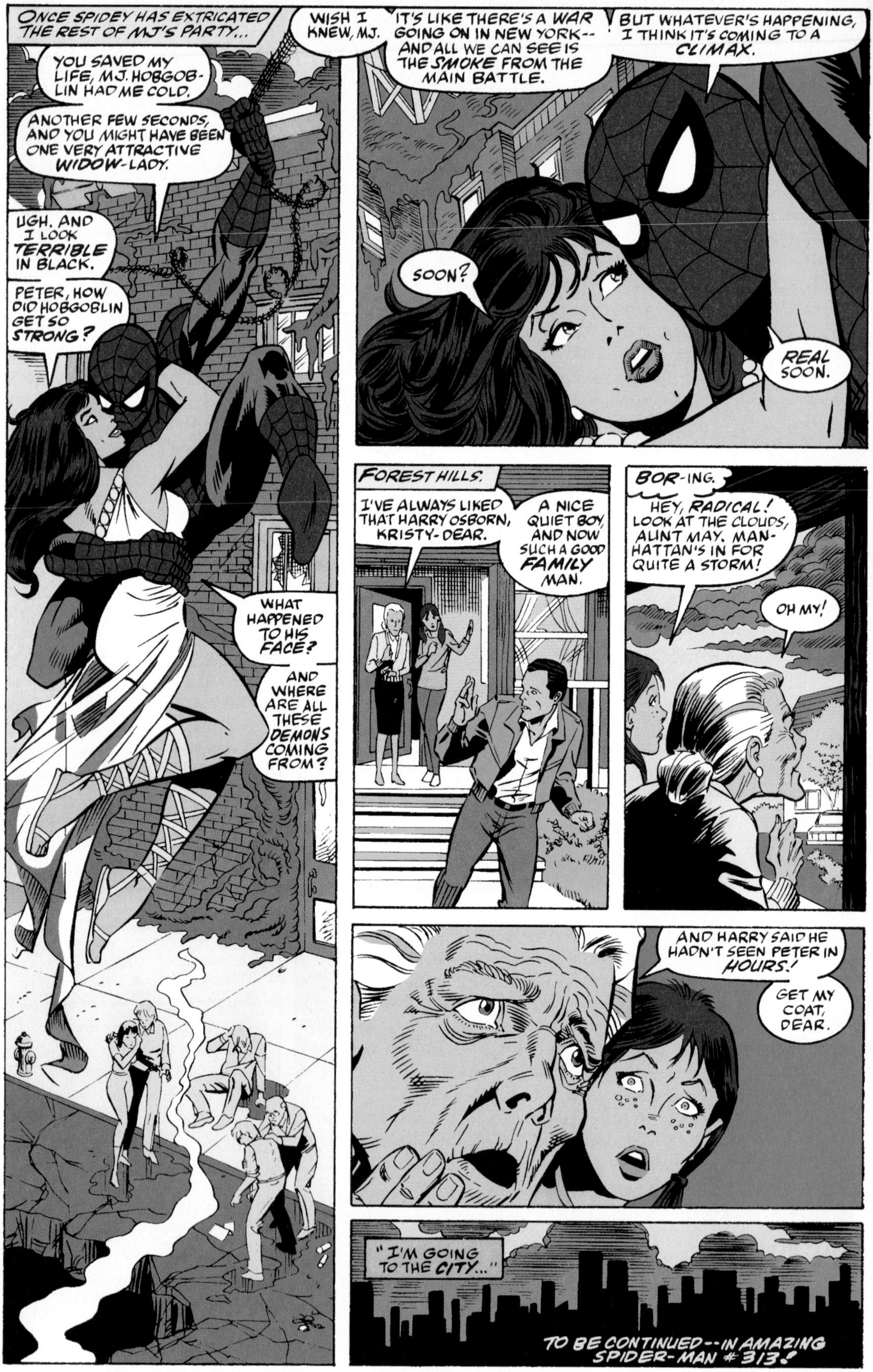

ONCE SPIDEY HAS EXTRICATED THE REST OF MJ'S PARTY...
YOU SAVED MY LIFE, MJ. HOBGOBLIN HAD ME COLD.
ANOTHER FEW SECONDS, AND YOU MIGHT HAVE BEEN ONE VERY ATTRACTIVE WIDOW-LADY.
UGH. AND I LOOK TERRIBLE IN BLACK.
PETER, HOW DID HOBGOBLIN GET SO STRONG?
WHAT HAPPENED TO HIS FACE?
AND WHERE ARE ALL THESE DEMONS COMING FROM?
WISH I KNEW, MJ.
IT'S LIKE THERE'S A WAR GOING ON IN NEW YORK-- AND ALL WE CAN SEE IS THE SMOKE FROM THE MAIN BATTLE.
BUT WHATEVER'S HAPPENING, I THINK IT'S COMING TO A CLIMAX.
SOON?
REAL SOON.
FOREST HILLS.
I'VE ALWAYS LIKED THAT HARRY OSBORN, KRISTY-DEAR.
A NICE QUIET BOY, AND NOW SUCH A GOOD FAMILY MAN.
BOR-ING.
HEY, RADICAL! LOOK AT THE CLOUDS, AUNT MAY. MANHATTAN'S IN FOR QUITE A STORM!
OH MY!
AND HARRY SAID HE HADN'T SEEN PETER IN HOURS!
GET MY COAT, DEAR.
"I'M GOING TO THE CITY..."
TO BE CONTINUED--IN AMAZING SPIDER-MAN #313!

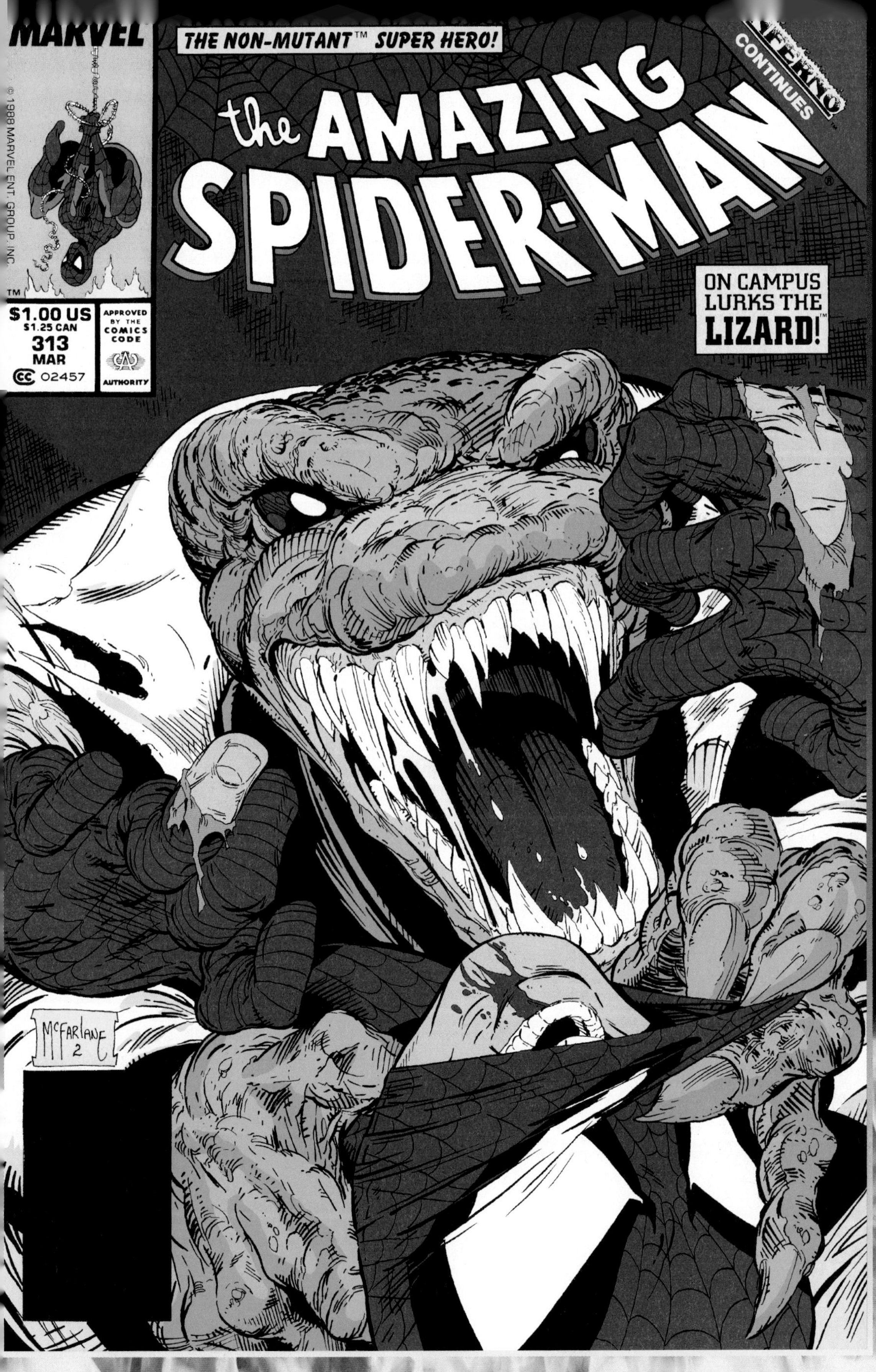
MARVEL
THE NON-MUTANT™ SUPER HERO!
CONTINUES
the AMAZING SPIDER-MAN®
ON CAMPUS LURKS THE LIZARD!™
© 1988 MARVEL ENT. GROUP, INC.
$1.00 US
$1.25 CAN
313
MAR
02457
APPROVED BY THE COMICS CODE AUTHORITY
McFARLANE 2

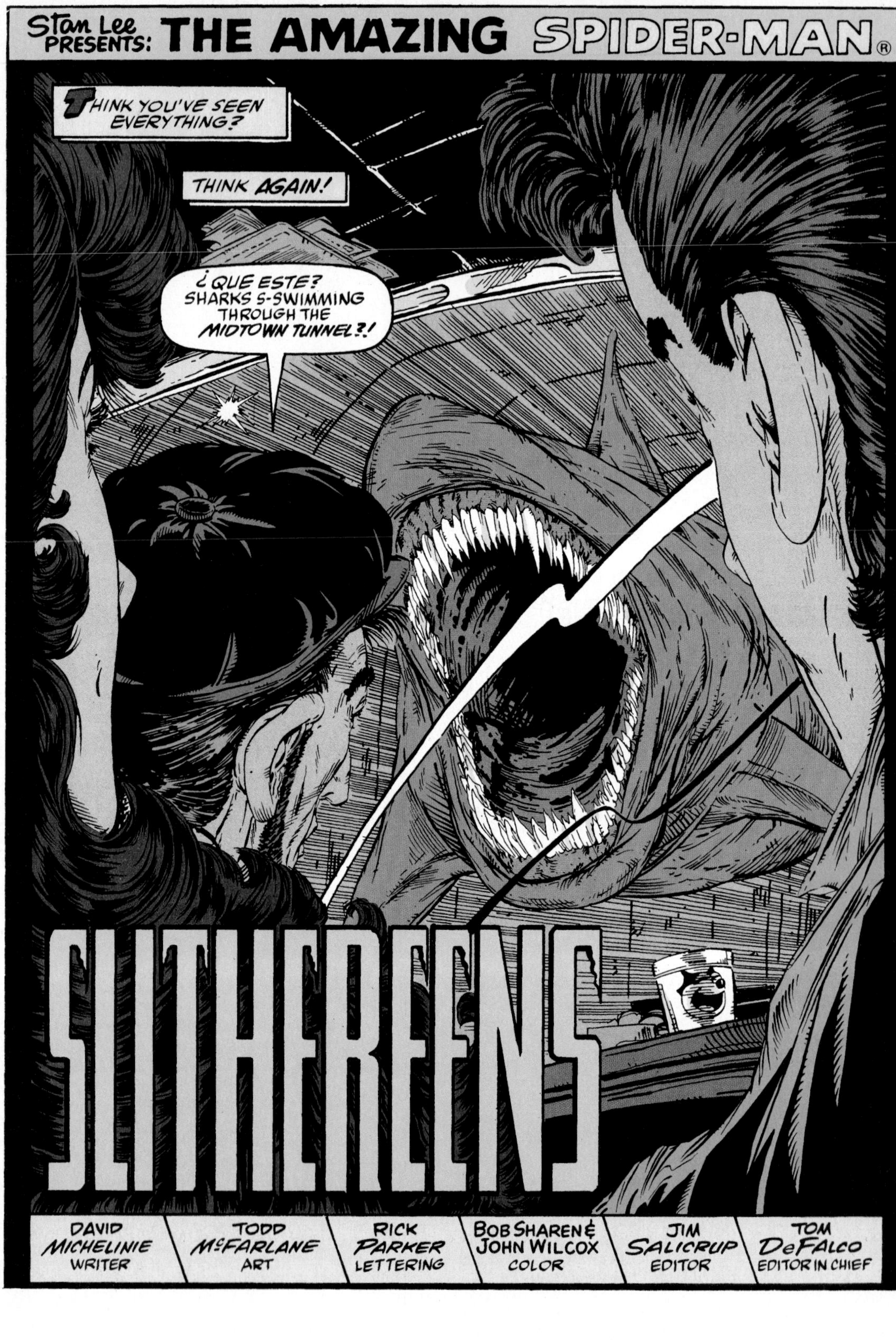
Stan Lee PRESENTS: THE AMAZING SPIDER-MAN®
THINK YOU'VE SEEN EVERYTHING?
THINK AGAIN!
¿QUE ESTE? SHARKS S-SWIMMING THROUGH THE MIDTOWN TUNNEL?!
SLITHEREENS
DAVID MICHELINIE WRITER
TODD McFARLANE ART
RICK PARKER LETTERING
BOB SHAREN & JOHN WILCOX COLOR
JIM SALICRUP EDITOR
TOM DeFALCO EDITOR IN CHIEF

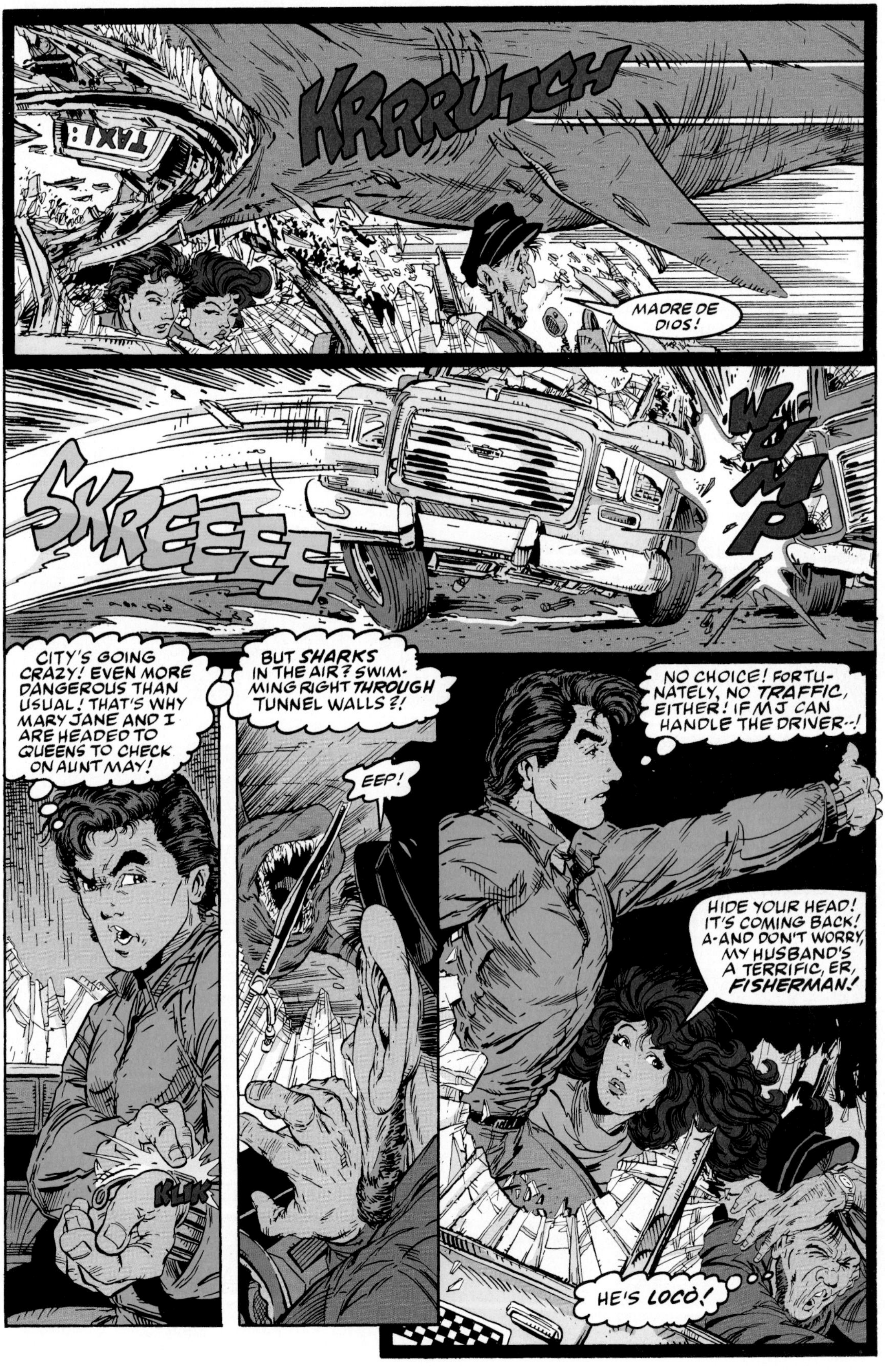

KRRRUTCH
TAXI
MADRE DE DIOS!
SKREEEEE
WUMP
CITY'S GOING CRAZY! EVEN MORE DANGEROUS THAN USUAL! THAT'S WHY MARY JANE AND I ARE HEADED TO QUEENS TO CHECK ON AUNT MAY!
KLIK
BUT SHARKS IN THE AIR? SWIMMING RIGHT THROUGH TUNNEL WALLS?!
EEP!
NO CHOICE! FORTUNATELY, NO TRAFFIC, EITHER! IF MJ CAN HANDLE THE DRIVER--!
HIDE YOUR HEAD! IT'S COMING BACK! A-AND DON'T WORRY, MY HUSBAND'S A TERRIFIC, ER, FISHERMAN!
HE'S LOCO!

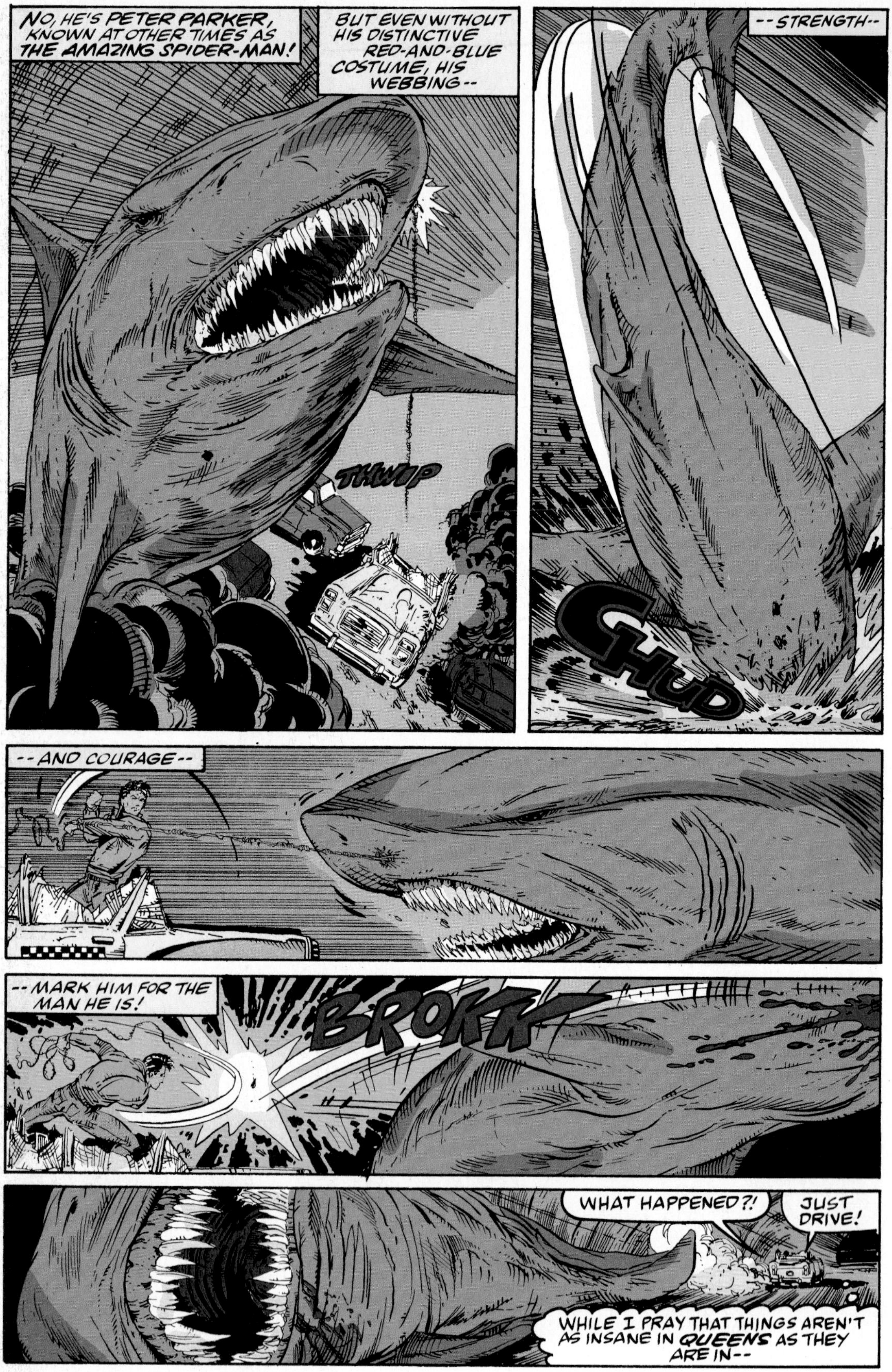
NO, HE'S PETER PARKER, KNOWN AT OTHER TIMES AS THE AMAZING SPIDER-MAN!
BUT EVEN WITHOUT HIS DISTINCTIVE RED-AND-BLUE COSTUME, HIS WEBBING--
THWIP
--STRENGTH--
CHUD
--AND COURAGE--
--MARK HIM FOR THE MAN HE IS!
BROKK
WHAT HAPPENED?!
JUST DRIVE!
WHILE I PRAY THAT THINGS AREN'T AS INSANE IN QUEENS AS THEY ARE IN--

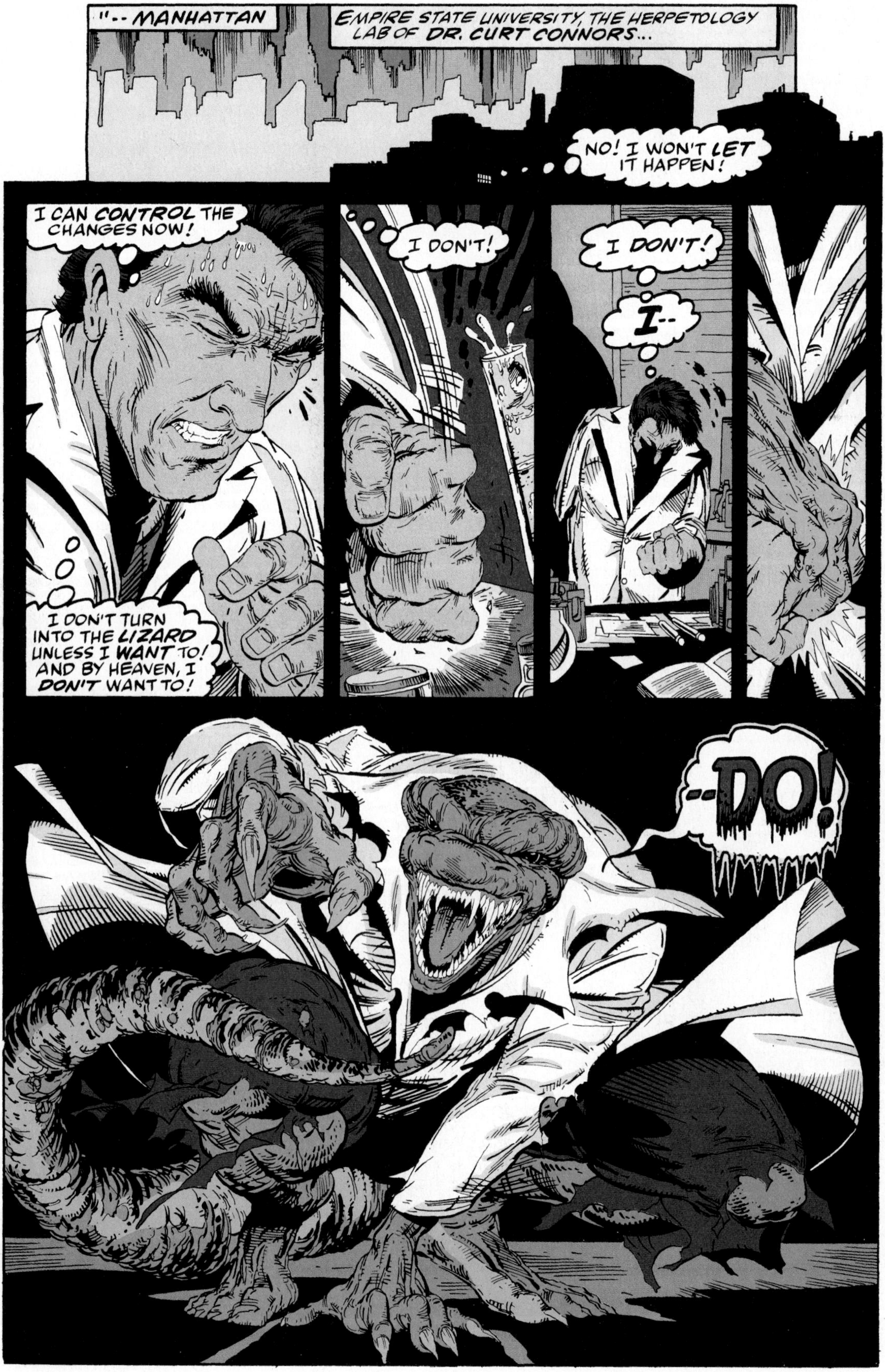

"--MANHATTAN
EMPIRE STATE UNIVERSITY, THE HERPETOLOGY LAB OF DR. CURT CONNORS...
NO! I WON'T LET IT HAPPEN!
I CAN CONTROL THE CHANGES NOW!
I DON'T TURN INTO THE LIZARD UNLESS I WANT TO! AND BY HEAVEN, I DON'T WANT TO!
I DON'T!
I DON'T!
I--
--DO!

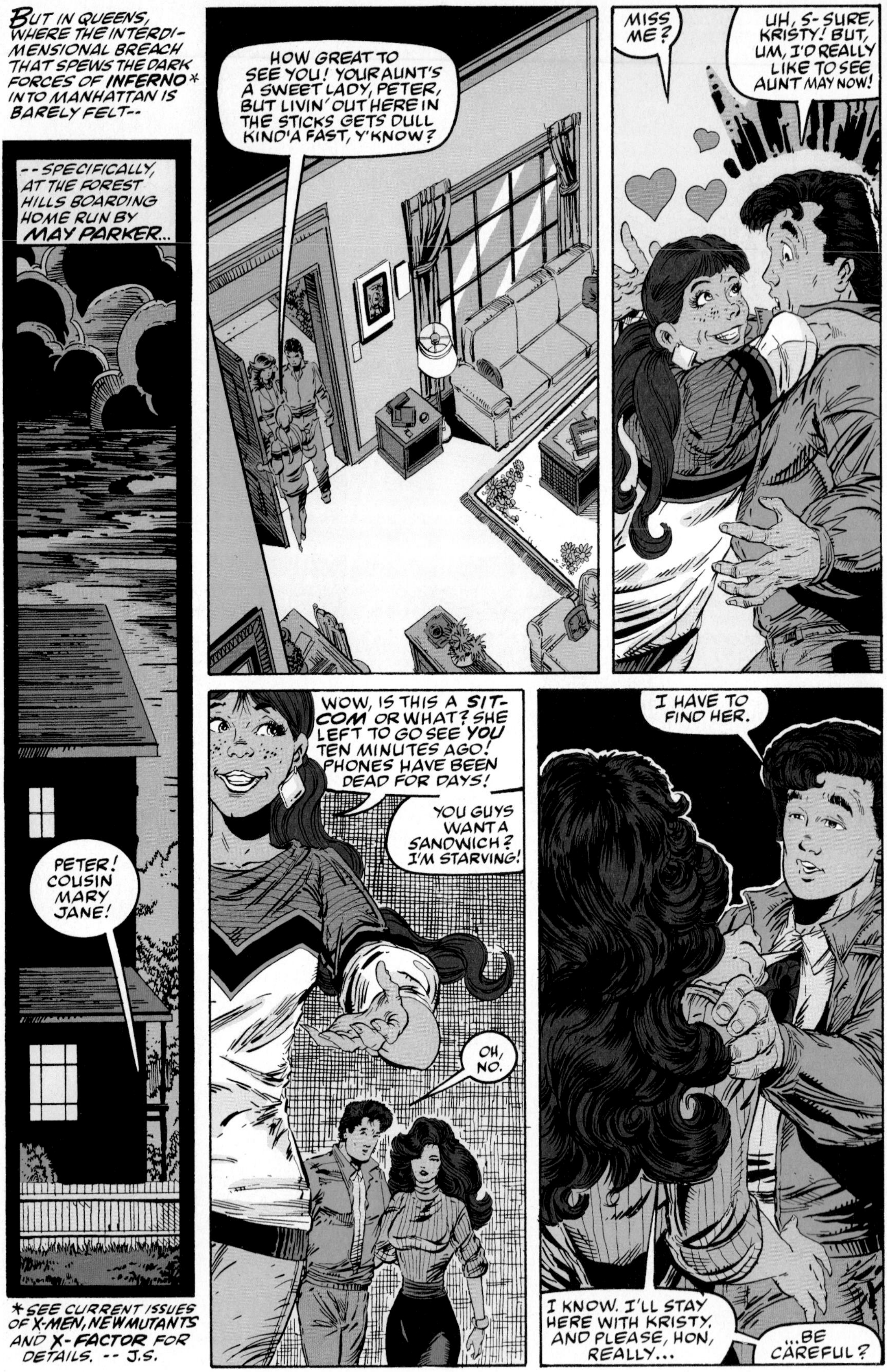
BUT IN QUEENS, WHERE THE INTERDIMENSIONAL BREACH THAT SPEWS THE DARK FORCES OF INFERNO* INTO MANHATTAN IS BARELY FELT--
--SPECIFICALLY, AT THE FOREST HILLS BOARDING HOME RUN BY MAY PARKER...
PETER! COUSIN MARY JANE!
HOW GREAT TO SEE YOU! YOUR AUNT'S A SWEET LADY, PETER, BUT LIVIN' OUT HERE IN THE STICKS GETS DULL KIND'A FAST, Y'KNOW?
MISS ME?
UH, S-SURE, KRISTY! BUT, UM, I'D REALLY LIKE TO SEE AUNT MAY NOW!
WOW, IS THIS A SIT-COM OR WHAT? SHE LEFT TO GO SEE YOU TEN MINUTES AGO! PHONES HAVE BEEN DEAD FOR DAYS!
YOU GUYS WANT A SANDWICH? I'M STARVING!
OH, NO.
I HAVE TO FIND HER.
I KNOW. I'LL STAY HERE WITH KRISTY. AND PLEASE, HON, REALLY...
...BE CAREFUL?
*SEE CURRENT ISSUES OF X-MEN, NEW MUTANTS AND X-FACTOR FOR DETAILS. -- J.S.

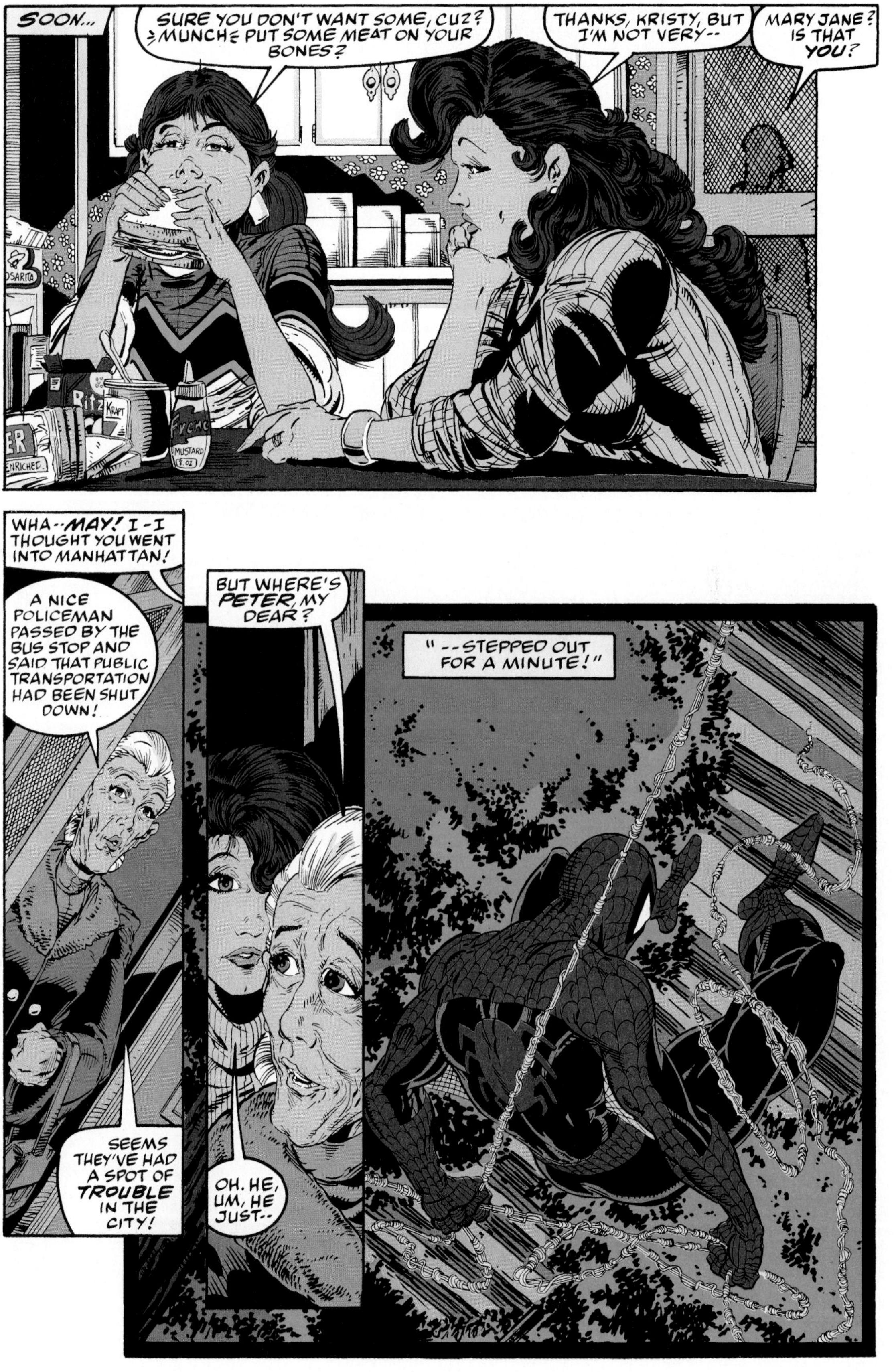
SOON...
SURE YOU DON'T WANT SOME, CUZ? ≥MUNCH≤ PUT SOME MEAT ON YOUR BONES?
THANKS, KRISTY, BUT I'M NOT VERY--
MARY JANE? IS THAT YOU?
RITZ
KRAFT
MUSTARD
ENRICHED
WHA--MAY! I-I THOUGHT YOU WENT INTO MANHATTAN!
A NICE POLICEMAN PASSED BY THE BUS STOP AND SAID THAT PUBLIC TRANSPORTATION HAD BEEN SHUT DOWN!
SEEMS THEY'VE HAD A SPOT OF TROUBLE IN THE CITY!
BUT WHERE'S PETER, MY DEAR?
OH. HE, UM, HE JUST--
"--STEPPED OUT FOR A MINUTE!"

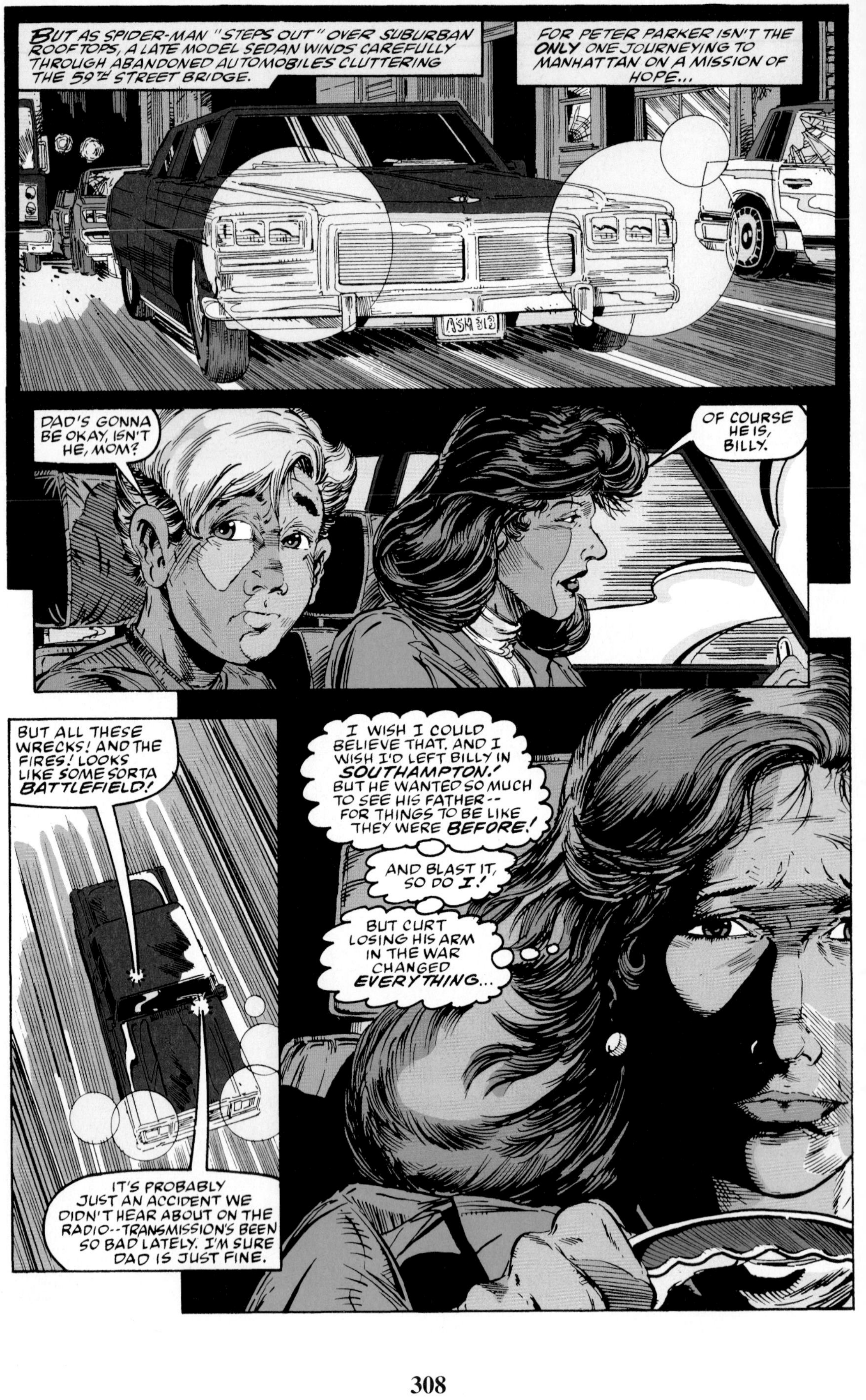

BUT AS SPIDER-MAN "STEPS OUT" OVER SUBURBAN ROOFTOPS, A LATE MODEL SEDAN WINDS CAREFULLY THROUGH ABANDONED AUTOMOBILES CLUTTERING THE 59TH STREET BRIDGE.
FOR PETER PARKER ISN'T THE ONLY ONE JOURNEYING TO MANHATTAN ON A MISSION OF HOPE...
ASM 313
DAD'S GONNA BE OKAY, ISN'T HE, MOM?
OF COURSE HE IS, BILLY.
BUT ALL THESE WRECKS! AND THE FIRES! LOOKS LIKE SOME SORTA BATTLEFIELD!
IT'S PROBABLY JUST AN ACCIDENT WE DIDN'T HEAR ABOUT ON THE RADIO--TRANSMISSION'S BEEN SO BAD LATELY. I'M SURE DAD IS JUST FINE.
I WISH I COULD BELIEVE THAT. AND I WISH I'D LEFT BILLY IN SOUTHAMPTON! BUT HE WANTED SO MUCH TO SEE HIS FATHER-- FOR THINGS TO BE LIKE THEY WERE BEFORE!
AND BLAST IT, SO DO I!
BUT CURT LOSING HIS ARM IN THE WAR CHANGED EVERYTHING...

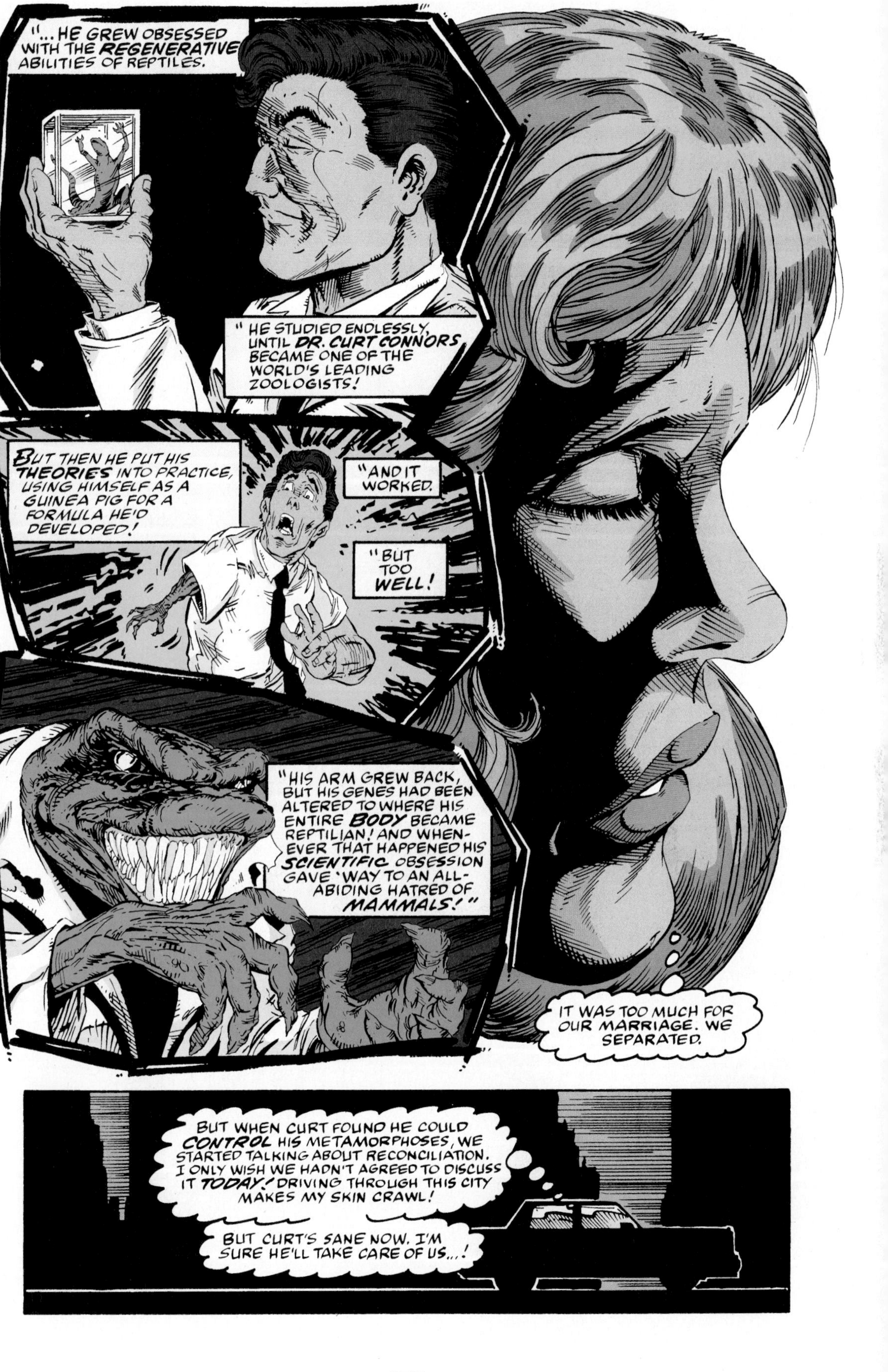
"...HE GREW OBSESSED WITH THE REGENERATIVE ABILITIES OF REPTILES.
"HE STUDIED ENDLESSLY, UNTIL DR. CURT CONNORS BECAME ONE OF THE WORLD'S LEADING ZOOLOGISTS!
BUT THEN HE PUT HIS THEORIES INTO PRACTICE, USING HIMSELF AS A GUINEA PIG FOR A FORMULA HE'D DEVELOPED!
"AND IT WORKED.
"BUT TOO WELL!
"HIS ARM GREW BACK, BUT HIS GENES HAD BEEN ALTERED TO WHERE HIS ENTIRE BODY BECAME REPTILIAN! AND WHENEVER THAT HAPPENED HIS SCIENTIFIC OBSESSION GAVE 'WAY TO AN ALL-ABIDING HATRED OF MAMMALS!"
IT WAS TOO MUCH FOR OUR MARRIAGE. WE SEPARATED.
BUT WHEN CURT FOUND HE COULD CONTROL HIS METAMORPHOSES, WE STARTED TALKING ABOUT RECONCILIATION. I ONLY WISH WE HADN'T AGREED TO DISCUSS IT TODAY! DRIVING THROUGH THIS CITY MAKES MY SKIN CRAWL!
BUT CURT'S SANE NOW. I'M SURE HE'LL TAKE CARE OF US...!

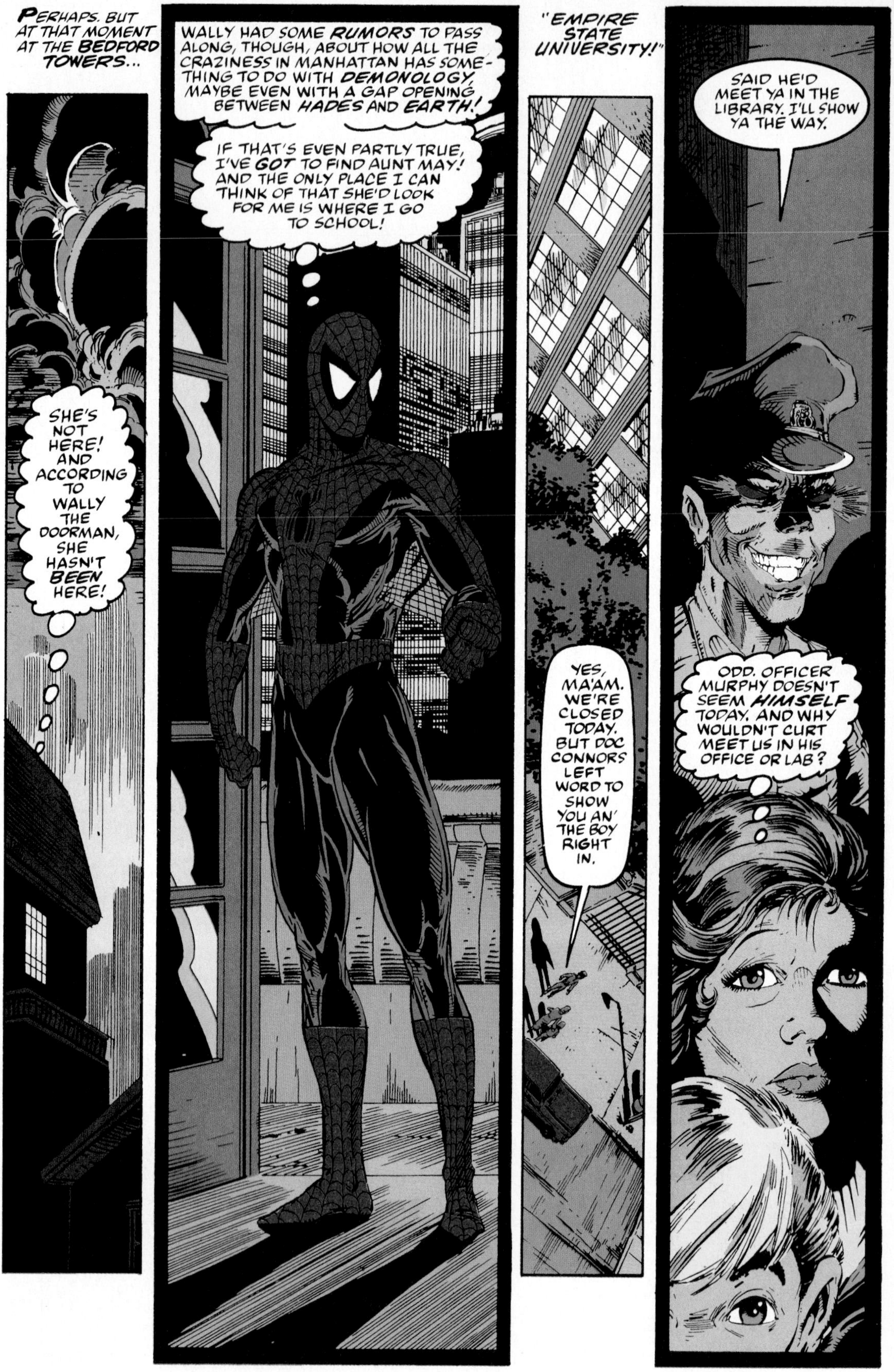
PERHAPS. BUT AT THAT MOMENT AT THE BEDFORD TOWERS...
SHE'S NOT HERE! AND ACCORDING TO WALLY THE DOORMAN, SHE HASN'T BEEN HERE!
WALLY HAD SOME RUMORS TO PASS ALONG, THOUGH, ABOUT HOW ALL THE CRAZINESS IN MANHATTAN HAS SOMETHING TO DO WITH DEMONOLOGY, MAYBE EVEN WITH A GAP OPENING BETWEEN HADES AND EARTH!
IF THAT'S EVEN PARTLY TRUE, I'VE GOT TO FIND AUNT MAY! AND THE ONLY PLACE I CAN THINK OF THAT SHE'D LOOK FOR ME IS WHERE I GO TO SCHOOL!
"EMPIRE STATE UNIVERSITY!"
YES, MA'AM. WE'RE CLOSED TODAY. BUT DOC CONNORS LEFT WORD TO SHOW YOU AN' THE BOY RIGHT IN.
SAID HE'D MEET YA IN THE LIBRARY. I'LL SHOW YA THE WAY.
ODD. OFFICER MURPHY DOESN'T SEEM HIMSELF TODAY. AND WHY WOULDN'T CURT MEET US IN HIS OFFICE OR LAB?

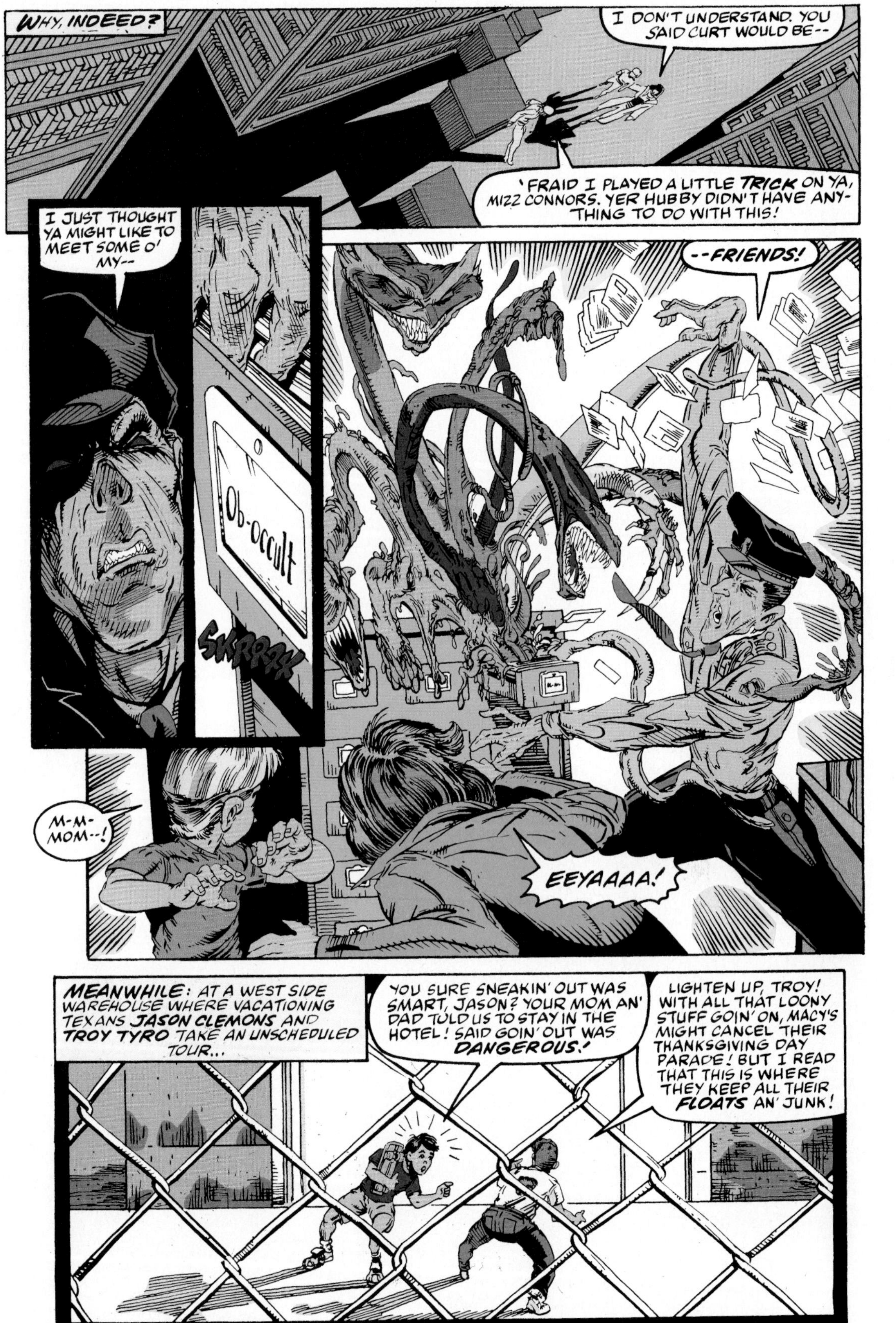
WHY, INDEED?
I DON'T UNDERSTAND. YOU SAID CURT WOULD BE--
'FRAID I PLAYED A LITTLE TRICK ON YA, MIZZ CONNORS. YER HUBBY DIDN'T HAVE ANYTHING TO DO WITH THIS!
I JUST THOUGHT YA MIGHT LIKE TO MEET SOME O' MY--
Ob-occult
SKROOK
--FRIENDS!
M-M-MOM--!
EEYAAAA!
MEANWHILE: AT A WEST SIDE WAREHOUSE WHERE VACATIONING TEXANS JASON CLEMONS AND TROY TYRO TAKE AN UNSCHEDULED TOUR...
YOU SURE SNEAKIN' OUT WAS SMART, JASON? YOUR MOM AN' DAD TOLD US TO STAY IN THE HOTEL! SAID GOIN' OUT WAS DANGEROUS!
LIGHTEN UP, TROY! WITH ALL THAT LOONY STUFF GOIN' ON, MACY'S MIGHT CANCEL THEIR THANKSGIVING DAY PARADE! BUT I READ THAT THIS IS WHERE THEY KEEP ALL THEIR FLOATS AN' JUNK!

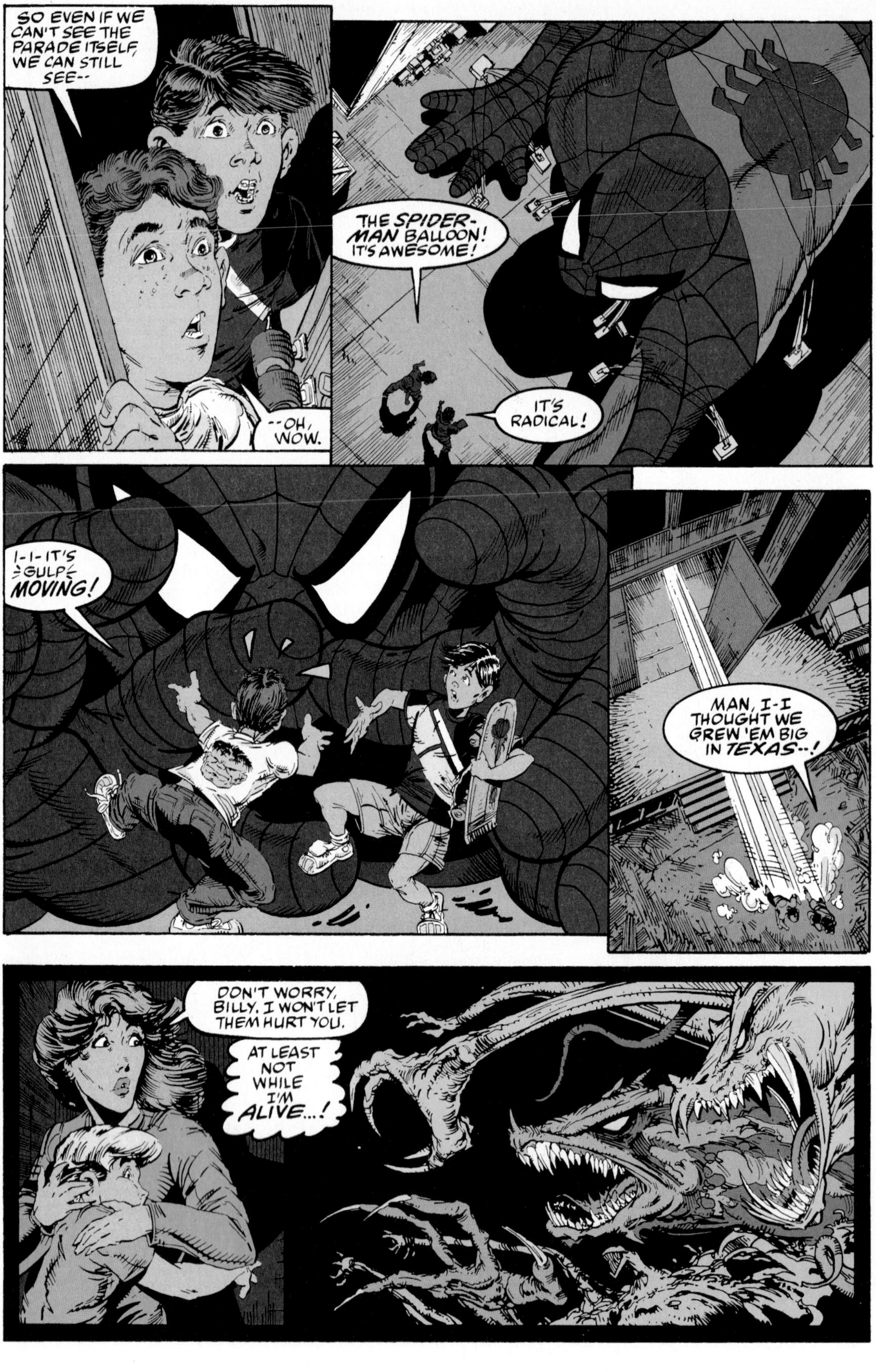
SO EVEN IF WE CAN'T SEE THE PARADE ITSELF, WE CAN STILL SEE--
--OH, WOW.
THE SPIDER-MAN BALLOON! IT'S AWESOME!
IT'S RADICAL!
I-I-IT'S ≥GULP≤ MOVING!
MAN, I-I THOUGHT WE GREW 'EM BIG IN TEXAS--!
DON'T WORRY, BILLY. I WON'T LET THEM HURT YOU.
AT LEAST NOT WHILE I'M ALIVE...!

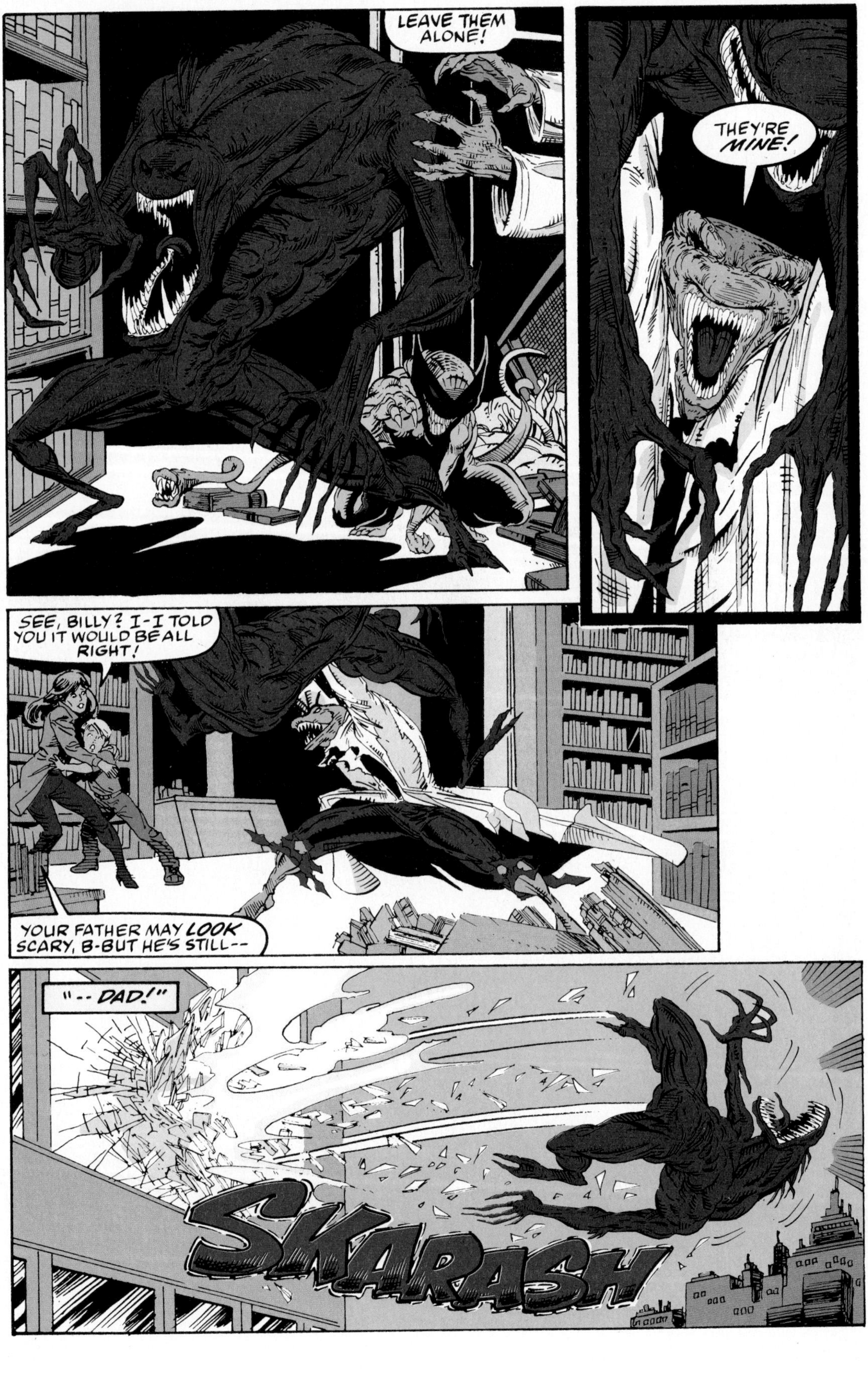

LEAVE THEM ALONE!
THEY'RE MINE!
SEE, BILLY? I-I TOLD YOU IT WOULD BE ALL RIGHT!
YOUR FATHER MAY LOOK SCARY, B-BUT HE'S STILL--
"--DAD!"
SKARASH

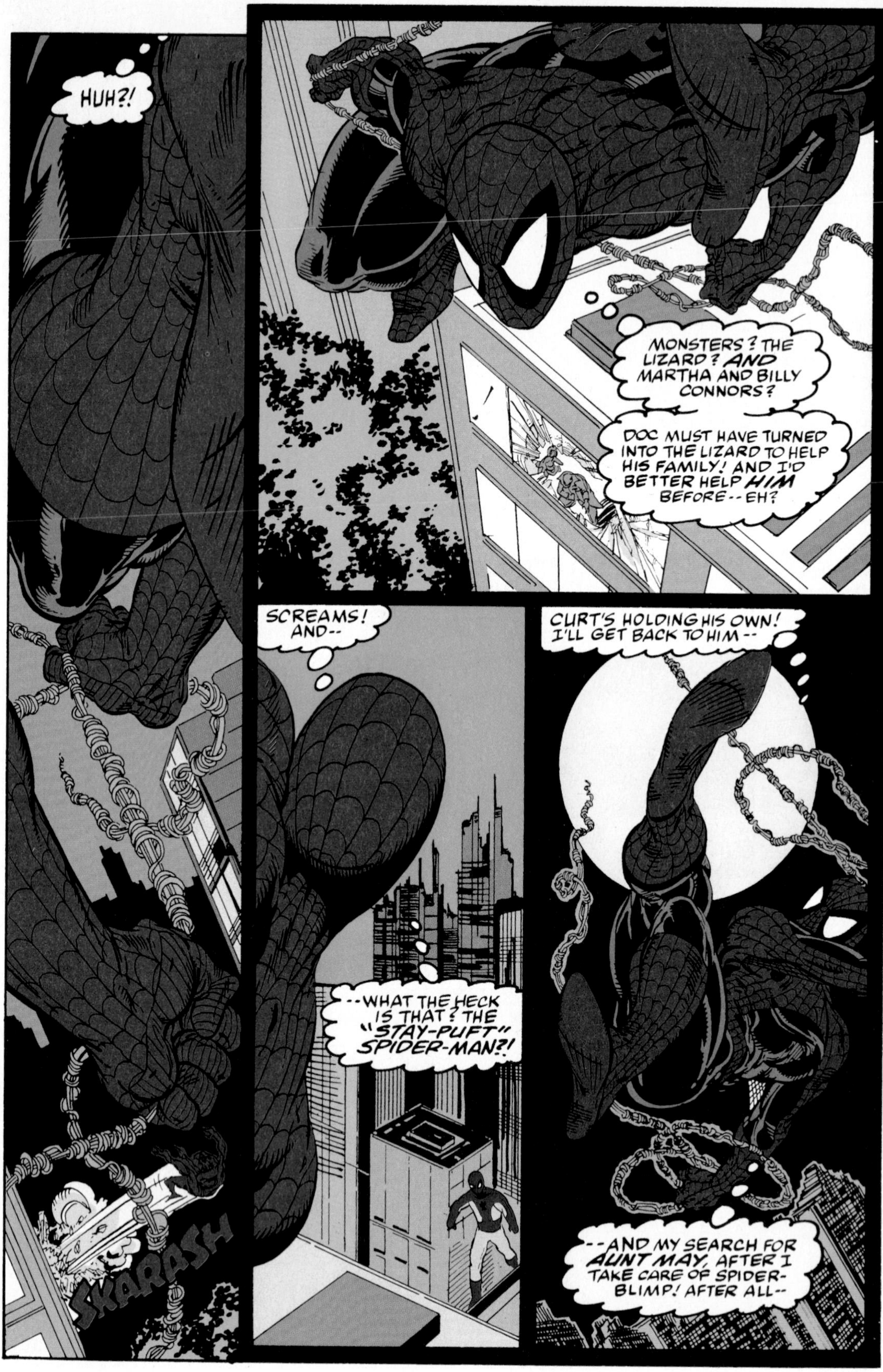
HUH?!
SKARASH
MONSTERS? THE LIZARD? AND MARTHA AND BILLY CONNORS?
DOC MUST HAVE TURNED INTO THE LIZARD TO HELP HIS FAMILY! AND I'D BETTER HELP HIM BEFORE--EH?
SCREAMS! AND--
--WHAT THE HECK IS THAT? THE "STAY-PUFT" SPIDER-MAN?!
CURT'S HOLDING HIS OWN! I'LL GET BACK TO HIM--
--AND MY SEARCH FOR AUNT MAY, AFTER I TAKE CARE OF SPIDER-BLIMP! AFTER ALL--

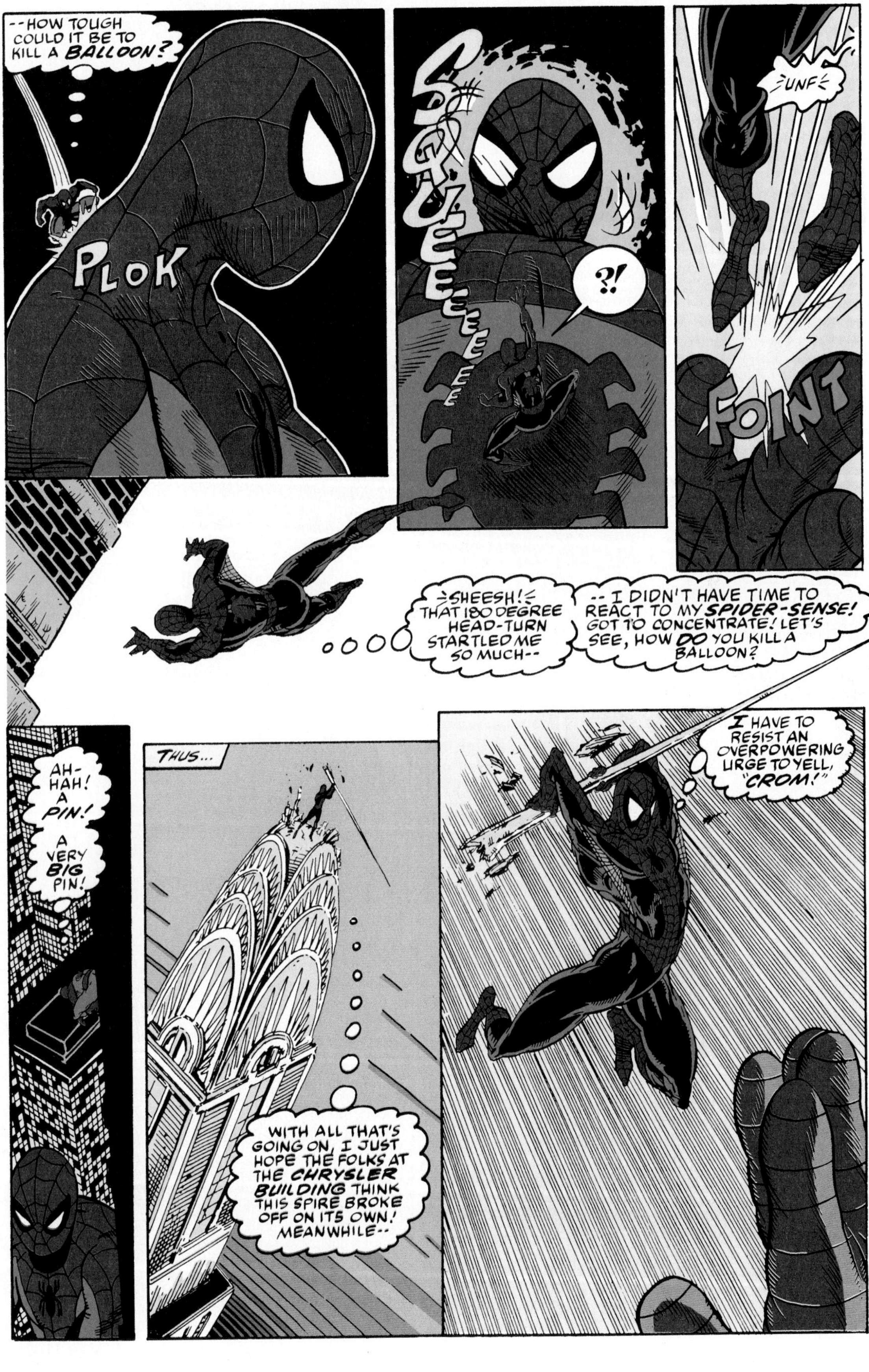
--HOW TOUGH COULD IT BE TO KILL A BALLOON?
PLOK
SQUEEEEEEEE
?!
UNF
FOINT
SHEESH! THAT 180 DEGREE HEAD-TURN STARTLED ME SO MUCH--
-- I DIDN'T HAVE TIME TO REACT TO MY SPIDER-SENSE! GOT TO CONCENTRATE! LET'S SEE, HOW DO YOU KILL A BALLOON?
AH-HAH! A PIN! A VERY BIG PIN!
THUS...
WITH ALL THAT'S GOING ON, I JUST HOPE THE FOLKS AT THE CHRYSLER BUILDING THINK THIS SPIRE BROKE OFF ON ITS OWN! MEANWHILE--
I HAVE TO RESIST AN OVERPOWERING URGE TO YELL, "CROM!"

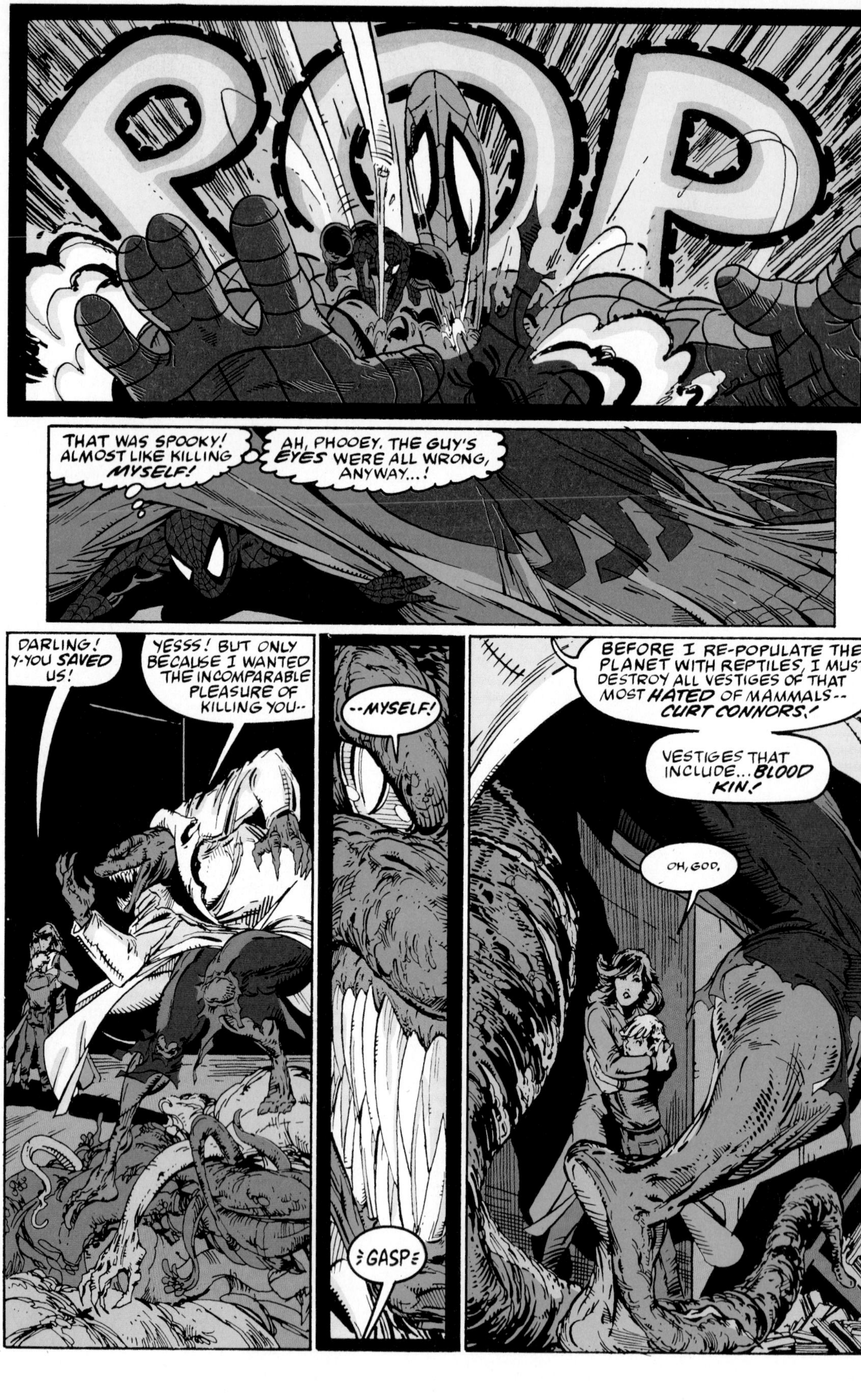
POP
THAT WAS SPOOKY! ALMOST LIKE KILLING MYSELF!
AH, PHOOEY. THE GUY'S EYES WERE ALL WRONG, ANYWAY...!
DARLING! Y-YOU SAVED US!
YESSS! BUT ONLY BECAUSE I WANTED THE INCOMPARABLE PLEASURE OF KILLING YOU--
--MYSELF!
GASP
BEFORE I RE-POPULATE THE PLANET WITH REPTILES, I MUST DESTROY ALL VESTIGES OF THAT MOST HATED OF MAMMALS-- CURT CONNORS!
VESTIGES THAT INCLUDE... BLOOD KIN!
OH, GOD.

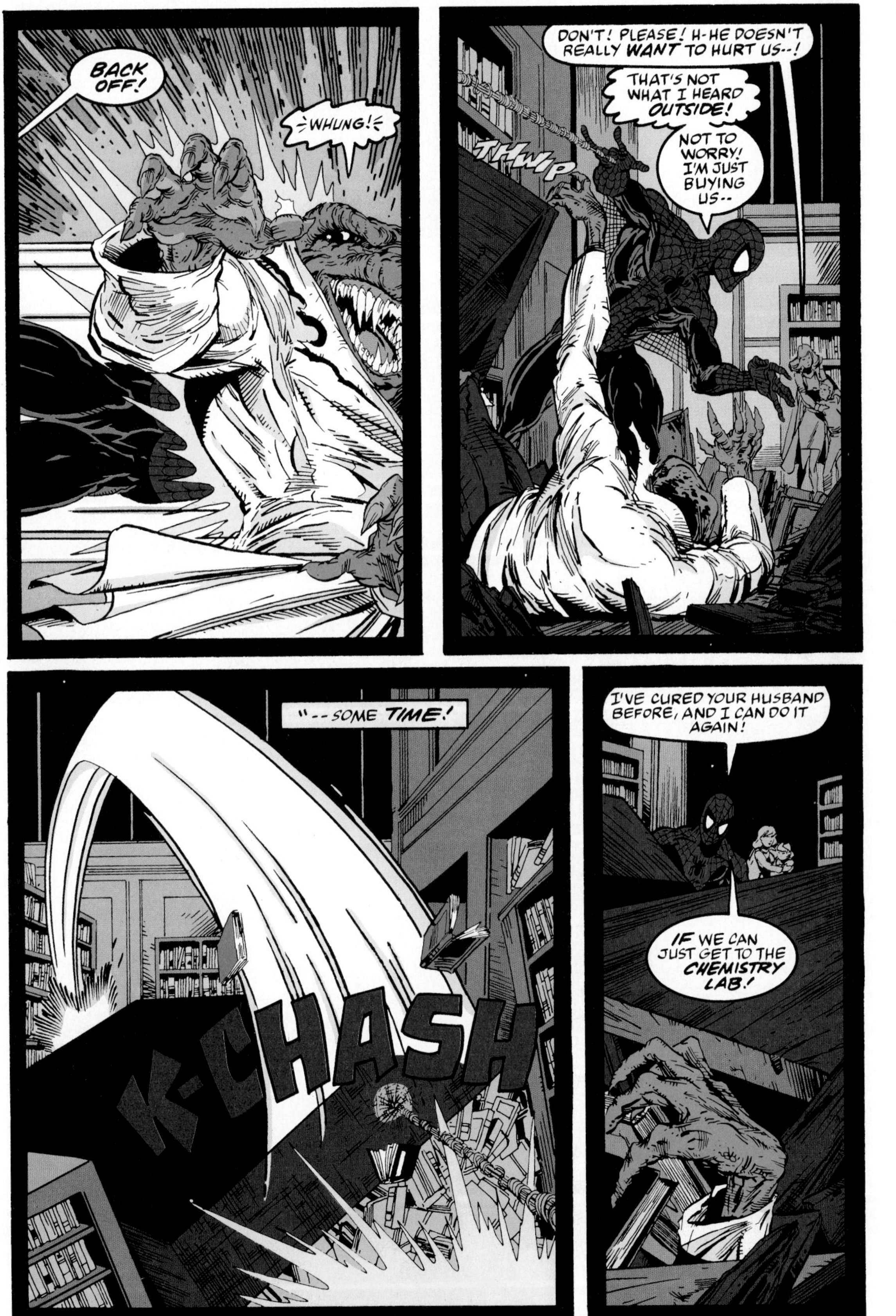

BACK OFF!
WHUNG!
DON'T! PLEASE! H-HE DOESN'T REALLY WANT TO HURT US--!
THAT'S NOT WHAT I HEARD OUTSIDE!
THWIP
NOT TO WORRY! I'M JUST BUYING US--
"--SOME TIME!
K-CHASH
I'VE CURED YOUR HUSBAND BEFORE, AND I CAN DO IT AGAIN!
IF WE CAN JUST GET TO THE CHEMISTRY LAB!

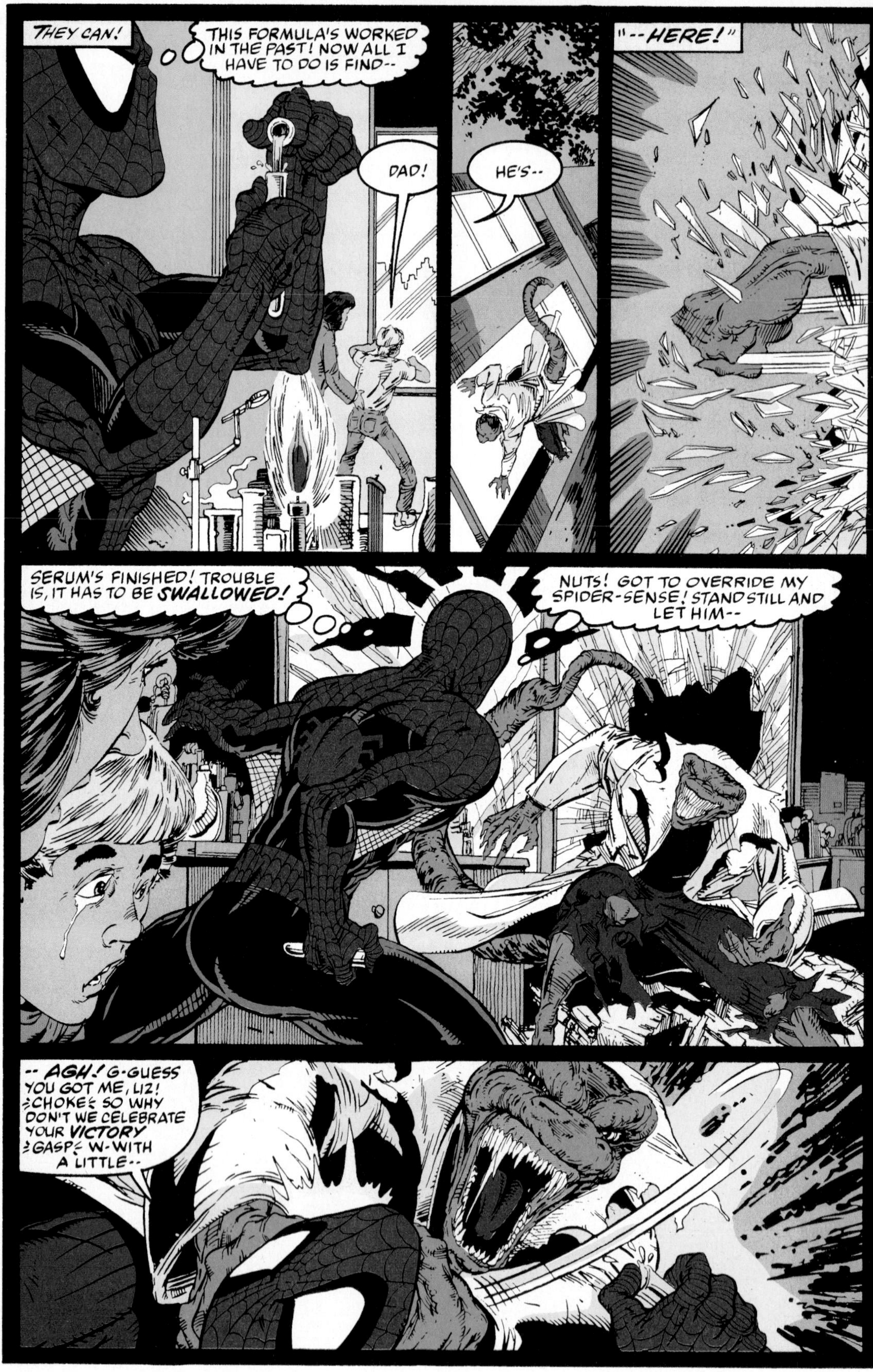
THEY CAN!
THIS FORMULA'S WORKED IN THE PAST! NOW ALL I HAVE TO DO IS FIND--
DAD!
HE'S--
"--HERE!"
SERUM'S FINISHED! TROUBLE IS, IT HAS TO BE SWALLOWED!
NUTS! GOT TO OVERRIDE MY SPIDER-SENSE! STAND STILL AND LET HIM--
--AGH! G-GUESS YOU GOT ME, LIZ! ≥CHOKE≤ SO WHY DON'T WE CELEBRATE YOUR VICTORY ≥GASP≤ W-WITH A LITTLE--

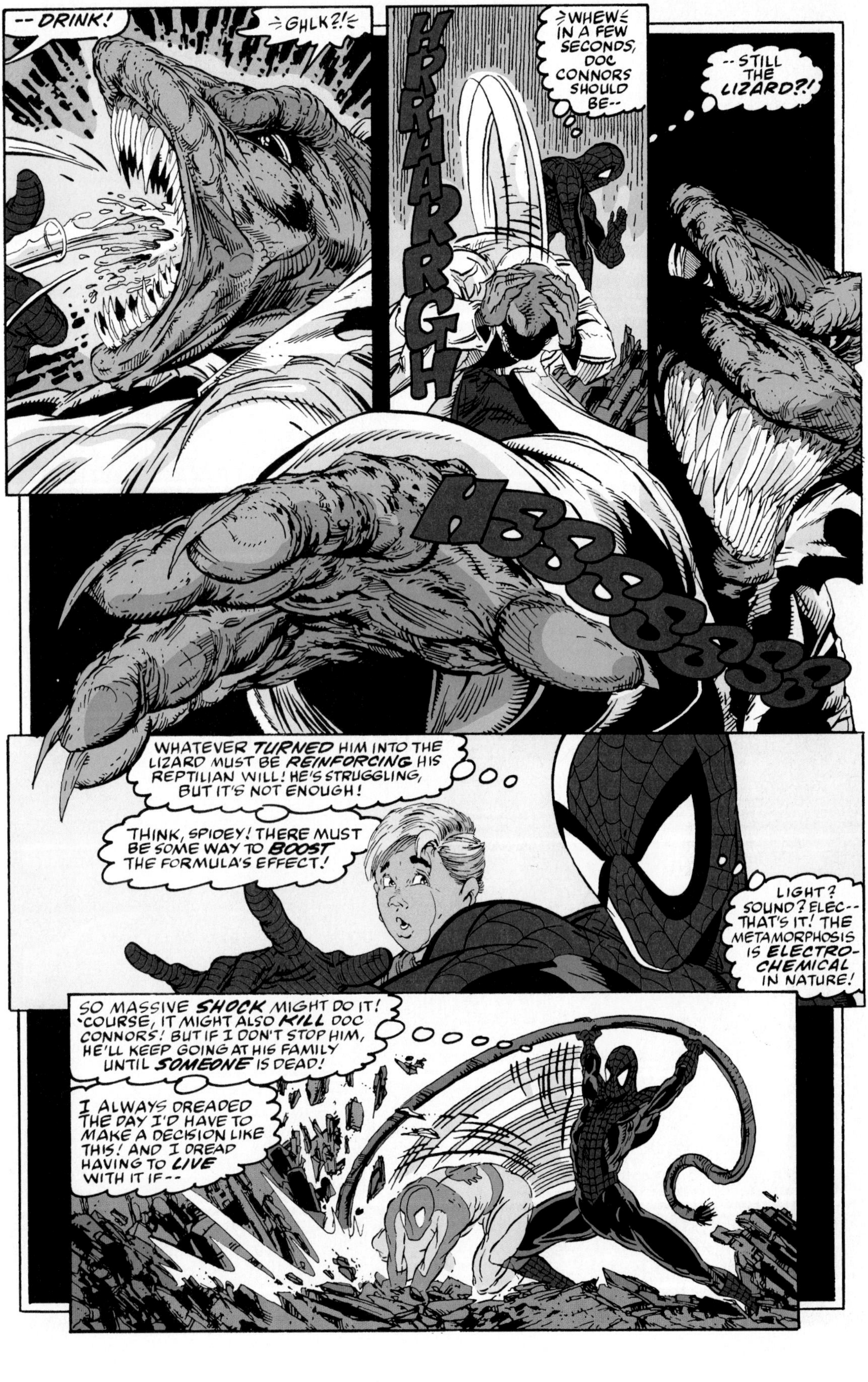
-- DRINK!
GHLK?!
HRRAARRGH
WHEW IN A FEW SECONDS, DOC CONNORS SHOULD BE--
-- STILL THE LIZARD?!
HSSSSSSSSS
WHATEVER TURNED HIM INTO THE LIZARD MUST BE REINFORCING HIS REPTILIAN WILL! HE'S STRUGGLING, BUT IT'S NOT ENOUGH!
THINK, SPIDEY! THERE MUST BE SOME WAY TO BOOST THE FORMULA'S EFFECT!
LIGHT? SOUND? ELEC-- THAT'S IT! THE METAMORPHOSIS IS ELECTRO-CHEMICAL IN NATURE!
SO MASSIVE SHOCK MIGHT DO IT! 'COURSE, IT MIGHT ALSO KILL DOC CONNORS! BUT IF I DON'T STOP HIM, HE'LL KEEP GOING AT HIS FAMILY UNTIL SOMEONE IS DEAD!
I ALWAYS DREADED THE DAY I'D HAVE TO MAKE A DECISION LIKE THIS! AND I DREAD HAVING TO LIVE WITH IT IF--

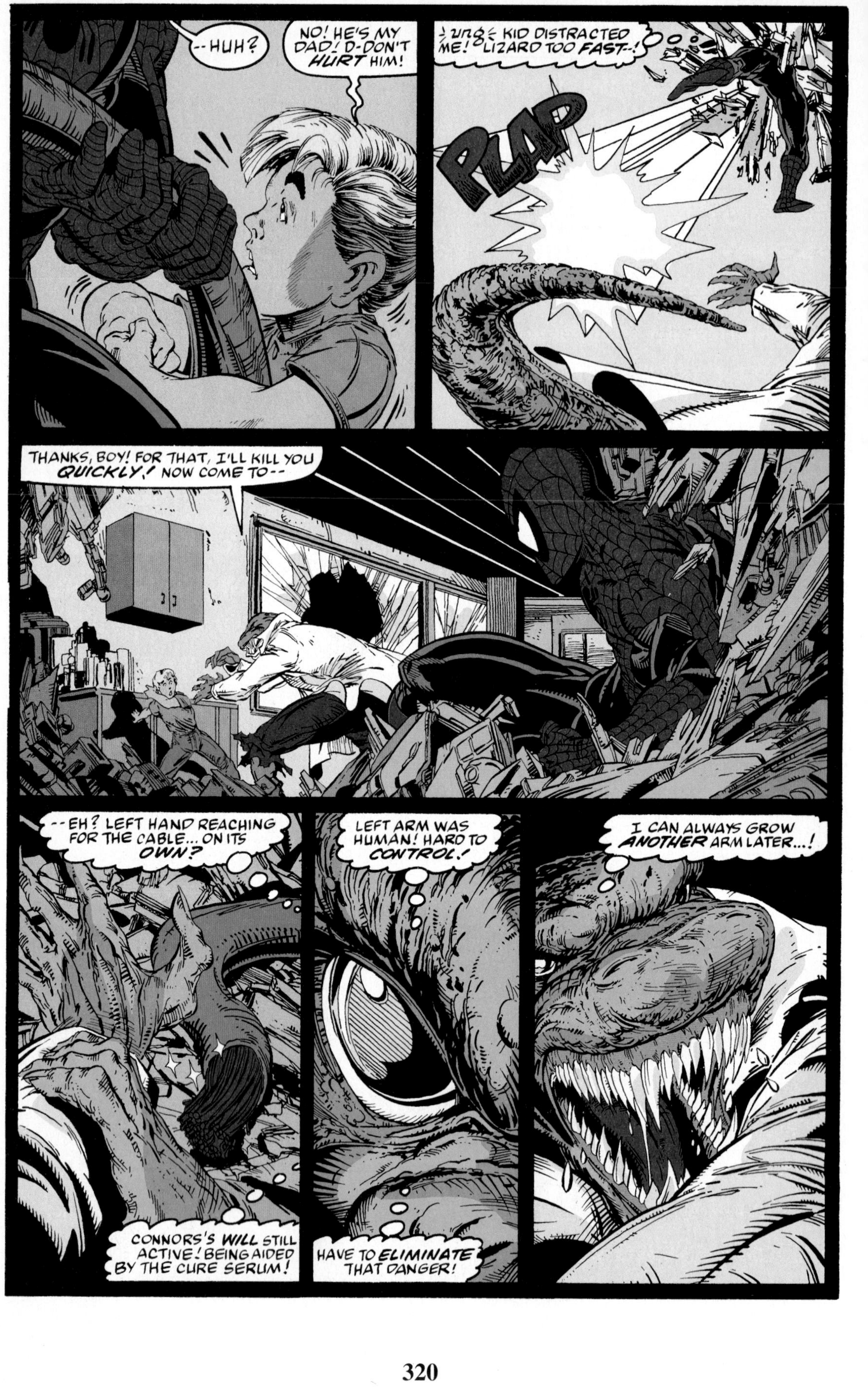

--HUH?
NO! HE'S MY DAD! D-DON'T HURT HIM!
ung KID DISTRACTED ME! LIZARD TOO FAST--!
PLAP
THANKS, BOY! FOR THAT, I'LL KILL YOU QUICKLY! NOW COME TO--
--EH? LEFT HAND REACHING FOR THE CABLE... ON ITS OWN?
CONNORS'S WILL STILL ACTIVE! BEING AIDED BY THE CURE SERUM!
LEFT ARM WAS HUMAN! HARD TO CONTROL!
HAVE TO ELIMINATE THAT DANGER!
I CAN ALWAYS GROW ANOTHER ARM LATER...!

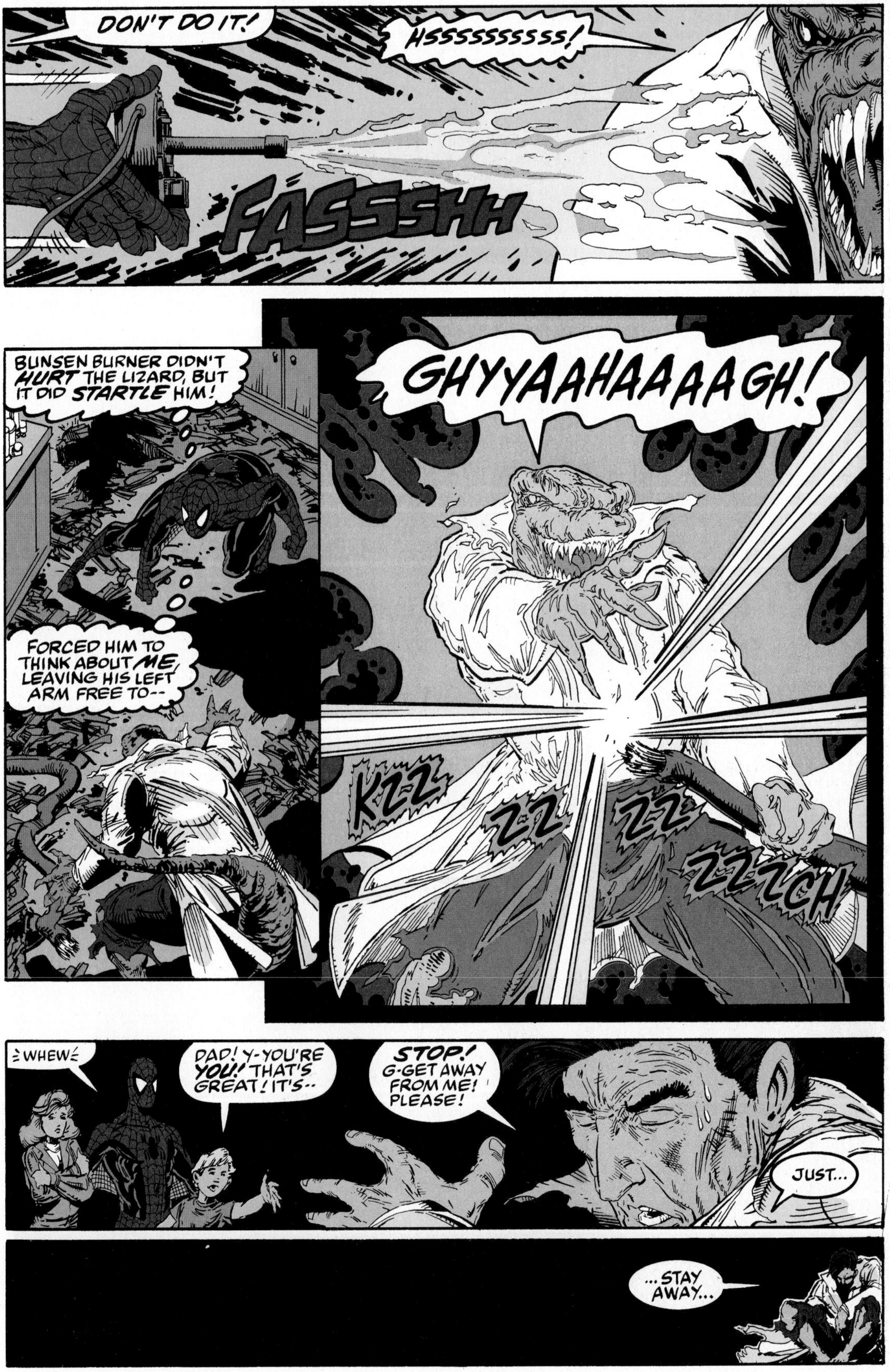
DON'T DO IT!
HSSSSSSSSSS!
FASSSHH
BUNSEN BURNER DIDN'T HURT THE LIZARD, BUT IT DID STARTLE HIM!
FORCED HIM TO THINK ABOUT ME, LEAVING HIS LEFT ARM FREE TO--
GHYYAAHAAAAAGH!
KZZ
ZZ
ZZ
ZZZCH
WHEW
DAD! Y-YOU'RE YOU! THAT'S GREAT! IT'S--
STOP! G-GET AWAY FROM ME! PLEASE!
JUST...
...STAY AWAY...

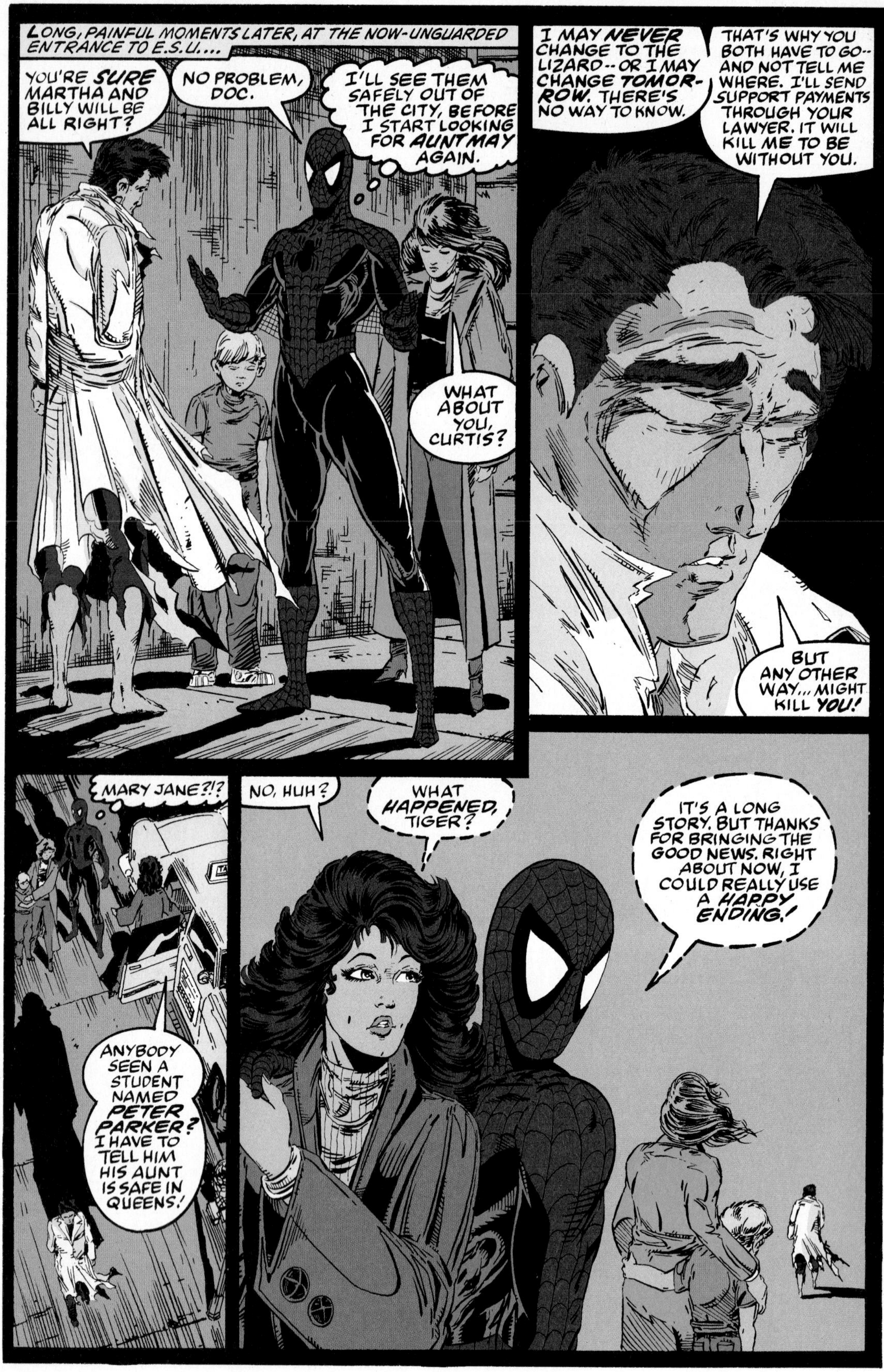
LONG, PAINFUL MOMENTS LATER, AT THE NOW-UNGUARDED ENTRANCE TO E.S.U....
YOU'RE SURE MARTHA AND BILLY WILL BE ALL RIGHT?
NO PROBLEM, DOC.
I'LL SEE THEM SAFELY OUT OF THE CITY, BEFORE I START LOOKING FOR AUNT MAY AGAIN.
WHAT ABOUT YOU, CURTIS?
I MAY NEVER CHANGE TO THE LIZARD -- OR I MAY CHANGE TOMORROW. THERE'S NO WAY TO KNOW.
THAT'S WHY YOU BOTH HAVE TO GO-- AND NOT TELL ME WHERE. I'LL SEND SUPPORT PAYMENTS THROUGH YOUR LAWYER. IT WILL KILL ME TO BE WITHOUT YOU.
BUT ANY OTHER WAY... MIGHT KILL YOU!
MARY JANE?!?
ANYBODY SEEN A STUDENT NAMED PETER PARKER? I HAVE TO TELL HIM HIS AUNT IS SAFE IN QUEENS!
NO, HUH?
WHAT HAPPENED, TIGER?
IT'S A LONG STORY. BUT THANKS FOR BRINGING THE GOOD NEWS. RIGHT ABOUT NOW, I COULD REALLY USE A HAPPY ENDING!

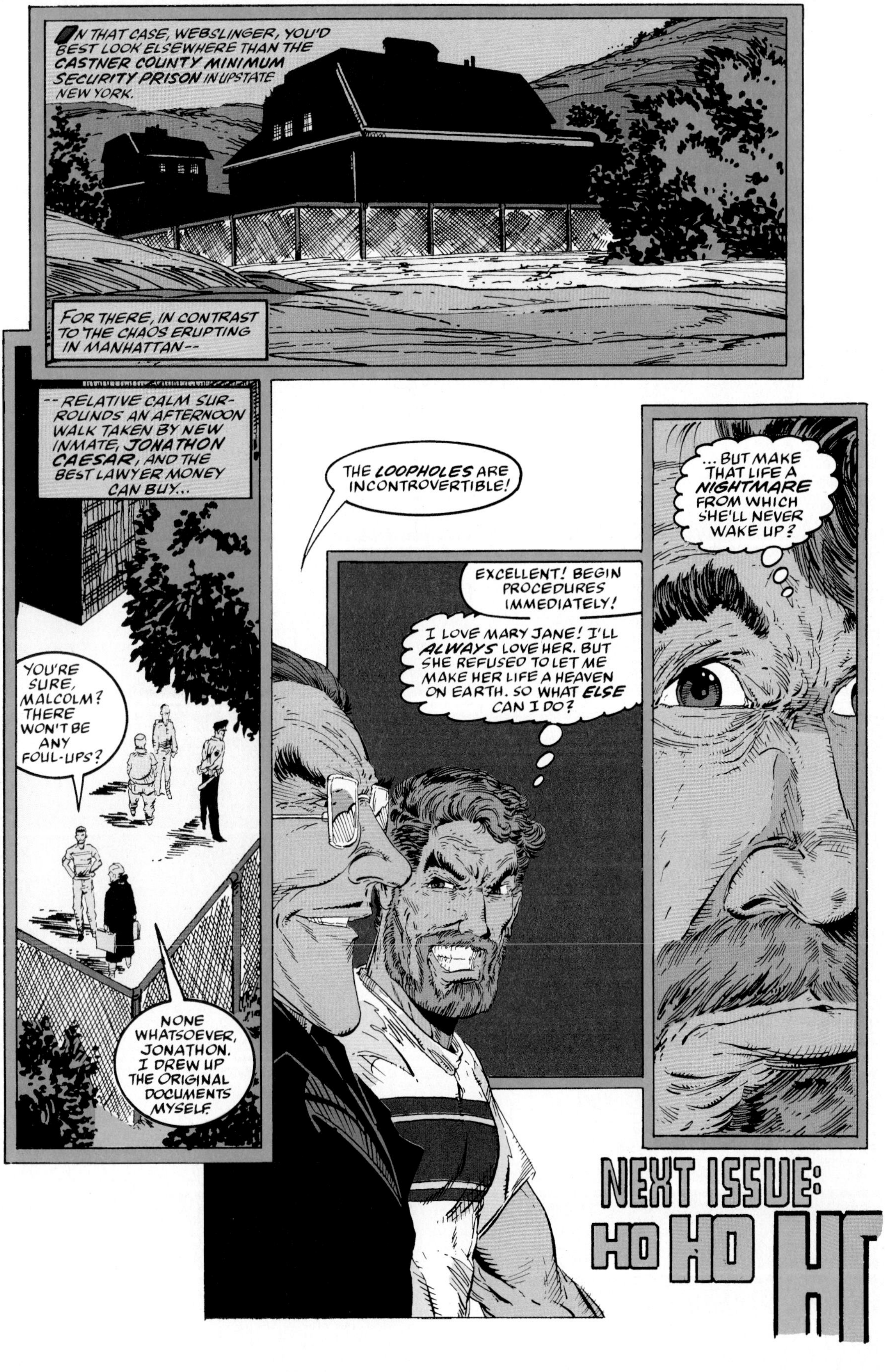

IN THAT CASE, WEBSLINGER, YOU'D BEST LOOK ELSEWHERE THAN THE CASTNER COUNTY MINIMUM SECURITY PRISON IN UPSTATE NEW YORK.
FOR THERE, IN CONTRAST TO THE CHAOS ERUPTING IN MANHATTAN--
--RELATIVE CALM SURROUNDS AN AFTERNOON WALK TAKEN BY NEW INMATE, JONATHON CAESAR, AND THE BEST LAWYER MONEY CAN BUY...
YOU'RE SURE, MALCOLM? THERE WON'T BE ANY FOUL-UPS?
NONE WHATSOEVER, JONATHON. I DREW UP THE ORIGINAL DOCUMENTS MYSELF.
THE LOOPHOLES ARE INCONTROVERTIBLE!
EXCELLENT! BEGIN PROCEDURES IMMEDIATELY!
I LOVE MARY JANE! I'LL ALWAYS LOVE HER. BUT SHE REFUSED TO LET ME MAKE HER LIFE A HEAVEN ON EARTH. SO WHAT ELSE CAN I DO?
...BUT MAKE THAT LIFE A NIGHTMARE FROM WHICH SHE'LL NEVER WAKE UP?
NEXT ISSUE:
HO HO H

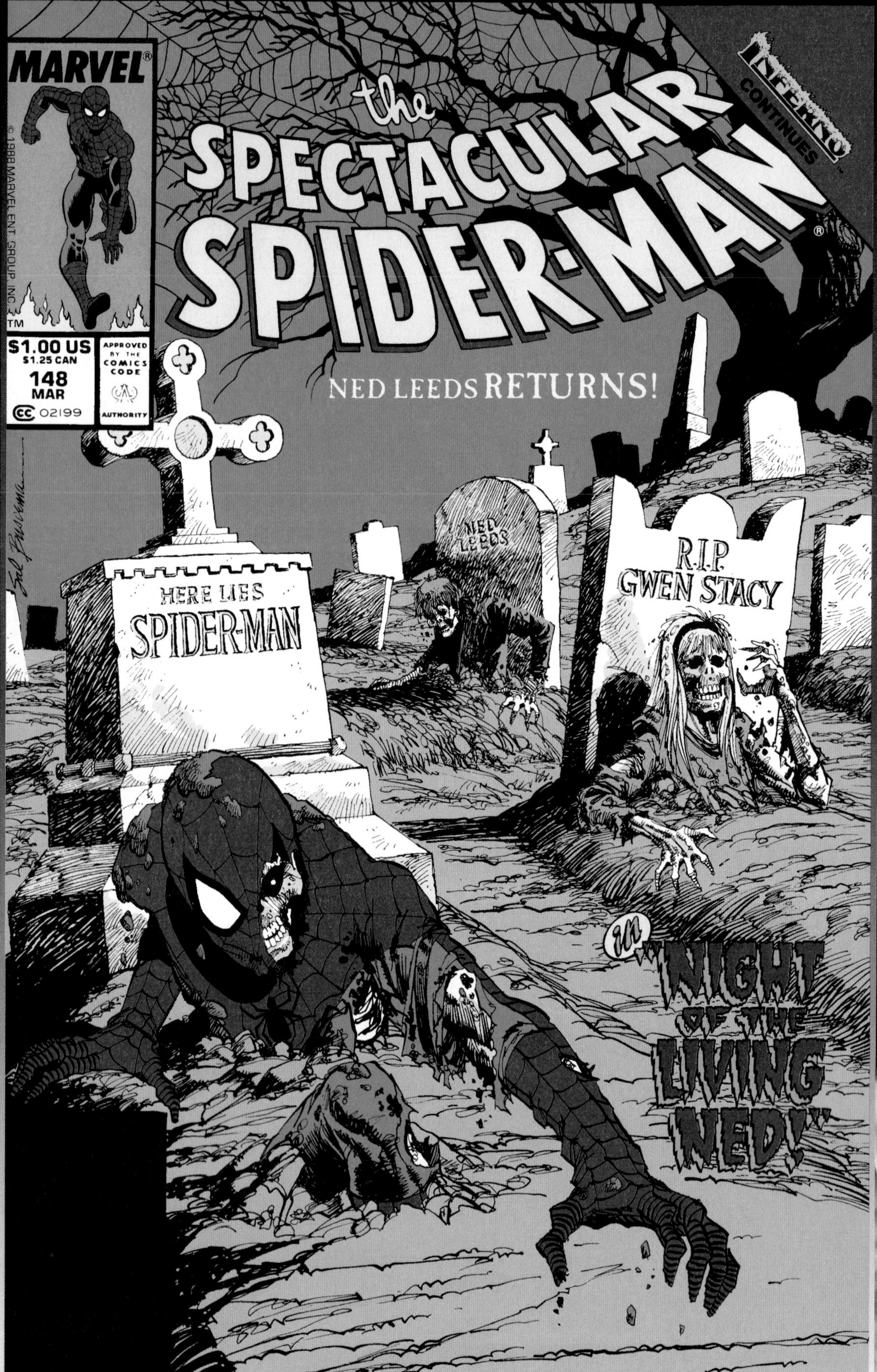
MARVEL®
© 1988 MARVEL ENT. GROUP, INC.
TM
$1.00 US
$1.25 CAN
148
MAR
CC 02199
APPROVED BY THE COMICS CODE AUTHORITY
the SPECTACULAR SPIDER-MAN®
INFERNO CONTINUES
NED LEEDS RETURNS!
HERE LIES SPIDER-MAN
NED LEEDS
R.I.P. GWEN STACY
in "NIGHT OF THE LIVING NED!"

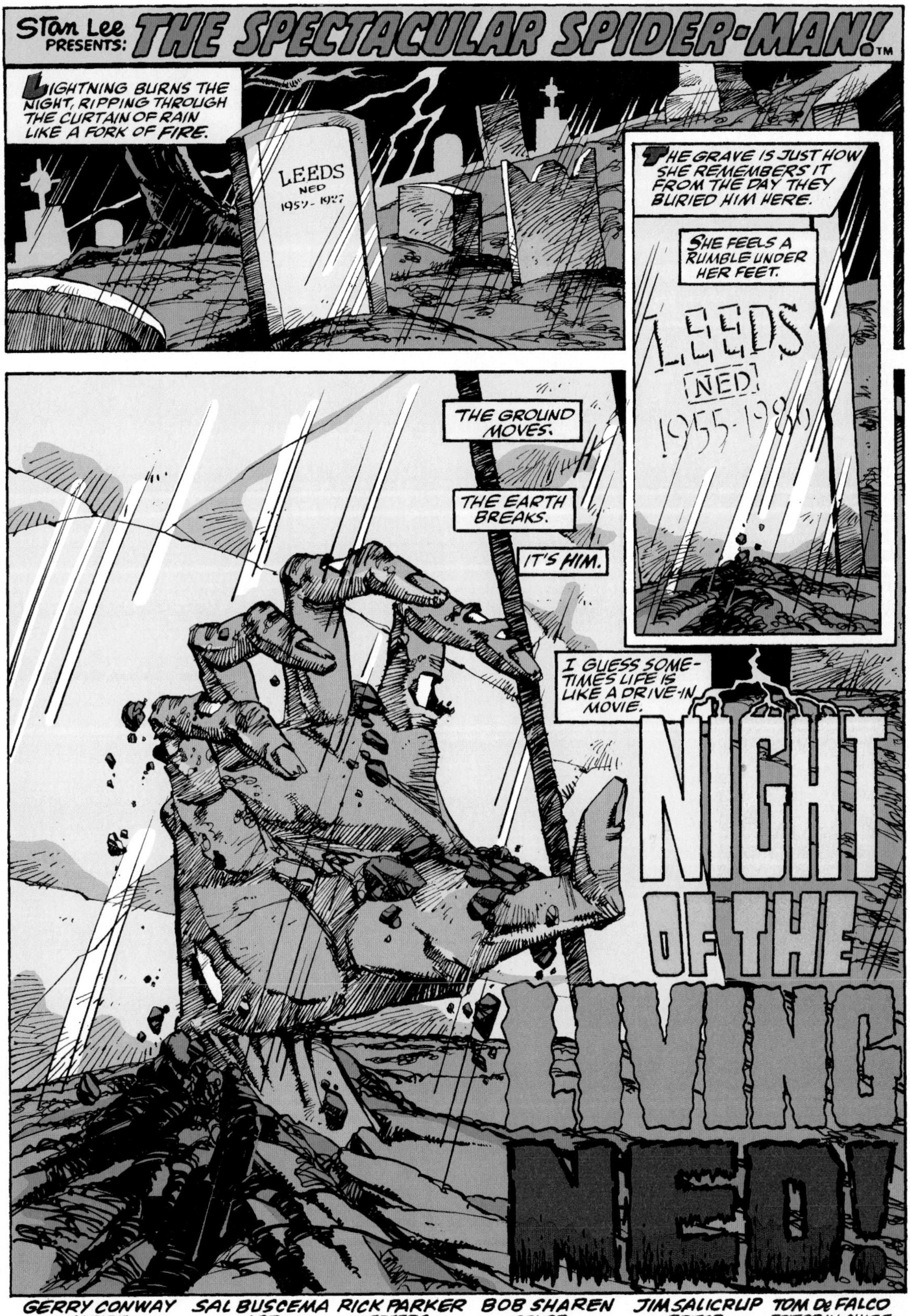
Stan Lee PRESENTS: THE SPECTACULAR SPIDER-MAN! TM
LIGHTNING BURNS THE NIGHT, RIPPING THROUGH THE CURTAIN OF RAIN LIKE A FORK OF FIRE.
LEEDS NED 1957-1987
THE GRAVE IS JUST HOW SHE REMEMBERS IT FROM THE DAY THEY BURIED HIM HERE.
SHE FEELS A RUMBLE UNDER HER FEET.
LEEDS NED 1955-1986
THE GROUND MOVES.
THE EARTH BREAKS.
IT'S HIM.
I GUESS SOMETIMES LIFE IS LIKE A DRIVE-IN MOVIE.
NIGHT OF THE LIVING NED!

GERRY CONWAY SCRIPT · SAL BUSCEMA ART · RICK PARKER LETTERS · BOB SHAREN COLOR · JIM SALICRUP EDITOR · TOM DeFALCO EDITOR IN CHIEF

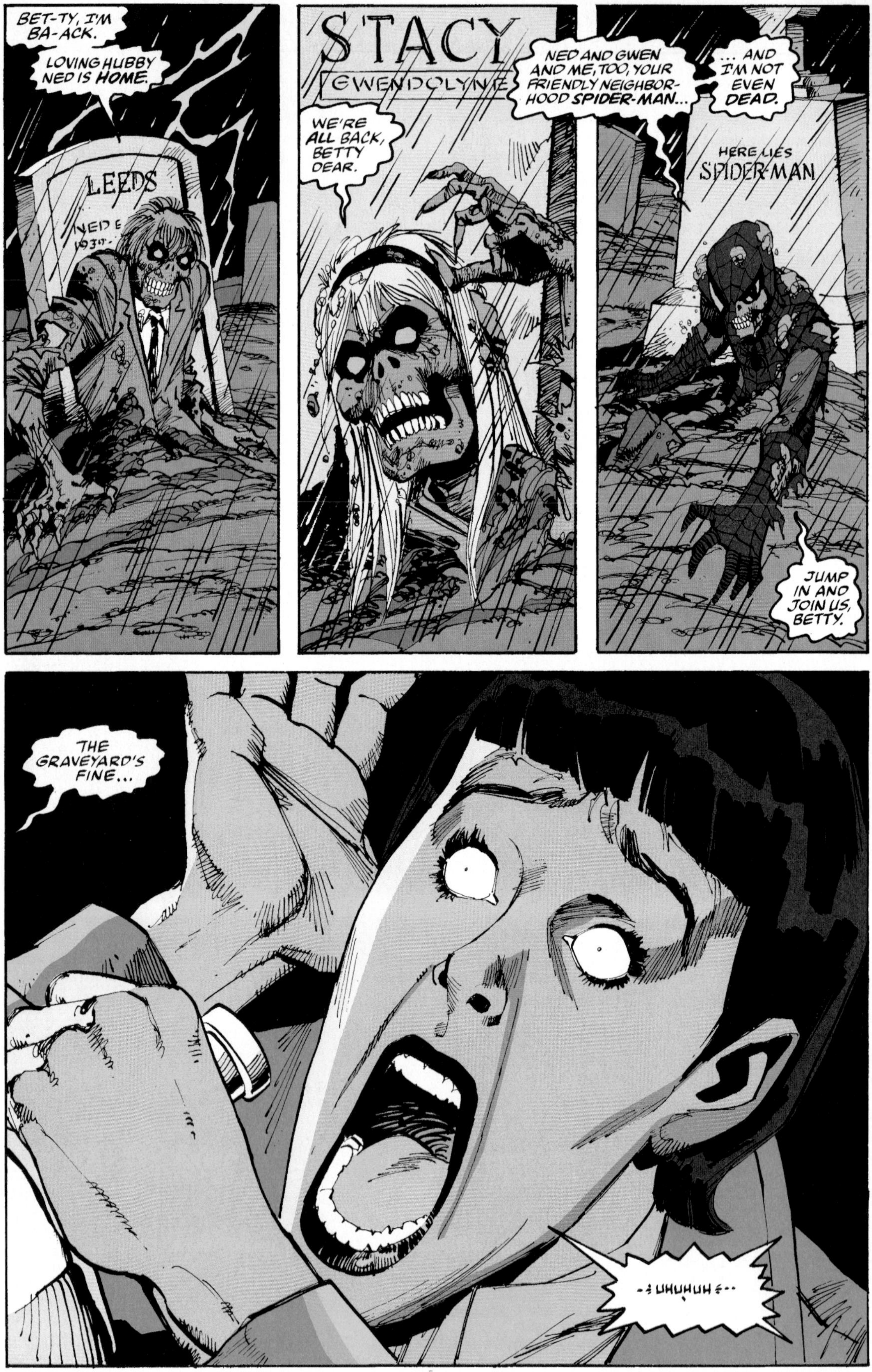
BET-TY, I'M BA-ACK.
LOVING HUBBY NED IS HOME.
LEEDS
STACY
GWENDOLYNE
WE'RE ALL BACK, BETTY DEAR.
NED AND GWEN AND ME, TOO, YOUR FRIENDLY NEIGHBOR-HOOD SPIDER-MAN...
... AND I'M NOT EVEN DEAD.
HERE LIES SPIDER-MAN
JUMP IN AND JOIN US, BETTY.
THE GRAVEYARD'S FINE...
UHUHUH

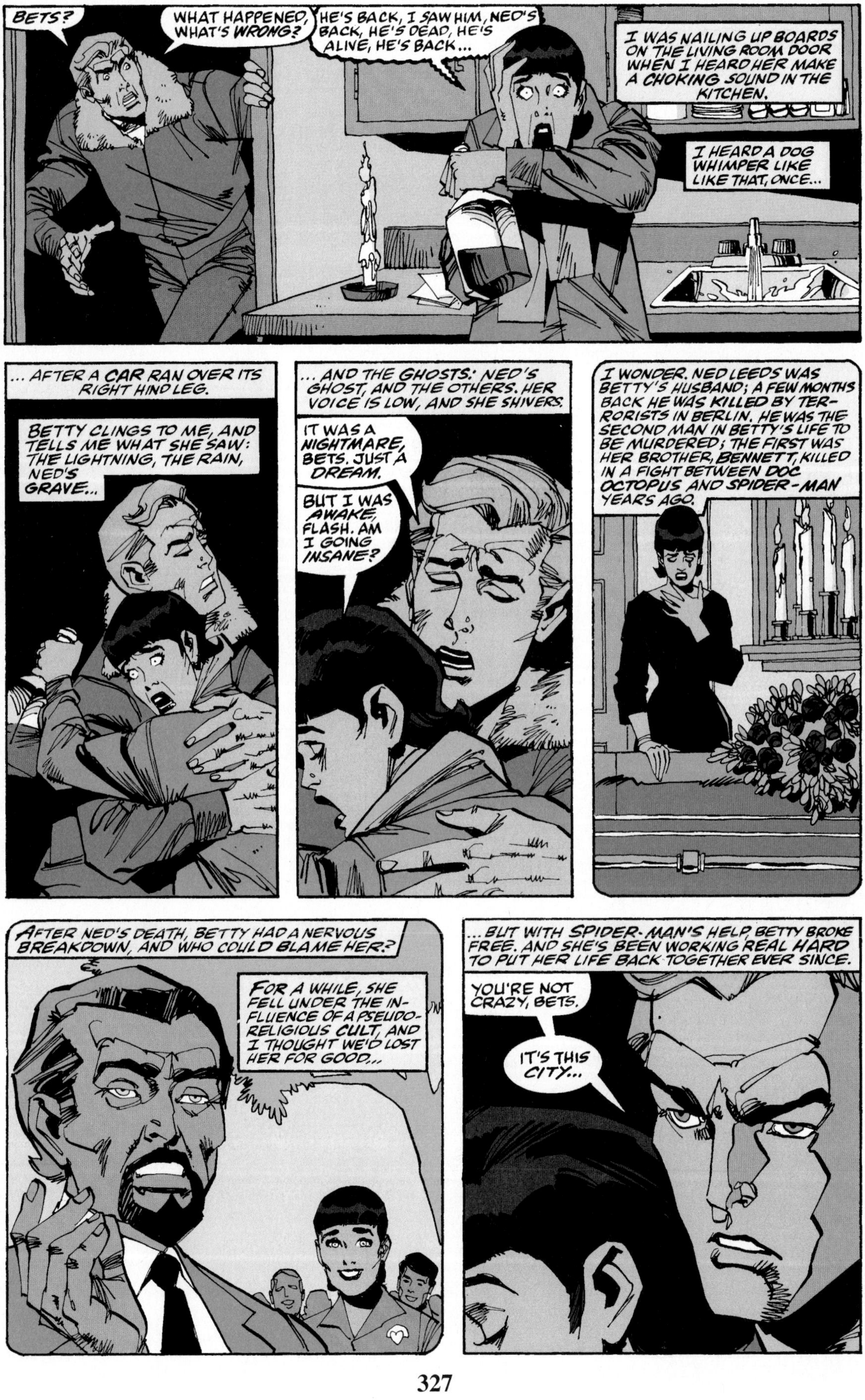
BETS?
WHAT HAPPENED, WHAT'S WRONG?
HE'S BACK, I SAW HIM, NED'S BACK, HE'S DEAD, HE'S ALIVE, HE'S BACK...
I WAS NAILING UP BOARDS ON THE LIVING ROOM DOOR WHEN I HEARD HER MAKE A CHOKING SOUND IN THE KITCHEN.
I HEARD A DOG WHIMPER LIKE LIKE THAT, ONCE...
... AFTER A CAR RAN OVER ITS RIGHT HIND LEG.
BETTY CLINGS TO ME, AND TELLS ME WHAT SHE SAW: THE LIGHTNING, THE RAIN, NED'S GRAVE...
... AND THE GHOSTS: NED'S GHOST, AND THE OTHERS. HER VOICE IS LOW, AND SHE SHIVERS.
IT WAS A NIGHTMARE, BETS. JUST A DREAM.
BUT I WAS AWAKE, FLASH. AM I GOING INSANE?
I WONDER. NED LEEDS WAS BETTY'S HUSBAND; A FEW MONTHS BACK HE WAS KILLED BY TERRORISTS IN BERLIN. HE WAS THE SECOND MAN IN BETTY'S LIFE TO BE MURDERED; THE FIRST WAS HER BROTHER, BENNETT, KILLED IN A FIGHT BETWEEN DOC OCTOPUS AND SPIDER-MAN YEARS AGO.
AFTER NED'S DEATH, BETTY HAD A NERVOUS BREAKDOWN, AND WHO COULD BLAME HER?
FOR A WHILE, SHE FELL UNDER THE INFLUENCE OF A PSEUDO-RELIGIOUS CULT, AND I THOUGHT WE'D LOST HER FOR GOOD...
... BUT WITH SPIDER-MAN'S HELP, BETTY BROKE FREE. AND SHE'S BEEN WORKING REAL HARD TO PUT HER LIFE BACK TOGETHER EVER SINCE.
YOU'RE NOT CRAZY, BETS.
IT'S THIS CITY...

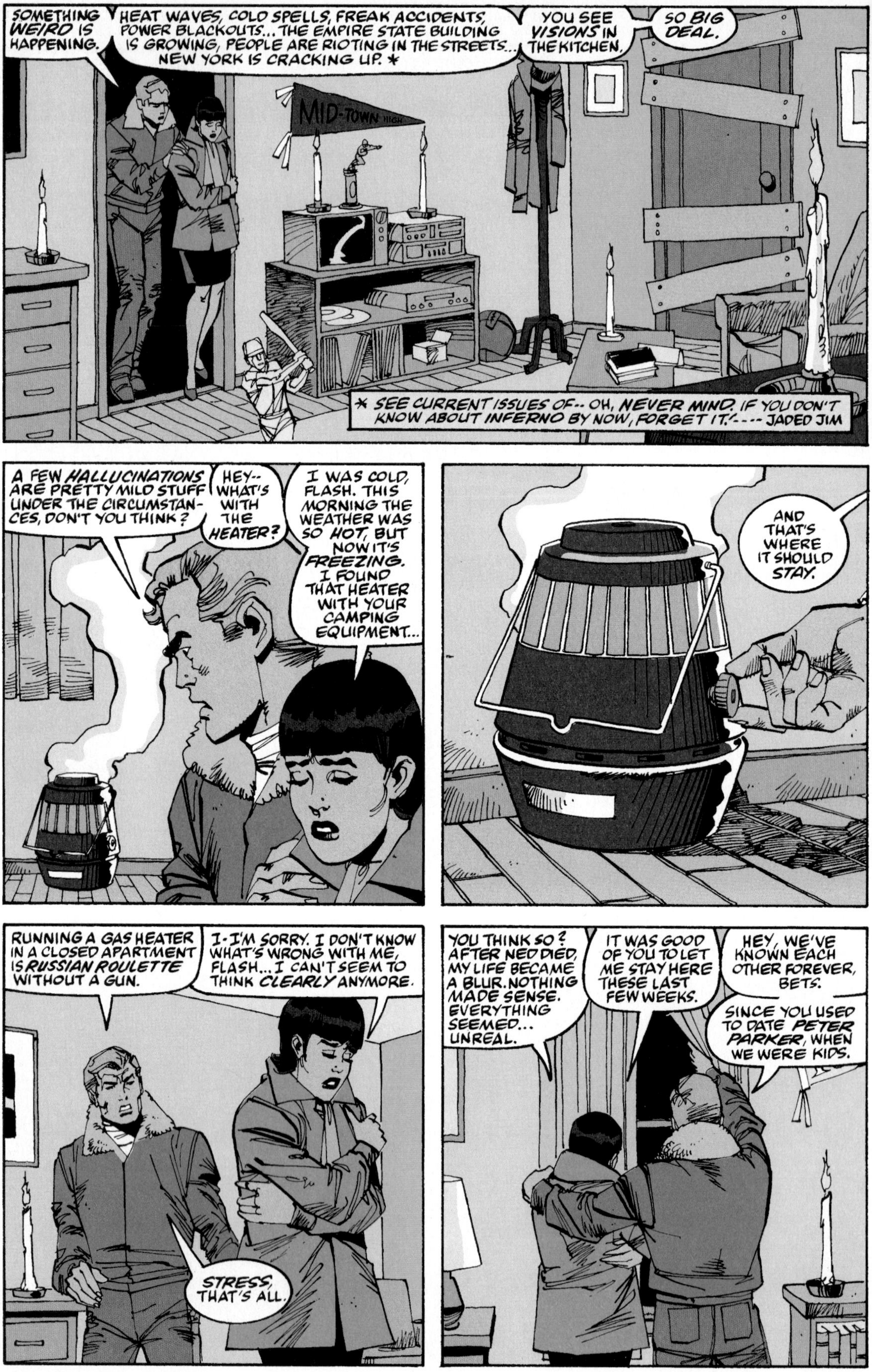
SOMETHING WEIRD IS HAPPENING.
HEAT WAVES, COLD SPELLS, FREAK ACCIDENTS, POWER BLACKOUTS... THE EMPIRE STATE BUILDING IS GROWING, PEOPLE ARE RIOTING IN THE STREETS... NEW YORK IS CRACKING UP. *
YOU SEE VISIONS IN THE KITCHEN,
SO BIG DEAL.
MID-TOWN HIGH
* SEE CURRENT ISSUES OF-- OH, NEVER MIND. IF YOU DON'T KNOW ABOUT INFERNO BY NOW, FORGET IT!---- JADED JIM
A FEW HALLUCINATIONS ARE PRETTY MILD STUFF UNDER THE CIRCUMSTANCES, DON'T YOU THINK?
HEY-- WHAT'S WITH THE HEATER?
I WAS COLD, FLASH. THIS MORNING THE WEATHER WAS SO HOT, BUT NOW IT'S FREEZING. I FOUND THAT HEATER WITH YOUR CAMPING EQUIPMENT...
AND THAT'S WHERE IT SHOULD STAY.
RUNNING A GAS HEATER IN A CLOSED APARTMENT IS RUSSIAN ROULETTE WITHOUT A GUN.
I-I'M SORRY. I DON'T KNOW WHAT'S WRONG WITH ME, FLASH... I CAN'T SEEM TO THINK CLEARLY ANYMORE.
STRESS, THAT'S ALL.
YOU THINK SO? AFTER NED DIED, MY LIFE BECAME A BLUR. NOTHING MADE SENSE. EVERYTHING SEEMED... UNREAL.
IT WAS GOOD OF YOU TO LET ME STAY HERE THESE LAST FEW WEEKS.
HEY, WE'VE KNOWN EACH OTHER FOREVER, BETS.
SINCE YOU USED TO DATE PETER PARKER, WHEN WE WERE KIDS.

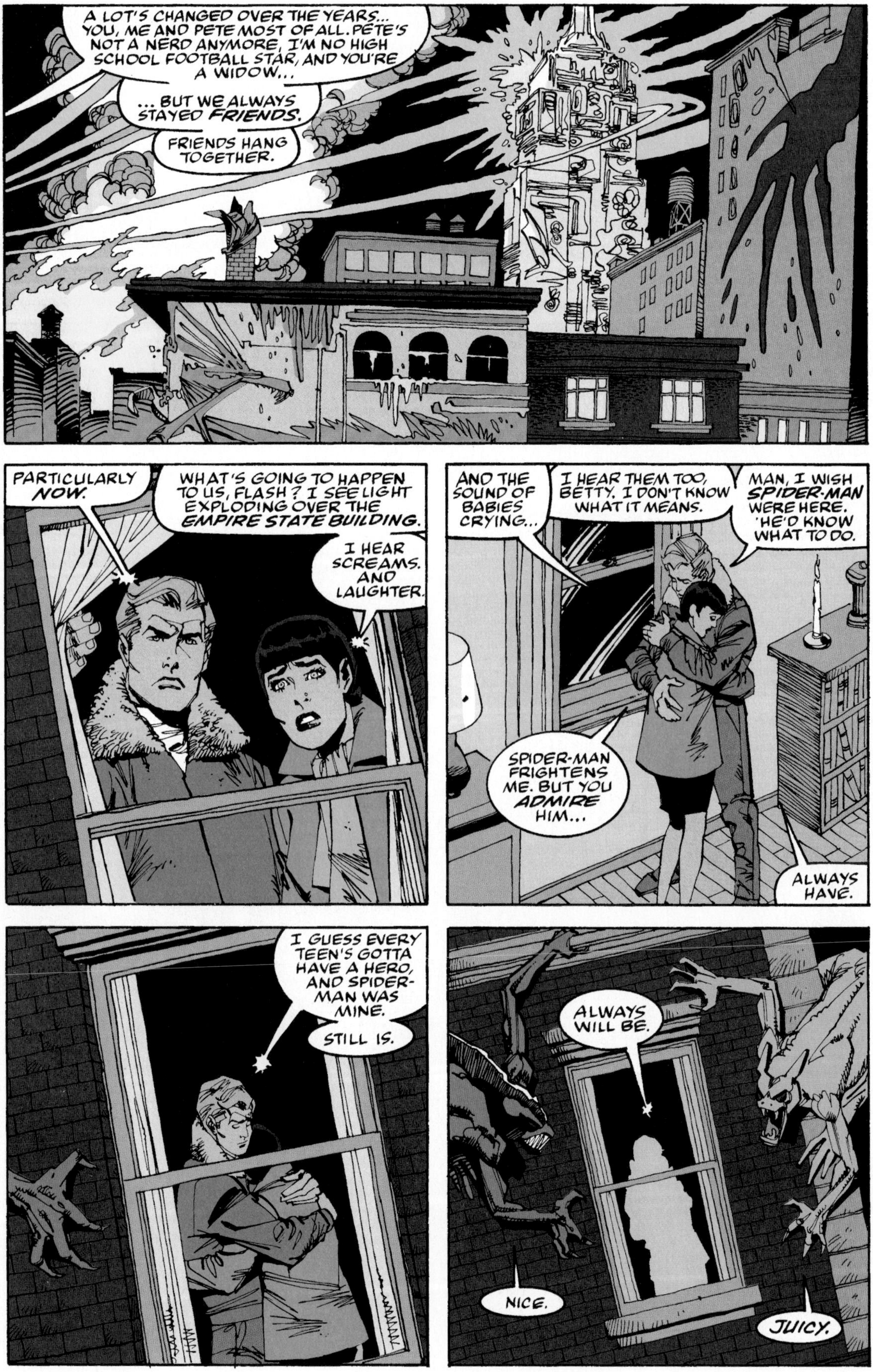
A LOT'S CHANGED OVER THE YEARS... YOU, ME AND PETE MOST OF ALL. PETE'S NOT A NERD ANYMORE, I'M NO HIGH SCHOOL FOOTBALL STAR, AND YOU'RE A WIDOW...
... BUT WE ALWAYS STAYED FRIENDS.
FRIENDS HANG TOGETHER.
PARTICULARLY NOW.
WHAT'S GOING TO HAPPEN TO US, FLASH? I SEE LIGHT EXPLODING OVER THE EMPIRE STATE BUILDING.
I HEAR SCREAMS. AND LAUGHTER.
AND THE SOUND OF BABIES CRYING...
I HEAR THEM TOO, BETTY. I DON'T KNOW WHAT IT MEANS.
MAN, I WISH SPIDER-MAN WERE HERE. 'HE'D KNOW WHAT TO DO.
SPIDER-MAN FRIGHTENS ME. BUT YOU ADMIRE HIM...
ALWAYS HAVE.
I GUESS EVERY TEEN'S GOTTA HAVE A HERO, AND SPIDER-MAN WAS MINE.
STILL IS.
ALWAYS WILL BE.
NICE.
JUICY.

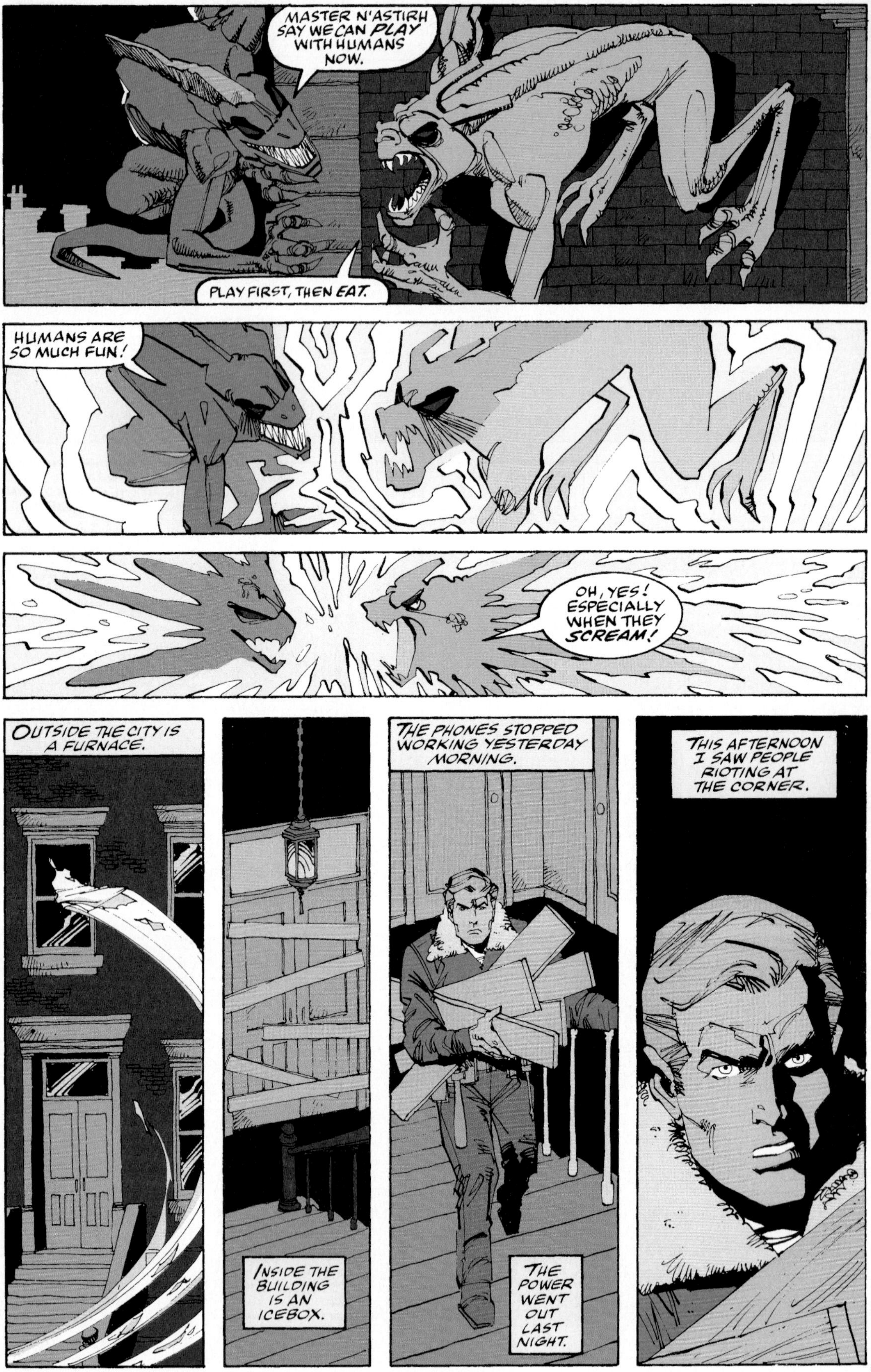
MASTER N'ASTIRH SAY WE CAN PLAY WITH HUMANS NOW.
PLAY FIRST, THEN EAT.
HUMANS ARE SO MUCH FUN!
OH, YES! ESPECIALLY WHEN THEY SCREAM!
OUTSIDE THE CITY IS A FURNACE.
INSIDE THE BUILDING IS AN ICEBOX.
THE PHONES STOPPED WORKING YESTERDAY MORNING.
THE POWER WENT OUT LAST NIGHT.
THIS AFTERNOON I SAW PEOPLE RIOTING AT THE CORNER.

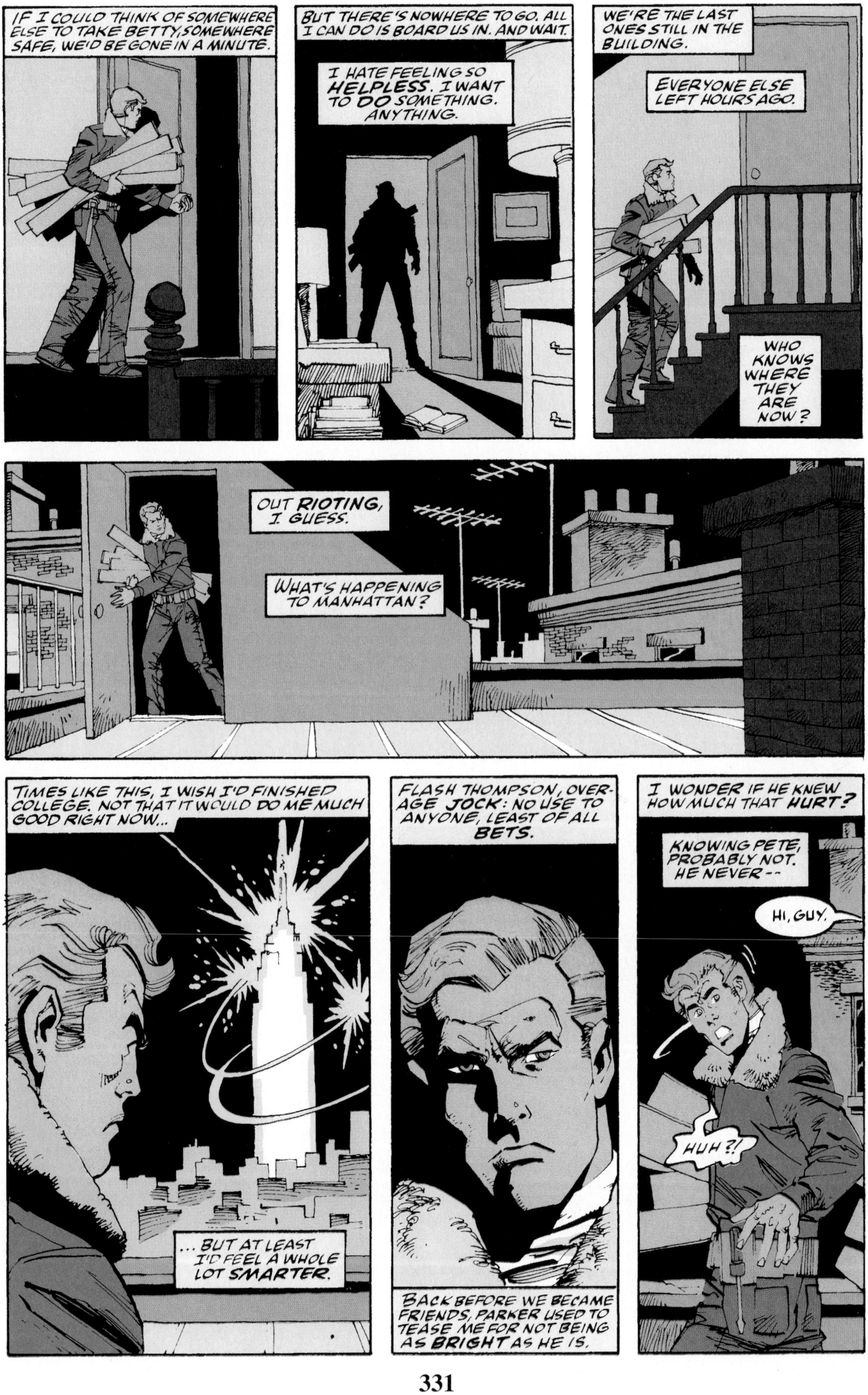
IF I COULD THINK OF SOMEWHERE ELSE TO TAKE BETTY, SOMEWHERE SAFE, WE'D BE GONE IN A MINUTE.
BUT THERE'S NOWHERE TO GO. ALL I CAN DO IS BOARD US IN. AND WAIT.
I HATE FEELING SO HELPLESS. I WANT TO DO SOMETHING. ANYTHING.
WE'RE THE LAST ONES STILL IN THE BUILDING.
EVERYONE ELSE LEFT HOURS AGO.
WHO KNOWS WHERE THEY ARE NOW?
OUT RIOTING, I GUESS.
WHAT'S HAPPENING TO MANHATTAN?
TIMES LIKE THIS, I WISH I'D FINISHED COLLEGE. NOT THAT IT WOULD DO ME MUCH GOOD RIGHT NOW...
...BUT AT LEAST I'D FEEL A WHOLE LOT SMARTER.
FLASH THOMPSON, OVER-AGE JOCK: NO USE TO ANYONE, LEAST OF ALL BETS.
BACK BEFORE WE BECAME FRIENDS, PARKER USED TO TEASE ME FOR NOT BEING AS BRIGHT AS HE IS.
I WONDER IF HE KNEW HOW MUCH THAT HURT?
KNOWING PETE, PROBABLY NOT. HE NEVER--
HI, GUY.
HUH?!

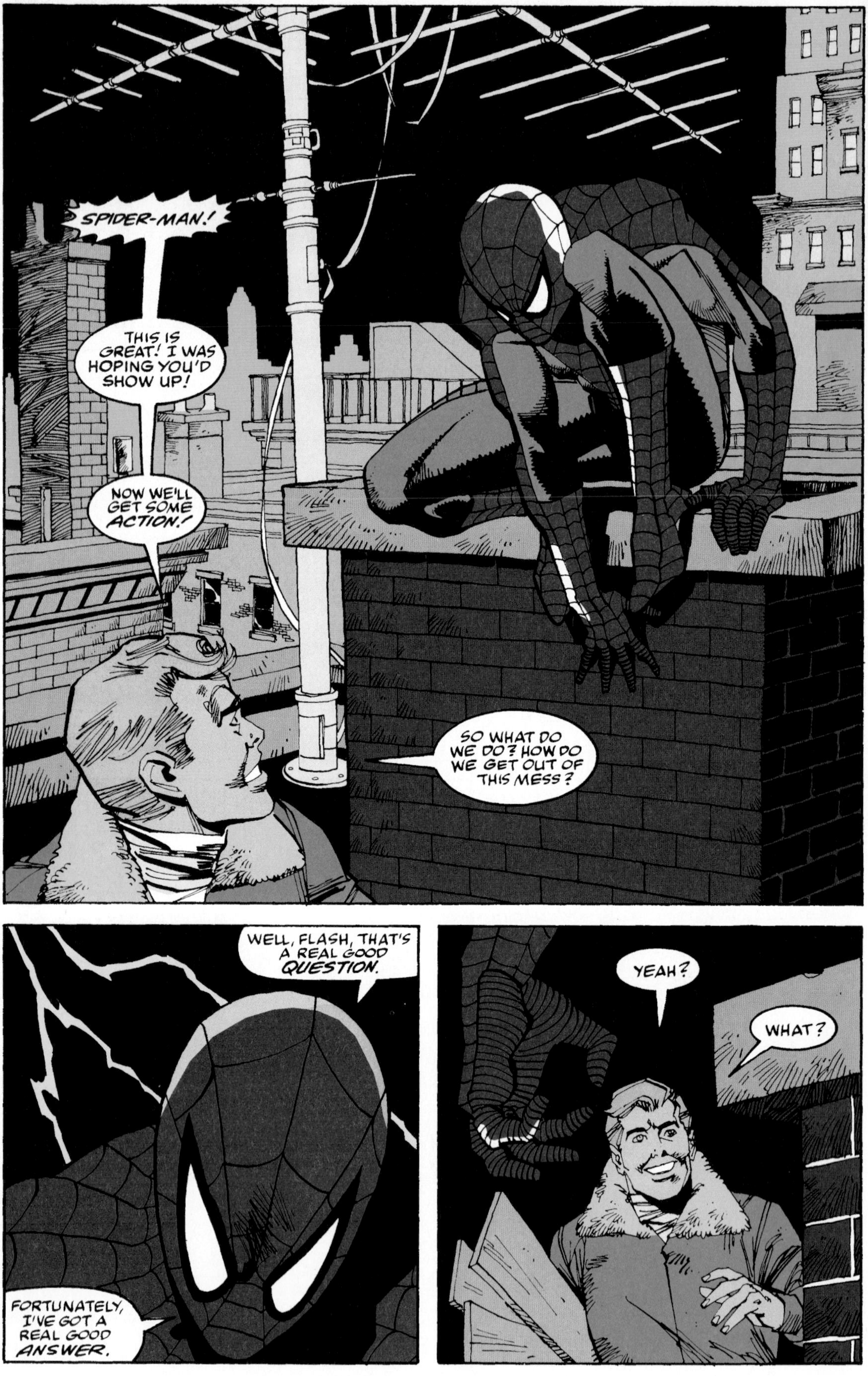
SPIDER-MAN!
THIS IS GREAT! I WAS HOPING YOU'D SHOW UP!
NOW WE'LL GET SOME ACTION!
SO WHAT DO WE DO? HOW DO WE GET OUT OF THIS MESS?
WELL, FLASH, THAT'S A REAL GOOD QUESTION.
FORTUNATELY, I'VE GOT A REAL GOOD ANSWER.
YEAH?
WHAT?

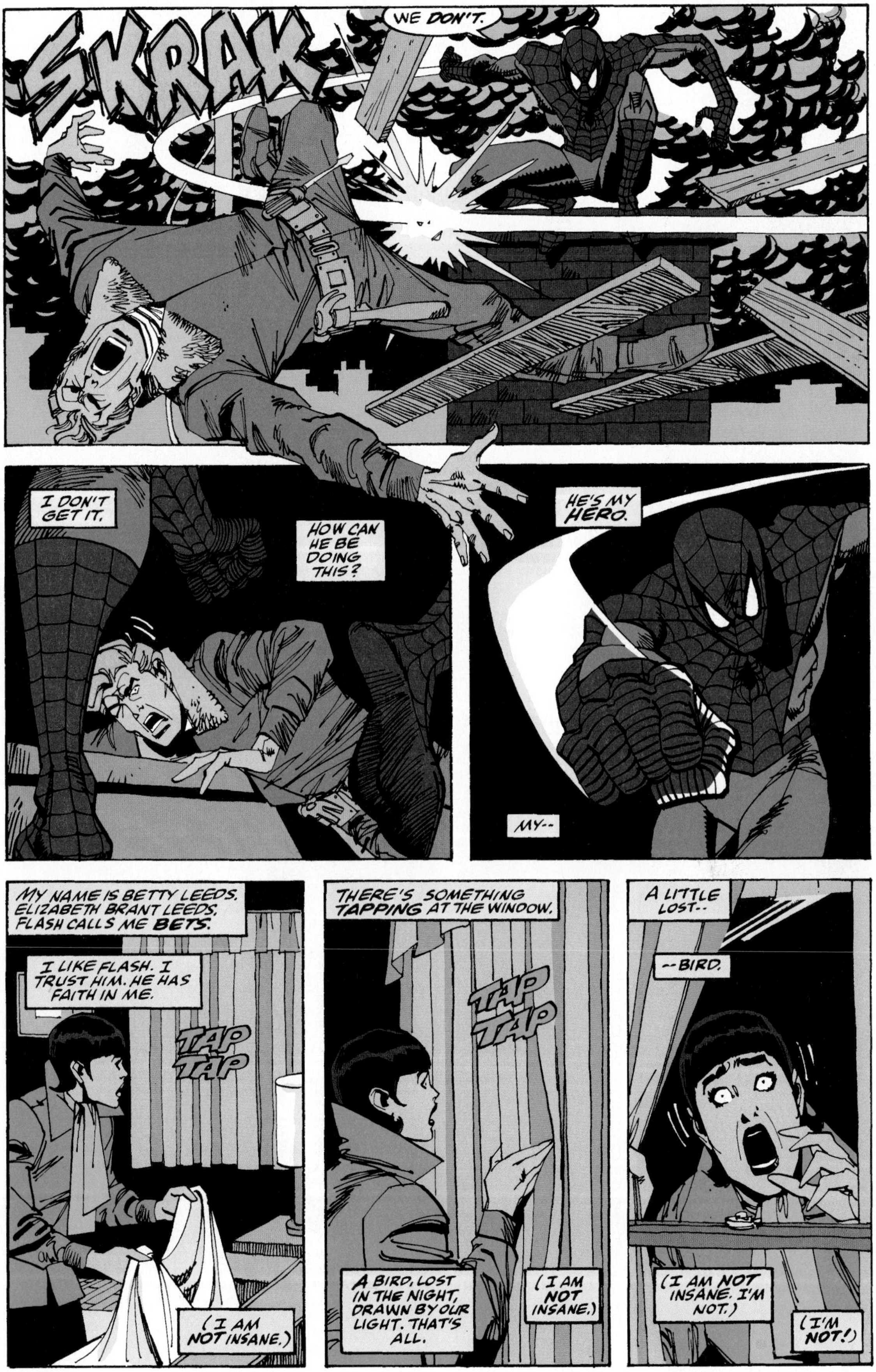
SKRAK
WE DON'T.
I DON'T GET IT.
HOW CAN HE BE DOING THIS?
HE'S MY HERO.
MY--
MY NAME IS BETTY LEEDS. ELIZABETH BRANT LEEDS. FLASH CALLS ME BETS.
I LIKE FLASH. I TRUST HIM. HE HAS FAITH IN ME.
TAP TAP
(I AM NOT INSANE.)
THERE'S SOMETHING TAPPING AT THE WINDOW.
TAP TAP
A BIRD, LOST IN THE NIGHT, DRAWN BY OUR LIGHT. THAT'S ALL.
(I AM NOT INSANE.)
A LITTLE LOST--
--BIRD.
(I AM NOT INSANE. I'M NOT.)
(I'M NOT!)

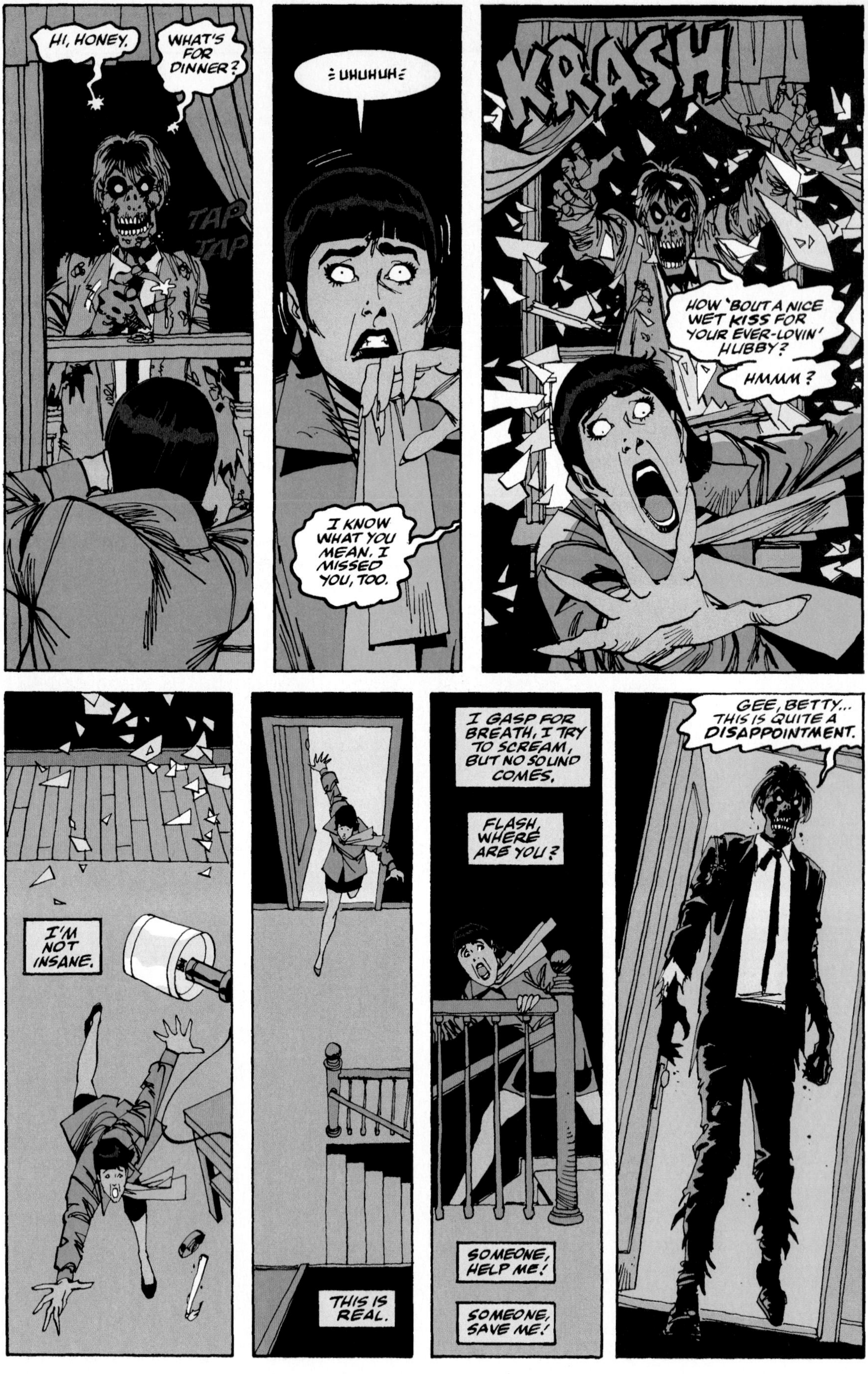
HI, HONEY.
WHAT'S FOR DINNER?
TAP TAP
UHUHUH
I KNOW WHAT YOU MEAN. I MISSED YOU, TOO.
KRASH
HOW 'BOUT A NICE WET KISS FOR YOUR EVER-LOVIN' HUBBY?
HMMM?
I'M NOT INSANE.
THIS IS REAL.
I GASP FOR BREATH, I TRY TO SCREAM, BUT NO SOUND COMES.
FLASH, WHERE ARE YOU?
SOMEONE, HELP ME!
SOMEONE, SAVE ME!
GEE, BETTY... THIS IS QUITE A DISAPPOINTMENT.

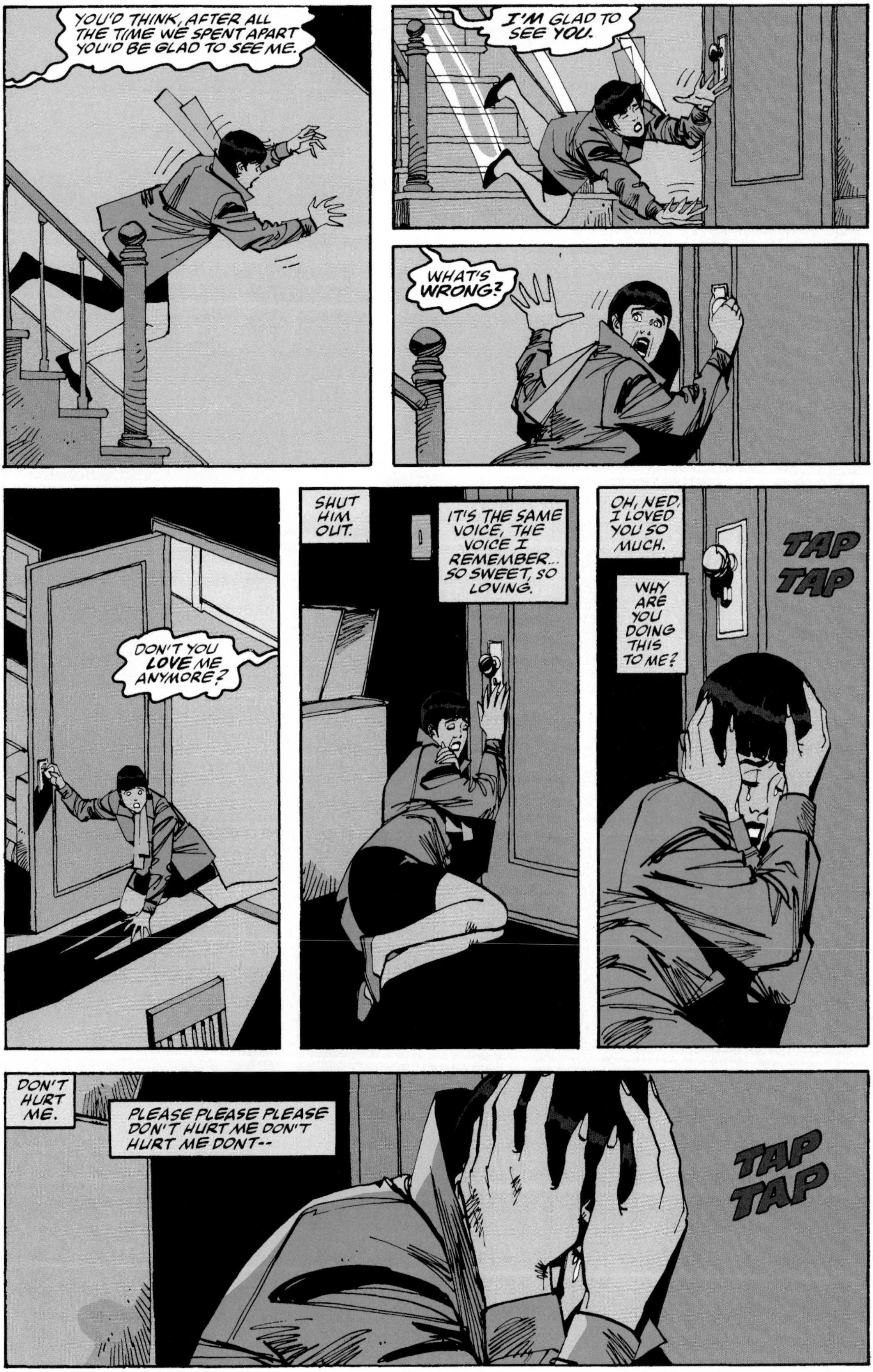
YOU'D THINK, AFTER ALL THE TIME WE SPENT APART YOU'D BE GLAD TO SEE ME.
I'M GLAD TO SEE YOU.
WHAT'S WRONG?
DON'T YOU LOVE ME ANYMORE?
SHUT HIM OUT.
IT'S THE SAME VOICE, THE VOICE I REMEMBER... SO SWEET, SO LOVING.
OH, NED, I LOVED YOU SO MUCH.
WHY ARE YOU DOING THIS TO ME?
TAP TAP
DON'T HURT ME.
PLEASE PLEASE PLEASE DON'T HURT ME DON'T HURT ME DONT--
TAP TAP

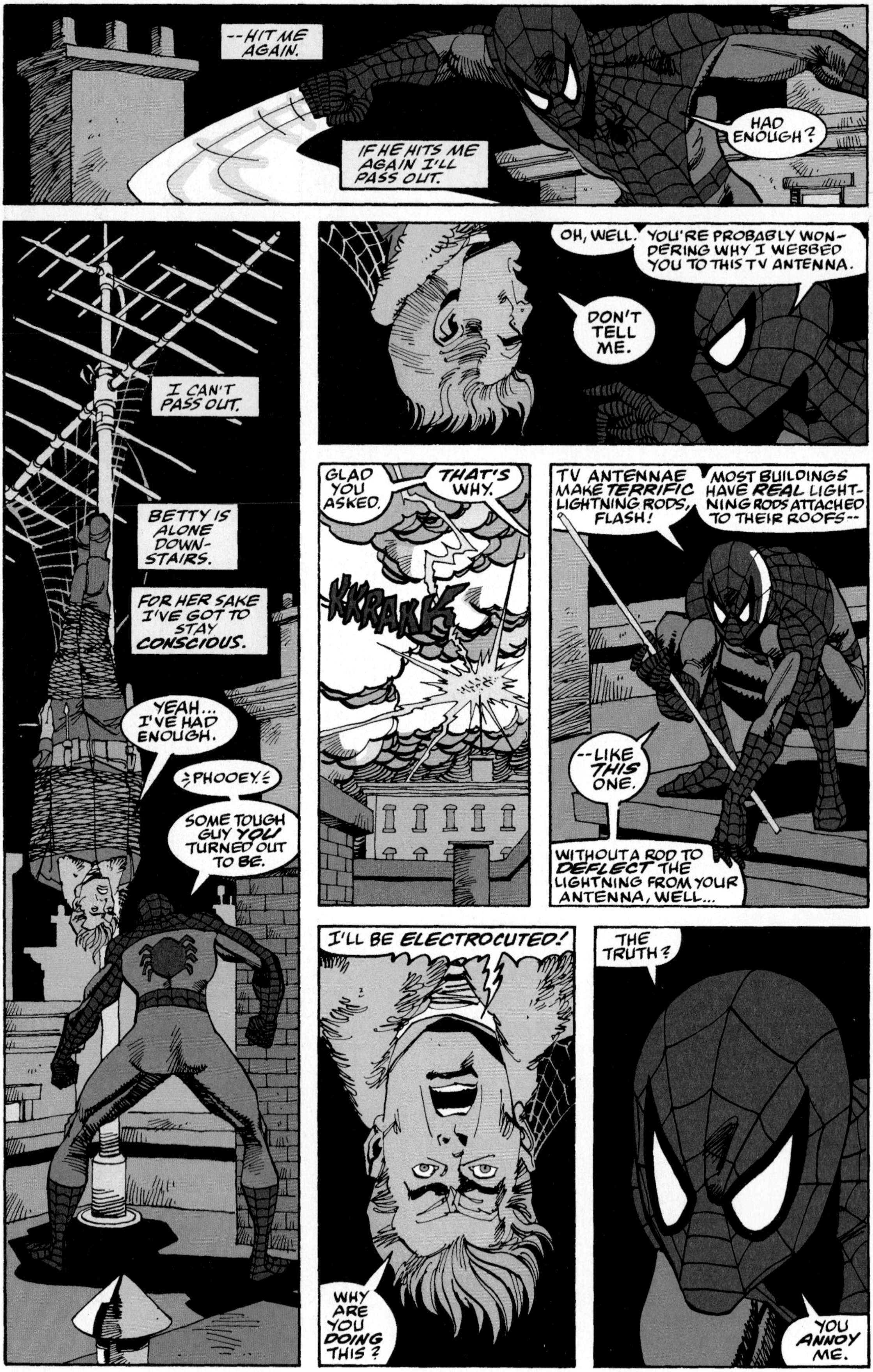
--HIT ME AGAIN.
IF HE HITS ME AGAIN I'LL PASS OUT.
HAD ENOUGH?
I CAN'T PASS OUT.
BETTY IS ALONE DOWN-STAIRS.
FOR HER SAKE I'VE GOT TO STAY CONSCIOUS.
YEAH... I'VE HAD ENOUGH.
PHOOEY.
SOME TOUGH GUY YOU TURNED OUT TO BE.
OH, WELL.
YOU'RE PROBABLY WON-DERING WHY I WEBBED YOU TO THIS TV ANTENNA.
DON'T TELL ME.
GLAD YOU ASKED.
THAT'S WHY.
KKRAKK
TV ANTENNAE MAKE TERRIFIC LIGHTNING RODS, FLASH!
MOST BUILDINGS HAVE REAL LIGHT-NING RODS ATTACHED TO THEIR ROOFS--
--LIKE THIS ONE.
WITHOUT A ROD TO DEFLECT THE LIGHTNING FROM YOUR ANTENNA, WELL...
I'LL BE ELECTROCUTED!
WHY ARE YOU DOING THIS?
THE TRUTH?
YOU ANNOY ME.

W-WHAT?

YOU HEARD ME.

THIS HERO-WORSHIP ROUTINE OF YOURS MAKES ME WANNA *BARF.*

TOOLS IN MY BELT. NOT MUCH HOPE, BUT I'VE GOTTA TRY.

HOPE HE DOESN'T SEE MY HAND MOVE.

KEEP HIM TALKING...

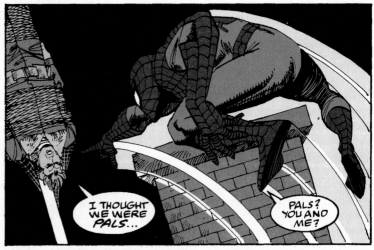

I THOUGHT WE WERE *PALS...*

PALS? YOU AND ME?

YOU MUST HAVE CAUGHT TOO MANY *TACKLES* DURING YOUR HIGH SCHOOL FOOTBALL CAREER, FLASH OLD CHUM.

EITHER THAT, OR YOU WERE *BORN* DUMB.

THINK ABOUT IT.

I'M A HERO...

...YOU'RE A *LOSER.*

HEROES DON'T HANG WITH LOSERS.

TALK.

KEEP TALKING.

DON'T LOOK AT MY HAND...

HEROES LIVE AND LOSERS DIE!

TIME TO *DIE,* FLASH, OLD SOCK...

...AND THEN IT'S TIME TO *EAT!*

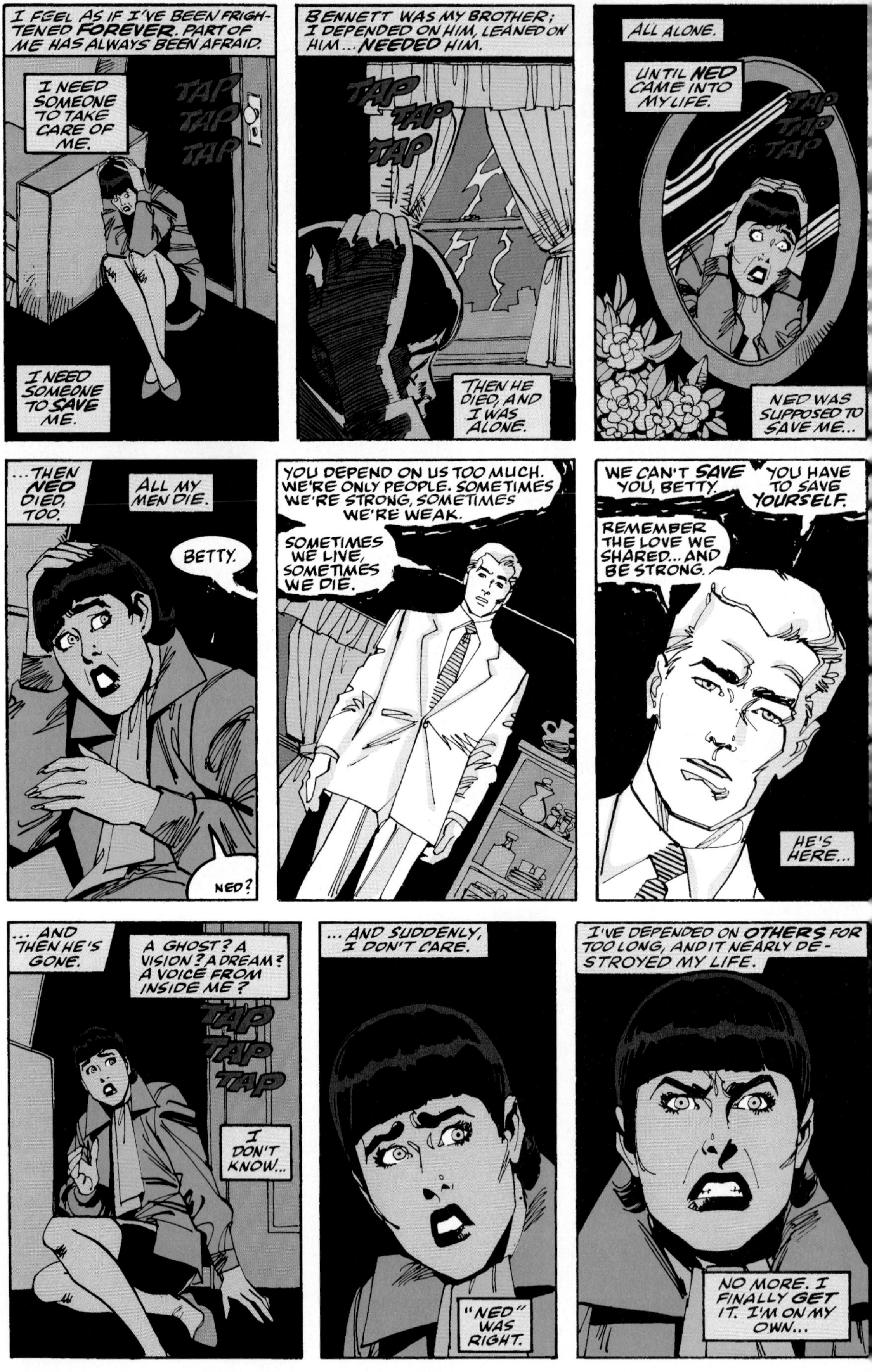
I FEEL AS IF I'VE BEEN FRIGHTENED FOREVER. PART OF ME HAS ALWAYS BEEN AFRAID.
I NEED SOMEONE TO TAKE CARE OF ME.
TAP TAP TAP
I NEED SOMEONE TO SAVE ME.
BENNETT WAS MY BROTHER; I DEPENDED ON HIM, LEANED ON HIM... NEEDED HIM.
TAP TAP TAP
THEN HE DIED, AND I WAS ALONE.
ALL ALONE.
UNTIL NED CAME INTO MY LIFE.
TAP TAP TAP
NED WAS SUPPOSED TO SAVE ME...
...THEN NED DIED, TOO.
ALL MY MEN DIE.
BETTY.
NED?
YOU DEPEND ON US TOO MUCH. WE'RE ONLY PEOPLE. SOMETIMES WE'RE STRONG, SOMETIMES WE'RE WEAK.
SOMETIMES WE LIVE, SOMETIMES WE DIE.
WE CAN'T SAVE YOU, BETTY.
YOU HAVE TO SAVE YOURSELF.
REMEMBER THE LOVE WE SHARED... AND BE STRONG.
HE'S HERE...
... AND THEN HE'S GONE.
A GHOST? A VISION? A DREAM? A VOICE FROM INSIDE ME?
TAP TAP TAP
I DON'T KNOW...
... AND SUDDENLY, I DON'T CARE.
"NED" WAS RIGHT.
I'VE DEPENDED ON OTHERS FOR TOO LONG, AND IT NEARLY DESTROYED MY LIFE.
NO MORE. I FINALLY GET IT. I'M ON MY OWN...

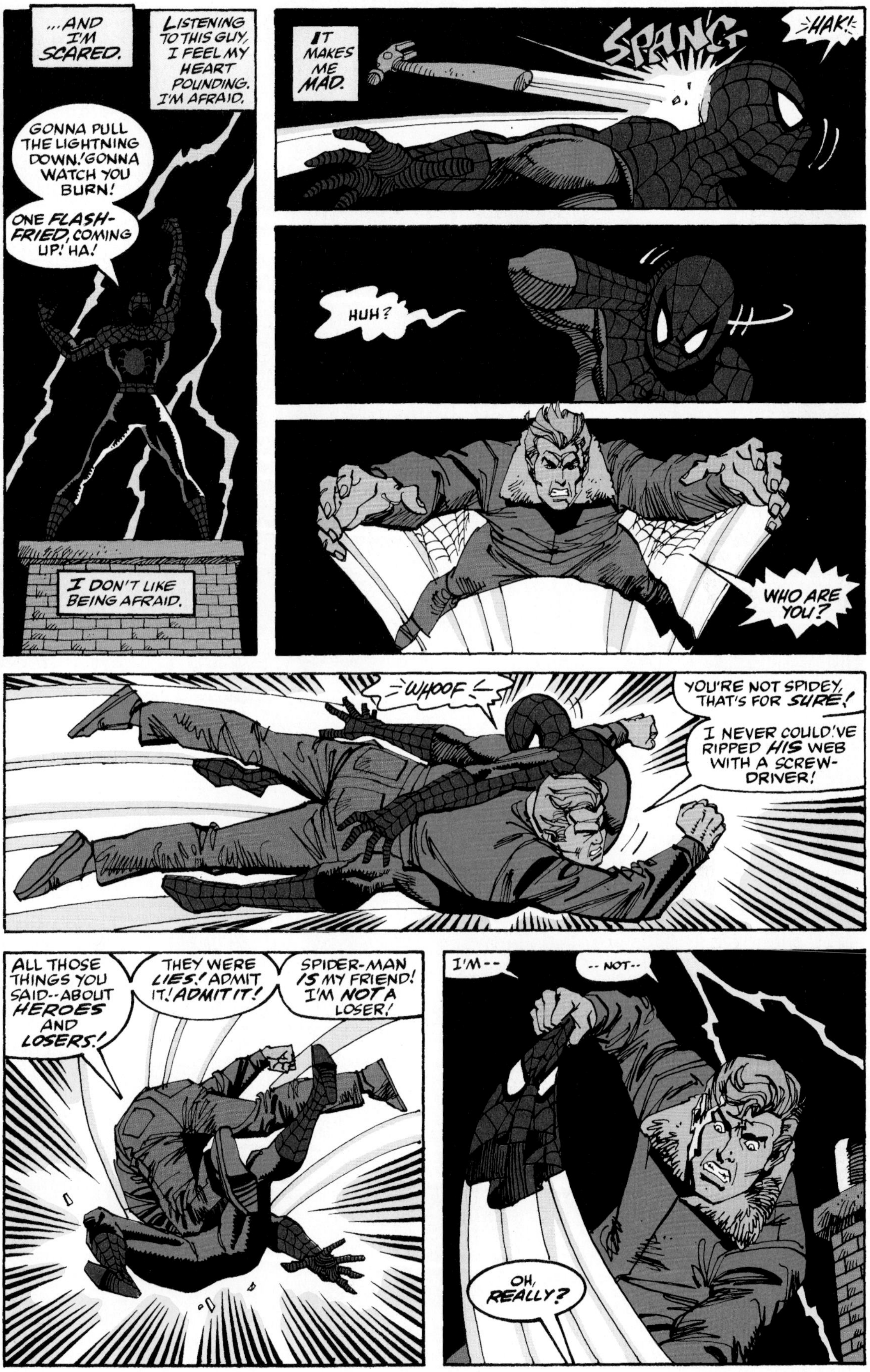
...AND I'M SCARED.
LISTENING TO THIS GUY, I FEEL MY HEART POUNDING. I'M AFRAID.
GONNA PULL THE LIGHTNING DOWN! GONNA WATCH YOU BURN!
ONE FLASH-FRIED, COMING UP! HA!
I DON'T LIKE BEING AFRAID.
IT MAKES ME MAD.
SPANG
HAK!
HUH?
WHO ARE YOU?
WHOOF
YOU'RE NOT SPIDEY, THAT'S FOR SURE!
I NEVER COULD'VE RIPPED HIS WEB WITH A SCREW-DRIVER!
ALL THOSE THINGS YOU SAID--ABOUT HEROES AND LOSERS!
THEY WERE LIES! ADMIT IT! ADMIT IT!
SPIDER-MAN IS MY FRIEND! I'M NOT A LOSER!
I'M--
--NOT--
OH, REALLY?

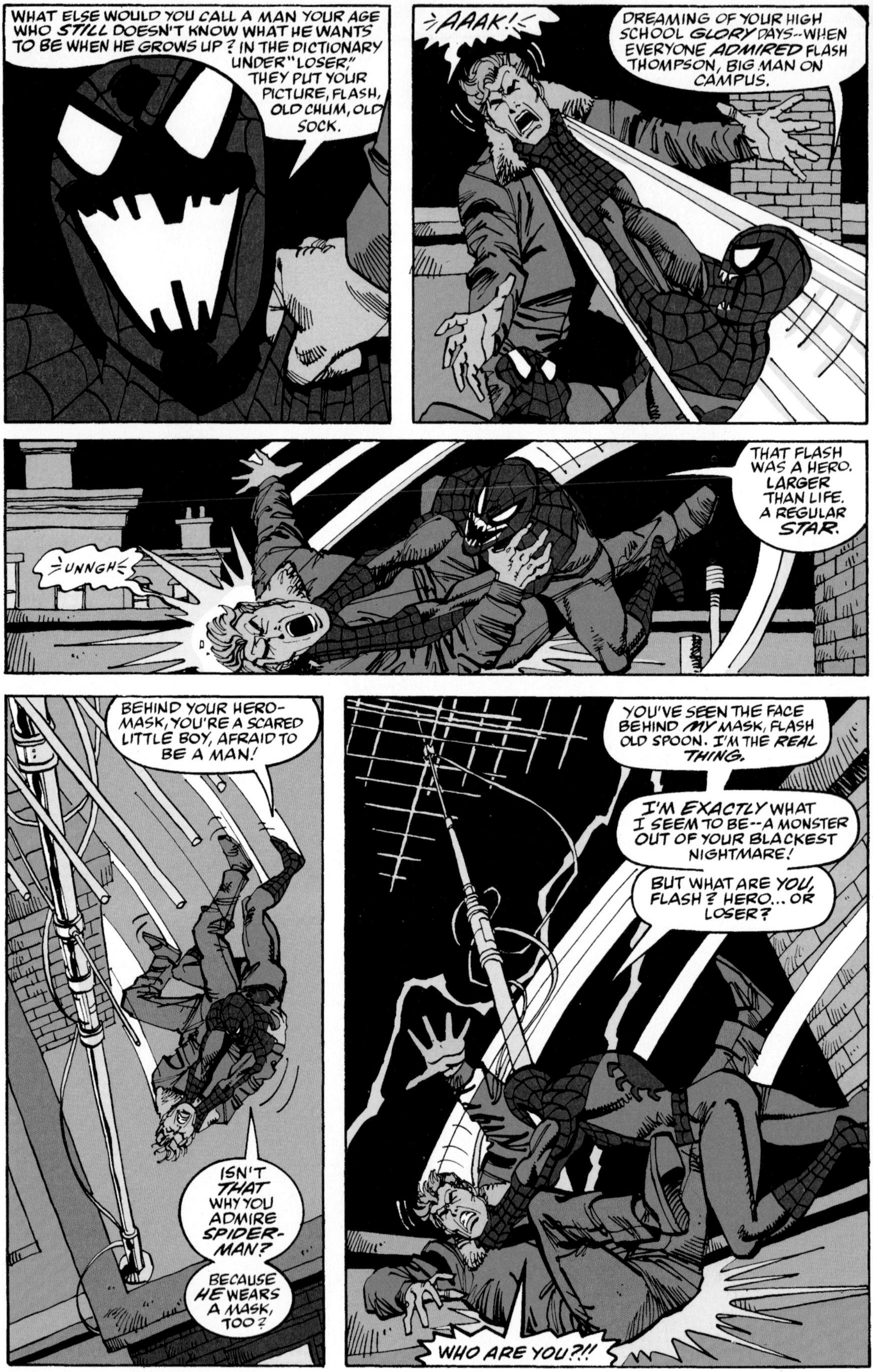
WHAT ELSE WOULD YOU CALL A MAN YOUR AGE WHO STILL DOESN'T KNOW WHAT HE WANTS TO BE WHEN HE GROWS UP? IN THE DICTIONARY UNDER "LOSER," THEY PUT YOUR PICTURE, FLASH, OLD CHUM, OLD SOCK.
AAAK!
DREAMING OF YOUR HIGH SCHOOL GLORY DAYS--WHEN EVERYONE ADMIRED FLASH THOMPSON, BIG MAN ON CAMPUS.
UNNGH
THAT FLASH WAS A HERO. LARGER THAN LIFE. A REGULAR STAR.
BEHIND YOUR HERO-MASK, YOU'RE A SCARED LITTLE BOY, AFRAID TO BE A MAN!
ISN'T THAT WHY YOU ADMIRE SPIDER-MAN?
BECAUSE HE WEARS A MASK, TOO?
YOU'VE SEEN THE FACE BEHIND MY MASK, FLASH OLD SPOON. I'M THE REAL THING.
I'M EXACTLY WHAT I SEEM TO BE--A MONSTER OUT OF YOUR BLACKEST NIGHTMARE!
BUT WHAT ARE YOU, FLASH? HERO... OR LOSER?
WHO ARE YOU?!!

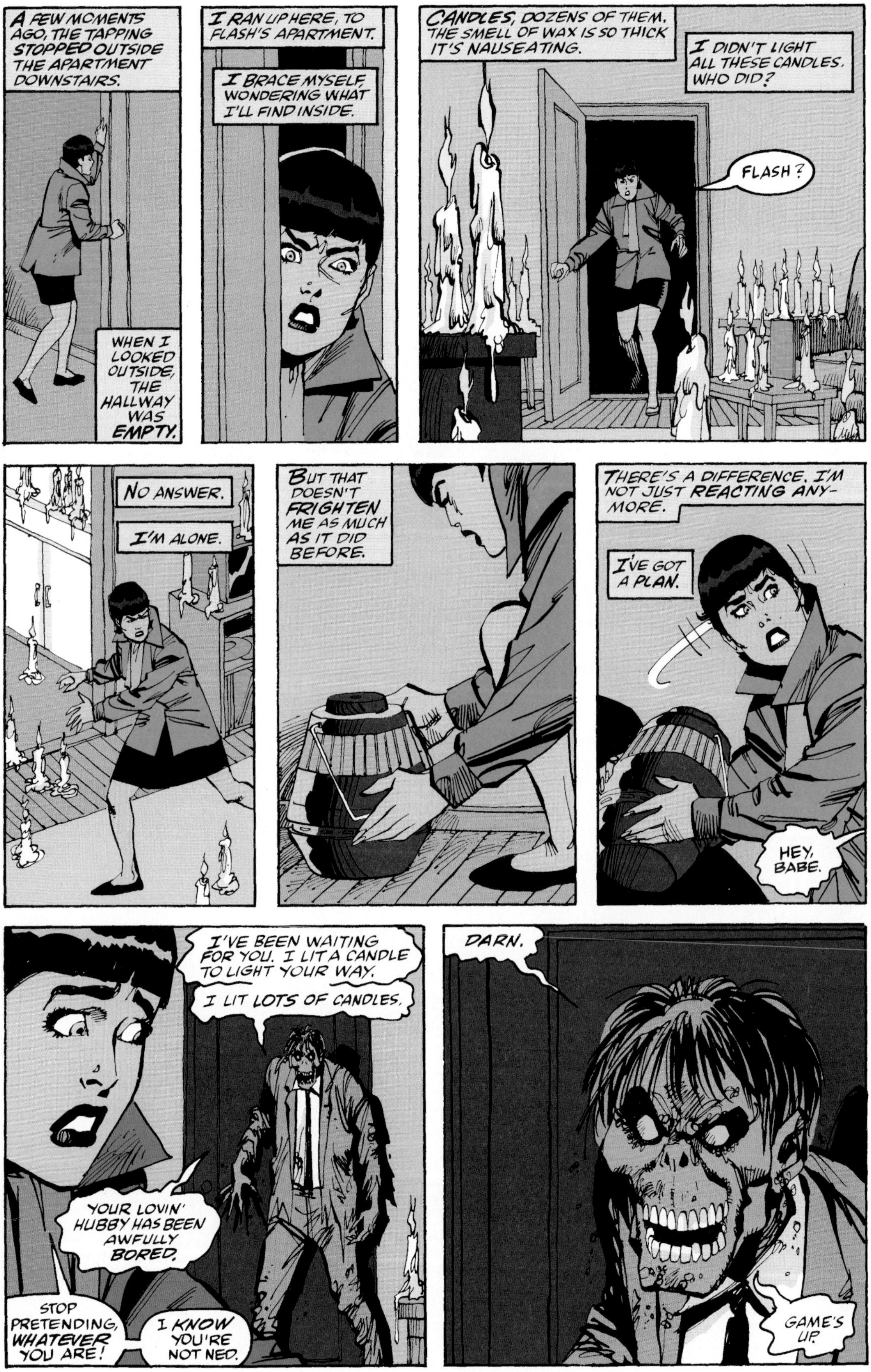
A FEW MOMENTS AGO, THE TAPPING STOPPED OUTSIDE THE APARTMENT DOWNSTAIRS.
WHEN I LOOKED OUTSIDE, THE HALLWAY WAS EMPTY.
I RAN UP HERE, TO FLASH'S APARTMENT.
I BRACE MYSELF, WONDERING WHAT I'LL FIND INSIDE.
CANDLES, DOZENS OF THEM. THE SMELL OF WAX IS SO THICK IT'S NAUSEATING.
I DIDN'T LIGHT ALL THESE CANDLES. WHO DID?
FLASH?
NO ANSWER.
I'M ALONE.
BUT THAT DOESN'T FRIGHTEN ME AS MUCH AS IT DID BEFORE.
THERE'S A DIFFERENCE. I'M NOT JUST REACTING ANY-MORE.
I'VE GOT A PLAN.
HEY, BABE.
I'VE BEEN WAITING FOR YOU. I LIT A CANDLE TO LIGHT YOUR WAY.
I LIT LOTS OF CANDLES.
YOUR LOVIN' HUBBY HAS BEEN AWFULLY BORED.
STOP PRETENDING, WHATEVER YOU ARE!
I KNOW YOU'RE NOT NED.
DARN.
GAME'S UP.

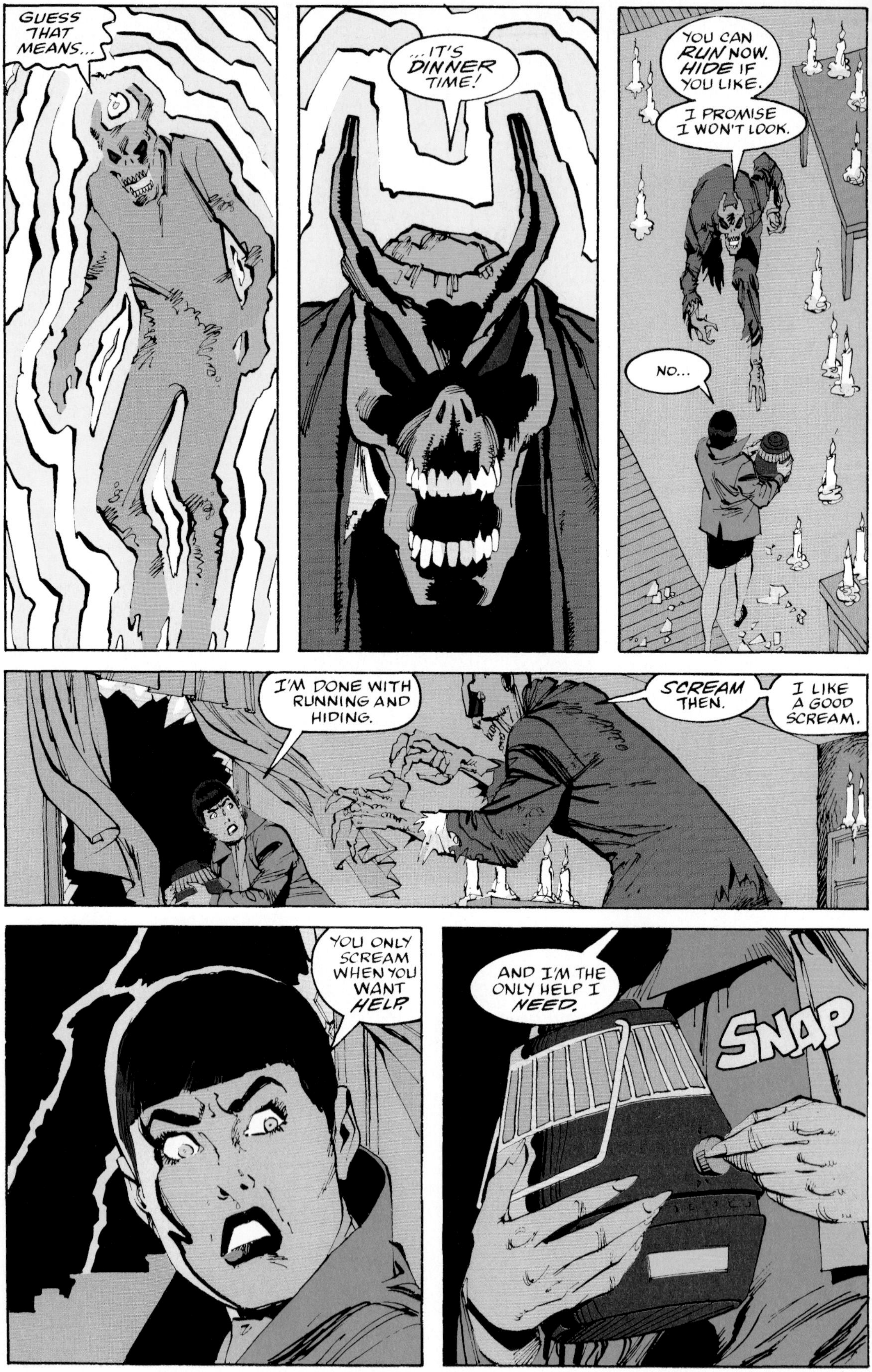
GUESS THAT MEANS...
...IT'S DINNER TIME!
YOU CAN RUN NOW. HIDE IF YOU LIKE.
I PROMISE I WON'T LOOK.
NO...
I'M DONE WITH RUNNING AND HIDING.
SCREAM THEN.
I LIKE A GOOD SCREAM.
YOU ONLY SCREAM WHEN YOU WANT HELP.
AND I'M THE ONLY HELP I NEED.
SNAP

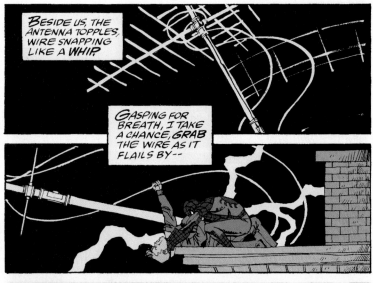

LIGHTNING BURNS THE NIGHT, RIPPING THROUGH THE CURTAIN OF RAIN LIKE A FORK OF FIRE.

BESIDE US, THE ANTENNA TOPPLES, WIRE SNAPPING LIKE A WHIP.

GASPING FOR BREATH, I TAKE A CHANCE, GRAB THE WIRE AS IT FLAILS BY--

-- AND PRAY.

I ALWAYS WANTED TO BE A HERO.

I GUESS SOMETIMES LIFE IS LIKE A DRIVE-IN MOVIE.

SKRASH

FLASH!

HUH?

343

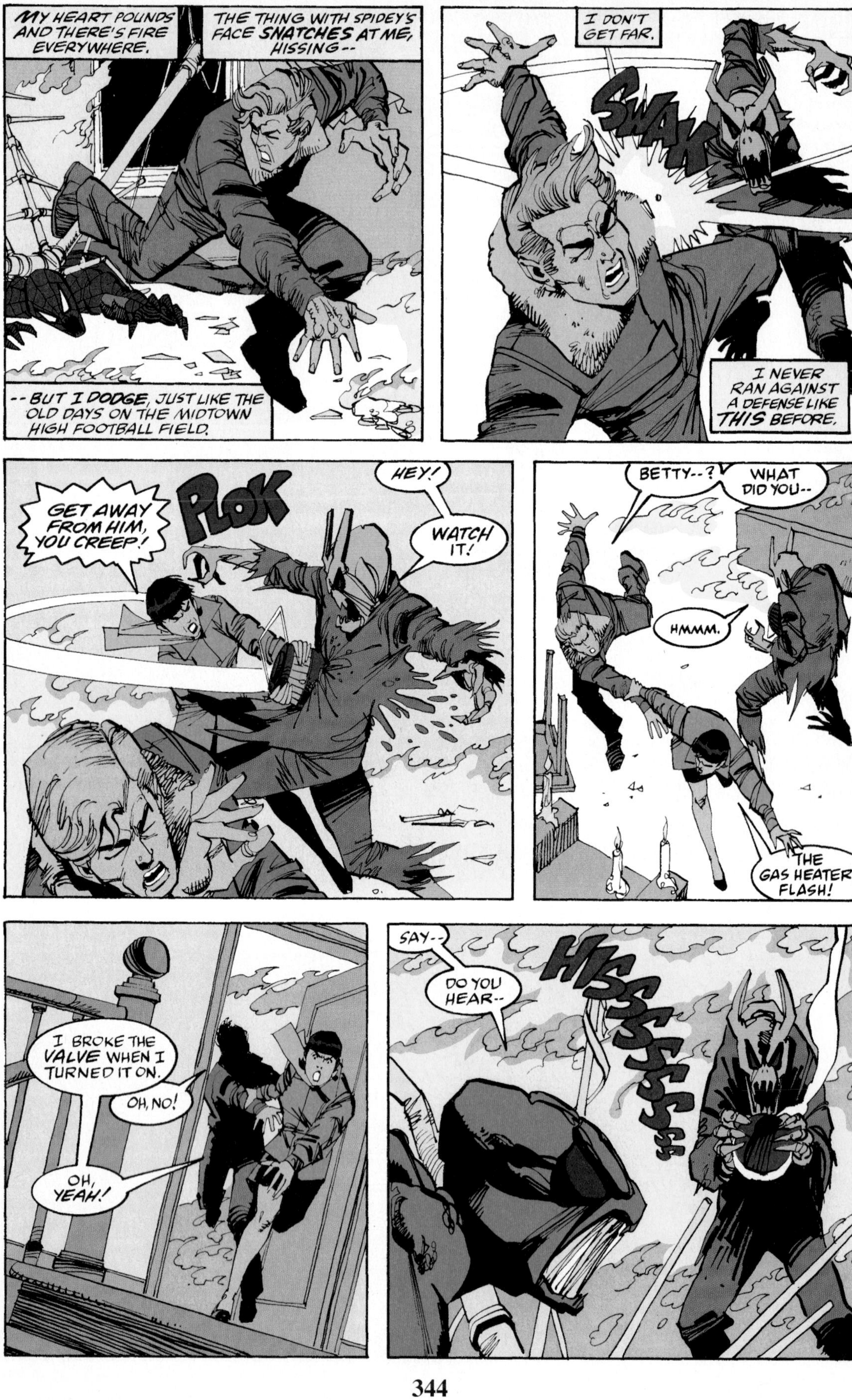
MY HEART POUNDS AND THERE'S FIRE EVERYWHERE.
THE THING WITH SPIDEY'S FACE SNATCHES AT ME, HISSING--
--BUT I DODGE, JUST LIKE THE OLD DAYS ON THE MIDTOWN HIGH FOOTBALL FIELD.
I DON'T GET FAR.
SWAK
I NEVER RAN AGAINST A DEFENSE LIKE THIS BEFORE.
GET AWAY FROM HIM, YOU CREEP!
PLOK
HEY!
WATCH IT!
BETTY--?
WHAT DID YOU--
HMMM.
THE GAS HEATER, FLASH!
I BROKE THE VALVE WHEN I TURNED IT ON.
OH, NO!
OH, YEAH!
SAY--
DO YOU HEAR--
HISSSSSSS

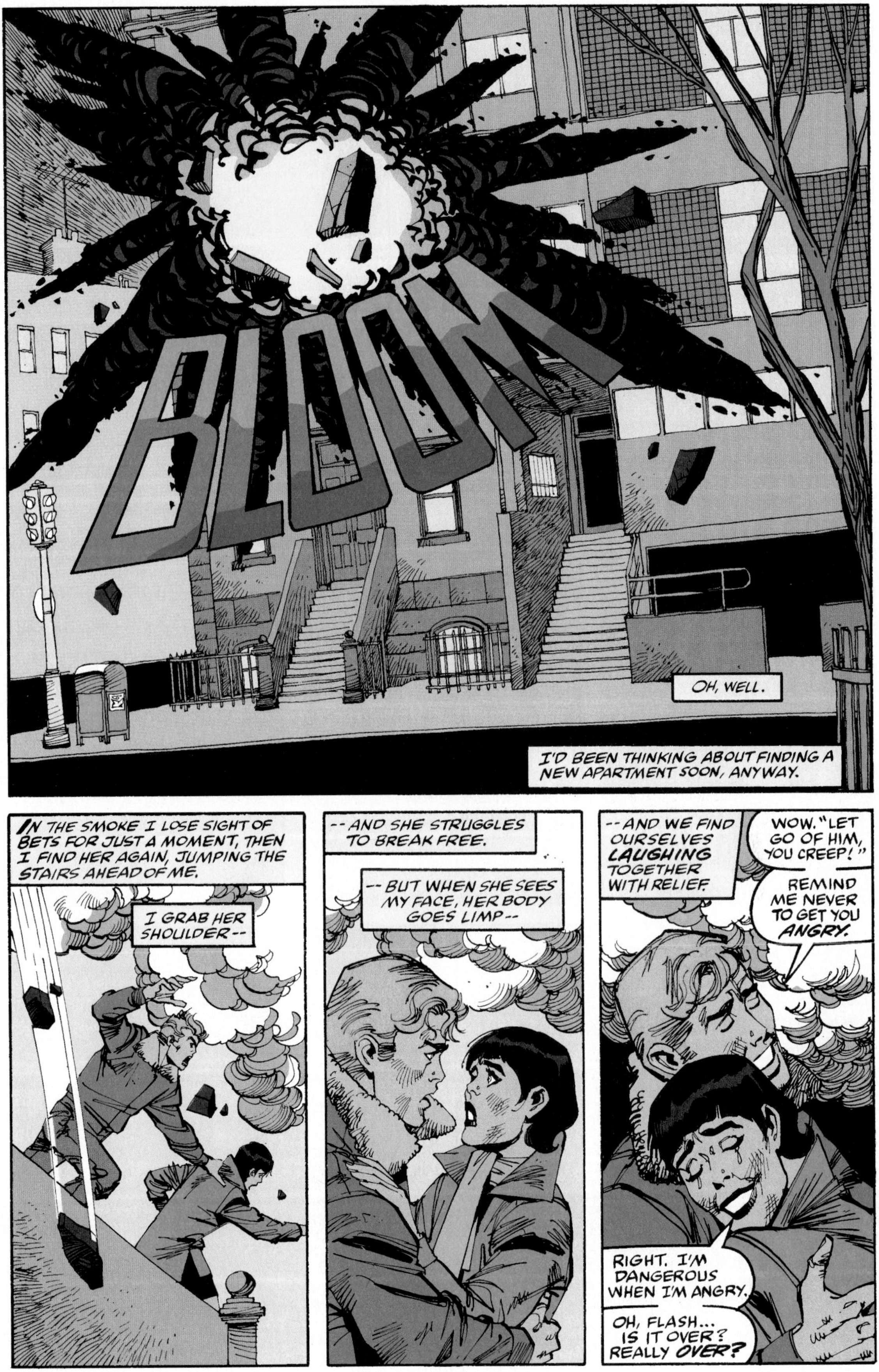
BLOOM
OH, WELL.
I'D BEEN THINKING ABOUT FINDING A NEW APARTMENT SOON, ANYWAY.
IN THE SMOKE I LOSE SIGHT OF BETS FOR JUST A MOMENT, THEN I FIND HER AGAIN, JUMPING THE STAIRS AHEAD OF ME.
I GRAB HER SHOULDER--
--AND SHE STRUGGLES TO BREAK FREE.
--BUT WHEN SHE SEES MY FACE, HER BODY GOES LIMP--
--AND WE FIND OURSELVES LAUGHING TOGETHER WITH RELIEF.
WOW. "LET GO OF HIM, YOU CREEP!"
REMIND ME NEVER TO GET YOU ANGRY.
RIGHT. I'M DANGEROUS WHEN I'M ANGRY.
OH, FLASH... IS IT OVER? REALLY OVER?

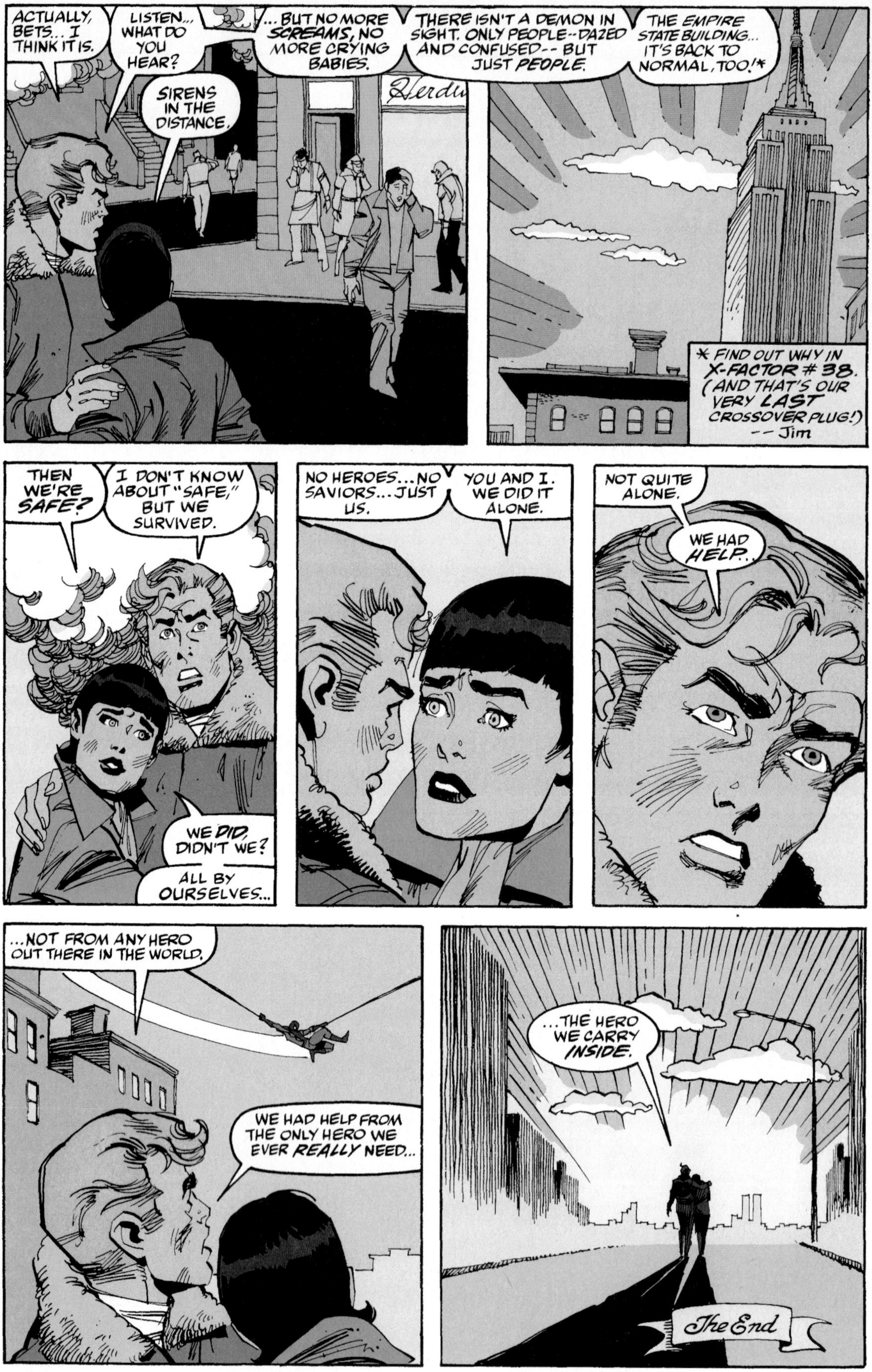
ACTUALLY, BETS... I THINK IT IS.
LISTEN... WHAT DO YOU HEAR?
SIRENS IN THE DISTANCE.
...BUT NO MORE SCREAMS, NO MORE CRYING BABIES.
THERE ISN'T A DEMON IN SIGHT. ONLY PEOPLE--DAZED AND CONFUSED-- BUT JUST PEOPLE.
THE EMPIRE STATE BUILDING... IT'S BACK TO NORMAL, TOO!*
* FIND OUT WHY IN X-FACTOR # 38. (AND THAT'S OUR VERY LAST CROSSOVER PLUG!) --Jim
THEN WE'RE SAFE?
I DON'T KNOW ABOUT "SAFE," BUT WE SURVIVED.
WE DID, DIDN'T WE?
ALL BY OURSELVES...
NO HEROES...NO SAVIORS...JUST US.
YOU AND I. WE DID IT ALONE.
NOT QUITE ALONE.
WE HAD HELP...
...NOT FROM ANY HERO OUT THERE IN THE WORLD.
WE HAD HELP FROM THE ONLY HERO WE EVER REALLY NEED...
...THE HERO WE CARRY INSIDE.
The End

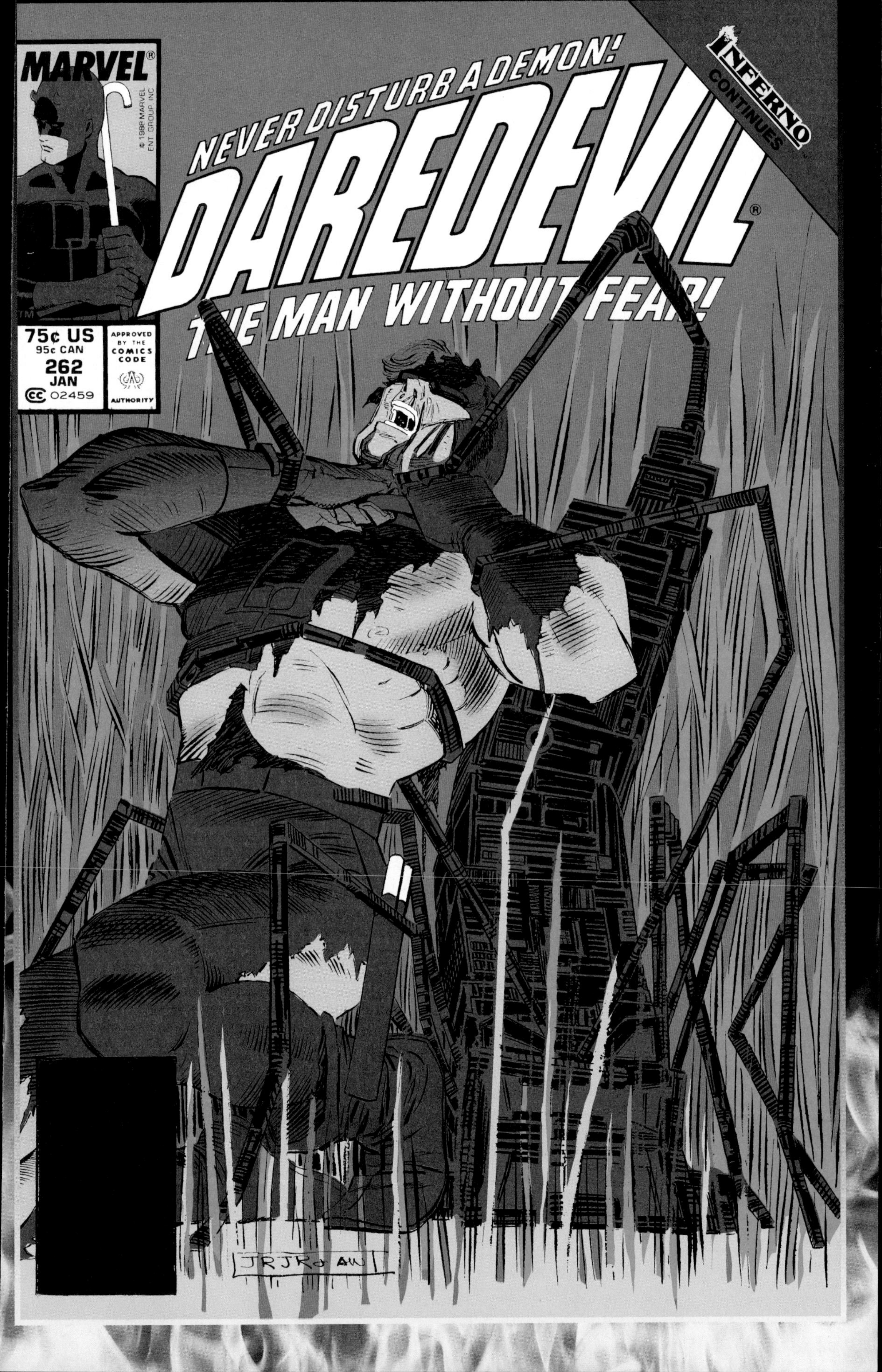
MARVEL
© 1988 MARVEL ENT GROUP INC
NEVER DISTURB A DEMON!
DAREDEVIL
THE MAN WITHOUT FEAR!
INFERNO CONTINUES
75¢ US
95¢ CAN
262
JAN
02459
APPROVED BY THE COMICS CODE AUTHORITY
JRJR & AW

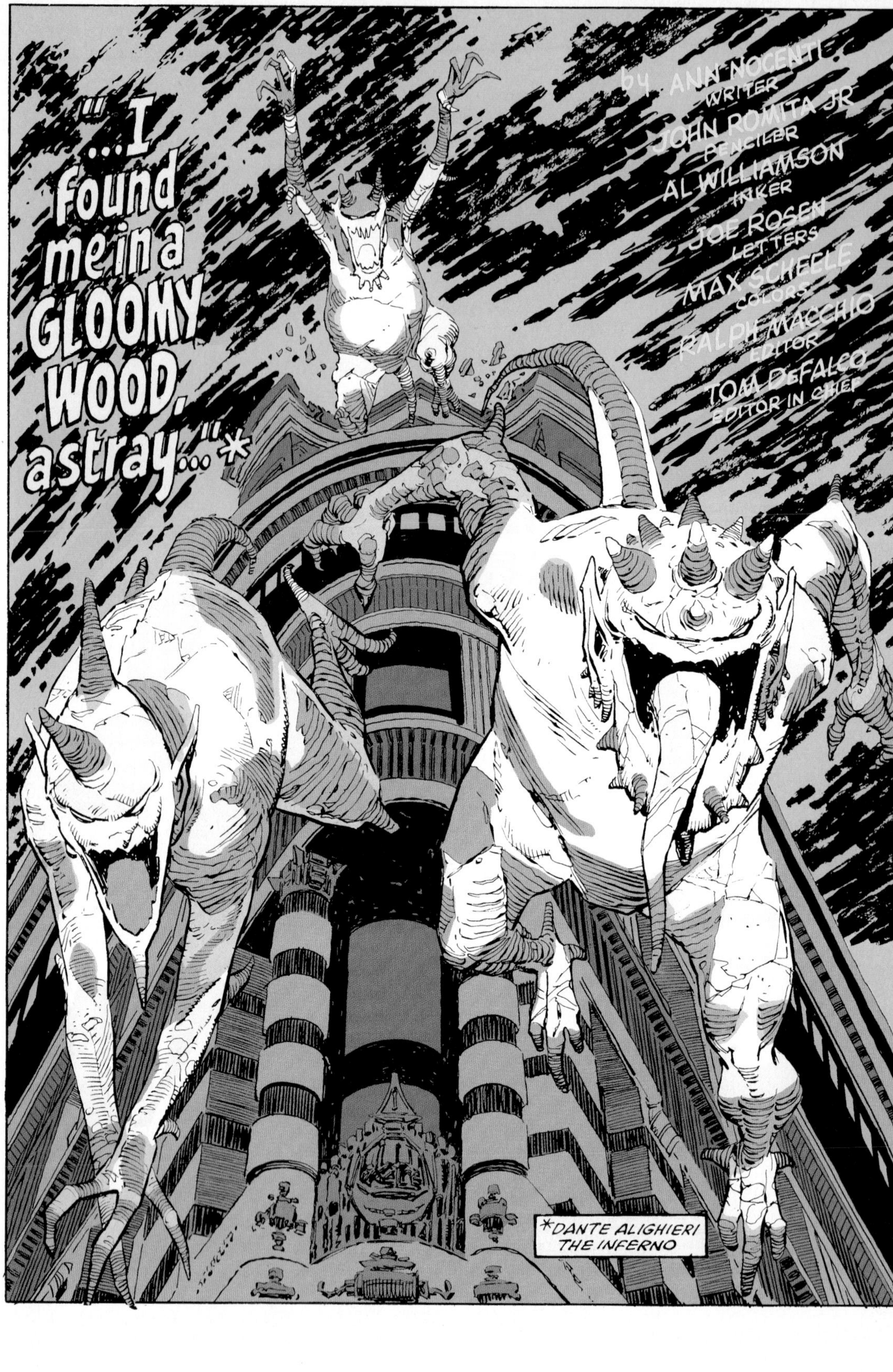
"...I found me in a GLOOMY WOOD, astray..."*
by ANN NOCENTI WRITER
JOHN ROMITA JR PENCILER
AL WILLIAMSON INKER
JOE ROSEN LETTERS
MAX SCHEELE COLORS
RALPH MACCHIO EDITOR
TOM DeFALCO EDITOR IN CHIEF
*DANTE ALIGHIERI THE INFERNO

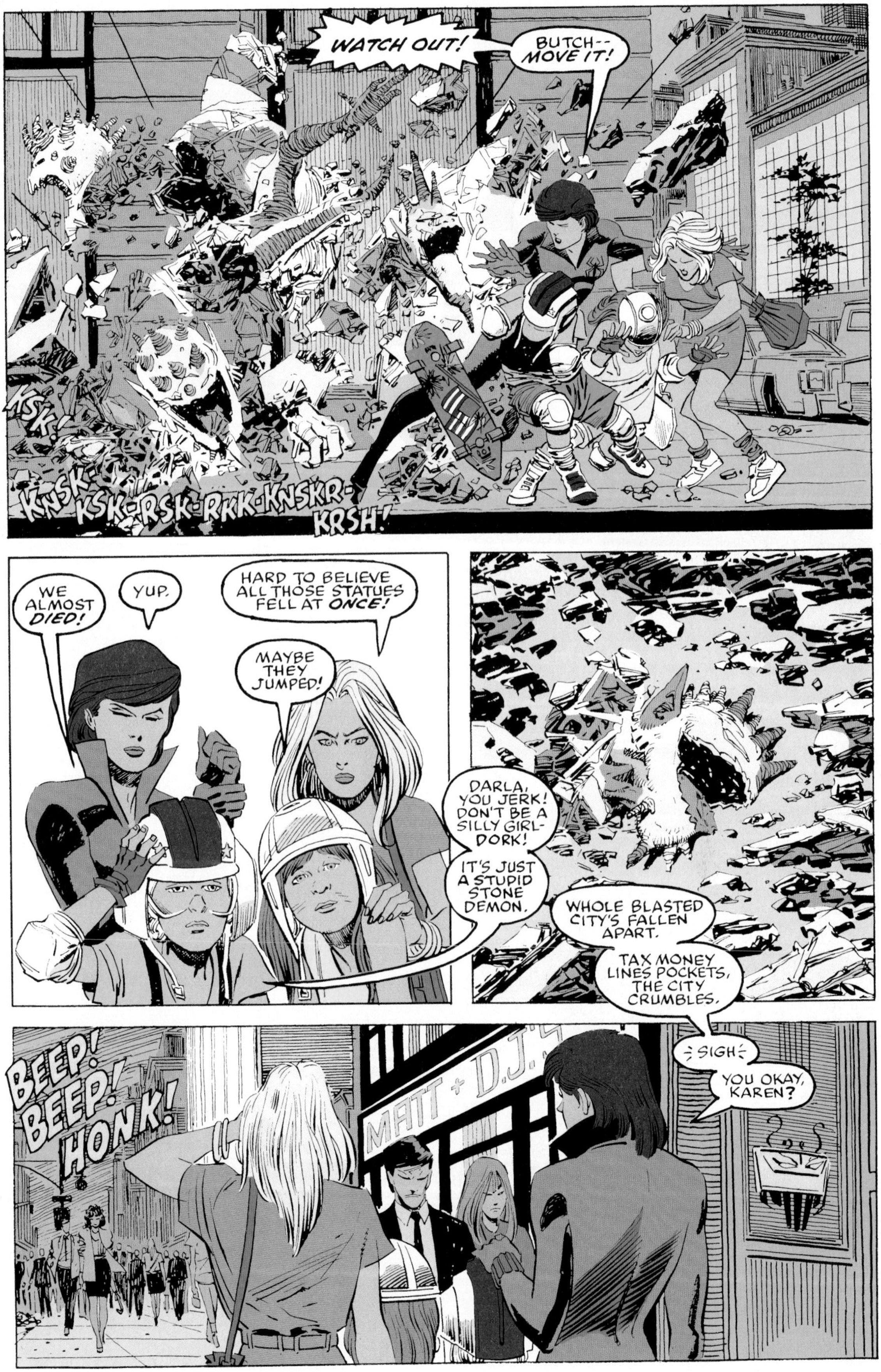
WATCH OUT!
BUTCH-- MOVE IT!
KSK!
KNSK-KSK-RSK-RKK-KNSKR-KRSH!
WE ALMOST DIED!
YUP.
HARD TO BELIEVE ALL THOSE STATUES FELL AT ONCE!
MAYBE THEY JUMPED!
DARLA, YOU JERK! DON'T BE A SILLY GIRL-DORK!
IT'S JUST A STUPID STONE DEMON.
WHOLE BLASTED CITY'S FALLEN APART.
TAX MONEY LINES POCKETS, THE CITY CRUMBLES.
BEEP! BEEP! HONK!
MATT + D.J.'S
SIGH
YOU OKAY, KAREN?

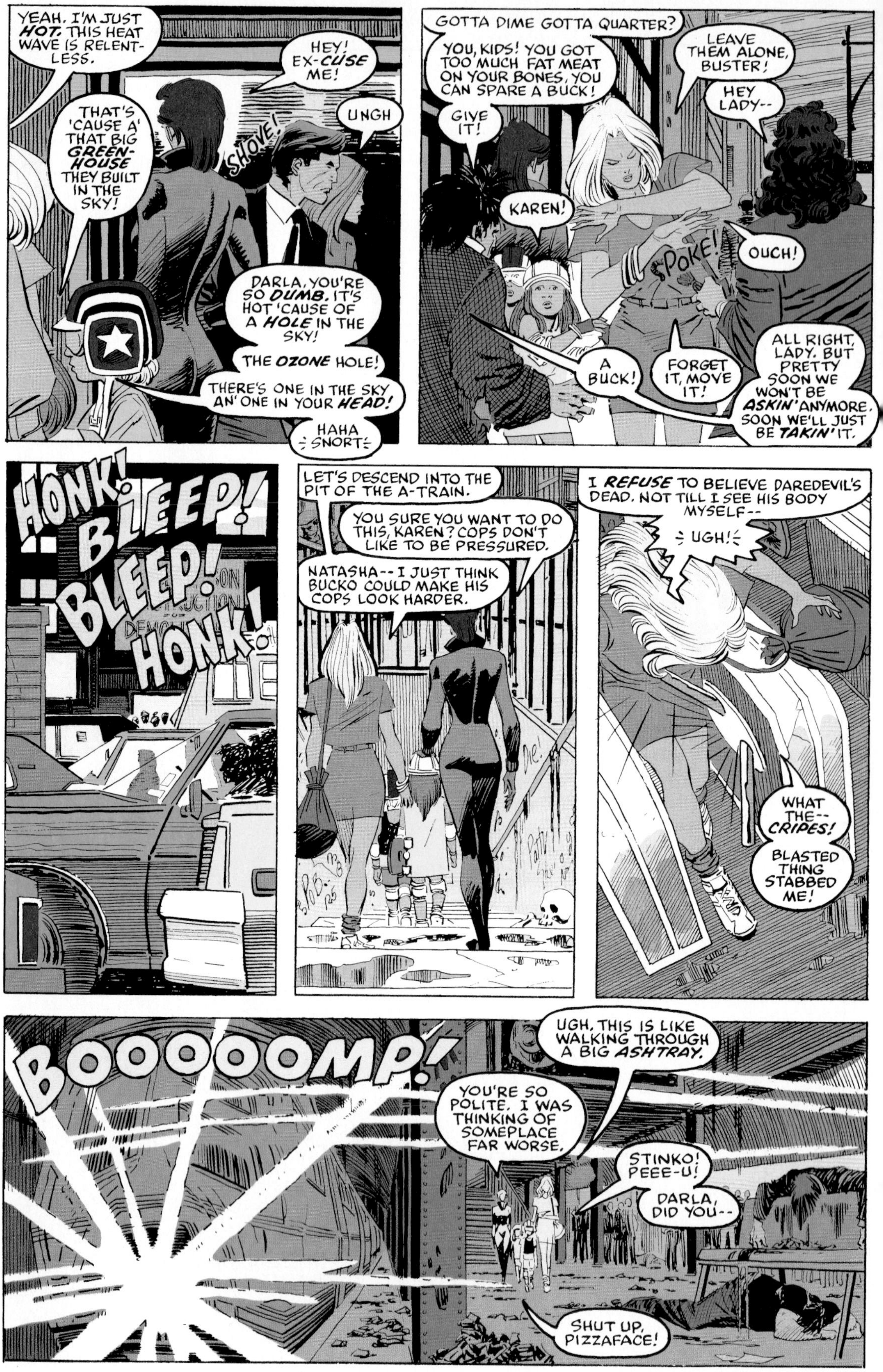

YEAH. I'M JUST HOT. THIS HEAT WAVE IS RELENTLESS.
HEY! EX-CUSE ME!
THAT'S 'CAUSE A' THAT BIG GREENHOUSE THEY BUILT IN THE SKY!
SHOVE!
UNGH
DARLA, YOU'RE SO DUMB. IT'S HOT 'CAUSE OF A HOLE IN THE SKY!
THE OZONE HOLE!
THERE'S ONE IN THE SKY AN' ONE IN YOUR HEAD!
HAHA SNORT
GOTTA DIME GOTTA QUARTER?
YOU, KIDS! YOU GOT TOO MUCH FAT MEAT ON YOUR BONES, YOU CAN SPARE A BUCK!
GIVE IT!
LEAVE THEM ALONE, BUSTER!
HEY LADY--
KAREN!
POKE!
OUCH!
A BUCK!
FORGET IT, MOVE IT!
ALL RIGHT, LADY. BUT PRETTY SOON WE WON'T BE ASKIN' ANYMORE. SOON WE'LL JUST BE TAKIN' IT.
HONK! BLEEP! BLEEP! HONK!
LET'S DESCEND INTO THE PIT OF THE A-TRAIN.
YOU SURE YOU WANT TO DO THIS, KAREN? COPS DON'T LIKE TO BE PRESSURED.
NATASHA-- I JUST THINK BUCKO COULD MAKE HIS COPS LOOK HARDER.
I REFUSE TO BELIEVE DAREDEVIL'S DEAD. NOT TILL I SEE HIS BODY MYSELF--
UGH!
WHAT THE-- CRIPES!
BLASTED THING STABBED ME!
BOOOOOMP!
UGH, THIS IS LIKE WALKING THROUGH A BIG ASHTRAY.
YOU'RE SO POLITE. I WAS THINKING OF SOMEPLACE FAR WORSE.
STINKO! PEEE-U!
DARLA, DID YOU--
SHUT UP, PIZZAFACE!

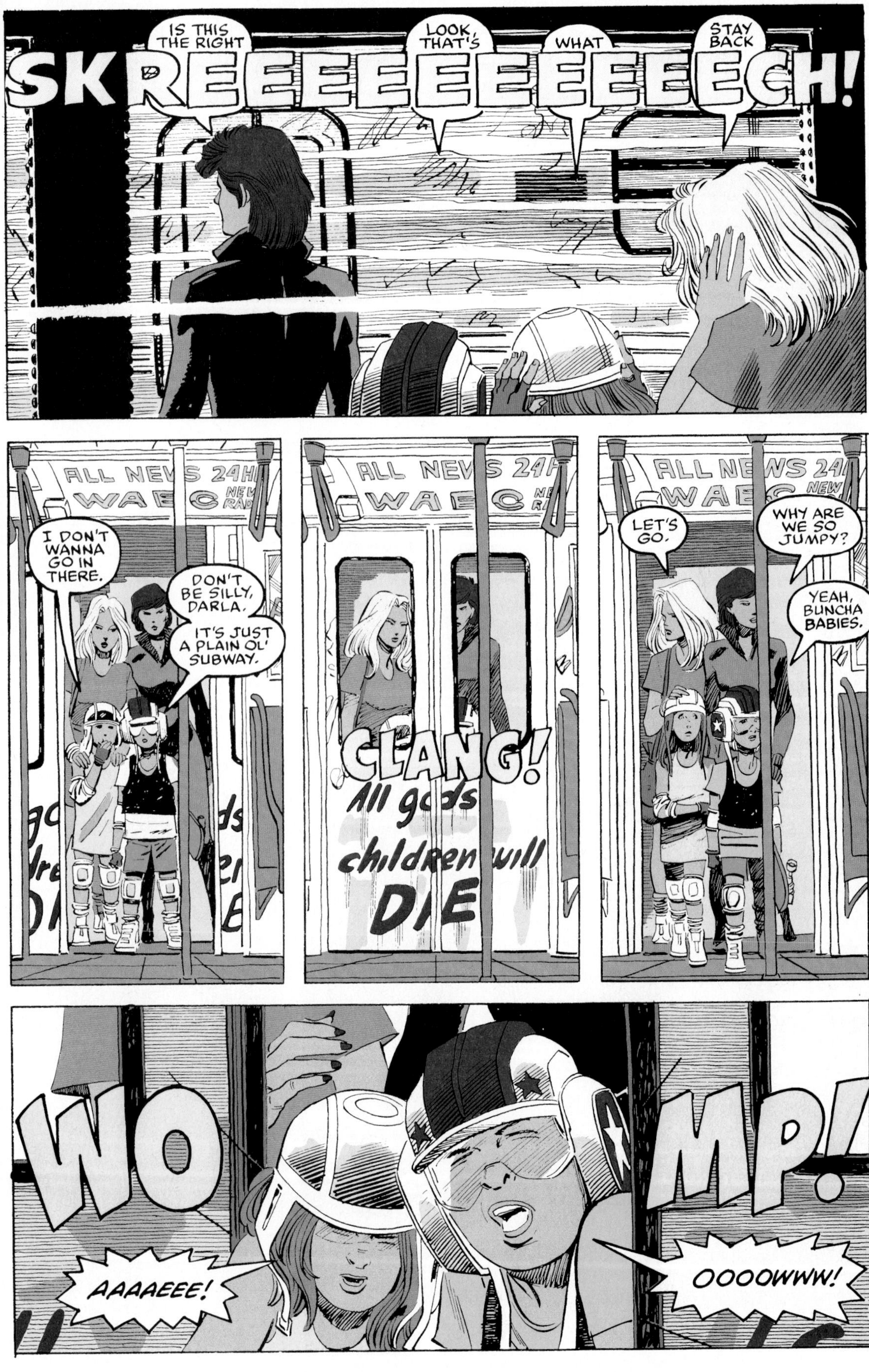
IS THIS THE RIGHT
LOOK, THAT'S
WHAT
STAY BACK
SKREEEEEEEEEEECH!
ALL NEWS 24H
WAEC
I DON'T WANNA GO IN THERE.
DON'T BE SILLY, DARLA.
IT'S JUST A PLAIN OL' SUBWAY.
CLANG!
All gods children will DIE
LET'S GO.
WHY ARE WE SO JUMPY?
YEAH, BUNCHA BABIES.
WOMP!
AAAAEEE!
OOOOWWW!

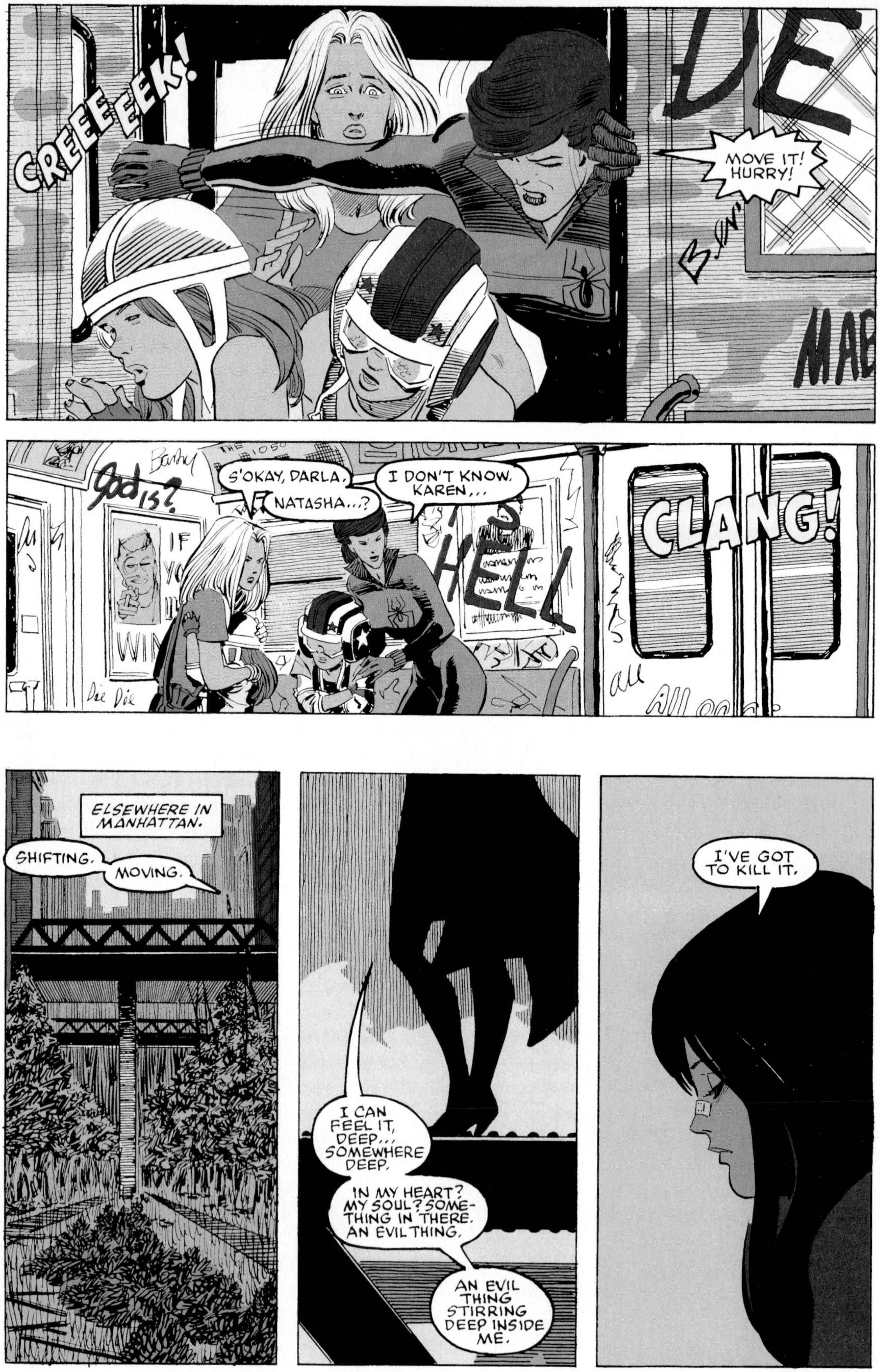
CREEEEEK!
MOVE IT! HURRY!
S'OKAY, DARLA.
NATASHA...?
I DON'T KNOW, KAREN...
CLANG!
ELSEWHERE IN MANHATTAN.
SHIFTING.
MOVING.
I CAN FEEL IT, DEEP... SOMEWHERE DEEP.
IN MY HEART? MY SOUL? SOMETHING IN THERE. AN EVIL THING.
AN EVIL THING STIRRING DEEP INSIDE ME.
I'VE GOT TO KILL IT.

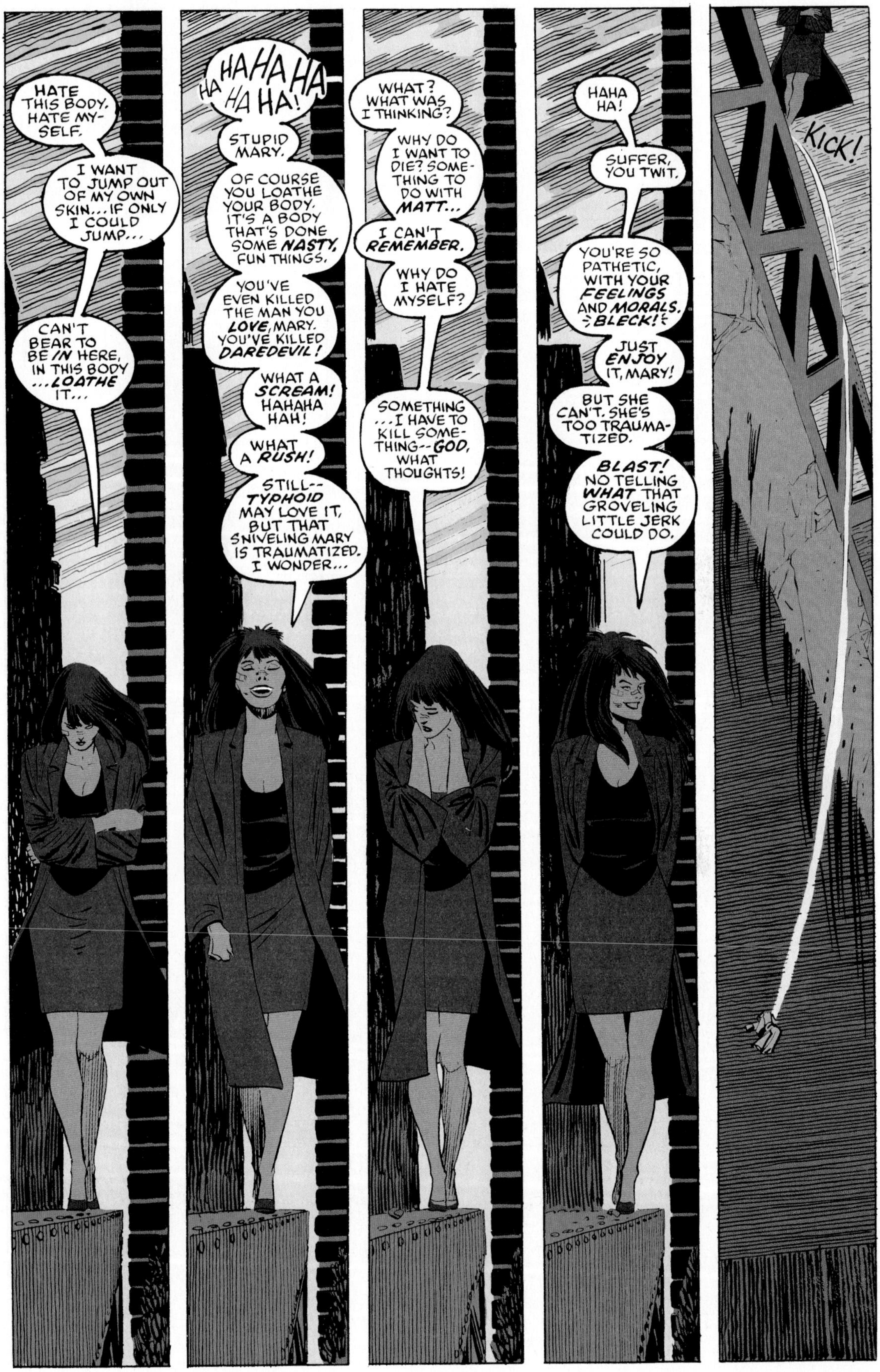
HATE THIS BODY. HATE MYSELF.
I WANT TO JUMP OUT OF MY OWN SKIN... IF ONLY I COULD JUMP...
CAN'T BEAR TO BE *IN* HERE, IN THIS BODY ...*LOATHE* IT...
HA HAHAHA HA HA HA!
STUPID MARY.
OF COURSE YOU LOATHE YOUR BODY. IT'S A BODY THAT'S DONE SOME *NASTY*, FUN THINGS.
YOU'VE EVEN KILLED THE MAN YOU *LOVE*, MARY. YOU'VE KILLED *DAREDEVIL!*
WHAT A *SCREAM!* HAHAHA HAH!
WHAT A *RUSH!*
STILL-- *TYPHOID* MAY LOVE IT, BUT THAT SNIVELING MARY IS TRAUMATIZED. I WONDER...
WHAT? WHAT WAS I THINKING?
WHY DO I WANT TO DIE? SOMETHING TO DO WITH *MATT...*
I CAN'T REMEMBER.
WHY DO I HATE MYSELF?
SOMETHING ...I HAVE TO KILL SOMETHING--*GOD*, WHAT THOUGHTS!
HAHA HA!
SUFFER, YOU TWIT.
YOU'RE SO PATHETIC, WITH YOUR *FEELINGS* AND *MORALS.* *BLECK!*
JUST *ENJOY* IT, MARY!
BUT SHE CAN'T. SHE'S TOO TRAUMATIZED.
BLAST! NO TELLING *WHAT* THAT GROVELING LITTLE JERK COULD DO.
KICK!

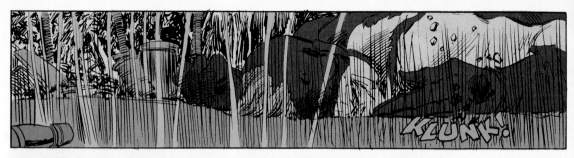

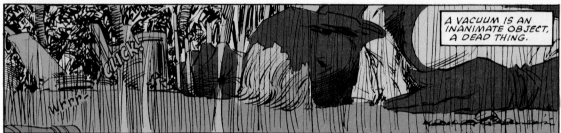

KLUNK!
A VACUUM IS AN INANIMATE OBJECT, A DEAD THING.
CLICK!
Wrrr-
A VACUUM CAN'T BREATHE OR THINK.
VROOM!
Wrrr-
VOOM!
A VACUUM HAS NO WILL.
A VACUUM IS AN ORDINARY, BORING, MUNDANE, DO-MESTIC OBJECT.
VRRR-RRR!
A VACUUM IS A HUNK OF STUPID METAL. A VACUUM CAN'T HURT YOU.
VOOM!

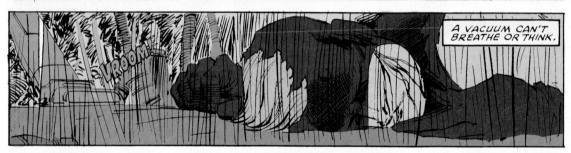

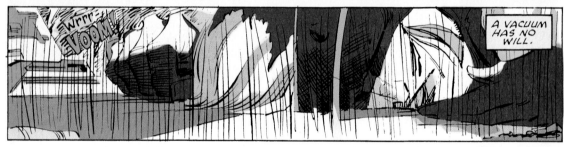

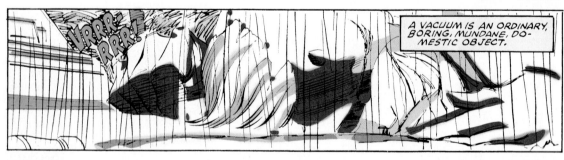

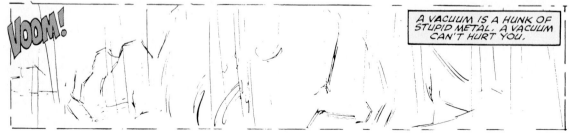

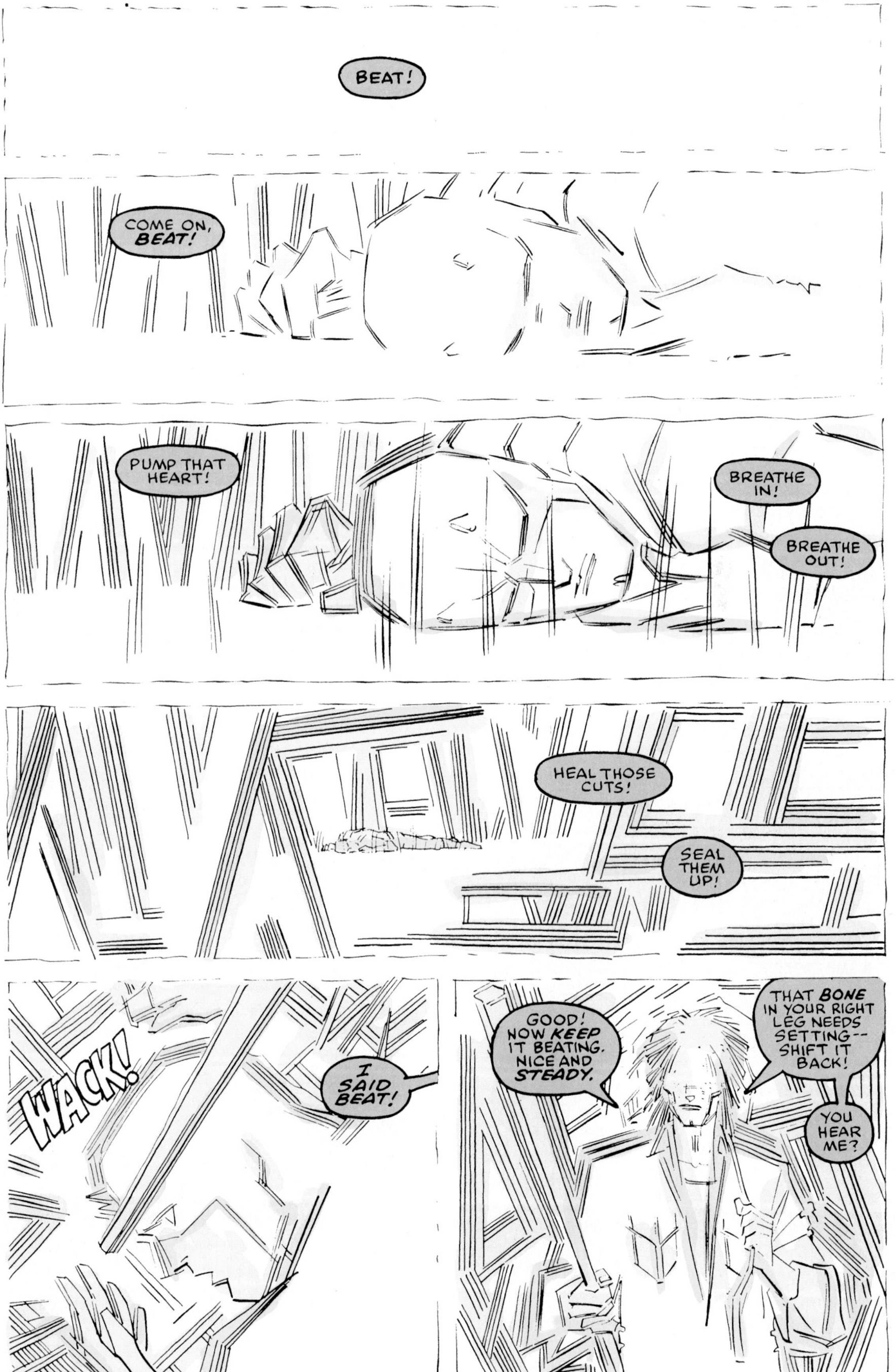
BEAT!
COME ON, BEAT!
PUMP THAT HEART!
BREATHE IN!
BREATHE OUT!
HEAL THOSE CUTS!
SEAL THEM UP!
WACK!
I SAID BEAT!
GOOD! NOW KEEP IT BEATING. NICE AND STEADY.
THAT BONE IN YOUR RIGHT LEG NEEDS SETTING-- SHIFT IT BACK!
YOU HEAR ME?

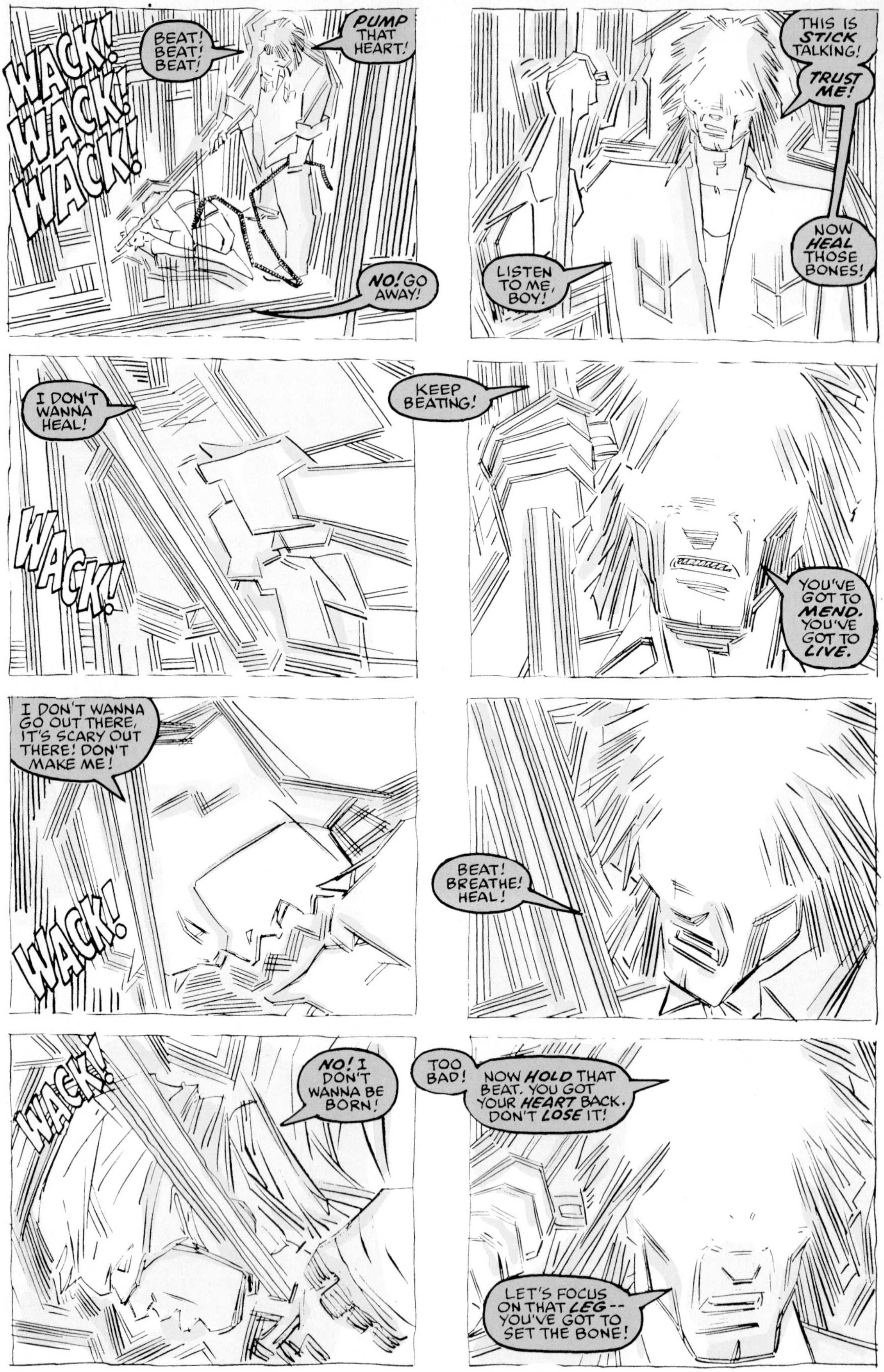
WACK! WACK! WACK!
BEAT! BEAT! BEAT!
PUMP THAT HEART!
NO! GO AWAY!
THIS IS STICK TALKING!
TRUST ME!
LISTEN TO ME, BOY!
NOW HEAL THOSE BONES!
I DON'T WANNA HEAL!
WACK!
KEEP BEATING!
YOU'VE GOT TO MEND. YOU'VE GOT TO LIVE.
I DON'T WANNA GO OUT THERE, IT'S SCARY OUT THERE! DON'T MAKE ME!
WACK!
BEAT! BREATHE! HEAL!
WACK!
NO! I DON'T WANNA BE BORN!
TOO BAD!
NOW HOLD THAT BEAT. YOU GOT YOUR HEART BACK. DON'T LOSE IT!
LET'S FOCUS ON THAT LEG-- YOU'VE GOT TO SET THE BONE!

I DON'T WANNA! I'M *DEAD,* I WANNA *STAY* DEAD!

I DON'T WANNA GO OUT THERE, I DON'T WANNA BE BORN!

WACK!

SHUT UP!

YOU FEEL IT? HEAL IT!

VRRRRRRRRRRRRRRRRRRRRRRR

STREET'S *BAD,* MAN. =*sniff!*=

LOTTA ACTION.

HANDS OFF!

HEY, BABY-- YOUCH!

SOMETHIN' IN THE *AIR,* MAN.

IT'S *OUR* TURN, *STREET'S* TURN.

REVOLUTION, MAN. *TAKE* IT. IT'S TIME TO *TAKE* IT ALL!

THE *RICH* BEEN GETTIN' *RICHER* FOR TOO LONG--

--*OUR* TIME'S COME!

WHY'D HE THROW THAT HYPODERMIC AT YOU, KAREN?

I DON'T KNOW, LET'S JUST GET OUT OF HERE.

WHY THEY ALL SO *MAD,* KAREN?

I DON'T KNOW, DARLA.

NEW YORK CITY'S ALWAYS BEEN AN *ANGRY* PLACE.

THE RICH BUILD HIGHER, MORE INSULATED TOWERS...

THE POOR GET FORCED OUT OF THEIR HOMES...

PLACE IS *RIPE* FOR A REVOLUTION...

SOONER WE GET TO THE POLICE STATION, THE BETTER.

15TH PRECINCT   15TH PRECINC

IT'S LIKE NEW YORK'S IN A *BAD MOOD...*

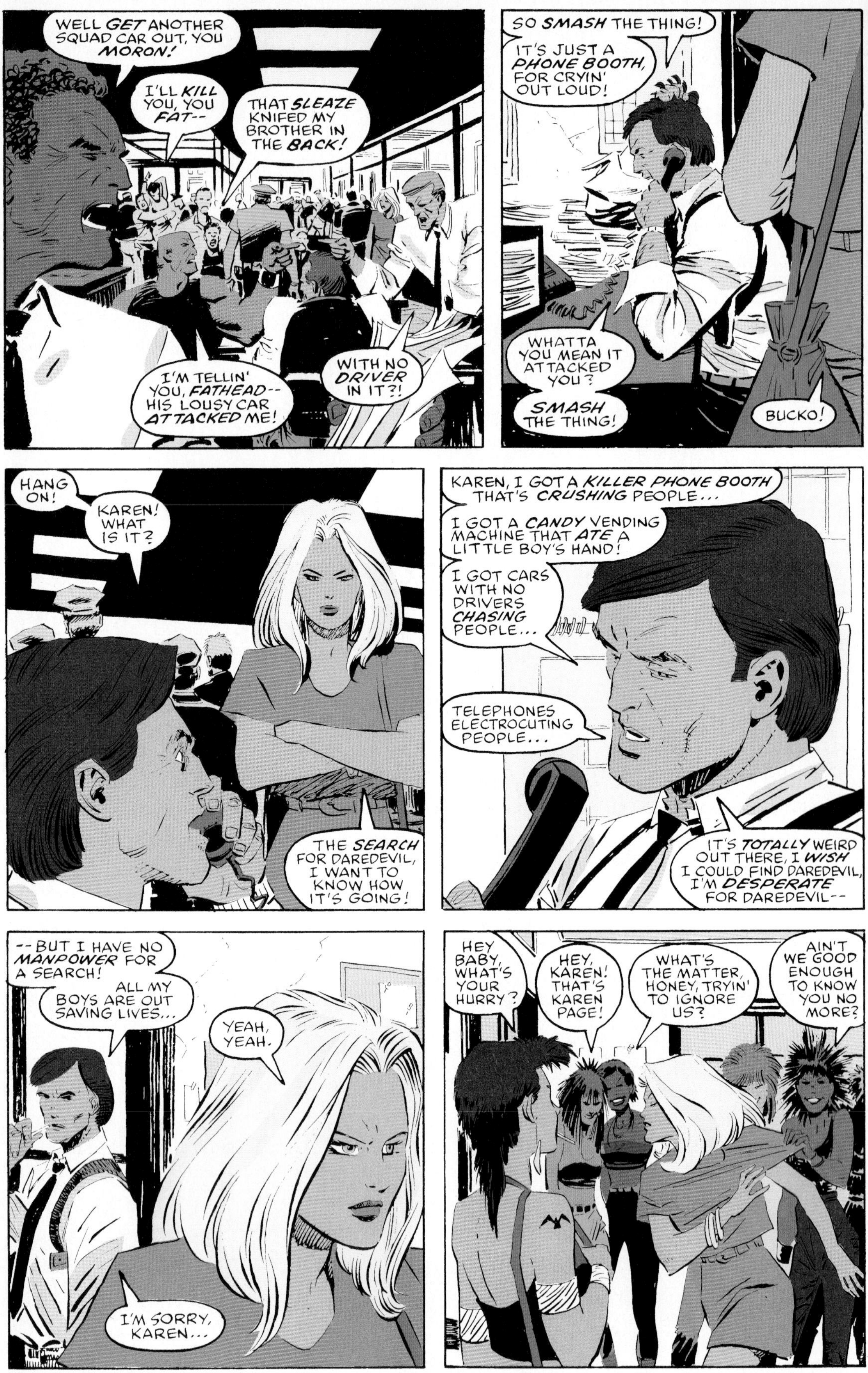
WELL GET ANOTHER SQUAD CAR OUT, YOU MORON!
I'LL KILL YOU, YOU FAT--
THAT SLEAZE KNIFED MY BROTHER IN THE BACK!
I'M TELLIN' YOU, FATHEAD-- HIS LOUSY CAR ATTACKED ME!
WITH NO DRIVER IN IT?!
SO SMASH THE THING!
IT'S JUST A PHONE BOOTH, FOR CRYIN' OUT LOUD!
WHATTA YOU MEAN IT ATTACKED YOU?
SMASH THE THING!
BUCKO!
HANG ON!
KAREN! WHAT IS IT?
THE SEARCH FOR DAREDEVIL, I WANT TO KNOW HOW IT'S GOING!
KAREN, I GOT A KILLER PHONE BOOTH THAT'S CRUSHING PEOPLE...
I GOT A CANDY VENDING MACHINE THAT ATE A LITTLE BOY'S HAND!
I GOT CARS WITH NO DRIVERS CHASING PEOPLE...
TELEPHONES ELECTROCUTING PEOPLE...
IT'S TOTALLY WEIRD OUT THERE, I WISH I COULD FIND DAREDEVIL, I'M DESPERATE FOR DAREDEVIL--
--BUT I HAVE NO MANPOWER FOR A SEARCH!
ALL MY BOYS ARE OUT SAVING LIVES...
YEAH, YEAH.
I'M SORRY, KAREN...
HEY BABY, WHAT'S YOUR HURRY?
HEY, KAREN! THAT'S KAREN PAGE!
WHAT'S THE MATTER, HONEY, TRYIN' TO IGNORE US?
AIN'T WE GOOD ENOUGH TO KNOW YOU NO MORE?

HOW'D IT GO?

KAREN?

WHAT'S THE MATTER?

SHE'S CRYIN'?

SHUSH!

I....

WHY...?

WHAT'S.... GOING ON?

DAREDEVIL'S GONE.... AND THE WHOLE *WORLD* IS FALLING APART!

I CAN'T... TAKE IT... ANYMORE....

WHERE IS HE?!

RRRrrrRRRrrrRRRrrrRRR   RRRRRR

WHY DON'T YOU WANT TO BE BORN?

BAD, BAD WORLD OUT THERE...

I'M JUST A LITTLE BOY! I CAN'T... *FIGHT* ANYMORE!

SO WHAT?!

I GET BEAT UP TOO MUCH!

SO WHAT?!

MY DADDY USED TO YELL AT ME! HE... WAS A FIGHTER, BUT HE SAID DON'T FIGHT!

I'M ONLY A BABY, AND... HE... *CONFUSED* ME!

OH, I SEE. YOUR *DADDY* RUINED YOU. IT'S *HIS* FAULT.

YOU HAD A TRAGIC, TRAUMATIZED CHILD-HOOD, SO NOW YOU HAVE A RIGHT TO *COLLAPSE?*

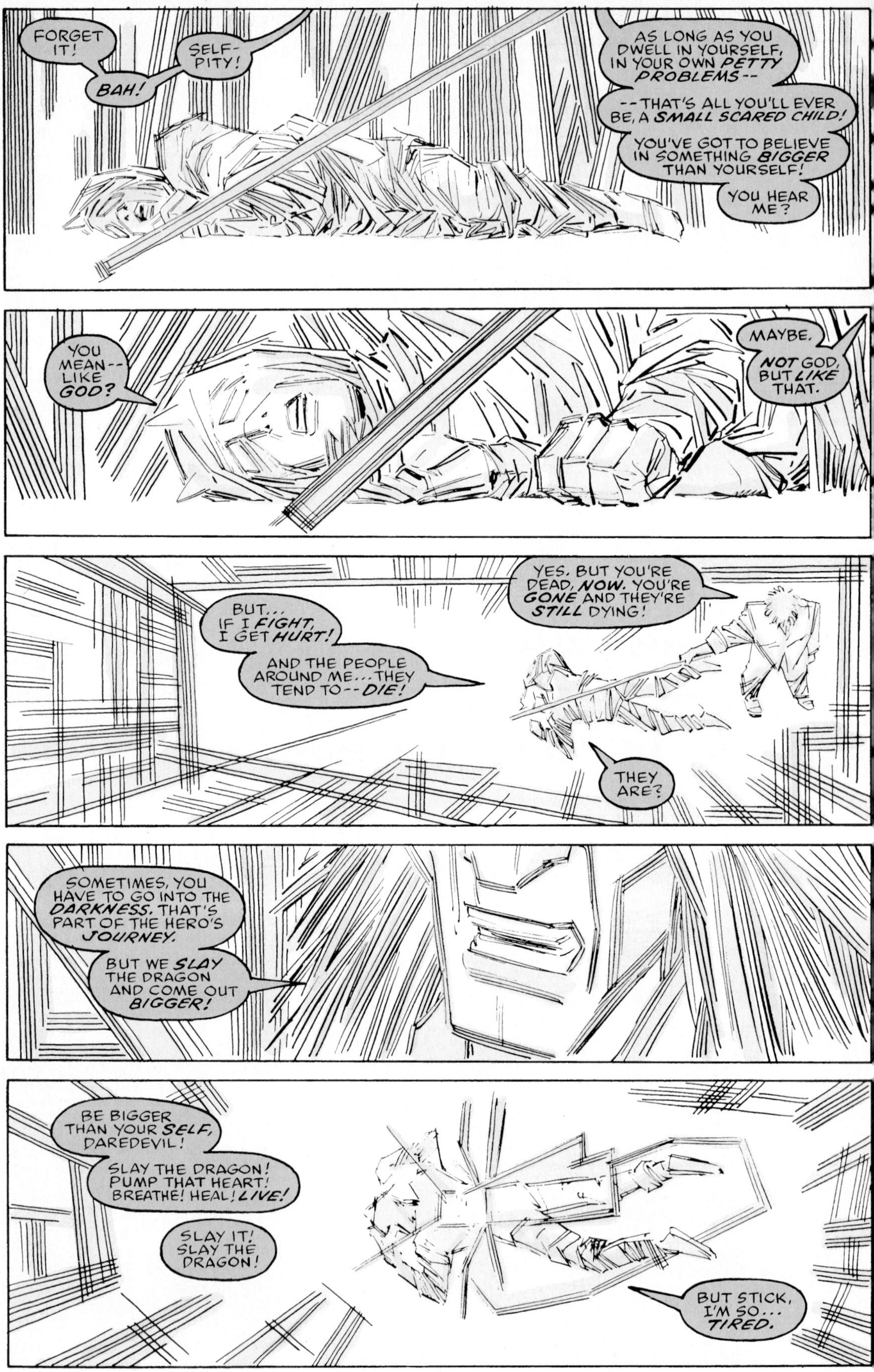
FORGET IT!
SELF-PITY!
BAH!
AS LONG AS YOU DWELL IN YOURSELF, IN YOUR OWN PETTY PROBLEMS--
--THAT'S ALL YOU'LL EVER BE, A SMALL SCARED CHILD!
YOU'VE GOT TO BELIEVE IN SOMETHING BIGGER THAN YOURSELF!
YOU HEAR ME?
YOU MEAN--LIKE GOD?
MAYBE. NOT GOD, BUT LIKE THAT.
BUT... IF I FIGHT, I GET HURT!
AND THE PEOPLE AROUND ME... THEY TEND TO--DIE!
YES. BUT YOU'RE DEAD, NOW. YOU'RE GONE AND THEY'RE STILL DYING!
THEY ARE?
SOMETIMES, YOU HAVE TO GO INTO THE DARKNESS. THAT'S PART OF THE HERO'S JOURNEY.
BUT WE SLAY THE DRAGON AND COME OUT BIGGER!
BE BIGGER THAN YOUR SELF, DAREDEVIL!
SLAY THE DRAGON! PUMP THAT HEART! BREATHE! HEAL! LIVE!
SLAY IT! SLAY THE DRAGON!
BUT STICK, I'M SO... TIRED.

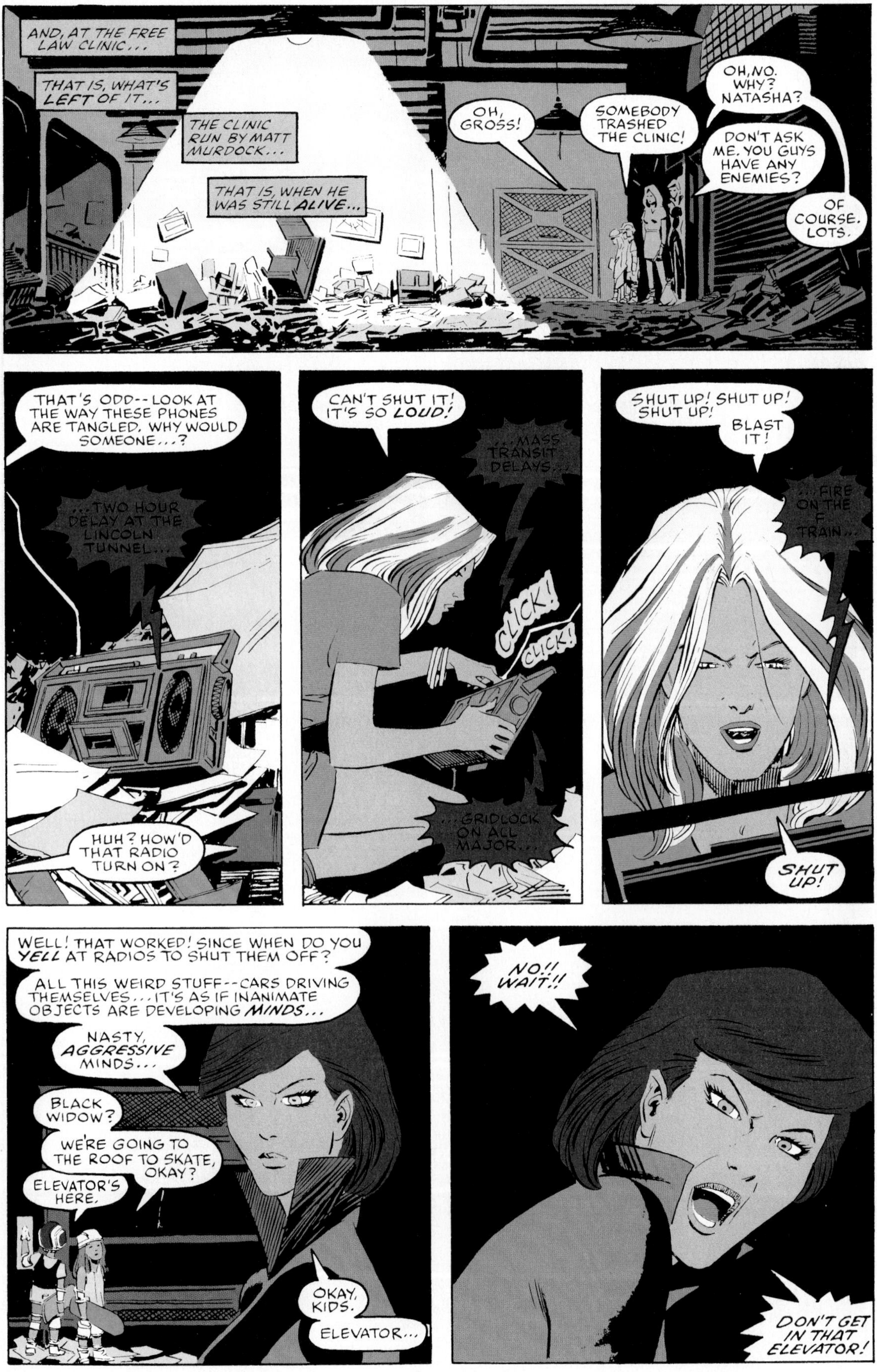
AND, AT THE FREE LAW CLINIC...
THAT IS, WHAT'S LEFT OF IT...
THE CLINIC RUN BY MATT MURDOCK...
THAT IS, WHEN HE WAS STILL ALIVE...
OH, GROSS!
SOMEBODY TRASHED THE CLINIC!
OH, NO. WHY? NATASHA?
DON'T ASK ME. YOU GUYS HAVE ANY ENEMIES?
OF COURSE. LOTS.
THAT'S ODD--LOOK AT THE WAY THESE PHONES ARE TANGLED. WHY WOULD SOMEONE...?
...TWO HOUR DELAY AT THE LINCOLN TUNNEL...
HUH? HOW'D THAT RADIO TURN ON?
CAN'T SHUT IT! IT'S SO LOUD!
...MASS TRANSIT DELAYS...
CLICK!
CLICK!
...GRIDLOCK ON ALL MAJOR...
SHUT UP! SHUT UP! SHUT UP!
BLAST IT!
...FIRE ON THE F TRAIN...
SHUT UP!
WELL! THAT WORKED! SINCE WHEN DO YOU YELL AT RADIOS TO SHUT THEM OFF?
ALL THIS WEIRD STUFF--CARS DRIVING THEMSELVES...IT'S AS IF INANIMATE OBJECTS ARE DEVELOPING MINDS...
NASTY, AGGRESSIVE MINDS...
BLACK WIDOW?
WE'RE GOING TO THE ROOF TO SKATE, OKAY?
ELEVATOR'S HERE.
OKAY, KIDS.
ELEVATOR...!
NO!! WAIT!!
DON'T GET IN THAT ELEVATOR!

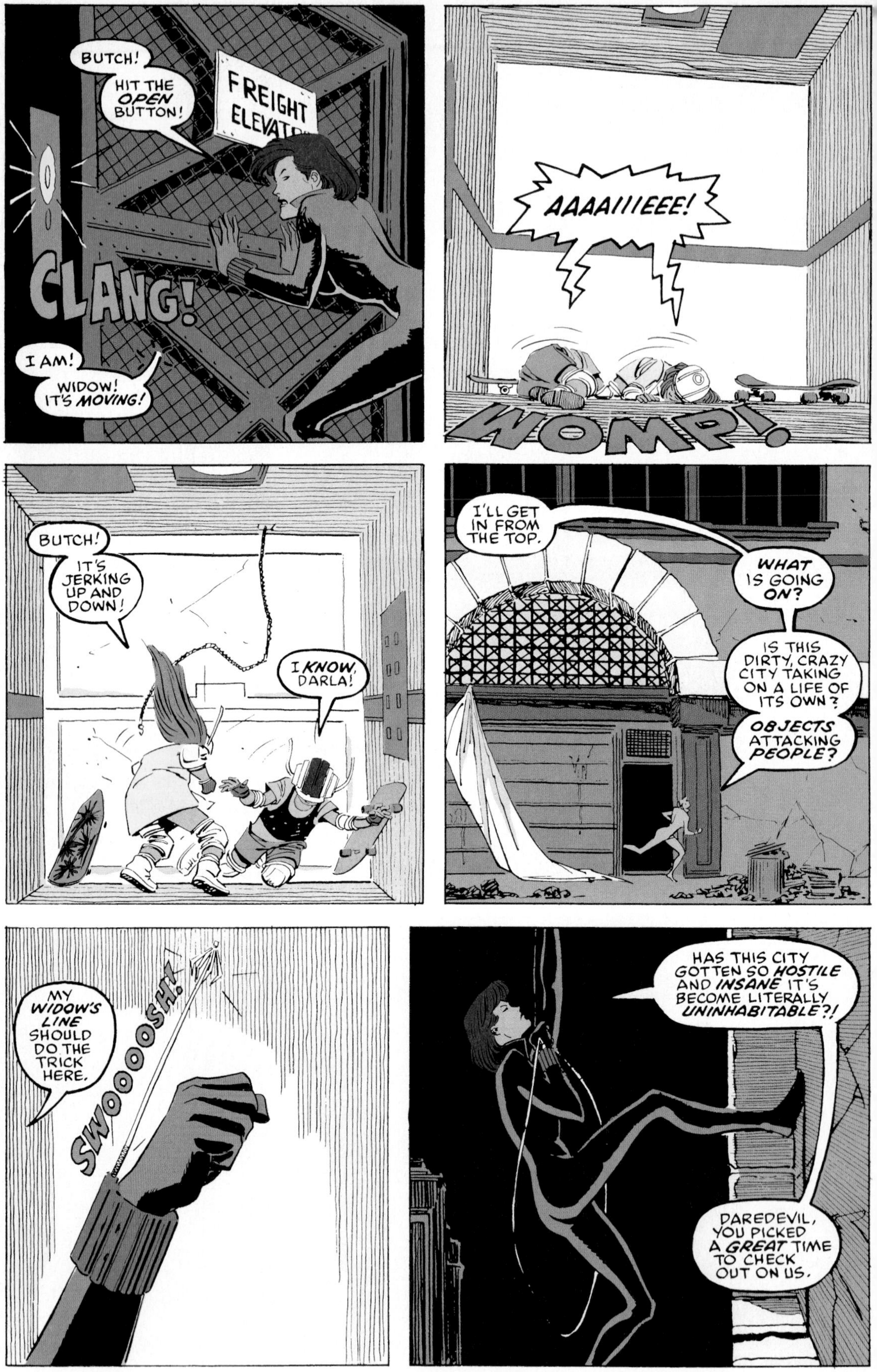

BUTCH!
HIT THE OPEN BUTTON!
FREIGHT ELEVAT
CLANG!
I AM!
WIDOW! IT'S MOVING!
AAAAIIIEEE!
WOMP!
BUTCH!
IT'S JERKING UP AND DOWN!
I KNOW, DARLA!
I'LL GET IN FROM THE TOP.
WHAT IS GOING ON?
IS THIS DIRTY, CRAZY CITY TAKING ON A LIFE OF ITS OWN?
OBJECTS ATTACKING PEOPLE?
MY WIDOW'S LINE SHOULD DO THE TRICK HERE.
SWOOOOSH!
HAS THIS CITY GOTTEN SO HOSTILE AND INSANE IT'S BECOME LITERALLY UNINHABITABLE?!
DAREDEVIL, YOU PICKED A GREAT TIME TO CHECK OUT ON US.

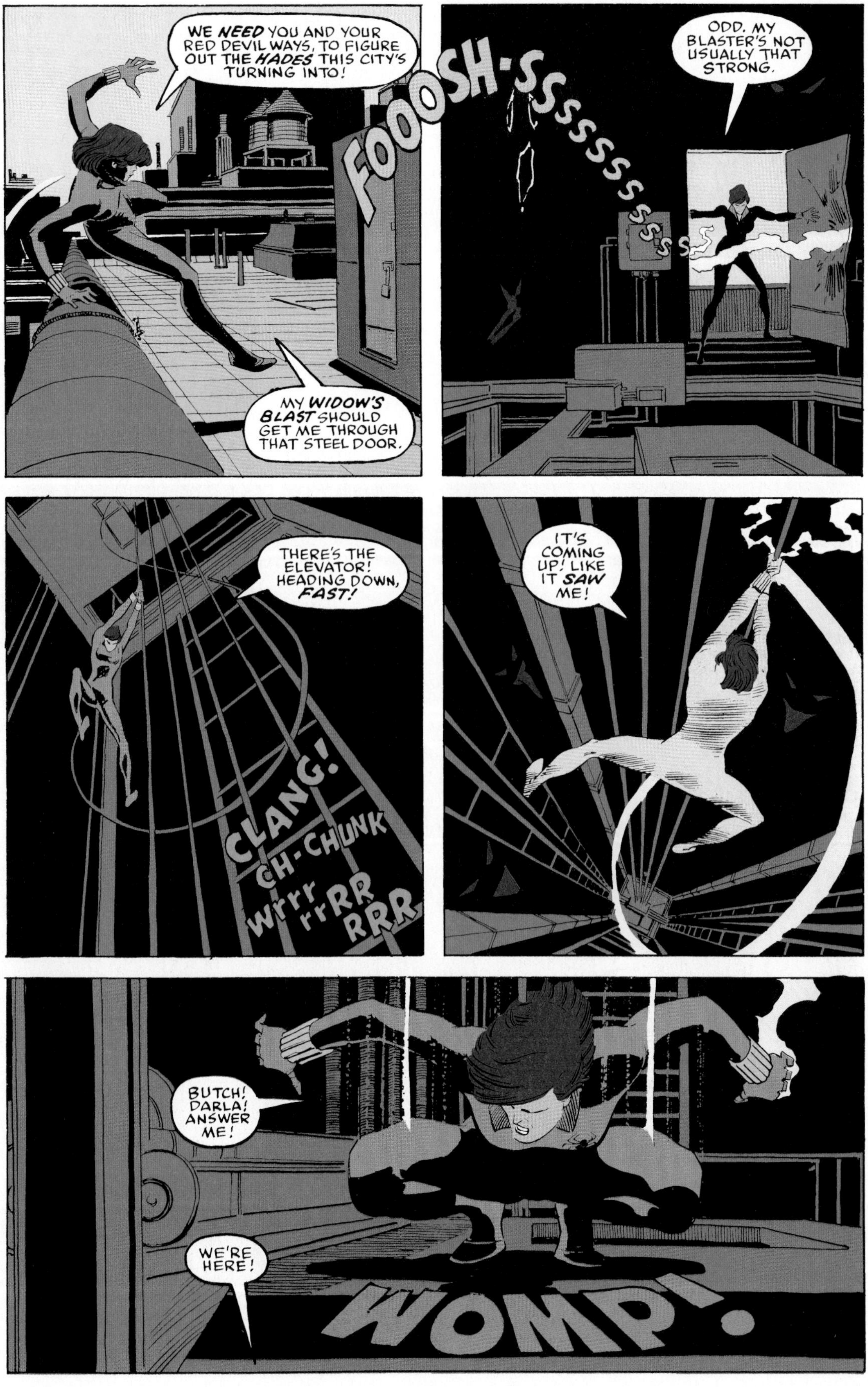
WE NEED YOU AND YOUR RED DEVIL WAYS, TO FIGURE OUT THE HADES THIS CITY'S TURNING INTO!
MY WIDOW'S BLAST SHOULD GET ME THROUGH THAT STEEL DOOR.
FOOOSH-SSSSSSSSSSSS
ODD. MY BLASTER'S NOT USUALLY THAT STRONG.
THERE'S THE ELEVATOR! HEADING DOWN, FAST!
CLANG!
CH-CHUNK
wrrr rrRR RRR
IT'S COMING UP! LIKE IT SAW ME!
BUTCH! DARLA! ANSWER ME!
WE'RE HERE!
WOMP!

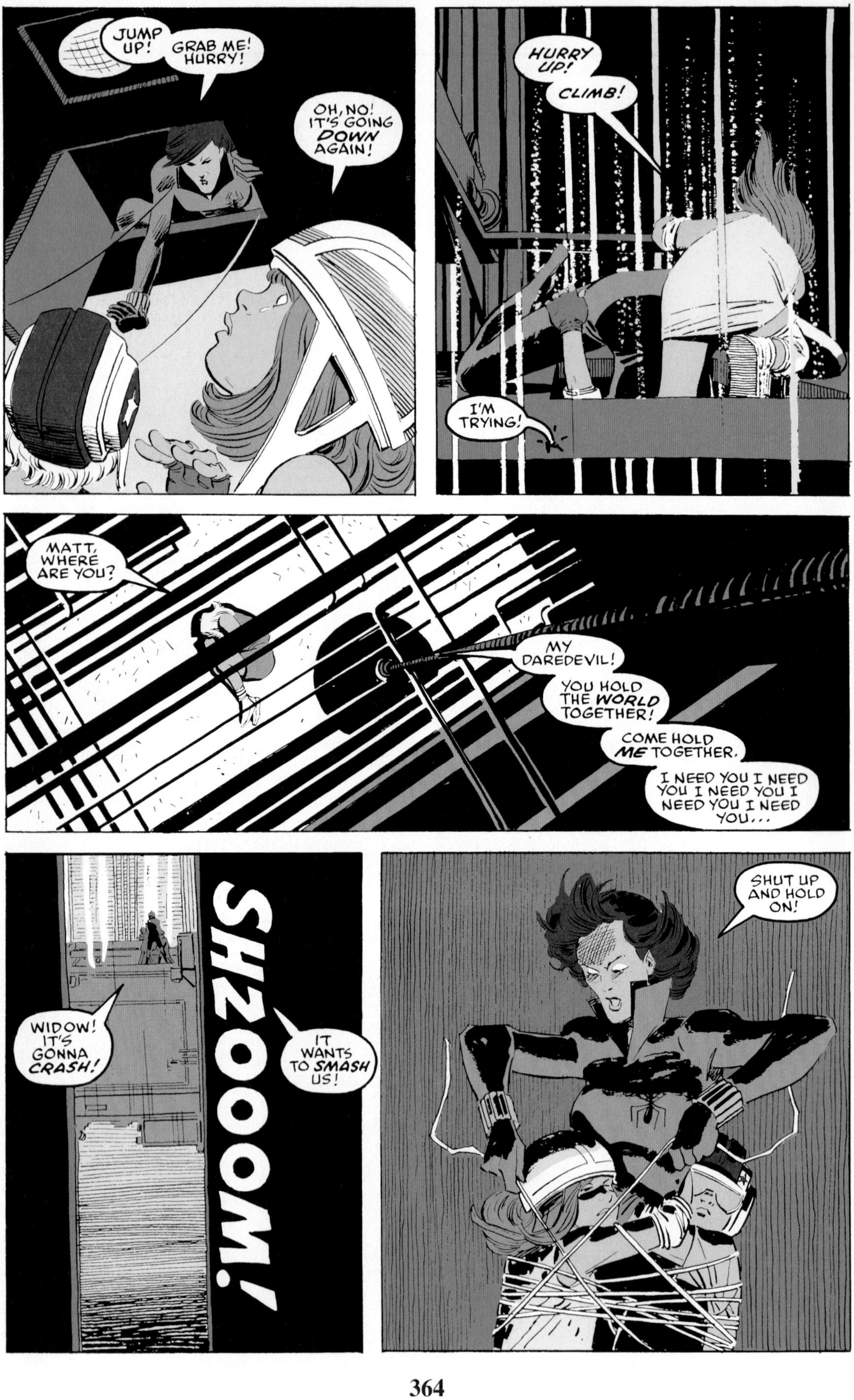
JUMP UP!
GRAB ME! HURRY!
OH, NO! IT'S GOING DOWN AGAIN!
HURRY UP!
CLIMB!
I'M TRYING!
MATT, WHERE ARE YOU?
MY DAREDEVIL!
YOU HOLD THE WORLD TOGETHER!
COME HOLD ME TOGETHER.
I NEED YOU I NEED YOU I NEED YOU I NEED YOU I NEED YOU...
SHZOOOM!
WIDOW! IT'S GONNA CRASH!
IT WANTS TO SMASH US!
SHUT UP AND HOLD ON!

FOOOOSH!

I CAN'T BREATHE!

JUST HOLD ON!

CLANK!

WIDOW-- I'M SLIPPING!

I... CAN'T BREATHE...

K-CHUNK!

HOLD ON!

GET READY--

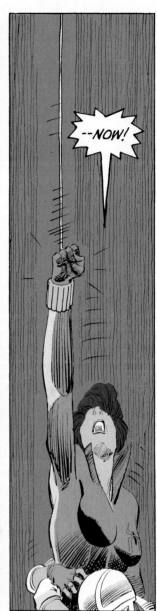

--NOW!

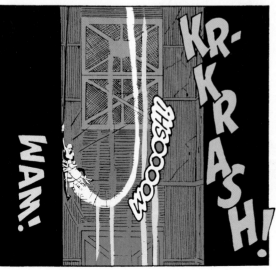

WAM!

KR-KRASH!

WOOOOSH!

LOOK AT IT! SMASHED LIKE AN ACCORDION!

THAT... THAT COULD HAVE BEEN US!

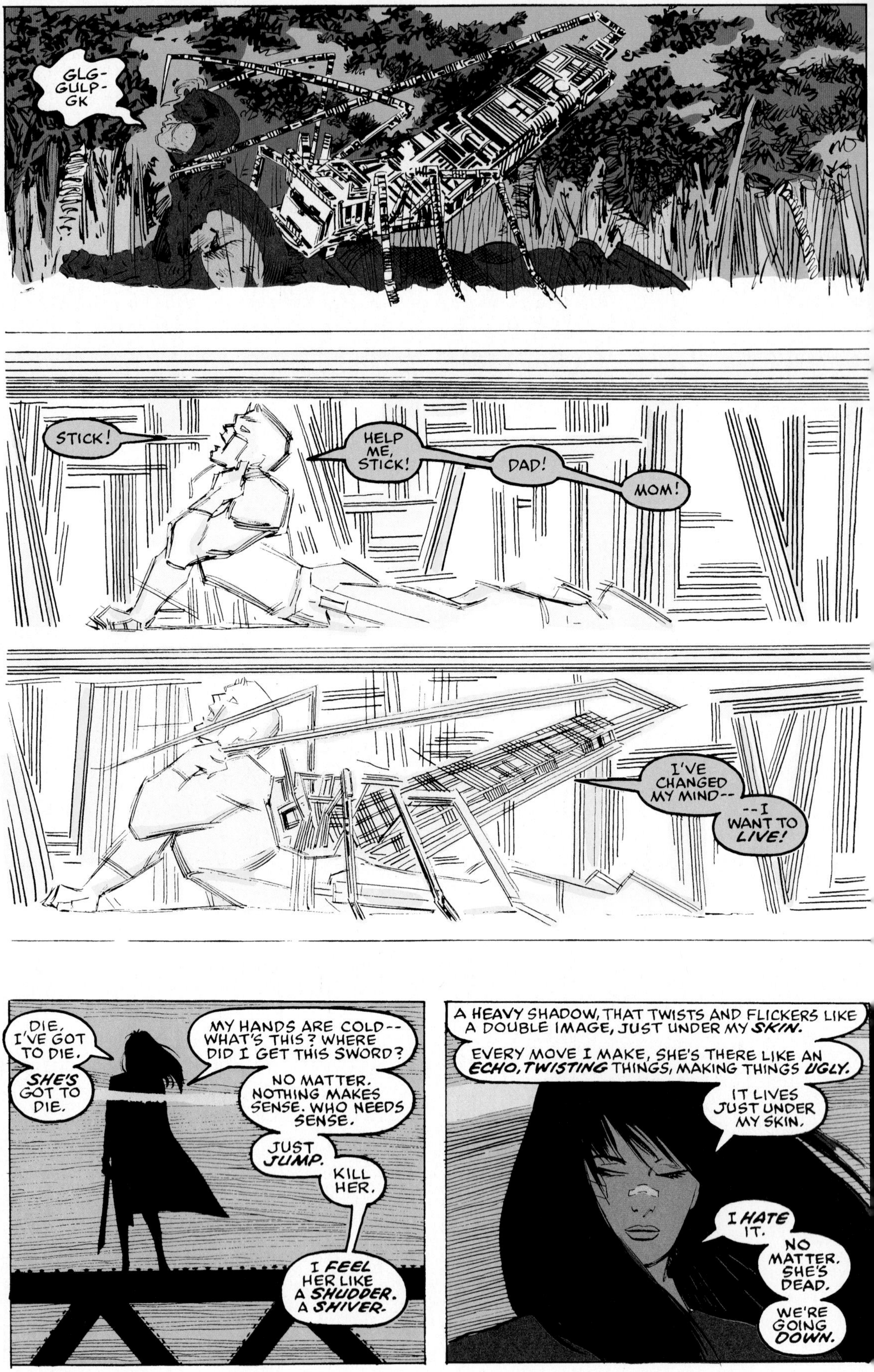
GLG-GULP-GK
STICK!
HELP ME, STICK!
DAD!
MOM!
I'VE CHANGED MY MIND--
--I WANT TO LIVE!
DIE. I'VE GOT TO DIE.
SHE'S GOT TO DIE.
MY HANDS ARE COLD--WHAT'S THIS? WHERE DID I GET THIS SWORD?
NO MATTER. NOTHING MAKES SENSE. WHO NEEDS SENSE.
JUST JUMP.
KILL HER.
I FEEL HER LIKE A SHUDDER. A SHIVER-
A HEAVY SHADOW, THAT TWISTS AND FLICKERS LIKE A DOUBLE IMAGE, JUST UNDER MY SKIN.
EVERY MOVE I MAKE, SHE'S THERE LIKE AN ECHO, TWISTING THINGS, MAKING THINGS UGLY.
IT LIVES JUST UNDER MY SKIN.
I HATE IT.
NO MATTER. SHE'S DEAD.
WE'RE GOING DOWN.

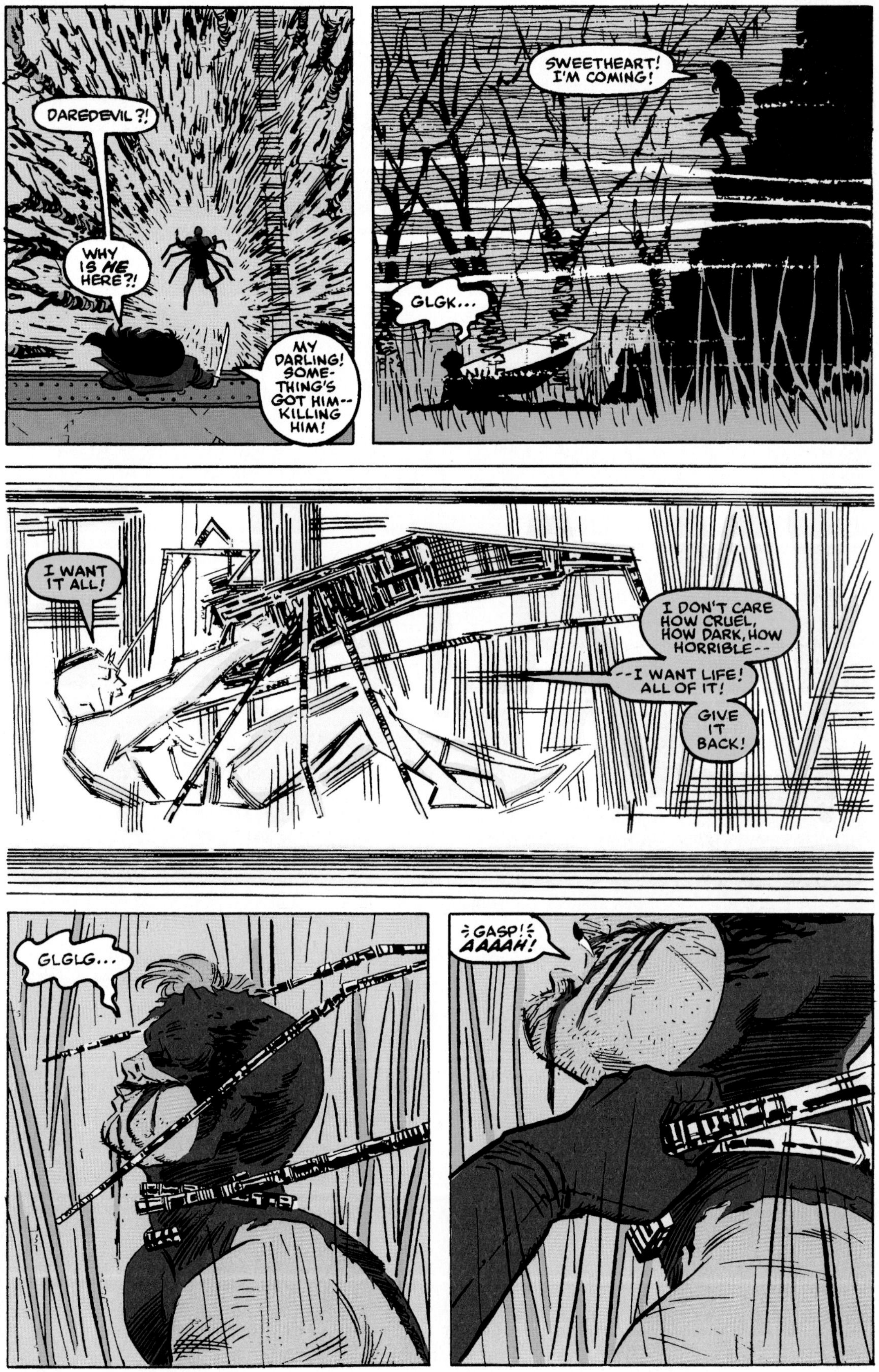
DAREDEVIL?!
WHY IS HE HERE?!
MY DARLING! SOMETHING'S GOT HIM-- KILLING HIM!
SWEETHEART! I'M COMING!
GLGK...
I WANT IT ALL!
I DON'T CARE HOW CRUEL, HOW DARK, HOW HORRIBLE--
--I WANT LIFE! ALL OF IT!
GIVE IT BACK!
GLGLG...
GASP! AAAAH!

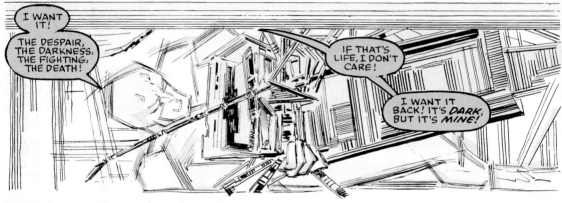

I WANT IT!

THE DESPAIR, THE DARKNESS, THE FIGHTING, THE DEATH!

IF THAT'S LIFE, I DON'T CARE!

I WANT IT BACK! IT'S *DARK,* BUT IT'S *MINE!*

PK-KOOM!

WHAT'S THAT-- OH!

CLANG!

PING!

SWOOSH!

CLINK!

VERY GOOD, MARY! *PROTECT* YOURSELF!

TOO BAD ONLY *TYPHOID* CAN SWING A MACHETE LIKE THAT!

YOU LET ME OUT, YOU FOOL!

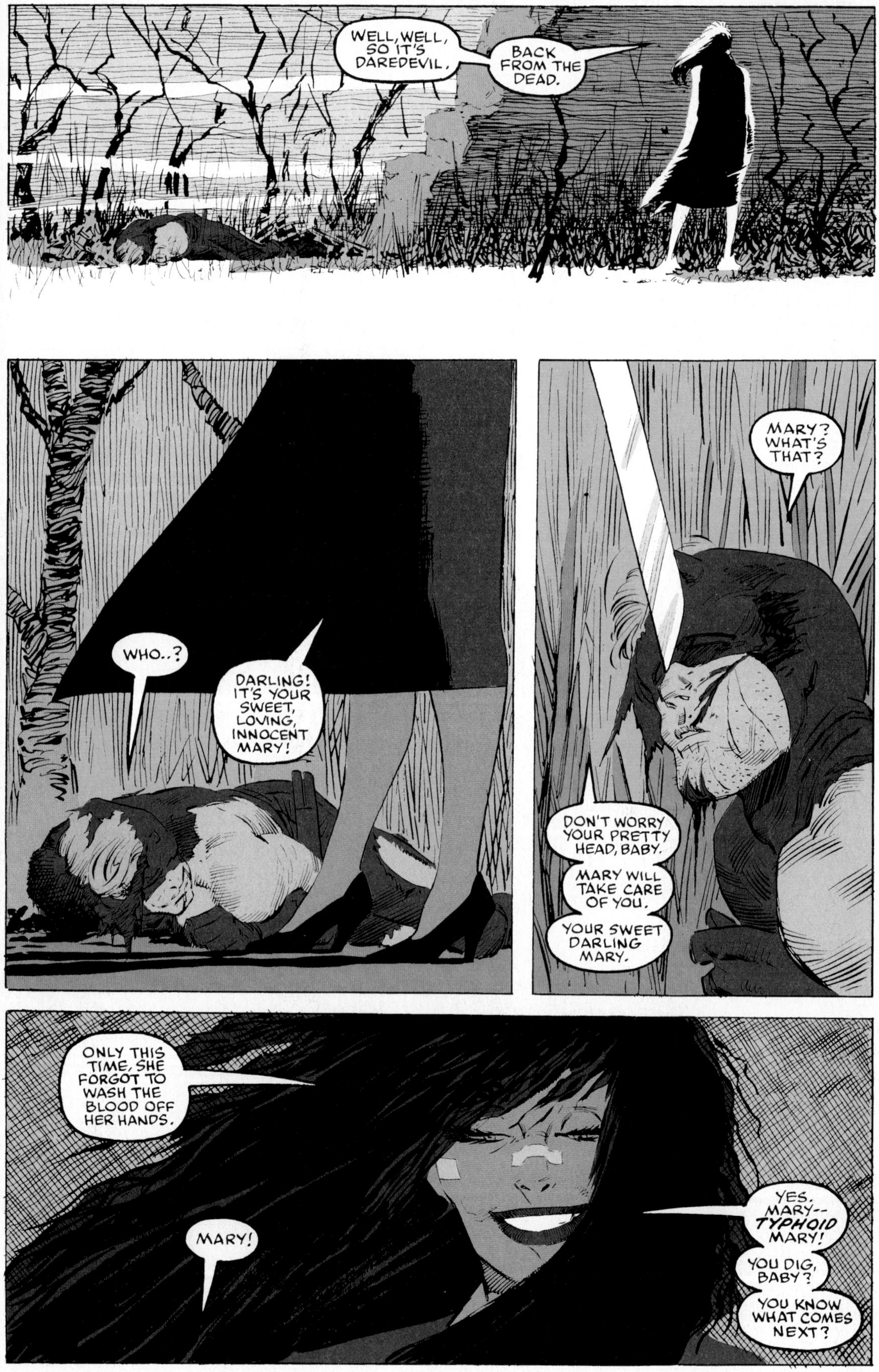
WELL, WELL, SO IT'S DAREDEVIL,
BACK FROM THE DEAD.
WHO..?
DARLING! IT'S YOUR SWEET, LOVING, INNOCENT MARY!
MARY? WHAT'S THAT?
DON'T WORRY YOUR PRETTY HEAD, BABY.
MARY WILL TAKE CARE OF YOU.
YOUR SWEET DARLING MARY.
ONLY THIS TIME, SHE FORGOT TO WASH THE BLOOD OFF HER HANDS.
MARY!
YES. MARY-- TYPHOID MARY!
YOU DIG, BABY?
YOU KNOW WHAT COMES NEXT?

END

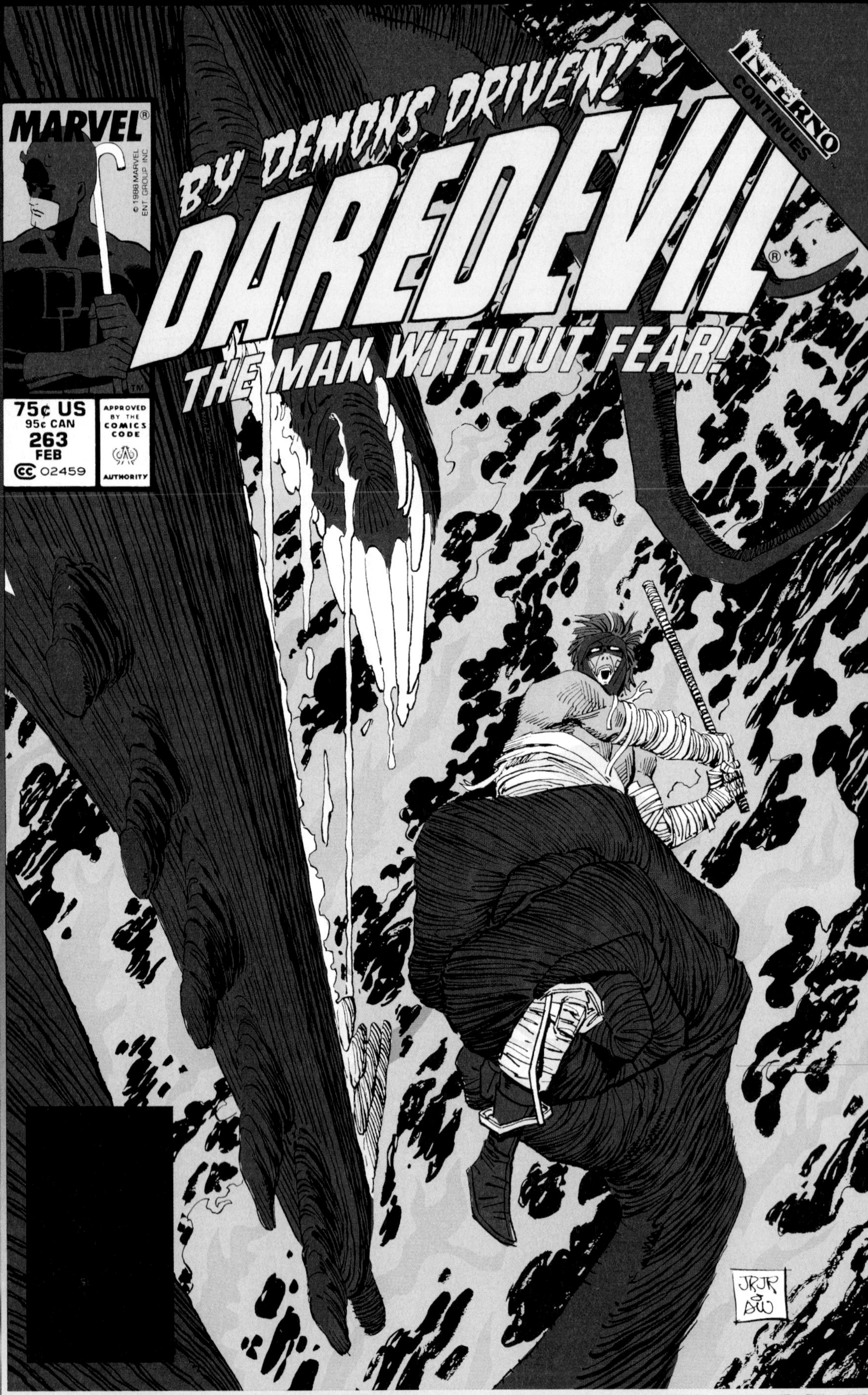
MARVEL®
© 1988 MARVEL ENT GROUP, INC.
75¢ US
95¢ CAN
263
FEB
CC 02459
APPROVED BY THE COMICS CODE AUTHORITY
BY DEMONS DRIVEN!
INFERNO CONTINUES
DAREDEVIL®
THE MAN WITHOUT FEAR!
JRJR & AW

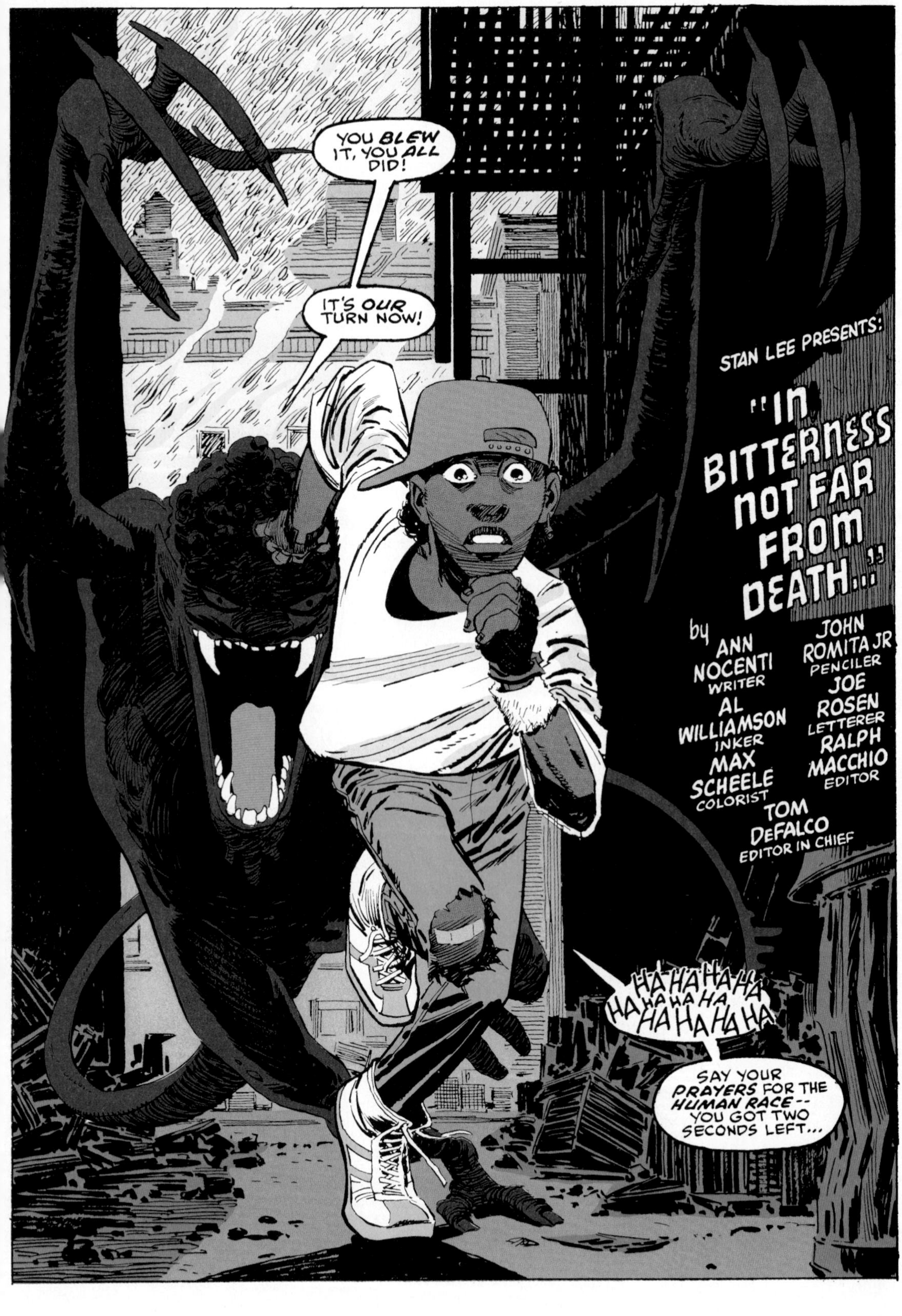
YOU BLEW IT, YOU ALL DID!
IT'S OUR TURN NOW!
STAN LEE PRESENTS:
"IN BITTERNESS NOT FAR FROM DEATH..."
by ANN NOCENTI WRITER
JOHN ROMITA JR PENCILER
AL WILLIAMSON INKER
JOE ROSEN LETTERER
MAX SCHEELE COLORIST
RALPH MACCHIO EDITOR
TOM DeFALCO EDITOR IN CHIEF
HA HA HA HA HA HA HA HA HA HA HA HA HA HA HA
SAY YOUR PRAYERS FOR THE HUMAN RACE -- YOU GOT TWO SECONDS LEFT...

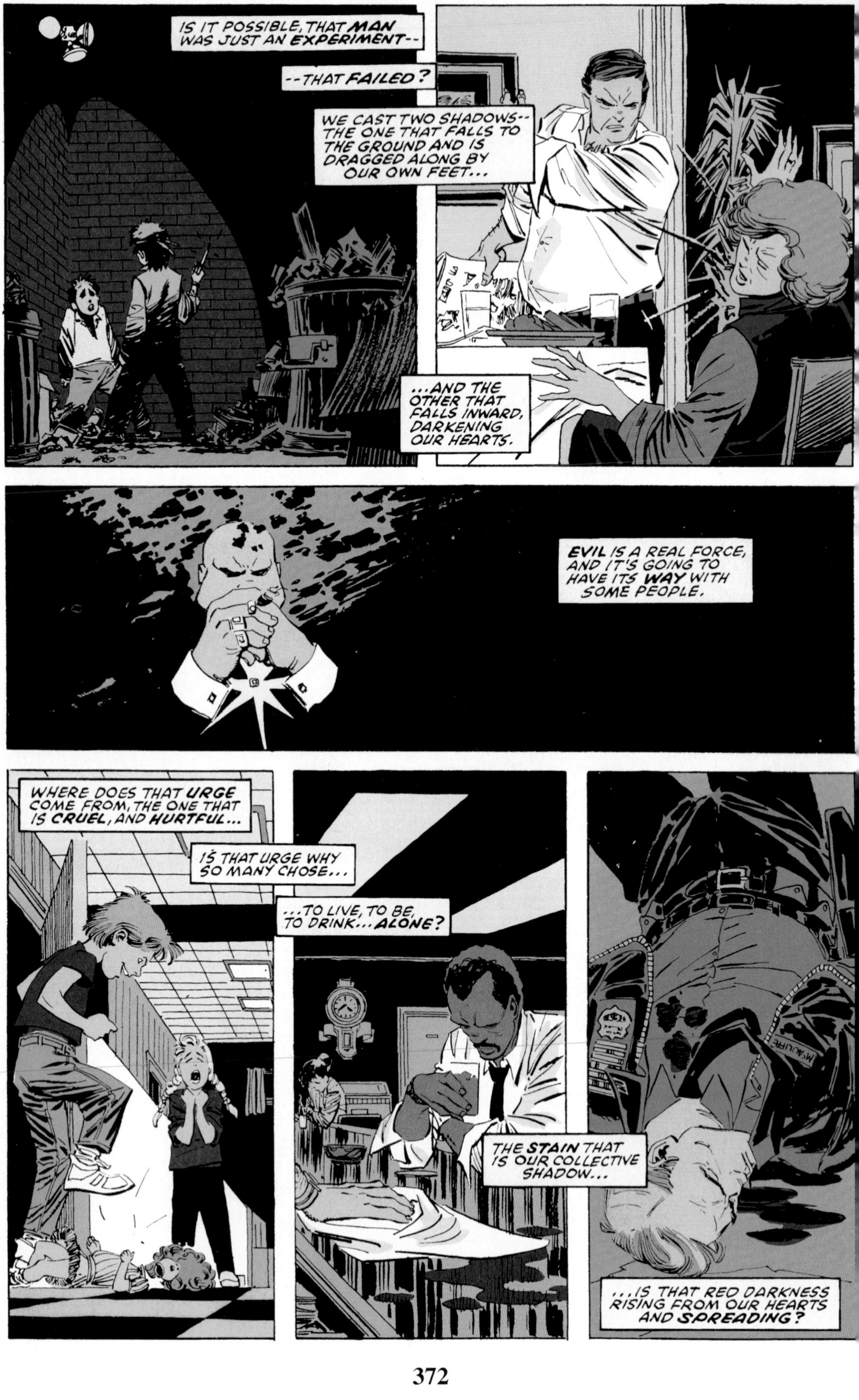
IS IT POSSIBLE, THAT MAN WAS JUST AN EXPERIMENT--
--THAT FAILED?
WE CAST TWO SHADOWS-- THE ONE THAT FALLS TO THE GROUND AND IS DRAGGED ALONG BY OUR OWN FEET...
...AND THE OTHER THAT FALLS INWARD, DARKENING OUR HEARTS.
EVIL IS A REAL FORCE, AND IT'S GOING TO HAVE ITS WAY WITH SOME PEOPLE.
WHERE DOES THAT URGE COME FROM, THE ONE THAT IS CRUEL, AND HURTFUL...
IS THAT URGE WHY SO MANY CHOSE...
...TO LIVE, TO BE, TO DRINK... ALONE?
THE STAIN THAT IS OUR COLLECTIVE SHADOW...
...IS THAT RED DARKNESS RISING FROM OUR HEARTS AND SPREADING?

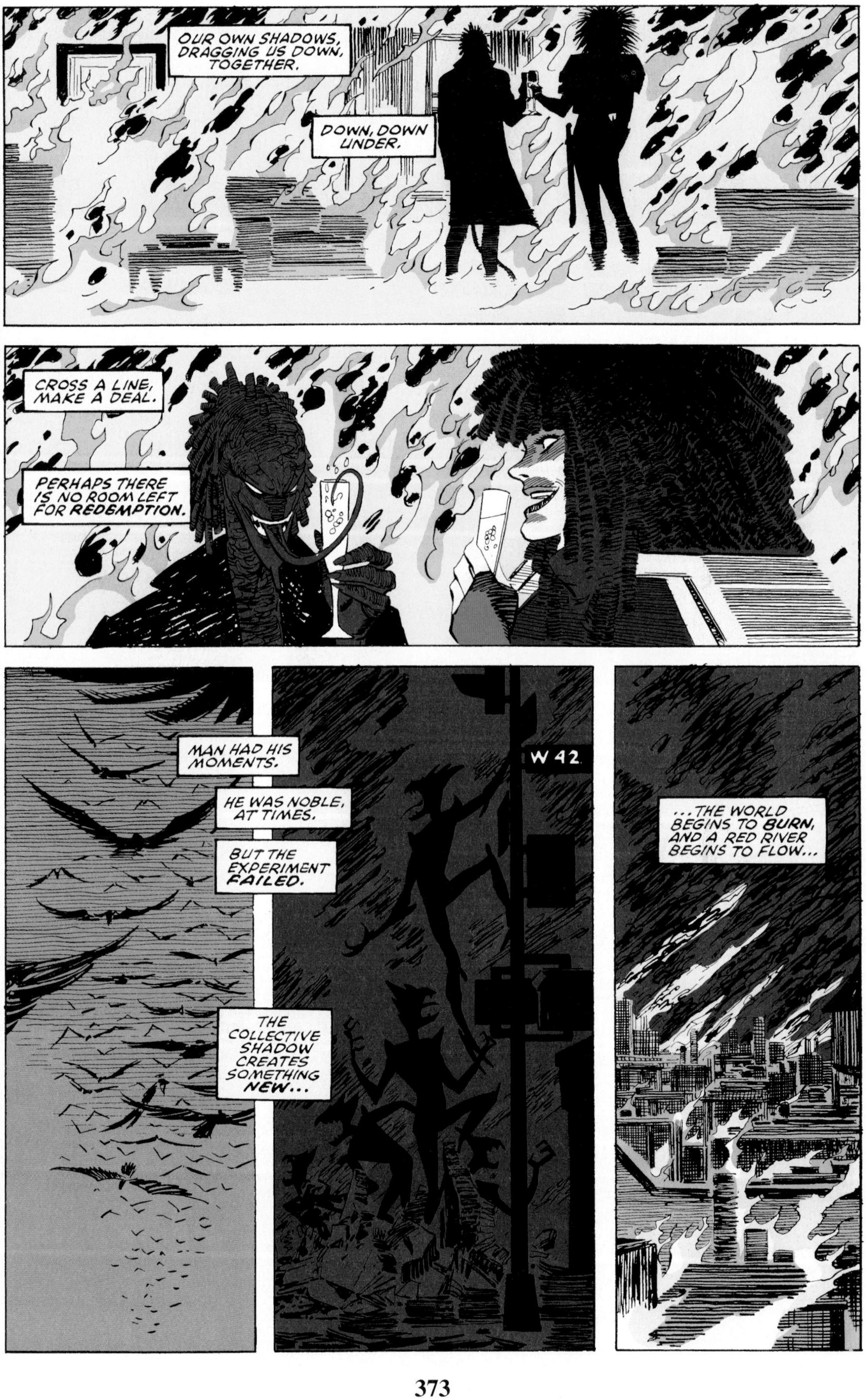
OUR OWN SHADOWS, DRAGGING US DOWN, TOGETHER.
DOWN, DOWN UNDER.
CROSS A LINE, MAKE A DEAL.
PERHAPS THERE IS NO ROOM LEFT FOR REDEMPTION.
MAN HAD HIS MOMENTS.
HE WAS NOBLE, AT TIMES.
BUT THE EXPERIMENT FAILED.
THE COLLECTIVE SHADOW CREATES SOMETHING NEW...
W 42
...THE WORLD BEGINS TO BURN, AND A RED RIVER BEGINS TO FLOW...

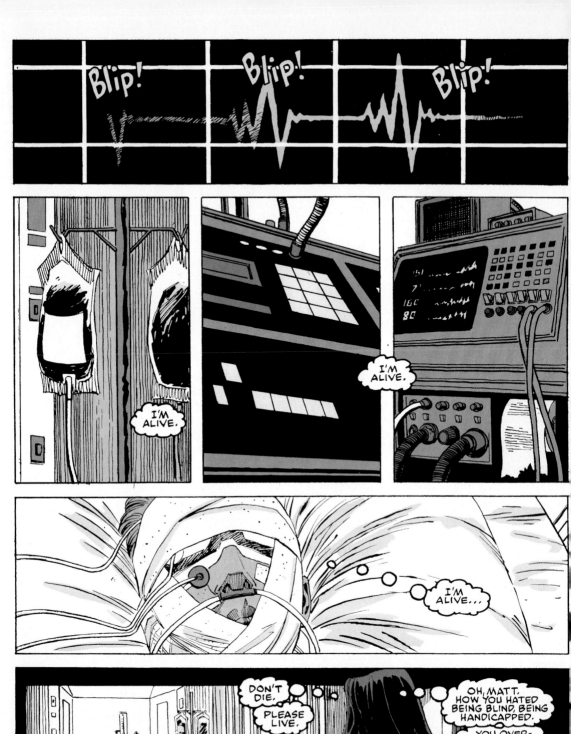

Blip! Blip! Blip!

I'M ALIVE.

I'M ALIVE.

I'M ALIVE...

DON'T DIE.

PLEASE LIVE.

OH, MATT. HOW YOU HATED BEING BLIND, BEING HANDICAPPED.

YOU OVER-COMPENSATED BY DEVELOPING ALL THOSE SUPER SENSES.

AND HERE YOU ARE, VULNERABLE AGAIN, TIED TO MACHINES.

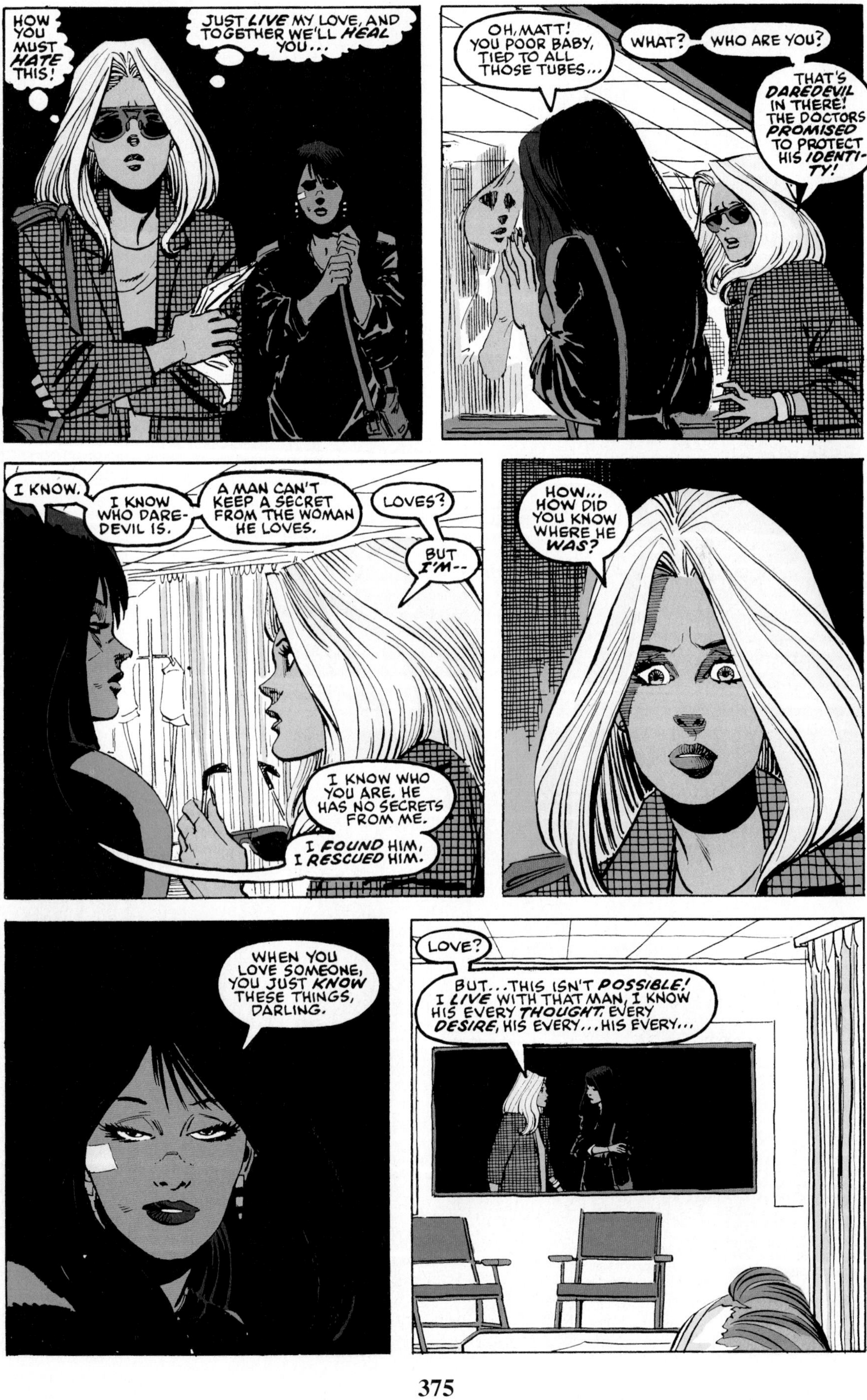
HOW YOU MUST HATE THIS!
JUST LIVE MY LOVE, AND TOGETHER WE'LL HEAL YOU...
OH, MATT! YOU POOR BABY, TIED TO ALL THOSE TUBES...
WHAT?
WHO ARE YOU?
THAT'S DAREDEVIL IN THERE! THE DOCTORS PROMISED TO PROTECT HIS IDENTITY!
I KNOW.
I KNOW WHO DAREDEVIL IS.
A MAN CAN'T KEEP A SECRET FROM THE WOMAN HE LOVES.
LOVES?
BUT I'M--
I KNOW WHO YOU ARE. HE HAS NO SECRETS FROM ME.
I FOUND HIM, I RESCUED HIM.
HOW... HOW DID YOU KNOW WHERE HE WAS?
WHEN YOU LOVE SOMEONE, YOU JUST KNOW THESE THINGS, DARLING.
LOVE?
BUT... THIS ISN'T POSSIBLE! I LIVE WITH THAT MAN, I KNOW HIS EVERY THOUGHT, EVERY DESIRE, HIS EVERY... HIS EVERY...

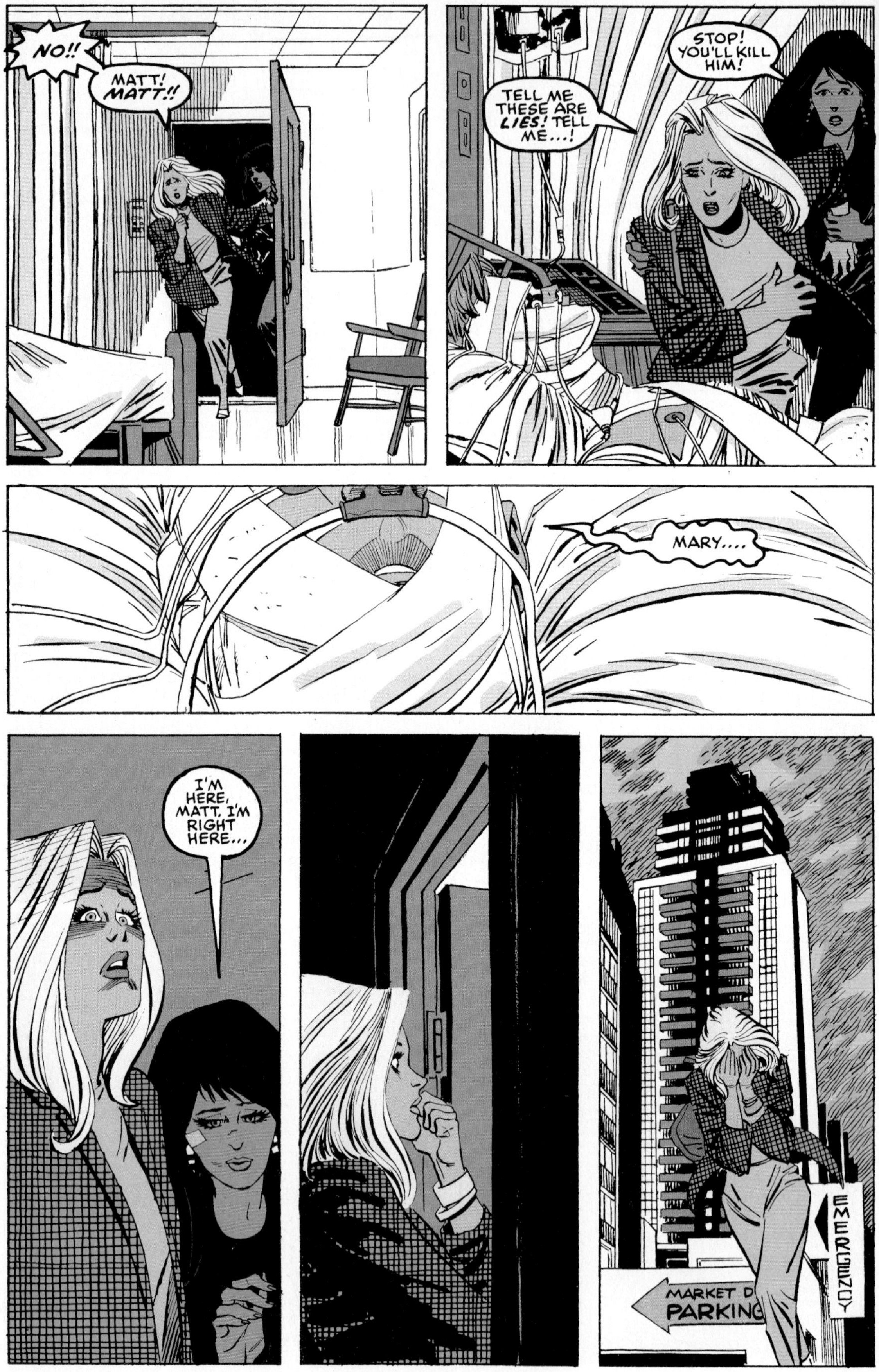
NO!!
MATT! MATT!!
STOP! YOU'LL KILL HIM!
TELL ME THESE ARE LIES! TELL ME...!
MARY....
I'M HERE, MATT. I'M RIGHT HERE...
EMERGENCY
MARKET D
PARKING

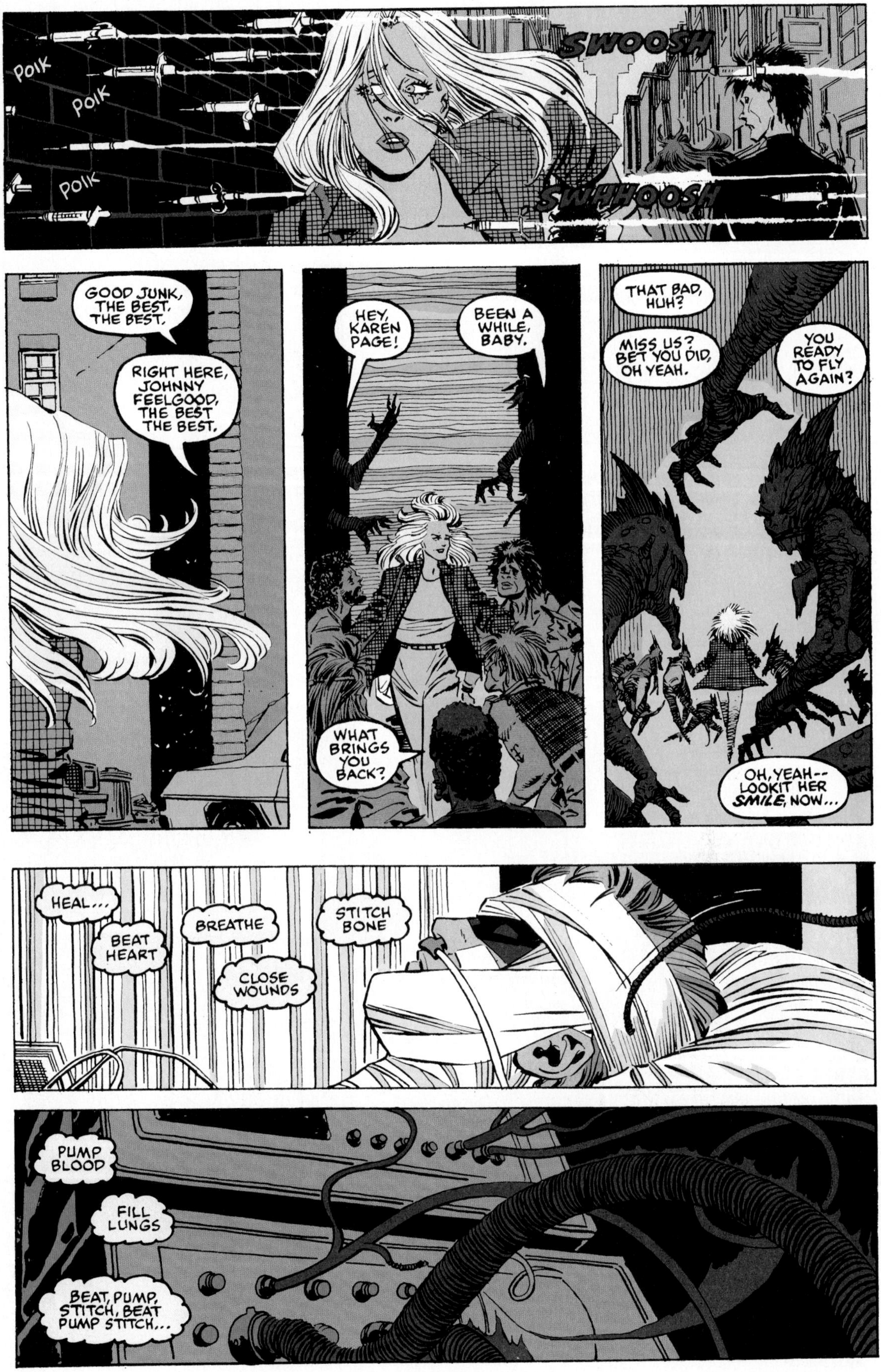
POIK
POIK
POIK
SWOOSH
SWHHOOSH
GOOD JUNK, THE BEST, THE BEST.
RIGHT HERE, JOHNNY FEELGOOD, THE BEST THE BEST.
HEY, KAREN PAGE!
BEEN A WHILE, BABY.
WHAT BRINGS YOU BACK?
THAT BAD, HUH?
MISS US? BET YOU DID, OH YEAH.
YOU READY TO FLY AGAIN?
OH, YEAH-- LOOKIT HER SMILE, NOW...
HEAL...
BEAT HEART
BREATHE
CLOSE WOUNDS
STITCH BONE
PUMP BLOOD
FILL LUNGS
BEAT, PUMP, STITCH, BEAT PUMP STITCH...

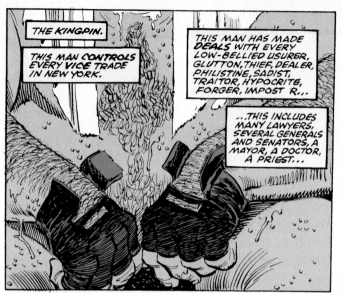

THE *KINGPIN.*

THIS MAN *CONTROLS* EVERY *VICE* TRADE IN NEW YORK.

THIS MAN HAS MADE *DEALS* WITH EVERY LOW-BELLIED USURER, GLUTTON, THIEF, DEALER, PHILISTINE, SADIST, TRAITOR, HYPOCRITE, FORGER, IMPOST R...

...THIS INCLUDES MANY LAWYERS, SEVERAL GENERALS AND SENATORS, A MAYOR, A DOCTOR, A PRIEST...

ALL MANNER OF MEN, FROM THE FIRST CIRCLE, DOWN TO THE NINTH.

NOT THAT ANY OF THIS *CONCERNS* HIM. HE DOESN'T *BELIEVE* IN ACCOUNTABILITY.

BUT SOME SMALL PART OF HIM, PERHAPS, EX- PECTED A DAY OF *RECKONING.*

KINGPIN, SIR! SORRY TO BARGE IN ON YOU LIKE THIS--

--BUT WE HAVE *SERIOUS* PROBLEMS!

IT SEEMS THE *X-MEN,* OR SOME SUCH MUTANT VIGILANTE TEAM, WERE FIGHTING A BATTLE--AND *LOST!*

CRAZY AS IT SOUNDS, SOME *CRACK* IN SPACE HAS ERUPTED UNDER MANHATTAN--AND *DEMONS* ARE POURING OUT!

NEW YORK IS BECOMING AN *INFERNO!*

I KNOW THIS SOUNDS LIKE SCIENCE FICTION, BUT IT'S *TRUE!*

WORST PART IS, THE DEMONS ARE TAKING OVER-- THE LOW LEVEL ONES ARE TAKING OVER THE VICE AND DRUG TRADES, THE HIGHER LEVEL ONES ARE ATTACKING BIG BUSINESS, CORPORATIONS!

WE'RE BEING INFILTRATED, *RUINED!*

AND... I...I... SIR?

I *KNOW* ALL THIS, YOU IDIOT.

I EX- PECTED IT.

AND I DON'T CARE.

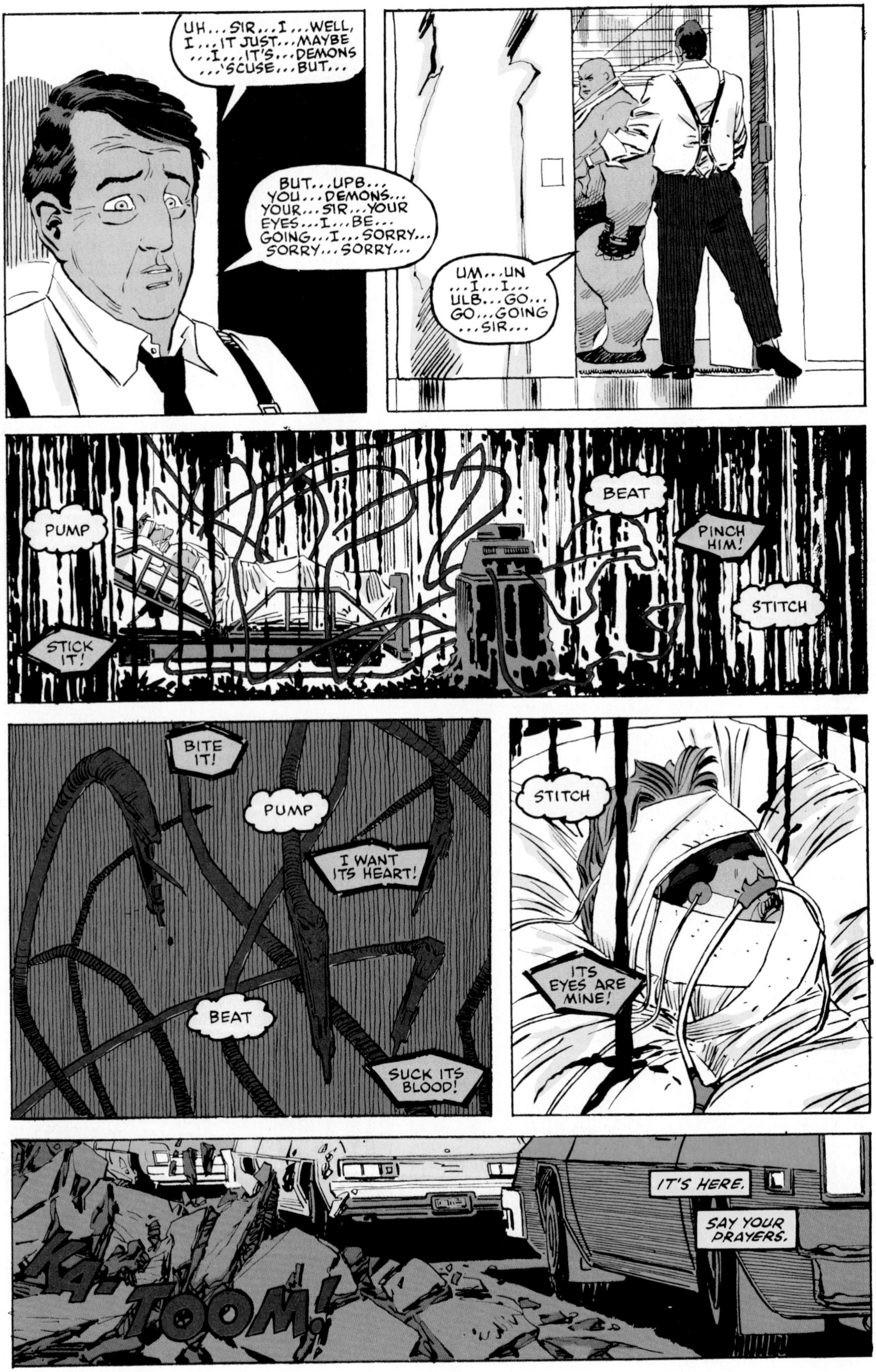
UH... SIR... I... WELL, I... IT JUST... MAYBE ...I... IT'S... DEMONS ...'SCUSE... BUT...
BUT... UPB... YOU... DEMONS... YOUR... SIR... YOUR EYES... I... BE... GOING... I... SORRY... SORRY... SORRY...
UM... UN ...I... I... ULB... GO... GO... GOING ...SIR...
PUMP
BEAT
PINCH HIM!
STITCH
STICK IT!
BITE IT!
PUMP
I WANT ITS HEART!
BEAT
SUCK ITS BLOOD!
STITCH
ITS EYES ARE MINE!
IT'S HERE.
SAY YOUR PRAYERS.
KA-TOOM!

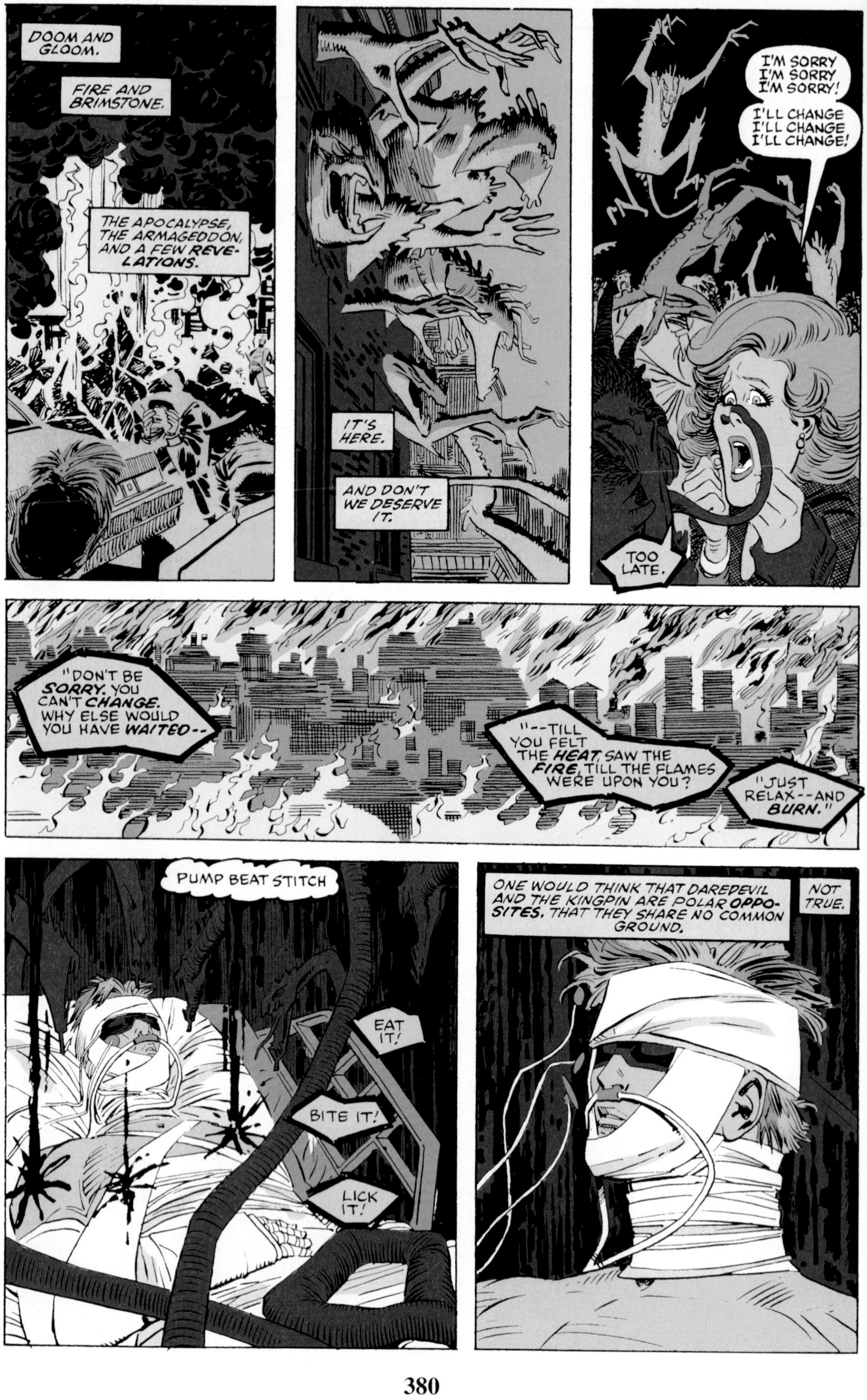
DOOM AND GLOOM.
FIRE AND BRIMSTONE.
THE APOCALYPSE, THE ARMAGEDDON, AND A FEW REVELATIONS.
IT'S HERE.
AND DON'T WE DESERVE IT.
I'M SORRY I'M SORRY I'M SORRY!
I'LL CHANGE I'LL CHANGE I'LL CHANGE!
TOO LATE.
"DON'T BE SORRY. YOU CAN'T CHANGE. WHY ELSE WOULD YOU HAVE WAITED--
"--TILL YOU FELT THE HEAT, SAW THE FIRE, TILL THE FLAMES WERE UPON YOU?
"JUST RELAX--AND BURN."
PUMP BEAT STITCH
EAT IT!
BITE IT!
LICK IT!
ONE WOULD THINK THAT DAREDEVIL AND THE KINGPIN ARE POLAR OPPOSITES. THAT THEY SHARE NO COMMON GROUND.
NOT TRUE.

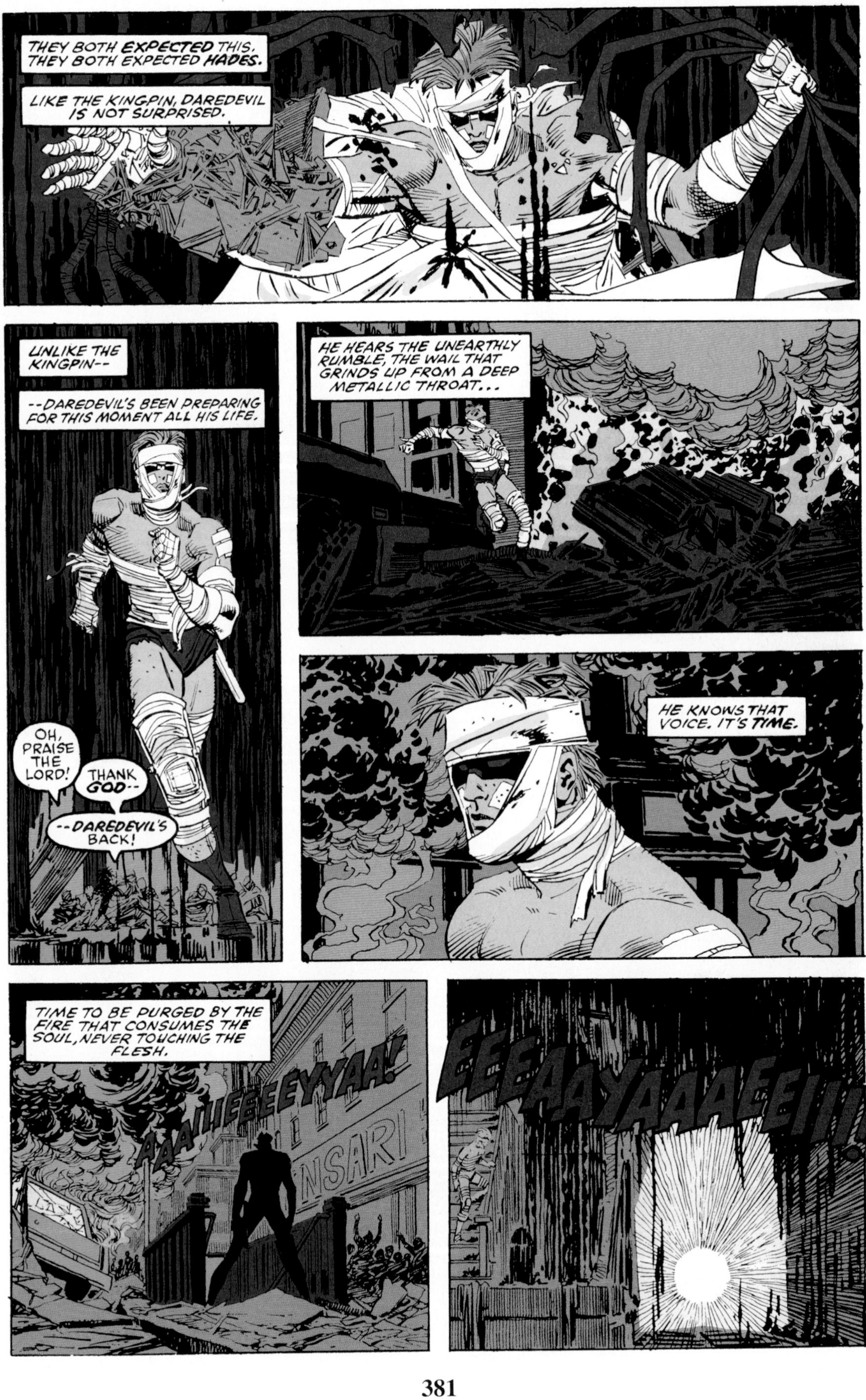
THEY BOTH EXPECTED THIS. THEY BOTH EXPECTED HADES.
LIKE THE KINGPIN, DAREDEVIL IS NOT SURPRISED.
UNLIKE THE KINGPIN--
--DAREDEVIL'S BEEN PREPARING FOR THIS MOMENT ALL HIS LIFE.
OH, PRAISE THE LORD!
THANK GOD--
--DAREDEVIL'S BACK!
HE HEARS THE UNEARTHLY RUMBLE, THE WAIL THAT GRINDS UP FROM A DEEP METALLIC THROAT...
HE KNOWS THAT VOICE. IT'S TIME.
TIME TO BE PURGED BY THE FIRE THAT CONSUMES THE SOUL, NEVER TOUCHING THE FLESH.
AAAIIIEEEEYYAA!
NSARI
EEEAAYAAAEEIII!!

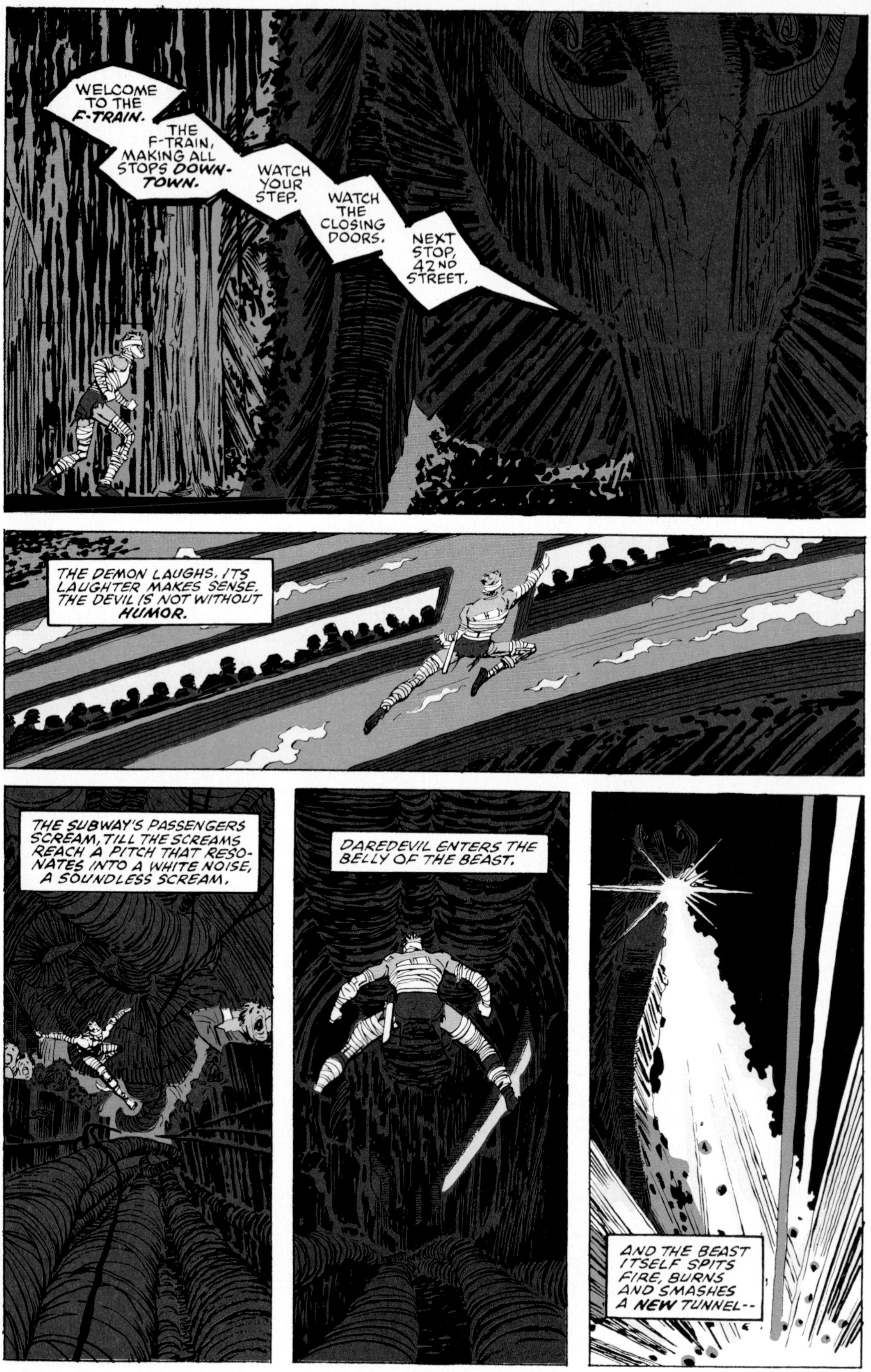
WELCOME TO THE F-TRAIN.
THE F-TRAIN, MAKING ALL STOPS DOWNTOWN.
WATCH YOUR STEP.
WATCH THE CLOSING DOORS.
NEXT STOP, 42ND STREET.
THE DEMON LAUGHS. ITS LAUGHTER MAKES SENSE. THE DEVIL IS NOT WITHOUT HUMOR.
THE SUBWAY'S PASSENGERS SCREAM, TILL THE SCREAMS REACH A PITCH THAT RESONATES INTO A WHITE NOISE, A SOUNDLESS SCREAM.
DAREDEVIL ENTERS THE BELLY OF THE BEAST.
AND THE BEAST ITSELF SPITS FIRE, BURNS AND SMASHES A NEW TUNNEL--

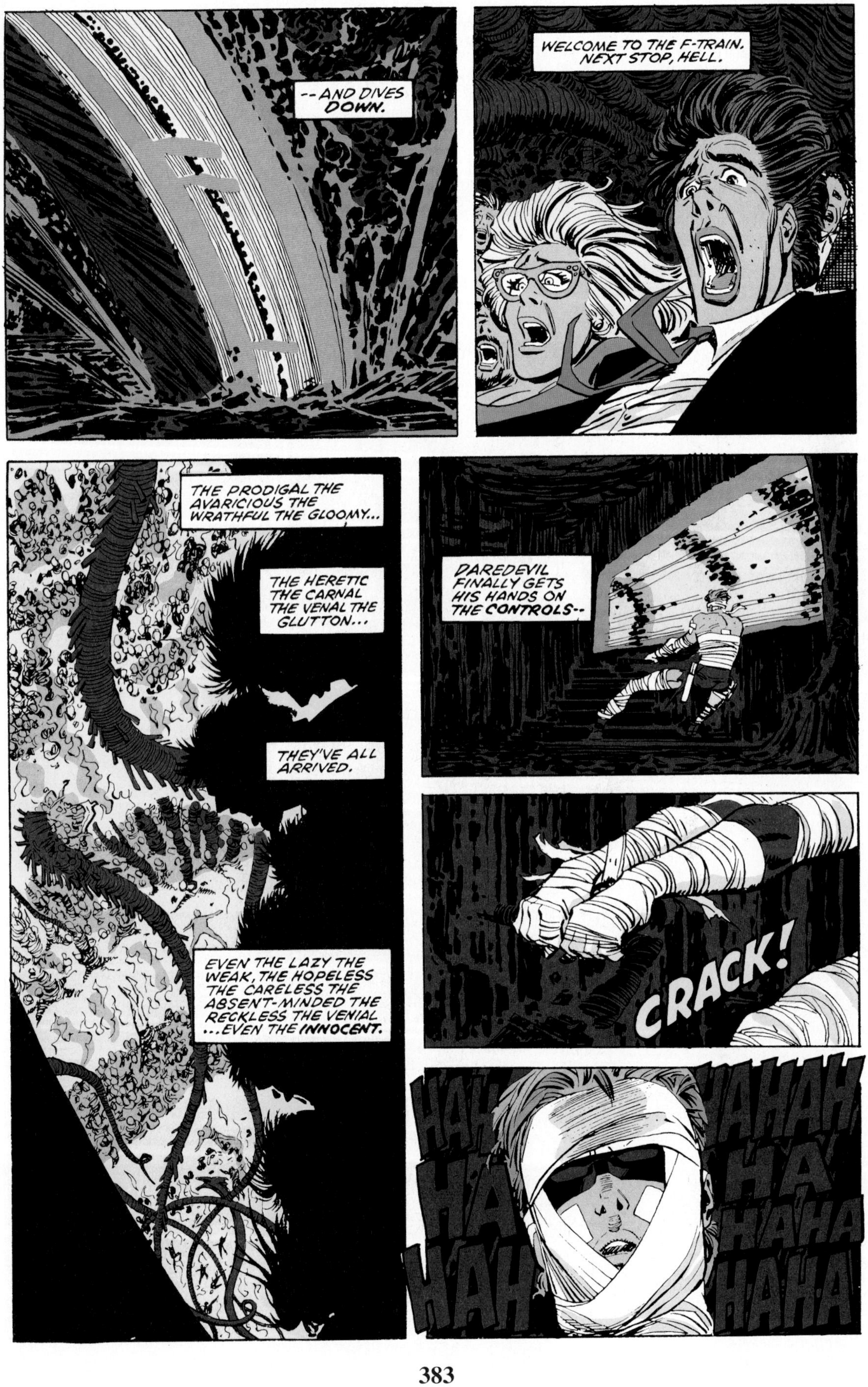
--AND DIVES DOWN.
WELCOME TO THE F-TRAIN. NEXT STOP, HELL.
THE PRODIGAL THE AVARICIOUS THE WRATHFUL THE GLOOMY...
THE HERETIC THE CARNAL THE VENAL THE GLUTTON...
THEY'VE ALL ARRIVED.
EVEN THE LAZY THE WEAK, THE HOPELESS THE CARELESS THE ABSENT-MINDED THE RECKLESS THE VENIAL ...EVEN THE INNOCENT.
DAREDEVIL FINALLY GETS HIS HANDS ON THE CONTROLS--
CRACK!
HAHA
HA
HAH
HAHAH
HA
HAHA
HAHA

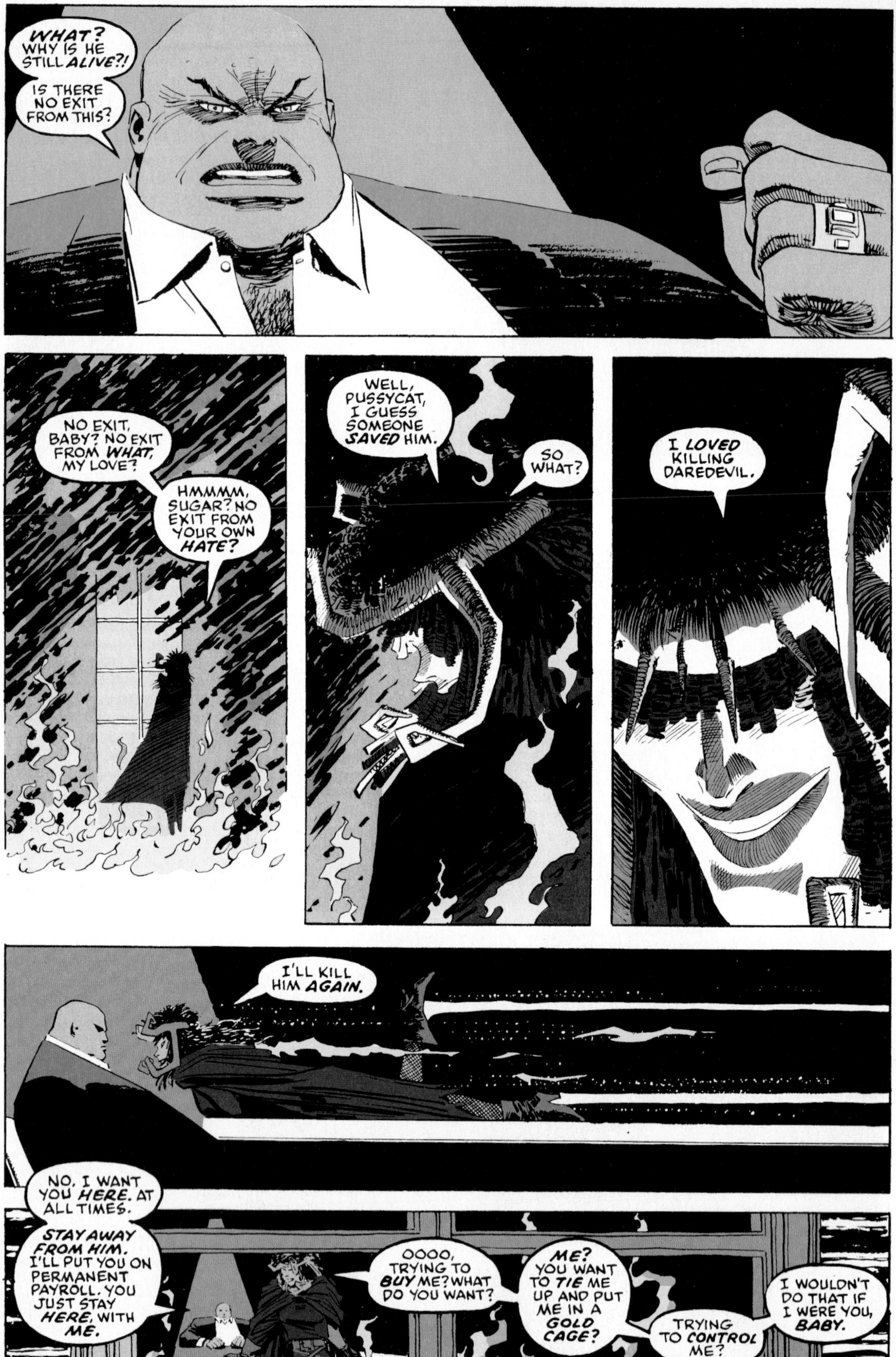
WHAT? WHY IS HE STILL ALIVE?!
IS THERE NO EXIT FROM THIS?
NO EXIT, BABY? NO EXIT FROM WHAT, MY LOVE?
HMMMM, SUGAR? NO EXIT FROM YOUR OWN HATE?
WELL, PUSSYCAT, I GUESS SOMEONE SAVED HIM.
SO WHAT?
I LOVED KILLING DAREDEVIL.
I'LL KILL HIM AGAIN.
NO, I WANT YOU HERE. AT ALL TIMES.
STAY AWAY FROM HIM. I'LL PUT YOU ON PERMANENT PAYROLL. YOU JUST STAY HERE, WITH ME.
OOOO, TRYING TO BUY ME? WHAT DO YOU WANT?
ME? YOU WANT TO TIE ME UP AND PUT ME IN A GOLD CAGE?
TRYING TO CONTROL ME?
I WOULDN'T DO THAT IF I WERE YOU, BABY.

YOU KNOW DARLING, SWEETIEPIE? YOU KNOW WHAT THEY SAY ABOUT *EVIL*?

THEY SAY IT CAN'T HURT YOU, CAN'T TAINT YOU TOUCH YOU HARM YOU.

UNLESS YOU *WANT* IT. UNLESS YOU *LET IT IN.*

WHAT IS THIS, TYPHOID?

HAHAHAHAAH

OH, BABY, DON'T *DO* THAT!

HELLO HELLO

HAHAHAHAHA

I THINK, KINGPIN, THAT *THIS* --IS YOUR *BOSS!*

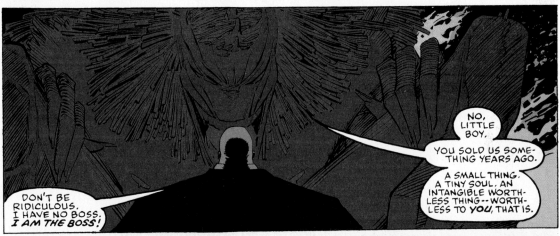

NO, LITTLE BOY.

YOU SOLD US SOMETHING YEARS AGO.

A SMALL THING. A TINY SOUL, AN INTANGIBLE WORTHLESS THING-- WORTHLESS TO *YOU*, THAT IS.

DON'T BE RIDICULOUS. I HAVE NO BOSS. *I AM THE BOSS!*

NO, KINGPIN, *SIR.*

DARLING BABY SUGAR SWEET KINGPIN, *SIR.*

HA HAHAH HAHA

YOU'VE BEEN WORKING FOR US FOR A LONG TIME NOW.

BUT YOU KNOW THAT.

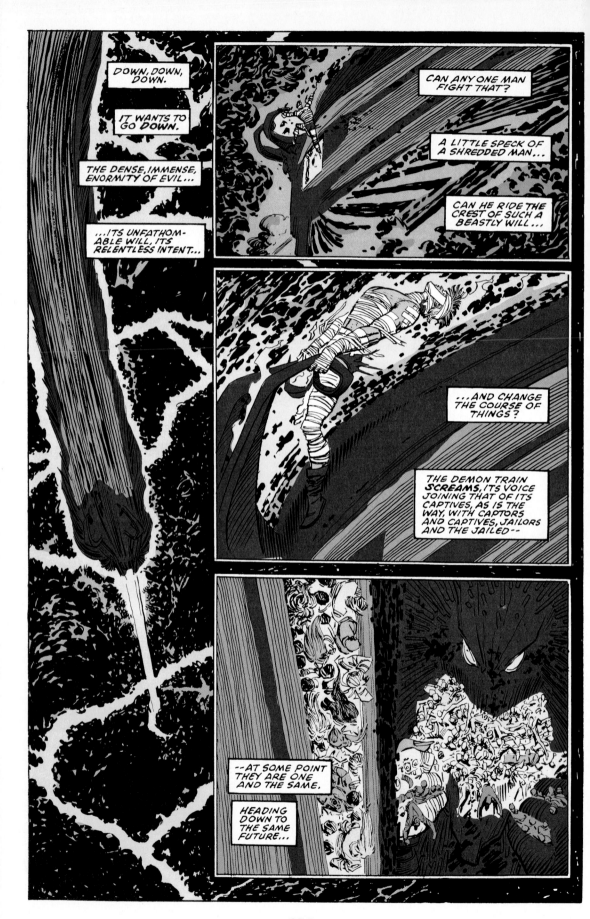

DOWN, DOWN, DOWN.

IT WANTS TO GO DOWN.

THE DENSE, IMMENSE, ENORMITY OF EVIL...

...ITS UNFATHOMABLE WILL, ITS RELENTLESS INTENT...

CAN ANY ONE MAN FIGHT THAT?

A LITTLE SPECK OF A SHREDDED MAN...

CAN HE RIDE THE CREST OF SUCH A BEASTLY WILL...

...AND CHANGE THE COURSE OF THINGS?

THE DEMON TRAIN SCREAMS, ITS VOICE JOINING THAT OF ITS CAPTIVES, AS IS THE WAY, WITH CAPTORS AND CAPTIVES, JAILORS AND THE JAILED--

--AT SOME POINT THEY ARE ONE AND THE SAME.

HEADING DOWN TO THE SAME FUTURE...

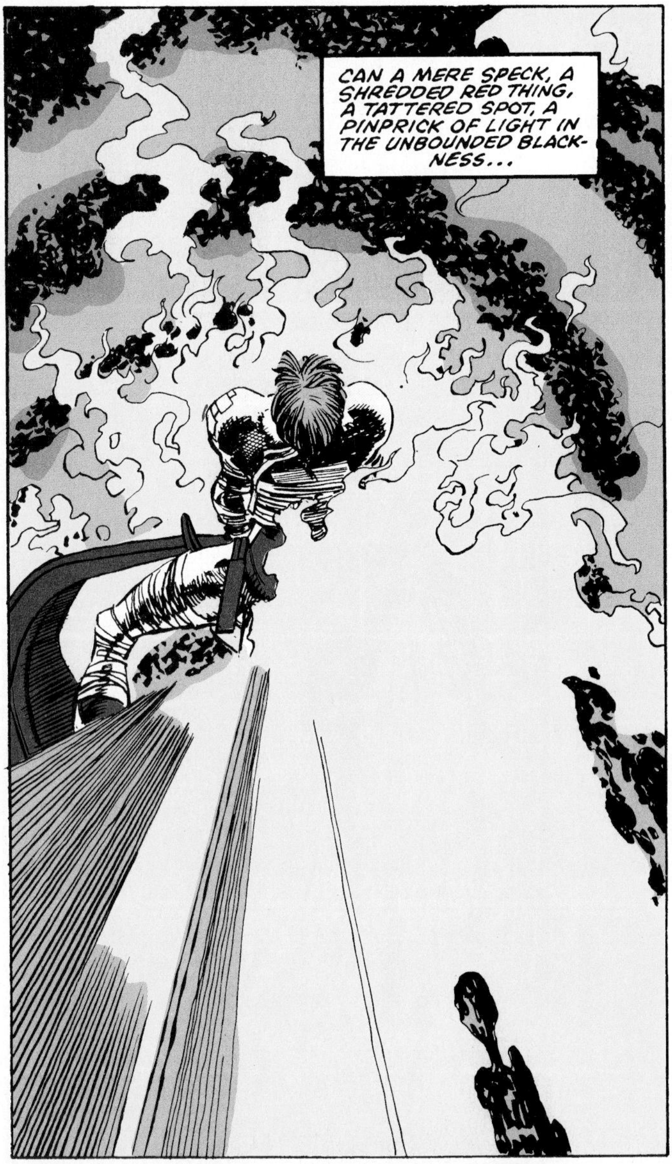
CAN A MERE SPECK, A SHREDDED RED THING, A TATTERED SPOT, A PINPRICK OF LIGHT IN THE UNBOUNDED BLACKNESS...

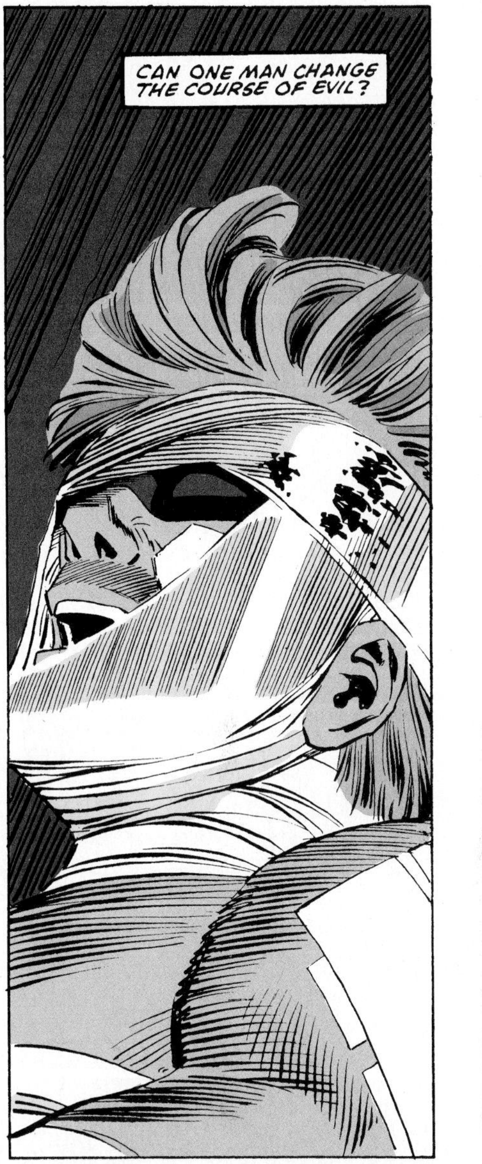
CAN ONE MAN CHANGE THE COURSE OF EVIL?

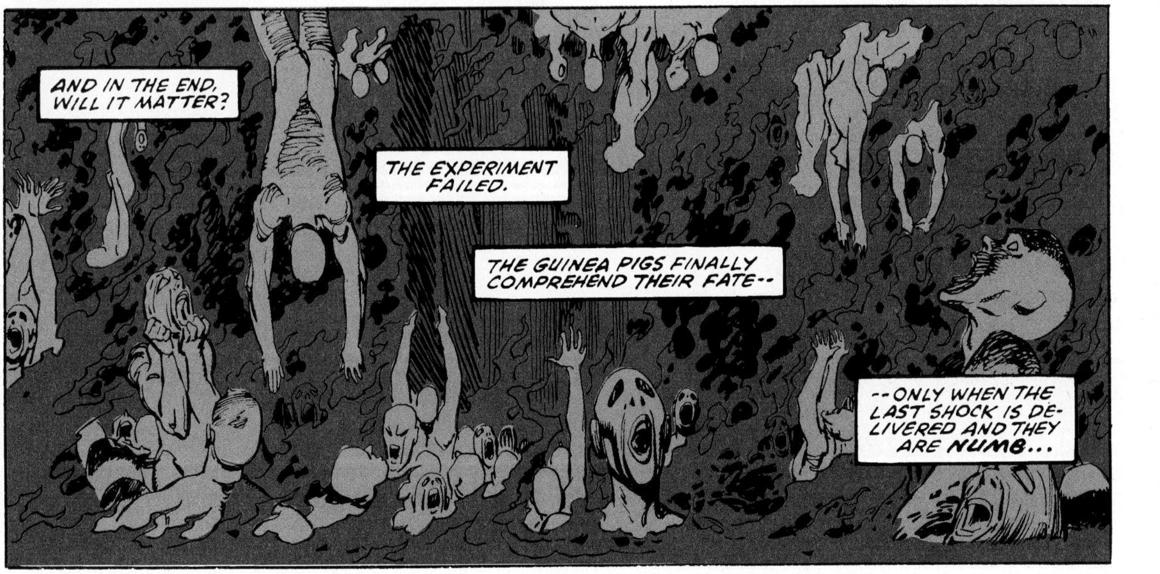
AND IN THE END, WILL IT MATTER?
THE EXPERIMENT FAILED.
THE GUINEA PIGS FINALLY COMPREHEND THEIR FATE--
--ONLY WHEN THE LAST SHOCK IS DELIVERED AND THEY ARE **NUMB**...

ONE MAN, ONE PINPRICK OF LIGHT, ONE SMALL AND GOOD ACT--

--GRABS THE DEMON BY THE HORNS AND TWISTS ITS WILL...

AND LIKE WRENCHING AN ARM BACKWARDS--

--SOMETHING SNAPS, AND CHANGES.

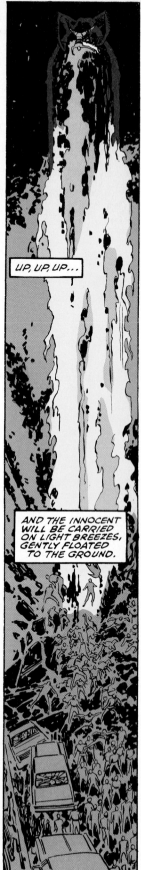

UP, UP, UP...

AND THE INNOCENT WILL BE CARRIED ON LIGHT BREEZES, GENTLY FLOATED TO THE GROUND.

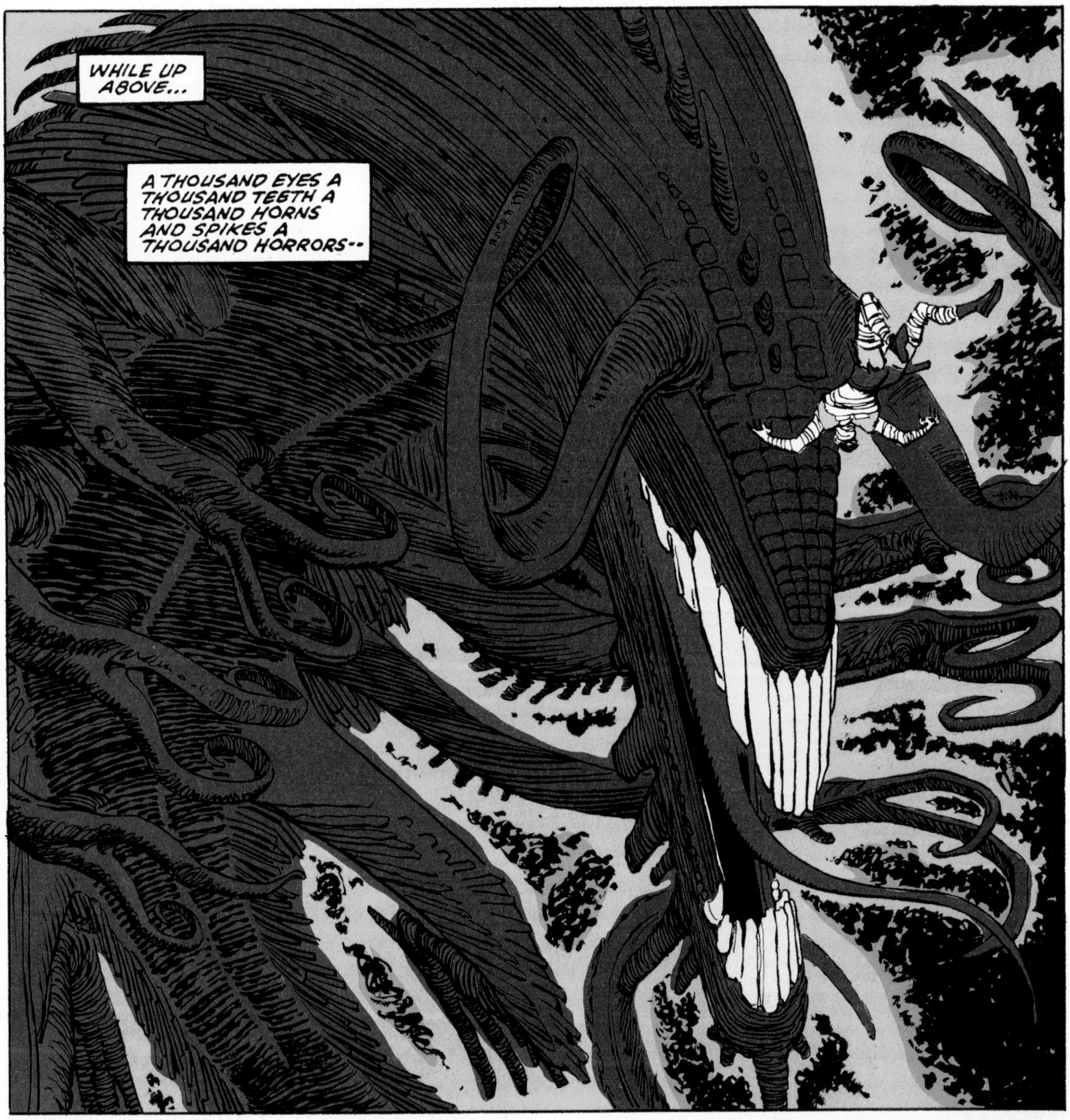
WHILE UP ABOVE...
A THOUSAND EYES A THOUSAND TEETH A THOUSAND HORNS AND SPIKES A THOUSAND HORRORS--
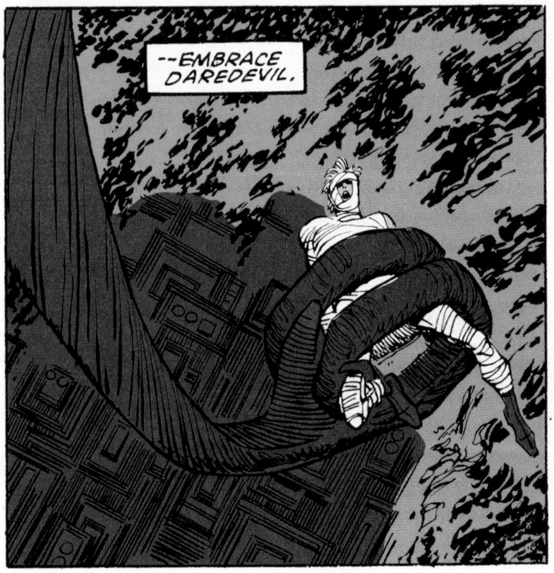
--EMBRACE DAREDEVIL.
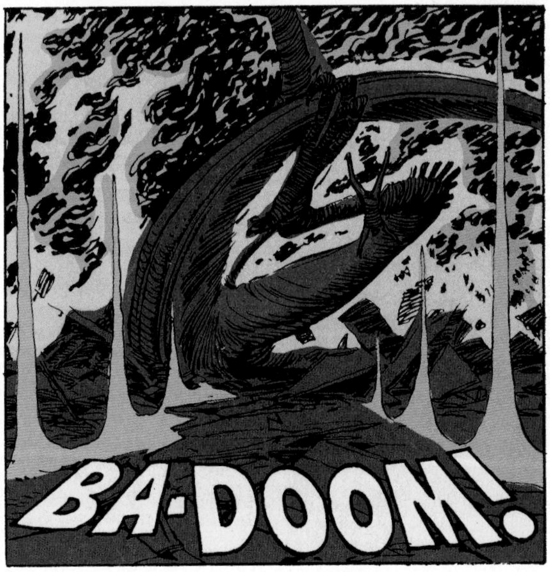
BA-DOOM!

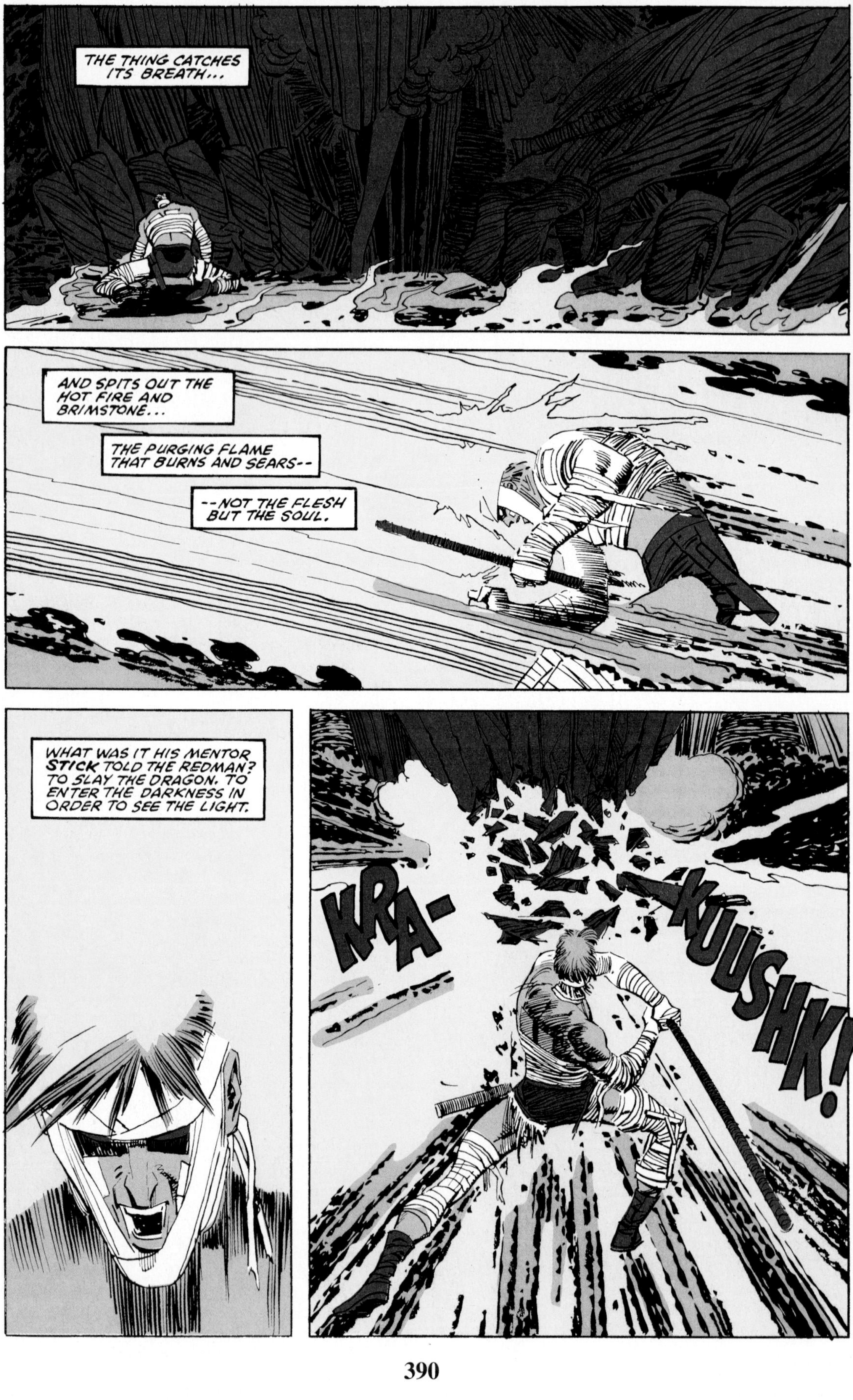
THE THING CATCHES ITS BREATH...
AND SPITS OUT THE HOT FIRE AND BRIMSTONE...
THE PURGING FLAME THAT BURNS AND SEARS--
--NOT THE FLESH BUT THE SOUL.
WHAT WAS IT HIS MENTOR STICK TOLD THE REDMAN? TO SLAY THE DRAGON. TO ENTER THE DARKNESS IN ORDER TO SEE THE LIGHT.
KRA-
KUUSHK!

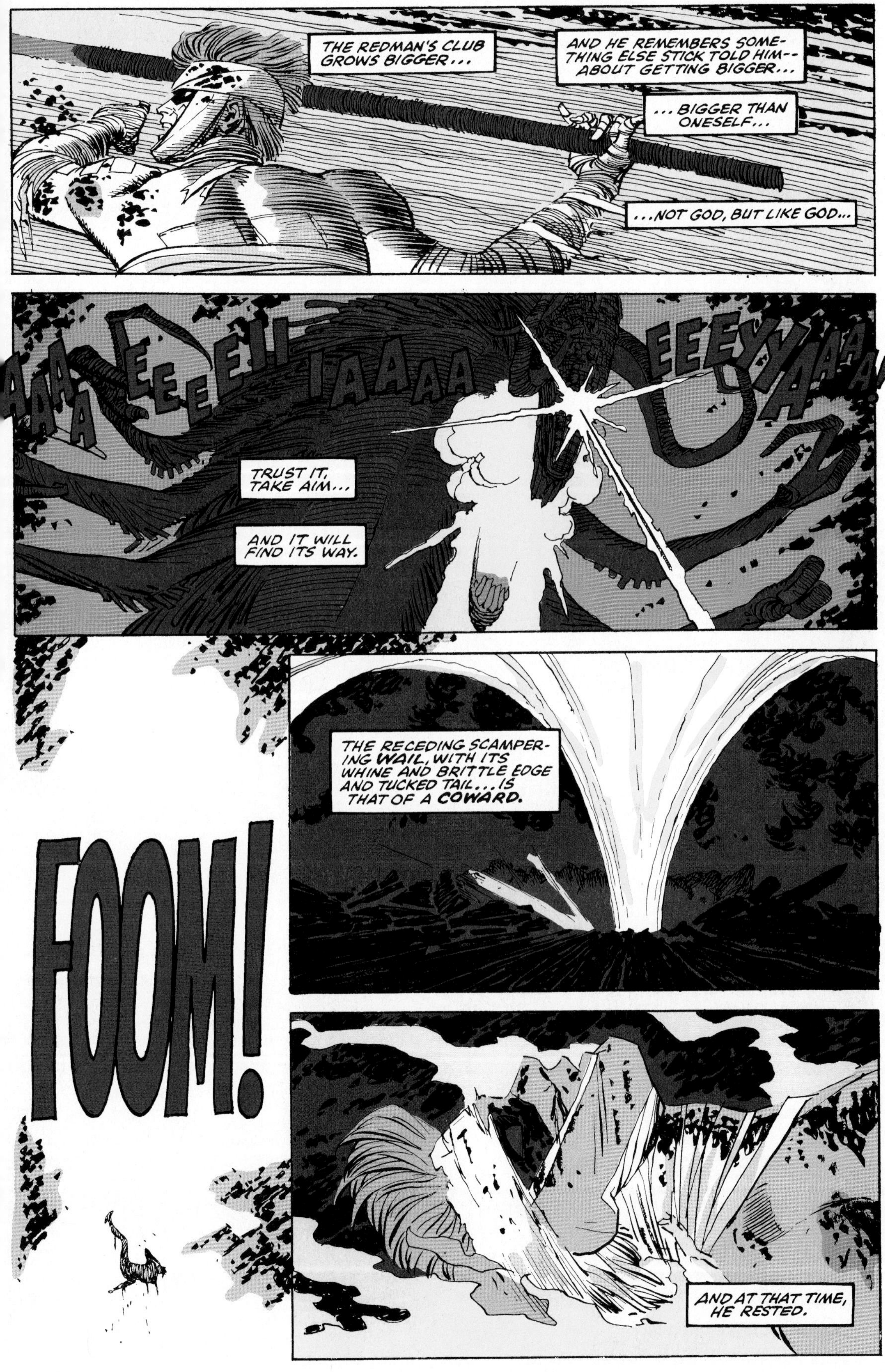
THE REDMAN'S CLUB GROWS BIGGER...
AND HE REMEMBERS SOMETHING ELSE STICK TOLD HIM--ABOUT GETTING BIGGER...
...BIGGER THAN ONESELF...
...NOT GOD, BUT LIKE GOD...
AAAAEEEEE!! IAAAAA EEEYYAAAA!
TRUST IT, TAKE AIM...
AND IT WILL FIND ITS WAY.
THE RECEDING SCAMPERING WAIL, WITH ITS WHINE AND BRITTLE EDGE AND TUCKED TAIL... IS THAT OF A COWARD.
FOOM!
AND AT THAT TIME, HE RESTED.

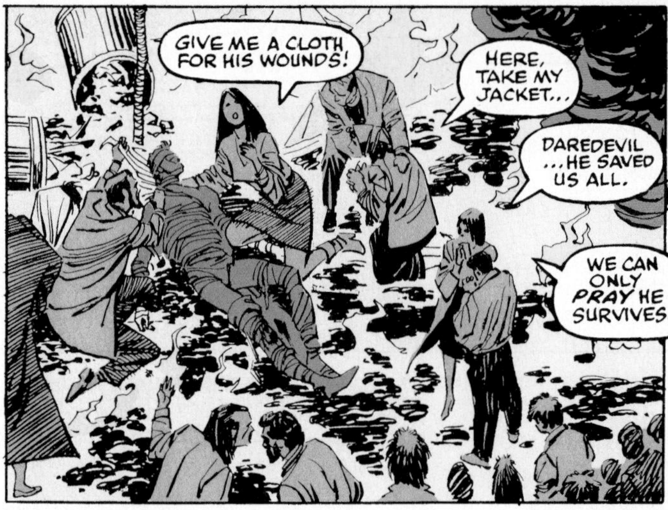
GIVE ME A CLOTH FOR HIS WOUNDS!
HERE, TAKE MY JACKET...
DAREDEVIL ...HE SAVED US ALL.
WE CAN ONLY PRAY HE SURVIVES...

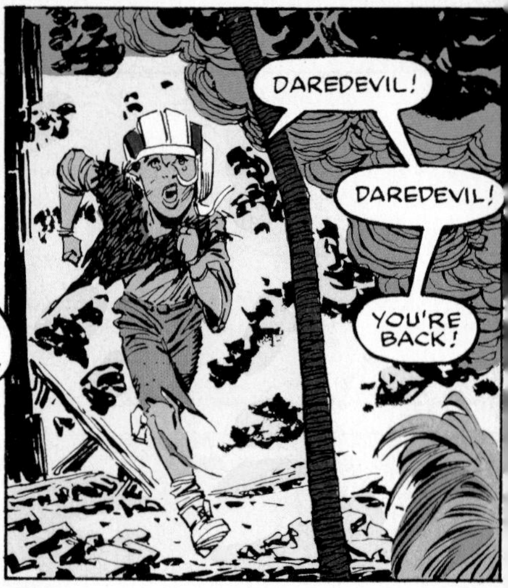
DAREDEVIL!
DAREDEVIL!
YOU'RE BACK!

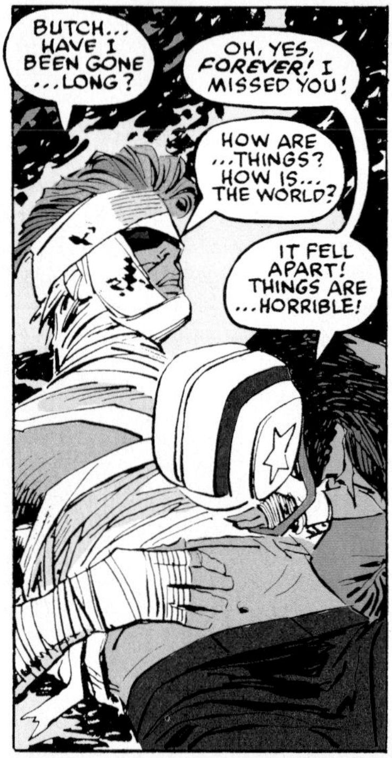
BUTCH... HAVE I BEEN GONE ...LONG?
OH, YES, FOREVER! I MISSED YOU!
HOW ARE ...THINGS? HOW IS... THE WORLD?
IT FELL APART! THINGS ARE ...HORRIBLE!

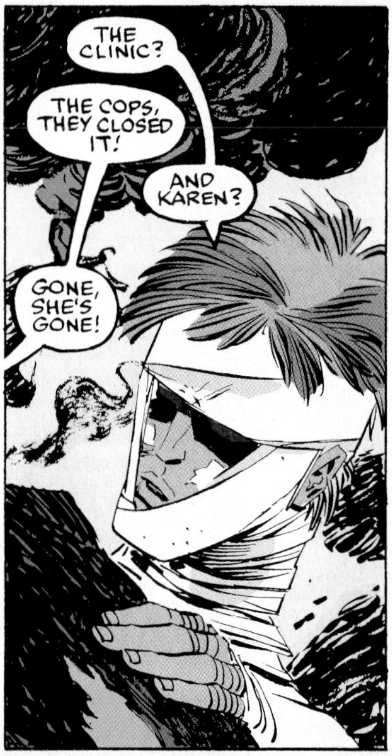
THE CLINIC?
THE COPS, THEY CLOSED IT!
AND KAREN?
GONE, SHE'S GONE!

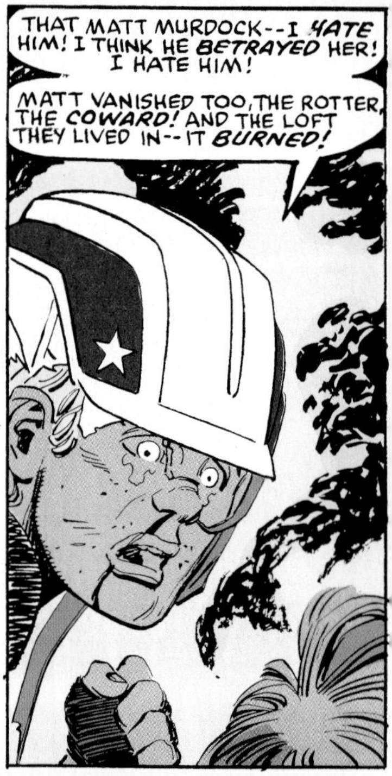
THAT MATT MURDOCK--I HATE HIM! I THINK HE BETRAYED HER! I HATE HIM!
MATT VANISHED TOO, THE ROTTER, THE COWARD! AND THE LOFT THEY LIVED IN--IT BURNED!

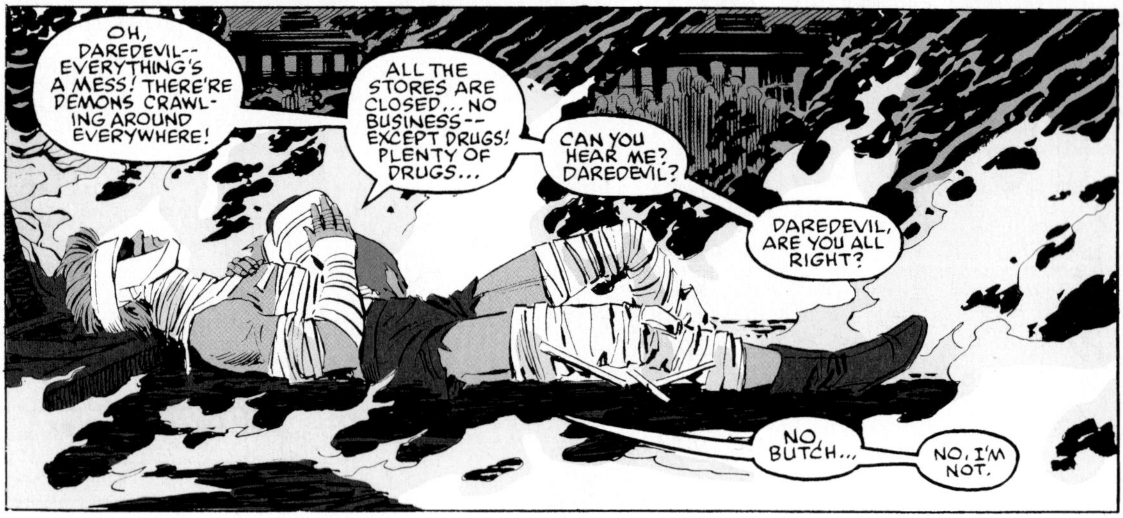
OH, DAREDEVIL-- EVERYTHING'S A MESS! THERE'RE DEMONS CRAWL-ING AROUND EVERYWHERE!
ALL THE STORES ARE CLOSED... NO BUSINESS-- EXCEPT DRUGS! PLENTY OF DRUGS...
CAN YOU HEAR ME? DAREDEVIL?
DAREDEVIL, ARE YOU ALL RIGHT?
NO, BUTCH...
NO, I'M NOT.

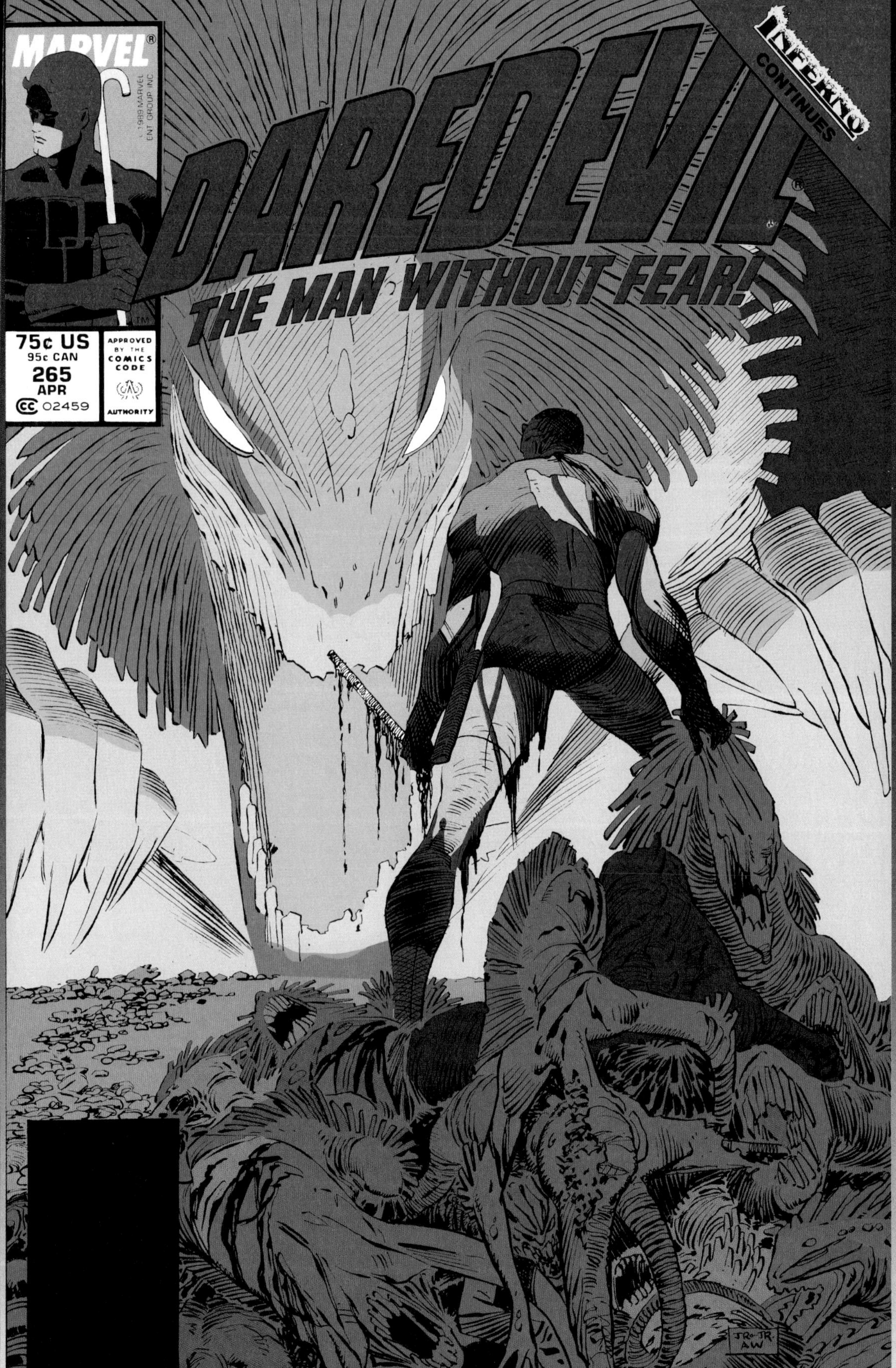
MARVEL®
© 1989 MARVEL ENT GROUP INC
INFERNO CONTINUES
DAREDEVIL®
THE MAN WITHOUT FEAR!
75¢ US
95¢ CAN
265
APR
02459
APPROVED BY THE COMICS CODE AUTHORITY
JR JR AW

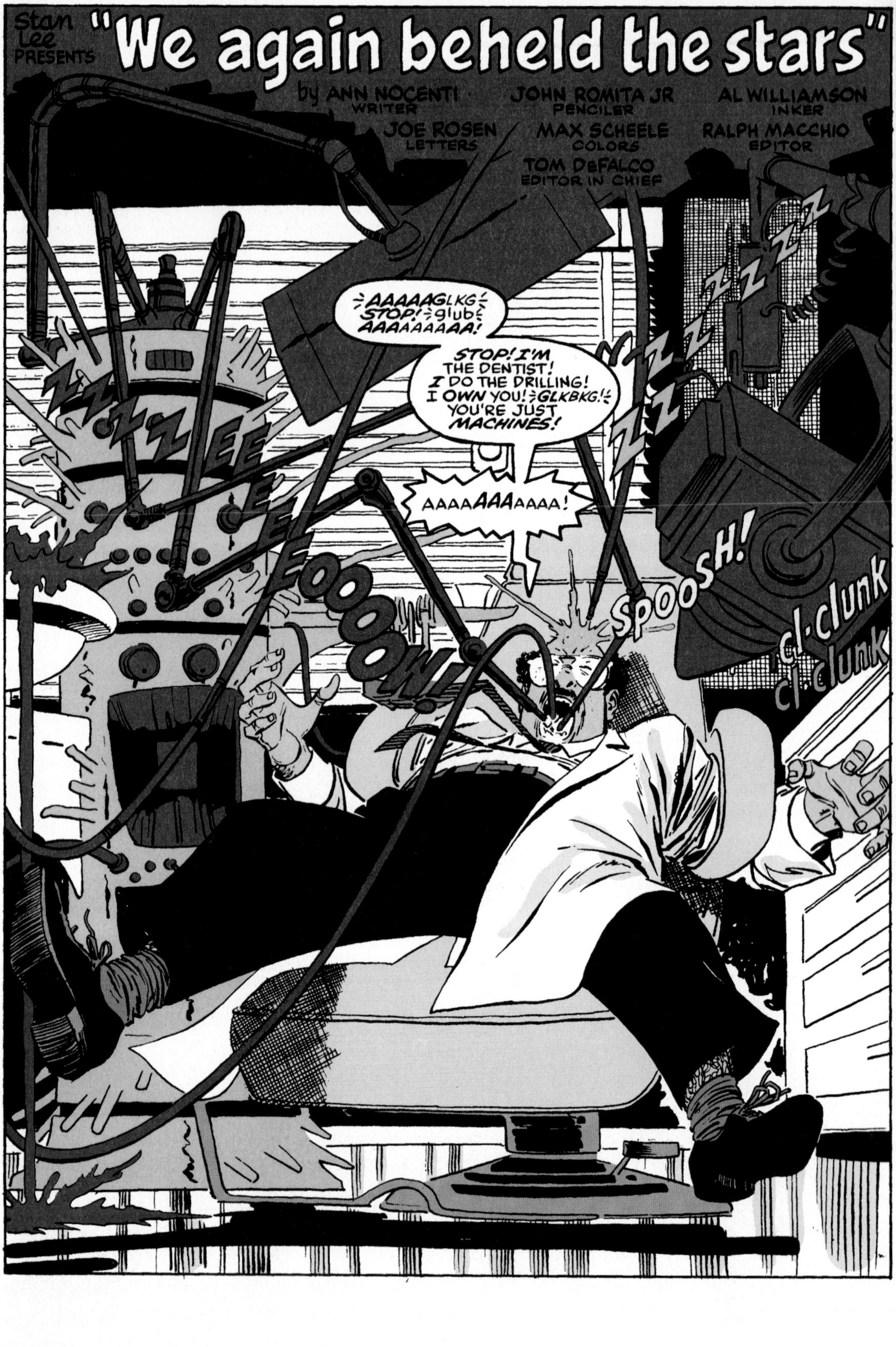

Stan Lee PRESENTS
"We again beheld the stars"
by ANN NOCENTI WRITER
JOHN ROMITA JR PENCILER
AL WILLIAMSON INKER
JOE ROSEN LETTERS
MAX SCHEELE COLORS
RALPH MACCHIO EDITOR
TOM DeFALCO EDITOR IN CHIEF
AAAAAGLKG STOP! glub AAAAAAAAA!
STOP! I'M THE DENTIST! I DO THE DRILLING! I OWN YOU! GLKBKG! YOU'RE JUST MACHINES!
AAAAAAAAAAA!
ZZZZZEEEEEOOOOOW!
ZZZZZZZZZZZ
SPOOSH!
cl·clunk
cl·clunk

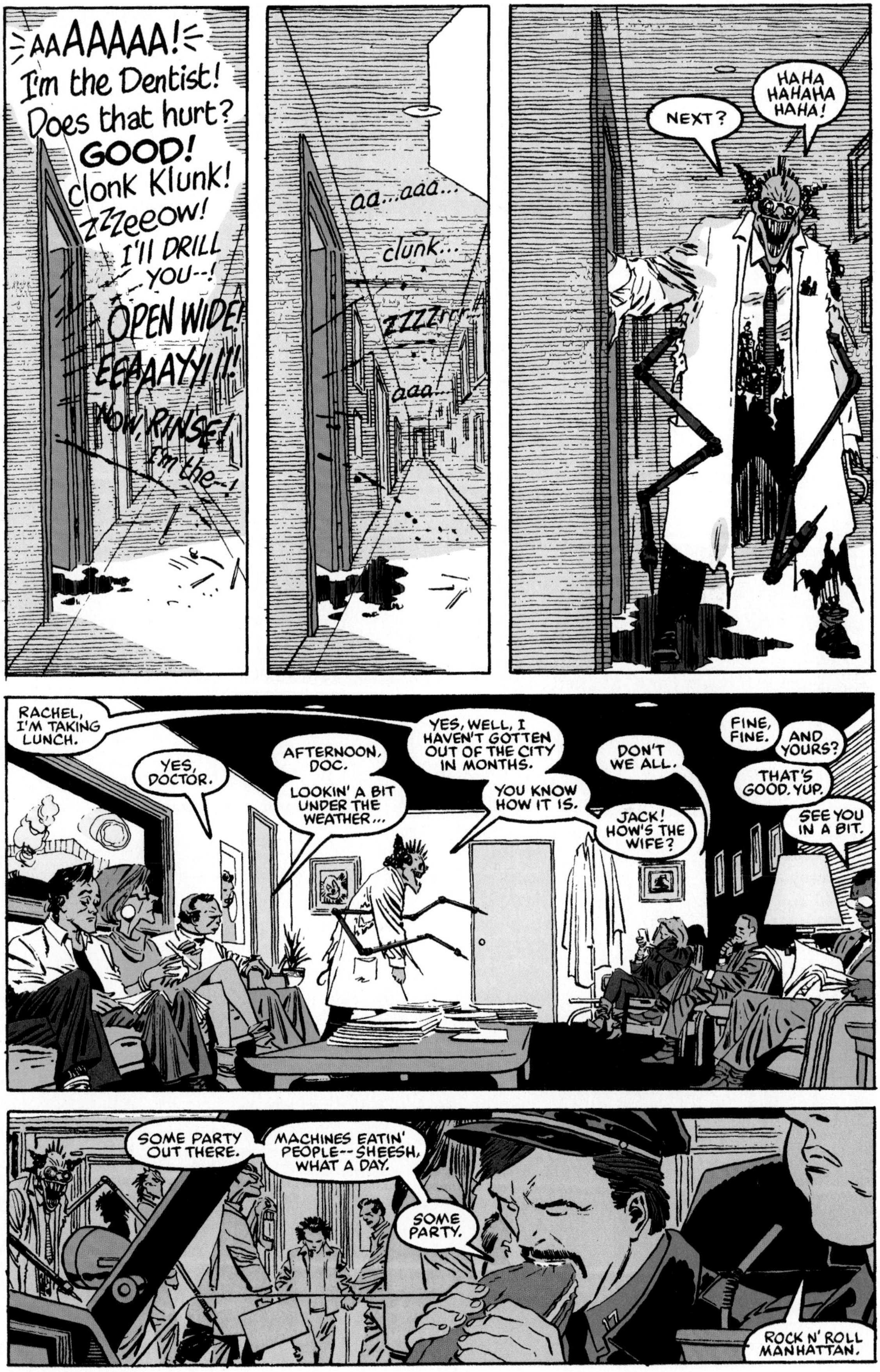
AAAAAAA!
I'm the Dentist!
Does that hurt?
GOOD!
clonk Klunk!
zzzeeow!
I'll DRILL YOU--!
OPEN WIDE!
EEAAAYY!!!!
NOW, RINSE!
I'm the--!
aa...aaa...
clunk...
zzzzrrr...
aaa...
NEXT?
HAHA HAHAHA HAHA!
RACHEL, I'M TAKING LUNCH.
YES, DOCTOR.
AFTERNOON, DOC.
LOOKIN' A BIT UNDER THE WEATHER...
YES, WELL, I HAVEN'T GOTTEN OUT OF THE CITY IN MONTHS.
YOU KNOW HOW IT IS.
DON'T WE ALL.
JACK! HOW'S THE WIFE?
FINE, FINE.
AND YOURS?
THAT'S GOOD. YUP.
SEE YOU IN A BIT.
SOME PARTY OUT THERE.
MACHINES EATIN' PEOPLE--SHEESH, WHAT A DAY.
SOME PARTY.
ROCK N' ROLL MANHATTAN.

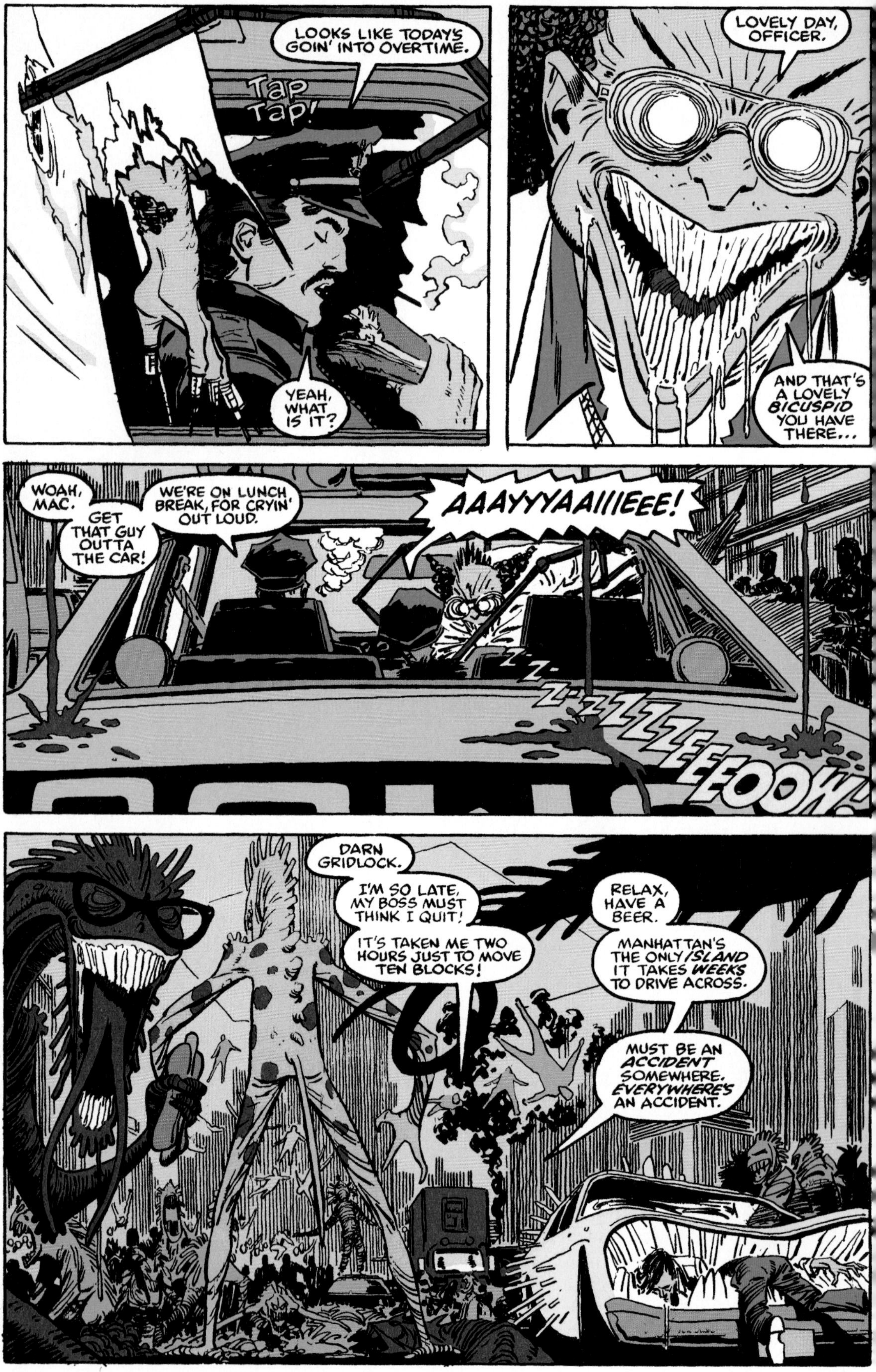
LOOKS LIKE TODAY'S GOIN' INTO OVERTIME.
Tap Tap!
YEAH, WHAT IS IT?
LOVELY DAY, OFFICER.
AND THAT'S A LOVELY BICUSPID YOU HAVE THERE...
WOAH, MAC.
GET THAT GUY OUTTA THE CAR!
WE'RE ON LUNCH BREAK, FOR CRYIN' OUT LOUD.
AAAYYYAAIIIIEEE!
ZZ-ZZZZZEEEOOW!
DARN GRIDLOCK.
I'M SO LATE, MY BOSS MUST THINK I QUIT!
IT'S TAKEN ME TWO HOURS JUST TO MOVE TEN BLOCKS!
RELAX, HAVE A BEER.
MANHATTAN'S THE ONLY ISLAND IT TAKES WEEKS TO DRIVE ACROSS.
MUST BE AN ACCIDENT SOMEWHERE. EVERYWHERE'S AN ACCIDENT.

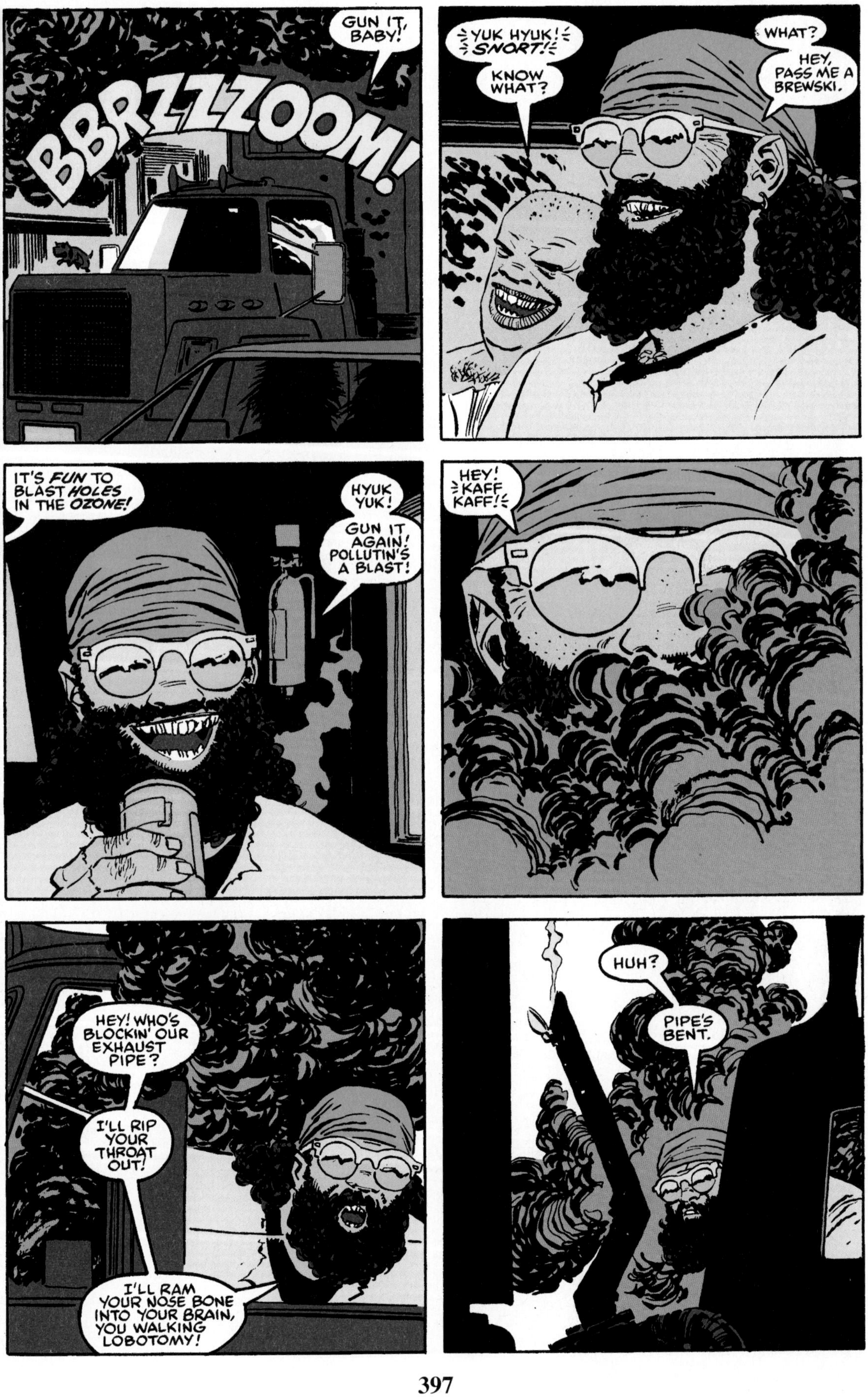
GUN IT, BABY!
BBRZZZOOM!
YUK HYUK! SNORT!
KNOW WHAT?
WHAT?
HEY, PASS ME A BREWSKI.
IT'S FUN TO BLAST HOLES IN THE OZONE!
HYUK YUK!
GUN IT AGAIN! POLLUTIN'S A BLAST!
HEY! KAFF KAFF!
HEY! WHO'S BLOCKIN' OUR EXHAUST PIPE?
I'LL RIP YOUR THROAT OUT!
I'LL RAM YOUR NOSE BONE INTO YOUR BRAIN, YOU WALKING LOBOTOMY!
HUH?
PIPE'S BENT.

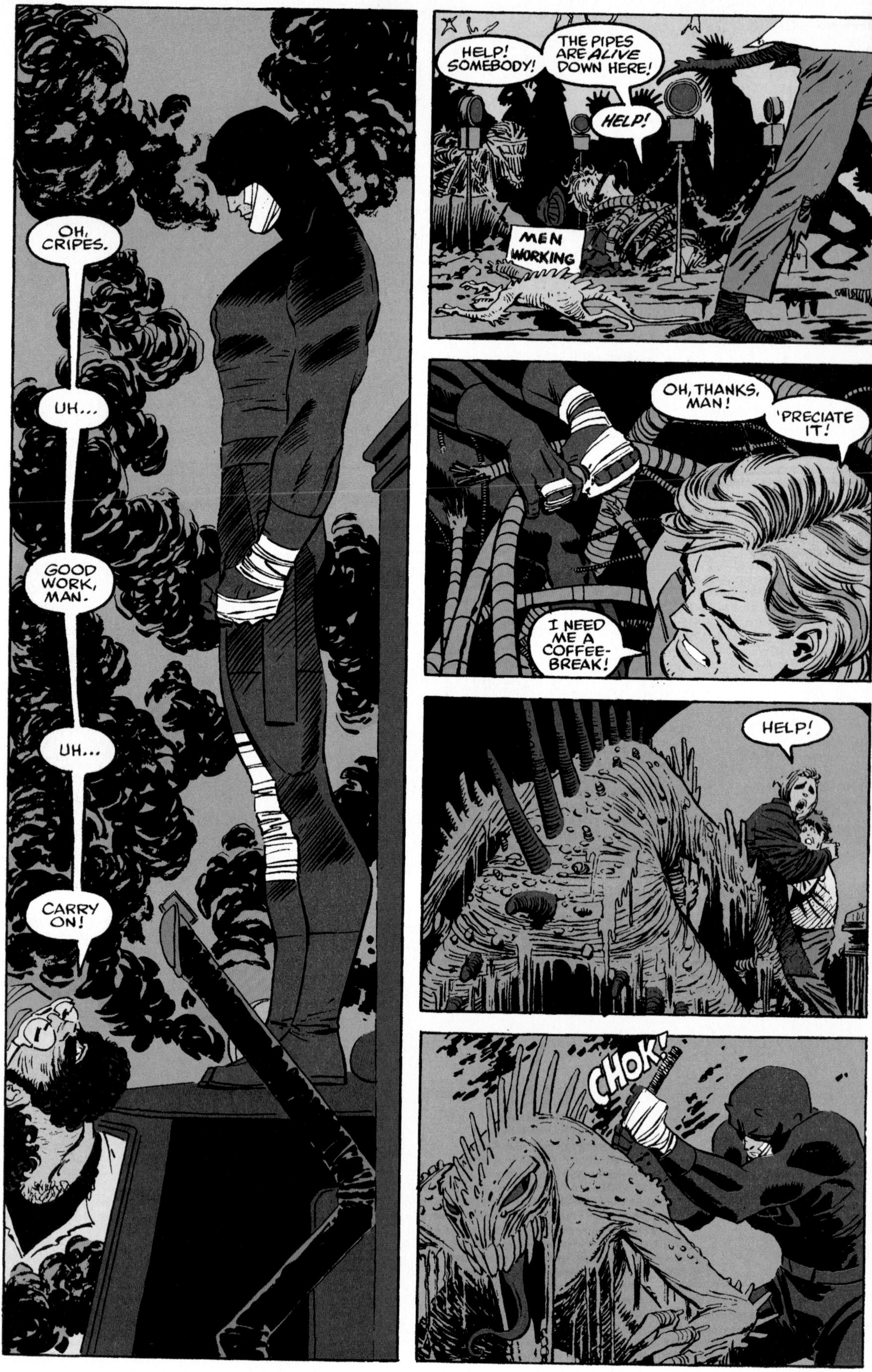
OH, CRIPES.
UH...
GOOD WORK, MAN.
UH...
CARRY ON!
HELP! SOMEBODY!
THE PIPES ARE ALIVE DOWN HERE!
HELP!
MEN WORKING
OH, THANKS, MAN!
'PRECIATE IT!
I NEED ME A COFFEE-BREAK!
HELP!
CHOK!

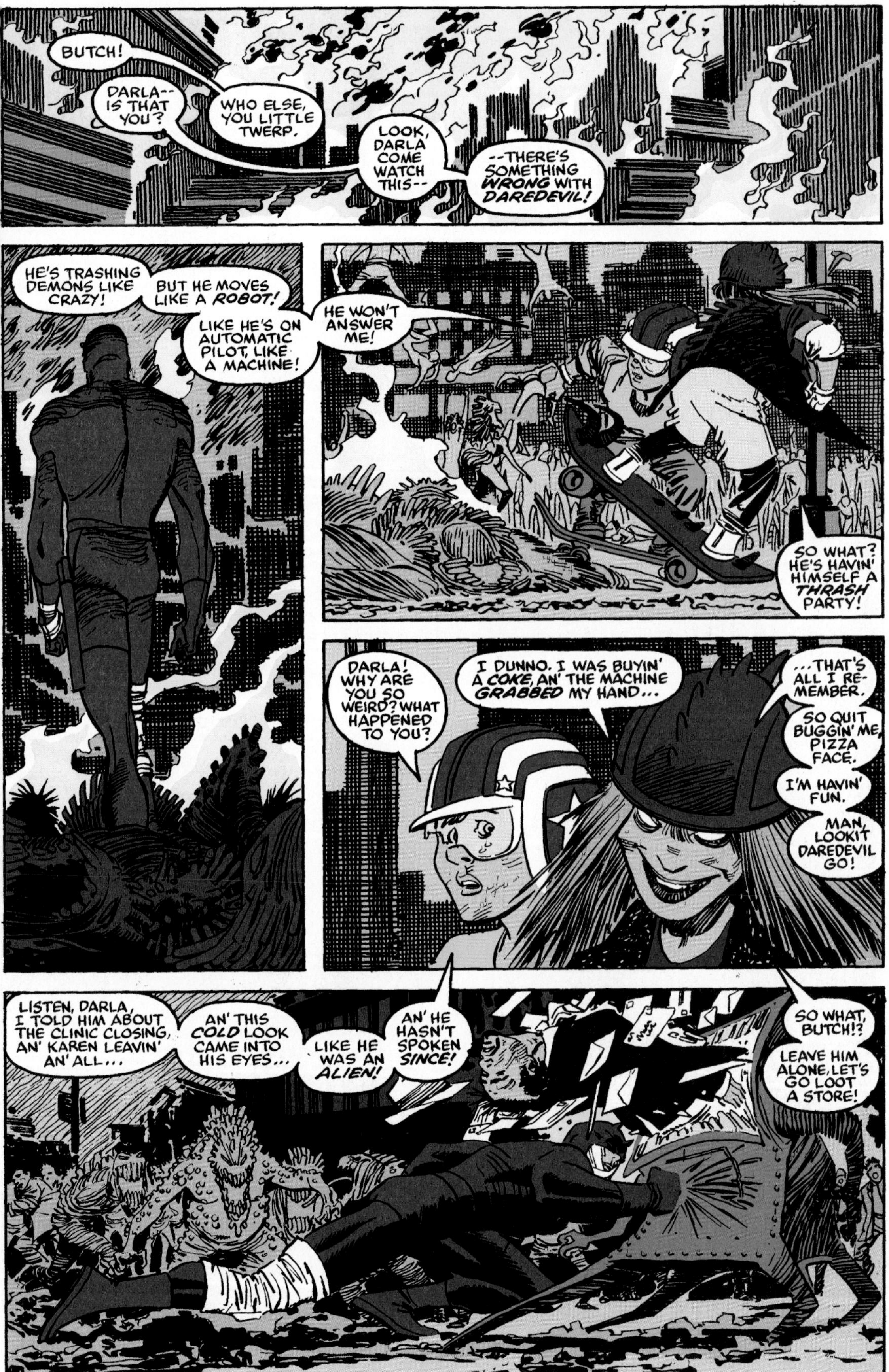
BUTCH!
DARLA-- IS THAT YOU?
WHO ELSE, YOU LITTLE TWERP.
LOOK, DARLA COME WATCH THIS--
--THERE'S SOMETHING WRONG WITH DAREDEVIL!
HE'S TRASHING DEMONS LIKE CRAZY!
BUT HE MOVES LIKE A ROBOT!
LIKE HE'S ON AUTOMATIC PILOT, LIKE A MACHINE!
HE WON'T ANSWER ME!
SO WHAT? HE'S HAVIN' HIMSELF A THRASH PARTY!
DARLA! WHY ARE YOU SO WEIRD? WHAT HAPPENED TO YOU?
I DUNNO. I WAS BUYIN' A COKE, AN' THE MACHINE GRABBED MY HAND...
...THAT'S ALL I REMEMBER.
SO QUIT BUGGIN' ME, PIZZA FACE.
I'M HAVIN' FUN.
MAN, LOOKIT DAREDEVIL GO!
LISTEN, DARLA, I TOLD HIM ABOUT THE CLINIC CLOSING, AN' KAREN LEAVIN' AN' ALL...
AN' THIS COLD LOOK CAME INTO HIS EYES...
LIKE HE WAS AN ALIEN!
AN' HE HASN'T SPOKEN SINCE!
SO WHAT, BUTCH!?
LEAVE HIM ALONE, LET'S GO LOOT A STORE!

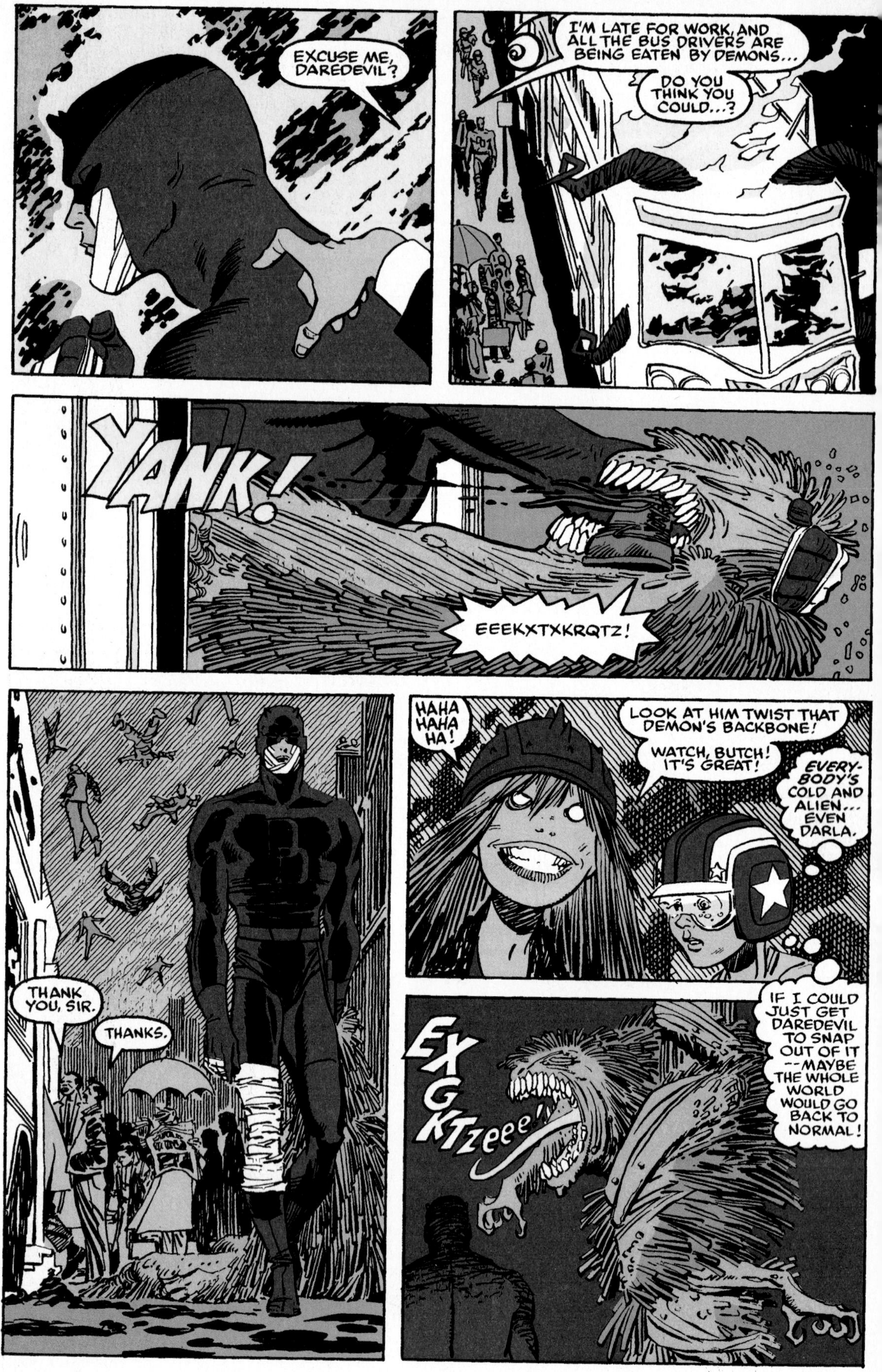

EXCUSE ME, DAREDEVIL?
I'M LATE FOR WORK, AND ALL THE BUS DRIVERS ARE BEING EATEN BY DEMONS...
DO YOU THINK YOU COULD...?
YANK!
EEEKXTXKRQTZ!
THANK YOU, SIR.
THANKS.
HAHA HAHA HA!
LOOK AT HIM TWIST THAT DEMON'S BACKBONE!
WATCH, BUTCH! IT'S GREAT!
EVERYBODY'S COLD AND ALIEN... EVEN DARLA.
EXGKTZeee!
IF I COULD JUST GET DAREDEVIL TO SNAP OUT OF IT --MAYBE THE WHOLE WORLD WOULD GO BACK TO NORMAL!

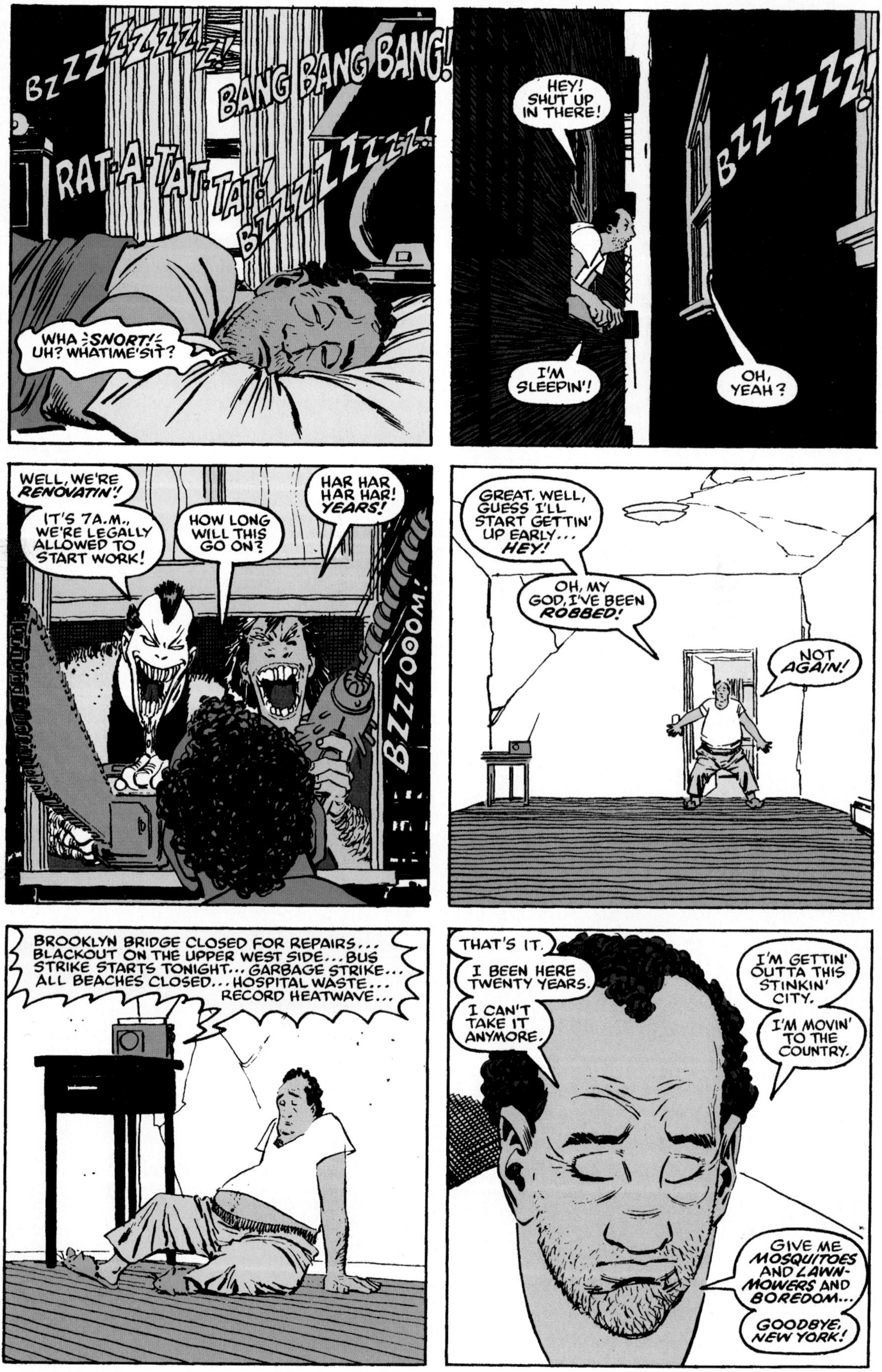
BzZZZZZZz!
BANG BANG BANG!
RAT-A-TAT-TAT-TAT!
BZZZZZZzzz!
WHA ~SNORT!~ UH? WHATIME'SIT?
HEY! SHUT UP IN THERE!
I'M SLEEPIN'!
BZZZZZZ!
OH, YEAH?
WELL, WE'RE RENOVATIN'!
IT'S 7A.M., WE'RE LEGALLY ALLOWED TO START WORK!
HOW LONG WILL THIS GO ON?
HAR HAR HAR HAR! YEARS!
BZZZOOOM!
GREAT. WELL, GUESS I'LL START GETTIN' UP EARLY... HEY!
OH, MY GOD, I'VE BEEN ROBBED!
NOT AGAIN!
BROOKLYN BRIDGE CLOSED FOR REPAIRS... BLACKOUT ON THE UPPER WEST SIDE... BUS STRIKE STARTS TONIGHT... GARBAGE STRIKE... ALL BEACHES CLOSED... HOSPITAL WASTE... RECORD HEATWAVE...
THAT'S IT.
I BEEN HERE TWENTY YEARS.
I CAN'T TAKE IT ANYMORE.
I'M GETTIN' OUTTA THIS STINKIN' CITY.
I'M MOVIN' TO THE COUNTRY.
GIVE ME MOSQUITOES AND LAWN-MOWERS AND BOREDOM...
GOODBYE, NEW YORK!

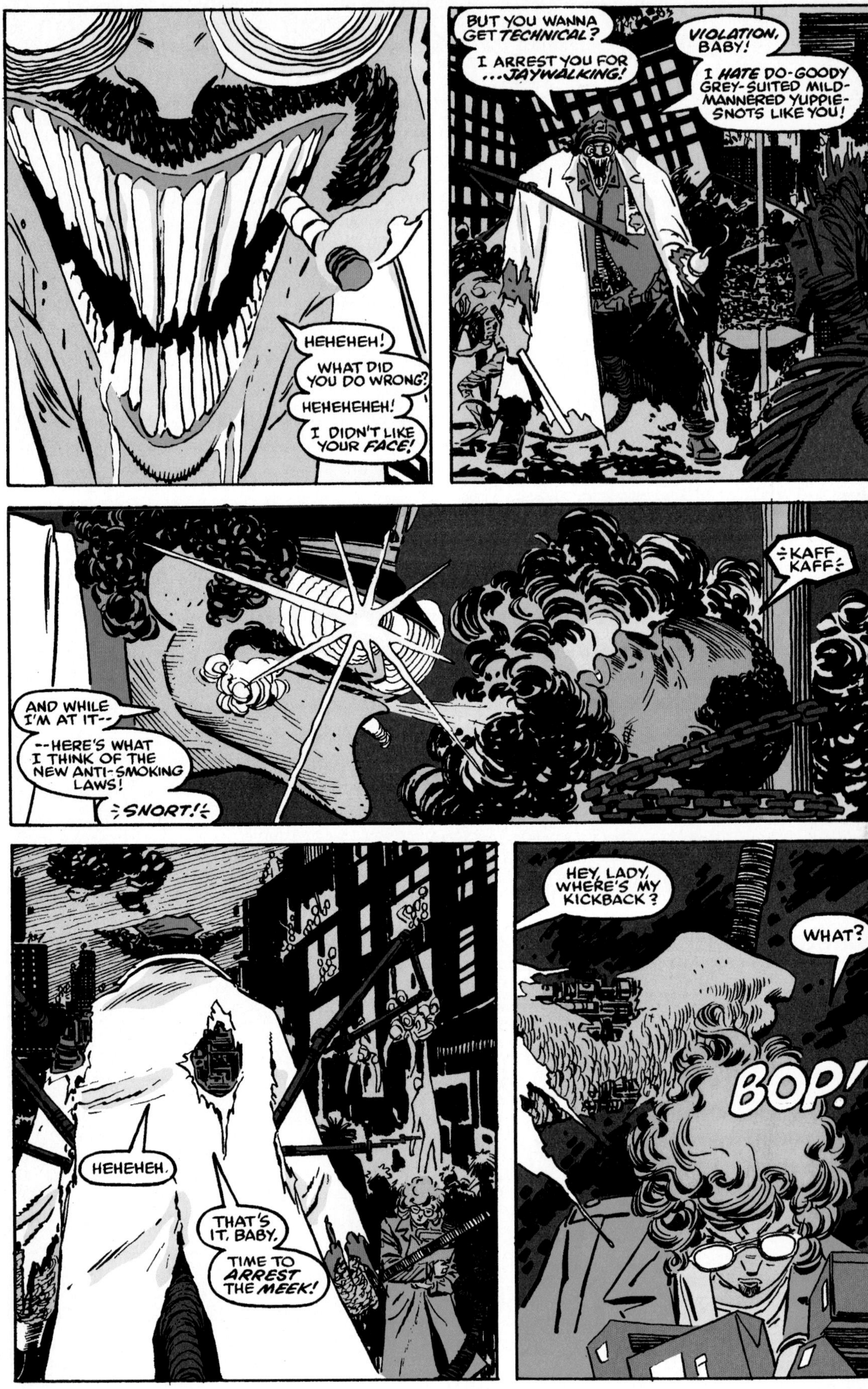
HEHEHEH!
WHAT DID YOU DO WRONG?
HEHEHEHEH!
I DIDN'T LIKE YOUR FACE!
BUT YOU WANNA GET TECHNICAL?
I ARREST YOU FOR ...JAYWALKING!
VIOLATION, BABY!
I HATE DO-GOODY GREY-SUITED MILD-MANNERED YUPPIE-SNOTS LIKE YOU!
AND WHILE I'M AT IT--
--HERE'S WHAT I THINK OF THE NEW ANTI-SMOKING LAWS!
SNORT!
KAFF KAFF
HEHEHEH.
THAT'S IT, BABY.
TIME TO ARREST THE MEEK!
HEY, LADY, WHERE'S MY KICKBACK?
WHAT?
BOP!

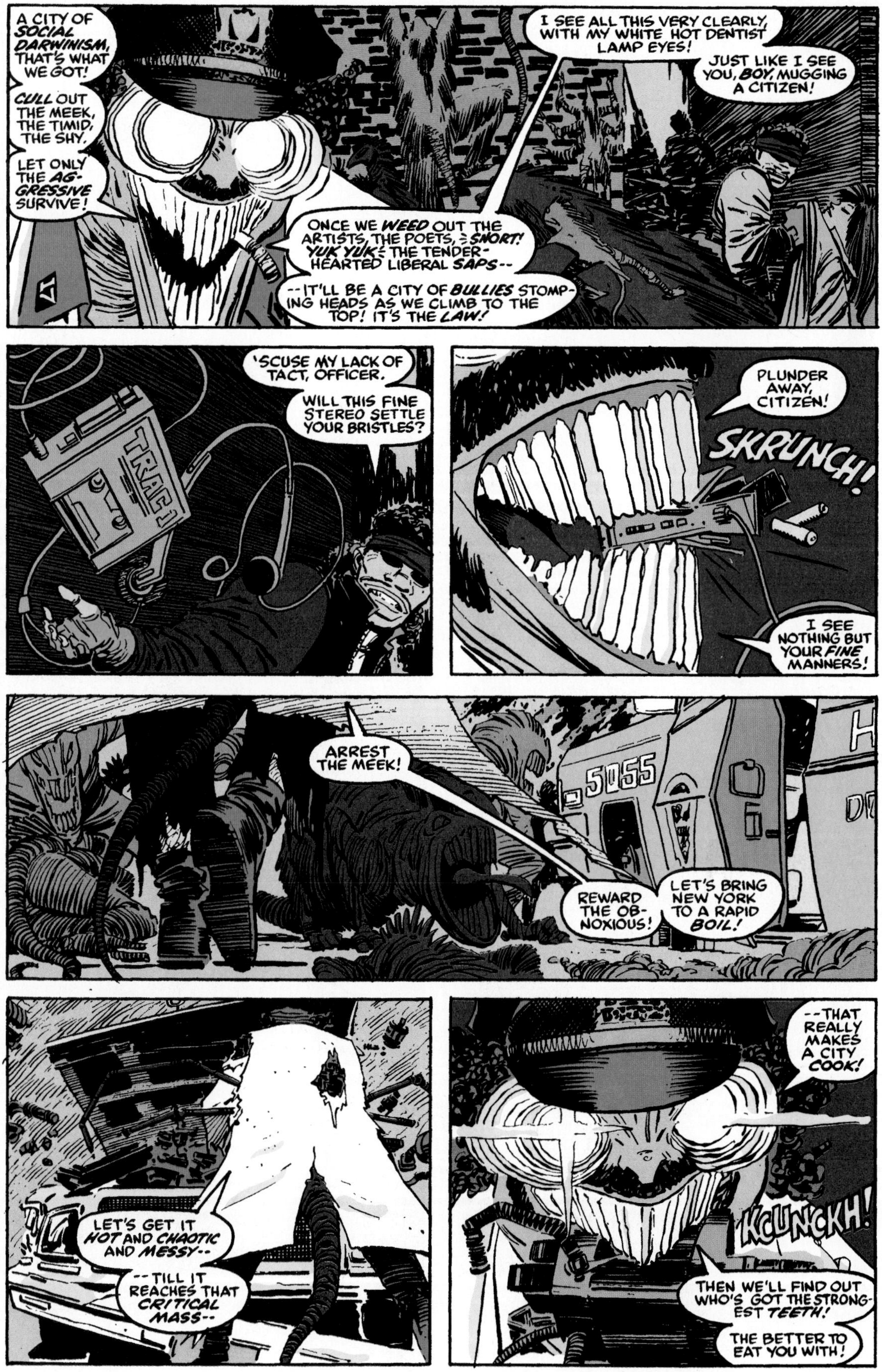
A CITY OF SOCIAL DARWINISM, THAT'S WHAT WE GOT!
CULL OUT THE MEEK, THE TIMID, THE SHY.
LET ONLY THE AG-GRESSIVE SURVIVE!
I SEE ALL THIS VERY CLEARLY, WITH MY WHITE HOT DENTIST LAMP EYES!
JUST LIKE I SEE YOU, BOY, MUGGING A CITIZEN!
ONCE WE WEED OUT THE ARTISTS, THE POETS, =SNORT! YUK YUK= THE TENDER-HEARTED LIBERAL SAPS--
--IT'LL BE A CITY OF BULLIES STOMPING HEADS AS WE CLIMB TO THE TOP! IT'S THE LAW!
'SCUSE MY LACK OF TACT, OFFICER.
WILL THIS FINE STEREO SETTLE YOUR BRISTLES?
TRAC
PLUNDER AWAY, CITIZEN!
SKRUNCH!
I SEE NOTHING BUT YOUR FINE MANNERS!
ARREST THE MEEK!
REWARD THE OB-NOXIOUS!
LET'S BRING NEW YORK TO A RAPID BOIL!
5055
LET'S GET IT HOT AND CHAOTIC AND MESSY--
--TILL IT REACHES THAT CRITICAL MASS--
--THAT REALLY MAKES A CITY COOK!
KCUNCKH!
THEN WE'LL FIND OUT WHO'S GOT THE STRONG-EST TEETH!
THE BETTER TO EAT YOU WITH!

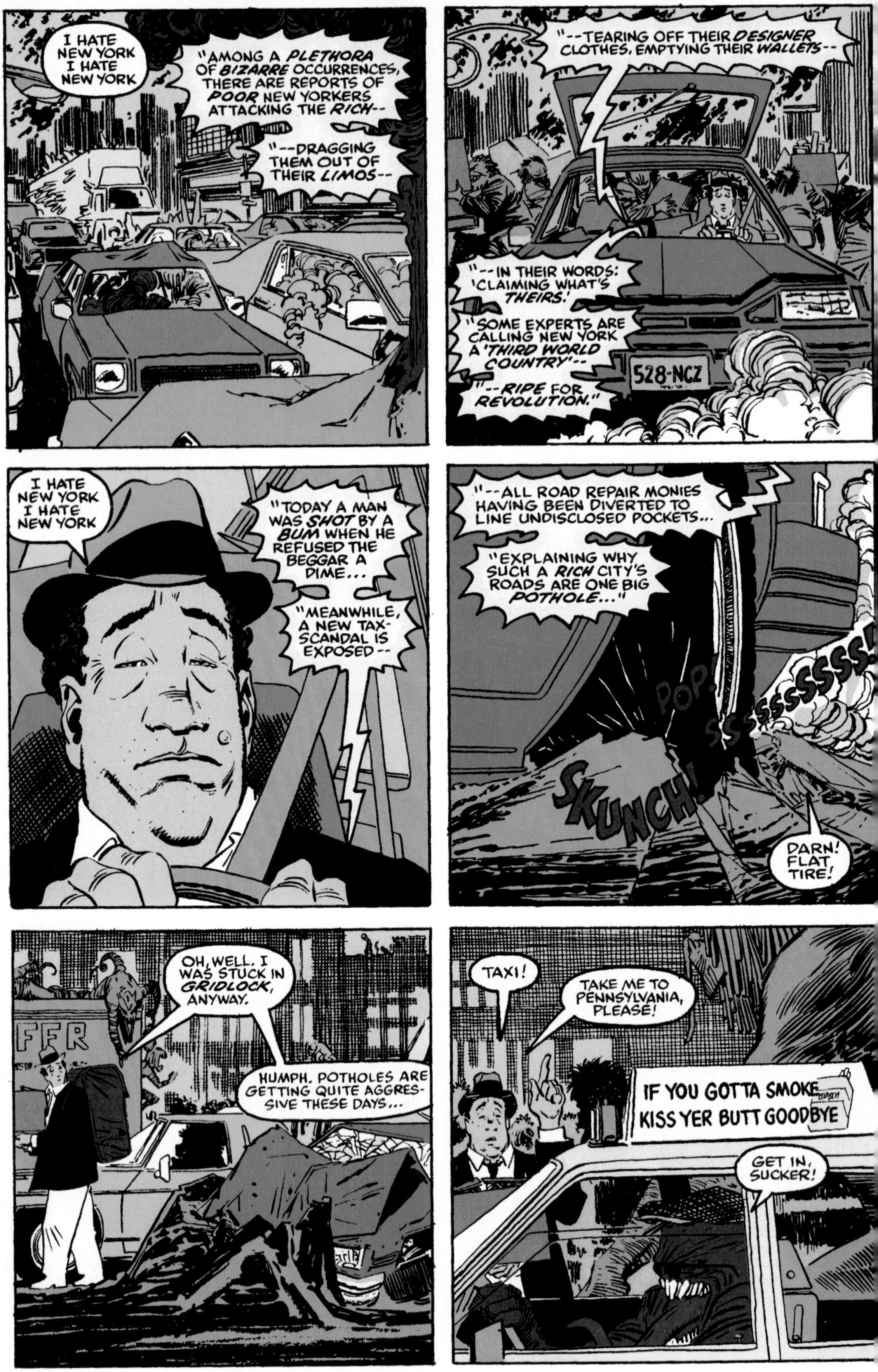
I HATE NEW YORK I HATE NEW YORK
"AMONG A PLETHORA OF BIZARRE OCCURRENCES, THERE ARE REPORTS OF POOR NEW YORKERS ATTACKING THE RICH--
"--DRAGGING THEM OUT OF THEIR LIMOS--
"--TEARING OFF THEIR DESIGNER CLOTHES, EMPTYING THEIR WALLETS--
"--IN THEIR WORDS: 'CLAIMING WHAT'S THEIRS.'
"SOME EXPERTS ARE CALLING NEW YORK A 'THIRD WORLD COUNTRY'--
"--RIPE FOR REVOLUTION."
528-NCZ
I HATE NEW YORK I HATE NEW YORK
"TODAY A MAN WAS SHOT BY A BUM WHEN HE REFUSED THE BEGGAR A DIME...
"MEANWHILE, A NEW TAX-SCANDAL IS EXPOSED--
"--ALL ROAD REPAIR MONIES HAVING BEEN DIVERTED TO LINE UNDISCLOSED POCKETS...
"EXPLAINING WHY SUCH A RICH CITY'S ROADS ARE ONE BIG POTHOLE..."
POP!
SSSSSSSSSSSS
SKUNCH!
DARN! FLAT TIRE!
OH, WELL. I WAS STUCK IN GRIDLOCK, ANYWAY.
HUMPH. POTHOLES ARE GETTING QUITE AGGRESSIVE THESE DAYS...
FFR
TAXI!
TAKE ME TO PENNSYLVANIA, PLEASE!
IF YOU GOTTA SMOKE KISS YER BUTT GOODBYE
GET IN, SUCKER!

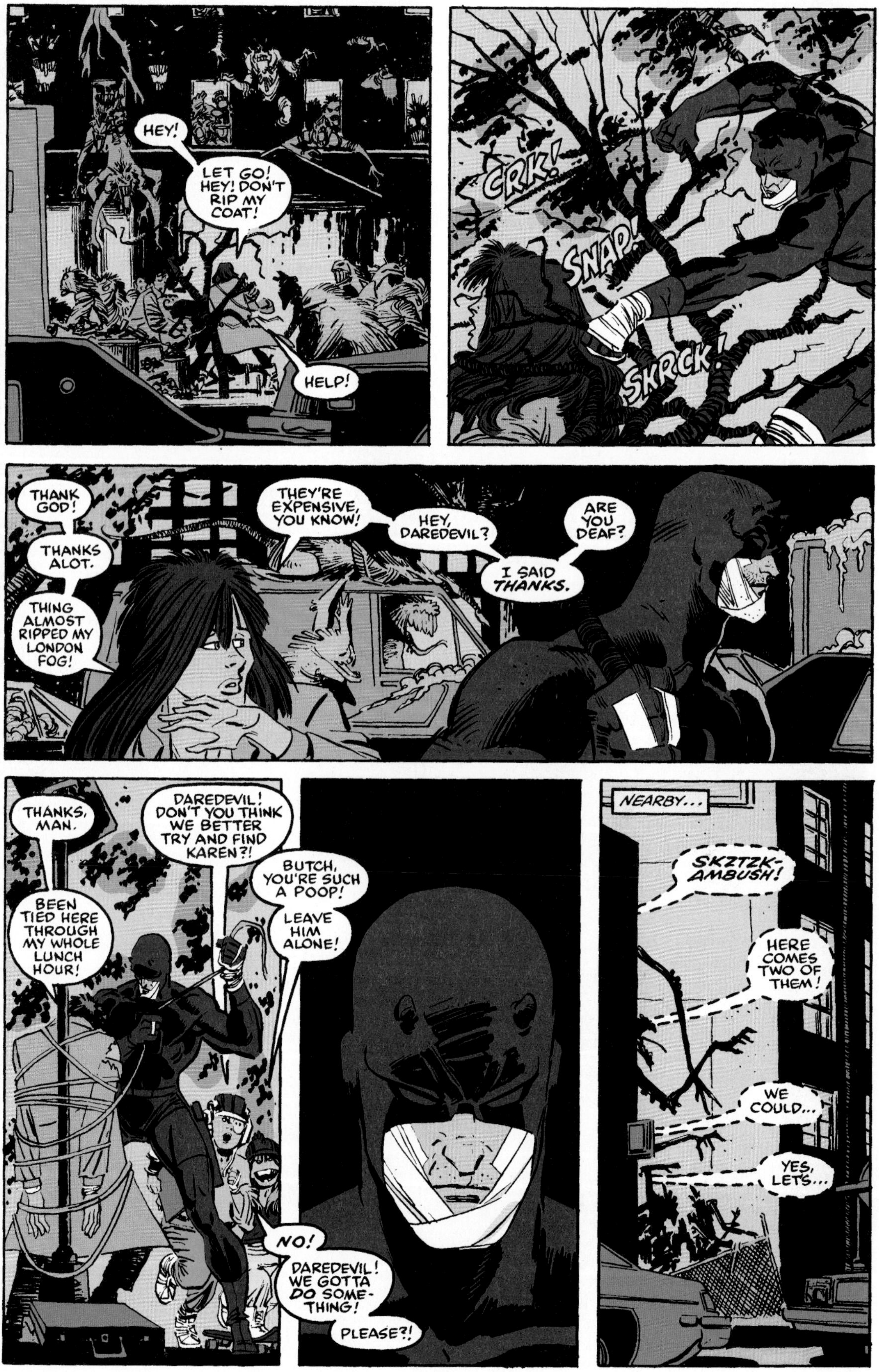
HEY!
LET GO! HEY! DON'T RIP MY COAT!
HELP!
CRK!
SNAP!
SKRCK!
THANK GOD!
THANKS ALOT.
THING ALMOST RIPPED MY LONDON FOG!
THEY'RE EXPENSIVE, YOU KNOW!
HEY, DAREDEVIL?
ARE YOU DEAF?
I SAID *THANKS.*
THANKS, MAN.
BEEN TIED HERE THROUGH MY WHOLE LUNCH HOUR!
DAREDEVIL! DON'T YOU THINK WE BETTER TRY AND FIND KAREN?!
BUTCH, YOU'RE SUCH A POOP!
LEAVE HIM ALONE!
NO!
DAREDEVIL! WE GOTTA *DO* SOMETHING!
PLEASE?!
NEARBY...
SKZTZK-AMBUSH!
HERE COMES TWO OF THEM!
WE COULD...
YES, LET'S...

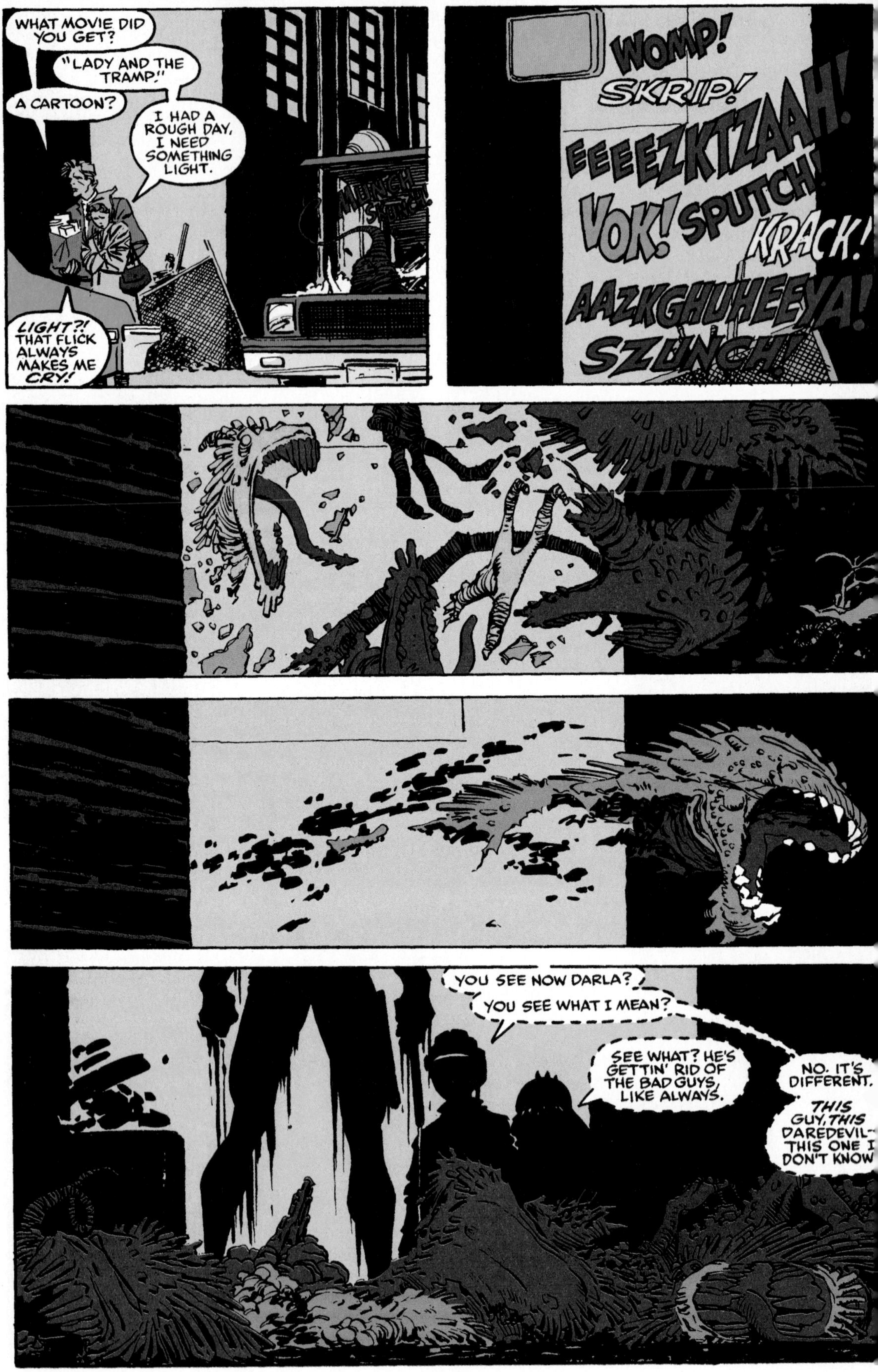
WHAT MOVIE DID YOU GET?
"LADY AND THE TRAMP."
A CARTOON?
I HAD A ROUGH DAY, I NEED SOMETHING LIGHT.
LIGHT?! THAT FLICK ALWAYS MAKES ME CRY!
WOMP!
SKRIP!
EEEEEZKTZAAH!
VOK!
SPUTCH!
KRACK!
AAZKGHUHEEYA!
SZUNCH!
YOU SEE NOW DARLA?
YOU SEE WHAT I MEAN?
SEE WHAT? HE'S GETTIN' RID OF THE BAD GUYS, LIKE ALWAYS.
NO. IT'S DIFFERENT.
THIS GUY, THIS DAREDEVIL-- THIS ONE I DON'T KNOW

WALLS DRIP WITH BAROQUE ANTHROPOMORPHIZED SHADOWS...

ANOTHER BUILDING BURNS.

STREETS SLINK WITH GIBBERING SLAVERING GROTESQUERIES...

ANOTHER BRIDGE COLLAPSES.

TRANSMOGRIFIED MACHINES BECOME BACCHANALIAN RINGMASTERS...

ANOTHER MAN FALLS TO THE GUTTER.

I HATE NEW YORK I HATE NEW YORK...

ROUGH DAY, BROTHER?

LET ME FIX YOUR TIE.

WHAT WAS THAT?

EEAAIIEEE

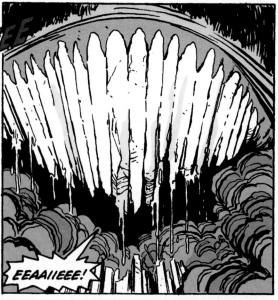

EEAAIIEEE!

VIOLATION, BABY!

WE'RE SMOKIN' NOW!

IT'S AN EIGHT-CYLINDER DAY--

--AN' MY ENGINE'S RUNNIN' HOT!

GONNA TAKE MY BABY FOR A DRIVE--

--AN' FILL THE SKY WITH MONOXIDE ROT!

UH-UH-UH....

SHUT UP, OR I'LL PULL YOUR TEETH, CITIZEN!

TSOOSH

TOOOT!

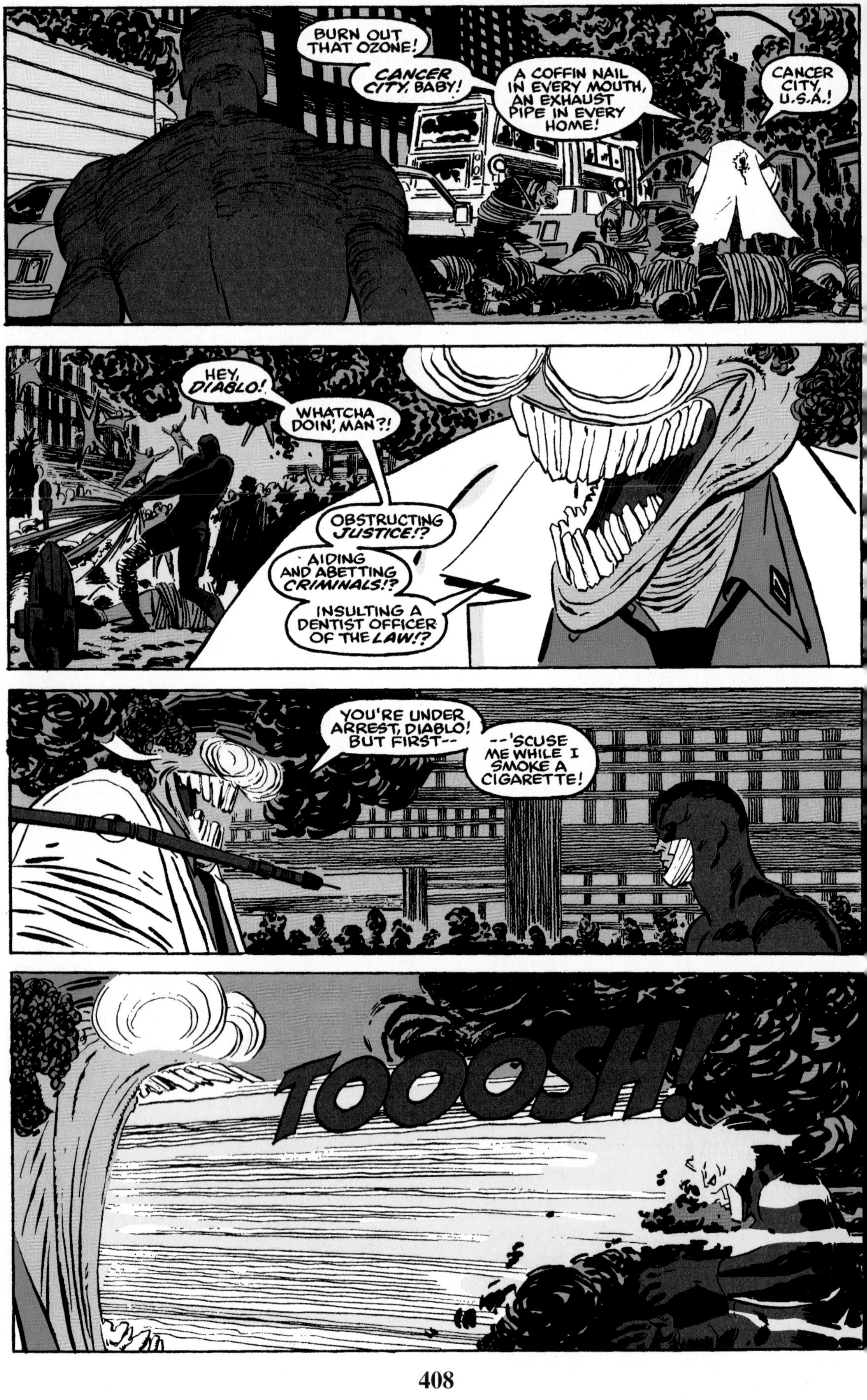
BURN OUT THAT OZONE!
CANCER CITY, BABY!
A COFFIN NAIL IN EVERY MOUTH, AN EXHAUST PIPE IN EVERY HOME!
CANCER CITY, U.S.A.!
HEY, DIABLO!
WHATCHA DOIN', MAN?!
OBSTRUCTING JUSTICE!?
AIDING AND ABETTING CRIMINALS!?
INSULTING A DENTIST OFFICER OF THE LAW!?
YOU'RE UNDER ARREST, DIABLO! BUT FIRST--
--'SCUSE ME WHILE I SMOKE A CIGARETTE!
TOOOSH!!

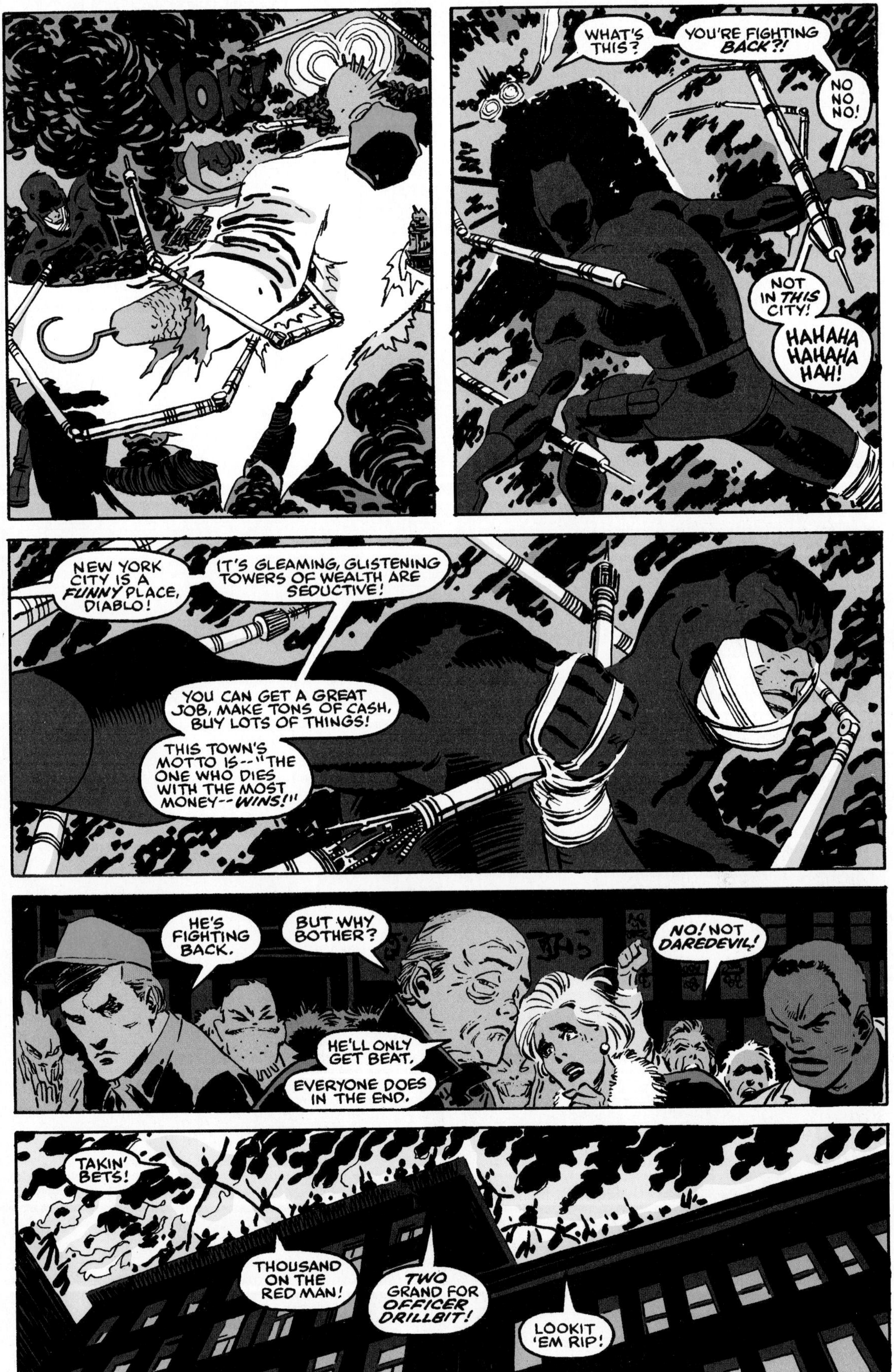
VOK!
WHAT'S THIS?
YOU'RE FIGHTING BACK?!
NO NO NO!
NOT IN THIS CITY!
HAHAHA HAHAHA HAH!
NEW YORK CITY IS A FUNNY PLACE, DIABLO!
IT'S GLEAMING, GLISTENING TOWERS OF WEALTH ARE SEDUCTIVE!
YOU CAN GET A GREAT JOB, MAKE TONS OF CASH, BUY LOTS OF THINGS!
THIS TOWN'S MOTTO IS--"THE ONE WHO DIES WITH THE MOST MONEY--WINS!"
HE'S FIGHTING BACK.
BUT WHY BOTHER?
HE'LL ONLY GET BEAT.
EVERYONE DOES IN THE END.
NO! NOT DAREDEVIL!
TAKIN' BETS!
THOUSAND ON THE RED MAN!
TWO GRAND FOR OFFICER DRILLBIT!
LOOKIT 'EM RIP!

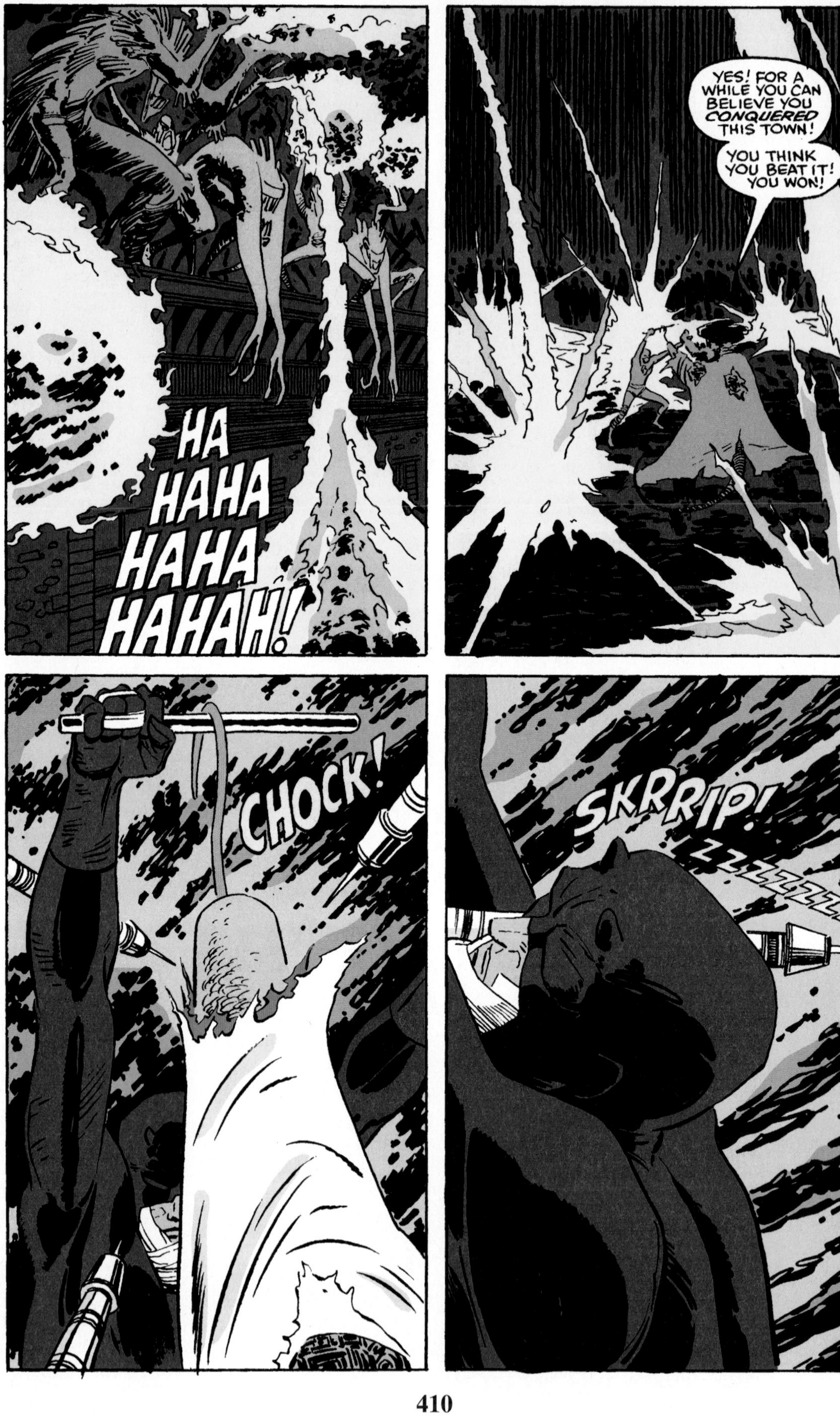
HA
HAHA
HAHA
HAHAH!
YES! FOR A WHILE YOU CAN BELIEVE YOU CONQUERED THIS TOWN!
YOU THINK YOU BEAT IT! YOU WON!
CHOCK!
SKRRIP!
ZZZZZZZZZ!

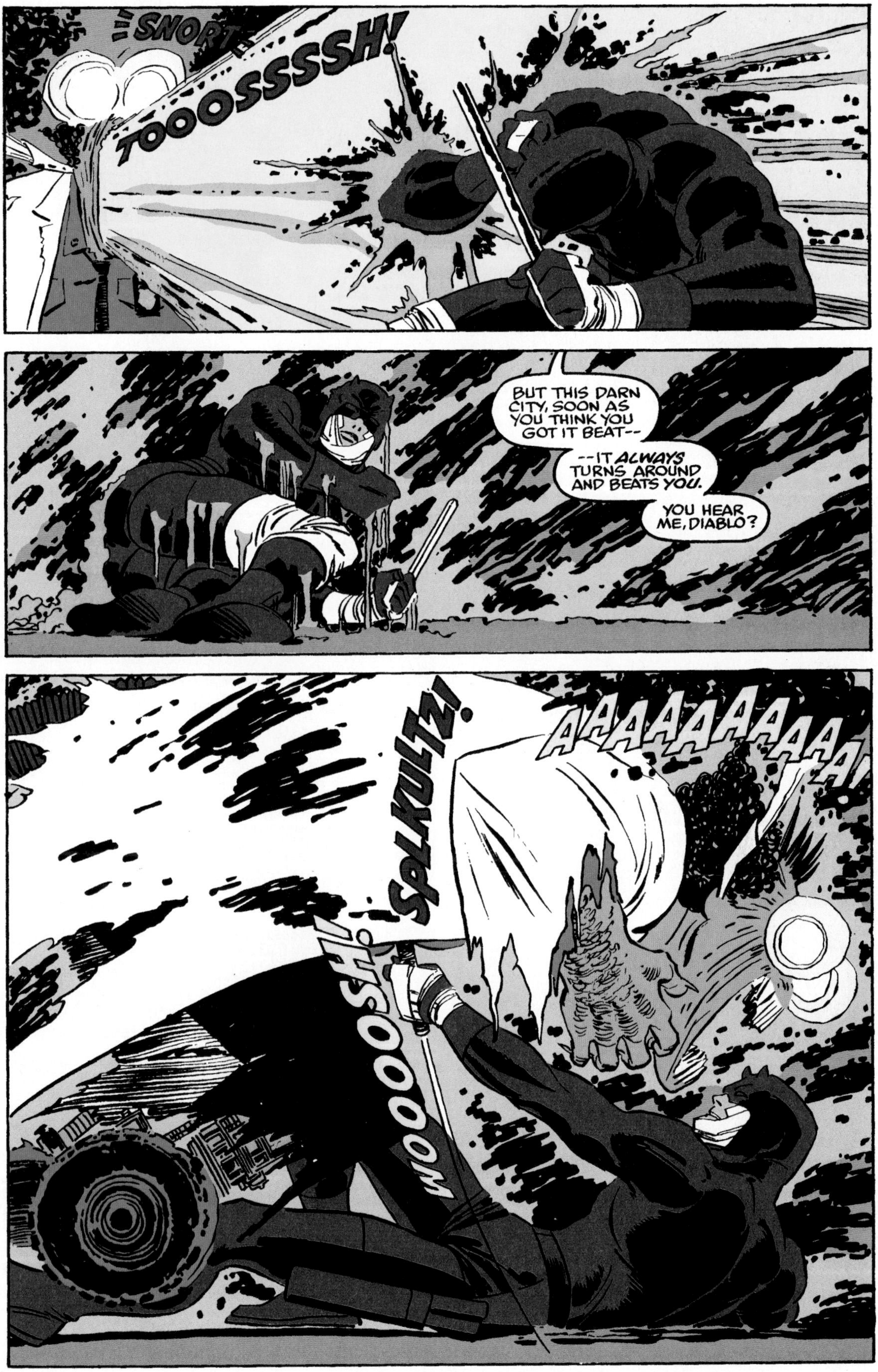
SNORT
TOOOSSSSSH!
BUT THIS DARN CITY, SOON AS YOU THINK YOU GOT IT BEAT--
--IT ALWAYS TURNS AROUND AND BEATS YOU.
YOU HEAR ME, DIABLO?
SPLKULTZ!
AAAAAAAAAA
WOOOOOSH!

HAHAHA HAH!

GOOD *SKEWER* JOB, DIABLO-- BUT IT DON'T MATTER.

THIS CITY'LL *GET* YOU, IF I DON'T.

IT *HAMMERS* YOU, DAY IN DAY OUT!

SKRIP!

ALL THE LITTLE HASSLES, ALL THE TENSION, THE SHEER CHAOS...

WOMP!

IT BEATS YOU NUMB, IN THE END.

BRUTALIZES YOU, DAY IN, DAY OUT. TILL YOU'RE SO HARD, YOU'RE INHUMAN.

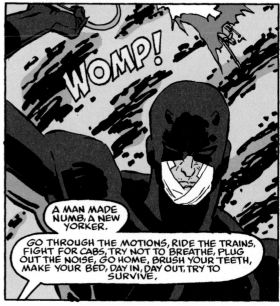

WOMP!

A MAN MADE NUMB, A NEW YORKER.

GO THROUGH THE MOTIONS, RIDE THE TRAINS, FIGHT FOR CABS, TRY NOT TO BREATHE, PLUG OUT THE NOISE, GO HOME, BRUSH YOUR TEETH, MAKE YOUR BED, DAY IN, DAY OUT, TRY TO SURVIVE.

WACK!

WHAM!

JUST LIKE YOU. A ROBOT, DOIN' YOUR JOB. COLD, EFFICIENT, EFFECTIVE.

NUMB. YOU FEEL NOTHING, DIABLO.

URK! NOTHING... GLKH

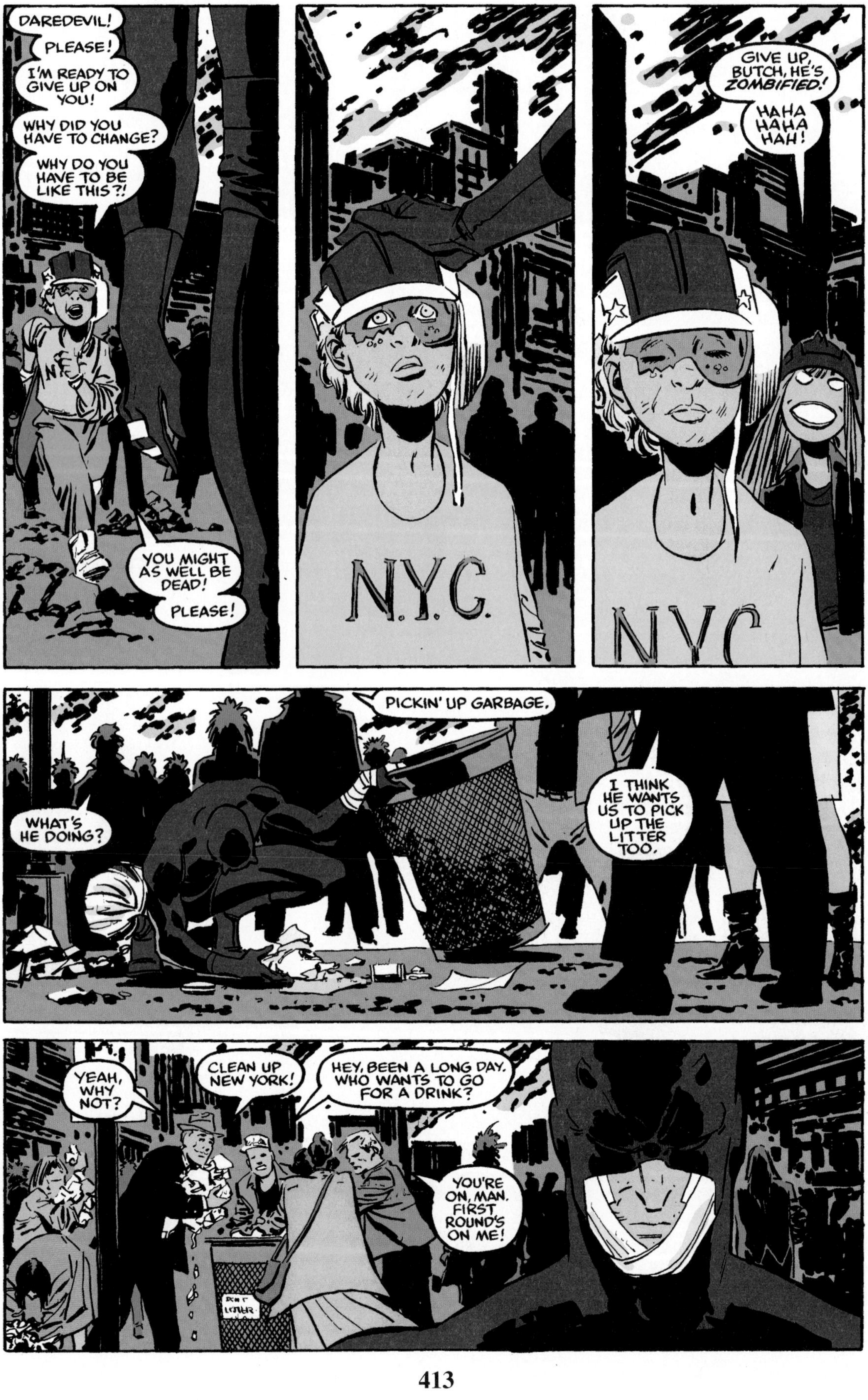
DAREDEVIL!
PLEASE!
I'M READY TO GIVE UP ON YOU!
WHY DID YOU HAVE TO CHANGE?
WHY DO YOU HAVE TO BE LIKE THIS?!
YOU MIGHT AS WELL BE DEAD!
PLEASE!
N.Y.C.
GIVE UP, BUTCH, HE'S ZOMBIFIED!
HAHA HAHA HAH!
N.Y.C
PICKIN' UP GARBAGE.
WHAT'S HE DOING?
I THINK HE WANTS US TO PICK UP THE LITTER TOO.
YEAH, WHY NOT?
CLEAN UP NEW YORK!
HEY, BEEN A LONG DAY. WHO WANTS TO GO FOR A DRINK?
YOU'RE ON, MAN. FIRST ROUND'S ON ME!

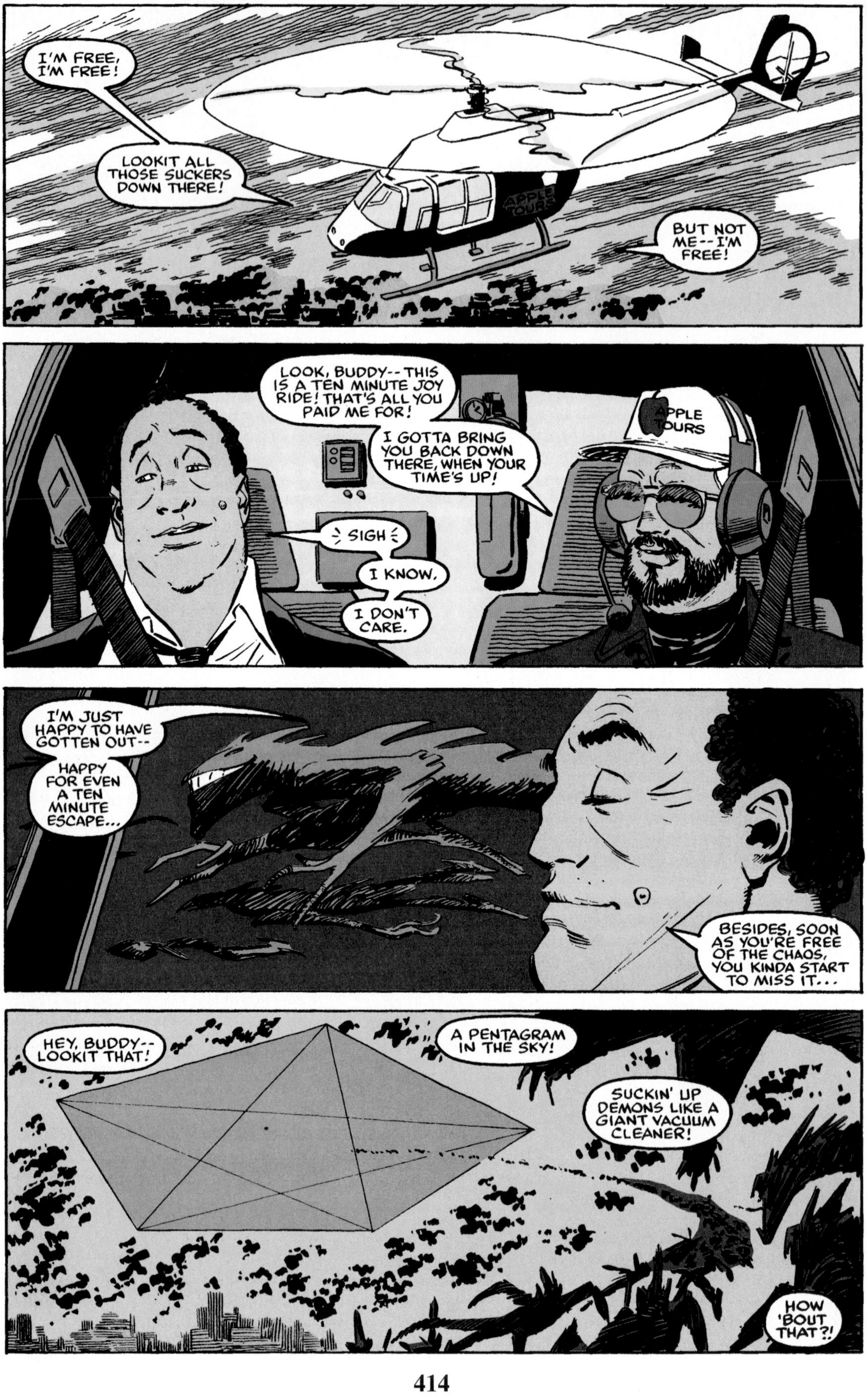
I'M FREE, I'M FREE!
LOOKIT ALL THOSE SUCKERS DOWN THERE!
APPLE TOURS
BUT NOT ME--I'M FREE!
LOOK, BUDDY--THIS IS A TEN MINUTE JOY RIDE! THAT'S ALL YOU PAID ME FOR!
I GOTTA BRING YOU BACK DOWN THERE, WHEN YOUR TIME'S UP!
APPLE TOURS
SIGH
I KNOW.
I DON'T CARE.
I'M JUST HAPPY TO HAVE GOTTEN OUT--
HAPPY FOR EVEN A TEN MINUTE ESCAPE...
BESIDES, SOON AS YOU'RE FREE OF THE CHAOS, YOU KINDA START TO MISS IT...
HEY, BUDDY--LOOKIT THAT!
A PENTAGRAM IN THE SKY!
SUCKIN' UP DEMONS LIKE A GIANT VACUUM CLEANER!
HOW 'BOUT THAT?!

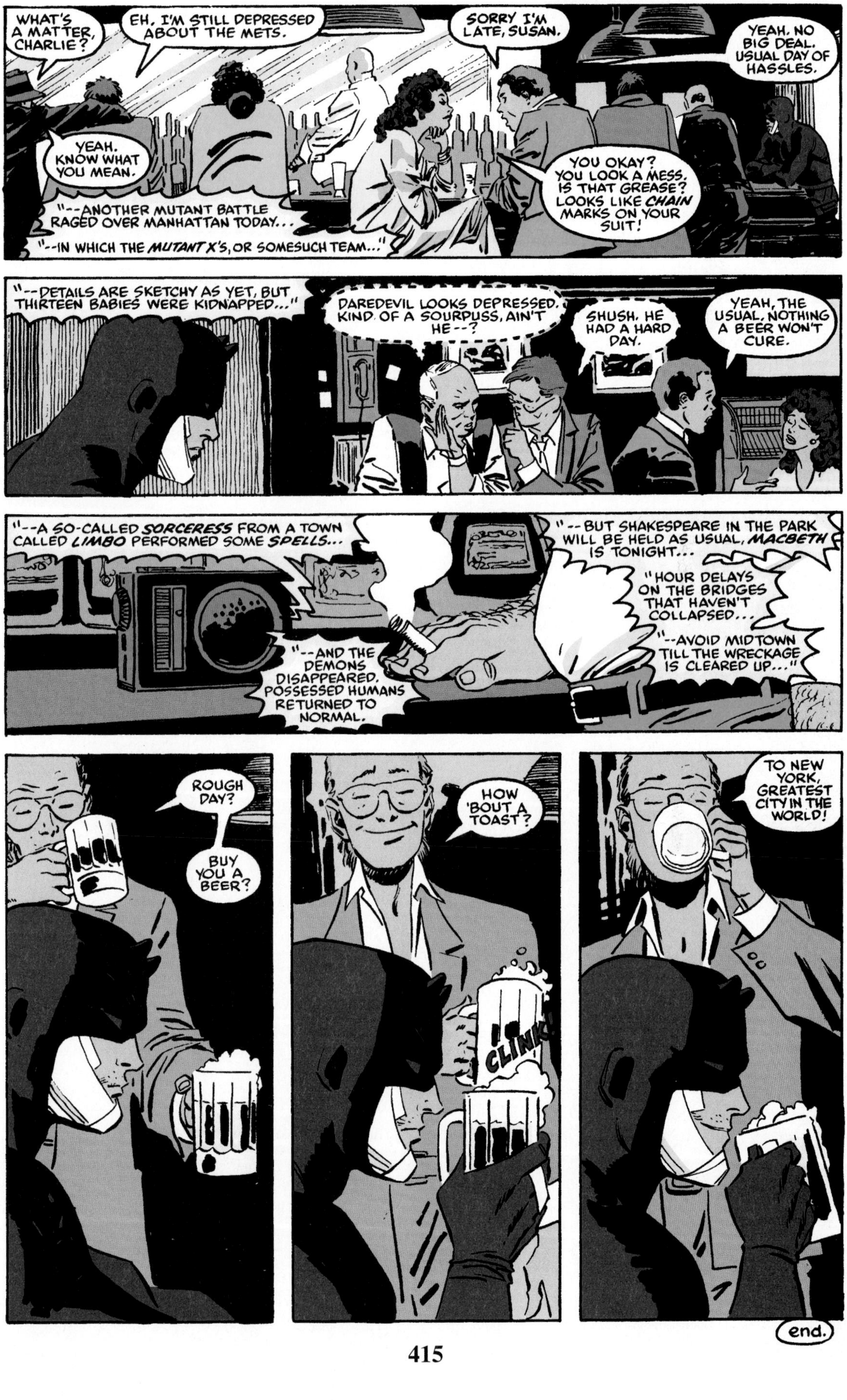
WHAT'S A MATTER, CHARLIE?
EH, I'M STILL DEPRESSED ABOUT THE METS.
SORRY I'M LATE, SUSAN.
YEAH. NO BIG DEAL. USUAL DAY OF HASSLES.
YEAH. KNOW WHAT YOU MEAN.
YOU OKAY? YOU LOOK A MESS. IS THAT GREASE? LOOKS LIKE CHAIN MARKS ON YOUR SUIT!
"--ANOTHER MUTANT BATTLE RAGED OVER MANHATTAN TODAY...
"--IN WHICH THE MUTANT X'S, OR SOMESUCH TEAM..."
"--DETAILS ARE SKETCHY AS YET, BUT THIRTEEN BABIES WERE KIDNAPPED..."
DAREDEVIL LOOKS DEPRESSED. KIND OF A SOURPUSS, AIN'T HE--?
SHUSH. HE HAD A HARD DAY.
YEAH, THE USUAL. NOTHING A BEER WON'T CURE.
"--A SO-CALLED SORCERESS FROM A TOWN CALLED LIMBO PERFORMED SOME SPELLS...
"--AND THE DEMONS DISAPPEARED. POSSESSED HUMANS RETURNED TO NORMAL.
"--BUT SHAKESPEARE IN THE PARK WILL BE HELD AS USUAL. MACBETH IS TONIGHT...
"HOUR DELAYS ON THE BRIDGES THAT HAVEN'T COLLAPSED...
"--AVOID MIDTOWN TILL THE WRECKAGE IS CLEARED UP..."
ROUGH DAY?
BUY YOU A BEER?
HOW 'BOUT A TOAST?
CLINK
TO NEW YORK, GREATEST CITY IN THE WORLD!
end.

Avengers #300 **also included the following short story and feature section.**

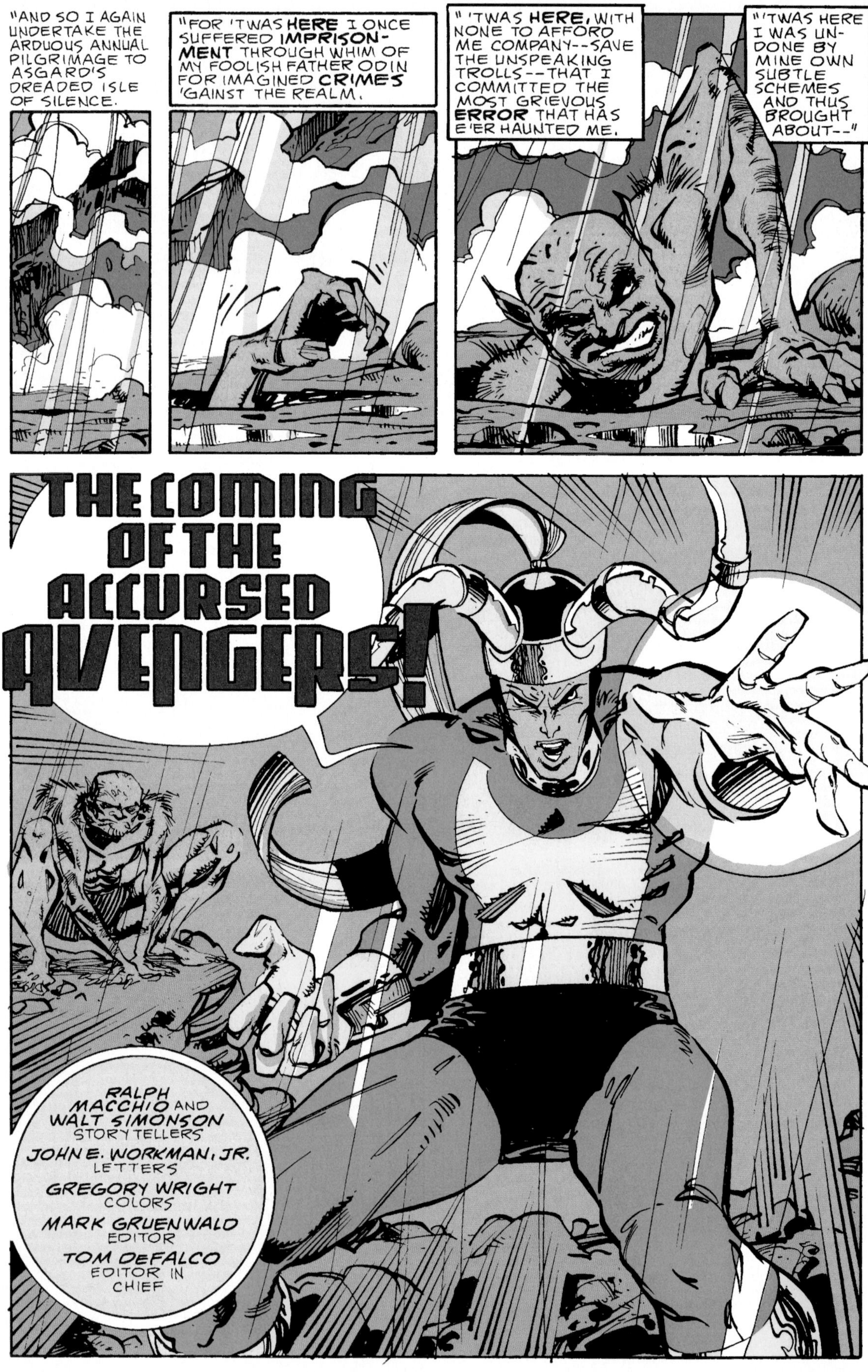
"AND SO I AGAIN UNDERTAKE THE ARDUOUS ANNUAL PILGRIMAGE TO ASGARD'S DREADED ISLE OF SILENCE.
"FOR 'TWAS HERE I ONCE SUFFERED IMPRISONMENT THROUGH WHIM OF MY FOOLISH FATHER ODIN FOR IMAGINED CRIMES 'GAINST THE REALM.
" 'TWAS HERE, WITH NONE TO AFFORD ME COMPANY--SAVE THE UNSPEAKING TROLLS--THAT I COMMITTED THE MOST GRIEVOUS ERROR THAT HAS E'ER HAUNTED ME.
"'TWAS HERE I WAS UNDONE BY MINE OWN SUBTLE SCHEMES AND THUS BROUGHT ABOUT--"
THE COMING OF THE ACCURSED AVENGERS!
RALPH MACCHIO AND WALT SIMONSON STORYTELLERS
JOHN E. WORKMAN, JR. LETTERS
GREGORY WRIGHT COLORS
MARK GRUENWALD EDITOR
TOM DEFALCO EDITOR IN CHIEF

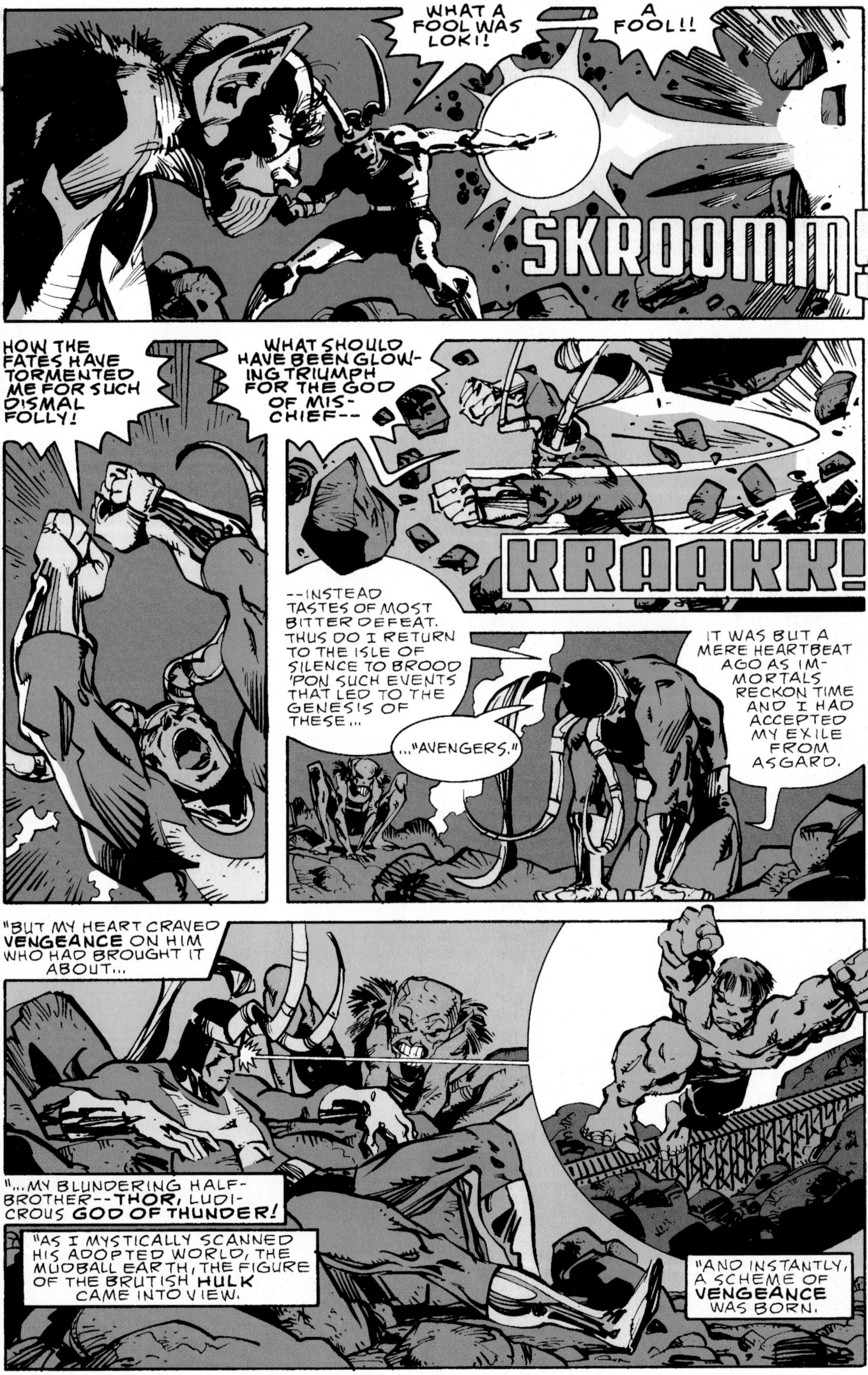

WHAT A FOOL WAS LOKI!
A FOOL!!
SKROOMM!
HOW THE FATES HAVE TORMENTED ME FOR SUCH DISMAL FOLLY!
WHAT SHOULD HAVE BEEN GLOWING TRIUMPH FOR THE GOD OF MISCHIEF--
KRAAKK!
--INSTEAD TASTES OF MOST BITTER DEFEAT. THUS DO I RETURN TO THE ISLE OF SILENCE TO BROOD 'PON SUCH EVENTS THAT LED TO THE GENESIS OF THESE...
..."AVENGERS."
IT WAS BUT A MERE HEARTBEAT AGO AS IMMORTALS RECKON TIME AND I HAD ACCEPTED MY EXILE FROM ASGARD.
"BUT MY HEART CRAVED VENGEANCE ON HIM WHO HAD BROUGHT IT ABOUT...
"...MY BLUNDERING HALF-BROTHER--THOR, LUDICROUS GOD OF THUNDER!
"AS I MYSTICALLY SCANNED HIS ADOPTED WORLD, THE MUDBALL EARTH, THE FIGURE OF THE BRUTISH HULK CAME INTO VIEW.
"AND INSTANTLY, A SCHEME OF VENGEANCE WAS BORN.

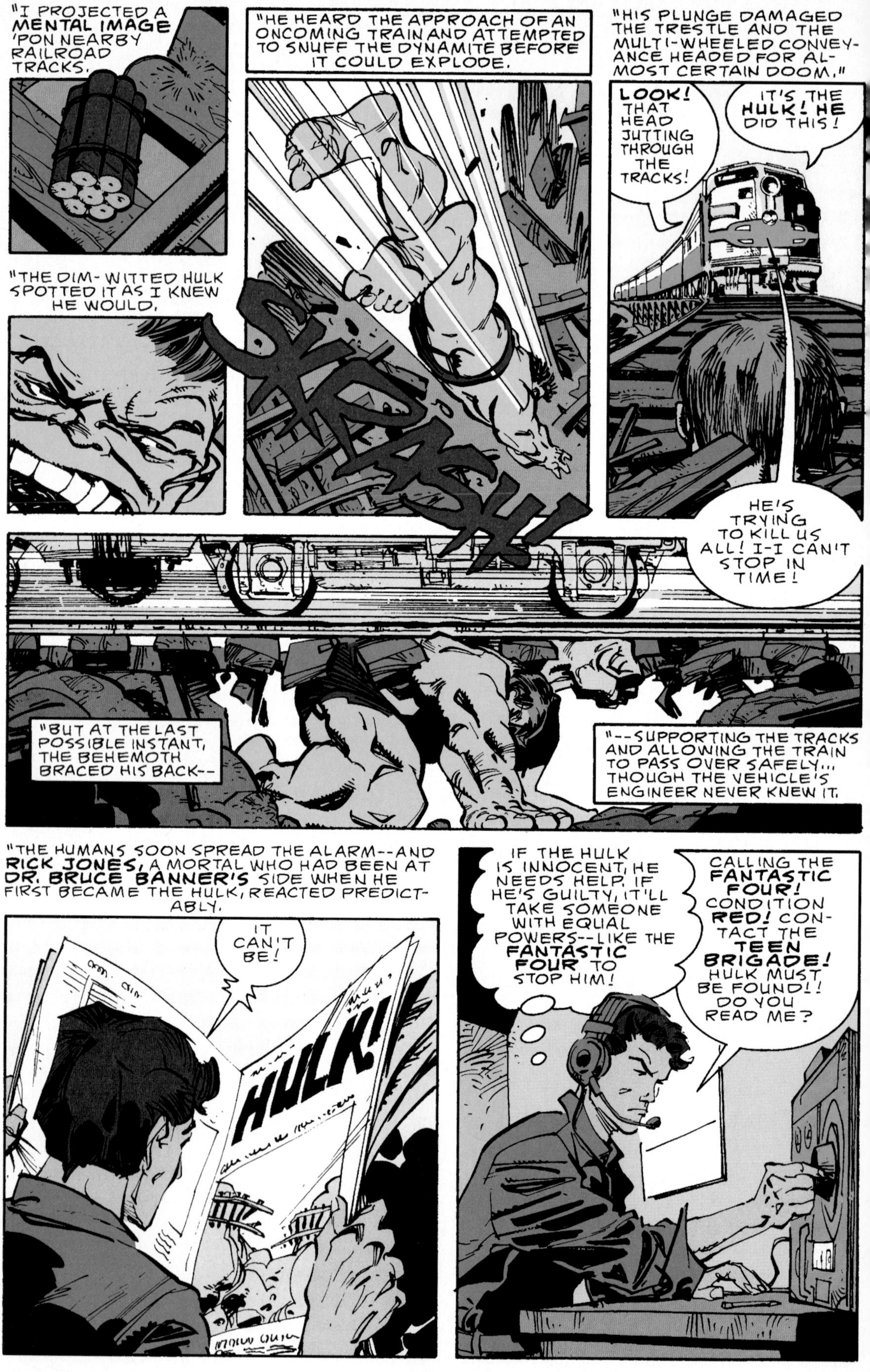

"I PROJECTED A MENTAL IMAGE 'PON NEARBY RAILROAD TRACKS.
"HE HEARD THE APPROACH OF AN ONCOMING TRAIN AND ATTEMPTED TO SNUFF THE DYNAMITE BEFORE IT COULD EXPLODE.
"HIS PLUNGE DAMAGED THE TRESTLE AND THE MULTI-WHEELED CONVEYANCE HEADED FOR ALMOST CERTAIN DOOM."
LOOK! THAT HEAD JUTTING THROUGH THE TRACKS!
IT'S THE HULK! HE DID THIS!
"THE DIM-WITTED HULK SPOTTED IT AS I KNEW HE WOULD.
SKRASH!
HE'S TRYING TO KILL US ALL! I-I CAN'T STOP IN TIME!
"BUT AT THE LAST POSSIBLE INSTANT, THE BEHEMOTH BRACED HIS BACK--
"--SUPPORTING THE TRACKS AND ALLOWING THE TRAIN TO PASS OVER SAFELY... THOUGH THE VEHICLE'S ENGINEER NEVER KNEW IT.
"THE HUMANS SOON SPREAD THE ALARM--AND RICK JONES, A MORTAL WHO HAD BEEN AT DR. BRUCE BANNER'S SIDE WHEN HE FIRST BECAME THE HULK, REACTED PREDICTABLY.
IT CAN'T BE!
HULK!
IF THE HULK IS INNOCENT, HE NEEDS HELP. IF HE'S GUILTY, IT'LL TAKE SOMEONE WITH EQUAL POWERS--LIKE THE FANTASTIC FOUR TO STOP HIM!
CALLING THE FANTASTIC FOUR! CONDITION RED! CONTACT THE TEEN BRIGADE! HULK MUST BE FOUND!! DO YOU READ ME?

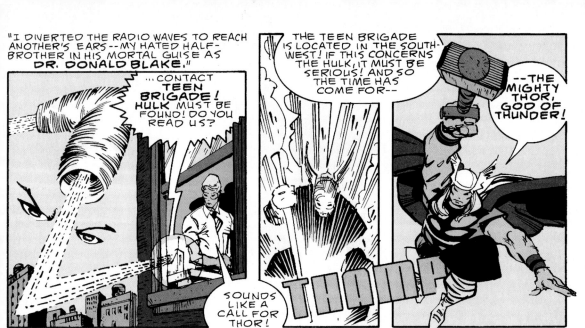

"I DIVERTED THE RADIO WAVES TO REACH ANOTHER'S EARS -- MY HATED HALF-BROTHER IN HIS MORTAL GUISE AS **DR. DONALD BLAKE.**"

...CONTACT **TEEN BRIGADE!** HULK MUST BE FOUND! DO YOU READ US?

THE TEEN BRIGADE IS LOCATED IN THE SOUTH-WEST! IF THIS CONCERNS THE HULK, IT MUST BE SERIOUS! AND SO THE TIME HAS COME FOR--

--THE MIGHTY **THOR, GOD OF THUNDER!**

SOUNDS LIKE A CALL FOR THOR!

THAMP

"OTHER SUPER-POWERED BUFFOONS ANSWERED THE SUMMONS, AS WELL,"

WOWEE! IT'S THOR!

IT WOULD SEEM THE GANG'S ALL HERE, EH, LADS?

WHY ART THOU SUR-PRISED? THOU DID SEND FOR ME!

"THE OTHERS' ARRIVAL COM-PLICATED AFFAIRS FOR ME! I NEEDED TO SEPARATE THOR FROM THE REST!

"A SIMPLE ILLUSION CAST OF THE HULK! NO NEED TO DISTURB THE OTHERS!"

IMPOSSIBLE! MY HAMMER--IT WENT RIGHT **THROUGH** HIM!

'TWAS MERELY A MENTAL IMAGE!

ONLY **LOKI** IS CAP-ABLE OF SUCH WIZARDRY! HE WAS WARNED NE'ER TO MEDDLE IN EARTHLY AFFAIRS!

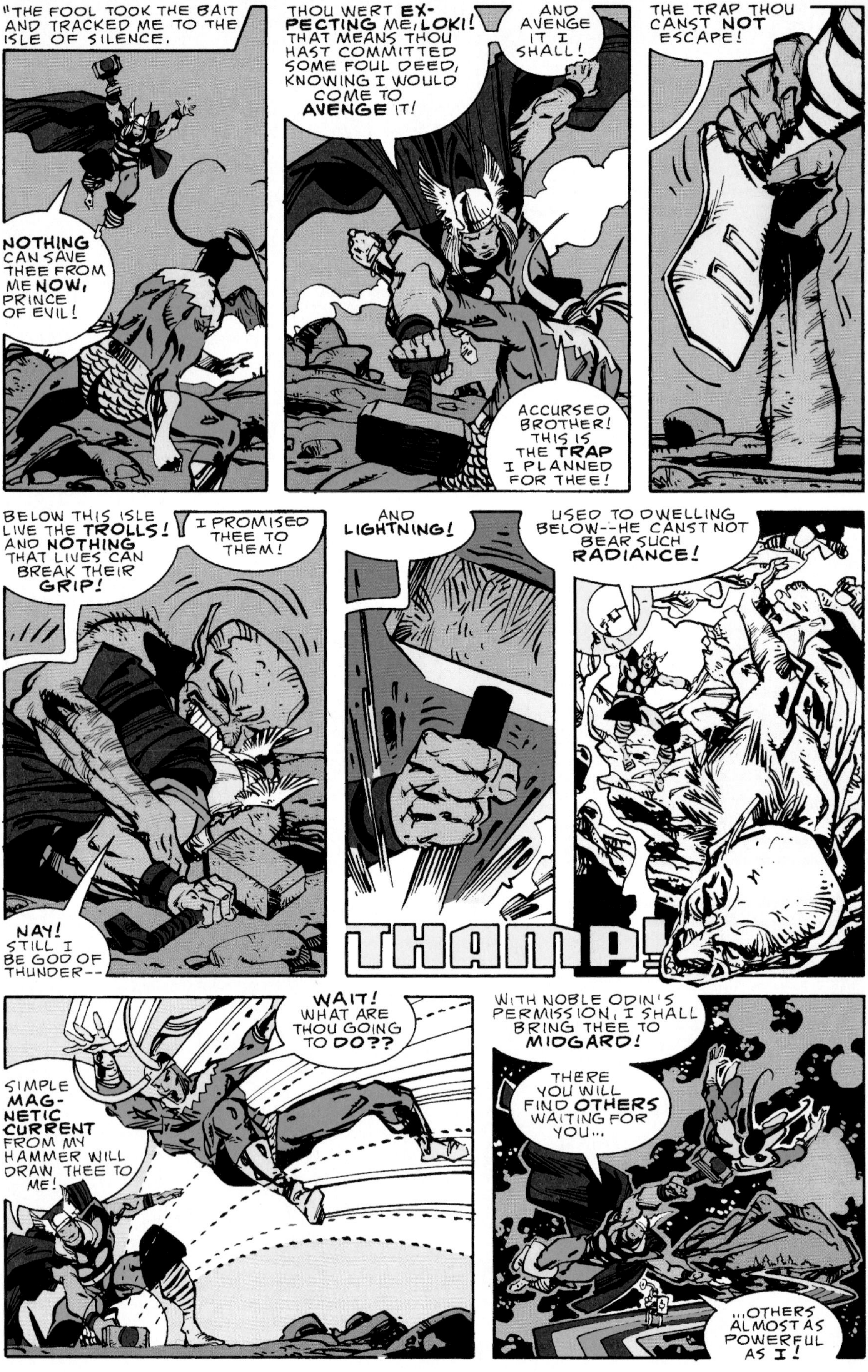
"THE FOOL TOOK THE BAIT AND TRACKED ME TO THE ISLE OF SILENCE.
NOTHING CAN SAVE THEE FROM ME NOW, PRINCE OF EVIL!
THOU WERT EXPECTING ME, LOKI! THAT MEANS THOU HAST COMMITTED SOME FOUL DEED, KNOWING I WOULD COME TO AVENGE IT!
AND AVENGE IT I SHALL!
ACCURSED BROTHER! THIS IS THE TRAP I PLANNED FOR THEE!
THE TRAP THOU CANST NOT ESCAPE!
BELOW THIS ISLE LIVE THE TROLLS! AND NOTHING THAT LIVES CAN BREAK THEIR GRIP!
I PROMISED THEE TO THEM!
NAY! STILL I BE GOD OF THUNDER--
AND LIGHTNING!
THAMP!
USED TO DWELLING BELOW--HE CANST NOT BEAR SUCH RADIANCE!
WAIT! WHAT ARE THOU GOING TO DO??
SIMPLE MAGNETIC CURRENT FROM MY HAMMER WILL DRAW THEE TO ME!
WITH NOBLE ODIN'S PERMISSION, I SHALL BRING THEE TO MIDGARD!
THERE YOU WILL FIND OTHERS WAITING FOR YOU...
...OTHERS ALMOST AS POWERFUL AS I!

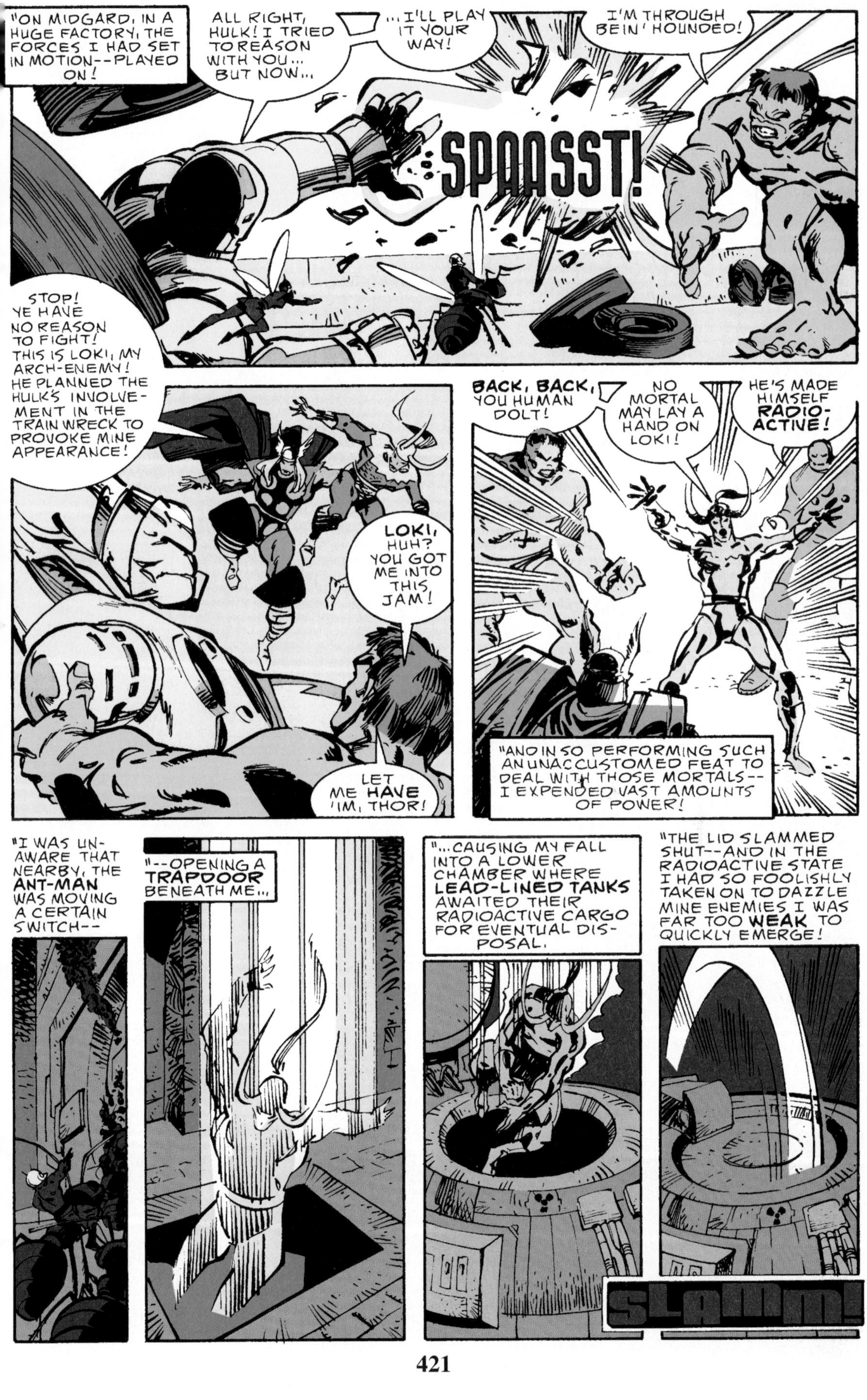
"ON MIDGARD, IN A HUGE FACTORY, THE FORCES I HAD SET IN MOTION--PLAYED ON!
ALL RIGHT, HULK! I TRIED TO REASON WITH YOU... BUT NOW...
...I'LL PLAY IT YOUR WAY!
I'M THROUGH BEIN' HOUNDED!
SPAASST!
STOP! YE HAVE NO REASON TO FIGHT! THIS IS LOKI, MY ARCH-ENEMY! HE PLANNED THE HULK'S INVOLVEMENT IN THE TRAIN WRECK TO PROVOKE MINE APPEARANCE!
LOKI, HUH? YOU GOT ME INTO THIS JAM!
LET ME HAVE 'IM, THOR!
BACK, BACK, YOU HUMAN DOLT!
NO MORTAL MAY LAY A HAND ON LOKI!
HE'S MADE HIMSELF RADIO-ACTIVE!
"AND IN SO PERFORMING SUCH AN UNACCUSTOMED FEAT TO DEAL WITH THOSE MORTALS-- I EXPENDED VAST AMOUNTS OF POWER!
"I WAS UNAWARE THAT NEARBY, THE ANT-MAN WAS MOVING A CERTAIN SWITCH--
"--OPENING A TRAPDOOR BENEATH ME...
"...CAUSING MY FALL INTO A LOWER CHAMBER WHERE LEAD-LINED TANKS AWAITED THEIR RADIOACTIVE CARGO FOR EVENTUAL DISPOSAL.
"THE LID SLAMMED SHUT--AND IN THE RADIOACTIVE STATE I HAD SO FOOLISHLY TAKEN ON TO DAZZLE MINE ENEMIES I WAS FAR TOO WEAK TO QUICKLY EMERGE!
SLAMM!

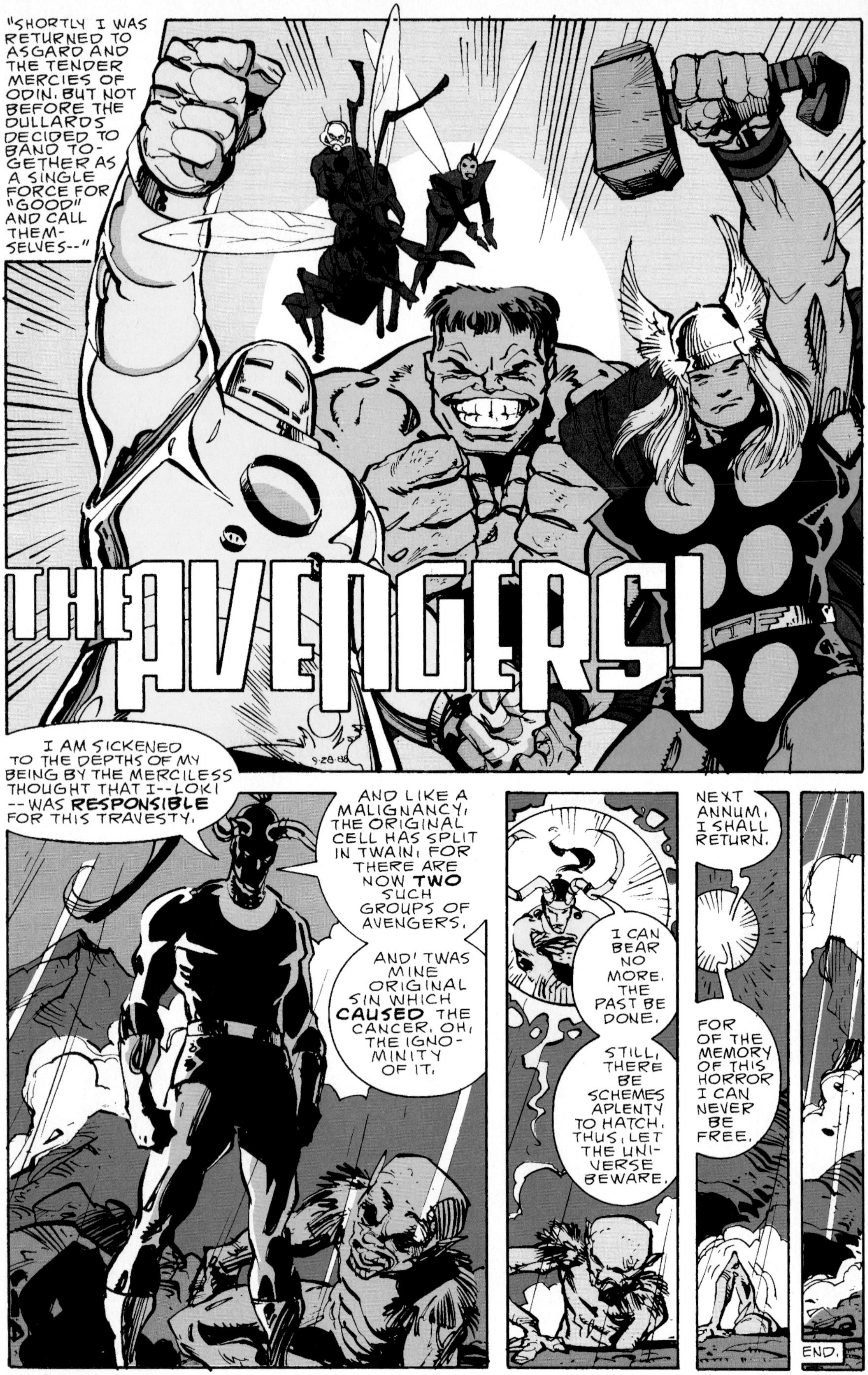
"SHORTLY I WAS RETURNED TO ASGARD AND THE TENDER MERCIES OF ODIN, BUT NOT BEFORE THE DULLARDS DECIDED TO BAND TOGETHER AS A SINGLE FORCE FOR "GOOD" AND CALL THEMSELVES--"
THE AVENGERS!
I AM SICKENED TO THE DEPTHS OF MY BEING BY THE MERCILESS THOUGHT THAT I--LOKI --WAS RESPONSIBLE FOR THIS TRAVESTY.
AND LIKE A MALIGNANCY, THE ORIGINAL CELL HAS SPLIT IN TWAIN, FOR THERE ARE NOW TWO SUCH GROUPS OF AVENGERS.
AND 'TWAS MINE ORIGINAL SIN WHICH CAUSED THE CANCER. OH, THE IGNOMINITY OF IT.
I CAN BEAR NO MORE. THE PAST BE DONE.
STILL, THERE BE SCHEMES APLENTY TO HATCH. THUS, LET THE UNIVERSE BEWARE.
NEXT ANNUM, I SHALL RETURN.
FOR OF THE MEMORY OF THIS HORROR I CAN NEVER BE FREE.
END.

AVENGERS MEMBERSHIP

AVENGERS ISSUES EACH APPEARED IN

THOR
1-16,51, 58, 66-71, 75-76, 84-88, 93-105, 109-135, 137-151, 159-160, 162, 165-168, 170-177, 179-181, 184-185, 189, 192-202, 210-216, 218-222, 224-235, 242-243, 249, 276-277, 279-285, 291-297, 299-300

Annuals
1, 7-13, 16

Giant-Sized
1-4

IRON MAN I
(Tony Stark)
1-10, 12-16, 51, 58, 66-71, 75-76, 79-82, 86-88, 93-135, 137-163, 165, 167-185, 189-191, 193-197, 199-202, 204-208, 210-222, 224-228, 231-233, 243, 250

Annuals
1, 6-11

Giant-Sized
1-4

ANT-MAN I
1, 93, 100, 223-224

(as GIANT-MAN)
2-16

(as GOLIATH I)
28-58

Annuals
1-2

(as YELLOWJACKET I)
63-74, 90-91, 137-141, 146, 150-157, 159-162, 164-167, 170-173, 175-177, 179-181, 189, 195-200, 211-214, 217

Annuals
6, 8-9

(as HANK PYM)
Annual
13

WASP
1-16, 28-60, 63-74, 83, 90-91, 100, 137, 141, 146, 150-157, 159-163, 167, 170-184, 186, 260-278

Annuals
1-2, 6, 8, 11-16

HULK
1-2, 100

Annuals
13, 17

CAPTAIN AMERICA
4-38, 42-46, 56, 58, 60, 69-72, 75-76, 78-82, 88, 93-104, 106-108, 110-119, 121, 125-126, 141-161, 163-164, 166-172, 174-178, 181-192, 194-201, 204-208, 210-214, 217-218, 220-222, 224-234, 237-238, 240-248, 250-285

Annuals
1-2 6-16

Giant-Sized
1

(as THE CAPTAIN)
298-300

Annuals
17

THOR
(Sigurd Jarlsen)
Founding Member

IRON MAN
(Anthony Stark)
Founding Member

ANT-MAN
(Henry Pym)
Founding Member

HULK
(Bruce Banner)
Founding Member

GIANT-MAN
(formerly Ant-Man)
Active AVENGERS #2

WASP
(Janet Van Dyne)
Founding Member

CAPTAIN AMERICA
(Steve Rogers)
Joined AVENGERS #4

HAWKEYE
(Clint Barton)
Joined AVENGERS #16

QUICKSILVER
(Pietro Maximoff)
Joined AVENGERS #16

SCARLET WITCH
(Wanda Maximoff)
Joined AVENGERS #16

SWORDSMAN
(real name classified)
Joined AVENGERS #19

GOLIATH
(formerly Giant-Man)
Active AVENGERS #28

HERCULES
(no alias used)
Joined AVENGERS #45

BLACK PANTHER
(T'Challa)
Joined AVENGERS #52

VISION
(no alias used)
Joined AVENGERS #58

HAWKEYE
16-62, 98-109, 130-135, 137, 142-146, 161, 163, 168, 170, 172-177, 181-185, 189, 198-204, 211, 221, 234, 239, 241-243, 246, 249-250, 253-254

Annuals
1-2, 8-10

Giant-Sized
2-4

(as GOLIATH II)
63-88, 90-97

QUICKSILVER
16-30, 36-49, 75-104, 110, 127

Annuals
1, 8

SCARLET WITCH
16-30, 36-49, 75-130, 140-161, 163-184, 186-190, 192, 197-198, 200-202, 204-211, 228, 231, 233-238, 240-255

Annuals
1, 6-10, 12

Giant-Sized
1-2, 4

SWORDSMAN
20, 100, 114-129

Giant-Sized
2

HERCULES
45-50, 100, 163, 173-174, 176, 249-250, 252, 254-285

Annuals
14-15, 17

BLACK PANTHER
52-65, 69-71, 73-88, 100, 105-119, 121-126, 160-161, 169, 173-177, 181, 211, 239

Annuals
2, 8

VISION
58-135, 140-161, 164, 167-185, 188-202, 204-211, 228-236, 238-255

Annuals
6-10, 12

Giant-Sized
1-4

BLACK KNIGHT
71, 84, 100, 260-297

Annuals
14-16

BLACK WIDOW
111-112, 239

MANTIS
114-135

Giant-Sized
1-4

BEAST
137-155, 157-161, 165-168, 170-172, 178-184, 186-190, 192-201, 203-214, 231, 239, 254

Annuals
6-11, 13, 17

MOONDRAGON
137-144, 147-151, 174-177, 181, 211, 219-220

Annual
7

YELLOWJACKET
(formerly Goliath)
Active AVENGERS #63

GOLIATH II
(formerly Hawkeye)
Active AVENGERS #63

BLACK KNIGHT
(Dane Whitman)
Joined AVENGERS #71

BLACK WIDOW
(Natasha Romanova)
Joined AVENGERS #111

MANTIS
(real name classified)
Joined AVENGERS #114

BEAST
(Henry McCoy)
Joined AVENGERS #137

MOONDRAGON
(Heather Douglas)
Joined AVENGERS #137

HELLCAT
(Patsy Walker)
Applied AVENGERS #144

JOCASTA
(no alias used)

MS. MARVEL
(Carol Danvers)
Joined AVENGERS #183

FALCON
(Sam Wilson)
Joined AVENGERS #184

WONDER MAN
(Simon Williams)
Joined AVENGERS #194

TIGRA
(Greer Nelson)
Joined AVENGERS #211

SHE-HULK
(Jennifer Walters)
Joined AVENGERS #221

CAPTAIN MARVEL
(Monica Rambeau)
Joined AVENGERS #231

HELLCAT
148-151

JOCASTA
170-171, 174-177, 181-182, 194-196,
202, 204-208, 210-211, 231-232

Annuals
10, 17

MS. MARVEL
(Carol Danvers)
171-172, 175-176, 181, 183-188,
190-198, 200

Annuals
8, 10

FALCON
183-194

Annual
17

WONDER MAN
152-154, 156-162, 164, 167,
173-182, 187-189, 192-201,
203-210, 239, 250, 253-255

Annuals
6, 8-10

TIGRA
212-216, 240-243, 250, 253-254

SHE-HULK
221-225, 227-321, 233, 235-238,
240-243, 246-247, 249, 254,
259, 278-297

Annuals
12-16

CAPTAIN MARVEL
(Monica Rambeau)
228-231, 233-238, 240-246,
248-252, 259-293

Annuals
12-16

STARFOX
231, 240-247, 249-261

Annual
12, 14

MOCKINGBIRD
239, 242-245, 249, 253-254

SUB-MARINER
262-272, 282-293

DR. DRUID
276-297

Annual
16

YELLOWJACKET II
(Rita Demara)
Annual
17

MR. FANTASTIC
299-300

INVISIBLE WOMAN
299-300

GILGAMESH
299-300

STARFOX
(Eros)
Joined AVENGERS #231

MOCKINGBIRD
(Barbara Morse Barton)
Joined WEST COAST
AVENGERS LS #1

IRON MAN II
(James Rhodes)
Joined WEST COAST
AVENGERS LS #1

THING
(Benjamin Grimm)
Active WEST COAST
AVENGERS #4

SUB-MARINER
(Namor McKenzie)
Joined AVENGERS #264

HENRY PYM
Resident scientist
Active WEST COAST
AVENGERS #1

FIREBIRD
(Bonita Juarez)
Active WEST COAST
AVENGERS #4

DOCTOR DRUID
(Anthony Druid)
Joined in AVENGERS #278

MOON KNIGHT
(Marc Spector)
Active WEST COAST
AVENGERS #21

MARRINA
(No alias used)
Active AVENGERS #286

YELLOWJACKET II
(Rita Demara)
Active AVENGERS
ANNUAL #17

MR. FANTASTIC
(Reed Richards)
Active AVENGERS #299

INVISIBLE WOMAN
(Susan Richards)
Active AVENGERS #299

"FORGOTTEN ONE"
(No alias used)
Active AVENGERS #300

With his assumption of command, Captain America has decided to increase the Avengers' staff of full-time support personnel in order to expand the scope and efficiency of the peace-keeping organization's activities and to maintain the Avengers' organizational integrity during crisis situations (such as the recent membership walkout). In the past, maintenance activities for Avengers headquarters and personal services for its members were performed by one man, Edwin Jarvis. Jarvis, primarily the butler, would frequently be obliged to hire caterers, mechanics, repairmen, computer programmers, laboratory assistants, groundskeepers, and special telephone operators as the need arose. The members of the Avengers themselves handled various operational functions such as information gathering and processing, the assessment of priorities, the briefing of military and law enforcement officials, the paperwork involved in criminal prosecutions, public relations coordination, etc. In Captain America's new plan, all these functions will be handled by full-time staff people under Edwin Jarvis's coordination. The following chart depicts those persons Captain America and Edwin Jarvis have hired or will hire in the next few months.

EDWIN JARVIS
Butler
TALES OF SUSPENSE #59

RAYMOND SIKORSKY
Government liaison
AVENGERS #235

PEGGY CARTER
Communications
TALES OF SUSPENSE #77

MICHAEL O'BRIEN
Security chief
IRON MAN #82

DONNA MARIA PUENTES
Administrator
CAPTAIN AMERICA #206

ARNOLD ROTH
Publicist
CAPTAIN AMERICA #270

GENJI ODASHU
Pilot
SHOGUN WARRIORS #1

JOHN JAMESON
Pilot
AMAZING SPIDER-MAN #1

M'DAKA
Vehicle maintenance
CAPTAIN AMERICA #342

KEITH KINCAID
Physician
THOR #136

INGER SULLIVAN
Lawyer
CAPTAIN AMERICA #332

ROBERT FRANK JR.
Groundskeeper
GIANT-SIZE AVENGERS #1

GILBERT VAUGHN
Physicist
MARVEL TWO-IN-ONE #53

TALIA KRUMA
Physicist
BLACK GOLIATH #1

WALTER NEWELL
Oceanographer
TALES TO ASTONISH #95

DIANE ARLISS NEWELL
Secretary
SUB-MARINER #5

FABIAN STANKOWICZ
Machinist
AVENGERS #221

JARVIS, EDWIN

Real name: Edwin Jarvis
Occupation: Butler
Identity: Publicly known
Legal status: Former citizen of the United Kingdom, now naturalized citizen of the United States with no criminal record
Other aliases: The Crimson Cowl
Place of birth: Unrevealed
Marital status: Unrevealed, now single
Known relatives: Mrs. Jarvis (mother)
Group affiliation: Employee of Anthony Stark and the Avengers
Base of operations: Avengers Mansion, New York City, later Avengers headquarters, Hydro-Base
First appearance: TALES OF SUSPENSE #59
History: Edwin Jarvis was the butler in the employ of millionaire inventor and industrialist Anthony Stark and worked in Stark's mansion in midtown Manhattan. Apparently Jarvis originally served Stark's parents, Howard and Maria Stark, and continued to work for Anthony Stark after their deaths. Before coming to the United States, Edwin Jarvis once served heroically in the United Kingdom's Royal Air Force as a pilot.

Jarvis was present at the mansion when the new team of superhuman adventurers, the Avengers, held their first meeting there (see *Avengers*). Anthony Stark, who, in his identity of Iron Man was a founding member of the team, donated the mansion to the Avengers for their use as a headquarters and set up the Maria Stark Foundation to cover the team's operational expenses (see *Iron Man*). Jarvis stayed on at the mansion to act as the Avengers' principal domestic servant.

Jarvis has served the Avengers loyally since the very beginning of the team's history. His duties include the maintenance of the Avengers' quinjets and specialized equipment and the supervision of work crews repairing damage to the Avenger headquarters, as well as normal household duties such as preparing the Avengers' meals. Presumably there are other members of the household staff to help Jarvis take care of such an enormous mansion, but Jarvis is the only servant who lives in the mansion itself.

Years ago the Avengers' enemy, Ultron, hypnotized Jarvis into helping him and the second Masters of Evil organization capture the Avengers and Avengers Mansion (see *Masters of Evil, Ultron*). Under Ultron's control, Jarvis even briefly assumed the guise of the Crimson Cowl, which Ultron himself used to conceal his true identity. Ultron caused Jarvis to believe he had betrayed the Avengers of his own free will to procure money to pay his ailing mother's hospital bill. Consumed by guilt, Jarvis revealed the location of Ultron's lair to the third Black Knight, thereby making possible the Avengers' rescue (see *Black Knight*). The Avengers took the repentant Jarvis back into their service. Months later Jarvis's memory cleared and he remembered that Ultron had hypnotized him into betraying the Avengers and told them so.

When the fourth Masters of Evil organization, led by the second Baron Zemo, seized control of Avengers Mansion, one of its members, Mister Hyde, brutally tortured Jarvis (see *Baron Zemo, Mister Hyde*). The Avengers finally defeated the Masters of Evil, but the Mansion had been left in ruins, and Jarvis was hospitalized. As a result of Hyde's treatment of him, Jarvis is now 90% blind in his left eye and must walk with a cane for the foreseeable

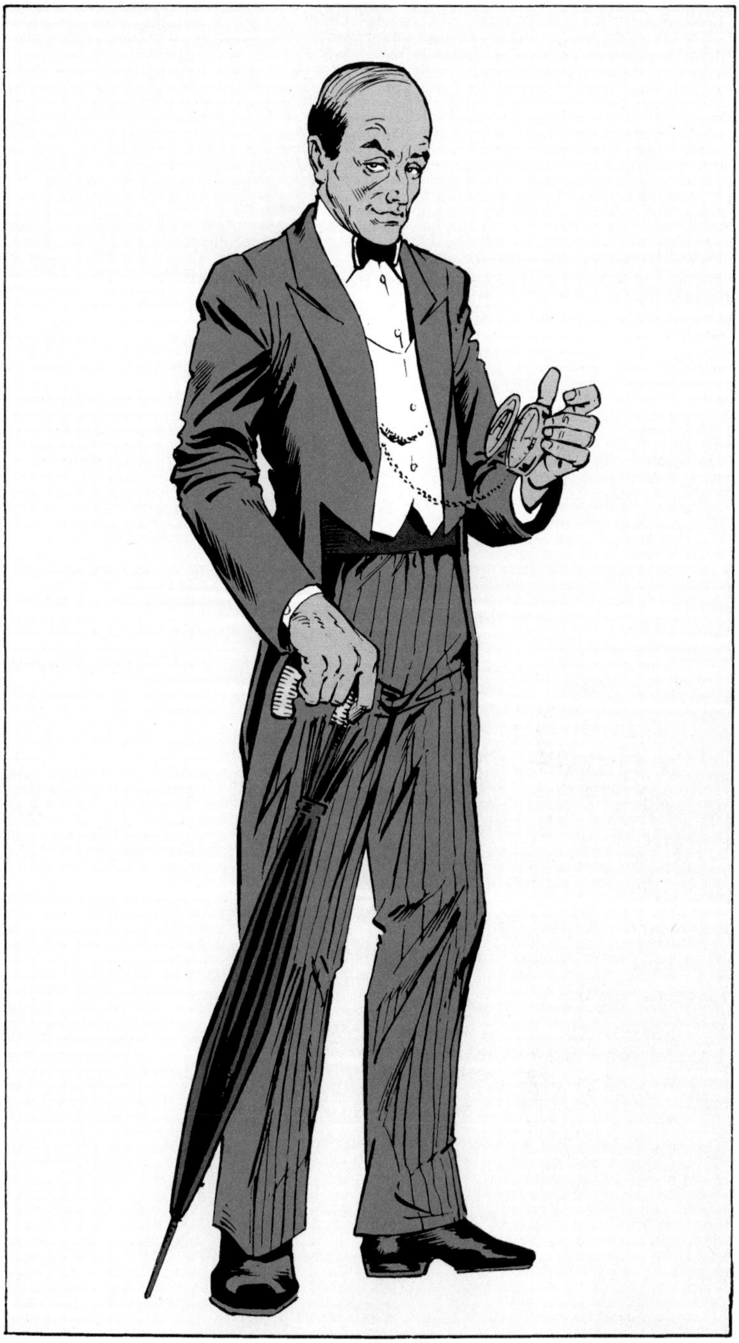

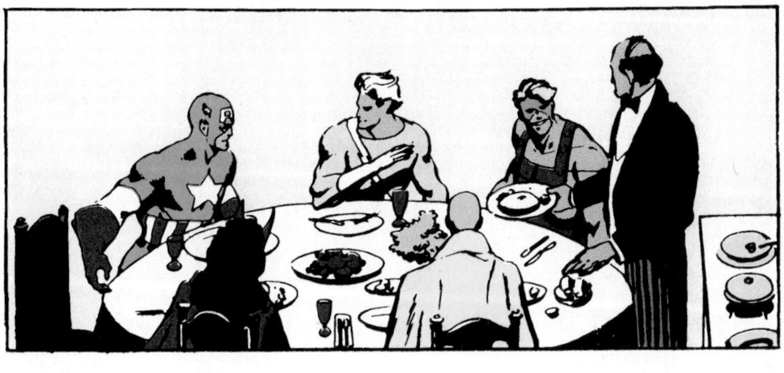

future due to the damage to his right leg.

Although he could have retired due to his injuries, Jarvis instead chose to return to his work with the Avengers. He now acts as the East Coast Avengers' principal domestic servant at their new headquarters on Hydro-Base (see *Hydro-Base*). His only known relative, his mother, still lives in New York City.

Height: 5′11″
Weight: 160 lbs.
Eyes: Blue
Hair: Black
Strength level: Edwin Jarvis possesses the normal human strength of a man of his age, height, and build who engages in moderate regular exercise.
Known superhuman powers: None
Other abilities: Edwin Jarvis is a good hand-to-hand combatant, and was boxing champion of the Royal Air Force for three years. Obviously, his recent injuries have hampered his fighting prowess.
Limitations: Due to injuries inflicted by Mister Hyde, Edwin Jarvis is 90% blind in his left eye and has a temporarily crippled right leg, requiring him to walk with a cane.

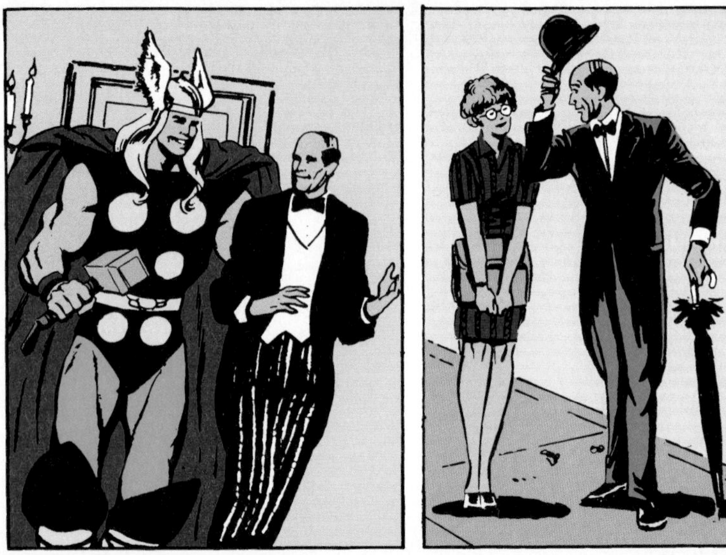

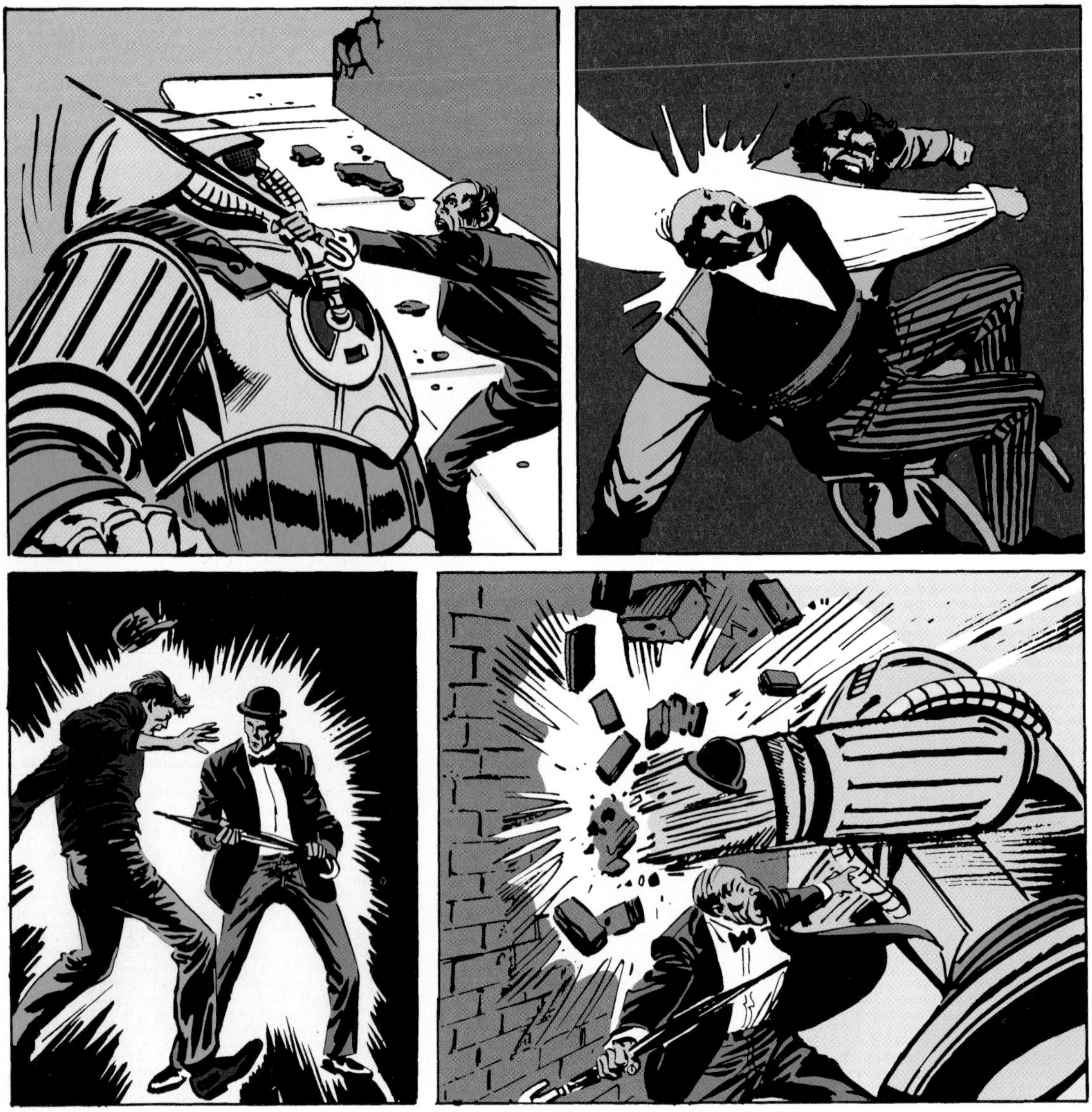

AVENGERS PARK

AT THE FORMER SITE OF THE AVENGERS MANSION

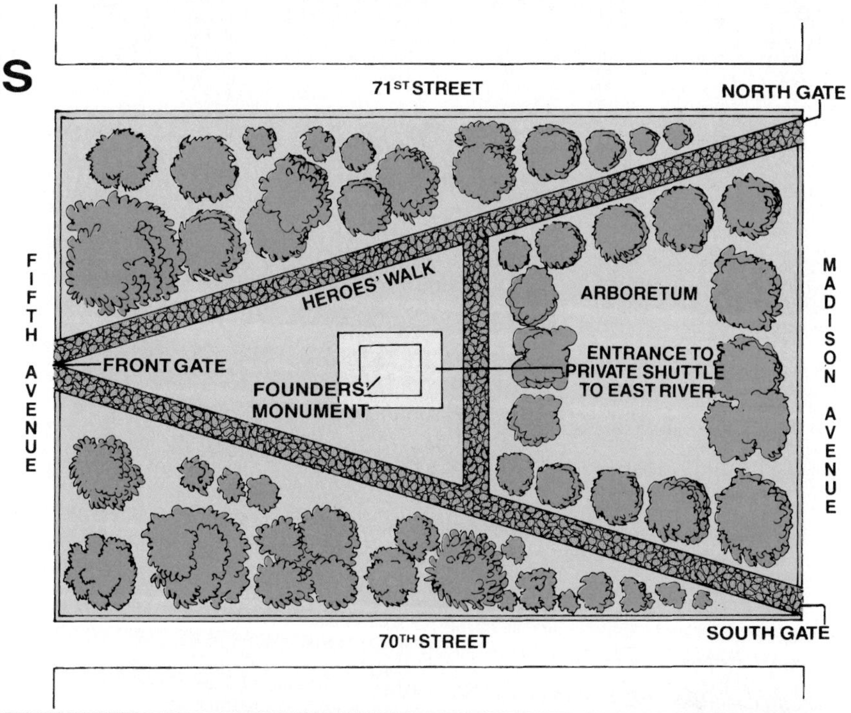
71ST STREET
NORTH GATE
FIFTH AVENUE
HEROES' WALK
ARBORETUM
MADISON AVENUE
FRONT GATE
ENTRANCE TO PRIVATE SHUTTLE TO EAST RIVER
FOUNDERS' MONUMENT
70TH STREET
SOUTH GATE

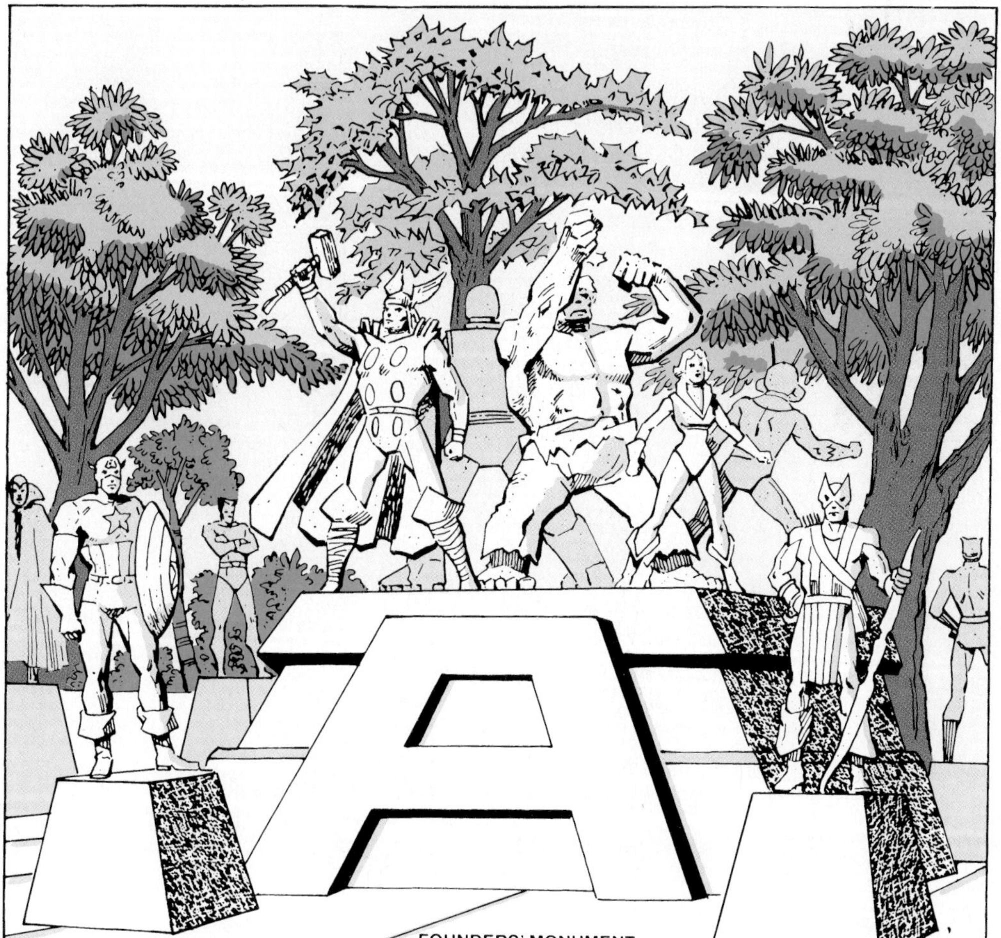

FOUNDERS' MONUMENT
(DETAIL)

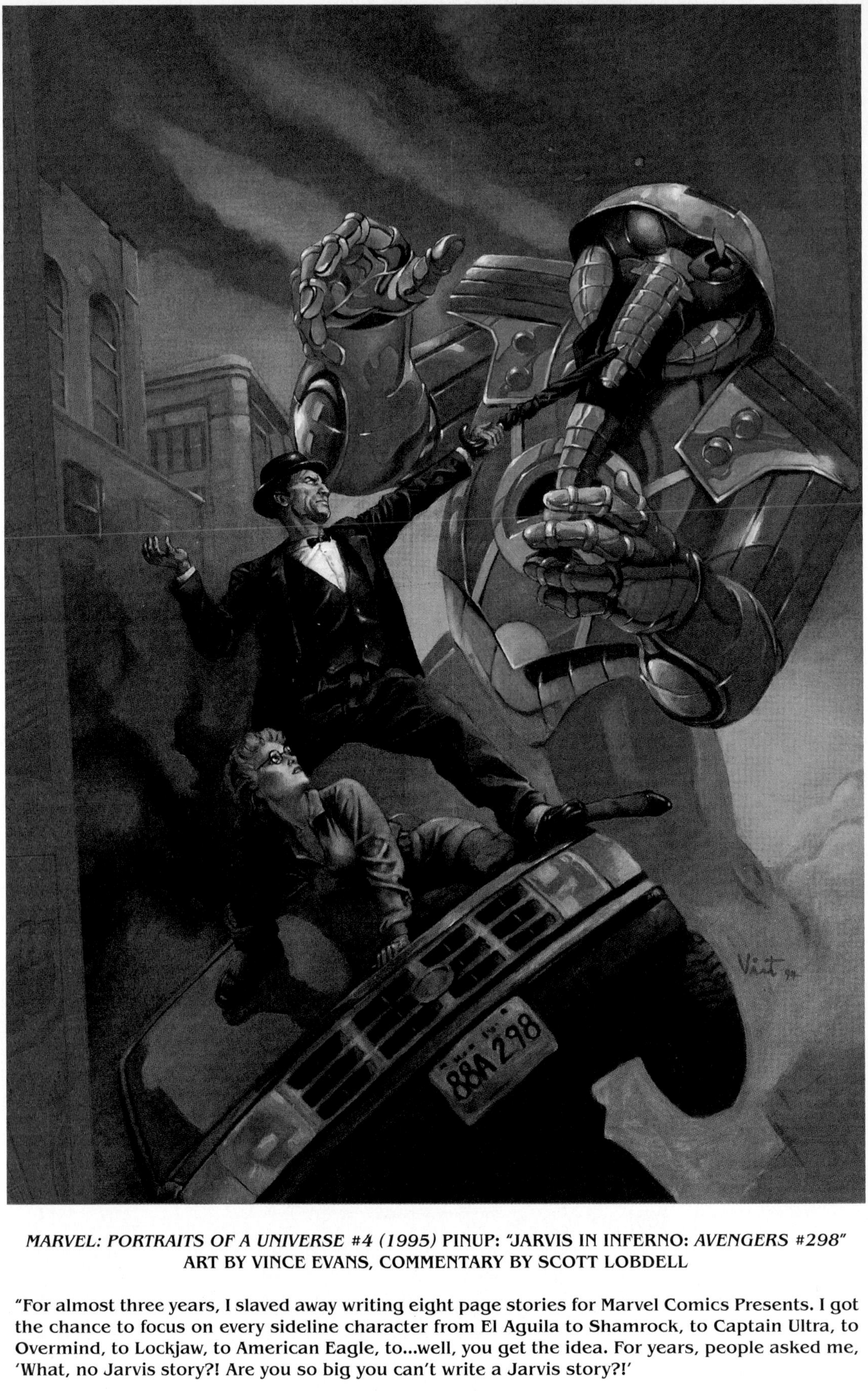
88A 298

MARVEL: PORTRAITS OF A UNIVERSE #4 (1995) PINUP: "JARVIS IN INFERNO: *AVENGERS #298*"
ART BY VINCE EVANS, COMMENTARY BY SCOTT LOBDELL

"For almost three years, I slaved away writing eight page stories for Marvel Comics Presents. I got the chance to focus on every sideline character from El Aguila to Shamrock, to Captain Ultra, to Overmind, to Lockjaw, to American Eagle, to...well, you get the idea. For years, people asked me, 'What, no Jarvis story?! Are you so big you can't write a Jarvis story?!'

"TRIPLE ANNIVERSARY"
EXCERPT FROM *MARVEL AGE* #70
BY PETER SANDERSON

In *The Avengers*, as everyone now knows, there has not actually been an Avengers team, all of the recent members having left for one reason or another. But *Avengers* writer Walter Simonson promises, "There will be a completely new team by the end of *Avengers #300*." Both *Avengers #299* and *#300* are tie-ins with the Inferno storyline that will then be going on in *X-Men*, *X-Factor* and various other series and that has been extensively covered in other *Marvel Age Magazine* articles. The heroes who will become the new team of Avengers will come together in the course of their individual efforts to battle the demons from the Inferno storyline who have been kidnaping babies. In *Avengers #300* those heroes join together to combat the demons.

But who are these heroes? Well, that we can't give away, but we can tell you that one of them is a character from the *Captain America* series, two others are longtime members of another famous Marvel super hero team, yet another is a member of one of the hidden races of the Marvel Universe, and the fifth is a character that no one should be surprised that Walter Simonson is using in THE AVENGERS!

By the way, 1988 also marks the twenty-fifth anniversary of *The Avengers*, which debuted with an issue cover-dated September, 1963 (the same month as *X-Men#11*).

The main story will be written by Walter and illustrated by John Buscema and Tom Palmer. Walter will draw a special feature that will be written by his predecessor as AVENGERS scripter, Ralph Macchio, and which recaps the origin of the Avengers from an unusual perspective. Ralph says, "Mark Gruenwald (editor of *The Avengers*) came to me one day, perplexed as he usually is, and said we have to do a short feature in *Avengers #300* about the origin of the Avengers, and I want to do it from the viewpoint of one of the characters. So we went through the founding members one by one, and he said, 'I can't figure out which one we should use.' So I said, 'Why don't we do it from Loki's point of view because it's his fault? He's the one who got all of them together to chase down the Hulk to get Thor in a lot of trouble.' And Mark said, 'Great idea. You write it.'"

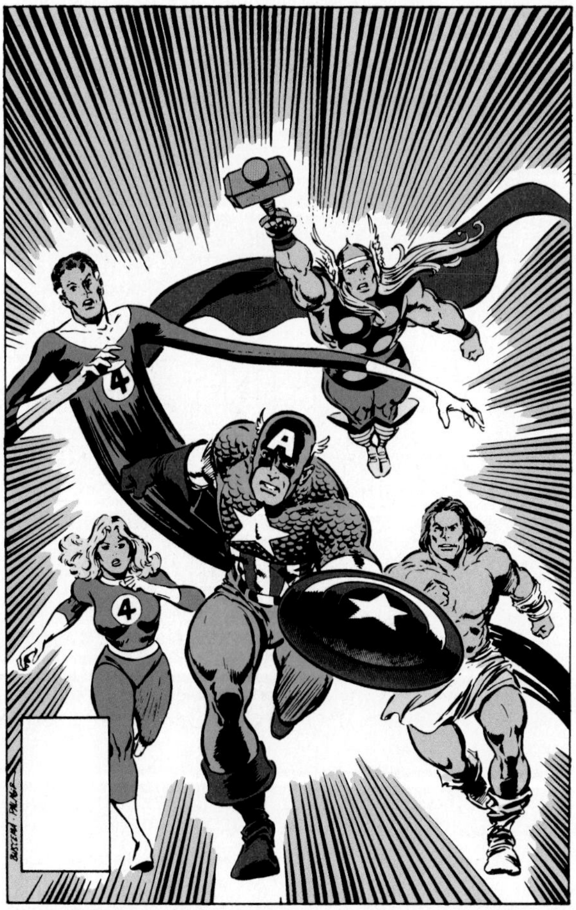

THE ORIGINAL VERSION OF *AVENGERS #300*'S COVER FEATURED STEVE ROGERS AS CAPTAIN AMERICA RATHER THAN THE CAPTAIN, AND GILGAMESH IN AN EARLIER COSTUME. ART BY JOHN BUSCEMA & TOM PALMER.

X-MEN: INFERNO CROSSOVERS HC COVER ART BY
TODD MCFARLANE & CHRIS SOTOMAYOR